Adobe® Acrobat® 8 PDF Bible

Adobe® Acrobat® 8
PDF Bible

Ted Padova

Wiley Publishing, Inc.

Adobe® Acrobat® 8 PDF Bible

Published by
Wiley Publishing, Inc.
10475 Crosspoint Boulevard
Indianapolis, IN 46256
www.wiley.com

Copyright © 2007 by Wiley Publishing, Inc., Indianapolis, Indiana

Published simultaneously in Canada

ISBN: 978-0-470-05051-4

Manufactured in the United States of America

10 9 8 7 6 5 4 3 2 1

1O/ST/QR/QX/IN

For general information on our other products and services or to obtain technical support, please contact our Customer Care Department within the U.S. at (800) 762-2974, outside the U.S. at (317) 572-3993 or fax (317) 572-4002.

Library of Congress Control Number: 2006939590

About the Author

Ted Padova is the former chief executive officer and managing partner of The Image Source Digital Imaging and Photo Finishing Centers of Ventura and Thousand Oaks, California. He has been involved in digital imaging since founding a service bureau in 1990. He retired from his company in 2005 and now spends his time writing and speaking on Acrobat and PDF.

For more than 17 years, Ted has taught university and higher education classes in graphic design applications and digital prepress at the University of California, Santa Barbara, and the University of California at Los Angeles. He has been, and continues to be, a conference speaker nationally and internationally at PDF conferences.

Ted has written more than 25 computer books and is one of the world's leading authors on Adobe Acrobat. He has written books on Adobe Acrobat, Adobe Creative Suite (versions 1 and 2), Adobe Photoshop, Adobe Photoshop Elements, Adobe Reader, Microsoft PowerPoint, and Adobe Illustrator. Recent books published by John Wiley and Sons include *Adobe Acrobat PDF Bible (versions 4, 5, 6, and 7)*, *Color Correction for Digital Photographers Only*, *Color Correction for Digital Photographers For Dummies*, *Microsoft PowerPoint 2007 For Dummies — Just the Steps*, *Creating Adobe Acrobat PDF Forms*, *Teach Yourself Visually Acrobat 5*, and *Adobe Acrobat 6.0 Complete Course*. He also co-authored *Adobe Illustrator Master Class — Illustrator Illuminated* and wrote *Adobe Reader Revealed* for Peachpit/Adobe Press.

For Karl and Susanna. May all your days together be as wonderful as you.

Credits

Acquisitions Editor
Kim Spilker

Project Editor
Katharine Dvorak

Technical Editor
Lori DeFurio

Copy Editor
Nancy Rapoport

Editorial Manager
Robyn Siesky

Business Manager
Amy Knies

Vice President and Executive Group Publisher
Richard Swadley

Vice President and Executive Publisher
Bob Ipsen

Vice President and Publisher
Barry Pruett

Project Coordinator
Patrick Redmond

Graphics and Production Specialists
Joyce Haughey
Jennifer Mayberry
Barbara Moore

Quality Control Technicians
Susan Moritz
Christy Pingleton

Media Development Project Supervisor
Laura Moss

Media Development Specialist
Kate Jenkins

Proofreading and Indexing
Techbooks

Wiley Bicentennial Logo
Richard J. Pacifico

Contents

Contents

Contents

Part II: Converting Documents to PDF   179

Chapter 7: Converting Files to PDF 181

Contents

Part III: Editing PDFs

Contents

Contents

Contents

Contents

Contents

Contents

Contents

A dobe Acrobat 8 PDF Bible is written for a cross-platform audience. Users of Microsoft Windows 2000 with Service Pack 2, Windows XP Professional or Home Edition, Tablet PC Edition, and Apple Macintosh computers running OS X v10.2.8, 10.3, and later will find references to these operating systems.

About This Book

Most of the chapters in this book include screenshots from Acrobat running under Windows. The user interface is closely matched between Windows and the Macintosh; therefore, Macintosh users will find the same options in dialog boxes and menu commands as found in the screenshots taken on a Windows machine. Where significant differences do occur, you'll find additional screenshots taken on a Macintosh to distinguish the differences.

How to read this book

I have to admit this publication is not a page turner that leaves you grasping for more time to finish up a chapter before retiring at night. After all, it's a computer book and inasmuch as my editors at Wiley always strive to get me to add a little *drama* to the text, few people will pick up this *Bible* and read it cover to cover. This book should be thought of more as a reference where you can jump to an area and read over the contents to help simplify your work sessions in Acrobat Standard (now available only on Windows in version 8.0) or Acrobat Professional version 8.0.

Because Acrobat is such a behemoth program and can do so many things for almost any kind of work activity, most people won't use every feature the program provides. You may be interested in converting files to PDF and setting up reviews, or you may devote more attention to the area of prepress and printing, or perhaps it's accessibility or PDF forms that's part of your work. Therefore, you may ignore some chapters and just want to jump to the area that interests you most.

Regardless of where you are in Acrobat experience, you should be able to gain much insight and skill at using the new version of Acrobat by studying in detail those areas that interest you most. However, don't completely ignore chapters that cover features you think you won't use. You can find many related concepts falling under headings that are not exclusively related to the general topic for each chapter. For example, you may not be interested in creating accessible PDFs for screen readers. However, the Accessibility chapter also includes coverage of document structures and tagging, which will be important if you need to get the content of a PDF back out to an authoring application.

Because many chapters may include features that relate to the work you want to perform, studying over the most important features of interest to you and skimming over those chapters that appear to be less beneficial for you works best.

To begin, I recommend you look closely at the section in the Introduction covering new features in Acrobat 8.0. No matter where you are in Acrobat skill, be certain to understand PDF navigation, as things have changed for moving around PDF files and creating cross-document links. Look closely at the Help documents and the Help features in Acrobat 8.0. Pay particular attention to Chapters 8, 12, 14, 19, 29, and 31. If you've read the *Adobe Acrobat 7 PDF Bible*, these chapters are all new in this revision of the book. In many other chapters of the book, the text has been completely updated and revised. Some chapters have been expanded to cover more depth in specific areas. For example, Chapter 33 on Adobe LiveCycle Designer has been expanded by more than 50 pages over the last book.

Throughout the book are sections called "Steps." If you find the contents of a given series of steps interesting, follow the steps to see whether you can replicate what is covered in that section. In this book, I've made an effort to expand steps greatly to provide you some tutorial assistance in understanding many concepts.

Icons

The use of icons throughout the book offers you an at-a-glance hint of what content is being addressed. You can jump to this text to get extra information, be warned of a potential problem, or amplify the concept being addressed in the text. In this book you'll find icons for the following:

CAUTION A Caution icon alerts you to a potential problem in using Acrobat, any tools or menus, or any supporting application that may be the origination of a document to be converted to PDF. Pay close attention to these caution messages to avoid potential problems.

CROSS-REF The Cross-Ref icon indicates a cross-reference to another area in the book where more information can be found on a topic. It is almost impossible to walk you through Acrobat in a linear fashion because it has so many interrelated features. Covering all aspects of a single feature in a contiguous section of the book just doesn't work. Therefore some common features for a command, a tool, an action, or task may be spread out and discussed in different chapters. When the information is divided between different sections of the book, you'll find a Cross-Reference icon that cross-references the current passage to another part of the book covering related information.

NEW FEATURE An icon appears throughout the book where a new feature in Acrobat 8 has been added to the program. Pay special attention to these icons to learn more about what has been added to Acrobat 8, Adobe Reader 8, and Adobe LiveCycle Designer 8.

NOTE A Note icon signifies a message that may add more clarity to a text passage or help you deal with a feature more effectively.

PDF WORKFLOW Where workflow solutions are particularly applicable, you'll see an icon indicating that the text describes tasks or features that apply to workgroups and workflows. This icon will be an important signal for people in large businesses, government, and education where large workgroups with common tasks exist.

PREPRESS Much support is offered in version 8.0 for the prepress and printing market. If you're a design professional, service bureau, or print shop, take note of these messages for information related to prepress and printing.

TIP Tips are handy shortcuts. They help you to more quickly produce results or work through a series of steps to complete a task. Some tips provide you with information that may not be documented in the Help files accompanying Acrobat Professional.

The book's contents

This book is about Adobe Acrobat Standard (on Windows) and Adobe Acrobat Professional on Windows and the Macintosh. All the content in the book applies to Acrobat Standard, unless you see a reference that a specific section applies only to Acrobat Professional. Acrobat Professional features are clearly marked throughout the book so you know when Acrobat Standard doesn't support a particular feature.

Just about everything that you can do with Adobe Acrobat is contained in the chapters ahead. This book is *not* about Adobe LiveCycle Designer, Acrobat PDF Forms, collaboration, PDF creation, Acrobat JavaScript, or some other aspect of Acrobat exclusively. Some Acrobat features can take a book this size alone to cover in their entirety. What this book does for you is provide you some exposure and understanding for *all* that Acrobat can do. You'll find chapters on Adobe LiveCycle Designer and Acrobat JavaScript, several chapters on PDF creation, and chapters on collaboration. However, any one of these areas is not exclusive to the content of the book.

I've made an effort to address many different uses for all types of users. This book covers Acrobat features and how to work with Adobe Acrobat Professional, Adobe Acrobat Standard, Adobe Reader, and companion products. Individual industries such as office occupations, digital prepress, engineering, enterprise workflows, and multimedia and Web publishing are covered. Regardless of what you do, you should be able to find some solutions for your particular kind of work. Whether you are an accounting clerk, a real estate salesperson, a digital prepress technician, an engineer, a Web designer, or a hobbyist who likes to archive information from Web sites, there's a reference to your needs and Acrobat will provide a solution.

To simplify your journey through the new release, the book is broken up into six separate parts. A total of 36 chapters address Acrobat features and some individual purposes for using the software. The six parts include the following:

Part I: Welcome to Adobe Acrobat. To start off, I offer some discussion on the PDF format and its new revision. Acrobat 8.0 has many new features and a new Getting Started window to help you find help fast. I cover tools, menus, and palettes to help you understand many Acrobat 8.0 features. This section covers the distinctions between different viewer types, navigating through PDFs, and using the Find tool and the Search panel to search PDF files.

Part II: Converting Documents to PDF. There are many different ways to create a PDF document and all these methods are thoroughly covered in Part II. I begin by discussing the ease of creating simple PDF files that might be used by office workers and travel through to much more sophisticated PDF file creation for more demanding environments. A new chapter devoted entirely to Microsoft applications has been added. In addition, I discuss how many application software manufacturers are supporting PDFs through direct exports from their programs. I discuss the Adobe Creative Suite and how you can integrate PDF with the CS applications. A bonus chapter on the CD-ROM in the CD version of the book has been added to detail more of what you can do with Acrobat Distiller for creating PDF documents. The advantages and disadvantages of using all these methods are also discussed.

Part III: Editing PDFs. This section covers editing, modifying, and enhancing PDF files for many different purposes. Also covered are how to modify content and how to flow content between Acrobat and authoring programs. New features for combining and packaging PDFs and redacting PDFs are added in special new chapters. I also discuss scanning in Acrobat and converting scans to text with Optical Character Recognition (OCR). Document repurposing is covered in this section for users who want to modify files for different output mediums. Another new chapter on all the enabling features available in Acrobat Professional is included in this section.

Part IV: PDF Interactivity. Part IV covers interactivity with PDF documents for workgroups through the use of Review and Comment tools, shared reviews, adding interactive elements such as multimedia, and links and buttons. I address the layer features in Acrobat Professional and include a chapter devoted to making PDF documents accessible.

Part V: PDF Publishing. This section covers distribution of PDF files in some of the more common means available today. I begin with security and authentication as your first step in document distribution and then move on to PDF workflows. I discuss creating PDFs for different kinds of distribution, such as presentations, and offer complete coverage of all the printing and prepress features. I also offer information about eBooks in Part V. Hosting your PDFs on the Web and sending them via e-mail are also covered in this section. New chapters have been added in this section that cover the new Acrobat Connect application and a chapter is devoted to printing color PDFs to desktop color printers.

Part VI: Acrobat PDF and LiveCycle Designer Forms. This section covers PDF forms and data. For Windows users I cover using Adobe LiveCycle Designer 8 in a much more extended and detailed chapter for forms authoring. All the new forms features for distributing forms, collecting form data, and running form field recognition are included in this section. An introduction to JavaScript and writing simple JavaScript routines is also included in this section.

Staying Connected

It seems like new products and new upgrades are distributed about every five minutes. If you purchase a software product, you can often find an updated revision soon after. Manufacturers rely more and more on Internet distribution and less on postal delivery. You should plan on making routine visits to Adobe's Web site and the Web sites of third-party product manufacturers. Any software vendor that has a Web site will offer a product revision for download or offer you details on acquiring the update.

Internet connection

With newer releases of computer software, an Internet connection is now essential. Programs, including Acrobat, prompt you routinely to check for updates over the Internet. To optimize your performance with Acrobat, you should run the software on a computer that has an Internet connection.

Registration

Regardless of whether you purchase Acrobat Professional, Acrobat Standard, Acrobat 3D, or Acrobat Elements, or download the free Adobe Reader software, Adobe Systems has made it possible to register the product. You can register on the World Wide Web or mail a registration form to Adobe. If you develop PDF documents for distribution, Adobe likes to keep track of this information. You will find great advantage in being a registered user. First, update information will be sent to you, so you'll know when a product revision occurs. Second, information can be distributed to help you achieve the most out of using Acrobat. Who knows — some day you may be asked to provide samples of your work that might get you a hit from Adobe's Web site. By all means, complete the registration. It will be to your benefit.

Web sites to contact

Obviously, the first Web site to frequent is Adobe's Web site. When Acrobat and the Acrobat plug-ins are revised, downloads for updates will become available. You can also find tips, information, and problem solutions. Visit Adobe's Web site at www.adobe.com. Also make use of the Help⇨Adobe Expert Support

menu command in all Acrobat viewers. This command opens a Web page where you can order technical support for a nominal fee. For acquiring plug-ins for Acrobat visit the Adobe Store where you can find a comprehensive list of plug-ins and demonstration software that works with Acrobat. Visit the Adobe Store at: `www.store.adobe.com/store`.

A wealth of information is available on the Acrobat Users Community Web site at `www.acrobatusers.com`. Here you can find tips, techniques, blogs hosted by some of the world's leading Acrobat professionals, and support for starting and maintaining a local Acrobat User Group. Be certain to routinely check Acrobat Users for up-to-date information and assistance. You can e-mail leading professionals who can help you solve problems.

Acrobat tips are available on many Web sites — all you need to do is search the Internet for Acrobat information. An excellent source for information as well as a comprehensive collection of third-party plug-ins is Planet PDF. You can visit them at `www.planetpdf.com`.

More Acrobat plug-ins can be found on ThePowerXChange Web site. Log on to `www.thepower exchange.com` Web site for a vast list of Acrobat plug-ins and demo software.

Another source of information, articles, tips, Acrobat and PDF information can be found at `www.pdfZone .com`. Visit the pdfZone Web site for up-to-date articles and interviews with industry leaders.

If learning more about Acrobat is your interest, you can find regional conferences sponsored by DigiPub Solutions Corporation. If you want to meet and discuss PDF issues with some of the world's experts, look for a conference in your area. You can find information at `www.pdfconference.com`.

The American Graphics Institute offers another PDF conference program. You can find out more information by logging on to `www.AGItraining.com`.

A new conference has popped up in the Midwestern part of the USA in Council Bluffs, Iowa. To find out more about the Acrobat Central Conference log on to `www.pdfcentralconference.com`.

The Open Publish conference in Sydney, Australia, is an annual conference for design and creative professionals. This organization hosts many PDF-related seminars and workshops annually. Find out more at `www.openpublish.com.au`.

In Japan try out the PDF Conference held in Tokyo. Visit `www.pdfconf.gr.jp` for more information.

Whatever you may desire is usually found on some Web site. New sites are developed continually so be certain to make frequent searches.

Contacting Me

If, after reviewing this publication, you feel some important information was overlooked or you have any questions concerning Acrobat, you can contact me and let me know your views, opinions, hoorahs, or complaints, or provide information that might get included in the next revision. (If it's good enough, you might even get a credit line in the acknowledgments!) By all means, send me a note. Send your e-mail inquiries to `ted@west.net`.

Chances are that if you have a problem or question about Acrobat, you're not alone and many others might be interested in your question and a response to the question. Send your questions directly to my blog on Acrobat Users at: `www.acrobatusers.com/blogs/tedpadova`. In addition to my blog, some very talented friends who know so much more than I do also host blogs on Acrobat Users. Visit `www.acrobat users.com/blogs` to see a complete list of the blog hosts.

If you happen to have some problems with Acrobat, keep in mind that I didn't engineer the program. Inquiries for technical support should be directed to the software developer(s) of any products you use. This is one more good reason to complete your registration form.

There you have it — a short description of what follows. Don't wait. Turn the page and learn how Acrobat can help you gain more productivity with its amazing new features.

Acknowledgments

I would like to acknowledge some of the people who have contributed in one way or another to make this edition possible. Mike Roney, my former acquisitions editor at Wiley who started out this project with me, and later my acquisitions editor, Kim Spilker, who helped me finish the project; my project editor, Katharine Dvorak, who was my project editor on the first *Acrobat PDF Bible* I wrote and who I was very pleased to have back with this edition; copy editor, Nancy Rapoport; and editorial manager, Robyn Siesky; as well as the rest of the Wiley crew who participated in the project.

What can I say about my Technical Editor, Lori DeFurio? Lori is perhaps the single best advocate for Acrobat and PDF, promoter, and solutions provider to people worldwide than any other individual on the planet. With an incredibly demanding schedule that takes her to all corners of the earth, Lori finds time to review more than a thousand pages of text and can find things as small as a period out of place in a manuscript. As Adobe's premiere Acrobat and PDF authority, her technical expertise in reviewing this book was invaluable to me. Lori is always my first contact when I don't understand something about Acrobat. This is the fifth book Lori and I have worked on together and my Acrobat books are always that much better because of Lori's contributions.

Much appreciation and thanks also go to my friend and colleague Leonard Rosenthal of Adobe Systems, who always stands ready to provide me with advice and assistance. Leonard graciously jumped in to help Lori with some of the technical editing on the printing chapters, and his comments were very helpful. A special thank you is extended to my friend and another colleague, Thom Parker of Windjack Solutions (www.windjack.com), who graciously helped me with questions related to Acrobat JavaScript. Thom's company also provided copies of Windjack Solutions' AcroButtons and AcroDialogs Acrobat plug-ins for the book's CD-ROM.

I feel very fortunate in having so much support from many people at Adobe Systems who were continually available for comments, suggestions, and favors over a four-month period of time while Acrobat 8.0 was in development. The energy and enthusiasm of the engineering and marketing teams throughout the development period made it evident that this is a group of people with passion and excitement for their work. A hearty thank you is extended to Rick Brown, senior Acrobat Product Manager, for his support, telephone conversations, and offering a quote you see appearing on the cover of the book; David Stromfeld, Product Manager, who spent time with me in a number of phone conversations and e-mails; Dov Isaacs for his insight, valuable perspectives, straightforward and no-nonsense responses to questions, Ali Hanyalolu for his support and advice for promoting Acrobat for educators, Greg Pisocky for adding some pointers on Acrobat and accessibility, Macduff Hughes for helping Lori and me out with some PostScript related issues, Bill McCoy for information on the new Digital Editions interface, and many other Adobe employees in the engineering and marketing divisions who graciously offered feedback and advice during the development of the Acrobat 8 family of products.

I'd also like to thank Kurt Foss, editor of Acrobat Users Community; Pooja Goyal of Adobe Systems; my colleagues on Acrobat Users, Carl Young, Jo Lou Young, Duff Johnson, Dimitri Munkirs, and Patty-Bing-You for much support in keeping up-to-date information available on the Acrobat Users Community Web site and for their willingness to help when I needed it.

Acknowledgments

Additionally, I'd like to thank another friend and colleague, Robert Connolly of pdfPictures.com, and his client Aruba Bonbini for permissions to include the Aruba Bonbini eBrochure on the book's CD-ROM. And again, I would like to thank my good friend Lisle Gates for permitting me to use his photos in several layouts.

Introduction

This book is the fifth edition of *Acrobat PDF Bible*. As a result of feedback from many users, this edition is an effort to include coverage of some topics missed in the last version and to add additional material where users asked for more detail. As you will see by browsing the contents of the book or launching the new version of all the Acrobat viewers, including Adobe Reader, Adobe Acrobat Standard (Windows only), and Adobe Acrobat Professional, there are many changes in the programs. As such, I've made an effort to cover as much of the new version as is possible in this single, comprehensive book.

What Is Adobe Acrobat?

We've come a long way in Acrobat evolution, and those users of Adobe Acrobat are familiar with the distinctions between the Adobe Reader software and Adobe Acrobat (either Standard or Professional). However, among the many users of Adobe Reader, there still exists some confusion about what Reader can and cannot do. When acquiring Adobe Reader, many folks think the viewing of PDF documents with Adobe Reader is the extent of Acrobat. Now in version 8, Adobe Reader can do much more in terms of editing PDF documents. In addition to editing features, Acrobat Professional 8.0 now includes the much desired options for enabling PDFs with special features for Adobe Reader users for saving form data and adding digital signatures.

For those who don't know the difference, I explain in Chapter 2 that Adobe Reader is only one small component of Acrobat. Other programs included in the suite of Acrobat software provide you with tools for creating, editing, viewing, navigating, and searching Portable Document Format (PDF) information. Regardless of your familiarity with previous versions of Acrobat, you should carefully review Chapter 2. In Chapter 4, you'll find some details on all the new features added to Adobe Reader and how you can add to PDF documents some new Reader Extensions that enable the Adobe Reader user much more functionality than was available in all versions prior to version 8.

Acrobat has evolved with many different changes both to the features it offers you and often to the names associated with the various components. In earlier versions of Acrobat, names such as Acrobat Professional, Acrobat Exchange, and then simply Acrobat were used to refer to the authoring application. Version 8.0 of Adobe Acrobat, fortunately, continues with the same product names as found in Acrobat 7. The high-end performance application is referred to as Adobe Acrobat Professional. In release 8, as was the case in version 7, there is also a lighter Acrobat version with many of the same features found in Acrobat 5.x. The lighter version, also the same as was available in Acrobat 7, is called Adobe Acrobat Standard. Now in version 8 of Acrobat, Acrobat Standard has been discontinued on the Mac and appears only on Windows. This program has all the features you find available in Acrobat Professional with the exception of forms authoring, high-end printing and prepress, enabling documents with Adobe Reader extensions, and some differences in tools and menu commands. As you follow the pages in this book, you can apply most of what is contained herein to either Acrobat Standard or Acrobat Professional, with the exception of Chapters 19 and 32, and Part VI where I talk about forms.

One more product you can purchase from Adobe Systems in the Acrobat family is Adobe Acrobat Elements. Elements is a low-cost PDF-creation tool designed for enterprises, and it requires that you purchase a site license of a minimum of 1,000 copies. The Adobe Acrobat Reader software remains a free download from Adobe Systems and offers you many more features than found with previous versions of the Acrobat Reader software.

Nomenclature

The official name for the new release of the high-end Acrobat product is Adobe(r) Acrobat(r) 8.0 Professional. You'll notice the registered marks appearing in the name. For the sake of ease and clarity, as you read through the book and see a reference to Acrobat, Adobe Acrobat, and Acrobat Professional (also called Acrobat Pro), please realize that the reference is to Adobe Acrobat Professional. For the other authoring application, the official name is Adobe(r) Acrobat(r) Standard. When referring to this product I may use terms such as Acrobat Standard or simply Standard. Where it makes sense I'll say it like it is supposed to be used; otherwise, I'll use an abbreviated name.

The official name for the lighter version is Adobe Acrobat Elements, and the free downloadable software is Adobe Reader. Again, for the purposes of communication and ease, I may refer to the applications as Elements or Reader. Please realize, however, that the official name should prevail when you communicate in writing about these products.

For Windows users, Acrobat 8.0 Professional also ships with Adobe(r) LiveCycle(r) Designer 8.0. You may find references to this product stated as LiveCycle Designer, Designer, or LCD. All of these references are made to the Adobe LiveCycle Designer product used for authoring dynamic XML-based forms.

Why is this important? Adobe Systems, Inc., has spent much time, labor, and money on developing branding for their products. With the different changes to product names and the different components of the software, some people using the products don't completely understand the differences or where the product came from. An Adobe Reader installer can appear on CD-ROMs distributed legitimately by users, and some end users may not know that it is a product available for upgrading at the Adobe Systems, Inc., Web site. Therefore, using the formal name can help users understand a little bit more about the software.

And there's a very good reason for helping Adobe Systems with the recognition and marketing of its products. If the product doesn't do well in the marketplace, you might one day see it disappear. You won't want that to happen because when you start working with the new release, you'll easily see many great new features and much more polish added to the programs. Adobe Systems has done well in bringing the entire Acrobat family of products to maturity and I'm certain you'll find many more new uses for Acrobat.

Above all, realize that *Adobe* is not a product. Adobe or Adobe Systems is a company. Making a reference to Adobe when you mean Acrobat or Adobe Reader is improper and promotes confusion. When referring to the products, be certain to include Acrobat, Standard, or Reader.

Adobe Systems and the Acrobat mission

Adobe Systems, Inc. began as a company serving the graphic design and imaging markets. With the release of PostScript, its first product, much development in the early years of its history was devoted to imaging programs, font libraries, and tools to help service graphic design professionals. When you speak to graphic designers and advertising people, they connect Adobe Systems with products such as Adobe Photoshop, Adobe Illustrator, Adobe InDesign, Adobe Premiere, and so on. With some of these flagship programs having long histories and large installed user bases, some people may think that a product such as Adobe Acrobat takes a back seat to the high-end graphics and multimedia programs.

Where does Acrobat fit into Adobe's mission and view of its product line? Adobe Chairman and CEO Bruce Chizen has been quoted as saying that he expects the Acrobat family of products to weather economic storms in the software market. Acrobat is Adobe's fastest-growing product, experiencing between 40 to 60 percent growth in year-over-year sales. Chizen has also stated that more than 60 percent of Adobe's worldwide sales and marketing personnel are devoted to Acrobat-related products from the Acrobat 5 life cycle to the present.

Adobe sees Acrobat as an integral part of its future and is investing much energy into Acrobat's growth. With more than 750,000,000 installed users of the Adobe Reader software, Acrobat and the PDF file format are among the most popular software products available today.

Acrobat has become a standard in many different industries. In the publishing market many large newspaper chains, publishing houses, and book and magazine publishers have standardized on the PDF format for printing and prepress. The prepress industry has long adopted PDF as a standard for commercial and quick-print houses. Almost every software manufacturer includes last-minute notes, user manuals, and supporting information in PDF format on CD-ROM installer disks. The U.S. federal, state, and city governments and the U.S. government contractor organizations have standardized on PDF for everything from forms, applications, notices, and official documents to intra-office document exchanges.

With the introduction of the Acrobat 6 product line, Adobe Systems expanded existing markets and targeted new markets. The features in Acrobat 6 and 7 Professional appealed to all kinds of engineering professionals. With the support for layers and direct exports from programs such as Microsoft Visio and Autodesk AutoCAD, engineers, planners, and architects welcomed the new additions to Acrobat. Now in Acrobat 8, users of Acrobat Professional can convert AutoCAD .dwg drawings to PDF complete with layers and comments without having AutoCAD installed on a computer. Enterprises, in which document flows include different workgroups for almost any industry, welcomed additions to the comment and review tools in Acrobat Professional. Additional enabling usage rights for Adobe Reader users in Acrobat 8 are another great feature for knowledge workers. The already standardized prepress market applauded new features for printing to high-end imaging devices without the use of third-party plug-ins. Seamless integration of JDF job ticketing with Acrobat and Creative Suite is now available in Acrobat 8 and the CS applications 2.3 and greater for the creative pro market. All the great new features in Acrobat 6 and 7 have now been amplified in version 8, and you find additional support for users in almost every industry. New Redaction tools and Bates Numbering will be welcomed additions for the legal community. Also, concurrent to Acrobat development, the Acrobat 3D product is continuing to be expanded with new features to suit the manufacturing industry. The list keeps growing and Acrobat keeps improving.

PDF workflows

A workflow can mean different things to different people. One of the nice aspects of working with Acrobat is the development of a workflow environment. Quite simply, workflow solutions are intended to get out of a computer what the computer was designed for: productivity in a more automated and efficient fashion. Editing page by page and running manual tasks to change or modify documents could hardly be called workflow solutions. Workflows enable office or production workers a means of automating common tasks for maximum efficiency. Batch processing documents, running them through automated steps, and routing files through computer-assisted delivery systems are among workflow solutions.

Acrobat provides workflow solutions in almost every industry and new features added to Acrobat 8 add some polish to an already great product. But the real advance in workflow activity is the introduction of Acrobat Connect. Now, instead of having documents flow across wide area networks, people can connect through real-time online events. The introduction of Acrobat Connect will not only ease a tremendous financial burden saving companies huge expenses for employee travel, but increase productivity in workflows through dynamic interaction.

New Features in Adobe Acrobat Professional

The changes to Acrobat in version 8.0 represent many more expanded and new features to an already impressive product. Just about everything you could do in the last version is still available in version 8.0, but there have been many additions to existing features and some new options for a variety of Acrobat uses. The user interface has greatly changed over all previous versions of Acrobat, adding more tools and commands and features and much easier methods for accessing tools.

In each chapter I've added a special icon to point out new features. Some new chapters have been added to this version that deal exclusively or mostly with new features. Chapters 3, 12, 14, 19, and 29 cover new features in much detail. The remaining chapters all cover some new features added to Acrobat and respective to the chapter topic.

Part I

Welcome to Adobe Acrobat

Chapter 1

Getting to Know Adobe Acrobat

To start off this large book on Adobe Acrobat, let's first take a look at what Acrobat is and what PDF is, and let's try to get a grasp on some of the many options you have for working with PDF files in Acrobat.

What Is Adobe Acrobat?

Assuming you know little about Adobe Acrobat, I start with a brief description of what Acrobat is and what it is not. As I explain to people who ask about the product, I usually define it as the most misunderstood application available today. Most of us are familiar with the Adobe Reader software, which is a product from Adobe Systems Incorporated that you can download free from the Adobe Web site (www.adobe.com/acrobat/readermain.html). You can also acquire the Adobe Reader from all the installation CD-ROMs for other Adobe software. You can even acquire Adobe Reader from other sources, as long as the Adobe licensing requirements are distributed with the installer program. The Adobe Reader, however, is *not* Adobe Acrobat. Adobe Reader is a component of a much larger product family that has evolved through several iterations over more than a decade.

You're probably a little more sophisticated and realize there is a major difference between the applications noted previously and you may wonder why I even spend any time discussing the difference between Acrobat and Adobe Reader. Unfortunately, many people still believe that Adobe Acrobat is the free Adobe Reader program.

To add a little more confusion, Adobe continues to market several Acrobat products in the Acrobat family. While Adobe Reader remains a free download from Adobe Systems, there are three additional commercial viewers — Acrobat Standard, Acrobat Professional, and Acrobat 3D. With the release of Acrobat 8, Acrobat Standard is now offered only to Windows users, and has been dropped from the Macintosh version. As I talk about Adobe Acrobat in this chapter, and

3

throughout the book, I'm referring to Acrobat Professional for both Windows and Macintosh and Acrobat Standard for Windows users only. Where the two programs differ in features, I point them out. I also mention when a feature is only available in Acrobat Professional.

> **NOTE** There are distinctions between the Acrobat Standard product (Windows) and the Acrobat Professional product in terms of tools and commands. Most editing tasks can be handled in either viewer; however, Acrobat Professional does provide more editing features than Acrobat Standard. Throughout this book I delineate the differences and point out when an Acrobat Professional feature cannot be accomplished in Acrobat Standard.

Adobe Acrobat (either Standard or Professional) in version 8 is the upgrade from Adobe Acrobat 7 (Standard or Professional) and both viewers are the subject of the remaining chapters of this book. Acrobat is the authoring application that provides you tools and commands for a host of features outlined in the following chapters. If you haven't yet purchased a copy of Acrobat, either the Standard version (Windows only) or the Professional version (Windows and Macintosh), you might want to look over Chapter 2 and observe some of the comparisons between the viewers. If fewer tools and features suit your purpose, you might find the Standard version satisfactory — but remember, Acrobat Standard is available only on Windows in version 8. Although some of the features differ between the viewers, they both provide many features for editing, enhancing, printing, and working with PDF documents.

Acrobat is an authoring application but it has one little feature that distinguishes it from almost any other authoring program. Rather than starting from scratch and creating a new document in Acrobat, your workflow usually involves converting a document, created in just about any program, to a Portable Document Format (PDF) file. Once converted to PDF you use Acrobat to edit and refine the document, add bells and whistles and interactivity, or prepare it for professional printing. In addition to the Acrobat program, Acrobat Professional ships with companion programs such as Adobe Acrobat Distiller and Adobe Acrobat Catalog, and Adobe LiveCycle Designer (Windows only). Acrobat Standard ships only with Acrobat Distiller. These companion products are used to convert PostScript files to PDF, create search indexes, and author XML-based forms.

> **CROSS-REF** For information related to Acrobat Distiller see Chapter 10. For more information on Acrobat Catalog, see Chapter 6. For more information related to LiveCycle Designer, see Chapter 35.

Acrobat solutions are greatly extended with other supporting programs from Adobe Systems and many different third-party vendors. If Acrobat can't do the job, chances are you can find a plug-in or companion program to handle all you want to do with a PDF file.

> **CROSS-REF** For information related to Acrobat plug-ins and companion products see Chapter 2.

What Is PDF?

PDF, short for *Portable Document Format*, was developed by Adobe Systems as a unique format to be viewed through Acrobat viewers. As the name implies, it is portable, which means the file you create on one computer can be viewed with an Acrobat viewer on other computers, handheld devices, and on other platforms. For example, you can create a page layout on a Macintosh computer and convert it to a PDF file. After the conversion, this PDF document can be viewed on a Linux or Windows machine.

Multiplatform compliance (to enable the exchange of files across different computers, for example) is one of the great values of PDF documents.

So what's special about PDF and its multiplatform compliance? It's not so much an issue of viewing a page on one computer created from another computer that is impressive about PDF. After all, such popular programs as Microsoft Excel, Microsoft Word, Adobe Photoshop, Adobe InDesign, Adobe FrameMaker, and Adobe Illustrator all have counterparts for multiplatform usage. You can create a layout on one computer system and view the file on another system with the same software installed. For example, if you have Adobe InDesign installed on a Macintosh computer and you create an InDesign document, that same file can be viewed on a PC with InDesign running under Windows.

In a perfect world, you may think the capability to view documents across platforms is not so special. Document viewing, however, is secondary to document integrity. The preservation of the contents of a page is what makes the PDF so extraordinary. To illustrate, suppose you have an InDesign document created in Windows using fonts generic to Windows applications. After it's converted to PDF, the document, complete with graphics and fonts intact, can be displayed and printed on other computer platforms. And the other computer platforms don't need the fonts, graphics, or original authoring application to print the file with complete integrity.

This level of document integrity can come in handy in business environments, where software purchases often reach quantum costs. PDF documents eliminate the need to install all applications used within a particular company on all the computers in that company. For example, art department employees can use a layout application to create display ads and then convert them to PDF so that other departments can use the free Adobe Reader software to view and print those ads for approval.

The benefits of PDF viewing were initially recognized by workgroups in local office environments for electronic paper exchanges. Today users have much more opportunity for global exchange of documents in many different ways. As you look at Acrobat and discover some of the features available for document comment and markup, comparing documents, support for layered files (which adds much more functionality to Adobe Reader), and preparing PDFs for screen readers, you'll see how Acrobat and the PDF have evolved with new technologies.

CROSS-REF The term "screen reader" is used extensively throughout this book. When you see a reference to "screen reader," I'm referring to either a hardware device or special software (JAWS, Kurzweil, and so on) used to convert visual information to audio format. For more information on screen readers and making documents accessible to the readers, see Chapter 25.

Document repurposing

The computer revolution has left extraordinary volumes of data that were originally designed to be printed on paper on computer systems. Going all the way back to UNIVAC, the number crunching was handled by the computer and the expression was the printed piece. Today, forms of expression have evolved to many different media. No longer do people want to confine themselves to printed material. Now, in addition to publishing information on paper, we use CD-ROMs, the Internet, file exchanges, and meeting sessions via the Internet between computers. Sometimes we use motion video, television, and satellite broadcasts. As high-speed access evolves, we'll see much larger bandwidths, so real-time communication will eventually become commonplace.

Technology will advance, bringing many improvements to bandwidth, performance, and speed. To enable the public to access the mountains of digital data held on computer systems in a true information superhighway world, files need to be converted to a common format. A common file format would also enable new documents to be more easily *repurposed*, to exploit the many forms of communication that we use today and expect to use tomorrow.

Acrobat Professional has added more tools for helping users repurpose documents. Tools for repairing problem files, downsizing file sizes, porting files to a range of different devices, and eliminating unnecessary data are part of the many features found in Acrobat Professional. In addition, the new PDF/A format available in Acrobat 8 is designed specifically for archiving documents. A standards committee has developed this format so documents viewed on computer systems 100 years from now will be compatible with future operating systems.

PDF and Adobe PostScript

The de facto standard for nearly all printing in the graphics industry has been Adobe PostScript. While PostScript is still the dominant printing language, this will slowly change because Adobe has recently announced support for PDF as the new print standard.

Okay, so how does PostScript relate to PDF? In the initial release of Acrobat, all PDF conversion began with a file that was created as a PostScript file. Users selected the Print command in an authoring program and printed the file to disk — thus creating a PostScript file. This file was then opened in the Acrobat Distiller program and Distiller converted the PostScript to a PDF.

Distiller is still a part of Acrobat. In some cases, creating a PDF from a PostScript file rather than through any of the many other means available may be preferable. It could be that you have a problem with exporting to PDF from a program, such as fonts not appearing embedded, or you may need to create a PDF for a special purpose such as printing and prepress. In such circumstances using Acrobat Distiller may be your best solution for generating a PDF document to properly suit the purpose.

CROSS-REF   **For information related to printing PostScript files and using Acrobat Distiller see Chapter 10.**

Printing to PostScript and opening PostScript files in Distiller is used much less today because now so many programs support PDF creation through one-button clicks or using the Save As command. However, many of these one-button clicks still use the Distiller application in the background to create the PDF file. You may not see Distiller launched when PDFs are created in the background, but the program is working away to convert your authoring application document to a PDF file.

PostScript can be a problem solver for you, and you may have an occasional need to use it even if your workflow does not require its use all the time. The more you know about PostScript and Acrobat Distiller, the more often you might be able to rescue problem files that don't seem to properly convert to PDF.

PDF versions

Acrobat is now in version 8. The version number indicates the number of releases of the product. PDF is a file format and with it you'll also find a version number. The PDF version relates to the specifications of the file format; for the end user it's usually not so important to understand all the specifications as much as it is to know what it does for you or what you can expect from it. If you create PDF documents for users of older Acrobat viewers and use the newer PDF format, your users may not be able to view your PDF files. Conversely, creating PDF files with the older version might prohibit you from using some newer features in the recent release.

PDF versions are typically referred to as Acrobat Compatibility. A PDF version 1.7 file, for example, is an Acrobat 8 compatible file. To understand how the PDF version relates to the Acrobat version, simply add the digits of the PDF version together. For example, PDF version 1.4 is Acrobat 5–compatible (1 + 4 = 5). PDF version 1.5 is Acrobat 6–compatible, and so on.

Each PDF version provides support for additional features. It's not as important to know all the features enabled by one version as it is to know which PDF version you need to use. For example, to optimize a PDF file for printing, you may need to use PDF version 1.3 (Acrobat 4–compatible). Or, if you want to embed movie files in a PDF, then you need to use an Acrobat 6–compatible file (PDF version 1.5). Or, you may want to add password security to a PDF that requires a newer Acrobat viewer to open a file using a password.

Rather than try to remember a long list of compatible features, you are generally informed when one PDF version is needed over another as you work through editing PDFs in Acrobat. In addition, when you know your user audience and the version of Adobe Reader or Acrobat that users have installed on computers, you'll know which Acrobat-compatible version of a PDF to create.

Understanding PDF Standards

PDF has been adopted as a standard file format in many industries, including engineering, legal, manufacturing, and prepress and printing. Even the United States Federal Government, has embraced PDF as a standard file format.

So what are *standards*? Without regulation and approved standards, the computer industry would be chaotic. Fortunately, an international committee known as the International Organization for Standardization (ISO) develops and approves standards for the technical industry. This international committee, an entity apart from Adobe Systems, has approved and developed substandards of the PDF format.

The PDF standards available now include the following:

- **PDF/X.** This standard is a subset of the PDF format used in the printing industry. PDFs meeting PDF/X compliance are typically reliable and, theoretically, can be accurately printed on almost any kind of PostScript device.

- **PDF/E.** This standard is a subset of the PDF format designed for engineers to insure that industrial designs and drawings comply with a PDF standard.

- **PDF/A.** This standard is a subset of the PDF format used for archiving documents. The standards committee wants to insure that the files you create today and save as PDF can be viewed by computers many years in the future. To do so, the PDFs you create for archival purposes can be saved as PDF/A documents.

- **PDF/UA.** Although, as of this writing, this subset of the PDF format is in an early draft stage, you may be hearing more about it in the near future — about one to two years from this writing. The goal of this proposed new standard is to provide universal access (UA) to all users including those persons working with assistive devices (see Chapter 25 for more on PDFs and assistive devices). The proposed new format is in the hands of the AIIMS Standards Board Committee that also proposed the PDF/X and PDF/A standards and submitted them to the ISO. People interested in participating on the committee can find more information at www.aiim.org/standards .asp?ID=27861.

Looking at the New User Interface

If you're an Acrobat user, the first thing you'll notice when you launch Adobe Acrobat 8 or Adobe Reader 8 is a new appearance for the user interface (UI). Many changes have been made to the Acrobat window, some

of which you may like and others you may not. I'll explain more about the user interface in later chapters where I discuss tools and viewing PDF documents. For now, let me share the reasons why Adobe has made the current significant changes to Acrobat 8.

Adobe Systems is a company committed to user feedback and responding to user needs. Most often, we find changes being made in Acrobat, and all of Adobe's products, as the result of a demand by a significant number of users. For instance, you might wonder why a great feature is removed from one version of the product. The answer may simply be that a number of IT managers were struggling with a security loophole caused by the feature.

The change in Acrobat's user interface was made because of a large demand by enterprise users who want Acrobat to appear similar to other programs used, such as the Office products and Web browsers. You may not agree, but Adobe can only respond to the majority and the majority is asking for something similar to the look and feel of the current release.

Such changes require all of us to become familiar with some new ways to move around a document and become familiar with the way your documents appear in an Acrobat window. As you can see in Figure 1.1, the Acrobat workplace has changed appearance. For those familiar with earlier versions of Acrobat, you'll notice some obvious changes in the user interface.

FIGURE 1.1

The new Acrobat 8 user interface

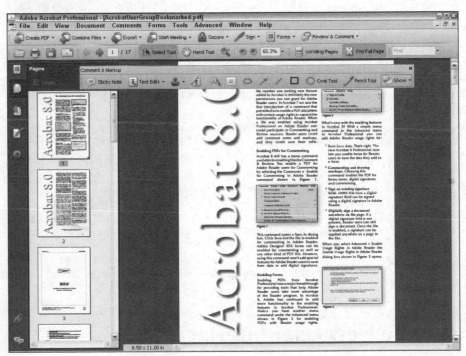

- **Color Scheme.** The Acrobat window has changed color because many users want to have more emphasis on the document page and less on the Acrobat workspace. The contrast in color between the background Document pane color emphasizes document pages more when the pages are white. White is the most common page color used by most users.

- **Elimination of the Status Bar.** You'll notice immediately that the familiar Status bar in Acrobat 8 is now absent. This decision was made to provide more viewing area for document pages. If you like having tools previously found in the Status bar in view, don't worry. I'll explain how to create a Status bar look in Chapter 5.

- **Icons in the Navigation pane.** Another obvious change in the user interface is the appearance of icons in the Navigation pane at the far left side of the Acrobat window. Again, this change was made to provide users more space in a crowded window. In earlier versions of Acrobat, we saw names for the Navigation panels, such as Bookmarks, Pages, Security, Comments, Attachments, and so on. These names took up quite a bit of real estate especially if you loaded a number of additional Navigation panels made available by selecting View ➪ Navigation Panels and selecting a panel from the submenu. After dragging a panel to the Navigation pane, the panels quickly begin to crowd the available space. By using icons, you can easily store more individual panels in the Navigation pane.

TIP If you want to begin to associate the icons with the Navigation panel names, just open the View ➪ Navigation Panels menu. All the Navigation panels are listed by icon and name, including the default Navigation panels you see when you first launch Adobe Acrobat.

- **Document windows with toolbars.** This user interface change was again made because of strong demand from users who wanted Acrobat to appear similar to other Windows and Macintosh programs. Although the view departs from Adobe's Creative Suite programs, Adobe found more users of Acrobat working in Microsoft Office and Internet Web browsers. Separate document windows with toolbars associated with each window was the demand and Adobe responded. You can choose in a preference setting whether to view PDF documents with or without toolbars attached to each document.

CROSS-REF Additional UI changes are discussed later in Chapter 5, along with some workarounds if you happen to prefer the old Acrobat viewer look.

Acrobat Environment

Acrobat provides you with features such as menu commands, toolbars, and palettes to accomplish work for whatever goal you hope to achieve with PDF documents. When you launch the program you see many of these features in the Acrobat window. Just so you know what is being referred to when I discuss accessing a feature in Acrobat, take a look at Figure 1.2 to understand the names used to describe the various areas of the new Acrobat workplace.

A **Title bar.** By default, the name of the file you open appears in the title bar. The title appearing in the title bar can change according to an option for displaying the Document Title in the Initial View properties.

CROSS-REF For information related to Initial View and displaying Document Titles, see Chapter 4.

B **Menu bar.** The menu bar contains all the top-level menu commands. These menu choices are also available from various actions associated with links and form fields when you choose the Execute a menu item command in the Actions Properties dialog box for links, form fields, and other features that permit associating an action with a command. When viewing files showing toolbars and menus for each open document, the Acrobat window appears as shown in Figure 1.2. This view can be toggled off in a preference setting.

FIGURE 1.2

The Acrobat Professional workplace contains menus, toolbars, and palettes.

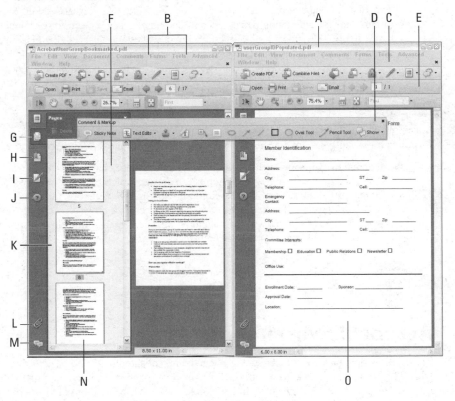

CROSS-REF For information related to link actions and the Execute a menu item command action type, see Chapter 22. For more information on actions with form fields, see Part VI. For making preference choices for viewing PDFs, see "Customizing the Acrobat Workplace" later in this chapter.

C **Toolbars.** A number of individual toolbars are nested below the menu bar. When preferences are set to view toolbars attached to each open document, you'll see multiple sets of toolbars. Toolbars are marked with a vertical separator bar at the left side of the toolbar. This bar can be selected and dragged to move it out of the Toolbar Well.

CROSS-REF For information related to working with toolbars, see the "Tools and toolbars" section later in this chapter.

D **Floating toolbar.** Toolbars can be opened by accessing the More Tools drop-down menu and selecting a toolbar name. When a toolbar is opened, it appears as a floating toolbar. Floating toolbars can be *docked* in the Toolbar Well.

E **Toolbar Well.** The Toolbar Well houses the toolbars. You can drag toolbars away from the Toolbar Well or add other toolbars and expand the Toolbar Well to house your new additions. When you drag a toolbar away from the Toolbar Well, the toolbar is "undocked" and becomes a floating toolbar. When you drag a floating toolbar and drop it in the Toolbar Well, the toolbar becomes "docked."

F **Palette pull-down menu.** Individual panels can be tucked away in the Navigation pane (see Navigation pane later in this list) or appear anywhere in the Acrobat window. Each palette contains its own menus accessible by clicking the down-pointing arrow. These menus are referred to as palette pull-down menus in all subsequent chapters.

G **Pages panel.** When you open the Pages panel, you'll see thumbnail images of each page in your document and you'll find many page-editing features available to you from the Pages panel palette pull-down menu.

CROSS-REF For information related to using the many options available in the Pages panel, see Chapter 16.

H **Bookmarks panel.** The second default panel appearing in the Navigation pane is the Bookmarks panel. If bookmarks are contained in the PDF document, they appear in the palette when the palette is open.

CROSS-REF For information related to creating bookmarks from authoring programs, see Chapter 9. For information related to creating and managing bookmarks in Acrobat, see Chapter 22.

I **Signatures panel.** If digital signatures are included in your PDF document, they can be viewed in the Signatures panel.

CROSS-REF For information related to digital signatures, see Chapter 26.

J **How To.** The How To pane has been moved in Acrobat 8 to the Navigation pane. In Acrobat 7, this pane appeared on the right side of the document window. The How To pane contains some help information related to many common PDF editing tasks. Users of previous versions of Acrobat will notice the How To pane has replaced the default appearance of the Layers pane.

K **Page thumbnails.** When the Pages panel is opened, page thumbnails of all the document pages appear within the Pages panel.

L   **Attachments.** The Attachments pane is used to show all file attachments in a document.

CROSS-REF To learn how to use file attachments, see Chapter 12.

M   **Comments panel.** When you open the Comments panel, the display of comments and reviews is shown horizontally at the bottom of the Acrobat window.

CROSS-REF To learn how to use the Comments panel options, see Chapter 20.

N   **Navigation pane.** The Navigation pane can be expanded or collapsed. The view in Figure 1.1 is an expanded view where the Bookmarks panel is the active pane. To open the Navigation pane you can click a panel to display the respective information associated with that panel in the expanded palette window. Clicking again on the panel collapses the view. You can also use the keyboard shortcut F4 to expand and collapse the Navigation pane.

O   **Document pane.** The Document pane is the container for PDF files you see in Acrobat. When no file is open, the Document pane is empty. When you open a PDF document, the document appears in the Document pane.

For more detail on specific menu commands, tools, and palettes, see the related chapters to discover the different options available to you. All of the items discussed here are explained in more depth in subsequent chapters.

Menus

As with any program operating on a computer system that supports a Windows type of environment, you'll notice menu commands at the top level of the Acrobat window. Users of previous versions will notice that Acrobat 8 features an additional menu that contains commands specific to creating PDF forms. If at first glance you don't see an option you used in Acrobat 7, poke around the menus. None of the Acrobat 7 features have been eliminated; they may just be in a different place or referred to by a different name.

File menu

The File menu is where you open and close documents, create PDF files, import and export certain data, access print commands, and find some other nifty new additions in Acrobat. The Mac and Windows operating systems display recent files in different menus. On the Mac in OS X you'll find recently viewed documents by choosing File ➪ Open Recent File. This command opens a submenu where you can access recent documents. On Windows, a list of the recently viewed documents is located at the bottom of the File menu, as shown in Figure 1.3.

CROSS-REF Note that a new menu command, Start Meeting, appears in the File menu. This command gets you started with Adobe Breeze as I explain in Chapter 29.

FIGURE 1.3

Recently opened files in Windows appear at the bottom of the File menu. Macintosh users can display a list of recently viewed files by choosing File ⇨ Open Recent File.

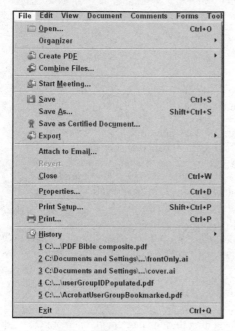

Edit menu

As shown in Figure 1.4, the traditional Cut, Copy, and Paste commands are located in the Edit menu along with other familiar commands from Acrobat 7. There are no changes to the Edit menu from Acrobat 7.

FIGURE 1.4

The Edit menu contains the same commands found in Acrobat 7.

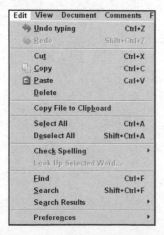

View menu

The View menu (see Figure 1.5) contains all the commands you'll use for viewing PDF documents. An addition to the View menu is the Reading Mode command. This command dismisses the Navigation pane and appears similar to the display you see when reading articles. The Wireframe command has changed to Line Weights you see at the bottom of the menu.

CROSS-REF For more information on using Reading Mode, see Chapter 5.

Document menu

The Document menu (see Figure 1.6) contains a collection of commands specific to document handling. Options in the Document menu have a few changes in Acrobat 8 compared to the options in Acrobat 7. Notice a new command — Enable Features in Adobe Reader, which appears in addition to Enable for Commenting and Analysis found in Acrobat 7 and used to enable PDFs for commenting in Reader. This new command now enables you to add both commenting and saving from data in Adobe Reader. The Paper Capture command has changed names to Scan to PDF and a new command exists for optimizing scanned PDF files. The OCR feature in Acrobat remains the same and is all available in the Text Recognition submenu. In addition to these new commands, we find the Examine Document command and Manage embedded index appearing in Acrobat 8.

CROSS-REF For information related to enabling PDFs for form data saving, see Chapter 19 where all the enabling features are discussed. For more information on examining documents, take a look at Chapter 19. For more information on embedding index files, look to Chapter 6 where I talk about search indexes and searching PDF files.

FIGURE 1.5

The View menu contains commands for viewing PDF documents and navigating through pages and different PDF files.

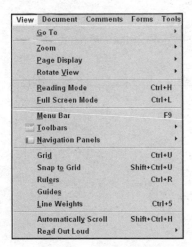

FIGURE 1.6

The Document menu reflects several changes in Acrobat 8.

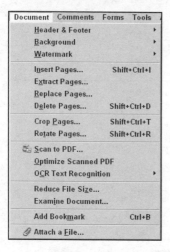

Comments menu

Some new menu commands in the Comments menu shown in Figure 1.7 include Send for Shared Review, Upload for Browser-Based Review, Search for Additional Services, and a number of different export commands for exporting comments to MS Word, AutoCAD, and to a data file.

CROSS-REF For details on working with comment reviews, see Chapter 21. For import/export commands and all other commenting features, see Chapter 20.

FIGURE 1.7

The Comments menu offers commands specific to review and markups.

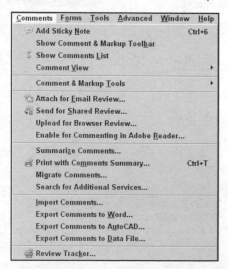

Forms menu

The Forms menu shown in Figure 1.8 is new to Acrobat 8. Here you'll find a number of different commands all used for working with PDF forms and Adobe Designer XML forms (Windows).

NEW FEATURE The new Run Form Field Recognition command is not only a special treat for forms designers, but it's one of the best new features added to Acrobat 8.

FIGURE 1.8

The Forms menu, new in Acrobat 8, contains commands specifically for working with forms.

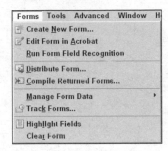

CROSS-REF For working with Acrobat PDF forms, see Chapters 33 and 34. For understanding more about Adobe Designer and XML forms (Windows only), see Chapter 35.

Tools menu

The Tools menu (see Figure 1.9) in Acrobat logically places access to many editing tools in a single convenient menu. You can access certain tools from the Acrobat toolbars (explained in the section "Tools and toolbars" later in this chapter) or you can use a context menu to access toolbars from the Acrobat Toolbar Well.

FIGURE 1.9

The Tools menu contains a collection of tools accessed from submenus. Select a tool group from the menu options to open a submenu.

Advanced menu

The Advanced menu (see Figure 1.10) contains a collection of menu commands considered to be advanced Acrobat features. A few of these tools are not available to users of Acrobat Standard such as Batch Processing, the new Redaction tools in Acrobat 8 Professional, and access to Acrobat Catalog. A few changes

have been made in this menu in Acrobat. You'll notice the Security commands have changed a bit and a new command exists for enabling PDFs with Adobe Reader usage rights. Also notice the Document Processing menu command. From the submenu you find many command that were positioned directly under the Advanced command such as Batch Processing, And JavaScript commands.

CROSS-REF For more information on using the Redaction tools, see Chapter 14.

FIGURE 1.10

The Advanced menu offers menu commands related to advanced editing features.

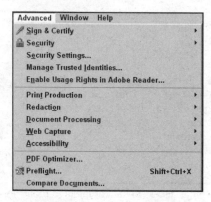

CROSS-REF For information related to Batch Processing, see Chapters 18 and 36. For information on using Acrobat Catalog, see Chapter 6. For information on using all the security commands see Chapter 26. For information on enabling PDFs with Adobe Reader usage rights, see Chapter 19.

Window menu

The Window menu (see Figure 1.11) provides menu commands to assist you in viewing documents.

FIGURE 1.11

The Window menu handles all the window views such as tiling, cascading, and splitting windows.

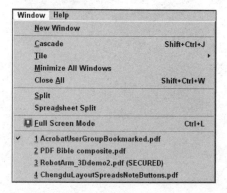

CROSS-REF For information related to window views and the split window views, see Chapter 5.

Help menu

The traditional help files added to your Acrobat folder at installation are found in the Help menu (see Figure 1.12). Various online help support is also located in this menu. You'll note that the Detect and Repair command found in earlier versions of Acrobat has changed to Repair Acrobat Installation.

CROSS-REF For information related to Help documents and Help menus, see the "Accessing Help" section later in this chapter.

Submenus

An extensive number of submenus appear in menus contained in the top-level menu bar and from many different tools contained in toolbars. Note that on individual toolbars you see a down-pointing arrow. Clicking the arrow opens a menu; some menus contain submenus. A submenu is denoted in Acrobat by a right-pointing arrow on the right side of a given menu command as shown in Figure 1.13. Select a command with one of these arrows adjacent to the command name and a submenu opens. In a few cases, you can find nested submenus where another right-pointing arrow may be visible in a submenu. If you want to access the second submenu, move the cursor to the menu option containing a right-pointing arrow. To make a selection from a submenu command, move the cursor to the desired menu command. When the menu command highlights, click the mouse button to execute the command.

FIGURE 1.12

The Help menu gives you access to Help information on selected topics as well as access to the complete Acrobat Help document.

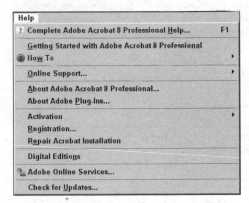

FIGURE 1.13

To access a submenu, move the cursor to the command containing a right-pointing arrow and slide the cursor over to the submenu options. Click the desired command in the submenu to execute the command.

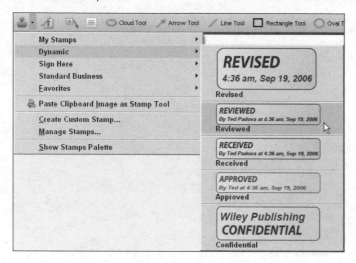

Context menus

Wherever you are in the Acrobat window—the toolbars, palettes, Document pane, or the Help menus—you can gain quick access to menu items related to your task by opening a context menu. Context menus pop up in an area where you either click the right button on the mouse or use an appropriate key modifier. In Windows, right-click the mouse button to open a context menu. On a Macintosh, when not using a two-button mouse, press the Control key and click the mouse button. Context menu options relate to the particular tool you have selected from a toolbar. By default the Hand tool is selected when you launch Acrobat and open a PDF document. When you right-click the mouse button (Windows) or Ctrl+click (Macintosh), a context menu pops up where you click the mouse as shown in Figure 1.14.

FIGURE 1.14

With the Hand tool selected, right-clicking (Windows) or Ctrl+clicking (Macintosh) the mouse button opens a context menu. From the menu, scroll the list and select the desired menu command.

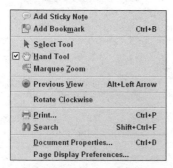

If you change tools in a toolbar and open a context menu, the menu options change to reflect choices with that particular tool. Likewise, a context menu opened on a palette offers menu options respective to the palette, as shown in Figure 1.15.

FIGURE 1.15

When a palette is open in the Navigation pane and you open a context menu, the menu options reflect tasks you can perform respective to the panel.

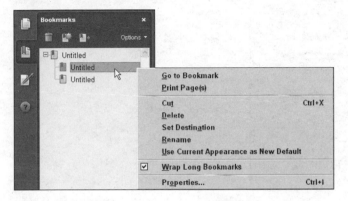

> **TIP** Opening a context menu on one of the icons in the Navigation pane opens a menu where you can add or remove panels from the pane. Additionally, you can hide the Navigation panel icons by opening a context menu in the Navigation pane and select Hide Navigation Pane Buttons. To bring back the Navigation Pane Buttons, press F4 on your keyboard or select View ➪ Navigation Panels ➪ Show Navigation Pane.

Context menus are a great benefit during your Acrobat sessions and using them helps you work much faster. Throughout this book I often make references to the different choices you have in selecting a tool or command. In most incidences, you find mention of context menus. Be certain you know how to open a context menu in Acrobat on your computer. For the remainder of this book, I'll mention opening context menus without walking through the steps for how to open the menu.

Keyboard shortcuts

Pressing one or more keys on your keyboard can also open menus and invoke different commands. When you become familiar with keyboard shortcuts that perform the same function as when using a menu or context menu, you'll find yourself favoring this method for making different menu selections or grabbing a tool from a toolbar. Fortunately, you can learn as you work when it comes to memorizing keyboard shortcuts. As I'm certain you know, several shortcut combinations are noted in menu commands. You can learn these shortcuts when you frequently use a particular command. However, the keyboard shortcuts you see in the menu commands are just a fraction of what is available in Acrobat for quick access to commands and tools. For a complete list of all keyboard shortcuts, look over the Complete Acrobat help document you open by selecting Help ➪ Complete Acrobat 8.0 Help.

> **NOTE** Pressing a single key to access a tool requires you to have your Preferences set to accept single keystroke shortcuts. See the steps for "Setting up the Acrobat environment" later in this chapter for the proper Preferences settings.

Tools, task buttons, and toolbars

Tools are grouped together in separate toolbars in the Toolbar Well below the menu bar. The default view when you launch Acrobat contains several toolbars visible in the Toolbar Well. You can remove various toolbars from the Well, move them around the Acrobat window, close them, and add different toolbars to the Toolbar Well.

NEW FEATURE **In addition to loading and unloading toolbars, a new feature in Acrobat 8 permits you to add or remove individual tools from any toolbar. Before you learn how to add and remove individual tools, let's first take a look at the Toolbar Well.**

The Toolbar Well, where the toolbars are contained, is collapsed and expanded according to the number of toolbars you add to it. When a toolbar is contained within the Toolbar Well, it is said to be *docked*. When a toolbar is dragged away from the Toolbar Well and rests atop the Acrobat window, it is said to be *undocked* and appears as a *floating* toolbar.

Task buttons

One of the many different toolbars in Acrobat is called the Tasks toolbar. This toolbar houses various Task buttons. In Figure 1.16 the tasks toolbar is shown with the label descriptions to describe each tool's purpose. Task buttons differ a little from other tools in that they all support pull-down menus where menu commands related to specific tasks are addressed.

FIGURE 1.16

The Tasks toolbar contains several Task buttons all containing pull-down menus.

The Tasks toolbar features commands for creating PDFs, working with comments and reviews, exporting PDFs to different formats, securing PDFs, working with forms, and digitally signing PDFs. The Tasks toolbar also features the new Task button containing commands for engaging in Acrobat Connect meetings. You'll find all these features covered in many of the following chapters.

Loading and unloading tools

The default tools you see in the Toolbar Well when you first open Acrobat is but a mere fraction of all the tools available to you. Fortunately in Acrobat 8, a nifty new window has been added to the program to help you easily manage tools.

It's important to realize that you have toolbars and tools. Tools appear as individual icons contained in a given toolbar. You can choose to show only one tool in a toolbar or all the tools that belong to a given toolbar and anything in between. The tools within toolbars can be added and deleted from the parent toolbar.

If you're familiar with earlier versions of Acrobat and you don't find tools loaded in the various toolbars, your first stop is to open the More Tools menu at the top right corner of your screen. Select More Tools from a context menu opened on the Toolbar Well and the More Tools window opens as shown in Figure 1.17.

FIGURE 1.17

Open the More Tools window to show/hide tools in toolbars.

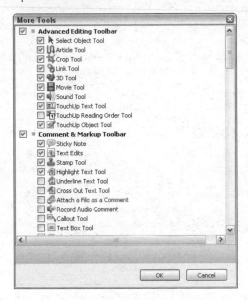

Place a check mark beside any tool to be shown in a toolbar docked in the Toolbar Well or opened as a floating toolbar. Figure 1.17 shows you a small portion of available tools that appear in a scrollable window.

NOTE Toolbars themselves can be shown or hidden using the More Tools window. If you remove a check mark adjacent to a toolbar name to hide the toolbar, the toolbar and all the tools are hidden, even if the individual tools are all checked.

Yet another way to add and remove tools to and from toolbars is to simply open a context menu on a toolbar. Right-click (Windows) or Ctrl+click (Macintosh) on a toolbar either docked in the Toolbar Well or as a floating toolbar and a pop-up menu provides options for adding or removing tools to/from that toolbar group.

In Figure 1.18 a context menu is opened on the Edit toolbar. When Show/Hide Tools is selected a submenu displays all toolbars. Select an item unchecked to open the respective toolbar or select a checked toolbar to remove hide it. Note that hiding a toolbar is temporary and only hides the toolbar from view in the Toolbar Well.

FIGURE 1.18

Open a context menu on a toolbar and select Show/Hide Toolbars to open a submenu where all toolbars can be opened or temporarily closed.

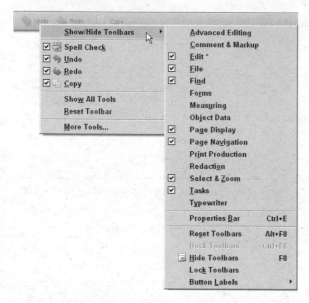

 If you want all tools within a given toolbar to be shown, select Show All Tools in the context menu.

The Show/Hide menu command in the context menu shown in Figure 1.18 provides the same commands you have available in the View ➪ Toolbars submenu. Either of these menus provides you a quick and easy way to show and hide toolbars.

The last menu item in the context menu shown in Figure 1.18 is used to open the More Tools window where you can add/remove tools among all toolbars.

Default toolbars

When you launch Acrobat for the first time or you set the toolbars to the default view, six different toolbars are docked in the Toolbar Well, including the Tasks toolbar discussed earlier in this section. The remaining default toolbars include:

■ **File toolbar.** These tools are used for general document handling. The default File tools activate commands for Open, Save, Print, and Email. When all the tools are loaded in the File toolbar the Create PDF from web page and Attach a File tools are added to the toolbar. In Figure 1.19 the default File toolbar appears on the left and the expanded File toolbar showing all tools appears on the right.

The File toolbar contains tools for document handling, such as opening PDF documents, saving documents, and printing files.

■ **Page Navigation toolbar.** The default tools in the Page Navigation toolbar shown on the left in Figure 1.20 contain tools for moving back and forth between PDF document pages. The numbers indicate what page you are currently viewing out of the total number of pages in the document. When the toolbar is expanded to show all tools as you see on the right in Figure 1.20, the First Page, Last Page, Previous View, and Next View tools are shown.

The Page Navigation toolbar, as the name implies, contains tools for navigating document pages.

■ **Page Display toolbar.** The Page Display toolbar is the home of many different tools used for page viewing, but only two of the tools appear in the default toolbar as shown in Figure 1.21 on the left. When you first open Acrobat, you see the Scrolling Pages and One Full Page tool. After expanding the toolbar to show all tools as shown on the right in Figure 1.21, the Single Page Continuous, Single Page, Two-Up, Two-Up Continuous, Full Screen Mode, Rotate Counterclockwise, Rotate Clockwise, and Line Weights tools are shown. Users of earlier versions of Acrobat will note that the tool names for Single Page, Continuous, Continuous – Facing, and Facing Pages have changed names to Single Page, Single page Continuous, Two-Up Continuous, and Two-Up respectively. In addition, these four tools previously appeared in a Status bar at the bottom of the Acrobat window in earlier versions of Acrobat. In Acrobat 8, the Status bar has been eliminated and all tools appear at the top of the Acrobat window.

The Page Display toolbar contains many tools used for page viewing.

■ **Select & Zoom toolbar.** The tools in this group are used to select text/images, move the page in the Document pane, and zoom in and out of pages in the Document pane. The left side of Figure 1.22 shows the Select tool followed by the Hand tool then the Zoom Out, Zoom In, and Zoom Value tools. When all tools are loaded the Actual Size, Fit Width, Fit Page, Pan & Zoom Window, Loupe tool, and Snapshot tool appear as shown in Figure 1.22 on the right.

FIGURE 1.22

Select & Zoom tools are used to select text/images, move a document around the Document pane, copy selections, and view the document page using a number of different zoom tools.

- **Find toolbar.** Of all the default toolbars, the Find toolbar shown in Figure 1.23 is the only one that does not have additional tools that can be added to the toolbar. However, a pull-down menu exists for making choices to refine your search for words in an open PDF document.

 For more information on searching PDFs, see Chapter 6.

FIGURE 1.23

The Find toolbar is used for searching words in a PDF document.

Managing default toolbars

In addition to loading and unloading tools within toolbars, the toolbars can be moved, docked, and undocked from the Toolbar Well. Here's a list of some of the things you can do with the default toolbars and any other toolbars you decide to view:

- **Undocking toolbars.** Toolbars can be relocated from within the Toolbar Well to another area within the Acrobat window. For example, you might find it more convenient to move a toolbar you frequently access during an editing session so it is positioned at the bottom of the Document pane. If so, just place the cursor on top of the vertical separator bar adjacent to the first tool in a toolbar and drag it away from the Toolbar Well. This vertical line is the *hot spot* used to select the toolbar instead of a tool in the group. Clicking anywhere else in the toolbar selects a tool.

- **Docking toolbars.** To dock a toolbar back in the Toolbar Well once removed, drag the toolbar, again by the vertical separator bar adjacent to the first tool, on top of the Toolbar Well. The toolbar snaps to an available position in the Well. If you drop the toolbar between two other toolbars, the toolbar you relocate back to the Toolbar Well snaps in position between the two docked toolbars.

  Toolbars can also be docked vertically on the left and right sides of the Document pane and at the bottom of the Acrobat window below the status bar. For example, if you drag a toolbar to the left of the Navigation pane and release the mouse button, the toolbar snaps to a docking station and the tools display vertically. In Figure 1.24 you can see toolbars docked on the left (A), right (B), and bottom (C) of the Acrobat window with one floating toolbar (D) in the Document pane.

FIGURE 1.24

Toolbars can be docked on all four sides of the Acrobat window and undocked from the Toolbar Well where they appear as floating toolbars.

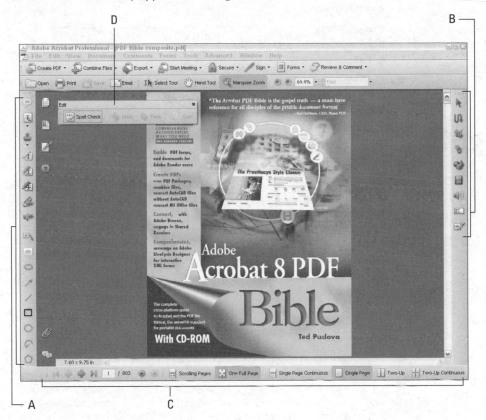

- **Resetting toolbars.** You can position toolbars around the Acrobat window and return them to the default positions with one menu command. This is particularly helpful if multiple users work on a single computer or you frequently change editing tasks that require using different tools during different editing sessions. In many cases it's easier to reset toolbars to the original default view, than open tools needed for a specific editing task. To set toolbars to their defaults, open a context menu from any toolbar or in the Toolbar Well by right-clicking (Ctrl+clicking on Macintosh), and select the menu item Reset Toolbars as shown in Figure 1.25. Alternately, you can press Alt/Option+F8.

FIGURE 1.25

To return toolbars back to the default view, open a context menu from any toolbar or in the Toolbar Well and select Reset Toolbars.

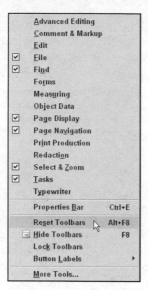

- **Hiding all toolbars.** Toolbars can be hidden from view to offer you more room when editing a PDF document or browsing the contents of PDFs. To hide the toolbars from view, open a context menu from the Toolbar Well and choose Hide Toolbars. When toolbars are hidden you won't have access to a context menu to get the toolbars back in view. Instead, choose View ➪ Toolbars ➪ Show Toolbars to make all toolbars reappear. (Note that using this menu command also hides toolbars.)

- **Hiding a single toolbar.** You can hide a toolbar after it has been undocked from the Toolbar Well. Click the X in the top-right corner of the toolbar (Windows) or the small circle on the top-left side of the toolbar (Macintosh) to close it, and it disappears from view. From a context menu opened on any toolbar or the Toolbar Well, you can open the toolbar and display it in the Acrobat window again. Toolbars can also be hidden by using the More Tools window, opening a context menu on the Toolbar Well and selecting a toolbar with a check mark to hide it, and selecting toolbars in the View ➪ Toolbars submenu.

- **Locking toolbars.** The vertical separator bar used to move toolbars disappears when you select Lock Toolbars from a context menu. The toolbars cannot be inadvertently moved after you lock them. To unlock the toolbars, open a context menu and select Lock Toolbars again. The check mark alongside the menu command becomes unchecked and the toolbars are unlocked in the Toolbar Well. If the toolbars are locked and you drag an undocked toolbar on top of the Toolbar Well, it won't dock. You need to first unlock the toolbars before you can redock them. Additionally, you need to unlock toolbars in order to use the Reset Toolbars command in a Toolbar Well context menu to return tools and toolbars back to the default position.

NOTE You can also lock toolbars that are undocked outside of the Toolbar Well. The separator bar on the toolbar disappears on floating toolbars the same as it does for toolbars docked in the Toolbar Well. However, locking undocked toolbars does not prevent you from moving them around the Acrobat window. You can click and drag the title bar for any undocked toolbar and move it to another location.

- **Setting new toolbar defaults.** If you decide to reposition your toolbars and want to keep them fixed as new defaults, Acrobat can do so for you automatically. Move the toolbars to the desired locations and go about your work. When you quit Acrobat and reopen the program, the toolbar positions remain as you last arranged them. Unfortunately, Acrobat does not have a Save Workspace command like you find in several Adobe Creative Suite applications.

TIP If you are unfamiliar with many Acrobat tools, you can change the tool labels to show you a more descriptive label for each tool that offers you a hint of what the tool does. To show more descriptive labels, open a context menu on the Acrobat Toolbar Well and choose Show Button Labels ⇨ All Labels. The toolbars expand and show a text description for each tool's name. Keep this option active until you are familiar with the tool names.

Understanding advanced toolbars

The default toolbars represent a fraction of the tools available to you in Acrobat. Many of the other toolbars remain hidden from view. The reason for this is obvious when you load all the toolbars in the Toolbar Well. You lose a lot of viewing real estate when all toolbars are docked in the Toolbar Well. Unless you have a large display monitor or a second monitor, working on a file in the Document pane when all toolbars are in view gives little room to see document pages. Fortunately, by managing the toolbars you can elect to show only the tools you want to work with and you can move them around the Acrobat window, allowing for the best view.

You open toolbars from menu commands in the Tools menu or by opening a context menu. If you're a seasoned Acrobat user, your first encounter with Acrobat viewers 6 and above might be a bit frustrating if you don't know how to access the tools you want to use. "Where is that Form tool?" you may ask. Don't worry; it's there. You just have to poke around and search for it or, better yet, look over the following descriptions to understand more about how these other tools are grouped into separate toolbars.

Opening advanced toolbars

For the purpose of discussion, I'll refer to the non-default toolbars as advanced toolbars. Acrobat does not refer to all these tools as advanced tools. Some of the tools labeled in the menu commands are not referred to as advanced tools. For clarity in this chapter, though, consider all the following toolbars as advanced toolbars.

You can use three methods for displaying toolbars not visible when you open Acrobat. You can open the View ⇨ Toolbars menu where you find a list of tools in submenus. Select a submenu item to open a toolbar as a floating toolbar in the Acrobat window. Another method is to open a context menu on the Toolbar Well and open toolbars from commands in the menu. A third option, and one that provides more options for viewing all tools and toolbars in a single window, is to use the More Tools menu command when you open a context menu on the Toolbar Well. As a matter of routine, you should use this option when preparing an Acrobat session that requires you to use several tools and toolbars. All tools except the Form tools (Acrobat Professional only) are accessible from the context menu.

Advanced Editing toolbar

The Advanced Editing toolbar shown in Figure 1.26 is one you'll use in just about all Acrobat editing sessions. Tools include the Select Object tool that is used to select content you add in Acrobat such as

comment markups and form fields. The Article tool is used to create article threads, the Crop, Link, 3D, Movie, and Sound tools follow. The TouchUp Text tool is used to edit text on a page and the last tool is the TouchUp Object tool that is used to select content that was originally created in an authoring program and converted to PDF.

 For more information about PDF editing using the Advanced Editing tools, see the chapters in Part III. To learn more about the Link tool, see Chapter 22. For using the Movie and Sound tools see Chapter 23. To learn how to use the TouchUp Order tool that follows the TouchUp Text tool, see Chapter 25.

FIGURE 1.26

The Advanced Editing toolbar contains a miscellaneous group of tools used for many different editing functions.

Comment & Markup toolbar

When you open either the View ⇨ Toolbars submenu menus or a context menu on the Toolbar Well, the first menu option after the default Advanced Editing toolbar is the Comment & Markup toolbar. Select the menu option and the Comment and Markup tools open in their own toolbar. Open a context menu on the toolbar and select Add/Remove Tools ⇨ Show All Tools. The toolbar appears as you see in Figure 1.27 when all tools are loaded.

FIGURE 1.27

Open the Comment & Markup toolbar and open a context menu on a tool and select Show All Tools to see all the comment and markup tools.

NEW FEATURE Now in Acrobat 8 you have the opportunity to load just the tools you want to use in a review session from both the former Commenting and the Drawing & Markup toolbars. Acrobat 8 nests all these tools together nicely in a single toolbar. This arrangement affords you the opportunity to view just those tools you commonly use in a review session — a great new feature. I won't go into all the tool names and explain their use now. You'll find a complete description in Chapter 20.

TIP When you select the Comment & Markup tools from the More Tools window and check the boxes for all tools, all the tools are loaded *except* the Paste a copied image as stamp tool. To show the tool in the Comment & Markup toolbar, open the Comment & Markup toolbar and open a context menu on any tool in the toolbar. Select Show All Tools and the Paste a copied image as stamp tool is added to the toolbar.

Edit toolbar

The Edit toolbar is the home of a miscellaneous group of editing tools, such as spell checking, copy, paste, undo, and redo. (See Figure 1.28.)

FIGURE 1.28

The Edit toolbar contains a miscellaneous selection of tools used for spell checking and editing.

Forms toolbar (Acrobat Professional only)

From a context menu in the Toolbar Well or the View ➪ Toolbars submenu select Forms toolbar to open the Forms tools. The eight forms tools shown in Figure 1.29 opens where you can access tools to create form fields.

NEW FEATURE   In addition to the same form tools you had available in Acrobat 7, a new tool is added to the toolbar to create bar code fields. In addition two other new tools are added to the Forms toolbar. The Edit Layout tool changes from a preview mode to a form editing mode and the Distribute tool used to distribute forms for an ad hoc data collection and enable the distributed forms for Adobe Reader users.

FIGURE 1.29

To access the Forms toolbar, open a context menu on the Toolbar Well and select Forms.

CROSS-REF   For more information on using the Forms tools and the new tools added to Acrobat 8, see Chapters 33 and 34.

Measuring tools

The Measuring tools include the Distance tool used for measuring linear distances, the Perimeter tool for measuring linear distances of angles and objects, and an Area tool for measuring the surface area of objects. The Measuring toolbar, shown in Figure 1.30, might be used for examining measurements in engineering and scientific drawings.

CROSS-REF   For more information about using the Measuring tools, see Chapter 24.

FIGURE 1.30

The Measuring toolbar offers three tools to measure distances and areas on a PDF page.

Object Data tool

The Object Data tool (see Figure 1.31) is used to select objects on a document page. When you select an object that has object data associated with it, the Object Data dialog box opens. This dialog box contains object metadata such as creation date, copyright information, color mode, resolution, and other file attributes similar to the kind of metadata you can view in programs such as Microsoft Visio, Microsoft Project, and AutoDesk AutoCAD.

CROSS-REF For a greater understanding about object and document metadata, see Chapter 5. For information on using the Object Data tool, see Chapter 9.

FIGURE 1.31

Use the Object Data tool to select objects and view file attributes associated with the selected object.

Print Production tools

The Print Production tools (see Figure 1.32) enable you to make adjustments on the PDF or alter the content. This toolbar contains tools for assigning traps, pre-flighting, converting colors, assigning color profiles, adding crop marks, cropping pages, fixing hairlines, transparency flattening, and assigning Job Definitions.

FIGURE 1.32

Use the Print Production tools to open dialog boxes where you can preview and change PDF documents to accommodate prepress and commercial printing.

CROSS-REF For more information on using Print Production tools and preparing files for commercial printing, see Chapter 32.

Redaction

A new toolbar has been added to Acrobat 8. The Redaction tools are particularly helpful for users working in the legal industry who need to remove text content from documents to protect sensitive data such as the names of minors, personal privacy information, and data breeching security policies. When you open the Redaction toolbar you'll see four tools to help you redact PDF documents as shown in Figure 1.33.

FIGURE 1.33

Redaction tools are used to remove sensitive information from PDF documents.

CROSS-REF For a complete explanation for redaction and using the Redaction tools, see Chapter 14.

Typewriter toolbar

The Typewriter tool was added to all Acrobat viewers in a maintenance upgrade during the Acrobat 7 life cycle. This toolbar, shown in Figure 1.34, contains tools for typing text on PDF documents. It's particularly helpful when filling out PDF forms that don't have form fields.

FIGURE 1.34

The Typewriter tool is used primarily for filling in forms that don't contain form fields.

 For more information on using the Typewriter tools, see Chapter 33.

Properties Bar

You use the Properties Bar (see Figure 1.35) in conjunction with several different tools. After you create comments, links, buttons, and similar content in a PDF document, the selected comment, link, button, and so on displays current properties such as colors, fonts, and line weights in the Properties Bar. You can make changes in the Properties Bar without visiting the Properties dialog box. You can quickly open the Properties Bar with a keyboard shortcut (Ctrl/⌘+E) or via a context menu opened on the Toolbar Well.

FIGURE 1.35

The Properties Bar offers a quick solution for editing item properties without the need for opening dialog boxes.

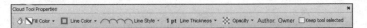

Customizing the Acrobat workplace

Whether you're an Acrobat pro or a new Acrobat user, seeing all those toolbars loaded and scattered across the Toolbar Well the first time can be very intimidating. As you poke around and possibly feel a little frustration when trying to identify the right tool icon to select the right tool for the task at hand, please realize that Acrobat is a multifaceted program serving a huge array of needs for different users. Not all the tools and features are designed for use in a single Acrobat session. You may be a PDF forms author and need only Basic tools, Navigation tools, Edit tools, and Form tools. In another session you may be a reviewer and only have need for the Comment and Markup tools. You might be an eBook author and need to work with many features for creating and viewing eBooks, or you might want to edit PDF pages and post modified PDFs on your Web site.

When learning all the tools and commands contained in Acrobat Professional, be certain to look over all the chapters where tools are discussed. Learn how to access toolbars and organize them in the Toolbar Well. When you begin a new Acrobat session, set up your environment so you can easily select a tool from toolbars you dock in the Toolbar Well.

As a starting point, you can configure Acrobat to provide you with immediate feedback related to tools selection and keyboard shortcuts. As you first start using Acrobat Professional, follow the steps in the next section to help you customize your environment for more efficient editing and less frustration. In this example, an environment for engaging in a commenting session is used. You can change the toolbars to meet needs in PDF editing or PDF creation, or add tools for some other kind of work you do.

STEPS: Setting up the Acrobat environment

1. **Return to toolbar defaults.** Open Acrobat. Position the cursor on any area in the Toolbar Well and right-click to open a context menu (Ctrl+click for Macintosh) and select Reset Toolbars.

2. **Open the More Tools window.** Open the More Tools menu. From a context menu opened from the Toolbar Well, select More Tools to open the More Tools window.

3. **Add the tools you intend to use to the Comment & Markup toolbar.** This is a personal choice. Look over all the Comment & Markup tools and check just those tools you intend to use. Be certain to check the box for the Comment & Markup toolbar so the toolbar shows up when you leave the More Tools window. (See Figure 1.36.)

FIGURE 1.36

The More Tools window

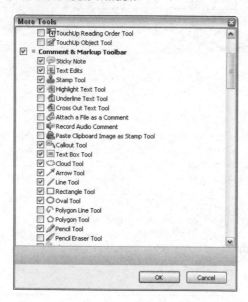

4. **Add some Edit tools.** While still in the More Tools window, scroll to the Advanced Editing Toolbar. One tool you'll use frequently in almost all editing sessions is the Select Object tool (denoted with an arrowhead icon). Click the check box for this tool. Other tools won't be used under most circumstances such as the Movie tool, Article tool, Link tool, and so on. Uncheck all the tools you anticipate not using.

5. **Add the Spell Check tool.** Scroll to the Edit toolbar and check the Spell Check tool.

6. **Exit the More Tools window.** When certain about the tools you think you'll use in a given editing session, click OK and all the toolbars open as floating toolbars.

7. **Open the Properties Bar.** Again open a context menu on the Toolbar Well and select Properties Bar from the menu options. Note that this tool is not available in the More Tools window and needs to be opened from a context menu or the View ⇨ Toolbars submenu.

8. **Dock the toolbars.** After opening all the toolbars you want to use for a given editing session return to the Toolbar Well context menu and select Dock All Toolbars. This command moves all the toolbars to the Toolbar Well, as shown in Figure 1.37.

FIGURE 1.37

Toolbars docked in the Toolbar Well include the A) File toolbar, B) Select & Zoom toolbar, C) Advanced Editing toolbar, D) Edit toolbar, E) Comment & Markup toolbar, and F) the Properties Bar.

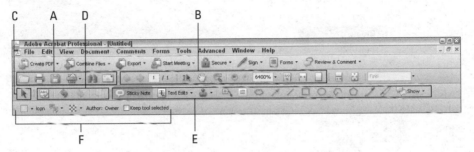

Tool Tips

When you select All Labels from a context menu or preference setting, you see tool descriptions on many tools. However, not all tools describe the tool with a label. For example, look at the Zoom In tool (the plus symbol). It should be apparent to you what the tool does by viewing the icon in the toolbar. Other tools' functions, however, may not be so apparent from viewing the tool icons. Fortunately, you have some extra help in the form of Tool Tips. To view a Tool Tip, place the cursor over a tool in the Toolbar Well or on a floating toolbar, and pause a moment before selecting the tool. A Tool Tip appears inside a yellow box directly below the cursor with a label describing the tool. In Figure 1.38 you can see the Tool Tip that appears when the cursor is placed over the Sticky Note tool. As you move the cursor over different tools, the Tool Tips change to reflect the description of the targeted tool.

FIGURE 1.38

Place the cursor over a tool and pause a moment before selecting the tool. A Tool Tip describing the tool opens below the mouse cursor.

As you become familiar with the tools, you can return to the context menu opened from the Toolbar Well and choose Button Labels ⇨ No Labels. When No Labels is active, your toolbars shrink and offer you more room in the Toolbar Well.

Palettes

Other tools available to you in all Acrobat viewers are *palettes*. Palettes are similar to toolbars in that they can be docked to a docking station called the Navigation pane; they can be undocked and floated around the Acrobat window; they can contain pull-down menus for selecting more options; a series of default palettes appears docked in the Navigation pane; and you can open additional palettes from menu commands.

A couple distinctions between toolbars and palettes are that palettes can be placeholders for information, and tools can appear inside a palette. Whereas tools are used in the Document pane, many palette operations take place directly in the palette. Toolbars remain relatively fixed in size, but palettes can be sized and stretched along the Acrobat window to provide you with more room to work within the palette or view the information contained within the palette. In addition, some palettes contain their own tools where edits can be made in the palette and dynamically reflected on the document page. Palettes help you organize content, view specific content across many pages, and provide some tools for global editing of PDF files.

Default palettes

As with toolbars, Acrobat displays a series of palettes docked in a well when you first launch the program. Palettes are contained in the Navigation pane along the left side of the Acrobat window. By default, the Navigation pane is collapsed; however, you can save PDF documents in such a manner where a palette expands when a file is opened in any Acrobat viewer. These settings are document-specific and can be toggled on or off for individual PDF documents.

 For more information about setting opening views for palette displays, see Chapter 4.

Pages

 Acrobat users have been familiar with the thumbnail view of each page since the early days of Acrobat. A mini view of each page in the active PDF document is displayed in the Pages pane, as shown in Figure 1.39. The Pages pane offers you menu options for arranging, deleting, inserting, and editing pages in a number of ways. You can zoom in to the thumbnail views as large or even larger than a page viewed in the Document pane.

FIGURE 1.39

Thumbnails are found in the Pages pane in all Acrobat viewers. The thumbnail view of document pages can be sized larger and smaller using context menu commands.

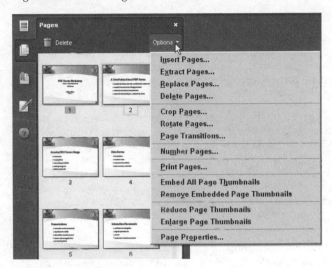

 CROSS-REF   For a complete description of working with pages (thumbnails), see Chapter 16.

Bookmarks

The second default palette panel in the Navigation pane is the Bookmark panel. You can save PDF documents in a manner where the bookmarks are visible when the file opens in Acrobat. A good example of such a file is a Help file. When you open a file such as the Adobe Designer FormCalc file, bookmarks are visible in an open Navigation pane, as shown in Figure 1.40. You can open and close the Navigation panel by pressing F4. You can also grab the vertical separator bar at the right edge of the Navigation pane and move it left and right to size the pane.

FIGURE 1.40

Bookmarks can be displayed in the Navigation pane when a file opens.

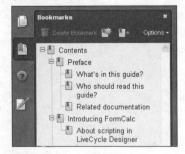

Bookmarks are navigation buttons that can launch a page, a view, or one of many different Action types similar to link and button actions. Anyone familiar with Acrobat already knows much about bookmarks and how to navigate pages by clicking individual bookmarks in the palette.

CROSS-REF To learn how to create and manage bookmarks and add actions, see Chapter 17.

How To

 The How To pane has been moved from where it appeared in Acrobat 6 and 7. In Acrobat 8, the How To pane is docked in the Navigation pane and its behavior is similar to other palettes. Here you find help information on some key Acrobat editing tasks. Click the links shown in Figure 1.41 and the help information is displayed in the pane.

CROSS-REF For more information on getting help in Acrobat, see the section "Accessing Help" later in this chapter.

Signatures

 Digital signatures help you manage signed documents; the Signatures panel enables you to perform tasks such as displaying signatures in the Signature pane, verifying signatures, clearing them, deleting them, and so on. All these editing tasks with signatures are still available in Acrobat Professional as is signature validation, which is also available in other Acrobat viewers.

CROSS-REF For a complete description of creating and managing digital signatures, see Chapter 26.

FIGURE 1.41

The How To pane provides help information on key Acrobat editing topics.

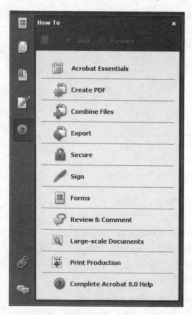

Attachments

 The Attachments pane (see Figure 1.42) in all Acrobat viewers is used to display, manage, and extract file attachments. You can attach files in Acrobat Standard and Professional and extract file attachments using all Acrobat viewers including Adobe Reader.

FIGURE 1.42

The Attachments pane provides options for managing file attachments. Attachments can be extracted from within Adobe Reader.

CROSS-REF For a complete description of adding file attachments to PDF documents, see Chapter 15. For more on extracting attachments from within Adobe Reader, see Chapter 3.

Comments

 The Comments palette shows you comments in an expanded horizontal view, just like the Attachments pane. When you click the Comments panel, you'll notice a number of pull-down menus (signified by down-pointing arrows at the top of the pane), a list of comments that can be expanded and collapsed, and a host of tools within the palette, as shown in Figure 1.43.

FIGURE 1.43

The Comments palette

CROSS-REF For a complete description of creating and managing comments, see Chapters 20 and 21.

Hidden panels

As with toolbars, you can choose to view additional panels through menu commands. You can choose to display a number of other panels in the Acrobat window and dock them in the Navigation pane. To open a hidden panel, choose View ➪ Navigation Panels. From the submenu, you'll find all the panels available. In Figure 1.44, the list shows Navigation panels available in Acrobat Professional.

Another way to access the Navigation panels is through a context menu. Right-click (Windows) or Ctrl+click (Macintosh) on the Navigation pane and a menu shows all the Navigation Panels. In order to see the panels, you must first open them from the Navigation Panels submenu and dock them in the Navigation pane. Once the panels have been docked, they appear in a context menu, as shown in Figure 1.45.

FIGURE 1.44

Open the Navigation Panels menu and a submenu displays all Navigation panels.

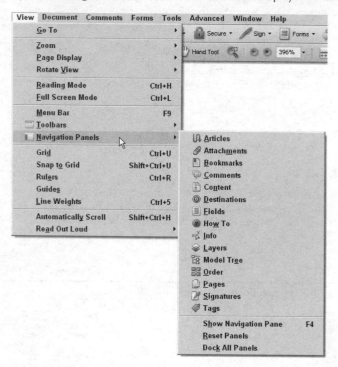

FIGURE 1.45

Once Navigation panels have been docked in the Navigation pane, they appear in a context menu opened from the Navigation pane.

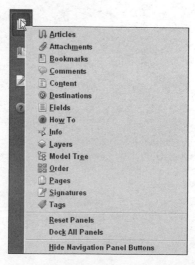

The list includes the default panels. If you select a default panel, the Navigation pane opens and the panel is selected. When you select a hidden panel, in other words, a panel other than those docked in the Navigation pane when you first launch Acrobat, the panel opens in the Acrobat window as a floating palette with one or more panels contained in the window. Drag a panel to the Navigation pane and it docks and then becomes visible in a context menu opened from the Navigation pane.

Articles

The first of the hidden panels listed in the Navigation Panels submenu is Articles. Choose View ➪ Navigation Panels ➪ Articles to open a floating palette. Articles enable you to create article threads to help users follow passages of text in a logical reading order. You won't find any new features added to the Article tool since Acrobat 5.

CROSS-REF For information on creating article threads and managing them, see Chapter 16.

Content

A palette designed for managing the structural content of PDF documents is found in the Content panel. When you choose View ➪ Navigation Panels ➪ Content, the Content palette opens in a floating palette as shown in Figure 1.46. Content features help you reflow tagged PDF files and manipulate the structure of tagged documents.

FIGURE 1.46

The Content palette opens in a floating palette where the structural content of the open file is reported.

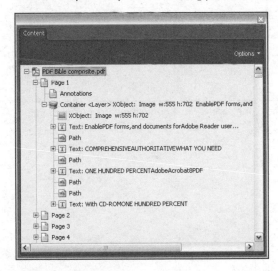

CROSS-REF For information on working with the Content palette and tagged PDF documents, see Chapter 25.

Destinations

Destinations work similarly to bookmarks, in that specific views are captured and listed in the panel. Clicking a destination opens the associated page in the Document pane, whereas clicking a bookmark opens the associated view (page and zoom).

CROSS-REF For information on creating destinations and managing them, see Chapter 22.

Fields

The Fields panel enables you to manage form fields on Acrobat PDF forms. You can list all form fields in the panel and execute menu commands from the pull-down menu and context menu opened from within the palette.

CROSS-REF For information about Acrobat forms, see Part VI.

Info

The Info panel displays the x,y position of the mouse cursor as you move it around the Document pane. From this panel you can choose to display from among three different units of measure — points, inches, millimeters, centimeters, and picas. No changes have been made to the Info palette in Acrobat viewers.

CROSS-REF For information on working with the Info panel, see Chapter 4.

Layers

If you create documents containing Adobe PDF layers, the Layers palette permits you to toggle layer views and work with layer properties. In Figure 1.47, the Layers palette is open showing visible and hidden layers.

FIGURE 1.47

The Layers palette enables you to manage layer visibility.

CROSS-REF To understand more about working with Adobe PDF layers, see Chapter 24.

Model Tree

 The Model Tree palette lets you examine information related to 3D drawings. You can review assets, hide and show drawing parts, toggle views, review comments, and more on 3D drawings. In Figure 1.48 you can see the model tree shown for a 3D image.

FIGURE 1.48

The Model Tree palette is designed to work with 3D drawings.

CROSS-REF   For more information about viewing 3D drawings and Acrobat 3D, see Chapter 2.

Order

 You use the Order panel to manage reading order of documents. This panel also relates to document accessibility, like the options available in the Tags panel. The Order panel enables you to add tags to a document, clear tags, and reorder a page's contents to change a reading order that might be read aloud by a screen reader.

CROSS-REF   For information on working with the Order panel, understanding screen readers, and document accessibility, see Chapter 25.

Tags

 Tagged PDF files provide more editing capability with PDF documents, and the files can be made accessible to adaptive devices such as screen readers. For adding, editing, and annotating tags in PDF documents use the Tags panel. Together with the Content panel options, you have much control over document accessibility.

CROSS-REF   To understand accessibility and the advantages of creating tagged PDF documents, see Chapter 25.

Palette menus

Each of the panels contains its own pull-down menu. When a panel is open in the Navigation pane or in a floating window, select the Options down-pointing arrow to open a pull-down menu, as shown in Figure 1.49. Menu commands found in panels may or may not be available from the top-level menu bar. Additionally, some panels, like the Attachments and Comments panels, offer you several pull-down menus.

FIGURE 1.49

Palette Options menus provide menu commands specific to each palette function.

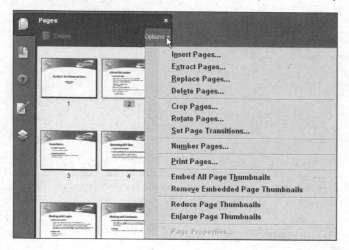

Context menus

Context menus can display different options for palette choices depending on where you open a context menu. If you move the cursor to an empty area when all text and objects in a palette are deselected and open a context menu, the menu options may be different than when you select text or an object in a palette. However, this is not always the case, because a few palettes provide you with the same options regardless of whether something is selected or not. In Figure 1.50 a context menu is opened within the Bookmarks panel. In this case you need to open the menu on a bookmark name. If you attempt to open a context menu in an empty area in the pane, no menu opens.

In Figure 1.51, a page in the Pages pane is selected and a context menu is opened on the page, as shown on the left side of the figure. On the right, a context menu is opened in an empty area in the pages pane. This figure illustrates the different menu options some panels have when selecting an object versus an open area in the pane.

FIGURE 1.50

A context menu opened on a bookmark.

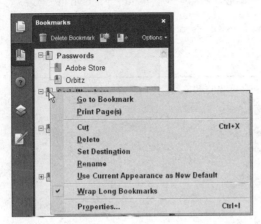

FIGURE 1.51

When a page is selected in the Pages palette and a context menu is opened, more menu choices are available than when no page is selected.

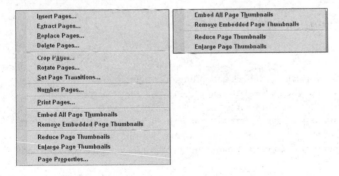

Accessing Help

You can see the number of different commands and tools available in Acrobat are extraordinary — and you haven't yet looked at all the submenu options or different preference options accessed from the top-level menu bar. With all these features available to you, your initial Acrobat sessions can sometimes be overwhelming. Fortunately, the great engineers and program designers at Adobe Systems thought about you and they decided to provide some help.

Help with learning more about Acrobat comes in several forms and you can choose from several help methods to find the one that works well in your workflow. This section covers different options for getting help in an Acrobat session.

Getting Started in Acrobat

When you first launch Acrobat, the Getting Started window opens, as shown in Figure 1.52. This window provides a number of different help items that ease you into the world of Acrobat and PDF.

FIGURE 1.52

When you first launch Acrobat 8, the Getting Started window opens.

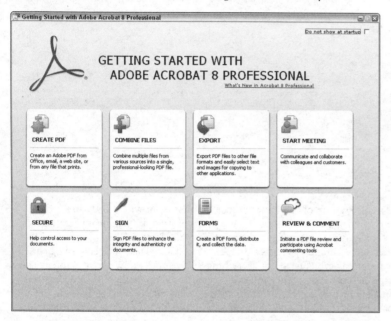

Click any one of the eight buttons in the Getting Started window and another pane respective to your selection opens where help information is provided.

CROSS-REF For more detail on the options in the Getting Started Window, see Chapter 4.

How To pane

The How To panel appears in the Navigation pane. Click the icon with a question mark and the How To pane opens. The topics in the How To pane are similar to those in the welcome screen. Click a topic listed in the pane and a second screen opens in the pane, providing another list of topics. Click on a topic and help information is provided in the pane, as shown in Figure 1.53.

FIGURE 1.53

Click different topics in the How To pane in the Navigation pane to explore help information.

Acrobat help

The How To window contains a select group of common Acrobat features about which you can find help within the listed topics on the Homepage. However, Acrobat is a monster program with many features and listing all the methods for working in the program is not the purpose of the How To help pane. To browse through a comprehensive help guide you need to access a different document. The comprehensive help guide contains more than 800 pages covering just about everything you want to know about Acrobat. There are, in essence, two flavors of the Acrobat Help guide. You can access the Complete Acrobat 8.0 Help document by selecting Help ➪ Complete Adobe Acrobat 8.0 Professional (or Standard) Help or you can open the Acrohelp.pdf file in Acrobat. These two documents are different in that the Complete Acrobat Help document is viewed in a separate executable application called the Adobe Help Viewer. The Acrohelp.pdf file is a standard PDF document contained in the Acrobat folder. Depending on which one you open, you have some different methods for viewing and navigation.

Complete Acrobat 8.0 Help

You open the Adobe Help Viewer window by selecting Help ➪ Complete Adobe Acrobat 8.0 Professional (or Standard) Help. The Adobe Help Viewer contains three tabs appear in the top of the window as shown in Figure 1.54. Click the Contents tab to show bookmarks, Index to see an alphabetical list of indexed topics, and Search to search for keywords.

Contents tab

By default the Adobe Help Viewer document opens with the Contents tab exposed as shown in Figure 1.54. In the Navigation pane you'll find a table of contents for the document shown in a very similar manner to the way bookmarks are listed in a PDF document. Click one of the bookmark topics listed in the Contents tab to see the respective bookmarked page in the Topic pane.

Search tab

You can use the Search tab to find any word(s) in the help document. Click the Search tab and the Navigation pane changes to display a field box where you type your search criteria. Type one or more words in the field box and click Search. The results then appear in the Search tab. All text appearing in red is linked to the page that opens in the Topic pane.

FIGURE 1.54

The Adobe Help Viewer opens as a floating window with three tabs — Contents, for listing bookmarks; Index, for an alphabetical topic list; and Search, for keyword searches.

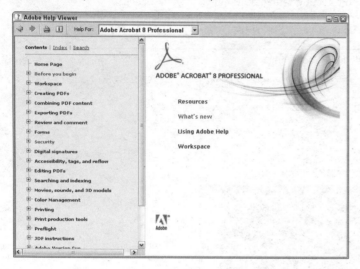

Index tab

The Index tab is an alpha index of topics. Click the text to open pages linked to the topics.

Navigating topics

The arrows at the top of the Navigation pane enable you to move forward and back to the pages you view during your search. The review history remains in memory until you close the document. If you close the help file, the review history is flushed from memory and you need to begin again to find information on the same topics. On the right side of the Topic pane is a scroll bar. Use the arrow keys and elevator bar to view documents as you do in any application document.

Printing topics

The Print tool located at the top of the Navigation pane opens the Print dialog box. In the Print dialog box you can choose to print a single page or a page range.

Adobe LiveCycle Designer

Adobe LiveCycle Designer is a separate executable program available to Acrobat Professional users on Windows only. Designer is used for creating dynamic XML forms. Designer also has a help document to assist you in learning the program. To access the Help file, select Help ➪ Adobe LiveCycle Designer Help or press the F1 key. The help document shown in Figure 1.55 opens.

Under the help menu you find other help options for accessing the Designer How To window and opening a scripting notation in the Adobe LiveCycle Designer help document with a link to a Web page on Adobe's Web site where more information about Adobe LiveCycle Designer can be found. In addition to menu commands under the Help menu you have sample files contained in the Adobe LiveCycle Designer 8.0 folder. Browse the folder contents to learn more about creating forms in LiveCycle Designer.

FIGURE 1.55

Press the F1 key in Adobe Designer to open the help document.

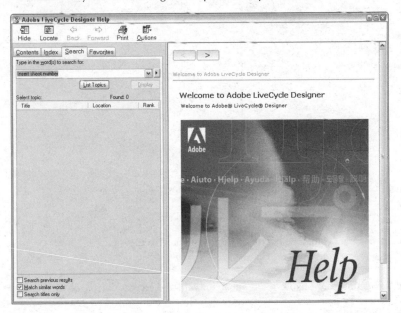

More help

In addition to the help file that covers working in Acrobat, some other help PDF files are located in the Help folder inside your Acrobat folder. These help documents are specific to certain tasks, such as pdfmark and Distiller parameters. To view the help documents, open your Acrobat folder and open the Help\ENU folder. The files are PDF documents and can be opened in any viewer.

Online help is available to you as well from Adobe Systems. If you choose Help ➪ Online Support and select one of the submenu items, your default Web browser launches and the Adobe Acrobat support page opens from Adobe's Web site. This Web page links to pages that are continually updated so be certain to make frequent visits to the Acrobat Online help Web pages.

> **NOTE** When accessing Adobe's Online Support, your Web browser opens in the foreground while Acrobat Professional remains open in the background. When you finish viewing Web pages and quit your Web browser, the Acrobat window returns to view.

Acrobat User Community

Adobe Systems sponsors a user group forum and supports the development of user groups internationally. Some of the world's leading experts on Acrobat participate through providing tips, articles, and hosting blog sessions. You can find some of the most up-to-date information at www.acrobatusers.com. Open the Adobe Acrobat User Community Web page and the opening page appears as shown in Figure 1.56. Here you'll find an easy to use Web site filled with many tips and solutions.

If you're interested in learning more about Acrobat, you may find a user group close to your home. If not, you can become one of the many people who start a local user group. You'll find great support from Adobe if you want to start a group. To learn more about the location of user groups and how to go about starting one, search the Adobe Acrobat User Community Web site.

FIGURE 1.56

Log on to www.acrobatusers.com to find up-to-date information on Acrobat and PDF.

Understanding Preferences

Preferences enable you to customize your work sessions in Acrobat. You can access a Preferences dialog box from within any Acrobat viewer and from within a Web browser when viewing PDFs as inline views. A huge number of preferences exist that all relate to specific tool groups or task categories, and it would not make as much sense to cover them here in the opening chapter as it would within chapters related to using tools and methods influenced by preference choices.

Some general things you should know about preferences is that they are contained in a dialog box as shown in Figure 1.57. You make a topic selection in the list on the left side of the dialog box and the related preferences are shown to the right side of the list. You make choices for preferences by selecting check boxes or making menu selections from pull-down menus. When you complete making your preference choices, click OK at the bottom of the dialog box.

Almost all the preferences you change in the Preferences dialog box are dynamic, which means you don't need to quit Acrobat and relaunch the program for a preference choice to take effect. Preferences remain in effect until you change them again. If you quit Acrobat and relaunch the program, the preferences you last made are honored by Acrobat. However, if for some reason the program crashes and you don't shut it down properly, any new preference changes will not be recognized when the program is launched again.

FIGURE 1.57

Press Ctrl/⌘+K to open the Preferences dialog box. Click a category on the left and the choices are reflected to the left of the categories list.

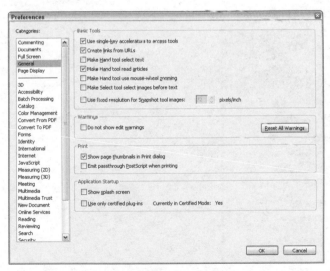

If you find some operation in Acrobat not working as you think it should, first take a look at the Preferences dialog box. In many cases you'll find a check box or menu command not enabled to permit you to perform a task. As you become familiar with specific tool groups and menu commands, make a habit of routinely visiting the Preferences dialog box so you understand all the toggles and switches that affect tool and viewing behavior.

Summary

This chapter offers you a general introduction for working in both Acrobat Standard and Acrobat Professional and helps you understand the environment, the user interface, and some of the many new features added to the commercial Acrobat products. At the very least, you should know how to go about finding help when you first start working in the program. Some of the more important points discussed in this chapter include the following:

- Adobe Acrobat is a multifaceted program designed to provide solutions for many different business professionals. Several types of Acrobat viewers exist, ranging in features to suit different user needs. The most sophisticated of the three viewers is Acrobat Professional, now in version 8. Acrobat Standard offers fewer tools and menu commands than Acrobat Professional and is now available only on Windows.

- PDF, short for Portable Document Format, was developed by Adobe Systems and was designed to exchange documents between computers and across computer platforms while maintaining file integrity.

- The PDF language format has changed version numbers along with the Acrobat viewers. The current PDF version is 1.7.

- Tasks are performed through the use of menus, tools, and palettes that can be accessed through mouse selections and keyboard shortcuts.

- The extensive list of tools appears in an abbreviated form when you open Acrobat and view the default toolbars. You can open additional toolbars from menu commands or the new More Tools window. You can dock toolbars in the Toolbar Well or float them around the Acrobat window.

- Palettes are similar to toolbars in that they can be docked and undocked from a well called the Navigation pane. Palettes contain pull-down menus, and some palettes contain tools.

- You can customize the Acrobat workplace to suit your work style through the use of different preference choices. When preferences, palettes, and toolbars are changed from their default views, the new views are saved when you quit your Acrobat session. They remain unchanged until you change them again or reset them to defaults.

- Acrobat Professional provides you extensive assistance through the use of help documents. You can gain immediate help on selected topics through choices in the How To pane or by expanding your list of categories to seek help in the Complete Acrobat 8.0 Help window. In addition to help documents, Adobe sponsors the development of local Adobe Acrobat user groups worldwide. To learn more visit www.acrobatusers.com.

- Preferences are settings that apply globally to Acrobat and influence the behavior of tools and menu commands.

Chapter 2

Using Acrobat Viewers

In Chapter 1 you got a feel for some of the tools and menu commands provided in Acrobat Standard and Acrobat Professional. If you're a PDF author and you use Acrobat Standard or Professional, knowing the capabilities of one viewer versus another is important for both job efficiency and productivity, as well as usefulness to the end user. You may want to add multimedia to a PDF document. Therefore, you need to know what authoring tool is needed to import video and sound. You may be sending out a document for review and want to solicit comments. Therefore, you need to know what viewer a user needs to send comments back to you.

At times you may find that neither Acrobat Standard nor Professional can help you do some editing tasks needed in your workflow. Fortunately, you have options for acquiring Acrobat plug-ins developed by third-party manufacturers that add much more functionality to the Acrobat tools and menu commands.

Many of the chapters ahead give you an idea of the distinctions between Acrobat Standard and Acrobat Professional and the tools accessible from one viewer versus the other. This chapter introduces you to the Acrobat viewers, points out some differences among them, and shows you how to use Acrobat plug-ins when you need more features than the viewers provide.

IN THIS CHAPTER

Understanding the differences among the Acrobat viewers

Using Acrobat plug-ins

Viewer Distinctions

Adobe Reader, Acrobat Standard (Windows only in version 8), Acrobat Professional, Acrobat 3D, and Acrobat Elements are designed to serve different users with different purposes. It should be obvious to you that Adobe Reader, as a free download from Adobe's Web site, is much more limited in features and performance than the products you purchase. It should also be obvious that because of the low cost of Acrobat Elements, it is much more limited in features than Acrobat Standard, Acrobat Professional, and Acrobat 3D.

For a general overview, take a look at the following descriptions of the Acrobat products.

Adobe Reader

Adobe Reader is available for download from Adobe's Web site free of charge. The Adobe Reader software is distributed for the purpose of viewing, printing, and searching, on PDF files created by users of Acrobat Elements, Acrobat Standard, Acrobat Professional or Acrobat 3D. Additionally, Adobe Reader is used for filling in forms on PDFs created with Acrobat Professional. The major features of Adobe Reader include:

- **Viewing and printing.** These features are common across all Acrobat viewers. You can view, navigate, and print PDF documents with Adobe Reader.

- **Forms completion and submission.** Adobe Reader enables you to complete forms but not save the form field data unless the forms carry special usage rights for Adobe Reader users. Forms are submitted through the use of buttons created on forms for e-mailing or submitting data to Web servers.

NEW FEATURE Forms and digital signatures can be saved from Adobe Reader if a PDF has been enabled with special rights. New in Acrobat is a feature to enable PDFs to save form data filled in with Adobe Reader. By default form field data cannot be saved. Only Acrobat Professional and Acrobat 3D provide this feature to enable PDFs with usage rights.

CROSS-REF For more information on enabling PDFs with usage rights, see Chapter 19.

- **Comment and Review.** PDFs can be enabled with usage rights for commenting and review in Acrobat Professional and Acrobat 3D only. Once enabled, Reader users can participate in a review workflow and save PDFs locally with comments and markups.

- **Reader Extensions Server.** If an organization uses the Adobe LiveCycle Reader Extensions Server product available from Adobe Systems to enhance PDF files, Adobe Reader users can digitally sign documents and save form data.

  A distinction exists between enabling PDFs with usage rights from within Acrobat Professional/Acrobat 3D and using the Adobe Reader Extensions Server. Licensing restrictions do apply when enabling documents and you should be aware of these restrictions. See Chapter 19, for all you need to know about enabling PDFs and licensing restrictions.

In addition to the preceding, Adobe Reader provides support for eBook services and searching PDF documents, as well as extended support for working with accessible documents.

CROSS-REF For more information on using tools in Adobe Reader, see Chapter 4.

Acrobat Elements

Acrobat Elements is available for site license purchasing of 100 or more copies on Windows only. The unit costs are very aggressive and are lowered with higher volume purchases. This product is intended to offer large companies and enterprises a means for employees to create PDF files. The primary features of Acrobat Elements include:

- **Viewing and printing.** For viewing PDFs, the Adobe Reader software is used as the viewer. Elements in and of itself is not an Acrobat viewer.

- **PDF creation.** The PDF creation capability available from Elements is limited to creating PDF documents from Microsoft Office products or printing files to the Adobe PDF printer.

Acrobat Standard versus Acrobat Professional

Acrobat Standard is available only on Windows in version 8 of Acrobat. The Macintosh version has been discontinued. Adobe Systems is a company that tries hard to respond to user needs, but there are limitations. If a product does not support the development costs, then it is likely to be discontinued. This is the case with Acrobat Standard on the Macintosh. Many users of Acrobat on the Mac acquire Acrobat Professional in a bundled purchase with the Adobe Creative Suite. Independent sales of Acrobat Standard were minimal on the Mac during the Acrobat 7 life cycle. Therefore, Adobe could not justify the development costs for continuing the product. On Windows, sales of Acrobat Standard were much greater, and therefore you see Acrobat Standard still available.

Acrobat Standard is the lightweight of the authoring programs. However, Acrobat Standard still offers many tools for PDF creation and authoring. Without going into every tool that differs between Acrobat Standard and Acrobat Professional, the major differences include the following limitations:

- **Form field authoring.** No form tools or form field authoring is available with Acrobat Standard. JavaScripts on form fields cannot be created in Acrobat Standard. However, if a JavaScript is contained in an area accessible to Acrobat Standard (such as Bookmark Properties or Link Properties), the JavaScript can be edited. You can also write JavaScripts on Page Actions in Acrobat Standard.

CROSS-REF For information on writing JavaScripts, see Chapter 36.

- **Professional printing.** Acrobat Standard does not provide options for soft proofing color, pre-flighting jobs, or commercial printing using such features as color separations, frequency control, transparency flattening, and so on. All these print controls are contained only in Acrobat Professional.

CROSS-REF For information on pre-flighting, soft proofing color, and commercial printing, see Chapter 32.

- **Adding Adobe Reader usage rights.** You can add usage rights enabling Adobe Reader users to add comments, extract file attachments to PDF documents, and in Acrobat 8 add usage rights for saving form field data and digital signatures in Acrobat Professional. Acrobat Standard does not support adding usage rights to PDF files for Reader users.

CROSS-REF For information on adding usage rights for Adobe Reader users, see Chapter 19.

- **Redaction.** The new tools for redacting documents are not available to Acrobat Standard users.

CROSS-REF For information on using the Redaction tools and redacting documents, see Chapter 14.

- **Batch processing.** Acrobat Standard does not support batch processing and running batch commands.

CROSS-REF For information on creating batch sequences, see Chapter 18.

- **Creating index files.** Acrobat Catalog is not part of Acrobat Standard. You can create index files only with Acrobat Professional through a menu command that launches Acrobat Catalog.

CROSS-REF For information on creating index files, see Chapter 6.

- **Creating PDFs.** Acrobat Standard offers support for an impressive range of file types that can be converted to PDF. However, Acrobat Standard doesn't support creating PDFs from certain file types such as AutoCAD, Microsoft Visio, and Microsoft Project. Acrobat Standard does use Acrobat Distiller, but the Acrobat Standard Distiller does not support PDF/X, PDF/E, and PDF/A compliance.

CROSS-REF For information on using Acrobat Distiller, see Chapter 8. For information on PDF/A and PDF/X, see Chapters 10 and 32.

- **Engineering tools.** Acrobat Standard does not support some features used by engineers and technical illustrators, such as merging and flattening layers.

CROSS-REF For information on using the measuring tools and working with layers, see Chapter 24.

The preceding items are some of the major differences between these two commercial viewers. You will discover subtle differences as you work with the programs. For example, Acrobat Standard doesn't support comparing documents, migrating comments, Bates numbering, show and snap to grids, convert .dwg and .indd files, does not contain the PDF Optimizer for repurposing files, and so on.

If your mission is to recommend the product for purchase or make the decision for your own use, be aware of the four primary distinctions between the products. Acrobat Standard does not support forms authoring, professional printing, engineering tools, or adding Adobe Reader usage rights for review and comment and forms data saving and digital signatures. If your work is in one of these areas, you need to purchase Acrobat Professional.

Acrobat 3D

Acrobat 3D is a commercial Acrobat product with all the features of Acrobat Professional. Its main focus is on the manufacturing segment and aimed at Engineering Design and Technical Publication workflows. Acrobat 3D additionally adds support for the Acrobat 3D Toolkit, 3D Capture for UNIX, and a conversion framework for converting and placing major CAD file formats into PDF files. This is a separate Acrobat product you can purchase for use with 3D drawings created in almost all major CAD formats. Among some of the features you find with Acrobat 3D are the following:

- **File conversion.** Acrobat 3D supports 3D drawing translations from all major 3D drawing programs including AutoCAD. These drawings can be imported directly into Acrobat 3D where comments, reviews, and markups can be applied and then shared with anyone using the free Adobe Reader.
- **Capture 3D files.** Acrobat 3D includes Acrobat 3D Capture so that you can convert any 3D drawing to PDF for use in Acrobat 3D.
- **Optimize, enhance, and animate.** Features in Acrobat 3D enable you to optimize drawings for faster display. You can add multiple views and materials and textures, multiple types of lighting and create animations such as exploded views, and more.
- **File compression.** 3D drawing files can be optimized for smaller file sizes.
- **3D drawing creation.** You can create simple 3D drawings directly in Acrobat 3D.
- **Photorealistic rendering.** You can render photorealistic images and create 2D raster and vector images.

There's much more to Acrobat 3D. If you're an engineer or technical artist working with CAD applications, you might want to check out some of the benefits of working with Acrobat 3D. This book does not cover Acrobat 3D features in the chapters ahead. To learn more about Acrobat 3D, take a look at the Acrobat 3D Corner on the Adobe Acrobat User Community Web site at www.acrobatusers.com/go/3D.

Using Plug-ins

All Acrobat viewers support a plug-in architecture. Plug-ins are installed during your Acrobat installation and loaded when you launch Acrobat. Many of the features you find when exercising commands and using tools are made possible by the use of plug-ins. To view the current plug-ins loaded with the viewer you use, choose Help ➪ About Adobe Plug-ins. The About Adobe Plug-Ins dialog box opens as shown in Figure 2.1.

FIGURE 2.1

The About Adobe Plug-Ins dialog box lists all the plug-ins accessible to your viewer.

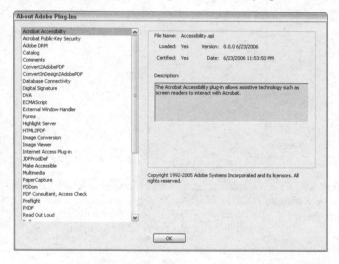

The list in the left side of the dialog box lists the names of the installed plug-ins. Click a name to see a description for the plug-in, including whether the plug-in is certified, the version number, creation date, text description, and dependencies. To examine different plug-ins, select them in the left pane and view the description on the right side of the dialog box.

Acrobat plug-ins are developed by Adobe Systems and third-party developers. All plug-ins developed by Adobe Systems are *certified* plug-ins. No third-party plug-ins are certified. Some features in Acrobat require that only certified plug-ins be loaded before the feature is enabled. Working with eBooks is one example where only certified plug-ins can be used.

NOTE Any time a document has Adobe DRM (Digital Rights Management) protection such as eBooks and/or documents protected with the Adobe Policy Server, the viewer is launched in *certified plug-in mode*. This mode loads only Adobe plug-ins and disables all third party plug-ins.

In order to instruct your Acrobat viewer to open with only certified plug-ins, open the Preferences dialog box by choosing Edit ➪ Preferences. Select General in the left pane and select the Use only certified plug-ins check box, as shown in Figure 2.2. When you quit your Acrobat viewer and relaunch the program, only certified plug-ins will load.

FIGURE 2.2

Select Use only certified plug-ins to open Acrobat to allow only certified plug-ins to load.

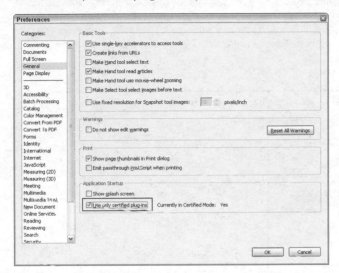

Plug-ins developed by third-party developers can also be loaded. The list of available resources for adding to Acrobat functionality in the form of add-ons and plug-ins is almost limitless. As you review all the chapters in this book and find that something you want to accomplish in your workflow is not covered, look for a plug-in developed by a third-party developer. Chances are that you can find a product well suited to do the job.

Plug-ins for Acrobat are far too numerous to mention in this book. For a single source where you can view a list of plug-ins, download demonstration copies, and make purchases, visit the Planet PDF store at www.pdfstore.com , the Adobe Store at www.adobe.com and click on the Store link, or The PowerXChange at: www.thepowerxchange.com. On several Web sites you'll find product descriptions and workflow solutions for almost any third-party product designed to work with Acrobat. When you visit one of the Web sites and review the products, be certain the product you purchase is upgraded to work with Acrobat 8.0 and the viewer you use. All products are listed with links to the manufacturer's Web sites, so you can find information on product descriptions, version numbers, and compatibility issues.

Installing plug-ins

Most plug-ins you acquire from third-party manufacturers are accompanied by an installer program. Installing plug-ins is easy. Open the folder for a plug-in you download from a Web site and double-click on the installer icon. The installer routine finds the plug-ins folder inside your Acrobat folder and the plug-in is loaded when you launch Acrobat.

If a plug-in is not accompanied by an installer program, you need to manually add the plug-in to your Acrobat plug-ins folder. On Windows, open the Program Files\Adobe\Acrobat 8.0\Acrobat\plug_ins folder. Copy the plug-in you want to install to this folder.

On the Macintosh, open your Applications folder. Open the Acrobat 8 Professional (or Standard) folder from within the Applications folder. Press and hold the Control key and click the program icon (Adobe Acrobat 8 Professional or Adobe Acrobat 8 Standard) to open a context menu, as shown in Figure 2.3. From the menu items, select Show Package Contents.

FIGURE 2.3

Open the Package Contents on the Macintosh to gain access to the Plug-ins folder.

When you open the Package Contents, the Contents folder appears in a single window. Double-click the folder to open it. Several folders appear within the Contents folder, one of which is named Plug-ins. Open this folder and copy your plug-in to it.

Uninstalling plug-ins

If your plug-in is not accompanied by an uninstaller program, you need to either disable the plug-in or physically remove it from the Acrobat plug-ins folder. A temporary solution is to disable third-party plug-ins by opening the Preferences dialog box, clicking on Startup, and selecting the check box for Use only certified plug-ins, as shown earlier in Figure 2.2.

To permanently remove a plug-in, open the plug-ins folder as described in the previous section, "Installing plug-ins," and drag the plug-in out of the Acrobat plug-ins folder.

CAUTION Some plug-ins are installed in their own folder. To remove a plug-in, drag the folder where the plug-in is installed out of the Acrobat plug-ins folder. Be certain not to remove the Acrobat plug-ins folder from within the Acrobat folder. Doing so disables all tools and menu commands using plug-ins.

Resolving plug-in conflicts

At times you may find a plug-in conflict among several third-party products or a plug-in that may have a bug. If your Acrobat functionality is impaired and you can't launch the program, hold down the Shift key while double-clicking the program icon to launch your viewer. All plug-ins are disabled when you use the modifier key. Open the Preferences dialog box again and select the Use only certified plug-ins check box. Quit and relaunch the program, and the offending plug-in is eliminated during startup.

If a plug-in is creating a problem, you may need to use a process of elimination to figure out which one it is by opening your plug-ins folder and removing all plug-ins. Then add several plug-ins at a time back to the plug-ins folder and launch your viewer. Keep adding plug-ins back to the plug-ins folder until you discover the plug-in that produces the error.

Working with plug-ins

There are many different plug-ins that provide you more features when working with Adobe Acrobat and Adobe Reader than can be covered in this book. To pick one out among the many is a hard choice. For your own workflow, visit the Planet PDF Store, Adobe Store, the PowerXChange, or the Acrobat User Community and explore various plug-ins available for download. Try to find a plug-in that offers at least a demo trial period and download it.

Almost all plug-ins come with a ReadMe file or user manual. Before installing a plug-in, be certain to review the installation recommendations by the developer. Install the plug-in and give it a try.

For a trial in using a plug-in, see Chapter 36 where using a third-party plug-in is discussed in more detail. Windows users can follow steps to install and use a plug-in by installing the AcroButtons and AcroDialogs plug-ins from the book's CD-ROM.

 See the book's CD-ROM for plug-in installers for AcroButtons and AcroDialogs developed by WindJack Solutions. These installers are for use on Windows only.

Summary

- The four Acrobat viewers include Adobe Reader, Acrobat Standard, Acrobat Professional, and Acrobat 3D. The tools that can create Adobe PDFs include Acrobat Elements, Acrobat Standard, Acrobat Professional, and Acrobat 3D.

- Adobe Reader is a free download from Adobe's Web site. All other products require purchase. Acrobat Elements is available only in site license quantities of 100 or more.

- Acrobat Standard offers fewer features than Acrobat Professional and is available in version 8 on Windows only. The primary limitations with Acrobat Standard are no support for Forms creation, commercial printing tools, engineering tools, or creating PDFs with Adobe Reader usage rights. These features are only available in Acrobat Professional or Acrobat 3D.

- Acrobat plug-ins are additions to Acrobat that offer features and tools for adding more functionality to Acrobat viewers. Plug-ins are installed with Acrobat from sources developed by Adobe Systems.

- Plug-ins are available from third-party software manufacturers. A complete list of plug-ins and demonstration products is available at the Planet PDF Store, the Adobe Store, and The PowerXChange.

Chapter 3

Getting Started in Adobe Acrobat

I n Chapter 1, I talked about getting help in Adobe Acrobat using many different help menu commands and I discussed a little bit about using the new
Getting Started with Adobe Acrobat welcome window. There's much more to
this welcome window, as well as different ways to access it, than I covered in
Chapter 1. Therefore, a separate chapter detailing the specifics of the welcome
and help options seems appropriate.

In this chapter, I talk about some of the links and options you have using the
Getting Started with Adobe Acrobat welcome window when you start up Acrobat
and when you begin to work on some different editing tasks.

IN THIS CHAPTER

Showing and hiding the Getting
Started window

Opening and searching files

Using the features buttons

Features descriptions

Getting Started Window

The window you see when you launch Acrobat viewers is the *Getting Started window*. Depending on the viewer you launch you'll see *Getting Started with Adobe
Acrobat 8 Professional* (or *Getting Started with Adobe Acrobat 8 Standard — Windows,*
or *Beyond Adobe Reader*). When you first launch Acrobat 8 Professional you see
the Getting Started window, as shown in Figure 3.1.

The same welcome window with some different options appears in all Acrobat
viewers in Acrobat version 8. Figure 3.1 shows the screen opened in Acrobat
Professional.

FIGURE 3.1

The Getting Started with Adobe Acrobat 8 Professional window opens when you first launch Acrobat 8 Professional.

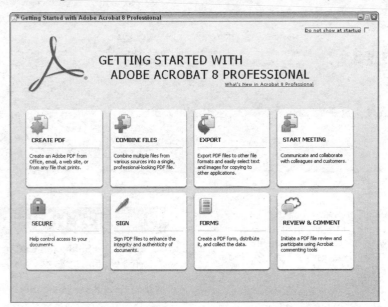

Navigating the Getting Started Window

When you first start using Acrobat 8, you'll want to take a look at the options available to you in the Getting Started window to access some help information. At some point, though, you'll want to bypass the screen when engaging in an Acrobat editing session. To stop the screen from opening on startup, check the box in the upper right corner where you see Do not show at startup. The next time you launch Acrobat, the Getting Started window won't open.

If at any time you want to reopen the window, select Help ⇨ Getting Started with Adobe Acrobat. The Getting Started window always opens on top of the Acrobat Document pane.

The Getting Started window contains eight task buttons that are links to other panes in the Getting Started window. When you click one of the buttons the second pane opens and displays information about the respective feature available in Acrobat.

On the second pane for any one of the eight individual task topics you find different icons and buttons that include:

- **Task action.** Click this button or the text adjacent to the button and Acrobat launches a dialog box or menu command to perform an action.

- **Task description.** Adjacent to this icon you find a short description explaining certain features available with the respective task.

■ **Task help.** Click the icon or the text description adjacent to the icon and the Adobe Help Viewer opens displaying help information related to the respective task.

■ **Home.** Click the Home button and you return to the first pane in the welcome window.

Using the Tasks Buttons

The eight tasks panes describe various options you have with the related topic and include buttons you can click to find help on the related task and buttons to get you started working with a given feature. These eight features include:

■ **Create PDF.** The Create PDF task provides you with help information as well as links directly to dialog boxes used for PDF creation. A description is provided in the central pane, as shown in Figure 3.2.

FIGURE 3.2

The Create PDF task pane provides help information and links to dialog boxes.

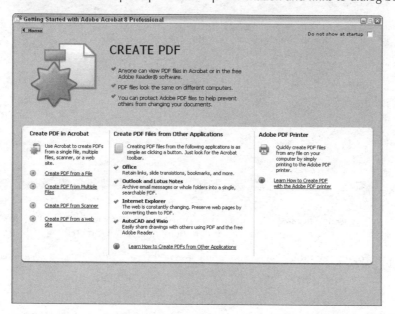

Clicking Learn How to Create PDFs from Other Applications opens the Adobe Help Viewer where creating PDFs using the Adobe PDFMaker is explained. Clicking Learn How to Create PDF with the Adobe PDF Printer links you to the Adobe Help Viewer where creating PDFs by printing to files is explained. Clicking one of the task action buttons opens menu commands found in the Create PDF task button pull-down menu.

CROSS-REF For more information on creating PDFs from other applications, see Chapters 8 and 9. For information on creating PDFs with the Adobe PDF Printer, see Chapters 7 and 10.

■ **Combine Files.** The new Combine Files feature is a great new addition to Acrobat 8. In the center of the Combine Files task pane shown in Figure 3.3 you see a list of descriptions for how combining files can be helpful for people working with legal documents, CAD drawings, Project Binders, and Sales Proposals. This is only an abbreviated list of descriptions for why you may want to use the Combine Files feature.

FIGURE 3.3

The Combine Files pane provides help information and links to dialog boxes related to combining files and creating PDF Packages.

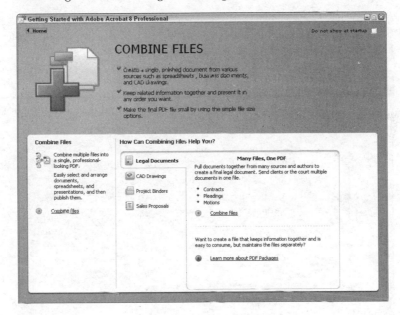

The Combine Files task links open the Combine multiple files into one PDF file dialog box. At the bottom of the task pane, you see a link to help information on creating PDF Packages.

CROSS-REF For more information on combining files and creating PDF Packages, see Chapter 12.

- **Export.** The Export tasks pane describes some file formats that you can export from Acrobat and several links to help information related to file exporting. As you can see in Figure 3.4, all the links in this task pane relate to providing help information. (When you see the text link begin with *Learn how to . . .*, the link is made to the Adobe Help Viewer document.)

CROSS-REF   For more information related to exporting PDF documents to other formats, see Chapter 11.

- **Start Meeting.** Start Meeting tasks shown in Figure 3.5 are related to Acrobat Connect sessions. You find help information related to Acrobat Connect and a link to the Welcome to Start Meeting dialog box where you can sign up for a free Acrobat Connect trial account.

CROSS-REF   For more information on Acrobat Connect and setting up a trial account, see Chapter 29.

FIGURE 3.4

The Export task pane provides help information related to exporting PDFs to other file formats.

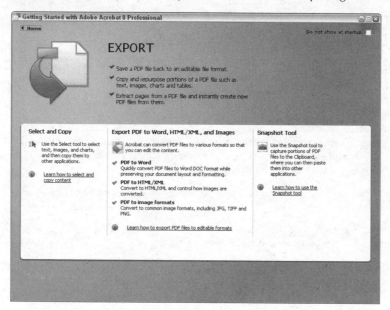

FIGURE 3.5

Start Meeting displays information related to Acrobat Connect.

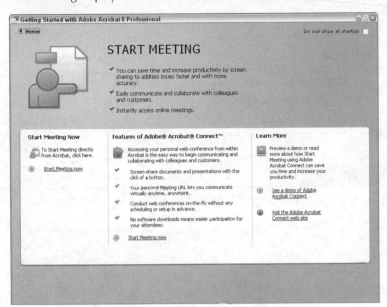

■ **Secure.** The Secure task pane contains information on securing PDF files. (See Figure 3.6.) Information is provided in the center of the pane for the many options Adobe offers you with PDF security and some links to help information that describes how to secure PDF files. Also, a link is made to the Create security envelope dialog box.

CROSS-REF For more information related to securing PDF files, see Chapter 26.

■ **Sign.** The Sign tasks pane shown in Figure 3.7 provides you with information links to help files related to digital IDs and digitally signing documents.

FIGURE 3.6

The Secure task pane provides information for adding security to PDF documents.

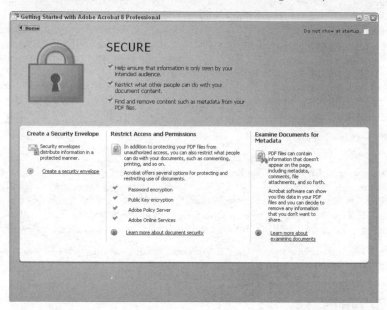

FIGURE 3.7

The Sign pane provides information related to digital signatures.

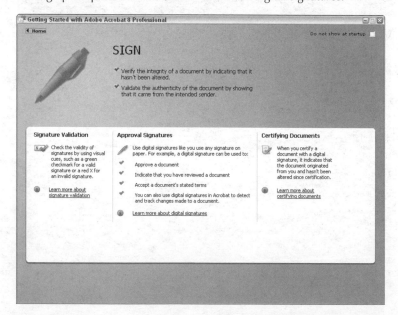

CROSS-REF For more information related to digital IDs and digitally signing PDFs, see Chapter 26.

■ **Forms.** A number of different links appear in the Forms task pane to pages in the Adobe Help Viewer and to dialog boxes for creating and editing forms. In Figure 3.8, you can see options for Browsing a template library (Windows), Convert an existing document, Scan a paper form, Create a new form, track forms, Distribute forms, and Compile data. All these links open dialog boxes or launch another program. On Windows, links to Create a new form and Browse the Template library launch Adobe LiveCycle Designer. On the Mac, you won't find the Browse the template library link, because Designer isn't supported. Other links are made to help files that provide more information on creating and editing forms.

CROSS-REF For information on working in Adobe Designer, see Chapter 33. For more information related to creating and editing PDF forms, see Chapter 34. For more information on collecting and compiling data, see Chapter 35.

■ **Review and Comment.** The last of the tasks panes is the Review and Comment pane shown in Figure 3.9. Here you find links to help information related to commenting and review sessions. The Start a shared review features action button opens a wizard that walks you through steps to create a review session. The task actions buttons at the bottom of the E-mail and Shared columns open wizards that walk you through steps for starting n e-mail-based review or a shared review.

CROSS-REF For more information related to commenting and markups, see Chapter 20. For more information on shared reviews, see Chapter 21.

FIGURE 3.8

The Forms task pane provides information for help with creating and editing PDF forms and links that open dialog boxes and Adobe Designer (Windows only).

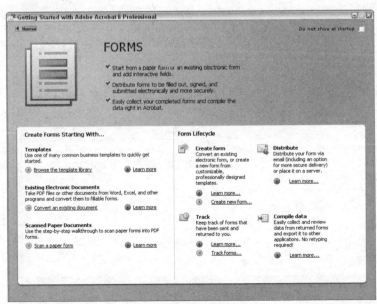

FIGURE 3.9

The Review & Comment task pane provides information for help with commenting and review sessions and links to a dialog box and a wizard to start and track reviews.

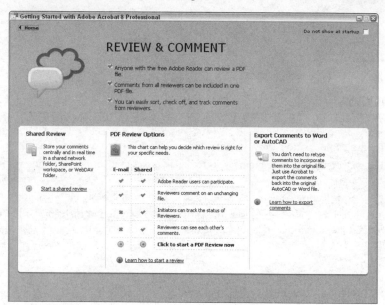

Opening the Tasks Descriptions from Tasks Buttons

If you look at the Tasks toolbar at the top of the Acrobat window you'll see the same tasks you find in the Getting Started window — that is, all but the last task button used for Send for Review. The first eight task buttons in the Tasks toolbar each have a menu command at the bottom of the task button drop-down menu that opens the Getting Started with Adobe Acrobat 8 Professional window and opens the pane respective to the task from which you select the menu command. In Figure 3.10, the menu command appears at the bottom of the Combine Files task button. As you can see, the menu command appears as Getting Started Combining Files. When you select this command, the Getting Started with Adobe Acrobat 8 Professional window opens and the Combine Files task pane is placed in view. Respectively, all the other task buttons menu commands, with the exception of the Send for Review task button, launch the Getting Started with Adobe Acrobat 8 window and open panes according to the task button menu item you select.

FIGURE 3.10

Task buttons contain menu items that open the Getting Started with Adobe Acrobat 8 window.

Summary

- The Getting Started with Adobe Acrobat welcome window appears in all Acrobat 8 viewers.
- The welcome window provides help information related to many different Acrobat features.
- The welcome window contains links to dialog boxes that support working within a particular feature.
- The Forms feature pane has a few links that open Adobe Designer on Windows.
- All the task buttons in the Tasks toolbar with the exception of the Send for Review task button contain menu commands to open the welcome window and the feature related to the task button menu item.

Chapter 4

Getting Familiar with Adobe Reader

A s a PDF author you need to be aware of the capabilities and the limitations of the Adobe Reader software. In some situations you can distribute PDF documents to users of the free Adobe Reader software for active participation in your workflow without all your clients and colleagues needing to purchase the full version of Acrobat Standard or Acrobat Professional. In other situations where the Adobe Reader software does not contain tools or commands to properly edit a file for a given workflow, you may need to recommend to others which commercial viewer they need to purchase. Regardless of where you are with PDF creation and editing, at one time or another you'll be called upon to explain some of the differences between the viewers.

Adobe Reader has matured as a product and the newest release offers users much more functionality than any previous version. Features that have long been requested by users such as being able to save form data and add digital signatures are now available in Adobe Reader 8. However, the features are document-specific and require at least one person in a workflow attempting to use these new tools to author a file in Acrobat 8 Professional.

This chapter covers most of what you need to know about Adobe Reader as both a user and as a PDF author preparing documents for Reader users.

Welcome to Adobe Reader

The first change you notice when launching Adobe Reader 8 is the welcome screen. The Beyond Adobe Reader welcome screen shown in Figure 4.1 opens when you first launch the program. Each time you launch Reader the same screen opens unless you check the box "Do not show at start up." If you dismiss the screen by checking the box for all subsequent launches of Reader, you can bring the screen back any time by selecting Help ➪ Beyond Adobe Reader. Alternately, you can also bring the Beyond Adobe Reader screen back by opening

a context menu on the Toolbar Well and selecting Beyond Adobe Reader. Another method for showing the Beyond Adobe Reader window is to load the Beyond Adobe Reader tool from the More Tools window. (See the section "Adobe Reader Tools" later in this chapter.)

On your first launch of Adobe Reader, the Beyond Adobe Reader welcome screen opens.

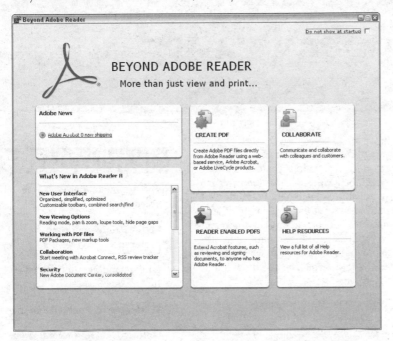

NEW FEATURE The Beyond Adobe Reader window is similar to the Getting Started with Adobe Acrobat window that opens when you launch Acrobat Standard and Acrobat Professional. Like the other Acrobat viewers, clicking one of the item links opens another pane in the window where some help information and directions are provided.

On the left side of the window are some topics related to what's new in Adobe Reader 8. On the right are four separate links to panes describing features in Adobe Reader 8.

Click Create PDF and you see the Create PDF pane shown in Figure 4.2. The information describes PDF creation for Adobe Reader users such as how to create PDFs online. In addition, information is provided for PDF creation in the Adobe Acrobat and Adobe Server products. Clicking the Learn more links opens your default Web browser and takes you to pages on Adobe's Web site where more information is provided about Acrobat and Adobe Server products.

Notice the Home link in the top-left corner of the Create PDF pane. Any time you click a link that opens another pane, you can easily return to the default Home page view in Beyond Adobe Reader by clicking Home.

FIGURE 4.2

Click Create PDF and the Create PDF pane opens with information provided on PDF creation alternatives for Adobe Reader users.

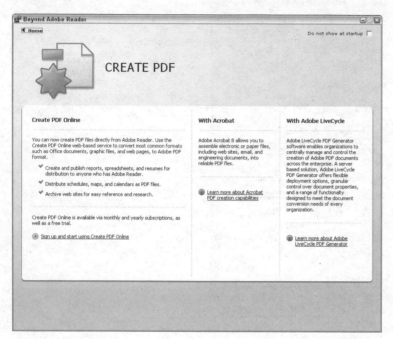

Click Home and you return to the opening screen. Click the Collaborate item on the Home page and the Collaborate pane opens as shown in Figure 4.3. This pane describes information related to review sessions and how Adobe Reader users can participate in reviews. In the center column, you see information related to tracking reviews. Like the Create PDF pane, click the Learn more links and your Web browser opens a page on Adobe's Web site where more information is provided about the topic.

NEW FEATURE In the right column some information is provided about Acrobat Connect and participating in online meetings. Again, clicking links in this area opens a Web page on Adobe's Web site where you can find more information on starting meetings and participating in online meetings.

CROSS-REF For more information on using Acrobat Connect and participating in online meetings, see Chapter 29.

Click the Home link and you return to the Home pane. In the lower-left corner, a link to information related to working with Adobe Reader–enabled files appears. Click Reader Enabled PDFs and the Reader Enabled PDF Files pane opens, as shown in Figure 4.4. This pane details information about files enabled with special usage rights and information on Adobe LiveCycle server products.

FIGURE 4.3

Click Collaborate and the Collaborate pane opens.

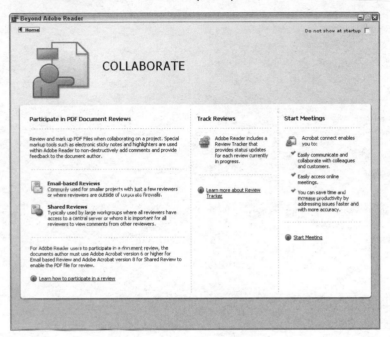

Like the other panes in the Beyond Adobe Reader screen, clicking links opens Web pages where more detail is provided about the respective items. Click the text links on the left side of the pane and the items expand providing some detail on Forms, Reviews, and Security. On the right side of the pane are links to Web pages where Reader enablement in Acrobat and Adobe LiveCycle Server products are explained.

CROSS-REF   For more information on enabling PDFs see the section "Enabling Adobe Reader usage Rights" later in this chapter and more in Chapter 19.

Click Home and click Help Resources and you see the final pane offering help information, as shown in Figure 4.5. For Adobe Reader users, you might want to refer the Reader user to this pane when viewing your PDFs. This pane offers some valuable help information on using Adobe Reader.

FIGURE 4.4

Click Reader Enabled PDF Files and the Reader Enabled PDF Files pane opens.

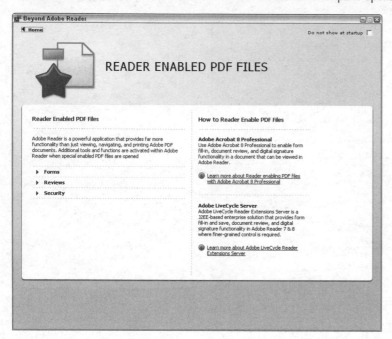

A variety of help topics appear in this pane. In the left column are some text descriptions and a few links that take the user to Web pages for online support and user forums. In the center column you see links for paid support programs. In the right column are Web links containing PDF documents providing information on Adobe Customization Wizard and Adobe PDF Security. Adobe Customization Wizard is particularly helpful for IT managers who want to customize Acrobat and Reader installations in large-scale deployments.

CROSS-REF For more information on Adobe PDF Security, see Chapter 26.

FIGURE 4.5

Click Help Resources and the Help pane opens.

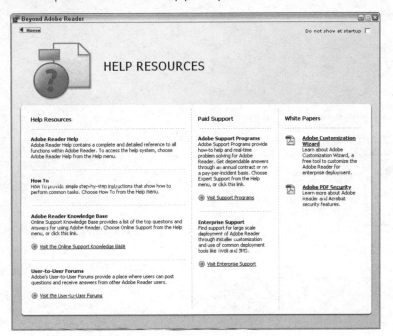

Setting Some Critical Preferences

Like the Acrobat viewers, Adobe Reader has an enormous number of different preference options designed to add more functionality to the program and to help you tailor your workspace and tools to suit personal workflows.

In previous versions of Acrobat you had at least one behavior common to all viewers in all versions prior to version 8. Acrobat and Reader were fixed environments where documents all opened in the same workspace. You could open multiple files, use the same tools and menus, bring documents forward in the Document pane, and all the views were maximized to fit your monitor size by default.

NEW FEATURE The view you're used to seeing in Acrobat viewers has changed. By default, documents now open in individual windows that are minimized and don't occupy the entire monitor size. When you open additional documents, the files open in separate windows, all having individual toolbars and menus attached to the individual files. Figure 4.6 shows how two PDF documents appear as a default in Acrobat Professional.

You may like the new look of the Acrobat viewers when working on PDFs. Personally, I found this to be the most aggravating view when working with my documents—especially in Acrobat Professional when I want to exchange content between documents. It may have its uses, but I personally like the traditional view of the Acrobat workspace. If you're like me, you'll want to immediately change the view. Fortunately, Adobe did not forget us old timers and added a preference setting for you to toggle the view.

FIGURE 4.6

By default, PDF documents open in separate windows and appear minimized on the screen.

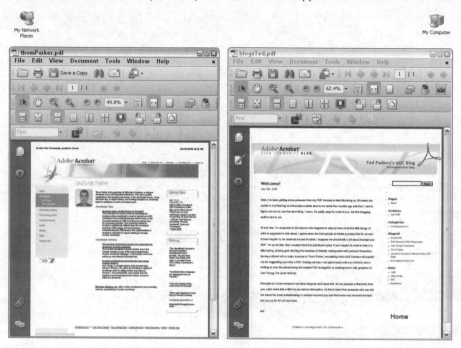

Open the Preferences dialog box by pressing Ctrl/⌘+K. In the Left pane of the Preferences dialog box, click Documents. Check the first check box in the right pane where you see Show each document in its own window (requires restart), as in Figure 4.7. Notice the label for the check box indicates you need to restart Acrobat before the preference item will take effect.

FIGURE 4.7

Click the Show each document in its own window (requires restart) check box in the Documents preferences.

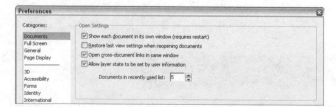

After you click OK, quit Adobe Reader (Ctrl/⌘+Q) and then relaunch the program. When you open two documents and tile the views, you see a workspace like you had available with earlier Acrobat viewers, as shown in Figure 4.8.

Preferences settings are detailed throughout this book in chapters that specifically relate to tools and commands. Just a couple of other preference options you want to start with in Reader include some settings to help you prepare for some of the features described in other chapters.

Open the Preferences dialog box (Ctrl/⌘+K) and click General in the left pane. Check Use single-key accelerators to access tools at the top of the right pane. When this check box is checked, you can access tools by pressing a key on your keyboard. For example, when another tool is selected, you can access the Hand tool by pressing the H key.

You'll also want to edit Identity preferences. When you engage in comment reviews and add comments in review sessions, you're prompted to edit your Identity preferences. To prepare your work environment, take time now to add your Identity information. Press Ctrl/⌘+K to open the Preferences dialog box and click Identity in the left pane. In the right pane, fill in the text boxes with your personal identity information as shown in Figure 4.9.

FIGURE 4.8

The traditional workspace shows multiple documents all having the same toolbars and menu commands and the files open in a maximized view.

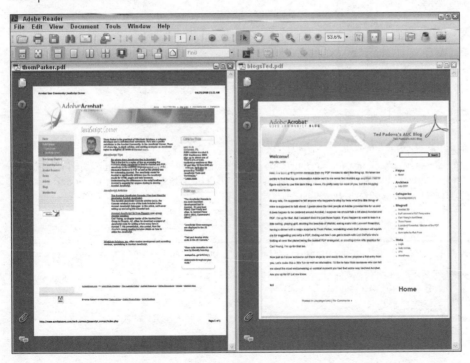

There are many more preferences you can adjust, but these few changes will get the Adobe Reader going for a good many viewing and editing sessions. After you make your edits in the Preferences dialog box, click OK, and then quit Adobe Reader. You'll want to quit and relaunch the program before doing anything else. In the unlikely event you experience a program crash after making preference changes, all your new preference changes are lost. The best way to guard against losing the preference changes is to quit and restart Reader *before* you experience a program crash.

FIGURE 4.9

Click Identity in the left pane and fill in the text boxes in the right pane to set up your Identity preferences.

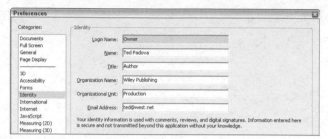

Adobe Reader Tools

What distinguishes Adobe Reader and other viewers is, in part, the tools. Knowing what the user can do with the Reader tools and what tools are not available in Reader is helpful if you intend to distribute documents to Reader users.

All tools available in Adobe Reader have counterparts in Acrobat Standard and Acrobat Professional. The Reader tools are the same in the other viewers; however, some of the Adobe Reader tools offer more limited features than the same tool used in the other viewers.

Loading tools and toolbars

Before you take a look at the individual tools you have available in Reader, you'll want to know how you go about loading tools and toolbars. A toolbar contains one or more tools that can be added or temporarily removed from a toolbar. You have one of two ways to access a window where toolbars are loaded and tools respective to a toolbar are added and removed.

NEW FEATURE   Select Tools ➪ Customize Toolbars or open a context menu on the toolbar window (right-click on Windows or Ctrl+click on the Mac) and select More Tools, as shown in Figure 4.10. Accessing either the Customize Toolbars or the More Tools menu command opens the More Tools window shown in Figure 4.11. The More Tools window is a new feature in all Acrobat viewers.

The More Tools window shown in Figure 4.11 is a scrollable window listing the various toolbars available to Adobe Reader. Below the bold type for most of the toolbars is a list of tools that can be loaded or unloaded from the respective toolbar. Click the check mark adjacent to a toolbar name and the toolbar opens as a floating toolbar in the Document pane. All tools marked with a check mark appear loaded in the toolbar. To hide tools from a given toolbar, uncheck the tools you want to remain hidden.

Notice that you can also load tools from a context menu and a few tools from the Tools menu. However, to customize the toolbars you need to open the More Tools window. Once a toolbar is opened in Reader, you can dock the toolbar(s) by opening a context menu from the Toolbar Well and selecting Dock Toolbars. The toolbars are then organized within the Toolbar Well.

FIGURE 4.10

Open a context menu on the Toolbar Well and select More Tools at the bottom of the menu to open the More Tools window.

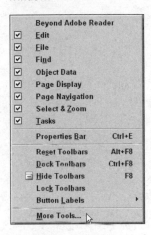

> **NOTE** If you set up your workspace to show each document in its own window, loading toolbars is respective to the window where you load the tools. Theoretically you can have several files open in Adobe Reader in its own window and you can have different tools appearing in each window.

FIGURE 4.11

Check the tools and toolbars you want shown in the Reader workspace.

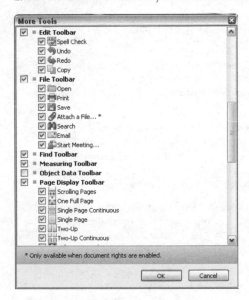

Getting familiar with the Reader tools

The first thing to understand about tools in Adobe Reader is that you have two different tool sets dependent on the kind of PDF file you open. In addition, you have a few different menu commands depending on the kind of PDF file you open.

If you open a PDF document with no special usage rights, you have fewer accessible tools and menu commands than when you open PDFs having special features. Notice that when you open the More Tools window, the second toolbar you see is the Comment & Markup toolbar. If you open a PDF file that isn't enabled for commenting, you can't open the Comment & Markup Toolbar. If you open a file that has special usage rights for Adobe Reader for commenting, then the Comment & Markup tools can be opened. These *optional* toolbars and tools are noted with an "*" to help you understand that they will only appear when the PDF allows the functionality to work.

Default tools

To start off a discussion on Adobe Reader tools, let's first take a look at the tools you have available when opening a PDF document with no special features. In this section, I refer to these tools as the default tools. Later, I'll talk about the additional tools you have available when opening files having special features.

CROSS-REF For more on PDFs with special features, see "Enabling Adobe Reader Usage Rights" later in this chapter. For enabling features with Acrobat Professional, see Chapter 19.

The Adobe Reader tools available to you when working on PDFs without special usage rights include the following:

- **Beyond Adobe Reader toolbar.** Open this tool and keep it docked in the Toolbar Well if you want to access the Beyond Adobe Reader window frequently.

- **Edit toolbar.** The Edit tools include Spell Check, Undo, Redo, and Copy.

- **File toolbar.** The File tools include Open, Print, Save a Copy, Search, E-mail, and Start Meeting. The Save a Copy tool saves a duplicate copy of the PDF document. You might use the tool for saving a PDF from an inline view in a Web browser. When files have been enabled with usage rights, the Save a Copy tool changes to the Save tool.

CROSS-REF For information related to using the E-mail tool, see Chapter 27. For information related to using the Print tool, see Chapter 31. For information related to using the Search tool, see Chapter 6.

- **Find toolbar.** The Find tool enables you to perform a text search in the open PDF document.

CROSS-REF For information related to using the Find toolbar, see Chapter 6.

- **Object Data toolbar.** The Object Data toolbar, explained in Chapter 1, is used to select objects (text, images, or vector) on a document page. When you select an object with this tool, the Object Data dialog box opens and displays information about an object that was originally supplied in an authoring program. The Object Data tool works only with objects where certain metadata were originally supplied in another program such as AutoCAD or Microsoft Visio.

- **Page Display.** The tools all relate to the document display in the Reader workspace. You can view pages as single page layouts, continuous, facing, and so on. The Full Screen tool takes you into Full Screen mode. Tools for rotating pages and viewing line weights at 1-pixel widths are also included in this toolbar.

CROSS-REF For more information on page layout views, see Chapter 5. For more on Full Screen mode, see Chapter 28. For more on rotating pages see Chapter 16.

- **Page Navigation toolbar.** This toolbar contains the First Page, Previous Page, Next Page, Last Page, Previous View, and Next View tools. Additionally, you can type a number in the text box to jump to a page.

CROSS-REF For information related to navigating PDF documents, see Chapter 5.

- **Select & Zoom toolbar.** The tools include Select, Hand, Marquee Zoom, Dynamic Zoom, Zoom Out, Zoom In, Actual Size, Fit Width, Fit Page, Pan and Zoom Window, Loupe, and Snapshot. The Select tool is used for selecting text and images, the zoom tools are used for page zooms, and the page layout tools are used for fitting the page to different sizes. New to Adobe Reader in version 8 are the Pan and Zoom Window and Loupe tools.

CROSS-REF For information related to using the Zoom, Loupe, and Pan and Zoom Window tools, see Chapter 5. For information related to using the Select tool, see Chapters 13 and 15. For more on page layout tools, see Chapter 5.

Tools available with enabled PDF documents

- **Comment & Markup toolbar.** All the tools in this toolbar are used for commenting on PDF documents enabled with special usage rights.

CROSS-REF For a comprehensive view of using all the Comment & Markup tools, see Chapter 20.

- **Measuring toolbar.** This toolbar contains tools also used for commenting. The tools are used for measuring distances and areas in engineering drawings.

CROSS-REF For more information on using the measuring tools, see Chapter 24.

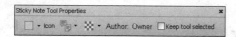

- **Properties Bar.** Even though Adobe Reader does have a Properties Bar you can open on PDFs that are not enabled with usage rights, none of the default tools have options that appear in the Properties Bar. The Properties Bar is used in PDF documents carrying usage rights for commenting. When used in conjunction with the Comment & Markup tools, you see comment properties appearing in the toolbar.

CROSS-REF For more information on using the Properties toolbar, see Chapter 20.

- **Tasks toolbar.** The Tasks toolbar includes the Sign and Review & Comment tasks. These tools work with documents enabled with usage rights.

CROSS-REF For more on using the Sign tool, see Chapter 26. Form more on using the Review & Comment tool, see Chapter 20.

- **Typewriter toolbar.** The Typewriter tool is used to type text on forms where no form fields are available.

CROSS-REF For more information on using the Typewriter tool, see Chapter 33.

In addition to the aforementioned tools, Adobe Reader contains tabs docked in the Navigation pane. To view all the Navigation Panels select View ➪ Navigation Panels. A submenu contains all the Navigation Panels you can access in Reader, as shown in Figure 4.12. Depending on the type of PDF you have open, some panels may or may not be accessible.

CROSS-REF For more information on using Navigation Panels, see Chapter 1.

FIGURE 4.12

Select View ➪ Navigation Panels to see the Navigation Panels available in Reader. When documents with special usage rights are open, the Document Extensions and Signatures panels are accessible.

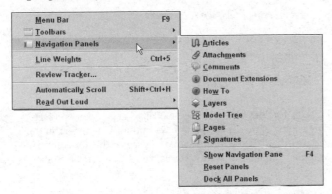

Enabling Adobe Reader Usage Rights

One of the best new additions to the Adobe Reader software is the ability to save form data and add digital signatures to PDFs that have been deployed with certain usage rights. To create a Reader-enabled document for certain usage rights, you need Acrobat Professional or Adobe LiveCycle Reader Extensions Server. In Acrobat Professional you can add usage rights that enable an Adobe Reader user to comment on a PDF file, save the comments, invite Reader users to participate in an e-mail–based review or shared review, save form data, and add digital signatures.

CROSS-REF For a complete description of using comment tools, starting an e-mail review, or starting a shared review, see Chapter 20. For more on saving form data from within Reader, see Chapter 33.

All the comment and forms usage rights are enabled in Acrobat Professional. When you want to distribute a document for Reader users to mark up and comment, choose Comments ➪ Enable for Commenting in Adobe Reader. The Enable Usage Rights in Adobe Reader dialog box opens as shown in Figure 4.13. Click the Save Now button and the PDF is enabled for commenting, saving form data, and adding digital signatures.

CROSS-REF For more on enabling PDFs with Reader usage rights, see Chapter 19.

FIGURE 4.13

With a simple menu command in Acrobat Professional you can enable PDFs for Adobe Reader users for commenting, saving data on forms, and adding digital signatures.

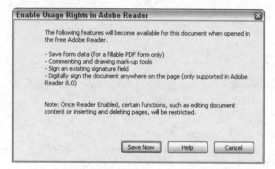

Commenting in Adobe Reader

Be certain you are aware of the fact that you need to grant a PDF document usage rights in Acrobat Professional by choosing Comments ➪ Enable for Commenting in Adobe Reader before a Reader user can make comments. When the file is enabled with usage rights, the Comment & Markup tools are accessible. If an Adobe Reader user opens a PDF document without usage rights enabled, the comment tools are not accessible.

Notice that Adobe Reader users have access to all comment and markup tools, as well as the ability to create and use custom stamps. When an Adobe Reader user marks up a document with the commenting tools, the file can be saved and the comments preserved. Documents enabled with usage rights also include a File ➪ Save command. By default, Adobe Reader permits saving an unedited copy of a PDF document only if usage rights are not enabled.

CROSS-REF For information on using the comment and markup tools and creating custom stamps, see Chapter 20.

Using file attachments

A file attachment is an external file that can be a PDF document or any other document saved from any program. The PDF acts as a wrapper container for the file attachment. File attachments can be extracted and saved to disk outside the PDF or opened in the native application in which the original document was created. In order to view a document in a native application, the original authoring program must be installed on your computer.

CROSS-REF For information on attaching and extracting files, see Chapter 20.

Another feature available in Adobe Reader is the ability to extract file attachments. Files can be attached to a PDF by a Reader user when a PDF document is enabled with usage rights for Adobe Reader users. When an Acrobat user attaches a file to a PDF, Adobe Reader users can extract the file attachments. A separate tab in the Navigation pane enables the Reader user to open, save, and search file attachments. Click the Attachments tab to open a panel where you can access tools to manage the attachments.

One great feature in all Acrobat viewers is the ability to attach any file type to a PDF document and secure the PDF with password protection. After a PDF has been encrypted with password security, the end user needs the access password in order to either open the PDF document or extract the attachment. With the process accessible to Adobe Reader users, business professionals in all industries will find much greater use for Adobe Reader 8.

CROSS-REF For information on adding permissions rights with Acrobat security, see Chapter 26.

Working with Forms in Adobe Reader

The other half of enabling PDF documents for Adobe Reader users involves adding usage rights for saving PDF forms and adding digital signatures. This feature has long been requested by many Acrobat users and has now been introduced in Acrobat 8.

NEW FEATURE When you select Advanced ➪ Enable Usage Rights in Adobe Reader and click the Save Now button your files are enabled for commenting, saving form data, and using digital signatures n Adobe Reader. As soon as you open a PDF with usage rights, you'll notice the Save command available in the File menu. Any form data you add to form fields can then be saved by the Reader user. In addition to saving form data, you can also create and use digital signatures on documents enabled with usage rights.

When you enable files for Reader users so the users can save form data, some restrictions apply. You need to be aware of the stipulations in the End User License Agreement (EULA) and the limitations detailed in this agreement.

CROSS-REF For more information on limitations related to PDF forms and special usage rights for Reader users, see Chapter 19.

Getting Help

In addition to help information you find in the Beyond Adobe Reader window, the Help menu provides a number of different options for help information and keeping the Reader product fine-tuned and updated. Click the Help menu and the menu options shown in Figure 4.14 appear.

The items in the Help menu are as follows:

- **Adobe Reader 8 Help.** Select this menu item and the complete online Help document opens. For just about any kind of help you need in working with Reader, this document provides you with detailed information on all Reader features.

- **Beyond Adobe Reader.** This menu item opens the Beyond Adobe Reader window.

- **How to.** This menu item opens the How To navigation panel where additional help information can be obtained for Adobe Reader Essentials and working with Large Document Formats.

- **Online Support.** Select this menu command and a submenu offers several choices for using Adobe's hosted services such as Create Adobe PDF Online and Protect PDF Online.

- **About Adobe Reader 8.** This menu item opens a screen showing you the current version of Reader installed on your computer. This command is particularly helpful when you want to know the current maintenance upgrade you have installed on your computer.

- **About Adobe Plug-ins.** If you have any plug-ins installed the plug-ins are displayed along with the Adobe default plug-ins. You can find plug-in descriptions and release dates in the About Adobe Plug-ins window.

- **Repair Adobe Reader Installation.** If you find performance or functionality problems, select this menu command. Adobe Reader has a self-healing feature that can often correct problems.

- **Purchase Adobe Acrobat.** When Reader users are ready to upgrade to Acrobat, they can click the menu command and order one of the Acrobat products online from Adobe Systems.

- **Adobe Online Services.** Another Web page view, the Adobe Online Services provides more information on Reader, Acrobat, and PDF.

- **Check for Updates.** If you suspect your version of Reader is not current, select this menu command to check for an update. If a newer version exists, you are prompted to install the newer version.

FIGURE 4.14

Click Help and the Help menu opens where additional help information and other services are accessed.

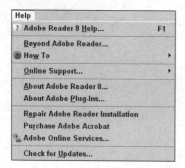

Adding More Functionality to Adobe Reader

You may look over the new Adobe Reader 8 and wish for more features or wonder why Adobe Systems didn't add more to the newest release. If the thought occurs to you, keep in mind that Adobe Systems offers the Reader software free of charge. Adobe Reader is certainly one of the most feature-rich applications that can be acquired without purchase.

If you want more from Adobe Reader, you do have other purchase options available to you from Adobe Systems. From PDF creation to saving form data for enterprise solutions, Adobe does make these features available to you in the form of online services and server-side applications.

Creating PDFs online

If your clients or colleagues don't have Acrobat Standard or Acrobat Professional and they need to create an occasional PDF file, they can download the free Adobe Reader software and choose File ➪ Create Adobe PDF Online. Create Adobe PDF Online is a Web service from Adobe Systems that permits users to upload documents of several different file types. The user uploads the file(s) to Adobe's Web site, where it is then converted to PDF and sent back to the user. A free trial period enables you to create your first five PDFs free of charge. After the fifth PDF creation, the cost is $9.99 (US) per month or an annual subscription of $99.99 (US) per year.

Create PDF Online supports many different file formats. The native document formats are as follows:

- **Microsoft Office.** All Microsoft Office files for Mac and Windows.
- **Other Microsoft formats.** Microsoft Publisher is supported.
- **Adobe formats.** Those programs not supporting direct export to PDF, such as earlier versions of PageMaker without the PDF plug-in, are supported. All Creative Suite programs now support export to PDF and using a service to create PDF files is not necessary.
- **AutoDesk AutoCAD.** AutoCAD is supported.
- **Corel WordPerfect Office formats.** Corel WordPerfect files can be converted to PDF.
- **Adobe PostScript formats.** Any program you use that's capable of printing can be printed to disk as a PostScript file. You can submit the PostScript file for conversion to PDF.
- **Text formats.** All ASCII (American Code for Information Interchange) and Rich Text Format (RTF) files can be converted to PDF.
- Image formats. Most of the common image formats such as Windows bitmap (.bmp), GIF (.gif), JPEG (.jpg/.jpeg), PCX (.pcx), PICT (Macintosh) (.pct/.pict), PNG (.png), RLE (.rle), and TIFF (.tif) can be converted to PDF.

In addition to Create PDF Online, Adobe also offers Create a Protected PDF Online where you can order PDF creation and security online. Adobe continually adds new services. To see the latest offerings for online services select Help ➪ Adobe Online Services.

CROSS-REF   **For information on converting native application documents to PDF, see Chapters 7 through 9. For information on printing PostScript files and converting PostScript files to PDF, see Chapter 10.**

Understanding Adobe Reader Extensions

The advanced tools in Adobe Reader for comment and markup, save forms, and digital signatures are features that are available through the Adobe LiveCycle Reader Extensions Server. For users of earlier versions of Acrobat, Reader Extensions enabled users of Adobe Reader versions below 7.0 to perform comment and markup, save forms, and digital signatures functions. The Adobe LiveCycle Reader Extensions Server is an enterprise solution intended for large companies that have the technology and resources to offer cost effective solutions for many users or those who want to automate processes like adding these enabling rights to PDFs. As an example, for 250 users, individual costs break down to about $60 (US) per user.

The addition of enabling documents for Reader users in Acrobat Professional to save form data and add digital signatures carries limitations in the End User License Agreement. For enterprise solutions where the needs exceed the licensing limitations, the Adobe LiveCycle Reader Extensions server offers unlimited use of PDF files enabled with usage rights.

For information about Adobe LiveCycle Reader Extensions Server, log on to Adobe's Web site at `www.adobe.com/products/readerextensions/main.html`. You'll find more information about the server-side software and how to acquire it for your company.

What We Lost in Adobe Reader 8

If you stop and think for a moment, software developers have to be struggling continually as a product is upgraded to determine what features need to be added and what features can be safely removed without creating problems for the user community. As we evolve with software development, it would be virtually impossible to retain all features while adding new features for any program. At some point the application would become so large, performance would greatly suffer. Currently, the download for Acrobat Professional on the Mac exceeds 1 gigabyte. To keep adding more features without eliminating the least used features would expand the program from 1 gigabyte to 2, then to 3 and so on as the program evolves. At some point the performance would deteriorate even on the most powerful computers.

As we upgrade software we will no doubt continually see some features eliminated in favor of newer features meeting more users' needs and conforming to new technology developments. Features lost in Reader 8 include the Picture Tasks tool and Digital Editions Bookshelf. You can no longer work with Pictures Tasks and the tool won't appear when you open image files, files created in Adobe Photoshop Album, or Adobe Photoshop Elements. The Digital Editions Bookshelf really hasn't been lost. It's actually been revamped and improved and is now called the Adobe Digital Edition Library. Some of the features you had with the Digital Edition Bookshelf don't appear in the Adobe Digital Edition Library, such as creating categories and subcategories. However, the new user interface makes reading eBooks and Digital Editions more pleasing and appealing.

CROSS-REF For more information on working with eBooks, Digital Editions, and the Adobe Digital Edition Library, see Chapter 30.

Adobe is a company that assesses each new product upgrade according to user feedback to determine what features are most often requested and what features are least used. This feedback shapes the development for the next product upgrade. If you find a particular feature eliminated in a product upgrade, then voice your complaint. If enough users ask for a feature, you'll see the feature return or be implemented in the next release. But be aware: A voice of one won't change the development of a product. Adobe can respond only to the majority of users.

Summary

- Adobe Reader usage rights are enabled in Acrobat Professional. When a PDF has been enabled with commenting, form data saving, and digital signatures usage rights, Reader users can comment and mark up a document, participate in an e-mail–based review, save comment updates, save data on PDF forms, and add digital signatures.

- File attachments can be extracted from within Adobe Reader. When usage rights have been enabled in a PDF document, Adobe Reader users can attach files to PDFs.

- Help and product performance options are available from menu commands in the Help menu.

- Adobe Systems provides an online service for converting files saved in a number of different formats to PDF. You can easily access the online service from within Adobe Reader by choosing File ➪ Create Adobe PDF Online.

- Adobe Reader Extensions Server is a J2EE-based server-side solution intended for automating the addition of user rights as well as meeting the needs for large-scale enablement requirements. With the Reader Extensions Server you can enable PDFs for using web services, spawning templates, decoding 2D barcodes, saving form data, and digitally signing PDFs from within Adobe Reader.

- Adobe Reader 8 no longer supports Picture Tasks or categorizing eBooks in a Digital Edition Bookshelf.

Chapter 5

Viewing and Navigating PDF Files

A crobat viewers provide you with many different kinds of tools to view pages and move around PDF documents. As a visitor to PDFs created by other PDF authors, you can use many tools within the program to browse pages and find information quickly. As a PDF author you can create viewing options and links to views you know will help the end user explore your files. In this chapter, I cover all viewing tools, pages, documents, and the different kinds of viewing options you have available in Acrobat viewers. I leave the authoring items and how-to methods to other chapters. For now, just realize this chapter is an abbreviated form of looking at a huge list of possibilities for viewing and navigation. The amplified explanations follow in several other chapters.

If you're familiar with Acrobat 7 viewers, you'll find little change with viewing options in Acrobat 8. Some of the tools have been reorganized a little, but their uses and the menu commands options are very similar to earlier versions of Acrobat.

Setting Up the Work Environment

At the beginning of all subsequent chapters, I begin the chapter by offering suggestions for setting up your work environment. As you can see in Chapter 1, all the Acrobat viewers contain many tools and palettes, and most of these tools and palettes are hidden when you first launch the program. Because Acrobat can do so many things for so many different working professionals, Adobe Systems didn't intend for you to use all the tools and palettes in each editing session. Therefore, you have the opportunity to open and hide different tools and palettes depending on the kind of edits you want to make. As you begin each chapter, look over the section related to setting up the work environment for suggestions on what tools and palettes should be loaded to follow along as you read a chapter.

Open a context menu (right click Windows or Control click Mac) on the Toolbar Well and select More Tools. Scroll to the Page Navigation toolbar and check all tools.

Scroll down to the File Toolbar and select the Organizer tool. Scroll further down to the Select and Zoom toolbar. Check all tools and make certain a check mark appears adjacent to the Page Display Toolbar.

Open a context menu on the Toolbar Well and select Dock Toolbars. Return to the context menu and select Button Labels ➪ All Labels. This view shows the names of tools within toolbars to help you become more familiar with tool names.

After loading toolbars and making choices in the context menu opened from the Toolbar Well, your Toolbar Well should look like Figure 5.1.

FIGURE 5.1

The Viewing and Page Display toolbars loaded in the Toolbar Well

As is explained in this chapter, several tools and menu commands provide a means for navigating pages and documents. When you're familiar with alternative methods, you can leave the Navigation toolbar hidden, especially if you're using other toolbars that occupy a lot of room in the Toolbar Well. If you're new to Acrobat, keep the Navigation toolbar open as you work through this chapter.

Arranging Toolbars in the Acrobat Window

Perhaps one of the most difficult things for most of us to experience is change. Once we become familiar with some form of standard, we like to keep things simple and uncomplicated. As I mentioned in Chapter 1, the Acrobat User Interface (UI) has changed appearance in Acrobat 8 compared to all earlier versions of Acrobat. With regard to toolbars and views, you can immediately see a difference in the UI in Acrobat 8.

If you want to regain a little of the familiar, there are a few things you can do to get the appearance of the Acrobat workplace similar to what you're familiar with in earlier viewers. Follow the steps here to design your Acrobat work environment to regain more of a familiar view as you had with earlier Acrobat viewers. Note that what follows in the steps below is a matter of personal preference.

STEPS: Organizing the Acrobat workplace

1. **Set Preferences.** A couple of Preference items will get you to a more familiar look when using Acrobat 8. Open the Preferences dialog box by pressing Ctrl/⌘+K. The preference items to change include the following:

   ■ **Minimized document views. Click Documents in the left pane to open the Documents preferences (Windows only).** If there's one thing I really hate about the new UI, it's having Acrobat windows minimized to a document's page size. Ten levels of toolbars get you a view like a page thumbnail in the Document pane. To prevent your files from defaulting to this view, remove the check from the box where you see Show each document in its own window

(requires restart). As the item description points out, you need to quit Acrobat and relaunch before the preference setting takes effect. This preference setting opens all your PDFs in a single window with one Toolbar Well. If the check box is enabled, each document you open has a separate Toolbar Well.

For the Mac users, unfortunately you're stuck with the minimized view in Acrobat and all PDF files open with separate Toolbar Wells. There is no preference option on the Mac to change the default view.

■ **Enable single key accelerators. Click General in the left pane to open the General preferences.** This option has always appeared off by default in Acrobat viewers since the preference was added to the General preferences. Check the box for Use single-key accelerators to access tools. Doing so means that when you're working on a document and you want to easily access the Zoom tool, you press the Z key. Pressing H gets you the Hand tool, and so on.

There are many more preferences that apply to specific editing tasks and they are covered when we come to specific features in Acrobat 8 in forthcoming chapters. For now, these preferences in Acrobat can help shape your editing environment for viewing and navigating PDF files. Remember though, these are all personal preferences and you can feel free to change items to suit your workflow.

■ **Always show document page size. Click page Display in the left pane to open the Page Display preferences.** In earlier versions of Acrobat, a document's page size was reported in the document window. This is a critical bit of information for engineers, creating pros, and others who work with files other than standard letter sizes. By default, the information is not displayed. In the Page Display preferences check the box for Always show document page size.

NOTE If you don't have the Always show document page size preference enabled, you can see document page sizes by moving the cursor to the lower left corner of a page. A pop-up display opens when the cursor is positioned in the lower-left corner reporting page sizes in the current established units of measure.

2. **What happened to the Status bar?** Another change in the UI in Acrobat 8 is the elimination of the Status Bar. Adobe removed the Status Bar because it often conflicted with your operating system status bar (the Status Bar on Windows and the Dock on the Mac). This new view provides you more room to view document pages and once you get used to viewing PDFs without the Status Bar, you'll find the removal of the Status Bar to be a nice addition to Acrobat. If you really want to return to a view similar to earlier Acrobat viewers, you can add toolbars and dock them at the bottom of the Acrobat window as shown in Figure 5.2. The point is that Adobe has provided you with the flexibility to customize the Acrobat workplace to suit your personal taste. As an initial default, I recommend you don't dock toolbars at the bottom of the Acrobat window and use the program. You'll soon find that working with keyboard shortcuts and tools in the Toolbar Well will satisfy all your viewing needs without having to load toolbars at the bottom of the Acrobat window.

3. **Quit Acrobat.** After you customize your toolbars and preference settings, quit Acrobat. Acrobat remembers the last settings you made to the toolbars arrangement. Just in case you start moving toolbars around for temporary views, you can return to your initial default by first quitting Acrobat, then restating the program.

4. **Relaunch Acrobat.** Open Acrobat and your settings will appear as you left them before quitting.

FIGURE 5.2

If you want to return to a view with a Status Bar, you can dock toolbars at the bottom of the Acrobat window.

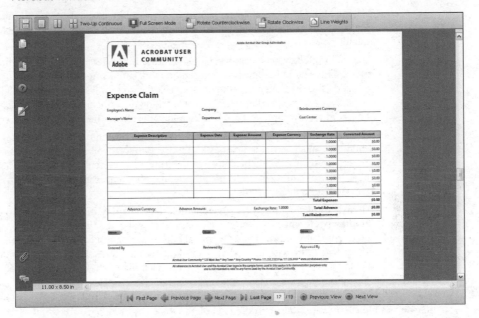

Understanding the *Why* for the Major UI Changes in Acrobat Viewers

When you first launch Acrobat you may be puzzled as to *why* Adobe changed the User Interface (UI) from viewing documents in a single window to multiple windows each with its own set of toolbars. Major changes like this are not simply the whim of a few engineers, but usually rooted in responding to many user requests.

Adobe has moved from an MDI (Multiple Document Interface) to an SDI (Single Document Interface) to keep up with other major applications software such as Microsoft Office. In an SDI interface, each document opens in its own application window. Programs such as Microsoft Internet Explorer and Microsoft Word are SDI applications. In MDI, there's one application window and documents are nested inside that window. Since the release of Acrobat 5 several years ago, Adobe has received many requests from users to move to an SDI.

In an SDI interface, you enjoy opportunities to better view multiple documents and view those documents across multiple monitors. You can open one document and hide toolbars while another document is viewed with toolbars in view. Evolving to an SDI also keeps Acrobat current with new developments with application's software and operating systems.

On Windows, Adobe provides you a choice for viewing files in an SDI or MDI. You control the viewing by opening the Preferences (Ctrl+K) and select Documents. In the right pane you can check the box for Show

each document in its own window (requires restart) to enable the SDI. If you want to return to an MDI, remove the check mark. Quit Acrobat and restart and the new preference option is enabled.

Unfortunately, on the Macintosh, you don't have a choice for switching from SDI to MDI. The program opens in SDI and remains with an SDI view. Part of the problem is the programming involved to switch interfaces on the Mac OS. As is the case with some other features in Acrobat, you find some distinctions between Windows and the Mac OS. The distinctions are not intentional by Adobe engineering, but rather, they are related to limitations and options inaccessible by the Mac OS.

Another major change in the UI is the appearance of the Acrobat Navigation panel icons and the background color in the Document pane. Adobe changed the Navigation tabs to icons to provide more viewing real estate in the Acrobat window, easy access to Navigation panels, and the ability to nest more panels in the Navigation panel. The background color change was made so documents would stand out in the Document pane and provide you with a viewing experience that clearly defines the document within the Document pane.

Major changes in a program all come with a price. The seasoned Acrobat user may initially balk at the changes and be somewhat disappointed. However, once you become familiar with the new look, you should find the many changes in the UI to be pleasing and you should realize the improvements. Adobe engineering devoted much time and research to UI enhancements during the development cycle of Acrobat 8 and what you see in the latest release is a result of many interviews with customers and much research into what users wanted to see in the current version.

Navigating PDF Documents

You can navigate pages in an Acrobat viewer via several means. You can scroll pages with tools, menus, and keystrokes; click hypertext links; and use dialog boxes to move through multiple documents and individual pages. Depending on how a PDF file is created and edited, you can also follow Web links and articles through different sections of a document or through multiple documents. All Acrobat viewers have many navigation controls and several ways to go about viewing and navigating PDF pages.

Navigation toolbar

The tools for navigation in Acrobat Professional and other Acrobat viewers shown in Figure 5.3 with All Labels viewed are as follows:

- **First Page.** In the current active document, the First Page tool returns you to the first page in the document.

- **Previous Page.** The Previous Page tool moves you back one page at a time.

- **Next Page.** The Next Page tool scrolls forward through pages one page at a time.

- **Last Page.** The Last Page tool moves you to the last page in the document.

- **Go to Previous View.** The Go to Previous View tool returns you to the last view displayed on your screen. Whereas the four preceding tools are limited to navigation through a single open document, the Go to Previous View tool returns you to the previous view even if the last view was another file.

- **Go to Next View.** The Go to Next View tool behaves the same as the Go to Previous View tool except it moves in a forward direction. Use of the Go to Previous View and Go to Next View tools can be especially helpful when navigating links that open and close documents. The Next Page and Last Page tools confine you to the active document; whereas the Go to Previous View and Go to Next View tools retrace your navigation steps regardless of how many files you have viewed.

Clicking one of the tools in the toolbar invokes the action associated with the tool. If you want to move through pages left or right, click the left or right arrows. If you want to go to the first or last page in the file, click the respective tools described earlier.

FIGURE 5.3

The Page Navigation toolbar shows the icon and name for each tool when the Button Labels ⇨ All Labels menu selection is made from a context menu command opened from the Toolbar Well.

Context menus

Acrobat viewers make use of context menu commands for page navigation. To use a context menu for moving forward and back in PDF pages and documents, select the Hand tool and click the right mouse button (Windows and two-button Macs) or Ctrl+click (Macintosh) to open the context menu as shown in Figure 5.4.

FIGURE 5.4

Context menus opened on a document page using the Hand tool offer navigation commands to move forward and backward one page at a time and to previous and next views.

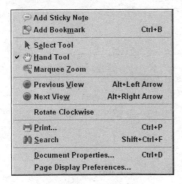

Navigation menu commands

The View menu contains all the page navigation commands contained in the Navigation toolbar. Notice that the View menu clearly describes viewing operations, and new users should be easily able to find menu commands associated with views.

Inasmuch as the View menu enables you to select menu commands that perform the same operations as those performed with the Navigation toolbar, you might opt for using the toolbar or keyboard shortcuts to navigate pages because other methods for page navigation are much easier than returning to menu commands. The real value in the View menu is all the other viewing commands you have accessible. The View menu contains many commands for viewing not only pages, but also toolbars and task buttons. When you choose View ⇨ Go To, the page navigation commands appear in a submenu, as shown in Figure 5.5.

FIGURE 5.5

The View menu contains many different commands for viewing pages, toolbars, and task buttons.

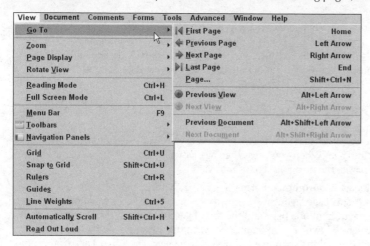

Those viewing commands, apart from the same options you have for navigation with the Navigation toolbar, include commands for viewing tools, for various page views, and alternatives to viewing such as the Reading mode, Read Out Loud, and scrolling pages automatically. Following is a list of what you can find in the View menu.

Go To

The commands that are equal to the actions you perform with the Navigation tools are contained in the Go To submenu. You can choose any of the Navigation commands in this menu and the results are the same as using tools and keyboard shortcuts. You'll probably avoid using the Navigation commands because using any one of the other methods to scroll through pages is so much easier. The exception is the Go To ⇨ Page command. When you select Go To ⇨ Page or press Shift+Ctrl/⌘+N, the Go To Page dialog box opens. Type a number in the text box and click OK and you jump to that page number.

Zoom

A submenu provides menu options for zooming to different views. For more information on using the Zoom options, see Zooming later in this chapter. In addition to zooming in and out with tools and commands, the View ⇨ Zoom submenu has a command for reflowing documents.

- **Reflow.** Document reflow enables users to view PDF documents on adaptive devices for the visually impaired and it is used when copying PDF files to handheld devices and tablets. When you reflow text onscreen or when using other devices, the text in the PDF wraps according to the zoom level of the page or the device viewing area. Therefore, when you zoom in on a paragraph of text and the text moves off the viewing area of your screen, you can use the Reflow command to make the text automatically scroll to your window size.

  Reflow only works with tagged PDF documents in Acrobat viewers earlier than version 7. Acrobat 7 and 8 viewers can reflow any PDF document whether it is a tagged file or not. When you copy PDF documents to handheld devices such as Palm Pilots, Adobe Reader for Palm software wraps text to fit the width of the screen for untagged as well as tagged documents.

 For information about tagging PDF documents, see Chapters 10 and 25.

Page Display

The Page Display view can be any one of four different layout types. Choices for page layout are contained in the View ⇨ Page Display submenu and also the Page Display toolbar. Depending on the way a PDF file has been saved and depending on what preference choices are made for the Initial View, a PDF layout may appear different on different computers according to each individual user's preference settings. Regardless of how you set your preferences, you can change the Page Display view at any time.

 For more information on setting Initial View preferences, see "Initial View" later in this chapter.

- **Single Page.** This layout places an entire page in view when the zoom level is set to Fit Page. When you press the Page Down key or the down-arrow key to scroll pages, the next page snaps into view.

- **Single Page Continuous.** Formerly labeled Continuous in earlier Acrobat viewers. This page layout view show pages in a linear fashion, where you might see the bottom of one page and the top of another page in the Document pane as you scroll down. The difference between this view and Single Page views is that the pages don't snap to a full page when viewed as Single Page Continuous.

- **Two-Up.** Formerly labeled Facing in earlier Acrobat viewers. This view shows two pages — like looking at an open book. When the zoom level is set to Fit Page or lower, only two pages are in view in the Document pane.

- **Two-Up Continuous.** Formerly Continuous–Facing in earlier Acrobat viewers. This page layout view displays a combination of the preceding two options. When the zoom level is zoomed out, the view displays as many pages in the Document pane as can be accommodated by the zoom level.

- **Show Gaps Between Pages.** When you select View ⇨ Page Display ⇨ Show Gaps Between Pages, the page views for Single Page, Two-Up, and Two-Up Continuous are displayed as you see on the left side of Figure 5.6. Remove the check mark by the menu command and the display shown on the right appears.

- **Show Cover Page During Two-Up.** When you view a document in a Two-Up page layout, page 1 and 2 are first shown in the Document pane. Click the Next Page tool and the Document pane shows you pages 3 and 4. If you want to show pages 2 and 3 together, select View ⇨ Page Display ⇨ Show Cover Page During Two-Up. If a document has more than two pages, the Two Columns and Two Pages views display the first page alone on the right side of the Document pane to ensure proper display of two-page spreads.

FIGURE 5.6

Show Gaps Between Pages is turned on in the left side and off in the right side of the figure.

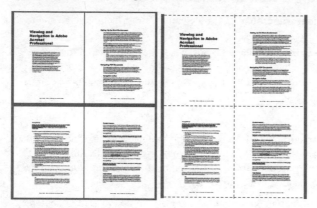

Rotate View

If your PDF opens in Acrobat with a rotated view, you can rotate pages clockwise or counterclockwise from two submenu commands. The same rotations are also available in the Page Display tools. Rotate View commands and tools rotate all pages in your PDF document and come in handy if the PDF pages are rotated on the initial view or if you want to view PDFs on eBook readers, tablets, or laptop computers. However, changes made with the Rotate View tools or the View menu commands are temporary and any saves you make do not record the rotated views. Another set of rotation commands is available in the Document menu. When you select Document ➪ Rotate Pages, a dialog box opens where you can choose Counterclockwise 90 degrees, Clockwise 90 degrees, or 180 degrees. When using the Document menu and the Rotate pages dialog box, the rotation views can be saved with the file.

Reading mode

When you open a PDF document you can choose to view the file in one of two modes where the Acrobat menu remains visible. The two views include the default editing mode and Reading mode. Another mode available to you is Full Screen mode; however, in this mode the menu bar is hidden.

CROSS-REF For more information on Full Screen mode, see Chapter 28.

NEW FEATURE The new Reading mode command changes the view of PDF files in the Acrobat window. To switch to Reading mode, select View ➪ Reading mode or press Ctrl/⌘+H. The screen view immediately changes to a different view. All toolbars are temporarily hidden and the Navigation panel likewise disappears. If you have floating toolbars open the toolbars are hidden when you enter Reading mode. Floating Navigation panels they remain in view when in Reading mode.

Reading mode provides you with more space dedicated to your document without the interference of the Toolbar Well and Navigation panel. This mode makes it especially easier to devote your attention to reading document pages on laptop and tablet computers.

To understand some of the advantages for using Reading mode, follow these steps:

STEPS: Changing a view to Reading mode

1. **Open a document in Acrobat.** Use a file you are most likely to read such as a manual, a book, or essay.

2. **Change the view to a Two Page layout.** Click the Two-Up tool in the Page Display toolbar in the Toolbar Well. Note that the tool should be visible if you loaded the tools mentioned in the section "Setting Up the Work Environment" at the beginning of this chapter.

CROSS-REF For more information on Page Layout views, see the "Page Layout" section later in this chapter.

3. **Open the Comment & Markup toolbar.** If you review a file or read an eBook, you might want to make some notes on the file. However, you can't stay in Reading mode if a toolbar is opened. Selecting a toolbar (View ➪ Toolbars ➪ Comment & Markup, for example) switches back to the standard edit mode as you see in Figure 5.7.

CROSS-REF For more information on using Comment & Markup tools, see Chapter 20.

FIGURE 5.7

The new Reading mode view provides you with a display where you can read books and manuals with more screen area dedicated to the document pages.

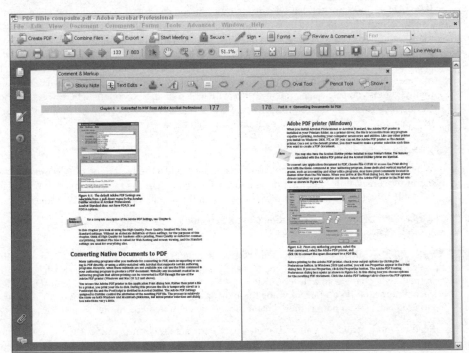

4. **Change the view to Reading mode.** After making edits with tools such as the Comment & Markup tools, you can return to Reading mode by pressing Ctrl/⌘+H.

5. **Scroll through the document pages.** Navigating pages in Reading mode is not a problem without having the Navigation tools available. Move the cursor to the elevator bar on the right side of the Document pane and click the mouse button. As you move the bar up or down, you see a thumbnail view of pages as you scroll as shown in Figure 5.8.

6. **Exit Reading mode.** Press Ctrl/⌘+H and you return to the default editing mode.

FIGURE 5.8

Click the elevator bar on the right side of the document pane and you'll see page thumbnails as you scroll pages.

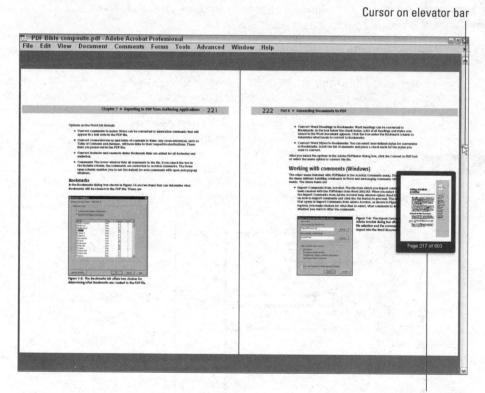

Cursor on elevator bar

Page thumbnail

Full Screen mode

Full Screen mode displays your documents without toolbars, menu bar, and Navigation panel. Many options exist for using Full Screen mode. See Chapter 28 for more information.

Menu Bar

Select View ⇨ Menu Bar or press F9 and the menu bar is temporarily hidden. To bring back the menu bar, press F9.

Toolbars

Open the View ➪ Toolbars menu command and a submenu displays all the toolbars and menu options you have when opening a context menu on the Toolbar Well. This menu is just an identical repeat for the same items contained in the context menu. To access the complete set of tools and options for loading and unloading tools from toolbars, select More tools at the bottom of either menu. Additionally you have options for selecting toolbars from the Tools menu. At the bottom of the Tools menu you find the Customize Toolbars command. Selecting this command is the same as selecting More Tools in either the View ➪ Toolbars submenu or a context menu opened on the Toolbar Well. Any one of the three menu selections opens the More Tools window.

Navigation Tabs

Choose View ➪ Navigation Panels and a submenu displays all the palettes that can be opened as floating palettes or docked in the Navigation panel.

 For a description of all the Navigation panels, see Chapter 1.

Grid (Acrobat Professional only)

If you need to examine drawings, a grid may help in your analysis. In Acrobat Professional, you can choose to view your file displaying a grid. Grids can be useful when you're authoring PDF files, particularly PDF forms. For viewing purposes they can be useful where relationships to objects require some careful examination. To show a grid, choose View ➪ Grid. By default, the grid displays in the Document pane with blue lines at fixed major and minor gridlines, as shown in Figure 5.9.

FIGURE 5.9

Choose View ➪ Grid or press the Ctrl⌘+U to access the grid. You can change the grid lines for major and minor divisions in the Preferences dialog box.

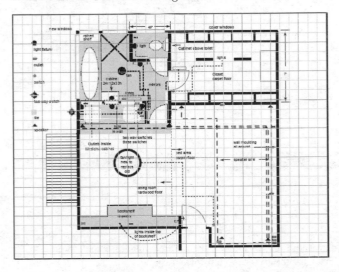

If you want to change the distances for the major gridlines and the number of divisions for the minor gridlines, open the Preferences dialog box and select Units & Guides in the left pane. The preference settings enable you to change the units of measure and attributes for the grid layout, as shown in Figure 5.10.

FIGURE 5.10

Preference choices for Units & Guides offer you options for changing the units of measure and the grid layout.

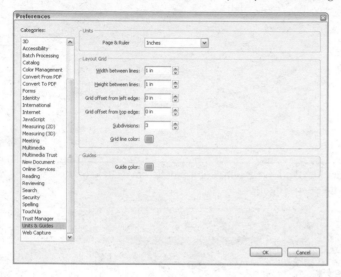

The Units & Guides preference settings are also used for changing attributes for the grid layout and rulers. The attribute choices include the following:

- **Page & Ruler Units.** Five choices are available from the pull-down menu. You can choose Points, Picas, Millimeters, Centimeters, or Inches. Whatever you choose here is reflected in the rulers when you display the rulers (View ➪ Rulers or press Ctrl/⌘+R). Choices here also affect the units of measure found in the Info palette discussed in Chapter 1.

- **Width between lines.** The horizontal distance between the major gridlines is determined in the field box for this setting. You can click on the arrows, enter a number between 0.03 and 138.889 in the field (when inches are selected for the unit of measurement), or press the up- or down-arrow keys to change the values.

NOTE The limit of 139.89 relates to inches. If you change the units of measure, the limits are roughly the same as the 139.89-inch limit. In points, the range measures between 2 and 10,000.

- **Height between lines.** You can change the major gridlines appearing vertically with this field. Use the same methods of changing the values here as for the lines for the Width option.

- **Grid offset from left edge.** Each grid has x and y coordinates indicating where the grid begins on a page. You set the x-axis in this field.

- **Grid offset from top edge.** Use this field to set the starting point of the y-axis.

- **Subdivisions.** The number of gridlines appearing between the major gridlines is determined in this field. The acceptable values range between 0 and 10,000 (when units are set to points).

- **Grid line color.** By default, the color for the gridlines is blue. You can change the grid color by clicking the color swatch. When you click the blue swatch for Grid Line color, a pop-up color palette opens, as shown in Figure 5.11. Select a color from the preset color choices in the palette or click Other Color. If you click Other Color, the system color palette opens, in which you can make custom color choices. The Windows and Macintosh system color palettes vary slightly, as shown in Figure 5.12.

FIGURE 5.11

Click the color swatch for the Grid line color to choose from a selection of preset colors, or select Other Color to open the system color palette.

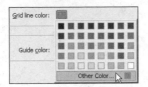

FIGURE 5.12

When you select Other Color, the Windows system color palette opens (left) or the Macintosh system color palette opens (right).

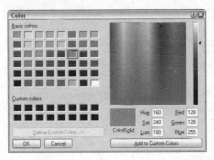

■ **Guide color.** Guides are created from ruler wells, and you can manually position them in the Document pane. If you have ruler guides and a grid, you'll want to change one color to easily distinguish the guides from the grid. Both default to the same blue. To change the guide color, click the Guide Color swatch and follow the same steps as described for Grid line color.

Snap to Grid (Acrobat Professional only)

When you choose View ➪ Snap to Grid, objects you draw snap to the major and minor gridlines. This feature can be particularly helpful with form designs and engineering drawings.

 For more information on Snap to Grid, see Chapter 34.

Rulers (Acrobat Professional only)

Acrobat Professional supports viewing rulers, and you can turn them on via the View menu or using the keyboard shortcut Ctrl/⌘+R. When you choose View ➪ Ruler or use the keyboard shortcut, rulers appear on the top and left side of the Document pane. Inside the top and left ruler is an inexhaustible supply of guidelines. To add a guideline on the document page, place the cursor within the top or left ruler, press the mouse button and drag away from the ruler in the Document pane. Continue adding as many guidelines as you want by returning to the ruler wells and dragging out more guidelines.

TIP You can also add guidelines by double-clicking a ruler. If you want guides positioned at 1-inch increments, as an example, move the mouse cursor to a ruler and double-click the mouse button on each 1-inch increment. Guidelines appear on the page in the Document pane with each double-click of the mouse button. If you attempt to create a guideline outside the page area, Acrobat sounds a warning beep. Guides are not permitted outside the page area.

If you want to move a guideline after it has been placed in the Document pane, select the Hand tool and place the cursor directly over the guideline to be moved. The cursor changes from a hand to a selection arrow. Press the mouse button and drag the line to the desired position.

TIP If you have multiple guidelines to draw on a page at equal distances, use the Units & Guides preferences and set the major guides to the distance you want between the guides. Set the subdivision guidelines to zero. For example, if you want guidelines two inches apart, set the major Height and Width guides to 2 inches and enter 0 (zero) in the subdivisions. Click OK and you save some time dragging guidelines from ruler wells.

To delete a guideline, click the line and press the Delete key on your keyboard. You can also click and drag a guideline off the document page and back to the ruler well to delete it. If you want to delete all guides on a page, open a context menu (see Figure 5.13) on a ruler and select Clear Guides on Page. If you select Clear All Guides, all guides drawn throughout your document are deleted.

FIGURE 5.13

To clear guides on a page or throughout all pages, open a context menu on a ruler and select Clear All Guides.

The context menu for rulers also enables you to hide the rulers; you can also use the shortcut keys Ctrl/⌘+R or revisit the View menu. Hidden rulers don't affect the view of the guides that remain visible. Notice that the context menu also contains choices for units of measure, which makes changing units here much handier than returning to the preference settings mentioned earlier. The context menu also offers the option to show and hide guides.

Guides

When you draw guidelines the View ⇨ Guides menu command is turned on. You can toggle the view of guidelines on and off by selecting View ⇨ Guides.

Line Weights

`Line Weights` Formerly labeled Wireframe in Acrobat 7, this item appears in both the View menu and the Page Display toolbar. When you zoom in and out of a drawing, the line weights zoom according to the zoom level. For example, a 1-point line zoomed in 400 percent produces a line weight view at four points. Zooming out reduces the line weight sizes to where lines can appear almost invisible. When you click the Line Weights tool or select View ➪ Line Weights, all lines appear at a one point size regardless of the zoom level.

Automatically Scroll

Automatic scrolling scrolls pages in the open file at a user-defined speed in all Acrobat viewers. When you select the command, Acrobat automatically switches the Single Page layout view to Single Page Continuous view and Two-Up views to Two-Up Continuous views. The pages in the document scroll up, permitting you to read the text without using any keys or the mouse. Attribute changes for automatic scrolling include the following:

- **Changing scrolling speed.** To change the scrolling speed, press a number key from 0 (being the slowest) to 9 (being the fastest) on your keyboard or press the up or down arrow keys to speed up or down in increments.

- **Reverse scrolling direction.** Press the hyphen or minus key.

- **To jump to the next or previous page and continue scrolling.** Press the right or left arrow, respectively.

- **Stopping.** To stop the scrolling, press the Esc key.

CROSS-REF For information related to page layout views, see the "Page Layout" section later in this chapter.

Read Out Loud

This command is a marvelous accessibility tool in all Acrobat viewers. You can have Acrobat PDF documents read aloud to you without having to purchase additional equipment/software such as screen readers. If you want to turn your back on the computer while doing some other activity, you can have Acrobat read aloud any open document. For entertainment purposes, you can gather the family around the computer and have an eBook read to you.

CROSS-REF For information on screen readers, see the sidebar "About Screen Readers" later in this chapter.

When you choose View ➪ Read Out Loud, a submenu opens with four menu commands. The menu commands all have keyboard shortcuts associated with them, but before you can use the commands you must first select Activate Read Out Loud in the submenu. The menu commands then become active as you see in Figure 5.14. For pausing and stopping the reading, you may want to remember these keyboard shortcuts. The commands include:

- **Activate/Deactivate Read Out Loud** (Shift+Ctrl/⌘+Y). Select Activate Read Out Loud when you start a Read Out Loud session. The menu name then changes to Deactivate Read Out Loud. Make this choice to stop reading out loud.

- **Read This Page Only** (Shift+Ctrl/⌘+V). The current active page in the Document pane is read aloud. Reading stops at the end of the target page.

- **Read To End of Document** (Shift+Ctrl/⌘+B). The reading starts on the active page and continues to the end of the document. If you want to start at the beginning of your file, click the First Page tool before selecting this menu command.

- **Pause/Resume** (Shift+Ctrl/⌘+C). After the reading begins, you see the Pause command active in the submenu. Select Pause or press the keyboard shortcut keys and Resume appears in the menu. Use the same menu command or shortcut to toggle Pause and Resume.

- **Stop** (Shift+Ctrl/⌘+E). To stop the reading aloud, select the command or use the keyboard shortcut.

FIGURE 5.14

To the Read Out Loud submenu commands provide options for audio output.

De_a_ctivate Read Out Loud	Shift+Ctrl+Y
Read This _P_age Only	Shift+Ctrl+V
Read To _E_nd of Document	Shift+Ctrl+B
Pa_u_se	Shift+Ctrl+C
_S_top	Shift+Ctrl+E

You change attribute settings for reading aloud in the Preferences dialog box, which you open by choosing Edit ➪ Preferences in Windows, Acrobat ➪ Preferences in Mac OS X, or use the keyboard shortcut (Ctrl/⌘+K). In the left pane shown in Figure 5.15, Reading is selected. The Reading preferences are displayed in the right pane. Preference settings include the following:

- **Reading Order.** Three choices are available from the Reading Order pull-down menu. When in doubt, use the default setting to Infer reading order from document (recommended).

  - **Infer reading order from document (recommended).** With this choice Acrobat makes some guesses about the order for what items are read on the page. If you have multiple columns and the layout is not clearly set up as a page with no layout attributes, the reading order may need some finessing. Acrobat will do its best to deliver the reading in an order compliant to the page layout.

  - **Left-to-right, top-to-bottom reading order.** Reading order delivers the reading ignoring any columns or heads that may be divided across a page. This choice might be best used for a book designed as text only in a single column.

  - **Use reading order in raw print stream.** Delivers words in the document in the order recorded in the print stream.

- **Override the reading order in tagged documents.** Tagged PDF documents contain structural information and they are designed to be accessible with reading devices so the proper reading order conforms to the way one would visually read a file. Tagged PDF documents have a designated reading order based on the tree structure. If the PDF document is a tagged PDF with a reading structure defined and you want to ignore the order, deselect the check box. You might make this choice if the tagged PDF does not accurately support the proper reading order and the delivery is more problematic than reading an untagged file.

- **Page vs. Document.** Choices include Only read the current visible pages, Read the entire document, or For large documents, only read the currently visible pages. The difference between the first and last command is when the last item is selected (For large documents, only read the currently visible pages), the field box below the pull-down menu becomes active where you can specify the number of pages to be read.

- **Confirm before tagging documents.** If a document is tagged before reading aloud, a confirmation dialog box opens confirming the file is a tagged document. When the option is checked you can confirm the options that will be used before Acrobat prepares an untagged document for

reading. Tagging can be a time-consuming procedure, especially for larger documents. This preference corresponds to the Confirm Before Tagging Documents option in the Accessibility Setup Assistant.

- **Volume.** You adjust volume settings in the Volume pull-down menu. Choose from 1 to 10 to lower or raise the volume.

- **Use default voice.** By default, the Use default voice check box is enabled. If you want to change the voice, deselect the check box and open the pull-down menu adjacent to Voice. The voice availability depends on voices installed with your operating system. Your text-to-speech default voice installed with your operating system is used. By default you may only have a single voice available. If you want additional voices, consult your operating system manual. If no additional voices are installed, you won't be able to change the voice. If you have multiple voices installed, select a voice from the pull-down menu.

- **Use default speech attributes.** The speech attributes are settings for the pitch and the speed the voice reads your file. If you want to change the pitch and/or reading rate, deselect the check box. Pitch can be changed to a value between 1 and 10. To completely understand what's going on with the pitch settings, experiment a little and listen to the various pitch changes with the voice you select from the Voice pull-down menu. Words Per Minute enables you to slow down or speed up the reading. The default is 190 wpm. If you want to make a change, type a new value in the field box.

- **Read form fields.** This setting is designed for use with Acrobat PDF forms. Check the box to have form field default values read aloud. If default text is added to a field, the text is read aloud. If the default text (or any text added to a text field) is replaced, the content of the form fields are read aloud.

CROSS-REF   For more information about setting form field default values, see Chapters 34 and 35.

FIGURE 5.15

To open Reading preferences, choose the Preferences command or press Ctrl/⌘ K. Click the Reading item in the list at the left side of the Preferences dialog box.

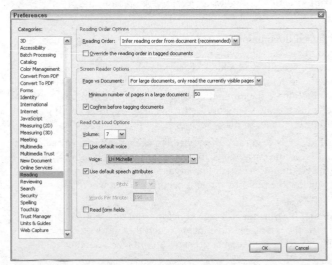

About Screen Readers

The term *screen reader* as used in this book refers to specialized software and/or hardware devices that enable the reading aloud of computer files. Software such as JAWS and Kurzwiel, and a host of other specialized software programs are sold to people with vision and motion challenges for the purpose of voice synthesizing and audio output. Many of these devices deliver audio output from proprietary formatted files or a select group of software applications. Some screen readers read raster image files saved in formats such as TIFF by performing an optical character recognition (OCR) on-the-fly and reading aloud text as it is interpreted from the image files. This method makes scanning pages of books and papers and having the scanned images interpreted by the readers easy.

Because Acrobat has implemented many tools and features for working with accessible files for the vision and motion challenged, screen reader developers have been supporting PDF format for some time. When a PDF is delivered to a reader and you select Read the entire document, the entire PDF file is sent to the reader before the first page is read. If you have long documents, you can choose to send a certain number of pages to the screen reader to break up the file into smaller chunks. When you select For long documents, read only the currently visible pages and the default of 10 pages is selected, ten pages are sent to the screen reader and the reading commences. After the pages are read, another ten pages are sent to the screen reader and read aloud, and so on.

CROSS-REF For more information on screen readers, tagged PDF files, and accessibility, see Chapter 25.

Scrolling

Anyone familiar with window environments is no stranger to scrolling. Fortunately, scroll bars behave in a standard fashion among computer platforms and various computer programs. Page scrolling works the same in an Acrobat viewer as it does in Microsoft Word (or any other Microsoft product for that matter), or any illustration, layout, or host of other applications that you may be familiar with. Drag the scroll bar up and down or left to right to move the document within the active window. Click between the scroll bar at the top or bottom of the scrolling column to jump a page segment or full page. The arrow icons at the top, bottom, left, and right sides allow you to move in smaller segments in the respective directions.

NEW FEATURE Acrobat 8 adds a little flair to scrolling. When you drag the elevator bar up and down, you get not only the page number and total pages in the file but a thumbnail preview of each page as you scroll the pages.

When you drag the scroll bar up or down in a multiple-page PDF file, a small thumbnail appears as well as a page number associated with the scroll bar position and the total number of pages in the document. (See Figure 5.16.) The readout is in the form of "*n* of *n* pages." The first number dynamically changes as you move the scroll bar between pages. This behavior works in all Page Layout modes.

CROSS-REF For information on auto scrolling, see the "Automatically Scroll" section earlier in this chapter.

FIGURE 5.16

When you click and drag an elevator bar used for page scrolling, a page thumbnail and a readout shows you page numbers and total pages.

Zooming

Zooming in and out of document pages is a fact of life with many different programs. Even when you type text in a word processor, you often need to zoom in on text that is set in a style suited for printing, but looks horrible at a 100% view on your computer monitor. The same holds true for spreadsheets, all the imaging and layout programs, and any kind of program where page sizes grow beyond a standard letter-size page.

Because Acrobat accommodates a page size of up to 200 × 200 inches, PDF documents sporting large page sizes need some industrial-strength zoom tools. Acrobat Professional contains a few more tools than other Acrobat viewers; however, all viewers enable you to zoom in and out of document pages using many tools consistent across all the viewers. The Zoom In and Zoom Out tools used in all viewers permit views from 8.33 percent to 6,400 percent of a document page.

Several tools are available for zooming. By default the Marquee Zoom and the Dynamic Zoom tools appear in the Select & Zoom toolbar docked in the Toolbar Well. If you load all the zoom tools in the Select & Zoom toolbar you can select from one of six zoom tools in Acrobat Professional. Four of the six tools are available in Acrobat Standard and Adobe Reader.

In all viewers, you can also zoom by clicking the Zoom In or Zoom Out buttons in the Zoom toolbar (represented by a + and – symbol) or editing the zoom percentage field in the toolbar — just type a new value in the field box and press the Enter/Return key to zoom. When you click the down-pointing arrow, the preset pull-down menu opens.

The View menu also has a Zoom To command. Select it and the Zoom To dialog box opens where you can select fixed zoom levels from a pull-down menu or type in a value from 8.88 to 6,400 percent. However, this menu command is redundant because you can also use the Zoom toolbar in the same manner.

TIP At first glance you may think that the menu command is useless and unnecessary. However, when viewing PDF documents where the menu bar is hidden or viewing files in Full Screen mode, you can use the keyboard shortcut Ctrl/⌘+M to open the Zoom To dialog box. You can then change zoom levels without making the menu bar visible or exiting Full Screen mode.

Marquee Zoom tool

 By default the Marquee Zoom tool appears in the Select & Zoom toolbar. This toolbar is loaded by default and appears when you open a context menu on the Toolbar Well and select Reset Toolbars.

NEW FEATURE The Marquee Zoom tool is new in Acrobat 8. In earlier Acrobat viewers you had the Zoom In and Zoom Out tools that performed the same function as the Marquee Zoom tool when using modifier keys. These two tools have been consolidated into a single tool.

Click the Marquee Zoom tool in the Select & Zoom toolbar and you have several ways you can use the tool using modifier keys that include:

- **Click and drag.** Drag the tool to create a marquee to zoom in to an area.
- **Alt/Option +click and drag.** Press the Alt/Option key to marquee and area and you zoom the page out.
- **Click.** Click the Marquee Zoom tool and the zoom jumps a fixed percentage.
- **Alt/Option +click.** Press the Alt/Option key and click and you zoom out at fixed percentages.

Zoom In tool

Zoom In The Zoom In tool is restricted to its fixed position in the Zoom toolbar. Click the Zoom tool in the Zoom toolbar and you zoom in to the same fixed preset zooms as when using the Marquee Zoom tool.

Zoom Out tool

Zoom Out The Zoom Out tool works in exactly the same way as the Zoom In tool, only it zooms out rather than in. It also has the same options associated with it as are associated with the Marquee Zoom tool when you press Alt/Option.

Dynamic Zoom tool

Dynamic Zoom When you first use the Dynamic Zoom tool you may feel like you're watching a George Lucas sci-fi movie. It's downright mesmerizing. This tool is available in all Acrobat viewers and is much handier than drawing marquees with the Marquee Zoom tool.

To use dynamic zooming, select the tool from the Select & Zoom toolbar. Click and drag up to zoom in and down to zoom out. Stop at the desired zoom level by releasing the mouse button. Acrobat displays a proxy view while zooming in and out and only refreshes the screen when you release the mouse button. Using this tool, therefore, is much faster because each zoom increment does not require a new screen refresh.

TIP You can easily toggle between the Marquee Zoom tool and the Dynamic Zoom tool using a modifier key. When the Marquee Zoom tool is selected, press the Shift key and the tool changes to the Dynamic Zoom tool. Release the Shift key and you return back to the Marquee Zoom tool.

Loupe tool (Acrobat Professional only)

Loupe If you use other Adobe programs, such as Adobe Photoshop, Adobe Illustrator, or Adobe InDesign, you know about the Navigator palette. In Acrobat Professional, the Loupe tool works similarly to the Navigator palette found in other Adobe programs but with a little twist. Instead of viewing a complete page in the Loupe Tool window, you see just the zoom level of your selection while the page zoom remains static. This tool can be a great benefit by saving you time to refresh your monitor when you change screen views.

To use the Loupe tool, click in the Select & Zoom toolbar or press Z on your keyboard and then Shift+Z to toggle the Marquee Zoom tool, the Dynamic Zoom tool, and the Loupe tool. Move the cursor to an area on a page you want to zoom to and click the mouse button. The Loupe tool window opens and displays the zoomed area you selected, as shown in Figure 5.17.

FIGURE 5.17

Click an area in the Document pane with the Loupe tool, and the target area is viewed at a zoom level in the Loupe window.

CROSS-REF When using keyboard shortcuts for accessing tools you need to enable the *Use single-key accelerators to access tools* preference setting. For more information on setting preferences for using keyboard shortcuts, see Chapter 1.

You can increase or decrease the magnification of the zoom area by adjusting the slider bar in the Loupe window or clicking the minus or plus symbols in the window. Clicking these symbols offers you smaller incremental changes than when using the same symbols in the Select & Zoom toolbar. If you want the Loupe tool to show a larger portion, you can resize the Loupe Tool dialog box by grabbing a corner of the box and dragging.

When you click in the Document pane with the Loupe tool, a rectangle appears around the area zoomed into the Loupe window (see Figure 5.17). You can place the cursor inside this rectangle and move it around the Document pane to view different areas at the same zoom level. As you zoom in, the rectangle reduces in size. At some point it would be impractical to select the rectangle on the page. If you can't find it, zoom out a little in the Loupe tool window until you see the rectangle on the page. Click and drag it to a new position and you can adjust your zoom.

Notice also in Figure 5.17 the four handles (squares) on the corners of the rectangle marking the Loupe tool zoom area. You can drag the handles in or out to zoom in or out, respectively.

If you have oversized documents that take a long time to refresh, using the Loupe tool helps speed up your PDF viewing. You can keep the document page in the Document pane at a reduced view while using the Loupe tool to examine areas in detail, which won't necessitate screen refreshes.

TIP The Loupe window displays the zoom level on an open document and remains fixed to that document until you target a new area. When you have multiple documents open, you can zoom in on one document and switch views in the Document pane to another document; the zoom display in the Loupe tool window remains fixed to the original document view. What you wind up with appears as if it's a picture-in-picture view such as you might see on a television set.

Pan & Zoom Window (Acrobat Professional only)

Whereas the Loupe tool displays the zoom view in its own window and the page in the Document pane remains static, the Pan & Zoom Window works in the opposite manner. The zoom level changes on the page in the Document pane while the original page view remains static in the Pan & Zoom Window. The zoom area is highlighted with a red rectangle in the Pan & Zoom Window. You can change the default red color of the zoom rectangle by opening the Line Color pull-down menu in the window and choosing from preset colors or choosing a custom color.

To use the Pan & Zoom Window, select the tool from the Zoom toolbar. The window displays a full page with the red rectangle showing the zoom area. If you open the Pan & Zoom Window when your PDF page is in Fit Page view, the page and the red rectangle are the same size.

To zoom a view in the Pan & Zoom Window, select one of the four handles on a corner of the rectangle and resize the rectangle by dragging in or out to zoom in or out, respectively. The page thumbnail view in the Pan & Zoom Window remains the same size while the rectangle is sized, as shown in Figure 5.18.

Also contained in the Pan & Zoom Window are navigation buttons. You can establish a zoom view and then scroll pages in your document with the page tools in the window. As you do so, the page views in the Document pane hold the same zoom level you set in the Pan & Zoom Window.

FIGURE 5.18

The Pan & Zoom Window displays a thumbnail view of the entire document page. The rectangle in the window shows the zoom level corresponding to the page zoom view.

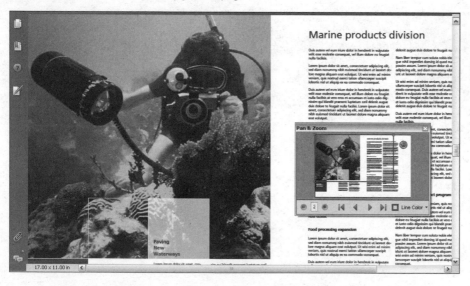

Zoom tool behaviors

A few specific differences exist between the Loupe tool and the Pan & Zoom tool that you should know. The Loupe tool targets an area on an open document and the zoom is fixed to that document while it remains open or until you target a new area. Regardless of the number of files you open, the Loupe tool window displaying your target view stays intact even if another document is brought to the front of the Document pane. If you close a file where the Loupe tool was set to view a zoom, the Loupe tool window clears and displays no view.

The Pan & Zoom tool always shows a target view of the active document brought forward in the Document pane. If you have multiple documents open, open the Pan & Zoom tool, then close a file, the page in view in the next file appears in the Pan & Zoom Window. If you close all files, the Pan & Zoom Window clears.

If you close a file during an Acrobat session, both the Loupe tool and the Pan & Zoom tool return you to the same views. The Pan & Zoom tool displays the opening page at the same zoom level as was last established in the window. The Loupe tool displays the same view last created with the tool. For example, if you zoom to 200% on page 25 of a file, close the file, and then reopen it, the Loupe tool window displays page 25 at 200% while the Document pane displays the opening page.

You can use both tools together to display different views in different documents. If the page in view in the Loupe window is not the current active document brought forward in the Document pane, you can still manage zooming on the hidden page. Use the slider between the minus/plus symbols to change zoom levels. In Figure 5.19, you can see the Loupe tool and the Pan & Zoom tool used together in different documents. The Loupe tool shows a zoom view on one page in a document while the Pan & Zoom tool shows a zoom view on a page in another document.

FIGURE 5.19

The Loupe tool and the Pan & Zoom tools show different zoom levels on different pages in different documents.

Changing Page Views

The page views for Actual Size, Fit Width, and Fit Page are static views that you want to access frequently when navigating through a PDF document. Acrobat viewers provide several ways to change a page view. Three tools appear in the Select & Zoom toolbar for toggling different page views. The different views include:

 ■ **Actual Size.** Displays the PDF page at actual size (a 100 percent view).

 ■ **Fit Width.** The data on a PDF page are displayed horizontally without clipping. If the page is large and data appear only in the center of the page, the page zooms to fit the data. The white space at the page edges is ignored.

 ■ **Fit Page.** Displays the page at the maximum size that fits within the viewer Document pane. If the Acrobat viewer window is sized up or down, the Fit Page view conforms to the size of the Document pane.

One of the keyboard shortcuts you'll want to remember is Ctrl/⌘+0 (zero). This enables you to view a page in a Fit Page view. As you browse pages in a PDF document, the page views are specific to the individual pages and not the document. Therefore, scrolling PDF files with different page sizes may require you to frequently change views if you want to see the full page in the Document pane. By using the keyboard shortcuts, you can reset page views much faster.

Page views can be established for the opening page according to user specified zoom views. Setting these attributes was referred to as Open Options in earlier versions of Acrobat. In Acrobat 6 and later, they are referred to as Initial View. These and other kinds of page views available in Acrobat are covered in the following section.

Setting Initial View Attributes

Initial View is the page view you see when you first open a PDF document. You can set several different attributes for an opening view and you can save your settings with the document. These views are document specific so they only relate to a document where you save the settings. When no settings have been saved with a file, the file is saved with a default view.

CROSS-REF   To understand more about default views, see "Understanding Initial View preferences" later in this chapter.

Coincidentally, even though previous versions of Acrobat provided you with options to save an initial view, most PDF authors rarely use them. You can find thousands of PDF files on the Internet and most of them have no settings enabled for an opening view other than the program defaults. I hope that by the time you finish this section, you can see some advantages for saving a particular initial view for the PDF documents you create and edit.

To set the attributes for the opening view, choose File ➪ Properties or use the keyboard shortcut Ctrl/⌘+D. The Document Properties dialog box opens, displaying a row of tabs at the top. Click the Initial View tab as shown in Figure 5.20.

FIGURE 5.20

To set the attributes for the opening view, choose File ➪ Properties and click the Initial View tab when the Document Properties dialog box opens.

Initial View settings are not available nor can they be changed in Adobe Reader even when usage rights have been added to the PDF. When Initial Views are saved from Acrobat Standard or Professional, PDFs open with the saved views in all Acrobat viewers.

Acrobat provides you with many different choices for controlling the initial view of a PDF opened in any Acrobat viewer. Settings you make on the Initial View tab can be saved with your document. When you establish settings other than defaults, the settings saved with the file override the user's default preference settings. The options on this tab are as follows:

- **Layout and Magnification.** The default opening page is the first page of a PDF document. You can change the opening page to another page and you can control the page layout views and magnification by selecting choices from the Layout and Magnification section. The choices include:

NOTE One reason you might want to open a PDF document on a page other than the first page is when you have a cover page or a title page that doesn't include content of interest to the reader. In such cases, you might want to open the PDF document on page two where a contents page or the first page of a section or chapter appears.

■ **Navigation panel.** Five choices are available from the Navigation panel pull-down menu. Select Page Only to open the page with the Navigation panel collapsed. Use the Bookmarks Panel and Page option to open the Bookmarks panel when the file opens. Use the Pages Panel and Page option to open the Pages panel where the thumbnails of pages are viewed. Use Attachments Panel and Page to open the Attachments panel when the file opens, and Use Layers Panel and Page to open the Layers panel when the file opens.

■ **Page Layout.** The default for Page Layout is noted in the pull-down menu as Default. When you save a PDF file with the Default selection, the PDF opens according to the default value a user has set for page viewing on the user's computer. To override the user's default, you can set a page layout in the opening view from one of six choices. Your options include:

Single Page. This option opens a single page view that appears the same as when you click the Single Page layout tool.

Single Page Continuous. The same as the Continuous page layout view in earlier versions of Acrobat. This view appears the same as when you click the Single Page Continuous tool.

Two-Up (Facing). The Two Pages (Facing) view shows the first two pages in a file beside each other in a two-page layout. When you scroll, subsequent pages snap to a page view. This view is the same as clicking the Two-Up tool.

Two-Up Continuous (Facing). The view appears very similar to Two-Up (Facing) but when you scroll pages, partial pages can be viewed in the Document pane. For example, the bottom of the previous page and the top of the next page may appear. In other words, this view doesn't snap pages to fit in the Document pane.

Two-Up (Cover Page). The initial view shows one page as in the Single Page view. When you scroll pages, however, the subsequent pages are displayed in a Two-Up (facing pages) view.

Two-Up Continuous (Cover Page). The initial page opens on the right side of the Document pane in a Single Page view. When you scroll pages, the scrolling is similar to the Two-Up Continuous view where facing pages are shown.

■ **Magnification.** Choose from preset magnification views in the pull-down menu. If you want the PDF document to open in a fit-in-window view, select Fit Page. Choose from other magnification options or edit the text box for a custom-zoom level. If Default is selected, the document opens according to user preference magnification settings.

■ **Open to page.** You can change the opening page to another page by entering a number in the Page number text box. This setting might be used if you want a user to see a contents page on page 2 in a document instead of a title page that appears on page 1.

■ **Window Options.** The default window for Acrobat is a full screen where the viewing area is maximized to occupy your monitor surface area. You can change the window view to size down the window to the initial page size, center a smaller window onscreen, and open a file in Full Screen mode. If you enable all three check boxes, the Full Screen mode prevails.

■ **Show.** From the pull-down menu choose either File Name or Document Title. If you select File Name, the title bar at the top of the Acrobat window shows the filename. If Document Title is used, the information you supply in the Document Properties dialog box for Document Title is shown in the title bar.

CROSS-REF Document titles are very important when you're archiving volumes of PDFs and creating search indexes. For information on creating document titles and how they are used, see Chapter 6.

■ **User Interface Options.** The Interface Options in the Initial View Document Properties dialog box have to do with user interface items in Acrobat viewers, such as menu bars, toolbars, and scroll bars. You can elect to hide these items when the PDF document opens in any Acrobat viewer. You can hide any one or a combination of the three items listed under the User Interface Options. When all three are enabled, the PDF appears as shown in Figure 5.21. If you elect to save files without any of the user interface items in view, then creating navigational buttons so users can move around your document is a good idea.

The window controls you see in Figure 5.22 include the scroll bars, the status bar, and the Navigation panel. If you hide the toolbars and menu bar but elect to leave the window controls visible, users can access tools for page navigation.

CAUTION If you elect to eliminate the toolbars and menu bar from view and later want to go back and edit your file, you need to use shortcut keys to get the menu bars and toolbars back. Be certain to remember the F9 key — F9 shows and hides the menu bar.

FIGURE 5.21

When toolbars, the menu bar, and window controls are hidden, navigating pages requires keyboard shortcuts or navigational buttons on the pages.

FIGURE 5.22

If window controls are visible, users can access tools for page navigation.

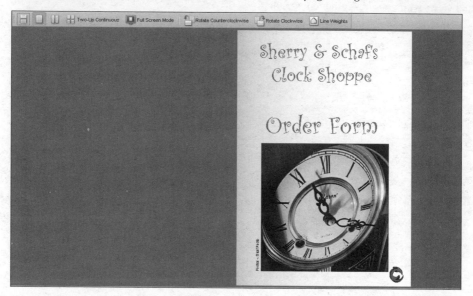

Understanding Initial View preferences

If you don't assign Initial View attributes in the Document Properties dialog box and save the file to update it, initial views are determined from individual user preferences. Because each user can set preferences differently, the same PDF may appear with a different page layout mode and a different zoom level on different computers. Depending on the design of your documents and how you want them viewed by end users, potential inconsistency in document views might make viewing difficult for those who view your files.

Users set initial view preferences in the Preferences dialog box. Open the Preferences dialog box by pressing Ctrl/⌘+K, and then click Page Display in the left pane. At the top of the right pane, a pull-down menu appears for Default page layout; at the bottom of the right pane another menu appears for Default zoom. You can select different page layout and default zoom views from the menus. In Figure 5.23, the Default page layout view is set to Single Page and the Default zoom is set to Fit Page. When you click OK to accept these changes, all PDF documents that have initial views set to Default will open on your computer with the views derived from your preference choices. Other users may choose different options from the pull-down menus, thereby displaying PDF documents with default views according to the choices they make in the Page Display preferences.

Be aware that the initial views you set in a PDF file from the Document Properties override the user preferences in the Page Display preferences pane. Therefore, you can control the initial views for all the PDFs you create. Doing so means your documents are viewed consistently across all computers regardless of the differences between individual user preference choices.

FIGURE 5.23

Changing the Default page layout to Single Page and the Default zoom to Fit Page opens all PDFs saved with default initial views with your new preference settings.

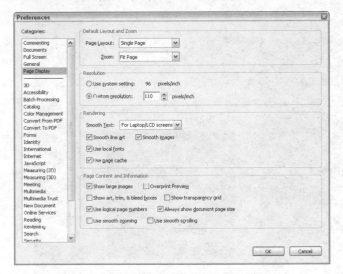

Saving the Initial View

When you decide what view attributes you want assigned to your document, you can choose one of two save options. The first option updates the file. Click the Save tool in the Acrobat File toolbar or choose File ➪ Save. Any edits you make in the Initial View properties activates the Save command. The Save command is inactive and grayed out by default until you make any changes to your file or reset any kind of preferences that can be saved with the document. The other option is to use Save As. When you select File ➪ Save As, you completely rewrite the file when you click the Save button in the Save As dialog box.

CROSS-REF You have different choices for saving files using either Save, Save As, or Save a Version a version. For a more complete understanding of saving, updating, and saving versions of PDFs, see Chapter 11.

Viewing Files with the Window Menu

If you open a PDF file and then open a second PDF, the second file hides the first document. If several PDFs are opened, the last opened document hides all the others. Fortunately, the Acrobat viewers have made it easy for you to choose a given document from a nest of open files.

When you load an Acrobat viewer with several open files, you can use tools to help you manage them. If you need to visually compare documents, several different viewing options are available.

The Window menu contains options for helping you manage document views, and in particular, multiple documents. The options you find in the Window menu won't be found with tools or in the status bar, so you'll find yourself visiting this menu frequently if you work with multiple open files in Acrobat or if you need to create more than one view in the same document.

Minimize and zoom views

By default when you open PDF files the Acrobat window appears minimized. In other words, the application window doesn't zoom to the full screen size. This behavior can be a blessing for those with large monitors who want to work in Acrobat and another application along side the Acrobat window or a curse for those who want to take advantage of a full screen size when working in Acrobat alone.

NEW FEATURE **You have control over your work environment in two separate areas. If you want to change the default view, open the Documents preferences (Ctrl/⌘+K) and remove the check mark where you see Show each document in its own window (requires restart). As the item suggests, you need to quit Acrobat and relaunch the program for the new preference to take effect.**

If you leave the preferences at the default, you can zoom the Acrobat application window by clicking the features button on the application window. Click the Maximize button represented by an X in the top-right corner (Windows) and the window zooms to a maximized view.

On the Macintosh, click the plus icon in the top-left corner of the application window and the application window zooms to a maximized view.

New Window

New Window was a new feature in Acrobat 7 Professional. When you open a document and select New Window, a duplicate view of your existing document is opened in the Document pane. You can change views and pages in one window while viewing different page views in another window. This feature is handy for viewing a table of contents in one window while viewing content on other pages in the same file.

When you select New Window, Acrobat adds an extension to the filename in the title bar. If you have a document open in Acrobat with a filename like Employee Application, and then select New Window, the title bar displays Employee Application:1 on one view and Employee Application:2 on the second view.

New Window can be particularly helpful when viewing PDF Packages. You can create a PDF Package and view two or more files within the package in new windows and tiled views.

CROSS-REF **For more information on PDF Packages, see Chapter 12. For more on tiling views see Tile later in this chapter.**

Cascade

If you have several files open and choose Window ➪ Cascade, the open files appear in a cascading view with the title bars visible much like you might view cascading Web pages. You can see the name of each file and easily select from any one shown in the Document pane. Click a title bar to bring a document forward.

After bringing a file forward, if you want to see the title bars in a cascading view again, choose Window ➪ Cascade again. The document currently selected in the foreground will appear first when you use this command.

The Window menu also lists the open files by filename at the bottom of the window. When you have multiple files open, the files are numbered according to the order in which they were opened, with the filename appearing in the list, as shown in Figure 5.24. Select any filename from the list in the Window menu to bring the file forward in the Document pane.

FIGURE 5.24

Acrobat lists all open files in the Window menu. To bring a document forward in the Document pane, choose the name of the file you want to view from the Window menu.

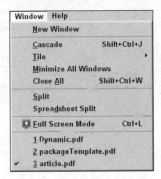

NOTE The view shown in Figure 5.24 appears when the Show each document in its own window (requires restart) check box is disabled in the Documents preferences. If the check box is checked in the Documents preferences, each tiled page appears with individual toolbar sets attached to the document.

Tile

You can also choose to have your documents tiled horizontally or vertically via the Tile submenu in the Window menu. When you choose Window ➪ Tile ➪ Horizontally or Vertically, the PDF files appear in individual windows arranged to fit within the Acrobat window in either a horizontal or vertical view. If you have more than three documents open at one time, the display for Tile Horizontally and Tile Vertically appear identical. With any number of documents displayed in tiled views, the Navigation panel is accessible for each document. Also, when you choose Window ➪ New Window and open a second view of the same document, and then tile the views, each window appears in the tiled documents. In Figure 5.25, a PDF Package is opened and a New Window is shown with the views tiled Vertically.

Tiling documents can be helpful when you need to edit documents and exchange pages between two or more PDF files or when you need to compare changes among documents.

CROSS-REF For information related to editing files, see the Chapters in Part III. For more information on comparing documents, see Chapter 20.

FIGURE 5.25

Tiling views neatly displays all open documents adjacent to each other within the Acrobat window.

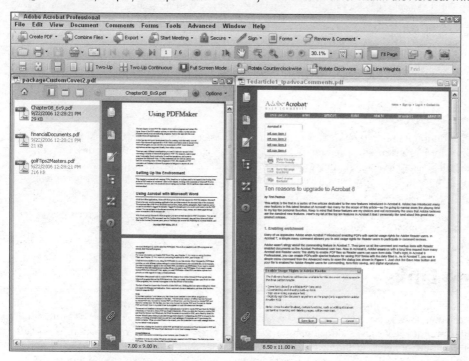

Close All

Select Close All or press Shift+Ctrl/⌘+W and all open windows close.

Split

Choose Window ➪ Split and the Document pane splits into two horizontal views of the active document, similar to the way you might see a split view in a word processing or spreadsheet program. The two views are independent of each other and offer you much flexibility. You can view the same page in two different zoom views or you can view two different pages at the same zoom level or different zoom views. You can view one pane in a Single page layout and the other pane in one of the other page layout options. You can also combine the Split and Tile option to view two or more documents, each with split views tiled horizontally or vertically. You can adjust the window division by moving the horizontal bar up or down, thereby showing a larger view in one pane and a smaller view in the other pane.

Spreadsheet Split

Spreadsheet Split is the same concept as using a Split view except you now have four panes. Just choose Window ⇨ Spreadsheet Split. Click inside the pane whose view you want to change and then zoom in and out and navigate pages as needed. Move the divider bars horizontally and vertically to size the panes to accommodate your viewing needs. Position the cursor at the intersection of the separator bars and you can move the bars vertically and horizontally together.

To remove the Spreadsheet Split view, return to the Window menu and select Spreadsheet Split again. The Document pane returns to the default view.

Full Screen Mode

Another viewing option found in the Window menu is the Full Screen Mode. Full Screen Mode displays your PDF document like a slide show and temporarily hides the menus, toolbars, and window controls. You can set up the Full Screen Mode for automatic page scrolling and then walk away from the computer — you'll have a self-running kiosk. You can give a presentation and automatically scroll pages or set preferences for pausing between slides.

CROSS-REF There's a lot to Full Screen viewing. To learn more about working with Full Screen views, see Chapter 23.

Viewing Links

For the purpose of discussion, links in Acrobat are *hot spots* where you click somewhere in the Acrobat window and some action takes place. With regard to viewing PDF documents, clicking the mouse button on a link takes you to another view, opens a document or Web page, or executes some sort of action. Links can be any one of a number of items, including elements on a PDF page such as buttons, articles, fields, and so on, or they can be part of the user interface such as thumbnails and links you create from options in palettes. In this chapter, I stick to link behavior in Acrobat as it relates to page viewing and locating links.

CROSS-REF For information on creating links and buttons that execute a variety of different actions, see Chapter 22.

Navigation panel

The Navigation panel contains the default panels discussed in Chapter 1. Most of these palettes are connected to certain capabilities for linking to views and other kinds of actions that can be invoked with the click of a mouse button. In some cases, a single click takes you to another view and in other cases a double-click takes you to another view. The palettes that contain some form of linking to views include:

CROSS-REF To learn more about the Navigation panels, see Chapter 1 and Chapter 3.

- **Pages.** To view thumbnails of each page, click the Pages panel in the Navigation panel. The page thumbnails are links to the respective pages. A single mouse click on a page thumbnail displays the respective page in the Document pane.

CROSS-REF For information on working with the Pages panel, see Chapter 22.

- **Bookmarks.** All Bookmarks in a PDF file are displayed in a list beside the Bookmarks panel. With a single click of the mouse button, a Bookmark may take you to another page or view, or invoke an action.

CROSS-REF For information on creating Bookmarks and setting link actions to them, see Chapter 22.

■ **Signatures.** The Signatures panel contains a list of all digital signatures in a PDF document. You can open the Signatures panel and navigate to pages where signatures have been added to the file.

CROSS-REF For information on creating digital signatures, see Chapter 26.

■ **How To.** The How To panel has been moved from the right side of the document window to the Navigation panel in Acrobat 8. Click an item in the How To panel and you see a help description respective to the selected item.

■ **Attachments.** The Attachments panel contains a list of all file attachments. Double-clicking an attachment, however, does not navigate to the page where the attachment is placed. Use the Attachments panel to search for the page where the attachment appears because double-clicking an attachment opens the attached file.

CROSS-REF For information on working with file attachments, see Chapter 12.

■ **Comments.** The Comments panel contains any annotations added to the open file. You can navigate to any page where a comment has been added by double-clicking on a comment in the Comments panel.

CROSS-REF For information on working with comments, see Chapter 20.

Navigation panels

The additional panels you can access from the View ⇨ Navigation Panels submenu described in Chapter 1 contain links to the content you create from various panel options. The panels not yet discussed that appear in the Navigation Panels submenu are as follows:

■ **Articles.** Article threads are like link buttons. You can create article threads in a PDF file and the threads are listed in the Articles panel. Use the panel to open an article thread and click the mouse button inside the article to follow the thread.

CROSS-REF For information on creating articles, see Chapter 22.

■ **Content.** Document content can be displayed in the Content panel. When you open the panel and select individual items, you can highlight the respective content item on the document page. In essence, the Content panel is linked to the content appearing on the PDF pages according to the natural reading order of the PDF file.

CROSS-REF For information on using the Content panel, see Chapter 25.

■ **Destinations.** Destinations are similar to Bookmarks and are linked to a specific location in an open PDF document or to secondary PDF documents. When you click a destination, the view associated with the destination opens in the Document pane.

CROSS-REF For information on destinations, see Chapter 22.

■ **Fields.** The Fields panel lists all form fields created in the open document. Click a field name in the panel and the field becomes highlighted in the Document pane.

CROSS-REF   For information on creating form fields, see Chapters 33 and 34.

■ **Info.** The Info panel offers pull-down menu choices for changing the units of measure in a document. Choose from Points, Inches, or Millimeters. The information displayed in the document page size text box reports the page size in the units selected from the Info panel. As you move the cursor around the Document pane, a read-out in the Info palette shows the cursor's x,y position on the page. For example, X: 3 and Y: 2 informs you the cursor is positioned 3 inches from the left side of the page and 2 inches up from the bottom of the page when the unit of measure is in inches.

In Acrobat 7 the page size appeared in the Status Bar at the bottom of the Document pane. In Acrobat 8 you don't have a status bar and by default the page size is not in view. You need to open the Page Display preferences and check the Always show document page size check box in order to view the page sizes that appear in the lower left corner of the Acrobat window as shown in Figure 5.26. If you don't have the check box enabled, the document page size appears only when moving the cursor to the lower-left corner of the Acrobat window.

CROSS-REF   For information on using rulers, guides, and measuring tools according to units of measure, see Chapter 24.

FIGURE 5.26

Check the Always show document page size check box in the Page Display preferences to view page sizes in the Document pane.

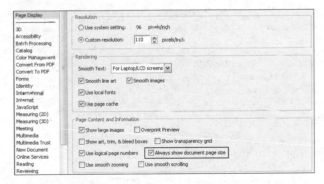

NOTE   Having the document page size appear by default without having to move the cursor in the lower left corner of the Acrobat window is a matter of personal choice. I find it helpful having the page size reported when I'm opening PDF documents. As a matter of consistency in viewing the screen shots in this book, I have this preference option turned on for all the figures in the remaining chapters of this book.

■ **Layers.** The Layers panel shows all Adobe PDF Layers contained in a document by layer names. If the panel is empty, no layers are contained in the file. You use the Layers panel to show and hide layers, set layer properties, and manage layers.

CROSS-REF For more information on using Adobe PDF Layers, see Chapter 24.

- **Model Tree.** Model Tree is used with 3D graphics within a PDF. You can examine content, change views, shading, and many different aspects of 3D models. The Model Tree is also opened with you use the Object Data tool.

- **Order.** When you click the panel and open the Order panel, the reading order of your pages is displayed in the panel and on the document pages. You can easily change the reading order by moving the references in the Order panel around much like you would reorganize Bookmarks.

CROSS-REF For information on using use the Order panel, see Chapter 26.

- **Tags.** Tags list all the structural content in a PDF document. You can highlight an element from within the Tags panel to locate a tagged element. Whereas the Contents panel identifies all the page content in any PDF file, the Tags panel only shows the structure and elements of tagged PDF files. Together with the Order panel, Tags are used with accessible documents.

CROSS-REF For information on using the Tags panel and making documents accessible, see Chapter 25.

Hypertext links

In an Acrobat viewer, hypertext references enable you to move around the PDF or many PDFs, much like surfing the Net. You've probably become so accustomed to clicking buttons on your desktop computer that link navigation is commonplace and needs little instruction. While invoking the action is nothing more than a click with the mouse, what it can do in Acrobat is simply remarkable. To help you gain an understanding of how Acrobat has employed hyperlinks, the following sections describe all the link actions as they can be created in Acrobat and executed in any viewer.

Hypertext references, or *buttons,* are easily identified in a PDF document. As you move the mouse cursor around the document window, a Hand icon with the forefinger pointing appears when you position the cursor over a button or a link. You click, and presto! — the link action is executed!

Link actions can be assigned to any one of several items in Acrobat. You can set a link action to links, fields, Bookmarks, and Page Actions. The action types available in Acrobat Standard and Acrobat Professional include:

NOTE All the Link Action types are available with both Acrobat Standard and Acrobat Professional. Form fields can only be created with Acrobat Professional. Link Actions can be assigned to links, Bookmarks, and Page Actions in both Acrobat Standard and Acrobat Professional.

- **Execute a menu command.** This action links to commands found in the Acrobat menus. Unfortunately, most of the Execute a menu command options have been removed in Acrobat 8. If you used these items in older PDFs, you now have to turn to JavaScript programming and completely rework your files. My personal opinion is that this is the single greatest loss with Acrobat 8.

  To be fair to Adobe, the changes made to Execute a menu item command are the result of many requests — particularly from enterprise users, who are concerned with security issues. To respond to these requests, Adobe was compelled to make the changes.

- **Go to a 3D view.** For PDF documents supporting 3D views, you can set an action to a specific 3D view.

- **Go to a page view.** The Go to a page view action opens another view on the existing page, a view to another page in the same document, a view to a named destination, or a view in another document.

- **Import form data.** This action imports data exported from other forms into the active document where form field names match those from where the data were exported.

- **Open a file.** The Open a file link opens any kind of document. PDFs open in Acrobat. Other file types require having the authoring program installed on your computer. For example, if the link is to a Microsoft Word document, you need Word installed on your computer to open the link.

- **Open a web link.** Opens a URL in your default Web browser.

- **Play a sound.** Plays a sound imported into the active PDF.

- **Play Media (Acrobat 5 Compatible).** Plays a movie file saved in formats compatible with Acrobat 5 and lower viewers. Note: Acrobat 5 compatible media cannot be embedded in a PDF document.

- **Play Media (Acrobat 6 and Later Compatible).** Plays movie files saved in newer formats compatible with Acrobat 6 through Acrobat 8 and movie clips can be embedded in PDFs using this compatibility.

- **Read an article.** This action navigates to the specified article in the open PDF document or another PDF document.

- **Reset a form.** All the fields or user-specified fields on a form are cleared of data.

- **Run a JavaScript.** Executes JavaScripts written in Acrobat.

 You can create JavaScripts with links, Bookmarks, and Page Actions in Acrobat Standard. The JavaScript Editor, however, is not accessible from a menu command in Acrobat Standard. For information on using the JavaScript Editor in Acrobat Professional, see Chapter 36.

- **Set layer visibility.** This action can be set to either hide or show a layer.

- **Show/hide a field.** With form fields, fields are hidden or made visible on a page.

- **Submit a form.** This action is used for submitting data in user-prescribed formats to a specified URL.

The preceding list is a simplified brief description of action types that can be associated with tools that support link actions.

 For more detail on how to create link actions and a host of attributes you can assign to them, see Part IV, "PDF Interactivity" and Part VI, "Acrobat PDF Forms."

Opening PDF Files

As with most computer programs you already use on either Windows or the Macintosh, you know that files are generally opened via the File ➪ Open command. In many programs, the keyboard shortcut used to open files is Ctrl/⌘+O. Acrobat uses the same menu and keyboard shortcuts to access the Open dialog box where you browse your hard drive, open folders, and ultimately select a file to open. When you double-click a filename or click the Open button when a file is selected, the file opens in Acrobat.

 All Acrobat viewers also offer you a tool to open files. Click the Open tool in the File toolbar and the Open dialog box appears just as if you had used the Open menu command or keyboard shortcut. Any one of these methods opens a PDF document or a document of one of many different file types that can be converted to PDF on-the-fly while you work in Acrobat.

CROSS-REF   For information related to opening files that are converted to PDF with the Open command, see Chapter 7.

Opening recently viewed files

When you launch Acrobat and view and/or edit PDF documents, Acrobat keeps track of the most recently opened files. By default, Acrobat keeps track of the last five files you opened. In the Startup preferences you can change the value to as many as ten recently viewed files. The files are accessible at the bottom of the File menu (Windows) or the File ⇨ Open Recent File submenu on the Macintosh. In Figure 5.27, you can see five filenames at the bottom of the File menu from Acrobat running under Windows.

FIGURE 5.27

The most recently viewed files appear in the File menu (Windows) or File ⇨ Open Recent File submenu (Macintosh).

You have another option for viewing files that were previously opened in an Acrobat session. As shown in Figure 5.27, the History menu command appearing over the recent file list offers you submenus for viewing files from a history as long as the previous 12 months. Until you clear the History by selecting the Clear History menu command, all the files you viewed over the last 12 months are displayed in a scrollable list. You can break down the history according to the files viewed Today, Yesterday, the Last 7 Days, the Last 14 Days, and the Last 30 Days, as well as the Last 12 Months.

Macintosh users can find the History submenu command appearing at the top of the list of files when you choose File ⇨ Open Recent File.

Using the Organizer

The Organizer is a tool similar in some respects to Adobe Bridge. Although not all features within Adobe Bridge are available in Acrobat's Organizer, it has many impressive tools and commands that help you manage and access documents from within Acrobat. To open the Organizer, choose File ⇨ Organizer ⇨ Open Organizer, click the Organizer tool in the File toolbar, or press Shift+Ctrl/⌘+1. (On Windows you can also choose File ⇨ History ⇨ Open Organizer.) When you select any of the options, the Organizer, shown in Figure 5.28, opens.

FIGURE 5.28

Click the Organizer tool or select Open Organizer from a menu command to open the Organizer window in Acrobat.

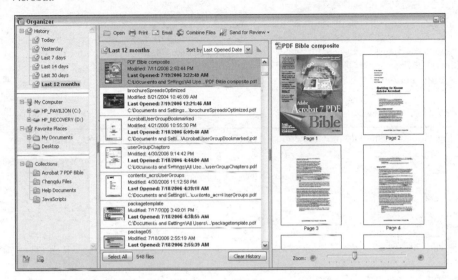

The Organizer window contains three panes, a number of tools, and menu commands that you select from context menus. When you first open the Organizer, you find three panes in the Organizer window divided by two separator bars. On the left side of the window is the Categories pane. In the center, you find the Files pane and the right side holds the Pages pane. You can adjust the size of the panes by clicking a separator bar and dragging it to the left or right. As one pane is sized down, the adjacent pane is sized up. You can adjust the size of the Organizer window by dragging the lower-right corner of the window.

Using the Categories pane

The Categories pane in the Organizer contains three types of categories. At the top of the pane is History followed by My Computer (Windows) or Macintosh HD (Macintosh) and at the bottom you find Collections. The History category offers you the same choices for viewing history as you find in the File menu in Windows as described in the earlier section "Opening recently viewed files." As you click one of the History options, the files listed in the Files pane reflect the history period you choose.

The My Computer/Macintosh HD category shows you a view of your hard drive and all servers and drives connected to your computer, similar to a Windows Explorer view or a Macintosh Finder view. You can select a folder, and all PDFs within that folder are listed in the Files pane regardless of whether they appear in the view history. Below your accessible hard drives and servers you find Favorite Places. If you keep documents within folders you frequently access, right-click (Windows) or Ctrl+click (Macintosh) to open a context menu over Favorite Places or click the *Add Favorite Place* button at the bottom of the Categories pane. (See Figure 5.29.)

The Browse For Folder dialog box opens (Windows) or the Select a folder to add to your favorite places dialog box opens on the Macintosh after clicking the Add to favorite place button. Adding Favorites in this fashion is similar to adding Favorites in your Web browser.

After you select a folder and click OK, the folder you selected appears at the bottom of the Favorite Places list.

Click the Add a favorite place button to add to the Favorite Places.

The Collections category works similarly to Favorite Places, except that instead of adding folders to a list, you can select individual files and add them to a collection. You can add files to collections from different folders on your hard drive. By default, Acrobat offers you three collections—Collection 1, Collection 2, and Collection 3.

You manage collections through the use of a context menu. Open a context menu from any collection name in the Collections category and the menu options appear as shown in Figure 5.30.

To manage collections, open a context menu on any collection name.

> Create a New Collection
> Rename Collection
> Delete Collection
> Add Files...

The menu selections should be self-explanatory. Select Create a New Collection to add another collection to the list. Select Rename Collection to rename a collection. Select Delete Collection to remove the collection. Click Add Files to add documents to your collection. After you add documents to a collection and click the collection name, all files added to the collection appear in the Files pane.

TIP After installing Acrobat you may want to rename the default collection names to more descriptive names used in your workflow. Open a context menu on each collection name and select Rename Collection. The collection name is highlighted and ready for you to type a new name.

Using the Files pane

The Files pane contains a list of all files derived from the choice you made in the Categories pane. For example, click a History category, and all files viewed within the selected history timeframe appear in a list sorted by metadata that you select from the Sort by pull-down menu. In addition to the file list you have tools at the top of the pane and context menu commands when opening a context menu on a file in the list.

Beginning with the tools at the top of the pane, you find the following:

- **Open.** By default, the first file in the pane is selected. Click the Open tool to open the selected file. If no file is selected in the pane, the Open tool, as well as all other tools, are grayed out. A condition where you might not have a file selected is when you click a collection that contains no file in the collection folder or when viewing a folder that contains no PDF documents. Otherwise, the first file, by default, is always selected when files are shown in the list.

- **Print.** Click a file in the list and click the Print tool to print the file. When you click Print, the PDF document opens and the Print dialog box opens in the foreground. Make your print attribute choices in the Print dialog box and click Print to print the file.

- **Email.** Select a file in the list and click the Email tool, and your default e-mail application opens with the selected file attached to a new e-mail message.

- **Combine Files.** Click this tool to open the Combine multiple files into one PDF file wizard. In the wizard window you can select PDF documents to combine into a single file or select a variety of different file formats that can be converted to a PDF. The tool works the same as selecting the Combine Files tool in the Tasks toolbar.

CROSS-REF To learn how to convert files to PDF with the Combine multiple files into one PDF file wizard, see Chapter 12.

- **Send for Review.** Select a file in the list and choose from the pull-down menu options to Send for Shared Review or Send by Email for Review.

CROSS-REF To learn how to send files for reviews and approval, see Chapter 20.

Below the tools is a pull-down menu used for sorting files. Files can be sorted on metadata contained within the file. From the pull-down menu you have several choices for sorting files.

Sorting by Filename is the default and lists files in an alphabetical ascending order. The Title, Subject, Author, and Keywords items are part of the Document Properties Description that you supply at the time of PDF creation from some authoring programs or that you later add in Acrobat. Creator and Producer are part of the Document Description supplied by Acrobat and relate to the original authoring program and the application producing the PDF file. Number of Pages, File Size, and Modified Date are data that Acrobat adds to the Document Properties derived from the structure of the file. The Last Opened Date sorts the files according to the last time you viewed them in Acrobat with the most recent file listed first and in descending order.

CROSS-REF To learn more about Document Descriptions and Document Properties, see Chapter 6.

You can also manage files from a context menu opened on a file in the list. This menu has commands to perform the same tasks handled by the tools at the top of the pane. In Figure 5.31 you can see the top portion of the menu, duplicating the tools' functions, such as Open, Print, Email, Combine Files, and Send for Review.

FIGURE 5.31

Open a context menu on a file listed in the Files pane and the menu options offer additional commands for managing files.

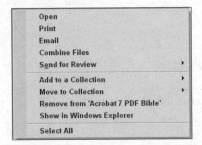

The Add to Collection menu item contains a submenu that lists all the collections in the Categories pane. As you add new collections to the Categories, they dynamically appear in the Add to Collection submenu. After you add a file to a collection, the context menu changes and displays a few more menu commands. Figure 5.31 shows the Move to Collection and Remove from 'Collection name' commands. The item within the single quotes denotes the collection name where a file has been added.

Select Move to Collection and the submenu displays all your collection names. Select a collection and the file is moved to the collection you choose in the submenu. Select Remove from '*n*' (where *n* represents the name of a collection) and a dialog box opens prompting you to confirm the deletion. When you delete a file from a collection, the file is deleted from the collection list but is not deleted from your hard drive.

The last menu item, Show in Explorer (Windows) or Show in Finder (Macintosh) takes you to Windows Explorer (Windows) or switches to Finder view (Macintosh) and opens the folder where the file is located.

Using the Pages pane

One of the great features of the Organizer is that it shows multiple pages in the Pages pane for all files containing more than one page. When you select a multipage document, all pages are displayed in thumbnail view in the Pages pane before you open the file. At the bottom of the pane is a zoom slider. Drag the slider left to display smaller thumbnails and to the right to make the thumbnail views larger. The minus and plus buttons display thumbnails smaller and larger, respectively, in zoom increments.

As you view multipage documents in the Pages pane, you can double-click any page thumbnail to open the respective page in Acrobat. Select a page thumbnail and open a context menu, and a single menu command appears enabling you to open that page.

Another nice feature in the Pages pane is the display of a Document Status icon that appears when you save files that have a special status or special feature. Such features might include a document saved with layers, a file in a commenting review, or a certified document. In addition to the Document Status icon, some files may display a security key representing files that have been password secured.

Bookmarking Web-hosted PDFs

As I explain in Chapter 27, Acrobat is well integrated with many different Web services and support. The Organizer is no exception when it comes to supporting Web-related services. You can add anything you can view in Acrobat as a PDF document to your Organizer. When you add a document to a collection from a Web-hosted PDF, the link is made to where the file is hosted. In this particular case, it's a link to a URL that you can create as easily as adding files from your hard drive to your collections.

The first step is to view a PDF document as an inline view in a Web browser. Both Apple Safari and Microsoft Internet Explorer are supported. When you view a PDF in a Web browser, many Acrobat tools appear below your browser's tools. In Figure 5.32, you can see the Organizer tool in the top-left corner of the Acrobat window inside Apple's Safari Web browser. When you click the Organizer tool, the Add to Favorites dialog box opens. Click a collection and click OK to add the link to your collection.

CROSS-REF   For more information on inline viewing in Web browsers, see Chapter 22.

When you return to Acrobat, you can view the URL link in the respective collection. Open the Organizer and click the collection name where you added the link. In the Files pane you see all documents added to the collection. Those files added from Web URLs appear with a different icon than standard PDF documents and the content of the page is not shown for these links, as you can see in Figure 5.33. You can add files from PDFs on your hard drive and view them from within a Web browser (something you might do when working with browser-based reviews), or from URL addresses on the Web. In the Files pane adjacent to the document icon, you see the URL address from where the document was retrieved.

FIGURE 5.32

Click the Organizer tool inside a Web browser to add the URL link to a collection.

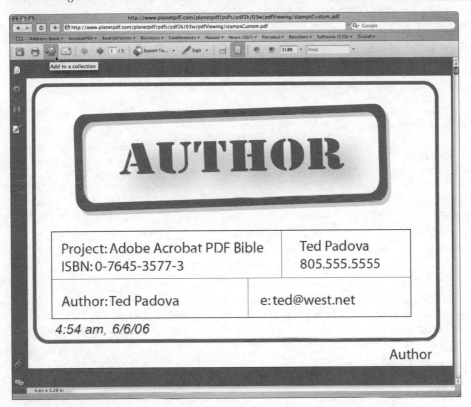

FIGURE 5.33

PDFs linked to URLs appear with a different document icon and a page preview is not available.

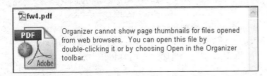

CROSS-REF For more information related to shared reviews, see Chapter 21.

Double-click any Web-linked file and your default Web browser opens, takes you to the URL, and loads the PDF in the browser window.

Summary

This chapter offers you a brief overview of how to go about moving around PDF documents, using viewing tools, palettes, and pages, as well as opening and managing files. As you can see, the list is long and there's quite a bit to understand in regard to viewing, navigating, opening, and managing files. Some of the more important points include the following:

- Page navigation tools are available in a toolbar not visible by default. You can place the toolbar in view and dock it to the left, right, top, or below the Document pane for easy access to navigation tools.

- Acrobat 8 contains no Status bar. You can simulate a Status bar view similar to earlier Acrobat viewers by docking tools at the bottom of the application window.

- The new Reading mode feature in Acrobat 8 optimizes your views for page content. You can easily scroll pages back and forth with simple mouse clicks.

- PDFs can be read aloud and pages can be autoscrolled without the need for any special equipment.

- PDF pages can be viewed in several different layout modes, with grids, guides, and rulers.

- Acrobat Professional contains six tools used for zooming views. The Marquee Zoom tool is a new tool in Acrobat permitting you to zoom in and out by drawing marquee selections. In addition to the Marquee Zoom, Zoom In, Zoom Out, and Dynamic Zoom tools are found in all Acrobat viewers; the Loupe tool and the Pan & Zoom are unique to Acrobat Professional.

- Initial Views of PDF documents can be displayed with pages and palettes, at different zoom levels, with or without menus, tools, and window controls. These settings are document specific and can be saved with different options for different documents. The settings are established in the Initial View document properties dialog box.

- Links are built into many different Acrobat tools and they can be assigned to items created in Acrobat. Different action types can be assigned to many tools and object elements.

- Acrobat 8 does not support most of the Execute a menu item commands found in all earlier versions of Acrobat.

- Links can be made to Web pages and URLs.

- PDF files are opened through menu commands or by using the Open tool. The most recently opened files are listed in the File menu (Windows) or the File ➪ Open Recent File submenu (Macintosh).

- The Organizer introduced in Acrobat 7 helps you manage files and access a file history of documents opened in Acrobat up to the previous 12 months. The Organizer enables you to view page thumbnails of PDF document pages before you open files and can be sorted on metadata, added to collections, and added to a Favorite Places list.

- You can add PDFs hosted on Web sites to collections in the Organizer.

Chapter 6

Searching PDF Files

Acrobat 8 continues with the search options you had available with Acrobat 7. You'll notice the Find tool and the Search pane are both present in this release; however, the Search pane has had a little cosmetic change and no longer appears nested in the previous How To pane. In Acrobat 8, you find the Search pane working as a floating window that opens on the left side of the Document pane.

You can find information contained in PDF documents either with the Find tool or the Search window for open documents. The search extends to PDFs scattered around your hard drive and all over the Internet and without the assistance of a search index. However, creating index files with Acrobat Catalog and searching the resultant index files is available to you for more sophisticated and much faster searches. In this chapter, I cover all the tools and features available in Acrobat viewers for searching through PDF files and creating and searching index files.

Setting Up the Work Environment

The Find toolbar is loaded by default when you open Acrobat. There's no real need to open the toolbar in the More Tools window if the toolbar is not present in the Toolbar Well. The toolbar automatically opens when you select a menu command or keyboard shortcut to use the Find feature. The Search window opens from a menu command; therefore, no special tool arrangement is needed when searching PDF documents.

For searching PDF documents you may want to load the Search tool. By default the tool is not loaded in the File toolbar. Open a context menu on the Toolbar Well and select More Tools. In the More Tools window, scroll down the File toolbar and check the box adjacent to the Search tool. Click OK and the Search tool is loaded in the File toolbar.

If you intend to engage in editing sessions, comment and review, printing files, and so on. The tool arrangement depends on your editing ambitions. For this chapter, I load the Edit toolbar and leave the other tools at the default.

Using the Find Toolbar

In order to use the Find toolbar, you must have a document open in the Document pane. If you have more than one document open, you can search only the active document appearing in the foreground.

Finding words in an open document can be handled in the Find toolbar. If the toolbar is not loaded in the Toolbar Well, select Edit ➪ Find or press Ctrl/⌘+F. The toolbar then opens as a floating toolbar.

Type a word in the field box in the Find toolbar and press the Enter/Return key. Acrobat searches the current active document and highlights the first occurrence of the found word. When a word is found, the Previous and Next buttons in the toolbar become active, as shown in Figure 6.1.

FIGURE 6.1

Enter the word(s) to be searched in the Find toolbar and press Enter/Return. The Previous and Next buttons appear in the toolbar.

Click the Next button in the toolbar, and Acrobat searches for the next occurrence and stops on the page where the word is highlighted again. Clicking Previous takes you to the last found word in the open document (if you click the button after the first search). When you click Next, and then click the Previous button, the search takes you to the previous found word. For example, if you search for a word in a 100-page document and the word appears on pages 5, 6, and 99, the first time you execute the Find, you stop at page 5. Clicking the Previous button takes you to page 99. However, if you click Next while on page 5, the next found word appears on page 6. Clicking Previous on page 6 takes you back to page 5.

The Find toolbar also includes a pull-down menu, as shown in Figure 6.2, containing several menu commands to assist you in narrowing your search.

FIGURE 6.2

Open the pull-down menu in the Find toolbar for more search options.

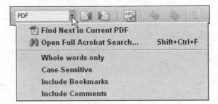

Click the down-pointing arrow to see the following menu commands:

- **Find Next in Current PDF.** The menu command finds the next occurrence of the found word just as it does when clicking the Find Next tool.
- **Open Full Acrobat Search.** Opens the Search window. This command performs the same function as clicking the Search tool or pressing the Ctrl/⌘+Shift+F keys.
- **Whole words only.** Returns words that match whole words only. For example, if you search for a word like "cat," this command avoids returning words such as catalog, catastrophe, category, and so on.
- **Case-Sensitive.** Finds words that match the letter case of the word typed in the Find toolbar.
- **Include Bookmarks.** Finds words in Bookmark descriptions.
- **Include Comments.** Finds words in comment notes.

You can choose one or any combination of the first four options to perform your search. For example, you can select Whole words only, Case-Sensitive, Include Bookmarks, and Include Comments, and Acrobat returns the first occurrence of only whole words matching the letter case in the search criteria whether it be in a Bookmark, comment note, or on a document page.

Using the Find toolbar also makes active two other menu commands. After invoking a find, the Next Result and Previous Result commands appear active in the Edit ➪ Search Results submenu. These commands are the same as using the buttons in the Find toolbar. They also are accompanied by keyboard shortcuts (Ctrl/⌘+G for Next Result and Ctrl/⌘+Shift+G for Previous Result. Note that the other two options in the submenu (Next Document and Previous Document) are grayed out when you use the Find toolbar. These commands are active only when you use the Search window.

Using the Search Window

You perform searches by accessing a menu command, clicking the Search tool, or by using shortcut keys. To search from the menu, choose Edit ➪ Search, or open a context menu with the Hand tool, and select Search. Click the Search tool in the File toolbar and the Search window opens. To use the keyboard shortcut, press Ctrl/⌘+Shift+F and likewise the Search window opens as shown in Figure 6.3. These all allow you to search for a word in an open document, in a collection of PDF files stored on your hard drive, or any type of external media. When you invoke a search, the Search window opens as a floating window. The window can be sized by dragging the lower-right corner out or in to size the width and height.

FIGURE 6.3

When you use the Search menu command or the Ctrl/⌘+Shift+F keyboard shortcut, the Search window opens as a floating window.

Basic search options

When the Search window is in view, you type a word or words to be searched for in the field box that appears at the top of the window. You are limited to the actual word(s) you want to find when you perform a simple search. You cannot use Boolean (AND, OR, and NOT) operators or any kind of search expressions if performing a simple search.

CROSS-REF For more sophisticated searches where you can use Boolean operators, see "Doing advanced searches" later in this chapter.

NOTE The area where you type words and phrases to be searched is in the field box following the text "What word or phrase would you like to search for?" in the Search window. Rather than describe this field box by name, the term "first field box" or "search field box" is used throughout this chapter. When you see such a reference, realize it refers to the area where you type words and phrases to be searched.

If you type more than one word in the search field box, the results are reported for the exact phrase. For example, if you search for "Adobe Acrobat Professional," all the occurrences of "Adobe Acrobat Professional" are reported in the results list. Individual occurrences of Adobe, Acrobat, and Professional are not reported. In other words, you don't need to place phrases within any quotes or special characters to find the results.

In the Search PDF window, you choose where you want to search and the options to narrow the search from the list following the first field box. The following sections describe several choices that are available.

Where to search

The question presented to you is "Where would you like to search?" Two radio buttons appear where you choose whether to search the current open file or search locally on your hard drive, a network server, or a media storage device attached to your computer such as removable media or CD-ROMs. If you select the

second radio button for "All PDF Documents in," you can narrow the search to a directory, drive, or media device by opening the pull-down menu and choosing from the hierarchy of drives and folders appearing in the menu options.

Acrobat also permits you to search through Bookmarks and Comments as the Find toolbar does. Check boxes appear below the pull-down menu for these items. If Bookmarks and Comments are to be part of your search, check the respective item(s). After you choose the options you want, click the Search button.

The results appear in the Search window, as shown in Figure 6.4. The total number of found instances for your search are noted at the top of the window and hot links appear in the scrollable list for the words found in the documents according to the search options you selected. Click any text and the respective document page opens in the Document pane with the first occurrence of the searched word highlighted.

FIGURE 6.4

The total number of occurrences in a single PDF or all occurrences in all documents searched is noted at the top of the window (1) and search results are reported in a scrollable list (2). Click any text in the Results list window to open a page (3) where Search found words matching your criteria.

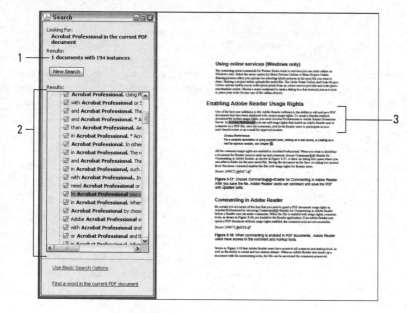

Navigating search results

Menu commands are also available for navigating through search results. Choose Edit ➪ Search Results to open a submenu where you find four menu commands used with searches. The Next Result and Previous Result items are discussed in the section "Using the Find Toolbar" earlier in this chapter. The other two items are as follows:

- **Next Document** (Ctrl/⌘+]): Click Next Document to bypass all found instances in the currently viewed file and open the next file listed in the Search results list.

- **Previous Document** (Ctrl/⌘+[): This command offers the opposite response as Next Document — it moves backward through previously viewed documents.

Next Result and Next Document are not available until you first invoke a search. Next Document becomes active only when a search result exists in two or more documents. Previous Result and Previous Document become active only after you have visited a result in a document more than once so as to retrace your steps backward to see previously viewed results.

If you search an open document and the search results are reported in the Search window, you're better off clicking results in the window than using menu commands. When you select any menu command, the Search window disappears (on Windows) when viewing documents in Acrobat in a maximized view. This is most annoying when you want to keep the Search window open. On the Mac you don't have to worry about using menu commands or opening files. The Search window remains in view at all times until you close it.

Stopping a search

When you start a new search, a button appears in the Search window so you can stop the search. Click Stop and the results found prior to stopping are listed in the scrollable list. If you click Stop, you need to search again starting at the beginning of the search to continue. Click the New Search button and the search starts over from the beginning of the file.

Displaying results

The results list is neatly organized for you in the Search window. If you search the open document, the search results report found words beginning at the front of the document and list occurrences as they are found on following pages. If you search multiple documents, the occurrences are listed in groups according to the individual documents where the words are found. The hierarchy is similar to that of Bookmarks. A plus symbol in Windows or a right-pointing arrow in Macintosh is shown for each document where results have been found. Click the icon, and the list expands the same way Bookmarks and comments expand. The icon changes to a minus symbol in Windows or a down-pointing arrow in Macintosh when a list is expanded. Click the icon again to collapse the list.

You can use Search or the Find toolbar to find words in the open document. Search offers more search criteria options and shows a list of results. As a general rule, using Search is much more efficient than using the Find toolbar.

For information on displaying Bookmarks, see Chapter 16. For information on displaying comments, see Chapter 20.

Searching files and folders

If you search through a large collection of PDF files, Search works away loading up the results window. Clicking a link to open a page where results have been found won't interrupt your search. You can browse files while results continue to be reported. To search a hard disk, a media storage device, a network drive, or a folder in any of these locations, open the pull-down menu below "All PDF Documents in" and select a folder location. The moment you select a folder, the "All PDF Documents in" radio button is activated.

The pull-down menu lists the drives and servers active on your system. If you want to search a particular folder, select the item denoted as Browse for Location (Windows or Macintosh) at the bottom of the pull-down menu. The Browse For Folder (Windows) or Choose a folder to search (Macintosh) dialog box opens as shown in Figure 6.5. Navigate your hard drive as you would when searching for files to open. When you find the folder to be searched, click the folder name and click OK.

When you click a file in the Results window, the Search window becomes hidden. If you want to show the Search window after clicking a file in the Results window, you can press Ctrl/⌘+Shift+F or use the Status bar (Windows) to open the window. On the Mac, the Search window remains open when you browse search results.

After you click OK in the Browse for Folder/Choose a Folder dialog box, the Search window returns. The search does not begin until you click the Search button. Before clicking Search, you can examine the name listed as the target folder. The selected folder is displayed in the Search window by folder name. If all looks as you expect, click Search.

FIGURE 6.5

Select the folder to be searched in the Browse For Folder (Windows) or Browse for Location (Macintosh) dialog box. Select the folder name and click OK (Windows) or Choose (Macintosh) to return to the Search window.

Searching PDFs on the Internet

In Acrobat 6 we had Search the Internet using Google in the Search window and as a separate tool. In Acrobat 7 we had Search the Internet using Yahoo! in the Search window and as a separate tool. In Acrobat 8 we have *nothing*. The ability to search files on the Internet from a click in the Search window has been removed in all Acrobat 8 viewers.

At first glance you may get a bit annoyed that you lost this feature in Acrobat and Reader. I can't give you a precise reason for the feature disappearing in Acrobat 8, but my hunch is that the problem lies more with the Web browser developers than it does with Adobe. It may be that Adobe just can't keep up with changes made by other developers when revisions are made to the browsers. To do so may be cost prohibitive and the functionality can easily be lost during an Acrobat version life cycle when developers upgrade their products.

For whatever reason we lost the ability to click a link in the Search window to search for PDFs on the Internet, you can still perform this kind of search. Using a search engine such as Google, just type your search word or phrase in the Search text box in the Google search engine, add a space, and then type *filetype:PDF*. For example if you want to search for Acrobat 8 and have only PDFs reported in your search results, type *"Acrobat 8" filetype:PDF*. The Google search results report only PDF documents containing your search phrase.

Not all search engines support the extension for searching for PDFs. If you use Yahoo or Ask.com, for example, you can't use the extension. In some cases, advanced search options in search engines can help you narrow a search to report PDFs with the found results. Check your favorite search engine for advanced options to see if searching PDFs is supported.

Performing advanced searches

In all Acrobat viewers, you can search PDF documents with selected criteria without the assistance of a search index. To take advantage of searching with advanced options, click the Use Advanced Search Options link at the bottom of the Search window. When you click the link, a series of advanced options appears in the Search window, as shown in Figure 6.6.

NOTE When you click the link to show the advanced search options, the link at the bottom of the Search window changes to Use Basic Search Options. Click this link to return to searching with the basic options.

Depending on whether you search an open PDF document or a collection of PDFs stored on drives and external devices, the Advanced Search Options change, offering you different options.

CROSS-REF Advanced search offers you options for searching index files as well as PDF files. For information on searching index files, see the section "Searching an index" later in this chapter.

FIGURE 6.6

Click Use Advanced Search Options to take advantage of more search options. When you select a folder of PDF files to search, the options in this figure are available.

Searching the open PDF file with Advanced Search Options

When you select the Current PDF Document from the Look In pull-down menu, the search options shown in Figure 6.6 are available to you. These options are as follows:

- **Whole words only.** When checked, the search results return whole words. If you search for "forgiven," the search ignores words like "for" and "give" that make up part of the whole word. If the check box is disabled, various stems and parts of a whole word are included with the search results.

- **Case-Sensitive.** Letter case is ignored if the check box is disabled. If enabled, then the search results return only words matching the precise letter case of the searched word.

- **Proximity.** Proximity is a powerful tool when performing searches. If you want to search for two independent words that may appear together in a given context — for example, *Acrobat* and *PostScript* — the Proximity option finds the two words when they appear within a range specified in the Search preferences. The default is 900 words. You can change the proximity range by opening the Preferences dialog box (Ctrl/⌘+K), click Search in the left pane and edit the Range of words for Proximity searches text box.

- **Stemming.** If you want to search for all words stemming from a given word, enable this option. Words such as "header" and "heading" stem from the word "head" in the English language. If you type "head" in the first field box and select the Stemming option, all PDFs containing the search criteria from the word *head* are listed.

- **Include Bookmarks.** When Bookmarks are checked, the search results report the found instances in the Bookmarks and the document pages.

- **Include Comments.** Text in comment notes and text on document pages are returned when this option is checked.

- **Include Attachments.** All PDF document file attachments are searchable. Select the Include Attachments check box and found results are reported in the Results list for all occurrences of the searched word. Clicking a search result opens the attached file in the Document pane.

If you open a PDF Package, the Search window changes to accommodate searching all files in the package. Select from the Look In drop-down menu In the entire PDF Package and Search will search all files in the package.

You can search PDF Packages using either the Basic search options or the Advanced search options. When searching package contents using Basic search options select the radio button for In the entire PDF Package, as shown in Figure 6.7. When using the Advanced options, select In the entire PDF Package from the Look In drop-down menu. Note that both these items are accessible only when you open a PDF Package.

FIGURE 6.7

Select In the entire PDF Package to search all files in the package.

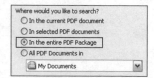

145

CROSS-REF   For more information on working with PDF Packages, see Chapter 12.

When all the search criteria have been established, click the Search button. The results are reported in the Search window like the searches performed with the Basic Search Options.

Searching multiple PDFs with Advanced Search Options

When you change the search parameters to search through a collection of PDF documents, the Advanced Search Options change, offering you more options to help narrow down your search, as shown in Figure 6.8.

FIGURE 6.8

Advanced Search Options offer you additional criteria when searching through multiple PDF documents.

These options are as follows:

- **Return results containing.** Four options are available from this pull-down menu:
    - **Match Exact word or phrase.** If you search for something like *Human Resource Forms*, only these three words together in a PDF document are returned as results. The results report the precise order of the words.
    - **Match Any of the words.** Using the same example, words such as Human, Resource, Forms, Human Resource, Resource Forms, Human Forms, and Human Resource Forms would be reported in the results. Any one of the words or any combination of words in a phrase is reported.

■ **Match All of the words.** In this case, all the words need to be contained in the document, but not necessarily in the order described previously. You might see returns such as Forms Human Resource returned from the search.

■ **Boolean query.** You can search PDF collections using Boolean expressions (AND, OR, NOT) without the assistance of a search index created with Acrobat Catalog. Note that Boolean queries are not available when you search an open document. You need to use the Advanced Search Options to search through a drive, external media, or a folder.

CROSS-REF For more detail on using Boolean queries, see the "Boolean queries" section later in this chapter. For more information on Acrobat Catalog, see the section "Creating Search Indexes (Acrobat Professional Only)" later in this chapter.

■ **Use these additional criteria.** Up to three check boxes offer you one or a combination of several different options to help you refine your search. The number of check boxes you have available depends on the vertical size of the Search window. If you reduce the size, you may see only a single check box, as shown in Figure 6.8.

From the first pull-down menu you select the primary category. The second pull-down menu to the right of each primary category helps refine that particular category. The options for each of the three check box pull-down menus are the same. You might, for example, choose Date Created from the first check box option and define the date from the options contained in the adjacent pull-down menu. You then might add another criterion and ask for the Keywords option. Adjacent to Keywords, you might specify that the file does not contain certain words. In the field box, you type any descriptions for the menu choices you make.

NOTE All the preceding items require that you supply at least one character in "What word or phase would you like to search for?" The options that follow enable you to search for specific content related to the option of choice and you do not need to supply a word in the first field box in order to execute a search. When you move around adjusting criteria, the Search button appears active or grayed out. If it is grayed out, you can't perform a search on the options you chose. In some cases, the missing option is a word or phrase that needs to be added to the first field box.

From the criteria selection pull-down menu, the choices available to you are as follows:

■ **Date Created.** If you look for PDF documents that you know were created before or after a certain date, use the Date Created menu option. You have four choices for options associated with this category available in the second pull-down menu adjacent to the first menu choice. These options are: Is exactly, Is before, Is after, and Is not. These four options are self-explanatory. When you make the choices from the two pull-down menus, your next step is to type the date criteria in the field box appearing below the pull-down menus. If, for example, you select Date Created and Is not, you then add the date you want to exclude from the search. As an additional aid to you, Acrobat offers a calendar when you select the pull-down menu from the field box, as shown in Figure 6.9 (Windows only). Make a date selection from the calendar and move to the option you want to change or click the Search button. If you click the month, a pop-up menu showing all months in a year opens. (Note that the calendar is not available on the Mac.)

■ **Date Modified.** The modified date searches for the date the PDF file was last modified. If you create a file on January 1, 2004 and then save some edits on July 1, 2004, the modified date is July 1, 2004. The manner in which you specify a date is the same as searching for the creation date.

FIGURE 6.9

After setting the date criteria from the pull-down menus, open the pull-down menu from the field box to open a calendar to help you find the date parameters to be searched. Click the month name and a pop-up menu opens showing all months in a year.

- **Author.** The information is derived from the Document Properties in the Description tab. Any data typed in the Author field are searched. This choice and the remaining options offer two menu options in the second pull-down menu. You can select from Contains or Does not contain. In essence, your search includes or excludes the data you supply in the field box immediately following the pull-down menu choices.

CROSS-REF For information related to document descriptions, see the "Document Descriptions" section later in this chapter.

- **Title.** Same as the Author search except the Title field is used in the document description.
- **Subject.** Same as the Author search except the Subject field is used in the document description.
- **Filename.** The name you provide for the PDF document is searched.
- **Keywords.** Same as the Author search except the Keywords field is used in the document description.
- **Bookmarks.** When you select this option, Acrobat searches for the words in both the PDF document and in Bookmarks. The results list includes the found words in both Bookmarks and pages.
- **Comments.** Same as Bookmarks, but the comment notes are searched. The results report the found words appearing in comment notes.
- **JPEG Images.** Narrows the search for files meeting the search text criteria and where JPEG images are contained within the PDF.
- **XMP Metadata.** Searches for words or phrases contained in the document metadata.
- **Object Data.** Certain images contain metadata created from an original authoring application, such as MS Visio, Microsoft Project, and AutoDesk AutoCAD. Select an object with the Object Data tool and click. The metadata information displayed in the Object Data dialog box is searchable as well as the data contained in the Object Data dialog box. If you know certain attributes for images contained in a file, you can narrow your search by searching the object metadata.

CROSS-REF For more information on XMP and object metadata, see "Searching Metadata" later in this chapter.

Below the Use these additional criteria pull-down menus are additional options. These options are the same as those used for the advanced searches on open PDF documents. Jump several pages back in this book to review the descriptions for the items listed at the bottom of the Search window.

Searching dates

To help you target the precise date with the field box and the calendar, Acrobat offers you several options. To change the year, you can edit the field box and type the year for the date to be searched. In the field box you can change dates by clicking the day, month, and year, and then use the up or down arrow keys to scroll dates. The dates revolve like an odometer. Select a day, and then click the month to highlight the value and press the arrow keys again until you find the correct month. Move to the year and follow the same steps to select the correct year. You can also select any one of the three values and type new values you want to search when the text is selected. The text you type replaces all selected text. Acrobat accepts only a legitimate value, so if you type a value not permitted for a date search, for example, entering 33 in the day field, Acrobat will not accept it.

To change dates with the calendar, click the down arrow in the pull-down menu adjacent to the date in the field box to open the calendar. For a month change, left-click in the title bar of the calendar on the month name. For example, if July appears listed in the title bar, click July. Be careful not to left-click the mouse below the title bar, because doing so selects a day and closes the calendar. When you left-click on the month name in the title bar, a pop-up menu displays the months of the year. Move the cursor to the desired month and left-click again.

NOTE You can also change months by scrolling the calendar backward or forward. Click the left arrow in the title bar to scroll backward or the right arrow to scroll forward. As you reach a year beginning or end, the next month in date order is opened. For example, scrolling backward from January 1996 opens December 1995.

When you click to select the desired month, Acrobat leaves the calendar view open so you can still make the year and day selections. To change the year in the calendar, left-click on the year in the title bar. The year becomes visible as editable text. You can edit the field or click the up or down arrows adjacent.

After you select the month and year, left-click on the desired day from the calendar displayed below the title bar. Acrobat supplies the new date in the field box, as shown in Figure 6.10, and closes the calendar.

FIGURE 6.10

Change the date for the calendar and the new date is shown while the current date is reported at the bottom of the calendar.

Searching metadata

The ability to search a document's metadata is a powerful tool in Acrobat. In order to use the tool, you need to know just a little bit about what *metadata* is.

Adobe Acrobat 5.0 and later contains metadata in XML (eXtensible Markup Language) format. In Acrobat 7 and 8 object metadata are accessible. The metadata of a file or an image is information related to the document structure, origination, content, interchange, and processing. Metadata might include, for example, the document author's name, the creation date, modified date, the PDF producer, copyright information on images, color space on images, and more. When you click Search, the search results report all files where the searched words are contained in a document's metadata.

XMP (eXtensible Metadata Platform) is an XML framework that provides all Adobe programs a common language for communicating standards related to document creation and processing throughout publishing workflows. XMP is a format, and document metadata viewed in XML source code can be exported to XMP format. Once in XMP, it can be exchanged between documents.

To take a look at the XML source code of the XMP metadata for a document, choose File ⇨ Properties and click the Description tab. In the Description tab click on Additional Metadata to open the dialog box shown in Figure 6.11. Click Advanced and expand the listed items by clicking the symbol adjacent to each listed item.

At the bottom of the dialog box are buttons used for replacing, appending, saving, and deleting data. Click Save to export the XMP data that can be shared in workflows across many different file types. For the purposes of searching information, any of the text you see in the source code in the Advanced list can be searched.

FIGURE 6.11

To see document metadata click the Additional Metadata button in the Description Properties dialog box.

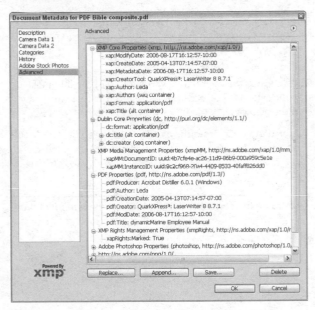

Searching layers

The search criteria discussed on the preceding pages works for documents containing layers. When you invoke a search in documents containing layers, Search automatically searches through all layers for the criteria you specify in the Search window. The results list contains items on any hidden layers as well as all visible layers. When you click a result associated with a hidden layer, Acrobat prompts you in a dialog box, as shown in Figure 6.12, asking whether you want to make the layer visible.

FIGURE 6.12

If searched words are found on hidden layers, Acrobat asks whether you want to make the hidden layer visible.

If you click Yes in the dialog box, the layer is made visible and the search stops at the found word. If you select No, the layer remains hidden and you are taken to the next search result.

Boolean queries

The Return results containing pull-down menu in the Search PDF window contains a Boolean query menu option for searching with Boolean expressions. Boolean expressions include AND, OR, and NOT. Acrobat recognizes these Boolean operators when you invoke a search. You can use all the previously listed criteria when you want to use the Boolean expressions option.

To search with Boolean expressions you need to search an index file. Boolean operators are not recognized when searching the current open document or when browsing folders.

CROSS-REF   For more on searching indexes, see the section "Creating Search Indexes (Acrobat Professional Only)" later in this chapter.

■ **AND operator.** Use AND between two words to find documents that contain both terms, in any order. For example, type Paris AND France to identify documents that contain both Paris and France. Searches with AND and no other Boolean operators produce the same results as selecting the All Of The Words option.

NOTE   When using Boolean operators, the text is not case-sensitive. Uppercase letters for the Boolean expressions are used here to denote a Boolean operator as opposed to text. You can use lowercase letters and the results are reported the same, as long as the Boolean query pull-down menu item is selected.

■ **OR operator.** Use to search for all instances of either term. For example, type email OR e-mail to find all documents with occurrences of either spelling. Searches with OR and no other Boolean operators produce the same results as selecting the Any Of The Words option.

■ **^ (exclusive OR).** Use to search for all instances that have either term but not both. For example, type cat ^ dog to find all documents with occurrences of either cat or dog but not both cat and dog.

- **().** Use parentheses to specify the order of evaluation of terms. For example, type white AND (whale OR Ahab) to find all documents that contain either white and whale or white and Ahab. (The query processor performs an OR query on whale and Ahab and then performs an AND query on those results with white.

- **NOT operator.** Use before a search term to exclude any documents that contain that term. For example, type NOT Kentucky to find all documents that don't contain the word Kentucky. Or, type Paris NOT Kentucky to find all documents that contain the word Paris but not the word Kentucky.

- **Multiple words.** Words appearing together such as "Acrobat PDF" can be included in quotes. You would supply "Acrobat PDF" in the field box (include the quotes) and all instances where these two words appear together are reported in the search results. If the words are not contained within quotes, the words "Acrobat," "PDF," and "Acrobat PDF" would all be returned in the search results. This behavior is similar to how you perform searches in Web browsers.

- **Searching and, or, not.** If you want to search for a term where these three words are part of the term, you can by distinguishing between words you search for and using operators. To search for something like "Ben and Jerry's" as a term, you would type "Ben and Jerry's" within quote marks. If you want to search for two terms and a Boolean operator you might use *"Ben and Jerry's" AND "Ice Cream" NOT yogurt.* The results report back to you the documents where the words "Ben and Jerry's" and "ice cream" are contained in the files and the words "Ben and Jerry's yogurt" are not reported in the search results.

 To learn more about searching with Boolean operators, search the Internet using Boolean searches as your search criteria in any search engine.

Search preferences

To open preference settings for Search, choose Edit ➪ Preferences (Windows) or Acrobat Preferences (Macintosh). In the left pane, select Search. The preference options available to you are shown in Figure 6.13.

FIGURE 6.13

Choose Edit ➪ Preferences to open the Preferences dialog box. Click Search in the list at the left to display preference settings for using Search.

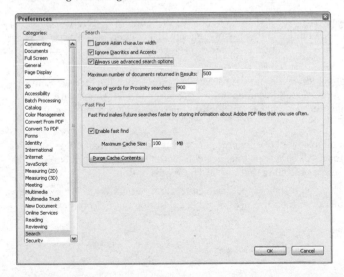

The preference choices listed on the right side of the dialog box are as follows:

- **Ignore Asian character width.** This setting ignores Asian character width and finds both half-width and full-width instances of Asian language characters.

- **Ignore Diacritics and Accents.** A diacritic is an accent mark like you might use on a word like "resumé" or the cedilla on a word like "façade" to indicate a special phonetic value. These and other accents are ignored during a search unless you check the box; so for example, if you have it checked Acrobat will find both "resume" and "resumé." If it is unchecked, Search looks for "resumé" only.

- **Always use advanced search options.** Sets the Advanced Search Options as the default. When the check box is enabled you don't need to keep clicking the Use Advanced Search Options button in the Search window. Enable this setting if you find yourself always using the Advanced Search Options.

- **Maximum number of documents returned in Results.** The acceptable range is between 1 and 10,000. Enter a value and the results are limited to this number.

- **Range of words for proximity searches.** When using Boolean operators, you might want to search for two words within a defined range of words. You can enter a value between 1 and 10,000. Both words need to be within the range when you use a Boolean expression such as AND.

- **Enable fast find.** Searches are logged by Acrobat in a memory cache. If you perform a search and later in another session perform a search on the same information, Acrobat returns to the cache for the information, thus speeding up the search. You can edit the cache size by editing the field box for the number of megabytes on your hard drive you want to allocate to the cache. Be certain you have ample hard drive space when enabling the cache and raising the cache size.

- **Purge Cache Contents.** The cache occupies as much memory as is available on your hard drive. If you want to clear the cache, click the button to erase all the contents.

After changing any settings in the Preferences dialog box, click OK. The changes you make are dynamically reflected in Acrobat and take effect the next time you perform a search.

Document Descriptions

Document descriptions are user-supplied data fields used to help you identify PDF files according to title, subject, author, and keywords. At the time you create a PDF document, you may have options for supplying a document description. In other cases, you may add descriptions in Acrobat either individually or with Acrobat's batch processing features.

CROSS-REF To learn how to create batch sequences, see Chapter 18.

After you add descriptions and save your files, the data added to these fields are searchable via advanced searches and index file searches. Developing an organized workflow with specific guidelines for users to follow regarding document descriptions significantly helps all your colleagues search PDFs much more efficiently.

To add a document description, choose File ➪ Document Properties. When the Document Properties dialog box opens, click the Description tab, as shown in Figure 6.14.

The four fields for document descriptions are as follows:

■ **Title.** The Title field in this example contains a description of a form. Other forms in a company using a similar schema might use titles such as W-2 Form, Travel Expense, Employee Leave, and so on in the Title field.

■ **Author.** In the example, the Author field contains the department authoring the form. Notice that an employee name is not used for the Author field. Rather than use employee names, use departments instead. Using departments is a much better choice because a company typically turns over employees more often than it renames departments.

■ **Subject.** In the example, the Subject field contains Form. The Subject here might be used to distinguish a Form from a Policy, Procedure, Memo, Directive, and so on.

■ **Keywords.** The first entry in the Keywords field is the form number used by the company to identify the form. Other words in the Keywords field are descriptors related to the form contents. If you want to add an employee author name, add it to the Keywords field.

FIGURE 6.14

You add document descriptions to the Descriptions tab in the Document Properties dialog box.

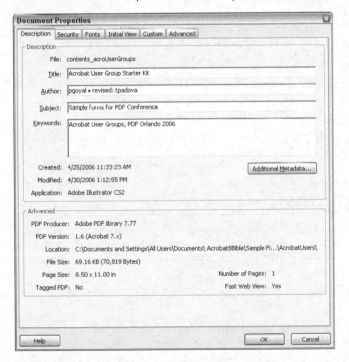

TIP Notice the Location item in the Document Properties. The text reports the location on your hard drive where the file is located. This test is a link. Click the text and your file is opened on the Desktop (Finder on Mac) showing you the folder location.

The reason the field information is important for any organization using a PDF workflow is that document description information can be used when a user searches a collection of PDF files. Each field is searchable by the summary title and the words contained in the fields. Therefore, a user can search for all PDF files where the Title field contains the word "Purchase" and the Subject field contains the word "Form." The search results display all PDF documents where the Title and Subject fields have these words contained in the document description.

As a comparison, imagine searching for the words "Purchase Order." The search would return all PDFs where these words appear in either the document summary or the text in the PDF files. "Purchase Order" might be used in memos, policies, procedures, and forms. The user might have to search through many PDFs in order to find the Purchase Order form, thus spending much more time trying to locate the right document.

Searching document descriptions

To search for document descriptions, you need to use either the advanced search or an index file search. Press Ctrl/⌘+Shift+F to open the Search window in an Acrobat viewer and click Use Advanced Search Options. Select a folder to search from the Look In pull-down menu.

CROSS-REF For searching index files, see the section "Searching an index" later in this chapter.

Under Use these additional criteria, select one of the description items from the first pull-down menu (Title, Author, Subject, or Keywords). Select either Contains or Does not contain from the pull-down menu adjacent to the first menu. Type the words to be searched in the field box below the pull-down menus. Continue adding additional description fields as desired. In Figure 6.15, two description fields are marked for the search.

FIGURE 6.15

Two description fields are identified. When you click the Search button, Acrobat searches the document descriptions for matches.

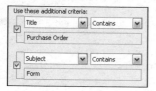

Note that no criteria need to be supplied in the first field box for specific words to be searched in the document. If you click Search in the Search window with the descriptions shown in Figure 6.15, all PDF files in the designated folder with the words "Purchase Order" in the Title field and "Forms" in the Subject field are returned in the results list for files matching the criteria.

Document descriptions and Boolean queries

You can add Boolean queries when searching document descriptions. You might know some content in PDF files as well as information contained in the document descriptions. In this case you address the additional criteria items in the same manner and add the Boolean query as discussed earlier in this chapter. In Figure 6.16, document descriptions are added to a Boolean query.

FIGURE 6.16

You can add Boolean queries to searches with additional criteria selections such as document descriptions.

When you click the Search button, the number of results returned in the Search window is significantly reduced compared to searching for individual words — especially when common words are contained in many PDF documents. What the document descriptions offer you is a method for targeting the exact file you're looking for as fast as possible. If you have 100 PDF documents in the search results list, looking through the list and finding the file you want will take some time. Compare that to two or three files listed. Obviously, the document descriptions offer significant time savings as you search PDFs from among very large collections.

Full-Text Versus Index Searches

This section represents a pivotal point in this chapter. What has been covered so far is information about finding content in PDF documents with a very elaborate *find* feature in Acrobat. The name used in Acrobat to refer to what has been discussed so far is "Search." Users of earlier versions of Acrobat may take this to mean using Acrobat Search as it was used in Acrobat viewers earlier than version 6.0. What has been covered thus far, however, is a Search of data files that was greatly improved in Acrobat version 6 and is more powerful in returning results in Acrobat version 8. To understand the difference between the preceding pages and what follows requires a little explanation.

In addition to full-text searches for documents, you can also create a separate index file and search one or more indexes at a time. Index files provide some benefit in that they are still a little faster than full-text searches, can be automatically assigned to PDF documents in the Advanced tab in the Document Properties, and can be automatically loaded from a CD-ROM, and multiple indexes can be searched so files can be scattered somewhat on your hard drive in different folders.

Search Index Procedures

I explain the details for working with search indexes in the remaining pages in this chapter. To provide you with an overall summary for how index file creation and management is dealt with in Acrobat, I give you a short summary of the procedures here.

Using index files to perform searches begins with using a current index file or creating a new one. Users who have been working with index files need to make sure that all your previous indexes are updated for compatibility with Acrobat 8.0 viewers.

Index files are created and updated with Acrobat Catalog with Acrobat Professional only. Catalog is available from a menu selection in the Advanced menu. In Acrobat 8, the menu item has changed location as well as the command name for opening Catalog. Select Advanced ➪ Document Processing ➪ Full Text Index with Catalog. You open Catalog and make a decision for creating a new index or opening an existing index file for rebuilding or editing in the Catalog window.

After an index file is created or updated, you load the index file into the Search window. Multiple index files can be loaded and searched. When you search index files, the results are reported in the Search window like all the searches discussed earlier in this chapter.

Earlier releases of Acrobat offered you options for various menu selections related to managing indexes and loading new index files. Earlier releases of Acrobat also offered you dialog boxes where results were reported and information about an index file could be obtained. In Acrobat 6.0 and 7.0 viewers, you handle all your index file management in the Search window. Menu commands are limited to viewing search results as described earlier in this chapter.

If you edit PDF documents, delete them, or add new documents to folders that have been indexed, you need to rebuild index files periodically. You can purge old data and re-index files in Acrobat Catalog. Index files can be copied to different hard drive locations, across servers, and to external media. When copying files, you need to copy all files and folders associated with the index file. Failure to copy all the files renders the index inoperable.

Creating Search Indexes (Acrobat Professional Only)

In order to search an index file, you must have one present on your computer, network server, some media storage device, or embedded in a PDF. When you install an Acrobat viewer, a help index file is included during your installation. You can use this file to search for words contained in any of the help documents. If you want to search your own files, you need to create an index. To create an index file, you use Acrobat Catalog.

NOTE Acrobat Catalog is available only in Acrobat Professional. Search indexes can be used by all Acrobat viewers including Adobe Reader.

To launch Acrobat Catalog from within Acrobat Professional choose Advanced ➪ Document Processing ➪ Full Text Index with Catalog. Catalog is robust and provides many options for creating and modifying indexes. After a search index is created, any user can access the search index in all Acrobat viewers to find words using the Search window. However, before you begin to work with Acrobat Catalog, you need to take some preliminary steps to be certain all your files are properly prepared and ready to be indexed.

Preparing PDFs for indexing

Preparation involves creating PDFs with all the necessary information to facilitate searches. All searchable document description information needs to be supplied in the PDF documents at the time of PDF creation or by modifying PDFs in Acrobat before you begin working with Catalog. For workgroups and multiple user access to search indexes, this information needs to be clear and consistent. Other factors, such as naming conventions, location of files, and optimizing performance should all be thought out and planned prior to creating an index file.

NOTE   Adding document descriptions is not a requirement for creating search indexes. You can index files without any information in the document description fields. Adding document descriptions merely adds more relevant information to your PDF documents and aids users in finding search results faster.

Document descriptions

Document description information should be supplied in all PDF files to be searched. As discussed earlier in this chapter, all document description data are searchable. Spending time creating document descriptions and defining the field types for consistent organization will facilitate searches performed by multiple users.

The first of the planning steps is to develop a flow chart or outline of company information and the documents to be categorized. This organization may or may not be implemented where you intend to develop a PDF workflow. If your information flow is already in place, you may need to make some modifications to coordinate nomenclature and document identity with the document summary items in Acrobat.

Document descriptions contained in the Title, Subject, Author, and Keywords fields should be consistent and intuitive. They should also follow a hierarchy consistent with the company's organizational structure and workflow. The document summary items should be mapped out and defined. When preparing files for indexing, consider the following:

- **Title.** Title information might be thought of as the root of an outline — the parent statement, if you will. Descriptive titles should be used to help users narrow searches within specific categories. The Title field can also be used to display the title name at the top of the Acrobat window when you select viewing titles in the Initial View properties.

CROSS-REF   For information on how to set document title attributes in the Initial View dialog box, see Chapter 5.

- **Author.** Avoid using proper names for the Author field. Personnel change in companies and roles among employees change. Identify the author of PDF documents according to departments, work groups, facilities, and so on.

- **Subject.** If the Title field is the parent item in an outline format, the Subject would be a child item nested directly below the title. Subjects might be considered subsets of titles. When creating document summaries, be consistent. Don't use subject and title or subject and keyword information back and forth with different documents. If an item, such as employee grievances, is listed as a Subject in some PDFs and then listed as a Title in other documents, the end users will become confused with the order and searches will become unnecessarily complicated.

- **Keywords.** If you have a forms identification system in place, be certain to use form numbers and identity as part of the Keywords field. You might start the Keywords field with a form number and then add additional keywords to help narrow searches. Be consistent and always start the Keywords field with forms or document numbers. If you need to have PDF author names, add them here in the Keywords fields. If employees change roles or leave the company, the Author fields still provide the information relative to a department.

To illustrate some examples, take a look at Table 6.1.

TABLE 6.1

Document Summary Examples

Title	Author	Subject	Keywords
Descriptive Titles Titles may be considered specific to workgroup tasks.	Department Names Don't use employee names in organizations; employees change, departments usually remain.	Subsection of Title Subjects may be thought of as child outline items nested below the parent Title items — a subset of the Titles.	Document numbers and random identifiers You can supply Forms ID numbers, internal filing numbers, and so on in the Keyword fields. If employee names are a *must* for your company, add employee names in the Keywords field box. List any related words to help find the topic.
Employee Policies	Human Resources	Vacation Leave	D-101, HR32A, H. Jones, policy, employee regulations
FDA Compliance	Quality Assurance	Software Validation	SOP-114, QA-182, J. Wilson, regulations, citations, eye implant device
Curriculum	English Department	American Literature	Plan 2010, Martha Evans, senior English, Emerson High, 11th grade
Receivables	Accounting	Collection Policy	F-8102, M-5433, Finance, collections, payments
eCommerce	Marketing	Products	M-1051, e-117A, golf clubs, sports, leisure

TIP Legacy PDF files used in an organization may have been created without a document description, or you may reorganize PDFs and want to change document summaries. To quickly (or efficiently) update these documents, you can create a batch sequence to change multiple PDF files and then run the sequence. Place your PDFs in a folder where the document summaries are to be edited. In the Edit Sequence dialog box, select the items to change and edit each document summary item. Run the sequence to update an entire folder of PDFs.

CROSS-REF For more information on creating batch sequences, see Chapter 18.

Managing Multiple PDF Documents

Books, reports, and manuals can be broken up into separate files and structured in a way that it still appears to the end user as a single document. Assuming a user reads through a file in a linear fashion, you can create links to open and close pages without user intervention. Create navigational buttons to move forward and back through document pages. On the last page of each chapter, use the navigation button to open the next chapter. Also on the last page of each chapter, create a Page action that closes the current document when the page is closed. (See Chapter 22 for creating links and Page actions.) If the end user disables "Open cross-document links in same window" in the Documents category in the Preferences dialog box, the open file still closes after the last page is closed. All the chapters can be linked from a table of contents where any chapter can be opened. If you give your design some thought, browsing the contents of books will appear to the end user no different than reading a book in the analog world.

File structure

The content, filenames, and location of PDFs to be cataloged contribute to file structure items. All the issues related to file structure must be thought out and appropriately designed for the audience that you intend to support. The important considerations are as follows:

- **File naming conventions.** Names provided for the PDF files are critical for distributing documents among users. If filenames get truncated, then either Acrobat Search or the end user will have difficulty finding a document when performing a search. This is of special concern to Macintosh users who want to distribute documents across platforms. The best precaution is to always use standard DOS file-naming conventions. The standard eight-character maximum filename, with no more than three-character file extensions (`filename.ext`), will always work regardless of platform.

- **Folder names.** Folder names should follow the same conventions as filenames. Macintosh users who want to keep filenames longer than standard DOS names must limit folder names to eight characters and no more than a three-character file extension for cross-platform compliance.

- **File and folder name identity.** In previous versions of Acrobat and Acrobat catalog you had to avoid using ASCII characters from 133 to 159 for any filename or folder name. Acrobat Catalog in earlier versions did not support some extended characters in this range, and you could experience problems when using files across platforms. (Figure 6.17 lists the characters to avoid.) Not in Acrobat 8 with more support for non-English languages, you don't need to be worried about file and folder identity that use special characters.

- **Folder organization.** Folders to be cataloged should have a logical hierarchy. Copy all files to be cataloged to a single folder or a single folder with nested folders in the same path. When nesting folders, be certain to keep the number of nested folders to a minimum. Deeply nested folders slow down searches, and path names longer than 256 characters create problems.

FIGURE 6.17

Extended characters from ASCII 133 to ASCII 159 used to be a problem when using Acrobat Catalog. In Acrobat 8 you'll find support for creating index files and searching files and folders containing these characters.

133	à	139	ï	144	É	149	ò	154	Ü
134	å	140	î	145	æ	150	û	156	£
135	ç	141	ì	146	Æ	151	ù	157	¥
136	ê	142	Ä	147	ô	152	_	158	_
137	ë	143	Å	148	ö	153	Ö	159	ƒ
138	è								

- **Folder locations.** Windows users must keep the location of folders on a local hard drive or a network server volume. Although Macintosh users can catalog information across computer workstations, creating separate indexes for files contained on separate drives would be advisable. Any files moved to different locations make searches inoperable.

- **PDF structure.** File and folder naming should be handled before creating links and attaching files. If filenames are changed after the PDF structure has been developed, many links become inoperable. Be certain to complete all editing in the PDF documents before cataloging files.

Optimizing performance

Searches can be performed very fast if you take a little time in creating the proper structure and organization. If you don't avoid some pitfalls with the way that you organize files, then searches perform much slower. A few considerations to be made include the following:

- **Optimize PDF files.** Optimization should be performed on all PDF files as one of the last steps in your workflow. Use the Save As optimizes for Fast Web View found in the General category in the Preferences dialog box and run the PDF Optimizer located in the Advanced menu (Acrobat Professional only). Optimization is especially important for searches to be performed from CD-ROM files.

CROSS-REF For information on PDF Optimizer, see Chapter 18.

- **Break up long PDF files.** Books, reports, essays, and other documents that contain many pages should be broken up into multiple PDF files. If you have books to be cataloged, break up the books into separate chapters. Acrobat Search runs much faster when finding information from several small files. It slows down when searching through long documents.

Creating search help

You can have multiple indexes for various uses and different workgroups. Personnel may use one index for department matters, another for company-wide information, and perhaps another for a research library. In a search, all relevant keywords will appear from indexes loaded in the Index Selection dialog box. When using multiple indexes, employees may forget the structure of document summaries and what index is needed for a given search.

You can create readme files and index help files to store key information about what search words can be used to find document summaries. You can create a single PDF file, text files, or multiple files that serve as help. Figure 6.18 shows an example of a PDF help file that might be used to find documents related to a company's personnel policies, procedures, and forms.

FIGURE 6.18

A PDF help file can assist users in knowing what keywords they need to use for the Title, Subject, Author, and Keywords fields.

Widget Company
Human Resources Index Description

Title: HR
Subject: Table
Author: Table
Keywords: Table

Title	Subject	Author	Keywords
Policy	PTO	HR	HR 501
Policy	Maternity	HR	HR 521
Procedure	Maternity	HR	HR 520
Form	Payroll	Accounting	FM 261
Policy	Bonus	Accounting	AC 245
Policy	Manual	Admin	AD 109
Procedure	Grievance	HR	HR 546
Policy	EAP	HR	HR 593
Policy	Hiring	HR	HR 506
Form	ID	HR	FM 505
Chart	HR	Admin	AD 117
Form	Leave	HR	FM 531
Procedure	Pay deduction	Accounting	AC 228
Policy	Benefits	Table	Table
Procedure	Extended Leave	HR	HR 564
Policy	Education Leave	HR	HR 568
Form	Insurance	HR	FM 533
Form	Dental	HR	FM 512
Policy	401K	HR	HR 555

In the top-right corner of Figure 6.18, the document summary for the help file is listed. The Title fields for this company are broken into categories for policies, procedures, forms, and charts. The Subject fields break down the title categories into specific personnel items, and the Author fields contain the department that authored the documents. Form numbers appear for all Keywords fields.

TIP **When creating help files that guide a user for searching document information, use a common identifier in the Subject, Author, and Keywords fields reserved for only finding help files. In Figure 6.18, the identifier is "Table." Whenever a user searches for the word "table" in the Author field, the only returns in the Search Results dialog box will be help files. When using the Title and Author field together, a user can find a specific help file for a given department. In the previous example, the Title is HR and the Author is Table. When these words are searched for the document information, the help file for the HR department is returned in the Search Results. If you reserve keywords for the document Summary fields, any employee can easily find information by remembering only a few keywords.**

Creating a new index file

After your files are optimized and saved in final form, it's time to create the search index. Choose Advanced ➪ Document Processing ➪ Full Text Index with Catalog to open the Catalog dialog box, as shown in Figure 6.19. In the dialog box you make choices for creating a new index file or opening an existing index file. Click the New Index button to create a new index file.

FIGURE 6.19

Click the New Index button in the Catalog dialog box to create an index file.

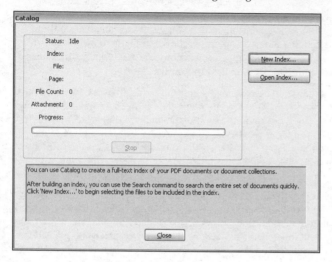

The New Index Definition dialog box shown in Figure 6.20 opens, in which you set specific attributes for your index and determine what folder(s) are to be indexed.

FIGURE 6.20

You set attributes for your new index file in the New Index Definition dialog box.

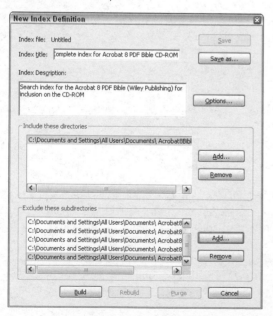

Index title

The title that you place in this field is a title for the index, but not necessarily the name of the file you ultimately save. The name you enter here does not need to conform to any naming conventions because in most cases it won't be the saved filename. When you open an index file, you search your hard drive, server, or external media for a filename that ends with a .pdx extension. When you visit the Search window and select Look In ⇨ Select Index, the Index Selection dialog box opens, as shown in Figure 6.21. What appears in the Index Selection dialog box is a list of indexes appearing according to the Index Title names. These names are derived from what you type in the Index Title field in Acrobat Catalog.

NOTE When you get ready to build a file, Acrobat prompts you for the index filename. By default the text you type in the Index Title field is listed in the File name field in the Save Index File dialog box. This dialog box opens when you click the Build button in the Catalog dialog box (see the section "Building the index" later in this chapter). In most cases where you supply a name as a description in the Index Title, you'll want to change the filename to a name consistent with standard DOS conventions (that is, eight-character maximum with a three-character maximum extension). Make this change when you are prompted to save the file.

CAUTION If you see an index name grayed out, the index is not available to your Acrobat viewer. You may have moved the index file to another location on your hard drive, deleted the file, or tried to search an index on a CD-ROM that is not mounted. In order to bring back the index and make it available to your viewer you need to delete the grayed out index name by clicking the Remove button and then add the file or rebuild and Add the file in the Index selection dialog box.

FIGURE 6.21

Choosing Select Index from the Look In pull-down menu in the Search window opens the Index selection dialog box. All loaded indexes are listed according to the index title supplied in Acrobat Catalog at the time the index was created.

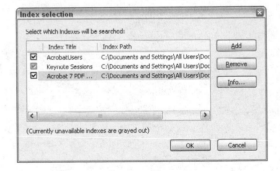

Index description

You can supply as many as 256 characters in the Index Description field. Descriptive names and keywords should be provided so that the end user knows what each index contains. Index descriptions should be thought of as adding more information to the items mentioned earlier in this chapter regarding document descriptions. Index descriptions can help users find the index file that addresses their needs.

When an index is loaded, the index title appears in the Select Indexes dialog box. To get more information about an index file, click the Info button shown in Figure 6.21. The Index information dialog box opens as shown in Figure 6.22. The Index information dialog box shows you the title from the Index Title field and the description added in Acrobat Catalog in the Index Description field.

FIGURE 6.22

The Index Description is contained in the Index information dialog box. Users can click on the Info button in the Index selection dialog box to see the description added in the Index Description field box in Acrobat Catalog.

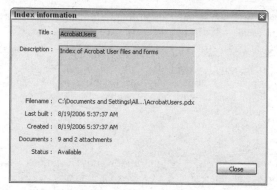

Include these directories

If you add nothing to the Include these directories field, Catalog won't build an index because it won't know where to look for the PDF files to be included in the index. Adding the directory path(s) is essential before you begin to build the index. Notice the first Add button on the right side of the dialog box in Figure 6.20. After you click Add, a navigation dialog box opens, enabling you to identify the directory where the PDFs to be indexed are located. You can add many directories to the Include these directories list. These directories can be in different locations on your hard drive. When a given directory is selected, all subfolders will also be indexed for all directory locations unless you choose to exclude certain folders. When the directories have been identified, the directory path and folder name will appear in the Include these directories field.

Exclude these subdirectories

If you have files in a subdirectory within the directory you are indexing and want to exclude the subdirectory, you can do so in the Exclude these subdirectories field. The folder names and directory paths of excluded directories appear in the Exclude these subdirectories field, as shown in Figure 6.20.

Remove

If you decide to remove a directory from either the Include these directories or Exclude these subdirectories lists, select an item in the list and click the Remove button. You can add or delete directories in either list prior to building an index or when modifying an index.

Saving index definitions

Two buttons appear at the top-right corner of the Catalog dialog box for saving a definition. If you begin to develop an index file and supply the index title and a description and want to come back to Catalog later, you can save what you type in the Index Definition dialog box using the Save As button. The Save button does not appear active until you have saved a file with the Save As option or you're working on a file that has been built. Saving the file only saves the definition for the index. It does not create an index file. The Save As option enables you to prepare files for indexing and interrupt your session if you need to return later. For example, suppose you add an index title and you write an index description. If you need to quit Acrobat at this point, click Save As and save the definition to disk. You can then return later and resume creating the index by adding the directories to be cataloged and building the index.

After you have saved a file you can update the file with the Save button. After a definition is saved, when you return to Acrobat Catalog, you can click the Open button in the Catalog dialog box and resume editing the definition file. When all the options for your search index have been determined, you click the Build button to actually create the index file.

Using Save As or Save is not required to create an index file. If you set all your attributes for the index and click the Build button, Acrobat Catalog prompts you in the Save Index File dialog box to supply a name for the index and save the definition. Essentially, Catalog is invoking the Save As command for you.

If at any time you click the Cancel button in the lower-right corner of the Index Definition dialog box, all edits are lost for the current session. If you add definition items without saving you'll need to start over when you open the Index Definition dialog box again. If you start to work on a saved file and click Cancel without saving new edits, your file reverts to the last saved version.

Setting options

To the right of the Index Description field is a button labeled Options. Click this button and the Options dialog box appears, allowing you to choose from a number of different attributes for your index file, as shown in Figure 6.23. Some of these options are similar to the Preference settings for Acrobat Catalog you made in the Preferences dialog box. Any edits you make here supersede Preference settings.

CROSS-REF   For information on setting catalog preferences, see "Setting Catalog preferences" later in this chapter.

FIGURE 6.23

Clicking the Options button adjacent to the Index Description field opens the Options dialog box. Here you can assign further attributes to the index file.

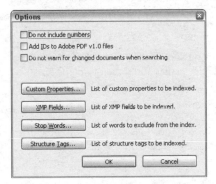

Do not include numbers

The first item in the Options dialog box is a check box for excluding numbers. By selecting the Do not include numbers option, you can reduce the file size, especially if data containing many numbers are part of the PDF file(s) to be indexed. Keep in mind, however, that if numbers are excluded, Search won't find numeric values.

Add IDs to Adobe v1.0 files

Because Acrobat is now in version 8.0, finding old PDF 1.0 files that need to be updated with IDs may rarely happen. If you do have legacy files saved as PDF 1.0 format, it would be best to batch process the older PDFs by saving them out of Acrobat 8.0. As software changes, many previous formats may not be supported with recent updates. For better performance, update older documents to newer file formats.

CROSS-REF For more information on batch processing, see Chapter 18.

If you have legacy files that haven't been updated and you want to include them in your search index, check the box. If you're not certain whether the PDFs were created with Acrobat 1.0 compatibility, check it anyway just to be safe.

Do not warn for changed documents when searching

If you create an index file, then return to the index in Acrobat Catalog and perform some maintenance functions, save the index, and start searching the index, Acrobat notifies you in a dialog box that changes have been made and asks whether you want to proceed. To sidestep the opening of the warning dialog box, check the Do not warn for changed documents when searching option.

Custom properties

The Custom Properties button opens the Custom Properties dialog box, as shown in Figure 6.24. Custom Properties are used when customizing Acrobat with the Acrobat Software Development Kit (SDK). This item is intended for programmers who want to add special features to Acrobat. To add a Custom Property to be indexed, you should have knowledge in programming and the PDF format.

You add Custom Properties to the field box and select the type of property to be indexed from the pull-down menu. You type the property values in the field box, identify the type, and click the Add button. The property is then listed in the window below the Custom Property field box.

FIGURE 6.24

You can add custom data fields to Acrobat with the Acrobat Software Development Kit.

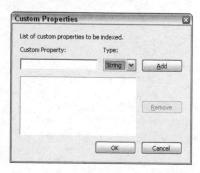

The types available from the pull-down menu are as follows:

- **String.** This is any text string. If numbers are included with this option they are treated as text.
- **Integer.** The integer field can accept values between 0 and 65,535.
- **Date.** This is a date value.

Support for programmers writing extensions and plug-ins, and working with the SDK is provided by Adobe Systems. Developers who want to use the support program need to become a member of the Adobe Solutions Network (ASN) Developer Program. For more information about ASN and SDK, log on to the Adobe Web site at `http://adobe.com/go/acrobat_developer`.

XMP Fields

Click XMP Fields and another dialog box opens in which you add to a list of XMP fields. The dialog box is virtually identical to the Stop Words dialog box shown in Figure 6.25. Type a name in the field box and click the Add button. All new XMP fields are added to the list window.

Stop Words

To optimize an index file that produces faster search results, you can add stop words. You may have words, such as the, a, an, of, and so on that would typically not be used in a search. You can choose to exclude such words by typing the word in the Word field box and clicking the Add button in the Stop Words dialog box. Click Stop Words in the Options dialog box to open the Stop Words dialog box shown in Figure 6.25. To eliminate a word after it has been added, select the word and click the Remove button. Keep in mind that every time you *add* a word, you are actually adding it to a list of words to be excluded.

FIGURE 6.25

You can eliminate words from an index file by adding words in the Stop Words dialog box. Adding a word to the list excludes it from the index file.

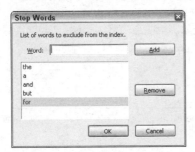

> **TIP** You can create an elaborate list of stop words and may want to apply the list to several index files, but Acrobat (as of this writing) does not include an ability to import or swap a list of words to be excluded from an index file. For a workaround, you can open any existing Index Definition field and change all attributes except the stop words. Add a new index title, a new index description, and select a new directory for indexing. Save the definition to a new filename and click the Build button. A new index is built using the stop words created in another index. In workgroups you can save an index definition file without adding directories and use it as a template so all index files have consistent settings for the stop words.

Structure tags

If you have a tagged PDF you can search document tags when the tags are included in the search index. Click Structure Tags in the Options dialog box to open the Tags dialog box shown in Figure 6.26. Tagged PDFs with a tagged root and elements can have any item in the tagged logical tree marked for searching. To observe the tags in a PDF file, open the Tags palette and expand the tree. All the tags nest like a Bookmark list. When you want to mark tags for searching, type the tag name in the Tags dialog box and click the Add button. You remove tags from the list window by selecting a tag and clicking the Remove button.

CROSS-REF For more information on tagged PDF documents and using the Tags palette, see Chapter 25.

FIGURE 6.26

You can mark tags for searches in index files by adding tag names in the Tags dialog box.

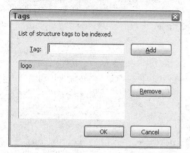

Building the index

After you've set all the attributes for the index definition, the index file is ready to be created. Clicking the Build button in the New Index Definition dialog box creates indexes. When you click this button, Acrobat Catalog opens the Save Index File dialog box where you supply a filename and target a destination on your hard drive. The default file extension is .pdx. Do not modify the file extension name. Acrobat recognizes these files when loading search indexes.

The location where you instruct Catalog to save your index file can be any location on your hard drive regardless of where the files being indexed reside. You can choose to save the index file inside or outside the folder that Catalog created during the indexing. Therefore you have an index file and a folder containing index resources. The relationship between the index file and resource folder locations is critical to the usability of the index. If you move the index file to a different location without moving the supporting folder, the index is rendered unusable. To avoid problems, try to create a folder either when you are in the Save Index File dialog box or before you open Catalog and save your index file to your new folder. Make the name descriptive and keep the index file together in this folder. When you want to move the index to another directory, another computer, or to an external media cartridge or CD-ROM, copy the folder containing the index and supporting files.

Click the Save button in the Save Index File dialog box, and Catalog closes the Index Definition dialog box, returns you to the Catalog dialog box, and begins to process all the files in the target folder(s). Depending on how many files are indexed, the time to complete the build may be considerable. Don't interrupt the processing if you want to complete the index generation. When Catalog finishes the progress bar stops and the last line of text in the Catalog dialog box reads "Index build successful." If for some reason the build is not successful, you can scroll the window in the Catalog dialog box and view errors reported in the list.

Stopping builds

If you want to interrupt a build, you can click the Stop button while a build is in progress. When building an index, Catalog opens a file where all the words and markers to the PDF pages are written. When you click the Stop button, Catalog saves the open file to disk and closes it with the indexed items up to the point you stopped the build. Therefore, the index is usable after stopping a build and you can search for words in the partial index. When you want to resume, you can open the file in Catalog and click the Rebuild button.

The Structure of Index Files

Users who have created index files in all earlier versions of Acrobat are no doubt familiar with the end product of creating a search index. As you may recall, the index file with a .pdx extension and nine subfolders containing all associated files were produced by Acrobat Catalog for every new index. The relationship between the index file and subfolders in terms of directory paths needed to be preserved in order for the index to work properly. When you copied an index file to another directory or source, you needed to copy all the files together and keep the same relative path between the files.

When you produce an index file in Acrobat Professional, you won't find the same nine folders created during the index build with Acrobat version 5 and earlier. Acrobat Catalog 6.0 through 8.0 creates a single folder where files with an .idx extension reside. The relative directory path is still a factor in relocating files, but in Acrobat 6.0 through 8.0, you need only copy an index file and a single folder to relocate your index and keep it functional.

The .pdx file you load as your search index file is a small file that creates the information in the .idx and .info files. The .idx files contain the actual index entries the end user accesses during a search. When you build an index, rebuild an index, or purge data from an index, the maintenance operation may or may not affect the .pdx file and/or .idx files depending on which option you choose. For specific information related to how these files are affected during index creation and maintenance, see the following pages for building, rebuilding, and purging index files.

Building existing indexes

When files are deleted from indexed folders and new files are added to the indexed folders, you'll want to maintain the index file and update it to reflect any changes. You can open an index file and click Build for a quick update. New files are scanned and added to the index, but the deleted files are marked for deletion without actually deleting the data. To delete invalid data, you need to use the Purge button. Purging can take a considerable amount of time even on small index files. Therefore, your routine maintenance might be to consistently build a file, and only periodically purge data.

Building legacy index files

When you open an index file created with an Acrobat Catalog version earlier than 6.0, a dialog box opens informing you the index is not compatible with the current version of Acrobat. In the dialog box you have three options: Create copy, Overwrite old index, and Cancel. Click the Create copy button to make a copy of the index file. A new index file is created leaving the original index file undisturbed. You can click the Overwrite old index button and the file rewrites, replacing the old index. If you choose this option your new index file won't be compatible with Acrobat viewers earlier than version 6.0. Clicking Cancel in this dialog box returns you to the Index Selection dialog box, leaving the index file undisturbed.

If you create a search index using Acrobat Catalog version 8, the index file is backward-compatible to Acrobat 6. All Acrobat viewers can use index files suited to the appropriate version.

If you know some users won't be working with the new Acrobat viewers, then be certain to make copies of your index files. Until all users have upgraded to a viewer 6.0 or higher, you may need to organize your indexes according to viewer versions.

TIP If you work in an organization where many users have different versions of Acrobat viewers, then keeping a complete installation of Acrobat 5.05 installed on a separate computer on your network is to your advantage. If you inadvertently overwrite index files or need to perform some task specifically related to Acrobat versions less than 6.0, you can use the older version to keep compatibility with other users. In addition, you can test many new files you edit in version 6.0 or higher to ensure they work with viewer versions less than 6.0. Ideally, all your colleagues, coworkers, and clients should upgrade to Acrobat 8.0. However, in a real world, we know some users are reluctant to let go of the familiar and convincing all users that upgrading Acrobat is the best solution may take some time.

Building index files from secure documents

In Acrobat versions lower than 6.0 you could not create index files from secure PDFs encrypted with either Acrobat Standard Security or Acrobat Self-Sign Security. Version 6.0 of Acrobat afforded complete access to secure files with Acrobat Catalog if the right permissions were applied. When applying Password Security in Acrobat 6 through Acrobat 8 you need to enable text access for screen reader devices in order to index a secure file. Creating an index does not compromise your security and doesn't affect all other permissions you set forth when the files are saved.

If you have legacy files that have been secured, you can index them like other files saved in earlier PDF format compatibilities. These files, and any other files you create with Acrobat Professional, can be used only by Acrobat viewers 6.0 and later.

CROSS-REF For more information on encryption and security, see Chapter 26.

Rebuilding an index

Rebuilding index files completely re-creates a new index. You can open an Acrobat 8.0–compatible index file and click Rebuild. The file rewrites the file you opened much like you would use a Save As menu command to rewrite a PDF document. If a substantial number of PDF documents have been deleted and new files added to the indexed folders, rebuilding the index could take less time than purging data.

Purging data

As indexes are maintained and rebuilt, you will need to perform periodic maintenance and purge old data. A purge does not delete the index file, nor does it completely rewrite the file; it simply recovers the space used in the index for outdated information. Purging is particularly useful when you remove PDF files from a folder and the search items are no longer needed. If you have built a file several times, each build marks words for deletion. A purge eliminates the marked data and reduces the file size. With a significant number of words marked for deletion, a purge will improve the speed when using Search. This operation might be scheduled routinely in environments where many changes occur within the indexed folders.

TIP When changing options for eliminating words and numbers from indexes or adding tags and custom properties in the Options dialog box, first open the index.pdx file in Catalog and purge the data. Set your new criteria in the Options dialog box and rebuild the index. Any items deleted will now be added to the index, or any items you want to eliminate will subsequently be eliminated from the index.

Setting Catalog preferences

Catalog preference settings are contained in the Preferences dialog box. Choose Edit ➪ Preferences and click the Catalog item in the left pane as shown in Figure 6.27. Notice that the Index Defaults items use the same settings as found in the Options dialog box from the New Index Selection dialog box. The top three options under Indexing in Catalog preferences are obtained only here in these preference settings.

FIGURE 6.27

Open the Preferences dialog box and click Catalog in the left pane to see the options settings for Acrobat Catalog.

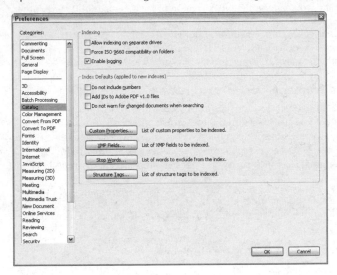

Indexing

The three options found in the Indexing section of the Catalog preferences are as follows:

- **Allow indexing on separate drives.** When creating index files where you want to include folders on network servers and/or computers on your network, select this item in the Catalog preferences. The indexing option includes indexing files only on local networks. Unfortunately, you can't index files on Web servers and use indexes from within Web browsers.

- **Force ISO 9660 compatibility on folders.** This setting is a flag that tells Catalog to look for any folders that are not compliant with standard DOS conventions (eight-character maximum with three-character maximum extensions) for folder/directory names. If Catalog encounters a folder name that is not acceptable, the processing stops and an error is reported in the Catalog dialog box. Folder names and directory paths are listed for all incompatible names. You can review the list and manually rename folders. After changing folder names, try to create the index again.

- **Enable logging.** A log file is created during an index build that describes the processing for each file indexed. The file is ASCII text and can be opened in any text editor or word processor. Any errors occurring during the build are noted in the log file. All documents and directory paths are also contained in the log file. If you don't want to have a log file created at the time of indexing, clear the check box to disable the logging. When you disable logging, you are prevented from analyzing problems when you close the Catalog dialog box.

Index defaults

The options listed in the Index Defaults area of the Catalog preferences are identical to the options you have available in the New Index Description Options dialog box described earlier in this chapter. These default/options settings exist in two locations for different reasons.

When you set the options in the Preferences dialog box, the options are used for all index files you create. When you elect to use the options from the New Index Selection Options dialog box, the settings are specific to the index file you create. When you create a new index file, the options return to defaults.

If you set a preference in the Catalog preferences and disable the option in the New Index Selection Options dialog box, the latter supersedes the former. That is to say, the New Index Selection Options dialog box settings always prevail.

Using Index Files

As I stated earlier, one reason you create index files is for speed. When you search hundreds or thousands of pages, the amount of time to return found instances for searched words in index files is a matter of seconds compared to Searching folders in the Search window.

Loading index files

To search using an index file, you need to first load the index in the Search window. From the Look In pull-down menu, choose the Select Index menu option, as shown in Figure 6.28.

The Index Selection dialog box opens after you make the menu selection. Click the Add button and the Open Index File dialog box opens. In this dialog box navigate your hard drive to find the folder where your index file is located. Click the index filename and click the Open button.

After selecting the index to load, you are returned to the Index Selection dialog box. A list of all loaded indexes appears in the dialog box. To the left of each filename is a check box. When a check mark is in view, the index file is active and can be searched. Those check boxes that are disabled have the index file loaded, but the file remains inactive. Search will not return results from the inactive index files. If an index file is grayed out as shown in Figure 6.21, the file path has been disrupted and Acrobat can't find the index file or the support files associated with the index. If you see a filename grayed out, select the file in the list and click the Remove button. Click the Add button and relocate the index. If the support files are not found, an error is reported in a dialog box indicating the index file could not be opened.

If you can't open a file, you need to return to the Catalog dialog box and click the Open button. Find the index file that you want to make active and rebuild the index. After rebuilding, you need to return to the Index selection dialog box and reload the index.

FIGURE 6.28

Your first step in using indexes is to load the index file(s) by choosing the Select Index menu option from the Look In menu in the Search window.

NOTE If you attempt to load an index file from a CD-ROM and the CD is not inserted into your CD-ROM drive, the index filename is grayed out in the Index Selection dialog box. After inserting the CD-ROM containing the index, the index filename becomes active. If you know index files are loaded from CDs, don't delete them from the Index Selection dialog box. Doing so requires you to reload the index file each time you insert a CD.

Attaching an index file to a document

You can associate an index file with a particular document. Open the Document Properties dialog box (Ctrl/⌘+D) and click the Advanced tab. Adjacent to the Search Index item is a Browse button. Click Browse and the Open dialog box appears. Navigate your hard drive to locate the index file created from a folder containing your document, select it, and click Open. When you save your file and reopen it, you can select Currently Selected Indexes in the Look In pull-down menu and your associated index file is automatically loaded for you.

Disabling indexes

If an index is to be eliminated from searches, you can deactivate the index by disabling its check box. In a later Acrobat session, you can go back and enable indexes listed in the Index Selection dialog box. You should always use this method rather than deleting an index if you intend to use it again in a later Acrobat session. However, at times you may want to delete an index file. If the index will no longer be used, or you relocate your index to another drive or server, you may want to completely remove the old index. If this is the case, select the index file to be deleted and click the Remove button. Indexes may be enabled or disabled before you select Remove. In either case, the index file is removed without warning.

If you inadvertently delete an index, you can always reload the index by clicking the Add button. Placing index files in a directory where you can easily access them is a good idea. To avoid confusion, try to keep indexes in a common directory or a directory together with the indexed PDF files. Acrobat doesn't care where the index file is located on your hard drive or server — it just needs to know where the file is located and the file needs to keep the relative path with the support files. If you move the index file to a different directory, be certain to reestablish the connection in the Index Selection dialog box.

Finding index information

When a number of index files are installed on a computer or server, the names for the files may not be descriptive enough to determine which index you want to search. If more detailed information is desired, the information provided by the Index Information dialog box may help identify the index needed for a given search.

PDF WORKFLOW Index information may be particularly helpful in office environments where several people in different departments create PDFs and indexes are all placed on a common server. What may be intuitive to the author of an index file in terms of index name may not be as intuitive to other users. Index information offers the capability for adding more descriptive information that can be understood by many users.

Fortunately, you can explore more descriptive information about an index file by clicking the Info button in the Index Selection dialog box. When you click the Info button, the Index information dialog box opens, displaying information about the index file, as shown earlier in Figure 6.22. Some of the information displayed requires user entry at the time the index is built. Acrobat Catalog automatically creates other information in the dialog box when the index is built. The Index information dialog box provides a description of the following:

- **Title.** The user supplies title information at the time the index is created. Titles usually consist of several words describing the index contents. Titles can be searched, as detailed earlier in this chapter, so the title keywords should reflect the index content.

- **Description.** Description can be a few words or several sentences containing information about the index. (In Figure 6.22, the description was supplied in Acrobat Catalog when the index was created.)

- **Filename.** The directory path for the index file's location on a drive or server is displayed with the last item appearing as the index filename.

- **Last built.** If the index file is updated, the date of the last build is supplied here. If no updates have occurred, the date will be the same as the created date.

- **Created.** This date reflects the time and date the index file was originally created, and is therefore a fixed date.

- **Documents.** Indexes are created from one or more PDF documents. The total number of PDF files from which the index file was created appears here.

- **Status.** If the index file has been identified and added to the list in the Index Selection dialog box, it will be Available. Unavailable indexes appear grayed out in the list and are described as Unavailable.

Searching an index

After your index file(s) is prepared and loaded in the Index selection dialog box, it is ready for use. You search index files in the Advanced Search window just as you search multiple files explained earlier in this chapter. From the Look In pull-down menu, select Currently Selected Indexes.

All the options discussed earlier for advanced searches are available to you. Select from the Return results containing pull-down menu, enter your search criteria, and select the options you want. Click the Search button and you'll find the search results reported much faster than using other search methods.

Index files can be created from PDF collections contained on external media where the index file can remain on your computer without the need for copying the PDF documents to your hard drive. When you insert a media disk such as a CD-ROM, your search index is ready to use to search the media.

Practice searching your new index file using different options and search criteria. To compare the difference between using a search index file and using the advanced search options, you can choose the Browse for Location menu item and search the CD-ROM for the same criteria. Go back and forth to see the differences between searching folders and searching an index file.

Searching external devices

A computer network server, another computer on your network, a CD-ROM, DVD-ROM, external hard drive, and a removable media cartridge are considered external to your local computer hard drive(s). Any of these devices can be indexed and the index file can be located on any of the devices you index. If you want to save an index file on a device different from where the PDF collection is stored, you need to be certain to open the Preferences dialog box for the Catalog preferences and enable the check box for Allow indexing on separate drives. This preference setting enables you to index across media devices.

NOTE When you want to write index files to read only media such as CD-ROMs and DVDs, you need to create the index file from PDFs stored on your hard drive. After the index file is created, copy the index file, the supporting files, and the PDFs to your media and burn the disc.

When you want to search an index, you can activate the index in the Index selection dialog box and invoke a search whether your external media is mounted and accessible or not. The search index returns results from the index .pdx file and the .idx files without looking at the PDFs that were indexed. You can examine the results of the search in the Search window and find the files where the search criteria match the PDF documents in the index collection.

If you want to open the link to the PDF document where a result is reported, you need to have the media mounted and accessible. If a network server or other computer contains the related files, the server/computer must be shared with appropriate permissions and visible on your desktop. If you use external media storage devices, the media must be mounted and visible on your desktop in order to view the PDFs linked to the search results. If you attempt to view a document when the device is not mounted, Acrobat opens an error dialog box.

If you see an error dialog box, click OK in the dialog box and insert your media, connect an external hard drive, or access a computer or network server. You don't need to quit Acrobat to make your device accessible. Wait until the media is mounted and then click a search result. Acrobat opens the linked page and you're ready to continue your search.

A search index file created on one computer can be moved or copied to another computer. To copy an index file to another computer, be certain you copy the index file (.pdx) and all supporting files in the folder created by Catalog. Be certain you maintain the same relative directory path for the index file and the supporting files. If an index file appears in a root folder and the supporting files appear in a nested folder, copy the root folder to other media. If you place the index file in the same folder as the supporting files, copy the single folder containing all files to your media.

You can load the index file and external media on another computer and perform the same searches as were performed where the index file was created. When distributing CD-ROMs and DVDs you can copy these index files to your media and all users can access the index files. If you access an index file on a network server and the PDF collection is stored on an external device such as a CD-ROM, you cannot open files from another computer unless the CD-ROM is mounted. You may see your network server, but the associated devices with the server need to be individually mounted in order to open PDF files remotely.

Working with Embedded Index Files

Index files can be scattered all over your hard drive and, at times, it can be a chore to load them in the Index selection dialog box. In addition, when sharing PDFs where indexes have been created requires you to either attach an index file to a PDF or send along your index to recipients of your PDFs. Again, the steps involved can be aggravating if you have to spend time finding the index files on your hard drive.

NEW FEATURE Acrobat 8 has simplified the steps for loading index files and sharing them. Now in Acrobat 8 you can embed an index file in PDFs. Embedding an index file is limited to a single PDF document and not a collection of PDFs. Therefore, it makes sense to embed an index file in a document having many pages or in PDF Packages. You won't gain any better performance embedding indexes in one page PDFs or files containing few pages.

When you embed an index file you bypass all the steps for creating an index using Acrobat Catalog. Indexes are automatically created and embedded by Acrobat Professional only through a simple button click in a dialog box.

To understand more about creating an index file and embedding it in a PDF document, follow the steps that follow.

STEPS: Creating and embedding index files

1. **Open a PDF document in Acrobat Professional.** Try to find a PDF having 500 or more pages or a PDF Package. Longer documents make index embedding more practical when using this feature. In this example I use a file containing 803 pages.

2. **Open the Manage Embedded Index dialog box.** Select Advanced ⇨ Document Processing ⇨ Manage Embedded Index. The Manage Embedded Index dialog box opens, as shown in Figure 6.29.

FIGURE 6.29

Select Advanced ⇨ Document Processing ⇨ Manage Embedded Index.

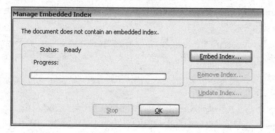

3. **Embed the Index.** Click the Embed Index button in the Manage Embedded Index dialog box.

4. **Click OK.** Click OK after Acrobat completes the index creation and your new index file is now embedded in your PDF. (See Figure 6.30.)

FIGURE 6.30

Click OK and your index is embedded in the PDF.

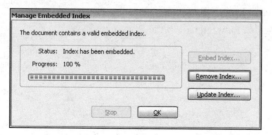

5. **Compare a search using the embedded index.** Open the original PDF without an index embedded in the document and press Ctrl/⌘+Shift+F to open the Search window. Select The Current PDF in the Look In drop-down menu and search for a work in the document. Notice the amount of time it takes to search all pages in the file.

   Bring the file with the embedded index forward in the Document pane or open the file if you closed it. Perform a search using The Current Document option in the Look In drop-down menu. Add the same search criteria in the Search window and search the document. You should see a noticeable difference in the speed for the returned results.

Summary

- Acrobat 8 includes a Find toolbar used for searching the current active document.

- Searching PDF files occurs in the Search window. When a search is requested, the Search window opens as a floating window.

- The Search window enables basic and advanced searches.

- Basic searches are used to search open PDF files but provide more options than the Find command.

- Advanced searches enable searching multiple PDFs locally, on external media, and across networks with the use of a search index file.

- Acrobat viewers 6.0 and greater support searching content of bookmarks and comments through advanced searches and index file searches. Acrobat 7.0 and 8.0 support searching file attachments.

- Searches for PDFs on the Internet are no longer built into Acrobat. If you want to search for PDFs on the Internet you need to use a Web search engine that supports searching for PDFs.

- Searches can be made with a variety of options, including Boolean queries, without the use of an index file.

- Search index files are created in Acrobat Catalog in Acrobat Professional only. Searching index files returns results for large collections of PDFs much faster than basic and advanced searches.

- Document descriptions can be searched with advanced searches and via index file searches.

- Index files can be built, rebuilt, and purged with Acrobat Catalog. Old index files created with PDF formats earlier than version 6.0 need to be rebuilt with Acrobat Catalog. Acrobat Catalog 8.0 index files are backward-compatible with Acrobat 6.0.

- Tags, XMP data, and object data can be searched with advanced searches and from index searches.

- Index files can be copied to other computers, network servers, and external media storage units. When copying search indexes, you need to duplicate all supporting files and the relative directory path(s) on the destination units.

- Index files can be embedded on a PDF-by-PDF basis in Acrobat 8. A single menu command creates and embeds an index in a PDF opened in the Document pane.

Part II

Converting Documents to PDF

Chapter 7

Converting Files to PDF

U nlike almost every other computer program, Acrobat was never designed to support creating new files and editing pages to add content. Where Acrobat begins is with file conversion to the PDF format. Users start with a document authored in another program and the resulting document is converted to PDF using either tools from within Acrobat or tools or commands within programs that support PDF conversion from native documents.

With Acrobat Standard and Acrobat Professional, the number of methods you can employ for converting documents to PDF is enormous. Any program file can be converted to PDF through a number of different methods offered by Acrobat, operating systems, and many different authoring applications. The method you use to convert a document to PDF and the purpose for which the PDF is intended require you to become familiar with a number of different options at your disposal for PDF file creation. This chapter begins a new part of the book entirely devoted to PDF creation. In this chapter you learn basic PDF conversion methods available in Acrobat Professional and Acrobat Standard. The following chapters in this part cover more advanced PDF creation methods.

Setting Up the PDF Creation Environment

You create PDF documents from within Acrobat primarily with default tools and with menu commands. In addition to the default tools, this chapter makes use of the Snapshot tool, the Edit toolbar, and the Create PDF From Web Page tool in the File toolbar. To regain the default toolbars, open a context menu on the Toolbar Well and select Reset Toolbars from the menu commands or press Alt/Option+F8.

Open the More Tools menu from a context menu on the Toolbar Well. Scroll down to the File toolbar and check the box for Create PDF from web page. Scroll further down the window to the Select & Zoom toolbar. Check the box for the Snapshot tool.

If you intend to edit documents after PDF creation, you need to open toolbars specific to your editing session. Depending on the type of edits you anticipate, open toolbars as needed after you finish converting files to PDF. For this chapter, click OK in the More Tools window and select Dock All Toolbars from a context menu opened on the Toolbar Well. Adjacent to the TouchUp Text tool in the Editing toolbar, click the down arrow to open the pull-down menu and select Expand this Button. The TouchUp Object tool becomes visible in the toolbar after making the menu selection.

Understanding How PDFs Are Created

You can use Acrobat Professional or Acrobat Standard to open various file formats in the viewer; the files are immediately converted to PDF. You can also print a file to the Adobe PDF printer, installed with your viewer, from just about any authoring program, and the native document is converted to PDF. It all sounds like simple stuff, but two very important distinctions exist between these methods of conversion for certain file types that you need to understand before you start converting files to PDF. Quite simply, opening some files in Acrobat Professional or Acrobat Standard does not involve any intervention from companion programs. On the other hand, using some file formats and using the Adobe PDF printer requires some help from the Acrobat Distiller software. To understand the fundamentals of document conversion you need to know a little bit about Acrobat Distiller.

CROSS-REF Acrobat Distiller is thoroughly covered in Chapter 10, where you'll find information on setting all the options Distiller offers you.

Acrobat Distiller accepts either a PostScript file or an Encapsulated PostScript (EPS) file that it processes to produce a PDF document. Through the processing mechanism, Distiller applies different options during conversion. These options can include image sampling, font handling, color control, PDF format compatibility assignment, document encryption, hypertext linking, and a host of other settings. Each of the settings is designed to produce PDF files for different purposes. Because so many different options can be applied to PDF conversion via the Distiller software, Distiller provides you the capability to save an assortment of specific settings to individual Adobe PDF Settings files. When you save the files to a specific location on your hard drive, you can access them from a pull-down menu in Acrobat Distiller or from within authoring programs where Adobe PDF Settings are used.

NOTE Adobe PDF Settings were referred to as Job Options prior to Acrobat 6.

In addition to custom settings you can save to Adobe PDF Settings files. Acrobat Distiller, when installed with Acrobat Professional, has nine settings, and Acrobat Standard has five settings. When you create a PDF file that calls upon Distiller to produce the PDF document, the Adobe PDF Settings last used by Distiller control the options for your resulting PDF document. The danger here is that if you intend to have a file created for printing, for example, and the settings are optimized for screen viewing, you wind up with a PDF document that won't be suitable for printing. Therefore, it is imperative that you know what settings are applied to PDFs created with the Acrobat Distiller software.

Prior to the conversion process you'll have an opportunity to make a choice for the Adobe PDF Settings that are applied during distillation. These choices may or may not be available depending on the type of files you convert to PDF. If the Adobe PDF Settings are not made available when you convert to PDF, the default settings in Acrobat Distiller are used. You need to be certain you open Acrobat Distiller and change the defaults when conversion of a particular file type does not open Acrobat Distiller. Regardless of where you

access the settings choices, the same options are always available. If you haven't saved any custom settings, the defaults appear as shown in Figure 7.1.

FIGURE 7.1

The default Adobe PDF Settings are selectable from a pull-down menu in the Acrobat Distiller window in Acrobat Professional. Acrobat Standard does not have PDF/X and PDF/A options.

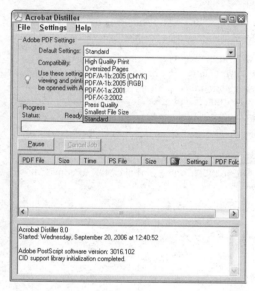

CROSS-REF For a complete description of the Adobe PDF Settings, see Chapter 10.

In this chapter we'll look at using the High Quality, Press Quality, Smallest File Size, and Standard settings. Without an elaborate definition of these settings, for the purposes of this chapter, think of High Quality for business office printing, Press Quality as suited for commercial printing. Smallest File Size as suited for Web hosting and screen viewing, and the Standard settings as suited for everything else.

Converting Native Documents to PDF

Many authoring programs offer you methods for converting to PDF, such as exporting or saving to PDF directly, or using a utility installed with Acrobat that supports certain authoring programs. However, when these methods are not available you can use the Print command in your authoring program to produce a PDF document. Virtually any document created in an authoring program that allows printing can be converted to PDF through the use of the Adobe PDF printer (Windows and Mac OS X10.2 and above).

You access the Adobe PDF printer in the application Print dialog box. Rather than print a file to a printer, you print your file to disk. During this process, the file is temporarily saved as a PostScript file and the PostScript file is distilled in Acrobat Distiller. The Adobe PDF Settings assigned to Distiller control the attributes of the resulting PDF file. The process is relatively the same on both Windows and Macintosh platforms, but initial printer selection and dialog box selections vary a little.

Adobe PDF printer (Windows)

When you install Acrobat Professional or Acrobat Standard, the Adobe PDF printer is installed in your Printers folder. As a printer driver, the file is accessible from any program capable of printing, including your computer accessories and utilities. Like any other printer you install on Windows 2000 with Service Pak 4, Windows XP Professional, Windows XP Home Edition, or Tablet PC with Service Pak 2, you can set the Adobe PDF printer as the default printer. Once set as the default printer, you don't need to make a printer selection each time you want to create a PDF document.

NOTE You may also have the Acrobat Distiller printer installed in your Printer's folder. The features associated with the Adobe PDF printer and the Acrobat Distiller printer are identical.

To convert any application document to PDF, choose File ⇨ Print or access the Print dialog box with the menu command in your authoring program. Some dedicated vertical market programs, such as accounting and other office programs, may have print commands located in menus other than the File menu. When you arrive at the Print dialog box, the various printer drivers installed on your computer are shown. Select the Adobe PDF printer in the Print dialog box, as shown in Figure 7.2.

FIGURE 7.2

From any authoring program, select the Print command, select the Adobe PDF printer, and click OK to convert the open document to a PDF file.

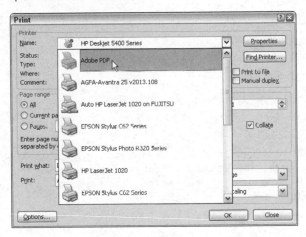

Before printing to the Adobe PDF printer, check your output options by clicking the Preferences button. In Windows 2000 and earlier, you will see Properties appear in the Print dialog box. If you see Properties, click the Properties button. The Adobe PDF Document Properties dialog box opens, as shown in Figure 7.3. In this dialog box you choose options for the resulting PDF document. Click the Adobe PDF Settings tab to choose the PDF options.

Set your PDF options in the Adobe PDF Printing Preferences dialog box in the Adobe PDF Settings pane.

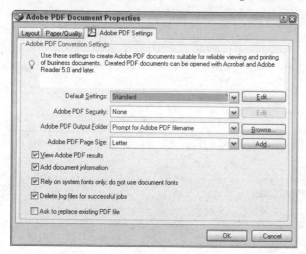

Choices you can make about the PDF file and handling the PDF conversion are contained in the Adobe PDF Settings window. Items you'll want to control include the following:

- **Default Settings.** This item relates to the discussion in the previous section concerning the Acrobat Distiller Adobe PDF Settings. The choices you have from the pull-down menu are the same nine preset choices (Acrobat Professional) or four choices (Acrobat Standard) provided with your Acrobat installation and any custom settings, if you've created them. It's important to make the proper choice for the options you want. When you print to the Adobe PDF printer, Acrobat Distiller is used in the background and applies the settings you specify in this dialog box.

CROSS-REF For a better understanding of Adobe PDF Settings, see Chapter 10.

- **Adobe PDF Security.** If you want to password-protect your document, you can apply security settings at the time the PDF is created. Choose the security options from the choices in the pull-down menu. The default choice for None results in PDF documents created without any password protection.

CROSS-REF To learn how to apply password protection to PDF documents, see Chapter 26.

- **Adobe PDF Output Folder.** Choose to save PDF files to a fixed folder and directory path or be prompted for a filename and directory path for the saved file.
- **Adobe PDF Page Size.** A pull-down menu offers an extensive list of page sizes derived from the printer driver and not the PPD (PostScript Printer Description file) for your printer. If you don't have a custom size that matches your document page, click the Add Custom Page button adjacent to the pull-down menu. The Add Custom Paper Size dialog box opens where you make choices for the custom page size and to add the new page option in the pull-down menu, as shown in Figure 7.4.

Acrobat accepts sizes up to 200 × 200 inches (5,080 × 5,080 millimeters/14,400 × 14,400 points). Enter your new custom page size in the units of measure desired and click the Add/Modify button. Your new page size is added to the Adobe PDF Page Size pull-down menu and selected for you after you click the Add/Modify button. If you want to delete a page after it has been created, click Add Custom Page in the Printing Preferences dialog box and select the page you want to delete from the Add Custom Paper Size dialog box. Click the Delete button and the page is deleted from both pull-down menus. Clicking Cancel (or pressing the Esc key) in the dialog box returns you to the Adobe PDF Document Properties dialog box without affecting any changes.

FIGURE 7.4

The Add Custom Paper Size dialog box enables you to create a page size up to 200 × 200 inches.

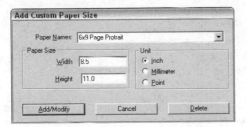

CROSS-REF Setting custom pages for the Adobe PDF Printer only makes the custom page sizes for this printer driver accessible. If using other methods for PDF creation such as using the PDFMaker tools in Office programs, you'll want to create custom page sizes in another preferences dialog box. For more information on creating custom page sizes and Microsoft Office programs, see Chapter 8.

- **View Adobe PDF results.** When the check box is enabled, the resulting PDF document opens in the Acrobat Document pane. If Acrobat is not open, the program launches after the PDF is created.

- **Add document information.** This item is a little misleading. You are not prompted in a dialog box to add document information. However, when using applications that support certain kinds of document information such as document title and author, the information from the native document is added to the Document Properties Description fields. The document properties in your native document are not translated precisely, though. You may have a Word file with custom properties set up in the Word Document Properties dialog box like a Title, Subject, Author, Keywords, and so on. When the Word file is converted to PDF you'll find your Title information in Acrobat to be the name of the saved Word file and the Author is your computer log-on name. Regardless of the custom properties you add to the Document Properties text boxes in Word, the results in Acrobat default to descriptions you can't control. If you remove the check box for this setting, all the Document Properties Descriptions in the PDF file are blank.

CROSS-REF For more information on document descriptions, see Chapter 6.

- **Rely on system fonts only; do not use document fonts.** What this check box does is control whether fonts are put into the PostScript stream that are sent to the Adobe PDF printer. Since 99.9% of the time those fonts are resident on your system, there is no value in having them also embedded in the PostScript stream - it just makes the process of printing to Adobe PDF slower. By default the check box to ON — it's faster. Leave this setting at the default.

CROSS-REF For more information on font management and font embedding, see Chapter 10.

- **Delete log files for successful jobs.** During PDF creation, the processing information is written to a log file in the form of ASCII text. You can open the log file in any text editor and review the steps used to produce the PDF. Each time a PDF is successfully created, the log file is deleted. In the event you want to review the PDF creation process logged in the text file, disable the check box and open the log file in a text editor.

- **Ask to replace existing PDF file.** If you elect to not have Acrobat prompt you for a filename, the PDF file is created using the authoring document filename. If you make changes in the document and want to create a new PDF document, the second creation overwrites the first file if the check box is disabled. If you're creating different versions of PDF files and want to have them all saved to disk, be certain to enable the check box.

After you review all the options in the Adobe PDF Printing Preferences dialog box, click OK. You are returned to the Print dialog box and are ready to create the PDF document. Click Print in the dialog box and the PDF is produced with the options you chose in the Adobe PDF Settings dialog box. If the check box was enabled for View Adobe PDF results, the PDF opens in Acrobat.

Because this method of PDF creation uses a printer driver, you can create a PDF document from virtually any application program. The only requirement is that the program is capable of printing. If you use programs such as Microsoft Office, other Adobe programs, certain CAD drawing programs, high-end imaging programs, or a host of other applications, you may have other methods for creating PDF documents depending on the level of PDF support for the program. It is important to understand when to use the Adobe PDF printer and other methods available to you from different applications. Before you integrate using the Adobe PDF printer into your workflow, be certain to review the next two chapters because they discuss other options for creating PDF documents.

CROSS-REF For more information on creating PDFs from Microsoft programs, see Chapter 8. For more information on exporting to PDF from Adobe programs, see Chapter 9.

Adobe PDF (Macintosh OS X)

Mac OS X and Adobe PDF are married at the operating system level and you can find several ways to convert your authoring files to the PDF format. The Acrobat-supported method uses the same type of printer driver you find on Windows. From any authoring program, select the Print command (most commonly accessed by choosing File ➪ Print). When the Print dialog box opens, select Adobe PDF 8.0 from the Printer pull-down menu. From the default selection for Copies and Pages, open the pull-down menu and select PDF Options, as shown in Figure 7.5.

FIGURE 7.5

PDF Options settings are available after you select the PDF Options pull-down menu command.

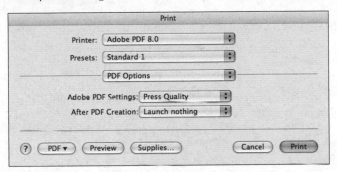

The dialog box changes so that you can access Adobe PDF Settings from a pull-down menu. The default selection is Use Default. If you leave this option active, the most recent settings selected in the Distiller application are used to produce the PDF file. The remaining options are the same as those discussed for Windows users. When you add new custom settings, they appear in the Adobe PDF Settings pull-down menus from the Print dialog boxes on Windows and Macintosh operating systems.

Another setting for viewing the PDF file appears in the pull-down menu: After PDF Creation. You can choose to view your PDF in the default Acrobat viewer or leave the default at Launch Nothing, which allows you to go about your work and view the PDFs later. After you choose the settings, click the Print button to convert the file to PDF using the Adobe PDF Settings you selected from the menu choices.

If you open the PDF pull-down menu at the bottom of the dialog box and select Save as PDF (see Figure 7.6), you create a PDF using the PDF engine built into Mac OS X. Checking this option also creates a PDF file, but the PDF creation is not an Adobe-based PDF creation method. This menu choice appears in a generic installation of Mac OS X, and creating a PDF this way is supported by the operating system without the use of Acrobat Distiller. When you use Save As PDF, the PDF is created using the native Mac OS X PDF creation tools, which provides adequate PDF creation of non-prepress documents. The PDF documents created using this method will work fine for office uses; however, they will be significantly larger than those created by Adobe Acrobat.

CROSS-REF For more information on PostScript and creating PostScript files, see Chapter 10.

FIGURE 7.6

Selecting the PDF pull-down menu and choosing Save as PDF creates a PDF file using Apple's OS X PDF creation tools.

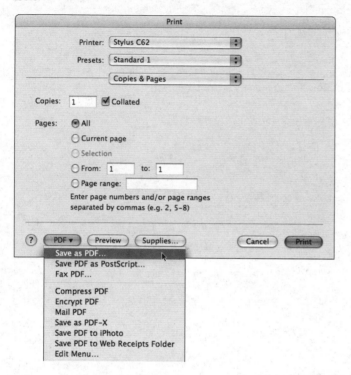

Save As PDF was designed by Apple to provide users with a PDF version of a document to send to people across the Internet for screen viewing and desktop printing. As a matter of practice, using the Adobe PDF printer is your best choice for creating PDFs suited for purposes other than screen displays.

CAUTION   A number of different clone printer drivers and clone PDF creators are distributed from developers and enthusiasts. Using a clone product can often produce unreliable PDF documents. If you purchased Adobe Acrobat, then be sure to use the tools Adobe has provided you for PDF creation. Adobe and many Adobe Partners that have licensed Adobe technology offer you the best results for reliable PDF creation.

Viewing PDFs on the Mac

Apple's OS X also supports an Apple developed PDF viewer called Preview. By default, double-clicking a PDF file opens the PDF in the Preview application. If you want to change the default viewer from Preview to Acrobat, select a PDF document and press ⌘+I to open the Document Info dialog box, as shown in the following figure.

From the Open with menu, select Adobe Acrobat Professional (or the viewer you want to establish as the default PDF viewer). Click the Change All button and all your PDF documents will open by default in Acrobat.

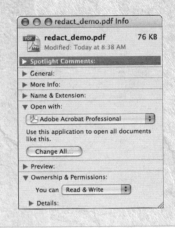

Creating Blank New Pages

Sometimes features added to programs are hidden in menu command and may be undocumented. When Acrobat 7 was introduced, a menu command was added to create a new PDF document from within Acrobat. I missed this addition in Acrobat 7 because it was so obscure and it never occurred to me that the command existed.

To create a blank new page in Acrobat 7, press the Shift key on your keyboard and select File ⇨ Create PDF ⇨ From Blank Page.

NEW FEATURE In Acrobat 8 the menu command to create a blank new page is not obscure and appears in the File ⇨ Create PDF submenu. Select File ⇨ Create PDF ⇨ From Blank Page and a new blank page opens in the Document pane.

Note that you must select the File ⇨ Create PDF menu command for From Blank Page to appear as shown in Figure 7.7. Using the Create PDF task button menu won't get you the option to create a new document. When you select the command, a single-page PDF is created. The page appears as a portrait standard letter-size page by default.

FIGURE 7.7

Select File ➪ Create PDF ➪ From Blank New Page and a blank page with a default text box a special toolbar opens in the Document pane.

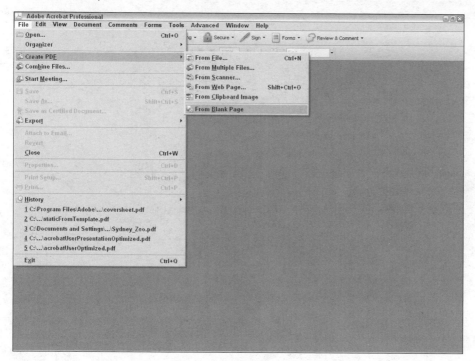

The blank page that is created appears with a default text box and a special toolbar used for setting type attributes for the text added to the text box. In addition, you have some preference options for selecting different page sizes, page orientation, and margins that define the size of the text box in the New Document preferences.

CROSS-REF Use of the type tools on blank new pages and setting preference options are all covered in Chapter 13.

Creating PDFs from Files

Adobe Acrobat, both Standard and Professional, offer you a number of options for converting application documents to PDF. For PDF creation supported by Acrobat, you don't need to leave the program to produce PDF files from a number of different file formats.

The Create PDF task button pull-down menu offers several different options for PDF creation, as shown in Figure 7.8. You use the first two menu options, From File and From Multiple Files, to convert files saved from authoring documents to the PDF format. Converting to PDF with either of these commands requires you to access files supported by Acrobat's Create PDF option. Although the number of file formats supported by Acrobat through the internal conversion process is greatly expanded in version 7.0, not all files can be converted with the Create PDF tool or menu option.

FIGURE 7.8

The Create PDF task button offers several different options for PDF file creation from within Acrobat.

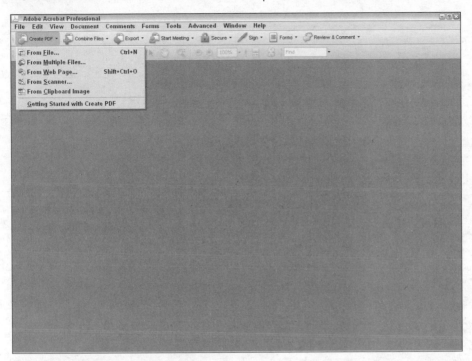

> **TIP**   You can also convert any file compatible with the Create PDF ⇨ From File menu command by dragging a document on top of the Acrobat window.

Supported file formats

To convert files to PDF from within Acrobat you first need to understand all the formats that are supported. You can try to convert any file format to PDF with the Create PDF tool. If the file format is supported, the document is converted to PDF and opens in Acrobat. If the format is not supported, a dialog box opens informing you the format is not supported. It won't hurt to try, but knowing ahead of time what formats are supported is better.

Many file formats that are acceptable to Acrobat can also have conversion settings defined by you. Options for the conversion settings are the same as you have available with the Adobe PDF printer, as discussed earlier in this chapter, and they're accessible in the Preferences dialog box. Before you begin converting files to PDF with the Create PDF tool, be certain to choose Edit ⇨ Preferences (Windows) or Acrobat ⇨ Preferences (Macintosh) or use (Ctrl/⌘+K) and click the Convert To PDF item in the left pane. On the right side of the Preferences dialog box you'll see a list of supported file formats, as shown in Figure 7.9 for Windows and Figure 7.10 for the Macintosh. As you can see at a quick glance, the Macintosh doesn't support as many file format conversions as Windows.

FIGURE 7.9

When using the Create PDF tool, you assign PDF Settings to different file formats in the Convert To PDF preferences. The Preferences dialog box lists all supported file formats in the Convert To PDF preferences.

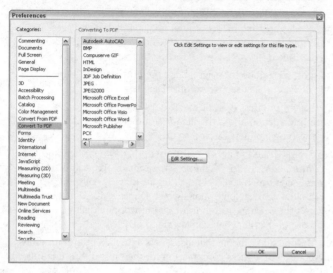

FIGURE 7.10

Fewer file formats are supported on the Macintosh.

The file formats that are supported by Acrobat include the following:

- **Autodesk AutoCAD (Windows only).** Autodesk's AutoCAD files can be opened in Acrobat directly. Layered files are preserved and opened with data on different layers when layer data are created in the AutoCAD file. AutoCAD is also supported with the PDFMaker utility, which installs Acrobat tools and menu options in the authoring application at the time you install Acrobat.

- **BMP.** Bitmap is a file format that can be saved from many image editing programs. Bitmap is also commonly referred to as a color mode in Photoshop. As a color mode, the file can be saved in other file formats. For example, a 1-bit bitmap image can be saved as a TIFF formatted file. In regard to Acrobat, the bitmap file format that is capable of rendering images in 1-bit, 4-bit, 8-bit, and 24-bit color depths can be opened as PDF. Furthermore a bitmap color mode saved as any of the compatible formats listed here can also be opened as a PDF.

- **CompuServe GIF.** CompuServe's Graphic Interchange Format (GIF) was developed years ago to port image files to and from mainframes and microcomputers. It remains a popular format for Web graphics, and the later version of GIF89a supports interlacing. If using Photoshop, you can either save in the CompuServe GIF87 format or use Photoshop's Save for Web command and choose the GIF89a format. Regardless of what format is used, Acrobat can import either as a PDF.

- **HTML.** Hypertext Markup Language files are documents written in HTML for Web pages. You can open any HTML file and the file and file links convert to PDF. Clicking an HTML link in a converted file in Acrobat appends the linked file to the open document.

- **InDesign.** New in Acrobat 8 is support for Adobe InDesign. Click the Edit Settings button and you can choose from all the Adobe PDF Settings used by Acrobat Distiller.

- **JDF Job Definition.** You find JDF files in prepress workflows. The resultant PDF produces a standardized XML-based job ticket with information about the file for commercial printing uses, such as page size, crop and bleed areas, trapping, colorspace, and so on.

- **JPEG.** Joint Photographic Experts Group (JPEG) images are also used for Web graphics and file exchanges on the Internet. JPEG compression is a lossy compression scheme that can degrade images rapidly when they are compressed at high levels. These files are already compressed. Adding further compression with the PDF conversion options won't compress files smaller than the original compression. Inasmuch as the Settings button is active in the Open dialog box, you can't actually get more compression out of the file when converting to PDF.

- **JPEG2000.** JPEG2000 is a newer compression scheme that also offers a lossless option for compressing images. You can use JPEG2000 with lossless compression for the most discriminating quality required in high-end printing.

- **Microsoft Office (Windows only).** Microsoft Office files are from the office programs of Excel, PowerPoint, Project, Visio, Word, and Publisher. Each of the Office programs is listed separately because you can edit different settings that apply to each respective program. On the Mac, you can convert Word, Excel, and PowerPoint files from within Acrobat, but you don't have access to settings options.

CROSS-REF For information related to settings adjustments with Microsoft Office programs, see Chapter 8.

- **PCX.** PCX files are native to the PC and were commonly used as an extension for PC Paintbrush. Adobe Photoshop can export in PCX format, but today it is rarely used for any kind of image representation. The advantage you have in opening PCX files in Acrobat is when converting legacy files saved in this format. Rather than your having to do a two-step operation of opening a PCX file in an image editor and saving in a more common format for file conversions, Acrobat can import the files directly.

- **PICT (Macintosh only).** The native Apple Macintosh equivalent to PCX (preceding bullet) is PICT (Picture). Photoshop supports PICT file exchanges in both opening and saving. However, Acrobat supports the format for conversion to PDF only via the From File or From Multiple Files commands.

- **PNG.** Portable Network Graphics (PNG — pronounced *ping*) is a format enabling you to save 24-bit color images without compression. The format was designed for Web use and is becoming more popular among Web designers. Older Web browsers need a special plug-in in order to view the images, which have slowed its wide acceptance. Interestingly enough, PNG images are saved from image editors without compression, yet Acrobat can apply image compression when converting to PDF. You can use all the compression options in the Adobe DF Settings dialog box with PNG images to reduce file sizes.

- **PostScript/EPS.** PostScript and EPS files were formerly converted only with Acrobat Distiller. In Acrobat 8 you can open the files in Acrobat using the Create PDF tool and Distiller works in the background, handling the conversion to PDF.

- **Text.** Text listed in the Convert to PDF preferences relates to plain text files. Unformatted text from word processors, text editors, and any file saved in a text-only format can be opened in Acrobat.

- **TIFF.** Tagged Image File Format (TIFF) is by far the most popular format among the print people regardless of platform. TIFF files originate from image editors and scans. When scanning text you can save it as a TIFF, import the file in Acrobat, and then convert the image file to rich text with Acrobat's Text Recognition feature.

CROSS-REF For more information on Scan to PDF and Text Recognition, see Chapter 17.

- **XPS.** XPS (XML Paper Specification) is a paginated representation of an electronic paper in an XML based format. XPS documents can be converted to PDF from within Acrobat in Acrobat 8. The Settings adjustments let you choose from any of the Adobe PDF Settings except the standards formats such as PDF/A and PDF/X.

CROSS-REF For more on PDF Standards formats, see Chapters 10 and 32.

Applying settings

Many of the file formats supported by Acrobat can have PDF Options or other settings applied during conversion. These settings are available to all formats except CompuServe GIF, HTML, JDF Job Definition, JPEG2000, and Text. Depending on the file type to be created, you can edit the settings and apply some different options. You edit settings by selecting a file type from those listed in the Preferences dialog box shown in Figure 7.8 and clicking the Edit Settings button. If the settings cannot be adjusted, the Edit Settings button is grayed out.

Settings options for the different file formats include the following:

- **Autodesk AutoCAD and PostScript/EPS.** Similar settings are available for these file types as well as many of the Microsoft Office files. One distinction between AutoCAD and PostScript/EPS is that the AutoCAD files can be converted with Bookmarks and Links, as shown in Figure 7.11. The Adobe PDF Settings and Security options are available to both file types. Click the Edit Settings button after selecting a file type to open the Adobe PDF Settings dialog box shown in Figure 7.11.

The Adobe PDF Settings dialog box offers options for files using PDFMaker and PostScript files.

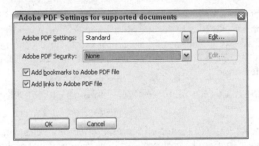

The Adobe PDF Settings enable you to make selections for the settings applied to Distiller during PDF file creation. These settings are the same as those you can access with the Adobe PDF Printer discussed earlier in this chapter. Adjacent to the pull-down menu for the Adobe PDF Settings is the Edit button. Clicking this button opens the Adobe PDF Settings dialog box where you can edit custom settings and save them as a new setting preference. The options in this dialog box are the same as you find when editing settings in Acrobat Distiller. Users of earlier versions of Acrobat can think of the Edit button as a way to open the Job Options dialog box.

CROSS-REF   For information on adjusting the Adobe PDF Settings, see Chapter 10.

The Adobe PDF Security pull-down menu offers options for adding password protection at the time the PDF file is created. By default, no security is added to PDFs converted from these file types. You have choices for using *None* for adding no security; *Reconfirm Security for each PDF,* which opens a confirmation dialog box after each file is converted to PDF; and a third option for *Use the last known security settings,* which uses the current default Adobe PDF settings for each file converted. Adjacent to the pull-down menu is the Edit button. Clicking this button opens the Acrobat Distiller – Security dialog box where you can further edit security options. Be aware that the first Edit button specifically handles the Adobe PDF Settings and the second Edit button handles the security options.

When you click OK in the Adobe PDF Settings dialog box, any new settings you added become new defaults. Every time you open one of these file formats in Acrobat the same settings are applied until you edit them again.

■ **BMP/JPEG/PCX/PNG/PICT (Macintosh only)/TIFF.** These file formats all use identical settings. Whereas many other file formats use the Acrobat Distiller application in the background and have Adobe PDF Settings applied during file conversion, these image file formats don't use Distiller and no Adobe PDF Settings are applied during file conversion. Different conversion settings can be applied from the same options lists to each of the file types individually. Therefore, a BMP file, for example, can be converted with one level of image compression and a TIFF file can be converted with another level of compression.

All of these file formats are image formats and the types of settings you apply to them relate to image options, such as file compression and color management. The same set of options available

from pull-down menus exists for all the different color modes listed in the Adobe PDF Settings dialog box shown in Figure 7.12.

NOTE Inasmuch as the Adobe PDF Settings dialog box appears the same for all image formats, some options may be grayed out depending on the type of file to be converted. For example, TIFF images can have compression applied during PDF conversion, whereas JPEG images cannot. Therefore, the compression options for JPEG images are grayed out.

FIGURE 7.12

Adobe PDF Settings for image files are available for file compression and color management.

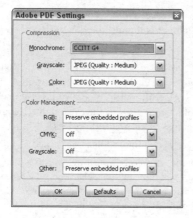

The top of the Adobe PDF Settings dialog box offers you options for file compression for monochrome (black-and-white line art), grayscale, and color images. The compression options you can select for each of these color modes include the following:

- **CCITT G4.** CCITT Group 4 compression is available only for monochrome images. This compression scheme, similar to the compression used by fax machines, works best for black-and-white images and results in smaller file sizes without data loss.

- **JPEG (Quality: Low/Medium/High/Maximum).** For grayscale and color images you can select from several compression options to specify the acceptable amount of data loss. Medium is sufficient for almost any kind of desktop printing and low-end output. High and Maximum are more suited for high-end printing and digital prepress. Use JPEG for files that need to be exchanged with users Acrobat versions below 6.0.

- **JPEG2000 (Quality: Minimum/Low/Medium/High/Maximum).** JBIG2000 is a newer compression scheme that offers much better compression and image quality than JPEG. For the amount of compression to be applied, select from the Quality settings for Minimum, Low, Medium, High, and Maximum. High and Maximum settings result in very little data loss that can be visibly seen in printed documents and high magnification levels onscreen. Medium is sufficient for any kind of desktop printing, and the minimum and low compression levels are

more suited to screen displays. Use JPEG2000 compression when exchanging files with users of Acrobat 6.0 and later.

- **JPEG2000 (Quality: Lossless).** JBIG2000 lossless offers the most compression without data loss for grayscale and color images.

- **ZIP.** ZIP compression is a lossless compression scheme. It works best where you have large areas of a common color — for example, a background with one color and a few foreground images with different colors.

The lower section of the Adobe PDF Settings dialog box handles Color Management. You have choices for applying settings to the three common color modes: RGB, CMYK, and Grayscale. The Other option at the bottom of the dialog box handles special color considerations such as spot colors you might find in duotones, tritones, and quadtones.

CROSS-REF For more information on color management and understanding different color modes, see Chapter 31.

The color management polices you can apply to each color mode are identical and they all include options from one of three choices.

- **Preserve embedded profiles.** If you work with images that have been assigned a color profile, choosing this option preserves the profile embedded in the document. Theoretically, no color changes occur when porting the files across platforms and devices.

- **Off.** If a color profile is embedded in an image, the profile is discarded.

- **Ask when opening.** If you select this option, Acrobat prompts you in a dialog box to use the embedded profile or discard it. You can make individual selections as you open files.

CROSS-REF For more detail on color management and working with color profiles, see Chapter 31.

- **Microsoft Office.** The Microsoft Office options include choices similar to those for Adobe PDF Settings and Adobe PDF Security, as found with the AutoCAD and PostScript/EPS settings listed earlier. In addition, you have options for enabling accessibility, adding Bookmarks from style sheets, converting an Excel workbook, and similar settings unique to each Microsoft program. In Figure 7.13 the options are shown for Microsoft Word.

FIGURE 7.13

Settings for Microsoft Office applications include options for enabling accessibility and converting heads and styles to Bookmarks.

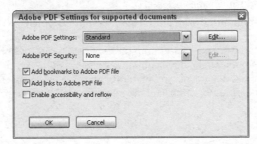

CROSS-REF   Specific uses for enabling accessibility and adding Bookmarks and links to PDFs from Microsoft Office applications are covered in Chapter 8 and Chapter 25.

After making choices for the options you want to use for file conversions, click the OK button in the Preferences dialog box. All the settings are set as new defaults until you change them. These settings are applied to documents you import from a file, from multiple files, and when you use the Open command in Acrobat.

Converting multiple files to PDF

The menu command you had available in Acrobat 7 for converting multiple files to PDF was Create PDF ⇨ From Multiple Files. This command has disappeared from the Create PDF task button and a new task button (Combine Files) now appears in Acrobat 8 for converting multiple files to PDF.

 In Acrobat 8 you can convert multiple files to PDF or combine multiple PDF documents together in either a PDF file or a PDF Package. There are so many options available when working with the Combine Files task button and menu commands, I added a chapter to cover all you need to know about working with this great new feature.

CROSS-REF   For more information on combining files into a single PDF document and creating PDF Packages, see Chapter 12.

Converting Clipboard images (Windows)

Suppose you have a map contained as part of a layout and you want to clip out the map and send it off to a friend for directions to an event, or perhaps you want to take a screenshot of an FTP client application to show log-on instructions, or maybe you want to clarify the use of a dialog box in Acrobat or another application. All of these examples and many more are excellent candidates for screen captures.

To capture a screenshot of the entire monitor screen in Windows, press the Shift+PrtScrn (Print Screen) or PrtSc keys. The keystrokes copy the current view of your monitor to the Clipboard. You can launch Acrobat or maximize it and select From Clipboard Image from the Create PDF task button pull-down menu. The Clipboard data opens as a PDF document in the Acrobat Document pane. If you have a menu or dialog box open, the screen capture includes the foreground items in the capture like the screenshots shown throughout this book. Screens captured on Windows through these methods create 96 ppi (pixels per inch) images; captures on the Mac are 72 ppi.

If you want to capture a dialog box without the background on Windows, use Alt+PrtScrn (or PrtSc). The dialog box screenshots in this book were all taken by using these key modifiers.

NOTE   Copying a screenshot to the Clipboard works with any program or at the operating system level when capturing desktop or folder views, accessories, or virtually any view you see on your computer monitor. Once data are on the Clipboard, you can open Acrobat and convert the Clipboard data to a PDF document.

Converting Clipboard images (Macintosh)

Converting Clipboard data on the Macintosh is handled exactly the same as when converting Clipboard data on Windows. However, if you want to first take a screen shot on the Mac, you use Acrobat instead of keystrokes.

NEW FEATURE   On the Mac version of Acrobat you have additional commands for capturing screen shots. These commands are not necessary on Windows where your keyboard can easily capture screen shots; but on the Mac, no keystrokes exist for capturing a screen and saving the captured data to the Clipboard. All Mac keystrokes used for capturing screen shots, record the data in a file saved to the Desktop.

To capture a screen to the Clipboard, select File ⇨ Create PDF ⇨ and choose one of the three screen capture items you see listed in the menu as shown in Figure 7.14:

- **From Screen Capture.** Selecting this option is the same as using ⌘+Shift+3. The entire monitor window is captured and converted to PDF.

- **From Window Capture.** Using this open is like pressing ⌘+Shift+4, and then pressing the Spacebar. A camera icon appears as the cursor. Move the icon on top of a window and click to capture just that window.

- **From Selection Capture.** Using this option is like pressing ⌘+Shift+4, but without following with pressing the Spacebar. A crosshair appears as a new cursor. Click and drag the area to capture and release the mouse button. The selected area is converted to PDF.

When you select one of the options for capturing a screen, the screen capture is made and the capture is converted to PDF and opened in Acrobat.

FIGURE 7.14

Select File ⇨ Create PDF and select one of the three screen captures to convert a screen, window, or selection to PDF.

Taking snapshots

In the default Select & Zoom toolbar, select the Snapshot tool and click on a PDF page. The entire page is copied to the Clipboard. You can then create a PDF file From Clipboard Image as described in the previous section. The page you create, however, is a raster image when you convert it to PDF. You lose all text attributes when copying a page in this manner. A better solution for converting an entire page is to use the Extract Pages command.

CROSS-REF For information on extracting pages, see Chapter 12.

 The advantage of using the Snapshot tool is when taking a snapshot of a partial page in Acrobat. You can select the Snapshot tool and drag a marquee in an area you want to copy. When you release the mouse button, the selected area is copied to the Clipboard. Choose Create PDF ➪ From Clipboard Image from the Create PDF task button to convert the selection to PDF. Again, you lose all type attributes, but you can use this method if retaining text is not an issue or if you want to crop an image. Using the Crop tool doesn't reduce the page size or file size of a PDF document. Using the Snapshot tool results in smaller file sizes when copying smaller sections of a PDF page.

Snapshots cannot be taken in password-protected files. If a file is encrypted you need to eliminate the file encryption before using the Snapshot tool.

CROSS-REF For additional information on creating Snapshots and setting resolution for snapshot captures, see Chapter 15. For information on using the Crop tool, see Chapter 16. For linking to snapshots, see Chapter 22. For information on file encryption, see Chapter 26.

Creating PDFs from blank pages

You're not likely to create some layouts in Acrobat but the possibilities are always there. Sometimes it's just as easy to assemble a few elements on a PDF page within Acrobat then it is to launch an editing program, assemble your document, and convert to PDF. It wouldn't be wise to create a document from scratch for commercial printing, but simple files you might use in a review session can work well.

Acrobat 8 offers you a menu command for creating blank new pages. In Acrobat 7 you had the menu command, but it was hidden and only made visible by using a modifier key. In Acrobat 7 press the Shift key and select File ➪ Create PDF ➪ From Blank Page. The From Blank Page menu submenu command was only available when you press the shift key. Using this command in Acrobat 7 resulted in creating a blank portrait US Letter sized page.

NEW FEATURE In Acrobat 8, the menu command isn't hidden and doesn't require using a modifier key. Select File ➪ Create PDF ➪ From Blank Page and a new blank page appears in the Document pane.

The difference between creating a blank new page in Acrobat 7 and a new blank page in Acrobat 8 is that the Acrobat 8 page isn't completely blank. A text box appears on the page. You can't delete the text box, resize it, or hide it. Acrobat, for the most part, expects you to use blank new pages created from this menu command as pages you'll use with type. Unfortunately, not all PDF authors are going to use a blank new page for type. You may want to add comments and markups, form fields, or place images on a page. If you attempt to add such items to the blank new page, the text box (that you can't hide or remove) can get in the way.

As an alternative to creating a blank new page using the Create PDF ➪ From Blank Page menu command, you can use the JavaScript Debugger to create a new page without any content on the page. Press Ctrl/⌘+J to open the JavaScript Debugger and type the following code:

```
app.newDoc();
```

Press the Num Pad Enter key or press Ctrl+Enter and a portrait US Letter size blank page appears in the Document pane. This page won't have a text box on the page.

 For more information on using the Create PDF ➪ From Blank Page and adding text to the page, see Chapter 13. For more on JavaScript, see Chapter 36.

Scanning to PDF

Click the Create PDF task button and select From Scanner. This option enables you to scan a document on your desktop scanner and convert to PDF. Acrobat 8 introduces a one-step method for scanning files and converting the scanned document to recognizable text. Select Document ➪ Scan to PDF and the same dialog box opens as when using the Create PDF ➪ From Scanner command.

 There's a lot to scanning from within Acrobat and converting scanned documents to recognizable text. Look over Chapter 17 where scanning and OCR conversion are covered.

Converting Web Pages to PDF

You use the Create PDF From Web Page menu command to convert Web pages to PDF. You can use the command or click the Create PDF From Web page tool in the File toolbar to convert Web pages hosted on Web sites or HTML files stored locally on your computer or networked servers.

Web Capture provides a complex set of preferences and tools with different options for converting Web pages, a Web site, or multiple sites to PDF. A captured Web site converts HTML, text files, and images to PDF, and each Web page is appended to the converted document. Conversion to PDF from Web sites can provide many opportunities for archiving information, analyzing data, creating search indexes, and many more uses where information needs to reside locally on computers.

Web pages containing animation such as Flash animation can be converted to PDF in Acrobat 6 and later. When animated pages are captured, the animation effects are viewed in the PDF file in any Acrobat viewer.

Understanding Web site structure

To understand how to capture a Web site and convert the documents to PDF, you need a fundamental understanding of a Web page and the structure of a site. A Web page is a file created with the Hypertext Markup Language (HTML). There is nothing specific to the length of a Web page. A page may be a screen the size of 640 × 480 pixels or a length equivalent to several hundred letter-sized pages. Size, in terms of linear length, is usually determined by the page content and amount of space needed to display the page. PDF files, on the other hand, have fixed lengths up to 200 × 200 inches. You can determine the fixed size of the PDF page prior to converting the Web site from HTML to PDF. After the PDF page size is determined, any Web pages captured adhere to the fixed size. If a Web page is larger than the established PDF page, the overflow automatically creates additional PDF pages. Hence, a single converted Web page may result in several PDF pages.

Web site design typically follows a hierarchical order. The home page rests at the topmost level where direct links from this page occupy a second level. Subsequently, links from the second level refer to pages at a third level, and so forth.

When pages are captured with Acrobat, the user can specify the number of levels to convert. Be forewarned, however; even two levels of a Web site can occupy many Web pages. The number of pages and the speed of your Internet connection determine the amount of time needed to capture a site.

Understanding captured pages structure

One or more levels can be captured from a Web site. You decide the number of levels to convert in the Create PDF from Web Page dialog box. PDF pages are converted and placed in a new PDF file or appended to an existing PDF file. One nice feature with Create PDF From Web Page is it can seek out and append only new pages that have not yet been downloaded.

After pages are converted to PDF they can be viewed in Acrobat. Any URL links on the converted Web page are preserved in the resultant PDF and can be used to append files to the PDF or open the link destinations in your Web browser. The file types that can be converted to PDF include the following:

- **Adobe PDF format.** Although not converted to PDF because they already appear in the format, PDF pages can be downloaded with Create PDF From Web Page.

- **FDF.** Form Data Format files can be captured and converted to PDF. An FDF file might be form data exported from a PDF form.

- **GIF Image Format (Graphics Interchange Format).** GIF images, as well as the last image in an animated GIF, can be captured when you convert a Web site to PDF. GIFs, like JPEGs within the HTML file, can also appear on separate PDF pages.

- **HTML documents.** HTML files can be converted to PDF. The hypertext links from the original HTML file are active in the PDF document as long as the destination documents and URLs have also been converted.

- **JPEG (Joint Photographic Experts Group) image format.** Images used in the HTML documents are also captured and converted to PDF. JPEGs may be part of the converted HTML page. When captured, they can be part of a captured HTML page and can also appear individually on PDF pages.

- **Plain text.** Any text-only documents contained on a Web site, such as an ASCII text document, can be converted to PDF. When capturing text-only files, you have the opportunity to control many text attributes and page formats.

- **PNG image format.** Portable Network Graphics (PNG) contained in Web pages can be converted to PDF just like GIF and JPEG images.

- **XDP.** Forms create with Adobe LiveCycle Designer can be saved in XDP (XML Data Package) that can be understood by an XFA plug-in.

- **XFDF.** XML-based FDF files typically exported from PDF forms can be converted to PDF.

- **Image maps.** Image maps created in HTML are converted to PDF. The links associated with the map are active in the PDF as long as the link destinations are also converted.

- **Password-secure areas.** A password-secure area of a Web site can also be converted to PDF. In order to access a secure site, however, you need the password(s).

Accepted file types and links

If a Web page link to another Web page or URL exists, it is preserved in the converted PDF document. Links to pages, sites, and various actions work similarly to the way they do directly on the Web site. However, if a PDF document contains a link to another PDF document, the converted file doesn't preserve the link. When the site is converted, the captured pages reside in a single PDF document. In order to maintain PDF

links that open other PDF documents, the destination documents need to be captured as individual pages or extracted and saved from the converted pages.

Links to other levels are also inactive if they have not been converted during the capture. You can append individual linked pages to the converted PDF document by clicking Web links. Selections for converting individual links can be made available in a dialog box opening after clicking a Web link. You can then append one or more links to the converted document. You can find the specifics on how to accomplish this task in "Appending pages" a little later in this chapter.

For executed animation, such as an animation from a GIF file or other programming application, the download contains only the last image in the sequence. A mouseover effect that changes an image is preserved in the converted PDF document as long as you download both the original image and the image associated with the mouseover. Additionally, you can capture sounds contained in documents.

You can also convert form fields to PDF, and field types such as radio buttons, check boxes, list boxes, and combo boxes often convert with the data intact. You might want to convert a form that has a list of countries and use the form field in your own PDF forms. The Acrobat implementation of JavaScript varies considerably from JavaScript written for Web pages, so many JavaScripts do not work in converted Web pages.

CROSS-REF For more information on form field types, see Chapters 33 and 34.

For Web pages that contain non-English characters, you need to have the appropriate resources loaded in order to download and convert the files. Japanese characters, for example, require installation of the Far East language files and additional system files. Using non-English characters requires you to make additional settings choices for Language Scripts. The options are available in the HTML Conversion Settings dialog box in the Fonts and Encoding tab. For making adjustments in the HTML Conversion Settings dialog box, see the section "Conversion Settings" later in this chapter.

Bookmarks in converted pages

After you convert a Web site to PDF, you can edit the document in Acrobat as you would any other PDF. Links to pages become editable links — that is, you can modify their properties. When a site has been converted to PDF, all the PDF pages contain Bookmarks linked to the respective pages, as shown in Figure 7.15. The first Bookmark is a regular (unstructured) Bookmark that contains the domain name from which the site was captured. All Bookmarks appearing below the server name are structured Bookmarks linked to the converted pages. With the exception of specific Web applications, you can edit these Bookmarks like any other Bookmarks created in Acrobat. Additionally, you can use structured Bookmarks for page editing by moving and deleting the Bookmarks and associated pages.

CROSS-REF For more information on Bookmarks, see Chapter 22.

FIGURE 7.15

A captured Web site converted to PDF displays the domain name server as a normal Bookmark and several structured Bookmarks.

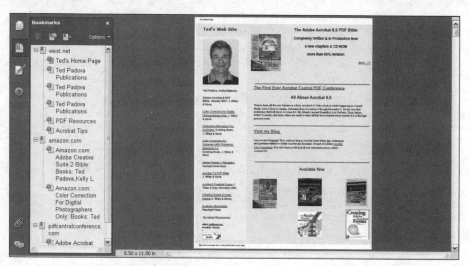

Capturing Web pages

To begin capturing Web pages, select From Web Page in the Create PDF task button pull-down menu, click the Create PDF from Web Page tool, or choose File ➪ Create PDF ➪ From Web Page. The Create PDF from Web Page dialog box opens, as shown in Figure 7.16.

FIGURE 7.16

When you select the From Web Page command, the Create PDF from Web Page dialog box opens.

In the Create PDF from Web Page dialog box, various settings determine many different attributes for how a Web page is converted to PDF and how it appears in the Acrobat Document pane. The first level of controls is handled in the Create PDF from Web Page dialog box. Additional buttons in this dialog box open other dialog boxes where you apply many more settings. If this is your first attempt at capturing a Web page, then leave the default values in the dialog box, as shown in Figure 7.16 and supply a URL in the URL field box. Click the Create button and watch the page appear in Acrobat.

CAUTION Be certain the Levels field box is set to 1 on your first attempt. Entering any other value may keep you waiting for some time depending on how many pages download from additional levels.

Depending on the site, the number of different links from the site to other URLs, and the structure of the HTML pages, you often need to wade through the maze of dialog boxes that control settings for the PDF conversion from the HTML files. You don't need to memorize all of these settings, but just use the following section as a reference when you capture Web pages.

Settings in the Create PDF from Web Page dialog box

The controls available to you in the Open Web Page dialog box begin with the URL you supplied in the Create PDF from Web Page dialog box when downloading the first Web page. This URL determines the site where the pages, which are converted, are hosted. After you enter the URL, the remaining selections you need to set include:

- **Get only *x* levels.** Appended pages can contain more than one level. The URL link may go to another site hosted on another server or stay on the same server. Select the levels to be downloaded by clicking the up or down arrows or entering a numeric value in the field box.

CAUTION A Web site can have two levels of extraordinary size. If the Home page is on the first level and many links are contained on the Home page, all the associated links are at the second level. If you're downloading with a slow connection, the time needed to capture the site can be quite long.

- **Get Entire Site.** When you select this radio button, all levels on the Web site are downloaded.
- **Stay on same path.** When this option is enabled, all documents are confined to the directory path under the selected URL.
- **Stay on same server.** Links made to other servers are not downloaded when this option is enabled.
- **Create.** When you're ready to convert Web pages from the site identified in the URL field box, click the Create button.
- **Browse.** Selecting this button enables you to capture a Web site residing on your computer or network server. Click Browse to open a navigation dialog box where you can find the directory where HTML pages are stored and capture the pages.
- **Settings.** Click this button to make choices for the conversion options. See "Conversion settings" later in this chapter.

TIP An alternative to using the Create from Web Page dialog box for a single Web page stored locally on your computer is to use drag and drop. Select the HTML document to convert to PDF and drag it to the top of the Acrobat window or program icon. If you have multiple HTML files to convert, you can also use the Create From Multiple Files menu command.

Although it may not be entirely practical, Web designers who are more comfortable with WYSIWYG (What You See Is What You Get) HTML editors than layout applications may find that creating layout assemblies in their favorite editor is beneficial. You can't get control over image sampling, but you can achieve a layout

for screen display. Create the layout in a program such as Adobe GoLive, Microsoft FrontPage, or Macromedia Dreamweaver. When you're finished with the pages, launch Acrobat and select Create PDF from Web Page. Click the Browse button in the Create PDF from Web Page dialog box and navigate to your HTML files. Click the Create button to convert your pages to PDF. You can send these pages as an e-mail attachment to a colleague or print them to your desktop printer. It may sound a little crazy, but some people just don't like to leave familiar ground.

CAUTION   Even though you may browse to a folder on your hard drive and convert a local Web site to PDF, any external links launch your Internet connection and capture pages on another site. If you want only local pages converted, be certain to click the Stay on same server button in the Create PDF from Web Page dialog box.

CROSS-REF   You can create Web pages from tools installed by Acrobat in Microsoft Internet Explorer in Windows only. For information related to converting Web pages to PDF from within Microsoft Internet Explorer, see Chapter 27.

Conversion settings

Clicking the Settings button in the Create PDF from Web Page dialog box opens the Web Page Conversion Settings dialog box, which has two tabs on which you supply file conversion attributes and page layout settings. The General tab deals with the file attribute settings, as shown in Figure 7.17.

FIGURE 7.17

The Web Page Conversion Settings dialog box offers controls for file types and how they will be converted to PDF.

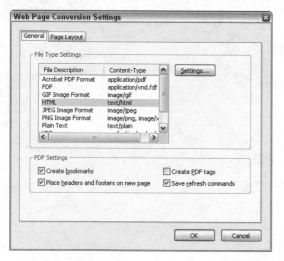

Under the File Description heading the file types are listed for those file types discussed in the "Understanding captured pages structure" section earlier in this chapter. Select any file type in the list. Only the file types for HTML and Text offer more options, which you access by clicking the Settings button on the right side of the dialog box. If you select a file type other than HTML or Plain Text, the Settings button is grayed out. At the bottom of the dialog box are four PDF Settings check boxes:

- **Create bookmarks.** When you enable this option, pages converted to PDF have structured Bookmarks created for each page captured. The page's title is used as the Bookmark name. If the page has no title, Acrobat supplies the URL as the Bookmark name.

- **Place headers & footers on new pages.** A header and footer are placed on all converted pages if this option is enabled. A header in the HTML file consists of the page title appearing with the <HEAD> tag. The footer retrieves the page's URL, the page name, and a date stamp for the date and time the page was downloaded.

- **Create PDF tags.** The structure of the converted PDF matches that of the original HTML file. Items such as list elements, table cells, and similar HTML tags are preserved. The PDF document contains structured Bookmarks for each of the structured items. A tagged Bookmark then links to a table, list, or other HTML element.

- **Save refresh commands.** When this option is enabled, a list of all URLs in the converted PDF document is saved. When the capture is refreshed, these URLs are revisited and new PDF pages are converted for any new pages added to the site. If you want to append new pages to the PDF, you must enable this item for Acrobat to update the file.

If you look again at the top of the dialog box, the two items for which you can edit additional settings include HTML and Plain Text files. When you select HTML in the File Description list and click the Settings button, a dialog box opens for HTML Conversion Settings, as shown in Figure 7.18.

FIGURE 7.18

When you select HTML in the File Description list and click the Settings button, the HTML Conversion Settings dialog box opens.

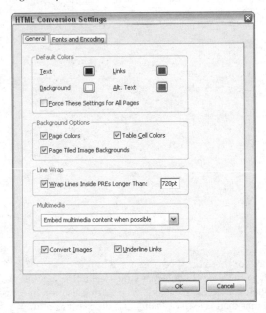

The two tabs in the HTML Conversion Settings dialog box are the General tab and the Fonts and Encoding tab. The first group of settings handles the general attributes assigned to the page layout:

■ **Default Colors.** Use this option to assign new default colors for Text, Background color, Links, and Alt Text. You can choose a color from a set of preset colors, or choose the option for custom colors, from a palette that opens after you click the swatch.

■ **Force These Settings for All Pages.** HTML pages may or may not have assigned color values. When no color is assigned for one of these items this setting defines the unassigned elements with the colors set in the Default Colors section. If this check box is enabled, all colors, including HTML-assigned colors, are changed to the Default Colors.

■ **Background Options.** These include settings for the background colors used on the Web page, tiled image backgrounds, and table cells. When these check boxes are enabled, the original design is preserved in the PDF document.

TIP If you find table cells, background colors, and tiled background images distracting when you're reading Web pages either in a browser or converted to PDF, disable the Background Options check boxes before converting to PDF. The original design is changed, but the files are easily legible for both screen reading and when printed.

■ **Line Wrap.** Enables you to choose a maximum distance for word-wrapping the text in an HTML file. When the <PRE> tag is used in HTML, the text is preformatted to preserve line breaks and indents. The field box for this option enables you to control the maximum length for text lines in inches.

■ **Multimedia.** Enables you to set options for handling multimedia clips. From the pull-down menu you can choose from three options:

▪ **Disable multimedia capture.** Movie and sound clips are ignored. Only the Web pages are converted to PDF and no links to the media are included in the capture.

▪ **Embed multimedia content when possible.** Acrobat viewers 6 and above enable you to embed multimedia clips in the PDF document. Selecting this option captures the Web page and embeds any multimedia files that meet the compatibility requirements of Acrobat. Be aware that embedded multimedia files are available only to Acrobat viewers 6.0 or later.

▪ **Reference multimedia content by URL.** The captured Web page contains a link to the URL where the multimedia files are hosted.

CROSS-REF For more about the new features for handling multimedia in PDF documents, see Chapter 23.

■ **Convert Images.** If checked, graphics are converted. If unchecked, the graphics are not converted.

TIP To produce faster downloads, disable the Convert Images check box. The number of pages to be converted is significantly reduced, thereby reducing the amount of time to capture a Web site.

■ **Underline Links.** Displays the text used in an <A HREF...> tag with an underline. This option can be helpful if the text for a link is not a different color than the body copy.

After you choose the General settings, click the Fonts and Encoding tab to open the Fonts and Encoding portion of the HTML Conversion Settings dialog box. The display appears as shown in Figure 7.19.

FIGURE 7.19

When you select the Fonts and Encoding tab in the HTML Conversion Settings dialog box, Acrobat offers options for font handling.

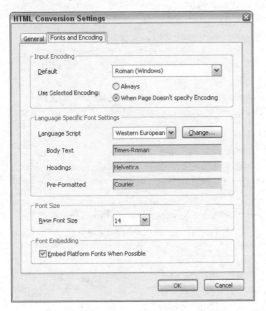

Options for font handling include the following:

- **Input Encoding.** Sets the Web page text encoding for body text, heads, and preformatted text. The default is consistent with the language you install. Other supported languages include Chinese, Japanese, Korean, and Unicode characters.

- **Body Text, Headings, and Pre-Formatted text.** The items appearing under the Language Specific Font Settings section contain editable fields for changing the text encoding and fonts used for the respective items. You make global changes by clicking the Change button, which opens a dialog box for font selections as shown in Figure 7.20. You choose fonts from all the fonts installed in your system. A pull-down menu is available for body text, headings, and preformatted text. You can assign fonts individually to each item.

FIGURE 7.20

When you click the Change button, a dialog box opens where you can select a system font and point size. The chosen font appears as the new default for text from font sets listed in pull-down menus for body text, headings, and preformatted text.

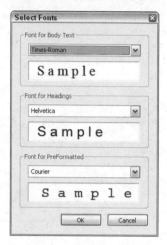

- **Base Font Size.** You choose font sizes for each of the three text items from pull-down menus or by editing the field boxes.

- **Embed Platform Fonts When Possible.** Fonts used to view the pages are embedded when the check box is enabled. File sizes are larger with embedded fonts, but file integrity is preserved and eliminates a need for font substitution. Embedded fonts ensure the display and print of the PDF documents precisely as seen in the Web browser.

After choosing all the settings for how to convert HTML files, click OK in the HTML Conversion Settings dialog box. The dialog box disappears and returns you to the Web Page Conversion Settings dialog box. The other file format to which you apply settings is Plain Text files. Select Plain Text in the File Description list and click the Settings button (refer to Figure 7.17). The Plain Text Conversion Settings dialog box opens, as shown in Figure 7.21.

FIGURE 7.21

In the Web Page Conversion Settings dialog box, select Plain Text in the File Description list and click the Settings button. The Plain Text Conversion Settings dialog box opens where you apply settings for ASCII text file conversion to PDF.

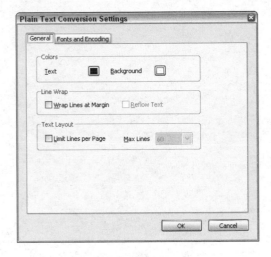

Choices in this dialog box are similar to the choices available in the HTML Conversion dialog box for the Color, Font, and Line Wrap items, which were just discussed. Line Wrap behaves similarly to the Pre-Formatted text discussed earlier in the chapter. One additional item appears in this dialog box:

- **Text Layout.** For large bodies of text, the number of lines on the page can be user-defined. Depending on point size, the standard number of lines on an 8.5 × 11–inch letter-sized page is 66. The default in Acrobat is 60 when the Text Layout check box is enabled. You can make a choice for the number of lines by editing the field box only after selecting the Limit Lines per Page check box.

You can also make font choices for plain text files. Click the Fonts and Encoding tab to reveal more options in the Plain Text Conversion Settings dialog box, as shown in Figure 7.22.

Options available in the Fonts and Encoding tab are similar to the font options you have with HTML page conversions. Make choices in this dialog box for text encoding, text font, and whether the fonts are to be embedded in the resulting PDF. After making changes in the Page Layout dialog box for Plain Text documents, click OK. Once again you return to the Web Page Conversion Settings dialog box.

FIGURE 7.22

Select the Fonts and Encoding tab to apply font options for plain text conversions.

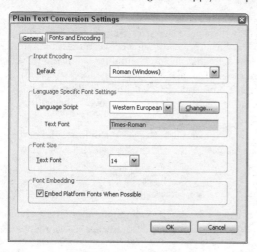

Page Layout conversion settings

All the settings discussed on the previous few pages were related to the General tab. In the Web Page Conversion Settings dialog box another option is available. Page layout offers you options for describing the physical size and orientation of converted pages. Click the Page Layout tab and the Web Page Conversion Settings dialog box opens, as shown in Figure 7.23.

FIGURE 7.23

The Page Layout options are available from the Web Page Conversion Settings dialog box when you select the Page Layout tab.

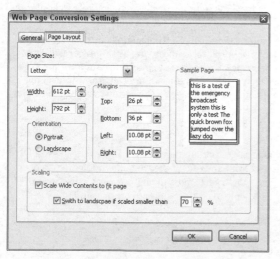

Page layout attributes enable you to force long HTML pages into more standard page sizes for viewing or printing. If an HTML page spans several letter-sized pages, you can determine where the page breaks occur and the orientation of the converted pages. Many options are available in the Page Layout tab of the Web Page Conversion Settings dialog box:

- **Page Size.** This pull-down menu provides a variety of default page sizes. Acrobat supports page sizes from 1-inch square to 200-inches square. You can supply any value between the minimum and maximum page sizes in the Width and Height field boxes below the pull-down menu to override the fixed sizes available from the pull-down menu. To make changes in the field boxes, edit the text, click the up and down arrows in the dialog box, or click in a field box and press the up and down arrow keys on your keyboard. Press Tab and Shift+Tab to toggle between the field boxes.

- **Margins.** In the four Margins field boxes, you can set the amount of space on all four sides of the PDF page before any data appear. You make the changes for the margin sizes via the same methods described in the preceding bullet.

- **Sample Page.** The thumbnail at the right side of the dialog box displays a view of the converted page when sizes are established for the Width, Height, and Margin settings.

- **Orientation.** You choose portrait or landscape orientation from the radio button options. If a site's Web pages all conform to screen sizes such as 640 × 480, you might want to change the orientation to landscape.

- **Scale wide contents to fit page.** Once again, because HTML documents don't follow standard page sizes, images and text can be easily clipped when these documents are converted to a standard size. When this option is enabled, the page contents are reduced in size to fit within the page margins.

- **Switch to landscape if scaled smaller than.** The percentage value is user definable. When the page contents appear on a portrait page within the limit specified in the field box, the PDF document is automatically converted to a landscape orientation. The default is 70 percent. If the default value is used, any vertical page scaled lower than 70 percent is auto-switched to landscape as long as the orientation is selected for Portrait.

PDF WORKFLOW If your workflow is dependent on capturing Web pages routinely, then you'll want to use the same conversion settings for all your Web captures. Educational facilities, government agencies, research institutes, and large corporate offices may have frequent needs for archiving research information found on the Web.

Unfortunately, Acrobat makes no provision for saving and loading Web Capture settings established in the dialog boxes discussed in the preceding pages. To develop a workflow suited to organizations or workgroups, your alternative may be setting up a single computer dedicated to the task of capturing data from the Web. The computer needs to be licensed for Acrobat, but using a single computer ensures all Web captures are performed with the same conversion settings. Users with any Acrobat viewer can retrieve the PDF files that are captured across a network or intranet.

Determining download status

After you choose all settings and options in all the dialog boxes pertaining to converting Web sites to PDF, you can revisit the Create PDF from Web Page command from any one of the three methods discussed earlier. As pages are downloaded and converted to PDF, the Download Status dialog box opens displaying, appropriately, the download status. After the first page downloads, this dialog box, shown in Figure 7.24, moves to the background behind the converted Web pages.

FIGURE 7.24

The Download Status dialog box appears momentarily and then disappears as Acrobat continues to download pages and convert them to PDF.

The dialog box actually remains open, but hides behind the PDF pages being converted as the download continues. If you want to bring the Download Status dialog box to the foreground, choose Advanced ➪ Web Capture ➪ Bring Status Dialogs to Foreground. The dialog box opens in the foreground while Acrobat continues to convert pages.

Appending pages

When a PDF file is open in the Document pane, you can append pages from URL links by choosing Advanced ➪ Web Capture and then selecting the appropriate choice from the submenu commands. You can also append pages via a context-sensitive menu. To open a context-sensitive menu, you must position the cursor over a structured Bookmark and right-click (Ctrl+click on the Macintosh). The context menu in Figure 7.25 includes options for appending Web pages and commands for handling pages. The submenu options from the Advanced ➪ Web Capture menu shown in Figure 7.26 relate to Web Capture features.

FIGURE 7.25

A context menu opened on a structured Bookmark offers options for appending pages as well as page-editing commands.

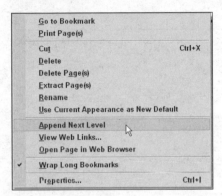

FIGURE 7.26

When you choose Advanced ⇨ Web Capture, the submenu displays options for treatment of Web captures.

To append pages to the open PDF, make choices from the following selections in the Web Capture submenu:

- **Append Web Page.** Selecting this option opens the Add to PDF from Web Page dialog box where you make attribute choices. The dialog box offers the same choices as originally displayed in the Create PDF from Web Page dialog box. When appending pages, you can change the attribute choices for all conversion options such as the URL, number of levels to be downloaded, and so on.

- **Append All Links on Page.** When you select this submenu option, no dialog box opens before the download commences. All Web links to other HTML pages are converted and appended to the PDF. Conversion settings are used from the last choices you made in the Create PDF from Web Page dialog box. If you need to change the conversion settings for links to other pages, you can use the View Web Links dialog box.

- **View Web Links.** The Select Page Links to Download dialog box opens when you select this menu command. This dialog box lists all Web links according to URL.

  The list contains an icon displayed at the far left of the URL list informing you that a link exists to the URL. You can select each of the items in the list. After you select a link, the Properties button on the right side of the dialog box becomes active. Click the Properties button and another dialog box opens. You'll notice in the next dialog box the options for conversion settings appear within three tabs. These options are the same as those you use with the Create PDF From Web Page command.

- **Page Info.** This option opens a dialog box displaying information about the current page viewed in the PDF file. As you scroll through pages, the page info changes according to the page viewed. The information supplied in the dialog box includes the original URL, title of the page, creation date, a description of the content, and the preferred zoom level for viewing.

When you open a context menu from a structured Bookmark, the menu options appear, as shown previously in Figure 7.25. The two choices from the menu commands for appending pages to the PDF are Append Next Level and View Web Links.

TIP You can also append Web pages by clicking a link in the PDF page. If the link destination is not contained in the PDF, the URL is contacted and the page is appended to the PDF. When you position the cursor over a link, the cursor displays a hand icon and index finger pointing upward. If a link has not yet been converted, the icon displays a plus (+) symbol inside the hand and a ToolTip shows the URL where you can find the link. If the link has been converted to PDF, no plus (+) symbol and no URL are shown. If you want to open a link in your Web browser, press the Control/Option key and click the link.

Refreshing Web pages

You use the Refresh pages command to update a previously captured site. If content has changed, the updated pages are downloaded. Any pages that haven't changed are ignored. To update a PDF file created with Web Capture, choose Advanced ➪ Web Capture ➪ Refresh Pages. The Refresh Pages dialog box opens, as shown in Figure 7.27. In order to update pages with the Refresh Pages command, the Conversion Settings in the original Web Page Conversion Settings dialog box must have the Save refresh commands check box enabled, as shown in Figure 7.17 earlier in the chapter.

FIGURE 7.27

The Refresh Pages dialog box offers options for updating pages in the open PDF file.

Updates occur according to options you select in the Refresh Pages dialog box. You have two choices for comparing the page to be downloaded with a page in the PDF document:

- **Compare Only Page Text to Detect Changed Pages.** If you are interested only in changes made to the text on Web pages, then select this radio button. Acrobat ignores new graphics, colors, backgrounds, and other non-text elements.

- **Compare All Page Components to Detect Changed Pages.** When enabled, this option downloads and converts pages where any changes have occurred.

If you want to selectively update different page links, then click the Edit Refresh Commands List button in the Refresh Pages dialog box. Another dialog box opens similar to the one opened with the View Web Links command, which is discussed in the "Appending pages" section of this chapter. When the Refresh Commands List dialog box opens, all links are selected by default. Options in this dialog box are similar to those found in the View Web Links dialog box.

If you want all links to be updated, leave the default alone and proceed with the download. If selected links are to be updated, click the desired link to update. For multiple links hold down the Shift key as you select the links. For non-contiguous selections in the list, hold down the Control key (⌘ key on Macintosh) and click the links to be included in the update. Click OK and exit the Refresh Pages dialog box. The download commences and the Download Status dialog box disappears. To view the status dialog box, bring it to the front by choosing Advanced ➪ Web Capture ➪ Bring Status Dialogs to Foreground.

TIP To compare Web pages for obvious changes prior to refreshing the page, visit the Web page in your browser. In Acrobat, choose Edit ➪ Preferences ➪ Internet. In the Internet Preferences, select Display PDF in Browser in the right pane. Click OK and click the URL link in the PDF file. The Web page opens in your Web browser. Compare this page to the PDF page to determine any discrepancies before downloading the pages.

Locating Web addresses

Acrobat 7 and 8 are intelligent viewers when it comes to detecting URLs in text on PDF pages. You don't need a link or button to click URL text and launch your default Web browser. Acrobat 7 and 8 do that automatically for you. If you prepare PDF files for users of earlier versions of Acrobat viewers, then you need to create links to URLs in text if you want users to click text to launch a Web page.

You can easily create links from URLs in text using a simple menu command. But don't do this if you know your entire audience uses a 7.0 viewer or above. The more links or buttons you add to a PDF, the larger your file size will be.

The text must have the complete URL listing including *http://, or https:*. After the Web link is converted, you can also click the link and append pages by using Web Capture. PDF authors may also create Web links for end users when distributing files to others.

To create Web links on pages containing URLs, choose Advanced ➪ Document Processing ➪ Create Links from. A dialog box opens, as shown in Figure 7.28.

FIGURE 7.28

The Create Web Links dialog box enables you to create Web links from text for user-defined page ranges in the open PDF file.

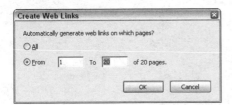

In the Create Web Links dialog box, you specify page ranges for where Acrobat should create the links. Acrobat performs this task quickly and creates all links where the proper syntax has been used to describe the URL. If you want to delete links from a PDF document, open the Remove Web Links dialog box by choosing Advanced ➪ Document Processing ➪ Remove All Links. The Remove Web Links dialog box opens and you can supply page ranges for eliminating Web links.

Setting preferences for Web Capture

To access the Web Capture preferences choose Edit ➪ Preferences. In the left pane, click Web Capture, and the preference settings shown in Figure 7.29 appear. You can set the additional attributes for Web Link behavior as well as options for converting Web pages to PDF.

FIGURE 7.29

The Web Capture Preferences dialog box opens when you choose Edit ➪ Preferences and click Web Capture in the list in the left pane.

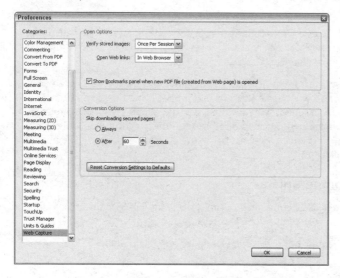

The options available in the Web Capture Preferences dialog box are as follows:

- **Verify stored images.** This pull-down menu contains options for verifying images stored on a captured Web site Once Per Session, Always, or Never. When you select the default setting, Once Per Session, Acrobat checks the Web site to see whether stored images have changed on the site. If changes have occurred, new pages are converted.

- **Show Bookmarks panel when new PDF file (created from Web page) is opened.** When this option is enabled, the converted PDF file is viewed with the Navigation pane open and the structured Bookmarks listed in the Bookmarks tab. When this option is disabled, the Navigation pane is closed, but the Bookmarks are still created.

- **Skip downloading secured pages.** Secured areas of a Web site can be downloaded, but you must have permission to access the password-protected areas and supply all passwords to gain access to the site. To avoid inadvertently attempting to download a secure area, you can elect to always skip secured pages or skip secured pages at specified intervals ranging between 1 and 9999 seconds.

- **Reset Conversion Settings to Defaults.** Clicking this button resets all options in the Conversion Settings dialog boxes to the default settings established when Acrobat was first installed.

Creating PDFs from Templates

One thing I've wanted for a long time as a feature in Acrobat has been the ability to create a PDF document from a template. Many different authoring applications support creating new files from templates, but not Acrobat — at least not the way I want to create a new PDF. You might want to reuse a purchase order form, an invoice form, a vacation leave slip, or other some such document you work with on an ongoing basis.

The nice thing about using templates is that they prevent you from inadvertently overwriting the original. Every time you open a template it's a fresh original; and when you click the Save tool, you're prompted to type a new name. This feature, as well as having your templates always stored in the same location, helps save time and aggravation.

Why hasn't Adobe added a command like Create PDF ➪ From Template? The primary reason is that not enough users have asked for this feature. I've asked Adobe for it for several years, but as a user of one, you can see how excited Adobe is to devote some engineering hours to the task.

But I'll bet many others have wanted such a feature in Acrobat, so I'm going to walk you through some steps so that you can actually create a workflow to create PDFs from template files. It might appear a little convoluted at first, but if you're like me, in the end it will save time over the hours you spend searching folders for files. The Adobe engineers didn't design this method to be used this way, but Acrobat is flexible enough that you can add some of our own personality in your workflow. If creating PDFs from Templates is of interest to you, look over the following steps.

STEPS: Creating PDFs from templates

1. **Create a PDF document for use as a template**. You can use any kind of PDF document you like. In my example I use a form created in Adobe Designer.

CROSS-REF For more information on creating forms in Adobe Designer, see Chapter 35.

2. **Add a document title.** Open the Document Properties (Ctrl/⌘+D) and click Description. In the Title field, type a descriptive title name to help identify your template.

CROSS-REF For more information on working with document properties and adding document titles, see Chapter 6.

3. **Save the PDF.** Select File ➪ Save As and save the file to a location where you can find it easily — such as the Desktop. For the filename, use any name that easily describes the document. In my example I used *tedsInvoice.pdf* for the file name. Quit Acrobat.

4. **Copy the document to a templates folder.** On Windows, open the DocTemplates folder. The path is C:/Program Files/Adobe/Acrobat 8.0/Acrobat/DocTemplates/ENU. Copy your template to the ENU folder.

   On the Macintosh open the Macintosh/Applications/Adobe Acrobat 8.0 Professional folder. Click the Adobe Acrobat Professional program icon once to select it. Open a context menu on the program icon (Ctrl+click) and select Show Package Contents. The folder that opens has two subfolders. Double-click the Contents folder to open it. Find the Resources folder and open it. Locate the en.lproj folder and open it. Inside this folder you find the DocTemplates folder. Open that folder and copy your template to this folder.

5. **Store the backup copy.** Copy your original file to a folder on your hard drive where you can easily return to it. If you upgrade your version of Acrobat, you can lose your DocTemplates folder. Try to keep some backup files in a folder location you can easily return to when upgrading the product.

6. **Launch Acrobat.** When Acrobat opens, click the Secure task button to open the pull-down menu and select Create Security Envelope, as shown in Figure 7.30. Creating a Secure Envelope was not designed for creating PDF files from custom templates, but we're going to fudge things a bit to create a workaround for not having a Create PDF From Template command.

CROSS-REF For securing PDFs with Create Secure Envelope, see Chapter 26.

FIGURE 7.30

Select Secure ⇨ Create Security Envelope to access your template.

7. **Add a file attachment.** The Create Security Envelope Wizard opens, as shown in Figure 7.31. The first pane requires you to add a file attachment. You can't progress in the wizard unless you identify a file to be attached to the envelope. Don't worry—you delete the file attachment later. Click the Add File to Send button and attach any PDF document in the Choose files to enclose dialog box.

FIGURE 7.31

Click the Add file to send button and select any PDF file to add as a file attachment.

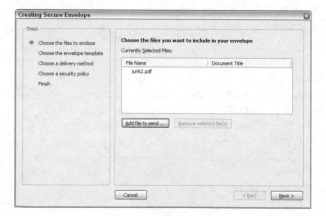

8. **Select your new template file.** Click Next and the second pane in the wizard opens. Here you'll find a list of default templates listed as template1.pdf, template2.pdf, and template3.pdf. Your new template should appear with any name you provide for your file name. If you added a document title to your file, the Document Title column lists your document title information. In my example, I used a form created in Adobe Designer. The Designer document title isn't reported in this wizard window, as you can see in Figure 7.32.

   Note that if you use forms created in Adobe Designer, the Document Title information isn't displayed in the Create Security Envelope Wizard.

9. **Choose the delivery method.** Click Next and you arrive at the Delivery Method pane in the wizard. Click the first radio button on the right side of the pane for Send the envelope later.

10. **Choose a security policy.** Click Next and the Choose a security policy pane opens in the wizard. For a custom template used in this example, no security is applied to the document. Just click Next and a warning dialog box opens. Click Yes in the warning dialog box and you arrive at the final pane in the wizard.

FIGURE 7.32

Select your template file.

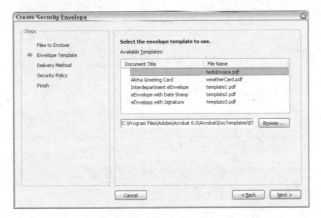

11. **Finish the template creation.** Click Finish in the last pane and your document opens in Acrobat.

12. **Delete the file attachment.** Click the Attachments pane (the paper clip icon) and open a context menu on the file attachment listed in the Attachments pane, as shown in Figure 7.33. Select Delete to delete the attachment. Remember, you had to add a file attachment in order to proceed through the wizard window.

CROSS-REF For more information on working with file attachments, see Chapter 12.

FIGURE 7.33

Delete the file attachment and your template is ready for use.

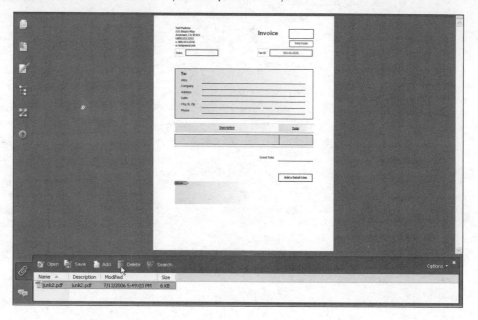

Your template is now ready for use. Make any changes you want on the file. When you click File ⇨ Save, a Save As dialog box opens prompting you to supply a filename. Your original file remains in the DocTemplates folder (until you upgrade Acrobat) and you can't inadvertently overwrite the file.

At first glance, working through these steps may seem a bit elaborate. However, once you create some template files and use them routinely you can quickly find a template and work with it.

Note that you can always store a number of files in the Organizer, but using the Organizer files doesn't give you the same features as using template files where you are prevented from overwriting the file. You can also set file properties to Read Only to prevent overwriting, so the Organizer comes a little closer to being a good tool for this kind of workflow. However, if you work in an enterprise environment where many people use the same templates, copying custom DocTemplates folders to all users' computers is much easier than configuring individual Organizer file links.

CROSS-REF For more information on using the Organizer, see Chapter 11.

Summary

- You can create PDF documents with the Adobe PDF printer. You can use the Adobe PDF printer to apply a variety of Adobe PDF Settings to the PDF conversion. Adobe PDF Settings are used by Acrobat Distiller and the Adobe PDF printer.

- You can use Acrobat to convert a variety of different native file formats to PDF using the Create PDF From File command. Multiple files can be converted to PDF and concatenated into a single document.

- You can use Acrobat to download Web pages and convert them to PDF. Web pages residing locally on hard drives can be converted to PDF. All Web page conversions preserve page and URL links.

- You can convert data copied to the system clipboard to PDF on both Windows and Macintosh. Acrobat 8 provides new commands for Macintosh users to capture screenshots and convert to PDF.

- Custom templates can be created using the Create Security Envelope features.

Chapter 8

Using PDFMaker with Microsoft Programs

T he last chapter covered PDF file creation from various programs and certain file types. Some of the PDF creation options you have from within Acrobat are also available directly from the authoring programs. Such is the case with the most popular Microsoft applications.

Adobe has devoted much development time to creating tools that easily convert most of the Microsoft applications to PDF and with certain other programs such as Autodesk AutoCAD discussed in Chapter 7 and Lotus Notes. With a one-button click in almost every Microsoft program you can convert your documents to PDF.

The common tool used in these programs is PDFMaker created by Adobe Systems and automatically installed in every program supporting the tool when you install Acrobat.

In this chapter you learn how to use the PDFMaker tool in the most popular Microsoft programs.

Setting Up the Environment

This chapter is concerned with creating PDFs; therefore, no toolbars need to be loaded in the Toolbar Well as far as PDF creation is concerned. Later in this chapter, working with comments in Microsoft Word is converted, but we'll load the Comment & Review tools when we come to that section. For now, don't be concerned about loading any toolbars. You'll load them when needed in the sections ahead.

Using Acrobat with Microsoft Word

Of all the Office applications, Microsoft Word gives you the best support for PDF file creation. Microsoft Word is the only word-processing application that provides access to the structural data of the document. The structural data of the Word document such as titles, heads, tables, paragraphs, figure captions, and so on can be converted to tagged Bookmarks. Tagged Bookmarks give you much more control over the PDF content. You can navigate to the element structures, and move, copy, extract, and delete pages through menu commands in the Bookmarks tab.

With Word, and all Microsoft Office programs you have several choices for PDF Conversion. You can use the Create PDF From File command, use the Combine Files command, drag and drop Microsoft Office files on the Acrobat Document pane, print to PostScript and convert the PostScript in Acrobat Distiller, and use a tool developed by Adobe called the Acrobat PDFMaker. This tool is installed in all Office programs and several other Microsoft programs.

CROSS-REF   For more information on Create PDF From File, see Chapter 7. For more on using Combine Files, see Chapter 12. For more on converting PostScript to PDF, see Chapter 10.

Of all the tools available to you, using PDFMaker is your best choice. Why? Because PDFMaker provides you with more options settings to control the attributes in the converted file. If, for example, you want bookmarks to appear in the converted PDF, you need to use PDFMaker. If you want to convert PowerPoint files with transitions and media effects, you need to use PDFMaker. If you want to create layered PDFs from Microsoft Visio, again, you need PDFMaker. Other PDF conversion options don't provide you with support for many of these attributes.

PDFMaker offers several tools to control PDF file creation from within Microsoft Word and all other Microsoft programs that use the PDFMaker tools. After you install Acrobat and later open Word (or other Office programs), two Acrobat icons appear on the far left side of the toolbar.

 The first of these two icons is the Convert to Adobe PDF tool. Clicking this icon opens a dialog box where you supply the filename and destination. Enter a name and choose a destination, and then click the Save button to create the PDF.

NOTE   In Acrobat versions 7 and below you had three tools installed in the Office programs on Windows and two tools installed on the Mac. The Windows version of Office had the Convert to Adobe PDF tool, Convert to Adobe PDF and Email tool, and the Convert to Adobe PDF and Send for review tool. On the Mac you had only Convert to Adobe PDF and Convert to Adobe PDF and Email. Now in Acrobat 8 two tools appear on both Windows and the Mac.

 The second tool installed in Microsoft Office Applications is Convert to Adobe PDF and Send for Review (Windows) or Convert to Adobe PDF and Email (Macintosh). When you click the Convert to Adobe PDF and Send for Review tool (Windows), the Word document is converted to PDF, and a Send by Email for Review Wizard opens where you proceed through three steps: 1) using the PDF you've just created, 2) inviting reviewers where you add the e-mail addresses of recipients, and 3) previewing the review invitation. When you click Finish in the wizard, your file is attached to an e-mail message window in your default e-mail program.

On the Mac, clicking the Convert to Adobe PDF and Email tool converts your Word document to PDF and attaches the resultant PDF as an Email attachment to a new e-mail message window.

CROSS-REF For more information concerning e-mail reviews, see Chapter 21.

In addition to tools, two menus (Windows only) are also installed with PDFMaker. The first is the Adobe PDF menu. The second is the Acrobat Comments menu.

You have the a few menu selections in the Adobe PDF menu that provide some additional PDF conversion options. From the Adobe PDF menu shown in Figure 8.1, the two tool options for Convert to Adobe PDF and Convert to Adobe PDF and Send for Review are also listed as menu commands. Notice in the menu you have two additional PDF conversion options. Convert to Adobe PDF and Email performs the same on Windows as the tool available on the Mac.

FIGURE 8.1

The Adobe PDF menu on Windows offers several options for creating PDFs from within Word.

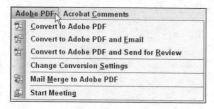

The second additional PDF conversion option on Windows in the Adobe PDF menu is Mail Merge to PDF. To use this feature you first need to create a data file and a mail merge document.

You can create a data file easily in Microsoft Excel. Just be certain to place labels in the first row at the top of an Excel worksheet such as name, address, city, state, zip, and so on. Save the file in native .xls format.

After creating a data file and a Word template document such as a letter, from the Task pane just select Mail Merge and follow steps in a wizard to create the merge document. Word provides you an easy wizard to help you create a letter, e-mail message, envelope, label, or directory. When the merge document is created, select Adobe PDF ➪ Mail Merge to Adobe PDF and the Adobe PDF Maker – Mail Merge dialog box opens, as shown in Figure 8.2.

In the Adobe PDF – Mail Merge dialog box identify data field that includes an email address. Note that the data below the head in the Excel worksheet must be a valid e-mail address. Type a Subject and then type the text you want to appear in the Message box. Optionally, you can specify a PDF filename by typing a new name in the text box. By default, the filename is PDFMailer. Click OK in the dialog box and your document is merged with the database file producing individual PDF documents attached to separate e-mail messages.

FIGURE 8.2

Select Adobe PDF ➪ Mail Merge to Adobe PDF and a dialog box opens where mail merge attributes are selected.

Changing conversion settings (Macintosh)

Windows users have an elaborate set of conversion settings they can address in menu commands when PDFMaker is installed on Windows. Macintosh users may look for the menus I mention, but they won't find them in OS X. Conversion settings for Macintosh users are much more limited than their Windows cousins and you need to choose your conversion options, as much as can be done, in the Distiller Adobe PDF settings.

CROSS-REF   For more on Adobe PDF Settings and Acrobat Distiller see Chapter 10.

When converting to PDF on the Macintosh, the PDFMaker uses a printer driver. As your first step in using the PDFMaker, open your Printer Setup Utility and select a PostScript printer. You can also select an Adobe PDF printer as shown in Figure 8.3. Click the Make Default icon in the Printer Setup Utility to establish the selected printer as the default. If you select a desktop color printer or other non-PostScript device you may see unexpected results in the PDFs created with the PDFMaker.

FIGURE 8.3

Select a PostScript printer or the Adobe PDF Printer driver and click Make Default to ensure the PDFMaker uses a
PostScript printer when converting to PDF.

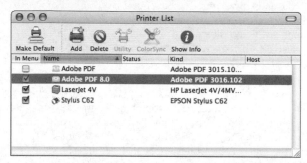

Changing conversion settings (Windows)

PDFMaker prints Word documents to disk and then converts them through Distiller's Adobe PDF Settings.
However, the Adobe PDF Settings used in Acrobat Distiller are only some of the attributes assigned to the
conversion process. You make the other assignments in Word before the file gets to Distiller. When you
choose Adobe PDF ➪ Change Conversion Settings, the Acrobat PDFMaker dialog box opens. In the dialog
box, four tabs offer attribute choices for how the PDF is ultimately created. The tabs are Settings, Security,
Word, and Bookmarks, as shown in Figure 8.4.

FIGURE 8.4

Select Adobe PDF ➪ Change Conversion Settings to open the Acrobat PDFMaker dialog box.

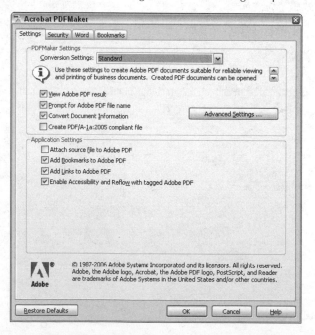

CROSS-REF Acrobat Distiller is covered in Chapter 10. All subsequent references to Distiller in this chapter are explained in more detail in Chapter 10.

Different programs support many different features. For example, Microsoft Visio and Autodesk AutoCAD both support layers. Programs such as Word, Excel, and PowerPoint do not support layers. Excel supports workbooks, Word supports style sheets, and PowerPoint supports media and transitions. When you open the PDFMaker in any program supporting the tool, you'll find different conversion settings options. Be aware that the dialog box you see in Figure 8.4 changes when opened in other programs. In Figure 8.4, the conversion settings options are specific only to Microsoft Word.

Settings

The Settings tab is the first of the four tabs where you select options. At the top of the Settings tab is a pull-down menu for Conversion Settings. From this menu, you choose the settings Distiller uses to convert the file to a PDF. If you want to edit the settings or create a new Adobe PDF Setting, click the Advanced Settings button to open the Adobe PDF Settings in Acrobat Distiller. The Distiller Adobe PDF Settings shown in Figure 8.5 enable you to make choices for attributes used to convert the document to a PDF.

FIGURE 8.5

The Settings tab offers you choices for selecting the Adobe PDF Settings used by Acrobat Distiller to convert the file.

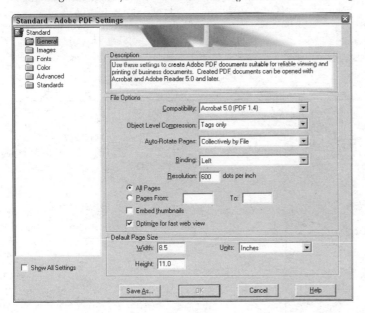

Options in the Settings tab are as follows:

- **View Adobe PDF result.** When the PDF is created, the document opens in Acrobat if this check box is enabled. If it's disabled, the PDF is created and the Word file remains in view.

- **Prompt for Adobe PDF filename.** If this check box is enabled, you won't inadvertently overwrite a file with the same name. Leaving this check box enabled is a good idea.

- **Convert Document Information.** This option ensures document information created in Word is added to the PDF Document Properties.

- **Create PDF/A-1a:2005 Compatible file.** Clicking this option automatically changes the Conversion Settings to the PDF/A-1b:2005(RGB) Adobe PDF Setting. The files are made compliant with PDF/A. Note that using PDF/A produces a PDF with Acrobat 5 compatibility; therefore, any features specific to PDF version 1.5 (Acrobat 6 and greater compatible) files are lost in PDF/A-compliant files.

- **Attach source file to Adobe PDF.** If you want to attach the Word file from which the PDF was created, enable this check box and the Word file is added as a file attachment.

- **Add Bookmarks to Adobe PDF.** Bookmarks are created from Word style sheets. Select this check box to convert styles and headings to Bookmarks. Make selections for what styles and headings to convert to Bookmarks in the Bookmarks tab.

- **Add Links to Adobe PDF.** This option ensures that hyperlinks created in Word are converted to links in the PDF document.

- **Enable Accessibility and Reflow with tagged Adobe PDF.** This option creates document structure tags. Accessibility for the visually challenged and developmentally disabled that are contained in the Word document are preserved in the PDF. Reflowing text enables the Acrobat user to use the Reflow view. As a matter of default, leave this check box enabled. Tagged PDF documents also help you export the PDF text back out to a word processor with more data integrity than when exporting files without tags.

NOTE If you enable accessibility and reflow, the file sizes of your PDF documents are larger compared to files exported to PDF without accessibility and tags. If you need to produce the smallest file sizes for specific purposes where you know accessibility and preserving structure are not needed, disable the check box.

Security

Click the Security tab to open options for security settings. Security options for permissions are available only for High-Bit encryption (128-bit RC4). If you choose to add security from the Word options, the PDF document is compatible with Acrobat 5.0 viewers and greater. If you need additional security controls available in Acrobat 6 and Acrobat 7 compatibility options, apply the security in Acrobat.

 For specific definitions of the security options, see Chapter 26.

Word

Click the Word tab to choose options for Word content, as shown in Figure 8.6.

FIGURE 8.6

The Word tab contains items specific to some of the content in Word that can be converted in the resulting PDF document.

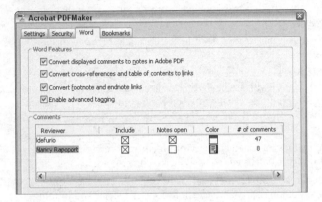

Options on the Word tab are as follows:

- **Convert displayed comments to notes in Adobe PDF.** Notes can be converted to annotation comments that will appear in a text note in the PDF file.

- **Convert cross-references and table of contents to links.** Any cross-references, such as Table of Contents and indexes, will have links to their respective destinations. These links are preserved in the PDF file.

- **Convert footnote and endnote links.** Bookmark links are added for all footnotes and endnotes.

- **Enable advanced tagging.** The tagging features available in Word exports to PDF have been split for accessibility with the Enable Accessibility and Reflow with tagged Adobe PDF files you see in Figure 8.4 and this option that adds settings *over and above* document accessibility. Checking this box adds document structure for character styles such as underlines, superscript, subscript, outline, strikeouts, and so on that can be useful when exporting PDF files back to text such as exporting to Word or RTF formats. The downside for selecting this check box is that the PDF conversion will take longer and the file sizes will grow. Unless you anticipate a need for adding this kind of document structure in your converted files, leave the check box unchecked.

- **Comments.** The lower window lists all comments by author in the file. If you check the box in the Include column, the comments are converted to Acrobat comments. The Notes open column enables you to set the default for note comments with open note pop-up windows.

> **TIP** If you have a document with comments added by several individuals and you want each person's comments appearing with different note colors, click the icon in the Color column to change color. Keep clicking the icon to continue changing color. Word scrolls through eight different colors as you keep clicking the mouse.

Bookmarks

In the Bookmarks dialog box, there are three items that can determine what Bookmarks will be created in the PDF file:

- **Convert Word Headings to Bookmarks.** Word headings can be converted to Bookmarks. In the box below the check boxes, a list of all headings and styles contained in the Word document appears. Click the box under the Bookmark column to determine what heads to convert to Bookmarks.

- **Convert Word Styles to Bookmarks.** You can select user-defined styles for conversion to Bookmarks. Scroll the list of elements and place a check mark for the styles you want to convert.

- **Convert Word Bookmarks.** Converts all Bookmarks created in Word to PDF Bookmarks.

Click the number appearing in the Levels column and a pop-up menu becomes visible. Click the down pointing arrow to open the menu and select the level of nesting for the bookmarks as shown in Figure 8.7. The nesting order you determine here in the Adobe PDFMaker settings dialog box determines the order of parent/child relationships in the Acrobat Bookmarks panel when the file is converted to PDF. (See Figure 8.8.)

CAUTION If you select the Convert Word Styles to Bookmarks check box and you have a number of style sheets in your Word document, you end up with a huge list of bookmarks. At some point the bookmarks will appear overwhelming and difficult to manage. Unless you have a definite need for converting styles in some Word documents, stick with the Convert Word Headings to Bookmarks option and convert the heads to Bookmarks.

After you select the options in the Acrobat PDFMaker dialog box, click the Convert to PDF tool or select the menu option to convert the file. In Figure 8.8, I converted a file having three levels of heads. Notice that when the Bookmarks panel is open, you see the Bookmarks nested into parent/child relationships.

CROSS-REF For more information on Adobe PDF Bookmarks and nesting bookmarks into parent/child relationships, see Chapter 22.

FIGURE 8.7

The Bookmarks tab offers three choices for determining what Bookmarks are created in the PDF file. Clicking a number in the Levels column permits you to determine parent/child relationships for bookmarks.

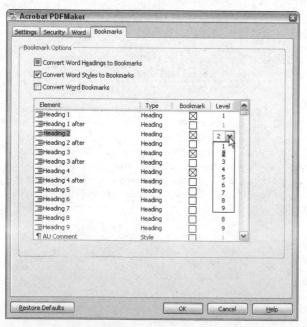

FIGURE 8.8

Bookmarks from subheads are nested as child bookmarks below the top-level heads according to the Level order specified in the Adobe PDFMaker.

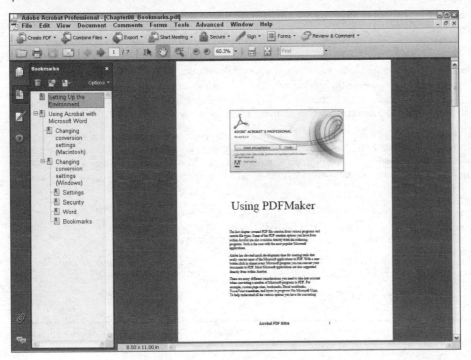

Working with comments (Windows)

The other menu installed with PDFMaker is the Acrobat Comments menu. The commands in the menu address merging your PDF comments back into the original Microsoft Word document. The menu items are as follows:

- **Import Comments from Acrobat.** This is a *round trip* process — that is to say you need to start with an Microsoft Word document, send it out to be reviewed, and then merge the received comments back into the Word file. In addition, when you created the PDF file in the first place, you must use PDFMaker. When you select the menu item, the Import Comments from Adobe Acrobat help window opens. Read the helpful tips on how to import comments and click OK to proceed. The next dialog box that opens is Import Comments from Adobe Acrobat, as shown in Figure 8.9. In the dialog box, you make choices for what files to select, what comments to import, and whether you want to filter the comments.

FIGURE 8.9

The Import Comments from Adobe Acrobat dialog box offers choices for file selection and the comment types to import into the Word document.

- **Continue Integration Process.** This continues the integration of PDF comments in the Word document for text edits such as inserts and deletions. If review tracking is on, you can merge tracked changes.

- **Accept All Changes in Document.** After the comment integration, select this menu command to accept the comments. Comments such as text marked for deletion are deleted; text marked with insertion adds the inserted comments, and so on.

- **Delete All Comments in Document.** All comments imported from the PDF document are deleted from the Word file.

- **Reviewing Toolbar.** This toggles the Microsoft Word Reviewing toolbar on and off, as shown in Figure 8.10. To hide the tools, uncheck the command by selecting it in the menu.

- **Show Instructions.** The dialog box that opens when you choose the Import Comments from Acrobat command (see the first bullet in this list) also opens when you choose the Show Instructions menu command.

FIGURE 8.10

When you select the Reviewing Toolbar option in the Acrobat Comments menu, the Microsoft Word comment and review tools are made visible in the Microsoft Word Toolbar Well.

To make the process for importing comments from Acrobat (or Exporting comments from Acrobat to Word), take a look at the steps that follow, which describe a workflow for exchanging comments in Word and PDF documents.

STEPS: Integrating Acrobat comments in Word documents (Acrobat Professional Only)

1. **Convert a Word document to PDF using the PDFMaker Convert to Adobe PDF Tool.** Be certain to use the PDFMaker to convert your Word file to PDF.

> **CAUTION** You must be certain to check Enable Accessibility and Reflow with tagged Adobe PDF in the Settings tab in order to export/import comments between Acrobat PDF and Word files.

2. **Mark up the PDF file in Acrobat using the Comment & Markup tools.** Be certain to use the Text Edits tools in the Comment & Markup toolbar to comment on the PDF file. Text Edit comments get merged directly into the Microsoft word document stream, whereas other comments are just applied as note comments in Word.

> **CROSS-REF** For more information on commenting and using the Text Edits tools, see Chapter 20.

3. **Initiate an export of comments to Word.** You can export comments from Acrobat to Word or Import comments in Word from a PDF file. In Acrobat you use the Comments ⇨ Export Comments to Word menu command. In Word you use the Acrobat Comments ⇨ Import Comments from Acrobat menu command. Either menu selection opens the Import Comments from Adobe Acrobat dialog box. If you start in Acrobat, Microsoft Word is launched and the Import Comments from Adobe Acrobat Wizard is handled from within Word. The first pane describes the process for integrating your PDF comments back to a Word document. Click OK after reading the help information.

4. **Choose files and comment types.** The second pane in the Import Comments from Adobe Acrobat Wizard provides options to choose your files and select the comment types you want to import, as shown earlier in Figure 8.9.

   Click the first Browse button to select the PDF file containing your comments. Click the second Browse button to select the Word file. Note that you must import comments from a PDF created from the Word file you intend to use for your comment imports.

   Below the Choose Files area in the first wizard pane is the Select Comment Types to Import. If you want all comments imported, click the All Comments radio button. Other options you have are shown in Figure 8.9.

   The last item in the first wizard pane is an option to turn on the Track Changes feature in Word. If you want your changes to be tracked and noted, check this box.

5. **Import the comments.** Click Next and your comments are imported into the Word document. You should see the Successful Import dialog box open, as shown in Figure 8.11.

6. **Integrate Text Edits.** Click the Integrate Text Edits button if you used the Text Edits tools in Acrobat to make comments. Another dialog box opens as shown in Figure 8.12 where you can selectively choose comments to integrate or click the Apply All Remaining button to integrate all Text Edits. Click Done after integrating comments and the comment imports are completed.

FIGURE 8.11

If your comments are successfully imported, the Successful Import dialog box opens.

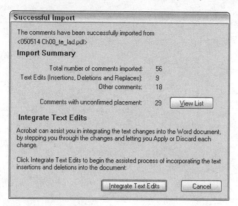

FIGURE 8.12

Click Apply to apply each comment as you review them in the New Text window or click Apply All Remaining to import all Text Edits comments.

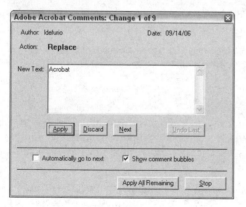

If you want to selectively import comments, you can filter the imported comments by selecting the Apply Custom Filters to Comments radio button in the Import Comments from Acrobat wizard pane shown in Figure 8.9. Click this radio button and click continue to open the Filter Comments pane shown in Figure 8.13.

In the Filter Comments pane you can select comments by authors you want to import, types of comments to import, and comments by status. Make the selections you want for importing comments and click OK. The comments are imported into the Word file and the Successful Import dialog box opens where you can view the list of those comments imported.

FIGURE 8.13

Click Apply Custom Filters to Comments and click Continue to open the Filter Comments pane.

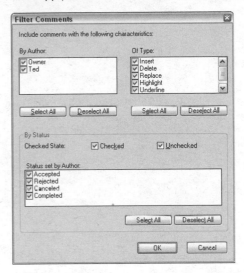

Once you complete importing comments, you can use the Reviewing toolbar tools to accept or reject comments. The comments are noted with callouts for easy recognition while reviewing the document in Word, as you can see in Figure 8.14.

NOTE If you select *Integrate Text Edits* then you "walk" through the document accepting or rejecting the text comments. The reviewing toolbar can be used for the non-Text Edits comments (like sticky notes, lines, clouds, and so on).

Working with custom page sizes

The most common page size and output for Word files is standard letter or A4 page sizes that are printed to desktop printers. On occasion, documents are created for output to commercial printing equipment. Manuals, reports, books, and more are sometimes designed for printing on commercial printing machines for offset press or on demand printing.

A few problems arise when Word files are created for this kind of output. The first problem is outputting documents using nonstandard page sizes. If you set up a document for a 7 × 9–inch page size for example, Word doesn't have a matching page size available in the print dialog box. As a result, you need to create a custom page size to format the document and print the custom formatted page size.

Second, files need to be printed with crop marks so the print shop knows where to cut the paper when it comes off press. As a word processor, Word is not designed for use as a page layout program. Professional layout programs such as Adobe InDesign have all the tools and features you need to print documents with crop marks and other attributes designed for output on commercial printing equipment.

FIGURE 8.14

After comments are imported into Word, use the Reviewing toolbar to accept or reject comments.

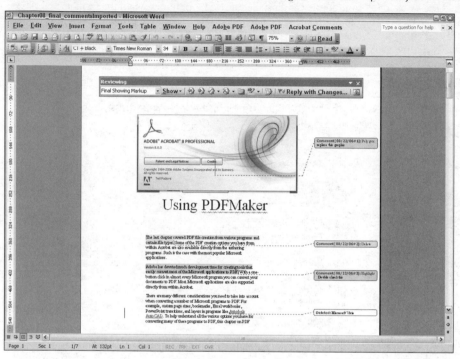

One solution is to take the Word document and import it into a program such as Adobe InDesign. But doing so requires a lot of work on your part. You have to reformat the document for a custom page size before you can print it. Fortunately, there's a much easier way. You can format the document in Word with a custom page size, export to PDF using PDFMaker, and use Acrobat to create the necessary crop marks and make the file print-ready.

The steps for setting up custom page sizes differ a little between Windows and the Macintosh. Let's first take a look at creating custom pages on Windows, and then I'll move on to creating custom page sizes on the Mac.

Creating custom page sizes on Windows

On Windows you have two different ways to configure Word for formatting and printing custom page sizes. You can use the Page Setup dialog box in Word to create a custom page size or you can add a custom page size to your printer driver. Adding a custom page size to the printer driver makes that page size available to all applications using the driver. Creating the custom page size in Word limits the page size to Word files.

For a more flexible use, create a custom page size in the Adobe PDF printer driver and you'll have the page size available for use with all applications. Here's how to do it.

STEPS: Creating custom page sizes in the print driver

1. **Open the Adobe PDF Properties.** From the Start menu select Settings ➪ Printers and Faxes. You should see icons for all printing devices installed on your computer when the Printers and Faxes window opens. Among the printer drivers, you'll find the Adobe PDF printer driver. Select this driver and either select File ➪ Properties in the Printers and Faxes window or right-click the Adobe PDF driver to open a context menu and select Properties as shown in Figure 8.15.

FIGURE 8.15

Open a context menu on the Adobe PDF Printer and select Properties.

2. The Adobe PDF Properties dialog box opens as shown in Figure 8.16. Note that the default tab selected in the Adobe PDF Properties dialog box is the General tab.

3. **Open the Printing Preferences.** In the Adobe PDF Properties dialog box, shown in Figure 8.15, click the Printing Preferences button. The Adobe Printing Preferences dialog box opens. In this dialog box, click Adobe PDF Settings, as shown in Figure 8.17.

4. **Add a new custom page size.** Click the Add button and the Add Custom Paper Size dialog box opens as shown in Figure 8.18.

FIGURE 8.16

The Adobe PDF Properties dialog box default view is the General tab.

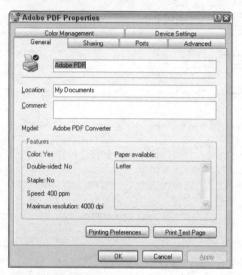

FIGURE 8.17

Click the Adobe PDF Settings tab in the Adobe PDF Printing Preferences dialog box.

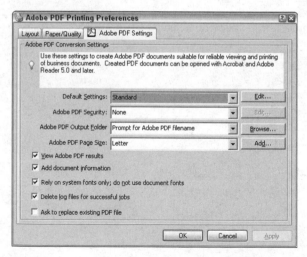

FIGURE 8.18

Click Add to open the Add Custom Paper Size dialog box.

5. **Edit the Custom Page Size.** Type the width and height values in the Width and Height text boxes and select the unit of measure from the three choices in the Unit section of the dialog box. Type a name for the custom paper size in the Paper Name text box. Use a name that defines the page size as you see in Figure 8.18.

6. **Save the new custom page size.** Click the Add/Modify button in the Add Custom Paper Size dialog box and you return to the Adobe PDF Printing Preferences dialog box. Click OK and your new custom page size is available each time you use the Adobe PDF printer driver.

7. **Set up a Word document with a custom page size.** Open Microsoft Word and open a file or create a new document. Select File ➪ Page Setup. In the Page Setup dialog box click Paper and from the Paper size pull-down menu select the custom page size you created, as shown in Figure 8.19. Your Word document will be reformatted for the new custom page size.

FIGURE 8.19

In Microsoft Word, choose File ➪ Page Setup and choose the new paper size in the Paper size pull-down menu.

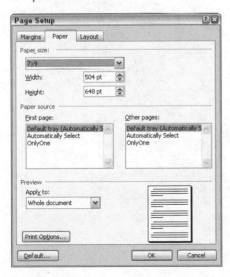

8. **Convert to Adobe PDF.** Click the Convert to Adobe PDF tool in the Word Toolbar Well. If you enabled View Adobe PDF result in the Acrobat PDFMaker Settings tab, the resulting PDF opens in Acrobat.

NOTE Creating custom page sizes is particularly important for programs such as Microsoft Visio, Microsoft Project, and AutoCAD where non-standard sizes are commonly used. Acrobat supports a page size of up to 200 inches square. Make certain you have the proper page size defined for the Adobe PDF printer before attempting to Convert to Adobe PDF.

Creating custom page sizes on the Macintosh

The process for creating custom page sizes on the Mac is much the same as on Windows, but the dialog boxes are a little different. For custom page size creation on the Mac, use the following steps.

STEPS: Creating custom page sizes on the Macintosh

1. **Open Microsoft Word.** You can create a custom page size on the Mac from within any program. Because we're talking about Word here, I'll use Word as my starting point with a document open in the Word window that I want to reformat for a custom page size.

2. **Open the Page Setup dialog box.** Select File ⇨ Page Setup to open the Page Setup dialog box. In the Page Setup dialog box select Adobe PDF 8.0 from the Format for pull-down menu. Open the Paper Size pull-down menu and select Manage Custom Sizes, as shown in Figure 8.20. Making the menu selection for Manage Custom Sizes automatically opens the Custom Page Sizes dialog box.

FIGURE 8.20

Format the page size for the Adobe PDF 8.0 printer driver and select Manage Custom Sizes from the Paper Size pull-down menu.

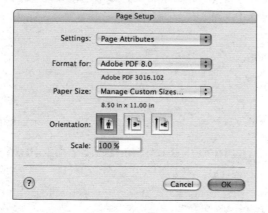

3. **Create a new custom page size.** Click the plus (+) symbol in the lower-left corner of the dialog box. Your new paper size is listed as Untitled. Double-click Untitled in the list to select the name, and type a descriptive name for your new page size. My preference is to use the paper sizes for names, as shown in Figure 8.21. Type the Width and Height values in the text boxes up in the top-right corner of the Custom Page Size dialog box.

FIGURE 8.21

Click the plus (+) symbol, type a name, and edit the Width and Height text boxes.

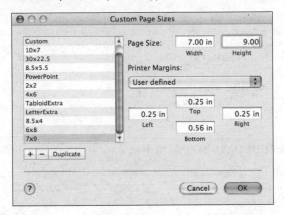

4. **Use a custom page size.** Click OK in the Custom Page Sizes dialog box and you return to the Page Setup dialog box. Select the Adobe PDF 8.0 printer and your new page size in the Paper Size pull-down menu. Your document is then reformatted for the custom page size.

5. **Export to PDF.** Click the Convert to Adobe PDF tool and your Word file is converted to PDF using the new custom page size.

CAUTION   If you begin with a document created on a standard letter page size or another page size and reformat the document to fit on another page size, you should review all document pages. As the document is reformatted you may find page breaks, headers and footers, tables, and other document elements needing some adjustments before converting to PDF.

Adding crop marks to PDFs

Regardless of whether your files are formatted for custom page sizes or standard page sizes, you need to add crop marks if your files are going to be printed on offset press or many on-demand printing devices. For some on-demand equipment such as Xerox DocuTechs and other devices that print on single sheet standard page sizes, you won't need to add crop marks.

When crop marks are needed for printing your files, follow these steps to add crop marks in Acrobat.

STEPS: Adding crop marks to PDF documents (Acrobat Professional Only)

1. **Open a document in Acrobat Professional.** For these steps you need Acrobat Professional. Acrobat Standard does not have a Print Production toolbar.

2. **Open the Print Production toolbar.** Open a context menu on the Acrobat Toolbar Well and select Print Production to open the Print Production toolbar. The Printer's Marks tool and the Crop tool shown in Figure 8.22 are needed to add printer's marks to your document.

FIGURE 8.22

Open the Print Production toolbar from a context menu opened on the Toolbar Well.

3. **Add Printer's Marks.** Click the Add Printer's Marks tool in the Print Production toolbar and the Add Printer's Marks dialog box opens. You can selectively add the type of marks you want to appear on your document by checking the various marks check boxes. In this example, I click the All Marks check box and all printer's marks are added to the file. For the Page Range, leave the default All selection checked if you want all pages to appear with the printer's marks as shown in Figure 8.23.

FIGURE 8.23

Check the boxes for the marks you want to appear on the PDF document and select the page range.

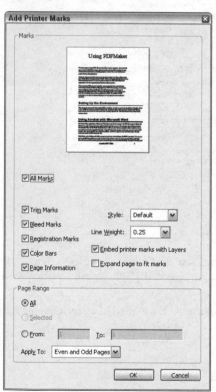

4. **Crop the pages.** When you click OK in the Add Printer Marks dialog box, you won't see any changes in your document — that's because the printer marks exist outside the page dimensions. You need to enlarge the pages so the crop marks are visible. To make the document pages appear larger, click the Crop Pages tool in the Print Production toolbar and the Crop Pages dialog box opens, as shown in Figure 8.24.

Click the Custom radio button and type a width and height larger than the page sizes. As a standard page size to accommodate crop marks, add 1 inch to the page width and height. In my example, my document is 7 × 9 inches. Therefore I added 8 inches for the width and 10 inches for the height. Over in the Page Range area of the Crop Pages dialog box, click All to apply your marks to all pages.

FIGURE 8.24

Click Custom and type the new dimensions for width and height. Click All to apply marks to all pages.

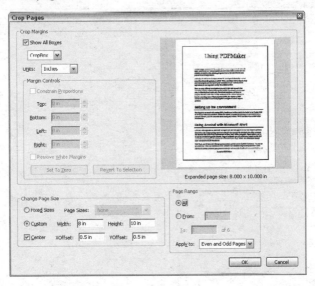

5. **Preview the PDF document.** Click OK in the Crop Pages dialog box and the printer's marks appear on all pages in the document. In Figure 8.25, the printer's marks are shown on the first page in my document.

CROSS-REF   For more information on using the Print Production tools, see Chapter 32.

FIGURE 8.25

Click OK in the Crop Pages dialog box and the printer's marks appear on pages in your PDF.

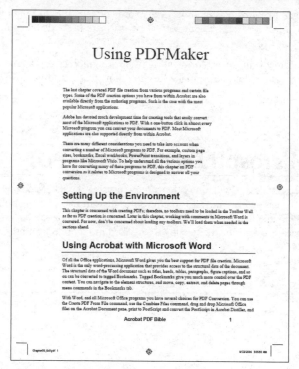

Using graphics in Word

Microsoft Word is first and foremost a word processing program. Inasmuch as many features have been added to the program to take it well beyond simple word processing, the program is not designed to be a layout program. Word lacks support for many features you find with layout programs such as supporting color management, printing color separations, controlling halftone frequency, and more.

CROSS-REF   For more information on terms used in commercial printing such as color profiling, color separations, and half toning, see Chapter 32.

As a matter of practice you should avoid creating files for press, and in particular for color separations, in Word. If it's an absolute must that you need to use Word for commercial printing, then you need to be aware of some things to avoid. These items include the following:

- **Use RGB images.** Be certain to not use Indexed color images in your Word files. Make certain all your images are edited and saved in an RGB color space and let the RGB to CMYK conversion take place at the time the files are printed.

- **Use TIFF format for raster images.** Avoid using GIF, JPG, PNG, PCX, PICT, BMP, and other file formats. Use only TIFF as the format to import photos and raster images.

■ **Use EPS for vector objects.** Again avoid using any other formats for vector objects and use only EPS for these graphics. Do not use the clip art you can import in Word. Create vector objects in a program such as Adobe Illustrator and save as EPS.

■ **Do not paste images in Word.** Pasting images in Word converts files to Windows Metafile (Window) or PICT (Macintosh). These file formats won't print properly on commercial printing equipment.

Again, I would caution you against using Word for printing files with graphics on commercial printing equipment. When you have no other alternative, make sure to follow the preceding tips.

CROSS-REF For more information on graphic file formats and commercial printing, see Chapters 7 and 32.

Converting Microsoft Excel Files to PDF

When converting Microsoft Excel files, as with any other program using the PDFMaker, you'll want to visit the Adobe PDF menu. As is the case with Word, this menu is installed in Excel when you install Acrobat. When you open the Adobe PDF menu and compare the menu choices with the same menu opened in Word, you see a few differences between the menu shown for Word in Figure 8.1 and the menu for Excel shown in Figure 8.26.

FIGURE 8.26

The Adobe PDF menu as shown in Microsoft Excel

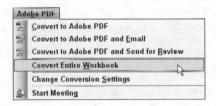

Notice the Mail Merge to Adobe PDF is unique to Word and doesn't appear in the Excel menu. In Excel you have an additional command for converting an entire workbook. Excel documents can have a single worksheet or many worksheets in a workbook. If you select the Convert Entire Workbook command, all worksheets in a workbook are converted to PDF.

Open the Acrobat PDFMaker dialog box by selecting Adobe PDF ➪ Change Conversion Settings. The Acrobat PDFMaker dialog box opens, as shown in Figure 8.27.

Compare Figure 8.27 with the Acrobat PDFMaker dialog box opened in Word in Figure 8.4. All the settings are identical in the Excel Acrobat PDFMaker dialog box as the same dialog box opened from Word with the exception of the last three items:

■ **Convert comments to notes.** Check this box when you want Excel comments converted to comment notes in the resultant PDF file.

■ **Fit worksheet to a single page.** Check this box to avoid tiling individual worksheet pages.

■ **Prompt for selecting Excel Sheets.** Check this box to individually select worksheets in a workbook you want converted to PDF.

FIGURE 8.27

Select Adobe PDF ⇨ Change Conversion Settings to open the Acrobat PDFMaker dialog box.

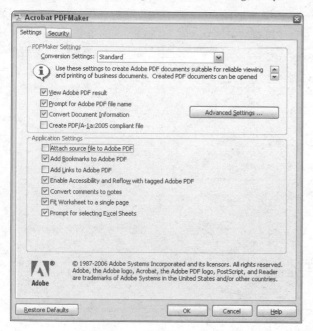

To understand a little more about converting Excel workbooks to PDF, follow these steps.

STEPS: Converting an Excel workbook to PDF

1. **Open an Excel workbook.** Try to use an Excel file having several worksheets in a workbook.

2. **Change conversion settings.** From the Adobe PDF menu, select Change Conversion Settings. In the Change Conversion Settings dialog box select the check boxes for Add Bookmarks to Adobe PDF and Prompt for selecting Excel Sheets. You can additionally make other choices such as Fit Worksheet to a single page if you like.

3. **Convert to PDF.** Click the Convert to Adobe PDF tool or select Adobe PDF ⇨ Convert to Adobe PDF.

4. **Select worksheets.** As soon as you make a choice to convert to PDF, a second Acrobat PDFMaker dialog box opens. Because you selected Prompt for selecting Excel Sheets in the first Acrobat PDFMaker dialog box, Acrobat prompts you to select the worksheets you want to convert to PDF.

   Click the Add All Sheets button if you want all sheets converted to PDF or individually select the sheets you want to convert and click the Add Sheets button. In my example I want to convert the first 5M sheet, the second 5M sheet, and the fourth 5M sheet you see listed in Figure 8.28. After making your selection(s), click the Convert to PDF button and your worksheet(s) is converted to PDF.

5. **View the PDF.** If you elected to view the PDF after conversion by selecting the View Adobe PDF result check box in the Acrobat PDFMaker dialog box, your file opens automatically in Acrobat. If you didn't check the box, open Acrobat and click the Open tool to locate and open your converted document. Click the Bookmarks panel and you should see bookmarks added for each worksheet in the converted workbook, as shown in Figure 8.29.

FIGURE 8.28

Select the sheets you want to convert and click the Add Sheets button.

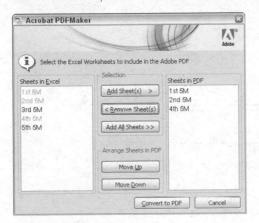

FIGURE 8.29

Click the Bookmarks panel and you'll find bookmarks associated with each worksheet in the converted workbook.

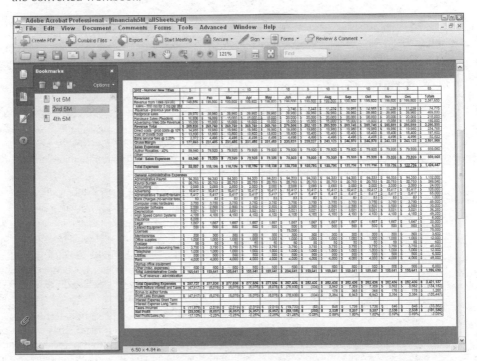

Converting Microsoft PowerPoint Files to PDF

When converting PowerPoint files to PDF, you won't find any special commands specific to PowerPoint in the Adobe PDF menu. However, PowerPoint Conversion Settings offer many more options than you find with either Word or Excel. To open the Adobe PDFMaker dialog box select Adobe PDF ➪ Change Conversion Settings. When the Acrobat PDFMaker dialog box opens you see six new items in the Applications settings that don't appear in the Word or Excel Acrobat PDFMaker dialog box.

The items shown in Figure 8.30 include the following:

- **Convert Multimedia to PDF Multimedia.** Imported media such as sound and video in PowerPoint files can be converted to PDF media.

- **Save Animations in Adobe PDF.** If you include animations such as moving text and objects in a PowerPoint presentation and you want the animations to appear in the resultant PDF document, check this box.

- **Save slide Transitions in Adobe PDF.** Slide transitions can be saved in the PDF file and viewed when you view the PDF in Full Screen mode in an Acrobat viewer.

- **Convert hidden slides to PDF.** Check this box if you have hidden slides in PowerPoint and you want the hidden slides to appear as pages in the resultant PDF.

- **Convert Speaker notes to Text notes in Adobe PDF.** Speaker notes are converted to PDF when you check this box.

- **PDF layout based on PowerPoint printer settings.** If you want the PDF page sizes to match the print settings in PowerPoint, check this box.

There are a number of options and reasons why you might want to convert PowerPoint slides to a PDF slide presentation. All you want to know about converting PowerPoint slides to PDF and viewing them in Acrobat is covered in a separate chapter later in the book where I talk about PDFs and presentations.

 **For more on PowerPoint conversions to PDF, see Chapter 28.**

Select Adobe PDF ⇨ Change Conversion Settings in PowerPoint to open the Acrobat PDFMaker dialog box.

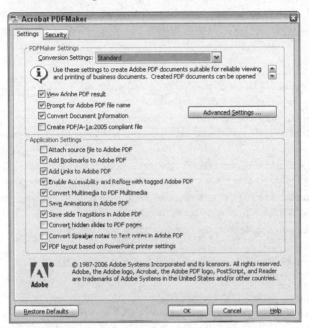

Converting Microsoft Publisher Files

Microsoft Publisher is Microsoft's effort at developing a more commercial and professional program designed for prepress and printing. Print shops and service bureaus shied away from Publisher in earlier versions for lack of essential tools such as adding printer's marks, color separation tools, and changing halftone frequency. However, Microsoft continued development of the product and the latest version of Publisher includes all the features needed for prepress and commercial printing.

When it comes to exports to PDF, Adobe supports some of the much needed file attributes required to print files on press. When you open the Acrobat PDFMaker from the Adobe PDF menu in Microsoft Publisher, the Acrobat PDFMaker dialog box displays some settings choices not found in any of the other Acrobat PDFMaker dialog boxes, as shown in Figure 8.31.

NOTE   When you first launch Microsoft Publisher after installing Acrobat, you are prompted in a dialog box for enabling macros. Because the Acrobat PDFMaker is a macro, you need to grant permissions for using the macro or you won't see the Adobe PDF menu or the Acrobat conversion tools.

FIGURE 8.31

The Acrobat PDFMaker opened from Microsoft Publisher

As shown in Figure 8.31 you have some unique settings that apply only to Microsoft Publisher. These settings include the following:

- **Conversion Settings.** The default Adobe PDF Setting is Press Quality. Like the other Acrobat PDFMaker dialog boxes, you can change the setting by clicking the Advanced Settings button.

- **Preserve Spot Color in Adobe PDF.** If spot colors are used in the Publisher file, you need to check this box to preserve the spot colors. If you fail to do so, spot colors are converted to CMYK.

- **Print Crop Marks.** As you can see by comparing this Acrobat PDFMaker dialog box with the others shown for Word, Excel, and PowerPoint, you see the first option for adding crop marks when a file is converted to PDF. This setting is very important if you have bleeds on pages in the Publisher document.

- **Allow Bleeds.** If bleeds are contained in the PowerPoint file, you must check the box to allow bleeds. When the box is checked, you have another setting to print separate bleed marks.

- **Preserve Transparency in Adobe PDF.** You can check the box to preserve transparency and let Acrobat flatten the transparency at print time.

The features added to the PowerPoint Acrobat PDFMaker are all related to commercial printing.

CROSS-REF   For more information on commercial printing and transparency flattening, see Chapter 32.

Microsoft Visio and PDF Creation

Engineers, technical professionals, and architects are among the many users of programs such as Microsoft Project, Microsoft Visio, and Autodesk AutoCAD. Each of these programs has an Acrobat PDFMaker to produce PDF documents. Inasmuch as you can either print PostScript or save as EPS from one or the other and distill the files in Acrobat Distiller, using PDFMaker is a much better choice.

AutoCAD and Visio offer options for converting the AutoCAD and Visio layers to PDF layers. It is critical to be certain that the Acrobat PDF Settings are enabled for converting layers with either program.

Like all the other Microsoft programs, Microsoft Visio has an Acrobat PDFMaker set of tools and menu commands. When you open the Adobe PDF menu, you see a single addition for Visio appearing as Convert all Pages in Drawing. Selecting this menu command converts all pages in the Visio file to PDF.

Additionally you have a Change Conversion Settings option in Visio like the other Microsoft programs. Select Adobe PDF ⇨ Change Conversion Settings and the Acrobat PDFMaker dialog box shown in Figure 8.32 opens.

FIGURE 8.32

The Acrobat PDFMaker opened in Microsoft Visio

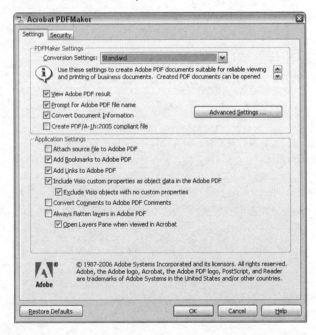

The settings unique to Visio are as follows:

- **Include Visio custom properties as object data in the Adobe PDF.** Programs such as Visio and AutoCAD support adding asset information on all the objects added to drawings. The metadata are hidden from view in the drawing itself. When the PDF is produced the object data are not visible in Acrobat in the document pane. However, a special tool known as the Object Data tool in Acrobat and the free Adobe Reader lets you view, search, count, select, and copy metadata. In

Acrobat you can also export the metadata as XML. Check this box if you want to use the Object Data tool in Acrobat to work with the metadata.

CROSS-REF For more on using the Object Data tool, see "Working with Object Data Tool" later in this chapter.

- **Convert comments to Adobe PDF Comments.** Comments added to a Visio file can be converted to Adobe PDF Comments.

- **Always flatten layers in Adobe PDF.** Microsoft Visio supports layers. If you want to retain layers in the resultant PDF, be certain to keep this check box unselected. You can keep the check box unselected as a default and when the need arises to flatten layers, you can handle layer flattening in Acrobat.

CROSS-REF For more on working with Adobe PDF layers, see Chapter 24.

- **Open Layers Pane when viewed in Acrobat.** If layers are created in the PDF, checking this box sets the Initial View in Acrobat to view Layers panel and Page where the Layers panel is opened when the PDF is opened in Acrobat.

CROSS-REF For more on setting Initial Views, see Chapter 5.

Notice that the default Conversion Settings in Figure 8.32 uses the Standard Adobe PDF setting. This setting is Acrobat 5–compatible. Acrobat 5–compatible PDFs do not support layers. In earlier versions of Acrobat you had to edit the conversion settings in the Acrobat PDFMaker dialog box and be certain you selected Acrobat 6 or greater compatibility. Failure to do so flattened layers in the resultant PDF. In Acrobat 8, you don't have to worry about changing your Adobe PDF Settings to Acrobat 6 or greater compatibility. When you click the Convert to Adobe PDF tool in Visio or select Adobe PDF ➪ Convert to Adobe PDF, you are presented first with a dialog box asking you if you want to Include Custom Properties. Click Continue and you proceed to an advanced Acrobat PDFMaker dialog box, as shown in Figure 8.33. Click the Retain all layers radio button and the file is created with the Visio layers converted to Adobe PDF layers.

FIGURE 8.33

When retaining layers in Visio files, click the Retain all layers radio button while converting to PDF.

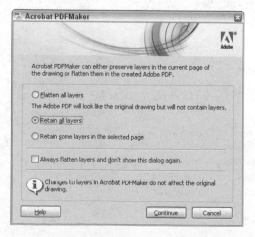

You may wonder whether Acrobat automatically changes the Acrobat Compatibility to 6.0 or above on the fly as the PDF is created. Miraculously, Acrobat actually creates an Acrobat 5–compatible file with layers intact. Although Acrobat 5 compatibility does not support Adobe PDF layers, the layers are indeed retained in the Acrobat 5–compatible file.

After converting a Visio document to PDF with layers, the file opens with the layers pane in view, as you see in Figure 8.34.

FIGURE 8.34

A Visio file converted to PDF with Adobe PDF layers

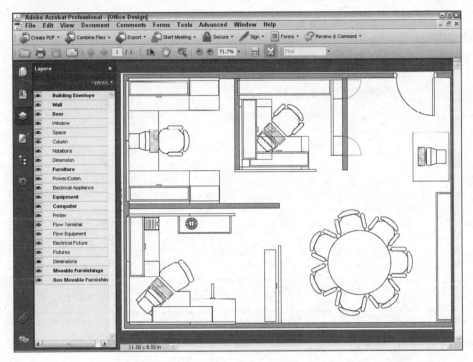

Working with object data

Engineering and scientific programs often enable you to describe objects in drawings that result in object data that can be added to the metadata in a PDF document. When using Acrobat PDFMaker you can view certain metadata in the resultant PDF file.

To view the data, open the Object Data tool from a context menu opened on the Acrobat Toolbar Well. Move to an object and click. The navigation pane opens to show the Model Tree, as shown in Figure 8.35. From the Options menu, you have a number of menu commands related to working with Object data.

FIGURE 8.35

Click an object and the Navigation pane opens showing assets identified in a drawing.

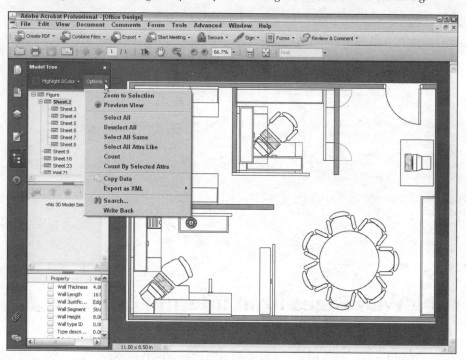

Objects in Visio are assigned custom properties for associating costs and comments with each milestone in a project. These data elements are added to the individual objects' metadata. As shown in the Options menu you have a number of commands available for copying data, selecting items, zooming views, counting objects, selecting similar objects, and so forth.

One command that can help you find assets in a drawing is the Search command. Select Search from either a context menu opened on the drawing or from the Model Tree panel and the Search pane opens. Type the object you want to search for and click the Search button. In Figure 8.36 I searched for Wall in my drawing. The results of my search are shown in the Results area in the Search pane.

As you can see in Figure 8.36, all Wall assets are identified with certain specifications all included as metadata in my drawing. This kind of information can be helpful for engineers and architects when analyzing drawings and determining costs, compliance with building codes, and so on.

FIGURE 8.36

Use the Search command for searching assets in a drawing.

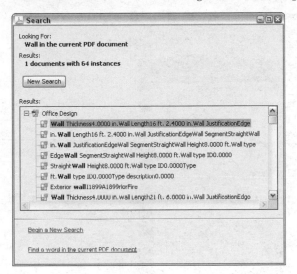

Converting Web Pages from Internet Explorer to PDF (Windows Only)

In Chapter 7, I talked about PDF conversion using the Create PDF From Web Page command. In Chapter 27 I talk about PDFs and the Web. But because this chapter is focused on using the Acrobat PDFMaker tool, I thought it best to talk about the Acrobat PDFMaker and Microsoft Internet Explorer here in Chapter 8.

If you're working in an Acrobat session and you want to convert one or more pages to PDF, it makes sense to use the Create PDF From Web Page command. You don't need to launch a Web browser and open a page you want to convert to PDF. You can do all that within Acrobat.

So why does Adobe supply yet another tool for Web page conversion to PDF? Because sometimes you browse the Internet and find a page you want to convert to PDF. Because you're already in a Web browser it makes sense to convert a Web page from the browser versus launching Acrobat and typing a URL in the Create PDF From Web Page dialog box.

As an example, let me share with you one Web page conversion I use routinely. When I book my airline tickets online, the ticket provider displays an itinerary showing my flight number, travel times, and travel dates. Of course the provider displays a print ready Web page that I can send off to my printer, but I'm prone to losing things and printing paper is a surefire target for a lost item in my travel bag.

As an alternative to printing Web pages, I just do a quick conversion to PDF and copy my PDF to the laptop I carry to conferences and as a backup to a flash drive. When I'm in a hotel, I just open the PDF to check on my departure when I finish up my travels.

You may find many other uses for converting Web pages to PDF. Perhaps a map to a location, a latest recipe you saw on Emeril's show, some research information you're collecting, a new product description you want to study, or many other similar uses. Personally, I find it much easier to locate a PDF file on my computer than that last piece of paper I printed to my desktop printer.

If you use Microsoft Internet Explorer on Windows, then you have the Acrobat PDFMaker installed in Explorer. Unlike all the other PDFMakers discussed thus far, the PDFMaker in Explorer doesn't support any changes to the conversion settings. However you do have a change in the menu options. In Explorer you can click the pull-down menu adjacent to the Convert Web Page to PDF tool in the Explorer toolbar to open the Adobe PDF menu and view the menu options, as shown in Figure 8.37. Notice in the menu you have a command for Adobe PDF Explorer and Preferences. Click the Adobe PDF Explorer Bar menu item and the left pane in the Internet Explorer window opens where you can view your hard drive, network server, and all media attached to your drive.

FIGURE 8.37

Select Adobe PDF Explorer Bar from the Adobe PDF pull-down menu adjacent to the Convert Web Page to PDF tool and the left pane opens showing your hard drive, any mounted servers, and all media attached to your computer.

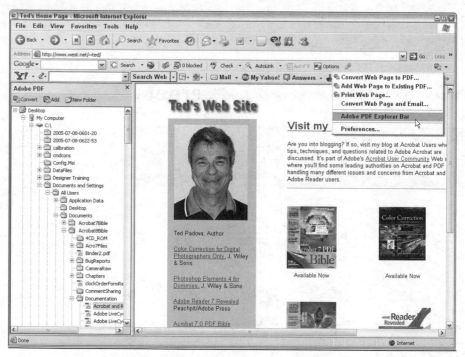

You can navigate folders and double-click a PDF document to open it in Explorer.

If you select Preferences, the Adobe PDF Preferences dialog box shown in Figure 8.38 opens. The four items in the Preferences dialog box should be self-explanatory.

Select Preferences in the Adobe PDF pull-down menu to open the Adobe PDF Preferences dialog box. By default all four items are checked.

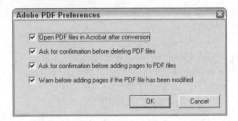

To convert a Web page to PDF, open a Web page in Internet Explorer and click the Convert Web Page to PDF tool. After conversion, the Web page opens in Acrobat. Notice that pages converted with Internet Explorer also include structured bookmarks like pages converted with the Create PDF From Web Page tool. If you open a context menu on a structured bookmark, you'll see the same menu options as you find with Web pages converted with the Create PDF From Web Page tool. Pages converted to PDF from Internet Explorer can also have additional pages appended to the converted file by selecting Append Next Level in a context menu, as shown in Figure 8.39.

Creating PDFs from the Acrobat PDFMaker in Internet Explorer produces structured bookmarks and menu options the same as when using the Create PDF From Web Page tool.

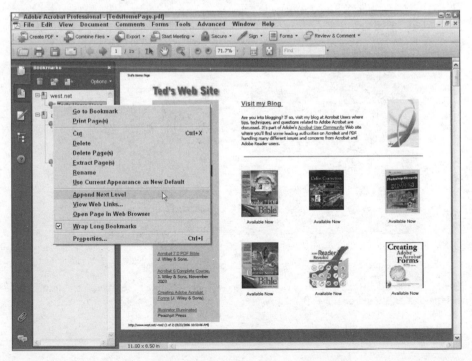

CROSS-REF For more information on structured bookmarks and options for appending Web pages, see Chapter 7.

TIP Macintosh users may feel a little left out when converting Web pages to PDF from within programs such as Apple's Safari. No PDFMaker exists on the Mac for Safari or Microsoft Internet Explorer. However, the Mac user can still create PDF documents from any Web browser. Just open a Web page and select File ➪ Print. In the Print dialog box click the PDF button to open a pull-down menu and select Save as PDF. Your Web page is converted to PDF when you save the file. You don't have an option for appending Web pages as the Windows users have when using the PDFMaker, but you can always use either the Create PDF From Web Page tool or navigate to other Web pages and print them to PDF.

Converting Microsoft Outlook E-mails to PDF

Whereas the Acrobat PDFMaker in Microsoft Internet Explorer may appear stale and without many new features or any kind of special menu commands, the Acrobat PDFMaker in Microsoft Outlook is a major development in Acrobat 8 and supports many unique features for PDF conversion.

Just click the Adobe PDF menu and look over the menu commands you find in Microsoft Outlook's Acrobat PDFMaker, as shown in Figure 8.40.

FIGURE 8.40

Click Adobe PDF to open the Adobe PDF Menu in Microsoft Outlook.

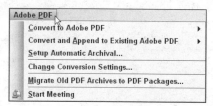

With the exception of Start Meeting all the commands in the Outlook Adobe PDF menu differ from all the other PDFMakers. The menu choices are as follows:

- **Convert to Adobe PDF.** Select this menu item and a submenu opens with two other menu choices. The first menu choice in the submenu is Selected Messages. You can select multiple messages for PDF conversion. When you convert the mail messages to PDF, the messages are combined into a PDF Package.

  The second menu choice is Selected Folders. Choose this item and the Convert folder(s) to PDF dialog box opens, as shown in Figure 8.41. The dialog box lists all your mail folders. You can select any of the folders where you want to convert the folder contents to PDF.

  But wait! There's more! Both these menu options are truly great new features in Acrobat 8. Selecting either submenu command creates a PDF Package of your selected files or your folder files. During the creation process a search index file is created and embedded in the PDF Package. Not only are the mail messages converted to PDF, but you can also preserve file attachments, package files with digital signatures, package file attachments protected with Acrobat Security, and package Adobe LiveCycle Designer XML forms attachments. Note that although you can add secure PDF files to a PDF Package you need a password to open all files that protect the file from opening with a password.

FIGURE 8.41

Select the mail folders for which you want to convert the contents to PDF.

When your PDF Package is created and you open the package in Acrobat, you see a view similar to Figure 8.42. Figure 8.42 shows the package contents listed at the top of the document pane. Click any one of the titles at the top of the list and your mails are sorted on the item you select. For example, clicking on Subject sorts your mails in alpha order according to subject. Click From and the sort changes to an alpha order according to those who sent you the mails.

CROSS-REF For much more thorough information on PDF Packages, see Chapter 12.

Not to be forgotten in the packages created from Outlook's Acrobat PDFMaker is the embedded index file produced with each package. When you open the Search pane and search while viewing any file in the package, your search is performed on the embedded index file. Searches are faster using the index file over searching documents, folders and using the Find toolbar.

CROSS-REF For a more information on embedded indexes and using Acrobat Search, see Chapter 6.

■ **Convert and Append to existing PDF.** If after creating a PDF Package you want to append files you later receive as new mails, select either Selected File or Selected Folders to append files or folder contents.

FIGURE 8.42

The PDF Package is viewed with the package contents listed at the top of the Document pane.

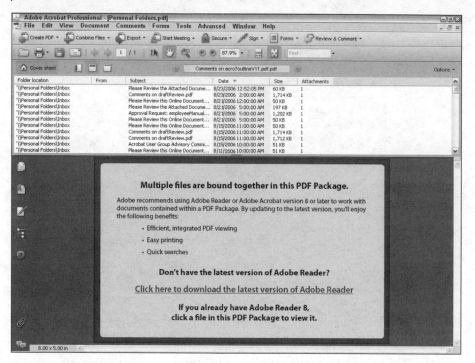

- **Set up automatic archival.** Another great new feature in Acrobat 8 and PDF packaging is the option for automatically archiving files. Select this menu command and the Acrobat PDFMaker dialog box opens with the Automatic Archival tab selected, as shown in Figure 8.43. In this dialog box you can specify the interval you want for your file archives, setting up a log file that records all the archive activity, embedding an index file, choose the folders you want to archive, and choose the host file you want to append your new documents to.

- **Change Conversion Settings.** Like the other PDFMakers, the Change Conversion Settings command opens the Acrobat PDFMaker dialog box. In addition to a few features you have with other PDFMakers, an option for including file attachments is provided as is a page layout area where you can define page sizes and margins, as shown in Figure 8.44. Notice the tab for Automatic Archival can also be selected from the Change Conversion Settings menu command and clicking the Automatic Archival tab.

FIGURE 8.43

Automatic Archival creates PDF Packages automatically at time intervals you specify.

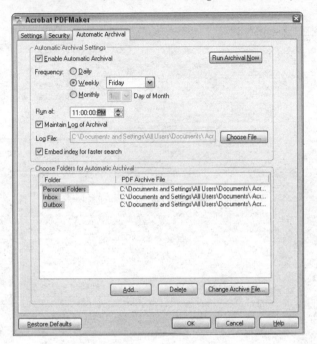

- **Migrate Old PDF Archives to PDF Packages.** If you created PDFs in Acrobat version 7 from the Outlook PDFMaker, you can migrate those older PDF documents into the newer PDF Package format. In PDF Archives crated with Acrobat 7 is was difficult to determine which attachments went with which e-mail. This new feature in Acrobat 8 makes your archives easier to work with.

In Chapter 7 you first saw support for the PDFMaker with Autodesk AutoCAD. In this chapter I covered many of the popular Microsoft programs that support the PDFMaker. But PDFMaker is not limited to these programs. If you use Microsoft Project, Microsoft Access, Lotus Notes, and some other applications, you find the PDFMaker available for use. The process is very much the same in all programs. Take a look at the Adobe PDF menu and select options for either Change Conversion Settings or Preferences to adjust settings for your PDF creation. In most cases the menu commands and settings adjustments are straightforward and intuitive.

FIGURE 8.44

Select Change Conversion Settings to open the Acrobat PDFMaker dialog box.

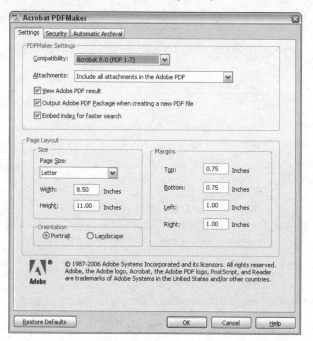

Summary

- Microsoft Office applications such as Word, Excel, and PowerPoint export directly to PDF with the assistance of PDFMaker. Office applications retain document structure and convert structured elements to Bookmarks and links in exported PDFs when Acrobat PDFMaker is used.

- Custom page sizes can be added to the Adobe PDF printer driver on both Windows and Macintosh.

- Printer marks and crop marks can be added with the Print Production tools to PDF files.

- The Microsoft Publisher PDFMaker supports some features used for commercial printing.

- Microsoft Visio files can be exported with Adobe PDF layers using the PDFMaker in Visio.

- Object Data contained in programs supporting the inclusion of certain metadata can be viewed using the Object Data tool.

- Microsoft Internet Explorer supports PDF creating with the PDFMaker very similar to PDFs produced with Create PDF From Web Page.

- Microsoft Outlook files can be converted to PDF and assembled in PDF Packages using the PDFMaker in Outlook.

Chapter 9

Exporting to PDF from Authoring Applications

Chapter 7 covered PDF creation from all the supported file formats contained in the Convert to PDF preferences. In Chapter 8 you learned about using the PDFMaker with Microsoft programs. Other PDF creation tools exist with programs such as QuarkXPress, CorelDraw, and Lotus Notes, and the list of programs supporting PDF creation continues to grow.

Where PDF exports from host applications are best is with Adobe's own Creative Suite applications. Many of the Adobe CS programs were created from the ground up using core PDF technology.

This chapter deals with PDF exports from the Creative Suite programs. Some options you find with exports to PDF in Adobe Programs are supported in other applications, but none have as comprehensive set of PDF export choices as do the Adobe programs. If you're a user of any one of the Creative Suite applications, then this chapter is for you.

IN THIS CHAPTER

Working with Adobe Creative Suite

Doing direct exports to PDF from design applications

Using Acrobat with engineering programs

Setting Up the Environment

This chapter is concerned with creating PDFs; therefore, no toolbars need to be loaded in the Toolbar Well. You can leave your toolbars in Acrobat set to the default view to follow what's covered in this chapter.

Working with Acrobat and the Adobe Creative Suite

The Adobe Creative Suite 2 (CS2) comes in two flavors. The Creative Suite Standard edition includes Adobe Illustrator CS, Adobe InDesign CS, Adobe Photoshop CS, and Adobe Version Cue. The Adobe Creative Suite Premium edition includes these four programs and adds Adobe GoLive, Adobe Dreamweaver,

and Adobe Acrobat. All the CS and CS2 applications support PDF documents with direct exports and imports. For the remainder of this chapter I'll refer to the CS and CS2 applications simply as the Creative Suite or CS programs. As of this writing the current version is CS2.3.

Acrobat and Adobe Photoshop

Adobe Photoshop CS supports creating and importing PDFs. When you create a PDF, you use the Save As command and save, and like all CS applications in the CS2 versions, the exports use Acrobat Distiller and Adobe PDF Settings to convert to PDF. When you import PDF documents that were not originally created in Photoshop, the files are rasterized. The process of rasterizing files converts all objects, such as type and vector objects, to raster images (pixels).

Saving to PDF from Photoshop

Creating a PDF file from Photoshop is nothing more than choosing the Photoshop PDF format from the Save dialog box. Photoshop supports many different file formats for opening and saving documents. In versions prior to Photoshop 6.0, you had to flatten all layers before you could save a document as a PDF file. In versions 6.0 and later, you can preserve layers and vector art. When you save a layered file from Photoshop CS as a Photoshop PDF and open it again in Photoshop, all layers are retained. Type and vector art work the same way. You can create type without rasterizing it and save the file as a PDF. Later, if you want to edit the file, you can reopen it and edit the type. What's more, you can search and edit the type in Acrobat when you save the file as PDF from Photoshop.

CAUTION   Flattening layers in Photoshop *always* rasterizes vector art and type. If you want to preserve vector art and type, you need to save the layered file as a Photoshop PDF document.

To save a multilayered Photoshop image, Photoshop document, or flattened image, you use the Save As command. In Photoshop CS, choose File ➪ Save As. The Save As PDF dialog box opens. This dialog box is the same when saving from all other CS applications. If you're familiar with Acrobat Distiller, the Save Adobe PDF dialog box and the various panes contained within appear similar to the tabs in Acrobat Distiller.

When saving as Photoshop PDF, the first pane in the Save Adobe PDF dialog box is the General settings, as shown in Figure 9.1. Options choices you make in the Save Adobe PDF dialog box include:

- **Adobe PDF Preset.** All the presets you create in Distiller are available from the pull-down menu. Any new presets created in Distiller are immediately made available to all CS programs.

- **Standard.** From the Standard pull-down menu you can select from the PDF/X subsets. PDF/A support is provided from the Adobe PDF Preset pull-down menu but not additional subsets are available from the Standard pull-down menu other than the PDF/X options.

- **Compatibility.** Acrobat compatibility choices are available from the Compatibility pull-down menu. You find compatibility choices dating back to Acrobat 4 compatibility with all subsequent compatibility choices up to the current version when Acrobat was last upgraded. Because Acrobat's development cycle usually is ahead of the CS programs, you find the most recent Acrobat compatibility choice for Acrobat not available until you see the next upgrade of the Creative Suite that follows the most recent upgrade to Acrobat.

- **Description.** This area in the General pane is a text description of the compatibility option you choose.

- **Preserve Photoshop Editing Capabilities.** If you choose to uncheck the Preserve Photoshop Editing Capabilities and later open the PDF in Photoshop, the file is rasterized and all layers are

flattened. Preserving Photoshop Editing Capabilities preserves layers and type. The type can be searched in Acrobat. If you don't need to preserve type and vector objects, remove the check mark and flatten the file. Flattened images result in smaller file sizes.

CROSS-REF For more on opening and rasterizing files in Photoshop, see the section "Acquiring PDF files in Photoshop" later in this chapter.

- **Embed Page Thumbnails.** As a general rule be certain to leave this option off. If for some reason you need to create page thumbnails, do it in Acrobat.

- **Optimize for Fast Web View.** Keep this option checked to optimize files. When downloading off the Web, files are downloaded much faster.

- **View PDF After Saving.** Checking this option launches your default Acrobat viewer and opens the file in Acrobat.

FIGURE 9.1

To export directly to PDF, use the Save or Save As dialog box in Photoshop. As with all other CS applications, the Save Adobe PDF dialog box opens.

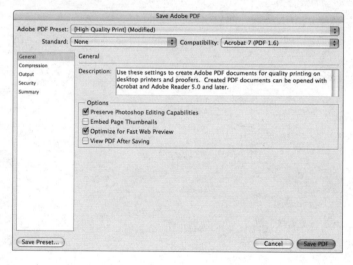

Click Compression in the left pane to open the compression choices. The options shown in Figure 9.2 include:

- **Compression.** In the Options area, leave Bicubic Downsampling To at the default. This option is likely to be the best choice for just about all your images. The two text boxes enable you to down-sample images. For Photoshop files you're best off changing resolution before you come to the save options. Leave these two text boxes at the defaults and use the Image ⇨ Image Size command in Photoshop to make resolution changes.

  Your choices include None, JPEG, JPEG2000, and ZIP. None adds no compression to the file. JPEG is a lossy compression scheme offering various levels of compression that you choose from the Image Quality pull-down menu. JPEG2000 requires Acrobat 6 compatibility or greater. Compression is greater with JPEG2000 than with JPEG. This compression scheme works with

transparent layers and alpha channels. ZIP compression is lossless. Files are not compressed as much as with JPEG, but the data integrity is optimal. ZIP compression is usually preferred for images with large amounts of a single color.

Convert 16 Bits/Channel Image to 8 Bits/Channel. Sixteen-bit images, such as those created with 16- or more bit scanners or digital cameras supporting Camera Raw and 16-bit, cannot be converted to PDF using the Create PDF ➪ From File command. Sixteen-bit images, however, can be saved from Photoshop as Photoshop PDFs and opened in Acrobat. To preserve 16-bit images, save with Acrobat 5 compatibility or later.

Tile Size. You're not likely to use Tile size because Acrobat supports document sizes up to 200-square inches and you can tile pages when printing PDF files from Acrobat. The option for tiling exists, but it's not something you'll find useful.

FIGURE 9.2

Click Compression to advance to the next pane in the Save Adobe PDF dialog box.

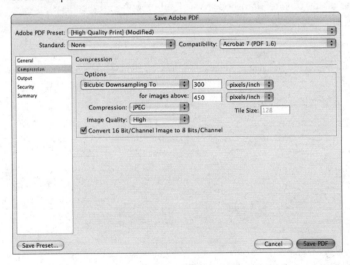

Click Output in the left pane and your choices appear, as shown in Figure 9.3.

You can handle color conversion and intent profiles here in the Save Adobe PDF dialog box, but you're most likely to handle these choices in your printer driver or layout program. The bottom half of the pane is only accessible if you select one of the PDF/X options in the Standards pull-down menu.

CROSS-REF For more on color handling and profile conversion, see Chapter 31. For more on PDF/X, see Chapters 10 and 32.

Click Security and the Security options are displayed. If you want security, click the check boxes and make choices for the security permissions you want to restrict.

The last pane displays a summary of the settings you chose to use to export to PDF. Click Save PDF and the file is saved as a Photoshop PDF file.

FIGURE 9.3

Output options offer choices for color profiling and color conversion.

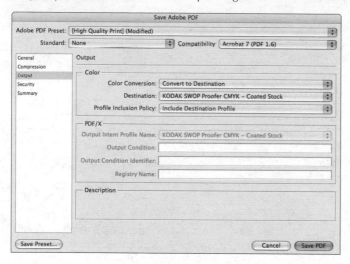

Working with Photoshop color modes

Photoshop provides a number of choices for the color mode used to express your image. You can open files from different color modes, convert color modes in Photoshop, and save among different formats available for a given color mode. File formats are dependent on color modes, and some format options are not available if the image data are defined in a mode not acceptable to the format.

 **See Table 9.1 later in this section for Photoshop PDF exports supported by the Photoshop color modes and relative uses for each mode.**

Color mode choices in Photoshop include the following:

■ **Bitmap.** The image is expressed in two colors: black and white. In Photoshop terms, images in the bitmap mode are referred to as line art. In Acrobat terms, this color mode is called monochrome bitmap. Bitmap images are usually about one-eighth the size of a grayscale file. The bitmap format can be used with Acrobat Capture for converting the image data to rich text.

■ **Grayscale.** This is your anchor mode in Photoshop. Grayscale is like a black-and-white photo, a halftone, or a Charlie Chaplin movie. You see grayscale images everywhere, including the pages in this book. I refer to this as an anchor mode because you can convert to any of the other modes from grayscale. RGB files cannot be converted directly to bitmaps or duotones. You first need to convert RGB to grayscale, and then to either a bitmap or duotone. From grayscale, although the color is not regained, you can also convert back to any of the other color modes. Grayscale images significantly reduce file sizes — they're approximately one-third the size of an RGB file, but larger than the bitmaps.

■ **RGB.** For screen views, multimedia, and Web graphics, RGB is the most commonly used mode. It has a color gamut much larger than CMYK and is best suited for display on computer monitors. A few printing devices can take advantage of RGB such as, film recorders, large inkjet printers, and some desktop color printers. In most cases, however, this mode is not used for printing files to commercial output devices, especially when color-separating and using high-end digital prepress.

- **CMYK.** The process colors of Cyan, Magenta, Yellow, and Black are used in offset printing and most commercial output devices. The color gamut is much narrower than RGB; and when you convert an image from RGB to CMYK using Photoshop's mode conversion command, you usually see some noticeable dilution of color appearing on your monitor. When exporting files to PDF directly from Photoshop or when opening files in other applications and then distilling them, you should always make your color conversions first in Photoshop.

- **Lab.** Lab color, in theory, encompasses all the color from both the RGB and CMYK color spaces. This color mode is based on a mathematical model to describe all perceptible color within the human universe. In practicality, its color space is limited to approximately 6 million colors, about 10+ million less than RGB color. Lab color is device-independent color, which theoretically means the color is true regardless of the device on which your image is edited and printed. Lab mode is commonly preferred by high-end color editing professionals when printing color separations on PostScript Level 2 and PostScript 3 devices. Earlier versions of PDFs saved from Lab color images had problems printing four-color separations. Now with Acrobat 6, you can print Lab images to process separations.

CROSS-REF For more information on printing color separations, see Chapter 32.

- **Multichannel.** If you convert any of the other color modes to Multichannel mode, all the individual channels used to define the image color are converted to grayscale. The resulting document is a grayscale image with multiple channels. With regard to exporting to PDF, you likely won't use this mode.

- **Duotone.** The Duotone mode can actually support one of four individual color modes. Monotone is selectable from the Duotone mode, which holds a single color value in the image, like a tint. Duotone defines the image in two color values, Tritone in three, and Quadtone in four. When you export to PDF from Photoshop, all of these modes are supported.

- **Indexed Color.** Whereas the other color modes such as RGB, Lab, and CMYK define an image with a wide color gamut (up to millions of colors), the Indexed Color mode limits the total colors to a maximum of 256. Color reduction in images is ideal for Web graphics where the fewer colors significantly reduce the file sizes. You can export indexed color images directly to PDF format from Photoshop.

TABLE 9.1

Photoshop Color Modes

Color Mode	Export to PDF	Screen View	Print Composite	Print Separations
Bitmap	Yes	Yes	Yes	No
Grayscale	Yes	Yes	Yes	No
RGB Color	Yes	Yes	Yes*	No
CMYK Color	Yes	No	Yes	Yes
Lab Color	Yes	Yes	Yes	Yes
Multichannel	Yes	No	No	No
Duotone	Yes	Yes	No	Yes
Indexed Color	Yes	Yes	No	No
16-bit	Yes	No	No	No

* When working with high-end commercial devices, CMYK is preferred.

Acquiring PDF files in Photoshop

PDF documents may be composed of many different elements depending on the design of the original file. If you design a page in a layout program for which you create text, import Photoshop images, and also import EPS illustrations, the different elements retain their characteristics when converted to PDF. Text, for example, remains as text, raster images such as Photoshop files remain as raster images, and EPS illustrations remain as EPS vector objects. Although the images, text, and line art may be compressed when distilled in Acrobat Distiller, all the text and line art remain as vector elements. In Photoshop, if you open an illustration or text created in any program other than Photoshop, the document elements are rasterized and lose their vector-based attributes. Photoshop rasterizes PDF documents much as it does with any EPS file.

In Photoshop, you have several methods of handling PDF imports. PDF documents opened in Photoshop are handled with the File ➪ Open command, File ➪ Place command, File ➪ Import command, and through a File ➪ Automate command. Each of the methods offers different options, so let's take the methods individually.

Opening PDF files in Photoshop

When you choose File ➪ Open, select a PDF file, click Open and the Import PDF dialog box appears. If your PDF document has multiple pages you can select one, all, or any number of pages to open. Press Ctrl/⌘ and click individual page thumbnails in the Import PDF dialog box shown in Figure 9.4 to select pages in a noncontiguous order. Click the first page, press the Shift key, and click the last page to select all pages.

FIGURE 9.4

The Import PDF dialog box enables you to pick the page number in a multi-page file to place in Photoshop.

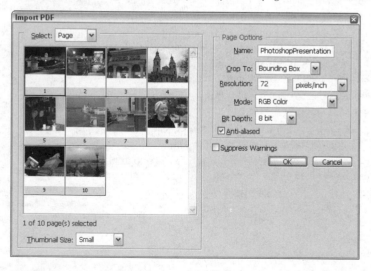

273

Options choices in the Import PDF dialog box include the following:

- **Crop To.** There are six choices you can make from the pull-down menu. For Photoshop files, the choices typically show no difference. Files are imported the same size no matter which option you select. The options are more significant when using Adobe InDesign.

- **Resolution.** The default resolution regardless of the size is 72 ppi. You can choose to supply a user-defined resolution in this dialog box. If the original raster images were at a resolution different from the amount supplied in this dialog box, the images are resampled. Text and line art will be rasterized according to the amount you define in the dialog box without interpolation.

> **NOTE**   Image resampling is a method for tossing away pixels (downsampling) or manufacturing new pixels (upsampling). Either way the process is referred to as *interpolation* where Photoshop makes some guesses as to which pixels to toss or which pixels to create.

- **Mode.** Choose a color mode — Grayscale, RGB, CMYK, or Lab color — from the pull-down menu.

- **Bit Depth.** Choose either 8- or 16-bit for the bit depth. If the PDF contains photos, changing an 8-bit depth file to 16-bit won't add more data to the file. Any tone adjustments using Photoshop's Levels and Curves result in the same data loss on 16-bit as you find with 8-bit images, if the original image file(s) was 8-bit.

> **TIP**   For much better tone separation, working with true 16-bit images results in less data loss and smoother tonal transitions. You can convert 8-bit images to 16-bit in Photoshop. Open a PDF using the 8-bit option. Once opened in Photoshop select Image ➪ Mode ➪ 16-bit. Next, select Image ➪ Image Size and downsample the image 50 percent. Select 71 percent for either the Width or Height and check the Resample check box. Use Bicubic for the method, click OK, and the image resolution is downsampled 50 percent. The pixels are compressed in a tighter relationship resulting in a true 16-bit image. The file now contains enough data to prevent data loss when making tone corrections with Levels and Curves.

- **Anti-Aliased.** Use this option to smooth edges of text, line art, and images that are interpolated through resampling. If you disable this option, text appears with jagged edges. Text in PDF files rasterized in Photoshop looks best when anti-aliased and when the display is more consistent with the original font used when the PDF was created.

- **Suppress warnings.** Check this box to open the files without your having to respond to any warning dialog boxes that might report problems with the pages.

One problem you may encounter when rasterizing PDF documents in Photoshop is maintaining font integrity. Photoshop displays a warning dialog box when it encounters a font that is not installed on your system, which presents problems when you attempt to rasterize the font. If such a problem exists, the font can be eliminated from the document or changed after you open the file in Photoshop and edit the type layer.

When files are password-protected, users are prevented from opening a PDF file in Photoshop or any other application without a password to open the file. If you attempt to open a secure document, an alert dialog box opens prompting you for a password.

CROSS-REF For information about Acrobat security, see Chapter 26.

PDF WORKFLOW If you want to convert catalogs and lengthy documents to HTML-supported files, the PDF to PSD conversion can be useful. You can set up Actions in Photoshop to downsample images, convert color modes, and save copies of the converted files in HTML-supported formats.

Placing PDF files in Photoshop

Instead of opening a PDF file through the File ➪ Open command, you can use File ➪ Place to add a PDF to an open Photoshop document. Placing PDFs in all versions of Photoshop prior to CS2 rasterized the placed file. In Photoshop CS2, placed PDF files retain all vector attributes. When you select Place, the Place PDF dialog box opens, as shown in Figure 9.5.

FIGURE 9.5

The Place PDF dialog box lets you pick the page number in a multi-page file to place in Photoshop.

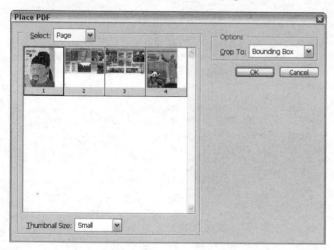

The file appears within a bounding box containing handles in each corner, as shown in Figure 9.6. Click and drag a handle to resize the placed image. You can size the image up or down in the Photoshop document window. When finished scaling, press the Enter (Windows) or Return (Macintosh) key. Pressing the key does not rasterize the file. All vector attributes are retained.

FIGURE 9.6

Placed PDF files retain all vector attributes.

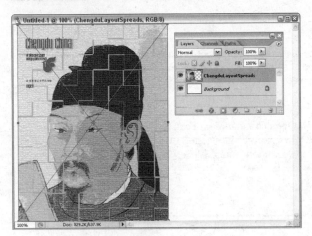

Using comments in Photoshop

Photoshop supports the use of Comment tools. You can create a note or sound attachment in Photoshop much like you do in Acrobat. The comment is an object and won't be rasterized with any other Photoshop data. You can delete the annotation at any time by selecting the Note icon or Attach Sound icon and pressing the Backspace (Windows) or Delete (Macintosh) key.

You can also import comments from PDF files into Photoshop. You must use the Comment Note tool because Photoshop does not support the other comment types available in Acrobat. If a Note is contained in a PDF document and you want to import the Note into Photoshop, choose File ➪ Import ➪ Annotations. Photoshop can import an annotation only from PDF formatted files.

CROSS-REF   For more information about comment notes and sound attachments, see Chapter 20.

Creating PDF presentations

All the features for Photoshop discussed thus far are derived from the top-level menu commands directly in Photoshop. You can also use Adobe Bridge to convert image files to PDF. Among options you find in Adobe Bridge is a command for converting image files to a PDF Presentation. In the Bridge window you can select files to choose in your presentation, invoke a menu command and Photoshop does the work to create a presentation complete with slide transitions and user defined time intervals. If you have Photoshop you also have Adobe Bridge. Open Adobe Bridge and follow the steps below to create a presentation.

STEPS: Saving a PDF presentation

1. **Select image files to include in a PDF Presentation.** Open Adobe Bridge and open the folder containing images you want to include in a presentation. You can add files from other folders, but your task is a little easier if you first copy all the files you want to include in the presentation to a common folder.

2. **Select Tools ⇨ Photoshop ⇨ PDF Presentation.** With the files selected in the Bridge window, open the menu command, as shown in Figure 9.7.

FIGURE 9.7

Choose Tools ⇨ Photoshop ⇨ PDF Presentation in the Adobe Bridge window.

3. **Set the Presentation attributes.** The PDF Presentation dialog box opens, as shown in Figure 9.8. Click Presentation for the Output Options and make a choice for the time interval for advancing slides by editing the Advance Every text box. If you want the presentation to run in a continuous loop, check Loop after last page. If you want transitions, select a transition effect from the Transition pull-down menu. Note that you can also click the Browse button if you want to add more files to your presentation than those viewed in the Bridge window.

FIGURE 9.8

Click Presentation and make choices for advancing slides and transition effects.

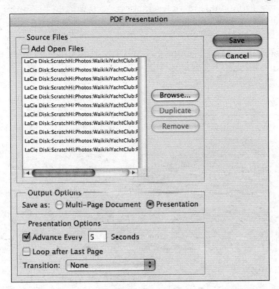

4. **Save the Presentation.** Click Save and the Save Adobe PDF dialog box, shown in Figure 9.1 at the beginning of this chapter, opens. Adjust settings as you like in the various panes in the dialog box. You might want to use some image downsampling in the Compression pane if you build a presentation from images taken with a digital camera. If you shot Camera Raw files with a camera of five or more megapixels, use the Compression options for lowering image resolution.

5. **View the presentation.** Click Save and Photoshop opens each image, samples the image, and converts to PDF. When the save is completed, open the file in Acrobat. Your presentation appears in Full Screen mode and slides change according to the interval specified in Step 3.

CROSS-REF For information on creating PDF presentations, see Chapter 28.

Adobe Illustrator CS

Adobe Illustrator, as with other Adobe programs, is built on core PDF technology. In fact, the native Adobe Illustrator file format is PDF, and as such it is one of the best applications supporting direct export to PDF.

Illustrator has evolved to a sophisticated integration with PDF and supports the following: transparency, editing capability, layers, blending modes, text, and filters. Further integration with the program in non-PDF workflows embraces exports for Web design where its current iteration supports one-step optimization for formats such as GIF, JPEG, PNG, SWF, and SVG.

Saving PDFs from Adobe Illustrator CS

To export PDF files from Adobe Illustrator, you use the File ⇨ Save command. The format options available to you include the native Illustrator format (Adobe Illustrator Document), Illustrator EPS (eps), Illustrator

Template (ait), Adobe PDF (pdf), SVG Compressed (scgz), and SVG (svg). Illustrator, choose File ⇨ Save from a new document window. A Save dialog box opens that enables you to name the file, choose the destination, and select one of the formats just noted.

Additional file formats appear in the Export dialog box (File ⇨ Export). Formats supported in this dialog box include BMP (bmp), Targa (tga), PNG (png), AutoCAD Drawing (dwg), AutoCAD Interchange File (dxf), Enhanced Metafile (emf), Macromedia Flash (swf) — soon to be labeled Adobe Flash, JPEG (jpg), Macintosh PICT (pct), Photoshop (psd), TIFF (tif), Text Format (txt), and Windows Metafile (wmf).

If you choose Adobe Illustrator (.AI) as the file format click Save, the Illustrator Options dialog box opens. In this dialog box you have an option to Create a PDF Compatible File. Check the box and click OK and your Illustrator document is saved in native format that can be opened directly in Acrobat. No other PDF conversion is necessary.

If you want to convert to PDF from a layered Illustrator document and have the layers appear in Acrobat, you need to save your Illustrator file as Adobe PDF. (*.PDF) When you select Acrobat PDF and click the Save button, the Save Adobe PDF dialog box opens with many similar settings found when saving Photoshop files.

A few differences appear in the Save Adobe PDF dialog box when you compare the options to Photoshop. These options are as follows:

- **General.** In the General tab you find two additional settings, as shown in Figure 9.9. The Create Adobe PDF Layers from Top Level Layers check box is active for Acrobat 6 compatibility files and later. Check the box when you want an Illustrator file exported to PDF with Adobe PDF Layers.

FIGURE 9.9

Two additional options appear in the Illustrator Save Adobe PDF General settings when comparing the options to those found in Photoshop.

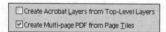

The Create Multi-page PDF from Page Tiles is used for creating multiple pages in Illustrator (see "Creating multi-page PDFs" later in this chapter).

- **Compression.** The appearance of the Compression pane is different than Photoshop but you have all the options for downsampling files and the same compression options as found in Photoshop.

- **Marks and Bleeds.** Click Marks and Bleeds in the left pane and the options in the right pane change to settings you can apply for setting printer's marks. Options are similar to those you find when setting marks in the Acrobat Print dialog box.

CROSS-REF For information on setting printer's marks in the Print dialog box, see Chapter 32.

- **Output.** The same color conversion and support for PDF/X compliance options are available to Illustrator as found in Photoshop. One option is added in Illustrator to mark the file if the source document uses trapping.

CROSS-REF For more information on trapping, see Chapter 32.

- **Advanced.** Illustrator has an Advanced pane where Font subsetting, overprint assignments, and transparency flattening options appear, as shown in Figure 9.10.

FIGURE 9.10

Advanced settings offer options for font embedding, overprinting, and transparency flattening.

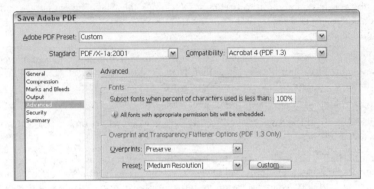

CROSS-REF For more on font subsetting and transparency flattening, see Chapter 10. For more on over-printing, see Chapter 32.

Saving layered files to PDF

You can save layered Illustrator CS files to PDF with Adobe PDF Layers. Creating layered PDF documents from Illustrator is supported in Illustrator CS version 1 and above. To create PDF layers you need an authoring program capable of creating layers and capable of saving or exporting to PDF 1.5 format (Acrobat 6 compatibility) and above — Illustrator CS does both.

When saving files with layers to PDF with Adobe PDF Layers, create the default layer view you want to appear in Acrobat. As shown in Figure 9.11, two layers in an Illustrator file are hidden and three layers are visible. The layer visibility you see in Illustrator is the same visibility you'll see in Acrobat when saving as PDF.

In Illustrator, choose File ➪ Save or Save As and select PDF as the format. In the Adobe PDF Options dialog box select Acrobat 6 or greater compatibility and check the box for Create Acrobat Layers from Top-Level Layers. If the box is not checked, you won't see layers in the resultant PDF document.

FIGURE 9.11

When saving to PDF with layers, create the layer view in the authoring program that you want to appear as the default view in Acrobat.

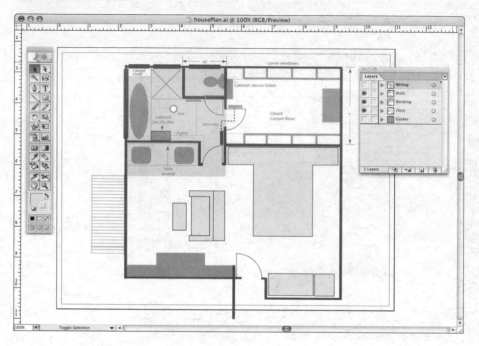

When you open the PDF in Acrobat, you see the same layer view as when the file was saved from Illustrator, as shown in Figure 9.12.

CROSS-REF For more information on working with layered files in Acrobat, see Chapter 24.

FIGURE 9.12

The default layer view in Acrobat appears the same as the view from Illustrator when the file was saved.

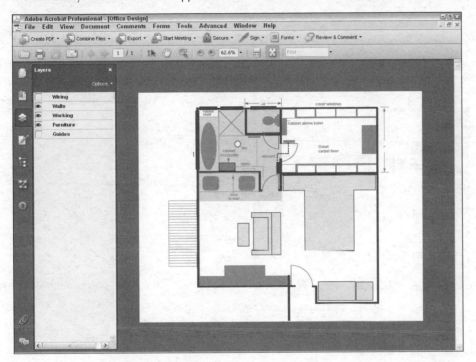

Creating multi-page PDFs

Quite often, with just about any application, users find ways to work with a program in a manner that was not intended by a developer. This is most apparent when looking at the way designers use Adobe Illustrator. Illustrator was created for artists who needed an electronic artboard to create illustrations and drawings. But when the program got to the hands of the graphic artists, it was frequently used as a page layout program. For years graphic artists pleaded with Adobe to offer support for multiple pages. No matter how many rich features were added to Adobe InDesign (which was created as a page layout program), the die-hard Illustrator users never abandoned their favorite tool. Today, great numbers of designers still first grab Illustrator to create page layouts.

It wasn't until Illustrator CS2 was released that Adobe responded. Perhaps not completely the way designers wanted to work with multiple pages, but in part, Illustrator now supports multiple pages. The only way you can create a multi-page document in Illustrator is when exporting to Adobe PDF.

Illustrator's approach to multiple page documents is quite different than any other application. If creating multi-page documents in Illustrator is your interest, follow the steps below:

STEPS: Creating multi-page PDFs from Adobe Illustrator

1. **Set up the page size.** For this demonstration I want to create four buttons to use in Acrobat as navigation buttons to move back and forth in a PDF document. Two buttons are needed for default appearances and two buttons will appear as rollovers so when the cursor appears over a

button, the button color or shape changes — much like you find in Web page designs. Rather than create four separate files, I want to create a single PDF document with four separate pages.

For buttons, my page size needs to be just large enough for all four buttons. When I select File ➪ New in Illustrator, I specify my page size for 2 inches by 2 inches. These dimensions are sufficient to create four pages each at 1-inch square. The Illustrator artboard can be set up as a single page only. The page will be tiled to produce individual smaller pages when you create the PDF file. Therefore, 2 square inches is large enough to create four separate pages each at 1-square-inch.

Note that you could create an artboard large enough to accommodate several letter or tabloid size pages if you want to use Illustrator for a traditional page layout.

2. **Create the button icons.** You can use font characters from Symbols, Wingdings, or other stylized fonts, draw shapes, or add symbols from the Symbols palette, and so on. In my example, I use some characters from the Symbol font that appear as left and right arrows. I copied the two characters and changed the color on the duplicated characters. All this is arbitrary. Feel free to use any design of your choice. The point is you need four images centered in four quadrants, as shown in Figure 9.13. Notice guidelines were drawn to help position the characters in each quadrant.

FIGURE 9.13

Create four shapes to be used as navigation buttons and position the shapes in the center of each quadrant on the 2 × 2 inch page.

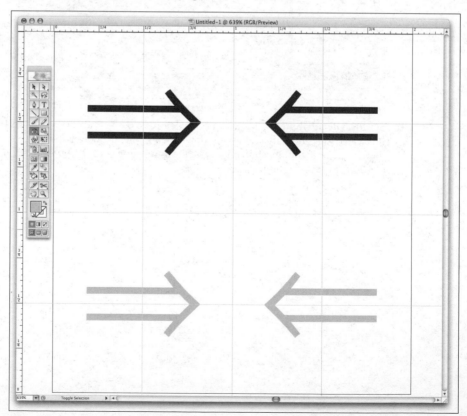

3. **Set Print Attributes.** Chose File ⇨ Print and select Adobe PDF for the Printer and AdobePDF 8.0 for the PPD at the top of the Print dialog box. Under the Media area, type 2 for the Width and Height and choose Custom for the size. The Print dialog box General settings should appear, as shown in Figure 9.14.

FIGURE 9.14

Set print attributes for Printer, PPD, and Size.

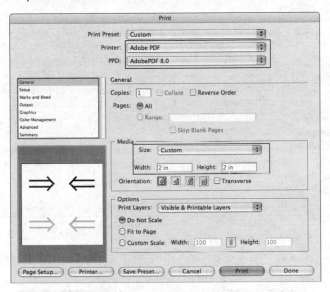

4. **Set the Tile attributes.** Click Setup in the left pane of the Print dialog box and select Tile Imageable Areas from the Tiling pull-down menu. The tiled pages should appear with dashed lines in the page thumbnail preview, as shown in Figure 9.15. If you don't see dashed lines, the file won't export as multiple pages.

FIGURE 9.15

Select Tile Imageable Areas and observe the preview to be certain the pages are defined with dashed lines.

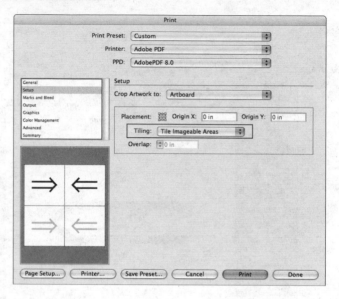

5. **Click Done.** Be certain to click Done and not Cancel or Print to preserve the settings.

6. **Save as Adobe PDF.** You must use the Adobe PDF (*.PDF) file format. A Native Illustrator .ai format won't produce multiple pages. Select File ⇨ Save As and choose Adobe PDF (*PDF) for the Type (Windows) or Format (Macintosh). Click Save and the Save Adobe PDF dialog box opens.

7. **Check Create Multiple-page PDF from Page Tiles in the General settings.** (See Figure 9.9 earlier in this chapter.) Click Save PDF and the file is saved.

8. **Open the PDF in Acrobat.** When the file opens, click the Pages pane. You should see four separate pages, as shown in Figure 9.16.

Open the file in Acrobat and click the Pages tab to view thumbnails of the pages in the document.

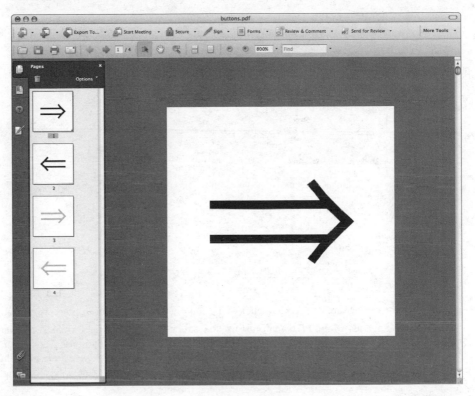

A file like the one created in these steps can be used as button faces with button form fields. Rather than have four separate files, you can choose any image in a multi-page document to add as a button face in Acrobat. In the Appearance settings in Button properties the Select Icon dialog box lists all pages in a PDF document. You can scroll the elevator bar on the right side of the dialog box to view different pages, as shown in Figure 9.17.

CROSS-REF For more information on creating button faces, see Chapters 22 and 34.

FIGURE 9.17

When assigning appearances in Button properties, you can choose any page in a multi-page document for a button appearance.

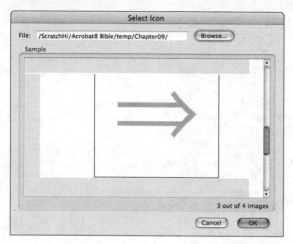

Saving SWF files

Acrobat versions 6 and above support many different kinds of media formats including Macromedia Flash SWF (soon to be Adobe Flash). Using Illustrator CS you can create vector objects as animated sequences to embellish PDFs such as forms, diagrams, electronic brochures, and similar documents where you want to add animation to amplify your messages. To understand a little more about saving SWF files from Illustrator and importing them in Acrobat, follow these steps:

STEPS: Exporting SWF files to Acrobat

1. **Create a sequence in Illustrator.** Either draw vector shapes in Illustrator or drag a symbol from the Symbols palette to the document page. The shape you create is on a layer. Duplicate the shape and paste it to a second layer. Continue adding new layers and shapes to complete a sequence. You can change size, rotations, or shape designs for each shape on a different layer. In my example shown in Figure 9.18, I created a shape on one layer and sized the objects up 25 percent on each new layer.

TIP To easily create a sequence for motion objects, drag a symbol from Illustrator's Symbols palette to the document page. Press the Control/Option key and click+drag to duplicate the shape. Press Control/⌘+D several times to repeat the duplication. Select all the objects and open the Layers palette fly-away menu. Select Release to Layers (Sequence) from the palette menu commands. All your objects are distributed to separate layers.

FIGURE 9.18

Add a shape to separate layers.

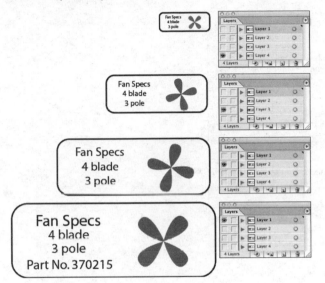

2. **Export to SWF.** Choose File ➪ Export. In the Export dialog box, select Macromedia Flash (swf) from the Format pull-down menu. Add a filename, select a target folder, and click the Export button. The Macromedia Flash SWF Format Options dialog box opens.

3. **Set the SWF file format options.** In the Macromedia Flash SWF Format Options dialog box shown in Figure 9.19 are choices for the frame rate, exporting HTML compatible files, and various appearance options. Make your choices here and click OK to continue the export to SWF.

4. **Save the Illustrator file.** When you export to a file format from Illustrator, your file is not yet saved. If you want to return to the document to make additional edits, save the file. Choose File ➪ Save and save the file as a .ai file with Create PDF Compatible File checked.

5. **Import the SWF file in Acrobat (Acrobat Professional only).** Open the Advanced Editing toolbar and select the Movie tool. Drag a rectangle on the document page where you want to import the SWF file. Click the Browse button in the Add Movie dialog box, locate your SWF file, and import it. When you import the movie, the first frame in the sequence appears within the movie rectangle, as shown in Figure 9.20.

6. **Play the movie clip.** Select the Hand tool and click the movie frame. Figure 9.21 displays the last frame in a sequence. The effect is that the message box appears to explode in view as the sequence is played.

FIGURE 9.19

Set options in the Macromedia Flash (SWF) Format Options dialog box.

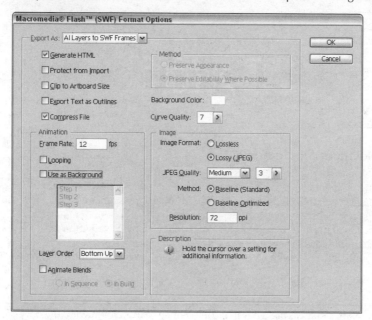

FIGURE 9.20

Select the Movie tool from the Advanced Editing toolbar and drag open a rectangle to import a movie clip.

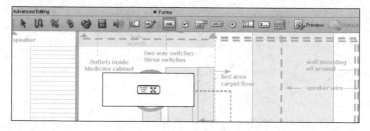

Whether you create SWF files from Illustrator or Adobe Flash, the SWF file imports in Acrobat are the same. Use the Movie tool in the Advanced Editing toolbar and locate an SWF file on your hard drive. Open the file choose Acrobat 6 compatibility. You can add play buttons in Acrobat to play, stop, pause, resume, and add JavaScripts for a variety of different play options. You can also convert Web pages containing SWF files to PDF. When Web pages are captured using Acrobat, the SWF files play as movies in the converted PDF.

CROSS-REF To learn more about importing SWF, movies files, and adding play buttons and Acrobat 5 and 6 compatibility, see Chapter 23. For more on capturing Web pages, see Chapter 7.

FIGURE 9.21

Select the Hand tool and click the movie box to play the sequence.

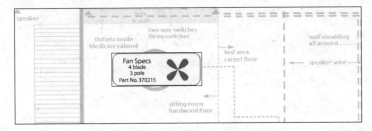

Opening Illustrator files in Acrobat

Illustrator native files do not need conversion to PDF to be viewed in Acrobat. Acrobat supports opening native Illustrator .ai documents. When you click the Open tool, choose File ➪ Open, or select Create PDF From File and select a native Illustrator .ai file, the file opens in Acrobat without conversion to PDF. All this is possible if the original Illustrator document was saved with an option for Create PDF Compatible File. When you save Illustrator files as native documents and click the Save button in the Save or Save As dialog box, the Illustrator Options dialog box opens, as shown in Figure 9.22. Under the Options, select the Create PDF Compatible File check box. You can then open the file in Acrobat without converting it to PDF.

FIGURE 9.22

Saving with PDF compatibility results in file types that can be opened in Acrobat without conversion to PDF.

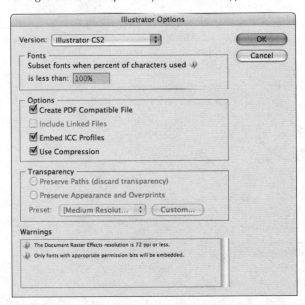

To export to PDF from InDesign, choose File ➪ Export. In the Export dialog box, select Adobe PDF from the Format pull-down menu and click Save. The Export Adobe PDF dialog box then appears, as shown in Figure 9.23. Options here provide some similar settings as you find with Adobe Illustrator and Adobe

Photoshop as well as a number of additional attribute choices for handling files designed for print, Web hosting, and screen viewing. You can export Bookmarks that appear in the resultant PDF file, export inter-activity with buttons and actions, export HTML and hyperlinks, and create PDF documents designed for commercial printing.

FIGURE 9.23

InDesign can export documents with options settings to accommodate files designed for print, Web hosting, and interactive screen viewing.

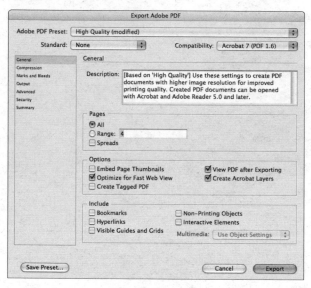

Exporting PDFs for print

The Preset pull-down menu offers you choices for several Adobe PDF Settings that determine how your PDF is created. Among those options are selections for PDF/X files. PDF/X is a format specifically designed for printing and commercial prepress. When you export to PDF/X, you resolve colorspace problems, transparency problems, and other potential problems faced when printing documents on commercial devices.

CROSS-REF For a detailed explanation of PDF/X and Adobe PDF Settings, see Chapter 10.

Exporting Adobe PDF Layers

Just as when exporting layers from Illustrator, you set the default layer view in InDesign that you want to appear in Acrobat as a default view. You can add interactive buttons in InDesign and export your interactive links that are also recognized by Acrobat. In the Export Adobe PDF dialog box shown in Figure 9.23, be certain to check the boxes for Create Acrobat Layers and the Include items such as Bookmarks, Hyperlinks, and Interactive Elements. Click the Export button to export your document to PDF. In Figure 9.24, a layered InDesign CS file with interactive buttons and imported video is prepared for export to PDF.

When you open the file in Acrobat, a modification of the button attributes sets a different layer visibility and plays the imported video, as shown in Figure 9.25. These kinds of design opportunities provide artists with tools to create effective presentations and electronic brochures that users who download the free Adobe Reader software can view.

FIGURE 9.24

A layout is prepared in Adobe InDesign with imported video, interactive buttons, and multiple layers.

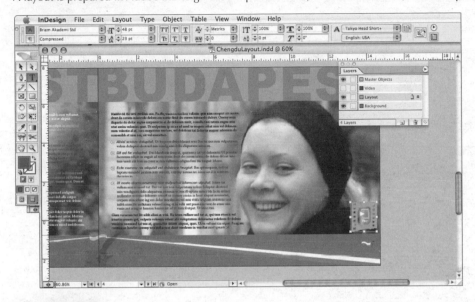

FIGURE 9.25

A slight modification to the button attributes changes layer visibility and plays the imported video.

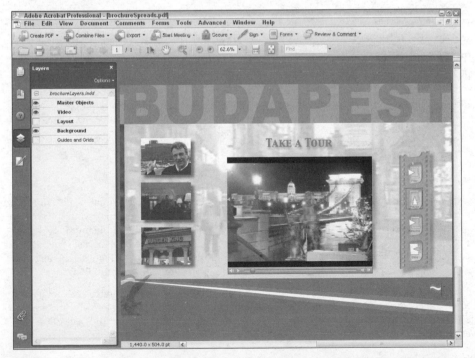

Adobe GoLive CS

Adobe GoLive CS is a powerful Web authoring tool. Inasmuch as you can convert Web pages to PDF and use the Create PDF From File command to convert HTML files locally on your hard drive to PDF, you may want to check a PDF view while working in GoLive. To complement the interoperability between the Creative Suite programs, you can export InDesign files to GoLive and export GoLive documents to PDF.

In GoLive, select PDF Preview at the top of the GoLive workspace to convert your file to a PDF view, as shown in Figure 9.26. The view you see is exactly how the GoLive file appears in Acrobat when it's opened as a PDF. If you want to save the document as a PDF after previewing it, choose File ⇨ Export ⇨ HTML as Adobe PDF. The Export Adobe PDF dialog box opens in which you can name the file and select a target folder.

 You must first preview your GoLive document as PDF before you can export the page to PDF.

There's much more to a seamless interoperability between the Creative Suite programs and Adobe Acrobat. If you want to learn more about all the CS applications, look at the *Adobe Creative Suite Bible* (Wiley Publishing; 2006) and *Adobe Creative Suite All-in-One Desk Reference For Dummies* (Wiley Publishing; 2004).

FIGURE 9.26

Preview GoLive files as PDF and export the preview to create a PDF file.

Using Acrobat with Non-Adobe Programs

A number of different application programs support PDF creation from file exports similar to the way Adobe handles exporting to PDF. Programs such as QuarkXPress, CorelDraw, and Adobe FreeHand (formerly macromedia FreeHand) all have their own options for exporting native files to PDF. Many attribute choices featured in the CS programs are also available in those non-Adobe programs that export to PDF. You may need to poke around in the export dialog boxes to find various settings adjustments.

If you use a program that doesn't support direct exports to PDF, you can either use the Adobe PDF print driver or print a file to PostScript and distill the PostScript file in Acrobat Distiller.

CROSS-REF For more information on using the Adobe PDF print driver, see Chapter 7. For more on using Acrobat Distiller, see Chapter 10.

Summary

- Adobe Creative Suite is a sophisticated solution for file interoperability. All the CS applications export directly to PDF.

- Adobe Photoshop can export directly to PDF as separate files and presentations. Photoshop can open single and multiple PDF documents created by any producer and preserve text and vector art when exporting to PDF.

- Adobe Illustrator exports Macromedia Flash SWF (soon t be named Adobe SWF) files that can be imported in PDF documents as movie files.

- Adobe Illustrator CS and Adobe InDesign CS export to PDF with layers intact.

- Adobe InDesign CS exports links, Bookmarks, and embedded media to PDF.

- Some non-Adobe programs offer export-to-PDF features similar to the CS applications. For those programs not supporting exports to PDF, you can use the Adobe PDF printer driver or print a file to disk as PostScript and use Acrobat Distiller to convert to PDF.

Chapter 10

Using Acrobat Distiller

ecause PDF file creation has been much simplified in Acrobat 8, you may bypass thoughts of learning what Acrobat Distiller does and how PDF documents are converted with the Distiller application. If you remember the PDF conversion steps discussed in the previous three chapters, the Adobe PDF Settings were mentioned many times. These settings apply to Acrobat Distiller, and also the conversion of documents for many options from within Acrobat and via exports from authoring programs. They all use the Adobe PDF Settings.

In order to successfully produce quality PDF documents, you need to have a basic understanding of how Acrobat Distiller works and what the settings control in regard to converting files to PDF. In some cases Distiller works in the background using Adobe PDF Settings you assign to the distillation process. Therefore, it is essential that you know how to change settings and understand what options are available to you. In this chapter I cover some advantages of using Acrobat Distiller and discuss how to change the Adobe PDF Settings.

Setting Up the Work Environment

You can access Acrobat Distiller in several ways. You can open Distiller from the Advanced menu command in Acrobat Standard and Acrobat Professional, you can launch Distiller from the desktop, or you can drag and drop files to the Distiller program application. None of these methods require loading special tools.

CROSS-REF For a description of the various ways to access Acrobat Distiller, see the section "Accessing Distiller" at the end of this chapter.

IN THIS CHAPTER

Understanding the basics of PostScript

Understanding Distiller Preferences

Controlling Adobe PDF settings

Saving and deleting settings files

Monitoring font folders

Creating Watched folders

Using non-Roman character sets

Distilling PostScript

When you convert files to PDF you typically create a PostScript file in other applications and convert the PostScript to PDF in Distiller. Therefore, the default view of the toolbars is all you need to follow the instructions throughout this chapter.

Understanding PostScript

Adobe PostScript is a *page description language* — that is, it describes the text and images on your monitor screen in a language. A raster image processor (RIP) interprets this language. Whereas PostScript is the language, the RIP behaves like a compiler. The RIP interprets the file and converts the text and images you see on your monitor to a bitmap image in dots that are plotted on a printing device. In the office environment, you won't see an RIP independent of a PostScript laser printer you use — but it exists. It's built into the printer. With high-end devices such as imagesetters, platesetters, large-format inkjet printers, on-demand printing systems, high-end composite color devices, and film recorders, the RIP is often a separate component that may be either a hardware device or software operating on a dedicated computer.

One of the reasons PostScript has grown to its present popularity is its device independence. When you draw a Bézier curve, rectangle, oval, or other geometric object in a vector art authoring application, the resolution displayed by your monitor is 72 pixels per inch (ppi). This image can be printed to a 300 dots per inch (dpi) laser printer or a 3,600 dpi imagesetter. Through the device independence of PostScript, essentially the computer "says" to the printer, "Give me all you can." The printer responds by imaging the page at the resolution it is capable of handling. When the file is ripped, the laser printer RIP creates a 300-dpi bitmap, whereas the imagesetter RIP creates a 3,600-dpi bitmap.

With all its popularity and dominance in the market, PostScript does have problems. It comes in many different dialects and is known as a *streamed* language. If you have a QuarkXPress file, for example, and import an Adobe Illustrator EPS file and a Macromedia EPS file, you'll wind up with three different flavors of PostScript — each according to the way the individual manufacturer handles its coding. If the same font is used by each of the three components, the font description resides in three separate areas of the PostScript file when printed to disk. PostScript is notorious for redundancy, especially with fonts.

About Imaging Devices

Imagesetters are high-end devices ranging from $10,000 to over $100,000 and are usually found in computer service bureaus and commercial print shops. Imagesetters use laser beams to plot the raster image on either sheet-fed or roll-fed paper or film. The paper is resin coated, and both paper and film require chemical processing through a developer, fix, and wash much like a photographic print. The material is used by a commercial printer to make plates that are wrapped around cylinders on a printing press. These prepress materials are an integral part of offset printing, and much of the printing performed today is handled from a form of digital output to material that is used to create plates for presses.

Direct-to-plate and direct-to-press systems bypass the prepress materials and expose images on plates that are used on print cylinders or directly to the press blankets where the impression receives the ink.

On-demand printing is a term describing machines that bypass the prepress process by taking the digital file from a computer directly to the press. Depending on the engineering of the output device, the consumable materials may consist of toner (as used in copy machines) or ink (as used on printing presses).

As a streamed language, PostScript requires the entire code to be processed by the interpreter before the image bitmap is created. Ever wonder why you need to wait while the RIP is churning for an endless amount of time only to eventually end up with a PostScript error or RIP crash? PostScript can't begin plotting the bitmap image until the entire PostScript stream has been interpreted.

PDF, on the other hand, is like a database file — it has a database structure. PDF eliminates redundancy with file resources. Fonts, for example, appear only once, no matter how many occurrences are used in imported EPS files. In addition, PDF takes all the dialectical differences of PostScript and converts them to a single dialect. Whereas a PostScript file containing many pages requires the entire file to be downloaded to the RIP and ultimately printed, a PDF file is page independent in that each individual page is imaged before proceeding to the next page. In short, PDF is much more efficient than PostScript for printing purposes.

Creating PostScript files

In some ways a PostScript file is very similar to a PDF file. If, for example, you create a layout in Adobe PageMaker, Adobe InDesign, Adobe FrameMaker, or QuarkXPress with images and type fonts, the document page can be printed to disk as a PostScript file. In doing so, you can embed all graphic images and fonts in the file. If you take your file to a service center, the file can be downloaded to a printing device. Assuming you created the PostScript file properly, the file prints with complete integrity.

On desktop printers, printing to a PostScript file is just like printing to a device. On printers in commercial imaging centers, there are additional requirements and considerations, including the following:

CROSS-REF The following items address PDF creation for the purpose of printing files on commercial printing equipment. For more information on commercial printing, see Chapter 32.

- **PPD device selection.** In past years it was essential for you to use a device PostScript Printer Description (PPD) file. Today your PPD selection can be either a device PPD, an Acrobat Distiller PPD, or the Adobe PDF Printer that doesn't offer you a separate PPD choice. In some cases, you'll find more success in using a Distiller PPD or the Adobe PDF Printer than using a device PPD, especially with PostScript clones and older printing devices.

- **Page size.** With desktop printers, you often have only one or two page sizes. With printers that have multiple trays or interchangeable trays, you select the appropriate page size for the tray used. With imaging equipment, you need to be certain the page size is properly selected to include all image data and printer's marks. Assume for a moment a document is created in the standard page size for a letter (8.5 × 11 inches). However, to accommodate printer's marks (registration and color bars), it turns out that the page area needs to be defined larger than a letter page. In the Paper Size area of the dialog box shown in Figure 10.1, the word "Custom" appears, indicating the page is a custom size. The thumbnail in Figure 10.1 shows how the page fits within the defined size. In this example, all data and printer's marks print within the defined page. If your page is too small, some clipping of the data occurs when printed or when a PDF file is generated.

- **Font inclusion.** You may need to specifically tell the host application to include fonts in the PostScript file. If the file is printed at a service center, you definitely need to include the fonts in the file you submit for output. If you distill the file in Acrobat Distiller, the fonts need to be loaded on your system in order for you to embed the fonts in the PDF file. When you have options in Print dialog boxes for font inclusion, always choose to embed the fonts.

- **Screening.** Halftone frequencies, or *line screens,* can be printed at different settings. With desktop printers the maximum line screen available for the device is often the default. 600-dpi laser printers, for example, most commonly use a maximum line screen of 85 lines per inch (lpi). With imaging equipment, you need to first know the requirements of the commercial printer and take

his/her advice depending on the paper, press, and prepress material. Therefore, if your file is ultimately printed at 133 lpi, you must enter this value in the Print dialog box of the application creating the PostScript file.

The page size was defined as a Custom size to include the printer's marks and page information.

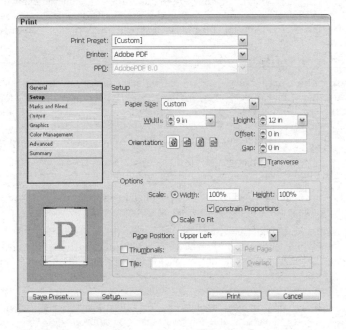

Setting the halftone frequency is an important issue only if the PostScript file is downloaded to an imaging device where the default screens are not overridden by a technician. For files printed from Acrobat directly to printing devices, the technician who prints the file also sets the frequency in the Acrobat Advanced Printing dialog box.

Screening can also be a particular type relative to the printing device and RIP. Stochastic screening, Crystal Raster, AGFA Balanced Screens, and others are available from a PPD selection for a particular device. For these settings you need to contact your service center for the precise screening options needed and use a device PPD.

■ **Color.** If separations are to be printed, you must make certain all identified colors are properly named in the host document. There is often an option in a Print dialog box to select separations. As you view a color list of potential separations, it is imperative to verify all colors appearing are those you specified in the document. If a spot color is in the current document, the color doesn't print unless it is an identified color in the Print dialog box. Fortunately, in Acrobat 7 a method is available for previewing separations. Before sending files off to a service center, make a habit of previewing files for printing in Acrobat.

CROSS-REF For information regarding separation previews and soft-proofing color, see Chapter 23.

Encoding

Encoding comes in two flavors: Binary and ASCII. Binary encoding results in smaller files and prints faster on PostScript Level 2 and PostScript 3 devices. As a default you'll want to use binary encoding if you see options in the Print dialog box to choose between ASCII and Binary. If no option is available for choosing between ASCII and Binary when you print a PostScript file, the file encoding defaults to Binary.

PostScript levels

PostScript originated sometime in 1976, and later it was updated to a version called Interpress at the Xerox Palo Alto Research Center (PARC). Interpress was designed for output to early laser printers. Xerox abandoned the project, and two of the staff at Xerox PARC decided to take it forth and develop it. In 1981, John Warnock and Chuck Geschke formed Adobe Systems Incorporated, and Adobe PostScript was their first product.

On March 21, 1985, the digital print revolution was founded when Apple Computer, Aldus Corporation, Adobe Systems, and Linotype collaborated on an open architecture system for electronic typesetting. Later that year Apple Computer introduced the LaserWriter printer that came with a whopping 13 fonts fried into the printer's ROM chips and a price tag of $6,500. If you were outputting to a PostScript device in 1987, when Adobe Illustrator first appeared, you may still be waiting for that 12K Illustrator file to spit out of your laser printer. PostScript Level 1 was a major technological advance, but by today's standards it was painfully slow. Many in the imaging world remember all too well still waiting at 3:00 a.m. for the final file to print after ripping over eight hours.

In 1990, Adobe Systems introduced PostScript Level 2, which was a more robust version of PostScript and a screamer compared to the first release. In addition to speed, PostScript Level 2 provided these features:

- **Color separation.** In earlier days, color was preseparated on Level 1 devices. PostScript Level 2 enabled imaging specialists to separate a composite color file into the four process colors, Cyan, Magenta, Yellow, and Black. Also, there was support for spot color in PostScript Level 2.

- **Improved font handling.** In the early days of PostScript imaging, there were more font nightmares than you can imagine. Font encoding for PostScript fonts handled a maximum of only 256 characters. Other font sets such as Japanese have thousands of individual characters. PostScript Level 2 introduced a composite font technology that handled many different foreign character sets.

- **Compression.** Getting the large files across a 10 Base-T network was also a burden in the Level 1 days. PostScript Level 2 introduced data compression and supported such compression schemes as JPEG, LZW, and RLE. The files are transmitted compressed, which means they get to the RIP faster, and then decompressed at the RIP. In a large imaging center, the compression greatly improved network traffic and workflows.

In 1996, Adobe introduced PostScript 3 (note that "Level" was dropped from the name). Perhaps one of the more remarkable and technologically advanced features of PostScript 3 is the inclusion of Web publishing with direct support for HTML, PDF, and Web content. PostScript 3 also provides the ability to create In-RIP separations. When you send a PDF file to an imaging center using PostScript 3 RIPs you can deliver composite color files that are sent directly to the RIP where they are separated at the imaging device.

Using Acrobat Distiller Preferences

Acrobat Distiller is launched from within Adobe Acrobat Standard or Adobe Acrobat Professional. As a separate executable application, Acrobat Distiller can also be launched from a desktop shortcut or alias or by double-clicking the program icon contained in the Distiller folder inside the Acrobat 8.0 folder.

> **NOTE**   Acrobat Distiller is accessible from the Advanced ➪ Print Production ➪ Acrobat Distiller menu command. The menu to open Distiller is now nested in a submenu in the Advanced menu. In Earlier versions of Acrobat, Distiller was accessed from within Acrobat via the Advanced ➪ Acrobat Distiller menu command.

When you first launch Acrobat Distiller, it looks like a fairly simple application. Examining the menus immediately tells you there's not much to do in the File menu. This menu is limited to opening a file, addressing preferences, and quitting the program. Distiller's real power is contained in the second menu item — the Settings menu. The commands listed in this menu offer all the control for determining how PostScript files are converted to PDF.

Before making choices in the Settings menu, look over the options in the Preferences menu. When you choose File ➪ Preferences on the Distiller Window (Windows) or the top-level Distiller ➪ Preferences (Macintosh), a dialog box opens. The options available are listed among three groups that include Startup Alerts, Output Options, and Log Files, as shown in Figure 10.2 for Windows and in Figure 10.3 for Macintosh.

FIGURE 10.2

Access Acrobat Distiller Preferences by choosing File ➪ Preferences. Preferences enable you to customize startup and output options.

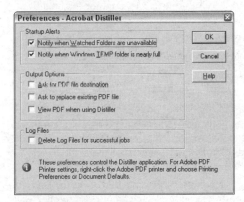

FIGURE 10.3

On the Macintosh, you select Preferences from the Distiller top-level menu.

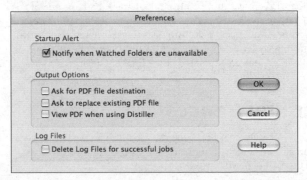

Startup Alerts

The two items listed in the Startup Alerts section of the Distiller Preferences dialog box have to do with your initial startup upon launching the Distiller application:

- **Notify when Watched Folders are unavailable.** This command enables Distiller to monitor a folder or directory on your computer or network server to automatically distill PostScript files placed in watched folders. In an office environment, you can have different users create PostScript files and send them to a server for automatic distillation.

CROSS-REF For more information on working with watched folders, see the "Creating watched folders" section later in this chapter.

- **Notify when Windows TEMP folder is nearly full (Windows only).** Distiller needs temporary disk space to convert the PostScript files to PDF documents. If the available hard disk space on your startup volume becomes less than 1 megabyte, Distiller prompts you with a warning dialog box. Leaving this preference setting enabled is always a good idea. The amount of temporary space required by Distiller is approximately twice the size of the PostScript file being distilled.

Output Options

Output Options relate to what you intend to do with the PDF both in terms of where it is saved and what to do after conversion:

- **Ask for PDF file destination.** When enabled, this option prompts you for the location of the saved file.

- **Ask to replace existing PDF file.** Selecting this option warns you if a PDF of the same name exists in the folder where the new PDF is saved. If you want to use different Adobe PDF Settings and create two PDF files, you may forget that you have a PDF with a filename the same as the new one you are creating. With this option, you are warned if Distiller attempts to overwrite your existing file.

- **View PDF when using Distiller.** After the PDF has been created, the default Acrobat viewer launches and the PDF opens in the Document pane.

TIP If you are running Adobe Reader and Adobe Acrobat Standard or Professional on the same computer, open the viewer you want to designate as the default viewer. When prompted to set the viewer as the default, click Yes in the dialog box. All subsequent PDF files are opened in the default viewer.

Log Files

A log file describes the sequence of steps used to produce the PDF file. The Log Files section offers an option for what to do with the log file: the Delete Log Files for successful jobs option. A log file is an ASCII text file detailing the distillation process. If an error is produced during distillation, the log file records the error even though the PDF is not created. Viewing the log file can be helpful in debugging problems with files not successfully being converted to PDF. If the PDF is successfully created, there would be no need to keep the log file on your computer. By default, you'll want to enable this check box to eliminate the clutter.

Editing Adobe PDF Settings

Distiller can be assigned some custom settings and you can also choose from some preinstalled Adobe PDF Settings. All Settings are selectable from a pull-down menu. If you need to create some custom settings you open the Settings menu and select Edit Adobe PDF Settings.

Using the Default Adobe PDF Settings

If your work can be satisfied using one of the preset settings, open the Default Settings pull-down menu, as shown in Figure 10.4. Select a setting you want to use and Distiller uses your selected setting as a new default. If you distill files from within Acrobat, the new default settings are used. Each time you open Distiller you see the new default you last selected in Distiller. Open a PostScript or EPS file and the file is converted to PDF using the settings appearing in the Distiller window as Default Settings.

The Default choices for Adobe PDF Settings when you install Acrobat are as follows:

- **High Quality Print.** The preset settings associated with this option are established for the highest-quality images for high-end digital prepress and printing. The lowest levels of compression and downsampling are used to preserve image quality.

- **Oversized Pages.** This option is designed specifically for PDFs of oversized pages that you might see from engineering drawings.

- **PDF/A-1b:2005(CMYK).** PDF/A is a standard for archival purposes. Acrobat Distiller does a check to assure PDF/A compliance; hence you have PDF/A as an option choice. The CMYK version of the PDF/A standard is used with CMYK files.

- **PDF/A-1b:2005(RGB).** The same as the first PDF/A standard mentioned in the last bullet, this standard is used with RGB files.

- **PDF/X-1a:2001.** For prepress and printing, PDF/X files are streamlined for print output. PDF/X is an ISO standard developed by a committee outside Adobe Systems. Although Adobe participates in the standards committee, the format is a collaborative effort between members of the ISO standards committee. PDF/X files result in PDF documents that eliminate data not essential for printing. It does not mean the file sizes are necessarily smaller, but they are optimized for printing and produce fewer problems than non-PDF/X files. The PDF/X-1a format supports process (CMYK) and spot color.

- **PDF/X-3:2002.** Like PDF/X-1a, the file format is a subset of the PDF format. PDF/X-3 files support ICC profile embedding. If working in a color-managed workflow, use this flavor of PDF/X.

- **Press Quality.** These settings are virtually identical to the settings for High Quality (see first bullet). The difference between the two is that when you use the High Quality settings, any fonts not available for embedding during distillation are noted in the log file but the PDF is produced without the embedded fonts. When you use Press Quality, the job cancels at the first encounter of a font not available for embedding and the PDF is not produced.

- **Smallest File Size.** The intent for this option is to produce files for Web hosting, e-mailing, and screen views. The name implies that the file sizes are very small, but in reality, you can create smaller file sizes by editing the downsampling of the images. The sampling resolution only downsamples files above 150 pixels per inch (ppi) to 100 ppi. You can create a new set for smaller file sizes and downsample all images to 72 ppi for Web hosting when the images don't need to be displayed above a 100% view.

- **Standard.** The general-purpose setting and quite often the default when accessing settings the first time in Acrobat is the Standard choice. For office desktop color printers, laser printers, photocopiers, and general-purpose printing, the settings create PDF files with no lower than 150 ppi resolutions and embed fonts when necessary.

If one of these preset conditions comes close to producing the type of PDF you want to create, but it doesn't exactly meet your needs, go ahead and select that preset option and then choose Settings ⇨ Edit Adobe PDF Settings to open a dialog box where you can make changes. When you finish editing the settings to your satisfaction, you have an opportunity to save your own custom preset file that you can access at a later time. There are six panes for which you can choose to change the settings — General, Images, Fonts, Color, Advanced, and Standards.

FIGURE 10.4

Open the Default Settings pull-down menu and select the Adobe PDF Setting you want to use to convert a PostScript or EPS file to PDF.

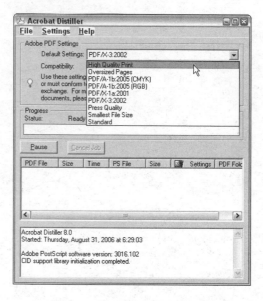

Each setting in the list of Default Settings has different attributes for PDF conversion assigned to the setting. You can modify the Default Settings or create new settings. The settings choices you have available are all accessed in the Adobe PDF Settings dialog box.

Changing Adobe PDF Settings

Select Settings ⇨ Edit Adobe PDF Settings in the Distiller window (Windows) or from the top-level menu bar (Macintosh). The Adobe PDF Settings dialog box opens, as shown in Figure 10.5. You have six categories from which to choose different settings options. The default is General, as shown in Figure 10.5, followed by Images, Fonts, Color, Advanced, and Standards. With the exception of the PDF/A Standard in the Standards tab, all settings are identical to the same settings in Acrobat 7.

FIGURE 10.5

The default Adobe PDF Settings for Press Quality

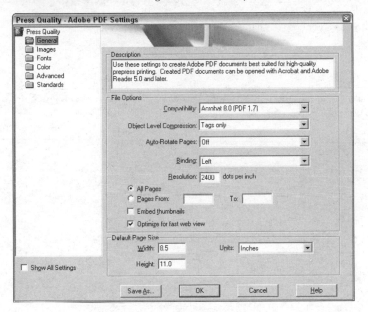

General settings

General settings are found under the General option in the Adobe PDF Settings dialog box (see Figure 10.6) and include the following options:

■ **Description.** A field box at the top of the General pane is editable and enables you to add a message description about the new settings you create. Place the cursor in the field box, highlight any existing text, and delete it. Type your new description in the field box. When you save the new setting, the description is saved along with your chosen options.

■ **Compatibility.** You have choices for Acrobat 3.0, 4.0, 5.0, 6.0, 7.0, and 8.0 compatibilities. Using earlier compatibility versions may affect the visibility of PDFs with earlier viewers. If you work in an enterprise where a large installed user base is using a particular version of Acrobat, create files for the compatibility version consistent with the site license of the Acrobat version. If you're creating files for mass distribution, think about forgetting Acrobat 3 and 4 compatibilities and focus on versions 5 through 8. Be aware that if you create Acrobat 6 through 8 compatible files and use new features such as embedding media clips or working with 2D barcodes, users of earlier versions won't be able to view your files. Excluding older versions is always a trade-off, and you need to clearly think about whom you want to target when distributing content.

■ **Object Level Compression.** Non-compressed objects are consolidated into streams for more efficient compression. You have choices for applying no compression (Off) or using Tags Only or Maximum (but there is no description in the Help file about what this means). You can reduce file sizes by selecting Tags only for Object Level Compression.

- **Auto-Rotate Pages.** You can have pages automatically or individually rotated during distillation. Choices from the pull-down menu include turning off rotation, rotating collectively by file, and rotating individually. When you select Collectively by File, Acrobat analyzes the text in the file and rotates pages based on the orientation of the majority of the text in the entire file. When you choose Individually, Acrobat rotates each page based on the majority of text on a given page. Selecting Off results in no page rotation.

- **Binding.** This setting relates to viewing pages in an Acrobat viewer with Two-Up and Two-Up Continuous page layouts and with thumbnails when viewed aside each other. In addition, the binding can affect other items like the direction of scrolling text across the screen and certain animated effects you add. By default, the binding is left-sided.

- **Resolution.** Settings for Resolution affect only vector objects and type in EPS files. The settings range between 72 and 4000 dpi. A handy Tool Tip appears when you click in the field box that shows the upper and lower limits of acceptable values. Lower resolution settings may create banding with gradients when files are printed. In practicality, you'll notice no visual difference if you change the resolution around the default of 600. Setting the resolution to 2400 adds less than 3K to your file size.

- **All Pages/Pages From.** You can choose to create a PDF within a specified range of pages from a PostScript file that has been printed to disk from a document containing many pages. If one page is having trouble converting to PDF, you can eliminate it from distillation by choosing a specified page range. The default, All Pages, distills all pages in the PostScript file.

- **Embed thumbnails.** Thumbnails add about 3K per page to your PDF file. Thumbnails are helpful when you're editing PDF files in Acrobat or browsing PDF files onscreen. However, because they create larger files, you'll want to eliminate thumbnails when producing PDF files for Web use or sending your PDF files across the Internet for output to printing devices. If you're using Acrobat viewers 5.0 and greater, thumbnails are displayed on-the-fly regardless of whether they have been embedded. Any legacy PDFs created with older PDF formats are also displayed with thumbnails without embedding when viewed in later viewers.

- **Optimize for fast Web view.** An optimized PDF file may be smaller than one created without optimization. All files intended to be used for screen views, CD-ROM replication, and Web usage should all be optimized. Optimized files are primarily designed for byte-serving on Web servers for page-at-a-time downloads. Generally, almost any printing device also accepts optimized files. As a default, keep this option On. Acrobat optimizes files by eliminating repeating elements and supplying pointers to where the first occurrence of an object is found in the file. Optimization also prepares files for page-at-a-time downloading from Web servers. If byte-serving capability exists on a server, the optimized files download pages as they are viewed.

- **Default Page Size.** Setting page sizes in these field boxes only applies to distillation of EPS and PostScript files where page boundaries are not specified. Whatever you enter in the field boxes when distilling PostScript files is ignored if the page boundary is included in the file. If you want to trim a page size or create a larger page size for an EPS file, you can establish the dimensions in the field boxes for width and height. The Units pull-down menu enables you to choose from four different units of measure.

FIGURE 10.6

The first Adobe PDF Settings that appear when you choose Settings ⇨ Edit Adobe PDF Settings are those under the General pane.

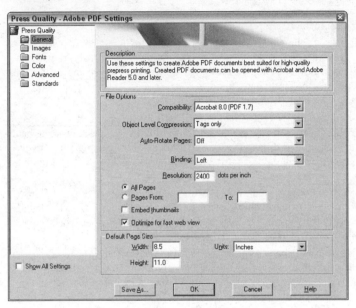

Images

Image settings are located under the second tab of the Adobe PDF Settings dialog box, as shown in Figure 10.7.

FIGURE 10.7

The second tab is Images.

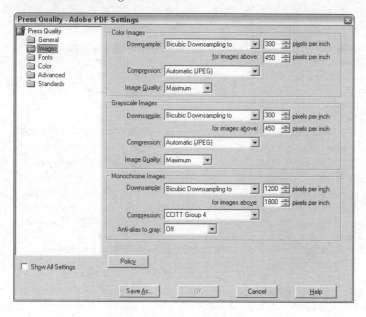

Color images

The first category handles color images used in your original file. You have choices for the sampling method and the amount of compression you want to apply. These include:

- **Downsample.** The Downsample pull-down menu offers choices for no sampling or three different sampling methods that include:

  - **Off.** This turns off all compression for color images.

  - **Bicubic Downsampling to.** A pull-down menu and two field boxes appear as your first choices in the Color Image section. Bicubic Downsampling is the default setting for all preset Adobe PDF Settings. Bicubic downsampling uses a weighted average to determine the resampled pixel color. The algorithm is much more mathematically intensive and, as a result, this method takes the longest time to complete distillation when files are downsampled. The upside is it produces the best image quality for continuous tone images. With this method as well as the other two choices for resampling images there are two field boxes where the amount of sampling is user defined. The values range between 9 and 2400 ppi. The "for images above" field box enables you to choose when an image is resampled.

  - **Average Downsampling to.** From the pull-down menu, the item following the Off selection is Average Downsampling to. When you resample an image by downsampling, the average pixel value of a sample area is replaced with a pixel of the averaged color. The field boxes to the right of the sampling method are for user-determined sampling amounts, used in the same way as the preceding Bicubic method.

  - **Subsampling to.** When Subsampling is specified, a pixel within the center of the sample area is chosen as the value applied to the sample area. Thus, downsampling noted previously, replaces pixels from averaged color values, whereas subsampling replaces pixels from a given

color value. Of the two methods, subsampling significantly reduces the amount of time to resample the image. Because all that averaging is taking place with downsampling, the calculations are more extensive, thereby increasing the distillation time. Subsampling, however, may result in more problems in the printed PDF file. Unless you have a large single-color background, you are better off choosing Bicubic downsampling when printing to hard copy.

- **Compression.** The pull-down menu enables you to select from Automatic (JPEG), JPEG, ZIP, or Off, depending on the compatibility setting you use. When you select Automatic, Distiller examines each image and automatically determines which compression to use (that is, either ZIP or JPEG). If an image has large amounts of a common color value, ZIP compression is used. If an image consists of smooth transitions of color, such as a continuous tone photograph, JPEG compression is used. If you want to apply the same compression to all images, you can select either the JPEG or ZIP options. Doing so eliminates any decision making by Distiller about the type of compression to be applied. When you select Off, no compression is applied. While you may want to downsample images as noted earlier with one of the downsampling options, you may not want to apply compression to the images.

- **Image Quality.** After you select the compression type, you have one of five choices (also depending on compatibility) for the amount of compression applied. Maximum relates to less compression, whereas Minimum relates to high compression. For high-end prepress, use the Maximum or High choice from the pull-down menu. For desktop color printers, use Medium quality; and for Web, screen, or CD-ROM replication, use Low quality. The Minimum setting might be used in some cases with screen or Web graphics, but continuous tone photographs often appear visibly degraded. You might use this setting to transfer files quickly across the Internet for client approvals and then later use a higher setting for the final production documents.

Grayscale

All the choices you have for color images are identical for grayscale images. You can use different settings for color and grayscale images by toggling through all the options. When the final PDF is produced, the sampling and compression for your images are respectively applied from choices made for each image type.

Monochrome images

Monochrome images include only two color values — black and white. Photoshop line art is a monochrome image. This is not to be confused with line art as we define it with vector art applications. The sampling methods available to you for monochrome images are identical to those described for color images. Compression settings, however, are much different. In addition to Off for applying no compression, the options include the following:

- **CCITT Group 3.** The International Coordinating Committee for Telephony and Telegraphy (CCITT) Group 3 compression is used by fax machines. The images are compressed in horizontal rows, one row at a time.

- **CCITT Group 4.** CCITT Group 4 is a general-purpose compression method that produces good compression for most types of bitmap images. This compression method is the default and typically the best method for bitmap images.

- **ZIP.** ZIP compression is more efficient than earlier versions of Acrobat that used LZW compression. ZIP achieves approximately 20 percent more compression. It should be used when large areas of a single color appear in an image.

- **Run Length.** The Run Length format is a lossless compression scheme particularly favorable to bitmap monochrome images. You can run tests yourself for the compression method that works best for you. Typically, CCITT Group 4 handles most of your needs when compressing these images.

- **Anti-Alias to gray.** Bitmap images may appear pixelated onscreen or, in some cases, when printed. By using anti-aliasing, images are rendered with a smoother appearance. You can choose the amount of anti-aliasing from the pull-down menu. Choices are for 2, 4, and 8 bits that produce 4, 16, and 256 levels of gray, respectively. If you use anti-aliasing with scanned type, small point sizes may appear blurry, especially with higher gray levels.
- **Policy.** Click the Policy button and the Adobe PDF – Image Policy dialog box opens as shown in Figure 10.8. The options in the dialog box enable you to control a job determined from decisions you make about image resolution. From the pull-down menus below each resolution item you can select from Ignore, Warn and Continue, and Cancel Job. If a given image is below a resolution value you add to one of the three field boxes for a given image type, you can instruct Acrobat to honor the choice(s) you make from the menu selections. Ignore is the default and no result occurs if images fall below a certain resolution. Warn and Continue opens a warning dialog box, informs you that Distiller found an image below the resolution you specify in one of the field boxes, and continues producing the PDF. Cancel Job stops all distillation if an image is found below the resolution setting(s).

FIGURE 10.8

The Adobe PDF – Image Policy dialog box enables you to set options for a job determined on decisions you make for image resolution.

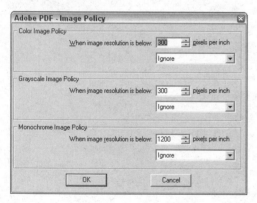

Guidelines for sampling images

Acrobat handles sampling appropriate for your output needs as long as the image sampling is equal to or greater than the requirements for the output. If image resolution is lower than the output needs, then Distiller isn't able to upsample images to provide the necessary resolution. Even though Distiller can effectively downsample images, you should observe a few rules.

First, you should sample the resolution for all images in a layout or design at the highest output requirement. For example, if you intend to use prepress and commercial printing, then the image sample needs a resolution to support commercial printing. In this regard, you want to sample images in Photoshop at the required resolution. Don't rely on Distiller to downsample images during distillation. The time you save can add up if you're converting many files with high-resolution images. When you open the Adobe PDF Settings and select the Images pane, select Off for the sampling items.

You use the second rule when repurposing images. If you have a PostScript file that has been printed for a higher order of output, like the commercial printing discussed earlier in this chapter, then you don't need to create a second PostScript file for another output destination. Use the same PostScript file and select the

sampling options appropriate for the output. Using this same example, if you now want to create a PDF for screen views, select Bicubic Downsampling to and set the resolution to 72 dpi.

Fonts

The distinctive advantage of using the Portable Document Format is that it maintains file integrity across computers and across platforms. One of the greatest problems with file integrity is the handling of fonts. Fortunately, Distiller provides the ability to embed fonts within the PDF so the end user won't need font installations to view and print PDF files. The Fonts pane, shown in Figure 10.9, offers options for setting font-embedding attributes during distillation.

FIGURE 10.9

The Fonts item in Adobe PDF Settings displays the control over font embedding available to you during distillation.

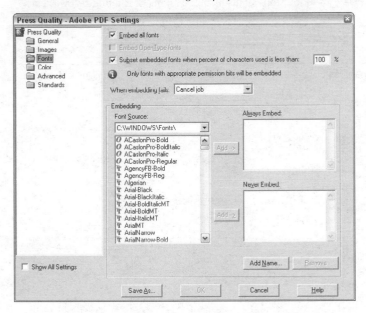

Options in the Fonts pane include the following:

- **Embed all fonts.** Unless you have a specific reason not to embed fonts, this option should always be enabled for file exchanges and printing. You might choose not to embed fonts when you want to reduce file sizes to the smallest possible size for Web hosting or if your documents will be exclusively in your organization and everyone has the fonts used.

CAUTION Many different font developers exist, and the permissions for use of fonts from these developers vary considerably. To legally include font embedding in a PDF file, you need to know whether the developer provides the permission for inclusion. Adobe original fonts that are owned by Linotype-Hell, International Typeface Corporation, AGFA, AlphaOmega, Bigelow & Holmes, Fundicion Typografica Neufville, and Monotype Typography, Ltd., as well as those in the Adobe library, can be used for font embedding without written releases. Fonts with licensing restrictions often appear with an explanation of the limitations of use. If in doubt, you'll need to check with the developer or distributor to inquire as to whether you can legally distribute PDF files that include certain fonts. Failure to do so may result in a copyright violation.

- **Embed OpenType fonts.** If the box is active, check the box to embed all OpenType fonts. The box is active only when using Acrobat 7 or greater compatibility.

- **Subset embedded fonts when percent of characters used is less than [ ].** Some PDF producers provide you an opportunity to subset PostScript, OpenType, and TrueType fonts. The difference between the subsetting in Distiller as opposed to other producers is your ability to determine when a font is subset. With Distiller, you can specify when you want subsetting to occur. The subsetting percentage has to do with the percentage of *glyphs* (special renderings) in the font. If 100% is selected, Distiller includes all information necessary to draw all the glyphs in the font. Lower percentages determine what characters among the set are embedded. Type 3, TrueType, and CID fonts are always embedded regardless of what value is supplied. (For font format descriptions, see Table 10.1 later in this chapter.)

  When two or more PostScript files are converted to PDF with Acrobat Distiller using font subsetting, Distiller gives the resulting PDF only one font subset. The result is a more efficient PDF document and produces smaller file sizes, especially when combining several PostScript files to produce a single PDF.

- **When embedding fails.** This pull-down menu offers three choices. Choose Ignore to ignore a failed font being embedded, in which case distillation continues. The Warn and Continue option displays a warning and then continues distillation. Choose Cancel to cancel the distillation if a font embedding error occurs. When sending files off to service centers for imaging or when font substitution is not desired, use this latter option as your default. If the PDF is not produced, you won't inadvertently forget there was a problem with font embedding.

- **Embedding.** The left side of the dialog box lists all fonts available for embedding. From the pull-down menu, you select from the different folders Distiller monitors for fonts. Distiller can monitor font locations on your computer. If you want to view the font list from another monitored folder, click the pull-down menu and select the folder. Regardless of what is listed in the Embedding list, Distiller can also embed fonts that were included in the PostScript file or all the folders listed for monitoring. The fonts to be embedded must be present in either the PostScript file or a monitored folder.

NOTE Fonts that have license restrictions are shown in the Font Source list with a padlock icon. If you select the font, the restriction attributes are displayed in the Fonts pane. You cannot move locked fonts to the Always Embed list.

- **Always Embed.** A list of fonts for always embedding appears to the right of the Embedding list. You add fonts to this list by selecting them from the Embedding list and clicking the right-pointing chevron (double arrows). You can select multiple fonts by pressing the Ctrl (Windows) key or ⌘ (Macintosh) key and clicking all the fonts to be included. If the fonts are listed in a contiguous display, press Shift+click. After selecting the font(s), click the right-pointing chevron. A good use for the Always Embed list might be for a font that appears in your company logo. Regardless of the type of document you create, you may want to always include your corporate font set in all your documents to avoid any font substitution.

NOTE The design of TrueType and OpenType fonts enables the type designer the ability to prevent font embedding. These fonts can be moved to the Always Embed list, but if they are designed without embedding permissions, they fail to embed in PDFs. Font embedding errors are reported in the log file, which you can view in a text editor. If a PDF is produced, you can choose File ⇨ Properties ⇨ Fonts to determine whether the font was embedded.

- **Never Embed.** This list operates the same way as the Always Embed list. You select fonts to be eliminated from the set of monitored fonts or fonts contained in a PostScript file. One use for this list might be to eliminate Courier, Times, Helvetica, and Symbol (the Base 13 fonts). Because they

are usually burned into ROM chips on most PostScript devices, you rarely have a problem either viewing them or printing documents containing these fonts.

> **NOTE** The Base 14 fonts are sometimes referred to as the Base 13 + 1 fonts. The Base 13 fonts consist of Courier, Helvetica, Times, and Symbol. Courier, Helvetica, and Times include Roman, bold, italic, and bold italic, thus resulting in four fonts for each family. The extra font added to the base set is Zapf Dingbats. The fonts shipped with Acrobat 6 and 7 are no longer the Base 14 fonts that were shipped with earlier versions of Acrobat. Acrobat 6 ships with a new set of Base fonts that include AdobePiStd (a replacement for Zapf Dingbats), Courier, Symbol, AdobeSansMM, and Adobe SerifMM. Acrobat Distiller 7 and 8 does not embed the Base fonts.

- **Add Name.** You can add fonts to the Always Embed list or the Never Embed list by entering the font name in a separate dialog box. To add a font name, you must type the name in the dialog box precisely as the font is identified. When you click the Add Name button in the Fonts pane, the Add Font Name dialog box opens where you enter the name in the field box. Two radio buttons exist for determining where the font is added. Select either the Always Embed list or Never Embed list as needed. Click Done, and the font appears in the appropriate list.

- **Remove.** If you add a font name to either the Always Embed list or the Never Embed list, and you want to delete that name, select the font name to be deleted and click Remove. You can't remove fonts from the Embedding list. The only time Remove is enabled is when you select a font name in either the Always Embed list or Never Embed list.

> **NOTE** The priority used by Distiller to decide whether to embed a font in the PDF follows an order to resolve ambiguity. The Never Embed list is viewed by Distiller as having the highest order of priority. If you place a font in the Never Embed list, it is not to be embedded even though you may add the same font to the Always Embed list.

Font types

Any PDF author will tell you the continuing problem with file displays and printing, as well as producing PDFs, relates to font handling. People swear at times that they have enabled all the appropriate controls for font embedding and PDF file creation, yet the resulting PDF either displays or prints with font substitution. Gathering as much knowledge as you can with regard to font evolution, design, engineering, and proper use helps you understand how to overcome problems and provide solutions for your workflow. To gain a little more understanding, look at the font types, formats, and their characteristics:

- **Type 0.** Type 0 (zero) is a high-level composite font format that references multiple font descendents. Type 0 fonts use an OCF (Original Composite Font) format that was Adobe's first effort in attempting to implement a format for handling fonts with large character sets. A good example of a font using a large character set is Asian Language font types. Today, the OCF format is not supported.

- **Type 1.** By far the most popular PostScript font today is the Type 1 font. These are single-byte fonts handled well by Adobe Type Manager (Windows and Macintosh OS X) and all PostScript printers. Type 1 fonts use a specialized subset of the PostScript language, which is optimized for performance. For reliability, use of Type 1 fonts presents the fewest problems when embedding and printing to PostScript devices.

> **NOTE** The one problem with Type 1 fonts is there isn't a means for flagging the font for *don't embed*. As a result, the end user can't determine font permissions for embedding Type 1 fonts. As of this writing Adobe is converting all its Type 1 fonts to OpenType fonts. OpenType fonts always have an extra bit to determine embedding rights. For more information on OpenType fonts, see "OpenType Font Format" later in this section.

- **Type 2.** Type 2 fonts offer compact character description procedures for outline fonts. They were designed to be used with the Compact Font Format (CFF). The CFF format is designed for font embedding and substitution with Acrobat PDFs.

- **Type 3.** Type 3 fonts are PostScript fonts that have often been used with some type-stylizing applications. These fonts can have special design attributes applied to the font such as shading, patterns, exploding 3-D displays, and so on. The fonts can't be used with ATM (Adobe Type Manager), and they often present problems when you're printing to PostScript devices. You should not use them when creating PDF files.

- **Type 4.** Type 4 was designed to create font characters from printer font cartridges for permanent storage on a printer's hard drive (usually attached by a SCSI port to the printer). PostScript Level 2 provided the same capability for Type 1 fonts and eventually made these font types obsolete.

- **Type 5.** This font type is similar to the Type 4 fonts but used the printer's ROM instead of the hard drive. PostScript Level 2 again made this format obsolete.

- **Type 32.** Type 32 fonts are used for downloading bitmap fonts to a PostScript interpreter's font cache. By downloading directly to the printer cache, space is saved in the printer's memory.

- **Type 42.** Type 42 fonts are generated from the printer driver for TrueType fonts. A PostScript wrapper is created for the font, making the rasterization and interpretation more efficient and accurate. Type 42 fonts work well with PDFs and printing to PostScript printers.

- **OpenType Font Format.** OpenType is a recent joint effort by Adobe Systems and Microsoft to provide a new generation of type font technology. OpenType makes no distinction between Type 1 and TrueType fonts. It acts as a *container* for both Type 1 and TrueType. OpenType doesn't care whether the font is Type 1 or TrueType; it uses the font inside the OpenType container accordingly. Font developers have a much easier way of porting font designs to a single format in production and mastering as well as across platforms. The OpenType format is supported with font embedding and distillation. Fonts eventually produced with this technology are as reliable as you find with Type 1 and Type 42 fonts. In addition OpenType offers a means for flagging the fonts for embedding permissions. To embed OpenType fonts in a PDF, use Distiller 8 and check the box for Embed OpenType fonts in the Fonts pane.

- **Compact Font Format.** CFF is similar to the Type 1 format but offers much more compact encoding and optimization. It was designed to support Type 2 fonts but can be used with other types. CFF can be embedded in PDFs with the PDF version 1.2 format and Acrobat 3.0 compatibility. Fonts supporting this format are converted by Distiller during distillation to CFF/Type 2 fonts and embedded in the PDF. When viewed onscreen or printed, they are converted back to Type 1, which provides support for ATM and printing with integrity.

- **CID-keyed Fonts.** This format was developed to take advantage of large character sets, particularly the Asian CJK (Chinese, Japanese, and Korean) fonts. The format is an extension of the Type 1 format and supports ATM and PostScript printing. Kerning and spacing for these character sets are better handled in the OpenType format. On the Macintosh you can find a utility called Make CID in the Distiller: Xtras folder. For Asian TrueType or Type 1 OCF formats, use the utility to convert the fonts to CID-keyed fonts. The first time Distiller launches with the Asian character set installed, you are prompted to convert any of these fonts found in monitored folders. If you want to manually convert the fonts you can double-click the application icon. On Windows, the Make CID application isn't available. Converted fonts can be copied across platforms, and Distiller running under Windows processes PostScript files created under Mac OS that have references to the character widths.

When distilling PostScript with Acrobat Distiller, font embedding and substitution are allowed as described in Table 10.1.

TABLE 10.1

Distiller Handling of Font Embedding and Subsetting According to Type Format

Font	Never Embed	Always Embed	Subset
Type 1	Yes	Yes	Yes
Type 2	No — Always embedded		No — Always subsetted
TrueType Type 42	Yes	Yes	No — Always subsetted
CIDFontType0	Yes	Yes	No — Always subsetted
CIDFontType1	No — Always embedded		No — Always subsetted
CIDFontType2	Yes	Yes	No — Always subsetted
OpenType*	Yes	Yes	No — Always subsetted

*OpenType Is supported only with Distiller 5.0 and greater.

Color

Adobe has been working on developing standard color viewing and file tagging for color spaces for some time. Releases of the latest software products continue to support sophisticated color-handling methods. Latest releases of products such as Adobe Illustrator and Adobe Photoshop have color control options consistent with the new color-handling features initially introduced in Acrobat 5. When making choices for color handling, your first decision is whether to convert color. After your conversion choice, you move on to working spaces and profile assumptions. If you tag a file for conversion, what profiles do you want to embed in the document? Under the Color Management Policies settings, you choose control for many conditions for prepress operations as well as onscreen viewing. As you view the Color pane in the Adobe PDF Settings, examine each of the controls available for color handling, as shown in Figure 10.10.

> **TIP**   A thorough coverage of color management is a complex subject and beyond the scope of this book. If you are confused about many issues discussed in this chapter or you want to work on developing a color-managed workflow, open any Acrobat viewer. Select the Search tool and click Search PDFs on the Internet. Add color management for the search criteria and select Match Exact word or phrase from the pull-down menu. Click the Search the Internet button. Many PDF documents are available on the Internet that define color management and discuss how to set up color-managed workflows. You can build a library of articles and essays on the subject and keep them readily available on your local computer.

FIGURE 10.10

Manage color profiles in the Color pane.

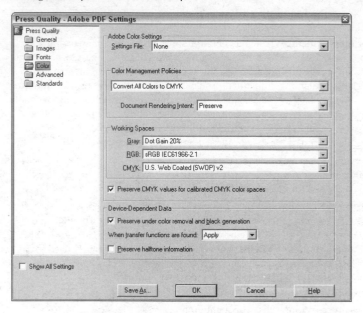

Adobe Color Settings

Working with a color management system requires you to make some decisions about how the color is viewed on your computer monitor and on the final output medium. In some cases the monitor view and output medium view are the same, such as Acrobat viewer files onscreen and Web files. You make the first of your color decisions from among the choices in the pull-down menu for Settings File. The choices available to you include the following:

- **Settings File.** When you select None from the pull-down menu, you can custom edit the Color Management Policies and Working Spaces choices. If you choose an option other than None, the Color Management Policies and Working Spaces options are grayed out. Other choices for Settings include prepress defaults, Photoshop emulation, defaults for Web graphics, and turning off color management. When color management and profile embedding is controlled by other programs such as Photoshop, leave the setting to None and turn off all color management for the choices discussed next.

Color Management Policies

If you select None from the Settings drop-down menu, the options for Color Management Policies and Intent are active. If you make any other choice from the menu, these items are grayed out. Choices for the Color Management Policies are different depending on what compatibility choice you select in the General pane of the Adobe PDF Settings dialog box. Acrobat 3.0 compatibility offers different options than the 4.0, 5.0, 6.0, 7.0, and 8.0 compatibilities. As you look at the following policy choices, keep in mind that the settings change according to the compatibility selection you made:

■ **Leave Color Unchanged.** Enable this menu item if you presume all color handling in the PostScript file is defined for your specific needs. No color conversion occurs and device-dependent colors remain unchanged. When you send files to color-calibrated devices, you should use this option. The presumption is the device specifies all color handling and the file is not to be tagged for color management.

■ **Tag Everything for Color Management.** When you choose Acrobat 3.0 compatibility or above, a color profile selected in the Working Spaces section is used to Tag Everything for Color Management, which embeds an ICC profile for the images, artwork, and text. The printed PDF file maintains the integrity of any documents containing embedded profiles; however, the view on your monitor screen assumes the color viewing space of the assumed profile selected respective to choices made in Working Spaces. When you choose Acrobat 3.0 compatibility, the option changes to Convert Everything for Color Management and no ICC profiles are embedded. Device-dependent color spaces for all color modes are converted to device-independent color spaces of CalRGB, CalGray, and Lab.

■ **Tag Only Images for Color Management.** The same holds true as noted in the preceding entry except only raster images are tagged for color management according to the same compatibility options selected in the General pane. Text and vector objects remain unaffected.

■ **Convert All Colors to sRGB.** Selecting this option converts all colors to sRGB. The RGB and CMYK color images are converted. When using Acrobat 3.0 compatibility, the RGB and CMYK images are converted to CalRGB (Calibrated RGB). Converting colors to sRGB is best used for screen and Web images. The file sizes are smaller and screen redraws appear faster. Grayscale images are unaffected by choices made for color tagging and conversion.

■ **Convert All Colors to CMYK.** This option provides RGB and spot color conversion to CMYK. If your job is to be printed as process color, select the menu item.

Below the Color Management Policies pull-down menu is the Document Rendering Intent pull-down menu, which you use for the Intent for how color will be mapped between color spaces. Choices for Intent include the following:

■ **Preserve.** The first of the Intent choices is Preserve. Preserve involves no color compensation.

■ **Perceptual.** Perceptual (Images) has to do with the mapping of pixels from one gamut to another. When you select this item, the image is mapped from the original pixels to the color gamut of the printer profile. All the out-of-gamut colors are remapped.

■ **Saturation.** Saturation (Graphics) maintains relative saturation values. If a pixel is saturated and out of the color gamut of the printer, it is remapped preserving saturation but mapped to the closest color within the printer's gamut.

■ **Absolute Colormetric.** This disables the white point matching when colors are converted. With no white point reference, you will notice a change in brightness values of all the remapped colors.

■ **Relative Colormetric.** This preserves all color values within the printer's gamut. Out-of-gamut colors are converted to the same lightness values of colors within the printable gamut.

Working Spaces

Profile management for working spaces involves your decisions for embedding profiles for the color space while viewing your images onscreen. If a color space is defined for a given image and viewed on one monitor, theoretically it can be viewed the same on other monitors if the color profile is embedded in the image. Working space definitions are applied only to images tagged for color management. Either of the two tagging options, Tag Everything for Color Management or Tag Only Images for Color Management, must be selected in order for a working space to be defined:

- **Gray.** Selecting None from this menu prevents grayscale images from being converted. The Dot Gain choices affect the overall brightness of grayscale images. Lower values lighten the image whereas values above 20 percent display grayscale images darker. Gray Gamma choices might be used for images viewed between computer platforms. A Gray Gamma of 1.8 is suited for Macintosh viewing whereas the higher 2.2 Gamma is better suited for Windows.

- **RGB.** If you use a color calibration system or monitor profile, you can select the respective profile from this pull-down menu. Choices available to you depend on profiles installed on your computer. If you have created custom profiles from Adobe Photoshop and saved them, they are listed as menu options. Default RGB profiles from Photoshop appear here after Photoshop is installed on your computer. The default option is sRGB IEC61966-2.1. If in doubt, use this option. It is becoming an industry standard and generally good for matching color between display and color output devices.

- **CMYK.** CMYK profiles also appear according to those stored in the respective folder according to platform as mentioned in the preceding bullet. Profile tagging is uniquely applied to images according to the color mode of the image. Thus, the Gray options apply only to grayscale images. RGB choices are applied to only RGB images whereas the CMYK choices tag only CMYK images. When using CMYK output for prepress you may have a profile embedded in the CMYK images. You can select None for this setting while changing the Gray and RGB working spaces, which preserves the color for output, enabling you to tag the other color modes for screen views. It would be unlikely that you would use RGB and CMYK images together for prepress, but you could set up the Adobe PDF Settings for consistent display of files regardless of the color mode used.

CMYK color spaces

A single check box — Preserve CMYK values for calibrated CMYK color spaces — appears for this item. Unless you select Convert All Colors to CMYK in the Color Management Policies, the item is grayed out. Check the box when it's active and the CMYK color space is preserved when profile embedding has been applied.

Device-Dependent Data

All options available under the Device Dependent Data section are applied to images intended for prepress and printing. Whatever choices you make here have no effect on screen views:

- **Preserve under color removal and black generation.** If you made changes to undercolor removal or black generation settings in Photoshop, these changes are preserved when the file is distilled. Disabling the check box eliminates any settings made in Photoshop.

- **When transfer functions are found.** If you embed transfer functions in Adobe Photoshop, you can preserve them by selecting Apply from the pull-down menu. If transfer functions have not been saved with your Photoshop file, it won't matter if Apply is used. Use Apply when you intentionally set them up in a Photoshop image and you have the settings confirmed by your printer. If you select Preserve, the transfer functions are preserved without applying them. You can eliminate transfer functions set in a file by selecting Remove from the pull-down menu. As a matter of default, if you don't use transfer functions or know what they are, select Remove from the pull-down menu. If you inadvertently save a Photoshop file as EPS and embed transfer functions, they are removed when the file gets distilled.

- **Preserve halftone information.** Preserving the halftone information does not disturb halftone frequencies embedded in documents, as well as custom angles, spot shapes, and functions specified. Depending on the service center you use, they may want to have you set halftone information in the PostScript file and preserve them in the PDF. For PostScript 3 devices, PDFs can be sent straight to the imagesetter and printed at the halftone frequency preserved in the file. Service centers using PostScript Level 2 RIPs won't care if the halftone frequency is preserved or not. They'll have to manually print the PDFs using the Print and Advanced Print Setup dialog boxes.

Advanced

Advanced settings contain a variety of options for job ticketing, document structure, and other items not found in the previous panes, as shown in Figure 10.11.

FIGURE 10.11

The Advanced Adobe PDF Settings offer a group of miscellaneous settings often not available with other PDF producers.

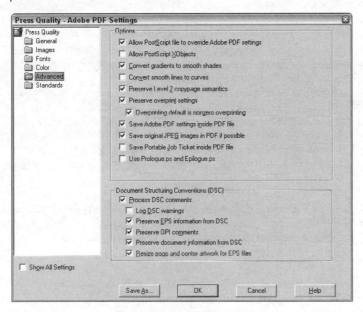

These options include:

- **Allow PostScript file to override Adobe PDF settings.** If you are certain the PostScript file you printed to disk has all the settings handled properly for output, enabling this option allows the PostScript file to supersede any changes you make in Adobe PDF Settings. Disabling the check box allows all Options specifications settings to take precedence.

- **Allow PostScript XObjects.** A PostScript XObject stores common information in a document, such as backgrounds, headers, footers, and so on. When PostScript XObjects are used, printing is faster, but requires more memory. If you disable the check box, XObjects won't be used and the memory burden is reduced.

- **Convert gradients to smooth shades.** This feature only works with Acrobat 4.0 compatibility and greater. Gradients are converted to smooth shades and appear much smoother when rendered on PostScript 3 devices. The appearance of the gradients is unaffected when viewed onscreen, but has noticeable differences when printing some files with more gray levels.

- **Convert smooth lines to curves.** Checking this box helps reduce file sizes significantly when creating PDFs from CAD drawing programs. Checking the box reduces the amount of control points used to build curves in CAD programs, resulting in much smaller file sizes and much faster displays on your monitor. You can experience similar results on files where the Auto Trace tool was used in Adobe Illustrator.

- **Preserve Level 2 copypage semantics.** This setting has to do with semantic differences between PostScript Level 2 and PostScript 3. If you are imaging to PostScript Level 2 devices, enable this option. If you're printing to PostScript 3 devices, disable this option. If you are sending files to an imaging center, ask the technicians which level of PostScript is used on their devices.

- **Preserve overprint settings.** Overprints manually applied in applications, such as illustration and layout programs, are preserved when you enable this option. Overprinting has an effect only when your files are color separated or possibly when you print composite color to proofing machines that display trapping problems from files printed as separations. If your workflow is consistent and you don't deviate between creating overprints and relying on a service center to perform them, then you could leave this item as a default for your high-end output needs. Enabling the check box has no effect on images where overprints are not present.

- **Overprinting default is nonzero overprinting.** When enabled, this option prevents objects with no color values specified as CMYK from knocking out other CMYK colors.

- **Save Adobe PDF settings inside PDF file.** This option embeds the Adobe PDF Settings used to produce the PDF inside the PDF document as a file attachment. Print shops can review the settings to diagnose problems that may have been produced during distillation. Open the Attachments pane to see the embedded file.

- **Save original JPEG images in PDF if possible.** Distiller decompresses JPEG files during distillation. If you select this option, the decompressed JPEG files are not recompressed by Distiller.

- **Save Portable Job Ticket inside PDF file.** Job tickets contain information about the original PostScript file and not the content of the PDF file. Information related to page sizes, page orientation, resolution, halftone frequencies, trapping information, and so on, is some of what is contained in job tickets. When printing PDF files, enable this option. If you produce PDF files for screen, Web, or CD-ROM, you can eliminate job ticket information.

- **Use Prologue.ps and Epilogue.ps.** There are two files, named prologue.ps and epilogue.ps, located in the Documents and Settings\All Users\Documents\Adobe PDF \Data folder (Windows) or Library\Application Support\Adobe PDF\Distiller\Data folder (Macintosh) when you install Acrobat. If you don't find the files installed in the location described here, search the Acrobat Professional 8 CD-ROM installer.

  In order to use the files, you must move them to the same folder as the Acrobat Distiller application, and both files must reside together in this location. The files contain PostScript code appended to a PDF file when it is created with Distiller. By default the files do not contain any data that affect distillation. They serve more as templates where you can write code to append data to the PDF. You use the prologue.ps file to append information to the PDF such as a note, cover page, or job ticket information. You use the epilogue.ps file to resolve PostScript procedure problems.

NOTE You can edit both of these files; however, you need to be familiar with the PostScript language to effectively change the files. When relocating the files, be certain to place a copy in the Distiller folder and leave the original in the Data folder, especially if you decide to edit either file. You can also use the files with watched folders, as explained a little later in this chapter. When using watched folders, place the prologue.ps and epilogue.ps files at the same directory level as the In and Out folders.

- **Process DSC comments.** Document structuring comments (DSC) contain information about a PDF file. Items such as originating application, creation date, modification date, page orientation, and so on, are all document-structuring comments. To maintain the DSC, enable this option. Because some important information such as page orientation and beginning and ending statements for the prologue.ps file are part of the document structure, you'll want to keep this item enabled as a default.

- **Log DSC warnings.** During distillation, if the processing of the document-structuring comments encounters an error, the error is noted in a log file. When you enable this check box, a log file is created. You can open the log file in a word processor or text editor to determine where the error occurred. Enable this option whenever document-structuring comments are processed.

- **Preserve EPS information from DSC.** This item is similar to the Process DSC comments option. If your file is an EPS file, enabling this check box preserves document-structuring comments.

- **Preserve OPI comments.** Open Press Interface (OPI) is a management tool used by many high-end imaging centers to control production. An OPI comment might include the replacement of high-resolution images for low-resolution FPO (for position only) files used in a layout program. OPI comments can include many different issues related to digital prepress such as image position on a page, crop area, sampling resolution, color bit depth, colors (in other words, CMYK, spot, and so on), overprint instructions, and more. If you're outputting to high-end imaging devices at service centers using OPI management, enable this option.

- **Preserve document information from DSC.** Document information items, discussed later in this book, include such things as title, subject, author, and keywords. Enabling this option preserves document information.

- **Resize page and center artwork for EPS files.** In earlier versions of Acrobat, distillation of a single-page EPS file, created from programs such as Adobe Illustrator, Macromedia FreeHand, or CorelDraw, used the EPS bounding box for the final page size. Many problems occurred when distilling EPS files directly as opposed to printed PostScript files. At times, a user would experience clipping and lose part of an image. With this option you have a choice between creating a PDF with the page dimensions equal to the artwork and having the artwork appear on the size of the original page you defined in your host application. When the check box is enabled, the page size is reduced to the size of the artwork, and the artwork is centered on the page. When the check box is disabled, the entire page appears consistent with the page size used in the host application.

Standards (Acrobat Professional only)

The Standards pane provides options for creating subsets of the PDF file in the form of PDF/X and PDF/A documents designed for printing and archiving, respectively. Click the Standards folder and select a Compliance Standard from the pull-down menu options. Although there are several options from which to choose, the categories are centralized around PDF/X and PDF/A.

PDF/X

As explained earlier, PDF/X is a subset of the PDF format developed by an ISO (International Organization for Standardization) standards committee outside Adobe Systems. Adobe is a participant on the committee and supports the development and advances in PDF/X standards.

PDF/X has gained much acceptance among commercial printing companies for the purposes of creating files suitable for printing. PDF is a reliable format for any kind of electronic file exchanges. However, files developed for viewing in Acrobat viewers, Acrobat PDF forms, Web-hosted documents, and so on, carry a lot of overhead not necessary for printing on commercial printing devices. The PDF/X compliance standard was developed to streamline documents by eliminating unnecessary data and optimizing files for print. The process of tailoring a PDF document for print by creating a PDF/X-compliant file does not necessarily reduce file size. In many cases, file sizes grow from a standard PDF to a PDF/X file.

The PDF/X options available to you in Acrobat Distiller produce either a PDF/X-1a:2002, PDF/X-1a:2003- or PDF/X-3:2002-, PDF/X-3:2003-compliant file. These file types are different versions of the PDF/X format. PDF/X-1a is designed to work well with both process and spot color, but no support is provided for color management or profile embedding. PDF/X-3 supports process and spot color and also supports color-managed workflows and ICC (International Color Consortium) profile embedding.

The PDF/X pane appears only in Acrobat Professional and is not available to Acrobat Standard users.

The two distinctions between the versions for PDFX-1a:2002, and PDF/X-1a:2003 have to do with versions of the same subset. PDF/X-1a:2002 is compatible with Acrobat 4.PDF/X-1a:2003 is compatible with Acrobat 5. The same applies to the version 2002 and version 2003 of the PDF/X-3 subset. If you select Acrobat compatibility for version 6, 7, or 8 in the General pane, you lose the ability to select either PDF/X format.

When you use PDF/X during distillation you are checking the file for PDF/X compliance. If the file does not meet the PDF/X standard you select (that is, PDF/X-1a or PDF/X-3), you can halt the distillation process much like halting distillation when fonts don't embed properly. If a file meets PDF/X compliance, you have much greater assurance that your PDF document will print on almost any kind of commercial printing device.

You create PDF/X-compliant files with Acrobat Distiller or an authoring program that specifically addresses PDF/X compliance when exporting to PDF. InDesign CS is one application that supports PDF creation with delivery of a PDF/X-compliant file. Other PDF producers such as PDFMaker used with Microsoft Office applications, Microsoft Project, Microsoft Visio, and Autodesk AutoCAD do not support PDF/X. If you want to print any of these files on commercial printing devices, print PostScript files and distill them with Acrobat Distiller and PDF/X enabled.

The options you have in the Standards pane in Acrobat Professional, shown in Figure 10.12, include the following:

- **Compliance Standard.** The pull-down menu contains options for all the PDF/X compliance versions, a setting for PDF/A compliance, and an option for None.

- **When not compliant.** Two menu choices are available from this pull-down menu. Select Continue to create the PDF file if the file does not meet PDF/X compliance. The PDF file is created and a log file is generated reporting problems. If you select Cancel Job, the PDF is not created and assures you of only producing files that meet the PDF/X standards.

- **Report as error.** Enabling this radio button reports the file noncompliant if a trim box or media box is missing on any page in the document.

- **Set TrimBox to MediaBox with offset (Inches).** When the radio button is enabled, the trim box is calculated against the media box for offset distances if neither is specified in the PostScript file. The trim box is always equal to or smaller than the media box. Edit the field boxes for determining the offset amounts that are analyzed.

- **Set BleedBox to MediaBox.** Uses the media box values for the bleed box if no bleeds are specified in the PostScript file. In many layout authoring programs you have options for specifying bleed areas. If no bleeds are defined in the print dialog boxes, the media box values are used.

- **Set BleedBox to TrimBox with offsets (Inches).** If the bleed box is not defined, the values specified in the field boxes are computed against the trim box.

- **Output Intent Profile Name.** If the file does not specify an output intent, such as SWOP coated for example, Distiller uses the intent you select from the pull-down menu. The field box is editable and you can type an output intent in the field box. If you don't require an output intent for the devices you use, select None. When the file is distilled and no intent was used when the PostScript file was printed, selecting None forces the job to fail compliance.

- **Output Condition Identifier.** This item is a reference name specified by the Output Intent Profile Name's registry. The name is automatically supplied for known Output Intent Profile Names. If a conditional identifier is used, then the parameter must be manually added.

- **Output Condition.** This field box is where you supply the intended output condition. The field value is not assessed for compliance. It is used by the service center for information purposes. If you leave the field blank, it has no effect on whether the job meets compliance.

- **Registry Name (URL).** This item is also informational. For certain profiles selected in the Output Intent Profile Name pull-down menu, you'll see a URL where more information is hosted on a Web site related to the profile.

- **Trapped.** Three options are available from the pull-down menu. PDF/X compliance requires that the trapped state be analyzed for True or False. If you select Undefined, you are checking the file against trapping. If it does not specify a trapping state the file fails PDF/X compliance. Insert True checks for a trapped state. If no trapping was added to the file, the file fails compliance. Insert False checks for no trapping. If trapping is applied to the file, the file fails compliance when this item is selected.

- **Help.** The five icons to the right of the items in the Default Values if Not Specified in the Document area of the PDF/X pane offer help information. Click one of the icons and a pop-up menu opens with a definition for the respective option.

- **Save As.** The Save As button captures all the settings you make for the Adobe PDF Settings and opens a dialog box that defaults to the Settings folder. If you change any item in one of the preset options and click OK in the Adobe PDF Settings dialog box, the Save As dialog box opens automatically to prompt you to save the new settings to a new file. Provide a filename and click the Save button to create a new settings file.

FIGURE 10.12

Click the Standards folder (Acrobat Professional only) to open the Standards pane.

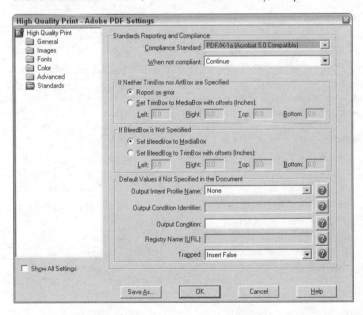

PDF/A

Adobe Systems has been working with international standards committees toward a goal of ensuring you that the documents of today can be electronically read 10, 20, even 100 years from now. One of the fruitions of these labors is the PDF/A-1b ISO standard developed for archiving purposes.

PDF/A files contain essentials in terms of document structure. The necessary essentials include raster images, fonts (embedded), and vector objects. Code used in documents such as JavaScript is deemed a nonessential ingredient as well as any form of security. Therefore, you cannot create PDF/A files containing any scripts or encryption. In general, you'll find PDF/A files are much leaner than other file standards such as PDF/X.

To select PDF/A-1b from the Compliance Standard pull-down menu you need to select Acrobat 5 or earlier compatibility in the General pane. When you select PDF/A-1b from the Compliance Standard pull-down menu the options in the PDF/A-1b pane appear as shown in Figure 10.13.

FIGURE 10.13

Select Acrobat 5 or earlier compatibility and select PDF/A-1b (Acrobat 5.0 Compatible) from the Compliance Standard pull-down menu.

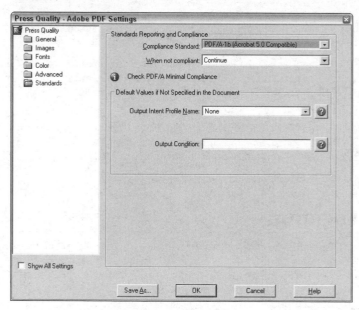

The few options you have include the same options for file handling when a file is not compliant as you have with PDF/X files. Under the Output Intent Profile Name pull-down menu are options for choosing the output intent like you see available in the Color pane. The Output Condition is a field box for user-supplied data.

Managing Adobe PDF Settings

You can manage Adobe PDF Settings via commands in the Settings menu, as shown in Figure 10.14. From the same Settings menu in Distiller (Windows) or top-level menu bar (Macintosh) click Settings to open the Settings menu.

FIGURE 10.14

Adobe PDF Settings are managed using commands in the Settings menu.

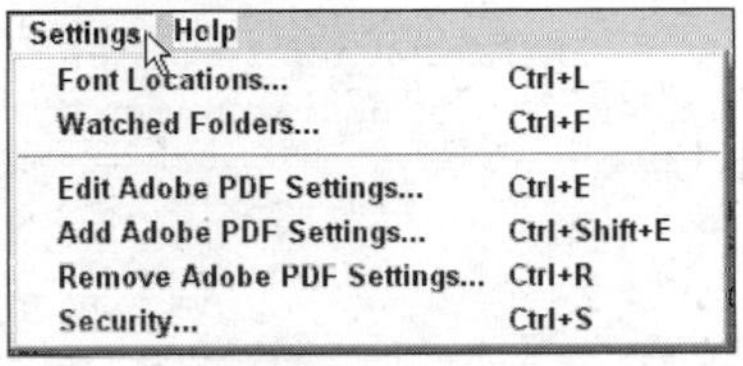

Settings	Help	
Font Locations...		Ctrl+L
Watched Folders...		Ctrl+F
Edit Adobe PDF Settings...		Ctrl+E
Add Adobe PDF Settings...		Ctrl+Shift+E
Remove Adobe PDF Settings...		Ctrl+R
Security...		Ctrl+S

The Add Adobe PDF Settings dialog box opens where you can load a settings file created by other users in your workflow or a settings file sent to you by a service provider. You can load settings files from any folder on your computer. When you add the file using the Add Adobe PDF Settings dialog box, the file is moved to a folder where Distiller retrieves the settings and lists them in the Default Settings pull-down menu.

Choose Settings ➪ Remove Adobe PDF Settings to open the Remove Adobe PDF Settings dialog box. The only settings you see displayed in the dialog box are custom settings files you added after your Acrobat installation. Select a file to remove and click Open. When you click Open, the file is discarded and doesn't appear in the Default Settings list in the Distiller window.

All additions and deletions for settings files can be accomplished through the menu commands. If you want to locate the folder where the settings files are located, look in C:\Documents and Settings\All Users\ Documents\Adobe PDF \Settings folder (Windows) or Library\Application Support\Adobe PDF \Settings folder (Macintosh).

Identifying Font Locations

Font embedding occurs when Adobe PDF Settings are enabled for font embedding and a font is contained in the PostScript file or loaded in the system with a utility such as Adobe Type Manager (Windows only), a third-party font utility, or the system folder where fonts are accessed. If fonts reside neither in the PostScript file nor are loaded in your system, Distiller offers another method for locating fonts. Choose Settings ➪ Font Locations. The Acrobat Distiller – Font Locations dialog box opens, as shown in Figure 10.15.

In this dialog box, you add folders of fonts that Distiller looks in when a font is neither contained in the PostScript file nor loaded in the system memory. Monitored font folders are listed in the window shown in Figure 10.15. To add a new folder, click the Add button. To remove a folder, select it in the list and click the Remove button.

A check box at the bottom of the dialog box enables you to resolve some problems that may occur when a TrueType font has the same name as a PostScript font. To eliminate embedding TrueType fonts with the same names as PostScript fonts, check the box at the bottom of the dialog box.

FIGURE 10.15

Distiller monitors fonts installed on your hard drive when the fonts appear in a list in the Acrobat Distiller – Font Locations dialog box.

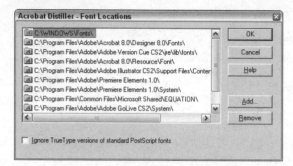

Using Watched Folders

Watched folders enable you to automate distillation of PostScript files in a business or production environment. You can easily develop a PDF workflow by hosting a server on a network where Acrobat Distiller is continually running in the background and watching a folder or many folders for the introduction of new PostScript files. When Distiller encounters a new PostScript file, the file is distilled in the background while foreground applications are running. The resulting PDF files are automatically moved to another folder or directory, and the PostScript files are either preserved or deleted automatically.

Licensing restrictions

Before moving on to working with watched folders, please look over this section carefully and try to understand the proper use and authorization of working with watched folders on networks. Adobe Systems grants you license for working on a single computer when installing Acrobat. When you create PDFs on your computer you can distribute them to anyone who uses an Acrobat viewer. Therefore, the PDFs you create can legitimately be distributed to anyone who acquires the free Adobe Reader software.

Creating PDFs, whether locally or on a network, assumes you have complied with the proper licensing agreements for use of the Acrobat Distiller application. Ambiguity arises when using the Distiller application on networks with watched folders. If you set up a watched folder on a network where multiple users access the watched folders, you need a site license to use the Acrobat Distiller application, you need to have a licensed copy of Acrobat Standard or Professional for each user, or you can purchase Adobe LiveCycle PDF Generator. Because Distiller is used by multiple users in this example, site licensing or individual purchases of the product is required.

Therefore, the licensing policies in this regard are related not to distribution, but rather, how the PDFs are created. As I move through the discussion on watched folders, keep in mind that when I make mention of using watched folders on networks, I'm assuming you are compliant with the proper licensing agreements.

Creating watched folders (Acrobat Professional only)

Watched folders can be individual folders, hard drive partitions, or dedicated hard drives. When you choose Settings ➪ Watched Folders, the Watched Folders dialog box opens, enabling you to establish preferences for the watched folders and distillation attributes.

The options available in the Watched Folders dialog box are as follows:

- **Path.** The list window displays all folders identified as watched folders. The name of the watched folder appears in the list as well as the directory path. In Figure 10.16, notice the directory path is shown.

- **Check watched folders every [ ] seconds.** This user-definable field accepts values between 1 and 9999 seconds. When Distiller monitors a watched folder, the folder is monitored according to the value entered in this field box.

- **PostScript file is.** Distiller automatically treats the PostScript file according to the options available in this pull-down menu. You can select the Deleted menu item, which deletes the PostScript file after distillation, or select Moved to "Out" folder, which moves the PostScript file to a folder entitled *Out*. If you intend to repurpose files for different uses, be certain to keep the PostScript file.

- **Delete output files older than [ ] days.** If you elect to keep the PostScript files in the Out folder, they can be deleted after the time interval specified in this field box. The acceptable range is between 1 and 999 days.

FIGURE 10.16

Watched folder preferences are established in the Acrobat Distiller – Watched Folders dialog box. When you open this dialog box, a reminder for the licensing restrictions appears at the bottom.

- **Add Folder.** To create a watched folder or add to the current list of watched folders, click the Add Folder button. A navigation dialog box opens. To add a folder to the watched folders list, the folder must first be created before you click the Add Folder button. Once you add a folder, Distiller automatically creates an In and Out folder inside your selected folder. Folders as well as

partitions and drives can be added to your list. On a network, remote folders, partitions, and drives can also be added to the list. If you want to select a folder, browse your hard drive and select the folder name after clicking the Add Folder button. If you want to have the entire hard drive watched, select the drive designation (C:\, D:\, E:\, and so on in Windows or Macintosh HD, Hard Drive, and so on with a Macintosh) and click OK in the Browse For Folder dialog box.

■ **Remove Folder.** To delete watched folders, select the folder name in the watched folders list and click the Remove Folder button. If a folder is moved or deleted from your hard drive, the next time you launch Distiller, a warning dialog box opens notifying you that Distiller cannot find the watched folder(s). Removal of watched folders must occur in the Acrobat Distiller – Watched Folder dialog box. If you inadvertently deleted a watched folder on the desktop, you need to delete the folder name in the watched folders list. Return to your desktop and create a new folder; then return to the dialog box and add the new folder to the list.

■ **Edit Security.** You can apply security to PDF files during distillation. Adding security during distillation is handy for multiple files created in PDF workflow environments. Security used on a watched folder is inherited from the Job Options settings. For example in the General pane if you select Acrobat 5.0 compatibility, the security settings available to you here, are compatible with 128-bit RSA. However, if you select Acrobat 7.0 and higher for your compatibility, the security is set to 128-bit AES.

CROSS-REF For more information on applying security to PDF documents, see Chapter 26.

■ **Clear Security.** Select any one or all of the watched folders in the list and click Clear Security. The Security is removed from the folders.

■ **Edit Settings.** The Edit Settings button becomes active when you select a watched folder name in the watched folders list. With a folder name selected in the list, click the Edit Settings button to open the Adobe PDF Settings dialog box. You can apply different settings to different watched folders. If, for example, you print PostScript files to disk and have them distilled for high-end output and Web page design, you will want compression and color modes distinctive for the output sources. You can set up two watched folders and have the same PostScript file distilled with the different settings. Editing settings here overrides Distiller's defaults and applies new options to the specific watched folder where the attributes are established.

■ **Load Settings.** All the settings contained in the Settings folder are available for loading and applying to watched folders listed in the window. Click Load Settings to open the Settings folder.

■ **Clear Settings.** This option removes any settings applied to a watched folder. If you leave the watched folder listed with no specific settings assigned to the watched folder, the current default Adobe PDF Settings are used.

PDF WORKFLOW Watched folders greatly help your PDF workflow and assist you in automating the smallest office environment to large offices with multiple networks and servers. When you install a site-licensed copy of Acrobat Distiller on a server, the burden of PDF creation is dedicated to the server and relieves individual workstations.

In identifying watched folders, you need only have the directory or folder created on a hard drive. After you identify the watched folder, Distiller automatically creates the other folders needed to execute distillation from watched folder files. The In folder created by Distiller is monitored. When a PostScript file is placed or written to the In folder, the distillation commences according to the interval you establish in the Watched Folder settings dialog box. Files can be placed into the In folder, or you can print to PostScript directly to the In folder from within an application.

Watched folders work well in cross-platform environments, too. In order to use a watched folder from one platform and have the distillation performed on another platform, you need to have the computers networked and have software installed that enables you to communicate between two or more computers on your network.

Working with Non-Roman Text

Acrobat provides great support for text created from character sets foreign to U.S. English and other Roman text alphabets. Eastern languages such as Russian, Ukrainian, and similar languages based on forms of Cyrillic characters require proper configuration for font access and keyboard layouts. After configuring and using the fonts in a layout application, be certain to embed the fonts in the PostScript file or have Distiller monitor the font's folder of the character set used. As is the case with any font embedded in the PDF, the document is displayed without font substitution. In Figure 10.17, I used a Cyrillic font in Microsoft Word. The file was printed to disk as PostScript and font embedding was used in Distiller's Adobe PDF Settings.

FIGURE 10.17

When fonts are properly configured from character sets foreign to Roman characters, the fonts can be embedded and viewed without font substitution.

Здравствуйте
Меня зовут Тед

Eastern language support is provided by Acrobat but requires much more in regard to configuration and proper installation of the Asian Language Support option (Windows) or the Asian Language Kit (Macintosh). As long as the language support respective to your platform is installed with the Acrobat installer, files can be printed as PostScript and embedded in the PDFs. PDFs with embedded Asian language options such as Traditional Chinese, Simplified Chinese, Japanese, and Korean (CJK) are displayed without font substitution.

When installing Acrobat for use with these languages, you need to use the custom installation and include the language support with the other Acrobat components. After the support is installed, font problems need to be resolved when you print to PostScript. PostScript fonts have fewer problems being embedded. TrueType fonts require special handling depending on the platform and type of fonts used. Special documentation for managing PostScript and TrueType fonts is included in the Acrobat documentation. For specific handling of Eastern Language support and TrueType fonts, review the documentation thoroughly before attempting to convert PostScript files to PDF.

Accessing Distiller

After all the controls have been established in the Adobe PDF Settings dialog boxes, you're ready to use the Distiller application. Files used with Distiller need to be PostScript files printed to disk or EPS files. You can access the Distiller application several ways:

- **Open from Distiller.** Find the Distiller application on your hard drive and double-click the application icon to launch Distiller. When the Distiller application window opens, choose File ⇨ Open. Navigate to the file you want to convert to PDF and select it in the Acrobat Distiller – Open PostScript File dialog box. Select multiple files by using the Shift key to select a contiguous group of files or Ctrl/⌘ to select a non-contiguous group. If the Preferences have been set up to ask for a filename or ask to replace a PDF, a navigation dialog box opens where you supply filename and destination.

- **Drag and drop to the application icon.** Either the application icon or a shortcut (alias in the Dock on Macintosh OS X) of the application can be used for drag-and-drop distillation. In this regard you can drag multiple PostScript files, EPS files, or a combination of both to either icon. Release the mouse button when the files are over the icon and Distiller launches and subsequently converts the file(s) to PDF.

- **Drag to the application window.** You can drag and drop a single file or multiple files on the Distiller application window. Launch Distiller to open the application window. Select a single file or multiple files and release the mouse button. All files are converted as individual PDFs.

- **Launch Distiller from within Acrobat.** To open Distiller from within Acrobat choose Advanced ⇨ Print Production ⇨ Acrobat Distiller. The Distiller application launches and opens in the foreground in front of the Acrobat window. Choose File ⇨ Open or use the drag-and-drop method to open the file.

- **Print to Adobe PDF printer.** From any authoring program, open the Print dialog box and select Adobe PDF. Execute the Print command and the file is distilled with the current default Adobe PDF Settings.

- **Use the Run command (Windows).** You can create PDFs with Distiller by accessing the Run command from the Windows status bar. Select Run and supply the directory path first for Distiller; then supply the path for the files to be converted. Syntax must be exact. Pathnames need to be contained within quotation marks and a space needs to separate the pathname for Distiller and the pathname for the file(s) to be converted. Filenames having spaces need to be contained within quotation marks. To distill multiple files enter the pathname and filename, and separate each file with commas. Inasmuch as Acrobat offers you this capability, you'll often find drag-and-drop methods much easier.

- **Exporting to PDF.** From many application programs, such as Microsoft Office, and illustration and layout programs as discussed in Chapters 7 through 9, Distiller is used to produce PDFs. When distillation is complete, the user is returned to the application document window.

- **Watched folders.** As described earlier in this chapter, copying a PostScript or EPS file to the In folder inside a watched folder prompts distillation at the interval specified in the Acrobat Distiller – Watched Folders dialog box. Distiller must be launched before distillation of files from watched folders occurs.

When Distiller is used in all the preceding circumstances other than the use of watched folders, the current Adobe PDF Settings selected in Distiller are used to produce the PDF. That is to say, if Distiller is launched and the Standard settings appear in the pull-down menu, the Standard settings are used to create the PDF. When using watched folders, the settings associated with the watched folder are used to produce the PDF. If no settings are assigned to the watched folder, the current default settings are used.

Summary

- PostScript is a streamed language that can contain many different dialects and is often redundant in describing page elements for imaging. PDF is a much more efficient file format, as it is structured like a database that offers logical order and eliminates redundancy.

- When creating PostScript files, the preferred PPD to use is the Acrobat Distiller PPD, or print to the Adobe PDF printer.

- Distiller Preferences enable you to establish settings for filenaming and overwriting.

- Acrobat Distiller has many Adobe PDF Settings enabling you to control font compression, image compression, color, high-end digital prepress output, PDF/X compliance, and PDF/A compliance. All Adobe PDF Settings are available to Acrobat Standard users except PDF/X and PDF/A compliance.

- Additional font monitoring is established in the Distiller Settings menu for identifying different font locations on your computer.

- Watched folders enable you to create PDF workflows that automate the PDF creation process. Watched folders can be contained on local or remote storage systems in network environments. Use of watched folders with multiple-user access on a network requires strict compliance with Adobe's licensing agreements.

- Acrobat enables you to supply security passwords at the time of distillation. Security levels are applied consistent with PDF compatibility.

- Eastern language character sets and Asian text are supported font-embedding features as long as font formats and font management are properly configured.

- Access to Acrobat Distiller is supported from within Acrobat 8.0, by using shortcuts or aliases, printer drivers, and through a variety of drag-and-drop procedures.

Part III

Editing PDFs

Chapter 11

Saving and Versioning Files

T o begin this section on editing PDF documents I'll start with saving files and exporting data. As you find in this chapter, Acrobat has Save tools and commands and supports exporting your PDF data in a variety of file formats. As you learned in Part II, files are not originally authored in Acrobat, but rather, they are converted to the PDF format. If you need to perform some major editing, it's always best to try to return to the original authoring application, make your edits, and then convert to PDF. In some cases however, you may not have an original authoring application document. In such circumstances, you may need to get the PDF data in a format that you can manipulate and edit in another program. Fortunately, Acrobat supports exporting to many different file formats that can be imported in other programs.

In addition to saving documents, you may find a need to create several versions of a file. If you plan on engaging in a review session, you may want to send several versions of a document to your review committee or share different versions in a workgroup. A nice feature in Acrobat 8.0 is support for the Version Cue workspace, in which you can save different document versions just like you find with all Adobe Creative Suite programs. In this chapter, you learn how to save PDF documents, update edits, and export data into other formats.

IN THIS CHAPTER

Using the Save commands

Saving data in different formats

Using Version Cue

Setting Up the Work Environment

The only tool used in this chapter is the Save tool, which appears in the default File toolbar. To return to default tools, open a context menu on the Toolbar Well and select Reset Toolbars or press Alt/Option+F8. The remaining tools used with this chapter are derived from menu commands.

Saving PDF Files

When you open a PDF document in any viewer, the Save tool in the File toolbar and the File ⇨ Save menu command are both grayed out. When you open the File menu and look at Save As, you notice the menu command is active.

 After you edit a file through the use of tools or menu commands, the Save tool and Save menu command become active.

You can use the File ⇨ Save As command at any time. As you edit PDF documents, they tend to become bulky and contain unnecessary information. To optimize a file and make it the smallest file size, choose File ⇨ Save As and select the default PDF format for the file type. If you save to the same folder location with the same filename, Acrobat rewrites the file as you use Save As. You should plan on using Save As and rewriting your file after your last edits. Doing so assures you of creating a smaller, more optimized file.

Another factor affecting optimized files is ensuring the default preferences are set to file optimization when using the Save As command. Open the Preferences dialog box (Ctrl/⌘+K) and click Documents in the left pane. In the Documents preferences pane, be certain the check box is enabled for Save As optimizes for Fast Web View. Enabling this option ensures that your files are always optimized when you use Save As.

Exporting Data

By default, when you use either Save or Save As, the file type is a PDF document. Using Save offers you no other option for changing the file type; but when you select Save As, you can choose to export your PDF document in one of a number of different file formats. If you need to update a file or export data from PDF files, choose File ⇨ Save As and choose a file format from the Save as type (Format on Macintosh) pull-down menu, as shown in Figure 11.1.

FIGURE 11.1

Choose File ⇨ Save As and choose the file format to be saved from the Save as type pull-down menu.

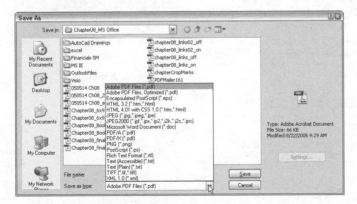

NEW FEATURE   In addition to using the Save As command, Acrobat 8 introduces a new task button for exporting PDF files to most of the file formats supported with the Save As command.

Click the Export task button and a drop down list of file formats to select from which the same file formats are supported in Save As dialog box opens. (Exceptions in the drop down list are the Adobe PDF Files (*.pdf) and Adobe PDF Files, Optimized (*.pdf) that are only found in the Save As dialog box). Using either the Save As dialog box or the Export menu commands results in file exports with options choices that are identical. You can use either command set to export in the following formats.

Selecting all but the Adobe PDF Files (*.pdf) and Text (Accessible) (*.txt) formats provides user-definable options in the Settings dialog box for the respective file type. When you select any of the formats other than the preceding two, the Settings button becomes active. Click Settings and the Save As Settings dialog box opens. The various options change according to the file format selected from the Save as type pull-down menu (Windows) or Format (Mac) in the Save As dialog box.

Adobe PDF files (*.pdf)

By default the Acrobat PDF Files (*.pdf) format is selected in the Save as type (Windows) or Format (Macintosh) pull-down menu. Saving as PDF without changing the filename updates the existing PDF by overwriting it.

Adobe PDF Files, Optimized (*.pdf)

Select this option and your file is optimized using the PDF Optimizer and saved in one step.

NEW FEATURE   **The Optimized PDF option in the Save As dialog box is new in Acrobat 8. Click the Settings button in the Save As dialog box and the PDF Optimizer dialog box opens. You can choose a preset or make custom adjustments in the PDF Optimizer; then click OK and click Save in the Save As dialog box. Your file is first optimized and then saved to disk.**

CROSS-REF   **For more information on using the PDF Optimizer, see Chapter 18.**

Encapsulated PostScript (*.eps) and PostScript (*.ps)

EPS files are saved as single page files. When multiple-page PDFs are saved to EPS, each page is saved as a new EPS document. PostScript files save the PDF to disk like you would print a file to disk as PostScript. PostScript files can then be re-distilled in Acrobat Distiller to convert back to PDF. You can also download PostScript files to PostScript printers through a downloading utility or a hot folder, which is used for sending files directly to the printer.

Many of the options for creating either an EPS file or a PostScript file are identical. You'll notice some differences as you travel through the many options found in the Save As Settings dialog box. Select either Encapsulated PostScript (*.eps) or PostScript (*.ps) from the Files of type (Format on Macintosh) pull-down menu and click the Settings button. The options appear in the Save As Settings dialog box. Shown in Figure 11.2 is the EPS Save As Settings dialog box.

FIGURE 11.2

Select Encapsulated PostScript (*.eps) or PostScript (*.ps) from the Save as type (Format on Macintosh) pull-down menu. Click the Settings button to open the Save As Settings dialog box. In this figure, Save as Encapsulated PostScript (*.eps) was selected.

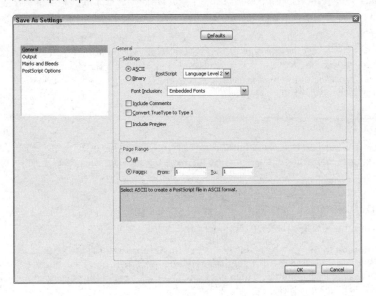

General settings

On the left side of the Save As Settings dialog box are several categories for choices you make on the right side of the dialog box. The first of the categories is the General settings where you set some general attributes for the way an EPS or PostScript file is saved. These settings are as follows:

- **Defaults.** The Defaults button at the top of the dialog box returns all settings to the original defaults. You can access this button at any time as you travel through the various option categories in the list at the left side of the dialog box.

- **ASCII.** PostScript files are encoded as ASCII (American Standard Code for Information Interchange). ASCII files are larger than binary files, which is the second option for encoding selections.

CROSS-REF For information on color separating EPS files and Acrobat PDF, see Chapter 32.

- **Binary.** Binary files are much smaller than ASCII files. Use binary encoding when the PostScript language level is 2 or 3.

- **PostScript.** Select the language levels from the pull-down menu choices. For ASCII encoding use Language Level 1 from the menu. For exporting EPS files to Adobe InDesign, you can use Language Level 2. If you're using Language Level 2 or 3, select binary encoding. Use PostScript 3 only when the output devices use PostScript 3 RIPs.

NOTE Users of previous versions of Acrobat had to either export PDF files to EPS, place PDFs in separating programs, or use third-party plug-ins to print color separations and print to high-end devices. These workarounds are all a part of the past. Acrobat Professional affords you almost all the printing controls you need for high-end printing. Forget about exporting EPS files if your only need is to print color separations or composites to high-end devices.

- **Font Inclusion.** You have three choices for font inclusion. Choose None to not embed fonts. Choose Embedded Fonts to keep the same fonts embedded in the PDF in the exported EPS file. Choose Embedded and Referenced Fonts to keep the PDF embedded fonts and fonts referenced from fonts loaded in your system. If you're using a font that is not embedded in the PDF document but is loaded as a system font, the font is embedded in the resulting PDF.

CROSS-REF   For more information about font embedding and limitations of font embedding, see Chapter 10.

- **Include Comments.** When the check box is enabled, any comment notes are included in the resulting EPS or PostScript document. When the PostScript document is distilled in Acrobat Distiller, the comment notes are retained in the resulting PDF document.

- **Convert TrueType to Type 1.** Check the box to convert TrueType fonts to Type 1 fonts.

CROSS-REF   For more information on TrueType and Type 1 fonts, see Chapter 10.

- **Include Preview (EPS file exports only).** The preview is a screen view of the EPS file. If this check box is not enabled, the EPS file appears as a gray box when you place the file in another program. The data are all there, but you won't be able to see the EPS image. When this check box is enabled, a preview is embedded in the EPS file. Preview image formats are TIFF on Windows and PICT on the Macintosh.

- **Page Range.** You can export all pages by selecting the All radio button or entering the page numbers for a range of pages to be exported. EPS files are exported as individual files for each page and automatically numbered by Acrobat.

Output

Click the Output item in the list on the left side of the Save As Settings dialog box and the options change, as shown in Figure 11.3.

FIGURE 11.3

Select Output and the options change to attribute settings designed for printing and prepress.

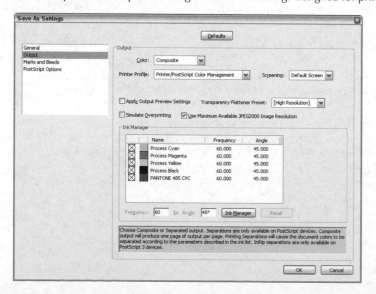

Output options enable you to control prepress output attributes, including the following:

- **Color.** The four choices for handling color in resulting EPS and PostScript file(s) are as follows:

  - **Composite.** Use this option to export the file as a composite image. If the file is a four-color image, you can still import an EPS file in a separating program and print separations. The intent for Composite is for use with composite color printing and printing separations to non-Adobe PostScript devices. For PostScript files, composites can be downloaded directly to PostScript 2 and 3 devices for in-RIP separating.

  - **Composite Gray.** If the files are grayscale, use Composite Gray.

  - **Separations.** This option creates a DCS (Desktop Color Separation) file, and each color as well as a composite are exported as separate files. If pre-separating the EPS file(s), be certain you use a program such as Adobe InDesign that supports DCS files, or you can directly download each plate to your RIP. For PostScript files, the file is separated. When you download the PostScript file, all colors print on separate plates.

CROSS-REF   For more information about DCS files, color separations, and RIPs, see Chapter 32.

  - **In-RIP Separations.** This option works only on Adobe PostScript 3 RIPs. A composite color image is printed to the RIP and the RIP color separates the composite file.

NOTE   Separations and In-RIP Separations are only active when you have your page setup set to a PostScript printer.

- **Screening.** You make choices for screening from this pull-down menu. Unless you have some special need for embedding half-tone frequencies in the EPS file, leave the Screening set to Default Screen and handle all your frequency control at the RIP. For PostScript files, set the screening as desired before downloading the file.

- **Printer Profile.** You can embed a printer profile in the EPS file(s) from the available choices in the pull-down menu. If you want to eliminate color management, select the option at the top of the menu choices for Same As Source (No Color Management).

- **Apply Output Preview Settings.** Select this option to simulate the output of one device on another. This option simulates the output condition defined in the Output Preview dialog box on the current output device.

- **Transparency Flattener Preset.** Choose from High Medium and Low resolutions for transparency flattening. Transparency is flattened according to your choice in the resultant EPS file.

- **Simulate Overprinting.** Overprints and knockouts can be soft-proofed onscreen for color-separated devices. The check box is grayed out unless you choose one of the separation items in the Color pull-down menu.

- **Use Maximum Available JPEG2000 Image Resolution.** For any raster images contained in the EPS file export, the file compression uses JPEG2000 at the maximum setting when this check box is enabled. If disabled, the original compression level at the time the PDF was created is used.

- **Ink Manager.** Clearing the box on the far left of each color plate eliminates the plate for separated files. Scroll the box to see any spot colors and you can select spot colors for conversion to CMYK color.

Marks and Bleeds

Select the Marks and Bleeds item in the list at the left of the Save As Settings dialog box and the options for adding printer's marks appear, as shown in Figure 11.4.

Select Marks and Bleeds to add printer's marks to the EPS/PS export.

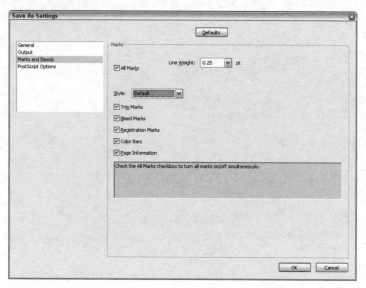

The options are as follows:

- **All Marks/Marks.** You can check the box for All Marks and all the check boxes below the Style menu are checked. You can toggle on or off all check marks to create just the marks you want to appear in the resultant file.

- **Line Weight.** From the pull-down menu, select line weights for the printer's marks from ⅛-, ¼-, and ½-inch choices.

- **Style.** You have choices for compatibility with authoring and illustration programs. Choose from different versions of InDesign, Illustrator, or QuarkXPress.

PostScript Options

Click the last item in the list for EPS/PS exports and the options shown in Figure 11.5 appear. The PostScript options offer you settings for embedded PostScript attributes in the EPS/PS file.

FIGURE 11.5

Select PostScript Options to add various PostScript printing attributes to the EPS/PostScript file(s).

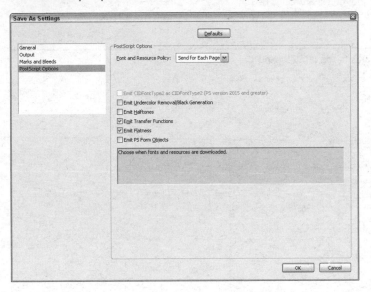

The PostScript options include the following:

- **Font and Resource Policy.** You determine how fonts download to a printer's RIP via three choices in the pull-down menu:

  - **Send at Start.** The entire font sets for all pages are downloaded to the printer's RIP. The file prints faster than any of the other methods, but puts a memory burden on the printing device to hold all the font matrices in memory during printing.

  - **Send by Range.** Fonts are downloaded from the first page where the fonts are used and stays in memory until the job is printed. The font downloading occurs as each font is found on a page that uses them. The job prints a little slower than when using the Send at Start option, but uses less memory initially as the job is printed.

  - **Send for Each Page.** Fonts encountered on a page are downloaded to the RIP, and then flushed as the next page is printed. The second page's fonts are then downloaded and flushed after printing, and so on. This method requires the least memory. Files print slower than when using either of the other two methods.

- **Emit CIDFontType2 as CIDFontType2 (PS Version 2015 and greater).** Use this option to preserve hinting in the original font when printing. The option is available only for Language Level 3 output.

- **Emit Undercolor Removal/Black Generation.** GCR/UCR removal is necessary only if the original document contained assignments in the PostScript file converted to PDF. If you want to remove any embedded settings for handling the amount of black or compensating for black generation with different inks, check this box. If you don't know what any of this means, checking the box or not won't have an effect on your own personal documents.

- **Emit Halftones.** If a halftone frequency was embedded in the original file, you can eliminate it in the exported document. Unless you want to use embedded frequencies, leave the box checked in case you accidentally preserved a frequency in the original file for EPS files. When printing PostScript files to high-end devices, you'll want to assign frequencies at the time the PostScript file is created.

- **Emit Transfer Functions.** The same criteria as the preceding bullet apply to transfer functions. If you intend to use embedded transfer functions, leave the check box disabled. Otherwise, keep it checked as a default.

- **Emit Flatness.** Flatness settings applied in Photoshop, Illustrator, or other illustration programs are generally applied to clipping paths in images and on vector objects to ease the burden of printing complex objects. When checked, the flatness settings applied in the original authoring program are honored.

- **Emit PS Form Objects.** This option relates to PS Form XObjects. XObjects are used to create a description of multiple smaller objects repeated several times such as patterns, brushes, backgrounds, and so on. Emitting the XObjects reduces the size of the print job; however, more memory is needed to RIP the file(s).

Click OK in the Save As Settings dialog box and click Save in the Save As dialog box. The PDF is exported in EPS or PostScript format, containing all the attributes you described for all the options listed earlier.

Because printing in Acrobat Professional takes care of all the print controls you need, exporting EPS files for printing is a task you won't need to perform unless there's some strange problem that needs to be resolved in a file that won't print. A more practical use for exporting EPS files from Acrobat is if you need to import a PDF file in another program that does not support PDF, but does support EPS. In such cases you'll find it helpful to understand all the options you have available for EPS exports.

You have many advantages in creating PostScript files from Acrobat. Files can be re-distilled in Acrobat Distiller with PDF/X formats for printing and prepress, sometimes as a workaround for repurposing documents, and for downloading directly to PostScript devices — particularly for print shops using imposition software that only supports PostScript and not PDF.

CROSS-REF For more information about PDF/X files, see Chapters 10 and 30.

HTML 3.2 (*.htm), HTML 4.01 with CSS 1.0 (*.htm), XML 1.0 (*.xml), and Text (Plain) (*.txt)

Options available for exporting PDFs to HTML files, HTML files with Cascading Style Sheets, Plain Text, and XML files all use the same attribute settings. Text is exported according to the encoding method you select and images are exported according to the format option you select. These settings are available when you select any one of the three file formats from the Save as type (Format on Macintosh) pull-down menu. Select a format and click the Settings button. The Save As *XXX* Settings dialog box opens, as shown in Figure 11.6.

The attribute settings are as follows:

- **Encoding.** Choose the encoding method from options for Unicode settings (UTF-8, UTF-16, or UCS-4), ISO-Latin-1, HTML/ASCII, or the default setting of Use mapping table default.

- **Generate bookmarks.** Generates Bookmark links to content for HTML or XML documents. Links are placed at the beginning of the resulting HTML or XML document.

- **Generate tags for untagged files**. Tags are temporarily created for file conversion for untagged documents. You need to select the check box for legacy untagged files or with files created with Acrobat 4 in order to complete the conversion. The tags are temporary for the conversion to work and are not added to the PDF. If you do not select this for legacy PDFs, you will not get the conversion.

- **Generate images.** Enable this check box for images to be exported as separate files.

- **Use sub-folder.** Images are saved to a subfolder below the directory where the HTML files are created. The default name for the folder is "images." In the field box you can change the folder name by editing the line of text.

- **Use prefix.** This option adds prefixes to image filenames. Check the box and supply the prefix text in the field box.

- **Output format.** Three options buttons enable you to determine the file format for the saved images. Choose from TIFF, JPG, or PNG.

- **Downsample to.** Images are downsampled to the setting selected from the pull-down menu. The settings are fixed with choices for 72, 96, 150, and 300 pixels per inch (ppi).

FIGURE 11.6

To set attributes for file exports for HTML, XML, or TXT files, select one of three file formats in the Save as type (Format on Macintosh) pull-down menu and click Settings. The dialog box is called Save As *XXX* Settings, where *XXX* is the format you selected.

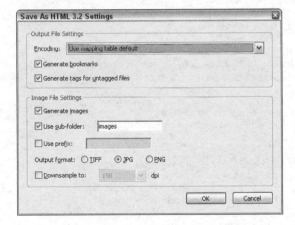

JPEG (*.jpg, .jpeg, .jpe), JPEG2000 (.jpf, *.jpx, *.jp2, *.j2k, *.j2c, .jpc), PNG (.png), and TIFF (*.tif, *.tiff)

You can export the PDF document as any one of the preceding image file formats. Each entire page, including text and images, is exported as a single image file. From the Settings dialog box, you choose options for image compression and color management. The options settings for exporting image file formats are the same as the options used when importing images in Acrobat with the Create PDF From File or From Multiple Files commands discussed in Chapter 7.

CAUTION When exporting PDF documents containing images, you cannot achieve a better resolution than the resolution in the source file. If you have, for example, a PDF document with a TIFF image where the image was originally sampled at 72 ppi, you cannot gain any resolution by saving the file from Acrobat as a TIFF file with 300-ppi resolution. The file is saved with the resolution you specify in the Save As *XXX* Settings dialog box, but image resolutions higher than source files are upsized with image interpolation. The results are often unusable and produce poor quality images. If you need image resolutions higher than the source images, you need to return to your scanner and scan images at higher resolutions. Recreate the original document and convert to PDF.

CROSS-REF For a better understanding of image resolutions required for printing, see Chapters 10 and 32.

Microsoft Word Document (*.doc) and Rich Text Format (*.rtf)

You can also export PDF files to Microsoft Word format and Rich Text Format files (RTF). The conversion settings include choices for image handling and sampling. Unlike HTML and XML files, exports to Word and RTF embed the images in the exported text files when you choose to export images. Acrobat does not offer an option for exporting images apart from the text data.

Be aware that although you can export PDF documents directly to Microsoft Word format, the integrity of your file depends on how well you created the PDF. If the PDF was created without tags and through less desirable PDF-creation methods, the ultimate file you produce in Word or RTF format may not be suitable for editing and converting back to PDF. Inasmuch as tags are added during conversion to PDF, the tagged structure is not retained in the resulting file.

CROSS-REF For more information on programs supporting exports to PDF as structured and tagged files, see Chapters 7, 8 and 25.

As a general rule you should keep native documents archived and return to them to perform any major editing tasks. As a workaround, you can use the export to Word and RTF formats for legacy files where no original documents are available. In some cases, you'll need to perform some extensive editing in either your word processor or page layout program.

Clicking the Settings button in the Save As dialog box for exports to Microsoft Word or RTF opens the Save As Settings dialog box. The settings are the same for RTF as for Word-formatted file exports (shown in Figure 11.7).

FIGURE 11.7

Select either Microsoft Word or RTF for the file export and click the Settings button. The options in both dialog boxes are identical.

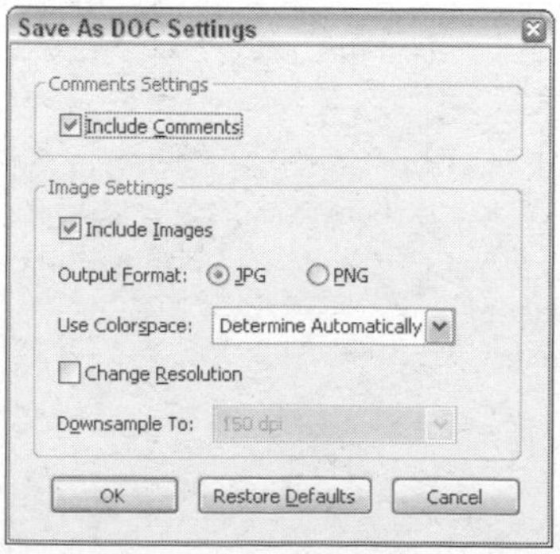

Settings for exporting to Microsoft Word or RTF formats include the following:

- **Include Comments.** Like EPS and PostScript files discussed earlier, Comment notes can be exported to Word or with RTF files. Select the box for Include Comments and the Comment notes are exported.
- **Include Images.** You can extract image files from the PDF and embed them in the .doc or .rtf file in either of two formats. Select JPG or PNG for the image file format.
- **Use Colorspace.** You have choices for colorspaces from a pull-down menu. Choose from Determine Automatically in which case Acrobat determines using either grayscale or color, or select Grayscale or Color from the menu options.
- **Change Resolution.** Downsampling and resolution issues are the same as those noted when exporting PDF documents to image formats.

CROSS-REF For more information on resolutions and sampling, see Chapter 18.

Text (Accessible) (*.txt)

Files are saved as text. For tagged PDF documents made accessible, all alternative text used to describe items like images and form fields that are contained in the document tags are converted to text. The alternate tags can be viewed in the Tags palette in Acrobat but won't necessarily appear in the document page. When you export PDFs as Accessible Text, the text is generated in the body of the document.

CROSS-REF For more information on document tags, see Chapter 25.

Saving Different Document Versions (Adobe Acrobat Professional and Creative Suite)

When you install Acrobat, the program is Version Cue–ready. However, creating a Version Cue workspace and administering Version Cue files requires installation of the Adobe Creative Suite. This section applies to users who have Adobe Creative Suite installed. There are two versions of Adobe Creative Suite. The Adobe Creative Suite Standard edition includes Adobe Photoshop, Adobe Illustrator, Adobe InDesign and Version Cue. The Adobe Creative Suite Premium edition includes all the Standard programs along with Adobe GoLive and Adobe Acrobat Professional. Either version supports Version Cue management.

For saving different document versions, you use Adobe Version Cue. Version Cue is a file versioning system that is tightly integrated into all the Adobe Creative Suite applications and supports Acrobat 7 and 8. Once enabled, the Version Cue file interface may be accessed from within all the standard file dialog boxes in Acrobat and all the CS Applications.

If you install Acrobat on one computer and another user on your network has installed either version of the Creative Suite, you can take advantage of saving and opening files in the Version Cue workspace. A key benefit of Version Cue is that it lets you set up projects that may be shared over a network. All files within these projects are version controlled, allowing all members of the team access to the very latest versions of each file. The versioning features also ensure that team members don't accidentally save changes over the top of other changes.

Using the Version Cue Workspace Administration utility (available only to Adobe Creative Suite users), you can control all aspects of Version Cue from an administration interface. This interface lets you create and edit the access properties for users and create and define properties for each project including which users have access and authentication and file locking.

Setting Up the Version Cue Workspace (Adobe Creative Suite users only)

Before Version Cue may be used, several steps are required to enable Version Cue for the various CS applications and Adobe Acrobat Professional and to turn the Version Cue system on.

NOTE   Version Cue was introduced with the introduction of the Creative Suite. If you purchased Acrobat 6 as part of the Creative Suite, Version Cue was not supported in Acrobat. You need to upgrade to Acrobat Professional version 7 in order to use Version Cue.

Enabling Version Cue and setting preferences (Adobe Creative Suite users only)

When the Adobe Creative Suite is installed, the Version Cue client is also installed by default, but even though Version Cue is installed, it is not active until you turn it on.

Version Cue's existence is a bit ambiguous. Unlike executable applications contained in your Programs folder (Windows) or Applications folder (Macintosh) you need to access Version Cue through the Control Panel (Windows) or the System Preferences (Macintosh). To turn on Version Cue, double-click the Version Cue icon to open the Version Cue Preferences dialog box, shown in Figure 11.8. The icon is found in the Control Panel folder and appears as a control panel item denoted as Adobe Version Cue (Windows) or under the Other category on the Macintosh at the bottom of the System Preferences dialog box.

FIGURE 11.8

The Version Cue dialog box includes a pull-down menu where you can turn Version Cue On or Off.

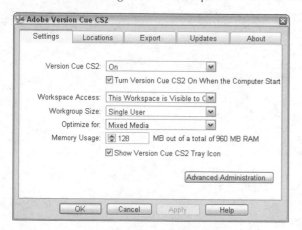

If you want Version Cue turned on automatically each time you start your computer, check the box for Turn Version Cue on When the Computer Starts.

The Workspace Access field offers menu options to make the workspace shared or private. The two options are This Workspace is Visible to Others and This Workspace is Private. To make the Version Cue workspace accessible to other users, leave the default at This Workspace is Visible to Others.

The next three preference choices are used to optimize the workspace and to specify the type of files that you'll be versioning. The Workspace Size may be set to Single User, Small (2–4 People), Medium (5–10 People), or Large (10+ People). By specifying the workspace size, Version Cue can make more connections available so users don't have to wait as long to gain access to the files. The Optimize for field lets you select the type of media files you'll most often be saving. The options include Print Media, which are typically fewer in number, but much larger; Web Media, which includes a large number of smaller files; and Mixed Media.

The Memory Usage field lets you specify the amount of memory on your local hard drive or on a network hard drive that is available for Version Cue to use. Increasing this memory value enables you to retrieve files very quickly, but leaves less memory available on your hard drive.

Specifying workspace folders (Adobe Creative Suite users)

When Version Cue is first enabled, two folders are created on your local system. One folder named Version Cue is located in the Documents folder on Macintosh systems or in the My Documents folder on Windows systems. This folder holds temporary working copies of the files that you are currently editing.

The other folders are located by default in a folder where the Creative Suite applications and Acrobat were installed. These folders, consisting of folders named Adobe Version Cue\data\ and Adobe Version Cue\ backups\, hold the actual versioned files and are referenced in the Locations panel of the Version Cue Preferences dialog box, shown in Figure 11.9.

CAUTION   If you look at the files located in the Data and Backup folders, you won't be able to find any recognizable file formats. Do not manually move or edit any of these files or Version Cue won't work properly.

FIGURE 11.9

The Locations panel of the Version Cue Preferences dialog box displays the location of the versioned files.

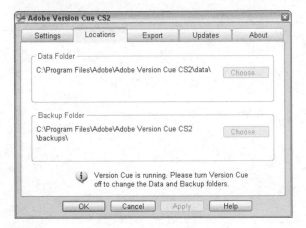

If you want to change the Data and Backups folder locations, you'll need to turn Version Cue off and click the Apply button before the Choose button in the Locations panel becomes active. Once active, you can click the Choose button to select a new directory location.

Enabling Version Cue within Acrobat Professional (Adobe Acrobat and Creative Suite users)

In Acrobat, Version Cue is not available unless you visit the Documents preferences and select Enable Version Cue file-version manager in the Documents pane. Other Creative Suite applications use various methods to enable Version Cue and some programs require you to quit the program and relaunch it before Version Cue is accessible. For a quick look at moving through the procedure for starting Version Cue, follow these steps.

STEPS: Setting up Version Cue for Acrobat Professional

1. **Turn Version Cue on.** If you're not an Adobe Creative Suite user, you must have your computer connected to a network where Version Cue is enabled by an Adobe Creative Suite user. For the Creative Suite users, open the System Preferences dialog box for Macintosh systems or the Control Panel dialog box for Windows systems and double-click the Version Cue icon (Macintosh) or Adobe Version Cue application (Windows). In the Version Cue dialog box, open the Version Cue pull-down menu and select On. Leave the remaining settings at the defaults and click OK.

2. **Enable Version Cue for Acrobat.** Within Acrobat, choose Edit ➪ Preferences (Windows) or Acrobat ➪ Preferences (Macintosh). Click the Documents item in the list at the left side of the dialog box. Check the box at the bottom of the Documents pane where you see Enable Version Cue file-version manager. Click OK in the Preferences dialog box.

3. **Open a PDF document.** Click the Open tool or press Ctrl/⌘+M and select a file to open. Open any PDF document you have handy.

4. **Open Version Cue projects.** Choose File ➪ Save As. In the Save As dialog box, Version Cue appears listed below your drives and network places.

   Note the button in the Save As dialog box where you see Use Adobe Dialog. Click this button and the dialog box changes, as you see in Figure 11.10. Click Version Cue and the Version Cue folders appear.

5. **Cancel out of the Save As dialog box.** Don't attempt to save a new project yet until you review the remainder of this chapter.

FIGURE 11.10

The Save As dialog box offers options for saving your document in a target Version Cue space.

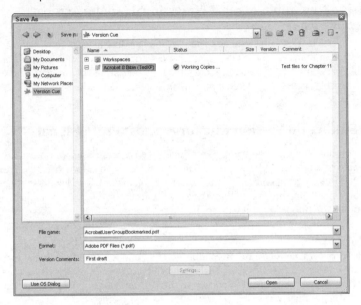

Working with Version Cue files (Adobe Acrobat and Creative Suite users)

When Version Cue is turned on and enabled for Acrobat (or any other Creative Suite application), you can access the Version Cue workspace by clicking the Version Cue button that appears at the bottom of any file dialog box. In addition to the Save As dialog box shown in Figure 11.11, you'll find the same Version Cue button in Open dialog boxes.

If you open the File menu, you can see two menu commands related to saving Version Cue projects. The Save As Version menu and Versions menu commands appear grayed out until you have a version of the active document saved in the Version Cue workspace. Opening a PDF document does not provide access to these menu commands until you use the Save As dialog box, click the Version Cue button, and save the file to a folder that Version Cue monitors.

Creating a Version Cue project

To manage your Version Cue workspace, you need to click the Advanced Administration button in the Version Cue dialog box. When you click the button, your default Web browser opens with help information and tools to manage your Version Cue projects. The first Web page appearing in your Web browser is a log-on page.

In order to access the Version Cue administration, you need to supply a log-on name and password. When you first work with Version Cue, the default log-on and password are both "system." Type **system** (lower-case) in the log-on field box and the password field box, click OK, and you are provided access to the Adobe Version Cue Workspace Administration page, as shown in Figure 11.11.

FIGURE 11.11

When you click Advanced Administration, enter **system** in the log-on and password field boxes, and click the log-on button to gain access to the administration settings.

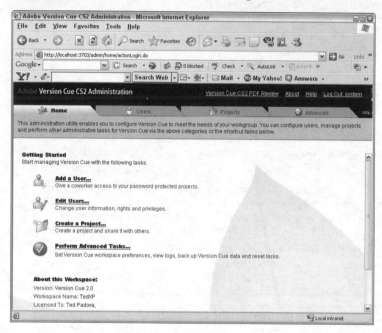

- **Home:** By default, the Home tab opens. The Home tab links to the following three options.

- **Users:** The Users tab offers options for managing the users added to your projects and lists all users working on the project in a list window. You can add a new user, delete an existing user, duplicate a user, and export a user list.

- **Projects:** The Projects tab is where you manage Version Cue projects and lists all active projects in a list window. You can create new projects, duplicate a project, back up a project, export a project, and delete a project in this pane.

- **Advanced:** The Advanced tab enables you to perform advanced tasks such as setting Version Cue preferences, importing Web workgroup server projects, exporting projects, performing maintenance tasks, and reviewing logging reports.

To create a new project, click the Create a Project link on the Home page or click the Projects link. You arrive at the New Project Web page where you can choose from creating a blank project, importing a project from a folder, importing a project from an ftp server, or importing a project from a WebDAV server. Click Blank and click the Next button to start a new project with an empty folder.

In the Create a Blank New Project pane you enter a name for your project and can assign permissions and comments. Click Next and you arrive at the Assigned Users pane. You can add new users in this pane and assign user privileges here. Click Save and the project is created as the Projects pane opens. Here you see a list of all active projects. In Figure 11.12 you can see one active project in the Projects pane.

FIGURE 11.12

All active Version Cue projects are displayed in the Projects pane.

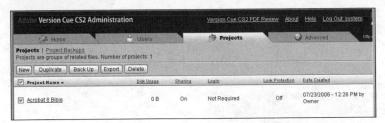

When you finish with the advanced administration, click the Log Off: system link in the title bar. You are returned to the log-on page. At this point, quit your browser and you're ready to save projects to your Version Cue folders.

The number of options in the Advanced Administration panes may at first appear a bit overwhelming. However, to begin, try to create a simple blank project folder using this section as a guide. You can also open the Adobe Version Cue dialog box from the Control Panel (Windows) or System Preferences (Macintosh) and click the Help button. Ample help is offered with Version Cue and most of the questions you may have can be answered in the Help pages.

Saving Version Cue files

When you save Version Cue files with the File ➪ Save command, the working copy is updated, but the actual versioned copy isn't updated until you use the File ➪ Save As or File ➪ Save a Version menu commands.

When you are ready to save a new version of the edited file to the Version Cue repository, choose File ➪ Save a Version. This command opens a simple dialog box, shown in Figure 11.13, where you can quickly type a Version comment and save the file. The version comment that you enter appears in the Version Cue file interface when you select the file.

When you use File ➪ Save As, the Version Cue file interface opens. The Version Cue file interface includes fields for naming the file, selecting a Format, and entering Version Comments. If you elect to save the file using the same filename, then a warning dialog box asks whether you want to save these changes as a new version or you can elect to save the file using a new name.

Understanding states

Each file that is saved is given a status that defines the state of the file. The available statuses include the following:

- **Available.** This status indicates that the file is available to be selected and edited.
- **Ready for Download.** This status indicates that the file is available to be copied to your local working file.
- **In Use By Me.** This status indicates that you are currently editing this file.
- **In Use By Me Elsewhere.** This status indicates that you are editing this file on a different computer.
- **In Use By User.** This status indicates that the file is currently being edited by another user. The user's name is listed.
- **Offline.** This status indicates that the file is unavailable because Version Cue has been turned off.

The status of a file opened using the Version Cue interface is displayed in the title bar of the document.

FIGURE 11.13

Choosing File ➪ Save a Version lets you enter comments for the file.

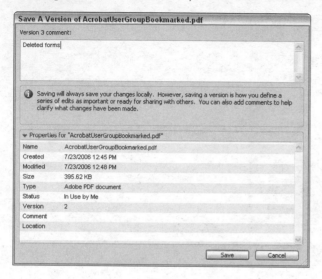

Adding files to a Version Cue project

The File ➪ Save As and the File ➪ Save a Version menu commands may be used to add single files to a Version Cue project.

To add multiple files to a project, copy all the files into their correct folders of the working project file in the Version Cue folder located in the Documents folder on Macintosh or in the My Documents folder on Windows. For example, your Acrobat documents or other Creative Suite application files should be put in the Documents directory under the project folder. If you're using Adobe GoLive, place these files in the Web-content and Web-data folders.

With the files added to the working directory, select the Synchronize menu command from the Project Tools pull-down menu. This command copies all the files added to the working directory to the Version Cue repository where they are accessed by all users.

Working with the Versions command

When a versioned file is opened in Acrobat or another Creative Suite application, you can gain access to the various versions by choosing File ➪ Versions. This command opens a dialog box, shown in Figure 11.14, where all the versions of the open file are listed along with their thumbnails, version numbers, and version comments.

Using this dialog box, you can select a version, delete a version, open a version, or promote a selected version to the Current Version. In Figure 11.14, note that Version 3 is promoted to the top level as the Current Version. When you open this document in Acrobat you see the Current Version appear in the Document pane. This particular file is an Acrobat PDF form. The promoted version has a watermark stamped as "draft." Version 2 is the form without form fields and without a watermark. Version 1 is the PDF form with form fields and without the watermark.

FIGURE 11.14

All the versions for an open file are accessible when you use the File ➪ Versions menu command.

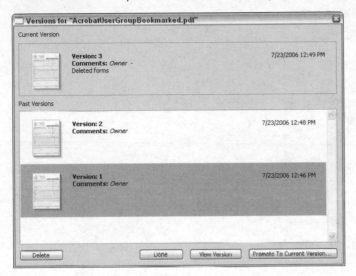

If you e-mail the example file as it appears in Figure 11.14 or send it for an e-mail review, the only version your recipients can view is the Current Version. You can collect comments, promote Version 1, edit the document, and save the file as a final document ready to distribute. To promote any version to the top level and make it the default view when it's opened in Acrobat, select any version and click the Promote To Current Version button. You can delete all other versions in a final file by selecting them and clicking the Delete button.

CAUTION When you save versions, you add to the original file size. Using Version Cue does not save you any hard drive space for storing files. When you post documents on the Web, write to CD-ROMs, or distribute final files, be certain to delete all unnecessary versions. Doing so reduces your file size.

Summary

- Using the Save As command and overwriting a PDF document optimizes it and can sometimes result in much smaller file sizes.

- Acrobat can save PDFs in a variety of different formats. Many formats have an elaborate number of options settings to set attributes for the saved files.

- Before you may use the Version Cue features, the Version Cue client must be turned on using the Version Cue Preferences dialog box, and Version Cue must be enabled for Acrobat and each Creative Suite application using their respective Preferences dialog boxes.

- The Version Cue file interface may be accessed using any of the file dialog boxes used to open, save, place, import, and export files.

- The Version Cue file interface lets you create new projects, search for files, sort files, view thumbnails, and view deleted files.

Chapter 12

Combining, Packaging, and Attaching PDFs

In Acrobat versions 6 and 7, we had a menu command for creating a single PDF from multiple files of different file formats. The Create PDF From Multiple Files menu command in the Create task button has been augmented with menu commands in the new Combine Files task button. A new feature introduced in Acrobat 8 is the PDF Packages command. These two new commands are like Create PDF From Multiple Files on steroids.

Read on to find out how to use Merge Files into Single PDF and Assemble Files into PDF Package and you'll learn why I rank these commands on my top ten list of the best new features in Acrobat 8.

IN THIS CHAPTER

Combining PDFs

Packaging PDFs

Using file attachments

Setting Up the Work Environment

Creating merged documents and PDF Packages requires no special tools loaded other than the default toolbars. However, later in this chapter I talk about adding file attachments that in some ways appear similar to files added in a PDF Package. Therefore, you'll want to load some commenting tools.

When you get to the section related to working with file attachments, open a context menu on the Toolbar Well and select More Tools. Scroll down to the Comment & Markup toolbar and check the box adjacent to Attach a File as a Comment and check the box adjacent to Record Audio Comment. Check the box adjacent to the Comment & Markup toolbar and click OK.

Open a context menu on the Toolbar Well and select Dock All Toolbars.

Note that if you want to work exclusively with combining files and creating PDF Packages, you don't need to bother using the Comment & Markup toolbar. In this chapter, the Comment & Markup toolbar is loaded in the "Working with File Attachments" section at the end of the chapter.

Combining PDFs

The new Combine Files command provides you with an easy and intuitive dialog box where you can add files from all file formats that can be converted to PDF from within Acrobat 8. You can combine a PowerPoint file, a Word File, PDF file, and any other file format compatible with the Create PDF From File command.

CROSS-REF For more information on the file formats supported by Acrobat for conversion to PDF, see Chapter 7.

Using a feature such as Combine Files provides you more flexibility than using the Document ➪ Insert Pages command for inserting PDFs into an open document. First off, when using Insert Pages, you need to first convert your files to PDF. If you have several files of different formats you need to employ a two-step operation — one for conversion to PDF and the other for combining PDFs into a single document.

The Combine Files command enables you to perform the same operation in a single step. What's more, you can neatly organize the order of your files in a dialog box before creating the composite document.

Combining files is handled from a task button in the Tasks toolbar. In Figure 12.1, you can see the drop-down menu and the menu choices you have in the Combine Files task button. The Merge Files into Single PDF command is used to merge files from a number of different formats including PDF into a single document. The Assemble Files into PDF Package command creates a different kind of merge, but essentially takes on an appearance almost like a single PDF.

CROSS-REF For more information on PDF Packages see" Creating PDF Packages" later in this chapter.

FIGURE 12.1

The new Combine Files task button provides two new commands in Acrobat 8 used for merging files and creating a PDF Package.

Combining files and folders

When you want to combine files into a single PDF document you can click the Combine Files task button or open the menu by clicking on the down-pointing arrow and selecting Merge Files into Single PDF. Either action opens the Combine Files dialog box. Before you use the command, there are a few restrictions you have with regard to the types of files you can combine. These restrictions include:

- **PDFs with security.** PDFs with security cannot be combined using this command.
- **Adobe LiveCycle Designer XML Forms.** Any form created in Adobe Designer cannot be added using this command.

CROSS-REF For more information on Adobe Designer XML forms, see Chapter 35.

- **Digital signatures.** You can add files using this command that have digital signatures, but the signatures are removed when you combine the files.

■ **Form fields.** Adding a form is no problem using the Combine Files command, but if you have different files using the same field names, the fields are merged into one field. For example, if you merge a form populated with data and another identical form with the fields left blank, the data are merged together. The order of the files to be merged is important. If you have two identical forms and merge them with the blank fields file listed in the first position, both forms are merged and the second form (populated with field data) now appears with empty fields. Conversely, if the populated fields file is in the top-most position in the list along with a file with blank fields, both documents appear with the same data when you combine them. In other words, forms with identical field names inherit data from the first form in a list of files you merge.

Before I go on to explain all the features available to you when merging files into a single PDF document, launch Acrobat and follow along to see how easy it is to merge files using this new command.

STEPS: Using the Combine Files Command

1. **Click the Combine Files task button.** Note that you don't need to open the pull-down menu and select Merge Files into Single PDF. Clicking the task button opens the same dialog box as using the Merge Files into Single PDF command.

2. **Select files to merge.** When you click the Combine Files task button the Combine Files dialog box opens. Click the Add button and select files you want to add to the file list in the first window in the wizard. You can click a file and add it to the file list and click Add again and locate files in different folders. If you have a folder containing all the files you want to combine, you can click the Add Folder button and locate a folder. All files within a folder are then added to the list.

    In Figure 12.2, I added four documents to my list: two PDF files, a PowerPoint slide presentation in native .ppt format, and an HTML document.

FIGURE 12.2

Click the Add button to add files to a list or click Add Folder to add a folder of files.

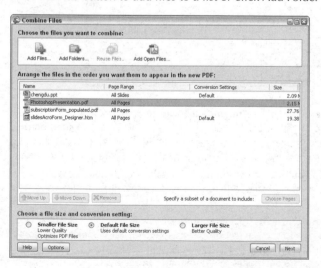

TIP Multiple files within the same folder can be added to your list. Click a file and press Shift and click to select a group of files listed in a contiguous order. Click and press Ctrl/⌘+click to select files in a noncontiguous order.

3. **Arrange the files in the order you want them to appear in the merged PDF document.** Click a file in the list and use the Move Up and Move Down buttons to arrange the files in the order you want them to appear in the resultant PDF document.

4. **Move to the second pane in the wizard.** Click Next and review the order of the files you want to merge. Any order you changed in the first pane in the wizard is reflected when you move to this next pane. In Figure 12.3, I changed the order of my file list. Note that if you merge files other than files in PDF format, the icons you see in the second pane are all PDF icons. Acrobat has not yet converted native files to PDF, but the appearance in the second pane shows you a post conversion view of the files. Be certain the Merge files into a single PDF radio button is active.

FIGURE 12.3

Click Next to move to the second pane in the wizard.

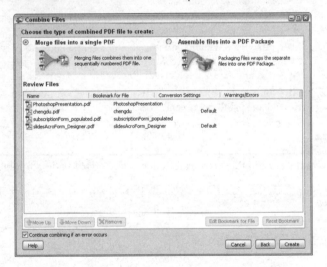

5. **Create the merged PDF document.** Click Create in the second pane in the wizard window. Any files you added to your list that need conversion to PDF are converted on the fly. The original authoring program opens and files are converted to PDF. Wait for Acrobat to complete the conversion and concatenation and you'll be prompted to save your composite document.

6. **Save the composite file.** When prompted to save the file, click Save. A Save As dialog box opens. Type a name for your file, navigate to the folder you want to use for your saved file, and click Save again.

7. **Review the resultant PDF file.** The composite file opens in the Acrobat Document pane. Click the Bookmarks tab in the Navigation pane. Notice that any bookmarks in your original PDFs containing bookmarks are preserved. Additional bookmarks are added to the file linking the first page of each separate document to a bookmark. In Figure 12.4, you see my composite document with the Bookmarks pane open.

CROSS-REF For more information on bookmarks, see Chapter 22.

FIGURE 12.4

Preview the composite file in the Document pane.

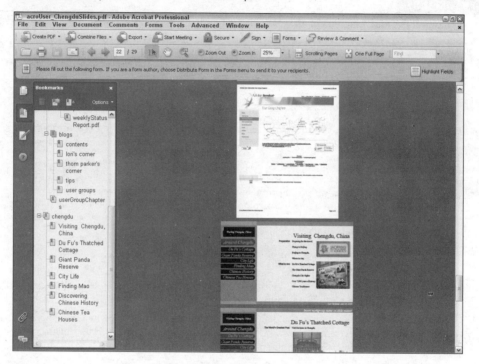

Using the Combine Files Wizard

There are a number of different buttons in the Combine multiple files into one PDF file wizard windows. Some of these buttons are quite intuitive and yet there are many different hidden options you might not first see when you start to combine files. As a matter of fact, there's so much involved with your options choices, I can't cover every detail for every feature. What I can do is point out some of the more obvious options and suggest to you ways to explore using context menus and double-clicks on files added to the wizard window. You'll be surprised at the number of choices Acrobat affords you.

NOTE Not all file formats are supported on the Macintosh. For a list of formats supported on the Mac click the Add button in the Combine Files dialog box and open the Show pull-down menu in the lower left corner of the Add Files dialog box. The formats discussed here for Microsoft Office files are among those file types not supported on the Mac.

Adding files to the wizard

As a first order of business, let's take a look at adding files to the wizard window when you first open the Combine Files dialog box. At the top of the first pane in the wizard are four buttons used to add files for combining into a single PDF document, as shown in Figure 12.5.

FIGURE 12.5

Four buttons at the top of the first pane in the wizard window are used for adding files to a list.

Your choices are as follows:

- **Add Files**. Use this button to open the Add Files dialog box. This dialog box behaves similar to an Open dialog box where you can navigate your hard drive and locate files to add to the list in the first pane.

NOTE If you select a secure PDF or a file created in Adobe Designer, the next pane in the wizard window reports a problem with your file choice and it is marked with an X. Acrobat informs you with one of two messages. A warning message appears when you try to combine files with digital signatures and files that have been secured. An error is reported when you try to combine Adobe LiveCycle Designer XML forms.

- **Add Folders**. Use this button to add a folder of files.

- **Reuse Files**. Click this button and the Reuse Files dialog box shown in Figure 12.6 opens. Once you've created a PDF by combining files, you can open the Reuse Files dialog box and use one or any number of files combined together in a previous file.

  On the left side of the dialog box you see a list of files used in a previous session that were combined to create a single PDF document. On the right you see files made available for reuse. Click a file in the right pane and click Add Files to reuse it. The file is then added to the list in the first pane in the wizard.

- **Add Open Files**. You can click the Combine Files task button without having a file open in the Document pane. You can also click the button when a file appears in the Document pane. If you have a file open when you open the wizard window, you can choose to add your open file to other files you add to the list.

FIGURE 12.6

Reuse Files enables you to select files used in a previous Combine Files session in a new session.

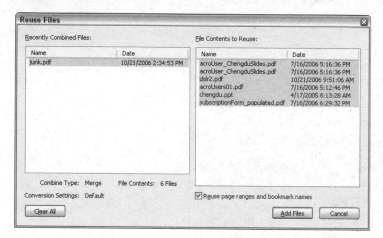

Organizing files

As you move below the file list in the first pane in the wizard window, a series of buttons appear for organizing pages in the file you ultimately create, as shown in Figure 12.7.

FIGURE 12.7

Buttons below the file list are used to organize pages.

Your options include:

- **Move Up.** Click a file and click the Move Up button and the file is reordered in the list. If the file you select is at the top of the list, the Move Up button is grayed out and unusable.

- **Move Down.** This button behaves the opposite of the Move Up button. Clicking the button moves a selected or several selected files down. When you select a file at the bottom of the list, the button is grayed out and unusable.

- **Remove.** As you might suspect, clicking this button removes any selected file(s) from the list.

- **Choose Pages/Sheets/Slides/Layouts/Sheet Selection.** This option is only available for multiple page documents and documents of certain file types. Most MS Office files are compatible with the Choose (*button text*) option. Click this button and the Preview Selected *button text* dialog box opens. The *button text* varies according to the file type you choose to add in the Combine Files dialog box. For MS Word files the button text is Choose Pages. With MS Excel the button text is Choose Sheets. AutoCAD files appear with Choose Layout. Microsoft Visio files appear with Sheet Selection. If you select a PowerPoint file, the button name changes to Choose Slides. Clicking any option opens a Preview dialog box like the one shown when I select Choose Slides with a PowerPoint file selected as shown in Figure 12.8.

 If you want to open the Preview and Select Pages/Slides dialog box, you can also double-click on a file in the list window.

 For simplicity, I'll refer to the item appearing in the Choose button as simply Choose button when describing options for choosing pages/sheets/layouts, etc. in the sections ahead.

FIGURE 12.8

Click Choose Pages to open a dialog box where pages in a file can be previewed.

Previewing files

Files of several different file types — primarily those of the Microsoft Office flavor and PDF documents — permit you to create a PDF preview, choose pages within the document to add to your resultant file, and also offer many different editing features. However, what you do in the Preview window cannot be saved. If you want to alter content you need to return to the original authoring program and make your edits, then export back to PDF.

CROSS-REF For more information regarding exporting to PDF, see Chapter 7. For information related to Microsoft Office and PDF creation, see Chapter 8.

Once again, I can't cover all the options available to you when previewing files, but here are some examples of the available options:

- **Microsoft Word.** Click a multipage Word document in the file list and click Choose Pages or simply double-click the Word document and the document opens in the Preview and Select Page Range dialog box. You can select specific pages you want added to the combined file by typing values in the Pages text box at the top of the dialog box. Noncontiguous pages are separated by commas and contiguous pages are separated by dashes. For example 1,3,7-9 denotes using pages 1, 3, and 5 through 7 for adding to the combined file.

In long documents, it would be helpful to see a view of the document pages so you know what pages you want to include in your combined file. The Preview and Select Page Range dialog box offers you just that. In addition, you can make a number of temporary edits through commands from a context menu, as shown in Figure 12.9.

FIGURE 12.9

Right-click (Windows) or Ctrl+click (Macintosh) to open a context menu where some editing commands appear.

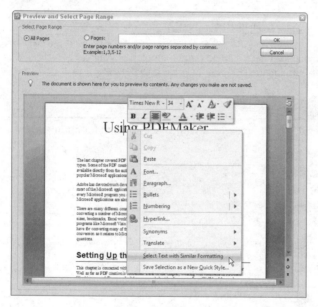

Be aware that any edits you make won't be applied to the combined file. Most of what you see available are commands designed to help you view files in many different ways. When opening a Word file in the Preview and Select page Range dialog box you have additional viewing options by clicking on icons in the lower-left corner of the window. The default view is a normal view represented by the icon on the far left. Moving from left to right, you have additional views that include Web Layout view, Print Layout view, Outline view, and Reading Layout view.

You can browse documents by tables, graphics, sections, comments, and much more. Just click the circle between the Previous and Next Page buttons represented by double arrowheads in the lower-right corner of the dialog box. A pop-up menu, shown in Figure 12.10, appears where you can choose to browse your file according to any one of 12 different options.

FIGURE 12.10

Click the small circle between the Previous and Next Page arrows to open a pop-up menu used for browsing different content.

- **Microsoft Excel.** Double-click an Excel Workbook file in the wizard window or click and select Choose Sheets. The Preview and Select Sheets dialog box opens, as shown in Figure 12.11. As with MS Word, you also have context menu commands. An entire workbook can be displayed and you can scroll the pages selecting only the pages you want to appear in your combined file.

FIGURE 12.11

A Microsoft Excel Workbook with a worksheet selected for adding to the Combine Files dialog box.

- **Microsoft PowerPoint.** You can choose from all of PowerPoint's numerous views in the Preview and Select Slides dialog box, which you open in much the same way as when opening Word and Excel files. In Figure 12.12, slides are shown in the Slide Sorter view. Additional choices for views are made in the lower-left corner by clicking on the icons. You can additionally view a PowerPoint file in a Normal view and a Slide Show view.

 If you view PowerPoint slides in Slide Show view all the tools are hidden. To bail out of Slide Show view, press the Escape (Esc) key.

PowerPoint files can also be viewed with content changes, but like other files, the changes are only temporary while in the Preview dialog box. From a context menu you have choices for adding and deleting slides, changing the slide design, changing animation schemes and changing transitions. Context menu options for PowerPoint files are shown in Figure 12.13. Displaying slides in the Slide Sorter View makes it easy to select just those slides you want to add to your single PDF document.

FIGURE 12.12

A PowerPoint file shown in a Slide Sorter view

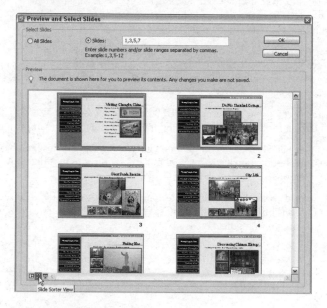

FIGURE 12.13

When viewing slides in the Slide Sorter View, you can easily select slides you want to include in your single PDF document.

Other similar options are available with Microsoft Visio files, Microsoft Project and Publisher files, and a number of different file formats including AutoCAD .dwg and .dwf files and InDesign .indd documents. (Note .indd files are also supported on the Macintosh). Your clue as to whether you have an option to open files in the Preview dialog box is whether you see an active Choose button in the first pane of the wizard. If the button is grayed out, you don't have the option to preview pages.

Conversion options

At the bottom of the first pane in the wizard window you have several buttons. The first set of radio buttons offers options for file optimization. Click the Smaller File Size and images will be downsampled to 150 ppi and compressed with a low quality JPEG compression scheme. The file size will typically be smaller than your original file unless you used lower resolution images and low quality JPEG compression. Click Default File Size to preserve the original file resolutions and the image size attributes will be the same setting identified in the Edit ➪ Preferences Convert to PDF Settings. Click Larger File Size to create a file with optimum results. You may not see much difference in file sizes between Default and Larger file sizes if you used high-resolution images and high quality JPEG compression.

NOTE Using Larger File Size does not upsample images. The image resolution won't be greater than the default resolution used when an image was saved. The primary change you experience with this option is when JPEG compression is set to Maximum Quality. If you saved your images with Medium Quality, the quality setting is changed.

These buttons affect files that need to be converted to PDF, and PDF documents. When PDF documents are included and you make a choice for the file size, the PDF Optimized is used to resample images.

CAUTION Creating Smaller File Sizes can result in much longer times to create a combined file. This option downsamples each image above 150 ppi and requires more time to produce the resultant PDF than the other two options.

At the very bottom of the wizard window the Help, Cancel, and Next buttons should be self-explanatory. Additionally, you have an Options button. Click the Options button and the Options for Conversion Settings dialog box opens, as shown in Figure 12.14.

FIGURE 12.14

Click the Options button at the bottom of the first pane in the wizard to open the Options for Conversion Settings dialog box.

The two options you have are making a document accessible and adding Bookmarks to the resultant PDF. Check the boxes for the options you want.

CROSS-REF For more information on accessibility, see Chapter 25.

Editing Bookmark names

Click Next in the wizard window and you arrive at the second pane where you can choose between merging your files into a single PDF document and creating a PDF Package.

Note that when the cursor appears over a filename, a tooltip provides you some information about the conversion options you have chosen as you can see in Figure 12.15.

A number of buttons in this pane are identical to those found in the first pane. However, the Edit Bookmark for File button is unique to this pane. Click Edit Bookmark for File and you can supply your own Bookmark names for each file combined or packaged.

To use the Edit Bookmark for File button, select a file in the list and click Edit Bookmark for File. The Edit Bookmark for File dialog box opens, as shown in Figure 12.16. Type a name for the Bookmark to bookmark the first page in the respective file and click OK.

FIGURE 12.15

Click Next and the second pane opens where you make a choice for creating a PDF from multiple files or a PDF Package.

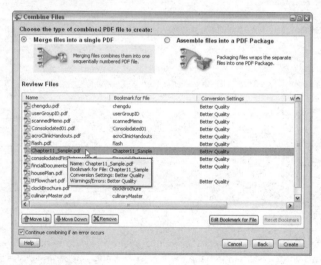

FIGURE 12.16

Type a name for the Bookmark in the Edit Bookmark for File dialog box.

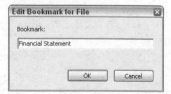

Previewing and saving combined files

Click the Create button in the second pane and Acrobat works away converting files to PDF format and combining them into a single PDF document. When the conversion and merging is completed, you see the wizard window change to the view shown in Figure 12.17.

Before you save the file, you can preview it by clicking on the navigation buttons below the preview thumbnail on the right side of the panel. In this example, 21 pages are contained in the resultant file. Clicking the next page button takes you to the next page. The last page button (far-right side) takes you to page 21.

After reviewing the file, you can choose to save it in one of two ways. First, start by clicking the Save button. This action opens the Save As dialog box. You can type a name for your file and click Save in the Save As dialog box and the file is saved.

FIGURE 12.17

After converting to PDF and merging files, Acrobat awaits your save instruction.

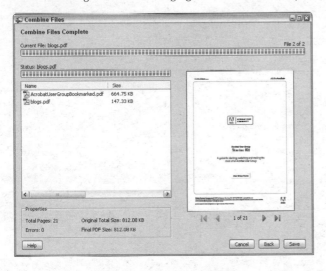

But what happens if you want to give your file a final review? Maybe you want to delete a page or make some edit before saving the file. You can do this without actually saving the file. Click Cancel in the Save As dialog box and you are returned to the view shown in Figure 12.17. Click Cancel again and click No in the warning dialog box that opens. The combined file appears in the Document pane and, as yet, is not saved. Be aware that the first time you see Figure 12.17, you must start by clicking Save to open the Save As dialog box, then click Cancel and Cancel again.

This might be living on the edge for a few users who get nervous about program crashes. If so, you can always execute the final save in the Save As dialog box and then go about your editing. I merely offer this clarity in the event you want to take control over when your file is ultimately saved.

Working with PDF Packages

The first time you launch Acrobat 8 and start poking around in the Combine Files task button you're likely to wonder why there are options for combining files into one PDF and why we have a PDF Package item. The answer is really quite simple. PDF Package enables you to do all the things you can't do when combining PDFs. Your options include:

- **Secure files.** PDF Package enables you to add secure files. In order to add a secure file to a package, you need the password(s).
- **Adobe Designer XML Forms.** PDF Package enables you to combine files that were created in Adobe Designer.
- **PDF Forms.** Actually this can be both PDF forms and XML forms. When you combine forms having identical field names, the data fields remain undisturbed.
- **Preserve original document format.** When you use Combine Files, any document other than PDF is converted to PDF as long as the file format is compatible with the Create PDF From File command. When creating a PDF Package, files appear with a PDF preview but they retain original file format attributes and can be exported from the package back to the original file format.

CROSS-REF PDF Packages can also be created from Microsoft Outlook emails and when compiling returned forms. To learn how PDF Packages are used with Microsoft Outlook, see Chapter 8. To learn more about compiling form data and creating PDF Packages, see Chapter 35.

When you create a PDF Package, you create a much different result than when merging files into one PDF document. PDF Packages are PDFs created with file attachments. The attachments appear in a new panel adjacent to the Navigation panel, but the files are all very similar to adding file attachments to a PDF document. One difference between a PDF having file attachments and a PDF package is that with adding file attachments you can add any file type as an attachment to a PDF. With PDF Packages you can add any file type, but during the processing to create the PDF package, all files are converted to PDF. The resultant document doesn't have contiguous pages that you scroll to navigate, but it also doesn't require you to open files quite like you need to do with file attachments in Acrobat 7. The package takes on a behavior as though it was a single document, but indeed the files you use in your package are separate documents.

CROSS-REF For more on file attachments see "Working with File Attachments" later in this chapter.

Once you open a PDF Package in an Acrobat 8 viewer you'll know it's a package immediately. PDF Packages add another sidebar to the Acrobat window. If you open a PDF Package in Acrobat 7, the files all appear in the Attachments panel as file attachments. Documents are not viewed in the Pages panel in Acrobat 8, although you can see individual pages of each file in the Pages panel. Rather, the files by default appear to the left side of the Navigation panel. One click on the file icon opens the first page of the document in the Document pane. File attachments are nestled together in the Attachments panel and they require you to double-click the file icon in order to open them.

Creating a package

To understand a little more about PDF Packages, let's first start by following some steps to create a package and then look at some of the attributes for working in the wizard used to create packages. The very same wizard you use to combine multiple files into one PDF file is used for creating PDF Packages. You can choose to select Assemble Files in PDF Packages from the Combine Files task button or you can use the Merge Files into a Single PDF command in the Combine Files task button. Also, just click the task button and you arrive at the same wizard window. Regardless of which menu command you use, the same Combine Files into a Single PDF wizard opens.

To use this wizard to create a PDF Package, follow these steps.

STEPS: Creating a PDF Package

1. **Click the Combine Files task button (or open the task button menu and select Assemble Files in PDF Packages).**

2. **Add files to the wizard list window.** Click the Add button and locate files on your hard drive you want to add to your package. Ideally, try to add a file that is password protected and a form created in Adobe Designer.

3. **Type a password for secure files.** If one of your files is password protected a Password dialog box opens prompting you for a password as you see in Figure 12.18. Type the password and click OK.

4. **Assemble the files into a package.** Click the Next button in the wizard window and click the Assemble files into a PDF Package radio button, as shown in Figure 12.19. This choice distinguishes your resultant file from a PDF file created from multiple files.

FIGURE 12.18

For secure files, type the password and click OK.

FIGURE 12.19

Click Assemble files into a PDF Package.

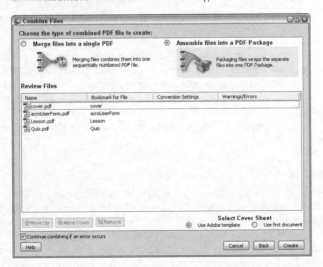

5. **Identify a template.** By default the Use Adobe template radio button is selected. Leave this radio button enabled to use the Adobe template.

6. **Create the package.** Click Create in the wizard.

7. **Save the file.** After Acrobat converts any files needed to be converted to PDF and assembles the document, click Save in the wizard window. The Save As dialog box opens next. Type a name for the file and click Save.

8. **Review the resultant document.** As you can see in Figure 12.20, the PDF Package appears a little different than other PDF files you open in Acrobat. On the far left is a list of files added to the package.

   Notice the Cover sheet icon above the file list on the far left of the Acrobat window. Click this button to open the Adobe template used when the file was created and you see the first page in your file appearing similar to Figure 12.21.

FIGURE 12.20

Review the PDF Package in Acrobat.

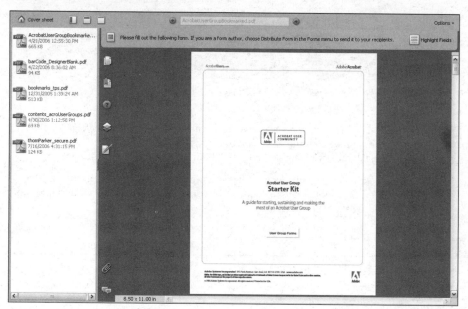

Click Cover sheet to open the first page in the document and view the default template.

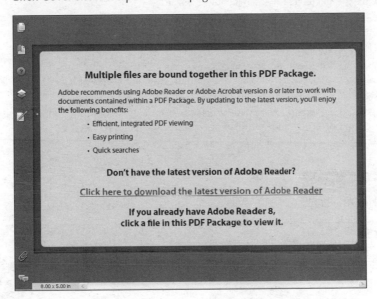

Viewing PDF Packages

All the buttons you see on the wizard window when creating a PDF Package are the same as those found when combining files with the exception of using a template. The differences between a combined file and a PDF Package lie in the viewing of the files and options you have for editing them.

Open a context menu on a file icon in the far left panel where the files in the package reside, as shown in Figure 12.22. From context menu commands, you have several options that differ from other PDF documents, including the following:

Open a context menu on a file icon.

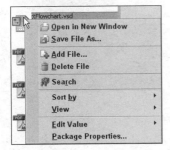

- **Open in New Window.** This menu option works the same as selecting Window ⇨ New Window. The same package opens in a new window in the Document pane.

- **Save File As.** Selecting this menu item saves the PDF document within a PDF package as a single PDF file.

- **Add File.** Clicking Add File adds a file to the package. The file is not converted to PDF. The file is added similar to the way you might add a file attachment, but the file doesn't appear in the Attachments panel.

- **Delete File.** Click an icon and click Delete File and the file is removed from the package.

- **Search.** Select this menu item and the Search window opens, as shown in Figure 12.23, enabling you to search the entire PDF Package for words typed in the text box at the top of the window.

- **Sort by.** From a submenu, as shown in Figure 12.24, you can sort the default package list by Index, Name, Description, date Modified, and file Size. If you add metadata to the PDF Package you'll, see additional items appear in the list.

FIGURE 12.23

Search options include searching in the entire PDF Package.

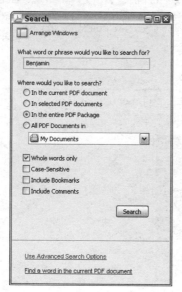

371

FIGURE 12.24

Sort by enables you to sort package contents.

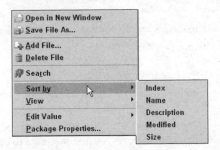

- **View.** The description information shown adjacent to the file icons in Figure 12.20 show the name, modified date, and file size. When you select the View command a submenu opens where you can toggle off/on these label descriptions.

- **Edit Value.** Click this menu item and a submenu opens with a list of the metadata fields you can edit. In Figure 12.25, I added a new Metadata field in the Document Properties after selecting Additional Metadata for a copyright field. When I choose Edit Value, my new Copyright item is displayed in the submenu.

FIGURE 12.25

After adding a metadata item, the Edit Value submenu displays the additional metadata item.

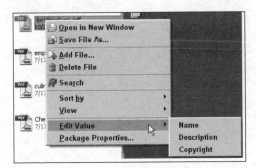

- **Package Properties.** Select Package Properties and the Package Properties dialog box opens, as shown in Figure 12.26. You can choose a number of options here for viewing, sorting, and modifying the package contents.

FIGURE 12.26

Open the Package Properties dialog box and make choices for viewing, sorting, and editing the package properties.

Three icons appear above the Navigation pane. (See Figure 12.27.) These icons are used to change the display of the package file names. By default, the left icon (View left) is selected, providing the view shown in Figure 12.27.

FIGURE 12.27

Click one of the three icons above the Navigation pane to change the package filenames display. The icons are from left to right View left, View top, and Minimize view.

Click the second (middle) icon (View top) and the display changes. (See Figure 12.28.) Click the third icon (Minimize view) and the files are shown by clicking the left and right arrows, as shown in Figure 12.29.

FIGURE 12.28

Clicking the middle icon (View top) shows files listed above the Document pane and all the metadata (or package properties) associated with the package.

Name	Description	Modified	Size ▲
ttFlowchart.vsd		4/19/2003 2:02:38 PM	116 KB
clockBrochure.pdf		7/17/2006 12:59:02 AM	1,218 KB
employeeManual.pdf		7/17/2006 12:59:43 AM	1,277 KB
culinaryMaster.pdf	Culinary Spread	7/17/2006 6:27:46 AM	3,501 KB
ChengduLayout.pdf		7/17/2006 12:59:38 AM	4,255 KB

Clicking the far-right icon (Minimize view) shows the current file in the Document pane by filename above the Document pane. Click the left and right arrows to toggle file views.

Creating a template for a PDF Package

Your choices for creating a template are only one of two. Either you use the template provided by Adobe shown in Figure 12.21 or use the first page in the first file as the opening cover page. Adobe hasn't provided an option for creating a custom template for our packages. But don't let that stop you. You can create your own custom template and use it with the PDF Packages you create. To create a custom template for PDF Packages, follow these steps.

STEPS: Creating a custom template for PDF Packages

1. **Create a document you want to use as a template.** Use your favorite authoring program to create the template and convert it to PDF.

2. **Add fields and links.** Open the file in Acrobat and add any data fields you want and links to any Web site or email address using tools in Acrobat. In my example shown in Figure 12.29, I added some URL links for users to acquire the latest version of Adobe Reader, a URL where I host a blog, a few web links to my Web site, and my email address. Additionally, I add a digital signature field so I could sign the package and a filed that calculates the date to datestamp the package.

CROSS-REF For more information on creating Web links, see Chapters 22 and 27. To learn how to write JavaScript code to datestamp a document, see Chapter 36.

3. **Enable the file in Adobe Reader.** If you want users to fill in any form data or add comment notes, select Advanced ➪ Enable Usage Rights in Adobe Reader and save the enabled document.

CROSS-REF For more information on enabling PDF documents with special features for Adobe Reader, see Chapter 19.

4. **Save the file and name it coversheet.pdf.** You must use this name for the template to be recognized by Acrobat.

5. **Move the coversheet.pdf file to the Combine Files/Enu folder.** On Windows the directory path is Program Files\Adobe\Acrobat 8.0\Acrobat\DocSettings\Combine Files\ENU. Replace the existing coversheet.pdf file with your new coversheet.pdf file.

   On the Mac, open the Applications folder and open the Adobe Acrobat 8.0 Professional folder. Select the Adobe Acrobat Professional program icon. Open a context menu (Ctrl+click) and select Show Package Contents. Open the Contents folder, then open the Mac OS folder. Open DocSettings and open the CombineFiles folder. Open the ENU folder and replace the coversheet.pdf file with your new coversheet.pdf file. The complete Mac directory path is: Macintosh HD\Applications\Adobe Acrobat 8.0 Professional\Adobe Acrobat Professional\Contents\MacOS\DocSettings\CombineFiles\ENU.

6. **Copy the file to a location where you keep backup files.** Be certain to keep a backup file. If you reinstall Acrobat, you'll need to use the backup copy to replace the default coversheet.pdf document.

7. **Create a PDF Package.** When you come to the Add button, add your template as the first document. Click Add to add the files you want in your package.

8. **Define the template.** Click Next and select Use Adobe template in the Combine multiple files into one PDF file wizard, as shown earlier in Figure 12.19. When you open your package, and click Cover sheet, your template appears as the cover as shown in Figure 12.30.

FIGURE 12.30

Create a custom template that can be used with all your PDF Packages.

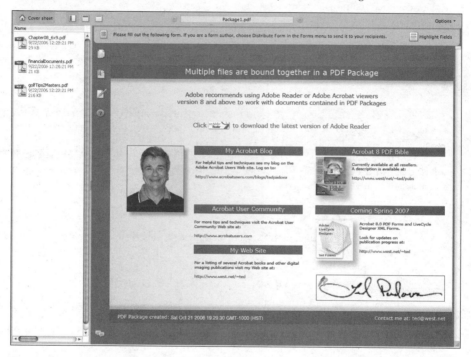

Working with File Attachments

File attachments enable you to attach any document file on your hard drive, a recorded sound, or a pasted image to an open PDF file. When you attach files, the file is embedded in the PDF document. Embedding a file provides other users the capability to view attachments on other computers and across platforms. At first it may appear as though the attachment is a link. However, if you transport the PDF document to another computer and open the attachment, the embedded file opens in the host application.

Users on other computers need the original authoring application to view the embedded file just like files added to PDF Packages. You can add file attachments in Acrobat Standard and Acrobat Professional. You can also add file attachments in Adobe Reader when PDFs have been created by using Adobe LiveCycle Reader extensions. If you open the Attachments panel (click the paper clip icon in the Navigation panel) in Adobe Reader, you cannot add file attachments. You can use the Add File for Comment command, but then the attachment is attached to a page vs. attached to the document.

There are two methods available to you when attaching files. You can use the Commenting toolbar and attach a file as a comment or use the Attach a File menu command from the Document menu. When files are attached using the Attach a File as a Comment, the PDF needs to be enabled with usage rights for Adobe Reader users to extract the file. Additionally, when Attach a File as a Comment is used, the file attachments show up in any comment summary you create in Acrobat.

CROSS-REF The commenting tools used for file attachments are discussed in this chapter. However, commenting is a huge topic and you'll find Chapter 20 devoted to all the other features all Acrobat viewers offer you for commenting.

When using the Attach a File menu command, any Adobe Reader user in version 7.0 and later can extract the file attachment without the file enabled with usage rights. Unlike using commenting tools, files attached using the menu command do not show up in comment summaries.

CROSS-REF For more information on adding usage rights to PDFs for Adobe Reader, see Chapter 19.

Regardless of what attachment you add to a document, the attachments appear in the Attachments panel in the Navigation panel. If you add a file attachment to a PDF in a PDF Package, the package files are shown in one of the three views shown in the section "Viewing PDF Packages" earlier in this chapter. Therefore, if you have a PDF Package and files have attachments within the package, you'll see the files in two different panels (that is, the PDF Package files in one of the three PDF Package views, and the attachments appearing in the Attachments panel).

Using the Attach tools

 To attach a file to a PDF document, select Document ➪ Attach a File. The Add Attachment dialog box opens where you can navigate your hard drive, locate a file to attach, select the file, and click Open. The file is attached to the open document and all users of all Acrobat viewers version 7.0 and later can extract the attachment.

To use the Attach File as a Comment tool, select the tool and click in the Document pane. The Select file to Attach dialog box opens, in which you navigate to a file and select it for the attachment. Any file on your computer can be used as a file attachment. Select a file and click Select. The File Attachment Properties dialog box opens with the Appearance tab in view as shown in Figure 12.31.

FIGURE 12.31

Select a file to attach and the File Attachment Properties dialog box opens.

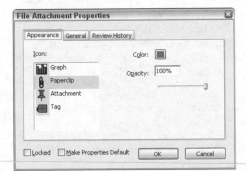

NOTE To use the Attach a File as a Comment feature, you need to load the Comment & Markup toolbar. See "Setting Up the Work Environment" at the beginning of this chapter for loading the tools necessary to follow along in this section.

The Appearance properties for file attachments offer you choices for icon appearances to represent file attachments. Choose from one of the four icon choices shown in Figure 12.30. By default the Paperclip icon is used.

The General tab shown in Figure 12.32 has editable fields used for Author name, Subject, and a Description. By default, the Author name is supplied by your Identity preferences.

CROSS-REF For information on editing Identity preferences, see Chapter 20.

FIGURE 12.32

The General properties offer choices for author name, subject, and a description of the attached file.

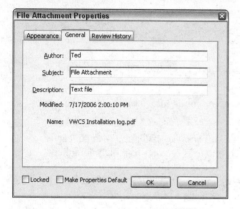

The Review History tab shown in Figure 12.33 is used for review sessions where information related to the review history and migration history are viewed.

CROSS-REF For information on review and migration history, see Chapter 21.

FIGURE 12.33

The Review History documents review and migration history.

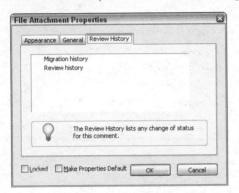

If you place the cursor over a file attachment icon, a tooltip displays the author name, file name, and the description information.

Attach a File as a Comment does not support an associated pop-up note. Double-clicking an attachment icon opens the file attachment.

NOTE You must have the original authoring application to open file attachments when the attachments are other than PDF.

You can use PDF documents like a security wrapper for any file you want to exchange with colleagues and coworkers. Use the Attach a File as a Comment tool and attach one or more files to a PDF document. Secure the PDF with Password Security and use the Email tool to send the file to members of your workgroup. You can protect the document with password security and prevent unauthorized users from opening your PDF or extracting attached files. In this regard you can use Acrobat to secure any document you create from any authoring program. Of course, you can also secure PDF Packages and use files within a package very similar to using file attachments.

CROSS-REF For more information on using Password Security, see Chapter 26. For more information about using the Email tool, see Chapter 27.

File attachments are embedded in PDFs, and double-clicking on the Attach File as a Comment icon provides you access to the file. If you want to save an embedded file to disk without opening the file, open a context menu and select Save Attachment. Acrobat opens a dialog box where you can navigate your hard drive and designate a location for the file to be saved to. Neither opening a file nor saving the attachment file to disk removes the file attachment. If you want to delete a file attachment, open a context menu on the attachment icon and select Delete Attachment or select the icon and press Delete or the Del key.

Record Audio Comment tool

 Sound comments are recorded from within the PDF document or from prerecorded sounds saved in .WAV (Windows) or .AIFF or .WAV (Macintosh). For recording a sound, you must have a microphone connected to your computer. The resulting sound file is embedded in the PDF when you use the Record Audio Comment tool.

Attaching prerecorded sounds

Select the Record Audio Comment tool and click on a PDF page. The Sound Recorder (Windows shown in Figure 12.34) or Record Sound (Macintosh shown in Figure 12.35) dialog box opens. Click Browse (Windows) or Choose (Macintosh).

FIGURE 12.34

To select a sound file to attach to the PDF (Windows), click the Browse button.

FIGURE 12.35

To select a sound file to attach to the PDF (Macintosh), click the Choose button.

The Select Sound File dialog box opens after you click Browse (Windows) or Choose (Macintosh). Navigate your hard drive and find a sound file to attach to the document. Select the sound file and click the Select button. Acrobat returns you to the Sound Recorder (Windows) or Record Sound (Macintosh) dialog box. At this point you can play the sound or click OK to embed the sound in the PDF. Click the right-pointing arrow (Windows) or Play (Macintosh) and you can verify the sound before importing it. After you click OK, the Sound Attachment Properties dialog box opens.

After the sound file has been embedded in the PDF document you can play the sound by opening a context menu on the Record Audio Comment icon and selecting Play File.

Recording sounds

Click the mouse button with the Record Audio Comment tool to open the Sound Recorder (Windows) or Record Sound (Macintosh) dialog box. Click the record button and speak into the microphone connected to your computer. When you've finished recording the sound, click OK (Windows) or Stop (Macintosh). The Sound Attachment Properties dialog box opens immediately after you stop the recording. The General properties are shown (Windows) in Figure 12.36 or Appearance properties (Macintosh) in Figure 12.37.

FIGURE 12.36

After you stop a recording, the Sound Attachment Properties dialog box opens (Windows).

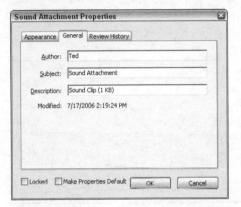

FIGURE 12.37

After you stop a recording, the Sound Attachment Properties dialog box opens (Macintosh).

When you close the Sound Attachment Properties dialog box, the sound can be played like imported sounds. Open a context menu and select Play File (or double-click on the Record Audio Comment icon). Because the sound becomes part of the PDF document, you can transport the PDF across platforms without having to include a sound file link. All sound files are audible on either platform once imported into PDFs.

 For more information on importing sound files, see Chapters 23 and 28.

Attachments and PDF Packages

You might first think that file attachments are unnecessary when you create PDF Packages. After all, you can add any file to a PDF Package, so why use a file attachment to add files to your document?

When you think about it though, there are some instances where file attachments might be helpful with PDF Packages. You might have a number of PDF documents where you want to send the original application

document along with the PDF version to colleagues and workgroup members. Attaching the original authoring document to each PDF in a package can help organize your files neatly.

Creative pros and engineers might make use of PDF Packages and file attachments. You might have several brochures or similar documents created in Adobe InDesign that you want to share with your workgroup. You can create a package from InDesign that saves your InDesign document, fonts, and images to a package file. You can then use the Attach a File command to attach the InDesign package files to the PDF versions of the documents. Similar kinds of workflows might be used with engineers creating technical drawings or mechanical engineers creating 3D images.

TIP   Because of potential virus problems .zip and .exe files are not recommended for use as file attachments. You can, however, attach Stuffit archives that can be extracted on both Windows and the Macintosh.

Another instance where a file attachment in a PDF Package might be helpful is when adding audio comments. PDF Packages don't support audio comments quite like using the Record Audio Comment tool. If you prefer adding notes in audio form to PDF documents, then using a recorded audio attachment might just be your solution.

If you ever find a need for adding file attachments to PDF Packages, there are a few things you should know about the structure of a PDF Package and attachments:

- Attachments, as well as comments, are attached to each file independently. In order to see an attachment either on a document page or in the Attachments panel, you need to place the respective PDF in view in the Document pane. Attachments made to files not in view are not shown in the Attachments panel. It's like having a separate Attachments panel for each PDF in a package.

- File attachments can be searched in a PDF Package. If you have attachments made to different PDFs, you can search all attachment files, as well as, all PDFs in a package. However, the search must be performed from a context menu item opened in the package panel. Searches invoked in the Attachments panel do not permit searching attachments other than within the PDF in view in the Document pane.

- Comment summaries are made specific to each PDF document. You cannot combine file attachments as comments made on different PDFs in a package to a single summary.

CROSS-REF   For more information on creating comment summaries, see Chapters 20 and 31.

- PDF Package files and file attachments are viewed in separate panes.

Using the Attachments panel

The Attachments panel docked in the Navigation panel appears by default. When you click the Attachments panel the panel opens horizontally like the Comments tab. The Attachments panel includes a list of file attachments contained in a document that were attached with either the Attach a File command or the Attach a File as a Comment tool.

File attachments can be added to PDF documents and PDF Packages. In Figure 12.38, file attachments were added to PDFs in a PDF Package. The Attachments panel is opened and a file attachment on a page in the last document in the PDF Package is in view.

FIGURE 12.38

Click the Attachments panel to open the Attachments panel where a list of all file attachments appear when added with either the Attach a File as a Comment tool or the Attach a File menu command.

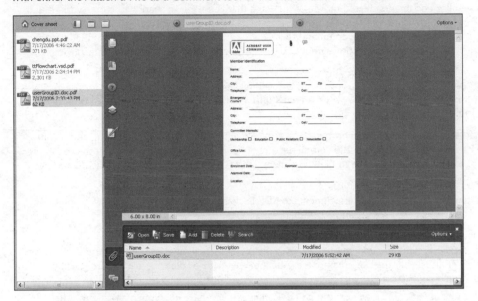

At the top of the Attachments panel, you find tools for the following:

- **Open.** Click an attachment listed in the panel and click Open. The attachment opens in the program that created the document.

- **Save.** Select an attachment and click Save to save the file to disk. Attachments are contained within PDF files and not accessible to authoring programs unless you open the file by using the Open tool or double-click on an attachment icon. Clicking the Save tool extracts the attachment and saves the extracted file to disk. (Note: Extraction does not delete the file attachment from the PDF.)

- **Add.** Add is the only tool accessible when an attachment is not selected in the panel. Click Add to open the Add Attachment dialog box where you can attach additional files. As new files are added as attachments, they are listed dynamically in the Attachment panel.

- **Delete.** Click an attachment and click the Delete tool to remove the attachment from the host document.

> **TIP**   If you inadvertently delete an attachment, you can choose Edit ➪ Undo and bring the attachment back. If you delete several attachments, you can select Undo several times and bring back each deleted attachment.

- **Search.** Clicking the Search tool opens the Search panel. You enter search criteria in the Search panel and click the Search Attachments button. Your Acrobat viewer searches all attached PDF files attached to files in the PDF Package.

CROSS-REF For more information on using Acrobat Search, see Chapter 6.

 ■ **Options.** From the Options pull-down menu in the panel or from a context menu opened on a selected attachment, you have additional choices from menu selections. Click the down-pointing arrow adjacent to Options or open a context menu and the menu appears, as shown in Figure 12.39.

FIGURE 12.39

The Options menu and context menu opened from selected attachments offer the same menu commands.

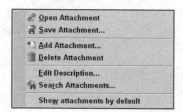

The menu commands for Open Attachment, Save Attachment, Add Attachment, Delete Attachment, and Search Attachments perform the same functions as their tool counterparts. The remaining two menu commands include Edit Description and Show attachments by default. Select Edit Description and a dialog box opens where you change the Description as you would edit a Description in the File Attachment Properties dialog box.

Select Show attachments by default and the Attachments panel opens each time you open the current document. Selecting this option is document specific and you need to save the file after making the menu choice. This menu item is the same as selecting the Attachments Panel and Page option in the Show pull-down menu in the Initial View pane for the Document Properties.

CROSS-REF For more information on setting Initial Views, see Chapter 5.

Summary

■ Separate files can be merged together in a single PDF file using the Combine Files task button.

■ A PDF Package is created with the same Combine Files task button menu. The second pane in the creation wizard provides radio button choices for creating a single file from multiple documents or a PDF Package.

■ PDF Packages can contain secure files and Adobe Designer XML Forms. Creating a single PDF from multiple files does not support secure files or Designer forms.

■ PDF Packages use either a default template or the first page in a package as a cover sheet.

■ You can create a custom template and use it as a cover sheet for a PDF Package.

■ File attachments can be added to PDFs and to files within PDF Packages.

- Attachments can be made as file attachment comments or using a menu command.
- If files are attached as comments, you can extract the attachments in Adobe Reader.
- If you attach files other than PDF, you need the original application program that created the document installed on your computer in order to open the attached file.
- File attachments are viewed according to the PDF file in the Attachments panel. When viewing file attachments made on PDFs in a PDF Package, only the attachments on the file in view can be seen in the Attachments panel.

Chapter 13

Editing Text

Ideally you should always return to an original document when you want to make changes on PDF pages that were converted from an authoring application. With all of Acrobat's impressive features, it is not designed to be used as a page layout program. The options you have in Acrobat for text editing are limited to tweaks and minor corrections. Inasmuch as Acrobat 8 has greatly improved text editing on PDFs, returning to your authoring program, editing the pages, and converting them back to PDF is a preferred method.

For minor edits and for purposes of editing PDF files where original documents have been lost or are unavailable, Acrobat does provide you tools and means for text editing. As you look through this chapter, realize that the pages ahead are intended to describe methods for minor corrections and text editing when you don't have an option for returning to an original document.

IN THIS CHAPTER

Editing text with the TouchUp Text tool

Adjusting text editing preferences

Using the Select tool

Looking up definitions

Setting text attributes in new blank pages

Setting Up the Text Editing Environment

For text editing, there are several toolbars that you'll want to make visible and dock in the Toolbar Well or float in the Document window, depending on what is handier for you. Toolbars you need for text editing include:

- **Reset Toolbars.** Open a context menu on the Toolbar Well and select Reset Toolbars to return the tools and toolbars to defaults.
- **Access the tools.** Open a context menu on the Toolbar Well and select More Tools.
- **Advanced Editing.** Check the check box for the Advanced Editing Toolbar. Uncheck all tools except the Select Object tool, the Crop tool, the TouchUp Text tool and the TouchUp Object tool.
- **File Toolbar.** Add the Organizer and Search tools to the File Toolbar.

- **Edit Toolbar.** Check the box for the Edit Toolbar and all tools are added by default.
- **Select & Zoom Toolbar.** For zooming in and out of the Document pane, use the Loupe tool. Add the Actual Size, Fit Width, and Fit Page tools.

Click OK in the More Tools window. Open a context menu on the Toolbar Well and select Dock Toolbars. After loading the toolbars, your Toolbar Well should look like Figure 13.1.

FIGURE 13.1

Load all editing tools in the Toolbar Well before beginning your text editing session.

Using the TouchUp Text Tool

TI TouchUp Text Tool   For minor text edits, the TouchUp Text tool on the Advanced Editing toolbar enables you to edit text along single lines of copy and edit bodies of text. Before you attempt to change text passages on a PDF page, you need to keep a few things in mind. Some of the considerations include:

- **Font embedding.** If you attempt to edit an embedded font, Acrobat prompts you in a dialog box to unembed the font. Text editing is only possible after a font is unembedded. Depending on the permissions granted by the font developer, some fonts can't be unembedded. If Acrobat informs you that font editing cannot occur, you need to make your changes in the original authoring document.

CROSS-REF   **For more information on font embedding, see Chapter 10.**

- **Tagged and untagged PDF documents.** Selecting text with the TouchUp Text tool was problematic with earlier versions of Acrobat. Blocks of text in untagged files were interpreted as separate passages and could not be selected in a contiguous area. Acrobat now has a more intelligent interpretation of text on a page and tagged, as well as untagged files, display no difference when selecting text. In Figure 13.2, a page of text is selected with the TouchUp Text tool in an untagged document.

  The ability to select lines of text, a paragraph, or multiple paragraphs with the TouchUp Text tool is not dependent on whether a PDF is tagged or untagged; but rather, it's dependent on the structure and content of a PDF. In some documents you can't select more than single lines of text like the file shown in Figure 13.3.

CROSS-REF   **For more information on tagged and structured PDF documents, see Chapter 25. For information on creating tagged PDF files, see Chapters 9 and 10.**

- **Property changes.** You can apply property changes for fonts, such as color, size, and other attributes, to text without unembedding the font.

FIGURE 13.2

The TouchUp Text tool in Acrobat 8 can select multiple blocks of text in untagged PDF files.

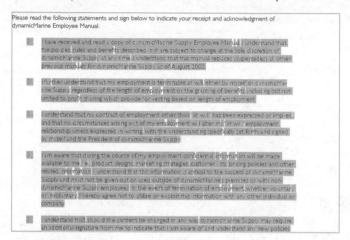

FIGURE 13.3

The TouchUp Text tool can select only single lines of text on a page in some PDF documents.

Fortunately, Acrobat alerts you ahead of time if you attempt to edit a PDF document with embedded fonts and those fonts aren't installed on your computer. To edit fonts on a page, select the TouchUp Text tool, and click and drag over a body of text to be changed. Acrobat pauses momentarily as it surveys your installed fonts and the font embedded in the PDF document. Enter your changes and the selected text is replaced with the new text you typed.

You'll be able to see onscreen whether your text editing results in an acceptable appearance and the edits are properly applied. If the text scrambles and you lose total control over the document page, you need to either find the original authoring document or export text from Acrobat into a word processor or layout program to make the changes.

PREPRESS Editing text passages are fine for screen displays when the text flows in an acceptable manner. For high-end printing and prepress you might be able to successfully make changes and minor edits without experiencing printing problems. However, for any kind of paragraph editing you are best off returning to the authoring application. You might get away with some edits in Acrobat, but eventually they will catch up with you. If you do make a spelling error change or other minor text edit, be certain to re-embed the font (see "Changing text attributes" later in this chapter).

In addition to selecting the Properties menu command, a context menu opened from a TouchUp Text tool selection offers menu commands for insertion of special characters. Four choices are available to you when you open a context menu and select the Insert menu command. From the submenu you can choose:

- **Line Break.** This choice adds a line break from the cursor insertion. This command is handy when creating new text on a page or when pasting text. Text lines may extend beyond the page width when creating new text or pasting text. You can create line breaks to keep text within a specific area of the page.
- **Soft Hyphen.** This choice adds a soft hyphen for text scrolling to a new line.
- **Non-Breaking Space.** To add spaces without line breaks, choose non-breaking space.
- **Em Dash.** To add an em dash (—) at the cursor insertion, choose em dash.

When text is selected and you insert a special character, the selected text is deleted and the new character is added. If you use special characters in some files, the results may be less than desirable. Line breaks can flow text into following paragraphs and the text can overlap, making the page unreadable. If you encounter such problems and the edits are necessary to make your files more readable, you must return the file to the authoring program, make the edits, and recreate the PDF document.

Changing text attributes

You can make many text attribute changes without unembedding fonts. You can change colors, point sizes in lines of text, character and word spacing, and other similar text attributes, as well as make changes related to the document structure. You make all of these changes in the TouchUp Properties dialog box.

To edit text properties, select the characters, words, or paragraph(s) you want to change. Be certain the text is highlighted and open a context menu, as shown in Figure 13.4. From the menu options, select Properties.

FIGURE 13.4

To change text properties, select the text to be changed with the TouchUp Text tool and select Properties from the menu options.

CROSS-REF Two tools enable text selection — the TouchUp Text tool and the Select tool. Always use the TouchUp Text tool context menu when opening the TouchUp Properties dialog box. The Select tool context menu does not provide access to the TouchUp Properties dialog box. For information related to using the Select tool, see "Using the Select Tool" later in this chapter.

After you select Properties from the context menu, the TouchUp Properties dialog box opens, as shown in Figure 13.5. The first two tabs relate to changing tags and document structure. Leave these alone for the moment and look at the third tab labeled Text. The properties contained on it relate to changing font attributes for the selected text.

FIGURE 13.5

Select the Text tab in the TouchUp Properties dialog box to make changes to font attributes.

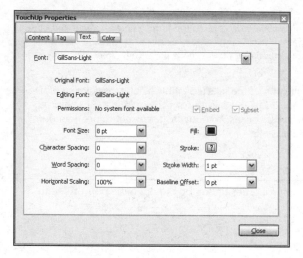

CROSS-REF For information on using the Content and Tag tabs, see Chapter 25.

Items contained in the Text tab include:

- **Font.** This pull-down menu contains a list of fonts for all the fonts loaded in your system and fonts embedded in the document. Keep in mind that just because a font is listed in the pull-down menu doesn't mean you can select the font. If the font is an embedded/subsetted font and you don't have a compatible font loaded in your system, Acrobat won't let you use that font. Fonts loaded in your system can be selected to replace fonts that are both embedded and not embedded.

NOTE The font list in the pull-down menu shows a line dividing the list at the top of the menu. All fonts appearing above the line are embedded fonts in the document. All fonts below the line are fonts loaded in your system.

- **Font Size.** You select a preset font size from this pull-down menu. If the desired size is not listed among the menu choices, select the font size in the field box and type a new value to change the size.

- **Character Spacing.** You can move characters in a line of text closer together or farther apart. The values shown in the pull-down menu are measured in em spaces. Choose from the menu choices or type a value in the field box. Using negative (–) values moves the characters together.

- **Word Spacing.** This option controls the space between whole words. You make choices for distance the same way you do for the preceding character spacing option.

- **Horizontal Scaling.** Sizing of individual characters (narrower or wider) is set according to the percentage of the original size. Values above 100% scale characters larger than the original font. Values below 100% result in smaller characters.

- **Embed.** Check the box to embed the selected font.

- **Subset.** Check the box to subset the font.

CROSS-REF For information on font embedding and subsetting, see Chapter 10.

CAUTION In order to legally embed a font, you must own a copy of the font to be embedded and comply with the licensing restrictions of the font manufacturer. Be certain to review the licensing agreement that came with your fonts to be certain embedding the font(s) is permitted. Some developers do not license fonts for embedding.

- **Fill.** The color swatch shows the default color of the selected font. Clicking the color swatch opens a pop-up menu, as shown in Figure 13.6. You select preset colors from the palette. When you click Other Color the system color palette opens. You can create custom colors from the system color palette and apply them to the text fill.

FIGURE 13.6

Click the color swatch in the TouchUp Properties dialog box to open the pop-up menu used for making color selections.

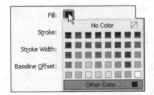

PREPRESS If you intend to print your PDFs for color separations, don't make color changes in Acrobat. Acrobat only supports RGB colors with no support for CMYK or spot colors using the TouchUp Properties dialog box. If color changes to text are needed, you would be best off returning to the original authoring application and make the color changes, and then recreate the PDF file. For more information on RGB, Spot, and Process color, see Chapter 32.

- **Stroke Width.** You change the weight (in points) of stroke outlines (if a font has a stroke) by making choices in the pull-down menu or by typing values in the field box.

TIP If you want to create outline text, select No color from the Fill Color pop-up menu and add a stroke color and width. When stroke fills are set to No color, the fills appear transparent and show the background color.

- **Baseline Offset.** You can raise or lower text above the baseline or below it. To move text up, enter positive values in the field box. To move text below the baseline, use negative values.

After making choices in the TouchUp Properties dialog box, click the Close button. The changes you make in the dialog box are reflected only on text you selected with the TouchUp Text tool.

Editing text on layers

You can edit text on layered PDF documents. When layer data are visible, you can use the TouchUp Text tool to select text and edit the properties as described in the section "Changing text attributes." If you have difficulty selecting text you can hide layers and select just the text on visible layers.

You can also select and edit text appearing on all visible layers. If text appears on all layers, the edits are applied to all layers. If text appears on a single layer, the text edits reflect changes only on the respective layer.

NOTE Engineers working in AutoCAD and Microsoft Visio can export drawings as layered files. When the PDF is opened in Acrobat, the layers created contain separate layer data. If you anticipate changing text, try to keep all the text on a single layer for a given drawing if it's practical. You can then hide layers and select all the text on the text layer. Make your edits and the changes are reflected only on the layer(s) that was edited.

CROSS-REF For more information on managing layers, see Chapter 24.

Adding new text to a document

You can also use the TouchUp Text tool to add a new line of text in a document. Select the TouchUp Text tool and press the Ctrl/Option key and then click the mouse button in the area you want to add new text. The New Text Font dialog box opens as shown in Figure 13.7.

FIGURE 13.7

Ctrl/Option+click on a document page when you have the TouchUp Text tool selected and the New Text Font dialog box opens. Select a font from the Font pull-down menu and select text alignment — Horizontal or Vertical — from the Mode pull-down menu.

From the Font pull-down menu, you can select any font loaded in your system. Fonts appearing below the horizontal line in the menu represent the current fonts loaded in your system. Fonts above the line are the embedded fonts in your PDF document. For an embedded font to be usable, it needs to be unembedded and available in your system.

From the Mode pull-down menu, you can select between Horizontal or Vertical alignment. Click OK in the dialog box and the cursor blinks at the location where you clicked the mouse button. The words "New Text" appear in a text field box. Type the text you want to add and open the TouchUp Properties dialog box by choosing Properties from a context menu. Select the check boxes for embedding and subsetting to embed the new text font in the document.

TIP Acrobat does not permit any edits on text where a font has been embedded and the font is not installed on your system. To resolve the problem, you can select the text, open the TouchUp Properties dialog box, and select a system font from the Font pull-down menu. After you change a font to one available to your system, you can make text edits.

Copying text with the TouchUp Text tool

The TouchUp Text tool is probably the last tool you want to use for copying text and pasting the text into other programs. I mention it here so you know what limitations you have in Acrobat for copying text with this tool. Inasmuch as the TouchUp Text tool enables you to copy multiple lines of text, you are limited to single paragraphs or short blocks of text.

To copy text with the TouchUp Text tool, click and drag the tool through the text block(s) you want to copy. The text is selected as you drag the mouse cursor. After making a selection, open a context menu and select Copy, as shown in Figure 13.8. Alternately you can press Ctrl/⌘+C.

FIGURE 13.8

Open a context menu on selected text and choose Copy.

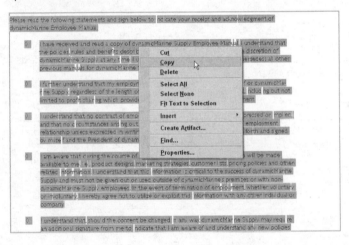

To paste text in a word processor or other application where pasting text is permitted, open the application and select the Paste command. Typically, you find Paste under the Edit menu. The text formatting of the pasted text can sometimes be better preserved if you copy text from tagged PDF documents.

Setting Text Editing Preferences

You have some options for preference choices when using tools for text editing. Using the TouchUp Text tool doesn't require you to make any preference changes. However, when using the Select tool you have some options in the General preferences settings. To open the Preferences dialog box, press Ctrl/⌘+K. When the Preferences dialog box opens, click General in the left pane. At the top of the right pane under the Basic Tools category are options that affect selecting text, as shown in Figure 13.9.

FIGURE 13.9

Open the Preferences dialog box and click General in the left pane. Under the Basic Tools category are options for handling text selections.

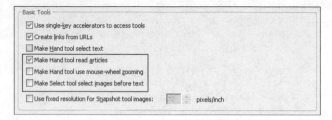

Selecting the order of objects

The Basic Tools options shown in Figure 13.9, reflects the order that objects are selected (consider a text block as an object as you review this section). When you check the box for *Make Select tool select images before text*, images are selected first when images and text occupy the same space on a page. You use the Select tool to click in an area and the selection is made according to the preference choice made in the Selection section of the General preferences. Selecting the *Make hand tool select* text check box and removing the *Make Select tool select images before text* reverses the order and, hence, text is selected before images when they both occupy the same space.

When I refer to occupying the same space, I'm talking about an image that may have a bounding box larger than the displayed image and text appears over the bounding box area, or when text is superimposed over an image.

Using the Hand tool for text selections

 If you're editing text on a page, you can choose to make text selections with the Hand tool instead of the Select tool or the TouchUp Text tool. The preference setting for using the Hand tool to select text is located in the General preferences as shown in Figure 13.9. Unfortunately, there is no context menu option for switching the Hand tool between selecting text and using the hand tool for moving the document page. You can see the menu options in Figure 13.10 when opening a context menu with the hand tool selected.

FIGURE 13.10

A context menu opened from the hand tool provides no option for switching the tool behavior between text selections and moving a document page around the Document pane.

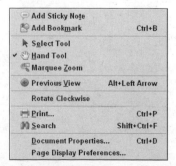

With the Hand tool, you can move a page around in the Document pane or scroll pages when viewing pages in views other than Single Page view. If you move the cursor above any text, quickly drag the page around the Document pane to move the page. If you wait a moment, the cursor changes and any dragging you do selects text. If you accidentally select text when you wanted to move the page, deselect the text by clicking outside a text block. This can be frustrating because if you don't click and drag fast enough, the hand tool will selected text when the respective preference option is selected. To disengage the text selection with the Hand tool, press the Spacebar on your keyboard. While the Spacebar is held down, the Hand tool returns to normal behavior and you can move the document page around the Document pane.

CAUTION If you enable text selection with the Hand tool and it's not working, you need to make an adjustment in the Accessibility preferences. Open the Preferences dialog box and click Accessibility in the left pane. Remove the check mark for *Always display keyboard selection cursor*. If this item is checked, the Hand tool preference options cannot be changed.

Using the Select Tool

Users of earlier versions of Acrobat prior to version 7 will immediately notice the absence of the Select Text tool, the Select Table tool, and the Select Image tool. All three of these tools, performing all three functions, have been combined in the form of the Select tool.

 The Select tool is a much better choice than the TouchUp Text tool for selecting text to be copied from a PDF document and pasted in an editor especially if you have multiple text blocks to copy. With this tool you can select multiple blocks of text and text in columns. However, you cannot make text edits with the tool like you do with the TouchUp Text tool.

To select text with the Select tool, click and drag the tool through the text on a page you want to copy. If a single column appears on the page, click just before the first character to be selected and drag down to the last character. Alternately, you can press the Alt/Option key and drag through a column of text to select it. Generally using the Alt/Option key enables you to create a more precise selection when columns are positioned close together. Acrobat won't copy the text in the adjacent column as long as you stay within the boundaries of the column you are selecting. Figure 13.11 shows text selected with the Select tool where only one column in a multiple-column layout is selected.

In conjunction with the Select tool, shortcut keys and mouse clicks provide several ways to make various text selections, including the following:

- **Select a word.** Double-click on a word, space, or character.
- **Select a line of text.** Triple-click anywhere on a line of text.
- **Select all text on a page.** Click four times (rapid successive clicks) to select all text on a page.
- **Select a column of text.** Click outside the text area and drag through the column or press the Alt/Option key as you drag the Select tool through a column of text.
- **Select a contiguous block of text.** Click and drag through the block of text or click the cursor at the beginning of the text to be selected, press Shift, and click at the end of the text block.
- **Deselect text.** Click outside of the text selection or press Ctrl/⌘+Shift+A.

Depending on choices you make for copying text, text pasted in other programs can retain certain formatting attributes. Your options for what you copy are derived from menu choices when you select text with the Select tool and open a context menu. When you select text and move the cursor within the text selection, a text selection icon appears above the selected text, as shown in Figure 13.12.

FIGURE 13.11

To select a column of text, use the Select tool and drag down the column length.

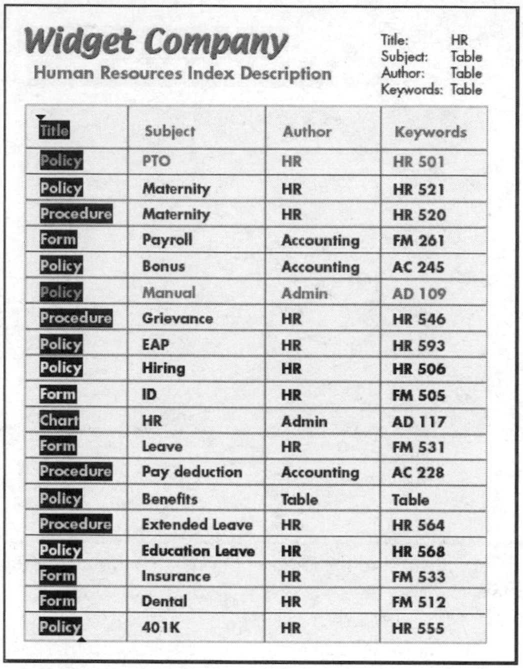

Widget Company

Human Resources Index Description

Title: HR
Subject: Table
Author: Table
Keywords: Table

Title	Subject	Author	Keywords
Policy	PTO	HR	HR 501
Policy	Maternity	HR	HR 521
Procedure	Maternity	HR	HR 520
Form	Payroll	Accounting	FM 261
Policy	Bonus	Accounting	AC 245
Policy	Manual	Admin	AD 109
Procedure	Grievance	HR	HR 546
Policy	EAP	HR	HR 593
Policy	Hiring	HR	HR 506
Form	ID	HR	FM 505
Chart	HR	Admin	AD 117
Form	Leave	HR	FM 531
Procedure	Pay deduction	Accounting	AC 228
Policy	Benefits	Table	Table
Procedure	Extended Leave	HR	HR 564
Policy	Education Leave	HR	HR 568
Form	Insurance	HR	FM 533
Form	Dental	HR	FM 512
Policy	401K	HR	HR 555

FIGURE 13.12

A text selection icon appears above a text selection.

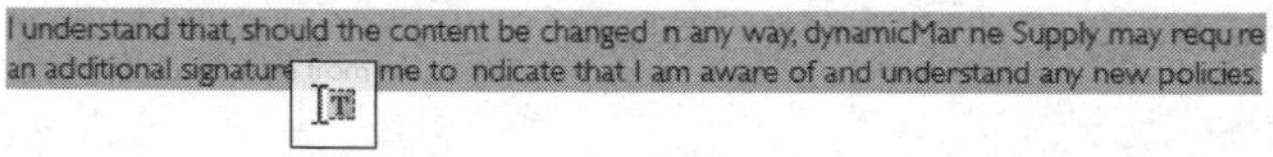
I understand that, should the content be changed n any way, dynamicMar ne Supply may requ re
an additional signatur me to ndicate that I am aware of and understand any new policies.

Move the cursor over the text selection icon and a pop-up menu opens, as shown in Figure 13.13. The menu does not open with a right-click (Windows) or Ctrl+click (Macintosh). If you open a context menu using right-click (or Ctrl+click on Macintosh), you see similar menu options as shown in Figure 13.14.

The options shown in both menus provide choices for marking text with a Highlight, Cross Out, Underline, Replace, and adding a note. These items are used for commenting on PDF files. Additionally, adding a Bookmark and creating a link appear in the context menu. The remaining options in both menus are used for copying and exporting text.

FIGURE 13.13

Move the cursor over the text selection icon and a menu opens.

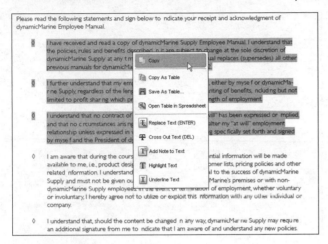

FIGURE 13.14

Open a context menu using right-click (Windows) or Ctrl+click (Macintosh) and the menu options are similar to the pop-up menu.

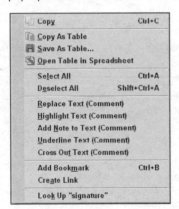

Copying text

Most often you'll find a difference when pasting text copied from tagged and untagged documents. In Figure 13.15, text was copied from an untagged file in Acrobat and pasted into a Microsoft Word document. Much of the text and paragraph formatting was lost when the data was pasted.

FIGURE 13.15

Text pasted from an untagged file loses much of the text and paragraph formatting.

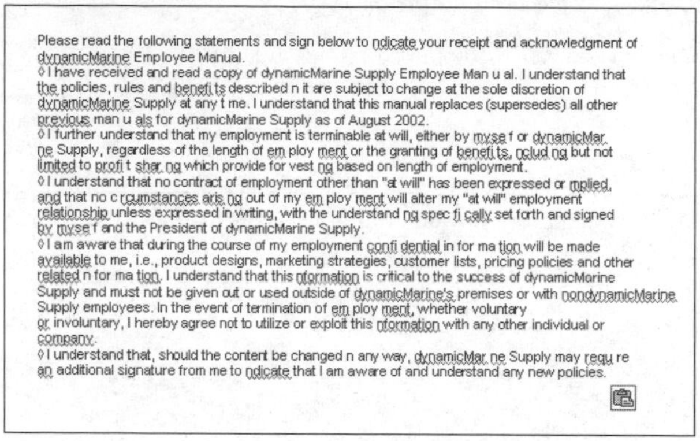
Please read the following statements and sign below to ndicate your receipt and acknowledgment of dynamicMarine Employee Manual.
◊ I have received and read a copy of dynamicMarine Supply Employee Man u al. I understand that the policies, rules and benefi ts described n it are subject to change at the sole discretion of dynamicMarine Supply at any t me. I understand that this manual replaces (supersedes) all other previous man u als for dynamicMarine Supply as of August 2002.
◊ I further understand that my employment is terminable at will, either by myse f or dynamicMar ne Supply, regardless of the length of em ploy ment or the granting of benefi ts, nclud ng but not limited to profi t shar ng which provide for vest ng based on length of employment.
◊ I understand that no contract of employment other than "at will" has been expressed or mplied, and that no c rcumstances aris ng out of my em ploy ment will alter my "at will" employment relationship unless expressed in writing, with the understand ng spec fi cally set forth and signed by myse f and the President of dynamicMarine Supply.
◊ I am aware that during the course of my employment confi dential in for ma tion will be made available to me, i.e., product designs, marketing strategies, customer lists, pricing policies and other related n for ma tion. I understand that this nformation is critical to the success of dynamicMarine Supply and must not be given out or used outside of dynamicMarine's premises or with nondynamicMarine Supply employees. In the event of termination of em ploy ment, whether voluntary or involuntary, I hereby agree not to utilize or exploit this nformation with any other individual or company.
◊ I understand that, should the content be changed n any way, dynamicMar ne Supply may requ re an additional signature from me to ndicate that I am aware of and understand any new policies.

Copying text from tagged PDF documents typically provides much better results, as shown in Figure 13.16.

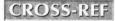

CROSS-REF **For information related to tagging PDF documents, see Chapter 25.**

FIGURE 13.16

Text pasted from a tagged file retains much of the text and paragraph formatting.

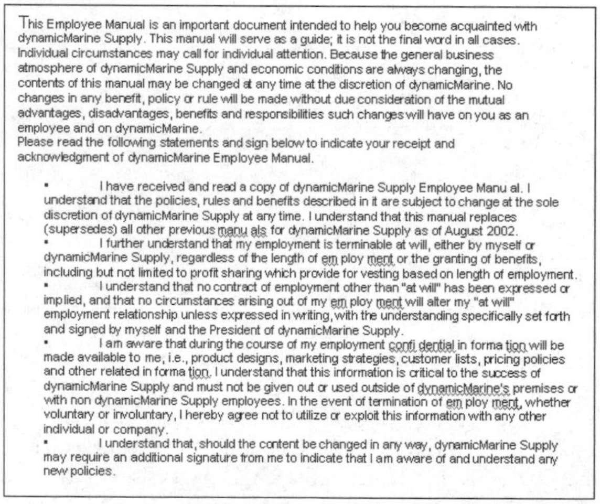
This Employee Manual is an important document intended to help you become acquainted with dynamicMarine Supply. This manual will serve as a guide; it is not the final word in all cases. Individual circumstances may call for individual attention. Because the general business atmosphere of dynamicMarine Supply and economic conditions are always changing, the contents of this manual may be changed at any time at the discretion of dynamicMarine. No changes in any benefit, policy or rule will be made without due consideration of the mutual advantages, disadvantages, benefits and responsibilities such changes will have on you as an employee and on dynamicMarine.
Please read the following statements and sign below to indicate your receipt and acknowledgment of dynamicMarine Employee Manual.

- I have received and read a copy of dynamicMarine Supply Employee Manu al. I understand that the policies, rules and benefits described in it are subject to change at the sole discretion of dynamicMarine Supply at any time. I understand that this manual replaces (supersedes) all other previous manu als for dynamicMarine Supply as of August 2002.
- I further understand that my employment is terminable at will, either by myself or dynamicMarine Supply, regardless of the length of em ploy ment or the granting of benefits, including but not limited to profit sharing which provide for vesting based on length of employment.
- I understand that no contract of employment other than "at will" has been expressed or implied, and that no circumstances arising out of my em ploy ment will alter my "at will" employment relationship unless expressed in writing, with the understanding specifically set forth and signed by myself and the President of dynamicMarine Supply.
- I am aware that during the course of my employment confi dential in forma tion will be made available to me, i.e., product designs, marketing strategies, customer lists, pricing policies and other related in forma tion. I understand that this information is critical to the success of dynamicMarine Supply and must not be given out or used outside of dynamicMarine's premises or with non dynamicMarine Supply employees. In the event of termination of em ploy ment, whether voluntary or involuntary, I hereby agree not to utilize or exploit this information with any other individual or company.
- I understand that, should the content be changed in any way, dynamicMarine Supply may require an additional signature from me to indicate that I am aware of and understand any new policies.

Copying multiple pages of text

If you view PDF files in a Single Page view, you can drag through the text on the page in view to select it. However, if you want to copy text on multiple pages, you need to change the view in a Scrolling mode. Zoom out of the document so you can see several pages in the Document pane and drag through the text

you want to copy. If you need to copy more pages than those in view, drag the cursor to the bottom of the Acrobat window. The document pages scroll to place more pages in view. Keep the mouse button pressed as the pages appear in view and release the mouse button on the last page you want to copy. In Figure 13.17, you can see a document in a Scrolling view and text selected on multiple pages.

To copy the text, select one of the Copy commands at the top of the pop-up or context menu or choose Edit ⇨ Copy.

FIGURE 13.17

Click Scrolling Pages in the Page Display Toolbar and drag the Select tool through multiple pages to select the text.

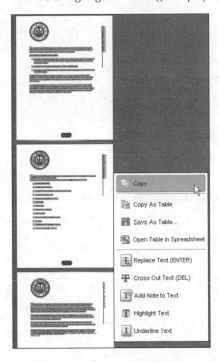

Using the Select All command

If you have a need to select all the text on a page or throughout a PDF document, you can use the Select All menu command. Depending on the tool you use and the page view mode, text selections behave differently. You must first determine whether you want to select all the text on a page or all text in the document. When selecting text on a PDF page, be certain the page layout view is set to a One Full Page layout. Click the Select tool and choose Edit ⇨ Select All or press Ctrl/⌘+A. All the text on a single page is selected. To copy the text you just selected, open a pop-up or context menu and select Copy. All the text is copied to the Clipboard and ready to paste into an editor.

If you want to select all text in a PDF document, change the page view to Scrolling Pages mode. Click the Select tool and choose Edit ⇨ Select All or press Ctrl/⌘+A.

 **TIP** In earlier versions of Acrobat you had to click the Select tool and click the tool in a block of text, then use the Select All command. In Acrobat 8, just click the tool and then press Ctrl/⌘+A to select all text. If you want to select all document content (text and graphics), click the TouchUp Object tool and press Ctrl/⌘+A. For more on selecting images and graphics, see Chapter 15.

This method only works when you use the Select tool. If you select all text using the TouchUp Text tool, the selected text is confined to a bounding box and you must first click in a bounding box area in order to use the Select All command. On any given page there can be one or more bounding boxes and using Select All only selects all text within a single bounding box. Regardless of which page layout view you choose, the TouchUp Text tool doesn't permit text selections across multiple pages.

Copying a file to the Clipboard (Windows only)

Clicking the Select tool and choosing the Select All command, selects all text in a document. You can also accomplish the same task by choosing Edit ⇨ Copy File to Clipboard. Open your word processor and you can paste the text into a new document.

If you don't see the menu command, you don't have OLE-compliant applications installed on your computer. Microsoft's OLE, (Object Linking and Embedding), is installed by default with Office applications on Windows. If the menu command does not appear, use the Select All menu command to achieve the same results.

Copying and pasting text in word processors is best achieved by exporting PDFs using the new Acrobat 8 Export task button. You can export files as Microsoft Word and RTF (Rich Text Format) by selecting menu options from the task button pull-down menu.

CROSS-REF For more on exporting PDF data, see Chapter 11.

Working with table data

You can copy and paste formatted text in columns and rows with the Select tool. If you want to paste data as tables or spreadsheets, Acrobat provides you options for copying table data and opening selected table data in a spreadsheet program.

Copying and pasting table data

Select a table using the Select tool and choose Copy As Table from a pop-up or context menu. Once copied to the Clipboard, you can paste the data in a word processing or spreadsheet program. When you paste the data in Microsoft Word, it appears as a table. Pasting in Microsoft Excel pastes the data in a spreadsheet document. If you use the Copy command, all data are pasted into a single cell in MS Excel. When selecting the Copy As Table command, the data are distributed into columns and rows in Excel.

Opening selected data in a spreadsheet document

To export a table directly to Microsoft Excel, select columns and rows of text. From a pop-up menu or a context menu, select Open Table in Spreadsheet. By default, Acrobat launches Microsoft Excel and the selected data appear in a new spreadsheet, as shown in Figure 13.18.

FIGURE 13.18

Select a table and choose Open in Spreadsheet from a pop-up menu or context menu and the data appear in a new spreadsheet in Microsoft Excel.

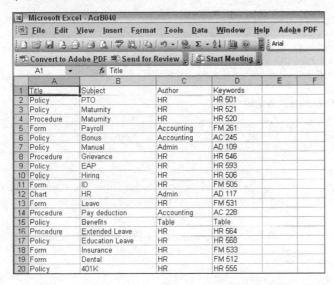

Saving data to a spreadsheet file

Another option you have for getting PDF data to a spreadsheet is to select the table with the Select tool and choose Save As Table from the Select tool pop-up or context menu. When you choose this command, the Acrobat Save As dialog box opens and offers you choices for saving your data in a variety of file formats. From the Save as Type (Windows) or Format (Macintosh) pull-down menu, select from the following:

- **Comma Separated Values (*.csv).** CSV-compliant applications can open files saved in this format. Microsoft Excel and Microsoft Access recognize CSV data, and you can open the files directly in Excel. If you use other applications recognizing the format, use CSV.

- **HTML 4.01 with CSS 1.0 (*.htm).** If you need to get table data to a Web page, you can save the data to HTML format.

- **Rich Text Format (*.rtf).** If you want to import data into programs such as word processing, accounting, and other applications that support RTF, save the file as RTF. If you want columns and rows of data without a table defined in the word processor, use the RTF format.

- **Text (Tab Delimited) (*.txt).** When you need to import data into a database management system (DBMS), export the data as tab delimited. Tab delimited tables import into programs such as FileMaker Pro with data in separate fields and records.

- **Unicode Text (Tab Delimited) (*.txt).** If you use some foreign language kits, Unicode might be a better choice for your file exports. Select Unicode and import the data into applications supporting Unicode text data.

- **XML 1.0 (*.xml).** Acrobat supports exporting tables in XML format. XML data can be exchanged between many programs. If your workflow uses XML, save in this format.

- **XML Spreadsheet (*.xml).** This is an XML format defined by Microsoft. Use XML Spreadsheet when using XML data with spreadsheet applications such as Microsoft Excel.

Click the Save button and the data are saved in the file format you select from the pull-down menu in the Save As dialog box.

Looking Up Definitions

Whether you're editing a PDF file or browsing documents, you can find the spelling and word definition for any text in an open document. This very nice little feature in Acrobat saves you time when looking up a definition. To employ the Look Up command from one of two context menus, use either the Hand tool or the Select tool and open a context menu. Text does not need to be selected, but the tool you use must be positioned over the word you want to look up. If using the Select tool, open the traditional context menu by right-clicking the mouse button (Windows) or Ctrl+clicking (Macintosh). From the menu choices, select Lookup "...", placing your selected word inside the quotation marks. In Figure 13.19, you can see the context menu opened when the word *supersedes* was targeted for a lookup.

FIGURE 13.19

Click a word with the Select tool or Hand tool. Open a context menu (right-click or Ctrl+click) and select Look Up ". . ." at the bottom of the menu.

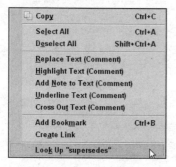

After you make your selection, Acrobat launches the default Web browser and the browser takes you to the Dictionary.com Web site. The Web page opens on the word selected in the PDF document. You can check for spelling errors, word definitions, pronunciation, and browse through a thesaurus. If you have an account for the Web site, you can click on the audio button to hear an audio pronunciation through your computer speaker(s).

Currently, Acrobat only supports U.S. English as a language. Regardless of whether you have a foreign language kit installed, Acrobat launches the Dictionary.com Web site.

Working with Text in New Blank Pages

Additional text tools and text editing features are available to you when creating a blank new page in Acrobat. A separate set of preferences and tools appear when you create a new blank page.

NEW FEATURE In Acrobat 8 a new feature is available to you for creating a new blank page. Although Acrobat is not intended to be an original document authoring program, this new feature addition to Acrobat is designed to offer a simple solution for creating documents when you want to write a memo, create a cover page for a PDF Package, or add some text to a page and send you document as a PDF to other users.

Setting text attributes

To create a blank new page in Acrobat 8 select File ➪ Create PDF ➪ From Blank Page. A new blank page opens in the document pane with a text box and a toolbar that loads automatically when the new page is created. The New Document Toolbar shown in Figure 13.20 opens when a new page is created or you can access the toolbar in the More Tools window. However, the tools in this toolbar can only be used in documents created from the New Blank Page command.

FIGURE 13.20

The New Document Toolbar tools are only available in documents created as blank new pages.

Tools you have available for formatting text only in the text box created on a new blank page include:

- **Text color.** The first tool in the New Document Toolbar contains a pull-down menu where a color palette opens. The choices you have for text colors are the same as you have available using the TouchUp Text Properties dialog box shown in Figure 13.6 earlier in this chapter.

- **Paragraph formatting.** The Left, Center, Right and Justified tools are used to format text alignment.

- **Fonts.** The pull-down menu displays all the fonts loaded in your system. Select a font and the font name is displayed in the text box. Adjacent to the pull-down menu is the Size pull down menu. Make a choice from fixed font sizes or type a font size in the text box. The sizes you can type in the Size text box range from 4 points to 300 points.

- **Text Style.** Text styles are from left to right in the New Document Toolbar: Bold, Italic, Underline, Strike-through, Superscript, and Subscript.

- **Indents.** The last two text tools in the New Document Toolbar are used for paragraph indenting. The Left Indent and Right Indent tools appear just before the Page Setup tool.

- **Page Setup.** Click the Page Setup tool and the Page Setup dialog box opens as shown in Figure 13.21. In the Page Setup dialog box you have options for selecting page sizes from a number of fixed page sizes by choosing an option in the Size pull-down menu. Additionally, you can choose an option for Portrait or Landscape pages in the Page area of the dialog box. Margins are set in the four text boxes at the top of the dialog box. Click the Always use these settings check box and your settings are applied as a new default each time you create a new blank page.

NOTE You cannot resize the text box added to a blank new page using any tool in Acrobat. All text box sizes are determined by the margin settings in the Page Setup dialog box or the New Document preferences.

FIGURE 13.21

Click the Page Setup tool and the Page Setup dialog box opens where page size and margins attributes are selected.

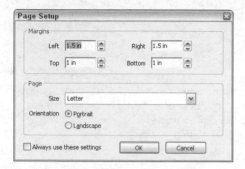

Setting preferences

Preferences can be set for the page attributes by clicking the Page Setup tool in the New Document toolbar or by selecting New Document preferences in the Preferences dialog box. Open the Preferences dialog box by pressing Ctrl/⌘+K and click New Document in the left pane. The options for page setup shown in Figure 13.22 are the same as when clicking the Page Setup tool in the New Document Toolbar.

FIGURE 13.22

Open Preferences and click New Document in the left pane to display the preference choices for creating new blank pages.

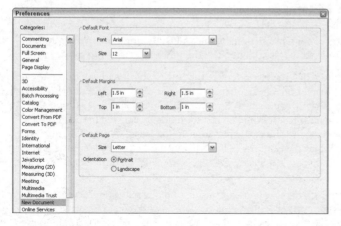

Using the PDF Editor

When you create a blank new page, Acrobat shifts the normal editing mode to a unique editor called the PDF Editor that is available only with blank new pages. By default a text box is created for you according to the preference options you made for page size and margins. Working in the PDF Editor differs from using other editing tools and commands in Acrobat when working in a normal edit mode.

Keyboard shortcuts in the PDF Editor

At first you may think there are anomalies when trying to use keyboard shortcuts when the Page Editor is active. Using Ctrl/⌘++ (plus sign) and Ctrl/⌘+- (minus sign) won't zoom a page. Ctrl/⌘+0 (zero) is consistent with using the standard edit mode for fitting a page in the Document pane. Using keyboard shortcuts for sizing text and changing font styles are all different in the PDF Editor than you have available in standard edit more. The keyboard shortcuts that are used with the PDF Editor include:

- **Bold text.** Ctrl/⌘+B.
- **Italicize text.** Ctrl/⌘+I.
- **Underline text.** Ctrl/⌘+U.
- **Increase text size.** Ctrl/⌘+] (right bracket).
- **Decrease text size.** Ctrl/⌘+[(left bracket).
- **Superscript text.** Ctrl/⌘+Shift++ (plus sign).
- **Subscript text.** Ctrl/⌘++ (plus sign).
- **Left Justify.** Ctrl/⌘+L.
- **Right Justify.** Ctrl/⌘+R.
- **Justified.** Ctrl/⌘+J.

Tools and commands in the PDF Editor

When you create a blank new page, the text box added to the page is not something you can delete. The Select Object tool and the TouchUp Text tool are not functional while in PDF Editor mode. While in the PDF Editor mode you have two new menu commands added to the Document menu:

- **Resume Editing.** If you click a tool like the Hand tool or the Select Object tool, you loose the text box on the new blank page. It's there, but appears invisible and you exit the PDF Editor. To switch back to the PDF Editor you can select Document ➪ Resume Editing. Click in the text box and you can type or edit text. You can also reenter the PDF Editor mode by clicking the Select tool and click inside the text box or click any one of the text tools in the New Document Toolbar. If you save a file created as a blank new page and reopen the file in another Acrobat editing session, select Document ➪ Resume Editing and you again gain access to the PDF Editor where text cane be added or edited in the default text box.
- **Prevent Further Edits.** You can lock the text you add to a text box by selecting Document Prevent Further Edits. The Prevent Further Edits dialog box opens as shown in Figure 13.23. Click Prevent Further Edits and the text box is locked and remains not editable. Be aware that when you click the Prevent Further Edits button in the Prevent Further Edits dialog box that you cannot regain an editing status, nor can you use the Edit ➪ Undo command. Selecting Document ➪ Resume Editing won't bring the text box back to the PDF Editor where any text editing can be performed.

FIGURE 13.23

To prevent a user from editing text in the blank new page text box, select Document ➪ Prevent Further Edits and click the Prevent Further Edits button when the Prevent Further Edits dialog box opens.

PDF Editor behavior

A few things you'll notice when using the PDF Editor as you add other content to the page such as comments, form fields, copy and paste text include:

- **Comments.** You can add comments to the text block on a blank new page. However, the comments are static and remain fixed to the coordinates when you first added a comment. For example, using a Text Edit tool or a markup comment tool to highlight text or mark text on the page stays in position where you added the comment. If you type text in the text box, the text flows but the comments remain in the original position.

- **Form Fields.** Form fields can be added to the page and appear aside or over a text box. When you engage the PDF Editor to add or edit text in the text box, the form fields, as well as comment notes are temporarily hidden.

- **Pasting text.** You can copy text from another PDF page or from a word processor or text editor and paste the text into the blank new page text box. To paste text in the text box, select Edit ➪ Paste or press Ctrl/⌘+V. Text pasted in the text box retains formatting from the copied text. If the text overflows the text box, you can't resize the box and text after the last visible line of text at the bottom of the box flows to a new page.

- **Copying text.** When you select text in the text box on a blank new page, you don't have access to commands when copying text like you do when copying text using the Select Text tool. To copy text use Edit ➪ Copy or press Ctrl/⌘+C.

- **Adding new text.** Text on a blank new page is restricted to the text box automatically added to the blank new page. You cannot use Ctrl/⌘ and click with the TouchUp Text tool either inside or outside the text box to create a new text box. Pasted text that extends beyond the text placeholder automatically flows to create new pages.

Alternate methods for creating blank pages

If you don't want the restrictions imposed by the PDF Editor when adding text to a page you can create blank page documents and add text using the Ctrl/⌘ key and click with the TouchUp Text tool. You have two methods you can use for creating blank new pages that include:

- **Create a blank PDF page.** Using any authoring program to create a blank new page. For example, create a new document in Microsoft Word or Adobe InDesign. Convert the file to PDF and open it in Acrobat. If you want to keep a blank page handy, you can add the blank page to your Organizer or create a page template.

CROSS-REF   For more information on creating pages from templates, see Chapter 7.

■ **Use a JavaScript.** If you don't have a blank page PDF document and you find the PDF Editor interfering with the work you want to perform in an editing session, you can create a blank new page using a JavaScript.

To create a new blank page using JavaScript, follow these steps:

STEPS: Create a blank new page using a JavaScript

1. **Open the JavaScript Debugger.** Press Ctrl/⌘+J to open the JavaScript Debugger.
2. **Clear the default text.** Click the trash icon in the JavaScript Debugger window to delete all of the default text.
3. **Type the code for creating a blank new page.** Even if you've never type a single line of JavaScript, this script is very easy and anyone can create a blank new page in Acrobat by typing one line of code. In the JavaScript Debugger type:

```
app.newDoc();
```

The previous code typed in the JavaScript Debugger as shown in Figure 13.24 is all you need to create a blank new page that defaults to a US letter sized portrait page.

FIGURE 13.24

JavaScript code in the JavaScript Debugger that is used to create a portrait US Letter sized page.

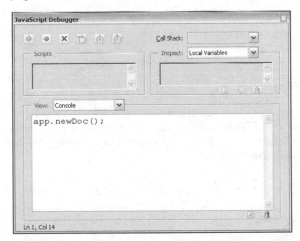

If you want a different page size and orientation you can add the size within the two () marks. For example, a page size of 6x4 inches could be created in a landscape view by typing the following line of code:

```
app.newDoc(432, 288);
```

The unit of measure is in points. To determine the number of points needed, multiply 72 times the size in inches. To create a landscape page, the larger value for the x-axis is typed first.

4. **Create the blank page.** With the cursor appearing inside the line of code, press the Num Pad Enter key. Note that if you use the Enter/Return key on the main keyboard you'll type a line break and not execute the code. If you have a laptop computer without a Num Pad, use Ctrl+Enter. After pressing the Num Pad Enter key (or Ctrl+Enter), your new blank page opens in the Document pane in Acrobat.

Summary

- You use the TouchUp Text tool to make minor edits on PDF pages. You can use the tool to change font attributes, add new lines of text, and access a Properties dialog box where you can select fonts to embed and subset.

- The TouchUp Text tool is not well suited for copying and pasting text data into other programs. Text selections are limited and text formatting is lost when pasting text into other programs.

- The Select tool can select text on a page, across multiple pages, and all text in a document.

- When pasting text copied from a Select tool selection in a tagged file, the text data retains much integrity and can be edited with minimum character and paragraph reformatting.

- Text can be edited on visible layers. You can't select text on hidden layers with the Select All command. Edits made to text appearing on all layers result in changes on all layers. Edits made to text on a single layer result in changes on a single layer.

- You also use the Select tool to select table data. You can copy and paste tables in other applications and save the data to a number of different file formats.

- Blank new pages using the File ➪ Create PDF ➪ From Blank Page menu command creates new pages with a text box and text tools that only appear when creating blank new pages.

Chapter 14

Redacting PDFs

This chapter covers an entirely new feature introduced in Acrobat 8 Professional only — the Redaction tools, which are used for removing data from PDF documents. In this chapter you learn about redaction, why and when it is necessary, and how to use all the new Redaction tools.

Setting Up the Work Environment

Load the Redaction and Advanced Editing tools for applying redactions to documents. You'll find Redaction tools in a separate toolbar and accessible from a context menu opened from the Toolbar Well, or select Tools ➪ Customize Toolbars to open the More Tools window. Alternately, you can select More Tools from the context menu. When the More Tools window opens, check the Advanced Editing Toolbar and scroll the list to the Redaction Toolbar and check the box adjacent to the toolbar name. You can selectively toggle individual tools within the toolbar in the More Tools window by checking and unchecking the tool names in the toolbar list. In this chapter, you look at all tools, so be certain check marks appear adjacent to all the tool names in the Redaction toolbar.

What Is Redaction?

Quite simply, *redaction* is the deletion of information from a document. You might want to use redaction to remove sensitive information for security purposes, to protect rights and privacy information, to eliminate classified information, to delete names of minors in legal documents, or to delete any other information you don't want viewed by others.

Redaction is much different than blotting out or hiding text, graphics, handwriting, or any other kind of marks. If you use tools like some of the comment tools to create markups that blot out some text and graphics in a document, the items

are not permanently deleted. It appears fine onscreen where you can't see items marked for deletion on a document page, but the PDF document still contains the original items. If the file is distributed, other users can access marked text and other data.

To understand why redaction tools are needed to permanently delete content from a PDF document, see the following steps.

STEPS: Understanding the need for redaction

1. **Open a PDF document in Acrobat.**

2. **Open the Comment & Markup tools.** Open a context menu on the Toolbar Well and select Comment and Markup. The Comment & Markup tools open in a floating toolbar.

3. **Mark out some text.** Select the Rectangle tool in the Comment & Markup toolbar. Draw a rectangle around some text. Alternately, you can use the Highlight tool so select text and hide it with a dark highlight color.

4. **Open the rectangle comment properties.** Right-click (Windows) or Ctrl+click (Macintosh) to open a context menu on the rectangle. Select Properties from the context menu.

5. **Edit the properties.** Click the Color swatch for both Color and Fill Color. From the color choices select Black, as shown in Figure 14.1. Click the Make Properties Default check box. The next time you draw a rectangle the rectangle will have the same style and fill color.

FIGURE 14.1

Set the Rectangle comment properties to black color and black fill.

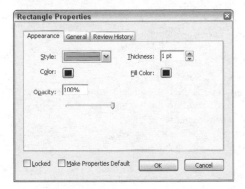

6. **Draw additional rectangles.** Using the rectangle comment tool, draw some additional rectangles to block out more text. In Figure 14.2, I have a text document with several markings where I don't want the text to be seen. Onscreen this is fine, but the text is not deleted and can be extracted by other users.

FIGURE 14.2

Text onscreen is blocked out, but the text can still be extracted.

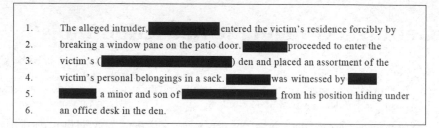

7. **Copy the text.** Click the Select tool and drag through the text to select it. Select Edit ⇨ Copy to copy the text, as shown in Figure 14.3. Note that you can also use the Search pane and search for text that you marked. You'll notice that the search results report all the hidden text.

FIGURE 14.3

Drag through all the text with the Select tool and choose Edit ⇨ Copy.

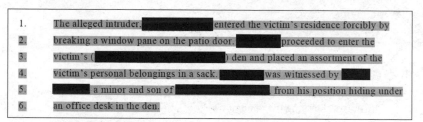

8. **Paste the text in a word processor.** In my example I open Microsoft Word and select Edit ⇨ Paste. As you can see in Figure 14.4, I was able to copy the text beneath all my comment markups.

FIGURE 14.4

When you paste all the text in a Word processor, the marked out text appears in the new document window.

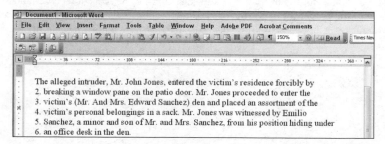

As shown in Figure 14.4, this form of redacting a document doesn't delete the marked text. You need another method to mark and eliminate data from PDFs. This is where the Redaction tools in Acrobat 8 come into play.

Getting a Grip on the Redaction Tools

Redaction is permanently deleting text, graphics, signatures, handwriting, and any other data you desire to remove from a document. In addition to marking and deleting text and other data that you can see, a good redaction tool also provides you a means for deleting certain metadata and hidden information in a file so all the content you decide you want to eliminate cannot be retrieved by anyone viewing your PDF files.

Acrobat 8 offers a few solutions for marking content for deletion, applying the redactions, eliminating metadata, and eliminating any hidden text. You first start a redaction session using the Redaction tools. When you open the Redaction toolbar by either selecting View ➪ Toolbars ➪ Redaction, choosing Advanced ➪ Redaction ➪ Show Redaction Toolbar, or selecting the toolbar in the More Tools window, the tools contained in the toolbar appear as you see in Figure 14.5.

FIGURE 14.5

The Redaction toolbar contains four tools.

The tools on the Redaction toolbar are as follows:

- **Mark for Redaction.** Use this tool to mark text and other data that you want to delete from a document. Marking the content does not yet delete it from the file.
- **Apply Redactions.** When you are ready to permanently delete content that you marked for deletion, click the Apply Redactions tool.
- **Redaction Properties.** Use this tool to set the redaction marking properties. You can mark content using the Mark for Redaction tool and the markings can be adjusted for color and other attributes in the Redaction Tool Properties dialog box. Click on the tool and the Redaction Tool Properties dialog box shown in Figure 14.6 opens.

  As you can see in the Redaction Tool Properties dialog box, you can select a color for your redaction marks, use text as an overlay, specify the font for the overlay text, set a number of different font attributes for the overlay text, and select from some redaction code standards. When you change the properties in this dialog box, the properties remain in effect for all redaction marks you make on a document until you again make settings adjustments in the Redaction Tool Properties dialog box.

FIGURE 14.6

Click the Redaction Properties tool and the Redaction Tool Properties dialog box opens.

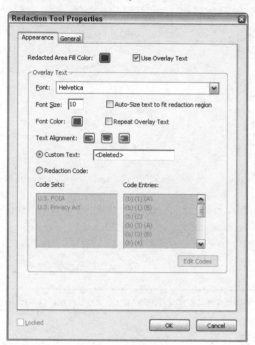

- **Search and Redact.** This tool is a powerful addition to the Redaction tools. Click the Search and Redact tool and the Search window opens as shown in Figure 14.7. Type a word or phrase in the first field text box and you choose a location. Your options include searching the open document or a folder location on your hard drive or network server. You can mark content for redaction in a collection of PDF documents contained in a common folder. Select the All PDF Documents in radio button. From the pull-down menu below the radio button select Browse for Location. The Browse For Folder dialog box opens where you select a folder containing files you want to redact.

  Click the Search and Redact button in the Search window and the Search window reports results of your search, as shown in Figure 14.8. As yet, no items have been marked for redaction. In the results list you see the reported results appearing next to check marks. If you want all items in the list to be redacted, click the Check All button. If you want to individually mark the results items, scroll the list checking all boxes adjacent to the items you want to redact.

CROSS-REF For more information on using the Search window, see Chapter 6.

FIGURE 14.7

Click the Search and Redact button and the Search window opens. Type a word or phrase and select either the open document or a folder of PDFs you want to mark for redaction.

FIGURE 14.8

Click Check All or individually check the items you want to redact in the open PDF or from a collection of PDF files.

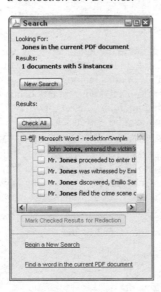

Redacting PDF Files

The tool set and options for redaction are very straightforward and intuitive. In the first section of this chapter you looked at marking files to hide content that didn't remove the items you marked. Let's compare that first effort with a true redaction that Acrobat 8 provides you by following some steps.

STEPS: Redacting a PDF document

1. **Open a file you want to eliminate some content from by using the Redaction tools.**

2. **Click the Mark for Redaction tool.**

   When you first click the Mark for Redaction tool, the Using Redaction Tools help dialog box opens, as shown in Figure 14.9. This dialog box provides you some instructions on redacting documents. If you don't want the dialog box to open in future redaction sessions, click the Don't Show Again check box.

   FIGURE 14.9
   _____

   When you first click the Mark for Redaction tool, the Using Redaction Tools help dialog box opens.

   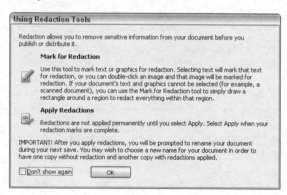

3. **Mark a graphic for redaction.** If you have a graphic in the file either as a vector object or an image file you can remove them just like removing text. In my example I have a logotype that is a graphic object. Clicking the Mark for Redaction tool changes your cursor to a crosshair when positioned over a graphic or an I-beam cursor when positioned over text. Draw a marquee around the object, as shown in Figure 14.10, or drag the I-beam cursor through text you want to redact.

    If you want to quickly mark a graphic object for redaction, select the Mark for Redaction tool and double click on the graphic.

4. **Mark text for redaction.** Drag the I-beam cursor through the first occurrence of text you want to redact. In my example I drag text through a name I want to remove from the file.

5. **Click the Search and Redact tool.** The Search window opens. Type any other occurrence of the text you want to redact. In my example, I type the same name as the first text marked for redaction. Click the Search and Redact button and the first occurrence of the word to be redacted is highlighted.

FIGURE 14.10

Draw a marquee around a graphic or select text to mark for redaction.

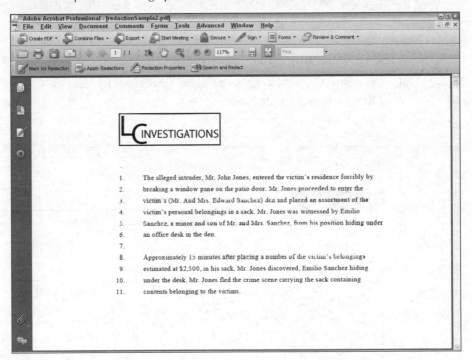

6. **Check all occurrences for redaction.** In the Search window, click the Check All button and all occurrences of the search results are now marked for redaction.

7. **Mark the search results for redaction.** After clicking the Check All button, the Marked Checked Results button appears in the Search window. Click this button and all occurrences of the search results are now marked for redaction, as you see in Figure 14.11.

8. **Continue marking all the content you want to eliminate in your document.** If you have other text or graphics you want to redact, follow the same steps outlined in Steps 3 through 7.

9. **Apply Redactions.** Click the Apply Redactions tool. A warning dialog box opens. Click Yes and the redactions are applied.

10. **Redact additional content.** After Acrobat redacts the items you marked, a dialog box opens confirming your action and prompts you to examine the document for additional content. Click Yes in the dialog box shown in Figure 14.12.

FIGURE 14.11

After clicking Check All or individually checking the items you want to redact in the open PDF or from a collection of PDF files, click the Mark Checked Results for Redaction button.

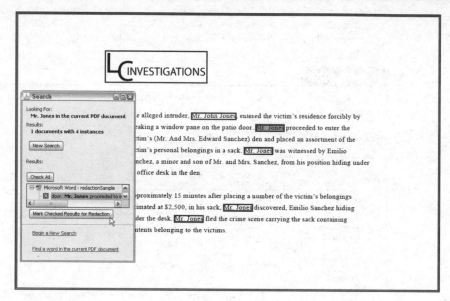

FIGURE 14.12

Click Yes to open the Examine Document dialog box.

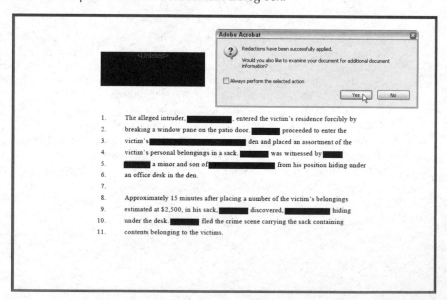

11. **Examine the document.** When you click Yes in the confirmation dialog box, the Examine Document dialog box opens. A number of different items can appear in your file that don't appear on the document pages. You might have metadata, hidden text, file attachments, hidden layers, bookmarks, and other items that use the same text you want to delete. To be certain all information is deleted from the document, the Examine Document dialog box provides a list of found items matching the items you deleted. Click the Remove all checked items button in the dialog box shown in Figure 14.13 and all the selected items are removed.

FIGURE 14.13

Click the Remove all checked items button in the Examine Document dialog box to elimi-nate any other occurrences of the text and graphics you want to delete.

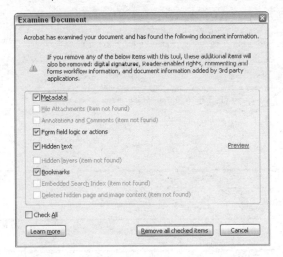

12. **Verify the redactions were made.** If you used objects with fills to redact the document, these objects are selectable and you can delete them. Select Tools ⇨ Advanced Editing ⇨ Touchup Object Tool to select the Touchup Object tool. Move the tool to one of your marks and click. Press the Delete (Del) key on your keyboard and the redaction frame is deleted. You can easily see that the redaction process did indeed remove the underlying content.

You should see that the text beneath the redaction frames has truly been deleted from your docu-ment. When you use the select tool and drag through the text, you'll notice that no selection appears where you redacted text (and/or objects) as shown in Figure 14.14. Alternately, you can verify redactions by opening the Search window and invoking a search for the words you redacted. You should see no results reported for all text that was redacted.

FIGURE 14.14

After removing redaction marks and selecting all the text, the redacted file shows you all the text/objects have been successfully deleted from the file.

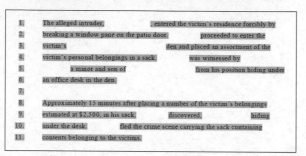

CROSS-REF Examine Document can also be helpful when you want to reduce file sizes. For more information on using the Examine Document dialog box, see Chapter 18.

Summary

- Redaction involves permanently removing data from a file.
- Acrobat 8 Professional only contains tools for redacting content, searching and redacting, applying redactions, and examining documents for content not visible on pages.
- Using tools other than the Redaction tools won't delete data from PDF files.
- Redaction marks can be modified for color changes, the use of text, and formatted text used to replace deleted data.

Chapter 15

Editing Images and Objects

I mages and objects, such as raster images from programs like Adobe Photoshop, vector images like those created in Adobe Illustrator, and text, can be edited in external editors and dynamically updated in a PDF document. The process involves launching the external editor from within Acrobat, making changes in the external editor, and saving the file. The file is treated like a link to the PDF where the edits are updated. Acrobat itself doesn't have any image editing tools, but you can use the external editors provided through companion programs to help out when you need to make modifications to objects in a PDF file.

Like editing text discussed in Chapter 13, image editing with Acrobat is intended to be a minor task for last-minute small changes. For major editing tasks, you should return to the original authoring program. In circumstances where you do not have an original document, you may need to extend the editing a little further by updating documents or exporting them for new layouts. In this chapter, you learn how to handle images and objects for editing and exporting purposes.

Setting Up the Editing Environment

Tools used for image editing are the same as those used in Chapter 13 for text editing. Refer to Chapter 13 to load the necessary tools and toolbars to follow along in this chapter. Your Toolbar Well should look similar to Figure 15.1.

FIGURE 15.1

Tools loaded for an image editing session

Selecting Images

Two tools in Acrobat enable you to copy images and objects. You can use the Select tool discussed in Chapter 13 to select images as well as text, and you also use the TouchUp Object tool to select images and objects. Objects can be vector-based artwork created in programs such as Adobe Illustrator and blocks of text that Acrobat interprets as objects. Only the TouchUp Object tool can be used to select objects; therefore, you cannot use the Select tool unless the item is an image such as a Photoshop file contained in the PDF document.

The distinction between text as text and text as an object can easily be understood in what you see selected in the Document pane. If you drag the Select tool through text, the text becomes highlighted. When you see the text highlighted, realize that the text is selected as text. When you click a text block with the TouchUp Object tool, you'll see a bounding box (border) around the text block but the text itself is not highlighted. When you see this view, you can be assured the text is selected as an object. In Figure 15.2, text is selected as text by dragging through it with the Select tool, and in Figure 15.3, multiple text blocks are selected as objects when dragging through text with the TouchUp Object tool.

FIGURE 15.2

Text selected with the Select tool is selected as text and highlighted.

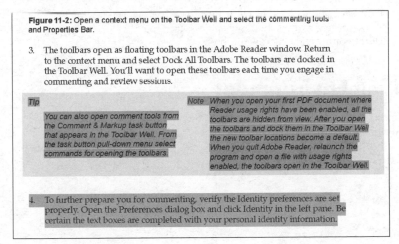

FIGURE 15.3

Text selected with the TouchUp Object tool is selected as an object and appears with a bounding box (border).

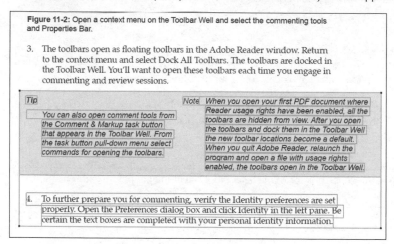

Each tool has different options and editing features associated with it. You use the Select tool, for example, when you want to select a photo image, copy it in Acrobat, and paste it in another program. Once copied to the Clipboard, you can also paste the image back into a PDF document, but the image is pasted as a Stamp comment. Double-click the image and an associated pop-up note appears like other comments, as shown in Figure 15.4.

The Select tool permits you to save an image as a separate file. Additionally, you can edit metadata for image files using this tool.

FIGURE 15.4

When pasting images copied with the Select tool, the pasted image appears as a Stamp comment.

The TouchUp Object tool permits you to copy an image in a PDF document and paste it back to the same document or another PDF document as an image. All the paste operations remain inside Acrobat, as you cannot copy with the TouchUp Object tool and paste an image or object into another program.

Furthermore, you cannot save an image file using the TouchUp Object tool as you can with the Select tool, but you can launch an external editor to edit either an image or object. When you want to edit images in Acrobat, the TouchUp Object tool provides you a number of different editing options — more so than the Select tool.

Using the Select tool

 In Chapter 13, you used the Select tool to select text and tables. You can also select images with this tool. As was covered in Chapter 13, you have some preference choices for handling selections when using the Select tool. If your last visit to the General preferences was to select text before images, you need to return to the General preferences by pressing Ctrl/⌘+K, click General in the left pane, and select Make Select tool select images before text in the Basic Tool Options, as shown in Figure 15.5.

FIGURE 15.5

Open the General preferences and select the check box for Make Select tool select images before text.

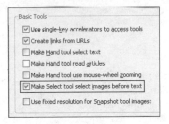

Click an image and click the Copy Image button shown in Figure 15.6. You need to place the cursor over the image after selecting it and pause a moment until the Copy Image button appears.

FIGURE 15.6

Pause a moment until you see the Copy Image button. Click the button and the selected image is copied.

You can also open a context menu after clicking an image and select Copy Image from the menu commands. The context menu offers you some other options for working with images selected with the Select tool, as shown in Figure 15.7.

FIGURE 15.7

Click an image and open a context menu.

Interactivity

From the context menu, you can add a Bookmark or link to the selected image. Click Bookmark from the context menu and the default view of the page is bookmarked. Click Create Link and the Create Link dialog box opens.

 **For more information on creating Bookmarks and links, see Chapter 22.**

Pasting images

As I said earlier in this section, images copied with the Select tool are pasted back into PDF documents as Stamp comments. The appearance onscreen looks like an image pasted into a document, but it remains a comment. If you want to print images pasted from content copied with the Select tool, you need to print using the Document and Stamps option in the Print dialog box.

 **For more information on printing documents and stamps, see Chapter 31.**

Use the Select tool to paste images into other programs. Pasted images in Acrobat appear as Stamp comments, but in other programs pasting is handled as you would expect when copying and pasting between other programs. The complete image is pasted into documents such as Microsoft Office files and other application documents.

CAUTION If you use professional layout and illustration programs designed for commercial printing, don't paste files in these applications. A preferred method is to save an image file from Acrobat and place or import the image in your design application.

Transforming pasted images

When you paste an image as a Stamp comment, you can size and rotate the image. From the four corners on a Stamp comment you see corner handles and in the top center you see another handle. Click and drag any corner handle to size the image up or down. No modifier key is required to proportionally resize a Stamp comment. All the sizing is kept to proportions without pressing the Shift key.

To rotate a Stamp comment, place the cursor over the middle top handle. When the cursor appears over this handle, the cursor changes to a semi-circle with an arrowhead, as shown in Figure 15.8. Click and drag when you see this cursor to rotate the Stamp.

FIGURE 15.8

Place the cursor over the top-center handle and click and drag to rotate the Stamp comment.

Saving image files

From a context menu opened by right-clicking (Windows) or Ctrl+clicking (Macintosh) you can save an image file when using the Select tool. Select Save Image As (shown in Figure 15.7) and the Save Image As dialog box opens. From the Save as type (Windows) or Format (Macintosh) pull-down menu you have options for saving in one of three file formats. Choose the default Bitmap Image Files (*.bmp), JPEG Image Files (.jpg), or TIFF Image Files (*.tif) format.

Saving as a bitmap file saves the file without compression and data loss. However, bitmap files may not retain all the data in the image. If you have images with clipping paths or drop shadows, for example, the saved image can appear significantly degraded, as shown in Figure 15.9.

NOTE A clipping path is a mask like a cookie cutter that cuts out all the image data outside the path. Without the clipping path and drop shadow the image in Figure 15.9 would have a white background around the image instead of transparent space.

JPEG files retain all data integrity; however, the downside to saving as JPEG is that the files are compressed and you end up with data loss. Use the TIFF format when you can and you'll save your files without data loss. As you can see in Figure 15.9, an image with a clipping path saved as a bitmap on the left is degraded compared to the correct detail shown in the TIFF export on the right.

TIP If you're not certain whether a BMP file will be saved, thus preserving all data integrity, you can select the image with the Select tool, copy the file to the Clipboard, and from the Create PDF Task Button drop-down menu, select Create File From Clipboard Image. Acrobat creates a separate PDF document and the image you see appears exactly as when saving as a BMP file. If the file looks good, save the PDF or return to the image and select Save Image As from a context menu.

Image Properties

Select Image Properties from a context menu and document metadata are reported for the image. If you shot an image with a digital camera, the data recorded by the camera is reported in the Image Information dialog box shown in Figure 15.10.

CROSS-REF For more information related to working with document metadata, see Chapter 17.

FIGURE 15.9

Saving files with clipping paths in bitmap format can present problems with image quality. Saving the same file as a TIFF (right) preserves data integrity.

FIGURE 15.10

Select Properties from a context menu using the Select tool, and the Image Information dialog box opens.

Recognize Text Using OCR

You may not see the Recognize Text Using OCR menu command when selecting images with the select tool. Images imported in a layout program won't give you the option for converting image data to recognizable text. If you have a scanned document and open the image in Acrobat, you might see this command. Use it for converting images to recognizable text.

CROSS-REF For more information on scanning and converting image data to recognizable text, see Chapter 17.

Using the TouchUp Object tool

You use the TouchUp Object tool for selecting objects on a page. You select photo images, drawings and illustrations, and blocks of text with the tool.

The TouchUp Object tool copies images and objects and pastes them back into a PDF or other PDF documents you open in Acrobat. You can click an image or object or marquee several images and/or objects to select multiple items. Acrobat interprets any text you click on with the TouchUp Object tool as an object. Hence, you can edit the object in an external editor or move the object(s).

CROSS-REF For information on external editing, see the section "Image and Object External Editing" later in this chapter.

You can also use the TouchUp Object tool to move or nudge objects. Click on a single object or marquee a group of objects on a page, and then click and drag the selection to a new location. You are limited to moving objects on a single page. You can't select an object on one page and drag it to another PDF page. For moving objects to different pages you need to cut the selection, move to another page, and choose Edit ➪ Paste. If you want to nudge objects, create a selection with the TouchUp Object tool and press the arrow keys on your keyboard to move the object right, left, up, or down.

NOTE If two or more images or objects are spaced apart and each object is selectable, you can click to select an object and Shift+click to select additional images/objects. If you have objects such as vector graphics where many paths are contained within the object or you have multiple overlapping objects, marquee the objects to be certain you select all you want to copy.

To copy and paste objects, including photo images, illustrations and vector objects, and text blocks, you use the TouchUp Object tool. To select a single object, click the object with the TouchUp Object tool. A keyline border shows the bounding box for the selected item. Open a context menu and you find menu options different from those available with the Select tool, as shown in Figure 15.11.

The menu offers several commands related to handling images and objects. Select Copy to copy the image to the Clipboard and select Cut to cut the image from the page and place it on the Clipboard. From either choice you can then paste the data on another PDF page or into another PDF document.

FIGURE 15.11

Select an image with the TouchUp Object tool and open a context menu. Select Copy from the menu choices to copy the selection.

| Cut |
| Copy |
| Paste |
Delete
Select All
Select None
Place Image...
Delete Clip
Set Clip
Flip Horizontal
Flip Vertical
Rotate Clockwise
Rotate Counterclockwise
Rotate Selection
Create Artifact...
Find...
Edit Image...
Show Metadata...
Properties...

Pasting images and objects

After copying with the TouchUp Object tool, choose Edit ➪ Paste or use a context menu opened with the tool and select Paste. When pasting data, the new image or object is pasted in the foreground. If you need to keep a stacking order intact, you need to carefully plan out copying and pasting images and objects. In more complex documents, it makes sense to return to the original authoring program as you do not have commands in Acrobat to paste in front, paste in back, and paste in place. These kinds of commands are found in design programs where you can easily control the stacking order of images and objects.

If you want to replace text, images, or objects on a page with a pasted block of text, an image, or an object, select the items you want to replace after copying the item you want to paste. Choose Edit ➪ Paste or use Paste from a context menu, and the pasted item replaces the selected items.

Place Image

Placing images is like using a Place command in a layout program. When you select the command, a dialog box opens where you can select an image on your hard drive and import the image in your layout.

NEW FEATURE Acrobat 8 now supports placing images much like layout programs. Click the TouchUp Object tool and open a context menu on a document page. The Place Image command appears when opening a context menu on a page or when selecting an image and opening a context menu. The Open dialog box appears where you can navigate your hard drive and locate the file you want to import in your PDF file. File formats supported using this command include Bitmap, BMP (*.bmp, *.rle, *.dlb); CompuServe GIF (*.gif), JPEG (*.jpg, *.jpeg, .jpe), JPEG2000 (.jpf, *.ipx, *.jp2, .j2k, .j2c, jpc), PCX (.pcx), PNG (.png), and TIFF (.tif, *.tiff). When one of these file formats is imported into a PDF document, Acrobat converts to PDF and imports the image.

CROSS-REF For more information on file formats, see Chapters 11 and 12.

TIP If you select an image on a PDF page with the TouchUp Object tool and select Place Image from a context menu, the selected image is replaced with the new image you select in the Open dialog box.

Delete Clip

The context menu opened with the TouchUp Object tool contains the Delete Clip menu command. You can delete a clipping path from an image or object that had the path applied in an image editor like Photoshop or an illustration program such as Adobe Illustrator. Deleting a path shows data outside the defined path. In Figure 15.12 you can see an image where a clipping path was created in Photoshop to hide edge artifacts on the left and after removing the clipping path on the right side of the figure where the artifacts are visible.

FIGURE 15.12

Selecting Delete Clip from a context menu removes clipping paths assigned to objects and images.

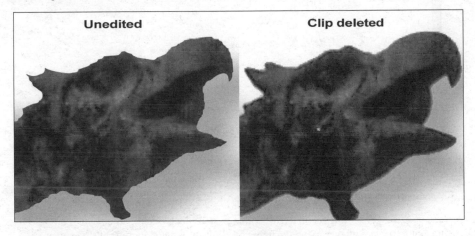

In Acrobat 8, Delete Clip also performs another function. You can set a clip on an image with NEW FEATURE or without a clipping path using the TouchUp Object tool context menu. Once a clip has been set, use the Delete Clip command to remove the clip. To completely understand the results, see the section "Set Clip" next.

Set Clip

Select the TouchUp Object tool, click an image on a PDF page, and from a context menu select Set Clip.

The Set Clip command enables you to clip (actually Crop) images. When using Set Clip you'll find three tools appear as you move the cursor around an image. The tools are shown in Figure 15.13.

FIGURE 15.13

The Scissors, Crop, and Move tools are used when setting a clip.

To crop an image, select the Set Clip command from a context menu opened from the TouchUp Object tool. The cursor immediately appears as the Scissors tool shown in Figure 15.14. This tool merely informs you that you are in Set Clip mode.

FIGURE 15.14

Select Set Clip from a context menu and the cursor changes to a scissors icon.

Move the cursor to one of the four handles you see on the four corners of the selected image. Place the cursor directly over one of the four handles. You may need to move the cursor around a bit or zoom into the document before you see the Crop tool shown in Figure 15.15. When you see the Crop tool, drag the corner in to crop the image. You can continue using the Crop tool as long as you don't click when the cursor changes from the Crop tool to another tool.

FIGURE 15.15

Move the cursor over a corner point to see the Crop tool. Click and drag to crop the image.

When your crop appears as desired, just click the mouse button and the cursor changes from the Crop tool to the Move tool, as shown in Figure 15.16. You can click and drag the cropped image anywhere on the page.

Now, let's return to the Delete Clip command. After you have cropped an image, you can return to the full-size image before the cropping. Just open a context menu again with the TouchUp Object tool and select Delete Clip. The image appears as you first opened your PDF document.

FIGURE 15.16

Click the mouse button and the cursor changes to the Move tool.

Rotations

Images can be rotated in many ways by using the context menu commands from the TouchUp Object tool. Open a context menu and five separate commands appear for rotating images.

NEW FEATURE   All the rotate options you find in the context menu are new in Acrobat 8. You can rotate images Horizontally and Vertically (180°), rotate Clockwise and Counterclockwise (90°), and rotate images using arbitrary rotations. The first four rotation options in the context menu should be self-evident. The more complicated rotation is Rotate Selection that requires a little explanation.

When you click an image with the TouchUp Object tool and choose Rotate Selection from the context menu, you won't see any change appear in the Acrobat window. Invoking the command changes modes from a scaling mode to a transformation mode. After selecting the command, move the cursor to one of the four corner handles. You need to wait for the cursor to change appearance to a line with two opposing arrowheads, as you see in Figure 15.17.

FIGURE 15.17

Select Rotate Selection and move the cursor to a corner handle.

Click and drag the cursor to rotate the image and you can make an arbitrary rotation as shown in Figure 15.18. When you rotate the image as you want it, click on the image and the rotation mode is disengaged.

FIGURE 15.18

Click and drag to rotate the image.

Scaling images

You won't find a menu command for scaling images in a context menu, but scaling images is available to you.

NEW FEATURE In Acrobat 8 you can easily scale images. Just select the TouchUp Object tool and click on an image. Move the cursor to a corner handle and drag the handle in or out to size an image down or up respectively. You can constrain proportions by pressing the shift key and dragging a corner handle.

Create/Remove Artifact

This menu command is used when working with tagged PDF documents and accessibility. Selecting the command opens the Create Artifact dialog box. Or, if an artifact has been created, you can remove an artifact by selecting Remove Artifact.

CROSS-REF For more on using the Create Artifact options, see Chapter 25.

Find

A number of search options are available that pertain to images. Select Find from a context menu and the Find Element dialog box opens, as shown in Figure 15.19. A number of options appear that relate to working with accessible files. You also have options for searching annotations and OCR Suspects.

FIGURE 15.19

Select Find and the Find Element dialog box opens.

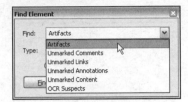

CROSS-REF For more information on accessibility, see Chapter 25. For more on annotations, see Chapter 20. For more on OCR Suspects see Chapter 17.

Show Metadata

Select this item and the same dialog box opens when you use the Select tool to select Image Properties.

Properties

Select an image with the TouchUp Object tool and select Properties from a context menu, and you arrive at the TouchUp Properties dialog box. When the TouchUp Properties dialog box opens, click the Color tab, as shown in Figure 15.20.

FIGURE 15.20

Click Color in the TouchUp Properties dialog box.

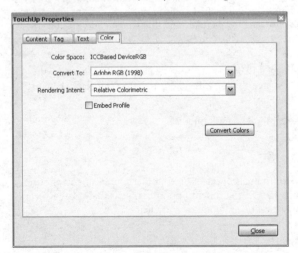

A number of tabs in the TouchUp Properties dialog box relate to accessibility and text editing, which are explained in Chapters 25 and 13 respectively. The one item in the Properties dialog box relating to image editing is contained in the Color tab.

NEW FEATURE The Color TouchUp Properties window provides you choices for converting color profiles. The current working color space is reported at the top of the dialog box. From choices in the Convert To pull-down menu, you can choose to convert color to a working space color or an output profile. Ideally, you should stick to the working space profiles and most often your choices will be either sRGB or Adobe RGB (1998). Output profile selections can be made in the Advanced Print Options dialog box.

CROSS-REF For more information on working with color workspaces and color output profiles, see Chapter 31.

If you want to change a color profile, make the choice for the new profile in the Convert To pull-down menu, select a Rendering Intent, and click Convert Colors. If you want the profile embedded in the image, click the Embed Profile check box before clicking Convert Colors.

CAUTION Be aware that if you embed a profile you need to make proper selections for printing files in both the Acrobat Print dialog box and switches in your printer driver. Be certain to carefully read Chapter 31 before converting color on your images.

As a matter of default, you'll want to keep the Rendering Intent at Relative Colorimetric. This choice is the best choice for raster image files. If you have vector images, you may want to use another rendering intent. For a comprehensive source on color management, see *Color Correction For Digital Photographers Only* (Wiley, 2006).

The item yet to be discussed in the context menu opened with the TouchUp Object tool is Edit Image. Selecting this command launches an external image-editing program, which is covered in the next section.

Image and Object External Editing

As demonstrated in the first part of this chapter, Acrobat offers you methods for copying and pasting images, moving them around the page, and exporting them to files. However, changing the physical attributes of images and shapes, other than transformations and scaling, is not something you can do in Acrobat. To modify certain appearances or attributes of raster and vector objects, you need to use an external editor. When you launch an editor from a menu command in Acrobat, you can make changes to images, text, and shapes and save your edits in the external editor. These saves are then dynamically updated in the PDF document. Acrobat treats external editing like many programs that support file links. When you edit linked files, the links are updated in the program where they are imported.

To access an external editor, you need to use the TouchUp Object tool. You cannot access external editors with any of the other selection tools.

TouchUp preferences

By default, Acrobat's external editors are Photoshop for image editing and Illustrator for object editing. When you install Acrobat, the installer locates these editors on your hard drive, if they are installed, and designates them as the default editors. If you install Photoshop and/or Illustrator after Acrobat, you need to instruct Acrobat where to look for the application files to use as your image/object editors.

Choose Edit ➪ Preferences to open the Preferences dialog box. Click the TouchUp item on the left pane of the Preferences dialog box. In the right pane are two buttons, as shown in Figure 15.21. Click Choose Image Editor to open the Choose Image Editor dialog box. The dialog box enables you to navigate your hard drive and locate Adobe Photoshop. Select the Photoshop application icon and click Open.

FIGURE 15.21

Select TouchUp in the preferences list and the Choose buttons appear on the right side of the dialog box. Click one of the buttons to navigate your hard drive and select the respective editor.

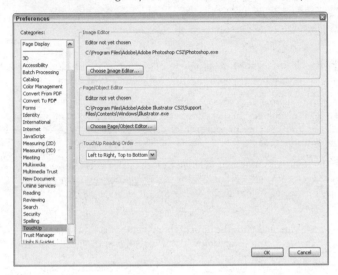

For page and object editing, Adobe Illustrator is the default tool. If you need to locate Illustrator, click the Choose Page/Object Editor button. Find the Illustrator application on your hard drive and select it in the Choose Page/Object Editor dialog box. Click Open and Adobe Illustrator is enabled as your page/object editor.

After identifying your editors, click OK in the Preferences dialog box. The choices you made are immediately available. If Acrobat loses contact with either program, you are prompted in a dialog box that external editing cannot be done. If you see warning dialog boxes open as you attempt to use an external editor, return to the Preferences and reestablish the connection to your editors.

Editing images in Adobe Photoshop

You launch Photoshop from Acrobat by selecting an image with the TouchUp Object tool and opening a context menu. From the menu commands, select Edit Image or press Control (Windows) or Option (Macintosh) and double-click. Depending on the speed of your computer and the amount of memory you have, Photoshop may take a few moments to launch. When the program opens, the image you selected is placed in a Photoshop document window.

You can change color modes and resolution, edit images for brightness and contrast, add effects, and just about anything else you can do in Photoshop to a single layer file. If you add type, add layers, or create transparency, you need to flatten all layers before saving the file. Layers added to a Photoshop file require you to use the Save As command to update the file. When you use Save As, the file is not updated in the PDF document. Flattening layers enables you to use the Save command that updates the PDF document when the file is saved. In Figure 15.22, a file in Photoshop was edited for color changes. Note that the file contains transparency and appears as a single-layer image. Because the file opened from Acrobat was a file on a single layer with transparency, all edits you make without creating additional layers enable you to still use the Save command.

FIGURE 15.22

You edit files in your image editor and dynamically update the PDF from which they originated.

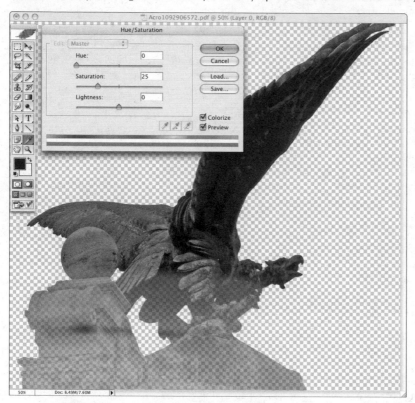

Photoshop updates the PDF document dynamically according to the edits you make with the Save command. If you add a layer to the file, you are prompted by Photoshop to Save As a new filename. Selecting Save As and writing to a new file disrupts the link. If you save in this manner, your PDF document won't update. If the file is saved without writing a new file, the updates are dynamically recorded in the PDF when you return to Acrobat.

Editing objects in Adobe Illustrator

Objects, for the purposes of discussing external object editing, can be vector objects such as illustrations created in Illustrator, CorelDraw, or Adobe Freehand. Objects can also be text. Both vector objects and text are edited in Adobe Illustrator when you select Edit Object(s) from a context menu with the TouchUp Object tool.

To edit a single object, select the object with the TouchUp Object tool and open a context menu. The Edit Image command changes to Edit Object in the context menu. Select Edit Object and Adobe Illustrator launches. Changes you make to the object are dynamically updated when you save the file just as the file saves discussed with image editing are updated. If selecting a single object on the PDF page is difficult, you can marquee a group of objects and select Edit Objects.

If no object is selected and you open a context menu with the TouchUp Object tool, the menu command changes to Edit Page. To easily access the Edit Page command, you can also open a context menu outside the page boundary. When you click outside the page area, the Edit Page command appears in the context menu. Select Edit Page and all objects are opened in Adobe Illustrator.

Be certain to not use the Save As command when editing objects. The procedures for saving files with object editing follow the same principles as described with image editing. Regardless of whether you edit a single object, multiple objects, or the entire page, the edits you make in Illustrator are updated in the PDF document only when you choose File ➪ Save.

Editing text in Adobe Illustrator

In some circumstances you may find editing text in an external editor to prove more satisfactory than editing text with the TouchUp Text tool. Editing text in Illustrator requires you to have embedded fonts loaded on your computer. Keep in mind that returning to an authoring application to apply major edits to documents is more advantageous than using the TouchUp Text tool. But, for those jobs where you don't have a document available and using the TouchUp Text tool just doesn't do the job, here's a little workaround you can try. I offer a disclaimer and tell you upfront that these methods may not always work, but I've found more often than not that you can successfully edit text in Illustrator for some minor edit jobs.

One problem you can face when editing text in Illustrator is the text blocks are likely to be broken up and lose their paragraph formatting attributes. You need to select the text, cut it from the page, and paste it back keeping the general size and position close to the original. You can then edit the text and choose File ➪ Save to update the PDF document.

Using Edit Page in Adobe Illustrator

If you want to edit an entire page in Illustrator, click the TouchUp Object tool on a document page without selecting an image. Open a context menu and select Edit Page. The entire page then opens in Adobe Illustrator.

You can also click the TouchUp Object tool and choose Edit ➪ Select All or press Ctrl/⌘+A. All objects and their respective bounding boxes are shown as selected. Open a context menu and choose Edit Objects. All the selected objects are then opened in Adobe Illustrator.

If you edit a page or all objects on a page in Illustrator, selecting File ➪ Save (Ctrl/⌘+S) updates the PDF document. If working on a single PDF page, you can just as easily select File ➪ Save As in Illustrator and save to a PDF file.

If you need to completely rework a PDF document, you can also open a PDF in Adobe Illustrator. Opening a file in Illustrator is the same as selecting Edit Page. All changes you make are dynamically updated in the PDF document after saving in Illustrator.

CROSS-REF For more information on editing PDF pages, see Chapters 9 and 16.

Using the Snapshot Tool

You use the Snapshot tool to create a marquee around any area on the document page. You can select text and graphics with the Snapshot tool. Select the tool from the Select & Zoom toolbar and click and drag a marquee around the area to be selected. When you release the mouse button, Acrobat takes a snapshot of the area within the marquee and copies it to the Clipboard. A dialog box opens to inform you the data has been copied to the Clipboard.

After you click OK in the Alert dialog box, the marquee is still active on the document page. You can open a context menu where you have options for copying the data or printing the selection. In addition, you can create a link to the snapshot by selecting Create Link in the context menu. These menu commands are the same as those shown earlier in Figure 15.7 earlier in this chapter.

CROSS-REF For more information on creating links from snapshots, see Chapter 22.

CAUTION Taking a snapshot of a page containing images and text or text creates only a bitmap of the selected area. All text is converted to a raster image. If you intend to preserve text and edit it later, don't use the Snapshot tool. The text is not editable from snapshot images.

The Snapshot tool provides paste functions equal to both the Select tool and the TouchUp Object tool. Once you take a snapshot you can paste the data back to the PDF document or to another application document. By default, the Snapshot tool places a copy of the snapshot on the Clipboard and makes the Clipboard data available to Acrobat. When you open a context menu on the snapshot and select Copy Selected Graphic, you can paste the data to other application documents.

Changing snapshot resolutions

By default, snapshot resolutions are 72 ppi (pixels per inch), which is sufficient for screen views at 100 percent. If you want to print files or zoom in to a document view above 100 percent, 72 ppi is not sufficient for rendering images that appear without obvious image degradation.

To understand how image resolutions affect image quality, try the following steps.

STEPS: Changing snapshot image resolutions

1. **Change Preferences.** Open the Preferences dialog box by pressing Ctrl/⌘+K. Click General in the left pane and check the box for Use fixed resolution for snapshots. In the resolution text box, type **72**, as shown in Figure 15.23.

FIGURE 15.23

Set the resolution for snapshots to 72 ppi.

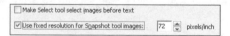

2. **Take a snapshot.** Open a file in Acrobat — preferably one with images and image resolutions above 200 ppi.

   Click the Snapshot tool. Drag a rectangle around the area you want to copy. When you release the mouse button, the data is copied to the Clipboard.

3. **Paste the data in an image editor.** Open an image editor such as Adobe Photoshop CS or Adobe Photoshop Elements. Paste the data in a new document window.

CROSS-REF For information on pasting data in an image editor, see the next section "Pasting snapshot data" later in this chapter.

4. **Zoom in on the document.** Zoom to at least a 200 percent view and notice the quality of the image. You should see poor image quality especially if you copy any text. In Figure 15.24, the pasted data includes both image and text.

FIGURE 15.24

Zoom to a 200 percent view after pasting the data in an image editor.

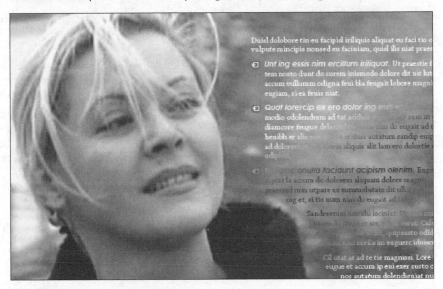

5. **Change preferences.** Return to the Acrobat Preferences dialog box as described in Step 1. Change the image resolution to 300 ppi.

6. **Take a Snapshot.** Try to take a snapshot as described in Step 2 in the same area of the PDF document as you took the first snapshot.

7. **Paste the data.** Paste the new Clipboard data in your image editor and zoom to the approximate same view as the first image you pasted in your image editor. Because the image resolution is much higher, the zoom will be much lower than a 200 percent view.

8. **Compare the two images.** Examine the second image you pasted at 300 ppi. You should see a noticeable difference in image quality. In Figure 15.24, compare the text with the text shown in Figure 15.25.

FIGURE 15.25

Paste the image copied at 300 ppi and compare the document with the first image pasted at 72 ppi.

Note that boosting image resolution in the Preferences won't help create better looking images than a value higher than the original image resolution. For example, if you convert to PDF using images at 72 ppi and try to take a snapshot at 300 ppi, you can't produce a better looking image. The image file is interpolated as you size it up just like sizing up images in image editing programs.

Pasting snapshot data

When you take a snapshot and paste the data in Acrobat, the pasted data becomes a Stamp comment just like using the Select tool. If you want to take a snapshot and paste as you can paste data using the TouchUp Object tool, you need to perform two operations.

First use the Snapshot tool to copy the area you want on a PDF Page. When the data are copied, choose the Create PDF From Clipboard command. A new PDF document is created from your snapshot.

If you now want to copy and paste the data, you can use the TouchUp Object tool, click the page, and copy the data. The copied data can then be pasted into any PDF file.

You can also paste snapshot data into other programs. If you use the Select tool to copy an image, the image is pasted at 72 ppi in another application. If using the Snapshot tool, you can adjust resolution and paste into another application document. Again, you need to have sufficient resolution in the original image to make this method worthwhile.

Exporting Images

If you need to completely overhaul a document and want to lay it out in an authoring program, you might want to copy and paste text into a word processor, format your text, save the file, and then import the text into a program best suited for layout design, such as Adobe InDesign CS. If your PDF document contains photo images, you need to export the images and add them to your layout. Having to individually export images with the Select Image tool would be tedious for a large layout project containing many images. Fortunately, Acrobat offers you a feature for exporting all images in a PDF with a single menu command.

Choose Advanced ➪ Document Processing ➪ Export All Images. The Export All Images As dialog box opens where you can make selections for filename, destination, and the format you want to use for the exported images. In the Export All Images As dialog box, open the pull-down menu for Save as type (Windows) or Format (Macintosh). Four format options are available from the menu choices — JPEG, PNG, TIFF, or JPEG2000. Select one of the format options and click the Settings button to assign file attributes to the exported images.

CROSS-REF For more information on image file format definitions, see Chapter 6.

When you select JPEG for the file type and click the Settings button, the Export All Images As JPEG Settings dialog box opens, as shown in Figure 15.26. The settings change according to the file type you select. Therefore, if you choose TIFF as a format, for example, you'll see changes for compression choices. The options for File Settings and Color Management are the same as those options discussed in Chapters 10 and 11. In addition to these settings, the Extraction item at the bottom of the dialog box enables you to eliminate certain files when the sizes are smaller than the size you choose from the pull-down menu.

From the pull-down menu you choose a preset option for an image's physical size. You might have icons or logos appearing on all pages constructed at .75-inch sizes. You can elect to exclude these images by selecting the 1.00 inches item in the pull-down menu. When you click OK in the Extract All Images As dialog box, all files above the size selected from the pull-down menu choice are saved as separate files in the specified format. If you want every image extracted, choose the No Limit item from the pull-down menu.

CROSS-REF For information on saving PDF files in other formats, see Chapter 11.

FIGURE 15.26

Make a choice for file format in the Export All Images As dialog box and click the Settings button. You choose options in the Export All Images As *(file format)* Settings dialog box for File Settings, Color Management, and Colorspace Conversion, and for eliminating image extractions falling below user-defined values.

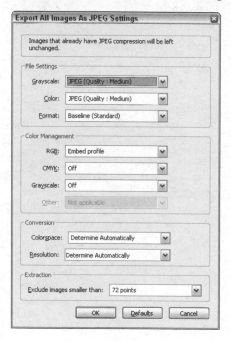

Summary

- You use the Select tool to select individual photo images on PDF pages. You can select only a single image with the tool. Selected images can be copied to the Clipboard.

- You can convert images copied with the Select tool to PDF with the Create PDF tool, and you can paste them into authoring programs.

- To select objects use the TouchUp Object tool. Objects include photo images, illustrative artwork, and text. Dragging a marquee enables you to select multiple objects. Pressing the Shift key and clicking an object toggles between adding or eliminating an object from a selection.

- You can paste objects and images copied with the TouchUp Object tool on PDF pages. You cannot paste them into authoring application documents.

- External editing is handled by selecting an image or an object and opening a context menu. From the menu options, select Edit Image/Object.

- The default image editor is Adobe Photoshop and the default object editor is Adobe Illustrator. Select editors in the Preferences dialog box by clicking the TouchUp item in the left list and clicking the Change button on the right side of the dialog box.

- You use the Snapshot tool to marquee an area on a page and select text, objects, and images within the selection marquee. Releasing the mouse button after you create a selection marquee copies the data within the marquee to the Clipboard.

- Image resolutions for snapshots can be changed in the General preferences dialog box.

- All images in a PDF can be exported as separate files with a single menu command. Choose Advanced ➪ Document Processing ➪ Export Images to open the Export All Images dialog box.

Chapter 16

Editing Pages

Chapters 13 and 15 covered editing content on PDF pages. Minor edits for text passages and images may be completed with the tools discussed in the earlier chapters. If you want to modify larger portions of a PDF document, then you'll want to know something about the tools Acrobat offers you for page editing. If you return to an authoring application and edit text, graphics, and layouts, you may want to update your PDF document according to the page edits made in other applications. Rather than recreate the entire PDF file, Acrobat enables you to selectively append, replace, delete, and extract pages in a PDF document.

In addition to the number of different page-editing tools found in earlier versions of Acrobat, the new version of Acrobat Professional offers some impressive features in the new revised Add Headers and Footers dialog box and adding backgrounds and watermarks in other dialog boxes. This chapter covers the page-editing tools in Acrobat and many new features that can help you modify documents.

Setting Up the Page-Editing Environment

For page-editing tasks, you need to use some viewing tools, advanced tools, and page-editing tools. Move the cursor to the Toolbar Well and open a context menu. From the menu options, select Reset Toolbars.

Open the More Tools window by selecting More Tools from a context menu opened on the Acrobat Toolbar Well. Click the check box for the Advanced Editing toolbar. Scroll down the window and click the check box for the Edit toolbar. Select the Organizer and Search tool in the File toolbar. Scroll to the Page Navigation toolbar and check all tools and the Page Navigation Toolbar check box. Scroll down to the Select & Zoom toolbar and check all but the Pan &

Zoom Window tool. Click OK and return to a context menu on the Toolbar Well and select Dock Toolbars. Your toolbar assortment should look something like Figure 16.1.

A toolbar arrangement that works well when editing PDF pages

Working with Page Thumbnails

Thumbnails are mini-views of PDF pages that can be displayed in various zoom sizes.

To see the thumbnail view of pages in an open document, click the Pages panel to open the pane, as shown in Figure 16.2. Thumbnail views are created on-the-fly when the pane is opened. Users of Acrobat 5 and below will remember the pane was referred to as Thumbnails. In Acrobat 6.0 viewers, the name was changed to the Pages panel and remains the same in Acrobat 7 and 8.

FIGURE 16.2

Click the Pages tab to open the Pages panel where thumbnail views of the pages are created on-the-fly.

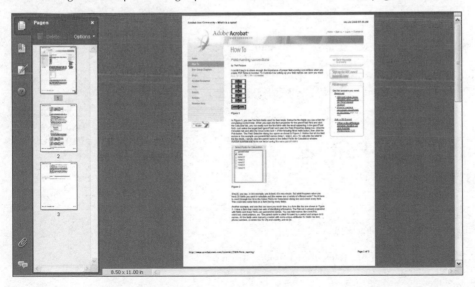

Navigating pages

The Pages panel can be used to navigate pages. Clicking a thumbnail takes you to the page associated with the thumbnail. The page opens in the Document pane at the currently established zoom view. You can zoom in or out of pages in the Pages panel by dragging the lower-right handle on the rectangle appearing inside the page thumbnail. The changing zoom levels are reflected in the zoom view in the Document pane. In Figure 16.3, a rectangle shows the current page view in the Document pane. Click on the handle in the lower-right corner and drag it into the center of the rectangle to zoom in on the page. Click and drag out to zoom out of the page.

FIGURE 16.3

Thumbnails in the Pages panel are linked to the pages in the Document pane. Click a thumbnail to navigate to the page link. Drag the red rectangle to zoom in or out of the page displayed in the Document pane.

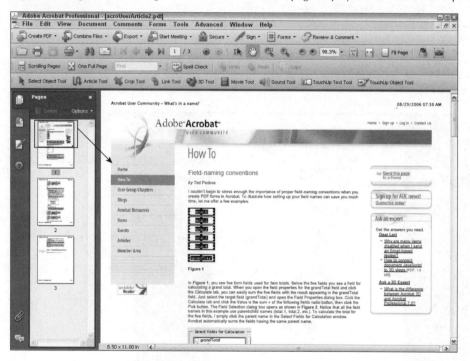

The Pages panel and the Document pane are two separate compartments in the open PDF document. Clicking in the Pages panel activates the pane. Conversely, clicking in the Document pane activates the area where you view pages. Unfortunately, Acrobat does not highlight any part of either pane to inform you when a pane is active. So you just have to remember to click first in the area you want to be active.

If you press the Page Down key or down-arrow key while the Document pane is active, the pages in the Document pane scroll. As each page is scrolled, the Pages panel likewise scrolls pages and the respective page thumbnails are highlighted. When you click in the Pages panel, you experience a different behavior. Pressing the Page Down key scrolls several pages down only in the Pages panel. The respective pages in the

Document pane are not scrolled. As you scroll through page thumbnails in the Pages panel, the Document pane remains fixed at its current view because as you scroll in the Pages panel, thumbnails are not actually selected. Instead, the selected thumbnail is linked to the view in the Document pane.

With reference to thumbnails, the term "selection" needs a little definition. When you click a page thumbnail, the number appearing below the page icon is shown selected (highlighted), and the thumbnail is further highlighted with a keyline border around the icon. Likewise, the respective page is placed in view in the Document pane. In essence, Acrobat communicates two selection messages to you. If you press the down-arrow key on your keyboard, the number below the thumbnail remains highlighted and the respective page remains open in the Document pane. However, the keyline border moves to the next page down, indicating the current thumbnail selection in the Pages panel. In Figure 16.4, page 2 in a PDF document is selected and page 2 is open in the Document pane. When the down-arrow key is pressed, page 3 becomes selected in the Pages panel, while page 2 remains as the page viewed in the Document pane.

FIGURE 16.4

Click the cursor in the Pages panel to activate the pane, and then press the down-arrow key. The keyline border shows the page selection in the Pages panel, while the highlighted page number on the previous page shows which page is in view in the Document pane.

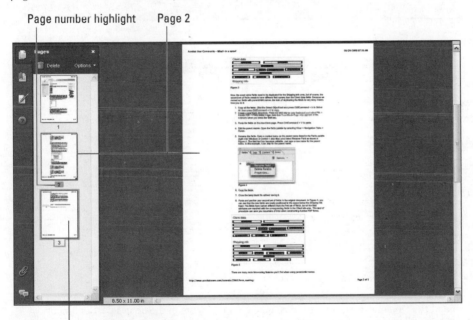

Page number highlight   Page 2

Page 3 selected in Pages panel

TIP You can use the Pages panel and the Document pane to compare pages in a PDF document. If you insert a new page that is similar to an existing page in the PDF file, click the thumbnail of one page to open it in the Document pane. Use the arrow keys (up or down) to navigate to the inserted page. Enlarge the thumbnail view so you can clearly compare the thumbnail to the page in the Document pane. For information on enlarging views and inserting pages, see the next section on changing thumbnail sizes.

Changing thumbnail sizes

In Acrobat 6 and later, you can reduce the size of pages to a mini-thumbnail view and enlarge the size up to a maximum thumbnail view of about 300 percent. The support for increased thumbnail views in the Pages panel enables you to quickly find a page in a PDF document.

You reduce or enlarge page thumbnail sizes through menu commands. A context menu opened in the Pages panel or the pane pull-down menu includes the Enlarge Page Thumbnails and Reduce Page Thumbnails commands. Before using these commands, you should understand opening context menus.

If you click in the Pages panel on a page thumbnail and open a context menu, the Enlarge Page Thumbnails and Reduce Page Thumbnails commands are available as options in a menu that contains many different commands for page editing. If you click outside the page thumbnails, but still in the Pages panel, a different menu opens with fewer commands. However, the same menu commands for enlarging or reducing page thumbnails are still present. Likewise, the pull-down menu adjacent to Options at the top of the Pages panel offers the same commands. Regardless of which menu you use, you can enlarge or reduce page thumbnail views.

To enlarge the size of the page thumbnails, click the mouse button outside the page thumbnails in the Pages panel and open a context menu. Select Enlarge Page Thumbnails from the menu options, as shown in Figure 16.5. Return to the menu and select the same menu command to enlarge again. Repeat the steps to zoom in to the desired view.

FIGURE 16.5

Open a context menu in the Pages panel and select Enlarge Page Thumbnails. Return to the context menu and repeat the steps several times to zoom in on a page thumbnail.

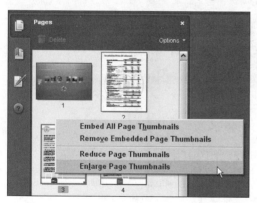

You'll notice that Acrobat makes no provision for selecting from among a number of preset zoom sizes. You need to return to the context menu or pull-down menu to successively increase or decrease page thumbnail views. If the zoom view in the Pages panel is larger than the panel width, click anywhere on the vertical bar on the right side of the pane and drag it to the right. The pane resizes horizontally to show more of the Pages panel while the Document pane is reduced in size. In Figure 16.6, I enlarged the thumbnail view, using repeated steps for enlarging the thumbnails, and I widened the panel so several large thumbnails could be viewed.

Embedding and unembedding thumbnails

Page thumbnails are created on-the-fly each time you open the Pages panel. In long documents, you may find your computer slowing down each time the Pages panel is opened and the thumbnails are recreated. If this proves to be a burden, you can choose to embed thumbnails when working with the Pages panel and avoid the delay caused by creating them.

Thumbnails add some overhead to your file. Each page thumbnail adds about 1K to the file size. Unless your files are to be viewed by users of earlier Acrobat viewers that don't support creating thumbnails on-the-fly; delete them as one of the final steps in your editing session.

To embed thumbnails, select the Embed All Page Thumbnails command from the pane Options menu or a context-sensitive menu. Thumbnails can also be created by batch-processing PDF files using a Batch Sequence or at the time of distillation when using Acrobat Distiller.

FIGURE 16.6

To size the Pages panel, click on the vertical bar on the right side of the pane and drag it to the right.

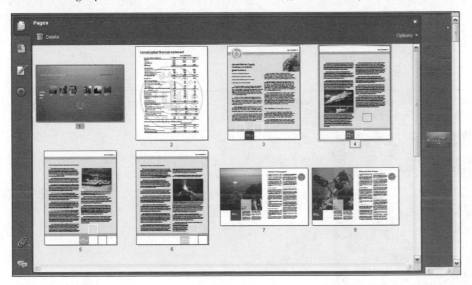

PDF WORKFLOW You can delete thumbnails from PDF documents either individually in Acrobat or by using the Advanced ➪ Document Processing ➪ Batch Processing command in Acrobat Professional. If your work environment is such that you do a lot of editing in Acrobat and often use thumbnails, you may want to create them during distillation. When thumbnails are embedded, screen refreshes for multiple edits in long documents are faster. After you finish editing jobs and want to post PDF files on the Web or create CD-ROMs, you can batch-process the files for optimization and delete the thumbnails. Run the Edit Batch Sequences command to optimize multiple files and remove thumbnails.

CROSS-REF For information on creating and running Batch Sequences, see Chapter 18.

To unembed thumbnails, open a context menu on a page thumbnail and select Remove Embedded Page Thumbnails. All embedded page thumbnails are removed from the document. This step can be particularly helpful when working with Adobe Illustrator files including the most current version of Adobe Illustrator CS. When Illustrator embeds thumbnails a bitmap representation of the page is created as a thumbnail and displays a poorly degraded image, as you can see on the left side of Figure 16.7. After the thumbnail is removed in Acrobat, the page thumbnail appears as you see it on the right side of Figure 16.7. Whenever you see thumbnail images with a degraded view, always check to see whether the thumbnail is embedded.

FIGURE 16.7

Adobe Illustrator exports thumbnails with a degraded bitmap view. Removing the thumbnail (shown right) improves the image quality.

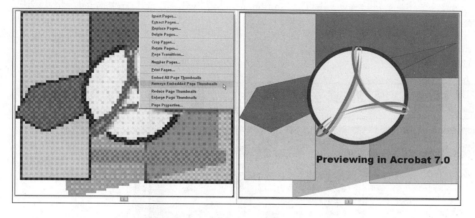

Organizing Pages

The Pages panel offers you a wealth of opportunity for sorting pages and reorganizing them. You can move pages around, copy and paste pages when you want to duplicate them, delete pages, print selected pages within a document, and a host of other options specific to page management.

Reordering pages

Acrobat provides you with a marvelous slide sorter where you can shuffle pages and reorder them in a page sequence suited to your needs. Now with an opportunity to view page thumbnails in much larger views, you can easily see the content of text-only pages when no visible icons or graphics are present to distinguish differences in page content. Reorganizing pages in earlier versions of Acrobat was a little more difficult because of having to view text pages in small thumbnail views; however, now you can manage page order more easily by zooming in on pages to clearly view the content.

To rearrange pages in a PDF document, open the Pages panel to the full width of your monitor by dragging the right side of the pane to the far right of the Document pane. Open a context menu in the Pages panel and select Enlarge Page Thumbnails. Repeat the steps to enlarge the thumbnail views to a size that enables you to read text comfortably on the pages.

Click on a page and drag the page to a spot between the pages where you want to relocate the selected page. When you move a page around the Pages panel, a vertical bar appears where the page will be located. If the highlight bar is positioned in the area where you want to relocate a page, release the mouse button. Figure 16.8 shows page 7 selected. The page is moved to the area after page 3. Notice the vertical highlight bar appearing to the right side of page 3.

> **TIP** If you want to move pages between pages not in view in the Pages tab, move a page down or up and the pages scroll to reveal hidden pages. Keep the mouse button depressed until you find the location where you want to move a page.

To select multiple pages, click a page to select it. Hold down the Shift key and click another page. If you want to select a block of contiguous pages, click the first page to be selected, hold down the Shift key, and click the last page within the group. All pages between the two selected pages are included in the selection. For noncontiguous selections, hold down the Ctrl/Option key to individually add random pages to a selection. After you make your selection, click one of the selected pages and drag to a new location to reorder the pages.

FIGURE 16.8

To move a page in a PDF document, click a thumbnail and drag it to the area where you want to relocate the page. When you see a vertical highlight bar appear in the desired location, release the mouse button.

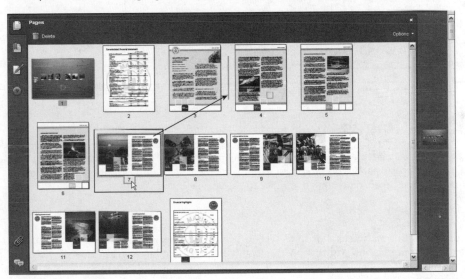

> **TIP** For a super slide sorter, open the Pages panel and view thumbnails in a large size. Place the mouse cursor over the vertical bar to the right of the Pages panel and drag to the right of your monitor screen. Press the F8 and F9 keys to hide the menu bar and toolbars. Resize the viewing window to fit the screen size. You'll get as much real estate on your monitor as possible. Shuffling pages is much easier in Acrobat than in almost any other program.

Copying pages

You can copy and paste pages within a PDF document or from one open PDF document to another. To copy a page with thumbnails, hold down the Ctrl/Option key as you drag a page to a new location in the same PDF file. Release the mouse button when you see the vertical highlight bar appear at the desired location. To copy a page from one PDF to another, open both PDF files and view them tiled either vertically or horizontally. The Pages panel must be in view on both PDF documents. Click and drag the thumbnail from one file to the Pages panel in the other document. The vertical highlight bar appears and the cursor changes, as shown in Figure 16.9. After the vertical bar is positioned at the desired location, release the mouse button, and the page drops into position.

CROSS-REF To learn how to tile PDF documents, see Chapter 4.

FIGURE 16.9

Dragging a thumbnail to a new location or copying between documents displays a vertical highlight bar where the page is placed.

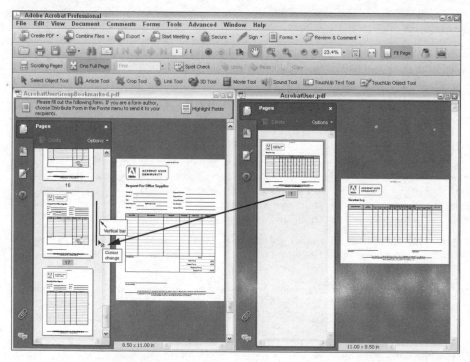

Removing pages

The previous example behaves like a copy-and-paste sequence. You can also create a cut-and-paste action whereby the page is deleted from one PDF document and copied to another. To remove a page and place it in another PDF file, hold the down Ctrl/Option key and then click-and-drag the page to another Pages panel in another file. The page is deleted from the original file and copied to the second file.

> **CAUTION** Be certain not to confuse the shortcut keys. If Control/Option is used in the page thumbnails on one document with click and drag, the page is copied. If using the same keys between two documents, the page is deleted from the file of origin and copied to the destination file.

To delete a page with the Pages panel, use a context-sensitive menu or the panel Options pull-down menu. Select a single thumbnail or Shift+click to select multiple thumbnails in a contiguous order (Ctrl/⌘+click for a noncontiguous order), and select Delete Pages from the context menu. This command opens the Delete Pages dialog box, as shown in Figure 16.10.

In the Delete Pages dialog box, by default the selected page is marked for deletion. You can make a change in the dialog box by selecting the From button and entering a contiguous page number range in the field box. The Selected radio button deletes all pages selected in the Pages panel. You can click and select pages in a contiguous or noncontiguous group. After you select the pages you want to delete, click OK. The selected pages are deleted from the document.

FIGURE 16.10

When you select Delete Pages from the Pages context menu, the Delete Pages dialog box opens. Click OK to delete the selected pages.

Modifying Pages

In this context, *modifying pages* refers to the PDF page in its entirety and not individual page elements. Rather than look at changing single items on a page, such as text and graphics, this section examines some of the features for structuring pages as an extension of the commands found in the Pages panel. Page editing discussed here relates to the insertion, extraction, and replacement of PDF pages.

> **NOTE** Most of the page-editing commands you have available in a context menu opened on a page thumbnail also appear in the Document menu. The commands for Insert Pages, Extract Pages, Replace Pages, Delete Pages, Crop Pages, and Rotate Pages appear in both menus.

Before you go about creating a huge PDF document with links and buttons, understanding how Acrobat structures a page and related links is imperative. Bookmarks and other links are often created within a PDF document as user-defined navigation. Acrobat handles thumbnails and the link to the respective pages without user intervention. You have no control over the links from a thumbnail to respective pages.

> **CROSS-REF** For information on creating Bookmarks and links, see Chapter 22.

With regard to links and Bookmarks, think of Acrobat as having a background and an overlay — the navigation items are placed on the overlay and page content is placed on the background (or layers in a PDF having Adobe PDF Layers). In regard to a single-layer PDF document, links appear as if on an overlay over the background. When viewing a PDF file, you don't see the navigation items independent of page content. This said, when you delete a page, all the links to the page are lost. Acrobat makes no provision to go to the page that follows a deleted page when links are deleted. Therefore, if you set up a Bookmark to page 4 and later delete page 4, the Bookmark has no place to go. Such links are commonly referred to as *dead links*.

When editing pages in Acrobat, you can choose to insert a page, delete a page, extract a page, and replace a page. If you understand the page structure, you'll know which option is right for your situation. Choices described in the Pages Options menu permit access to each of the following options by enabling you to select commands from the Document menu, or by proving a context-sensitive menu (as shown earlier in Figure 16.7) while clicking a thumbnail in the Pages panel.

CAUTION The menu commands for page editing are available only when you work with PDF documents that are not password protected, which prohibits page editing. If you attempt to edit pages in a secure PDF document, Acrobat prompts you for a password if the file is password protected. This behavior applies to all the options listed here.

The page-editing options in a context menu opened on a page thumbnail (not the empty space in the Pages panel) include the following:

- **Insert Pages.** When you select this option, the Select File to Insert dialog box opens. Select a file to insert, and click the Select button in the dialog box. The Insert Pages dialog box opens next, enabling you to choose the location for the insertion regardless of the current page viewed (see Figure 16.11). You can choose to insert a page either before or after the page in view, within a page range, or before or after the first or last page. Inserted pages do not affect any links in your document. All the pages shift left or right, depending on whether you select the Before or After option.

FIGURE 16.11

The Insert Pages dialog box enables you to locate the page that precedes or follows another page for the target location.

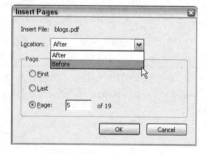

- **Delete Pages.** When you delete a page, you delete not only its contents but also its links. If a link or Bookmark is linked to a view in the deleted page, all links to the page become inoperable. When creating a presentation in Acrobat with multiple pages, you must exercise care when deleting pages to be certain links aren't broken.

Select a single thumbnail or multiple thumbnails in the Pages panel. Pages can be selected in a contiguous or noncontiguous selection. Open a context menu or the Options pull-down menu and select the Delete Pages command. The Delete Pages dialog box opens where you can delete the selected pages by leaving the default Selected radio button active or by selecting a page range and clicking OK.

Acrobat opens a warning dialog box to confirm your choice. If you change your mind and want to keep the pages, click the Cancel button. To continue with the page deletion, click OK.

> **TIP** If you begin an editing session and work on files where you insert and delete pages frequently, you may find the confirmation dialog box annoying. To eliminate the dialog box opening every time you delete a page, open the Preferences dialog box (Ctrl/⌘+K). Click General in the left pane and select the box for Do not show edit warnings in the right pane. When you return to the Document pane, all subsequent page deletions are performed without the warning dialog box opening. Be certain to exercise care when targeting pages for deletion if you are not using the edit warnings. When you want to bring back the edit warnings, open the General preferences and click Reset All Warnings.

- **Extract Pages.** Extracting a page is like pulling out single or multiple pages and creating a new PDF file with them. Extracting pages has no effect on Bookmarks or links for the destination pages in the original document unless you delete pages when extracting them. All links are operable for pages among the extracted pages. For example, if you extract ten pages with Bookmarks to each page, all the Bookmarks within the extracted pages are functional in the new file. If you have a Bookmark to a page not part of the extraction, the link is not operational.

  When you select the Extract Pages command, the Extract Pages dialog box opens, as shown in Figure 16.12. You supply the page range in the From/To field boxes and check boxes exist for Delete Pages After Extracting and Extract Pages As Separate Files. You can select these two options individually or together when extracting pages.

  Pages are extracted and deleted from the original file when you select Extract Pages and you check the box for Delete Pages After Extracting. The new pages open in the foreground as a single PDF document and remain unsaved until you use the Save or Save As command.

  The other option you have in the Extract Pages dialog box is Extract Pages As Separate Files. Check this box to extract pages and save them to your hard drive instead of having them open in the Document pane. When you select the page range and click OK after checking the box to create separate files, a Browse For Folder dialog box opens, enabling you to select a target folder for the saved files. Check the box for Delete Pages After Extracting and pages are deleted from the original file after the new files are saved. Each page you select for extraction is saved as a separate file.

FIGURE 16.12

If you want to delete the pages extracted from the original file, check the box for Delete Pages After Extracting. Checking the box for Extract Pages As Separate Files saves each page as a separate PDF to your hard drive.

- **Replace Pages.** This option affects only the contents of a PDF page — the overlay is unaffected. If you have links going to or from the replaced page, all links or interactive content are preserved. When editing PDF documents where page contents need to be changed, redistilled, and inserted in the final document, always use the Replace Pages command.

Replace Pages is particularly helpful when recreating Acrobat PDF forms. If you create a form in an authoring program and add all the form fields in Acrobat, and then later decide you want to edit the form design, replacing the old design with a new design preserves the form fields.

You can click a single page thumbnail or select multiple pages in a contiguous order and open a context menu. Select Replace Pages to open the Select File With New Pages dialog box. Navigate to the file containing pages that are to replace pages in the open file, and click Select.

The Replace Pages dialog box opens. In the Original area of the dialog box shown in Figure 16.13, you select the page range in the open document for the target pages to be replaced. In the Replacement section of the Replace Pages dialog box, you select the first page number of the document selected in the Select Pages to Replace dialog box. The readout to the right of the field box automatically displays the range of pages that are targeted for replacement. At the bottom of each section, notice the filename listed for the open document and the selected document.

If you disabled the edit warnings, the pages are replaced according to the selection made in the Replace Pages dialog box. If the edit warnings are not disabled (in this case, the check box isn't selected in the General preferences dialog box), a confirmation dialog box opens. Click OK to replace the pages.

TIP You can replace pages through drag-and-drop operations when viewing two documents in tiled views and when the Pages panel is opened for both documents. When you drag a page or a number of selected pages, move the cursor in the target document on top of the number below the thumbnail for the first page to be replaced. Rather than place the cursor between pages where the highlight bar is shown, be certain to drop the selection on top of the page number. The target page is highlighted in black when the cursor appears directly over the page number.

FIGURE 16.13

Specify the page range for the pages to be replaced in the first two field boxes. Enter the page number for the first page in the target file.

You can approach page editing in Acrobat in many ways. Using the Pages panel helps you access menu commands quickly. You can also access the commands just discussed with the Pages panel collapsed by choosing the commands from the Document menu. In addition, you can open multiple documents, view them with horizontal or vertical tiling, and drag-and-drop pages to accomplish the same results. To help in understanding how page editing with tiled views is accomplished, try following these steps for a little practice.

Appending Pages to PDF Documents

If you want to create a PDF document by combining multiple files that may have been created from multiple authors and multiple authoring programs, you can choose some alternatives in Acrobat that permit you to concatenate files to form a single PDF document.

When you use the Insert Pages command, the Select File to Insert dialog box enables you to select multiple files stored in a single folder. You can select multiple files by holding down the Shift key and clicking on the target files in a listed order from within a folder, or pressing the Ctrl/⌘ key to select files in a noncontiguous order.

However, when you use the Insert Pages command, the order of the files are appended to the open PDF file, which does not follow the same file order you viewed in the list in the Select File to Insert dialog box. You have no control over rearranging the order or selecting additional files from within separate folders. Additionally, you can't add PDFs having security, forms created in Adobe Designer, or digital signatures. You can't retain form field data in multiple PDF forms having identical form data field attributes.

A much better alternative to use when appending pages is the new Acrobat 8 Combine Files task button and in some cases the new Assemble Files into PDF Package option. Combining files permits you to establish the page order for the files you combine into one PDF document. It also enables you to choose specific pages within each PDF to add to a single PDF document. The Assemble Files into PDF Package option permits you to assemble files into one document when you need to add PDFs having security, adding files with digital signatures, adding PDF forms created in Adobe LiveCycle Designer, and when aggregating forms among files having identical field names.

To review a thorough coverage on combining files using the new Acrobat 8 Combine Files task button and creating PDF Packages, see Chapter 12. For a complete description on merging multiple e-mails together in a PDF Package, see Chapter 8.

STEPS: Editing pages with thumbnails

1. **Open two PDF documents where pages need to be arranged in a third document.** As an example for page editing, assume you have two files that need selected pages merged in a new, third file. Some of the pages need only to be copied to the new file and some pages need to be copied and deleted from the source document.

2. **Create a new blank page.** Select File ➪ Create PDF ➪ From Blank Page.

3. **Tile the page views.** Choose Window ➪ Tile ➪ Vertically (or Ctrl/⌘+Shift+L). Click the Pages panel in each file to open the panes. The two files you opened and the new file you created should appear similar to Figure 16.14.

4. **Replace a page.** The new document you created contains a blank page. One of the cover pages in the opened files is used as the cover in the new document. Select a page from one of the open document's Pages panel and drag the page to the top of *number 1* in the new document. When the page is targeted for replacement, the entire page is highlighted in black, as shown in Figure 16.14.

FIGURE 16.14

The two opened files and the new file appear with the Pages panels open. Drag a thumbnail image to the target file and place the cursor on top of the page number. Release the mouse button when the page turns black.

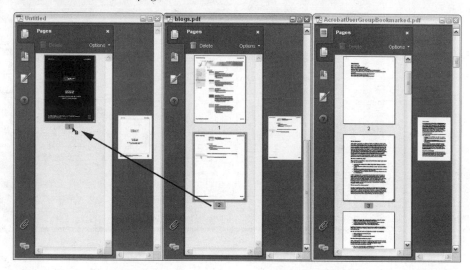

5. **Insert pages.** Select a page in one of the open documents. Press the Ctrl/⌘ key and click on pages in a noncontiguous order. Release the modifier key and drag one of the selected pages below the title page in the new document. Wait until you see a highlight bar appearing below the page before releasing the mouse button.

6. **Extract pages with deletion.** Move to the second open file. In this document you copy pages to the new document while deleting them from the source document. Click on a contiguous or noncontiguous group of pages to select them. Press the Ctrl/Option key and drag the pages to the new document's Pages panel. Pages are inserted in the new file and deleted from the source document.

7. **Close the original source documents.** Click the close button or choose File ➪ Close to close the documents. If you want to save the file where you extracted and deleted pages, save the document and close the file.

8. **Sort the pages.** Open the Pages panel by dragging the right side of the pane to the right side of the Acrobat window. Open a context menu and select Enlarge Page Thumbnails. Repeat the steps to enlarge pages until you have a comfortable view of the page content. Click and drag pages around the Pages panel to reorder the pages, as shown in Figure 16.15.

9. **Save the file.** Choose File ➪ Save As. Supply a filename and select a destination in the Save As dialog box. Click the Save button.

FIGURE 16.15

Open the Pages panel and move the pages to the desired order.

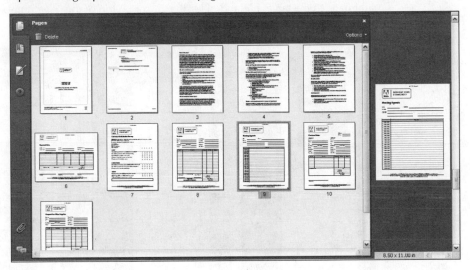

Save your work periodically if you have a major editing job. When you create a new file with the Create PDF ➪ From Blank Page command, Acrobat creates a new Untitled document, but the file is not actually saved to disk until you save the file. Save the file after a few edits; then repeat the Save command as you work on the file. When you finish the job, choose File ➪ Save As and rewrite the file. Page editing can add a lot of unnecessary data to a file during an editing job. When you rewrite the file, much of the redundancy is eliminated and the file size is reduced.

CROSS-REF For information on rewriting files with the Save As command, see Chapter 11.

Cropping Pages

Crop Tool In the Advanced Editing toolbar, you find the Crop tool. Cropping pages in Acrobat is performed with the Crop tool, Document ➪ Crop Pages, the Crop tool on the Print Production toolbar, or by selecting a menu command from the Pages panel. You can select the Crop tool and draw a marquee in the document window to define the crop region, double-click on the Crop tool in the Advanced Editing toolbar, or select the Crop Pages command from a context menu or panel menu in the Pages panel. Regardless of which manner you select to crop pages, the Crop Pages dialog box opens, as shown in Figure 16.16.

FIGURE 16.16

The Crop Pages dialog box displays a thumbnail image of the document page and offers options for crop margins and page ranges.

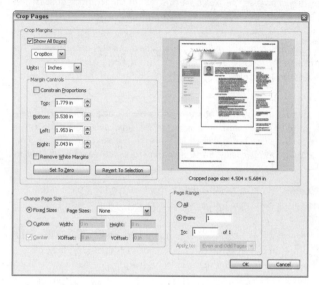

 **To quickly access the Crop Pages dialog box, double-click the Crop tool.**

If you don't use the Crop tool from the Advanced Editing toolbar, the Crop Pages dialog box opens with no crop zone specified. You can edit the margins numerically where a keyline border displays the crop area dynamically as you change the margins. When you use the Crop tool, open a rectangle marquee and move the mouse cursor inside the rectangle. The cursor changes to a selection arrow, indicating that you can double-click the mouse button to open the Crop Pages dialog box. The Crop Pages dialog box enables you to refine the page cropping. You can select from the following options:

- **Crop Margins.** Four radio button options are available. When you choose one of the options, the keyline border displaying the crop region changes color according to the option selected. The four options are as follows:

  - **CropBox.** This is the default selection. It is shown with a black keyline for the cropped page when displayed or printed.

  - **ArtBox.** The Art box is shown with a red rectangle. The Art box size includes the entire bounding box for the page size.

  - **TrimBox.** The Trim box is shown with a green rectangle. Trim areas are usually determined by the printer's marks indicating the finished paper size. The paper trim is made inside the bleed box.

  - **BleedBox.** When you select the Bleed option, the keyline showing the crop area is blue. Bleeds allow colors to extend off the finished page size to account for paper trimming sizes.

- **Show All Boxes.** Displays the Crop, Trim, Bleed, and Art boxes.

- **Units.** From the pull-down menu select a unit of measure. The options include Points, Picas, Millimeters, Centimeters, and Inches.

- **Margin Controls.** Choices for margins are available for each side of the page. In the field boxes for each side, you can use the up or down arrows and watch a preview in the thumbnail at the top of the dialog box. As you press the up or down arrow, the margin line is displayed in the thumbnail. If you want to supply numeric values, enter them in the field boxes.

- **Constrain Proportions.** Check the box to keep proportions constrained. As you edit one text box in the Margin Controls, Acrobat supplies the same value in the remaining text boxes. For example, if you add one inch in the Top text box, Acrobat adds 1 inch to the Bottom, Left, and Right text boxes.

> **TIP**   To quickly adjust margins you can click in any field box and press the up and down arrow keys on your keyboard. The margins jump in increments according to the units selected from the Units pull-down menu. Press the Shift key and arrow keys and the margins jump to the next whole unit. For example, when inches are used for the units of measure, pressing Shift plus an arrow changes the amount in whole inches.

- **Remove White Margins.** Acrobat makes an effort to eliminate white space on the page outside any visible data. Acrobat's interpretation is confined to true white space. If a slight bit of gray appears as a border, it is not cropped.

- **Set to Zero.** This choice resets the crop margins to zero. If you change the dimensions with either of the preceding settings and want to regain the original dimensions of the crop boundary, click the Set to Zero button. From here you can redefine the margins. This button behaves much like a Reset button in other image editing programs.

- **Revert To Selection.** If you open a crop range and open the dialog box, and then change the margins or click the Set to Zero button, the crop rectangle is restored to the size it was when the dialog box was opened. That is, it's restored to the original crop area. The view displays the crop area within the current page. In other words, the thumbnail preview displays the entire page with the crop area indicated by a red rectangle.

- **Change Page Size.** You can change page sizes to standard fixed sizes by selecting options from the Page Sizes pull-down menu. You can also click the Custom radio button and the field boxes for Height and Width become active. Change values in the field boxes to create custom page sizes. When you add printer's marks to a page or document, you can crop the page(s) larger than the page size to accommodate adding printers marks.

> **CROSS-REF**   For more information on adding printers marks and cropping pages, see Chapters 8 and 32.

> **TIP**   If you want to see a larger view of what's happening on your PDF document while making adjustments in the Crop Pages dialog box, such as changing the page sizes, move the dialog box aside, and the background display in the Document pane dynamically updates to reflect many changes made in the Crop Pages dialog box.

- **Page Range.** Pages identified for cropping can be handled in the Page Range options. If All is selected, all pages in the PDF file are cropped according to the sizes you specify in the dialog box. You can target specific pages for cropping by entering values in the From and To field boxes. You select choices for Even and Odd Pages, Even Pages Only, and Odd Pages Only from the *Apply to* pull-down menu. The Selected option is available when you select page thumbnails in the Pages palette. If you select pages in the Pages palette, use the Document ➪ Crop Pages menu command. Using the Crop tool can deselect page thumbnails and the Selected option appears grayed out when the Crop Pages dialog box opens.

When creating PDFs for slide presentations or screen views, you may occasionally have an unwanted white border around the pages. This appearance may result from creating pages in layout or illustration programs when the image data doesn't precisely match the page size. To polish up the pages and eliminate any white lines, double-click the Crop tool or select the tool and double-click on the page. In the Crop Pages dialog box, select Remove White Margins and then select All for the page range. When the pages are cropped, the excess white lines are removed.

Cropping pages does not eliminate data from the PDF document regardless of whether you use the Save or Save As command. If you return to the Crop Pages dialog box either after cropping or after cropping and saving, reopen the file and select Set To Zero. The PDF page is restored to the original size.

If you want to eliminate the excess data retained from the Crop tool, you can open the PDF in either Adobe Photoshop (for raster only images) or Adobe Illustrator (for PDFs having images and objects and/or text). Both programs honor the cropped regions of PDF files cropped in Acrobat. When you open a cropped page in either program, resave it as a PDF. Open the PDF in Acrobat. When you use the Crop tool and select the Set To Zero button, the page no longer has data remaining outside the page dimensions. The new file size saved from Photoshop or Illustrator is smaller due to elimination of the excess data. If you crop raster images such as photos, you can save the PDF in an image file format such as TIFF. After saving the file, use the Create PDF From File command and open the TIFF image in Acrobat. The cropped region is eliminated and the file size is reduced proportional to the cropped image size. (Note that alternately you can export image files from Acrobat in TIFF or JPEG format, the select Create PDF From File and convert back to PDF. The excess cropped areas are eliminated when you use this method too).

Rotating Pages

PDF documents can contain many pages with different page sizes. You can have a business card, a letter-sized page, a tabloid page, and a huge poster all contained in the same file. Depending on the authoring program of an original document and the way a PDF is created, you may experience problems with pages appearing rotated or inverted. Acrobat offers you tools to rotate pages for viewing and printing solutions to correct such appearance problems.

You rotate pages with the Document ➪ Rotate Pages menu command or in the Pages panel via context or Options menus. When you select Rotate Pages through any of these methods, the Rotate Pages dialog box opens. You choose the direction of rotation from a pull-down menu that enables you to rotate the page three different ways, as shown in Figure 16.17. Options in the Rotate Pages dialog box include the following:

- **Direction.** Three choices appear from the Direction pull-down menu. Select from rotating pages clockwise 90 degrees, counterclockwise 90 degrees, or 180 degrees. Selecting clockwise or counterclockwise repeatedly rotates the page in 90-degree rotations.

- **Page Range.** Select All to rotate all pages in the PDF document.

- **Selection.** If you select page thumbnails in the Pages tab and select Rotate Pages from a context menu or by selecting Document ➪ Rotate Pages, the Rotate Pages dialog box offers you an option for rotating selected pages.

- **Pages.** Enter the page range you want to rotate in the From and To field boxes.

- **Rotate.** The pull-down menu for Rotate offers selections for Even and Odd Pages, Even Pages Only, or Odd Pages Only. The last pull-down menu offers choices for Portrait Pages, Landscape Pages, or Pages of Any Orientation.

> **NOTE** Rotate Pages is a menu command found in the menus discussed previously. When you rotate pages with a menu command, the pages are rotated and you can save the PDF with the new rotated appearances. You also have tools in the Page Display toolbar used for rotating views. When you use these tools to rotate a view, the page rotation is a temporary view and cannot be saved.

FIGURE 16.17

The Rotate Pages dialog box offers options for rotating pages in a range or by selecting even or odd pages. The Even/Odd choices can be helpful when printing to devices requiring page rotations for duplexing.

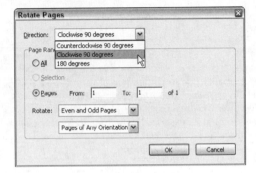

Rotating PDF elements

When you rotate a page, all page content is rotated. If you have any layers, visible or hidden, they are rotated. Acrobat provides no means for rotating individual layers.

If you create comments on a page and later rotate the page, the comment notes rotate at the point of origin, but the note displays are not rotated. For example, if you create a comment note in the top-left corner of a page and rotate the page 90 degrees counterclockwise, the note icon on the page is rotated, eventually ending up in the lower-left corner of the page. However, the open note is viewed at the default view with the note text in its original orientation.

Form fields behave differently than notes. If you create a form field containing text, the field and contents are rotated with the page.

Minimizing rotation problems

Among the major problems with PDF page rotation involves creating PDFs from layout programs. Layout programs such as Adobe InDesign or QuarkXPress enable you to transverse pages in the Print dialog box. This control is implemented for digital prepress and printing to high-end printing devices. In addition, many device PostScript Printer Description files (PPDs) used with high-end devices include transverse page options for page size selections.

CROSS-REF For more information on commercial printing and PPDs, see Chapter 32.

As an example, a portrait page that prints transversed is rotated 90 degrees to conserve media on roll-fed devices. If you print files to disk as PostScript and distill the files in Acrobat Distiller, don't transverse the pages. When transversed pages are opened in Acrobat, even though the auto rotate feature is enabled during distillation, Acrobat interprets the page coordinates with a 90-degree rotation. The end result is a zero point (0,0) located in the lower-right corner of the page. This interpretation can lead to problems when you're trying to define x,y coordinates for JavaScripts, replacing pages, and copying and pasting data between documents.

If you set up a landscape page in a layout program, print the file as a portrait page with the horizontal width described in field boxes for custom page sizes. Print the file to disk and distill in Acrobat Distiller. The end product is a PDF that winds up with the proper page orientation and is interpreted by Acrobat with the zero point (0,0) located in the default lower-left corner.

PREPRESS Design and print professionals who seek to print files from PDFs can create the PDFs without transversing pages. When printing the PDFs for prepress, use the Acrobat Print dialog box to control printing and select device PPDs from within Acrobat. If you need to repurpose documents for Web or screen presentations, you can use the same file created for prepress without having to reprint and redistill the authoring document.

CROSS-REF For more information on printing PostScript and using Acrobat Distiller, see Chapter 10.

Creating Headers and Footers

Headers and Footers can be used for adding page numbers, dates, and any custom data you want to add to a header and footer appearing on all or a range of pages.

The Add Header and Footer dialog box has been greatly improved in Acrobat 8. When you select Document ⇨ Header and Footer ⇨ Add, the Add Header and Footer dialog box opens, as shown in Figure 16.18. At first launch you can see a more improved dialog box compared to earlier versions of Acrobat. You'll notice the Add Header and Footer dialog box is the same dialog box you use when adding Bates numbers (see "Using Bates numbering" later in this chapter).

TIP The Add Header and Footer dialog box offers no provision for batch processing files. When you open the dialog box you're limited to adding headers and footers to the document open in the Document pane. If you want to add headers and footers to multiple documents, use the Advanced ⇨ Document Processing ⇨ Batch Processing command. Create a new batch sequence and use the Add Header and Footer command. For more on Batch Processing, see Chapter 18.

FIGURE 16.18

Select Document ➪ Add Header & Footer to open the Add Header and Footer dialog box.

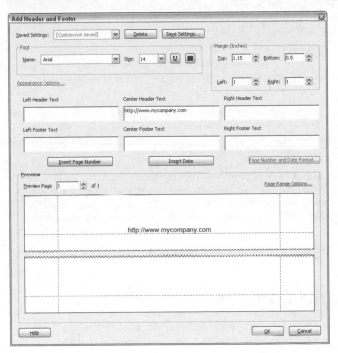

You create page headers and footers in this dialog box. Options exist for adding a date stamp, a page number, and a custom text description. In Figure 16.18, I added a Web address as a header to apply to all pages in my open document. Options for adding footers are identical to the settings provided for adding headers. Among your choices in the Add Headers and Footers dialog box are the following:

- **Saved Settings.** You can select options from the pull-down menu. By default no settings are listed in the menu. Make your settings adjustments in the dialog box and click Save Settings. Name your settings and they are added to the Saved Settings menu. If you want to delete a saved setting, select the setting and click the Delete button.

- **Font (Name).** All the system fonts available to you from your operating system are displayed in a pull-down menu. Click the down-pointing arrow and make your font choice. You can assign a different font to each line of text in the listed items in the six boxes below the menu.

- **Font (Size).** Font sizes can be assigned individually to each line of text. If you want custom text to appear larger than a date or page number, select the item after clicking an Insert button and choose a font size from the pull-down menu. You select a font from preset point sizes. You cannot edit the field box to add a point size other than the preset sizes.

- **Margins.** The four Margins field boxes are editable. You can physically position a header or footer at any location on a page. If you add a header, the options relate to the top, left, and right field boxes. Footers relate to all but the top field box. Entering values in the lower field box has no effect on the position where the text is added when adding headers. If you use top = 5 inches,

left = 3 inches, and select the left alignment radio button, the text is added 5 inches from the top and 3 inches from the left side.

Although a header or footer extending beyond the space shown in the Preview area (denoted by dashed lines) disappears from the preview, you can move data outside the guidelines by adding values in the Margins text box and click OK. When you view the PDF file, the data appear at the coordinates you described in the Margins text boxes.

■ **Appearance Options.** Six boxes are shown for adding data. The top row of three boxes is used for adding headers. The second row of three boxes across is used for adding footers. You can type custom text in any one of the six boxes.

■ **Insert Page Number.** Click the box in the Appearance Options where you want a date to appear and type the code used for a date format. The same five date formats you have available with page numbering are also available in the Add Headers and Footers dialog box. To select a date format, you can click the Page Number and Date Format link to the right of the Insert Date button (See Page Number and Date Format).

■ **Insert Date.** Follow the same steps as when adding a page number. First click in the box where you want the data to appear, then choose a date format and insert it.

■ **Page Number and Date Format.** The blue text is like a button. Click the text and the Page Number and Date Format dialog box opens, as shown in Figure 16.19. From pull-down menus you select formats for Date, Page number, and a page to start adding the header and/or footer.

FIGURE 16.19

Click Page Number and Date format to open the Page Number and Date Format dialog box.

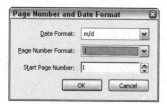

■ **Page Range Options.** By default, all pages are used when you add a page header and/or footer. You can control page ranges by clicking the Page Range Options blue text. Clicking the text opens the Page Range Options dialog box shown in Figure 16.20. Select Pages from and type values in the text boxes. From the subset pull-down menu you have All Pages, Even Pages Only, or Odd Pages Only.

FIGURE 16.20

Click Page Range Options to open the Page Range Options dialog box.

■ **Preview.** The Preview Page text box and up/down arrows permit you to scroll through the document. Below this item are the preview boxes for headers and footers. You cannot type in either of the boxes. They are used only for previewing data added in the top six boxes.

Click OK after adding data to a header and/or footer and the data are applied to your selected page range.

Updating headers and footers

Acrobat 8 makes it much easier to update and remove header/footer data than earlier versions of Acrobat. If you add or delete pages, the headers and footers are not dynamic and do not change when adding or deleting pages. You need to reedit the headers and footers to renumber pages deleted from a document or add header/footer data to pages inserted in your document. From the Document ➪ Header & Footer menu select Update. The Update Header and Footer dialog box opens. Options in this dialog box are identical to the Add Header and Footer dialog box.

The Update Header and Footer dialog box displays the exact same settings you used when you first added a header and/or footer. Just click OK if you want the update to be exactly the same as your original assignment of headers and footers, and the file is updated.

Removing headers and footers

In earlier versions of Acrobat the only way you could remove a background was to open the Add Header and Footer dialog box and return all settings to defaults, and then click OK. Acrobat essentially replaced your headers and footers with nothing. Now in Acrobat 8 you have a menu command specifically used for removing headers and footers. Select Document ➪ Header & Footer ➪ Remove. A dialog box opens prompting you to confirm the action. Click OK and your headers and footers are removed.

Numbering Pages

In Acrobat, page numbers appear in the Page Navigation toolbar at the top of the Acrobat window and in the Pages panel. When you open the Go To Page dialog box (View ➪ Go To ➪ Page or Ctrl/⌘+Alt/Option+N) and enter a value in the status bar and press Enter/Return, you may find that the destination page does not correspond with the page number you supplied in the dialog box. This is because certain documents may be numbered in sections where front matter, such as a table of contents, foreword, preface, and other such items precede the page numbering in a document. This is particularly true of books, pamphlets, essays, journals, and similar documents using numbering schemes other than integers for the front matter.

Numbering individual PDF documents

Pages in a PDF file can be renumbered using the Page Numbering dialog box that you access with a simple menu command. Open the Pages panel and open a context menu on a page thumbnail. From the menu options, select Number Pages. The Page Numbering dialog box opens, as shown in Figure 16.21.

FIGURE 16.21

The Page Numbering dialog box offers options for numbering pages.

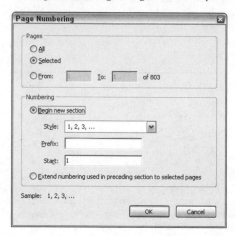

The Page Numbering dialog box offers options for selecting a range of pages and renumbering them in sections or throughout the entire document. The choices available to you include:

- **Pages.** This area of the dialog box asks you to specify the page range. If you want to renumber all pages with the same numbering scheme, select the All radio button. You might use this option when numbering pages numerically with integers.

  If you enable the radio button for Selected, only the pages selected in the Pages panel are affected. By default the Selected radio button is enabled if you click on a page or a page's thumbnail in the Pages panel and open the dialog box. If no page thumbnail is selected, the default radio button selection is From.

  Enable the From radio button and supply a page range in the field boxes to select a page range numerically according to page position in the document. That is to say, pages 1 to 10 are interpreted as the first 10 pages in the file regardless of the page numbering scheme used before you open the dialog box. Perhaps you want to create a separate scheme for a document's front matter. Specifying the scheme in the Numbering section of the dialog box renumbers the selection. Click OK to accept the changes. If you want to renumber another section, return to the dialog box and select a new section and new scheme. Repeat the process for all changes in page numbering according to different sections.

- **Numbering.** This portion of the dialog box offers you options for determining the page-numbering scheme you want to use. From the Style pull-down menu select a number style — the choices are shown in Figure 16.22.

  - **Style.** If None is selected, no page number is assigned to the page. The readout in the status bar would appear similar to this: (10 of 100). The numbers within the parentheses represent the original page number order preceded by a blank space where no number (None) is specified. If you want to add a prefix, you could add alphanumeric data to the Prefix field box and supply a prefix with no number. Using the same example, the readout would appear something like this: A000 (10 of 100), where A000 is the prefix and no number follows.

The remaining options in the Style pull-down menu are specific choices for styles of page numbers. If you have front matter where you want to use Roman numerals, you can choose between the two styles shown in Figure 16.22. Alpha characters offer you options for upper-case or lowercase letters, and integers are also available. You can combine these options with special characters by typing data in the Prefix field box.

FIGURE 16.22

Select number styles from the Style pull-down menu.

- **Prefix.** Type any character, number, or combination of numbers and characters in the field box for a prefix value. The prefix precedes the numbering scheme defined in the Style pull-down menu.
- **Start.** The Start item is used to indicate the number a new section starts with. Typically you use 1 to start a new section, but you can begin sections with any number you want to type in the field box. Upon occasion you may have a document where page insertions might be added later. You can number pages in a section leaving room for new additions to be made later in another editing session.
- **Extend numbering used in preceding section to selected pages.** For this option you need to select a range of page thumbnails in the Pages panel, and then open the Page Numbering dialog box. Selecting the radio button and clicking OK removes the currently assigned numbers and extends the previous section. For example, you may have Appendix A numbered A-1 through A-10. You later decide to combine Appendix B with Appendix A. Appendix B might be numbered B-1 through B-10. To extend the previous B numbered pages, you select the page thumbnails in the Pages panel, open the dialog box and select this radio button. When you click OK, pages formerly numbered B-1 through B-10 are changed to A-11 through A-20.

Using Bates numbering

Bates numbering is a method to keep multiple documents in a recognizable order. The legal industry uses Bates numbering when identifying legal documents in court cases. During the discovery phase of a case in litigation, there might be an enormous number of documents submitted as evidence. A Bates numbering system is used to provide an arbitrary unique identifier for each document. The numbers are typically numeric, but they can also be alphanumeric. There is no standardized algorithm used for a Bates numbering schema in a court case for assigning numbers to documents, however, the numbers are generally eight or more characters in length. An example of a schema that might be used to disclose documents in the legal environment is shown in Figure 16.23.

NEW FEATURE A new feature in Acrobat 8 now permits you to add Bates numbers to documents. Rather than open a PDF document in Acrobat and number each file individually, the Bates numbering feature lets you batch process multiple files and add unique numbers in a numeric order to multiple files without opening them.

An example of Bates numbers that might be used in a court case.

Company	Sequence	Length <char>	Example	Multi-page divider	Example Muli-page divider
Universal Gas & Electric	numeric	10	2005684511	slash /	1001453289/5049
Small Town USA	numeric	8	15678907	slash /	10296733/002194
ACE Construction	alphanumeric	11	ACE45876302	space dash	ACE04876932 -1189
Edwards Trust	alphanumeric	9	ETU45632	space asterisk	ETU94560 *1022
ATC	numeric	8	08145633	not applicable	Start Bates: 45350001 End Bates: 45350871
Ewings & Sons	numeric	10	0258942356	not applicable	Start Bates: 0250000001 End Bates: 0250009657
GC Equipment Corporation	numeric	7	2034537	dash	5635891-56890

To see how the new Bates numbering feature works in Acrobat, follow these steps.

STEPS: Adding Bates numbers to multiple PDFs

1. **Open the Bates Numbering dialog box.** Select Advanced ➪ Document Processing ➪ Bates Numbering ➪ Add. The Bates Numbering dialog box shown in Figure 16.24 opens.

2. **Select files to number.** Click the Browse button and select files you want to add to the Bates Numbering dialog box shown in Figure 16.24.

Click the Browse button to locate and add files you want to number.

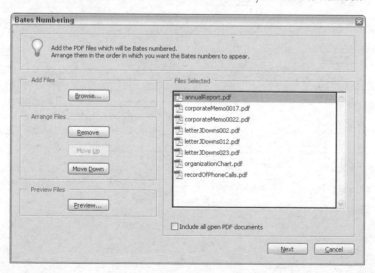

3. **Order the documents.** Click a document and click the Up or Down buttons to organize the files in the order you want them to appear. Because the Bates numbering system uses no standardized algorithm and the numbers are arbitrary, you don't need to worry about organizing files according to dates, topics, and so on. Simply make some order arrangement that you want based on whatever criteria you elect to use.

 TIP If you want to preview documents before adding numbers, click the Preview button.

4. **Click Next.**

5. **Add the number schema for the select documents.** When you click Next, a lightly modified version of the Add Header and Footer dialog box opens as shown in Figure 16.25. You can align the numbers left, center, or right by clicking in the Left, Center, or Right Header or Footer text box and then click the Insert Bates Number button.

When you click Insert Bates Number, the Bates Numbering System dialog box opens. Add the total digits (including alpha characters if you use alpha characters for a number schema) in the Number of Digits text box. You have an option to type the start number, a prefix, and a suffix. Click OK and the Bates number is shown in the field box respective to your selection. In Figure 16.25, I added a three character prefix and six numbers for my numbering schema.

FIGURE 16.25

Click inside the text box where you want your Bates numbers to appear and click Insert Bates Number. Add the numbering schema in the Bates Numbering System dialog box and click OK. Your Bates Numbering schema then appears in the text box.

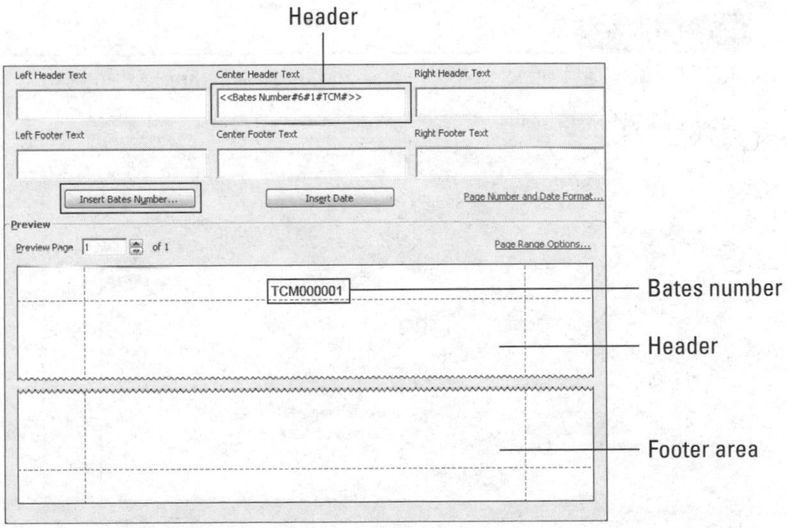

Header

Left Header Text	Center Header Text	Right Header Text
	<<Bates Number#6#1#TCM#>>	

Left Footer Text	Center Footer Text	Right Footer Text

[Insert Bates Number...] [Insert Date] Page Number and Date Format...

Preview

Preview Page [1] of 1 Page Range Options...

TCM000001 — Bates number

— Header

— Footer area

6. **Add the numbers to your selected documents.** Click OK in the Add Headers and Footers dialog box and the numbers are added to all the selected PDFs. In Figure 16.26, you see one of several files where I added a Bates number. Each number in all documents is a unique number following the schema I identified in the Add Header and Footer dialog box.

FIGURE 16.26

A file where the Bates number was added as a footer

Removing Bates numbers

When you select Document Processing ⇨ Bates Numbers, the submenu offers two menu commands. The first command is Add numbers as was used in the previous steps. Your second option is to Remove numbers. Click Remove and the same Bates Numbering dialog box shown earlier in Figure 16.24 opens. You follow the same process for removing Bates numbers as you do when adding them. Click the Add button and add the files you want to appear without the Bates numbers. You can choose the same files to remove Bates numbers from all documents or a selection of files within the same group you want to remove numbers. Click Next and Acrobat removes numbers only from the selected files in the Bates Numbering dialog box.

Packaging files with Bates numbers

If you want to group documents according to a certain Bates numbering schema, first use the Bates Numbering dialog box and add Bates numbers to all your PDF documents. Next, use the Assemble Files into a PDF Package option in the Combine Files task button menu. Create a PDF Package and all your files are assembled in one package with Bates numbers. In Figure 16.27, you can see an example of a PDF Package with Bates numbers.

CROSS-REF For information on how to create PDF Packages, see Chapter 12.

FIGURE 16.27

Bates numbers as they appear in a PDF Package

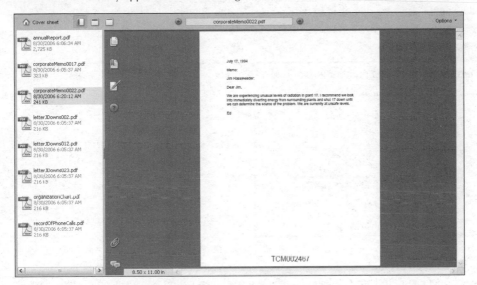

Adding Watermarks and Backgrounds

You add watermarks and backgrounds in different dialog boxes in Acrobat 8, but the attributes for both items are almost identical. A few options are different in the Add Watermark dialog box where you can add custom data in addition to importing files. You can also add a watermark in front of or behind page data. Backgrounds are only added behind page data.

Adding backgrounds

To add a background to a PDF document, choose Document ➪ Background ➪ Add/Replace. The Add Background dialog box opens, as shown in Figure 16.28.

FIGURE 16.28

Choose Document ➪ Background Add/Replace to open the Add Background dialog box.

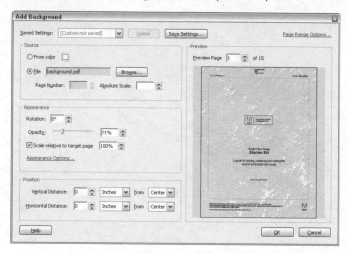

Choices you have for adding backgrounds include the following:

- **Saved Settings.** The options here are the same as when adding headers and footers. See the section "Creating headers and footers" earlier in this chapter.

- **Page Range Options.** Click the text and the Page Range Options dialog box opens. The same dialog box with the same options is opened as when adding headers and footers. See the section "Creating headers and footers" earlier in this chapter.

- **Source.** Choose From color or File to add a background color or import a file.

NEW FEATURE Click the From color radio button and a color palette opens where you make a color choice to apply as a background color. This is a new feature in Acrobat 8.

Click File and click the Browse button. The Browse dialog box opens where you select a file to import. File types supported include PDF documents, BMP, and JPEG. Note that choices for adding text along with a background are not available in Acrobat 8. Because the Add Watermark feature appears in a different dialog box, all text options are available only in the Add Watermark dialog box.

- **Appearance.** Several different options are listed in the Appearance settings. These include:
  - **Rotation.** You can rotate backgrounds in 1-degree increments by typing values in the Rotation text box or clicking the up and down arrows.
  - **Opacity.** Opacity adjustments are made by moving the slider, typing values in the text box, or clicking the up and down arrows. In Figure 16.29, objects were rotated in two separate documents. The object on the left was rotated +45 degrees. The object on the right was rotated +135 degrees with an opacity of 20%.

FIGURE 16.29

Rotations of 45 and 135 degrees. The figure on the right is adjusted for a 20% opacity.

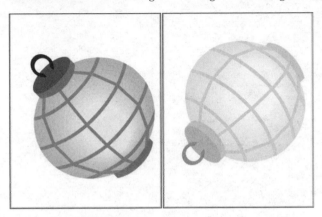

- **Scale relative to target page**. By default, the scaling is set to 100%. Type a value in the text box for scaling up or down to the desired value.

- **Appearance Options**. Click the Appearance Options blue text and the Appearance Options dialog box opens, as shown in Figure 16.30. In the dialog box you can toggle on and off showing backgrounds when printing and when displayed on your monitor.

FIGURE 16.30

Click the Appearance Options blue text to open the Appearance Options dialog box. Check the boxes to show or hide a background when printing and when displaying on screen.

- **Position**. Set options for the position of the background by typing values in the text boxes for Vertical Distance and Horizontal Distance. From the first set of pull-down menus, select a unit of measure. The second set of pull-down menus lets you position the vertical and horizontal placement from Top, Center, and Bottom. In Figure 16.31, the position of an object with the Vertical Distance menu options is shown first and the Horizontal Distance menu options is shown second. It also shows how the objects fall on a page when making the menu choices.

- **Preview Page**. In the preview area, you see a page preview of an imported background (or background color if you click the From color radio button). The Preview Page text box is used to type a page number and the respective page appears in the Preview window. You can toggle through all pages and view the page previews before applying a background. Click OK in the Add Background dialog box and the background is added to pages in the selected page range.

FIGURE 16.31

Nine different positions are available from the pull-down menu choices for Vertical and Horizontal placements.

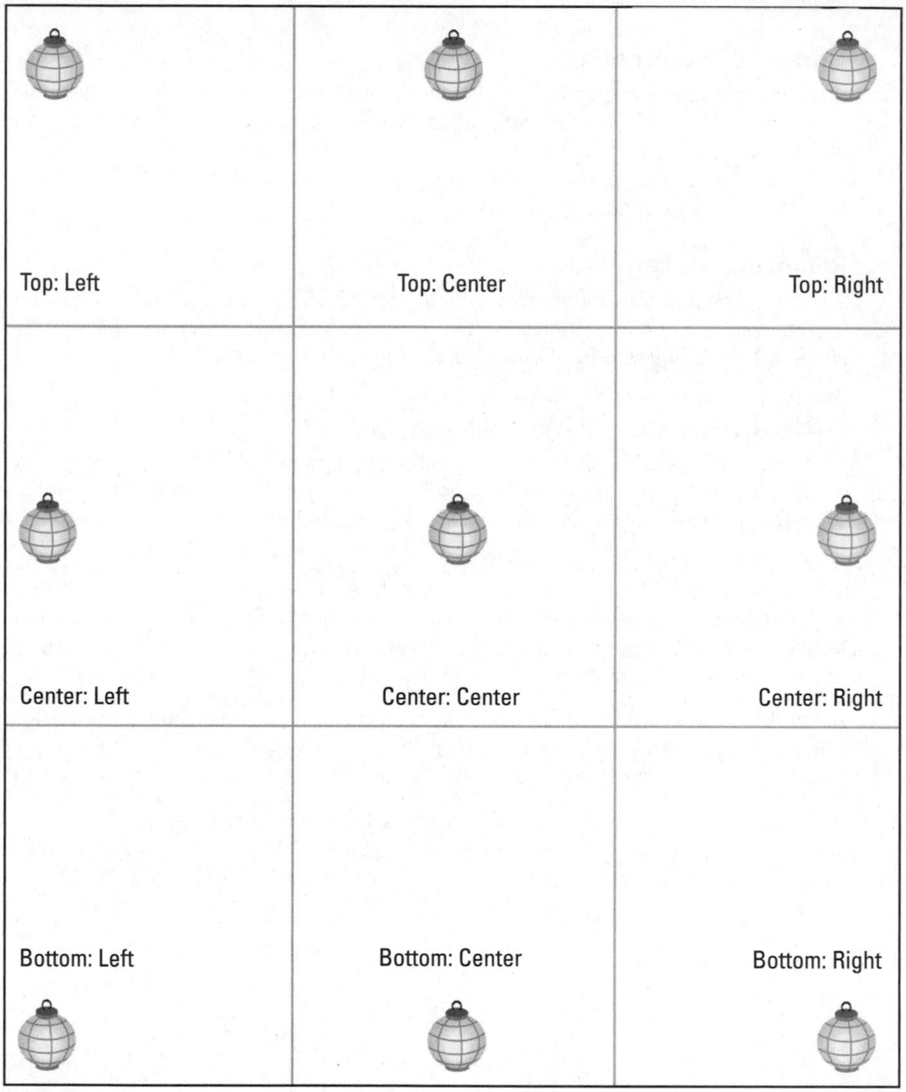

Top: Left	Top: Center	Top: Right
Center: Left	Center: Center	Center: Right
Bottom: Left	Bottom: Center	Bottom: Right

Replacing backgrounds

From the Document ➪ Background menu, the item for adding backgrounds and replacing backgrounds opens the same dialog box. Select Document ➪ Background ➪ Add/Replace and follow the same steps used for adding a background. If a file contains a background, the new background you select from either a color or a file replaces the old background.

Updating backgrounds

If you add a background to a PDF file from an image file, and then edit the image file and select Document ➪ Background ➪ Update, Acrobat won't update the edited background. A dynamic link is not made from Acrobat to the image file. If you want to update a background imported from an image file, you need to click again on the Browse button and identify your edited image file. Add it as you add a new background and the PDF background is updated.

Removing backgrounds

As with the menu command for removing headers and footers, you also have a new command in Acrobat 8 for removing backgrounds. To remove the current background, select Document ➪ Background ➪ Remove and a dialog box opens. Click OK and the background is removed.

Adding watermarks

Select Document ➪ Watermark ➪ Add to add a watermark to a PDF. Watermarks generally appear on top of page data, but in Acrobat 8 you can chose to have a watermark appear on top or behind the page data. The Add Watermark dialog box that opens, as shown in Figure 16.32, is similar to the Add Background dialog box.

The Add Watermark dialog box contains a few different options than the Add Background dialog box. The first noticeable difference is the Source area in the Add Watermark dialog box. The first item and the default selection is Text. You have a text box where text is typed in the Add Watermark dialog box. Below the text box are some options for changing text attributes.

As yet, however, you don't have an option for creating outline text that would be helpful when creating watermarks. The only way to create outline text is to first create it in an illustration program such as Adobe Illustrator and import the text as a graphic in the Add Watermark dialog box.

In the appearance area of the Add Watermark dialog box, you find options for fixed rotations as well as arbitrary rotations. The Location options enable you to place your watermark behind or in front of the page data. The remaining choices are the same as those found in the Add Background dialog box.

FIGURE 16.32

Select Document ⇨ Watermark ⇨ Add to open the Add Watermark dialog box.

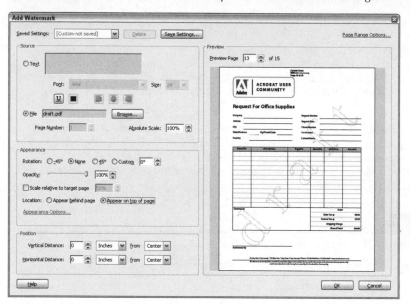

TIP Graphics placed behind page data only appear in transparent areas on the page. To quickly check what areas are transparent (as opposed to opaque), open the Preferences dialog box (Ctrl/⌘+K) and click Page Display in the left pane. Click the Show transparency grid check box in the right pane and click OK. All the areas appearing with transparency are shown in the Document pane.

To create a watermark on a PDF document, follow these steps.

STEPS: Adding a watermark to a PDF document

1. **Open a file in Acrobat.** Use any PDF document that you want to appear with a watermark.
2. **Open the Add Watermark dialog box.** Choose Document ⇨ Watermark ⇨ Add. The Add Watermark dialog box opens.
3. **Type text in the Text box.** In my example, I typed Draft in the text box I'll use for watermarking draft documents.
4. **Set Font attributes.** Select a font from the Font pull-down menu, select a font size, and click the color swatch and choose a color. Note that if you select a particular hue in the color palette and you want that hue to appear lighter, you can reduce opacity with the Opacity slider. For example, to make a light gray, select the default black color and set the opacity to 20 to 30 percent.
5. **Edit appearance settings.** In my example, I want the text rotated so I clicked the 45° radio button. I reduced the opacity of my black color selection to 30% and then I clicked the Scale relative to target page check box. This action scaled my text to fit the page size. Note that if you scale text to fit a page, any font size you select in the Source area of the dialog box works.

6. **Edit the location.** Determine whether you want your watermark on top of the page content or behind it. In my example, I want the watermark to appear behind my page data so I clicked the Appear behind page radio button.

7. **Preview pages.** Click the Preview Page arrows or type values in the text box to scroll through the pages you want to apply your watermark.

8. **Set Appearance Options.** Click the Appearance Options blue text to open the Appearance Options dialog box. Check the boxes to either show or not show the watermark when printing and screen viewing. Another check box is available to keep the watermark position and size constant on different page sizes. Check this box if you're working with files that have different page sizes and click OK.

   ■ **Set the Page Range.** Click the Page Range Options blue text in the top-right corner of the dialog box to open the Page Range Options dialog box. If you want all pages to appear with a watermark, you don't need to open this dialog box. If you want a page range less than all pages, type the page numbers in the from and to text boxes and click OK. My final settings adjustments are shown in Figure 16.33.

FIGURE 16.33

The Add Watermark dialog box after making settings adjustments

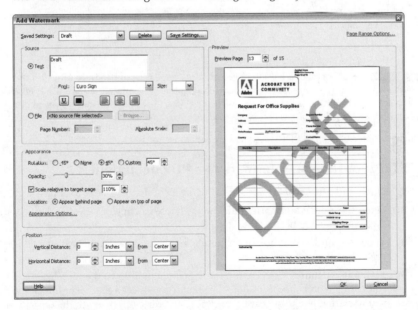

   ■ **Save the settings.** If this is a watermark you intend to reuse with other documents, you can save the settings and use them whenever you want to apply the same watermark. Click the Save Settings button at the top of the dialog box and the Save Settings dialog box opens. Type a name for your new setting and click OK. The new setting now appears under the Saved Settings pull-down. In Figure 16.34, I added my new Draft settings to the menu.

FIGURE 16.34

The Settings menu after I saved my Draft custom setting

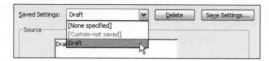

- **Click OK.** The watermark is applied to the page range you chose in the Page Range Options dialog box.

CROSS-REF If you don't want anyone to tamper with watermarks added to your PDF files such as changing or deleting them, you can secure your file against editing pages using Acrobat Security. For more information on how to secure PDFs, see Chapter 26.

Removing and updating watermarks

The options for removing and updating watermarks are the same as removing and updating Backgrounds. Select Document ➪ Watermarks and the submenu commands appear for Add, Update, and Remove. If you want to modify a saved setting, choose Document ➪ Watermark ➪ Update. Edit your settings and click OK. Acrobat updates all pages containing watermarks. Clicking Remove in the Watermark submenu opens the same dialog box as when removing backgrounds. Click OK and all watermarks are removed.

Note that if you want to remove backgrounds or watermarks from selected pages in a file while keeping backgrounds/watermarks on some pages, clicking the Remove menu item removes all watermarks/backgrounds from your document. You then need to add the watermarks/backgrounds to pages where you want them to appear.

When adding watermarks and backgrounds, you can't select pages in the Pages panel and apply watermarks/backgrounds to selected pages in the panel. You must use the Page Range dialog box to apply watermarks/backgrounds to a page range. Acrobat makes no provision for adding these items to noncontiguous pages. You have to individually apply watermarks/backgrounds to pages in a noncontiguous order.

TIP If you want to add a watermark or background on a form enabled with Adobe Reader usage rights, first apply the watermark or background to a PDF, and then enable the file with usage rights. If you attempt to add a watermark or background to an enabled file, you need to save a copy of the file, add the watermark or background, and then re-enable the file again. (For more information on enabling files with Adobe Reader extensions, see Chapter 19.)

Summary

- You can enlarge or reduce page thumbnails through successive menu commands in the Pages panel.
- You can open the Pages panel to full screen size where you can sort and reorder pages.
- Page thumbnails can be used to navigate pages and zoom in on pages.
- To copy pages in a PDF document and between PDF documents you can use page thumbnails.

- Page thumbnails are created on-the-fly when you open the Pages panel. If you want to speed up the screen refreshes when opening the Pages panel, you can embed thumbnails from a menu option in the Pages panel and delete them after your editing sessions.

- Pages are inserted, deleted, extracted, and replaced through menu commands from the Pages panel context menu or the pane pull-down menu.

- You crop PDF pages with the Crop tool. When you crop a page, the page view is reduced to the crop region, but all the original data in terms of page size is still contained in the file. You can return to the Crop Page dialog box and undo crops even after a file has been saved.

- You can rotate PDF pages in 90- and 180-degree rotations via menu commands in the Rotate Pages dialog box.

- Enabling a preference setting for viewing logical pages helps you navigate to pages numbered with integers.

- Opening the Page Numbering dialog box from a context menu in the Pages panel enables you to renumber pages in a PDF file.

- To number multiple PDF documents with consecutive numbering, use the Bates Numbering dialog box. To add page numbers to a collection of PDFs without consecutive numbers use the Batch Processing command.

- To add page numbers to a PDF document use the Add Header and Footer dialog box.

- You can add different headers and footers to different pages in a PDF document. Each time the content for headers and footers changes, you open the Add Header and Footer dialog box, add the content, and specify the page range.

- To add a background to a document use the Add Background dialog box. To add a watermark to a file, use the Add Watermark dialog box.

- Backgrounds and watermarks can be updated and removed using new menu commands introduced in Acrobat 8.

- After you save a PDF with a watermark and/or background, the data are embedded in the PDF document. In Acrobat 8, you can always return to a document and remove backgrounds and watermarks.

Chapter 17

Scanning and OCR Conversion

elcome to the world of one-stop scanning and text recognition. Anyone who scanned documents in earlier versions of Acrobat will appreciate the new one-step operation for scanning a text document and performing text recognition via Acrobat's Optical Character Recognition (OCR) engine. Now in Acrobat 8, you click a button to perform a scan and your document is converted to PDF with recognizable text automatically.

When performing a scan in either Acrobat Standard or Acrobat Professional, you are not limited to scanning documents for text conversions. Acrobat enables you to scan photos and images that might have some other uses. Therefore, this chapter covers all the aspects of scanning from within Acrobat using the Scan to PDF command and the Text Recognition commands.

Setting Up the Scanning Work Environment

For scanning and text recognition tasks, you need access to the TouchUp Text tool. First, reset the tools from a context menu opened from the Toolbar Well and choose Tools ➪ Advanced Editing ➪ Show Advanced Editing Toolbar. When the toolbar opens, dock it in the Toolbar Well. Note that if you want to eliminate some tools from the Advanced Editing toolbar such as the Movie tool, the Sound tool, and other tools not likely to be used when scanning documents, you can open the More Tools window and choose the toolset you want in the Advanced Editing toolbar.

During text recognition, you may want to create several views that enable you to zoom in to see words requiring edits. Tools handy for displaying different views are found in the Page Display toolbar. Open the Customize Toolbars window and check the boxes for Single page continuous and One Full Page as well as the Page Display Toolbar check box and click OK. Dock the toolbars in the Toolbar Well by opening a context menu on the Toolbar Well and select Dock All Toolbars.

IN THIS CHAPTER

Setting up a scanner

Scanning documents

Working with scanning settings

Scanning workflows

Correcting OCR errors

Copying and pasting OCR text

Scanning forms

Configuring Scanners

Before you can scan a page in Acrobat, you need to configure your scanner and be certain it functions properly. After you complete your installation of Acrobat, it should recognize your scanner immediately. If all the scanner hardware is in place and operational and Acrobat still does not recognize your scanner, the next step is to be certain the scanner's software is recognized by Acrobat. If Acrobat doesn't see your scanner, you may need to relocate software to another location on your hard drive or acquire a software update from your scanner manufacturer.

You get access to your scanner in Acrobat through one of two methods: TWAIN software or Acquire plug-ins.

TWAIN software

TWAIN (Technology With An Important Name) software is manufacturer-supplied and should be available on the CD-ROM you receive with your scanner. In Windows, the TWAIN files are stored in the \WINNT\twain_32 folder. When you install scanner software, the TWAIN driver should find the proper folder through the installer routine. On the Macintosh you'll find TWAIN resources in the System\Library\Image Capture\TWAIN Data Sources folder.

Many scanner manufacturers produce the equipment but use third-party developers to write the software. Adobe has certainly not tested the Scan plug-in with all scanner manufacturers and all software developers. Theoretically, the TWAIN software should work in all cases. If you have problems accessing your scanner from within Acrobat, but can perform scans in other applications, then you most likely have a problem with the TWAIN software. If this is the case, contact your scanner manufacturer and see whether it has an upgrade or whether you can get some technical support. In many cases, you can download upgrades for registered software on the Internet.

Adobe Photoshop plug-in software

Acrobat 8.0 supports Acquire plug-ins to use with Adobe Photoshop. More prevalent than TWAIN drivers, Photoshop plug-ins are available from just about every scanner manufacturer. If you use Adobe Photoshop or Adobe Photoshop Elements, you may need to copy your Photoshop Acquire plug-in to your Acrobat plug-ins folder. On Windows, copy the Photoshop Acquire plug-in and open the Acrobat\plug_ins\PaperCapture folder and paste your Acquire plug-in.

Mac OS X requires you to expand the Acrobat 8.0 Professional or Acrobat Standard package in order to paste your Photoshop Acquire plug-in. To do so, follow these steps:

1. **Open your Acrobat 8.0 Professional folder and select (not double-click) Acrobat 8.0 Professional.**

2. **Ctrl+click to open a context menu, and select Show Package Contents.** The Contents folder appears in the Acrobat 8.0 Professional folder.

3. **Double-click the Contents folder and double-click the Plug-ins folder that comes into view.**

4. **Double-click again to open the PaperCapture folder and drag your Photoshop Acquire plug-in into this folder.** (Option+click+drag to copy the plug-in to the target folder.) When you close the folders, the package is restored.

Understanding Scanning Essentials

At this point you should have your scanner and Acrobat configured properly. Before I begin discussing how to use your scanner with Acrobat, take a moment to understand some of the essential issues to deal with in performing clean, accurate scans. A few items need to be discussed: the hardware and hardware-related issues; the types of scans to be produced; and understanding your scanner capabilities. A few moments here saves you much time in producing the best scans you can expect from your equipment.

CROSS-REF Preparing documents for scanning is discussed later in this chapter in the section "Preparing a document."

The hardware issue to consider is your scanner. The single most important issue with scanner hardware is keeping the platen clean. If you have dust and dirt on the glass, these particles show up in your scans. Keep the platen clean, and use a lint-free cloth to clean the glass. If you use a solvent, always apply the solvent to the cloth and not the scanner glass.

Preparing a document

Just as your scans can benefit from careful attention to your scanner, exercising a little care with the source material can help produce clean scans. Bits of dust, improperly aligned pages, poor contrast, and degraded originals affect your ability to create scans capable of being read without many errors by the text recognition software. A little preparation before scanning saves you much time in trying to clean up poorly scanned images.

Photocopying originals

Sometimes you can improve image and text contrast by photocopying original documents. Try some experiments to test your results. Placing photocopies of large, bulky material on the scanner bed ultimately results in better scans than when using the original material.

Ensuring straight alignment

If you have documents with frayed edges or pages torn from a magazine, trim the edges and make them parallel to the text on the page. Precise placement of pages on the scanner bed facilitates clean scans. Even though Acrobat has a recognition capability within a 14-degree rotation, the straighter the page, the better the results. Acrobat 8 actually rotates a scan 180 degrees, but the text recognition may experience problems. As a matter of practice, be certain to keep the source material rotated in the proper portrait view on the scanner platen.

CAUTION Be certain to observe copyright laws when scanning published material. If you scan text from books and magazines, you need to obtain permission from the publisher before using the material.

Try to remember the axiom "garbage in, garbage out" when you approach any kind of scanning. The better the source material, the better your scanned results. Exercise a little care in the beginning, and your Acrobat scanning sessions move along much faster.

Using Scan to PDF

As I mentioned in the beginning of this chapter, Acrobat 8 offers you one-step scanning and OCR conversion. Before getting into all the options in dialog boxes and what they mean, try following these steps to produce your first text scan in Acrobat 8.

STEPS: Scanning a text document

1. **Place a document on the scanner platen.** Be certain your scanner is configured and operational.

2. **Select Document ⇨ Scan to PDF (or Open the Create PDF task button pull-down menu and select From Scanner).** The Acrobat Scan dialog box opens, as shown in Figure 17.1.

FIGURE 17.1

The Create PDF From Scanner dialog box opens after you select Create PDF From Scanner.

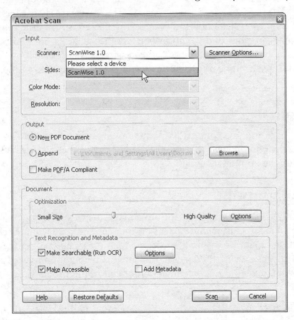

3. **Select your scanner.** The first task is to be certain your scanner appears listed on the Scanner drop-down menu in the Acrobat Scan dialog box. If you don't see your scanner here, then you have a configuration problem. Assuming everything is working okay, select your scanner as shown in Figure 17.1.

4. **Select the Output.** If you have a document open in the Document pane, you can append your document with the new scan. If you want to create a separate document, click New PDF Document in the Output section of the Acrobat Scan dialog box. If you want to make your scanned document compliant with the PDF/A standard, click the check box Make PDF/A Compliant.

CROSS-REF For more information on the PDF/A standard, see Chapter 1.

5. **Set Document Optimization.** The default optimization setting is set to Automatic. For a first time effort, leave the Optimization setting at the default. If you want to check to see if Automatic is selected, click Options and another dialog box opens where you'll see a check box for Automatic.

6. **Adjust Text Recognition and Metadata.** Check the box for Make Searchable (Run OCR). This check box informs Acrobat to use the OCR engine to convert the scanned image to recognizable text. Check Make Accessible to add tags and make your document accessible.

CROSS-REF For more information on accessible documents see Chapter 25. For more information on metadata, see the section "Text recognition and metadata options" later in this chapter.

7. **Click Scan.** You click the Scan button and your TWAIN or plug-in software is loaded. When you arrive at your scanner software, you have more choices for the scan attributes.

8. **Set the scanner attributes.** The most important attributes are the resolution and cropping area. When your scanner plug-in opens set the resolution to 300 ppi (pixels per inch) and check the preview thumbnail to be certain the document area you want to scan is not clipped. In Figure 17.2, you can see the resolution setting and the preview area in a scanner plug-in window.

FIGURE 17.2

Set the resolution to 300 ppi (A) for your first scan and set the crop area to include the entire document page (B).

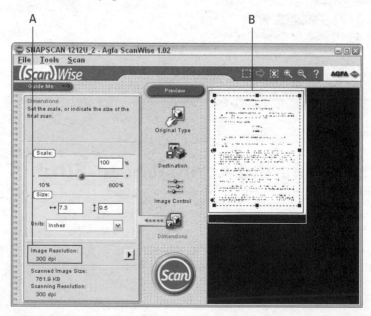

9. **Click Scan.** Now when you click Scan or your scanner plug-in button label to start a scan, the scanner begins to work. When the scanner finishes, a dialog box opens in Acrobat asking if you want to scan more. Click the Scanning Complete radio button and click OK to return to Acrobat.

10. **Check the document for recognizable text.** Click the Select tool in the Editing toolbar and drag through the document. You should see the text selected as you drag, as shown in Figure 17.3.

FIGURE 17.3

The scanned document appears in Acrobat with selectable text.

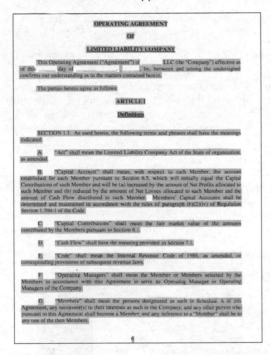

Understanding the Acrobat Scan Attributes

The Acrobat Scan dialog box has a number of different options for preparing your scanner and the files you ultimately save to PDF. These options fall into several different categories.

Input options

Beginning at the top of the Acrobat Scan dialog box, as shown in Figure 17.1, Input options include:

- **Scanner.** The drop-down menu is used to select your scanner. When the scanner is online and recognized by Acrobat you'll see the scanner plug-in software name appear in a drop-down menu. Some scanning software may not enable you to see other options such as Color Mode and Resolution in the Acrobat Scan dialog box. If these items are grayed out, you'll need to make the choices in the scanner plug-in. When you first select Acrobat Scan, a dialog box informs you that the Native Scanners Interface can't be hidden. In such a case, you need to make choices in your plug-in software.

- **Color Mode.** If the box is not grayed out, you can make choices for color or grayscale scanning. With text scans you can reduce file sizes by choosing grayscale.

- **Resolution.** If your Resolution option is not available in Acrobat Scan, choose it from your plug-in software. Use at least 200 ppi for scans. If you find problems with Optical Character Recognition, increase the resolution to 300 ppi.

- **Scanner Options.** For scanning options, click the Scanner Options button and the Scanner Options dialog box opens, as shown in Figure 17.4. You can choose Native Mode or Memory Mode from the drop-down menu. Both modes prompt you to save your file in a Save dialog box. For faster scanning of multiple pages, choose the Memory Mode option. For User Interface, choose between options in Acrobat or your scanner's interface. If the drop-down menu is grayed out, choices such as resolution and color mode need to be made in your scanner's interface. Paper size is automatically selected in your scanner's interface if you see this item grayed out. Invert Black and White Images is self-descriptive.

FIGURE 17.4

Click Options to open the Scanner Options dialog box.

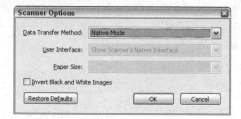

Output options

The second section of the Acrobat Scan dialog box handles options for file output. The options include:

- **New PDF Document.** Click this radio button when you want to create a new PDF from the scanned image.

- **Append.** This option enables you to append scanned pages to a file. The file can be opened in the Acrobat Document pane or in a file on your hard drive. If you want to append the scan to a file on your hard drive, click the Browse button to select the file.

- **Make PDF/A Compliant.** Check this radio button to make a PDF/A compliant file.

Document options

Document options offer settings for file optimization, file compression, and image enhancements. Options choices are made in the Optimization Options dialog box. Click Options in the Document area and the Optimization Options dialog box opens, as shown in Figure 17.5.

By default, the Automatic item is selected in the Optimization Options dialog box. When this radio button is selected, all the other items are grayed out. Click Custom Settings and all other options are accessible, as shown in Figure 17.5.

FIGURE 17.5

Click Options in the Document area of the Acrobat Scan dialog box to open the Optimization Options dialog box.

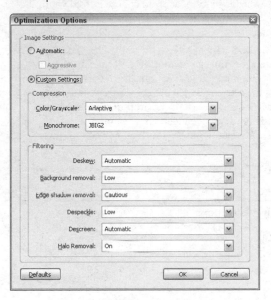

Your custom choices include:

- **Compression.** For color/grayscale images, choose from Adaptive or JPEG for file compression. JPEG files result in smaller file sizes, but you experience data loss. In many cases the data loss may have no effect on appearance or Acrobat's ability to recognize text. If you do experience problems, try using Adaptive compression.

  Monochrome images are compressed with three different compression schemes depending on the choice made from the pull-down menu. JBIG2 is a JPEG compression scheme with little data loss. You can also use Adaptive like that used for color/grayscale images and CCITT Group 4, which is a common compression used by fax machines. When applying compression to images, try the defaults (Adaptive for color/grayscale and JBIG2 for monochrome) first. If your scans are presenting with visual problems or Acrobat has difficulty in recognizing text, experiment with the other settings.

  You can adjust the quality slider for the amount of compression applied to the scans. As you move the slider left, the file size is smaller but the image quality is reduced. Move the slider toward Higher if you experience problems with text recognition.

- **Deskew.** Acrobat automatically straightens crooked scans when Deskew is set to automatic. To turn off the deskewing, select Off from the pull-down menu.

- **Background removal.** Removes background data. Use this option and choose from Low, Medium, High, or Off from menu choices. When text has drop shadows or original paper copies show dust and dirt, play with the amount settings to sharpen the text.

- **Edge shadow removal.** If you want to scan in grayscale or color mode, Acrobat can eliminate levels of gray where shadows appear around type. For cleaner text scans, enable this option. Note that you need to have crisp, clean originals to see much of a difference between scanning with the option enabled versus disabled. Two settings are used for Cautious and Aggressive as well as Off. Use Aggressive for more removal.

- **Despeckle.** This item and descreen are particularly helpful when scanning documents that have been printed and subject to moiré patterns (a condition common when scanning printed documents) or when scanning documents with dust and dirt.

- **Descreen.** Use Descreen like Despeckle mentioned previously when scanning printed documents and screened type.

- **Halo Removal.** Artifacts creating halo effects around type can be cleaned up by setting this option to On.

Custom settings should be necessary only if your scans have some visual artifacts or you have trouble recognizing text. A lot depends on the quality of your originals and the font used on the hard copy. If you desire minimal cleanup or fewer errors in the recognized text, try playing with the settings to find the options that work best for the job at hand.

Text recognition and metadata options

If scanning for OCR, check the box for Make Searchable (Run OCR). If you want to scan images, remove the check mark from this option. Likewise, check Make Accessible for documents you want tagged and made accessible. For searchable text, you have more choices when you click the Options button. Clicking this button opens the Recognize Text – Settings dialog box. As shown in Figure 17.6, you have three choices for PDF Output style, which determine how the text recognition is performed:

- **Primary OCR Language.** By default, Acrobat installs 34 language dictionaries available for OCR. If you scan documents from any of the supported languages, select the appropriate language in the pull-down menu in the Recognize Text — Settings dialog box.

- **PDF Output Style.** As shown in Figure 17.6 your options are as follows:
  - **Formatted Text & Graphics.** The bitmapped image is discarded and replaced with searchable text and graphics. If there is an instance where the OCR engine does not have confidence, the original bitmap is left in place and the best guess is placed behind, mimicking the "Searchable Image" style.
  - **Searchable Image.** Text is also placed behind the original image, preserving the integrity of the original documents. The image scan is compressed to reduce file size. Some of the quality of the original scan is lost.
  - **Searchable Image (Exact).** This option keeps the image scan in the foreground with text placed in the background. The appearance of the scanned image does not change. Text is added on a hidden layer that gives you the capability of creating indexes and performing searches. Use this option when you don't want to change a document's appearance, but you do want to be able to search the text of that document. Something on the order of a legal document or a certificate might be an example of such a document.

NOTE See the "PDF Image Versus PDF Formatted Text & Graphics" sidebar in this chapter for more detail on the differences among the PDF Output Styles.

- **Downsample Images.** This option enables you to downsample images or keep them at the original scanned resolution. If None is selected, no downsampling is applied to images. The remaining options offer downsampling values at 600 dots per inch (dpi), 300 dpi, 150 dpi, and 72 dpi.

Open the PDF Output Style drop-down menu and choose from one of three options for performing the OCR.

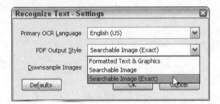

After you make choices in the Recognize Text – Settings dialog box and click OK, you return to the Acrobat Scan dialog box. The last choice here is the option for Add Metadata. When you check Add Metadata, the metadata options are addressed after you complete a scan. After the scan is completed and the dialog box opens, you're presented with a dialog box to add metadata. The first dialog box opening is shown in Figure 17.7.

When Add Metadata is selected in the Acrobat Scan dialog box, the Document Properties dialog box opens.

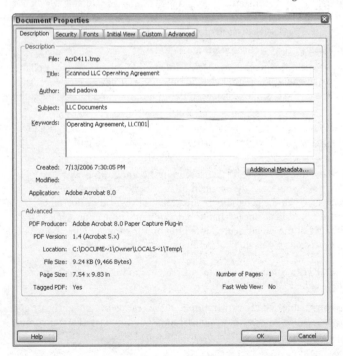

The Document Description tab is opened in the Document Properties dialog box where the Title, Author, Subject, and Keywords metadata are added. This dialog box is the same as you see when selecting File ➪ Properties or pressing Ctrl/⌘+D.

CROSS-REF For more information on using Document Descriptions, see Chapter 6.

Additional metadata can be added to your document by clicking the Additional Metadata button in the Description tab in the Document Properties dialog box. After clicking Additional Metadata, the dialog box opens as shown in Figure 17.8.

FIGURE 17.8

Additional Metadata offers options for a number of field boxes where descriptions can be added as metadata.

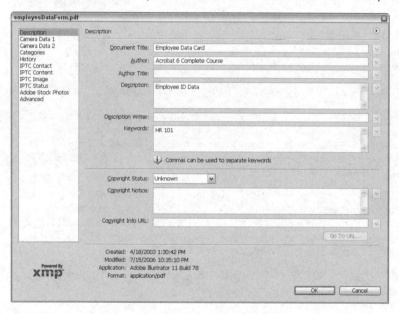

Anyone familiar with Adobe Photoshop will recognize the options for adding metadata to images. You begin with the Description information shown in Figure 17.8. The other categories on the left side of the dialog box offer options for adding detail descriptions for an image. For example, the Camera Data pane provides field boxes for camera model, f-stop, shutter speed, ISO setting, lens, flash, and so on. Obviously, these settings won't apply to scanned images, but image files taken with digital cameras and saved as PDF from Photoshop have this data automatically supplied in the Document Metadata dialog box.

NOTE If you save a digital camera image file from Photoshop as PDF, the document metadata appears populated with the camera information and file attributes. If you use Create PDF From File, you loose the metadata in the image file.

Metadata is valuable when you have large collections of files because the metadata is searchable. The more information you add to the metadata dialog boxes, the easier it is to search for files in large collections of documents.

CROSS-REF For more information on searching PDFs, see Chapter 6.

PDF Image Versus PDF Formatted Text & Graphics

When you search OCR pages with either Searchable Image (Exact) or Searchable Image, the pages are image files with searchable text. The original file is an image file produced from your scan designed to be viewed as an original, unaltered document. This option enables you to electronically archive documents for legal purposes or when unaltered originals need to be preserved.

When you convert a document with Recognize Text Using OCR, the OCR conversion places text behind the scan. The intent is for you to be able to archive files and search them either through using the Search pane to search files on your hard disk or by searching an index where these documents have been catalogued.

The text behind PDF Image is not editable with Acrobat. However, Adobe Acrobat Capture 3.0 does have tools to edit text in a PDF Image file. If Recognize Text Using OCR misinterprets a word, you cannot make corrections to the text. The text is selectable, and you can copy the text and paste it into a word processor or text editor. If you want to examine the OCR suspects, paste the text into a word processor and review the document. Or buy a copy of Adobe Acrobat Capture 3.0 to do the edits from within the PDF file.

To copy text from a PDF Image format select the Select tool. Click the cursor anywhere in the text and choose Edit ⇨ Select All (Ctrl/⌘+A). Open a context menu and select Copy File to Clipboard. Open a word processor and choose Edit ⇨ Paste. You may find the number of suspects to be too many to be usable. If you want to improve the OCR conversion, return to the Create PDF From Scanner dialog box and rescan the file with a higher resolution or different scanning mode.

PDF Formatted Text & Graphics files (previously referred to as PDF Normal in Acrobat 5 and earlier) are scanned documents converted to text. When you select Formatted Text & Graphics in the Recognize Text dialog box, the file conversion is made to a PDF Formatted Text & Graphics document. Recognize Text reads the bitmap configuration of words and converts them to text. This text can be edited and altered on a page. When you make text corrections, you see the changes reflected on the document page.

When capturing pages, be certain to view the options and know the difference between capturing pages as PDF Scanned Image and PDF Formatted Text & Graphics.

Creating Workflow Solutions

Scanning individual pages for limited use can easily be handled by the methods described previously. As you scan documents, you need to attend to feeding papers under the scanner lid and manually clicking buttons to continue scanning. If you need to convert large numbers of pages to digital content, you may want to explore other solutions. Depending on how much money you want to spend, you may want to invest in a commercial-grade scanner with a document feeder.

Some scanners support automatic document feeders. If your workflow demands scanning volumes of papers, acquiring a good scanner with an automatic document feeder is a great advantage. When you scan in Acrobat, scanned pages are successively appended to a PDF. Therefore, you can leave a stack of papers in the scanner feeder and leave it unattended. Scanning can be performed automatically overnight. When you return to your computer, the PDF file is complete with recognized text and ready for saving to your hard disk. The only downside to this operation is that if your computer crashes, you lose everything because Acrobat won't save your PDF on the fly as new pages are appended.

A more expensive solution, but not out of the question for workflows needing automated means of capturing pages, is to purchase Adobe's stand-alone product, Adobe Acrobat Capture. Combined with a scanner and document feeder, the conversion of scanned images to text is handled in a single operation. You have other solutions from third-party vendors that support industrial-strength scanning and OCR conversion with the capability of converting the final file to PDF format.

PDF WORKFLOW Users in government and educational workflows seeking to scan volumes of text for document accessibility will find purchasing auto document feeding scanners and Adobe Acrobat Capture, or other software capable of batch scanning and OCR conversion, to be a much more effective means for converting publications and documents to accessible PDFs. Some hardware screen readers use proprietary software to read TIFF image files for document accessibility. Acrobat PDF is a much better solution over TIFF images and proprietary formats, as once converted to PDF, the document content is searchable and much smaller. If scanning textbooks and government papers is your task, PDF is a much better file format for document accessibility.

Using Text Recognition

You may have files scanned as image files and want to convert them to recognizable text, which is similar to performing OCR tasks in earlier versions of Acrobat. You first scan files as image scans, and then use a menu command to run the OCR engine.

If you don't have a scanner or you're looking for a more efficient way to scan documents and recognize text, you can use a digital camera and a copy stand. A digital camera fires off images ten to one over a flatbed scanner and you can import the images directly into Acrobat and run the Text Recognition command. If using a digital camera be certain to shoot JPEG images and not Camera Raw. Acrobat converts JPEGs to PDF via the Create PDF From File or the Combine multiple files into one PDF commands. Camera Raw conversion is not supported.

If you have scanned image files or digital camera files and you want to convert to searchable text, perform the following steps.

STEPS: Converting image files to searchable text

1. **Open files in Acrobat.** Use the Create PDF From File or the Combine Files task button to convert image files to PDF.

CROSS-REF For more information on converting image files to PDF, see Chapter 7.

2. **Recognize text.** Select Document ➪ OCR Text Recognition ➪ Recognize Text Using OCR to open the Recognize Text dialog box shown in Figure 17.9.
3. **Set the PDF Output Style.** Click the Edit button in the Recognize Text dialog box to open the Recognize Text – Settings dialog box. (This is the same dialog box shown earlier in this chapter in Figure 17.6.) From the PDF Output Style pull-down menu, select Formatted Text & Graphics. If you don't make this selection, you can't change misspelled words later. Click OK and you return to the Recognize Text dialog box.
4. **Run the OCR engine.** Click OK and Acrobat starts the OCR engine to convert the image file to recognizable text.

FIGURE 17.9

Choose Document ➪ OCR Text Recognition ➪ Recognize Text Using OCR to open the Recognize Text dialog box.

5. **Check for suspect words.** After Acrobat completes the text recognition, select Document ➪ OCR Text Recognition ➪ Find First OCR Suspect. The Find Element dialog box opens as shown in Figure 17.10. Suspect words are reported in the Suspect text box. If the word is correct as it is reported in the Suspect text box, click Accept and Find to move to the next suspect. If the word is incorrect, type the correct spelling in the Suspect text box and click Accept and Find to change the spelling and move to the next suspect. Continue moving through the document until you correct all suspects.

FIGURE 17.10

Type the correct spelling in the Suspect text box and click Accept and Find.

> **NOTE** You may be prompted by a dialog box informing you that the font in the document is not found and font substitution is needed. Click OK in the warning dialog box to use font substitution and continue correcting the misspelled words.

6. **Save the PDF.** Select File ➪ Save As to optimize the file and update your corrections.

Understanding suspect words

A *suspect* word is one that the OCR Engine interprets differently from the closest match found in the Primary OCR Language Dictionary. The word is suspect because it may or may not be a correct interpretation. You might have proper names, industry terminology, abbreviations, and so on that the OCR Engine marks as suspects. Simply because the word(s) is marked as a suspect doesn't necessarily require changing the word. Therefore, when you review suspects, you have two choices: Either change the word to a correct spelling or inform Acrobat to leave it as is and move to the next suspect.

After the Recognize Text dialog box disappears, the converted page(s) doesn't appear any different from before you began the OCR conversion. In order to see any words that may have been misinterpreted during the conversions, you need to access a menu command and tell Acrobat you want to view the suspect words. You have two choices in the OCR Text Recognition submenu.

NOTE In order to correct OCR suspects in Acrobat, you need to convert pages with the Formatted Text & Graphics PDF Output Style.

If you choose Document ⇨ OCR Text Recognition ⇨ Find First OCR Suspect, Acrobat shows the first word that it interprets as a suspect, which means the interpretation of OCR Engine did not exactly match a word in its dictionary. The suspect word is highlighted in the document pane.

If you choose Document ⇨ OCR Text Recognition ⇨ Find All OCR Suspects, all the suspect words are highlighted with a red border across all pages converted. At a glance you can see the number of suspects that need to be reviewed.

TIP When examining suspect words you should plan on zooming in to the suspects. If you prefer to view a page in a zoomed out view, select the Loupe tool to zoom in on suspect words. You can keep the page view in a smaller view while zooming in on suspects with the Loupe tool.

To leave a word unedited, you can choose either Find Next or Accept and Find. If the OCR engine recognized a graphic (such as a signature) as text you can also select "Not Text" to return it to the original bitmap image. If you choose Find Next, the bitmap image of the text stays in place and the text behind the bitmap stays as is. When you click the Accept and Find button, the bitmap is thrown away and the word behind the bitmap is promoted to the text location. As you work with the text corrections, realize that you have two layers. The bitmap is the scanned image and Recognize Text created the text below the scanned image. Therefore, as you edit the text corrections you can choose to throw away the bitmap image on top of the text layer or choose to preserve it. To make a correction, edit a suspect word and click Accept and Find. The new text you edited is promoted to the text layer while the bitmap is thrown away.

PDF WORKFLOW If you want to develop a workflow in an office environment, you may want to have several machines perform the function of scanning documents and have other computers perform OCR functions. You can scan images in software such as Adobe Photoshop and save your files in either an image format or as Photoshop PDFs. The scans can be routed to other workstations used for the OCR conversion.

Reducing suspects

When you begin a new Acrobat session and want to scan many pages with OCR Text Recognition, scanning one or two pages representative of the pages you want to convert and examining the number of suspects in your sample scan is a good idea. If the suspects outnumber the number of correct interpretations, editing the suspect words could take you more time than typing the document in a word processor. At some point the ratio between the number of suspects to correct words can make capturing pages more of a burden than providing you a solution.

If the number of suspect words is extraordinary, you may want to scan another few pages using different settings. For example, increase the image resolution or scan in a different color mode. Change the attributes in the Acrobat Scan dialog box or adjust settings in your Acquire plug-in to produce scans more suitable for capturing pages. Run Text Recognition and examine the suspects. When a scan results in fewer suspects, you can then go about scanning the remaining pages. In Figure 17.11, I scanned a page at 200 ppi and converted the page with Recognize Text Using OCR. After viewing the number of suspects, I decided to scan the page again with a higher resolution. The results of my OCR suspects with a higher resolution were significantly reduced, as you can see in Figure 17.12.

FIGURE 17.11

I scanned a page using Create PDF From Scanner and converted it with Recognize Text Using OCR. After I chose Document ⇨ OCR Text Recognition ⇨ Find All OCR Suspects, I determined that the number of suspects made this job too difficult to edit in Acrobat.

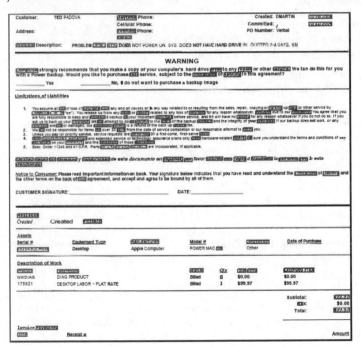

FIGURE 17.12

I scanned the same page from Figure 17.11 at a higher resolution and converted it again. Fewer suspects were found and the job of correcting the suspects was more manageable.

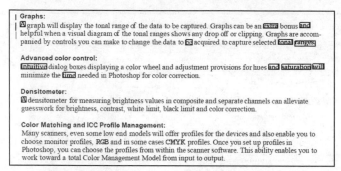

Exporting OCR text

If you want to take your scanned text to a word processor for editing and integration with other text documents, Acrobat provides an easy way to transfer data to word processors. After scanning a document with Scan to PDF with Make Searchable (Run OCR) or after running Text Recognition Using OCR on an image file, follow these steps to export your text to Microsoft Word.

STEPS: Exporting recognized text to Microsoft Word

1. **Select all text.** Click the Select Text tool in the Select & Zoom toolbar and click on the document page. Choose Edit ➭ Select All or press Ctrl/⌘+A.
2. **Copy text with formatting.** Move the cursor to the icon (it appears similar to the TouchUp Text icon) you see in the selected text to open a menu, as shown in Figure 17.13. Click the menu command where you see Copy with Formatting.

FIGURE 17.13

Select Copy With Formatting from the pop-up menu.

3. **Launch Microsoft Word.** Press Ctrl/⌘+N to create a new blank page in Word.

4. **Paste the text.** In Word, select Edit ➪ Paste or press Ctrl/⌘+V. The text is pasted with formatting as you see in Figure 17.14.

FIGURE 17.14

Text is pasted into a new Word document with formatting

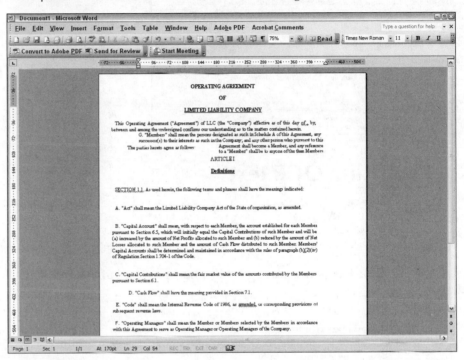

> **NOTE**   Be certain you use the Copy with Formatting command. If you select Copy and paste into Word, the document appears without formatting, as shown in Figure 17.15.

> **CROSS-REF**   For more information on exporting PDF data, see Chapter 11. For more information on working with Acrobat and Microsoft Word, see Chapter 8.

FIGURE 17.15

Text pasted into Word without formatting

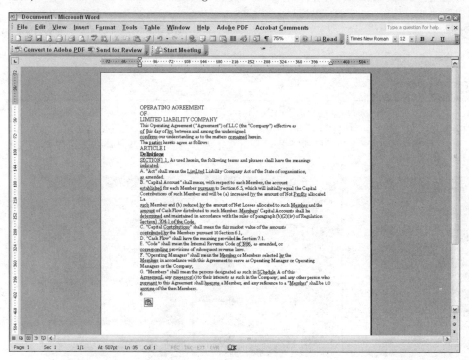

Scanning Paper Forms

If you scan paper forms that you want populated with form fields in Acrobat or Adobe LiveCycle Designer and you want to use Run Form Field Recognition in Acrobat or the Create a New Form Assistant from within Acrobat, you need to start with a form that has sufficient resolution for the form fields to be recognized by Acrobat. If the resolution and image contrast isn't sufficient for Acrobat to recognize form fields, your results will vary and you will often find very few fields created by Acrobat on low resolution scans.

CROSS-REF For more information on using Run Form Field Recognition in Acrobat see Chapter 34. For more information on creating forms in Adobe LiveCycle Designer, see Chapter 33.

Developing a workflow for scanning forms using your scanner and Acrobat requires some practice and testing. Scanners vary considerably with quality, options, and resolution choices. The first thing you need to do is run a series of tests to determine what settings are optimum for recognizing fields automatically in Acrobat. Some considerations include:

- **Resolution.** More is generally better when it comes to scanning forms. Almost all desktop scanners support two resolutions. Optical resolution is the true resolution of your scanner. You may have a 600 ppi (pixels per inch) scanner that supports an optical resolution of 600 ppi. You scanner is also supports an interpolated resolution. For the 600 ppi scanner, the interpolated resolution is likely to be 1200 ppi. A 1200 ppi optical resolution scanner often supports an interpolated resolution of 2400 ppi, and so on.

Interpolated resolution is best suited for line art drawings. Since most office forms are black and white, your scan resolution for forms at the highest interpolated resolution of your scanner usually produces the best results when it comes to recognizing form fields. In Figure 17.16 you can see three scans I created using Scan to PDF. The form on the left is a 150 ppi scan. In the middle is a 300 ppi scan and on the right is a 600 ppi scan. Although the Forms ➪ Run Form Field Recognition command isn't perfect, you can see that the 600 ppi scan produced more fields when the command was run in Acrobat.

FIGURE 17.16

Three scans after selecting Forms ➪ Run Form Field Recognition. On the left is a 150 ppi scan, in the middle is a 300 ppi scan, and on the right is a 600 ppi scan. The scans were performed on a scanner with an optical resolution of 600 ppi and an interpolated resolution of 1200 ppi.

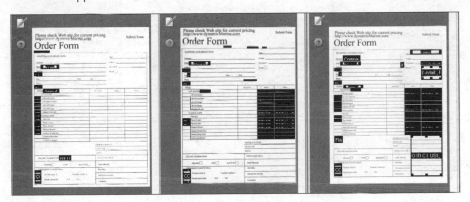

NOTE   The sample form used in these figures is a complex form having rows and columns of fields. Run Form Field Recognition provides you with a start in a complex form. You can expect to do some editing in Acrobat or Adobe LiveCycle Designer to polish up the fields and add fields where the auto recognition of form fields missed adding fields to the form. In much simpler forms, the Run Form Field Recognition command does a superb job of automatically populating a form. See Chapter 34 for more on Run Form Field Recognition.

- **Color Mode.** Black and white art is generally scanned in a line art (bitmap) color mode. However, when it comes to OCR Text Recognition and ultimately using Run Form Field Recognition, the anti-aliasing of grayscale scans most often provide you with better results. In Figure 17.17 you can see a 1200 ppi scan using the scanner's Line Art mode and on the right you see a 1200 ppi scan using the scanner's Grayscale color mode. The grayscale scan produced more form fields than the Line Art scan, and at 1200 ppi, there are a few more fields recognized than the 600 ppi scan shown in Figure 17.16.

FIGURE 17.17

A line art scan (left) produces fewer recognized fields than a grayscale scan (right).

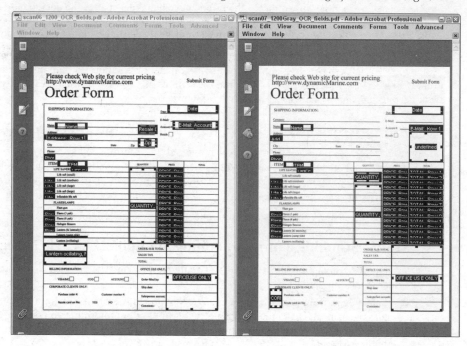

- **Make Searchable (Run OCR).** When you use Scan to PDF for scanning forms that you want to use the Run Form Field Recognition command, be certain to check the box for Make Searchable (Run OCR) in the Acrobat Scan dialog box. (See Figure 17.1 earlier in this chapter.) Using Forms ➪ Run Form Field Recognition produces no results if you attempt to run the command on a scan that hasn't been converted with the OCR Engine.

- **Clean Up.** Ideally, you're best off using Scan to PDF and achieve optimum results using the controls in your scanner software for brightness, contrast, color mode choices, and scanning resolution. However, if your scanner software doesn't produce good results when recognizing form fields on your scans, you may be able to do a little image editing to adjust brightness and contrast. You'll need a program like Adobe Photoshop or Adobe Photoshop Elements to adjust Levels (Photoshop and Elements) and Curves (Photoshop only).

  If you do plan to do some image editing to adjust your scans' brightness and contrast, turn off Make Searchable (Run OCR) if using Scan to PDF. After editing a scan in Photoshop or Photoshop Elements, save as a Photoshop PDF file, open in Acrobat and choose Document ➪ OCR Text Recognition ➪ Recognize Text Using OCR. After running the OCR Engine, you can then choose Forms ➪ Run Form Field Recognition.

> **TIP** If the quality of your original forms is poor and you can't adjust contrast in Photoshop or Elements sufficiently to convert text with the OCR Engine and ultimately recognize fields, you can use Photoshop or Photoshop Elements to improve image brightness. Duplicate the Background layer in the layers palette in either program. For the layers blending mode, change the default Normal to Multiply. Add more duplicate layers using the Multiply blending mode until you see enough brightness in areas such as text, lines, boxes, etc. Flatten the layers and make your final adjustments in the Levels dialog box.

Plan to do a lot of testing if you need to scan many forms and populate them with form fields in Acrobat or Adobe LiveCycle Designer. Try scanning forms with different resolutions to pinpoint the resolution setting that works best for your forms. After you find the settings that work best, then go about scanning the forms you need to prepare in Acrobat.

Scanning forms for Adobe LiveCycle Designer (Windows only)

If you want to work in Adobe LiveCycle Designer for editing a form, you have two choices when you start with a scanned document. One option is to use Scan to PDF and use the Run Form Field Recognition command, save your file and open the document in Designer. The other option is to use the Create a New Form Assistant in Acrobat.

To use the Create a New Form Assistant in Acrobat (Windows only), follow these steps:

STEPS: Scanning a form for editing in Adobe LiveCycle Designer

1. **Open Acrobat and select Forms ➪ Create New Form.** The Create a New Form Assistant opens as shown in Figure 17.18.

2. **Select Scan from paper in the Create a New Form Assistant.** Click the Continue button and a message pane opens in the Create a New Form Assistant informing you that the form will be edited in Adobe LiveCycle Designer. Click OK and you arrive at the first step in the Create a New Form Assistant.

FIGURE 17.18

Select Scan from paper and click Continue.

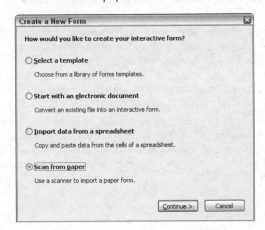

3. **Click the Start Scanning Process button.** Clicking this button, shown in Figure 17.19, opens the Acrobat Scan dialog box. Click the Make Searchable (Run OCR) check box and click Scan to open your scanner software. Set the controls in your scanner software that you've tested for proper resolution, color mode, and brightness/contrast adjustments. When the scan is complete the Acrobat Scan dialog box opens with two options for scanning more pages or completing your scanning. Click OK in the dialog box if you have no more pages to scan and you return to Step 1 in the Create a New Form Assistant. Click Continue to move to the next step.

FIGURE 17.19

Click Start Scanning Process to begin scanning your form.

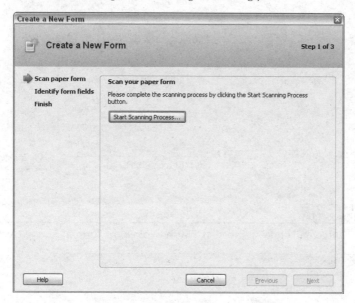

4. **Select Auto Field Detection.** To automatically populate form fields, select the first radio button you see in Figure 17.20. This choice is similar to selecting Forms ⇨ Run Form Field Recognition in Acrobat. Click Next and the auto form field recognition is run and you arrive at Step 3 in the Create New a Form Assistant.

5. **Finish.** Click Done in the last step in the Create a New Form Assistant and the New Form Assistant Wizard opens in Step 3. Add an email address to the Return email address text box, as shown in Figure 17.21, and click Finish.

6. **Edit the form in Adobe LiveCycle Designer.** The form opens in Adobe LiveCycle Designer with the form fields added as recognized in Acrobat. (See Figure 17.22.) At this point you need to modify fields and add those fields that were missed by the form field recognition option.

FIGURE 17.20

Select Run Auto Field Detection and click Next.

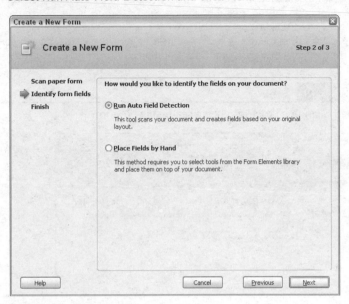

FIGURE 17.21

Add a return email address and click Finish to open the form in Adobe LiveCycle Designer.

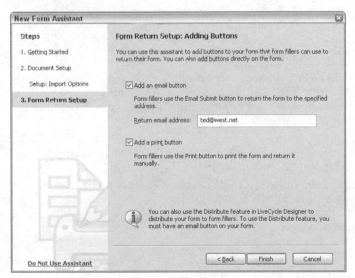

FIGURE 17.22

The form opens in Adobe LiveCycle Designer with form fields.

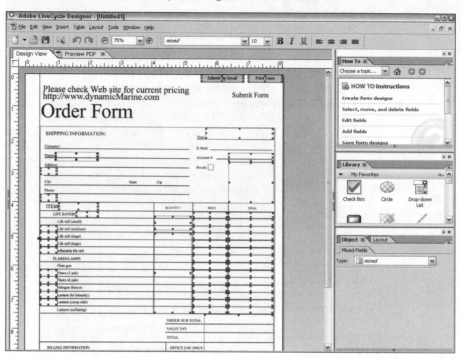

CROSS-REF For more information on editing forms in Adobe LiveCycle Designer, see Chapter 33.

Using a digital camera in lieu of a scanner

If you have a number of forms you want to scan from paper and convert to either Acrobat PDF forms or Adobe LiveCycle Designer XML forms, you can often save much time by shooting paper forms with a good quality digital camera. After properly setting up a camera, you can shoot a dozen paper documents or more in the same time as it takes to scan forms — and the ratio broadens when you need to scan forms at 1200 ppi or higher.

To use a digital camera, you need to consider some of the following:

- **Camera type.** You may find some point and shoot cameras providing you with satisfactory results, but the best results will come from a DSLR (Digital Single Lens Reflex) camera and a good quality macro lens.

- **Copy stand.** For best results, either buy or create a makeshift copy stand. Outfit the stand with daylight lights and use cross lighting to avoid shadows.

■ **Save as JPEG and Raw.** When running tests with your camera, save files to your camera's media card in JPEG and Camera Raw file formats. You can test the images to see if the JPEG files will produce good results when running form field recognition. If you don't get the results you find with JPEG as you do when using Camera Raw images, then you can set up some defaults in the Camera Raw converter in either Photoshop Elements or Adobe Photoshop to automate preparing Raw files for Acrobat.

■ **Set up an Action in Photoshop.** If you work with Adobe Photoshop, you can create an Action to automate image correction and saving files to Photoshop PDF format. You can let an Action run overnight if you have a huge number of files to convert to PDF forms.

■ **Set up a nested Batch Sequence in Acrobat.** Two things need to be accomplished for preparing forms for editing in Acrobat or Adobe LiveCycle Designer. You need to Recognize Text Using OCR and Detect Form Fields (one of the new built-in Batch Sequence options available in Acrobat 8 is the Detect Form Fields Sequence). Open the Batch Sequences dialog box (Advanced ➪ Document Processing ➪ Batch Sequences) and create a new sequence. Select Recognize Text Using OCR and add it to the right pane in the edit Sequence dialog box. Next, select Detect Form Fields in the Edit Sequence dialog and click the Add button to add the item as a second sequence. (See Figure 17.23.) Run the sequence on a folder of forms and the files are converted with the OCR Engine and form fields are added to the documents. You can open the resultant files in either Acrobat or Adobe LiveCycle Designer for editing.

FIGURE 17.23

Create a batch sequence for Recognize Text Using OCR and Detect Form Fields on files you save from Photoshop or Photoshop Elements.

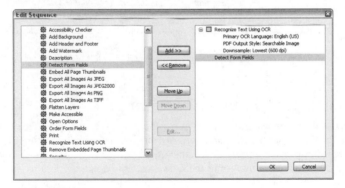

CROSS-REF   For more information on creating Batch Sequences, see Chapter 18.

If you have just a few forms, it makes no sense to go through the trouble for setting up a copy stand, shooting forms with a digital camera, editing the forms in Photoshop or Photoshop Elements and creating a batch sequence. However, if you have 20, 50, 100 or more forms to convert from paper to electronic forms, you'll find that using a digital camera will save you time more than 10 to 1 over scanning forms.

Summary

- Create PDF From Scanner uses TWAIN drivers or Adobe Photoshop Acquire plug-ins.

- Properly preparing the scanner and documents for scanning in Acrobat improves the quality of the scans. The scanner platen should be clean, the documents should be straight, and the contrast should be sharp.

- When scanning images in Acrobat, use the scanning software to establish resolution, image mode, and brightness controls before scanning. Test your results thoroughly to create a formula that works well for the type of documents you scan.

- Workflow automation can be greatly improved by purchasing Adobe's stand-alone product Adobe Acrobat Capture. When using Adobe Acrobat Capture with a scanner supporting a document feeder, the scanning and capturing can be performed with unattended operation.

- Acrobat Capture is a stand-alone application for optical character recognition used for converting scanned images into editable text.

- Text can be converted and saved as a PDF Formatted Text & Graphics, where you can edit text and change the appearance of the original scan. Text can be converted with Optical Character Recognition and saved using the Searchable Image option, which preserves the original document appearance and adds a text layer behind the image.

- OCR suspects are marked when the OCR Engine does not find an exact word match in its dictionary. Text editing is performed in the Find Element dialog box.

- To import text into Microsoft Word, use the Copy with Formatting command to preserve text formatting.

- Scanned paper forms can be populated with form fields using the Run Form Field Recognition command in Acrobat.

- Digital cameras can be used in lieu of a scanner and can often speed up the scanning process.

Chapter 18

Repurposing and Batch Processing

PDF documents designed for one purpose, such as for commercial printing, might need to be repurposed for other output intent such as Web hosting or for copying to CD-ROMs. Rather than going back to the original authoring program and recreating PDFs for each purpose, you can use tools in Acrobat that enable you to downsample file sizes and strip unnecessary content. The resulting documents can then be more efficiently viewed on Web sites or exchanged via e-mail.

You may have several files that need to be repurposed or some other kind of edit you make using menu commands. Rather than open each file independently and apply menu commands, you can create batch sequences that apply commands to several files in one operation.

In this chapter, you learn how to repurpose PDF documents using some Acrobat tools and methods for downsizing file sizes and eliminating content unnecessary for other viewing purposes. In addition, you take a look at automating tasks by creating batch sequences.

Setting Up the Environment

To downsize files and optimize them for other output circumstances, you don't need to access any special tools. The menu commands offer all the means for repurposing files. Therefore, set up your Acrobat work environment by opening a context menu on the Toolbar Well and selecting Reset Toolbars from the menu options.

Reducing File Sizes

Reducing file sizes often occurs with downsampling images — that is to say, reducing the image resolution of all raster images or compressing images with

higher compression options. In addition, you can reduce file sizes by eliminating redundant backgrounds; eliminating objects such as form fields, comments, Bookmarks, and destinations; unembedding fonts; and/or compressing the document structure. You can handle file-size reductions at the time of PDF creation when you control file compression, image sampling, and font embedding for PDFs designed for a specific output purpose. However, if you create PDFs for one purpose, such as commercial printing, and later want to host the same file on a Web site, you need to either create a new PDF document specifically for the new purpose or use Acrobat tools to create smaller file sizes more suited for other output purposes. Fortunately, several means are available to you for squeezing file sizes down and optimizing PDFs for multiple purposes.

CROSS-REF For more information on understanding terms such as "downsampling" and "resampling," see Chapter 10.

Downsizing cropped images

If you scan a document in Acrobat using the Scan to PDF command without making the file searchable, the scanned image is sampled according to settings you apply when scanning pages. After a scan opens in Acrobat, you may have a need to crop the scan using tools in Acrobat.

When you use the Crop tool in Acrobat, the cropped image data remains in the file; data is not eliminated. To reduce file sizes when cropping images, choose the File ⇨ Save As menu command and save as a TIFF file. After saving the file, open it in Acrobat to convert back to PDF. The result is a document in which the cropped area is completely eliminated from the file. Choose File ⇨ Save As and overwrite the file to optimize it.

CROSS-REF For more information on cropping PDF documents, see Chapter 16.

Using the Reduce File Size command

Both Acrobat Professional and Acrobat Standard offer a menu command that enables you to reduce file sizes. Open a document and choose Document ⇨ Reduce File Size. The Reduce File Size dialog box opens, as shown in Figure 18.1.

FIGURE 18.1

Choose Document ⇨ Reduce File Size to open the Reduce File Size dialog box, where you select options for Acrobat version compatibility.

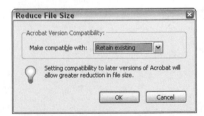

NOTE The Reduce File Size command has been moved from the File menu in Acrobat 7 to the Document menu in Acrobat 8.

The Reduce File Size dialog box offers a pull-down menu with options for selecting Acrobat compatibility. The default is Retain existing, which means that the original PDF compatibility will not be changed when the file is reduced in size. If your PDF documents are to be viewed by Acrobat users of version 4 or later, choose the Acrobat 4 and later compatibility. If all users are using Acrobat 6 through 8 viewers, use Acrobat 6, 7, or 8 compatibility, respectively. You might use Acrobat 4 compatibility for printing purposes because all the transparency will be flattened in Acrobat 4–compatible files.

CAUTION If you want to use many of the new features available in Adobe Reader 8, such as enabling documents for commenting and markup and form field saving, you must use Acrobat 8 compatibility. For more information on using Adobe Reader with usage rights enabled, see Chapter 19. For information on commenting, see Chapter 20.

After you make the menu selection and click OK, the Save As dialog box opens. Provide a filename and save the file to disk. As a matter of practice it's a good idea to write a new file to disk in case the file reduction fails and you need to return to the original file to try another method of file reduction.

Examining documents

PDF files can contain artifacts and unnecessary elements that were either left behind from the original authoring program or that are not necessary for viewing content on the Web or screen viewing.

NEW FEATURE To determine if unnecessary elements are contained in a file, you can examine the document using the Examine Document dialog box. Select Document ⇨ Examine Document and the dialog box shown in Figure 18.2 opens.

FIGURE 18.2

Select Document ⇨ Examine Document to open the Examine Document dialog box.

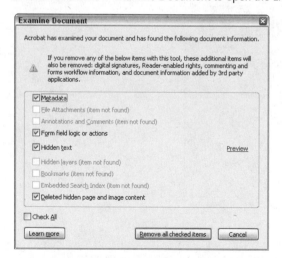

Eliminating some items can help reduce your file size. To see how items are eliminated from a PDF file, follow these steps.

STEPS: Eliminating items from a PDF file

1. **Open a PDF in Acrobat.** Try to use a file that was created with Acrobat 7 or 8 compatibility and contains several high-resolution images. Check the file size by opening the Document Properties (Ctrl/⌘+D). Click the Description tab and note the file size.

2. **Examine the document.** Select Document ⇨ Examine Document to open the Examine Document dialog box shown in Figure 18.2.

3. **Preview the file.** Check all check boxes that are active in the Examine Document dialog box and click the Preview link.

4. **Search for hidden text.** A dialog box opens, as shown in Figure 18.3, after clicking the Preview link. Click the Show Only Hidden Text radio button and scroll through the document by clicking on the arrow buttons. Reexamine the file by clicking the Show Both Hidden and Visible Text and scroll through the pages. Showing both visible and hidden text gives you an idea for the location of any hidden text on pages.

FIGURE 18.3

Using the Preview, you can locate hidden text in a file.

5. **Remove items.** Click OK in the Preview window and you return to the Examine Document dialog box. Click Remove all checked items. Acrobat shows a progress bar as items are removed from the file.

6. **Save the file.** When Acrobat finishes removing items, another dialog box opens reporting the results. Click OK in the dialog box shown in Figure 18.4 and select File ⇨ Save As. Click Save to rewrite the file. If saving a copy, use another filename and click Save.

FIGURE 18.4

FIGURE 18.4

A dialog box opens informing you of successful elimination of the items checked in the Examine Document dialog box.

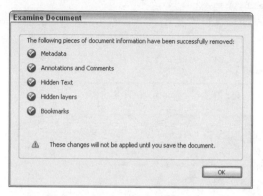

7. **Check the file size.** Press Ctrl/⌘+D to open the Document Properties dialog box. Click Description and check the file size. (See Figure 18.5.) You should notice a reduction in file size. The amount of the reduction depends on the elements contained in the original file and how much was eliminated. In some cases, your file size reduction may be very slight.

FIGURE 18.5

Check the file size in the Description properties.

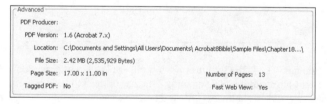

Using PDF Optimizer (Acrobat Professional only)

Examining documents and eliminating items supported in the Examine Document dialog box might get you only a slight file reduction. A more aggressive tool is the PDF Optimizer that can significantly reduce file sizes — especially files with high-resolution images.

With PDF Optimizer you make the choices from a number of different settings in the PDF Optimizer dialog box for what data is affected during optimization. The PDF Optimizer also offers you an option for analyzing a file so you can see what part of the PDF document occupies higher percentages of memory.

For a fast look at how to use the PDF Optimizer, use the steps that follow. Later in this chapter I'll point out the various options you have when using the PDF Optimizer.

STEPS: Using PDF Optimizer

1. **Open a PDF file in Acrobat.** Try to use the same file you used in the section "Examining documents" earlier in this chapter. If you followed the steps in that section, you should know the current file size of the document you saved in Step 7.

2. **Open the PDF Optimizer.** Select Advanced ➪ PDF Optimizer to open the dialog box shown in Figure 18.6.

FIGURE 18.6

Downsample files to 72 ppi for all images above 108 ppi.

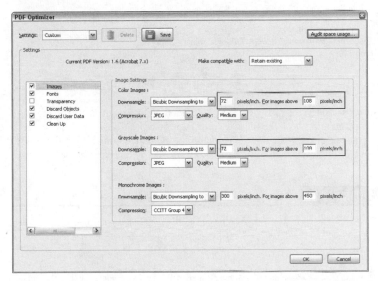

3. **Downsample images.** The PDF Optimizer has a number of different panes that offer settings for a number of different file attributes. The opening pane has options for downsampling files. Where you see Color Images and Grayscale Images you find text boxes where sampling amounts are edited. Type **72** and **108** for the sampling amounts for both sets of text boxes, as you see in Figure 18.6.

   Click on the listed items on the left side of the dialog box, and you are offered a number of other choices for changing and removing data. For now, just use the defaults after changing the resolution amounts for color and grayscale images.

4. **Save the file.** Click OK and you are prompted to save your file. Type a new filename and click Save. The PDF Optimizer displays a progress bar as it optimizes the file.

5. **Examine the file size.** After the PDF Optimizer completes its task, open the Description properties. Press Ctrl/⌘+D and check the file size. You should see a substantial reduction in file size.

When you want to get the most out of reducing file sizes, you'll note that you can use both PDF Optimizer and Examine Document. Whether you first use one or the other method is unimportant. The final results are exactly the same file size.

TIP You can also open the PDF Optimizer when saving files. Select File ⇨ Save As and choose Save as Optimized from the Save as type (Windows) or Format (Macintosh) drop-down menu when the Save As dialog box opens. Click the Settings button in the Save As dialog box and the PDF Optimizer window opens. You can choose a preset or make custom settings for the way you want to optimize your file. Click Save and the file is optimized and saved to disk. (For more on saving files, see Chapter 11.)

Auditing space usage

As a matter of practice the first step you want to perform when optimizing files with the PDF Optimizer is to analyze a file so you can see what content occupies the larger amounts of memory. Analyzing a document and using the PDF Optimizer are handled in the PDF Optimizer dialog box, which opens when you choose Advanced ⇨ PDF Optimizer and which is shown in Figure 18.6.

Click the button labeled Audit space usage. Depending on the size and complexity of the document, the analysis can take a little time. When the analysis completes, the dialog box shown in Figure 18.7 opens.

FIGURE 18.7

After the analysis is completed, the Audit Space Usage dialog box opens, where space usage according to different objects/elements is reported as a percentage of the total space.

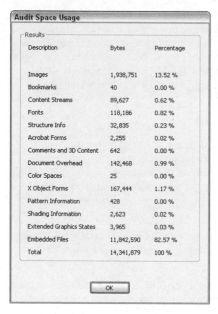

Description	Bytes	Percentage
Images	1,938,751	13.52 %
Bookmarks	40	0.00 %
Content Streams	89,627	0.62 %
Fonts	118,186	0.82 %
Structure Info	32,835	0.23 %
Acrobat Forms	2,255	0.02 %
Comments and 3D Content	642	0.00 %
Document Overhead	142,468	0.99 %
Color Spaces	25	0.00 %
X Object Forms	167,444	1.17 %
Pattern Information	428	0.00 %
Shading Information	2,623	0.02 %
Extended Graphics States	3,965	0.03 %
Embedded Files	11,842,590	82.57 %
Total	14,341,879	100 %

In the example shown in the preceding figure, notice that most of the document space is used for embedded content (83.22 percent). Most of the embedded content relates to embedded images. If the image resolution in this document is higher than images suited for screen viewing at 72 pixels per inch (ppi), then downsampling the images by reducing resolution would compact the file and make it significantly smaller. If you have documents designed for print and want to repurpose the documents for Web viewing, image downsampling is likely to be one of the things you'll want to adjust in the PDF Optimizer.

Optimizing files

Using the PDF Optimizer, you control a number of different attributes that contribute to a document's structure and content. By adjusting the number of different options found in the PDF Optimizer dialog box you have the opportunity to produce documents much smaller than when using the Examine Document menu command. The options found in the PDF Optimizer include a Settings option, an option for changing PDF compatibility, and categories listed on the left side of the dialog box. Click on one of the items listed in the left pane and the right pane changes much like when using the Preferences dialog box. These categories include Images, Fonts, Transparency, Discard Objects, Discard User Data, and Clean Up.

Settings

This item appears first in the PDF Optimizer, but it's the last setting you address. When you open the PDF Optimizer, the default is Standard. Select Custom or make changes to any setting and the Save button becomes active. When you click Save, Acrobat prompts you to save your new settings as a preset. After saving, the name you define for the preset is added to the pull-down menu. When you return to the PDF Optimizer in another Acrobat session, you can select from the number of different presets and click OK to optimize files with the same settings defined for the respective preset.

If you want to clear a preset from the pull-down menu, select a preset in the menu and click the Delete button.

Make compatible with

From a pull-down menu you select Acrobat compatibility levels. You can make your optimized document compatible with Acrobat 4, 5, 6, 7, and 8. The Retain existing menu command keeps the compatibility the same as the source file. When the need arises to serve users with earlier compatibility files, change the menu command to the desired compatibility level. By default, Retain Existing is selected in the menu. If you change from Acrobat 5 to Acrobat 6 or 7, some other attribute settings in the PDF Optimizer change to reflect choices supported by newer versions of Acrobat.

Images

To reduce file size with the PDF Optimizer, use the first set of options found in the left pane; the default Images pane appears, as shown in Figure 18.6. You can make choices for downsampling color, grayscale, and bitmap images by typing values in the field boxes for the sampling amounts desired. To the right of the downsampling amount, another field box is used to identify images that are downsampled. This box instructs Acrobat to look for any image above the setting defined in the field box and downsamples the file to the amount supplied in the first field box.

CROSS-REF The Images pane offers choices for the downsampling method. The default method is Bicubic Downsampling. Leave the choice for Bicubic Downsampling at the default selection. To learn more about the other methods and what they mean, see Chapter 10.

The Compression pull-down menu offers choices for Retain existing, JPEG, JPEG2000 (an additional setting available when Acrobat 6 through 8 compatibility is selected), and Zip compression. The Retain existing setting honors the original compression used when the PDF was created.

CROSS-REF For more information on the JPEG, JPEG2000, and Zip file formats, see Chapter 7.

For either form of JPEG compression you have additional choices for the amount of compression from the Quality pull-down menu. If you choose a JPEG compression and use Minimum for the Quality choice, your images may appear severely degraded. As a general rule, Medium quality results in satisfactory image quality for Web hosting. If you try one setting and the images look too degraded, you can return to the original file and apply a different Quality setting; then examine the results.

Zip compression is a lossless compression scheme, which means that files are compressed without data loss. For Acrobat 4 and 5 compatibility, Zip offers a good choice when you want to maximize image quality. When using Acrobat 6 through 8 compatibility, you can select JPEG2000 for a better compression result and select Lossless from the Quality pull-down menu, which will save all the image data.

Fonts

Fonts won't always appear in a list in the Fonts pane when you click the word Fonts on the left side of the PDF Optimizer. Only fonts that are available for unembedding are listed on the left side of the Fonts pane. If no fonts appear in the list, you can move on to the Transparency settings. If fonts are listed in the box in the left side of the pane, select the fonts to unembed and click the Unembed button adjacent to the right chevron.

In the right box are fonts listed for unembedding. If you want to keep the font embedded, select it in the right box and click the Retain button adjacent to the left chevron. To select multiple fonts in either window, press Shift+click to select a list in a contiguous group, or press Ctrl/⌘+click to select fonts in a non-contiguous group.

Transparency

Transparent images and objects can be flattened in Acrobat 8 for all PDF documents created in Acrobat 5 and greater. If you select Acrobat 4 compatibility, transparency is automatically flattened because Acrobat 4 compatibility does not support transparency. When you select all other compatibility versions, you have options for flattening the transparency.

 **For information on using transparency-flattening settings, see Chapter 32.**

Discard Objects

Discarding items such as comments, form actions, JavaScript actions, cross references, and thumbnails affects document functionality as you might suspect. If the respective items are eliminated, any PDF interactivity created with these items is also eliminated. If you know that one or any group of these items won't have an effect on the way the repurposed document is viewed or printed, enable the check boxes for the items you want to remove.

 **Acrobat 8 provides a new feature in the Discard Objects pane for flattening form fields. For more on using this option see "Redistilling PDFs" later in this chapter.**

Discard User Data

Comments, multimedia, file attachments, hidden layers, and more are listed in the Discard User Data pane. Like Discard Objects, if you choose to eliminate the items, the result can affect the way PDFs are viewed and remove some interactivity. Pick and choose these items wisely to retain the kind of interactive features you want in the resultant file.

Clean Up

Click on Clean Up in the left pane and you find a list of items checked by default that can be used safely without affecting the functionality of your document. Select the box for Remove unreferenced named destinations if the check box is not checked. Settings such as removing invalid Bookmarks, links, and destinations won't affect the document viewing but removing the unnecessary items helps reduce file size. As a matter of practice, leave all the options in this pane checked.

After you make your preferred settings in the PDF Optimizer, click the Save button if you want to save the settings as a new preset or click OK to start the optimization process.

Redistilling Files

In each version of *Acrobat PDF Bible* dating back to version 4 of Acrobat, I've included some various reasons why you might want to export a PDF file back to PostScript and redistill the file. This is often referred to as *refrying* a PDF.

Before Acrobat 8, you might have used this method of document repurposing when you had a number of form fields for which you didn't need the field objects, but you wanted to retain the data within fields in a repurposed document. All previous versions of Acrobat couldn't perform this operation using the PDF Optimizer. In other cases, the PDF Optimizer was broken upon the first release of a new Acrobat version. In Acrobat 7, for example, I used the PDF Optimizer on a 10+MB file and the optimized file turned out a 295MB file. This wasn't fixed until the release of Acrobat 7.05. The only option I had to repurpose my document was to refry the PDF.

NEW FEATURE Acrobat 8 offers an option in the PDF Optimizer to flatten form fields. (See Figure 18.8.) Doing so retains the form data but discards the field objects. On files with columns and rows of fields, you can produce a substantially lower file size after optimizing it and flattening the fields.

FIGURE 18.8

Acrobat 8 provides an option to flatten form fields in the PDF Optimizer.

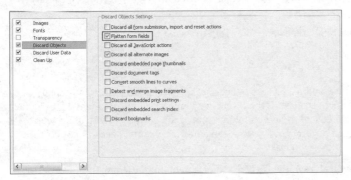

I'm happy to report that the PDF Optimizer seems to be working very well in the first release of Acrobat 8. With the flatten form field option and the efficiency of the PDF Optimizer, there now appears to be very little reason to export a PDF document to PostScript and distill the PostScript in Acrobat Distiller.

CROSS-REF For information on creating PostScript files from PDF documents, using Acrobat Distiller, and making choices for Adobe PDF Settings, see Chapter 10.

Obviously it's impossible to test PDF Optimizer on every kind of file. At times you may find an anomaly in a file where the PDF Optimizer just won't work. I haven't found it so far in Acrobat 8, but it is possible. Therefore, as a last resort workaround, it may be worthwhile knowing a little about exporting to PostScript and using Acrobat Distiller to repurpose a PDF.

As a first effort in repurposing PDF files, users of Acrobat 8 Professional should try the PDF Optimizer. If the results don't satisfactorily downsize a file, you can select File ➪ Save As and choose PostScript (*.ps) for the file type. Launch Acrobat Distiller and select a PDF Setting; then open the PostScript file to distill it. Note that because Acrobat Standard doesn't offer the PDF Optimizer, this method of repurposing PDF files may be the only option you have.

TIP If you have interactive elements in a document such as Bookmarks, form fields, destinations, and so on and want to preserve the interactive elements when redistilling PDFs, realize that all such items are lost in the new file created with Acrobat Distiller. To regain Bookmarks, form fields, and so on, open the original file in Acrobat. Choose Document ➪ Replace Pages. Locate the new file created with Acrobat Distiller in the Select File With New Pages dialog box and replace all pages in the file. Choose File ➪ Save As to write a new optimized file to disk. The new file uses the optimized pages and the old file's interactive elements. You'll see a little increase in the file size because of the interactive elements, but the overall file size will be much smaller in your new file compared to the original file.

Batch Processing PDF Files

If you have multiple files that need to be refined for distribution on network servers, Web sites, or CD-ROM, then you'll want to create a batch sequence. *Batch sequences* are a defined series of commands in a specific order that can be run on multiple files. You create the batch sequence from a list of executable functions and determine the commands and order of the sequence.

Batch sequences help you automate tasks in Acrobat that might otherwise take considerable time, such as manually applying a common set of commands on many different files. After you develop one or more sequences, you can run the sequence(s) on selected PDF files, a folder of PDF files, or multiple folders of PDF files.

Tasks such as setting opening views of PDF documents, adding document descriptions, adding page numbers, or running the PDF Optimizer can be applied to multiple files you might want to distribute on CD-ROM or on Web sites. Before distributing files, you can run a batch sequence as a final step in your production workflow to be sure all files have common attributes.

Creating a batch sequence

To create a new sequence, choose Advanced ➪ Document Processing ➪ Batch Processing. The Batch Sequences dialog box opens, as shown in Figure 18.9. The dialog box lists several sequences that are predefined for you when you install Acrobat. From the list in the dialog box you can run a sequence, edit one of the listed sequences, rename a sequence, or delete any one or more sequences from the list. The first button in the dialog box is used to create a new sequence where you choose what commands you want to run from a list in other dialog boxes.

FIGURE 18.9

Choose Advanced ➪ Document Processing ➪ Batch Processing to open the Batch Sequences dialog box.

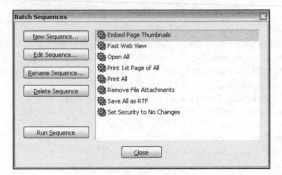

Click New Sequence and the Name Sequence dialog box shown in Figure 18.10 opens. The first step in creating a batch sequence is to provide a name for the sequence. The name supplied in the dialog box ultimately is added to the list in the Batch Sequence window. When you want to run the sequence you can open the Batch Sequences dialog box, select any one of the sequences you added to the list, and click the Run Sequence button.

FIGURE 18.10

The first step in creating a new sequence is naming the sequence. You add the names of new sequences to the list in the Batch Sequences dialog box.

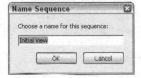

Type a name in the field box and click OK. The next dialog box that opens is the Edit Batch Sequence – Initial View dialog box shown in Figure 18.11. Three items are listed in the dialog box. The next step (the Batch Sequence dialog box actually lists this step as the first step in creating a sequence) is to click the Select Commands button. After you make choices for the commands added to the sequence, you are returned to this dialog box to make choices for items 2 and 3 where you identify the input location of files and the destination (output) location.

FIGURE 18.11

The Edit Batch Sequence – Initial View dialog box opens after you provide a name such as *Initial View* for a new sequence. Click the Select Commands button to choose the commands executed in the sequence.

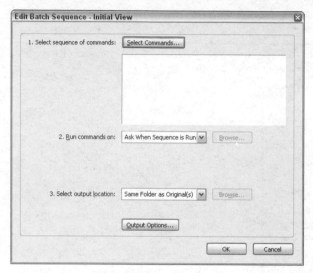

The Edit Sequence dialog box opens for you to make choices for the commands added to your new sequence. From the scrollable list on the left side of the dialog box, select a command and click the Add button to move the command to the right side of the dialog box. If you want more than one set of commands applied to your sequence, select a command and click the Add button; then select additional commands and click Add. In this example, I added a command for setting the Initial View by adding the Open Options item in the Document list. Click the icon adjacent to the sequence command and the options are displayed, as you see in Figure 18.12.

FIGURE 18.12

Select a command in the left window and click the Add button. Click the icon adjacent to the command name and a list expands displaying the options.

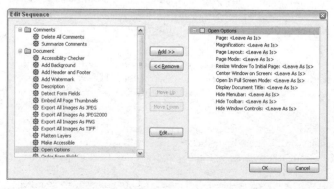

After the commands are added to the right window, you can make attribute choices for each command. From those commands in the right window, either select the command or double-click on the name to open dialog boxes where you make attribute choices. In Figure 18.13 I adjusted the Set Open Options dialog box where I made changes to the Initial View and the Window Options.

FIGURE 18.13

Initial View options are selected in the Set Open Options dialog box. To open the dialog box, double-click the command in the right window in the Edit Sequence dialog box or click the Edit button.

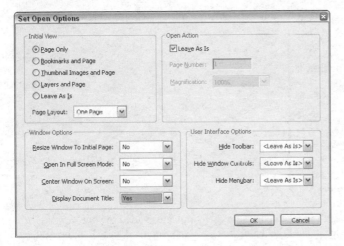

The settings applied for the Initial View are applied globally to files when you run the sequence. You can run the sequence on a folder of files if you want the files to share common attributes.

To finish creating your sequence, click OK and click OK again in the Edit Sequence dialog box. Your new sequence is added to the Batch Sequences dialog box that opened first when you selected Batch Sequences from the Advanced menu.

Setting output options

When you click the Output Options button in the Edit Batch Sequence dialog box, you'll find choices for filenaming and output formats as well as file optimization. Select the Output Options check box when you create a new sequence in the Edit Batch Sequence dialog box and the Output Options dialog box opens, as shown in Figure 18.14.

You can add a suffix or prefix to filenames by clicking the Add To Original Base Name(s) button and editing the field boxes for Insert Before and Insert After. If you enter data in the Insert After field box the data is added before the filename extension. Select the box for Do not overwrite existing files to ensure that you won't inadvertently overwrite the original files.

The Save File(s) As pull-down menu offers choices for the file formats to be exported. The default is Adobe PDF. If you want to save files in text formats (Word, RTF, XML, text only, and so on), you can make the choice for the text format from the pull-down menu options. Additionally, PostScript, EPS, image formats, HTML, and XML formats are available. One great new feature in Acrobat 8 is the option for saving PDF documents compatible with specifications such as PDF/A and PDF/X. Choose one of these formats and you can convert a collection of PDFs to a PDF/A or PDF/X standard.

CROSS-REF For more information on the PDF/A and PDF/X PDF standards , see Chapter 10.

FIGURE 18.14

Output Options offer you choices for naming the processed files as well as saving in different formats and optimizing files with the PDF Optimizer.

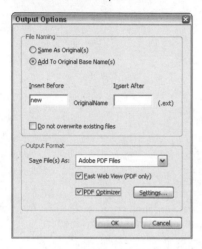

You'll note that the Save As options in the Output Format Save File(s) pull-down menu offers the same options as when you choose the File ➪ Save As command. The one option not available to you when saving files with a batch sequence is saving to your Version Cue workspace.

CROSS-REF For more information on using Version Cue, see Chapter 11.

Running sequences

Presuming you created a sequence and added the new sequence, you can open the Batch Sequence dialog box by choosing Advanced ➪ Batch Processing and selecting the sequence you want to run. Click the Run Sequence button in the Batch Sequence dialog box and the Run Sequence Confirmation dialog box opens, as shown in Figure 18.15.

A list of commands appears in the dialog box where you can review the settings for each command by click-ing the icon adjacent to the sequence commands to display the settings as discussed earlier in this chapter. If all the settings are appropriate for the sequence you want to run, click OK and the Select Files to Process dialog box opens. You can select a file or a contiguous or non-contiguous group of files by using Shift+click or Ctrl/⌘+Shift and click a folder or a group of folders for processing. Click the Select button, and the sequence runs. If you created a sequence to toggle open a dialog box for supplying unique data for each file, the dialog boxes open. Make changes in any dialog boxes, click the OK buttons, and the sequence contin-ues. Files are saved according to the choices you made in the Output Options dialog box or the choice made from the Select output location pull-down menu in the Edit Batch Sequence dialog box.

After running a sequence, examine the files to ensure all files are created with the options you expect them to have. If there are any errors and you saved the new set of files without overwriting the original set, you can edit the sequence and run the edited version on the original files.

FIGURE 18.15

Click Run Sequence in the Batch Sequences dialog box and the Run Sequence Confirmation dialog box opens. Click the icon adjacent to the command name to open a list of the settings.

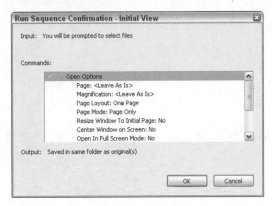

Editing sequences

If you create a sequence for one purpose and want to modify the sequence for another processing venture, you can edit the attributes of a command, add new commands, or delete commands from the original sequence. To edit a sequence, choose Advanced ➪ Document Processing ➪ Batch Processing. In the Batch Sequences dialog box, select the sequence you want to edit and click the Edit Sequence button. The Edit Batch Sequences dialog box opens.

In order to edit the commands, add new commands, or delete commands, you first need to click the Select Commands button. The Edit Sequence dialog box opens where you can add new commands or edit existing commands by following the information in the earlier section on creating sequences.

If you want to delete a sequence and all the commands associated with the sequence, click the Delete Sequence button in the Batch Sequences dialog box. This action removes the sequence from the list. If you delete commands in the Edit Sequence dialog box and keep a modified version of a sequence listed in the Batch Sequences dialog box, you may want to rename a sequence to more closely relate to the modified version. Click the Rename Sequence button in the Batch Sequence dialog box and edit the name in the Name Sequence dialog box.

Creating custom sequences

The batch sequences you create are chosen from the list of commands in the Edit Sequence dialog box. If you want to add a command that doesn't exist in the list in the Edit Sequence dialog box, you can create custom sequences from commands you add with JavaScripts.

JavaScripts offer you an infinite number of possibilities for automating commands and sequences applied to a group of PDF documents. As an example, suppose you want to add a Stamp comment to an assorted collection of PDFs designed to be documents in draft form. After the files have been stamped with a Draft icon from the Stamp comment, you disperse the documents, collect feedback, and use another batch sequence to delete all comments from the documents. The sequence for deleting comments is a preset installed with Acrobat. Adding Stamp comments, however, is something you need to do with a JavaScript. Use the steps that follow to add a JavaScript to a batch sequence, and in particular, to add a Stamp comment to a collection of PDF files.

STEPS: Creating a JavaScript batch sequence

1. **Create a new batch sequence.** Choose Advanced ⇨ Document Processing ⇨ Batch Processing. In the Batch Sequences dialog box, select New Sequence. When the Name Sequence dialog box opens, type a name for the sequence. In this example I use Add Stamp. Click OK.

2. **Select Execute JavaScript and add it to the list of sequences to be executed.** In the Edit Batch Sequence dialog box, click Select Commands to open the Edit Sequence dialog box. In the Edit Sequence dialog box, select Execute JavaScript from the list on the left and click the Add button to move the command to the right window.

3. **Add the JavaScript code to execute the action.** Select the command in the right pane and click the Edit button (or double-click on the command). The JavaScript Editor dialog box opens. In the JavaScript Editor, type the following code. (The same code is shown as it should appear in the JavaScript Editor in Figure 18.16.)

NOTE Line numbers in the code below are for reference only. Do not type the numbers in the JavaScript Editor.

```
1. /* adds a stamp to the first page */
2. var annot = this.addAnnot ({
3.    page:0,
4.    type: "Stamp",
5.    name: "Draft",
6.    rect: [400, 700, 600, 790],
7.    popupOpen: false,
8.    author: "Ted",
9.    contents: "First Review",
10, });
```

FIGURE 18.16

Type the code in the JavaScript Editor dialog box.

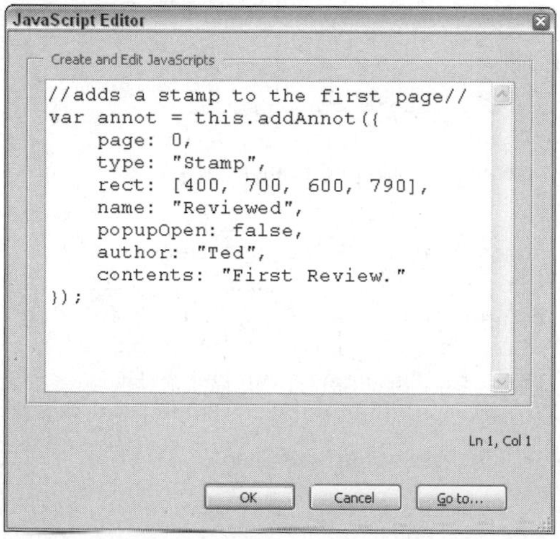

NOTE The coordinates for the position of the note are set for a standard US Letter size page (8.5 × 11 inches, portrait view). If you run the sequence on documents with different size pages or orientation, the results may not show the stamp on a page.

4. **Save the JavaScript.** Click OK in the JavaScript Editor dialog box. Click OK in the Edit Sequence dialog box to return to the Edit Batch Sequence dialog box. The script is saved when you exit the JavaScript Editor dialog box.

5. **Set the Output Options.** Leave Run commands on at the default for Ask When Sequence is Run. In the Select output location pull-down menu, select the option you want to use for the saved files location. If you want to be prompted at the time the sequence is run, select Ask When Sequence is Run. Click OK in the Edit Batch Sequence dialog box and the sequence is added to the list of Batch Sequences.

6. **Run the sequence.** Select the Add Stamp sequence in the Batch Sequences dialog box and click Run Sequence. (If you closed the Batch Sequences dialog box after the last step, choose Advanced ➪ Document Processing ➪ Batch Processing to reopen the dialog box.)

7. **Examine the results.** Select a single file to process when the Select Files to Process dialog box opens. You should see a Stamp comment in the top-right corner of the document page. Double-click the Stamp icon to open the pop-up note window, the note contents are shown in Figure 18.17.

FIGURE 18.17

The Stamp comment is added to the first page of all documents processed with the Add Stamp routine created in the JavaScript Editor.

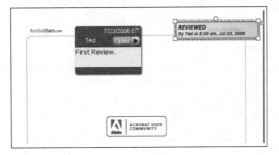

CROSS-REF For more information on creating stamps and using pop-up note windows, see Chapter 20.

The preceding steps create a Stamp comment (from the Stamp comment you last used in Acrobat) (Line 2) at the coordinates (Line 6) — note that the page size where the stamps are added is a standard US Letter 8.5 × 11 inches in portrait view. The note pop-up window is closed by default (Line 7), and the content of the note pop-up is *First Review* (Line 9). You can change the position of the note by editing the coordinates in Line 6, change the contents in Line 9, or change the stamp type in Line 4. The code can be easily modified or you can copy and paste the code in the JavaScript Editor if you want to create other similar sequences.

CROSS-REF For more information on writing JavaScripts, see Chapter 36.

Summary

- File sizes can be reduced with the Reduce File Size menu command. If you're cropping image files in Acrobat, save the cropped image to an image format; then open the file in Acrobat to convert back to PDF.

- Examine Document offers some options for deleting content from files to help reduce file size.

- The PDF Optimizer is used to reduce file sizes and eliminate unnecessary data in PDF files. PDF Optimizer can often reduce file sizes more than when using the Reduce File Size command.

- Selecting options in the Discard Objects pane in the PDF Optimizer other than the default options can interfere with the PDF functionality. Care must be exercised in selecting options to prevent potential problems.

- The new Flatten form fields option in the Discard Objects pane discards field objects while retaining data for optimizing forms when the fields are no longer needed.

- In some cases, saving a PDF file to disk and redistilling with Acrobat Distiller can reduce file sizes. Redistillation can be used with Acrobat Standard where no PDF Optimizer is available.

- Batch sequences help you automate processing multiple PDF documents. From a standard set of sequence options you can create batch sequences for a limited number of actions. When custom options are needed, you can add JavaScripts for processing files with custom settings.

Chapter 19

Enabling Features for Adobe Reader

Enabling features for Adobe Reader or adding *special features* for Reader users is a means whereby certain features not appearing in the default Adobe Reader program can be added to PDF documents. This enabling function can be handled by one of two applications. You can use a server product such as the Adobe LiveCycle Reader Extensions Server (LCRE) or Adobe Acrobat 8 Professional.

In Acrobat 7, a single enabling feature was introduced that added these special features to permit Adobe Reader users participation in e-mail–based reviews. When a PDF document was enabled for commenting and markup, all the comment tools appeared in Adobe Reader, they we usable, and the comments could be saved from Reader.

In Acrobat 8, Adobe has introduced more enabling features such as those for saving form data and adding digital signatures. These options are not part of Adobe Reader. But when opening an enabled file in Reader, you can take advantage of the special features for saving form data and adding digital signatures.

> **NOTE** This chapter deals exclusively with Adobe Acrobat Professional. Users of Acrobat Standard do not have features for enabling PDF documents.

Setting Up the Enabling Work Environment

Enabling PDF files with Reader extensions is handled through menu commands. No special toolbars need to be loaded to enable PDF files. Return to the default view by opening a context menu and selecting Reset Toolbars.

IN THIS CHAPTER

Using server products

Understanding licensing restrictions

Adding special features for Adobe Reader

Editing files enabled with usage rights

Adobe LiveCycle Reader Extensions Server

To get a grasp on enabling PDF files and to better understand what limitations you have for adding special features to PDFs, you should know a little something about Adobe's server product used for adding special features. The Adobe LiveCycle Reader Extension Server (LCRE) is a server product sold to enterprises and large organizations. The cost of the product begins at $30,000 and goes up from there depending on the use.

At first blush you might think the cost is extraordinary. But stop for a moment and think about an organization like the US Internal Revenue Service (IRS) that uses LCRE. The IRS processes millions of forms annually for income tax reporting. In an analog world where the IRS needs to print millions of tax forms and distribute them worldwide, the costs per form rise well above a more affordable solution such as the Reader Extensions Server.

You and I as individual users of Acrobat are not likely to purchase LCRE, but we may have an occasional need to work with forms that need to be enabled for Adobe Reader users. This being the case, Adobe recognized the gap between independent PDF authors and workers within small workgroups vs. IT managers enabling forms for mass distribution. Hence, the enabling features have been enriched in Acrobat 8 Professional.

Restrictions for Enabling Features

As logic would have it, you're no doubt thinking there must be some restriction or limitation on enabling PDF files in Acrobat 8. After all, how could Adobe hope to sell one product that starts at $30,000 when a user could find the same thing purchasing a copy of Acrobat Professional?

There are indeed limitations and they are all spelled out in the End User License Agreement (EULA) you agree to when installing Acrobat. Just in case you are confused about language in the agreement after reading it, let me paraphrase the licensing agreement and amplify some of the conditions. In addition to what is covered in this chapter, you should carefully read the agreement and understand the limitations of use.

Audience

Prior to Acrobat 8 there was no opportunity for users to enable features in PDF files that permit Adobe Reader users the ability to fill in form data, save the data, and digitally sign documents. Adobe recognized a clear distinction between users who have occasional and limited needs vs. enterprises that distribute PDF forms to many thousands of people.

Small to medium businesses might have needs for people to fill out small batches of forms for travel expense claims, purchase orders, personal time off forms, and so on. Some of the data such as data compiled from expense forms might need to be exported to an Excel spreadsheet and integrated into an accounting program.

You might also have an annual charity golf tournament with a few hundred participants, a small annual conference with less than 300 registrants, or other similar need to distribute forms and collect data.

These kinds of examples fit within Adobe's EULA and target audience. On the other hand, if you have a commercial Web site and you're collecting PDF forms for point of sale purchases where the numbers of potential customers may be in the thousands, then this kind of use for your PDF-enabled forms is a clear violation of the licensing agreement.

Licensing restrictions

The language in the EULA suggests that you can enable PDF forms with forms saving and digital signatures for Adobe Reader users for up to 500 instances of a given document. The document usage can be one of two ways. You can distribute an unlimited number of enabled forms, but you can only aggregate up to 500 forms — something like hosting a form on your Web site where you might get less than 500 registrants for something like a conference. The other instance is distributing forms to 500 named individuals and you can aggregate any number of those forms — something like expense accounts that people fill out and return monthly.

> **NOTE**   For an up to date description of the Acrobat EULA or any other Adobe product, visit:
> `www.adobe.com/products/eulas`. **On the opening Web page you'll find links to Acrobat and other Adobe products specifying the conditions of the license agreements.**

Enforcing the restrictions

Adobe uses no special coding or technology to ensure users are complying with the licensing agreement. Adobe believes that the enforcement for restricting users to the limitations is vested in the amount of work people need to perform. For limited use, the enabling features in Acrobat 8 are among the top ten best new features in Acrobat and serve a need for many PDF authors. However, the kind of use an LCRE user needs to process volumes of forms such as parsing data and routing data to databases is something to be found only in the server products from Adobe.

There remains a clear distinction between industrial strength use and limited use, not only in the licensing agreement, but also in practicality. The new enabling features do not diminish the need for the Adobe LiveCycle Reader Extensions Server. Quite the contrary: Workgroups that begin to work more with enabling PDFs with Reader extensions are likely to experience needs for evolving to more sophisticated uses that can only be satisfied using LCRE.

Enabling PDF Documents with Reader Extensions (Acrobat Professional only)

In Acrobat 8 Professional you can enable PDFs with special usage rights for adding comments and markups and save the comments once added in Adobe Reader. You can enable PDF forms, adding features for Adobe Reader users permitting the Reader user to save form data and add digital signatures.

PDF files can be enabled for either Comment & Review or commenting and form saves/digital signatures. How you go about enabling files from Acrobat is handled through menu commands. You choose from one of four menu commands for adding special features to PDF documents for Adobe Reader users. Furthermore, enabling files can be performed only in Acrobat Professional.

Enabling PDFs for Commenting

The first of the four menu commands you can use to enable PDF files for Adobe Reader users is Comments ➪ Enable for Commenting in Adobe Reader. The first time you select this command an application alert dialog box opens informing you that certain editing functions normally available to Acrobat users will be restricted. If you check the Don't show again check box as shown in Figure 19.1, the dialog box won't appear when enabling future documents.

FIGURE 19.1

The first time you enable a file for commenting in Adobe Reader an application alert dialog box opens.

Click OK in the application alert dialog box and a Save As dialog box opens. Type a new name for your file to avoid overwriting the original and click the Save button. The PDF is now enabled with Adobe Reader usage rights for commenting and markup.

When an Adobe Reader user opens the enabled PDF document, the Comment & Markup tools are all accessible, as shown in Figure 19.2. You can add the same kind of comments as you can with either Acrobat Standard or Acrobat Professional. After adding comments, the Reader user also has access to a File ⇨ Save command. This command is not available unless a file has been enabled. Selecting File ⇨ Save permits the Reader user the opportunity to save all comments added to the PDF.

FIGURE 19.2

Adobe Reader users can add and save all comments and markups on PDF files enabled for commenting.

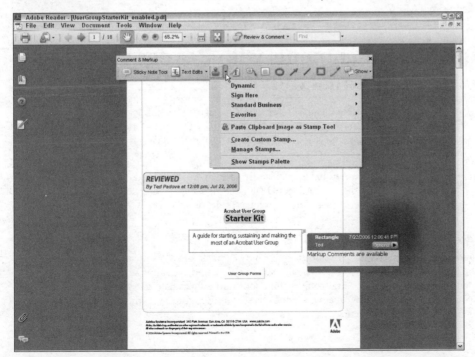

CROSS-REF For more information on limitations of Adobe Reader, see Chapter 4. For more information on comment and markup, see Chapter 20.

Enabling PDFs for Comment & Review

Enabling PDFs for Comment & Review provides essentially the same usage rights as when enabling for Commenting in Adobe Reader. You click the Review & Comment tool in the Tasks Toolbar to open a drop-down menu. From the menu items, select Attach for Email Review. The Send by Email for Review Wizard opens in the first of three steps, as shown in Figure 19.3.

FIGURE 19.3

Click the Review & Comment task button and choose Attach for Email Review.

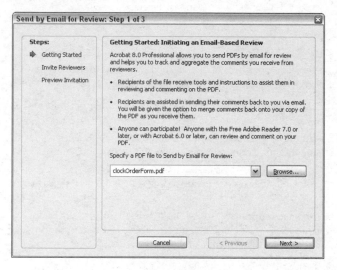

The first pane in the wizard states that users of Adobe Reader 7.0 and above can participate in the review. Click through the wizard panes and your PDF document is attached to an e-mail message window. When you send the e-mail to an Adobe Reader recipient, the Reader user sees the same comment options as shown earlier in Figure 19.2.

CROSS-REF For more information on comment reviews, see Chapter 21.

Enabling PDFs for form saves

The third of the four menu options provides you a complete set of enabling features for Adobe Reader users. Select Advanced ➪ Enable Usage Rights in Adobe Reader, and the Enable Usage Rights in Adobe Reader dialog box opens, as shown in Figure 19.4.

FIGURE 19.4

Select Document ⇨ Enable Features in Adobe Reader and a dialog box opens informing you of the features that you can enable.

Click Save Now and all the features listed in the dialog box are enabled in the PDF file for Adobe Reader users. This option provides a complete set of enabling features, including the following:

- **Save form data (for fillable PDF form only).** Adobe Reader users can add data to PDF forms containing form fields and save the edited file.

- **Commenting and drawing mark-up tools.** The same comment and markup tools are available to Adobe Reader users as when enabling files for Comment & Markup and Review & Comment. All comments can be saved.

- **Sign an existing signature field.** Adobe Reader users can add a digital signature to a signature field on a form and save the edits.

- **Digitally sign the document on the page (supported in Adobe Reader 8 only).** As the text implies, this feature is available only to users of Adobe Reader 8 and above. A Reader user can sign a document without the appearance of a signature file and save the edits.

When you click Save Now, the file is enabled with the usage rights.

CROSS-REF For more information on fillable form fields, see Chapters 33 and 34. For more information on using digital signatures, see Chapter 26.

Sending files for Shared Reviews

One of the most popular and requested features from users during the Acrobat 6 and 7 life cycles has been a means for sharing comments other than the options Adobe made available with Browser-Based Reviews. In local environments as well on Web servers, users wanted a way to comment on documents and have all the comments viewed by all participants in a review in a collaborative workflow.

NEW FEATURE Adobe has responded to the users' needs by introducing the Send for Shared Review command. Open the Review & Comment task button menu and select Send For Shared Review. The Send PDF for Shared Review Wizard opens and walks you through steps to set up a shared review. The first pane in the wizard window provides you an option for enabling the PDF with Reader usage rights.

When sending PDFs for Shared Reviews (or sending a location where the file is located in a file folder on a server or Web site) be certain to keep the check box checked in the Send PDF for Shared Review Wizard for Enable Reviewers with Adobe Reader to Participate as shown in Figure 19.5. As you progress through the wizard and save your file the PDF is enabled with Adobe Reader usage rights where users of Adobe Reader can comment and markup PDFs in a collaborative work environment.

CROSS-REF For more information on Shared Reviews, see Chapter 21.

FIGURE 19.5

When sending documents for Shared Reviews, be certain to keep the check box checked for Enable Reviewers with Adobe Reader to participate so all users of Reader can collaborate on the file.

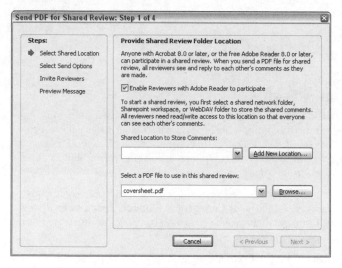

Distributing Forms?

The last of the four menu commands you can use to enable PDF documents is the Distribute Form command found in the Forms menu. When you select Forms ➪ Distribute Form, the Form Distribution Options wizard opens as shown in Figure 19.6. Your first step is to choose whether you want to e-mail the form or save the form and e-mail it later. When you choose the Send now via email option, your form is enabled with Adobe Reader usage rights and attached to a new e-mail message in your default e-mail program. If you choose the Save and send later option, the form is enabled with Reader usage rights and it is added to the Forms Tracker History pane. You can easily find the form for later distribution by selecting Forms ➪ Track Forms and click the History item in the left pane. Double-click the file listed in the right pane and you can click the Distribute button in the Forms toolbar to send the form via e-mail.

CROSS-REF For more information on using the Distribute Form command and the Distribute Forms Options wizard, see Chapter 35.

FIGURE 19.6

Select Forms ➪ Distribute Form to open the Form Distribution Options wizard and apply Adobe Reader usage rights.

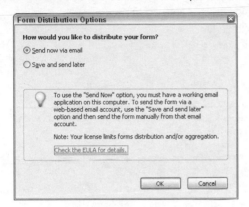

What about Adobe Designer Forms?

Anyone working with forms created in Adobe LiveCycle Designer knows you have limited editing possibilities when opening the forms in Adobe Acrobat. You cannot enable a form with Reader Extensions directly in Adobe LiveCycle Designer per se. You can select File ➪ Distribute Form in Adobe LiveCycle Designer, but doing so launches Acrobat and opens the Form Distribution Options dialog box. All enabling features of Designer forms are handled within Acrobat Professional.

You can open any form created in Designer in Acrobat 8 Professional and use the same menu commands used for all enabling features as you do when enabling files for Comment & Markup, Comment & Review, and Enable Features in Adobe Reader (save form and digital signatures), and by using the Distribute Form command.

When you enable a form using the Comments ➪ Enable Commenting in Adobe Reader command, you don't have an option for enabling form saves and commenting in the same file. Likewise, you don't have an option to add a digital signature if a digital signature field is not contained on the form. When you use the Advanced menu for Enable Usage Rights in Adobe Reader or the Distribute Form command, both commenting and form saves and using digital signatures are enabled in the PDF for Reader users.

 For more information on Adobe LiveCycle Designer, see Chapter 35.

Editing Enabled PDF Files

Upon occasion you may enable a PDF document using any one of the enabling options available in Acrobat 8 Professional and then later decide you want to edit the file. When you enable a PDF document and try to edit it in Acrobat, an application alert dialog box opens as shown in Figure 19.7.

FIGURE 19.7

If you try to edit an enabled file in Acrobat, an alert dialog box opens informing you that you can't edit the file.

Modifying an enabled PDF file

To edit an enabled file in Acrobat you first need to save a copy of the document. When you open non-enabled PDF files, the File menu lists commands for Save and Save As. When you open an enabled file in Acrobat you find the commands Save, Save As, and Save a Copy. The addition of the Save a Copy command is unique to enabled PDF files and only this command will remove the restrictions applied when the PDF was enabled. The usage rights are removed when you save a copy, so after editing you need to re-enable the form.

Select File ➪ Save a Copy and the Save a Copy dialog box opens as you see in Figure 19.8. Click the Save a Copy button and a second Save a Copy dialog box opens where you can name the copy and select a folder where you want to save it. Once you save a copy, your copy file is not open in the Acrobat Document pane. It's merely saved to disk. Your original file remains open and it's not editable. Close the open file, then select File ➪ Open or click the Open tool in the Toolbar Well. When the Open dialog box appears, select the copy file and open it in Acrobat. You can edit this file and enable it after you complete your editing tasks.

FIGURE 19.8

Click the Save a Copy button to save an editable copy of the enabled PDF document.

You'll find that most of the kinds of editing you typically perform on a PDF document aren't available with enabled documents. Items such as changing any of the Document Properties (Description, Security, Initial View, Custom and Advanced), adding headers and footers, changing backgrounds, adding comments, editing form fields, changing JavaScripts, and so on, are all unavailable to you when working on an enabled PDF document. To edit any of these items select File ➪ Save a Copy and open the copy file.

CROSS-REF For more information on changing Document Properties, see Chapter 6. For more information on adding headers and footers and changing backgrounds, see Chapter 16. For more information on adding comments, see Chapter 20. For more information on editing form fields, see Chapter 34. For more information on editing JavaScripts, see Chapter 36.

Working with enabled files and PDF Packages

When you create PDF Packages, you may want to edit an enabled PDF document after you create the package. If you select File ➪ Save a Copy, your enabled document is saved as a copy outside the PDF Package while the original enabled file remains within the package. In order to update the PDF Package with an edited copy, you need to delete the original enabled PDF document from the PDF Package and then add the edited file that you re-enable back into the PDF Package. It's not as confusing as it sounds and here's how you do it.

STEPS: Editing an enabled PDF in a PDF Package

1. **Assuming you created a PDF package with a PDF that has been enabled with reader usage rights**, click the enabled PDF in the PDF Package pane to bring it into view in the Document pane.

2. **Save a Copy.** Select File ➪ Save a Copy and save a copy of the enabled PDF document. Note that when you select File ➪ Save a Copy only the PDF in view in the Document pane is saved as a copy. The entire PDF Package is not saved.

3. **Delete the enabled PDF from the PDF package.** Open a context menu on the PDF you just saved as a copy in the PDF Package and from the menu commands, select Delete File as shown in Figure 19.9. Alternately you can open the Options menu on the far right side of the document window and select Delete File.

Open a context menu by right-clicking (Ctrl+click on the Mac) on the enabled file icon in the PDF Package panel and select Delete File to remove it from the PDF Package.

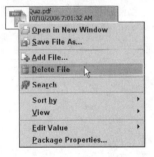

4. **Save your PDF Package.** Select File ➪ Save Package As and save the PDF Package when the Save As dialog box opens. Just to be safe, you might want to save the PDF Package with a different name and avoid overwriting the original file. It something goes awry, you can return to the original and start over.

5. **Edit the enabled file you saved as a copy.** Perform all the edits you need to make on the copy file and then re-enable the file by selecting one of the enabling options discussed in the section, "Enabling PDF Documents with Reader Extensions (Acrobat Professional Only)."

6. **Open the PDF package.** If you closed the PDF Package file in step 4, select File ➪ Open and open the package in Acrobat.

7. **Add the enabled PDF document to the package.** Open a context menu from any location in the PDF Package panel and select Add File. Note that you don't need to select a PDF icon in the PDF Package panel to open the context menu. Just open the context menu from any open area in the PDF Package panel. (Note that newly added documents to a PDF Package are added to the bottom of the list).

8. **Save the PDF Package.** Select File ⇨ Save PDF Package As to open the Save As dialog box. You can save the file using the same file name to overwrite the file. Your PDF Package is now updated with the most recent version of your enabled PDF document.

These steps are used when you find yourself overlooking some edit you need to make on a PDF file that is ultimately enabled with Reader extensions. More often than not you'll find you need to make some sort of edit on a PDF form before it is deployed. When you work with PDF forms and PDF Packages, it's a good idea to plan ahead and develop a workflow that provides you with some flexibility when you need to make some edits on enabled PDF forms.

As an example for planning ahead, assume you want to create a PDF Package containing a document enabled with reader usage rights. Further assume that you want to add some navigational links, buttons, or bookmarks in the PDF Package and specifically you want to add these items on the enabled PDF form. You know ahead of time that you can't introduce links, buttons, bookmarks, and so on, in a document that has been enabled. Therefore, you know you first need to create the PDF Package with the non-enabled document and after all the elements have been added to the PDF Package, you then need to replace the document with the enabled PDF.

To develop a workflow that accommodates the need for creating links, buttons, bookmarks, and so on, on an enabled PDF within a PDF Package, follow these steps.

STEPS: Adding interactive links in a PDF Package containing enabled PDFs

1. **Create two copies of the document(s) you want to enable.** Enable one of the files and leave the other document in its native format without enabling.

2. **Create the PDF Package.** Be certain to create the PDF Package using the copy of the document you did not enable.

3. **Add the interactive links you want to appear in the PDF Package.** If you want to create links from PDF pages in one document to open another PDF within the same PDF Package, use the Go to a page view action for bookmarks, links, and buttons.

4. **Perform any additional edits that need to be made on the file that needs to be enabled.** For example, if you need to change the Initial View, modify form fields, add comments, and add JavaScripts, complete all the edits you want to make before saving the final file.

5. **Replace the page(s) that needs to be enabled.** After finishing all your edits, be certain the page you want to replace is in view in the Document pane and select Document ⇨ Replace Pages. When the Replace Pages dialog box opens, select the file you enabled and replace the current file in the PDF Package. All the edits you made on the original document(s) remain intact (bookmarks, links, buttons, Initial View, comments, JavaScripts) and only the enabled PDF replaces the current document.

6. **Save the package.** Select File ⇨ Save Package As and overwrite the original file.

CROSS-REF For more on PDF Package creation, see Chapter 12. For learning how to add JavaScripts and create pop-up menus for navigation links with enabled PDFs in a PDF Package, see Chapter 36. For more information on overwriting PDF files, see Chapter 11.

After you've followed the steps for both methods used in editing PDF Packages you may ask yourself "why didn't I use Replace Pages in the first series of steps?" In other words, why not just edit a file, enable it and replace the existing enabled file with a modified enabled file? The reason is quite simply that the Document ⇨ Replace Pages command is not available when working on a PDF that has been enabled with Reader usage rights. In order to use the second series of steps listed earlier, you need to first create the PDF package without enabled documents.

Summary

- The Adobe LiveCycle Reader Extensions Server (LCRE) is a server product used for enterprise enabling features for Adobe Reader users.

- The End User License Agreement (EULA) specifies the limitations you have for enabling PDFs with Reader extensions. When enabling forms for form saves for Reader users from within Acrobat, you are limited to 500 instances of use for unknown users. For known users, such as within a company of less than 500 employees, there is no limit to the number of uses of enabled forms.

- PDFs can be enabled for Comment & Markup and Comment & Review in Acrobat Professional only.

- Acrobat 8 Professional provides a new feature for enabling PDF files for saving form data and digital signatures for Adobe Reader users.

- Forms created in Adobe Designer can be enabled for commenting, form data saving, and digital signatures.

- Enabled PDF documents can be deleted from and added to PDF Packages. When modifying an Enabled PDF within a PDF Package you need to delete the enabled file and add a modified enabled PDF back into the package.

- When you know ahead of time that you need to make edits on an enabled PDF document within a PDF Package, start by creating the PDF Package with non-enabled PDFs. Use the Document ⇨ Replace Pages command to replace the non-enabled PDF with the enabled PDF after adding links, buttons, bookmarks, and so on, in the PDF Package.

Part IV

PDF Interactivity

Chapter 20

Review and Markup

A dobe Acrobat is the perfect tool for workgroup collaboration. With sophisticated tool sets and a number of menu options, Acrobat provides you the ability to comment and mark up PDF documents and share your annotations with users dynamically on Web sites or through file exchanges on servers or via e-mail. For example, you can mark up documents, send your comments to a group of colleagues, ask for return comments, and track the review history. Where PDF documents may be too large to efficiently exchange files in e-mails, you can export comments to smaller data files or summarize them and create new PDF documents from comment summaries that can be sent to members of your workgroup. You can compare documents for changes, for comment status, and for errors and omissions and as with Acrobat 7 Professional you can add usage rights in Acrobat 8 Professional to documents so Adobe Reader users can participate in reviews.

The review and comment tools and methods in Acrobat are extraordinary in number. Because Acrobat provides these great tools doesn't necessarily mean you'll use all of them in your daily work activities. The best way to decide what tools work best for you and your colleagues is to review this chapter thoroughly and pick and choose the tools you favor and the features in review and markup that work best in your environment. In this chapter, you learn how to use all the comment tools and compare documents for reviewing purposes.

DF WORKFLOW All the tools and features discussed in this chapter are related to workflow environments. Regardless of what industry you work in, the many features related to review and comment and comparing documents can be applied to virtually all environments with two or more individuals collaborating on common projects.

Setting Up the Review and Comment Environment

You may be a user who adds comments infrequently with a few comment tools located in the Comment & Markup toolbar. However, to decide what tools work best in your workflow, you might want to add all the tools for review and markup to the Toolbar Well and look over all the tools available in your viewer.

To set up the review and comment work environment, open a context menu on the Toolbar Well and select Reset Toolbars to return to the default toolbar view. Return to the context menu and select More Tools to open the More Tools window (or select Tools ➪ Customize Toolbars). In the More Tools window, click the Advanced Editing toolbar and be sure to check the Select Object tool and the TouchUp tools. Check the Comment & Markup toolbar and add check marks to all the tools in this toolbar. Scroll down and check the Edit toolbar to add all the Edit tools. Scroll down and pick and choose the Select & Zoom toolbar tools you want to use. Be certain to add the Snapshot tool.

Return to the context menu and select the Properties Bar. Again return to the context menu opened from the Toolbar Well and select Dock All Toolbars. After docking toolbars, your Toolbar Well should look similar to the one shown in Figure 20.1.

FIGURE 20.1

A view of toolbars set up for comment and review

Notice that the tools are grouped together in logical collections. In a real-world scenario, you might only use tools from a single group and not need to load all the tools in the Toolbar Well. If you work on a small monitor, you can see how expanding all the tools and the Comments panel can eat up a lot of screen real estate very quickly. If the view of your pages in the Document pane is too small to comfortably annotate files, close the less frequently used tools to open up more space in the Document pane.

 Additional comment tools include the Measuring tools. These tools are often used with engineering and CAD drawings. For more information about the Measuring tools, see Chapter 24.

Setting Commenting Preferences

Acrobat provides an elaborate set of preference options that enable you to control comment views and behavior. As you draw comments on PDF pages you may see pop-up windows, connector lines across a page, changes in page views, and a host of other strange behaviors that might confuse you. Before you begin a commenting session, you should familiarize yourself with the commenting preferences and plan to return to the preference settings several times to completely understand how you control comment behavior in Acrobat.

Open the preference settings by pressing Ctrl/⌘+K or choosing Edit ⇨ Preferences (Windows) or Acrobat ⇨ Preferences (Macintosh). In the left pane, select Commenting. In the right pane, you'll see a long list of preference settings, as shown in Figure 20.2. Take a moment to review these settings before you begin a commenting session.

Open the Commenting Preferences by pressing Ctrl/⌘+K or choosing Edit ⇨ Preferences. When the Preferences dialog box opens, select Commenting in the left pane.

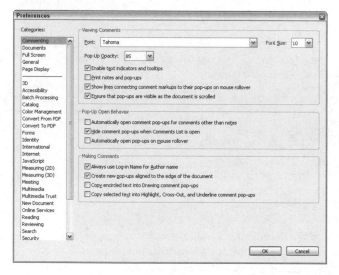

- **Font (Windows only).** The comment tools are used to mark up text and create icons, symbols, and graphic objects on pages. Most of the comment tools have associated pop-up notes where you type remarks in a note window. By default the font used for the note text is Tahoma. To change the font, select another font from the pull-down menu. All fonts loaded in your system are available from the menu choices. The fonts you use are not embedded in the file. If you exchange PDFs containing comment notes with other users, the fonts default to another user's preference settings.

  Note that changing font and arbitrary font sizes is not available on the Mac. On the Mac the default Tahoma font is used and sizes are limited to Small, Medium, and Large.

- **Font Size.** Font point sizes range from 4 points to 144 points. You can type a number between these values in the field box or select one from the preset point sizes from the pull-down menu. Changing font size applies to note pop-up windows you see on your computer. If you change font size and share the file with other users, fonts appear in sizes set by individual user preferences.

- **Pop-up Opacity.** A pop-up note background color is white. At 100 percent opacity the note is opaque and hides underlying page data. You can change the opacity of pop-up notes for a transparent view so the background data can be seen when a pop-up note window is open. You adjust the level of transparency by typing a value in the field box or selecting one from the preset choices in the pull-down menu. The default is 85 percent.

■ **Enable text indicators and tooltips.** Turns on or off tooltips when the Hand tool approaches a comment icon. The tooltip reports text contained in a comment note when the note is collapsed.

■ **Print notes and pop-ups.** Enabling this check box prints the pop-up note contents for all pop-up note windows regardless of whether they are opened or collapsed.

■ **Show lines connecting comment markups to their pop-ups on mouse rollover.** When you place the cursor over a comment markup, a series of dashed lines appear between the comment mark and the pop-up note, as shown in Figure 20.3. Users of earlier versions of Acrobat will immediately notice that the connector lines in Acrobat 8 appear as a series of dashed lines instead of a shaded triangle.

FIGURE 20.3

When the preference setting is enabled, connector lines are displayed on a mouseover between the comment and the associated note window.

■ **Ensure that pop-ups are visible as the document is scrolled.** If a comment note extends beyond one page in a continuous page view, the note is visible when scrolling pages.

■ **Automatically open comment pop-ups for comments other than notes.** As you create comments with drawing tools, the Text Box tool, or Pencil tool, the pop-up note windows are collapsed by default. If you want a pop-up note window opened and ready to accept type when creating comments, check the box.

■ **Hide comment pop-ups when Comments List is opened.** The Comments List is contained in the Comments panel. When you open the Comments panel, the list shows expanded comment notes with the content displayed in the pane. To hide the pop-ups in the Document pane when the Comments panel is opened, enable the check box. If you set this item as a default, you can expand comments in the Comments panel by clicking icons to see the content of the pop-ups.

■ **Automatically open pop-ups on mouse rollover.** Pop-up note windows can be opened or closed. Double-clicking a collapsed pop-up note window, opens the window. If you want to have a pop-up note window open automatically as the cursor is placed over a comment icon, select this check box.

■ **Always use Login Name for Author name.** Another set of preferences appears when you click on Identity in the left pane. The Login Name specified in the Identity preferences is used for the author name on all comments when this check box is enabled. If you are a single user on a workstation, setting the Identity preferences and enabling this check box saves you time creating comments when you want to add your name as the author name.

■ **Create new pop-ups aligned to the edge of the document.** By default, the top-left corner of a pop-up note window is aligned to the top-left corner of the comment icon. If you enable this check box, no matter where you create the note icon, the pop-up notes are aligned to the right edge of the document.

■ **Copy encircled text into Drawing comment pop-ups.** When proofreading a document and using the Markup tools you mark text with the Rectangle tool, Circle tool, or Cloud tool. When this preference option is checked, the text you surround with one of these tools is placed in a comment note.

■ **Copy selected text into Highlight, Cross-Out, and Underline comment pop-ups.** This enables the text selected with the Highlight Text, Cross Out Text, and Underline Text tools to automatically appear in the pop-up note window.

As you can see, there are many different preference settings. How you want to view comments and the methods used for review and comment is influenced by the options you set in the Commenting preferences. Take some time to play with these settings as you use the tools discussed in this chapter.

Looking at the Comment & Markup Toolbar

Users of Acrobat Professional, Acrobat Standard, and Adobe Reader (when a file is enabled with usage rights) can access the Comment & Markup tools.

NEW FEATURE Users of earlier versions of Acrobat will notice that all Comment & Markup tools are now added to a single toolbar. In earlier versions of Acrobat, you had the Comment & Markup toolbar and the Drawing Markups toolbar. Now in Acrobat 8, all commenting tools with the exception of the Measuring tools are contained in a single toolbar.

The commenting and markup tools arranged in a single toolbar are shown in Figure 20.4.

FIGURE 20.4

All commenting and markup tools are nested together in a single toolbar.

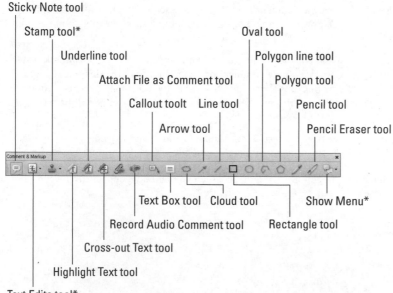

* Denotes more options in pull-down menu

CROSS-REF For more information on using the Measuring tools, see Chapter 24.

The Comment & Markup toolbar essentially contains two tool subsets. The Commenting tools begin with the Sticky Note tool on the far left of the toolbar and move to the right to the Record Audio Comment tool. The Markup tools begin with the Callout tool in the middle of the toolbar and extend to the far right to the Pencil Eraser tool. While the Commenting tools are generally used for text documents, the Markup tools are used more with drawings and diagrams. All tools are accessible in any kind of PDF document you want to mark up with comments and you can use any tool to mark up text and drawings.

Using the Comment & Markup Tools

The Comment & Markup tools are intended for use by anyone reviewing and marking up documents. Much like you might use a highlighter on paper documents, the commenting tools enable you to electronically comment and mark up PDF documents. A variety of tools with different icon symbols offer you an extensive library of tools that can help you facilitate a review process.

Most comment tools have a symbol or icon that appears where the comment is created. They also have a note pop-up window where you add text to clarify a meaning associated with the mark you add to a document. These pop-up note windows have identical attributes. How you manage note pop-ups and change the properties, works the same regardless of the comment mark you create, with the exception of the Callout and Text Box tools. I explain how to use the Sticky Note tool in this section. All the features described for the Sticky Note tool are the same as when handling note pop-up windows for all the comment tools that accommodate note pop-ups.

Using the Sticky Note tool

 The Sticky Note tool is the most common commenting tool used in Acrobat and the oldest of the commenting tools dating back to Acrobat 3. To create a comment note, select the Sticky Note tool in the Comment & Markup toolbar and drag open a note window. When you release the mouse button, the note pop-up aligns to the top-left corner of the note icon.

You can also select the Sticky Note tool and click the mouse button or open a context menu and select Add Sticky Note. Using either of these options adds a note comment on the right side of the document page away from the note icon if the Create new pop-ups aligned to the edge of the document preference option is checked in the Commenting preferences. If you disable the preference option, using either of these methods positions the note popup close to the right side of the note icon.

TIP You can also add notes to a page via menu commands. To add a note to a page, choose Comments ➪ Add Sticky Note. A comment note is added to the center of the page in view. For example, if the document is viewed in a Fit Page view, the note appears in the center of the page. If the document view is zoomed in to show only the top third of the page, the comment note appears in the center of the top third in view.

Note Nomenclature

The tool you use to create notes is the Sticky Note tool. In earlier versions of Acrobat, this tool was called the Note tool. When referring to the tool throughout this chapter, I refer to it by its proper name in Acrobat 8 (Sticky Note tool). When you add comments from most of the other commenting tools, the tools have an associated note pop-up window. Throughout this chapter, I refer to this window as the pop-up note window or simply refer to it as a note or note window.

The official name for the toolbar where you select tools for comments and markups is called the Comment & Markup toolbar. For simplicity and ease of reading, I often refer to the tools in this toolbar as the commenting tools. When you see a reference to the commenting tools, realize that I'm talking about both comment and markup tools.

When, you can click without dragging and release the mouse button, a pop-up note window is created at a fixed size according to your monitor resolution. The higher you set your monitor resolution the smaller the pop-up note window appears. On an 800 × 600 display, the window size defaults to 360 × 266 pixels. In Figure 20.5, I drew a comment note with the Sticky Note tool in the center of the page. On the left side of the page, I clicked the Sticky Note tool. Notice the center note is aligned with the note icon, whereas the icon on the left is linked to the note pop-up on the far right side of the page. Note also that because my cursor is not placed over either note, no connector lines appear between the Sticky Note icon and the pop-up note window.

FIGURE 20.5

When clicking and dragging the Sticky Note tool, the pop-up note aligns to the top-left corner of the note icon. When clicking with the Sticky Note tool, a pop-up window is created at a fixed size away from the icon.

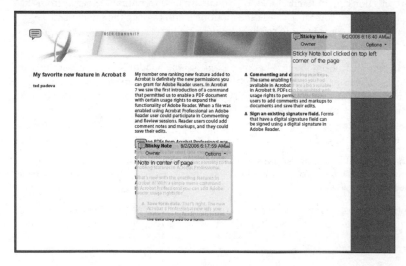

To add text to the pop-up note, begin typing. Acrobat places an I-beam cursor inside the pop-up note window immediately after creating the note. For font selection and font sizing, you need to address the Commenting preference settings discussed earlier in this chapter.

Managing notes

The color of a note pop-up and the note icon is yellow by default. At the top of the note pop-up the title bar is colored yellow and the area where you add the contents is white. The title bar contains information supplied by Acrobat that includes the subject of the note, the author, and the date and time the note is created. You can move a note pop-up independently of the note icon by clicking and dragging the title bar.

CROSS-REF The Subject of a note by default is titled *Sticky Note*. The default Author name is derived from either your computer logon name or your Identity depending on how your preferences are established. For information on how to change the Subject and Author in the title bar, see "Sticky Note tool properties" later in this chapter.

You delete note popup windows and Sticky Note icons either by selecting the note icon and pressing the Delete/Backspace or Del key on your keyboard or through a context menu selection. If you use a keystroke to delete a note, you must be certain to select the icon, then press the Delete/Backspace or Del key. Selecting the title bar in a note pop-up and using the same keys won't delete the note.

To resize a note pop-up window, grab the lower-right corner of the window and drag in or out to resize smaller or larger, respectively. Note pop-ups containing more text that can be viewed in the current window size use elevator bars so you can scroll the window much like you would use when viewing pages in the Document pane. Only vertical elevator bars are shown in the popup windows. As you type text in the window, text wraps to the horizontal width, thereby eliminating a need for horizontal scroll bars. As you size a note popup window horizontally, the text rewraps to conform to the horizontal width.

You open context menus from either the note icon or the note popup window. When opening a context menu from the note popup window, you have two choices: open the context menu from the title bar or open the context menu from inside the note window (below the title bar). Depending on where you open the context menu, the menu selections are different. Opening a context menu from the title bar or from the note icon shows identical menu options. You can also use the Options menu to open the same menu as when opening a context menu inside the note window. Click the right-pointing arrow adjacent to Options and the menu opens.

In Figure 20.6, I opened a context menu from the title bar on a pop-up note window. The menu options are the same as if I had opened the context menu from the note icon. In Figure 20.7, I opened the context menu from inside the note popup window. Depending on edits you make in the note window and whether you have text selected, menu options change. In Figure 20.7, text was selected in the note window that adds the Cut, Copy, and Paste commands to the context menu. In both menus, you can select Delete to remove the note popup menu and the note icon.

TIP If you accidentally delete a note or several notes, you can select Edit ➪ Undo to bring back the note and Sticky Note icon. Successively select the Undo command and you can bring back several Sticky Note icons and note windows.

The context menus are similar and most commands existing in the smaller menu are the same as those found in the larger menu. If two notes are selected, additional menu commands appear in a context menu.

FIGURE 20.6

This context menu is opened from the note popup window title bar. From the menu options, select Delete to remove the note icon and the note popup menu.

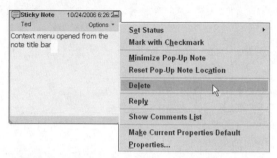

FIGURE 20.7

When you open a context menu from the note popup window below the title bar, menu options change. If you select text in the note window, additional commands are added to the context menu.

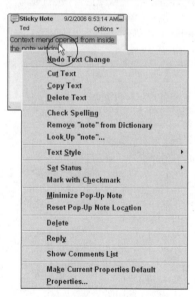

Click the Select Object tool in the Advanced Editing toolbar and open a context menu on one of the note icons. You see different menu commands when two or more comment icons are selected as shown in Figure 20.8. The options you have in the context menu are the same as those you find when opening a context menu on two or more form fields.

CROSS-REF Most of the context menu commands you see when two or more comment icons are selected should be self-explanatory. For a detail description of the menu commands, see Chapter 34.

FIGURE 20.8

Drag the Select Object tool through comment icons to select two or more. Open a context menu and new menu commands appear for organizing comments.

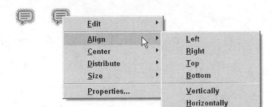

In Figure 20.7, you see a long list of menu commands. Let's take a look at these commands; the same commands found in the context menu shown in Figure 20.6 operate the same way.

- **Undo Text Change.** When you type text in the popup menu and delete it, you can select the Undo Text Change command to regain your text. Deleting a comment note can also be undone. Because deleting a comment note eliminates an opportunity to open a context menu from the note popup window, you need to choose Edit ⇨ Undo. If text was added to a popup note window and you delete the note, choosing Edit ⇨ Undo returns the note and the text in the note popup window.

- **Redo Text Change.** If you type a block of text and select Undo, you can later select Redo and bring the text back.

- **Cut Text/Copy Text.** These items work as you might assume from using any text editor or word processor. The commands relate to typing text in the note popup window. You can also highlight text and use key modifiers (Ctrl/⌘+C for Copy; Ctrl/⌘+X for Cut; Ctrl/⌘+V for Paste).

- **Delete Text.** Select text and choose Delete Text. The selected text is deleted.

- **Check Spelling.** When you select Check Spelling in the note popup menu, the Check Spelling dialog box opens. When the dialog box opens, click the Start button and Acrobat checks the spelling for all the text typed in the note popup. When Acrobat finds a misspelled word, it is highlighted and a list of suggestions that closely match the spelling are shown in the lower window. Select a word with the correct spelling and click the Change button.

- **Remove "..." from Dictionary.** This menu item is active only when you have a word selected in the note popup window and that note is contained in your custom dictionary. It's a nifty little feature in Acrobat. Because Acrobat automatically spell checks text you type in the comment note popup window by matching your words to those found in its dictionary, words not matched are underlined in red with a wavy line similar to those used in programs such as Microsoft Word. If you want Acrobat to alert you whenever you type a specific word, remove that word from the dictionary. Then Acrobat displays the word with a red underline each time you use it.

  When would you use this feature? Assume for a moment that you want to use a generic reference to users as opposed to a masculine or feminine reference. Highlight the word *he* or *she* and open a context menu from the note popup window. Select Remove "*he*" from Dictionary. Each time you type the word *he*, Acrobat underlines the word because it can't find a match in the dictionary. When you review your notes, you might substitute *s/he* for the word *he*.

■ **Look Up "...".** The default menu command is *Look Up Definition*. When a word is selected, the menu command changes to Look Up *selected word*. For example, if you select a word like *reply*, the menu command changes to Look Up "reply." Select the menu command, which launches your Web browser, opening to the Dictionary.com Web site where the word is searched and a definition is displayed on the Web page.

CROSS-REF For more information on looking up a definition and the Dictionary.com Web site, see Chapter 13.

■ **Text Style.** From a submenu, select from Bold, Italic, Underline, Superscript, Subscript, or Clear Formatting). Select any one of the formatting options to apply to selected text. You can combine format changes by selecting text and a format option, and then return to the context menu and select another option, and so on.

■ **Set Status.** Two submenu items are listed when you select Set Status. The Migration submenu command has three additional submenu options for migrating comments (comments can be migrated when you make document revisions and you want to migrate comments from an earlier PDF to a revised PDF). The Review submenu command enables you to choose from various status settings such as None, Accepted, Cancelled, Completed, and Rejected.

CROSS-REF For more information on migration and reviews, see Chapter 21.

■ **Mark with Checkmark.** Whereas the Set Status items are communicated to others, a check mark you add to a comment is for your own purposes. You can mark a comment as checked to denote any comments that need attention, or that are completed and require no further annotation. Check marks are visible in the Comments panel and can be toggled on or off in the pane as well as the context menu. Check marks can be added to comments with or without your participation in a review session. You can choose to have your comments sorted by those with check marks and those comments without check marks.

■ **Minimize PopUp Note.** Selecting this command closes the note window. Click back on the Sticky Note icon and the note window opens again. The same close action is also available by clicking the minimize icon in the top-right corner of the note popup window.

■ **Reset Popup Note Location.** If you move a note popup window, selecting this menu command returns the note popup to the default position.

■ **Delete.** Deletes the comment popup note and the note icon.

■ **Reply.** When participating in a review, you select the Reply command to reply to comments made from other users. A new window opens in which you type a reply message. From the popup bar you can review a thread and click the Reply button to send your comments to others via e-mail, to a network folder, or to a Web-hosted server.

CROSS-REF For more information on comment reviews, see Chapter 21.

■ **Show Comments List.** Selecting this item opens the Comments panel. Any comments in the open document are expanded in a list view in the Comments panel. When the Comments panel is open, this option toggles to Hide Comments List.

■ **Make Current Properties Default.** Any attributes you changed in the Properties dialog box (see Properties below) such as changing the Author name or Subject can be set to new defaults. After making settings choices, select this menu item and all subsequent notes you add will use the same new defaults.

■ **Properties.** Opens the Properties dialog box.

Sticky Note tool properties

Each comment created from any tool supporting a popup note has properties that you can change in a properties dialog box. Properties changes are generally applied to note pop-up windows and icon shapes for a particular tool. In addition, a variety of properties are specific to different tools that offer you many options for viewing and displaying comments and tracking the history of the comments made on a document.

With respect to note pop-ups and those properties assigned to the Sticky Note tool, you have choices for changing the default color, opacity, author name, and a few other options. Keep in mind that not all property changes are contained in the properties dialog box. Attributes such as font selection and point sizes are globally applied to note pop-ups in the Comment preferences.

 **CROSS-REF** For information about Commenting preferences, see "Setting Commenting Preferences" at the beginning of this chapter.

Additionally, you have many options available to you in the Properties Bar. If you want certain attributes to be changed for a given comment type, fist look at the Properties Bar after selecting a comment tool to see if a property you want to change exists in the toolbar.

In the Sticky Note tool you find attributes for changing pop-up note color, text color, icon shapes, and a variety of font styles. It is easier to change these attributes using the Properties Bar rather than the Properties dialog box. For other properties changes, such as comment author, subject, opacity settings, and editing the review history, you need to use the Properties dialog box.

You open the properties dialog box from a context menu. Be certain to place the cursor on a popup note title bar or the note icon before opening a context menu. Select Properties from the menu choices and the Sticky Note Properties dialog box opens, as shown in Figure 20.9.

NOTE When you create a comment with any of the Comment tools, the Hand tool is automatically selected upon releasing the mouse button. You can select a comment mark/icon or popup note with the Hand tool or the Select Object tool. Use either tool to open a context menu where the menu options enable you to select Properties. However, other menu items vary between the two context menus. For information regarding menu options from context menus opened with the Select Object tool, see the discussion on Drawing Markup tools later in this chapter.

TIP To keep a comment tool selected without returning to the Hand tool after creating a comment, check the box in the Properties Bar for Keep tool selected.

FIGURE 20.9

Select Properties from a context menu and the Sticky Note Properties dialog box opens.

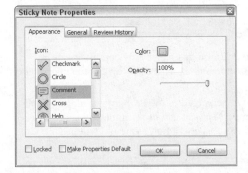

The Sticky Note Properties dialog box contains three tabs. Select a tab and make choices for the items contained in the dialog box. For pop-up note properties, the items you can change include the following:

■ **Appearance.** Options in the Appearance tab relate to the note icon appearances and the pop-up note window appearance.

    ■ **Icon.** From the scrollable list, select an item that changes the Note icon appearance. Selections you make in this list are dynamic and change the appearance of the icon in the Document pane as you click on a name in the list. If you move the Note Properties dialog box out of the view of the note icon, you can see the appearance changes as you make selections in the list. Fifteen different icons are available to choose from, as shown in Figure 20.10. The same options are also available in the Properties Bar. Click the Icon button in the Properties Bar and a pull-down menu opens where the same choices are listed.

FIGURE 20.10

You select icon shapes from the Icon list in the Appearance tab in the Note Properties dialog box or in the Icon pull-down menu in the Properties Bar. You can choose from 15 different shapes.

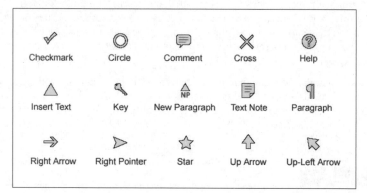

■ **Color.** Click the color swatch to open the pop-up color palette shown in Figure 20.11. You select preset colors from the swatches in the palette. You add custom colors by selecting the Other Color item in the palette, which opens the system color palette. In the system color palette, make color choices and the new custom color is applied to the note.

FIGURE 20.11

Click the color swatch to select from preset colors or select Other Color to open the system color palette where you select custom colors.

Changing color in the Appearance properties affects both the color of the note icon and the pop-up note title bar. If you mark up and review documents in workgroups, different colors assigned to different participants can help you ascertain at a glance which participant made a given comment.

For a quick change in note colors, use the Properties Bar where you see the same color attributes found in the Properties dialog box in the Properties Bar Color pull-down menu.

■ **Opacity.** Global opacity settings are applied in the Commenting Preferences dialog box. You can override the default opacity setting in the Appearance properties for any given note pop-up window.

Additionally, opacity adjustments can be made in the Properties Bar by choosing fixed opacity percentages from the Opacity pull-down menu. One distinction between adjusting opacity in the Properties dialog box and making adjustments in the Properties Bar is that the Properties dialog box enables you to choose different opacities at 1% increments. The Properties Bar is limited to fixed opacity settings in 20% increments.

■ **Locked.** Select the Locked check box to lock a note. When notes are locked, the position of the note icon is fixed to the Document pane and cannot be moved when you leave the Note Properties dialog box. All other options in the Note Properties dialog box are grayed out, preventing you from making any further attribute changes. If you lock a note, you can move the pop-up window and resize it. The note contents, however, are locked and changes can't be made to the text in the pop-up note window. If you want to make changes to the properties or the pop-up note contents, return to the Note Properties dialog box and uncheck the Locked check box.

■ **General.** Click the General tab to make changes for items appearing in the note pop-up title bar. Two editable fields are available, as shown in Figure 20.12. The changes you make in the Author and Subject fields are dynamic and are reflected in the Document pane when you edit a field and tab to the next field. You can see the changes you make here before leaving the Note Properties dialog box.

FIGURE 20.12

Make changes to the Author name and the pop-up note Subject in the General preferences.

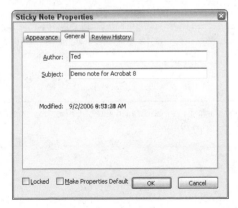

■ **Author.** The Author name is supplied by default according to how you set your Commenting preferences. If you use the Identity preferences, the Author name is supplied from the information added in the Identity preferences (see "Setting Commenting Preferences" earlier in this chapter). If you don't use Identity for the Author title, the name is derived from your computer log-on name. You might see names like Owner, Administrator, or a specific name you used in setting up your operating system.

If you want to change the Author name and override the preferences, select the General tab and edit the Author name. The name edited in the General preferences is applied to the selected note. All other notes are left undisturbed.

■ **Subject.** By default, the Subject of a note for the Sticky Note comment is titled *Sticky Note* appearing in the top-left corner of the pop-up note title bar. When you use other comment tools, the subject defines the tool used. For example, when using the Highlight tool, you'll see *Highlight* as the subject, using an Approved stamp comment places *Approved* in the Subject field, and so on.

You can change the subject in the General properties by typing text in the Subject line. You can add long text descriptions for the Subject; however, the text remains on a single line in the pop-up note properties dialog box. (The total characters you can type for the Subject field is 255.) Text won't scroll to a second line. The amount of text shown for the Subject field relates to the horizontal width of the note window. As you expand the width, more text is visible in the title bar if you add a long Subject name. As you size down the width, text is clipped to accommodate the note size.

Text added to both the Author and Subject text boxes are searchable using Acrobat Search when you check the box in the Search panel for Include Comments.

CROSS-REF For more information on using Acrobat Search, see Chapter 6.

■ **Modified.** This item is informational and supplied automatically by Acrobat from your system clock. The field is not editable. The readout displays the date and time the note was modified.

■ **Review History.** The Review History lists all comment and status changes in a scrollable list. The list is informational and not editable.

CROSS-REF For more information on review history, see Chapter 21.

After making changes in the Note Properties dialog box, click the OK button to apply the changes. Clicking on the close box or pressing the Esc key cancels any changes you make to note properties.

TIP The Properties dialog boxes for all Comment tools are not dynamic in Acrobat 8. You need to exit the Properties dialog box before making any other edits in your document or accessing any tool or menu command.

Setting default properties

A great new feature in Acrobat 8 is an option for changing certain comment tool defaults as an application level default. If you use the Make Current Properties Default menu command from a context menu opened on a comment tool or comment pop-up note, the new default is only applied in your current Acrobat session. Quit Acrobat and all the defaults are lost.

NEW FEATURE In Acrobat 8, you can globally change defaults for comment and markup tools and retain the new defaults in subsequent Acrobat sessions. To set these defaults, open a context menu on a tool in the Comment & Markup toolbar and select Tool Default Properties. A properties dialog box for the selected tool opens. Make any settings changes, click OK in the Properties dialog box and your new defaults remain in effect until you change them again or select Reset Toolbar from the same context menu. (Note that the context menu opened on a tool in the Comment & Markup toolbar that also displays commands for selecting each and every tool in the Comment & Markup toolbar as well as opening the Customize Toolbars window.)

Using the Properties Bar

If you set up your work environment to view the Properties Bar while working in a review session, you can address several properties options from it. The attributes you can change for Sticky Notes have all been mentioned in the "Sticky Note tool properties" earlier in this chapter.

One additional item you have in the Properties Bar, shown in Figure 20.13, is the More button. This button appears for all comment markups that support options in the Properties Bar. Click the More button after selecting a comment icon and the Properties dialog box opens.

FIGURE 20.13

You can change some properties options in the Properties Bar. To open the toolbar, open a context menu on the Toolbar Well and select Properties Bar.

TIP If you're proofreading a document and you prefer another term or word, you can find word definitions or access a thesaurus by opening a context menu with the Hand tool and selecting Add Note. Type a word in the note pop-up window and highlight the word. Open a context menu from the highlighted word and select LookUp ". . .". The Dictionary.com Web site opens in your Web browser with the word definition, and access to a thesaurus, and an encyclopedia on the open Web page.

Working with the Text Edits tools

The Text Edits tools can be acquired from several menu locations. When you load the Comment & Markup toolbar, the Text Edits tools are all located in a pull-down menu adjacent to the Sticky Note tool in the toolbar. The Text Edits tools are the only comment tools you won't find in the Comments ➡ Comment & Markup Tools submenu. The Text Edit tools can be used for any kind of review session; however, they were designed to be used for comments that you want to export to source documents that originated in programs such as Microsoft Word and Autodesk AutoCAD.

CROSS-REF For more information on exporting comments to Microsoft Word, see Chapter 8.

To use the tools, click the Select tool and click or select text in the Document pane. A blinking cursor or selected text needs to appear in a document before the Text Edits tools can be selected. When text is selected, you have access to all the tools in the Text Edits pull-down menu, as shown in Figure 20.14.

As you move to text you want to mark, drag the cursor to highlight text to be annotated. When text is selected, open the Text Edits pull-down menu and select the tool you want to use for your edit.

FIGURE 20.14

Use the Select tool to click on a body of text or select text where you want to add a comment. Open the Text Edits pull-down menu and select the tool respective to the type of edit you want to make.

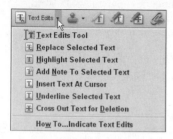

The Text Edits tools include:

- **Text Edits Tool.** You'll notice the Text Edits tool looks like the Select tool. This tool is not used to make a comment in the document. Click the tool and a dialog box opens where you find help information on using all the other Text Edits tools.

> **NOTE** All the tools below the Indicate Text Edit tool are grayed out unless you select the Select tool and click or click and drag in a text block. Selecting either option without a cursor insertion on the document page or without highlighting text does not enable any of the Text Edit tools.

- **Replace Selected Text.** Use this tool to mark text for replacement. The line appears similar to the Cross Out Text for Deletion mark, but the caret at the end of the mark distinguishes this tool from the aforementioned one. A note pop-up window opens where you can add comments. The note contents do not include the text marked for replacement.

- **Highlight Selected Text.** This tool works like the Highlight tool and similar to a yellow highlighter you might use on paper documents. Select the Highlight tool and drag across a block of text. The text is highlighted and a note pop-up window enables you to add comments.

- **Add Note to Selected Text.** Select a word, a paragraph, or a body of text. When you release the mouse button a note pop-up window opens in which you add a comment. Selecting the text does not include the selected text in the pop-up note.

- **Insert Text At Cursor.** Select the menu command and move the cursor to the document page. The cursor appearance changes to an I-beam, informing you that text can be selected. Rather than selecting text, clicking the cursor at a specific location is the method most often used with this tool. The intent is to suggest to a reviewer that text needs to be inserted at the cursor position. When you click on a document page, a caret is marked on the page at the insertion location and a note pop-up window opens. Type the text to be inserted in the note pop-up.

- **Underline Selected Text.** Use this tool to underline the selected text. A note pop-up window opens where you can add comments.

- **Cross Out Text for Deletion.** Select text and the text mark appears as a strikethrough. The symbol is used to mark text that needs to be deleted. A note pop-up window opens where you can add comments.

- **How To . . . Indicate Text Edits.** The How To panel opens with the Text Edits help page in view.

Working with the Highlight tools

 The three tools appearing after the Stamp tools are the Highlight tool, the Underline tool, and the Strikethrough tool. When you have comments that are to be exported to MS Word documents, don't use these tools because the comments made with the tools cannot be exported to MS Word. Use the Text Edits tools for highlighting, strikethrough, and underlining. Where these three tools are helpful are when you want the text you mark to be added to a comment note. Especially if you have long passages of text, you'll want to have the text added to a note where you can easily make some corrections/suggestions. The tools have their place, but if you don't need text added to the comment note popups, then always opt for using the Text Edits tools for the same types of markups.

Attaching Files as Comments

The next tool in the Commenting toolbar lineup is the Attach File as Comment tool. You use this tool to attach files as comments. Users of Adobe Reader can open your attached files without any special usage rights added to the file for Adobe Reader users. The Attach File as Comment differs somewhat from another tool you have available for adding file attachments to PDFs. For detail information related to using the Attach File as Comment tool and using the Attachments panel for adding file attachments to PDFs, see Chapter 12.

Recording audio comments

Next on the Commenting toolbar you find the Record Audio Comment tool. This tool is used to add audio to a PDF document. You need to have a microphone properly set up on your computer and you can use audio recordings in lieu of or addition to other comments you add to a document. For more information on using the Record Audio Comment tool and adding rich media to PDF files, see Chapter 23.

Using the Stamp tool

 The Stamp tool is part of the Commenting tools, but it differs greatly from the other tools found in the Comment & Markup toolbar. Rather than mark data on a PDF page and add notes to the marks, Stamps enable you to apply icons of your own choosing to express statements about a document's status or add custom icons and symbols for communicating messages. Stamps offer a wide range of flexibility for marking documents similar to analog stamps you might use for stamping approvals, drafts, confidentiality, and so on. You can use one of a number of different icons supplied by Acrobat when you install the program, or you can create your own custom icons tailored to your workflow or company needs.

CROSS-REF All the features related to the Stamp tool, including creating your own custom stamps, are treated in Adobe Reader the same as Acrobat Standard and Acrobat Professional when PDFs contain usage rights for Adobe Reader. To learn more about usage rights with Adobe Reader, see Chapters 4 and 19.

Whether you use a preset stamp provided with your Acrobat installation or create a custom stamp, each stamp has an associated note pop-up window where you add comments. You select stamps from menu options in the Stamp pull-down menu where stamps are organized by categories. Add a stamp to a page by clicking the Stamp tool after selecting a stamp from a category; or you can click and drag the Stamp tool to size the icon. After creating a stamp, you access Stamp properties by opening a context menu and selecting Properties.

Selecting stamps

Using a stamp begins with selecting from among many different stamp images found in submenus from the Stamp tool pull-down menu. Click the down-pointing arrow and the first three menu commands list categories for stamps installed with Acrobat. If you have at least one Custom stamp added to your stamps library, then the custom category you added appears in addition to the three default categories. Notice in Figure 20.15 I added a custom category called Acrobat Users.com that appears at the top of the Stamps pull-down menu. Selecting one of menu items opens a submenu where you select specific stamps from the respective category, as shown in Figure 20.15.

FIGURE 20.15

Select the pull-down menu from the Stamp tool and select a Stamp category. Select a subcategory and slide the mouse over to the Stamp name. Release the mouse button and the selection becomes the new default stamp.

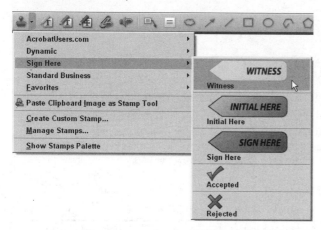

Adding a stamp to a page

The stamp name you select in the menu becomes the new default stamp. When you click the Stamp tool or click and drag open a rectangle with the Stamp tool, the default stamp is added to the document page. Stamps are created by default with the pop-up note window collapsed unless you enable the Commenting preferences for *Automatically open comment pop-ups for comments other than notes*. To open the pop-up note window, click the mouse button on the stamp image. The pop-up note opens and appears the same as other pop-up note windows for other Comment tools.

If you want to resize a stamp after creating it on a page, select the Hand tool and click the stamp icon to select it. Move the cursor to a corner handle and the cursor changes shape to a diagonal line with two opposing arrowheads, as shown in the lower-left handle in Figure 20.16. Drag the handle in or out to resize the stamp.

NOTE Stamps are always proportionately sized when you drag any one of the corner handles. You don't need to drag handles with a modifier key to proportionately size the image.

NEW FEATURE Stamps can also be rotated. Click the top center handle and the cursor changes to a circle with an arrowhead, as shown in Figure 20.16. Drag left or right and the stamp icon rotates. You can rotate stamps in arbitrary 1-degree rotations or in constrained 45-degree rotations. To perform an arbitrary rotation, drag the center handle left or right. To constrain rotations to 45 degrees, press the Shift key and drag the center handle left or right. When you rotate a stamp, the note pop-up remains fixed in the same view as when you first open the note.

FIGURE 20.16

To resize a stamp, drag a corner handle using the Hand tool and drag in or out to size the icon. To rotate a stamp, drag the top center handle left or right to rotate counterclockwise or clockwise respectively. Pressing the Shift key constrains rotations to 45 degrees.

CROSS-REF   Another new feature in Acrobat 8 is the ability to size and rotate images and objects. For more information on scaling and rotating items in Acrobat, see Chapter 15.

Acrobat offers you an assortment of stamps you can select from the category submenus in the Stamp tool pull-down menu. These stamps are created for general office uses and you'll find many common stamp types among the sets. The three categories of stamps and their respective types and icons are shown in Figure 20.17.

FIGURE 20.17

Choose stamps from three categories. The stamps installed with Acrobat are general office stamps used in many traditional workflows.

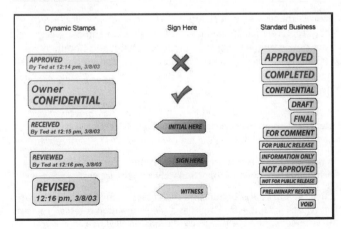

Resizing Stamps

The stamps you find installed by Acrobat are all vector art images created in Adobe Illustrator. When you resize vector art images, the display quality remains the same no matter how large you size the stamp.

When creating custom stamps you can use a program such as Adobe Illustrator and use vector art for your stamp design. You can also create custom stamps from Photoshop files. These files, however, are raster art. If you size raster artwork above a 100% actual view size, you can see distortion in your stamp image.

If you plan on using photographs or other artwork created in Adobe Photoshop, be certain to anticipate the largest size you might need to size up a stamp icon. When you view a Photoshop image created at 72 ppi (pixels per inch), the largest size you can see on your monitor without distortion is a 100% actual size view. If you size the stamp up 200% or more you'll notice image degradation and the image is likely to display jagged edges.

If you anticipate sizing stamps up to a 400% view, for example, create your stamps from Photoshop images at 288 ppi. This calculation is determined by taking 72 ppi and multiplying times 4 ($72 \times 4 = 288$). Hence, when you size the stamp up to 400%, the actual size view is 72 ppi. As size increases, resolution decreases.

If you plan your work and anticipate the size you might use for custom stamps created from Photoshop files, you can avoid any display problems when viewing files in Acrobat. The sizing issues only have to do with physically sizing a stamp image containing raster artwork. If you use zoom tools in Acrobat, the stamps appear at the same size no matter what zoom level you view a document page.

You should think of these stamps as a starter set and use them for some traditional office markups when the need arises. The real power of stamps, however, lies in creating custom stamps where you can use virtually any illustration or photo image.

Changing stamp properties

You change stamp properties in the Stamp Properties dialog box. You have the same options in the Stamp Properties as those found in the Note Properties dialog box, with one exception. In the Note Properties dialog box, you make choices for the icon appearance from a list in the dialog box. Because stamps have appearances determined before you create the stamp, no options are available for changing properties for the stamp image. The color options in the Stamp Properties dialog box apply to comment notes and not the stamp images. Opacity settings, however, can be applied to the stamp image.

If you want to change the appearance of a stamp, you need to delete the stamp and create a new stamp after selecting the category and stamp name from the category submenu. You delete stamps by opening a context menu and selecting Delete, or selecting the stamp icon and pressing the Backspace/Delete or Del key.

Creating custom stamps

You might create custom stamps with a company logo or personal identification so users in your workgroup or recipients of your files can see at a quick glance that files received are coming from you. You might use a custom stamp for approving documents in a review session, asking others to review one of your documents, or use stamps for other business uses such as marking documents for signatures, confidentiality, time stamping, or other similar tasks.

To understand how custom stamps are created, follow these steps:

STEPS: Creating a custom stamp

1. **Create the stamp icon image.** Using your favorite authoring program capable of exporting to one of the formats supported by creating a custom stamp, create an icon or image you want to use for your stamp. My tool of choice for creating custom stamps is Adobe Illustrator — but feel free to use the program you like to create your stamp image.

   File formats compatible with custom stamp creation are shown in Figure 20.18.

   FIGURE 20.18

   File formats compatible with creating custom stamps

   ```
   Acrobat PDF Files (*.pdf)
   Autodesk AutoCAD (*.dwg,*.dwf,*.dst)
   BMP (*.bmp,*.rle,*.dib)
   Compuserve GIF (*.gif)
   HTML (*.html,*.htm,*.shtml)
   InDesign (*.indd)
   JPEG (*.jpg,*.jpeg,*.jpe)
   JPEG2000 (*.jpf,*.jpx,*.jp2,*.j2k,*.j2c,*.jpc)
   Microsoft Office Excel (*.xls)
   Microsoft Office PowerPoint (*.ppt)
   Microsoft Office Visio (*.vsd)
   Microsoft Office Word (*.doc,*.rtf)
   Microsoft Publisher (*.pub)
   PCX (*.pcx)
   PNG (*.png)
   PostScript/EPS (*.ps,*.eps,*.prn)
   Text (*.txt,*.text)
   TIFF (*.tif,*.tiff)
   XPS (*.xps)
   ```

2. **Select an image to use as the new custom stamp.** Open Acrobat and select Create Custom Stamp from the Stamp tool pull-down menu. The Select Image for Custom Stamp dialog box opens. Click the Browse button in the dialog box and select your image file in the Open dialog box. Click Open and you return to the Select Image for Custom Stamp with a preview of your new stamp, as shown in Figure 20.19.

   FIGURE 20.19

   Select a file and an image preview is shown in the Select Image for Custom Stamp dialog box.

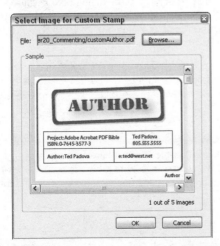

3. **Create a new stamp category.** Click OK in the Select Image for Custom Stamp dialog box and you arrive at the Create Custom Stamp dialog box. The Category text box appears with the default text: *<type here to name a new category>*. Select the text and type a new category name. (Note you can also select a category from the pull-down menu and add your new stamp to an existing category.) In my example, I typed My Stamps for a new category.

4. **Name your stamp.** Tab to the Name text box in the Create Custom Stamp dialog box and type a name for your stamp. I used the name Author for my stamp, as shown in Figure 20.20.

FIGURE 20.20

Type a Category and Name for your new custom stamp.

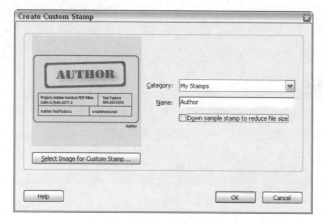

If you want to downsample a large image file, check the Down sample stamp to reduce file size check box. If you want to change your design and not use the image shown in the preview, you can click the Select Image for Custom Stamp button and locate another image.

When all the attributes are assigned for your new stamp, click OK.

5. **Use your new stamp.** Open the Stamp pull-down menu and you should see your new stamp category. Select the category name and the new stamp appears in a submenu, as shown in Figure 20.21. Click the new stamp and click in a document to apply the stamp.

FIGURE 20.21

Select the stamp from the new category submenu and click in a document to add the stamp.

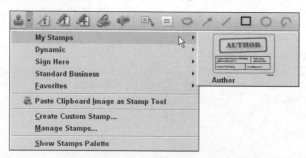

Appending stamps to a new category

After creating a custom stamp and adding a new category, the next time you open the Create Custom Stamp dialog box, you have a choice for adding a new category or appending a new stamp to your existing category. Here's how you append a stamp to an existing category:

STEPS: Appending stamps to an existing category

1. **Select Manage Stamps from the Stamp tool pull-down menu.** The Manage Stamps dialog box opens, as shown in Figure 20.22.

2. **Click Create.** Click the Create button and the Select Image for Custom Stamp dialog box opens.

3. **Add a new stamp.** Follow the same steps for adding a stamp as you do when creating a new stamp. When you arrive at the Create Custom Stamp dialog box, select the category you want to add your stamp from the Category pull-down menu. Type a name for your stamp and you arrive at the Manage Custom Stamps dialog box, as shown in Figure 20.22. In Figure 20.22, I appended a stamp to the My Stamps category.

FIGURE 20.22

The Manage Custom Stamps dialog box shows all stamps appended to categories.

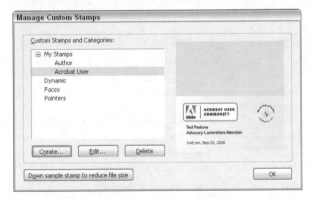

4. **Click OK.** Your new stamp appears listed in the category submenu.

In the Manage Custom Stamps dialog box, you have several tools for managing stamps. Click the Create button to append stamps to a category or create new categories. Select a stamp and click Edit to modify an appearance, category name, or stamp name. Select a stamp and click Delete to remove a stamp from a category or select a category and click Delete to remove an entire category. Click a stamp and click the Down sample stamp to reduce file size, if you want to downsample images. Apply edits and click OK. When you return to the Stamp tool pull-down menu, the additions/deletions are shown when you open the menu.

Pasting a clipboard image as a stamp

Yet another Stamp tool in Acrobat is the Paste Clipboard Image as Stamp tool. Any data you copy to the Clipboard can be pasted as a stamp. You might want to copy an image and text together in a document to make a comment about a layout design or the relationship between a drawing and image. In a comment pop-up note, you can add annotations describing your point.

To paste data back in a document as a stamp comment you need to first copy data, then paste it as a stamp comment. Listed below are the steps to copy data and paste the Clipboard data as a stamp.

STEPS: Pasting image data as a stamp comment

1. **Open a document in Acrobat containing both images and text.** For this example, we'll look at copying an image and a text passage.

2. **Take a snapshot.** Select the Snapshot tool from the Select & Zoom toolbar. Marquee an area you want to capture for your stamp image. When you release the mouse button, the data are copied to the Clipboard.

3. **Open the Stamp tool pull-down menu and select Paste Clipboard Image as Stamp Tool.** The cursor changes to load the Stamp tool cursor.

4. **Add the stamp to a document page.** With the cursor gun loaded as a new stamp, click and drag open a rectangle where you want the stamp to appear.

 You can also press Ctrl/⌘+V to paste any Clipboard data as a stamp.

5. **Add a comment note.** Select the Hand tool and click the stamp icon and a pop-up note window opens. Type a message in the note window, as shown in Figure 20.23.

FIGURE 20.23
Click the stamp icon with the Hand tool and type a comment in the note pop-up window.

Snapshot area

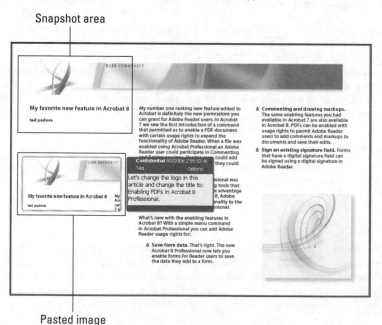

Pasted image

TIP If the Paste Clipboard Image as Stamp command is grayed out, you don't have an image copied to the Clipboard. To verify content on the Clipboard, open the Create PDF Task Button pull-down menu. If the From Clipboard Image menu item is grayed out, no data exist on the Clipboard.

Attaching files

File attachments enable you to attach any document file, recorded sound, or pasted image on your hard drive to an open PDF file. When you attach files, the file is embedded in the PDF document. Embedding a file provides other users the capability to view attachments on other computers and across platforms. At first it may appear as though the attachment is a link. However, if you transport the PDF document to another computer and open the attachment, the embedded file opens in the host application. Users on other computers need the original authoring application to view the embedded file. You can add file attachments in Acrobat Standard and Acrobat Professional. You can also add file attachments in Adobe Reader when PDFs have been created with usage rights for Adobe Reader.

CROSS-REF For more information on using the File Attachments tools and the File Attachments panel, see Chapters 12 and 26.

Using the Markup Tools

As I mentioned earlier in this chapter when introducing the Comment & Markup tools, the tools in the Comment & Markup toolbar can be categorized into two subsets. All the previous pages in this chapter dealt with the comment tools from the Sticky Note tool through the Attachments tools. Beginning with the Callout tool and moving to the right in the Comment & Markup toolbar, you have tools that fit into the Markup tools category.

Markup tools offer you a range of different tools that can be used with technical drawings, manuals, brochures, design pieces, as well as routine office memos and other such documents. These tools deviate from the standard highlighter and Text Edits tools in that they tend to be used as graphic enhancements for communicating messages. If you're an engineer or technical writer, you may be inclined to use all the tools. If you're a business professional, you may pick and choose certain tools when reviewing and marking up documents. At the least, Acrobat provides a tool for just about any user in any environment when it comes to review and markup.

Callout tool

 The Callout tool is used to note attention to an object, block of text, image, or other element on a page where you want to focus comments about a specific item. Notice in Figure 20.24 the Callout in the upper-right corner of the figure.

Cloud tool

 The Cloud tool is used like the Polygon Line tool where you click, release the mouse button, and move the cursor, click, and move the cursor again, and continue until you draw a polygon shape. Return to the point of origin and release the mouse button and Acrobat closes the path. The paths appear as a cloud shape. The shape can be filled and stroked. In Figure 20.24, a shape was drawn with the Cloud tool and an opacity of 25 percent was applied so the underlying area could be viewed with transparency.

Line tools with inline text

You use the Line tools with inline text like the Dimension tool was used in earlier versions of Acrobat to mark or comment about the distance between two points. The mark is drawn with two lines at right angles to the distance line, as shown in Figure 20.24. After you draw a line you can reshape it, changing the angle or the length of the two lines at right angles or the distance line.

Text Box tool

You use the Text Box tool for creating large blocks of text. You have more control over fonts, text attributes, and flexibility with the Text Box tool than when using a Note comment. Notice in Figure 20.24, text in the Text Box and the options available in the Properties Bar at the bottom of the Toolbar Well. As text is selected in the Text Box, you have an abundant number of font attribute choices in the Properties Bar.

FIGURE 20.24

Markups shown are the 1) Cloud tool, 2) Callout tool, 3) Line tool, and 4) Text Box tool.

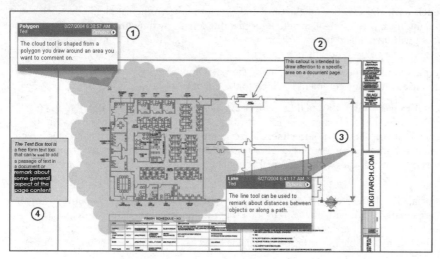

In the Text Box Properties dialog box, you can change opacity for text boxes, background colors, and line styles for borders. The remaining options are similar to properties for other comment tools.

Drawing tools

The Line tools are used for creating straight lines. You might use Line tools with or without arrowheads to illustrate points of interest, point out where background elements need to be moved, point to an object, or similar kinds of notations. These tools include:

- **Arrow tool.** The Arrow tool can be used with arrowheads, although applying arrowheads is a matter of user preference. You can draw straight lines on a 360-degree axis.

- **Line tool.** The Line tool can have the same attributes assigned as the preceding Arrow tool, making them indistinguishable from each other. The intent is for the Arrow tool to provide you with a line for arrowheads, whereas the Line tool remains without arrow-

heads. When marking up a document and using both line tools, you don't need to keep addressing the Line Properties dialog box each time you want to toggle on or off arrowheads. It's a matter of user preference, though, as you can choose to add or eliminate arrowheads from either tool.

- **Rectangle tool.** Use this tool to draw rectangle or square shapes. To keep the object constrained to a square, hold down the Shift key as you click and drag.

- **Oval tool.** Using this tool involves the same process as the Rectangle tool for constraining objects to circles. Oval shapes are drawn without adding the Shift key.

- **Polygon Line tool.** The Polygon Line tool also creates straight lines, but the lines are connected as you click the cursor to move in another direction. When you finish drawing a shape or lines with angles, double-click the mouse button to complete the line.

- **Polygon tool.** Use the same sequence of clicking and moving as described earlier for the Cloud tool. When you release the mouse button back at the point of origin, the shape closes with flat edges instead of semi-circles like the Cloud tool.

- **Pencil tool.** You use the Pencil tool to draw freeform lines. Whereas all the line tools draw straight lines, you use the Pencil tool for marking a page by drawing with a pencil, as you would with pencil and paper. The properties for pencil markings include choices for line weights, line colors, and line opacity settings.

Pencil comments are one contiguous line. If you stop drawing by releasing the mouse button, click, and drag again, a new comment is added to the document.

- **Pencil Eraser tool.** The Pencil Eraser tool erases lines drawn with the Pencil tool. Lines drawn with other tools cannot be erased with this tool. When you draw a line with the Pencil tool and erase part of the line, the remaining portion of a Pencil comment is interpreted as a single comment. Broken lines where you may have several smaller lines remaining after erasing part of a Pencil comment are considered part of the same comment.

A note pop-up is associated with the entire group of Drawing tools. You can access tool properties by opening a context menu on a mark drawn with any tool. In the Properties dialog box for the respective tool, you can change stroke and fill colors and opacities. For strokes, you can change line weights. As with other comment tools, you also have available in the Properties dialog box General attributes options and Review History options.

Drawing tools and context menus

One addition to an open context menu on one of the drawing tools is the Flip Line command. If you have an arrowhead on one side of a line and you want the direction to be pointing in the opposite way, open a context menu and select Flip Line.

Line tool properties

Many of the same Sticky Note properties — color assignment, opacity, author, subject, and reviewing — are available for line tools. Additional line tool properties include line weights and end caps. More options are available for end caps in the Properties dialog box than in the Properties Bar. In Figure 20.25, the line attributes are compared between settings with the Properties Bar on the left and the Properties dialog box on the right.

Line styles are the same in both the Properties Bar and the Properties dialog box, as shown in Figure 20.26.

FIGURE 20.25

Line settings available in the Properties Bar and the Properties dialog box

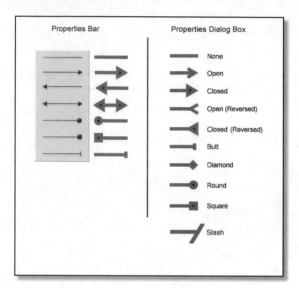

FIGURE 20.26

Line Style properties are the same in the Properties Bar and the Properties dialog box.

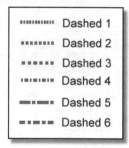

Managing line comments

To move drawing objects, align them, or reshape them, you need to select an object with the Hand tool. If you experience difficulty selecting a line, it may be because the Make Hand tool select text check box for the Hand tool preference option is selected. If selecting drawing tool objects is awkward, open the Preferences dialog box (Ctrl/⌘+K) and select General in the left pane. Disable the check box for Make Hand tool select text.

TIP If you want to keep the Hand tool preferences set to select text with the tool and you have difficulty selecting markups, open the Comments tab and click a comment to select it.

 **CROSS-REF** For more information on using the Hand tool for text selections, see Chapter 13.

Click an object and handles appear either at the line ends or at each end of line segments around polygon objects. (See Figure 20.27.) You can drag any handle in or out to resize or reshape objects. To move an object, click on a line or a fill color and drag the shape.

FIGURE 20.27

To reshape objects, select the Hand tool, click on a handle (square shape on a line), and drag to change the shape.

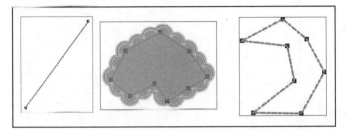

Drawing tools comments can be copied, cut, pasted, deleted, aligned, distributed, and sized. Use the Select Object tool and open a context menu while one or more objects are selected. Choose a menu command for the operation desired.

 TIP When selecting objects with the Select Object tool, you can draw a marquee through objects to select them. You don't need to completely surround comments within a marquee to select them.

Using the Show Menu

You can adjust several settings for comments and comment pop-up notes in the Show tool contained in the Comment & Markup toolbar. Options for the pull-down menu are also found in the Comments panel. Open the pull-down menu to see the menu commands shown in Figure 20.28.

FIGURE 20.28

The Show tool pull-down menu offers commands for working with comments and comment note pop-ups.

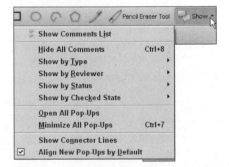

From the menu selections, you have the following choices:

- **Show Comments List.** Select this command to open the Comments panel. You can also open the Comments panel by clicking the Comments tab.

- **Hide All Comments.** Selecting the command opens a warning dialog box indicating that all replies in a review will be hidden. Click OK in the warning dialog box and all comments are hidden from view, but still attached to the document. Return to the menu and Show All Comments.

- **Show by Type.** You can selectively show comments by type. Choices from the submenu include All Types, Notes, Drawing Markups, Text Editing Markups, Stamps, and Attachments. You can select multiple types by returning to the submenu and making additional selections. For example, if you want to show Notes, Stamps, and Attachments while hiding Drawing Markups and Text Editing Markups, select Notes, return to the menu, and select Stamps. Notes remain selected when you make the second selection. Return again and select Attachments and all three types remain in view while the other types remain hidden from view.

- **Show by Reviewer.** You can choose to show comments by one or more reviewers for documents retrieved from a review session. The method of selecting multiple reviewers follows the same behavior as with Show by Type.

- **Show by Status.** Also used with review sessions, you can show comments by selected Review status and by Migration status.

CROSS-REF For information on Status assignment, see "Using the Comments panel" later in this chapter. For information on the Migration options, see Chapter 21.

- **Show by Checked State.** You can check comments for your own personal use. Comments are either Checked or Unchecked in the Comments panel. From the submenu options, you can choose to show all checked comments, unchecked comments, or both.

- **Open All Pop-ups.** Opens all pop-up notes.

- **Minimize All Pop-ups.** Closes all pop-up notes.

- **Show Connector Lines.** When the mouse cursor appears over a comment, connector lines are shown from the comment to the comment note. If you don't want to show the connector lines, select this command. By default, connector lines are shown.

- **Align New Pop-ups by Default.** By default, comment notes are aligned to the right side of the document page. When this menu item is checked, the comment notes appear aligned together on top of each other. Removing the check mark from this option causes note pop-ups to align with the note icon.

Using the Comments Menu

A menu dedicated to comments appears at the top-level menu bar. Open the Commenting menu and you find several commands redundant with the Show pull-down menu and a single command not available in other menus.

Unique commands in the Comments menu include:

- **Commands for Comment Reviews.** Several commands appear for comment reviews such as Attach for Email Review, Send for Shared Review, Upload for Browser-Based Review, Migrate Comments, and Review Tracker. Note that Review Tracker is also accessed in the Comments panel.

CROSS-REF For information on all the commands related to reviews, see Chapter 21.

- **Enable for Commenting in Adobe Reader.** When you chose this command and save the PDF file, the file is enabled only for commenting. No provision is made for saving form data or adding digital signatures.

CROSS-REF For information on enabling PDFs for commenting in Adobe Reader, see Chapter 19.

- **Summarize Comments.** You also have the same commands available in the Comments panel. See "Using the Comments Panel" later in this chapter.

- **Print with Comments Summary.** This command is also available in the Comments panel. See "Using the Comments Panel" later in this chapter.

- **Search for Additional Services.**

- **Importing and exporting comments.** You have the same commands available in the Comments panel. See "Exporting and Importing Comments" later in this chapter.

CROSS-REF For more information on importing and exporting comments, see Chapter 8.

Using the Comments Panel

The Comments panel conveniently contains many tools and options for managing comments. By default, the Comments panel opens horizontally across the bottom of the Acrobat window like the Attachments panel and lists all the comments created in a PDF document. If you toggle views between several PDF files, the Comments panel dynamically updates the list of comments to reflect comments on the file active in the Document pane or in two document panes.

Depending on the size of your monitor, you'll find that viewing the panel occupies substantial space in the Acrobat window. If you're working on a small monitor, the amount of room left over for viewing pages, after loading toolbars in the Toolbar Well and expanding the Comments panel, can be very skimpy. Fortunately, you can view the panel docked in the Navigation pane and control the size by dragging the horizontal separator bar at the top of the panel down to reduce size, as shown in Figure 20.29.

You also have a choice for floating the panel by undocking it from the Navigation pane and resizing the panel. To undock the Comments panel, click on the tab and drag it to the Document pane. You can resize the panel by dragging the lower-right corner in or out to reduce or expand the size.

Either way you choose to view the Comments panel, you'll find using it to be a great asset when reviewing documents and participating in review sessions. At first it may be a struggle to find the right size and location for the panel, but with a little practice you'll find the many tools contained in the panel much easier to access than using menu commands.

FIGURE 20.29

Drag the separator bar up or down to resize the Comments panel.

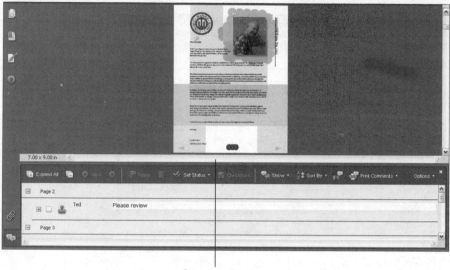

Seperator bar

Viewing comments

The Comments panel lists all the comments contained in the active document. By default the comments are listed by page. In a multi-page document, you'll see Page 1, Page 2, Page 3, and so on displayed in the list on the left side of the panel.

You can view the list of comments expanded or collapsed. In Figure 20.30, you see the list expanded. Expanded lists show comments in a hierarchy as Bookmarks are shown in the Bookmarks pane. You can expand individual pages that contain comments by clicking on the plus (+) symbol (Windows) or the right-pointing arrow (Macintosh). To expand all comments, click the Expand All button in the Comments panel toolbar shown in Figure 20.30. Conversely, you can collapse all comments by clicking the Collapse All button. Note that in Figure 20.30 the minus (–) symbol shows the Collapse All tool but the text is not shown because of a lower resolution monitor view.

Comments are listed in a hierarchical order. If you have several comments on a page and you click on the icon to the left of the comment to expand the page comments, you see the Comment icon, author, and content of a note pop-up. You can further expand each comment in the expanded list by clicking on the plus (+) symbol (Windows) or right-pointing arrow (Macintosh). When further expanded, the comment subject and the creation date are displayed in the pane.

FIGURE 20.30

Comments are ordered in a hierarchical list. By default, comments are viewed nested in a page order. The first three pages are expanded while the individual comments remain collapsed.

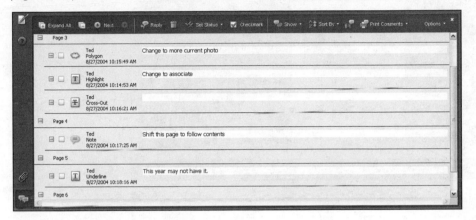

Sorting comments

 You can change the default Page sorting to any of the following:

- **Type.** Comments are sorted together by the type of comment contained on pages. All Note comments appear together, highlight comments together, stamps together, and so on.
- **Page.** The default. Comments are listed together successively by page.
- **Author.** If a document has comments from several different authors, the comments are listed by author and sorted in an alphabetical order by author name.
- **Date.** The creation date is the sort order with the most recent date appearing first in the list.
- **Color.** Comments are sorted according to the color settings made in the comment Properties dialog boxes.
- **Checkmark Status.** You can check a comment for your own personal method of flagging a comment. Checking comments might be made for you to alert yourself to review comments, perhaps mark them for deletion, or to spend more time in a later editing session reviewing the comments made by others. The choice for what the check mark signals is a personal choice. When you view comments according to Checkmark Status, all unchecked Comments (Unmarked) are listed first followed by comments marked with a check mark.
- **Status by Person.** The menu option includes a submenu where you can select an author. Select an author name from the submenu and comments are sorted with the comments for the selected author appearing first. The unchecked comments are listed next by author name. You must have Status set on at least one comment to activate this command.

Navigating comments

The up and down arrows in the Comments toolbar enable you to move back and forth between comments. Click the down-pointing arrow to move to the next comment in the list. Click the up-pointing arrow to navigate to a previous comment. The arrow tools are grayed out when comments are collapsed. In order to use the tools you need to have one or more groups of comments expanded and have a comment selected.

Double-clicking a comment in the list takes you to the page where the comment appears. When you double-click the comment in the Comments panel, an associated pop-up note also opens. You must uncheck Hide comment popups when Comments List is open for the note popups to open from clicking the notes in the Comments panel.

Searching comments

 You can search the contents of comment pop-up notes. To find a word in a pop-up note, select the Search comments tool. Enter the search criteria and click Search Comments. You can also open the full or generic Search pane and select the Include Comments check box. The Search pane offers you the same search options used for searching open PDF documents. You can match case, search for whole words only, and other search criteria. The results of your search, however, return words found in the document as well as words found in comment pop-up notes.

When a word is found in a comment pop-up note, the page where the note appears opens and the pop-up note opens with the found word highlighted.

 For more information on using the Search pane, see Chapter 6.

Printing comments

 The Print Comments tool does more than print the comments in a document to your printer. When you select the Print Comments tool, a pull-down menu opens where you can choose from two menu options. These menu commands include the following:

- **Print Comments Summary.** Use this command to create a summary page as a new PDF file and print the summarized comments to your default printer. The comment summary is a temporary file that Acrobat creates while you print the summarized comments. After completing the print job the summary is deleted by Acrobat.

- **Create PDF of Comments Summary.** Use this command to create a new PDF document that summarizes the comments in your document, rather than print a file to your printer. You can save this file and keep it around to review a summary of the comments.

From each of the menu commands, Acrobat defaults to "Document and comments with sequence numbers on separate pages." If you want to print pages with comments configured with different settings, select from one of four radio button options for the way you want to view a summary. The radio button options appear in the Summarize Options dialog box that opens when you select either menu command in the Print Comments menu.

 For details in regard to working with comment summaries, see the section "Creating Comment Summaries" later in this chapter.

Deleting comments

In addition to the context menus used when creating comments, you can delete them from within the Comments panel. Select a comment in the pane and click on the Trash icon to delete the selected comment. After deleting a comment, you have one level of undo available to you. If you change your mind after deleting a comment, choose Edit ⇨ Undo. You can also undo selecting multiple comments and clicking on the Trash icon. Choose Edit ⇨ Undo successively if you change your mind after deleting multiple comments. In the event you lose the Undo command, you need to choose File ⇨ Revert to bring back the comment. Be certain to update your PDF file after reviewing any comment deletions. The Revert command reverts to the last saved version of the file.

Marking comments

`Checkmark` The Checkmark tool is used to flag comments for a special purpose. You can select a comment in the Comments list in the panel and select the tool to checkmark the current selection. You can also apply checkmarks to comments by clicking in the open checkmark box when a comment is expanded. Between the expand/collapse icon and the comment icon is a check box. Click the box to checkmark a comment. When viewing an expanded comments list, you do not need to select comments in order to mark the check boxes.

Setting comment status

`Set Status ▾` Marking a comment with a check mark, described in the preceding section, is a method for you to keep track of comments for your own purposes. The Set Status tool is used to mark a comment's current status that is intended for use in comment reviews and when shared with other users. From the tool pull-down menu you have two subcategories for marking the status of a comment. Under Review you have five choices: None, Accepted, Cancelled, Completed, and Rejected. Under Migration you have three choices: None, Not Confirmed, and Confirmed. These options are the same as those you have in the Show tool pull-down menu.

CROSS-REF For more information on using the status marks in review sessions, see Chapter 21.

Editing comment pop-up notes

A very handy feature available to you when viewing comments in an expanded list is the ability to edit note pop-up text. Rather than navigating to each page containing a comment and opening the associated note pop-up window to make your edits, you can delete, change, or modify text listed in the Comments panel.

When you select the note pop-up text in the Comments panel, the note pop-up window opens in the Document pane. In order for the note popup window to open when you click a comment in the Comments panel, you need to make certain the Commenting preference option for Hide comment pop-ups when Comments List is open is unchecked. You don't need the comment popup note open to make edits in the Comments panel, but if you want to examine note popups on the document pages, disable this preference option.

As you make changes in the Comments panel, changes are dynamically reflected in the pop-up note window. If you edit text in the pop-up note window, the text edits are reflected in the Comments panel.

Exporting and Importing Comments

If you ask a colleague to comment on a document, you can bypass the e-mail, shared, and browser-based reviews by having a reviewer export comments and e-mail the exported file to you. When you export comments from a PDF document, the data are exported as an FDF or XFDF file. The data file results in much smaller file sizes than PDF documents and can easily be imported back into the original PDF or copy of the original PDF document.

To export comments from a PDF document, choose Comments ➪ Export Comments. Three menu commands exist for exporting comments. Choose Comments ➪ Export Comments to Word to export the comments directly to a Microsoft Word document. Choose Export Comments to AutoCAD to export comments directly to an AutoCAD .dwg file. The third option is Export Comments to a Data File. When you choose

this option you can select either FDF or XFDF as your file format. Using these two formats, you can import the data file comments back into your PDF document. Choose Comments ➪ Import Comments to import the data file comments into your PDF file.

CROSS-REF For information on exporting Comments to AutoCAD files, see Chapter 7. For exporting to MS Word files, see Chapter 8.

Exporting/importing comments to and from a file

When you export comments to a file, the Export Comments dialog box opens. The dialog box behaves similarly to a Save As dialog box where you select a destination folder, provide a filename, and click a Save button. Acrobat provides a default name by using the PDF filename with an .fdf extension. You can use the default name or change the name in the File Name field box. From the Save as Type (Windows) or Format (Macintosh) pull-down menu, you can select between FDF formatted files and XFDF (XML-based FDF file). The default is FDF.

Click Save in the Export Comments dialog box. The resulting file can be exported to a user who has the same PDF document from which the FDF file was created. If you receive an FDF file and want to load the comments, choose Comments ➪ Import Comments. The Import Comments dialog box opens. Navigate to the location where the data file is located and select it. Click the Select button and the comments are imported into the open PDF document.

NOTE You have three file format options — not only FDF and XFDF for export, but also PDF. If someone sends you a PDF with comments, you can import those comments directly to your version without having to export them from your reviewer's copy and then import into your copy.

When you import comments in a PDF document, all the comments are imported in the exact location where they were originally created. If you delete a page in a PDF file and import comments, Acrobat ignores comments where it can't find matching pages. Note pop-ups and icons are matched with the way they appear in the file from which the comments were exported.

Exporting selected comments

You can select comments and choose to export only the selected comments to an FDF file. Open the Comments panel and select comments according to the sort order listed in the Comments panel. The default is by page. Select a page in the list and open the Options pull-down menu from the Comments panel toolbar. Select Export Selected Comments from the menu options.

The Export Comments dialog box opens. Navigate your hard drive to find the folder where you want to save the FDF or XFDF file, provide a name for the file, and click the Save button.

TIP When exporting all comments leave the filename for the FDF or XFDF exported file at the default provided by Acrobat. When exporting Selected Comments, be certain to edit the filename. By default, Acrobat uses the same name. If you elect to export all comments and then want to export selected comments, you might mistakenly overwrite files with the same filename. By getting into a habit of being consistent when naming files, you'll prevent potential mistakes.

Filtering Comments

You can further enhance the features available to you for review and markup, exporting and importing comments, and viewing comments in the Comments panel, by filtering comments in groups. Filtering

comments temporarily hides comments you don't want to use at the moment. You can choose to display all comments by an author, a date, a reviewer, selected types of comments, and a range of other criteria. When comments are filtered, exporting comments or creating comment summaries (explained in the next section) is applied only to those comments currently viewed. Any hidden comments are excluded from the task at hand.

 You manage the comment filter via the Show pull-down menu. The options in the Show pull-down menu in the Toolbar Well are identical to the menu options in the Show tool pull-down menu in the Comments panel.

 To understand more about the Show menu options, see the section "Using the Show menu" earlier in this chapter.

TIP If you know ahead of time that you want to export edits back to Microsoft Word, you can mark only those comments received from reviewers that you intend to export to Word. When the review session is completed, choose Show ➪ Hide All Comments. Open the menu again and choose Show by Type ➪ Text Editing Markups. Return to the menu and choose Show by Checked State ➪ Checked. Export the comments, and only the Text Edit comments with the items you checked during the review are exported to Word.

The remaining menu options include non-filtering menu choices such as opening/closing note pop-ups, showing connector lines, aligning icons and pop-up notes, and accessing the Comment preferences. You can also make these menu selections from other tools and menus as described earlier in this chapter.

Creating Comment Summaries

If you create an extensive review from many participants over a period of time, the number of comments may become too many to comfortably manage in the Comments panel or on the document pages. Or you may have a need to create a comment summary you want to distribute to users after filtering out comments that you don't want included in a summary. Furthermore, you may want to print a hard copy of comments that show the PDF pages with connector lines to a summary description. You can accomplish all these tasks and more when you create comment summaries.

To create a comment summary, you need to have a PDF document open in the Document pane and comments in view in the Comments panel. The pane can be open or collapsed. Comments can be filtered according to the sorts and filtering you want to apply, but at least one comment with the criteria must exist for a summary report to contain comment information.

If the Comments panel is collapsed, you create a comment summary by opening the Comment menu and select Summarize Comments. If the Comments panel is open, you can choose the menu command from Options menu.

When you select Summarize Comments from either menu command, the Summarize Options dialog box opens, as shown in Figure 20.31.

FIGURE 20.31

Select Summarize Comments from the Comments menu or a context menu in the Comments panel to open the Summarize Options dialog box.

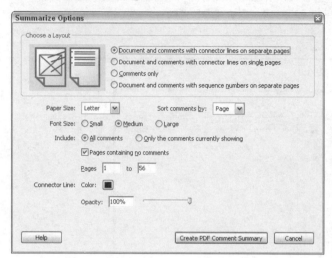

The first four radio buttons in the dialog box offer you choices for the way the summary pages are created and the page layout view, which may contain single page views or Continuous – Facing Pages views. The resulting summaries are created as separate PDF documents.

Choices for creating a comment summary in the Summarize Options dialog box include:

- **Document and comments with connector lines on separate pages.** This option creates a comment summary with each summary page aside the respective document page with connector lines from each comment on a page to the summarized item in a new summary. When the summary is created, Acrobat automatically switches to a Two-Up Continuous layout. If you don't want a continuous view and you want the pages to snap to fit in the Document pane, select View ➪ Page Display ➪ Two-Up. In Figure 20.32, you see a Document and comments with connector lines on separate pages summary shown in a Two-Up view.

- **Document and comments with connector lines on single pages.** The summary is similar to the preceding option; however, the PDF document and the summary are created together on a single landscape page. The size of the paper is determined by the setting specified in the Paper size drop-down menu. One advantage for this summary view compared to the preceding summary is the comments, connector lines, and summary data require a little less room on your monitor to view the original file and the summary information. Furthermore, if you export summaries for other users, the summarized information and original file are assembled together in a single document.

- **Comments only.** Only the summarized data are assembled together on single pages. The comment summaries are shown in a hierarchy according to the sort order you select in this dialog box. The page layout is a single page view.

■ **Document and comments with sequence numbers on separate pages.** Summaries are created similarly to the method described in the preceding bullet, but with the addition of sequence numbers assigned to each comment according to the sort order and the order in which the comments were created. The page layout view is Two-Up Continuous, which shows the comments with sequence numbers and the resulting summary in the opposing page view.

FIGURE 20.32

A summary shown in a Two-Up view

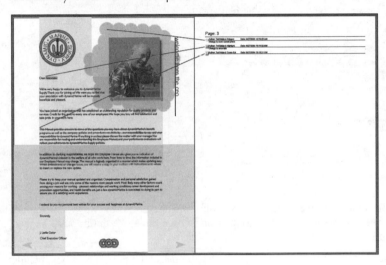

■ **Paper size.** From the pull-down menu, select a paper size according to the sizes available for your selected printer.

■ **Sort comments by.** From the pull-down menu you can choose from four different options. The default is a sort according to Page. If you want another sort order, choose from Author, Type, or Date from the pull-down menu options. The sort order selected in the Summarize Options dialog box supersedes the sort order selected in the Comments panel.

■ **Font Size.** Applies to the font used in the comment summary description on the newly created pages. Depending on the size selected, the summary pages may be fewer (Small) or more (Large). The point size for small is 5 points, for medium 6.75 points, and for large 9 points.

■ **Include.** All comments summarizes all comments on the PDF pages regardless of whether the comments are in view or hidden. The Only the comments currently showing option creates a comment summary from the comments visible in the Comments panel.

■ **Pages containing no comments.** Check the box if you want pages containing no comments included in the summary. Disable the check box and only pages with comments are included in the summary.

■ **Pages.** Specify the page range for the summary in the text boxes.

■ **Connector Line Color.** Click the color swatch and you can choose a color for connector lines from the pop-up color palette.

■ **Opacity.** Applies an opacity setting for the connector lines.

Comment summaries are particularly useful when sending PDF documents to Adobe Reader users. Although Reader users can see comments you create in a PDF document, they cannot create comment summaries. You can create a summary for a Reader user and append the new document to the existing PDF file, then send the file to other members in your workgroup.

Comparing Documents

If you set up a review for users to provide feedback on a document, you may incorporate recommended changes in a file. As you work on modifying files, you may end up with several documents in different development stages. If you aren't quite certain which document contains your finished edits, you may have a need to compare files to check for the most recent updates. Acrobat's Compare Documents feature (Acrobat Professional only) provides you a method for analyzing two files and reporting all differences between them.

To compare two documents choose Advanced ➪ Compare Documents. The Compare Documents dialog box opens. You can open the dialog box without any file open in the Document pane or open both files to compare and then select the menu command. In Figure 20.33, I have two files titled dynamicMarine Employee Manual.pdf and employee ManualCommentsEnabled.pdf. Because these two files are similar documents, I'm not certain which document contains revisions. Therefore, the documents are selected for comparison to check the differences.

FIGURE 20.33

Choose Advanced ➪ Compare Documents to open the Compare Documents dialog box.

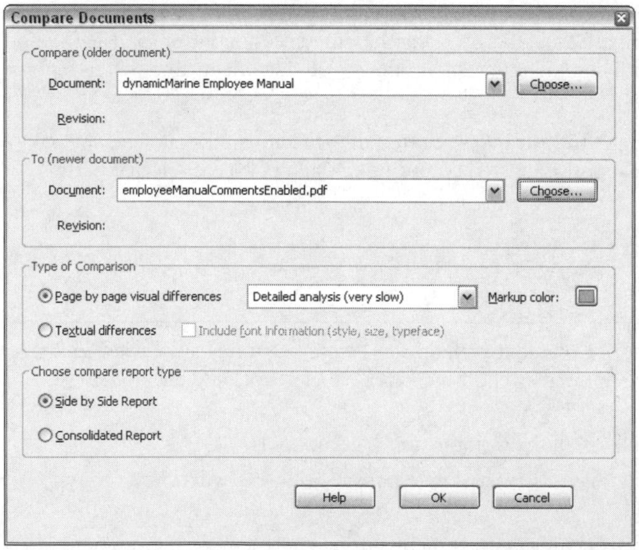

The Compare Documents dialog box contains the following options:

- **Document.** The first two items are used to identify the documents for comparison. If no files are open in the Document pane, click the Choose button and select a file in the Open dialog box that appears. Click the second Choose button and open a second file. If you have the two documents to be compared open in the Document pane before opening the Compare Documents dialog box, the pull-down menus show you both open files. Select one file in the top pull-down menu and the second file in the next pull-down menu.

- **Page by page visual differences.** Three options are available from pull-down menu choices. Depending on which item you choose, the reports are more or less detailed and the speed in which the documents are compared relate to how much detail you want to analyze. A detailed analysis takes more time than the other two options. From the menu, choose Detailed analysis, or Normal analysis, or Coarse analysis. Small visual differences between documents are reported when choosing the Detailed analysis (very slow) option. The resulting report shows differences in very small graphics. The Coarse analysis ignores small graphics that may appear on one document or another, and the Normal option falls somewhere in between the other two.

- **Textual differences.** Selecting this radio button deselects the preceding radio button selection. Use this option if your only interest is in comparing text in the document while ignoring graphics and the layout or reading order. If you want to compare fonts between documents, select the Include font information (style, size, typeface) check box. This option is very handy for reviews where you have moved chunks of text around in a document, but have not really changed the words. It's good for legal documents, chapters, articles, and so on.

- **Markup color.** A report is created with markups. You can choose what color is used for the markups by clicking on the color swatch and selecting a preset color or a custom color.

- **Choose compare report type.** After comparing two files, Acrobat creates a report. The type of report can be either a Side-by-Side Report with the two documents displayed in a Two-Up Continuous Page layout and comparison marks showing the differences, or a Consolidated Report where differences are marked with comment notes in a single PDF document. Choose the report type and click OK.

Acrobat compares the documents according to the attributes selected in the Compare Documents dialog box. When the comparison is finished, the report is created according to the report type selected in the Compare Documents dialog box.

Summary

- Acrobat provides an extensive set of Comment preferences. Before beginning any review session you should review the preference settings by choosing Edit ➪ Preferences and clicking on Commenting in the left pane.

- A single toolbar in Acrobat 8 contains all the Comment & Markup tools.

- Most comments created in Acrobat have associated note pop-up windows where you can type comments.

- You access comment properties by opening context menus from a note icon or pop-up note title bar.

- You can create custom stamps in Acrobat from a variety of different file formats.

- The Comments panel lists all comments in a PDF document. Additional tools are available in the Comments panel where you can mark status changes in comments, check comment status, and filter comments.

- You can enable usage rights for Adobe Reader users to participate in comment reviews from Acrobat Professional.

- Comments can be filtered and sorted to isolate authors, types, dates, and other criteria. When exporting comments, only the sorted comments in view in the Comments panel are exported.

- Comments exported from a document can be imported into a matching PDF file, a Word file, and an AutoCAD file.

- When exporting comments from Acrobat as a file, the comments data are saved as FDF or XFDF and result in smaller file sizes.

- Comment summaries are displayed in one of four different report styles. When a summary is created it can be sorted upon creation and saved as a separate PDF file.

- The Compare Documents command enables you to locate differences for text and images between two PDF documents. Reports are generated with comments describing found differences.

Chapter 21

Working with Review Sessions

Throughout this book, I address the use of PDFs on the Web. As I discussed in Chapter 9, you can download selected Web pages or entire Web sites and have all the HTML pages converted to PDF. In Acrobat 7 and 8 you can convert media, animation, and sound to PDFs with the animated pages appearing the same in Acrobat viewers as when you see them on Web sites.

Coming ahead in Chapter 30, I talk about eBooks and downloading eBooks; in Chapter 34 I talk about submitting form data; and in other chapters you find similar discussions on Acrobat PDFs hosted online. In short, the Web plays a major role with much of your Acrobat activity.

This chapter builds on information covered in Chapter 20 where I discussed using the commenting tools, menus, and Comments panel. In this chapter I cover commenting through Attach for Email Review and Send for Shared Reviews, which are, again, another use for PDFs and the Internet.

Setting Up the Commenting for Reviews Environment

Commenting in review sessions requires use of the same tools discussed in Chapter 20. If you haven't read Chapter 20, take a moment to read how to load commenting tools and open the Comments panel. The tools you need to follow along in this chapter are the Comment & Markup tools and the Properties Bar. Load these tools as explained in Chapter 20.

Creating an Attach for E-mail Review

The abundant number of comment tools, properties, and menu commands are nothing more than overkill if all you want to do is add some comments on PDF

pages for your own use. Acrobat is designed with much more sophistication when it comes to commenting, and the tools provided to you are intended to help you share comments in workgroups.

Comment and review among workgroups is handled in two ways. You can set up an Attach for E-mail review and exchange comments with your coworkers and colleagues where PDFs and data are exchanged through e-mail, or you can set up a Send for Shared review where comments are uploaded and downloaded by participants to a shared folder on a network or Web server in the review process.

Adobe's Acrobat team wanted to make it almost seamless for any user to not only start a review session but participate in a review session. With the ability to enable documents with usage rights for Adobe Reader users, anyone with the free Adobe Reader software can participate in a review.

CROSS-REF   For more information on adding usage rights to PDFs, see Chapters 19 and 20.

Initiating an Attach for E-mail review

An Attach for Email Review is a method for you, the PDF author, to share a document that needs input from other members of a workgroup (in an e-mail exchange), such as a proposal or draft document, and ask them to make comments for feedback. As comments are submitted, you can track comments from others and make decisions about how the comments are treated. Decisions such as accepting or rejecting comments are part of this process. The comment exchanges between you and your workgroup members are handled through e-mail exchanges. When using this kind of review, the review initiator is the only person who sees comments from all the reviewers.

When you send a file for review, the PDF contains information about you, the author/initiator, who's invited to the review and where the original is located on your system. When a recipient receives the e-mail inviting him or her to review your document, the attachment to the e-mail is a PDF the recipients use to make comments. The recipients open the PDF e-mail attachment in Acrobat or Adobe Reader and make comments. When a reviewer finishes commenting, the reviewer sends the data back to the PDF author. The data sent from the reviewers can either be the FDF data or both the data and the PDF document (choices are made in Reviewing preferences discussed later in this chapter). If you start with a large PDF file, the comment exchanges using FDF data require much less data transfers as the comment data are typically much smaller than original PDF files.

When reviews are initiated, you *must* send the PDF file to all reviewers. You can then make a decision in the Reviewing Preferences for whether the PDF or an FDF file is returned back to you. In the Preferences dialog box, click Reviewing and type a value in the Send comments as FDF for files greater than text box. The default is 5MB. Therefore, FDF data are returned for all files greater than 5MB. You can raise or lower the number by typing a new value in the text box. This setting is applied only to comments returned back to you. If you have a PDF greater than 5MB — or any file size for that matter — you must first send the PDF document to the recipients.

When comments are returned to you either in PDF or FDF form, double-click the file attachment in your e-mail application. Double-clicking either file type appends comments from recipients to your original PDF you used when you invited recipients to participate in a review.

NOTE   Before initiating a review, be certain to add your e-mail address in the Identity preferences. If you don't add the Identity preferences Acrobat prompts you in a dialog box and opens the Identity preferences for you. You can't proceed until you fill in the preference text boxes. Open the Preferences dialog box and select Identity. Add your personal identity information including your e-mail address. The e-mail address supplied in the Identity preferences is used when e-mailing PDFs from within Acrobat.

To understand how to start an e-mail–based review, follow these steps.

STEPS: Initiating an e-mail–based review

1. **Open a document in Acrobat Professional.** Opening a document is optional as you can begin a review without a document open in the Document pane. In this example, I start with a document open in Acrobat Professional. If using Acrobat Standard, you can initiate an e-mail–based review, but you cannot enable the document with usage rights for Adobe Reader users. If using Acrobat Professional you have an option for enabling the document for Reader users to participate in your review.

2. **Initiate the review.** If you want to make a comment on your document you can do so, but you need to be certain to save all your updates. After saving the file, select Attach for Email Review from the Review & Comment task button pull-down menu. The Send by Email for Review: Step 1 of 3 wizard page opens, as shown in Figure 21.1. This is the first of three panes appearing in the wizard when you initiate a review.

   By default, documents active in the Document pane are specified in the field box in the first pane. If you change your mind or you start a review without a document open in Acrobat, click the Browse button and browse your hard drive to locate a file.

 You can also access the same menu command by choosing Comments ⇨ Attach for Email Review.

FIGURE 21.1

To start a review session, open the PDF to be used for the review and choose Attach for Email Review from the Review & Comment task button pull-down menu or the Comments menu.

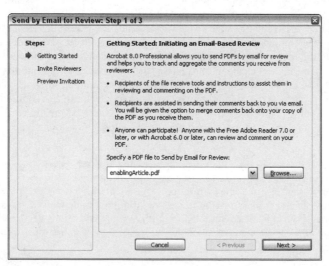

3. **Invite reviewers.** After identifying the file to send out for review, click the Next button to open the Send by Email for Review: Step 2 of 3 pane, as shown in Figure 21.2. The Address Book window will contain a list of recipients for your review. Type in the e-mail addresses for the people you want to participate in the review or click Address Book to launch your e-mail address book to select reviewers to invite.

FIGURE 21.2

Add e-mail addresses for the review participants.

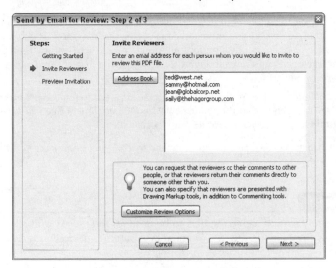

4. **Enable the PDF for Adobe Reader usage rights.** Click the Customize Review Options button to open the Review Options dialog box shown in Figure 21.3. If you want Adobe Reader users to participate in the review, keep the default check box checked for Also allow users of Free Adobe Reader 7.0 or later to participate in this review. Click OK and you return to the Step 2 pane. Additionally, you can specify who will receive the review comments; the default is the e-mail address you specified in the Identity properties. However, you can add additional names or change it to a name of a co-worker or administrator. For more information on working with an Address Book in review sessions, see the sidebar, "Managing an Address Book for Review Sections."

NOTE In Figure 21.3 you can see a light bulb in the dialog box. Whenever you see this image, be certain to read the text warning aside the image. This is particularly important when enabling PDFs with Adobe Reader usage rights. Some features on PDFs are disabled when the files are enabled with usage rights. For example, if you send a form out for review (using the Comments menu) and enable the document with usage rights, all form fields are disabled for both Acrobat and Adobe Reader users. To enable PDFs for both comment and review and form fill-in and saving, you need to use the Advanced menu and select Enable Usage Rights in Adobe Reader.

FIGURE 21.3

Click the Customize Review Options button to open the Review Options dialog box.

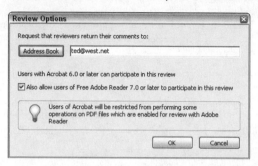

5. **Preview the invitation.** Click Next and you arrive at the Send by Email for Review: Step 3 of 3 pane, as shown in Figure 21.4. This pane displays a preview of the e-mail message you are about to send to reviewers. You can edit the Invitation Message Subject or Invitation Message by typing in the respective text boxes. Click Send Invitation when the preview appears as you like to start the e-mail process.

FIGURE 21.4

Preview the message to be sent to reviewers and click Send Invitation.

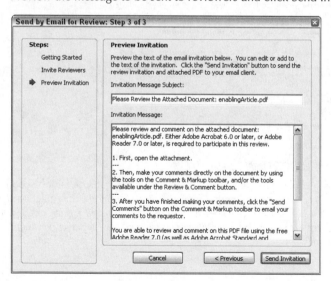

6. **Send the invitation.** If your e-mail program does not immediately send the invitation to reviewers, open your default e-mail program and click the Send (or Send/Receive) button to commence the e-mail initiation. In Figure 21.5, an invitation is displayed in Microsoft Outlook showing the recipients in the To field, the Subject of the e-mail, and a file attachment in the Attach field. The message is derived from the Send by Email For Review dialog box. Note that before initiating a send, you can still edit the message. Click the Send (or Send/Receive) button and the e-mail and attachment are sent to the reviewers.

FIGURE 21.5

If your default e-mail program does not send the message, open the program and click the Send (or Send/Receive) button.

Participating in a review

Participants in a review include you — the PDF author and review initiator, and the people you select as reviewers. In your role, you field all comments from reviewers. If you use the Attach for Email Review to send comments back to users, Acrobat does permit you to reply to users' comments. A review session is designed for a single set of responses; however, if you want, you can exchange comments back and forth between you and the reviewers.

Managing an Address Book for Review Sessions

When you open the Address Book from the Invite Reviewers section, shown earlier in this chapter in Figure 21.2, when using Microsoft Outlook as your default mail program, or from the Review Options dialog box shown in Figure 21.3, several options are available to manage addresses that you can use in future review sessions. The Address Book, shown here, offers the following:

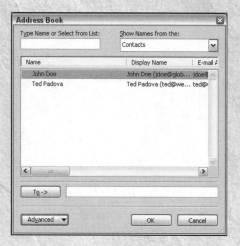

- **Show Names from the.** Choices appear from a pull-down menu. If using Microsoft Outlook the choices are Outlook Address Book and Contacts. You can choose to use either your e-mail program's address book or a contact list you create in Acrobat.

- **Type Name or Select from List.** Type a name to be added to your recipients list or select a name from the left list window.

- **To.** Click a name in the Name list and click the To-> button to copy the name to the To list window. All addresses you list in the right window are added to a review session when you click OK.

- **Advanced.** From the Advanced pull-down menu, select New to add a new contact and the Contact dialog box opens as shown in the following figure.

continued

continued

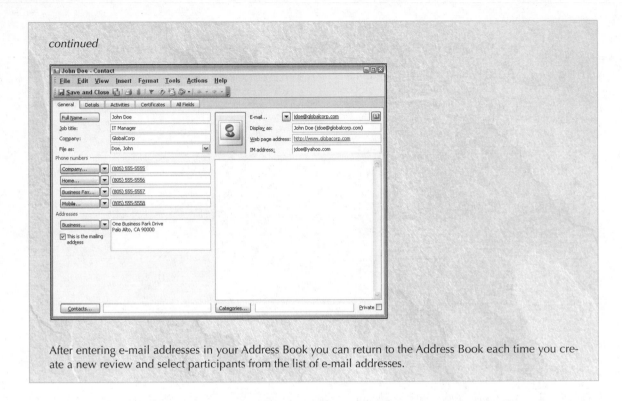

After entering e-mail addresses in your Address Book you can return to the Address Book each time you create a new review and select participants from the list of e-mail addresses.

Before you begin a review, be certain to save any edits made on the PDF. If you insert pages, delete pages, or perform a number of other edits without saving, the comments retrieved from others will appear out of place and make it difficult to understand where comments are made from the reviewers. Also, be certain to keep the original PDF in the same folder. If you decide to move the PDF to another folder, be certain to keep track of the location where the PDF resides. As you update comments, Acrobat needs to keep track of the directory path where the original PDF can be found. If Acrobat can't find the PDF, you are prompted to search for it.

During a review period you and your recipients use tools in Acrobat designed for use with e-mail reviews. When starting an e-mail review, the first time you access the Attached for Email Review menu command, the PDF is sent to recipients. All subsequent comment exchanges between you and reviewers are handled with other tools. Be certain to not return to the Attach for Email Review command if you decide to respond to user comments. Doing so sends another PDF to a recipient.

Recipient participation

A recipient receiving your e-mail with the PDF attachment can open the attachment directly within the e-mail message. Double-clicking the e-mail file attachment launches Acrobat and loads the PDF in the Document pane.

NOTE   Reviewers make comments with any of the comment tools discussed earlier in this chapter and in Chapter 20. After a reviewer completes a review session, the reviewer clicks the Send Comments button in the Comment & Markup toolbar, as shown in Figure 21.6.

FIGURE 21.6

When working on a PDF in review, the Send Comments tool is added to the Comment & Markup toolbar to the right of the Show tool.

When the reviewer sends a response to the PDF author, the PDF author's e-mail address is automatically supplied in the To field in the e-mail program. The reviewer clicks Send and either a PDF or FDF are sent back to the PDF author. Again the file type is determined in the Reviewing Preferences.

Author participation

As comments are submitted from reviewers, you'll want to track reviews and decide to mark them for a status. If you want to reply to the recipients you can elect to send a reply to recipient comments; however, in many cases you'll want to make corrections and start a new review session. If you send a reply, each comment is treated as a separate thread in Acrobat. Rather than your having to select different tools to make responses scattered around a document page, Acrobat keeps each thread nestled together to make following a thread easier. Replies are contained in Note pop-up windows. If you want to reply to a comment, open a context menu on the note pop-up and select Reply or select Reply from the Options pull-down menu on a comment note. Additionally you can click the Reply tool in the Comments panel.

 **For more on using Reply with note comments, see Chapter 20.**

 **You can open a context menu on a comment in the Comments panel and select Reply to reply to a comment.**

Updating comments

You send a file to recipients for review. The reviewers then send comments back to you. Your original document needs updating to reflect the new additions added by other reviewers. When you receive an e-mail attachment, the comment data are submitted back to you. Only a single PDF resides on your computer. If you want to merge the data sent by other reviewers with your existing PDF document, double-click the file attachment sent back to you. Acrobat updates the original PDF document with the new comments.

Asking new reviewers to participate

You may begin a review and later decide you want to add new users to participate in the review. You can add new reviewers to a review at any time. To add a reviewer, open the Review Tracker from the Comments menu, the Review & Comment Task Button, or the Options pull-down in the Comments panel. The Review Tracker opens in a separate window. From the Manage pull-down menu, select Add More Reviewers. The same dialog box opens as when you initiate a review. Add the recipient's e-mail address and any additional message in the Invitation Message window and click OK.

Using the Review Tracker

The Review Tracker is a separate window that opens on top of the Acrobat window where you find menu commands to help manage e-mail–based, browser-based, and Shared reviews. To open the Review Tracker, select Review Tracker from the Review & Comment task button or choose Comments ➪ Review Tracker, or from the Options pull-down menu in the Comments panel select Review Tracker. All three menu items open the Review Tracker shown in Figure 21.7.

FIGURE 21.7

The Review Tracker window provides information and tools for working with documents in review.

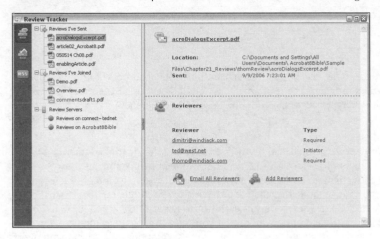

Viewing documents in the Review Tracker

The left pane in the Review Tracker lists all documents you have in review. From the list, select a filename and open a context menu. From the menu choices select Open. The respective file opens in the Document pane.

 Three categories appear in the left pane in Figure 21.7. All reviews I initiated are listed in the Reviews I've Sent list. Expand the list to see reviews by filename. The Reviews I've Joined list contains all reviews sent to me by another review initiator. Review Servers include Shared reviews from shared folders on a network or on a Web site. (See "Working with Shared Reviews" later in this chapter.) Additional categories can appear in the Review Tracker depending on the work you perform for reviews. You might also have categories for Offline Documents and Updated Reviews if you have any files where you added comments offline or updated reviews.

From a context menu opened on a document listed in the Reviews I've Sent list shown in Figure 21.8, you have the following commands:

- **Open.** Opens the selected file the same as clicking the Open tool.

- **Email All Reviewers.** Select this option and your default e-mail application is opened with the To field populated with all review participants. This command is a review reminder for participants to receive an e-mail from you to remind them to send back comments.

- **Add Reviewers.** Also launches your default e-mail application with an automated message to invite other reviewers. The selected PDF file used for initiating the original review is added as a file attachment.

- **Remove From Review Tracker.** Removes the selected file from the review category the same as clicking the Remove tool.

- **Send To Folder.** From the submenu you can create a new folder that is added to the menu. When you return to the Send To Folder command, the submenu shows a list of folders where you can nest reviews to organize the documents in a hierarchical order.

FIGURE 21.8

Open a context menu on a file listed in the left pane of the Review Tracker for more options.

On Windows a collapsed list is marked with a plus (+) symbol. On the Macintosh a collapsed list is marked with a right-pointing arrowhead. Click this symbol and the list is expanded. If a list is already expanded, a minus symbol (Windows) or down arrow (Macintosh) appears. Click this symbol and the list is collapsed.

Forms Tracker

The Forms Tracker lists all forms you have distributed. You can open forms from the list shown when you click on the Forms Tracker icon and click the Open button that appears in the right pane. Select a form in the list and click the Remove button in the right pane. Another option you have is to search for text in the list of forms shown in the Forms Tracker. Type the search criteria and click Search in the right pane.

CROSS-REF For more information on using the Forms Tracker, see Chapter 35.

RSS (Subscriptions)

Click the RSS button and you open the Subscriptions pane in the Review Tracker. RSS (Really Simple Syndication) is a lightweight XML format designed for sharing headlines and other Web content. The Tracker allows you to manage subscriptions using RSS feeds.

You might want to list RSS feeds that provide you with technical support for solving problems with a program like Adobe Acrobat. You can subscribe to a subscription and receive up-to-date information from the service.

This is a valuable tool at your hands in the Review Tracker and you should use the steps that follow to add an Acrobat subscription to the Subscriptions pane right after installing the program.

STEPS: Adding an RSS Subscription to the Review Tracker

1. **Search the Internet for a service.** Open your Web browser and search for an RSS feed. In my example I search for an Adobe RSS site. In the Google search engine I type Adobe RSS feeds. The search engine reports a list of links meeting my search criteria. The first item reported in the search engine is a link to Adobe RSS Feeds. Click the link and a Web page listing RSS feeds from Adobe is opened in the Web browser, as shown in Figure 21.9.

FIGURE 21.9

Adobe lists a number of RSS feeds hosted on their Web site. Among one of the most popular feeds is a service on Acrobat.

2. **Click the Acrobat feed.** Adobe lists the most popular RSS feeds that they host. One of those is the Acrobat service. Click Acrobat and the Acrobat RSS service opens in your Web browser.

3. **Copy the URL.** Copy the URL from your Browser's Location bar.

4. **Open the RSS Subscriptions in the Review Tracker.** You can keep your Web browser open and switch to Acrobat and open the Tracker by selecting Comments ➪ Review Tracker.

 If you opened the Review Tracker before you browse Web sites, your Tracker window is a separate item in your Windows status bar. You can click the Review Tracker to return to the window.

5. **Click RSS** in the left pane in the Review Tracker to open the Subscriptions.

6. **Subscribe to a service.** Click the Subscribe button and the Add Subscription dialog box opens. Subscribe to a service and Acrobat automatically adds the URL in the Add Subscription dialog box, as shown in Figure 21.10.

FIGURE 21.10

Paste the URL you copied in your Web browser in the text box.

7. **Click OK.** The Subscription is added to the Review Tracker Subscription Services, as shown in Figure 21.11.

FIGURE 21.11

The Subscription service is added to the RSS Subscriptions pane.

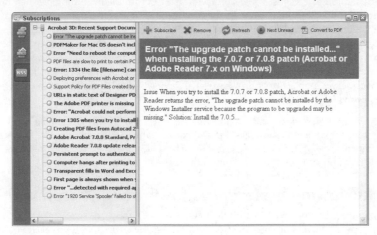

In the top right of the RSS Subscriptions pane, the following tools are available:

- **Subscribe.** Click the Subscribe button when you want to add more subscription services. You can collapse the list in the left pane and scroll through different services you subscribe to.

- **Remove.** Select a service in the left pane and click the Remove button to delete the service from the list.

- **Refresh.** When you open RSS your subscriptions are automatically updated. If you have Acrobat and the Review Tracker open with the RSS pane in view and you want to check for new feeds, click the refresh button and your subscription is updated to the current minute.

- **Next Unread.** Click the Next Unread button to view the next item in the left pane.

- **Convert to PDF.** If you want to archive a particular thread, click the PDF button. The item is immediately converted to PDF and opened in the Document pane. This can be a valuable asset if you find some issues going on with Acrobat that require a configuration on your computer to avoid a problem. You can combine files into a single PDF file or a PDF Package and search the archived documents.

CROSS-REF   For more information on Combining files and creating PDF Packages and searching PDFs, see Chapters 12 and 6.

PDF creation from the Review Tracker

What's different about the RSS reader in the Acrobat Review Tracker is that you can convert an RSS feed to PDF. Open a context menu on a subscription or article and select Convert To PDF or click the Convert to PDF button in the Review Tracker window. The feed/article converts to PDF and opens in the Document pane. You can take a converted feed along with you on a plane trip and read posts to a blog or news in a feed on your laptop computer. You might want to attach a PDF created from a news feed to an article or document you prepare for review. A number of different uses are available to you when converting RSS subscription files to PDF.

Working with Shared Reviews

Working with Shared Reviews just got easier in Acrobat 8. From the beginning of when Browser-Based Reviews where introduced in Acrobat 5, Adobe has been trying to simplify review sessions for people to comment on documents in real-time where all participants can see each other's comments. We've seen simplicity added in each release of Acrobat and now in Acrobat 8 things have gotten much better. Essentially, you have two types of Shared Reviews you can set up and participate in. The Send for Shared Review feature, new in Acrobat 8 let's you use an Acrobat viewer to participate in a review. When you set up a review hosted on a Web server, you set up a Browser-Based Review where participation in the review is handled within a Web Browser.

NEW FEATURE Send for Shared Review is a new feature in Acrobat 8. It works similar to the Browser-Based reviews we had in Acrobat 7 but the configuration for shared reviews and many options you have are all new in Acrobat 8. Shared reviews can be hosted in folders on local computers, network servers, or on a Web server and you're not dependent on the browser vendors.

Setting Reviewing preferences for browser-based reviews

You have two choices to work with Shared Reviews. You can choose to share reviews locally on your computer and on network servers or you can choose to share reviews on a Web server. If you decide to share reviews locally and on networks servers, you don't need to worry about any special configurations. Acrobat 8 makes it very easy to set up a shared review by opening a Send by Shared Review Wizard that walks you thought all the steps needed to begin the review. (See "Working in a Shared Review" later in this chapter for information on Send for Shared Review.)

If you elect to share comments on Web servers, you need to configure your Acrobat viewer properly for Browser-Based reviews. To set up the configuration, choose Edit ➪ Preferences (Ctrl/⌘+K) and click Reviewing in the left pane in the Preferences dialog box. The Reviewing preferences appear in the right pane, as shown in Figure 21.12.

In the Shared Reviews section of the Reviewing preferences you have options for setting time intervals for automatically checking for new comments. From the Online Comments Repository select the Server Type from options in the pull-down menu.

On both Windows and the Macintosh, you have choices for Custom, Network Folder, None, and WebDAV. All options other than Network Folder and None require assistance from your system administrator. In order to properly configure a server, your network administrator can obtain assistance from Adobe help documents hosted online at Adobe's Web site. Special documents designed for configuring Web servers are made available to users. If you want to configure a WebDAV server, for example, log on to http://developer.adobe.com/acrobat. The Adobe Developer Center provides instructions on configurations for WebDAV servers. If you use other server types, you can search the Adobe Developer Center by clicking the Search button on the Adobe Home page.

No longer is there a difference for options between the Macintosh and Windows. All services are equally supported on both platforms.

For sharing a folder on a server, open the Server Type pull-down menu and select Network Folder. The Browse for Folder dialog box opens, as shown in Figure 21.13. You'll see a list of all your mounted volumes. Locate the server where your comment exchanges will be made and select the folder you want to use for starting a browser-based review. Click OK and your folder location is identified.

FIGURE 21.12

Open the Preferences dialog box and click Reviewing in the left pane.

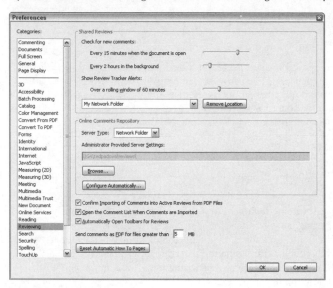

FIGURE 21.13

Locate the folder on a network identified for sharing browser-based reviews.

The three check boxes at the bottom of the Reviewing preferences relate to behavior in your Acrobat window when you participate in a shared review. The last item has to do with e-mail reviews where you have a choice for when FDF data or a PDF are sent back to you. At the default 5MB level, FDF data are exchanged for any PDF larger than 5MB. You can raise or lower this value by typing in the text box. The value range is between 0 and 1,000MB.

Click OK in the Preferences dialog box and your configuration is complete.

NOTE   At best, working with browser-based reviews is IT intensive, non-intuitive, and difficult to set up. browser-based reviews are dependent on browser vendors and not all browsers work the same. If you want to work in a shared review, bother setting up preferences and identify a repository for your review comments. Using the new Send for Shared Review Wizard to set up shared reviews simplifies the process and takes the complexity out of configuring a repository and initiating shared reviews.

Working in a Shared Review

Send for Shared Review is a much easier solution for engaging in reviews where all participants can exchange and see each other's comments.

You work in shared review sessions as an author of a document or a participant. Once you publish a document for review as an author, your commenting takes on the same role as participants. Each individual in the review process works on a PDF document and exchanges comments that are published to the network folder and merged with each individual's PDF document. Inside the shared folder is an XML file that collects the comments, but a copy of the PDF file is used on each participant's hard drive or you can send recipients a link to where the original PDF document can be found.

To understand the process of engaging in shared reviews, follow these steps.

STEPS: Starting a Shared Review

1. **Open the Review & Comment task button pull-down menu and select Send For Shared Review.** The Send for Shared Review Wizard opens.

2. **Identify the file to be shared in the review.** In the first wizard pane shown in Figure 21.14, click the Browse button and locate the file you want to share in the review. Click Add New Location and select Network Folder. Type a name for a new folder that Acrobat will create to host your review document. Click Next and you can browse your hard drive to locate the parent folder that will host the subfolder where your review document is located. Click Add Folder and you return to the first pane in the Add Shared Folder Location Wizard. Click Next and you arrive at the second pane in the wizard.

NEW FEATURE   By default, the check box is checked for enabling the file for Adobe Reader participants. Now in Acrobat 8, Adobe Reader users can participate in shared reviews. Be certain to leave the check box enabled all the time so you can include Reader users when you start a review or maybe later when you invite additional reviewers.

FIGURE 21.14

Locate the file to be shared and click Next.

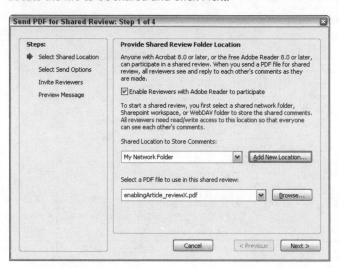

3. **Determine how the PDF will be shared with other users.** In the second pane of the Send PDF for Shared Review Wizard shown in Figure 21.15, you make a choice for how the recipients will receive the file.

Select Attach the PDF file to the message & save a copy locally and the PDF is added to an e-mail message you send to all recipients. Send a link to the PDF in the message sends a URL link that the reviewers can click to download the PDF and start the review session. The third option is Do not send email invitation, just save the file locally. You could use this choice if you wanted to send the file later or store the file on a server where other users could copy the file to their computers (see Figure 21.15).

FIGURE 21.15

Make a choice for how the PDF will be distributed.

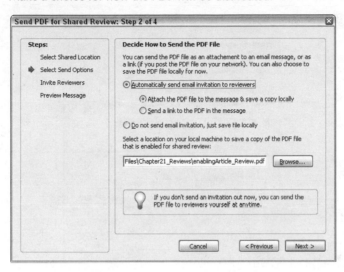

Choose an option and click Next. If you have a large PDF document, such as a four-color brochure or engineering document of several megabytes, use the Send a link to the PDF in the message option, otherwise choose the first option that attaches the PDF document to the e-mail message.

4. **Invite Reviewers.** Add the e-mail addresses of the reviewers who will participate in the review. You can also identify a deadline date for when the review will be terminated. Add a date as shown in Figure 21.16.

FIGURE 21.16

Add recipients and a deadline in the third pane of the Send PDF for Shared Review Wizard.

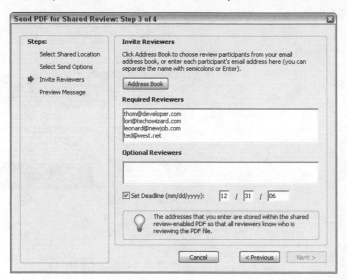

5. **Preview the Message.** Click Next and you can review the message that will be sent to the participants. Click Finish and an e-mail message is created in your default e-mail program. If you chose to send the PDF document, the PDF is attached as an e-mail attachment. Click the Send button in your e-mail and all recipients receive either the PDF document or a URL or network location where the PDF file is stored.

6. **Exchange comments.** All the tools you need for sending and retrieving comments automatically appear in the Acrobat window. When you add comments to the document, click the Publish Comments button and your comments are added to the data file in the shared folder. To check for new comments click the Check for New Comments button in the Document message bar. If new comments have been added to the data file, a message box opens and informs you of how many comments have been added to the file. Click the text in the message bar where you see Click here to add them, as shown in Figure 21.17.

FIGURE 21.17

When adding comments from reviewers, click the Click here to add them text in the pop-up message bar.

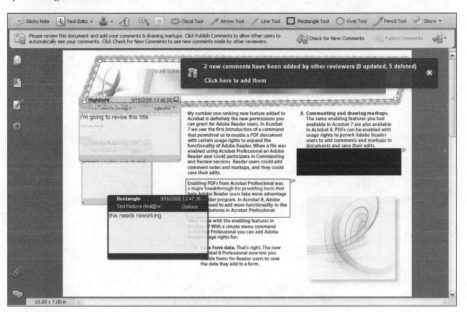

7. **Send comments.** When you want to send comments, add your comments on the document and click the Publish Comments button in the Document message bar shown in Figure 21.17. Your comments are uploaded to the shared folder and a pop-up message confirms the upload, as you see in Figure 21.18.

FIGURE 21.18

After publishing new comments, a pop-up message bar confirms the upload.

8. **Reply to comments.** You reply to comment threads in a shared review just as you do in an e-mail–based review. Open the Options pull-down menu on a comment note and select Reply. Type your response in the Reply area of the comment note, as shown in Figure 21.19.

FIGURE 21.19

Select reply from the Options menu and you can reply to comments made from other recipients.

9. **Save the file.** Click the Save button and your comments are saved. You can quit Acrobat and later go online again and publish or retrieve additional comments.

PROXY Reviewers

One of the coolest things that Shared Reviews can offer is PROXY. Imagine an Adobe (or any company) employee wants to invite you to participate in a review. The Adobe employee uses a shared folder to start a review. However, access to the Adobe Web server is limited to only Adobe employees.

An employee decides to add you to the review, but you don't have access to the shared folder on the Adobe network. You receive the PDF via e-mail and try to *connect* to the shared folder and, of course, you can't. Using Shared Review still makes it possible for you to add your comments to the document.

Participating is such a review provides you new options on the status bar (see Figure 21.20) where you select Send Comments. Instead of accessing the secure network folder limited to Adobe employees, your comments are e-mailed to the review initiator who can then inject these comments to the review and (here's the cool part) — they show up as "Reviewer name (Adobe employee) by your name" making it clear that the Adobe employee made the comment but you added it to the review cycle.

FIGURE 21.20

When participating as a PROXY reviewer, click Send Comments in the status bar and your comments are e-mailed to the review initiator.

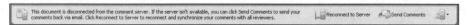

Working offline

Acrobat also offers you an opportunity to work offline when sharing comments on any kind of server. You may be temporarily away from an Internet connection or network connection and want to organize comments and later submit them. To work offline, open the pull-down menu on the Server status button on the top-right corner of the Document Message Bar, as shown in Figure 21.21. Select Work Offline and you can add comments while disconnected from the server.

NOTE If you open a document that is in a shared review and you don't select Work Offline and you are disconnected from the Internet, Acrobat automatically puts you in an offline state. The Document Message Bar will change to reflect your offline status.

FIGURE 21.21

Select Work Offline from the Server status pull-down menu to add comments to the PDF file while working offline.

When you want to (or able to) go back online you first see the Welcome window where you can open the PDF document and the Welcome to Shared Review dialog box opens, as shown in Figure 21.22. The dialog box reports any new activity in the review session. Notice the Changes since you last viewed the file section of the dialog box. Click OK button you can click Publish Comments for any comments added to the document while you were offline. Click the Check for New Comments button and you can retrieve any new comments added to the data file.

FIGURE 21.22

When you open a document in a shared review, the Welcome to Shared Review dialog box opens.

Migrating Comments

You might have an edit you make on a document in review and want to populate the document with comments made in the review sessions. Acrobat provides you a method to import new or unresolved comments to a PDF after the document has been revised using the Migrate Comments feature. This feature attempts to place comments in the correct location by searching specific word groupings and structural elements in the revised PDF.

 **Results may be less reliable in untagged PDFs that lack the internal structure necessary to correctly place imported comments in a revised document.**

In order to migrate comments from one file to another, you need both documents open in Acrobat. Bring the document you want to import comments into forward in the Document pane. Select Comments ⇨ Migrate Comments and the Migrate Comments dialog box opens, as shown in Figure 21.23. Select the other file open in the Document pane in the From pull-down menu and click OK. Your file gets populated with all the comments from the file in review.

FIGURE 21.23

Select the file containing comments in the From pull-down menu and click OK to import the comments from the review file.

If you open the properties on a comment markup and check the Review history, you should see a list of the Migration history in the dialog box, as shown in Figure 21.24. All comment migration is listed in the Review History tab for assessing the dates and times you migrated comments.

FIGURE 21.24

The Review History in the comment properties shows a list of Migration history.

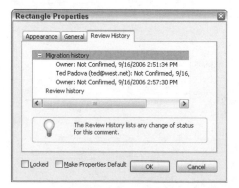

Summary

- You can initiate e-mail and shared reviews in Acrobat and participate in reviews in any Acrobat viewer. For Adobe Reader participation, documents need to be saved from Acrobat Professional with Reader usage rights.

- The Tracker lists all documents initiated from Attach for Email Reviews, Send for Shared Review, Upload for Browser Review, forms that have been distributed, and RSS Subscriptions.

- Send for Shared Review is a new feature in Acrobat 8 that simplifies the opportunity to engage in reviews where all participants, including users of Adobe Reader, can share reviews and view all reviewer comments.

- When files are enabled with Adobe Reader usage rights, the Adobe Reader users can participate in ad-hoc review workflows.

- Migrating Comments is used for moving comments from a review in progress to an updated version of the reviewed document that might have been modified during the review cycle.

Chapter 22

Links and Actions

O ne of the truly great features Adobe Acrobat offers is the ability to create interactive documents containing hot links that invoke many different actions. Acrobat provides you with many tools and methods for making your PDFs come alive, and Acrobat helps you refine documents for user navigation and interactivity. Regardless of whether you post PDFs on Web servers, communicate via e-mail, replicate CD-ROMs, or work with documents on local network servers, Acrobat offers tools and features that help you create dynamic documents.

In this chapter, you learn how to create links with a variety of Acrobat tools, and you learn some of the differences between several methods for linking views. With hypertext links originating from various elements such as bookmarks, page actions, links, and destinations, you have a number of action tools that provide you with an almost limitless opportunity for handling views and relationships between documents. This chapter covers creating hot links and all the different actions you can associate with links.

Setting Up the Links and Actions Environment

Reset the toolbars (open a context menu on the Toolbar Well and select Reset Toolbars). Open the More Tools dialog box (open a context menu on the Toolbar Well and select More Tools) and scroll down to the Advanced Editing Toolbar. Select all tools and select the Advanced Editing Toolbar check box. Move down to the File Toolbar and check the box for the Organizer. Scroll to the Page Display toolbar and select the tools you want to use for page displays. If you want the Navigation tools accessible, check the Page Navigation toolbar. Move to the Forms toolbar (Acrobat Professional only) and select the box to show the forms tools. Scroll to the Select & Zoom toolbar and select the Actual Size, Fit Width, and Fit Page tools.

Click OK to open the toolbars not loaded by default. Another toolbar that can be helpful when creating links and buttons is the Properties Bar. Open a context menu on the Toolbar Well and select Properties Bar. Return to the context menu and select Dock All Toolbars. When finished, your Acrobat application window should look like Figure 22.1.

 **NOTE**   Acrobat Form tools are available only in Acrobat Professional.

FIGURE 22.1

Toolbars loaded for editing PDFs with interactive links and buttons

Working with Bookmarks

If you use programs that support exporting to PDF with structure, you can add bookmarks automatically at the time PDF files are created. Programs such as Microsoft Word, Microsoft Excel, Microsoft PowerPoint, Microsoft Visio, Autodesk AutoCAD, Adobe PageMaker, Adobe InDesign, Adobe FrameMaker, and QuarkXPress support bookmark creation from style sheets when you use export tools in the authoring programs. Ideally, in a workflow environment where these programs are used, it is advantageous to create bookmarks from authoring applications when permitted by the program and when the bookmark action relates to page views. In other programs, or when editing PDFs with bookmarks, you may need to reassign bookmark actions, order bookmarks in a hierarchy, or create additional bookmarks.

CROSS-REF   For more information regarding bookmark exports from authoring programs, see Chapters 8 and 9.

The most common bookmark action in Acrobat is navigating page views. Whereas analog bookmarks mark pages, the electronic bookmarks in a PDF document enable you to navigate to different pages and different zoom views. You can capture various page views and zoom in on images, text, tables, and so on in Acrobat as bookmark destinations. In a broader sense, you can use bookmarks to invoke actions such as opening/closing files, opening secondary files, executing menu commands, submitting forms, playing sounds and movies, executing JavaScripts, and a host of other related actions.

Creating bookmarks

As long as you understand the sequence of steps, creating bookmarks is easy. Creating a bookmark is like capturing a snapshot. The process involves navigating to the page and view you want to capture and then creating the bookmark. Therefore, if you want to capture page 13 of a document in a Fit Page view, you navigate to page 13, click on the Fit Page tool, and then create the bookmark.

You create bookmarks from several options. When the page view is in place, open the Options menu in the Bookmarks panel and select New Bookmark. You can also open a context menu on a page and select Add Bookmark from the menu options. In Figure 22.2 the Bookmark Options menu is shown.

FIGURE 22.2

To create a bookmark, navigate to the desired page view and select New Bookmark from the Options pull-down menu in the Bookmarks panel (left).

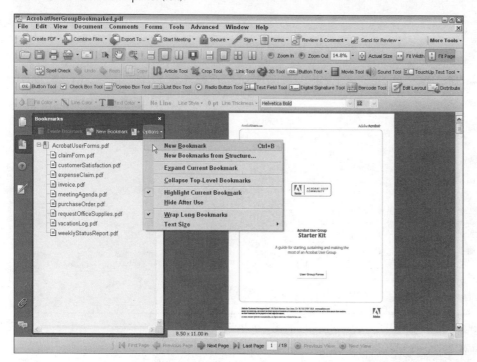

 Click on the Bookmarks panel to access the Options menu for bookmarks. Using a context menu, you can create a bookmark when the Navigation panel is collapsed. When you create a bookmark from a context menu while the panel is collapsed, the Navigation panel opens and the Bookmarks panel is placed in view.

If you open the Options menu without selecting a bookmark in the Bookmarks panel, the menu options appear as shown in Figure 22.3. However, if you first select a bookmark and then open the Options menu, the menu commands change to menu commands shown in Figure 22.4.

You have fewer menu options when selecting a bookmark in the Bookmarks panel and opening a context menu than when opening the Options pull-down menu. In Figure 22.4, a context menu was opened from a selected bookmark.

 By default, the items Paste under Selected Bookmark and Paste after Selected Bookmark are grayed out. You need to select Cut from the menu options to make the two Paste commands active.

FIGURE 22.3

If you select a bookmark in the Bookmarks panel and then open the Options menu, the menu offers additional commands as compared to opening the menu without selecting a bookmark.

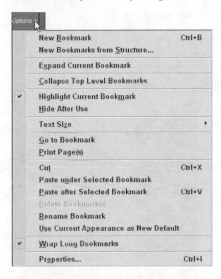

FIGURE 22.4

If you select a bookmark in the Bookmarks panel, the context menu is as shown here.

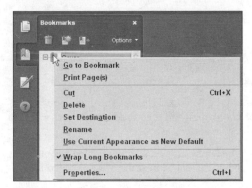

You can also use shortcut keys to create a bookmark when the Bookmarks panel is either opened or closed. Press Ctrl/⌘+B on your keyboard to create a bookmark. In all of these methods, a bookmark defaults to the name Untitled. Acrobat highlights the Untitled bookmark name after the bookmark is created. You type a name and press the Enter or Return key when you are finished typing.

On pages where text corresponds to names you want to use for bookmarks, Acrobat helps simplify the naming process. Select the Select tool and highlight the text you want to use as your bookmark name. From a context menu, select Add Bookmark. The bookmark is created and the highlighted text is used as the bookmark name. The stages of creating a bookmark in this manner are: 1) the page view is in place, 2) text is selected on the page and a context menu opened, 3) Add Bookmark is selected from the menu options (see Figure 22.5), and 4) the bookmark is created using the selected text for the bookmark name. You can also use the Options menu or modifier keys to create a bookmark while text is selected.

FIGURE 22.5

To automatically name a bookmark, select text with the Select tool and create the bookmark.

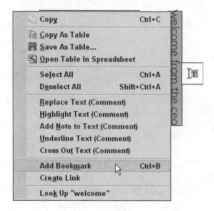

Managing bookmarks

Bookmarks created in a document appear in the Bookmarks panel in the order they are created, regardless of the page order. For example, if you create a bookmark on page 15, and then create another on page 12, the bookmarks are listed with page 15 before page 12 in the Bookmarks panel. At times you may want to have the Bookmarks list displayed according to page order. Additionally, bookmarks may appear more organized if they are nested in groups. If you have a category and a list of items to fit within that category, you may want to create a hierarchy that expands or collapses. Fortunately, Acrobat enables you to change the order of bookmarks without recreating them. Additionally, you can categorize the bookmarks into groups.

To reorder a bookmark, select either the page icon or bookmark name in the list and drag it up or down and left or right. A triangle with a dotted line appears when you drag a bookmark, as shown in Figure 22.6. To nest a child bookmark below a parent bookmark, drag straight up. The triangle and line show you the target area for the bookmark.

FIGURE 22.6

The triangle indicates where a bookmark is to be reordered.

If you have a parent bookmark with several child bookmarks nested below it, you can move the parent to a new location. Drag the parent bookmark and all child bookmarks below it move with the parent. If you want to remove a child bookmark from a nest, click and drag the bookmark to the left and either down or up to the location desired.

In addition to moving bookmarks, you can cut and paste them. Select a parent or child bookmark, and from a context menu or the Bookmark panel Options menu, select Paste under Selected Bookmark or Paste after Selected Bookmark. When you choose Paste under Selected Bookmark the cut bookmark(s) is pasted as a child Bookmark under the selected bookmark. Pasting after a selected bookmark pastes the cut bookmark(s) after the selected parent and all child bookmarks.

Multiple nesting is also available with bookmark organization. A bookmark can be subordinate to another bookmark that is itself nested under a parent bookmark. To subordinate a bookmark under a child bookmark, use the same method as described previously for creating the first order of children. As you drag right and up slightly, you can nest bookmarks at several levels.

You can also relocate multiple bookmarks at one time. To select several bookmarks, Shift+click each bookmark in a group. As you hold down the Shift key, you can add more bookmarks to the selection. If you click one bookmark at the top or bottom of a list and Shift+click, all bookmarks between are selected. For a non-contiguous selection, Ctrl/⌘+click. Once selected, drag the bookmarks to a new location in the list. Their order remains the same as it was before the move.

By default, new bookmarks appear at the end of a bookmark list. If you want to place a bookmark within a series of bookmarks, select the bookmark you want the new bookmark to follow. When you select New Bookmark from the bookmarks Options menu, from a context menu, or press Ctrl/⌘+B, the new bookmark is created at the same level after the one you selected.

Renaming bookmarks

If you create a bookmark and want to change the bookmark name, select the bookmark to be edited from the Bookmarks panel. From the Options menu, select Rename. Acrobat highlights the name in the Bookmarks panel. Type a new name and press the Return or Enter key on your keyboard to finish editing the bookmark name. You can also click the cursor anywhere in the Document pane to finish editing the name.

You can rename bookmarks by clicking on a bookmark name and clicking again on the bookmark. You can also use a context menu, but be certain you first select the bookmark; then open a context menu to select the menu option for Rename. When you click on a bookmark, you go to the associated bookmark view. Clicking a second time informs Acrobat you want to edit the name. To select the text, click and drag across the part of the name you want to edit or press Ctrl/⌘+A to select all text. When you type a new name, the selected text is deleted and replaced with the new text you type.

Structured bookmarks

Structured bookmarks retain document structure in files generated from Microsoft Word, Web page captures, and programs supporting PDF creation with tags. You can use structured bookmarks to navigate PDF pages, reorganize the pages, and delete pages. If you create PDFs without tags, you can add structure to a document by choosing Advanced ➪ Accessibility ➪ Add Tags to Document. After you have a structured document and you create bookmarks, more options are available to you. For example, moving a bookmark in the Bookmarks panel moves only the bookmark; the page associated with the bookmark is unaffected. When you move a structured bookmark, the page associated with the bookmark is moved. The same holds true for bookmark deletions, extractions, and printing.

Depending on whether you have a bookmark or a structured bookmark, context menu commands and the Options menu commands appear differently. When you open a context menu from a standard bookmark, the menu commands appear as shown in Figure 22.4. When you open a context menu from a structured bookmark, the menu commands are as they appear in Figure 22.7. Notice the items that relate to Print Pages, Delete Pages, and Extract pages that are available when you open a context menu from a structured bookmark.

These menu commands are available when you open a structured bookmark context menu.

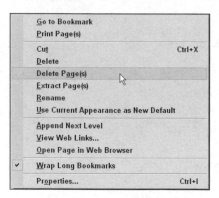

When you create a bookmark, the destination for the bookmark is a link to a page view. In the context menu for standard bookmarks, you see the menu command for Set Destination. You can navigate to a new page and select this command to change the bookmark link to a new view. With structured bookmarks, you capture the page structure (a page view, a table, a head, and so on). In the context menu, be certain to select Delete and not Delete Page(s) if you want to delete a bookmark. The Delete command deletes just the bookmark. Delete Page(s) deletes the bookmark and the page associated with the bookmark.

Bookmark appearances

Both bookmarks and structured bookmarks contain menu options for Use Current Appearance as New Default. This menu choice is like a bookmark style sheet where you first select the appearance of the bookmark in terms of font style and color; then you select this menu option to set the attributes as a new default. For example, change the bookmark to small text, italicized, in red; then open a context menu and select Use Current Appearance as New Default. All subsequent bookmarks you create use the same style until you change the default.

The Wrap Long Bookmarks option from either menu creates a word wrap for the bookmark name in the Bookmarks panel. By default Bookmarks are wrapped. If you want more Bookmarks to appear in the vertical list, you can unwrap them. An unwrapped Bookmark appears as you see in Figure 22.8. When the cursor is placed over a Bookmark, a tooltip displays the entire bookmark name. When the Bookmark is wrapped, it appears as you see in Figure 22.9. Notice that fewer Bookmarks are shown in Figure 22.9 than Figure 22.8, but the Bookmarks in the second figure are neatly contained in the bookmark panel for easy reading.

FIGURE 22.8

When Wrap Long Bookmarks is selected in a Bookmarks context menu, bookmark names are wrapped to the panel width and shown in multiple lines of text. This display appears by default.

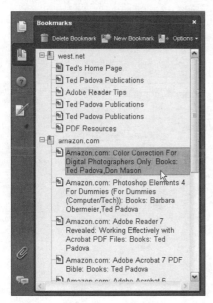

FIGURE 22.9

When a Bookmark name is longer than the panel width, a tooltip shows the complete name extended beyond the panel width.

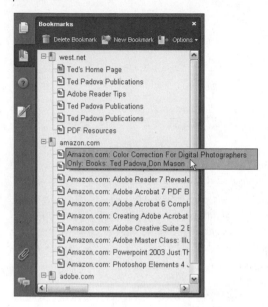

If you open the Options menu, you have more choices for how the bookmarks appear in the panel. In Figures 22.8 and 22.9, bookmarks are expanded. The minus (–) symbol (a down-pointing arrow on Macintosh) shows all nested child bookmarks below it. Click on the symbol and the bookmark collapses to hide all child bookmarks below the parent. If you want to show all top-level bookmarks expanded, select Expand Top-Level bookmarks from the Options pull-down menu. To collapse the bookmark list, select Collapse Top-Level bookmarks from the same menu. The latter menu command is dynamic and is accessible only in the menu if you have first expanded bookmarks.

Select Hide After Use from the Options menu if you want to hide the Bookmarks panel after you select a bookmark. To change text sizes, make selections from the Options pull-down menu. Select Size and choose from one of the three submenu items for Small, Medium, or Large point sizes.

Bookmark properties

The Options pull-down menu offers you choices for text sizes. For other text attribute changes you need to use the Bookmark Properties dialog box. Select Properties from a context menu and the Bookmark Properties dialog box shown in Figure 22.10 opens.

The Bookmark Properties dialog box opens when you open a context menu from either a standard bookmark or a structured bookmark.

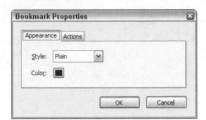

You select type styles from the Style pull-down menu. Select from Plain, Bold, Italic, or Bold & Italic. Clicking the Color swatch opens the color pop-up window where you select preset colors or custom colors. You can capture changes from these style options when you select the Use Current Appearance as New Default menu command previously discussed.

The Actions tab enables you to change bookmark actions. By default, the bookmark action is set to open a view within the active PDF document. You can assign many other actions to bookmarks in the Actions properties.

CROSS-REF For assigning bookmark actions, see the section "Working with the Link Tool" later in this chapter.

Using the Properties Bar

The Properties Bar also offers options for appearance settings. (Remember, we loaded that toolbar when we set up our editing environment at the beginning of the chapter.) Using the Properties Bar is a trade-off. On the one hand, it's so much easier to make changes to Bookmark appearances using the toolbar; but on the other hand, it takes up a row in the Toolbar Well. If your monitor is large enough and your viewing space adequate to comfortably see page content, then take a look at the options your have in the Properties Bar shown in Figure 22.11.

Select a Bookmark and the Properties Bar reflects options for editing Bookmark appearances.

When you select a Bookmark, options in the Properties Bar include the following:

- **Color.** Click the Color down arrow and the color palette opens where you can assign a preset color or a custom color to a Bookmark name.
- **Text.** Click Plain and a pull-down menu opens displaying font attribute choices.
- **More.** Click the More button and you get a quick launch of the Properties dialog box, as shown in Figure 22.10.

All in all, the Properties Bar is helpful when you need to make Bookmark appearance and property changes. If the Toolbar Well isn't too crowded, keep this toolbar open when you make edits for Bookmarks and other types of link options.

Setting bookmark opening views

If you create bookmarks in a document and want the document to open with the Bookmarks panel open, you can save the PDF document in a manner where the Bookmarks panel opens in the Navigation panel each time the PDF is opened.

Choose File ➪ Properties or press Ctrl/⌘+D to open the Document Properties dialog box. Click the Initial View tab. From the Navigation panel pull-down menu, select Bookmarks Panel and Page, as shown in Figure 22.12. Save the file after making the properties change. The next time you open the document, the Bookmarks panel opens.

FIGURE 22.12

Choose Bookmarks Panel and Page from the Navigation panel pull-down menu.

CROSS-REF For more information on setting Initial Views, see Chapter 5.

The width of the Bookmarks panel is a user default specific to Acrobat on the end user's computer and not the file you save. If you open the Bookmarks panel to a wider view than the default, each time you open a PDF with the bookmarks in view, the Bookmarks panel is opened at the width you last adjusted. If you save the file with the Initial View showing Bookmarks and pages, Acrobat does not take into consideration your Bookmarks panel width. Other users who open your files see the Bookmarks panel sized to their personal panel width default sizes. This default is made from the last time you adjusted the panel size.

Working with Articles

Acrobat offers a feature to link text blocks together for easy navigation through columns of text. User-specified ranges of text can be linked together, thereby forming an article. Articles help a user navigate through a PDF file, enabling the user to read logical sequences of paragraphs throughout a document. Working with articles is particularly helpful when you view PDF files on the World Wide Web. PDF files can be downloaded a page at a time in a Web browser. If you have a column or group of paragraphs of text that begins on page 1 and continues on page 54, an article thread can assist a reader in jumping from page 1 to page 54 without his or her having to download the remaining pages in the document.

Viewing and navigating articles

You need to know a few basics on navigating through an article in a PDF.

 To determine whether articles exist, choose View ➪ Navigation Panels ➪ Articles. A panel opens with tabs for Articles, as shown in Figure 22.13.

> **TIP** If you want to move the Articles panel to the Navigation panel, click the panel and drag it to the top of the Navigation panel. The Articles panel can remain in the Navigation panel for all subsequent Acrobat sessions as long as you leave it docked in the panel when you quit Acrobat.

FIGURE 22.13

To determine whether articles exist in a document, open the Articles navigation panel.

Article Tool The Articles panel displays any articles existing in the PDF file in the panel list. If you select the Article tool from the Advanced Editing toolbar, the article definition boundaries are shown. In Figure 22.14, the Article tool is selected. The defined article is contained within a rectangular box with an identifier at the top of the box. In this example, 1-1 indicates that this is article number 1 and box number 1. If the article is continued on another page, the subsequent boxes read 1-2, 1-3, 1-4, and so on, indicating they are continuations of the same article thread. If you create a second article, the article begins with numbers 2-1, indicating the second article in the document and the first box of the second article.

Article properties

The article properties are contained in a dialog box that opens immediately after you create an article or double-click an article with the Article tool. The Properties dialog box shown in Figure 22.15 is informational. When you view Article Properties, information supplied at the time the article was created is displayed for four data fields. The Title, Subject, Author, and Keywords fields are the same as those found in the Document Information dialog box. Inasmuch as the data for these fields are identical to that found in document information, Acrobat Search does not take advantage of the article properties information. Properties are designed to help you find information about an article before you jump to the page where the article is contained. All the fields are editable when you open the Article Properties dialog box.

FIGURE 22.14

Select the Article tool and the article boundaries are shown on pages.

FIGURE 22.15

The Article Properties dialog box displays user-supplied information for Title, Subject, Author, and Keywords fields. These fields are not searchable with Acrobat Search.

Viewing articles

Articles are viewed at the maximum view established in the Preferences dialog box. When you view an article, you select the Hand tool and click an article thread. The screen view jumps to the maximum view assigned in the Page Display Preferences. By default, the zoom is set to an 800% view or a view that accommodates the complete width of a column of text. In most situations this view is much larger than needed for comfortable viewing. In earlier versions of Acrobat you could choose Edit ➪ Preferences and click General in the left panel. From the Max Fit Visible Zoom pull-down menu select a zoom view comfortable for reading on your monitor. However this preference setting has been removed in Acrobat 8 viewers and you no longer have control over zoom levels when reading articles.

NEW FEATURE In order to read articles you need to have a preference option enabled in the General preferences dialog box. Open Preferences (Ctrl/⌘+K) and click General in the left pane. Check Make Hand Tool read articles in the right pane. If the check box is disabled, the Hand tool won't recognize articles.

Alternately, you can open the Articles panel by choosing View ➪ Navigation Panels ➪ Articles. The Articles panel can remain open as an individual panel, or you can drag it to the Navigation panel and dock it. The panel pull-down menu in the Articles panel offers only one option. If you select Hide After Use from the panel pull-down menu, the panel disappears when you view an article. If you want to have the panel remain open, but want more viewing area in the document, dock the Articles panel in the Navigation panel.

Double-click an article to jump to the first view in the thread. Acrobat places the top-left corner where the article begins in view. You immediately see a right-pointing arrow blink on the left side of the first line of text. Once an article is in view, select the Hand tool and position the cursor over the article (be certain the General preferences are set up to read articles with the Hand tool). The cursor changes to a Hand tool icon with an arrow pointing down. As you read articles, the cursor changes according to the direction Acrobat takes you when you're reading an article. For example, if you're viewing a column up instead of down, the cursor changes to inform you which direction you're going. The different cursor views are shown in Figure 22.16.

FIGURE 22.16

When you view articles, different cursors inform you ahead of time the direction you need to navigate.

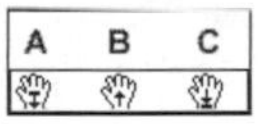

You can use several keyboard shortcuts to help you navigate with the Article tool. The cursor changes according to the following modifier keys:

- **Click.** The first click zooms to a zoom level up to 800%. If you read columns of text, you may find the zoom level lower such as 200%. Click the cursor again to continue reading down a column. Click at the end of an article box, and the view takes you to the beginning of the next column.
- **Shift+click.** Moves backward or up a column.
- **Ctrl+click or Option+click.** Moves to the beginning of the article.
- **Return or Enter.** Moves forward down the column or to the top of the next column.
- **Shift+Return or Shift+Enter.** Moves up or to the previous column.

Defining articles

You define articles by drawing rectangular boxes around the text you want to include as part of your article thread. While you're using the Article tool, the rectangular boxes are visible. When the tool is not active, the rectangular boxes are invisible.

Click and drag open a rectangle surrounding the column where you want to begin a new article. When you release the mouse button, the rectangular box displays on the page. At each corner and side of the article box are handles that you can grab and move to reshape the box. Notice that the lower-right corner of the article box contains a plus (+) symbol. When you finish your edits, deselect the Article tool to exit edit mode. You can return to edit mode and add more columns after reselecting the Article tool. Click the aforementioned plus symbol to let Acrobat know you want to extend the article thread (see the later section, "Combining articles" for more on extended article threads).

TIP You can create article threads at the time the PDF file is either exported or distilled with Acrobat Distiller. Many layout applications support creating articles prior to exporting to PDF. In some cases, you may want to have a single article thread to help user navigation through your document. To practice, identify an article in one of the programs discussed in Chapter 6 and then export to PDF either through the program's export feature or by printing to PostScript and later distilling in Acrobat Distiller.

Ending an article thread

When you reach the end of the article, Acrobat needs to know you want to finish creating the thread. To end an article thread, press Return, Enter, or Esc. Acrobat prompts you with a dialog box in which you supply the Title, Subject, Author, and Keywords fields for the article properties. This dialog box appears immediately after you define an article. Supplying the information at the time the dialog box opens is a good idea because then you won't need to worry about returning to the Article Properties dialog box for last-minute cleanup.

Deleting articles

You might want to delete a portion of an article thread or an entire article. To delete either, select the Article tool and click an article box. Press the Backspace (Delete) key on your keyboard or open a context menu and select Delete from the menu options. A dialog box opens providing options for deleting the currently selected box or the entire article. Or to delete the entire article from within the Article panel, select the article and click the Trashcan icon, or open a context menu and select Delete.

If you select the Box button in the Article dialog box, the deletion eliminates the article box within the article thread you selected when you pressed the Backspace (Delete) key on the keyboard. Clicking the Article button deletes all boxes in the thread across all pages in the document.

Combining articles

At times you may want to join two articles to create a single article. To join two articles, you must first have them defined in the PDF document. Move to the last column of the first article and click the plus symbol in the last box. This click loads the Article tool. Next, move to the beginning of the article to be joined to the first article and Ctrl+click or Option+click inside the first box. While you press the shortcut keys, the cursor icon changes, as illustrated in Figure 22.17.

FIGURE 22.17

When you press the Ctrl or Option key while clicking the mouse button, the cursor changes to an icon, informing you that the selected articles are to be joined.

The numbering at the top of each box in the second article changes after the articles are joined. For example, if you have two articles, the first numbered 1-1, 1-2, 1-3, and the second article numbered 2-1, 2-2, the new numbering for the second article changes to 1-4 and 1-5. Article 2 takes on the attributes of article 1 and assumes the next order of the article boxes. In addition, the properties identified in the second article are lost. Because the continuation of the thread is from article 1, all attributes for article 1 supersede those of article 2. You can select multiple articles and join them all together in a single article by following the same steps.

> **TIP** When combining two articles, always start with the article containing the attributes to be retained. For example, in the preceding case, to retain the attributes of article 2, select the plus symbol at the end of the last column in Article 2 and click. Ctrl+click or Option+click in the first box for Article 1. When the two articles are combined, the attributes of Article 2 are retained.

Working with the Link Tool

Links are no mystery to any user who has browsed the Web. Buttons and text that open other Web pages and invoke various actions are something that's commonplace to any computer user. With Adobe Acrobat Standard and Professional, you have many tools to create hypertext links that ultimately appear very similar to the kinds of links you find on Web pages.

Link Tool You use the Link tool to create links from a rectangle drawn with the tool to other pages, other documents, and a host of other link actions you can define in the Link Properties dialog box. The area within a link rectangle is the hot spot for invoking a link action. Links used with tools such as Bookmarks and Form Field buttons have the same attribute choices for the actions associated with the objects created with the respective tools.

> **TIP** You can also create a link without drawing a rectangle when you want a link to appear from text on a page. Use the Select tool and drag across some text to select it. From a context menu, select Create Link. A rectangle is automatically created for you around the selected text. You then target the link destination and the link action is created.

When creating links with the Link tool, you encounter two dialog boxes used to establish link actions. For link actions used in opening a view, opening a secondary document, or opening a Web page, the action choices are contained in the Create Link dialog box, which opens when you click and drag open a link rectangle and release the mouse button. If you want to assign different link actions, you create a custom link and make attribute choices in the Link Properties dialog box. The Create Link dialog box requires you to make all option choices in the dialog box before you can access any commands in the Document pane. The dialog box is static, which means you need to cancel out of the dialog box or click OK to use menus, shortcut keys, or select objects on a page in the Document pane. When you work with the Link Properties dialog box you can access tools and menu commands, and select items such as buttons and other links on pages while the dialog box remains open.

Creating links for page navigation

To help you understand how to use the Link tool, it might be helpful to walk through some steps first before you go on to read over all the attribute choices you have for links. To follow the steps that follow, you should have two documents. In one document you'll create a link to another file, and in the other document you'll create a link to a specific page in another file. To see how all this comes about, try following these steps.

STEPS: Creating links to page views

1. **Open a file in Acrobat.** For these steps you should have two documents. The first document should be a multiple-page file.

2. **Navigate to a page other than the opening page.** Use the Next Page tool or press the Page Down key on your keyboard to open a second page in the document. If you want to open another page, press Next Page or Page Down to scroll pages. Find a page other than the opening page. In my example, I start on page 2.

3. **Create a link.** Select the Link tool in the Advanced Editing toolbar and draw a rectangle with the tool in the area you want the link to appear. You should have text or an icon on the page that makes it intuitive for a user to know a link exists: a graphic, blue text, or some other indication that clicking in an area will invoke an action much like you might see on a Web page.

4. **Identify the link attributes.** When you click the link tool and draw a link rectangle, the Create Link dialog box opens. Click Open a file and click Next. The steps are shown in Figure 22.18.

5. **Select a file to open.** The Select File to Open dialog box appears after clicking Next in the Create Link dialog box. Navigate your hard drive and locate the file you want associated with the link. Click Select in the Select File to Open dialog box.

CAUTION You should copy all PDFs that are linked to the same folder. If you create links to files scattered on your hard drive and then relocate the files, Acrobat will lose the link destinations. When copying files to the same folder, you can relocate your folder on your hard drive, network server, or CD-ROM without disturbing the link destinations.

FIGURE 22.18

1) Click the Link tool and draw a link rectangle. 2) The Create Link dialog box opens. 3) Click Open a file, and 4) click Next.

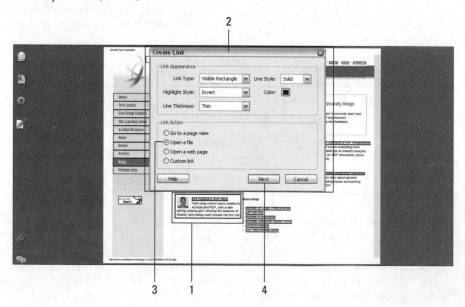

6. **Set the Open Preferences.** After identifying a file to open, the Specify Open Preferences dialog box (formerly known as Window Preferences in earlier versions of Acrobat) appears. Click Existing Window, as shown in Figure 22.19. Making this choice opens your target link while the file containing the link closes.

FIGURE 22.19

Select Existing window to open a file. The current open document closes in the Document pane as the new file opens.

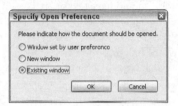

7. **Save the file.** Select File ➪ Save or click the Save tool in the File toolbar to save your edits. Because this file will close when the new file opens, you need to be certain your edits are saved.

8. **Open the linked file.** Select the Hand tool and click the link. The target file should open in the Document pane.

9. **Create a second link.** Select the Link tool and draw a link rectangle. Select Go to a page view in the Create Link dialog box. Click Next to open the Create Go to View dialog box.

10. **Select the target page to open.** While the Create Go To View dialog box (shown in Figure 22.20) is open, you have complete access to all the tools and menu commands in Acrobat. Just leave the dialog box in view and click the Open tool or select File ➪ Open. Locate the file you added a link to in Step 1 and open it. Navigate to the page containing your original link by clicking the Next Page tool or the Page Down key on your keyboard. When the page is in view at the zoom level you want, click Set Link.

FIGURE 22.20

Open the target page and click Set Link.

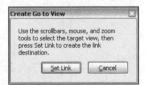

11. **Save your edits.** When you click Set Link, you are returned to the page from which the link originated (your second file in this example). Click the Save tool or select File ➪ Save to save your edits.

12. **Test the links.** Close all documents and open the file containing the first link. Click the link and the second file opens. Click the link on that page and the first file opens, but this time the page that opens should be a page other than the first page in your document.

Note that you created two different links in these steps. The first link used the Create Link dialog box and you opened a file. When the file was opened you arrived at the default view on the first page in the file. The second link opened a page other than the opening page (in my example it was page 2). To link to specific document pages in secondary files you need to use the Go to a page view option and set the link in the Create Go to View dialog box.

The steps outlined here are but a fraction of the many different attribute choices you have for creating links and choosing actions. A host of other actions are available to you when you create custom links. Read on to find out more about creating different kinds of links.

Linking to views

In the Create Link dialog box (opened when you draw a link rectangle with the Link tool) you make one of four radio button selections. The first three radio buttons enable you to specify link attributes in the Create Link dialog box shown back in Figure 22.18. If you select the fourth radio button and click OK, the Link Properties dialog box opens where you select different actions for the link behavior.

The first three radio button choices offer you options for selecting a page view or a file to open. Options shown in the Create Link dialog box include the following:

- **Go to a page view.** Use this option to link to a page in the open document or create a cross-document link that opens a page in another document. When you click the Next button, the Create Go to View dialog box opens as shown earlier in Figure 22.20. While the dialog box remains open you have access to menu commands and tools. Navigate to a page in the open document or click the Open tool, open a second file, navigate to the desired page, and click Set Link.

- **Open a file.** Select this option if you want to open a PDF document or any file from another authoring program. When you click the Next button, the Select File to Open dialog box opens and allows you to select any file on your system. If you select a file other than files that can be opened in Acrobat, you (or your customer) must have the native authoring program installed in order to click on the link and open the file. If you select a PDF document, you link to the Initial View in the secondary document.

> **CROSS-REF** Initial View is typically the first page in a PDF document, but it can be changed to another page in the Initial View properties. For more information on setting the Initial View, see Chapter 5.

- **Open a web page.** When you select this radio button, the Edit URL field is enabled. You type a URL in the Edit URL field to link to a PDF hosted on a Web site. When you add a URL, be certain to supply the complete Web address, including `http://www`. After you add a URL, the address becomes a new default. Each time you create a new link, the last URL added to the Edit URL field box is inherited and appears in the field box.

- **Custom Link.** Custom Link in and of itself contains no properties. You select this radio button if you want to set a different action for a link. If you select Custom Link and click OK, the Link Properties dialog box opens.

> **TIP** URLs in text on PDF pages don't require links. Acrobat versions 7 and 8 are intelligent and they interpret URLs created in authoring programs from text with either `http://www.` or `www.` prefixes as URLs. When you place the Hand tool over URL text in a document, the Hand tool shows an icon with a Hand and a W inside the Hand indicating a live Web link. Click the link and your default Web browser opens the linked page. For earlier versions of Acrobat having URLs in text, you need to create URL links in the PDF files.

CROSS-REF For more information on creating Web links, see Chapter 27.

Editing a link action

If you create a link using any one of the first three radio buttons in the Create Link dialog box and later want to edit the link, you are not returned to the Create Link dialog box. The Create Link dialog box opens only after you first use the Link tool to create a link.

To change a link action, use either the Link tool or the Select Object tool. Double-click the mouse button with either tool to open the Link Properties. If you select the Hand tool and click on a link, the link action is employed.

Link appearance properties

The link appearance applies to the rectangle drawn when you drag the Link tool on a page in the Document pane. Default appearances are established from the last appearance settings made for the link properties. To change properties, you have two choices. You can use the Properties Bar (described in "Setting Up the Links and Actions Editing Environment" at the beginning of this chapter) or the Link Properties dialog box.

When using the Properties Bar, you make changes to link appearances for the items contained across the bar, as shown in Figure 22.21.

FIGURE 22.21

Select a link with the Link tool or the Select Object tool to enable the options in the Properties Bar.

The choices in the Properties Bar include the following:

- **Color.** The Color pop-up window opens when you click on the square at the far left side of the Properties Bar. Choices for color apply to strokes only and the options are the same as you find when changing colors in Note properties.

CROSS-REF For more information on changing Note properties, see Chapter 20.

- **Line Style.** You have choices from the pull-down menu for No Line, Solid, Dashed, and Underline. No lines might be used when you have a graphic image or text on a page and a link is apparent to a user. For example, if text appears blue and underlined, you might use No Line for the line style.
- **Line Thickness.** The default shown in Figure 22.21 is 1 pt. You have choices for Thin, Medium, or Thick that translate to 1 point, 2 points, or 3 points, respectively. The line weight you choose appears in the Properties Bar. If you select No Line in the Line Style menu, 0 pt is listed in the Properties Bar.
- **Highlight Style.** Use this option to display highlights when the mouse button is pressed. When you select the Hand tool and click on a link, the highlight is shown within the link rectangle while the mouse button is pressed. You can choose from No Highlight, Invert, Outline, and Inset.
- **More.** Clicking the More button opens the Link Properties dialog box just as a context menu command does.

Note that when you click the Link tool in the Advanced Editing toolbar and before you create or select a link, the Properties Bar becomes active. You can make choices for Color, Line Style, Line Thickness, and Highlight Style. But the More button is not active unless you select a link. When you click the Link tool before selecting a link and make appearance changes, the changes become a new default and will remain as a default until you change them again. If you quit Acrobat and relaunch the program, the default changes you made are still honored.

Link properties

To open the Link Properties dialog box, you can open a context menu and select Properties; double-click on a link with the Link tool or the Select Object tool; select a link and press the Enter or Return key; or, with a link selected, click the More button in the Properties Bar. A right-click in Windows or Ctrl+click on Macintosh opens a context menu where you can select Properties to open the Link Properties dialog box.

When the Link Properties dialog box opens, you have options nested in two tabs: the Appearance tab and the Actions tab. By default, the Appearance tab is placed in view, as shown in Figure 22.22.

FIGURE 22.22

Two tabs exist in the Link Properties dialog box where you select appearance and actions options.

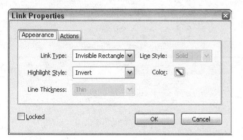

The same options offered in the Properties Bar for appearance settings are available in the Appearance tab with the addition of the Link Type and a check box for Locked. Link Type is a choice you have in the Create a Link dialog box as well as here in the Link Properties. Choose from Visible Rectangle or Invisible Rectangle to make the link rectangle visible or hidden.

If you enable Locked, the link rectangle is locked to position on the document page and cannot be moved; however, when you select the Hand tool and click on a locked link, the action associated with the link still executes. Locking a link also disables all option choices in the Properties Bar and the Link Properties dialog box for that link. If you need to change properties for a locked link, open the Appearance tab and disable Locked.

NEW FEATURE Notice the Link Properties dialog box uses OK and Cancel buttons instead of a Close button as was used in Acrobat 7. For some reason, Acrobat 7 deviated from previous versions of Acrobat in not offering you an option to make some attribute changes, and then to click Cancel if you changed your mind. The only way to exit the Link Properties dialog box in Acrobat 7 was to click Close. This resulted in a change to the link properties whether you wanted it or not. Now in Acrobat 8, we return to the options for clicking OK to accept changes and Cancel to dismiss the dialog box without making any changes.

In Acrobat 7 where you had a Close button used to dismiss the dialog box, you also had the opportunity for dynamic creation of links. While in the Link Properties dialog box you could access menu commands and

tools. You could create several links while keeping the Link Properties dialog box open. In Acrobat 8, we return to the same options you had in Acrobat prior to version 7. No dynamic editing is available. You need to create a link, assign properties, and click OK. Clicking OK closes the Link Properties dialog box and you need to start over with creating a second link. Moreover, you don't have access to the menus or tools while the Link Properties dialog box is open.

NOTE   Link Properties behavior for creating links and assigning actions is the same when creating form fields. You need to click OK in form fields' properties dialog boxes before you can create additional fields.

Link actions properties

Click on the Actions tab to assign an action to a link. The default link action is Execute a menu item (the top item in the Actions list). Open the Select Action pull-down menu and you find a scrollable list of Action types, as shown in Figure 22.23. After you create a link with another action type, the new action becomes the default.

The Select Action pull-down menu offers a number of actions you can assign to a link. You can select an action and repeat a selection for a different action to nest action types that are executed in the order displayed in the Actions window. In Figure 22.24, three separate actions are associated with the same link. When you click the link with the Hand tool, a page opens, a Web link opens that launches your default Web browser, and a menu item is executed to quit Acrobat.

FIGURE 22.23

Click the Select Action pull-down menu to view all the Action types.

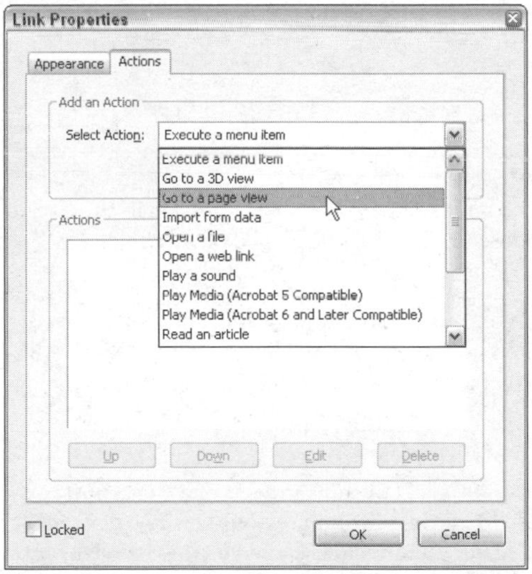

FIGURE 22.24

Action items can be nested in the Link Properties. The order of link execution is the same as the order listed in the Actions window.

From the pull-down menu, you can choose action types such as the following.

Go to a 3D View

If you have a PDF containing a 3D drawing, you can create links and buttons to open different views in the drawing such as wireframe, shading, and various other views. The Add this action option opens the Select a 3D View dialog box where the views are selected.

Go to a page view

You add the action and the Create Go to View dialog box opens. Navigate to a page in an open document or a secondary document and click Set Link.

You can also link to pages in secondary documents using the Go to a page view in the Link Properties dialog box.

Execute a menu item

All versions of Acrobat prior to Acrobat 8 provided options for executing almost all the menu commands you see from the top-level menus.

NEW FEATURE Now in Acrobat 8, instead of using pull-down menus in a Menu Item dialog box, the Menu Item dialog box opens where you select from a list organized by menus with more limited commands. A number of different menu commands have been eliminated from the Execute a Menu Item action in Acrobat 8, including several items that relate to changing PDF content such as adding bookmarks; creating page templates; adding headers, footers, watermarks, and backgrounds; adding comments and markups; and using Forms menu commands. The Advanced menu commands have also been eliminated.

Adobe's reasoning for this is that it's answering user demand for the capability to protect files against document changes that an end user may not be aware of. For example, if you create a button that creates a Bookmark or comment, adds a form field, and so on, the end user may not be aware that the button action altered the document. You are now just limited to executing a selected set of menu commands, as shown in Figure 22.25.

FIGURE 22.25

Select menu commands from the Menu Item dialog box when using the Execute a menu item action type.

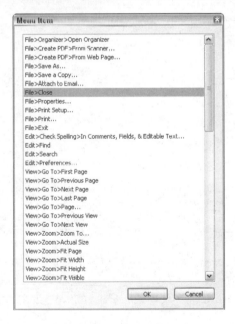

Import form data

When you select the Import form data option and click Add, the Select File Containing Form Data dialog box opens. Select the file containing the form data you want to import and click the Select button. Imported form data is from files saved in FDF (Form Data File) or XML format that are exported from PDF documents. When you click the Select button, the data matching identical form fields is imported. Using Import form data limits you to importing data saved only in FDF format. If you use the Forms ➪ Manage Form Data ➪ Import Data menu command, data can be imported when saved as FDF, XFDF, XML, FormFlow99 Data Files(.xfd), and TXT. Note that you must have at least one form field on the page for this to work.

Open a file

You use Open a file to open any file on your computer. When you select the action type and click the Add button, the Open dialog box opens. Browse your hard drive and select the file you want to open. If the file is not a PDF file, you (or your customer) need to have the authoring application that created the file installed on your computer in order to execute the link action. Creating the link does not require you to have any external programs installed on your computer.

Open a web link

The Open a web link option enables you to associate a link action to a Web address. Web links can be contained in PDF documents locally on your computer or within a PDF page where the PDF is hosted on a Web server. If a Web link is contained locally in a PDF document, selecting the link launches the browser configured with Acrobat and establishes a URL connection. Acrobat remains open in the background while the Web browser appears in the foreground. Always use the complete URL to identify a Web address.

When you specify a URL in the Edit URL dialog box that opens after you click the Add button in the Link Properties, you can add custom viewing in the URL address for the way you want to open a PDF document. For example, if you want to view a page other than the opening page you can add to the URL a request for opening any page number. To open a specific page, enter this text:

http://www.*mycompany.com/myDoc*.pdf#page=3

In this example the file myDoc.pdf opens on page 3 in the Web browser. In addition to opening a specific page, you can add other viewing parameters such as zoom levels, page modes such as viewing layers or bookmarks, named destinations, and so on.

CROSS-REF For more information on setting viewing options with Web links, see Chapter 27.

Play a sound

You can create a button to play a sound in a PDF document. When you select the Play a sound action and click the Add button, the Select Sound File dialog box opens for you to locate a sound file on your hard drive and import the sound. Acrobat pauses a moment while the sound is converted to a format usable in Acrobat viewers. After it's imported in the PDF, the sound can be played across platforms. When the link button is selected, the sound plays. Sounds imported with the Play a Sound action and those added with the Record Audio Comment tool support only Acrobat 5 media. If you use the Sound tool you can choose to import either Acrobat 5– or Acrobat 6–compatible sounds.

CROSS-REF For importing sounds with the Sound Attach tool, see Chapter 12. For information on using Acrobat 5– and Acrobat 6–compatible sound and media, see Chapter 23.

Notice the Advanced Editing toolbar contains a Sound tool. You can use the Sound tool to import sounds. In addition, you can use the Record Audio Comment tool to import sound files. Playing sounds from any of these tools is identical. The Sound tool and the Record Audio Comment tool are limited to adding sounds on a page where a user needs to click or double-click a button to play the sound. The link action is more versatile as you can add sounds with nested link actions, page actions, and form fields. Sound files are supported from files saved as AIFF or WAV.

CROSS-REF For information on using the Sound tool, see Chapter 23, and for information on using the Attach Sound tool, see Chapter 12.

Play media (Acrobat 5 compatible)

To select the Play Media action type, a media file must be present in the PDF file. If there is no media file present, a dialog box opens informing you no media is on the page to select. You import media clips with the Movie tool and at least one movie file needs to be present before you can create a link with the Play Media action type. After a movie is contained in a PDF file, create a link and select the action type. After you click Add, the Play Media (Acrobat 5 Compatible) dialog box opens. If you have several media clips in the PDF document, the Select Media pull-down menu lists all the clips by filename. Select a file and choose from one of four action types in the Select Operation pull-down menu shown in Figure 22.26. You may choose to play a movie, stop a movie, pause a movie during the play, or have it resume after it has been paused.

FIGURE 22.26

When the Play Media (Acrobat 5 Compatible) dialog box opens, select a media clip from the Select Media pull-down menu and select the play option from the Select Operation pull-down menu.

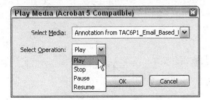

Play media (Acrobat 6 and later compatible)

Playing Acrobat 6–compatible media clips requires you to first import a movie (or import a sound). When you import a movie with the Movie tool or import a sound with the Sound tool, you have a choice for importing the media as an Acrobat 5– or Acrobat 6–compatible file. Acrobat 6 allows you to embed Acrobat 6–compatible media in the PDF document. All previous versions of Acrobat treated movie files as links. When you transport PDFs with Acrobat 5–compatible movie files, you need to send the movie file along with the PDF, whereas Acrobat 6–compatible files offer you a choice for importing the movie and embedding the file in the PDF document.

After you have imported a media clip with the Movie tool as an embedded file or a file link, select the Play Media (Acrobat 6 and Later Compatible) action and click the Add button. The Play Media (Acrobat 6 and Later Compatible) dialog box opens as shown in Figure 22.27. The operations available with Acrobat 6–compatible imports are the same as those used with Acrobat 5–compatible imports, with the exception of being able to add a Custom JavaScript and Play from beginning.

To add a JavaScript, select Custom JavaScript from the Operation to Perform pull-down menu and click the Specify JavaScript button. Other dialog boxes open for specifying a rendition if you choose to do so and the JavaScript Editor dialog box opens where you write a custom JavaScript.

You can use media clips saved in a variety of formats compatible with Acrobat 5 or the newer formats supported with Acrobat 6. When you use the Play Media (Acrobat 6 and Later Compatible) action type, the file you select does not require Acrobat 6 compatibility for newer file types per se. However, Acrobat 6 compatibility enables you to embed files and use custom JavaScripts, and provides support for newer compression schemes.

FIGURE 22.27

In addition to offering the same operations available with Acrobat 5–compatible imports, Acrobat 6 compatibility provides an option for adding a custom JavaScript.

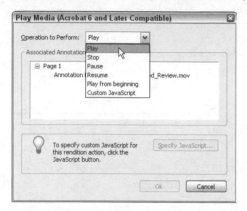

When you use Acrobat 6 compatibility, be aware that users of earlier versions of Acrobat won't be able to use your PDF documents. If you need to work with users of older versions of Acrobat viewers, be certain to use Acrobat 5 compatibility.

CROSS-REF For more information on Acrobat 6–compatible file formats, see Chapter 23.

Read an article

When you select Read an article as the action type for a link, the Select Article dialog box opens when you click the Add button. If no articles are present in the PDF document, you receive a dialog box alerting you that there are no articles present and you can't use this link action. When articles are present, select the article you want to associate with the link from the listed articles in the Select Article dialog box. When you select the link in the navigation mode, Acrobat opens the page where the first box in the article appears. Additionally, the cursor changes to the Article icon that enables you to continue reading the selected article.

Reset a form

The Reset a form link action relates to PDF documents with form fields. When a form is filled out, you can reset the form to remove all data contained in the form fields. Acrobat provides an opportunity to clear the data from all fields or from selected fields you identify individually. A Reset a form dialog box opens, enabling you to select the fields to clear.

CROSS-REF For more information on resetting forms, see Chapter 34.

Run a JavaScript

JavaScript adds great opportunity for making PDF documents interactive and dynamic. You can add JavaScripts to link button actions as well as form fields. When you select Run a JavaScript and click the Add button, the JavaScript Editor dialog box opens. You type the code in the dialog box, or copy and paste code from a text editor to the JavaScript Editor. Click OK to commit the JavaScript.

Set layer visibility

For PDF documents containing layers, you first create the layer view you want in the Layers panel.

 Open the Layers panel and show the layers you want displayed when a user clicks on the link. In Figure 22.28, four layers are hidden, as shown in the Layers panel. When you use the Set layer visibility action type, the layer view at the time you create the link is what is shown to the user when he or she clicks the link. This behavior works similarly to bookmarks in which you place in view in the Document panel your resultant view, and then create the bookmark. Layer visibility works the same. Set the visibility you want, and then set the link.

FIGURE 22.28

When using the Set layer visibility action type, you first show the layer view you want to display to assign it to the link action.

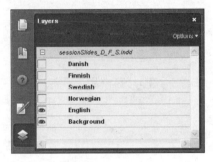

After setting your layer view for the display when the user clicks the link, create a link and click the Custom Link button. Select Set layer visibility from the Actions pull-down menu and a dialog box opens, informing you the current layer state has been captured, as shown in Figure 22.29.

FIGURE 22.29

When you add the Set layer visibility action type, a dialog box opens, informing you that the layer state has been captured.

CROSS-REF   For more information on layer visibility, see Chapter 19.

Show/hide a field

The Show/hide a field action enables the user to allow selected form fields to be visible or hidden. Forms can be created to display and hide form fields for help menus and informational items, to protect data, and

so on. You can make a hidden field visible by opening the Show/Hide Field dialog box and selecting the Hide radio button. Within this dialog box the options for both hiding and showing fields are enabled through radio buttons.

CROSS-REF For more information on working with Acrobat PDF forms, see Part VI.

Submit a form

Form and comment data contained in PDF documents can be transported on the World Wide Web. When a user completes a form, the data can be submitted to a URL as a Form Data File (FDF), HTML, or XML data. Additionally, the entire PDF can be submitted. The PDF author can then collect and process the data. Using form and comment data with Web servers has some requirements you need to work out with the ISP hosting your Web site. If you use forms on PDF Web pages, include a button that submits data after the user completes the form. Using the Submit a form action enables you to identify the URL where the data is submitted and determine which data type is exported from the PDF document. If comment data is to be submitted, a check box enabling comment delivery appears in the dialog box.

CROSS-REF For more information on submitting PDF forms to Web servers, see Chapter 34.

Managing links

Acrobat 8 provides many menu options for link management. You can copy/paste, align, and distribute links and more through the use of a context menu. If you need to apply these editing tasks to multiple links, select the Select Object tool and click and drag through the links you want to manage. If you attempt to use the Link tool, you can select only a single link.

After selecting a link with the Link tool or selecting multiple links with the Select Object tool, open a context menu as shown in Figure 22.30. The context menu offers several menu categories with submenu items used for managing links.

FIGURE 22.30

Select a single link with the Link tool or multiple links with the Select Object tool and open a context menu. Select a menu category and select from the submenu items the command you want to use.

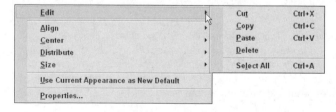

The menu items include the following:

- **Edit.** The Edit menu contains several items in a submenu for cut/copy/paste, and are accessible in the top-level Edit menu. You can delete a link or group of links by selecting Delete.
- **Select All.** Select All deserves some special comment. When you select a link with the Link tool or choose Edit ➪ Select All, all links are selected on a page. If you click on a link with the Select

Object tool and choose Select All from the Edit submenu, all objects selectable with the Select Object tool are selected on the page. For example, if you have links and form fields, Select All selects all links and form fields on the target page. If you want to edit the links for deletion, alignment, copying, and so on, be certain to click on the Link tool and then use Edit ➪ Select All.

- **Align.** You can align multiple links Left, Right, Top, Bottom, and along the vertical and horizontal centers. Choose the respective submenu command for the alignment option of your choice.

- **Distribute.** If you have a row or column of links and you want to position them equidistant from each other, choose the Distribute command and select from either Vertically or Horizontally. Vertically distributes a column and Horizontally distributes a row of link objects.

- **Size.** As you create link rectangles, you may draw the links at different sizes. To resize links on a given page to the same size, select one of the links with the Link tool. Using a context menu, select Select All, move the Link tool to the target size link rectangle, and open a context menu. (The target link rectangle is displayed with a red keyline and red handles while the other rectangles in the selected group are highlighted blue.) Select from the submenu Height, Width, or Both. The selected link rectangles are resized to the size of the target link.

- **Properties.** Use this option to open the Link Properties dialog box. If you select more than one link rectangle, the link actions shows Varies in the action list if the link actions are different among other selected links. You can apply common appearance settings to all selected links or you can edit actions if the actions are all the same among the selected links.

Working with Page Properties

A page action is like a link button that invokes an action when a page is opened or closed in the Document pane. You don't have to click on anything because the trigger for executing the action type is handled by Acrobat when the page opens or closes. All the action types available with links are the same actions that are associated with page actions.

To create a page action, open the Pages panel. Select a page with the Hand tool and open a context menu. From the menu options select Page Properties. The Page Properties dialog box opens with two sets of properties types available. The default page properties options are contained in the panel for Tab Order, but these settings don't have anything to do with setting a page action, so I'll skip them for the moment.

CROSS-REF For information related to setting tab orders, see Chapter 34.

It is the second tab in the Page Properties dialog box that is used for setting page actions. Click on the Actions tab shown in Figure 22.31, and the options for defining actions to page behavior are displayed. Two areas are used for applying a page action to any page in a PDF document. You first select the trigger for either Page Open or Page Close and then select the action from the Select Action pull-down menu. The options in this menu are the same as you have available with link actions.

FIGURE 22.31

Open the Page Properties dialog box from a context menu on a page thumbnail. Click the Actions tab to open the page actions options settings.

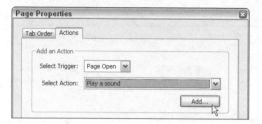

Page actions help you make your PDF documents more automated. You might select a sound to play when a file opens, as shown in Figure 22.31. You may want to set layer visibility, play a movie, or execute a menu item. Of all the options available for action types, with page actions you have the addition of an infinite number of choices when running JavaScripts. You might want to run a script that analyzes the Acrobat viewer version when a user opens a PDF document and alerts the user that Acrobat 6 is needed to properly view your document if the user opens the file in a viewer version earlier than Acrobat 6. This example and many more options are available to you when running JavaScripts from page actions.

CROSS-REF To see examples of JavaScripts that analyze Acrobat viewer versions and viewer types, see Chapter 36.

Creating Destinations

A destination is a specific location in a document. Whereas a bookmark and a link may link to page 5 in a file, a destination links to the location where page 5 resides. If you delete page 5, bookmarks and links have no place to go and the links are often referred to as *dead links*. If you delete page 5 where a destination has been created, the destination remains at the same location — that is, following page 4 and preceding page 6. Furthermore, if you insert a page after page 4, the bookmarks and links are linked to page 6. All pages shift to make room for a new page, but the links from bookmarks and links remain fixed on a specific page. With destinations, if you insert a page after page 4, the destination takes you to the new page 5.

You can also use destinations when you want to use JavaScripts for creating pop-up menus, creating smart forms, and adding other interactive features.

It all sounds pretty nifty but there's a downside to using named destinations. Adding many destinations in a PDF document adds a lot of overhead to the file size. Destinations can make a PDF bulky and slow if they are used extensively. Destinations should not be thought of as a substitute for bookmarks and links, but rather, a complement for creating interactive documents when other methods don't support the same features.

Destination tools

 You create, organize, and display destinations within the Destinations panel. To open the panel, choose View ⇨ Navigation Panels ⇨ Destinations. If you want to use the Destinations panel frequently in an Acrobat session, you can drag the panel away from the panel and place it in the Navigation panel. As a panel in the Navigation panel it is visible and easily accessible until you remove it by dragging it out of the panel.

The panel contains a few icons and a pull-down menu, as shown in Figure 22.32. In addition to the panel tools, context menus offer several menu options. You create, edit, and manage all destinations through this panel.

FIGURE 22.32

Open the Destinations panel by choosing View ⇨ Navigation Panels ⇨ Destinations. Several icons and a list of destinations appear in the panel.

The options are as follows:

- **New.** Click the New icon or a context menu option to create new destinations. You create a destination by first navigating to the page and view, and then creating the destination, much like you create bookmarks.

- **Delete.** You can use the Trashcan icon in the panel, as well as a menu command available when opening a context menu on a selected destination to delete the destination.

- **Sort by Name.** Open the Options pull-down menu and select Sort by Name. Destinations are sorted alphabetically by name. Alternately, you can click on Name or Page in the Destinations panel title bar and sort by Name or Page.

- **Sort by Page.** Open the Options pull-down menu and select Sort by Page. Destinations are sorted by page number.

- **Go to Destination.** Open a context menu on a destination and select Go to Destination. When you invoke the command, Acrobat opens the destination page.

- **Set Destination.** Also from a context menu opened in the Destinations panel, Set Destination can reassign a new target destination. First navigate to a new view, and then select Set Destination.

- **Rename.** From a context menu opened on a destination name, select Rename. The name becomes highlighted and ready for you to type text for a new name.

Creating a pop-up menu

You can use destinations to create a pop-up menu on a page that displays menu options for navigating to other pages and other files. To create a pop-up menu that links to other pages, you create destinations and then add some JavaScript to a link or button field. When a user selects a menu item, the page destination opens in the Document pane.

Follow these steps to experience how easy it is to create an application pop-up menu.

STEPS: Creating application pop-up menus

1. **Open the Destinations panel.** Open a PDF file with multiple pages. Select View ➪ Navigation Panels ➪ Destinations.

2. **Create destinations.** Navigate to each page and set the view using the Zoom tools. Click New in the Destinations palette for each page view you want to capture. As you create new destinations, type a name for each destination in the Destinations panel. In my example, I created five destinations, as you can see in Figure 22.33.

FIGURE 22.33

After you add destinations, the Destinations panel displays the names you used when creating each new destination. The destinations are sorted by name in the list. To sort the list by page number, select Sort by Page from the Options pull-down menu.

3. **Create the JavaScript.** After you have finished adding new destinations, you need to do a little programming. If you haven't used the JavaScript Editor, don't panic. These steps are no more complicated than following a few simple directions.

CROSS-REF For a better understanding of using JavaScript and the script created here, see Chapter 29.

Select the Link tool and click and drag open a link rectangle. Ideally, it's best to have some text or an icon on the page indicating that a button or link is present. If you don't use button faces and icons, you can also simply use a keyline border to show where the link appears on the page. In the Create Link dialog box, select Custom link and click OK. The Link Properties dialog box opens. Click Actions and from the Select Action pull-down menu, select Run a JavaScript.

Click Add and the JavaScript Editor opens. In the JavaScript Editor, type the following code:

```
1. var c = app.popUpMenu
2. (["category_1", "item_1", "item_2", "item_3"],
3.  ["category_1", "item_1", "item_2", "item_3"],
4.  ["category_1", "item_1", "item_2", "item_3"]);
5. this.gotoNamedDest(c);
```

See the sidebar, "Analyzing the Script," later in this chapter for a detail explanation of the code. In my example, the code appears as you see in Figure 22.34.

NOTE The items category1, category 2, and so on, are used to describe a category you want to appear in your pop-up menu. Something like *Accounting, Human Resources, Manufacturing,* etc. The items listed in the code (item1, item2, etc.) would be the destination names. You might use something like *Accounting Policies, Accounting Procedures, HR Polices, HR Procedures,* and so on, as the destination names.

FIGURE 22.34

JavaScript code to create an application pop-up menu

4. **Exit the JavaScript Editor and Link Properties.** Click OK in the JavaScript Editor and click OK in the Link Properties dialog box.

5. **Test the pop-up menu. Select the Hand tool and click the link.** You should see a pop-up menu similar to Figure 22.35. In this example, I included two items in the first category to appear in a submenu. In Figure 22.35, User Groups and Forms are labels. The submenus open Chapters and ClaimForm items that are the destinations.

FIGURE 22.35

If the pop-up menu was created properly, you should see submenu items listed when selecting a category.

Contents

Analyzing the Script

In the script, the first line of code sets a variable c for a pop-up menu. Regardless of what your destinations are named or the contents of your PDF, copy this line of code into your JavaScript Editor exactly as you see it.

Lines 2 to 4 contain the categories and submenu commands that link to the destinations you created. Here's where you need to modify your code. Where you see "category x," replace the name with a category title of your choosing. You might want to use names such as Personnel, Administration, and Finance, or you can use category names such as Designs, Illustrations, and Photos, or any other combination of names that relate to the categories you want to use. Notice that line 2 begins with an open parenthesis, (, followed by a left bracket, [. These characters are important to include in your code.

In lines 2 through 4 are three item numbers contained in quotes and separated by commas. These names need to be the same as your destination names. Type the destination names exactly, including letter case, as you created them in your Destinations panel. The order in which you add the names is unimportant. Also notice that after the last destination name and quote mark, no comma is inserted. Lines 2 and 3 end with a comma and line 4 ends with a semicolon. It is also important to type these characters just as you see them in the sample code.

Line 5, the final line of code, is the instruction to take the user to the destination selected from the menu options. Type this line exactly as you see it into your JavaScript Editor.

To modify JavaScript code, select the Link tool and double-click the link. In the Link Properties dialog box select the item denoted as Run a JavaScript in the Actions list and click the Edit button. The JavaScript edit dialog box opens where you can make changes to the code.

In this example, destinations are used to navigate pages in a PDF document via a pop-up menu. If the design of your PDF documents better suits pop-up menus, you have many options when using JavaScripts. You can also create pop-up menus with JavaScripts that open other PDF documents or specific pages in other PDF documents, and that execute many different menu commands.

CROSS-REF For an example of a pop-up menu that opens secondary PDF documents, see Chapter 29.

Working with Buttons (Acrobat Professional only)

In the previous section you saw how to use the Link tool to navigate pages and open files. When links are created, you need some kind of icon or text that lets a user know that a link button exists. If you add links on a page in empty white space with no border keyline, users won't know where or when to click on a link button. If you want to use images or icons for button appearances, you can use another form of link tool with the Button tool that supports importing icons.

Creating a button field

Using form fields instead of links has some advantages. You can add image icons to button fields, use rollover effects, and copy and paste fields across multiple pages, and you have all the same action types accessible as those used with bookmarks, links, and page actions.

CROSS-REF The discussion of button fields in this chapter is limited to creating button fields with actions similar to those discussed in this chapter when creating link actions. For a more thorough discussion on using form fields in Acrobat, see Part VI.

OK Button Tool The Button tool appears by default in the Advanced Editing toolbar. Select the tool and click and drag open a rectangle. The Button Properties dialog box opens by default with a default name in the General tab. Acrobat automatically names the field for you beginning with Button1, then Button2 for the next button you create, then Button3, and so on. When you open the Properties dialog box you can change the field name in the General tab. Highlight the default name and type a new name. In this example, I want to create some navigation buttons. The name of the button I'll use is goNext, as shown in Figure 22.36.

FIGURE 22.36

Type a name for the button field in the General tab.

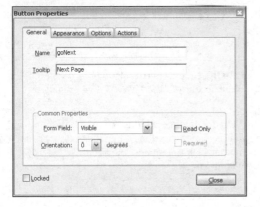

Button faces are handled in the Options tab. Click the Options tab and select Icon Only from the Layout pull-down menu. Click the Choose Icon button and the Select Icon dialog box opens. From this dialog box you need to access yet another dialog box by clicking the Browse button. The Open dialog box opens to a view where you can navigate your hard drive and select a file to import as your button face. Any file format compatible with the Create PDF from File tool is acceptable. Select a filename in the Open dialog box and click Select. Acrobat returns you to the Select Icon dialog box where you can see a preview of the imported file, as shown in Figure 22.37.

The Select Icon dialog box displays a thumbnail preview of the imported file. Click OK to return to the Button Properties dialog box.

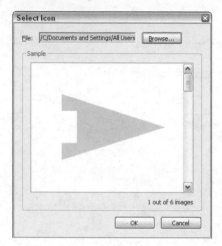

If the preview looks like the file you want to use as a button face, click OK to return to the Button Properties dialog box. Click the Actions tab where you assign the action type associated with your button. In this dialog box you make a choice for the trigger action. The default is Mouse Up, which means when the mouse button is released the action executes. Leave the Select Trigger menu option at the default and open the Select Action pull-down menu.

Select Execute a menu item from the pull-down menu. Click the Add button and the Menu Item dialog box opens. Select View ⇨ Go To ⇨ Next Page, as shown in Figure 22.38.

Add a menu item to navigate to the next page.

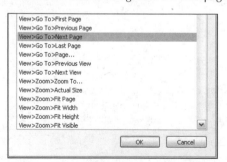

Now repeat the preceding steps to create a second navigation button for moving to previous pages and using different icons to represent moving backward in the PDF file.

To move a button field, select either the Button tool or the Select Object tool. In the example here, two buttons are created to provide navigation back and forth between pages as shown in Figure 22.39. If you want to move the two buttons together, you need to use the Select Object tool. Drag the buttons to an area on the page where you can easily click the buttons to navigate pages.

FIGURE 22.39

Two buttons used to navigate forward and back through document pages.

Duplicating buttons

At this point, the obvious advantage of using a button field over a link is when you want an image or icon appearance used with the button. Another advantage for using button fields over links is the ability to duplicate button fields across pages. The hard part is finished after you create the fields and add the button faces. The next step is to duplicate buttons so you don't have to copy/paste them on each page.

With the button fields in place, select the Select Object tool and click and drag through both fields. Be certain to click and drag outside the first field so as not to select it while dragging. When both fields are selected, open a context menu and select Duplicate, as shown in Figure 22.40.

FIGURE 22.40

Open a context menu on selected buttons and choose Duplicate.

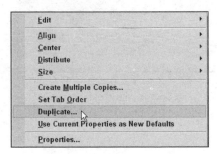

When you release the mouse button, the Duplicate field dialog box opens as shown in Figure 22.41. In the dialog box, select the page range for the duplicated fields. If you created fields on the first page, enter **2** in the first field box and enter the last page number in the second field box. Click OK and the fields with the same field properties are duplicated across the specified pages.

FIGURE 22.41

Enter the page range in the Duplicate Field dialog box and click OK. The fields are duplicated on the pages you specified.

Click the buttons to navigate pages. Notice that each button appears in the same relative position on each page.

The important thing to remember as you work with bookmarks, links, page actions, destinations, and fields is that each is designed for different purposes. Although you can create the same results with one method or another, at times you'll favor one method over the others for a particular editing assignment. Acrobat offers many tools and features for creating dynamic interactive documents, often limited only by your imagination. The more time you invest in learning all that Acrobat affords you, the more impressive results you'll produce.

Summary

- You can name, organize, and create bookmarks with different appearance properties. You can move, reassign, and delete standard bookmarks without affecting page content. When you delete or move structured bookmarks, the respective pages are deleted or moved.

- Bookmarks support the same actions you can apply to links. Actions enable you to view pages, open documents, create Web links, and write JavaScripts and other types of commands that act as hypertext links.

- Article threads enable viewers to follow passages of text in a logical reading order.

- Links support many different actions from page navigation to running JavaScripts. Links can be copied and pasted and the link properties are retained in the pasted objects. Links cannot be duplicated across PDF pages and links do not support content files with colors or images.

- Acrobat supports opening user-defined pages in external PDF documents via link actions.

- You select link properties in the Create Link dialog box, from a context menu command, or by double-clicking on a link. All link actions are changed in the Link Properties dialog box.

- You make links from text by selecting text with the Select tool and selecting Create Link from a context menu.

- All the actions assigned to links can also be assigned to page actions. Page actions are established in the Page Properties dialog box accessed by opening a context menu on a page thumbnail and selecting Properties.

- Page actions are invoked when a page opens or a page closes.

- Destinations are similar to bookmarks. Destinations do not support actions. Destinations tend to make file sizes larger than when using bookmarks and links.

- You can use destinations, together with a JavaScript, to create pop-up menus.

- You can assign form field buttons different button faces from external files.

- Form fields can be duplicated across multiple pages. Duplicated fields are placed on all pages in the same relative position as from where they were duplicated.

Chapter 23

Multimedia and PDFs

Acrobat offers a wide range of possibilities with animation, motion, and sound. You can import sound files in PDFs, import movie files, convert Web pages with Flash animation, convert PowerPoint files with motion objects, and create animation by writing JavaScript routines. With the exception of writing JavaScripts, you create animation and sound in other applications and import them in PDF documents.

Movie files and sounds added with the Sound tool are only available in Acrobat Professional. Acrobat Standard does not have these tools and you have no way of adjusting properties for movie and sound files with Acrobat Standard. However, after you've added movie and sound files in Acrobat Professional, all Acrobat viewers, including Adobe Reader, can play the movies and sounds.

In this chapter you learn how to import multimedia files into PDF documents and create some motion effects by writing JavaScripts in Acrobat Professional.

Setting Up the Multimedia Environment

You import sound and video files with the Movie and/or Sound tools available from the Editing toolbar. To open the toolbar, select Tools ➪ Editing ➪ ShowEditing Toolbar, open a context menu on the Toolbar Well and select Editing, or use the Customize Toolbars window and check the Editing toolbar. When the toolbar opens, right-click to open a context menu from the Toolbar Well and select Dock All Toolbars.

Working with Sound Files

You import sounds in Acrobat in one of two ways. You can use the Record Audio Comment tool and record or import a message in the form of a comment. Once recorded, the sound is embedded in Acrobat and not accessible for importing via an action. The other method of handling sound in PDF documents is to import sounds from files saved on your hard drive. By importing sounds you can invoke a sound with various action types; for example, using a page action to play a sound when the user opens or closes a page or clicks a button or link field.

CROSS-REF   For information on using the Record Audio Comment tool and setting action types, see Chapter 20. For more information on action types, see Chapter 22.

You import sound files with the Sound tool found on the Editing toolbar. Be certain to understand the difference between creating an audio comment and importing a sound with the Sound tool. Using the Record Audio Comment tool enables you to record a sound or import a sound file from your hard drive. Using the Sound tool enables you to import a sound from a file saved in a format compatible for importing sounds, but does not offer you an option for recording a sound. Before you can use the Sound tool, you need to either acquire or edit sounds and save them to a file format recognized by Acrobat.

Creating sound files

If you are so inclined you can purchase a commercial application for editing sound and saving recordings that Acrobat can recognize. If recording sounds is an infrequent task and does not warrant the purchase of expensive commercial software, you can find sound recording applications as shareware and in the public domain that can satisfy almost any need you have for using sounds on PDF documents.

Web sites change frequently, so you may need to do a search for public domain and shareware applications for your computer platform. As of this writing you can find sound-editing programs at www.freeware files.com (Windows) or www.macupdate.com (Macintosh). You can find applications that enable you to record sounds and save them in formats acceptable to the platform you use that can then be recognized by Acrobat. The most common of the file types recognized by Acrobat is .wav for Windows and .aiff for Macintosh.

NOTE   You can import video and sound files that are compatible with Apple QuickTime, Flash Player, Windows Built-In Player, RealOne, and Windows Media Player. Windows media files need to be converted to QuickTime if you're importing a Windows Media file on a Mac. Windows needs a QuickTime installation in order to import QuickTime files on Windows. Sound files saved as .wav and .aiff can be imported in Acrobat running on either platform.

Be certain you have a microphone properly connected to your computer according to your computer's user manual. Launch the sound-editing application you downloaded from a Web site or use a commercial application if you have one available. Most programs offer you a record button similar in appearance to a tape recorder or VCR. Click the Record button and speak into the microphone. When finished recording, click the Stop button. Depending on the application, you may be prompted in a dialog box to save the file or you may see a window where you can further edit the sound, as shown in Figure 23.1.

FIGURE 23.1

To record sounds and save the sound to a file available for importing in Acrobat, use a sound-editing program.

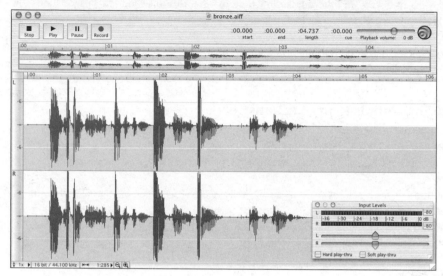

If a dialog box does not prompt you to save the recording, select Save or Save As from a menu option. Typically the commands are under the File menu, but these may vary depending on the program you use. When you save the file, be certain to save in a format acceptable to Acrobat. A .wav (Windows) or .aiff (Macintosh) file format can be imported in Acrobat, but be careful of any file compression applied to the file when saved. You may need to test various compression options in order to find a format that Acrobat can recognize. After choosing the format, supply a name for the file with the proper extension, as shown in Figure 23.2.

FIGURE 23.2

After editing a sound, save the file in either .aiff (Macintosh) or .wav (Windows) format.

Adding sounds to page actions

A sound might be added to a Page Open or a Page Close action to provide informational instructions to complete a form, play a music score, or other similar function. In order to add a sound to a page action, you must have the sound file saved to disk as described in the preceding section. To add a sound to a page action, follow these steps:

 **NOTE**   Acrobat Standard does support importing sounds on page actions, Bookmarks and with links. Although you have no Sound tool in Acrobat Standard, you can use an action to import sounds.

STEPS: Adding sounds to page actions

1. **Open the Page Properties.** Be certain your sound file is available in a directory on your hard drive and click on the Pages tab in the Navigation pane. From a context menu opened on the page where you want the sound to play, select Page Properties. The Page Properties dialog box opens.

2. **Set the action trigger.** Click the Actions tab and select either Page Open or Page Close from the Select Trigger pull-down menu.

3. **Set the action type.** Open the pull-down menu for Select Action and choose Play a sound from the menu options as shown in Figure 23.3.

FIGURE 23.3

Choose Play a sound from the Select Action pull-down menu.

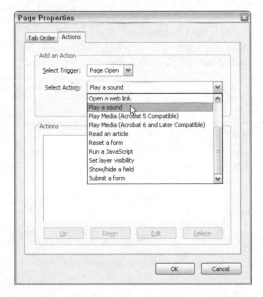

 **NOTE**   By default, the Play a sound menu item in the Select Action pull-down menu may not be in view. Scroll the menu down to show the command.

4. **Add the action to the page trigger.** Click the Add button in the Page Properties dialog box to add the sound to your PDF.

5. **Select the sound file.** The Select Sound File dialog box opens. Navigate your hard drive to find the sound to import, select it, and click the Select button. After importing the sound, click Close in the Page Properties dialog box.

> **NOTE** Acrobat may pause momentarily. The sound file imported in Acrobat is converted during the import. When a sound is imported in a PDF file, the sound can then be played across platforms. Therefore, a .wav file can be played on a Macintosh computer and an .aiff file can be played on a Windows computer.

6. **Save the file.** Choose File ➪ Save As and rewrite the file to disk. Close the file and reopen it to test the page action.

After you save the PDF file and reopen it, the sound is played. You can also test the sound by scrolling a page in the PDF file and returning to the page where the sound was imported. The action is dynamic and the sound plays before you save the PDF file.

Adding sounds to form field actions

Of the mouse behavior types, you may find that Mouse Enter, On Focus, or On Blur behaviors work equally as well as using a Mouse Up or Mouse Down trigger. As an example, you might have a descriptive message display when the user places the cursor over a button field and before he or she clicks the mouse. Or you may want to invoke a sound when the user tabs out of a field as a reminder to verify data entry in a PDF form. In these situations and similar uses, the sound is played from a mouse behavior related to a data or button field. To understand how to use sound actions with data fields, follow these steps:

> **NOTE** Acrobat Standard does not support Forms tools. You can substitute a button field for a link with Acrobat Standard and import sounds on a link action.

STEPS: Adding sounds to form fields

1. **Open a PDF document with form fields.** In Figure 23.4, I use a form with several check boxes. I want to create a sound when the user places the cursor over one of the check boxes or tabs to the field.

FIGURE 23.4

Four check boxes are to be configured to play a sound on a Mouse Enter trigger.

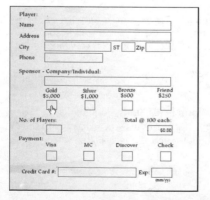

2. **Open the field properties.** Choose the Select Object tool in the Editing toolbar and double-click on the field you want to edit. If no fields exist in your document, create a check box field. The field type properties dialog box opens, which in this case is the Check Box Properties dialog box.

CROSS-REF For more information on creating form fields in Acrobat Professional, see Chapter 34.

3. **Select the mouse trigger.** In the Check Box Properties dialog box, click the Actions tab and select Mouse Enter as the Select Trigger, as shown in Figure 23.5.

4. **Add a sound action to the field.** Open the Select Action pull-down menu and select Play a sound.

5. **Select the sound file.** Click the Add button to open the Select Sound File dialog box. Select the file to import and click the Select button.

FIGURE 23.5

Choose Mouse Enter from the Select Trigger pull-down menu.

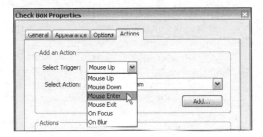

6. **Close the Check Box Properties dialog box.** Check to be certain the mouse trigger is set to Mouse Enter (or another trigger you chose to use). Click Close in the Check Box Properties dialog box.

7. **Test the sound.** Select the Hand tool and place the mouse cursor over the check box where you added the sound. (Note: To play the sound by tabbing to the field, use the On Focus mouse trigger.)

When the mouse enters one of the check boxes, the respective sound plays. The sound plays completely even if the cursor leaves the field. Sounds added to forms either for page actions or field actions can be played from any Acrobat viewer.

TIP A sound continues to play to completion. If you want to stop the sound while editing a document, select the Select Object tool or press the R key on your keyboard to activate the Select Object tool. (Note: You need to enable Use single-key accelerators to access tools in the General Preferences to use key modifiers to select tools.)

Using the Sound tool

Sound Tool Importing sounds with page actions, form fields, links, bookmarks, and so on limits your import options to fewer file formats and limits the attributes you can assign to the imported file. In essence, you import the file and play the sound. Not much else is available when you use the Select Action

command. Another method for importing sound files in PDF documents is with the Sound tool. When you use the Sound tool to import sounds, your options are much greater for the kinds of files you can import and attributes you can assign to the imported sounds.

To import a sound with the Sound tool, select the tool from the Editing toolbar and just double-click on a document page or drag open a rectangle on a document page. The area contained within the rectangle becomes a trigger to play the sound. When you release the mouse button, the Add Sound dialog box opens, as shown in Figure 23.6.

TIP You can manage sound and movie links similarly to links and form fields where context menu options enable you to size, align, copy, paste, and distribute fields. You can access these menu commands when you select sound and movie links in a group together with links and form fields. For more information on managing links and form fields, see Chapters 22 and 34.

FIGURE 23.6

When you use the Sound tool, the Add Sound properties offer you different file format import options, embedding choices, and appearance choices.

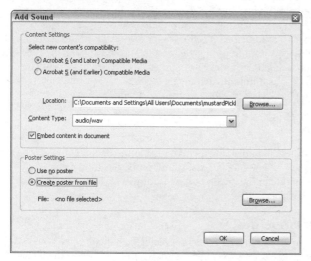

You set the attributes for sound imports when you initially use the Sound tool. Double-clicking or clicking and dragging the Sound opens the Add Sound dialog box when you release the mouse button. In the Add Sound dialog box you have the following options:

NOTE Initial settings you apply to an imported sound are handled in the Add Sound dialog box. If you later want to edit the sound settings, the changes are made in either the Movie Properties (for Acrobat 5 or earlier compatible files) or the Multimedia Properties (for Acrobat 6 or later compatible files) dialog box. Either of these dialog boxes opens when you open a context menu on a sound rectangle using either the Sound tool or the Select Object tool and select the Properties command. The Multimedia Properties dialog box offers you many more settings options than the Add Sound dialog box. For more information on the Multimedia Properties options, see Acrobat 6 Multimedia Properties later in this chapter.

- **Compatibility.** From the radio button choices you decide whether the sound import is Acrobat 6 (and later) or Acrobat 5 (and earlier) compatible. If you select Acrobat 5 (and earlier) compatible, the format options are limited to .wav and .aiff formats. If you use Acrobat 6 (and later) compatible media, the sound may not play with earlier Acrobat viewers depending on the file types you import and attributes assigned to the sound.

- **Browse.** Click the Browse button to locate the sound you want to import.

- **Content Type.** By default, the type of the file you import is listed automatically in the field box. By clicking the down arrow you can open a pull-down menu where all compatible file formats are listed. A total of 46 different file formats are supported. When you import files, let Acrobat interpret the file format and leave the format unchanged. If you select a sound for which Acrobat does not know the Content Type, Acrobat prompts you to click in a dialog box to select a content type.

- **Embed content in document.** Using Acrobat 5 compatibility automatically embeds sound files. If you use Acrobat 6 compatibility you can choose to link the sound file to the PDF or embed the sound in the PDF document. If you disable the check box for Embed content in document, you need to send the sound file to a user as well as the PDF in order for other users to play the sound.

- **Poster Settings.** If you select Acrobat 5 (and earlier) this option is not available. The rectangle you create appears similar to a button field. If you leave the default at Use no poster, then noting appears inside the sound rectangle. If you select Create poster from file, you can fit a graphic to the rectangle; for example, something similar to using button faces for form field buttons. You click the Browse button to select the file you want to use for the poster. You can choose any file type that is compatible when using the Create PDF From File command. If the file type is other than PDF, Acrobat converts the file to PDF as it imports the image. If you're using a multi-page PDF document for the poster, the first page in the PDF document is used for the poster.

CROSS-REF For information on creating button faces, see Chapter 22.

Click OK after selecting options in the Add Sound dialog box. When you return to the document page, the rectangle is visible. You assign additional properties when you open the sound properties from a context menu. When the properties dialog box opens, the title of the dialog box is Multimedia Properties if Acrobat 6 (or later) and Movie Properties if Acrobat 5 (or earlier).

Acrobat 5–compatible Movie (Sound) Properties

If you're using an Acrobat 5-compatible sound import, the Movie Properties dialog box opens when you select Properties from a context menu opened from the sound rectangle. As shown in Figure 23.7, the dialog box contains three tabs used for selecting more options than were available in the Add Sound dialog box.

TIP When you use either the Sound tool or the Movie tool and create a sound or movie field, the first dialog box that opens is the Add Sound or Add Movie dialog box. While selecting options in the dialog box, you have no opportunity to select objects on the document page or use menu commands. However, after you create a sound or movie field and open the Properties dialog box, working with it is similar to working with Link Properties and Form Field Properties windows where you can access both objects on the page and menu commands. When editing properties for sound and movie files, you don't need to close the Properties window to select and edit additional fields.

FIGURE 23.7

When working with Acrobat 5 (and earlier) media, to open the Movie Properties dialog box, use the Sound tool, the Movie tool, or the Select Object tool and select Properties from a context menu.

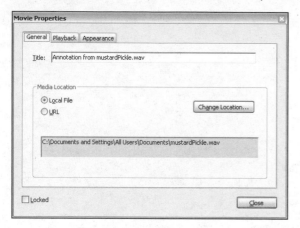

General properties

The default properties are the General Movie Properties. In this dialog box, you make the following selections:

- **Title.** By default, the title of the sound clip is the filename. Edit the title name in the field box to change the title.

- **Media location.** Local files are stored on your hard drive. Although the sound file is embedded in the PDF, you can change the sound to another file by clicking the Change Location button. Click the button and the Select Multimedia File dialog box opens. Select another file and click the Select button and the sound is changed to another file. If you select URL, another dialog box opens asking you to specify a URL where a sound file is located. If importing sounds, you need to add the sound filename as part of the URL when using Acrobat 5 compatibility. When you deselect the option to embed the file with Acrobat 6 compatibility, the directory path is all you need to address in the line where the URL is specified.

Playback

The Playback tab offers options settings for playing sound clips and movies, as shown in Figure 23.8.

FIGURE 23.8

Click the Playback tab to set options for playing sounds.

- **Show player controls.** If this check box is enabled, a control palette opens when a sound is played. In the control palette you have a button to play/pause and a slider. Click and drag the slider to move forward or backward in the sound file. In Figure 23.9, the sound rectangle appears without a poster. The Show Player Controls check box was checked in the Movie Properties dialog box and the player controls are shown after you click once inside the rectangle. Below the rectangle is the player control. The sound is currently stopped. Clicking on the right pointing arrow with the Hand tool continues the play.

- **Use floating window.** With sounds, the sound file is fixed to a location. With video clips you can select the Use floating window option to float a video clip in a window centered in the Acrobat window. If you select floating window for a sound file, the player control opens in a floating toolbar. In Figure 23.10, player controls are very similar to those shown in Figure 23.9. When Use Floating Window is added in the Playback tab in the Movie Properties dialog box, the player control appears as a floating window.

FIGURE 23.9

Player Controls are displayed when you check the Show Player Controls check box in the Movie Properties Playback tab.

FIGURE 23.10

When Use floating window is checked, the player controls open in a floating toolbar.

One reason you might use a floating window with a sound file is if you place the sound rectangle on a page where you don't want the rectangle visible to the end user. For instance, something like a tiny rectangle in the top left corner of the page. If you add a page action to start the sound to play and you want the end user to stop or pause a sound, add the floating window. The window opens in the center of the page irrespective of where the sound rectangle is placed. The viewer of your PDF file can then pause, stop, and resume play.

- **Size.** For sound imports, the Size pull-down menu and field box are disabled. These options relate to sizing video clips, explained in the "Playback" section later in this chapter.

- **Play.** From the pull-down menu you can choose to play a sound Once; play a sound once and Keep the player open; Loop through the sound and continue playing it over and over again; and play Forward and backward, which provides an interesting way of hearing your voice played backward. The latter option is best used for video clips without sound.

Appearance

Many of the options for appearance settings are the same as those found for link and form field appearances. Click on the Appearance tab and make choices for the appearance of the rectangle border and the contents of the rectangle as shown in Figure 23.11.

- **Type.** From the Type pull-down menu select from Visible Rectangle or Invisible Rectangle. If Invisible Rectangle is selected, the following options for Width, Style, and Color are grayed out.

- **Width.** The same three choices for link and form field rectangle widths of Thin, Medium, and Thick are listed in the pull-down menu.

- **Style.** Two choices appear for either setting the rectangle to a solid line or a dashed line.

- **Color.** You can choose from the same color options you have available for links and form fields by clicking on the color swatch and selecting either preset or custom colors.

- **Option.** The Option pull-down menu applies to movie files. If you select Put in Document from the pull-down menu when using a sound file, the menu defaults back to Don't Show. With sound files you cannot show a poster image because the sound contains no graphic data.

FIGURE 23.11

Click the Appearance tab to change border colors and the poster image.

- **Colors.** The Colors pull-down menu and field box are disabled for sound files.
- **Locked.** The Locked check box is accessible from all tabs. When you select the Locked check box the sound rectangle is locked to position on the document page and the attributes are locked. If you want to make any edits on the Movie Properties dialog box, you first need to uncheck the Locked item.

Acrobat 6–compatible Multimedia (Sound) Properties

If you elect to use Acrobat 6 compatibility, the options in the Add Sound dialog box are the same as discussed in the "Using the Sound tool" section earlier in this chapter. After you create a sound, import and select Properties from a context menu, a different set of property options appear in the Multimedia Properties dialog box. In Figure 23.12, the Multimedia Properties dialog box shows the default Settings tab options.

Settings

The Settings tab offers options for labels and renditions. By default the Settings tab is placed in view when you open the Multimedia Properties. As you can see in Figure 23.13, the Appearance tab is consistent with the Movie Properties dialog box, but the other two tabs (Settings and Actions) offer options much different from those found with Acrobat 5–compatible sound files. In the Settings tab you have options for the following:

- **Annotation Title.** Add a title for the sound in this field. The title supplied here can be different from the filename.
- **Alternate Text.** When creating accessible files for vision- and motion-challenged users, you can add alternate text that can be read by screen-reading software.
- **Renditions.** A good number of options available when editing renditions apply to movie clips. For information on setting rendition options for sound files, see the section "Adding a rendition" later in this chapter.

FIGURE 23.12

Select Properties from a context menu to open the Multimedia Properties dialog box for Acrobat 6–compatible sounds.

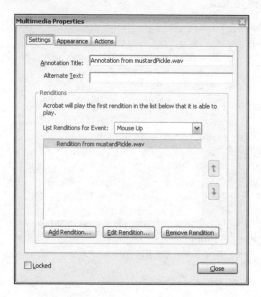

FIGURE 23.13

The Appearance tab offers options for setting the field rectangle appearance and a button to access the Change Poster Options dialog box.

Appearance

The Appearance tab (shown in Figure 23.13) in the Multimedia Properties dialog box offers options similar to those found in the Movie Properties for defining the attributes of a rectangle border for Type, Width, Style, and Color. In addition to these settings, other options include:

- **Annotation is hidden from view.** The annotation added to the field box in the Settings tab is visible by default. To hide the annotation, enable this check box.

- **Change Poster Option.** Options for the poster image are similar to those used with Acrobat 5–compatible files. The settings appear in a dialog box, shown in Figure 23.14. When you click the button for Change Poster Option, you find the following three options:

  - **Use no poster.** This choice is the same as selecting Don't Show in the Movie Properties dialog box. No poster is shown in the sound field.

  - **Retrieve poster from movie.** Also a similar choice as you find in the Movie Properties dialog box. With sound files a dialog box opens informing you that no support for a poster is retrievable from sound files. For movie files the poster is retrieved from the first frame in the movie file.

  - **Create poster from file.** The Movie Properties dialog box used with Acrobat 5–compatible files offers you an option for Retrieve From Movie as the third choice in the pull-down menu. This choice is the same as the preceding option and pulls the first frame in the movie clip as the poster image. With Acrobat 6 compatibility, the Create poster from file option enables you to use a PDF or file compatible with the Create PDF From File command as the poster image. To add a poster from a file, click the Browse button and select the file you want to import.

FIGURE 23.14

When you click the Change Poster Options button, a dialog box opens, offering three choices for poster displays.

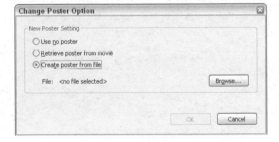

Actions

The Actions tab offers you options for setting an action on mouse triggers much like you apply actions to links, Bookmarks, page actions, and form fields. Options from the Select Trigger pull-down menu differ slightly from those you select for links, Bookmarks, page actions, and form fields. The same triggers are available for video and sound files. Additionally you have the same options for selecting an action, and you can manage actions such as changing the order, adding additional actions, deleting actions, and so on.

The options in the Actions tab include:

- **Select Trigger.** Open the pull-down menu and you see the trigger actions like those shown in Figure 23.15.

FIGURE 23.15

Open the Select Trigger pull-down menu in the Actions tab to select a mouse trigger.

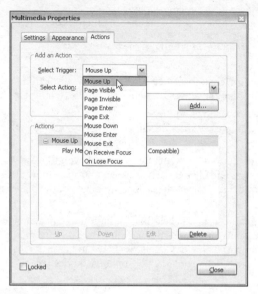

CROSS-REF For more information on selecting trigger options, see Chapter 23.

- **Mouse Up.** The behavior is identical to the same trigger used for other items such as page actions, links, and buttons where actions are applied.

- **Page Visible.** A current page active in the Document pane can be different than page visibility. When using Continuous page layout, Facing Pages, or Continuous – Facing Pages, you can have one page active while other pages are visible in the Document pane. When this trigger is selected, the media clip plays dependent on page visibility and not necessarily the current page.

- **Page Invisible.** If a page is not visible in the Document pane, the media clip can be played on an action such as a button, link, or Bookmark.

- **Page Enter.** This trigger is like setting a page action. When the page becomes the current page, the media plays.

- **Page Exit.** The opposite of the preceding option. When you scroll to another page, the media clips play.

- **Mouse Down.** When the mouse button is pressed down, the trigger is invoked.

- **Mouse Enter.** When the mouse cursor enters the focus rectangle, the media clips play.

- **Mouse Exit.** Opposite of the preceding option where the sound or video plays when the mouse cursor exits the focus rectangle.

- **On Receive Focus.** This trigger is similar to the On Focus mouse trigger used with form field buttons. Pressing the Tab key activates the focus rectangle and the media clip plays.

- **On Lose Focus.** The opposite of the preceding option and like the On Blur mouse trigger where a media clip plays when you tab out of the field.

■ **Select Action.** From the Select Action pull-down menu, you can select any action type that is also available to links, fields, Bookmarks, and page actions. You might nest different actions and use the Select Action menu to add additional actions. For example, you might play different media clips with a single mouse trigger, play a media clip and then open a URL to display a Web page in your Web browser, change a layer view, or any number of other actions.

CROSS-REF For more information on Select Action options, see Chapter 22.

■ **Add.** When you select an action, click the Add button to include the action in the Actions list window. New actions are added at the end of the action list in the Actions list window.

■ **Actions.** The Actions list window shows all the trigger options and actions assigned to the sound or video clip. You can add multiple actions with different triggers and view all the additions in the Actions list.

■ **Up/Down.** The buttons at the bottom of the Actions tab enable you to reorder multiple actions. Select an item in the Actions list and click the Up or Down button to move the selected action before or after other items in the list. When the actions are invoked, the play is in the order shown in the Actions list.

■ **Edit.** Select an item in the Actions list and click the Edit button to edit action item attributes. If you select a sound or video file in the Actions list and click the Edit button, the Play Media (Acrobat 6 and Later Compatible) dialog box opens as shown in Figure 23.16. From the pull-down menu, you make choices for changing the play options. Notice you also have an option for writing a custom JavaScript.

FIGURE 23.16

When you select Edit in the Actions tab for media files, the Play Media (Acrobat 6 and Later Compatible) dialog box opens. Make choices in the dialog box for play options you want to change.

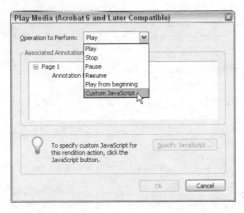

■ **Delete.** If you want to delete an item in the Actions list, select the item to be removed and click the Delete button.

■ **Locked.** Check the Locked check box and the media rectangle is locked to position on the document page. You can't move a media placeholder when the Locked check box is checked. To unlock the media placeholder, open the Multimedia Properties dialog box and uncheck the box for Locked.

Creating Movie Files

As with sound files, video files require that you create video clips in other authoring programs. No tools or features are contained in Acrobat for editing movies. However, after you create video clips in authoring applications, you have the wealth of import options and play opportunities similar to those used with sound files.

Video editing at the high end is handled by sophisticated software such as Final Cut Pro, Adobe Premiere, Adobe After Effects, and other similar professional programs designed to offer you limitless choices for editing video and audio channels. On the low end, you have some impressive features in programs that cost very little. For Windows, Adobe's marvelous consumer image editor — Adobe Photoshop Elements is a low-cost editing program that offers you options for exporting to PDF slide shows, embedding sound files, and mixing slides and video clips. The great advantage of using Photoshop Elements for media creations is that the program exports direct to PDF along with side transitions and imported sounds that open directly in Acrobat in Full Screen Mode.

For Macintosh users, Apple's own iMovie is a free application shipping with System X that produces QuickTime movies. iMovie supports PDF imports as well as still photos and video clips. If you happen to be a cross-platform user, the combination of using Photoshop Elements 4 and iMovie offers you a sophisticated editing environment where you can produce PDF presentations and displays for just any purpose.

CROSS-REF Discussion in this chapter is related to multimedia authoring and working with video and sound in PDF documents. For additional information related to creating presentations and other application support for various kinds of animation, see Chapter 28.

NOTE Since Photoshop Elements 3 was introduced the product shipped as a Windows only program. The first introduction of Photoshop Elements 4 also supported Windows only. After the release of the Windows version, Adobe created Adobe Photoshop Elements 4 for the Mac, providing Macintosh users with the same media export options as Windows users. As of this writing, Adobe Photoshop Elements 5 ships on Windows only.

There are other programs that also enable you to create movie files. You can use Adobe Premiere Elements (Windows only), Microsoft Media Maker (Windows only), Final Cut Express HD (Macintosh only), and a number of different shareware programs that enable you to edit digital video clips. Regardless of the video editor you use, you can import video clips in PDF files from a huge range of supported video formats.

Importing Movies

Movie Tool Use the Movie tool in the Editing toolbar to import movies. To import a movie, you create a movie link in the same way you create a link with the Sound tool. Select the Movie tool from the Toolbar Well and double-click the mouse button or click and drag open a rectangle. When you release the mouse button, the Add Movie dialog box opens, as shown in Figure 23.17.

Select the compatibility you want to use and click the Browse button to locate the movie to import. Import a movie file by clicking Select and click OK in the Add Movie dialog box. The movie is imported in the current document.

TIP In Acrobat 7 or 8, when you double-click the mouse button or click and drag open a rectangle, the movie frame defaults to the size to which the video was compressed. If you want to size the frame up or down, press the Shift key and drag one of the four handles with the Movie tool or the Select Object tool to reshape the rectangle. Be aware that if you size up the movie frame from the default size, the video looks distorted when played.

The Add Movie dialog box offers you options for selecting the content compatibility for either Acrobat 5 (or earlier) compatible media or Acrobat 6 (and later) compatible media.

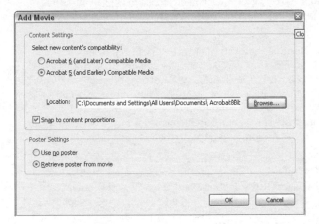

Acrobat 5–compatible movies

Figure 23.18 shows the Add Movie dialog box options for Acrobat 5–compatible movies. You have options for selecting either Acrobat 5 or Acrobat 6 compatibility like you do with sound imports. When you select the Acrobat 5 (and Earlier) Compatible Media radio button, the dialog box reduces in size and displays only the options available when using Acrobat 5 or earlier compatibility.

Add Movie

You make choices in the Add Movie dialog box when you first create a movie field. After creating the field, you can make changes and select attributes in the Movie Properties dialog box that are similar to the Sound properties choices. In the Add Movie dialog box, you select from the following:

- **Compatibility.** Click on the compatibility for either Acrobat 5 or Acrobat 6-compatible media. If you select Acrobat 5 compatibility the movie clips cannot be embedded in the PDF file — the files are linked to the PDF. Therefore, you need to send the PDF and the movie file to other users or host both on a Web site in order for users to view the movies. If you use Acrobat 6-compatible media, you have a choice to either embed the media in the PDF or link the media to the PDF. If using Acrobat 6–compatible media and embedding movie clips in a PDF, Acrobat users with viewers earlier than Acrobat 6 won't be able to see your movie files.

- **Location.** On local drives, the location of the movie file is added to the Location field box. When you first import a movie, identify the movie in the Add Movie dialog box and leave the Location at the default. After you create the movie rectangle, you can change the location to a URL for Web-hosted documents in the Movie Properties dialog box.

NOTE   If you move a movie file on your hard drive to another location, the path to the file is broken and the movie won't play. To reset the directory path, click the Browse button, find the movie file, and click Select in the Select Movie File dialog box.

- **Snap to content proportions.** When enabled, the movie remains proportional as you drag open a rectangle, preventing distortion when the movie is played. The media file's original dimensions are preserved no matter how large you draw the rectangle.

- **Poster Settings.** Select the Use no poster option to show a blank video frame. Select the Retrieve poster from movie option to show the first movie frame in the movie rectangle when the movie is not playing.

Acrobat 5 Movie Properties

After you import a movie with Acrobat 5 compatibility, you can make further attribute choices in the Movie Properties dialog box. Select either the Movie tool or the Select Object tool and open a context menu. From the menu options, select Properties. The Movie Properties dialog box opens, as shown in Figure 23.18.

FIGURE 23.18

The General Movie Properties are identical to the Sound Properties.

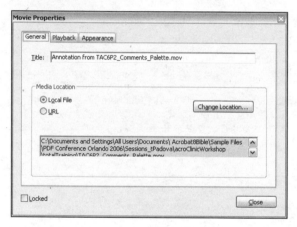

General

Notice that options in the General tab are identical to the Sound Properties. For further definition of the options refer to the section "Using the Sound Tool" earlier in this chapter.

If you want to link the movie to a URL location, select the URL radio button. The Enter URL dialog box opens where you add the URL. Be certain to include the complete URL address, beginning with *http://*.

Playback

Playback options are also identical to the options found with Sound files with the exception of the pull-down menu for Size. This option is only available for video files. From the menu options, you make choices for the size of the video frames during playback, as shown in Figure 23.19. If you choose a size above the Default (1x) size, the video may be distorted when played.

FIGURE 23.19

Playback options are identical to the Sound properties with the exception of the Size options. Choose the playback size from the menu choices.

If you choose Full Screen from the menu choices, the video plays at the largest possible size on your monitor in a separate window. However, the video playback does not change the view to Full Screen mode.

Options for showing the player controls and using a floating window are handled a little differently than when enabling the same options for sound files. The player controls are fixed at the bottom of the video clip for viewing movies either with or without a floating window. When you choose Floating Window for a video file, the media opens in a floating window with the player controls fixed at the bottom of the floating window. In Figure 23.20 you can see the video frame playing with the player controls visible at the default size of the video. In Figure 23.21 the player controls are enabled as well as floating window.

FIGURE 23.20

Player controls are enabled and the floating window option is disabled.

FIGURE 23.21

Player controls are enabled and the floating window option is enabled.

Appearance

Appearance options are also the same as those discussed for Sound properties. In the Appearance options, you have access to showing the movie poster in the file when the movie is still and not playing. If you choose to Put the Poster in the Document, you can also make choices for the color display of 8-bit (256 colors) or 24-bit (millions of colors).

Acrobat 6–compatible movies

If you decide to use Acrobat 6 compatibility, you need to do it when you use the Movie tool to draw the field. If you create a movie field and specify Acrobat 5 compatibility, and then change your mind and want to use Acrobat 6 compatibility, you need to delete the first movie field by clicking on it with the Movie tool or the Select Object tool. Press the Backspace/Delete key on your keyboard or open a context menu and choose Edit ⇨ Delete. Double-click the mouse button with the Movie tool and select Acrobat 6 compatibility and the dialog box changes to reflect the Acrobat 6–compatible options, as shown in Figure 23.22.

FIGURE 23.22

Select the Movie tool and draw a rectangle or double-click in the Document pane. In the Add Movie dialog box, select Acrobat 6 (and later) Compatible Media.

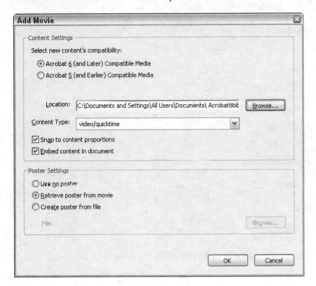

Add Movie

Select Acrobat 6 (and Later) Compatible Media and you'll notice the dialog box expands to offer more options than when you use Acrobat 5–compatible files. The settings are the same as those discussed in the section "Acrobat 6–Compatible Multimedia (Sound) Properties." When adding movies you have options for the poster view in a still frame while the movie is not playing. Select from Use no poster, Retrieve poster from movie, or Create poster from file. These options are the same for sounds with the exception of the Retrieve poster from movie. Whereas sound files produce an error when you make this menu choice, movie files retrieve the first frame in the video for the poster image.

After making choices in the Add Movie dialog box, access more options in the Multimedia Properties dialog box. Click OK after selecting the Acrobat 6–compatible settings. Open a context menu with either the Movie tool or the Select Object tool and choose Properties from the menu options.

Acrobat 6 Multimedia Properties

The Multimedia Properties dialog box shown in Figure 23.23 contains the same options found when you open Acrobat 6–compatible sound files properties. The first stop is the Settings tab, where you see options for annotation text and alternate text. The items below the text fields contain options for renditions. Because I didn't cover renditions earlier in the sounds discussion, I address the options you have for adding renditions here.

FIGURE 23.23

Open a context menu and select Properties to open the Multimedia Properties dialog box.

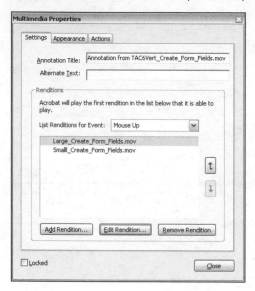

Understanding renditions

When you import a sound or video, the rendition of the clip is assigned to a Mouse Up trigger and plays according to the properties you enable for the play options. By default imported sounds and videos have a single default rendition. When using Acrobat 6–compatible media options, you have an opportunity to add different renditions to the same media clip or multiple media clips. For example, you may have a rendition that plays full screen from a large file and you may want to add an alternate clip of a duplicate movie with a smaller file size. If hosting the media on a Web site you can assign what media clip is downloaded to a user's computer based on the end user's connection speed. The movie field remains the same, but the attributes contain two different renditions for the same field.

You have options for editing existing renditions after importing a media clip or you can add new renditions to an imported file. When you add new renditions, they are listed in the Settings tab in the Multimedia Properties dialog box.

Adding a rendition

By default a rendition is listed in the lower window in the Settings properties. To add a rendition, click the Add Rendition button. A pull-down menu opens where you make choices for one of the following:

- **Using a File.** For local files select Using a File. The Select Multimedia File dialog box opens where you navigate your hard drive and select the file to use. This option might be used to select a duplicate file smaller or larger in size than the original rendition.

- **Using a URL.** If you want files downloaded from Web sites, select Using a URL. The Add a New Rendition Using a URL dialog box opens where you add the URL address for where the file is located. When you add the URL, a pull-down menu opens where you can select the content type for the media format.

■ **By Copying an Existing Rendition.** If you want to use the same rendition as one listed in the Settings list window for the purpose of duplicating the rendition and providing alternate attributes, select By Copying an Existing Rendition. The Copy Rendition dialog box opens in which you select the rendition to copy from a pull-down menu. The new rendition is not actually *copied*, but rather points to another file and adds about 4K to your file size.

Select any one of the three options and click the Edit button to open the Rendition Settings dialog box.

Editing a rendition

You can choose to edit an existing rendition or edit the new rendition you added to the media file (see the preceding section). If you want to edit an existing rendition, click the Edit Rendition button from the Settings properties. If you've added a new rendition, it now appears in the list window, so you can select it and click the Edit button. In either case, the Renditions Settings dialog box opens, as shown in Figure 23.24.

FIGURE 23.24

Select a rendition and click the Edit button. The Rendition Settings dialog box opens.

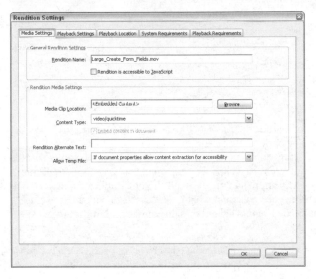

A considerable number of options are available in the various tabs of the Rendition Settings dialog box. By default, the dialog box opens at the Media Settings tab. The various tabs and choices you have include:

■ **Media Settings.** Make choices from the Media Settings tab for the rendition name, the media location and content type, and the rendition for alternate text, and choose from the Allow Temp File pull-down menu for various options related to accessibility. If the media is to be made accessible to JavaScript, be certain to check the box for enabling JavaScript.

■ **Playback Settings.** Click the Playback Settings tab to make choices for the player window visibility, volume settings, showing player controls, continuous looping, or times played. In the list at the bottom of the Playback Settings tab, click the Add button to add the type of media players you want users to use for playing the media. You have an option for enabling all players and a setting for the preferred player.

- **Playback Location.** Make choices on this tab for where the media is played, such as in the document, floating window, or full screen. If you select floating window, you have many different choices for document size and position.

- **System Requirements.** From a pull-down menu you have choices for connection speeds. If you want a particular rendition to be downloaded for all users with 384K connections or greater, you can make the choice in this dialog box. In addition you have choices for screen displays, captions, subtitles, and language.

- **Playback Requirements.** Based on options you selected in the other settings tabs, a list is displayed in the last settings tab. Each item has a check box for enabling a required condition. Check all the boxes for those items you want to make a required function.

Click OK in the Rendition Settings dialog box when you're finished setting the options in the various settings tabs. If you need to add another rendition with some alternate options to the last rendition you edited, copy the rendition and make the necessary edits. You can list as many different renditions as you like to provide much flexibility for your viewer audience and the systems they use.

CROSS-REF There are a considerable number of options in the Renditions Settings dialog box. For more information on editing Renditions, refer to the Acrobat Help document.

Appearance

The Appearance tab in the Multimedia Properties dialog box offers the same options as those you find when editing Sound Properties. Options are available for poster display in the Change Poster Option dialog box when you click the Change Poster Option button shown in Figure 23.25. The poster options are the same as those available as discussed in the "Acrobat 6–Compatible Media (Sound) Properties" section described earlier in this chapter.

FIGURE 23.25

Click the Change Poster Option button to change the poster image.

Actions

The Actions tab also offers the same choices as those available with sound files for adding an action to the media clip. You can choose an action from the Select Action pull-down menu the same as when using action types with Acrobat 5 media.

Creating Play Buttons

As I explain in Chapter 28, you can create presentations from programs such as Microsoft PowerPoint where animated effects from PowerPoint appear in PDF documents in Full Screen mode. You can add media clips to a presentation while showing slides in Full Screen mode and set up some buttons to play, pause, and stop the media clips. You can add media to other PDF files such as electronic brochures, advertising materials, educational materials, and so on. Regardless of the content, adding some play buttons makes it much easier for the end user to start, pause, resume, and stop video and sound.

CROSS-REF For more information on converting PowerPoint files to PDF, see Chapter 28.

PowerPoint is a good tool to use when converting to PDFs for presentations, but any authoring tool that supports creating the design you want works well. If you intend to add media and play buttons in the final PDF, you might add the necessary design elements that work well with the content you'll add in Acrobat. As an example, take a look at Figure 23.26. This file was created in Adobe InDesign. The drop shadow in the center of the document is added in InDesign. A movie file with a poster will eventually appear atop the drop shadow. On the right, you see where buttons will be added in Acrobat to start, pause, resume, and stop the video.

FIGURE 23.26

To add play buttons to documents you are designing, create icons and design elements in your authoring program before converting to PDF.

To understand how play buttons are added to a PDF document, follow these steps:

STEPS: Adding play buttons to PDF documents

1. **Open a PDF document in Acrobat Professional.** Note that Acrobat Standard does not support importing media, therefore, the following steps can only be performed in Acrobat Professional. Use a PDF document converted from PowerPoint or any other PDF you want to use with imported media. In this example, I'll use the file shown in Figure 23.26.

2. **Select the Movie tool and double click on the document page where you want to import the media.** The Add Movie dialog box opens.

3. **Select the Acrobat compatibility you want to use.** In this example I use Acrobat 6 (and later) compatible media and choose to embed the media in the PDF file.

4. **Click Browse and locate the file you want to import.** Select the file in the Select Movie File dialog box and click Select. You are returned to the Add Movie dialog box.

5. **Click OK and the movie is imported.** Use the Select Object tool to move the movie frame to position. If you need to size the frame, drag one of the four corner handles in to size down, or out to size up. (See Figure 23.27.)

FIGURE 23.27

Use the Select Object (or Movie) tool to position and size the video frame.

6. **Using either the Movie tool or the Select Object tool, open a context menu and select Properties.** The Rendition Settings dialog box opens. By default, the Playback Location is set to In Document, which plays the video within the movie frame you create with the Movie tool.

7. **If you want to use a floating window, click the Playback Location tab in the rendition settings dialog box.** Then select Floating Window from the Playback Location pull-down menu.

8. **Click the Appearance tab.** If you open the Rendition Settings, click OK to return to the Multimedia Properties dialog box and then click Appearance. Click Change Poster Option in the Appearance tab to open the Change Poster Option dialog box. Choose a poster option you want to appear on the movie frame when the movie is not playing. If you use a design element in your layout, click Use No Poster. To retrieve the first frame of the movie for a poster, click Retrieve poster from movie. If you have a file on disk you want to use for a poster image, click Create Poster from file then click the Browse button to locate the file. Click OK and then click Close to close the Movie Properties dialog box.

9. **Select the Button tool and create a button on the page by dragging open a rectangle.**

10. **Name the button in the General tab in the Button Properties dialog box.** If you didn't design a layout that includes a label for Play, click the Options tab and type *Play* in the Label text box. If you have an icon or label that clearly shows the end user that the button is used to play the movie, skip this step and move to the next step.

11. **Click the Actions tab and open the Select Actions pull-down menu.** Select Play Media (Acrobat 6 and later–compatible) from the menu options.

12. **Click Add in the Button Properties dialog box.** The Play Media (Acrobat 6 and later–compatible) opens, as shown in Figure 23.28.

FIGURE 23.28

When you select the Play Media (Acrobat 6 and later compatible) option from the Select Action pull-down menu, a dialog box opens where you make choices for the play action from a pull-down menu.

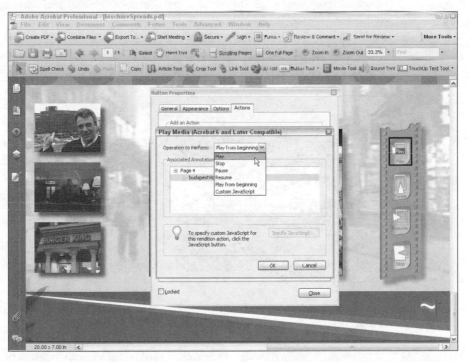

13. **Select Play from the Operation to Perform pull-down menu.** Then click OK in the Play Media (Acrobat 6 and later–compatible) dialog box, shown in Figure 23.28.

14. **Add additional buttons for stopping, pausing, and resuming the play by following Steps 8 through 11.** Be certain to change the name for the button and type descriptive names for the labels.

15. Press Ctrl/⌘+L to set the viewing mode to Full Screen.

16. Click the buttons and the media plays, stops, pauses, and resumes according to the buttons you click.

CROSS-REF For more information on creating button fields, see Chapters 34. For more information on Full Screen mode and button actions, see Chapter 28.

Summary

- Sound files can be imported with either Acrobat 5 or Acrobat 6 compatibility. Acrobat 5–compatible sound imports can be used with earlier Acrobat viewers. Acrobat 6–compatible sounds are only available to Acrobat 6 or later viewers. Acrobat 6 compatibility offers more options for attribute settings and file format compatibility.

- You can add sounds to page actions, links, Bookmarks, and form fields or by using the Sound tool.

- Importing sounds on actions or with the Sound tool requires you to have access to a sound file. You create and save sound files from sound-editing programs. A number of sound-editing programs are available as freeware or shareware on the Internet.

- You can edit movie files in multimedia authoring programs. Among low-cost alternatives for creating movie files are Adobe Photoshop Elements and Apple Computer's iMovie. You can save Photoshop Elements files direct to PDF. You save iMovie files in QuickTime format and import them in PDFs with the Movie tool.

- Movie and sound files can have several renditions. Renditions offer you many options for assigning attributes to sound and media clips as well as providing end users with alternatives for downloading different versions of the same file.

- You can create button fields to play, pause, and stop movies in Full Screen mode without showing the player controls.

- You can embed Acrobat 6–compatible media files in PDF documents. Acrobat 6–compatible media files offer much more support for importing different file formats.

- A poster is a still image that shows inside a sound or movie field. Posters for movie fields can be retrieved from a movie. Posters for sound and movie fields can be created from files including all file formats supported by the Create PDF From File menu command.

Chapter 24

Working with Layers

L ayers are an integral part of many professional imaging applications and specialized technical programs, such as AutoCAD and Microsoft Visio. In Acrobat versions 6 through 8 you can view native layered documents and toggle on and off different layer views.

With the introduction of the Adobe Creative Suite, support for Adobe PDF layers has been integrated into Adobe Illustrator CS and Adobe InDesign CS. As we advance in time and software development, more applications are supporting exports to PDF with layer data.

Design and creative, scientific, and engineering professionals can find many uses for communicating ideas and concepts with layered documents. To help simplify the viewing of layered documents, you can add interactive buttons for guiding users through various layer views. In this chapter, you learn about what constitutes a PDF with layers, how to manage them, and how to create links to different layer views.

Setting Up the Work Environment

Viewing layers requires no special set of toolbars — the tools you need are dependent on what you intend to do with a PDF containing layers when you begin editing. If, for example, you intend to review and comment layered documents, you'll open the Commenting tools. In this chapter, I explain how to add links to layer views and use the Measuring tools. To prepare for this, you need to open the Advanced Editing toolbar and the Measuring toolbar, and it's also a good idea to open the Properties Bar. To open these tools, select the More Tools command from a context menu opened on the Toolbar Well and check the Advanced Editing toolbar in the More Tools window. Scroll down to the Measuring toolbar and check the box to display it. Click OK and open a context menu on the Toolbar Well and select the Properties Bar. Open the context menu again and choose Dock All Toolbars.

As explained later in this chapter, the Measuring tools offer you options for annotating measurements. For some commenting issues, you may want to open the Comment & Markup toolbar. However, you won't need to use the Comment & Measurement tools to follow along in this chapter. Another option you may find helpful is a grid. To set up the grid, you might want to determine the distances for major and minor grid lines. These settings are available in the Preferences dialog box. Select Units and Guides in the left pane in the Preferences dialog box and define the grid height and width values as well as the offset and subdivisions.

After opening the toolbars, your work environment should look like Figure 24.1.

FIGURE 24.1

Open the Advanced Editing toolbar, the Measuring toolbar, the Properties bar, and dock the toolbars in the Toolbar Well.

You may also need to load the Layers panel if not currently shown in the navigation pane. Select View ⇨ Navigation Panels ⇨ Layers. Drag the Layers panel to the Navigation pane to dock it.

Understanding Layers

Acrobat supports the creation of layered documents from several authoring programs. Among the programs supporting the PDFMaker are Microsoft Visio, Microsoft Project, and Autodesk AutoCAD. In regard to exporting to PDF with Adobe PDF layers, you can use Adobe Illustrator CS and Adobe InDesign CS. Other Creative Suite programs such as Adobe GoLive CS and Adobe Photoshop CS do not support layered PDFs. When layers are created in these programs, the document can be converted to PDF with Adobe PDF layers and viewed in all Acrobat viewers 6.0 and above with the layers intact. The creation of Adobe PDF layers requires Acrobat Professional; however, after the PDF creation, layers can be viewed in any Acrobat 6.0 or later viewer, including Adobe Reader.

There are two important points to understand when creating layered PDF files. First, you must begin with an authoring program that supports layers. Adobe Illustrator, Adobe PageMaker, Adobe InDesign, CorelDraw, Autodesk AutoCAD, and Microsoft Visio are some of the popular imaging programs that support layers. Second, the authoring application must export to the PDF 1.5 format or above (Acrobat 6 compatibility or later). Just because the authoring program supports layers is no guarantee that your resultant PDF will contain layers.

If you use a program that enables you to create and save layered documents and the program does not currently export to Acrobat 6 or later compatibility, log on to your software manufacturer's Web site and see whether a new version of the program is available and whether the latest release exports to PDF v1.5 or higher.

Layer Visibility

When you open a layered document in Acrobat and the Layers palette is open in the Navigation pane, you see a list of all the layers contained in the document and an eye icon adjacent to each layer name when the respective layer is in view. A layer's visibility is either on or off, as shown in the Layers palette.

Initial visibility is determined from the visibility shown in the original authoring program when the PDF is created. In Figure 24.2 you see a layered document with three layers visible as indicated by the eye icons in the Layers palette. The remaining layers in the document are hidden and the hidden state is expressed in the Layers palette by the absence of an eye icon adjacent to the layer names.

FIGURE 24.2

The initial visibility of layers in this file shows three layers in view as indicated by the eye icons. Those layers were no eye icon appears are hidden.

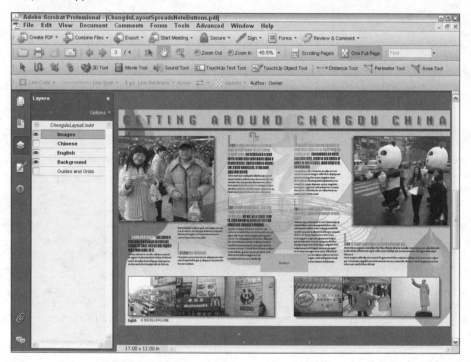

Setting initial visibility

The initial layer visibility is the default view of visible layers when you open a PDF document. The layers in view when you open a layered PDF document are determined from the visibility of the layers in view in the original authoring application. If layers are hidden in the authoring application, the Initial View in Acrobat viewers shows the same layers hidden as well. The Initial View or *state* is the same view displayed in the authoring application at the time of PDF creation. As you browse a file in an Acrobat viewer and turn on and off different layer views, you may want to return to the initial state. You return to the default view with

the Reset to Initial Visibility menu command in the Options pull-down menu in the Layers palette, as shown in Figure 24.3. Select this command to return to the layer views you saw when you first opened the PDF document.

FIGURE 24.3

To return to the default layer visibility, open the Options pull-down menu in the Layers palette and select Reset to Initial Visibility.

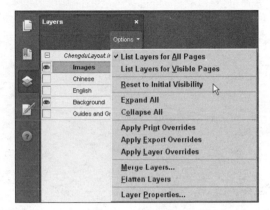

Showing/hiding layers

You show and hide individual layers by clicking on the eye icons in the Layers palette. When an eye icon is hidden, the respective layer is hidden. If you want to display a hidden layer, click in the box adjacent to a layer name; the eye icon appears, and the layer is made visible in the Document pane.

At times, you may have pages in a PDF with different layers associated with different pages. If you want to display all layers on the page in view in the Document pane while hiding layers on other pages in your document, select List Layers for Visible Pages in the Options pull-down menu. All layers not contained on the pages in view in the Document pane are hidden. If the same layer spans more than one page and you select this menu command, the layer is made visible only when the layer is contained on the active page.

When you change layer visibility in the Layers palette and save the PDF document, the layer visibility is not recorded when you save the file. When you open a file after saving with a different layer view, you are still returned to the initial visibility from your first editing session. To create a new default Initial View, you need to change the Layer properties.

Initial Views

You can open the Layers palette when the PDF is opened in the Document pane by setting the Initial View in the Document Properties. Choose File ➪ Document Properties and click the Initial View tab. From the Navigation tab pull-down menu, select Layers Panel and Page. Save the PDF document. When you reopen the file, the Layers palette is expanded to show the layers.

CROSS-REF For more information on Initial Views, see Chapter 5.

Layer Properties

Layer properties are specific to each layer. To open the Layer Properties dialog box, you must have a layer selected in the Layers palette. Click on a layer name and open a context menu (or choose Options ⇨ Layer Properties). The context menu contains two menu options — one for Show Layer and the other for Properties (unless it is a locked layer, in which case Properties is the only option). Select Properties to open the Layer Properties dialog box, as shown in Figure 24.4.

FIGURE 24.4

To open the Layer Properties dialog box, select a layer in the Layers palette, open a context menu, and select Properties from the menu options.

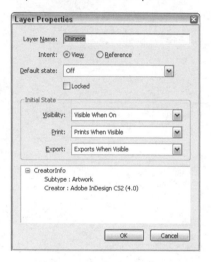

You adjust layer properties for individual layers only. Acrobat does not permit you to select multiple layers. If you need to make changes in visibility for several layers, you must open the Layer Properties dialog box independently for each layer or alternately, return to the original authoring program and set the default layer visibility and convert to PDF. When you open the Layer Properties dialog box, the layer name appears in the dialog box for the respective layer contained in the Layers pane. Two radio buttons exist for the Intent. By default you see View selected, which is normal viewing mode. Select View to allow the layer to be turned on or off. If you click Reference, the remaining items in the dialog box are disabled and the eye icon in the Layers tab disappears. All layer attribute choices are disabled and the behavior is similar to locking a layer. You use View to keep the layer on at all times, which permits editing layer properties. When a layer is set to the Reference Intent, the layer name appears in italics.

Changing the default state

The Default state pull-down menu contains menu options for either On or Off. The menu choice you make here determines the layer visibility when a file is opened. If you want to change the default state, select On or Off from the pull-down menu. When you click OK in the Layer Properties dialog box and save the PDF document, the default visibility changes according to the views you set in the Layer Properties.

Locking visibility

When you select the Locked check box, you lock the layer visibility (either on or off). A lock icon appears in the Layers tab and prevents you from turning the visibility on or off from the tab. You need to return to the Properties dialog box and disable the check box to return visibility control to the Layers tab. You might use Reference and Lock, and then secure a PDF file to prevent users from seeing information on a given layer.

 For more on securing PDF files, see Chapter 26.

Changing the initial state

Initial State settings include Layer Visibility, Print, and Export. The default state described previously enables you to determine whether a layer is visible or hidden when a PDF document opens. To apply the individual settings for layer states, you enable a preference setting. Open the Preferences dialog box and select Documents in the left pane. Check the box for Allow layer state to be set by user information, as shown in Figure 24.5

FIGURE 24.5

Open Preferences and click Documents in the left pane. Check Allow layer state to be set by user information.

Open Settings

☐ Show each document in its own window (requires restart)
☐ Restore last view settings when reopening documents
☑ Open cross-document links in same window
☑ Allow layer state to be set by user information
☑ Allow documents to hide the menu bar, toolbars, and window controls

Documents in recently used list: 5

Remember files in Organizer History for: Last 12 months ▼ (requires restart)

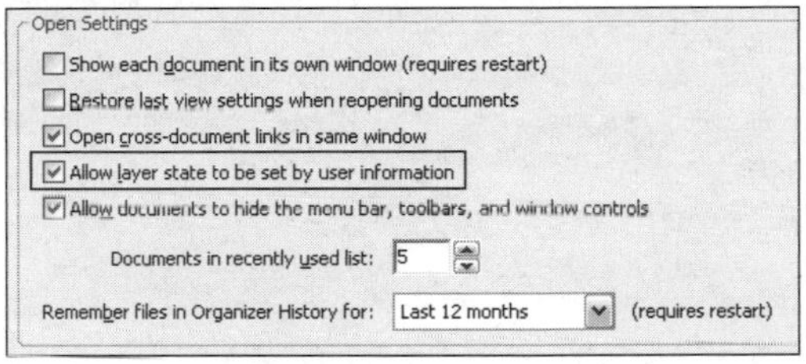

When this preference option is enabled, the layer state options chosen from the Initial State pull-down menus override the layer visibility set from the Default State pull-down menu. For example, if the default state is set to On and the preference item is deselected, the PDF opens with the layer visible. If you enable the preference settings and select Always Visible from the Visibility pull-down menu, the layer is always visible regardless of whether you have the default state On or Off.

The options for initial states include the following:

- **Visibility.** Three choices are available from this pull-down menu. They include Visible When On, Never Visible, and Always Visible. The first option displays a layer according to whether you have the eye icon visible in the Layers palette. When toggled on, the layer is visible. When toggled off, the layer is hidden. Never Visible hides the layer data regardless of whether the default state is on or off. Always Visible always shows the layer.

- **Print.** You may have a watermark or message that you want to eliminate or display on a printed page. The three choices, Prints When Visible, Never Prints, and Always Prints, are similar to the options for visibility. Printing a layer does not require the layer to be in view in the Document pane at the time you print the file if Always Prints is selected.

- **Export.** This setting applies to exporting PDF documents back into authoring programs using a Save As command and selecting a file format compatible with your intended authoring program. Export provides you the same three options when exporting layer data as are available for printing. You can eliminate layers exported by selecting Never Exports or hide or show a layer and choose Exports When Visible. Likewise, you can choose to always export a layer regardless of the visibility and print settings by selecting Always Exports.

CROSS-REF For information on exporting PDF data back to authoring programs, see Chapter 9.

The window at the bottom of the dialog box displays information according to the initial state(s) you select from the pull-down menu. When you open the Properties dialog box you can see, at a glance, the options for each initial state. At the bottom of the scrollable list is information related to the authoring document that was exported to PDF. By default when the initial state is set to Visible When On, you see no view information in the window at the bottom of the Properties dialog box. Change the Visibility to Never Visible or Always Visible. Click OK and when you open the Layers Properties dialog box, a new category labeled "View" appears at the bottom of the window. Below the category name you see ViewState: ON or ViewState: OFF depending on the respective visibility choice you made after changing the initial state.

A good real-world condition for setting a layer state to be visible when printing is when you want to use a watermark or stamp on printed copies. If you want the watermark or stamp to be hidden when viewing the PDF in Acrobat, set the layer visibility for Print to Prints When Visible. If you distribute the document and want all users to print a watermark or some symbol, secure the document with Acrobat security and other users won't be able to avoid printing the file without the mark. In Figure 24.6 you see a PDF file as it prints. The watermark is not visible when viewed onscreen.

CROSS-REF For more on creating and using watermarks, see Chapter 16.

Overriding defaults

In your original authoring program you can create PDF documents with layers that aren't visible in the Layers palette. You can also hide layers in the Default State or the Initial State pull-down menus. If you change defaults to hide layers in the Layers palette, you can change layer visibility in the Options menu. If the Options menu shows a menu item for overriding a layer state grayed out, the menu choice is not available. To change the options, you need to return to the Layer Properties dialog box.

Open the Options pull-down menu to see the following three options for overriding defaults:

- **Apply Print Overrides.** When selected, this option overrides any options you made for not printing layers. When you select this menu item in the Options palette, when you print the PDF all the layers are printed.
- **Apply Export Overrides.** When selected, this option overrides any options you made for exporting layer data. When you select this option, all layer data are exported.
- **Apply Layer Overrides.** Layer Overrides relates to the layer visibility. When this option is enabled, all layers are visible in the Document pane, but the individual layer visibility options are no longer available to you. You cannot click on an eye icon for hiding a layer when the override is enabled. To individually show or hide a layer, you need to deselect the Apply Layer Overrides menu option and use the Layers palette for showing/hiding layers.

Watermarks on separate layers can appear on a printed document but are not visible when a PDF is in view in the Document pane.

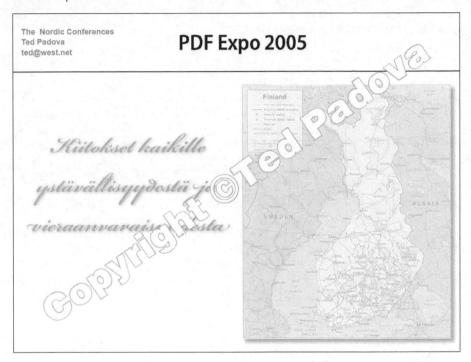

Managing layers

You can edit layers in that you can name, merge, and flatten them. However, you cannot rearrange layers in Acrobat. To rename a layer, select the layer in the Layers palette and click a second time on the layer name. The layer name is highlighted. Begin typing, and the text you type replaces the highlighted text. You can click and drag across a layer name and edit a portion of the text much like you might change names in Bookmarks. You can also edit layer names in the Layer Properties dialog box. If you are changing properties and decide you also want to change a layer name, select the name in the Layer Name field in the Layer Properties dialog box and edit the name.

Merging layers

You can merge layers whether they are visible or hidden. All layer merging takes place in the Merge Layers dialog box and is available only to users of Acrobat Professional. To open the dialog box, select Merge Layers from the Options pull-down menu in the Layers palette. The Merge Layers dialog box opens, as shown in Figure 24.7.

Regardless of whether a layer is visible or hidden, the list in the Layers to be merged column on the left side of the dialog box includes all layers in the document in a scrollable window. You can merge visible layers with hidden layers. To merge layers, select the layers to be merged into a single layer from the list on the left

and click the Add button. You can select multiple layers by holding down the Shift key for a contiguous selection or by using the Ctrl key (Windows) or ⌘ key (Macintosh) to randomly select layer names in a noncontiguous group.

FIGURE 24.7

To merge layers, select Merge Layers from the Options pull-down menu. The Merge Layers dialog box opens where all layers (visible and hidden) are listed in the Layers to be merged column.

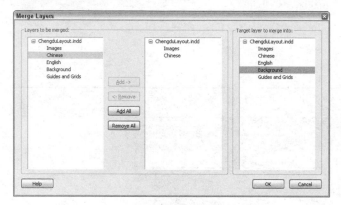

When the layers to be merged are visible in the center column, select the target layer in the Target layer to merge into column. The name you select here is the name listed in the Layers palette and contains all the data from the other layers. The properties associated with the target layer become the properties in the merged layer. After you merge layers, all previous layer names are removed from the Layers palette.

When adding layers to the list in the center of the dialog box (add list), you can move the target layer to the add list or elect to not move the target layer to the list. For example, if you have Text as a target layer where you want to merge Text02 and Text03 together with Text, you can add Text to the center window or not add Text to the list. When you select Text as the target layer and click OK, Text01 and Text 02 are added to Text regardless of whether Text was added to the center column.

TIP   If you want to merge a group of layers to a new layer name, you can edit the name of one of the layers to be merged in the Layers palette. Click, and click again, on the layer name in the Layers palette to edit the layer name. Open the Merge Layers dialog box and merge the desired layers to the new target layer name.

Flattening layers

Users of Acrobat Professional can flatten a group of layers or all layers in a PDF document into a single layer. Neither the merging layers option discussed earlier nor the flattening layers option is available to Acrobat Standard users. You may want to flatten layers to simplify printing a document, exchange a PDF with users of an Acrobat viewer earlier than version 6, or reduce the file size. When layers are flattened, the layer visibility is taken into account. If you have four layers and two layers are visible, the flattened PDF document results as a combination of the visible layers only. Be certain about what layer data you want to remain visible before selecting the Options menu and choosing Flatten Layers, as you won't be able to undo the operation and regain the data that was discarded from the hidden layers.

Creating Layer Visibility Buttons

You may have a document in which you want to create navigation buttons to help a user easily navigate through different layer views. Having some buttons that link to different layer views can help users understand the document structure and quickly navigate different views.

Creating buttons for layer visibility is much like creating Bookmarks. You first establish the view you want as the destination view of a link action and then you create the link button. Figure 24.8 shows a document displayed in the Navigation pane at the initial layer visibility.

CROSS-REF   For more information on creating form fields, see Chapter 34.

FIGURE 24.8

The open document is viewed at the default layer visibility with the Layers palette open.

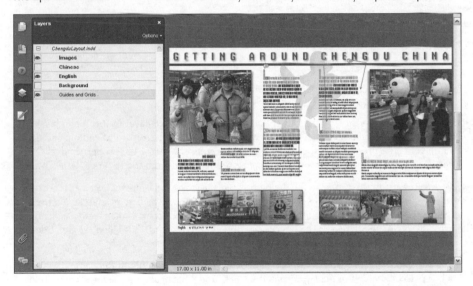

To create the view that you want to display when a user clicks on a button, use the Layers palette to toggle on or off different views. Then create a button using the Button tool. Select the Actions tab in the Button Properties dialog box and select Set layer visibility from the Select Action pull-down menu. In Figure 24.9 you can see the new visibility in the Layers palette; the Chinese language layer is visible as well as the Images and Background layers. This view is different from the Initial View shown in Figure 24.8. After setting the view, create a button field and select Set layer visibility in the Select Action pull-down menu, as shown in Figure 24.9.

CROSS-REF   You can also assign layer visibility to links, Bookmarks, and page actions. For more information on showing visibility and assigning actions, see Chapter 22.

After clicking OK, you can select the Options pull-down menu and choose Reset to Initial Visibility to return to the default view. You can select the Hand tool and click the button to see the new view displayed in the Document pane.

The most difficult part of the process is keeping in mind that you first need to set the visibility you want as the result of clicking the button. After you create a few buttons, the process becomes second nature and creating links to layer visibility will become as easy as creating Bookmarks.

FIGURE 24.9

Use the Layers palette to set the visibility for the resultant view. Select Set layer visibility from the Select Action pull-down menu of the Button Properties dialog box. The link action captures the current view.

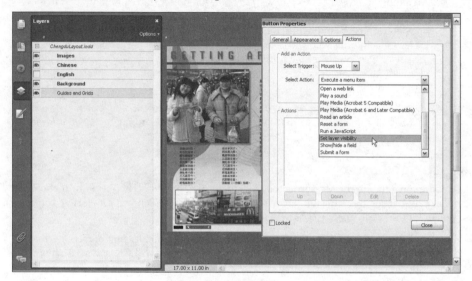

> **TIP** If you want more control for working with layers such as creating layers in existing PDF documents, you can find third-party plug-ins supporting more features for working with layers. Plug-ins such as ARTS PDF Stratify extend the editing of PDF documents with features not supported in Acrobat. Search the internet for tools that work with PDF layers or visit www.artspdf.com/arts_pdf_stratify.asp for more on ARTS PDF Stratify.

Using Measuring Tools

Although using the Measuring tools is not specific to PDF documents containing layers, it can be a great help to users creating engineering drawings and CAD documents for measuring distances and surface area in layered documents. Therefore, I included the use of these tools along with layers. Keep in mind that you can use these tools in any PDF document you open in Acrobat regardless of whether layers are present. Measuring tools, however, are not available in Acrobat Standard. This complete section on using the Measuring tools is relevant only to Acrobat Professional users.

The following are the three tools available to you in the Measuring toolbar:

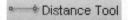

- **Distance tool.** You use the Distance tool to measure linear distances between two x,y coordinates on a document page. To use the tool, click and release the mouse button. Move the cursor to a different location and click again. The measurement is calculated when you make the second click and can be recorded in a comment note.

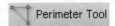

- **Perimeter tool.** You use the Perimeter tool to measure the outside perimeter of any angle or polygon object. To use the tool, click and release the mouse button. Move the cursor and click again. Repeat the steps to continue along a path (right angle, triangle, or polygon). When finished, make the last click and keep the mouse stationary. Click a second time when you see a small circle appear aside the cursor. The second click on the destination point informs Acrobat you're finished measuring. As each segment is drawn, the Distance Tool dialog box opens where measurement information is reported.

- **Area tool.** You use the Area tool with any polygon object (three or more sides) to measure the surface area contained within the perimeter. When using the tool, you need to draw line segments and return to the point of origin to close the path. Acrobat Professional informs you when you reach the point of origin by adding a small circle to the cursor. When you use the Area tool, the circle appears only when you reach the point of origin. After you click at the point of origin, the surface area is calculated within the path you draw.

NEW FEATURE Measuring tools are now available in Acrobat 8 Standard (Windows only) . When PDFs are enabled with Adobe Reader usage rights for commenting, the Measuring tools also show up in Adobe Reader 8.

Measuring surface area

Click the mouse button on a tool in the Measuring toolbar and a dialog box associated with the tool opens, such as the Perimeter Tool dialog box shown in Figure 24.10 when using the Perimeter tool. Here you can make settings choices for the following:

- **Scale Ratio.** Choose a value for the first field box that equals a particular unit of measure you select from the pull-down menus. For example, if you want to scale a drawing at a 5:1 ratio, enter 5 in the first field box and 1 in the second field box.

- **Measuring Markup.** The measurement data and a comment can be contained in a comment note. The comment for the note is derived from the text you type in the Measuring Markup field box. Check the box and type a line of text. The assessment of the measurement is also reported in the comment note. Acrobat automatically supplies this value.

From the Options pull-down menu, you can access the menu commands shown in Figure 24.11.

FIGURE 24.10

The Perimeter Tool dialog box reports information related to a perimeter measurement where you can make settings adjustments before measuring a distance.

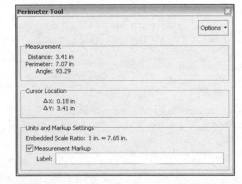

FIGURE 24.11

Click Options to open the pull-down menu.

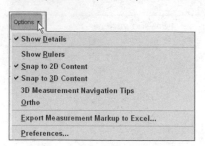

The commands include the following:

- **Show Details.** When Show Details is not selected you see just the measurement coordinates. When this option is selected, the dialog box expands to show x,y coordinates, Scale Ratio information, and the Measuring Markup comment.

- **Show Rulers.** Select the menu command to show/hide rulers.

- **Snap to 2D Content.** When you place the cursor above a line on a drawing, a small square snaps to the line when you have Snap to Content checked. Uncheck the item and no square appears below the cursor. This item is similar to lines drawn when snapping to a grid.

- **Snap to 3D Content.** When viewing 3D drawings, you can use the measuring tools on 3D objects and drawings.

- **Ortho.** When you select this option, your ability to draw is constrained to 90-degree angles.

- **Export Measurement Markup to Excel.** All measurement data that was recorded as a comment (that is, the Measuring Markup option was selected) is exported as a .csv file compatible with Microsoft Excel. When you select this menu command, the Export Measurement Markup dialog box opens where you type a filename and navigate to a destination folder.

- **Preferences.** Select Preferences and the Preferences dialog box opens with the Measuring pane in view. You can set some defaults such as Snap to Content or Use Scale and Units from Document, set markup and not colors, and drawing properties.

To use any one of the measuring tools click on a document page, set the attributes for your measurements in the respective dialog box, and move to another location and click again. If you use the Distance tool, click the mouse button at the destination; using the Perimeter or Area tool, move the mouse and click the next coordinate. For the Perimeter tool where you measure an angle or two sides of an object, click at the destination and click again to end the measurement. For area measurements continue clicking and moving the mouse until you end up at the point of origin. Click the mouse when you see a small circle at the lower-right side of the cursor. When you finish a measurement, the tool's dialog box reports measurement data.

Because the measurement tools are annotation tools, you also have available comment notes and properties settings much the same as when adding comments to a PDF document. To open the Comment & Markup properties for a measurement, open a context menu using either the Select Object tool or the Hand tool and select Properties. The Properties dialog box offers options for note properties such as other comment notes. (See Figure 24.12.)

CROSS-REF For more information on working with note properties, see Chapter 20.

FIGURE 24.12

Open Properties from a context menu and the note properties for the measurement are shown.

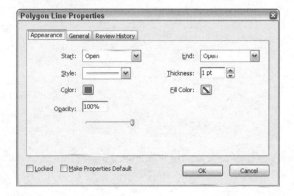

Changing markup appearances

Use the Properties Bar to change appearance attributes for the lines you draw with the Measuring tools. You can change line color and line width, assign arrowheads, and set transparency with the Properties Bar shown in Figure 24.13. In order to enable Properties Bar options. You need to switch from a measurement tool to the Hand tool or Select Object tool. Click the measurement line with either tool to select it and make appearance changes in the Properties Bar. Notice the More button in the Properties Bar. When you click More, it opens the same Properties dialog box shown earlier in Figure 24.12 where you can make similar appearance changes.

FIGURE 24.13

Select a line with the Hand or Select Object tool and use the Properties Bar to adjust appearances for markups created with the Measuring tools.

Measuring Preferences

A number of preference options exist for measuring 2D and 3D objects. When you click one of the Measuring tools, a dialog box opens particular to the tool. Open the Options menu shown in Figure 24.11 and select Preferences. The Preferences dialog box is the same dialog box you access when pressing Ctrl/⌘+K. However, the preferences associated with the object you are measuring (either 2D or 3D) are automatically selected in the left pane as you see in Figure 24.14 when a 2D object is measured.

A number of the preference options appear similar to the options you find in the tools' dialog boxes, the Properties Bar, and the Properties dialog box. You can make choices for default appearances for leaders, labels, line ends, captions, line color, snapping to content, and so on.

FIGURE 24.14

Select Options ⇨ Preferences to open the Preferences dialog box.

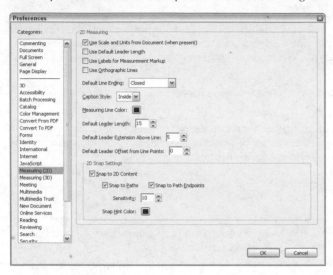

The same holds true for the 3D measurements. When measuring a 3D object and you select Options ⇨ Preferences, the Measuring (3D) preferences open, as shown in Figure 24.15.

FIGURE 24.15

3D preferences offer options for default appearances similar to the options you have in the Options menu, Properties Bar, and Properties dialog box.

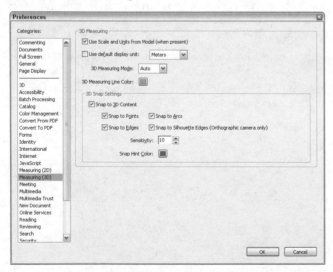

Comments, measurements, and layers

When you add measurement lines on layered documents and open pop-up notes, the lines and notes are visible on any layer in the document. When you hide all layers, the lines and pop-up notes are still visible.

If you have text that appears on all layers, you can edit the text regardless of what layer is visible. For example, adding a header to a document and selecting the TouchUp Text tool to change the text properties is one condition where the text is visible on all layers. Regardless of what layers are in view, you can edit the text; the changes are reflected in all layer views.

CROSS-REF   For information on using the TouchUp Text tool, see Chapter 13.

If you want objects in terms of PDF content to appear on separate layers, you need to return to your authoring application and create the objects on specific layers. Objects and data created in Acrobat cannot become a part of individual layers or toggled on and off in the Layers palette.

Summary

- The PDF 1.5 and above formats support layers from authoring applications that are capable of creating layered files and exporting with Acrobat 6 or greater compatibility.

- You can view and hide individual layers in Acrobat. The initial visibility the layers in view and what layers are hidden are determined at the time the PDF is created.

- Saving files after showing and hiding layers does not change initial visibility. You change initial visibility in the Layer Properties dialog box, where you toggle layers on and off.

- You change layer states for visibility, printing, and exporting data in the Layer properties. Layers can be printed or exported without visibility.

- You merge and flatten layers using menu commands from the Options pull-down menu in the Layers palette.

- Measuring tools enable you to measure distances, perimeters, and surface area. Distances and area are displayed in the Measuring Tools dialog box and distances can be recorded in comment notes.

- Measurings can be exported to Microsoft Excel.

- Measuring distances to scale is available by selecting options for scale values and units of measure in the Measuring Tools dialog box.

- You can create link buttons to display different layer visibility. To create a link action to a view, you first create the desired view in the Layers palette and then set the link action in the Link or Button Properties dialog box.

Chapter 25

Accessibility and Tagged PDF Files

A dobe Acrobat 8 is compliant with United States federal code regulating document accessibility for vision- and motion-challenged persons. This means that screen readers can intelligently interpret the PDFs you create; in other words, PDF files can be read aloud in a reading order as a sighted person would read a document. Through an extensive set of keyboard shortcuts available in Acrobat, almost anyone with vision or motion challenges can share your documents and read them.

In order for a document to be accessible, you must use authoring applications capable of delivering a document's structure to Acrobat. Hence, you need to know something about the internal structure of documents and what programs to use to create the structure required by Acrobat to make a document accessible. Not all the content in a document travels through the PDF creation process with information necessary to make a document completely accessible. Therefore, you need to perform some work in Acrobat to either add accessibility or to polish up a document for delivery to a screen reader in a form that makes sense to the user. In this chapter, I cover how to make documents accessible from authoring programs, as well as how to use Acrobat tools to make existing documents accessible.

Setting Up the Work Environment

The essential tools for working with document accessibility include the Tags panel, Content panel, and Order panel. To view the panels, you need to have a document open in Acrobat. When you start working with accessibility in a document, select View ➪ Navigation Panels ➪ Tags. The Tags panel opens in a palette that also includes the Content, Order, and Fields tabs. You can drag the tab for each panel to the Navigation pane to dock them among the other tabs in the "'free" or "open'" region below the How To panel and above the Attachments tab. Click the Close box in the top-right corner of the palette to close the palette containing the Fields tab.

NEW FEATURE Additionally, you have a new panel in Acrobat 8 you can load in the Navigation pane called Accessibility Report. Reports are shown in this pane instead of the How To pane, as was the case in earlier Acrobat viewers. You don't need to load the pane, because it opens automatically in the navigation pane when you run a Full Check for accessibility.

The TouchUp tools are important not only for editing text and objects, but the TouchUp Reading Order tool was specifically designed to work with reading order on accessible documents. Be certain to load the TouchUp tools. Select Tools ⇨ Customize Toolbars or open a context menu on the Toolbar Well and select More tools. Check the check box in the Advanced Editing toolbar for TouchUp Reading Order Tool. Pick and choose other tools in this toolbar you expect to use, and click OK. To dock the toolbars, select Dock All Toolbars from a context menu opened from the Toolbar Well.

Creating Accessible Documents

The terms "document accessibility," "structure," and "tagged PDFs" may be a mystery to you. If the term "accessibility" is new, then you need to begin with an understanding of what accessible documents are before working with them. After you know more about document accessibility, you can move forward to look at how to create an accessible document, and then look at how you can edit accessible documents. Therefore, the three areas to work with are understanding accessibility, creating accessible documents from authoring programs, and finally, working with accessible documents in Acrobat

Understanding accessibility

Sighted people can view a document on the computer or read a printed page and easily discern the difference between titles, subtitles, columns, graphic images, graphic elements, and so on. With regard to Acrobat PDFs, you can easily see the difference between background designs, button links, Bookmarks, animation, and form fields, and you typically see visual clues to know where buttons and fields exist.

Screen Readers

I use the term "screen reader" extensively in this chapter. When I use this term, I'm referring to tools created by third parties to read open documents aloud in Acrobat and other programs or from files in various formats saved to disk.

Screen readers range in price from $99 to over $1,000. The advantage of using third-party products with Acrobat PDF files is that they can read aloud single words as well as spell out words character by character. Through keyboard controls, users choose reading rates, audio output levels, voices, and navigation.

Screen readers are typically software programs installed on either Mac OS or Windows. More programs support Windows than Macintosh operating systems, but developers have been increasing their support for both platforms. In past years, PDF documents were not supported by many developers. Today, much more support exists for reading PDF documents with the Adobe Reader software.

For a complete list of screen readers that have been tested with Acrobat, log on to Adobe's Web site at http://access.adobe.com. From Adobe's Web page you'll find URL links to vendor sites as well as general information about accessibility.

With regard to screen-reading devices, which depend on software to generate audio output from an Acrobat PDF file, the software readers aren't intelligent enough to distinguish differences based on visual clues. For example, a screen reader may interpret a three-columned document as one continuous column and read the text from left to right across all three columns row by row. Obviously the output is useless to the end user working with a screen reader. Screen readers interpret headings, subheadings, and tables the same as body copy, and they offer no distinction in the structure unless the screen reader software has some clue that these items are different from the body text.

Some authoring programs provide you an opportunity when creating the PDF file to retain the underlying structure of a document in the resulting PDF file. With a series of tags and retention of the document structure, screen readers use alternate text to make distinctions in the document much like the visual user would interpret a page. The document flow, alternate text for graphic elements, distinctions between headings, and so on, can all be managed in Acrobat when the internal document structural tree is included in the PDF export. When files are not exported with the document structure, you can use Acrobat commands to add structure to PDFs. In order to make it possible for people with screen readers to navigate your PDF documents correctly, the underlying structure must be present.

PDF files fall into three categories when you are talking about a document's structure:

- **Unstructured PDF files.** Unstructured PDF documents could not be interpreted by screen readers with complete document integrity in earlier versions of Acrobat. For example, when you exported the PDF to other formats such as a Rich Text Format (RTF), the basic paragraph structure was preserved, but tables, lists, and some text formatting were lost. In Acrobat 8, unstructured documents can be interpreted by screen readers with accuracy. What remains as an unstructured document when using Acrobat 8 are image files converted to PDF such as scanned documents. These files clearly are not structured.

- **Structured PDF files.** Structured PDF files can be read by screen readers, but the reliability is much less than the next category of tagged PDF documents. When you export structured PDF files to other formats, more structural content is preserved, but tables and lists can be lost. Additionally, structured documents, such as the unstructured documents discussed previously, do not support text reflows for different-sized devices.

- **Tagged PDF files.** Tagged PDFs contain both the document structure and a hierarchical structure tree where all the internal structure about the document's content is interpreted. Tagged PDFs have the highest reliability when you're repurposing files for screen reader output and saving files in other formats such as RTF, HTML, XHTML, and XML. In addition, tagged PDF files support text reflow for viewing on different-sized screens and devices and accommodate any zoom level on a monitor.

CROSS-REF For more information on exporting PDF content, see Chapter 9. For more on document structure, see "Understanding Structure" in this chapter.

NOTE Structured documents were introduced with Acrobat 4 (PDF 1.3) and tagged documents were introduced with Acrobat 5 (PDF 1.4). PDFs created prior to version 1.3 had no document structure and PDFs created before version 1.4 could not be tagged. With later versions of Acrobat, document structure and tagging could be added to these PDFs from within Acrobat.

The goal for you when creating PDF documents for accessibility is to be certain you use PDF documents that are not only structured, but also tagged PDFs. After you create tagged PDFs, you can work with the structure tree and modify the contents for optimum use. In terms of making Acrobat PDFs accessible, you must consider several criteria to optimize files for effective handling by screen readers:

- **Assessing accessibility.** Fortunately, Acrobat provides tools for determining whether a PDF file is an accessible document. As a first order of business you should plan on assessing a file for accessibility. If you work with legacy files or files that are created from authoring programs that don't support the export of the document structure, be certain to make the document accessible before beginning an editing session.

CROSS-REF For adding accessibility to PDF files from within Acrobat see the section "Making existing PDFs accessible" later in this chapter.

- **Logical reading order.** The text should follow a logical flow. You need to properly define column text in terms of the path that a screen reader follows (that is, down one column; then begin at the top of the second column, and so on). You should also mark headings and subheadings for distinction.

- **Alternative text descriptions for image and graphic elements.** Those familiar with HTML know that you can code an HTML document with alternate tags so users with text-only browsers can understand the structure of Web pages. The same principle for accessible documents applies. Alternate text needs to be inserted so the screen reader can interpret graphic elements.

- **Form field descriptions.** Form fields need to be described with text to inform a user with a screen reader that a form field is present.

- **Field tab order.** Setting the logical tab order for fields on a form is important for the visual user. With screen readers it is essential. The logical tab order for fields should be strictly followed.

- **Document security.** If documents are secured with Acrobat security, you must use 128-bit encryption compatible with Acrobat 5 and above. If you use compatibility less than Acrobat 5 or 40-bit encryption, the PDF is rendered inaccessible.

- **Links and interactivity.** Use form fields for link buttons with descriptions so the user knows that another destination or a link action is invoked if he or she selects the field.

- **Document language.** Screen readers typically deliver accessible documents in only one language. To protect your documents against inoperability with new releases, specify a document language when creating accessible PDFs. Document language specification is also important when using tools in Acrobat for checking accessibility.

CROSS-REF For more information on field tab order, see Chapter 34. For more information on document security, see Chapter 26. For more information on links and interactivity, see Chapter 22.

Adding accessibility in authoring applications

Not all authoring programs currently support accessibility. This phenomenon may change with new upgrades to software, so what is said today may change tomorrow. As of this writing the programs offering the best support for document accessibility include Microsoft Word version 2000 or higher, Adobe PageMaker 7.0 or higher, Adobe FrameMaker, Adobe LiveCycle Designer, and Adobe InDesign 2.0 or higher. If you use other authoring applications, you do have the option to make documents accessible with Acrobat Standard and Acrobat Professional.

When converting Microsoft Word files to PDF, be certain to use the PDFMaker in the Word toolbar or from the Adobe PDF menu in Word. Set up the conversion settings for enabling accessibility and reflow with tagged PDF documents. This option is available in the Settings tab in the Acrobat PDFMaker dialog box. Select the "Enable Accessibility and Reflow with tagged Adobe PDF" check box.

CROSS-REF For more on creating PDF files with accessibility and tags from Microsoft Office applications, see Chapter 8.

When creating documents with text, images, charts, diagrams, and so on, using a professional layout program often works better than a word processor. Adobe InDesign CS is an ideal tool for creating layouts that you need to make accessible. When you design a document for accessibility, be precise about how you add elements on each page. The order in which you lay out documents can have an effect on the order of the exported structure. For example, adding a block of text, and then importing an image, may result in the text appearing first in the structure tree and the image following the text even if you move the elements so the image appears first on the page. The only way to observe the results of how the document structure ultimately converts to PDF is to practice and examine the tags structure tree in Acrobat versus your layouts. You can develop a workflow that minimizes the work in Acrobat to properly create the structure needed for optimum performance when read by a screen reader.

 If you arrange objects in an authoring program like Adobe InDesign and the reading order is not following the viewing order, you can cut either text or images and paste them back into the document. If, for example, an image should be first in the structure tree followed by text, but the order is reversed when you examine the tags in Acrobat, cut the text block and paste it back into the document in InDesign. Recreate the PDF and you'll find the order changed according to the order that the elements were last placed on the page. This method is not always a precise solution for reordering elements, but can often be used to resolve problems.

Making existing PDFs accessible

If you have PDF documents either from legacy files or from files converted from authoring applications that do not support exports to PDF with tags, you can use Acrobat commands to add structure to the document and make the files accessible. The first step is checking a document for accessibility. If the document contains no tags, then you can add tags in Acrobat Standard or Acrobat Professional.

Performing a Quick Check

To determine whether a document is accessible, you can perform a Quick Check. In Acrobat Standard or Acrobat Professional choose Advanced ➪ Accessibility ➪ Quick Check (or press Shift+Ctrl/⌘+6). In Adobe Reader, choose Document ➪ Accessibility Quick Check (or press Shift+Ctrl/⌘+6). This method of checking the PDF is a quick analysis to determine whether tags exist in the file. When the check is completed, a dialog box opens informing you of the accessibility status. If the document is not accessible, the dialog box message states that the document is not structured and reading problems may occur.

NOTE Document accessibility can be checked in Adobe Reader. Making a document accessible, however, requires Acrobat Standard or Acrobat Professional.

Performing a Full Check (Acrobat Professional only)

Acrobat Professional offers you a more sophisticated analysis where more file attributes are checked and a report is created in a file or by adding comments to the open PDF document, or both. To use the Full Check option, follow these steps.

STEPS: Checking accessibility in Acrobat Professional

1. **Choose Advanced ➪ Accessibility ➪ Full Check.** The Accessibility Full Check dialog box, shown in Figure 25.1, opens.

2. **Check the box for Create Accessibility Report and Create comments in document.** Checking these boxes creates a report and adds comment notes in the document pertaining to the results of the analysis. All errors found during the check are reported in comment notes.

FIGURE 25.1

When you run a Full Check in Acrobat Professional, you can choose options for what content to check.

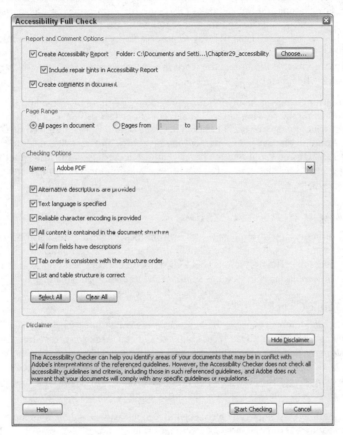

3. **Select the Checking Options for the items you want to check.** Enable the check boxes in this section for items you want to check. In this example I selected all the check boxes.

4. **Click the Browse button.** Identify the location for the report file if you want a report saved to an HTML file, which you can view in the Accessibility Report panel.

5. **When you set all the attributes, click Start Checking.** Acrobat opens a dialog box similar to Figure 25.2, reporting the findings.

FIGURE 25.2

After running the Full Check, the findings are reported in a dialog box.

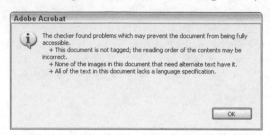

NEW FEATURE After completing the check, the Accessibility Report pane (new in Acrobat 8) opens and displays a more detailed report as shown in Figure 25.3. If you selected Create comments in document, comment notes may appear reporting problems in untagged documents.

FIGURE 25.3

The Accessibility Report pane shows you a detailed report of the full accessibility check findings.

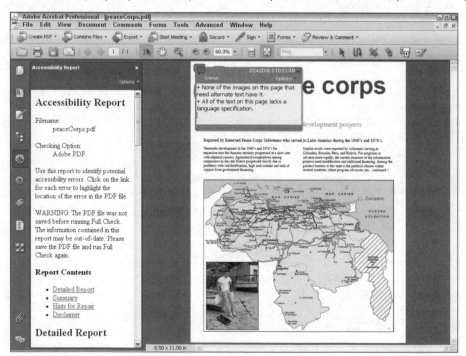

An Accessibility report is also saved to your hard drive in HTML format. If you click the Browse button in the Accessibility Full Check dialog box, you can target a location for the saved report. By default, the report is saved to your My Documents folder (Windows) or your Documents folder (Macintosh). Open your Web browser and select File Open. Navigate to the folder where the report is found and open the file. The report is displayed in the browser window.

The links in the HTML document link directly to the PDF file and highlight the item associated with the link. Click a link in your Web browser and the PDF file opens in the foreground with the respective item highlighted, as shown in Figure 25.4. You can correct problems by clicking links in the Web browser and correcting the problems in the PDF document.

FIGURE 25.4

Click a link in the Web browser and the referenced item in the PDF is highlighted.

- 1 images(s) with no alternate text. (How to Add Alternate Text)
  1. No alternate text
- 1 element(s) that are not contained within the structure tree. (How to Add Tags)
  1. Inaccessible page content

Click link in Web browser and problem item in the PDF is highlighted.

Adding accessibility

Keep in mind you are always best served by adding accessibility at the time a PDF document is created from authoring programs supporting exports to PDF with accessibility and tags. If you have files for which either returning to the authoring program is impractical or the authoring program is incapable of exporting to PDF as tagged files, choose Advanced ⇨ Accessibility ⇨ Add Tags to Document. Or from the Tags panel in the Navigation pane, select Add Tags to Document from the Options pull-down menu. Immediately after you select the menu command from either Acrobat Standard or Acrobat Professional, a slider bar opens displaying Acrobat's progress in adding tags to the document. After completion, no confirmation dialog box opens to report the status. If problems were encountered while adding the tags, a dialog box opens, reporting the problems found.

After adding the tags, you can return to the Quick Check or Full Check menu command and check the document for accessibility.

If a file has tags and you choose Advanced ⇨ Accessibility ⇨ Add Tags to Document, Acrobat opens a dialog box informing you that the file already has tags. Adding tags is not permitted using the menu command. If you are unhappy with the current tagging, you can remove all tags from the document, and then reapply with this method. To remove all tags, open the Tags panel in the Navigation pane. Select the topmost tag (typically labeled "Tags") and select Delete Tag from the Options pull-down menu.

Understanding Structure

To understand more clearly the need for creating accessibility and adding tags to a document, look at Figure 25.5 as an example. This document contains several items that need attention to make the file accessible and comprehensible when read by a screen reader.

FIGURE 25.5

A document with images, illustrations, and text in multiple columns needs to have the structure modified for proper reading by a screen reader.

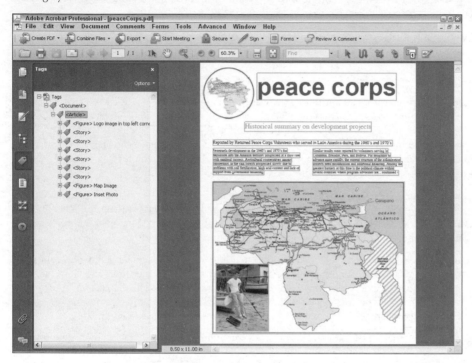

In Figure 25.5 the items of importance in terms of accessibility include the following:

- **The first element on the page is a logo.** A screen reader won't interpret the logo unless you add some alternate text to the document describing the object. Adjacent to the logo on the right side is text that a screen reader can read after you make the document accessible. If the text does not read properly, the two lines of text need to be modified for the proper interpretation by the screen reader.

- **The two lines of text are in a single column.** These lines should be read in logical order without any problems. They are shown here to illustrate the difference between the two lines and the two columns following.

- **The text is blocked in two columns.** Unless the structure is established for the screen reader to read down one column before moving to the second column, the screen reader defaults at a left-to-right reading order, reading across both columns.

- **Item four is a large map.** Alternate text for the illustration is needed for the screen reader to explain what graphic appears on the page.

- **Item five is an inset photo.** The alternate text for the map can describe the photo or the photo can have an alternate text description. Either way, you need to create the alternate text for the screen reader to fully interpret the graphics.

When you export to PDF from authoring programs with tags, the structure of the document for the blocks of text in logical reading orders is preserved. In the example in Figure 25.5, the single and double-column text is typically not a problem when the file is read by a screen reader. Images, however, need some form of manual editing. Even the best source exporting with tags wouldn't be able to describe the visual elements in the layout. These are subjective items that need a description.

If using a program such as Microsoft Word, you can add alternate text in Word before the file is exported to PDF. In other applications you need to create the alternate text in Acrobat.

Using the Tags palette

When you export a document from an authoring program with tags or use the Add Tags to Document menu command, a *structure tree* is created in the PDF file. The structure tree is a hierarchical order of the elements contained in the file. Elements may be in the form of heads, subheads, body text, figures, tables, annotations, and other items identified as separate individual structural elements. The hierarchy contains a nested order of the elements with parent/child relationships. A heading, for example, may have a subhead. The heading in this case is a parent element with the subheading a child element.

When a document contains tags, you view the tag elements and the structure tree in the Tags panel. Open the Tags panel and click on the top item. By default, you see an icon labeled Tags with a plus (+) (Windows) or right-pointing arrow (Macintosh) symbol adjacent to it. Click the symbol and you open the tree at one level. Other child elements are nested below.

The Tags palette may have an extensive list of elements depending on your document length and complexity. If you want to edit an element or find it in the document, you need some help from Acrobat to find out exactly what tag in the Tags palette is related to what element on a given page. The help comes in the form of a menu command in the Tags palette. Click the down-pointing arrow adjacent to Options in the Tags palette and select Highlight Content. The content is highlighted as shown earlier in Figure 25.5.

When you return to the structure tree, the items you select are highlighted on the respective elements on pages in the Document pane. Click an element and Acrobat navigates to the page where the content is located. The object is highlighted with a keyline border, as shown in Figure 25.5.

Adding alternate text

In the example in Figure 25.5, the logo appearing at the top of the page is an image file. When a screen reader reads the document, no specific instructions are contained in the document to interpret this image. As an option, you can create alternate text so a visually challenged person knows a graphic element exists on the page. To add alternate text in a tagged PDF document, follow these steps.

STEPS: Adding alternate text to tagged elements

1. **Open a tagged PDF file.** Or add tags to a document. Open the Tags panel in the Navigation pane. Note: If you didn't set up the working environment as described in the beginning of the chapter, choose View ➪ Navigation Panels ➪ Tags to open the Tags panel.

2. **Open the structure tree.** Click the Tags Root icon to the left of the text. On Windows a plus (+) symbol appears adjacent to the text. On the Macintosh, a right-pointing arrow appears next to the text. Clicking the icon opens the tags tree.

3. **Select Highlight Content.** If you haven't selected the menu command for highlighting content, open the Options palette in the Tags panel and select Highlight Content.

4. **Find the element for which the alternate text is to be added.** In this example, the figure below the second paragraph (<P>) was selected. When you click the Figure tag, the logo at the top-left

corner of the page is highlighted. Alternately, you can also select the TouchUp Object tool, click an object on the page, and select Find Tag from Selection from the Tags palette Options pull-down menu.

5. **Open the element's properties.** Select the TouchUp Object tool from the Advanced Editing tool-bar you opened earlier. If you do not have this tool available, choose Tools ⇨ Advanced Editing ⇨ TouchUp Object Tool. Click the element and open a context menu. Select Properties from the menu options.

6. **Add alternate text.** Click the Tags panel. Add a title for the tag by typing a title in the Title field box. The title is not necessary for, nor read by, the screen reader. Add the text you want the screen reader to read out loud in the Alternate Text field. Select the pull-down menu for Language and select a language. The edits made in this example are shown in Figure 25.6.

7. **Close the TouchUp Properties dialog box.**

FIGURE 25.6

Fill in the fields for a title and alternate text, and select a language in the TouchUp Properties dialog box.

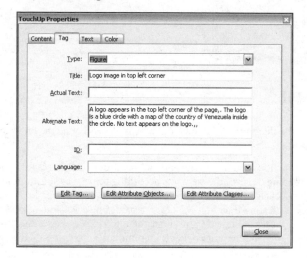

Using the Content tab

The Content tab contains a hierarchical list of the objects in the PDF file. Objects are listed in the order in which they appear on the page, similar to the logical structure tree in the Tags palette. Click the Content tab to open it in the Navigation pane and you see a view similar to Figure 25.7. Click an object and move it up or down to change the order of the objects.

The Content tab can be helpful when you want to navigate to and highlight a content item listed in the tab. Click an item such as a text item or figure and the page appears in the Document pane with the respective item selected.

In addition to physically reordering objects, a number of menu commands are available from the Options pull-down menu. Among the menu commands is an option to create a New Container. Notice in Figure 25.5 all the tags are nested within containers. You can select a tag and select New Container to add alternate text to any area in the document.

FIGURE 25.7

Click objects and drag up or down to reorder the objects in the Content pane.

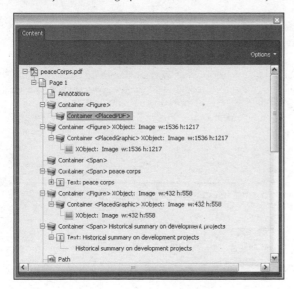

Using the Order tab

You use the Order tab to correct reading order problems. After you create a tagged PDF document, Acrobat infers the reading order from the document structure. You may need to change the order for text and images to create a more logical flow in the document.

 You use the Order tab in conjunction with the TouchUp Reading Order tool. Select the tool and open the Order tab. Acrobat lists the reading order of the elements according to page as shown in Figure 25.8. To reorder the elements or regions, click and drag a tag up or down to change the reading order. Each tagged object is numbered on a page indicating the order the tags are read. From the Touchup Reading Order dialog box you can change the attributes of tags and renumber them to change the reading order. Figure 25.8 shows the tagged elements and the reading order defined by numbers adjacent to each tagged object.

Checking accessible tags

You can check your work easily in Acrobat by having Acrobat read the document. Choose View ➪ Read Out Loud ➪ Read This Page Only. The default text-to-speech voice installed on your computer reads the text as a screen reader would interpret it. If you prepare files for screen readers, you can use Acrobat's built-in reading engine to read aloud the text in the document and the alternate tags you add to the file.

Although the Read Out Loud menu command is not intended to replace screen readers, the feature in all Acrobat viewers offers you a good means for checking files that meet accessible standards.

FIGURE 25.8

To change reading order, click and drag tags up or down in the Order tab.

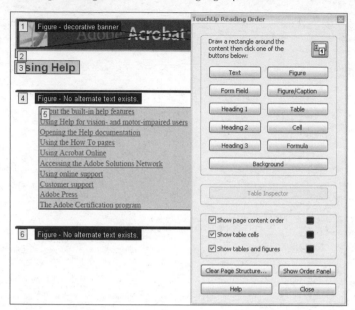

TIP You can save PDF files as accessible text. Select File ➪ Save As and select Text (Accessible).txt from the Save as Type (Windows) or Format (Macintosh) pull-down menu. The saved text is saved in the same reading order as when you read a document aloud.

CROSS-REF For more information on Read Out Loud and controlling voices and reading speeds, see Chapter 5.

In addition to using Acrobat's built-in function for reading documents aloud, you can acquire a low-cost plug-in from a third-party developer without purchasing a screen reader. PDFAloud, marketed by textHELP Systems (www.texthelp.com), is more robust than Acrobat's Read Out Loud command. With PDFAloud you can read text a word, sentence, or paragraph at a time. The plug-in also offers you synchronized colored highlighting while the text is read.

Viewing Accessible Documents

Some accessibility requirements extend beyond text-to-speech reading. Individuals with assistive devices for visual impairments can view documents when text is zoomed and when text color significantly contrasts with background colors. You can modify the display of documents on your screen by adjusting preferences for Accessibility in the Preferences dialog box, or you can customize viewing by choosing Advanced ➪ Accessibility ➪ Setup Assistant (in Adobe Reader, select Document ➪ Accessibility Setup Assistant.), which opens the Accessibility Setup Assistant dialog box, shown in Figure 25.9.

FIGURE 25.9

The Accessibility Setup Assistant contains options for screen displays and reading orders.

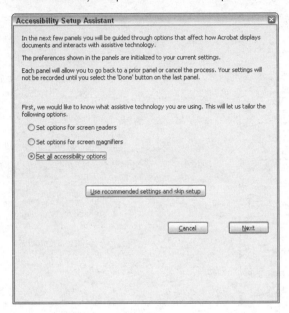

You make attribute choices in a pane and click the Next button to advance through the Accessibility Setup Assistant. You can make choices for color displays, text smoothing, zoom displays, reading orders, and page delivery by moving through the panes. When you finish, these selections will be set in the Accessibility Preferences for you.

Summary

- Screen readers can interpret accessible PDF files and create audio output for people with vision and motion challenges.

- Adobe PDFMaker for Microsoft products, including Word, Excel, Visio, and so on; Adobe PageMaker 7 and higher; and Adobe FrameMaker, Adobe LiveCycle Designer, Adobe InDesign 2.0 and higher are capable of creating tagged and accessible PDF forms.

- You can add tags to PDF documents from a menu command within Acrobat Standard and Acrobat Professional.

- You check files for accessibility with the Quick Check command in Adobe Reader, Acrobat Standard, and Acrobat Professional or with a Full Check in Acrobat Professional.

- Tagged documents contain a structure tree. Elements in the tree locate respective elements in the document if you enable the Highlight Content menu command.

- You can add alternate text to elements in Acrobat by addressing the element's properties.

- You can make text and background color changes in the Accessibility Preferences dialog box or via the Accessibility Setup Assistant.

Part V

PDF Publishing

Chapter 26

Authentication and Security

A crobat PDF documents can be secured using a host of different security methods and encryption tools to prevent unauthorized users from opening files and changing documents. Acrobat Security combined with digital signatures enables you to protect data and secure files for just about any purpose. There's much to learn about using Acrobat Security and digital signatures, and it's important to know what levels of security are available to you and what kinds of security you can apply in many different circumstances. This chapter covers a broad description of security and digitally signing PDF documents and the methods you use to protect files against unauthorized viewing and editing.

Setting Up the Work Environment

You add security to a PDF document through menu commands and the Secure Task button that appears in the Tasks toolbar when you return to the default view. If all you want to do is add security to PDFs, you can open a context menu and select Reset Toolbars from the menu options.

If you want to add digital signature fields on a form where users can digitally sign documents, you need to use the Forms tools or use a document created in Adobe LiveCycle Designer that contains signature fields. Documents can be signed without using signature fields, but when you want to add a field for signing the document, you'll want to work on a form created in Adobe Designer with signature fields or have the Form tools available in Acrobat Professional.

For the examples in this chapter, open a context menu on the Toolbar Well and select Forms Toolbar. In addition to the Forms tools, add the Properties bar by opening a context menu on the Toolbar Well and selecting Properties Bar from the menu. After the toolbars open, dock them in the Toolbar Well.

CROSS-REF For information on creating signature fields, see Chapters 33 and 34.

IN THIS CHAPTER

Adding password security to PDFs

Creating signature profiles

Certifying documents

Securing files with Create PDF Online

Using digital signatures with PDF Packages

Using Trusted Identities

Verifying electronic signatures

Using security envelopes

NOTE   Use of the Forms tools is available only in Acrobat Professional; however, Acrobat Standard and Adobe Reader users (when using enabled files) can create digital signatures and signature fields. Signature fields can be created in Adobe LiveCycle Designer, which is available only on Windows. Windows users can use LiveCycle Designer or Acrobat for adding Signature fields and security. Macintosh users need to add signature fields in Acrobat Professional.

Restricting the Opening and Editing of Files

Acrobat security comes in many different forms, allowing you to secure PDF files against user viewing and/or editing in many ways based on the level of security you assign to a PDF document. However, depending on what level of security you apply to a file, the document may or may not be able to be opened by users of earlier versions of Acrobat. Therefore, when you add security it is critical to know your audience and what versions of Acrobat they are using to view files.

Methods of security available in Acrobat include three types of restrictions. You can secure a file against opening and editing by using Password Security at different levels of encryption. You can also secure files using public key certificates, or if your organization is using Adobe LiveCycle Policy Server you can apply security policies from here. You should think of the first method (Password Security) as security you might apply globally to PDFs when you want the public to have a password to open your PDFs or you want to restrict certain Acrobat features, such as content editing or printing. In this regard, you secure documents for what is referred to as *unknown* users. You can further delineate securing individual files into two categories. You can secure documents by applying security settings that you select via options in security windows, or you can create a security policy in which the same level of security and encryption attributes are applied to documents each time you secure files.

Think of the second method (Certificate Security) as restrictions you want to apply for a selected group of people, or what are referred to as *known* users. You might want to restrict opening documents or PDF editing for a group of co-workers, colleagues, or individuals with whom you have direct communication. This method requires the use of digital IDs and public key certificates. This form of security also uses a security policy you create from public key certificates derived from users' digital IDs.

The third method is securing files with the Adobe Policy Server. The Adobe Policy as a product is not covered in this book. Please see the Acrobat Help Guide for more details or information. Adobe Policy Server enables you to apply server-based security policies to PDF documents. One of the great benefits for using a policy server is that you can encrypt documents for limited time use.

NEW FEATURE   What is covered in this book is the new Acrobat 8 feature where you can submit files to Adobe on a fee-per-file basis using the Protect an Adobe PDF File with the Create PDF Online service. For personal and small business uses, this new feature enables you to submit PDFs to Adobe where the Adobe Policy Server is used to encrypt the PDFs. For more information on using Create Adobe PDF Online see the section, "Protect an Adobe PDF File," later in this chapter.

Keep in mind that Security Policies can be used with either Password Security or Certificate Security.

The discussion on Acrobat Security starts with the first method of applying security for a more global environment for unknown users. Later in this chapter encryption using a security policy with public key certificates for known users is covered along with digital signatures.

Using password security

To secure an open document, choose File ➪ Properties. Click the Security tab in the Document Properties dialog box. Notice the Security Method pull-down menu. Four options are listed in the menu for different security methods. The default selection is No Security. Open the pull-down menu and select Password

Security. The Password Security – Settings dialog box shown in Figure 26.1 opens. Depending on which compatibility option you select from the Compatibility pull-down menu, the bottom of the dialog box activates additional options or removes options. In Figure 26.1, you can see that when choosing Acrobat 7 compatibility, all options are available in the dialog box. If you select an earlier version, such as Acrobat 3 compatibility, some options are grayed out, such as two of the options in the Select Document Components to Encrypt section.

FIGURE 26.1

Depending on what level of compatibility you choose, the options available for Password Security will change.

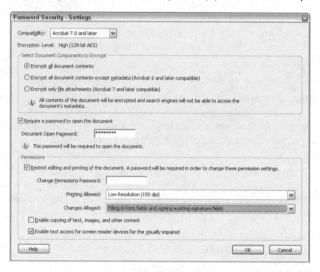

Creating a Policy for Adding Security

If you've used earlier versions of Acrobat, accessing the Document Properties dialog box is something you are probably familiar with. It's a fast and easy way for adding document security and it's okay when you have a single document you want to secure and never again want to secure additional documents with the same permissions and restrictions. In Acrobat 7 and 8, Adobe Systems has made securing PDF documents much easier when you want to routinely secure PDF files using the same permissions settings. The preferred method for securing files in Acrobat 7 and 8 is to create a *Security Policy*.

To create a security policy you use the Secure Task button pull-down menu and select Manage Security Policies from the same menu. Either choice opens a dialog box where you create a new policy. You step through a New Security Policy Wizard where you make choices for the security method you want to use and make choices for the permissions you want to assign to a document.

Once you create the policy, you can easily apply the same policy when you want to secure additional documents without the need to select the different permissions options each time you apply security. For more detail information on creating and using security policies, see "Using a security policy" later in this chapter.

You add Password Security via this dialog box any time you want to restrict users from opening a file and/or making changes to the content. Users must know the password you add in this dialog box in order to open a file and/or make changes. The options available to you include the following:

- **Compatibility.** The options from this pull-down menu include Acrobat 3, Acrobat 5, Acrobat 6, and Acrobat 7 compatibility. If you select Acrobat 7 compatibility and save the PDF document, users need an Acrobat 7 viewer or greater to open the file. The same holds true when saving with Acrobat 5 compatibility. Users need Acrobat 5 or greater to view PDFs created with Acrobat 5 compatibility.

- **Encryption level.** Below the Compatibility pull-down menu, Acrobat informs you what level of encryption is applied to the document based on the compatibility choice made in the pull-down menu. If you select Acrobat 3 from the Compatibility pull-down menu, the encryption level is 40-bit encryption. Acrobat 5 and Acrobat 6 compatibility are encrypted with 128-bit RC4 encryption. Acrobat 7 and 8 supports 128-bit AES. All the higher encryption levels offer you more options for restricting printing and editing.

  - **Encrypt all document contents.** This option applies encryption to all document contents.

  - **Encrypt all document contents except metadata (Acrobat 6 and later compatible).** Use this option to apply encryption to all document contents except document metadata. As the item name implies, this level of security is compatible with Acrobat 6 and later. This is a good selection if you want to have the metadata in your secure documents available for a search engine.

  - **Encrypt only file attachments (Acrobat 7 and later compatible).** Use this option to encrypt file attachments but not the PDF document. This option is only compatible with Acrobat 7 and above. You might use this when sending an eEnvelope or a PDF Package where you want to encrypt the contents only.

CROSS-REF For more information on encrypting eEnvelopes, see the section "Using Secure PDF Delivery" later in this chapter. For more information on PDF Packages, see Chapter 12.

TIP Encrypting only file attachments is a nifty feature that was introduced in Acrobat 7. As an example for using this feature, you might have a document such as a memo you want to distribute to all employees. Attached to the memo you might have a financial report, draft company policy document, or some other file you want to have reviewed by management personnel only. All company personnel can see the memo, but only those who have a security password can open the file attachments. You can likewise secure files in a PDF Package. The entire package, or individual files within the package, can be secured.

- **Require a password to open the document.** Select this check box if you want a user to supply a password to open the PDF document. After selecting the check box, the field box for Document Open Password becomes active and you can add a password. Before you exit the dialog box, Acrobat prompts you in another dialog box to confirm the password. Note: if you select Encrypt only file attachments (Acrobat 7 and later compatible), you must enter a password to be able to open the attachment(s).

- **Restrict editing and printing of the document. A password will be required in order to change these permission settings.** Select this check box if you want to restrict permissions from the items active in the Permissions area of the dialog box. You can use this with or without a Document Open Password.

- **Change Permissions Password.** Fill in the field box with a password. If you also have a Document Open Password, the passwords must be different. Acrobat opens a dialog box and

informs you to make different password choices if you attempt to use the same password for opening the file and setting permissions.

■ **Printing Allowed.** If you use Acrobat 3 compatibility, the options are available to either enable printing or disallow printing. The choices are None and High Resolution. Even though the choice reads High Resolution, the result simply enables users to print your file. With Acrobat 5, 6, and 7 compatibility, you have a third choice for enabling printing at a lower resolution (150 dpi). If you select Low Resolution (150 dpi) from the menu options, users are restricted to printing the file at the lower resolution. This choice is typically something you might use for files intended for digital prepress and high-end printing, eBooks or eContent, or to protect your content from being printed and then re-scanned.

■ **Changes Allowed.** From this pull-down menu you make choices for the kinds of changes you allow users to perform on the document. Acrobat 3 compatibility offers you four choices; Acrobat 5, 6, and 7 compatibility offers you five choices. These options include the following:

   ■ **None.** This option prevents a user from any kind of editing and content extraction.

   ■ **Inserting, deleting, and rotating pages.** This option is not available when using Acrobat 3 compatibility. Users are permitted to insert, delete, and rotate pages. If you create PDFs for eBooks, allowing users to rotate pages can be helpful when they view PDFs on tablets and portable devices.

   ■ **Page layout, filling in forms, and signing existing signature fields (Acrobat 3 only).** Select this option to enable users to extract pages, insert pages, and also perform actions on form fields.

   ■ **Filling in form fields and signing existing signature fields.** If you create Acrobat forms and want users to be able to fill in the form fields and digitally sign documents, enable this check box. Forms are useless to users without the ability to fill in the form fields.

   ■ **Commenting, filling in form fields, and signing existing signature fields.** You might use this option in a review process where you want to have users comment on a design but you don't want them to make changes to your file. You can secure the document against editing, but allow commenting and form field filling in and signing. When you enable form filling in with this option or the Filling in form fields and signing existing signature fields option, users are restricted against changing your form design and cannot make edits other than filling in the fields. A good example of using this option might be having your customers fill out a form, and also add comments to describe their selections.

   ■ **Any except extracting pages.** With this option, all the permissions are available to users except extracting pages from the document and creating separate PDFs from selected pages.

■ **Enable copying of text, images, and other content and access for the visually impaired.** This option is available when selecting Acrobat 3.0 and later. If you restrict permissions for any of the previous pull-down menu options, users aren't allowed to copy data. You can add permission for content copying by enabling this check box. Enable copying of text, images, and other content: The setting above was replaced with two settings in Acrobat 5.0 and higher security. This setting restricts the user from copying information from your PDF.

■ **Enable text access for screen reader devices for the visually impaired.** This option is available for all versions except Acrobat 3 compatibility. As a matter of practice, checking this box is always a good idea. If you check this box, you can restrict all editing features while permitting users with screen reading devices the ability to read your files. If the check box is not enabled, screen readers and other devices designed for accessibility are not able to read the PDF document and all the options for using the View ⇨ Read Out Loud menu command are grayed out. Furthermore, users

Understanding Password Encryption

When you encrypt a file with password security, it's important to understand that tools exist that can be used to decrypt files. Just about anything that can be encrypted using a password can be broken given enough time with the right tools. Software applications used for decryption run through cycles combining different characters to arrive at the right combination that accesses the encrypted file.

If you use a three-character password, the amount of time to break your password by a sophisticated decryption tool might be a matter of a few hours. As you add characters to the password, the decryption tool requires more time to explore all combinations of characters. If you add 10 to 12 characters to a password, the most sophisticated tools on the fastest computers can take decades of constant running to come up with the right combination of characters to break a password.

As a matter of practice when assigning permissions for sensitive material, always use no fewer than eight characters to secure a file. Adobe Systems has provided a sophisticated tool that enables you to protect your content if you observe a few simple rules.

can index your files with Acrobat Professional by using Acrobat Catalog when this check box is enabled, regardless of the other items you prevent users from accessing.

CROSS-REF For more information on screen readers and accessibility, see Chapter 25. For more information on creating index files, see Chapter 6.

After you make choices for the password permissions, click OK, click OK again in the Document Properties dialog box, and then save your file to apply the security. If you close the document without saving, the security settings are not applied.

Using a security policy

Security policies are settings you save that are later used when securing documents — similar to creating style sheets in word processors or layout programs. The three different options for creating a security policy are as follows:

- **Use passwords.** This option is the same as applying a password to a document via the Document Properties Security pane. The difference between applying password security in the Password Security – Settings dialog box shown in Figure 26.1 and adding a security policy is that the latter is more efficient when you're applying the same security settings repeatedly to multiple documents. If you use the Password Security – Settings dialog box you need to set options each time you secure a document by selecting check boxes and making choices from pull-down menus. When you use a security policy, the options you choose are captured and saved as part of the policy; you just use the policy each time you want to encrypt documents with the same settings.

- **Use public key certificates.** Use this option to share files with users who have a public certificate. These certificates include ones you've added to your Trusted Identities list, or by searching directories you have access to. You can create a policy that applies different permissions to different users. Using this policy ensures that every document is encrypted with the same settings for the recipients.

- **Use the Adobe LiveCycle Policy Server.** If you have access to an Adobe LiveCycle Policy Server, you can create a security policy that is enforced by connecting to the Adobe Policy Server. PDF documents and attachments can be secured for a selected group of users or for a period of time

you determine when creating the policy. When a policy changes or expires on the server, the documents tied to the policy respect these changes as well.

To make the process of creating a security policy a little more clear, try the following steps to create a policy using password security.

STEPS: Creating a password security policy

1. **Open the Managing Security Policies Wizard.** You open the Managing Securities Policy Wizard by selecting Manage Security Policies from the Secure Task Button pull-down menu. You can access the wizard with or without a file open in the Document pane.

2. **Create a new policy.** In the Managing Security Policies Wizard, click the New button to open the New Security Policy Wizard pane, as shown in Figure 26.2. You have three options from which to choose. The default is Use passwords as shown in Figure 26.2. Leave the default settings as is and click the Next button. The Use the Adobe LiveCycle Policy Server is grayed out if you don't have access to an Adobe LiveCycle Policy Server or you have not subscribed to the hosted Protect PDF service from Adobe Systems.

FIGURE 26.2

Click New in the Managing Security Policies Wizard to open the New Security Policy dialog box.

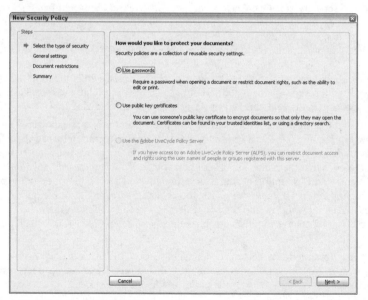

3. **Add a name and description for the new policy.** Type a Policy name and Description in the respective field boxes in the General Settings panel of the New Security Policy Wizard as shown in Figure 26.3. Select the box for Save passwords with the policy. The name and description you add

in the second pane appears when you access the Managing Security Policies dialog box. Try to add information in the field boxes that describe the settings you use when creating the policy.

NOTE If you want to periodically change passwords, leave the check box unchecked. Each time you use the policy, Acrobat prompts you for a new password.

FIGURE 26.3

Name the policy and add a text description.

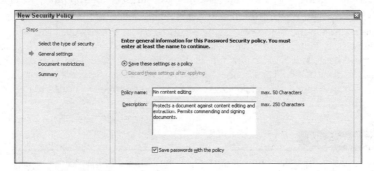

4. **Add the security settings.** Click Next, and you arrive at the Document restrictions panel of the New Security Policy dialog box. This is the same dialog box you see in the Password Security – Settings dialog box shown earlier in Figure 26.1. Here you set the attributes for the security to be applied when using the policy. In my example, I selected Acrobat 7 compatibility; checked the box for "Restrict editing and printing of the document. A password will be required in order to change these permission settings"; added a password; selected None from the Print allowed pull-down menu; set the Changes allowed pull-down menu to Filling in form fields and signing existing signature fields; and checked the last check box in the dialog box.

5. **Review the policy.** Click Next, and the last pane (Summary) appears with a Finish button as shown in Figure 26.4. Click Finish to create the policy. You are returned to the Managing Security Policies dialog box where your new policy is listed in the policy list window, as shown in Figure 26.5. Notice that the name and description you added when creating the policy now appear in the Name and Description headings. Additionally you see a description of the policy details and encryption components for the policy you created. If creating multiple policies, select a policy name in the top window and the policy details and encryption components in the lower half of the dialog box change to reflect attributes for the selected policy. Click the Finish button to save the policy.

6. **Secure a document.** By default the Managing Security Policies dialog box opens as shown in Figure 26.5. Your new policy is listed in this dialog box. If you have a document open in the Document pane, you can apply the policy to the open document.

   Select the policy you created and click the Apply to Document button. Acrobat opens a dialog box informing you that you need to save your file after applying the policy to complete the security. Click OK and save the file. Your file is now secure using the permissions you identified for the policy.

FIGURE 26.4

Review the policy in the Summary pane.

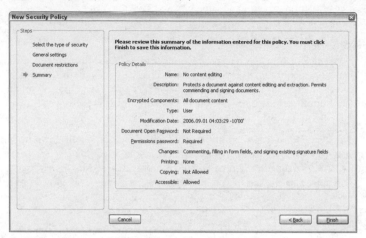

FIGURE 26.5

Select the policy you want to use for securing a document and click the Apply to Document button.

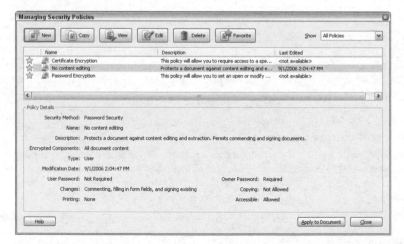

If you work with documents where you need to add different permissions depending on the document content and the users with whom you want to distribute your files, you'll want to add additional policies each designed with different permissions. As you add additional policies, you can choose what policy you want to use to secure a document in one of two areas. Open a document and open the Secure task button. The pull-down menu shows your policy added as a Favorite by default and appearing in the task button pull-down menu. Select the menu command and click Yes when prompted in a dialog box. Save your file and the policy is applied to the document.

The second area you find your policy listed is in the Managing Security Policies dialog box shown earlier in Figure 26.5. You open this dialog box by selecting Manage Security Policies from the Secure task button pull-down menu and the Managing Security Policies dialog box opens. Select the policy and click Apply to Document. Click Yes when prompted in a dialog box and save the file.

Managing security policies

You can add several policies using different permissions settings. Each time you create a new policy, it appears in the Managing Security Policies dialog box. Each time you want to secure documents with the same settings, open the Managing Security Policies dialog box and select a policy from the list. Click the Apply to Document button and the open document is secured with the settings created from the selected policy.

The Secure task button lists all your Favorites at the top of the pull-down menu. You add or delete Favorites in the Managing Security Policies dialog box. Select Manage Security Policies to open the Managing Security Policies dialog box. In the far left column you see a star icon adjacent to policy names. You may also see no appearance of a star icon adjacent to a policy name, as shown in Figure 26.6.

FIGURE 26.6

Select a policy and click the Favorite button. The policy is then listed in the Secure task button pull-down menu.

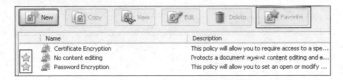

To make a policy a Favorite, select a policy where you see no star icon and click the Favorite button. When you add a Favorite the policy is added to the Secure task button pull-down menu. If you want to remove a Favorite from the menu, open the Managing Security Policies dialog box and select the policy you want to remove. If it's already a Favorite, the policy appears listed with a star icon adjacent to the policy name. Click the Favorite button and the policy is removed from the Favorites list in the Secure task button pull-down menu.

Copying and editing policies

If you want to create a policy that's based on an existing policy, you can copy the policy in the managing Security Policies dialog box and modify the policy attributes. Assume for a moment you want to add password protection to open a file and use all the same attributes of an existing policy that doesn't restrict the permissions to prompt for a password when a file is opened.

Select the policy you want to duplicate and click the Copy button. Acrobat opens the Creating a New Security Policy from an Existing Security Policy Wizard. This wizard offers the same options as shown earlier in the New Security Policy Wizard (see Figure 26.2 earlier in this chapter) for the General Settings, Document Restrictions, and Summary. In the General Settings pane, type a new name for the new policy and type a description. Click Next and set the permissions for the policy. Click Next and the Summary pane opens. Review the permissions and click Finish. Your new policy is added to the Managing Security Policies dialog box.

Select a policy and click the Edit button and you get the same wizard options as when copying files. You can modify a policy name and description and edit the permissions for an existing policy.

Viewing and deleting policies

Select a policy and click the View button. The Viewing a Security Policy Wizard opens where you can review settings for a given policy. In this wizard you can't make any changes to the policy. If you need to change settings, use the Edit button.

Select a policy and click the Delete button. Acrobat prompts you in a warning dialog box to confirm the action. Click Yes and the policy is deleted. Click No and the policy remains without changes.

Understanding Digital IDs

A digital ID is a file that you create in Acrobat or acquire from a third-party signature provider. Your ID, also known as a *credential* or *profile*, is password protected and used to electronically sign or certify documents. Before you can digitally sign a document you need to create or acquire your own personal ID.

Digital IDs have two components important to understand — your personal or private digital ID and your public certificate. When you create a digital ID with Acrobat you are creating your private ID and your public certificate. The public certificate is a file you share with other users so they can encrypt files that they send to you. In order to open such encrypted files you need to supply the password used when you created your personal profile.

As a matter of understanding the security involved when using digital signatures, realize that, unless you choose to save a password when you create a policy, every time you want to sign a document, you need to supply your password. Therefore, anyone having access to your computer cannot sign or certify a document on your behalf unless the user has your password. When a file is encrypted using your public certificate, the file is opened only when you supply your password. Again, anyone having access to your computer cannot open a document encrypted with your public certificate unless that user has access to your password. Private digital signature IDs are used to sign and decrypt documents. Public Certificates are used to encrypt documents and validate signatures.

As mentioned earlier, each digital ID has two components — the private ID and the public certificate. The private ID can be used to either digitally sign a PDF or to decrypt documents encrypted with the public certificate, and conversely, the public certificate can be used to encrypt documents or to validated digital signatures.

Digital IDs can be created in Acrobat or acquired from other parties. They can then be accessed locally from your computer or from a remote server. For a quick look at the options available when working with digital IDs and public certificates, select Advanced ➪ Security Settings and the Security Settings dialog box shown in Figure 26.7 opens. This dialog box is used to manage and create digital IDs. You also use this dialog box to configure servers, time stamp digital IDs, and Adobe LiveCycle Policy Servers.

As shown in the dialog box, the options you have for working with digital IDs and configuring server access include the following:

- **Digital IDs.** There are three types of IDs available that include:
  - **Roaming ID Accounts.** A new feature in Acrobat 8 permits you to host your ID on a Web site server. You can access your ID anywhere in the world by logging on to the server that contains your roaming ID and digitally sign documents using any one of your IDs available on the server. Roaming ID accounts are available to both Windows and Macintosh users.
  - **Digital ID Files.** Available on Windows and Macintosh, this form of ID is similar to what you had available in earlier versions of Acrobat when using Acrobat Certificate Security. You can select 'Add ID'(which opens the Add Digital ID dialog box to find an existing digital ID, create a new Acrobat Self-Sign, or get a 3rd party certificate).

- **Windows Digital IDs.** This ID is available only on Windows. The ID is installed in the Windows Certificate Store where it is also available to other Windows applications. This digital ID is protected by your Windows logon password.

- **PKCS#11 Modules and Tokens.** PKCS#11 encryption is used on hardware devices such as smart cards. You acquire the module from your device manufacturer.

- **Directory servers.** This option is used to enable you to locate specific digital ID certificates from network servers for encrypting documents using Certificate Security. Directory servers can be added by importing a configuration supplied by a System Administrator, or by entering the parameters required to configure the server.

- **Time Stamp Servers.** This option is used if you will be adding time stamps to documents. As with Directory Servers, Time Stamp Servers are added by importing a configuration from a system administrator or by adding parameters required to configure the server.

- **Adobe LiveCycle Policy Servers.** Adobe LiveCycle Policy Server (`www.adobe.com/products/server/policy/main.html`) is a Web server–based security solution provided by Adobe Systems that provides dynamic control over PDF documents. Policies created with Acrobat or Adobe LiveCycle Policy Server are stored on the server and can be refreshed from the server. Once you've configured an Adobe Policy Server, all polices maintained on this server are available to you. You must log into Adobe Policy Server to use these policies. This option also requires that you access a URL provided by a System Administrator and add the server to your list of Adobe Policy Servers.

FIGURE 26.7

Open the Security Settings dialog box to create new Digital IDs and manage your existing IDs.

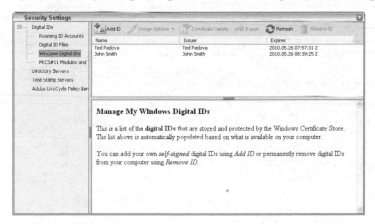

726

Using Third-Party Signature Handlers

Digital signature handlers, tokens, biometrics, hardware solutions, and other similar products are available from third-party providers and offer you many different options for securing PDF documents depending on the product and manufacturer. To find information on acquiring third-party products for signature handling, take a look at a new area on Adobe's Web site at `http://partners.adobe.com/security`. On the Adobe Web pages you find links to digital signature and document control vendors worldwide.

If you use Acrobat for languages other than US English, go to your local Web page and log on to Adobe's Web site. You might use, for example, a URL such as `www.adobe.com.fr/security` for a French language document page. This page includes a link to security partners supporting the localized products.

When you create a digital ID in Acrobat by choosing Advanced ⇨ Security Settings, the Security Settings dialog box opens. Select Directory Servers and click New. The Edit Directory Server dialog box opens where you identify a third party server and provide log on information and password.

Creating a personal digital ID

Digital IDs can be created with or without custom appearance settings. The appearance of your signature has no effect on the kind of security you add to a signature. If you want to create a custom signature appearance, it's usually best to first create the appearance, and then create the digital ID.

Creating a custom appearance

Appearances for your digital IDs are created in the Security preferences. Open the Preferences dialog box (Ctrl/⌘+K) and click Security in the left pane. The right pane changes as shown in Figure 26.8.

FIGURE 26.8

Click Security in the left pane in the Preferences dialog box and the right pane changes where you can add a new appearance for a digital ID.

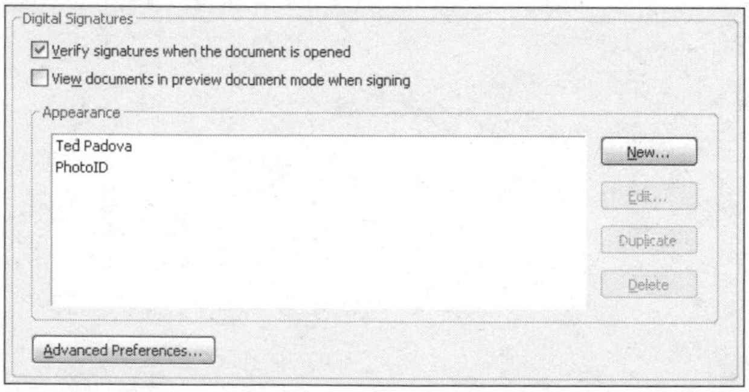

Two preferences dialog boxes are used for creating an appearance and setting some attributes for your signatures. These include:

- **Security Preferences.** You use the Security Preferences to create digital ID appearances for your personal digital IDs. If you want to add a logo, analog signature, symbol, or some text to an ID, you can do so by clicking the New button and choosing from various settings in the Configure Security Appearance dialog box.

- **Advanced Preferences.** If you have an ID configured such as the two shown in Figure 26.8, the ID(s) appears listed in the Appearance list in the Security Preferences dialog box. Select an ID and click Advanced Preferences to open another dialog box where a number of options exist for verifying signatures, creating them, and on Windows settings for Windows Integration. A number of different options exist in three tabs (Windows) or two tabs (Macintosh). For a detailed description of each item, consult the Acrobat Help document.

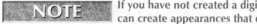 **NOTE** If you have not created a digital ID yet, you will not see anything listed in this box, but you still can create appearances that can later be used with a digital ID.

To understand how to create a custom appearance for a digital ID, follow these steps:

STEPS: Creating a custom digital ID appearance

1. **Open the Security preferences.** Press Ctrl/⌘+K. Click on the Security item in the left pane.
2. **Click New to open the Configure Signature Appearance dialog box.**
3. **Configure the appearance.** Type a Title in the Title text box. This title will appear as the name for your appearance and one you'll select when configuring a digital ID. If you want to use a graphic, click the Imported graphic radio button and click File to open the Select Picture dialog box. Locate and select the graphic you want to use for the appearance. (Note that the file can be any file type supported by the Create PDF From File command.)

   Select the text items you want to display on your signature by checking boxes in the Configure Text area of the Configure Signature Appearance dialog box. In my example, I removed all check boxes, as shown in Figure 26.9.
4. **Click OK in the Configure Signature Appearance dialog box.** The signature is listed by Title in the Security preferences. Click OK in the Preference dialog box and your appearance for a signature is now configured.

FIGURE 26.9

Type a title in the Title text box, import a graphic, and check the boxes you want to use for text appearances.

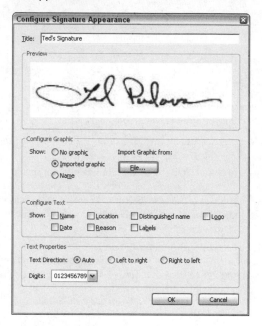

Creating a digital ID

The steps used to create a signature appearance are optional. You don't need to use a custom appearance when creating a digital ID. If you do create a signature appearance, you can use it when creating a new ID.

To understand how digital IDs are created, follow these steps.

STEPS: Creating a digital ID and appearance

1. **Open the Security Settings dialog box.** Click Advanced ➪ Security Settings. The Security Settings dialog box, shown earlier in this chapter in Figure 26.7, opens.

2. **Create a Self-Signed digital ID.** Click Add ID in the Security Settings dialog box. The Add Digital ID Wizard opens, as shown in Figure 26.10. Select the Create a self-signed digital ID for use with Acrobat and click Next.

FIGURE 26.10

Click Add ID in the Security Settings dialog box and the Add Digital ID dialog box opens.

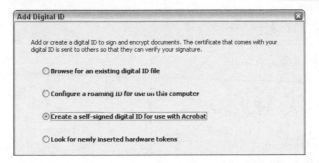

3. **Select the area you want to store your ID.** The next pane has two options for where you can store your digital ID. Select the first radio button (New PKCS#12 digital ID file to create a password protected ID on either Windows or the Mac. Select the second radio button (Windows Certificate Store) if you want your ID made available to Acrobat and Windows applications. Click Next to arrive at the new pane in the wizard.

4. **Add Identity Information.** The next pane opens with text boxes for you to supply identity information. If you added Identity information in the Identity preferences, the information is transposed to the pane shown in Figure 26.11. If you want to use special characters, non-Roman languages, or non-ASCII, check the box for Enable Unicode Support.

FIGURE 26.11

Add identity information if all fields are not completed in your Identity preferences.

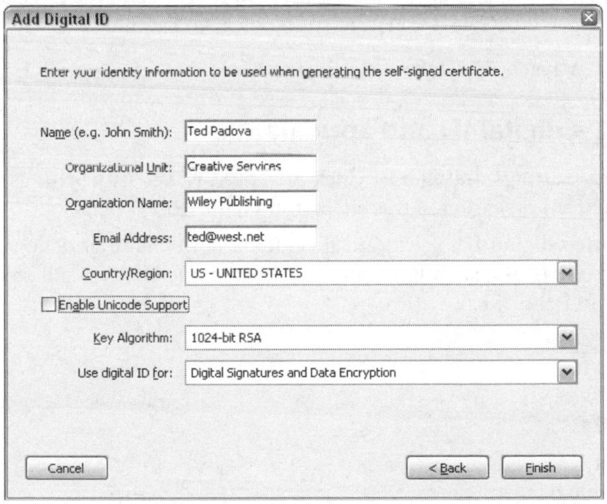

5. **Choose where you want to store the ID and type a password.** Click Next in the wizard and click the Browse button to locate a folder where you want to save the ID (for New PKCS#12 digital ID files). Type a Password in the Password text box and type the Password again in the Confirm Password text box.

6. **Click Finish.** Click Finish in the Add Digital ID dialog box and you return to the Security Settings dialog box. Your new digital ID is now ready to use.

Notice as yet, we have not selected an appearance for the digital ID. You can store multiple appearances in the Security preferences and each time you sign a document, you can choose which appearance you want to use for your signature. You might, for example, sign documents internally in your company using one appearance and with the same ID sign documents coming from other sources outside your company with another appearance.

Managing multiple IDs

If you create several IDs used for different purposes, you may have a need to remove old IDs and add new IDs. In the Security Settings you have options for assigning attributes to your IDs, adding new IDs, and removing IDs. Choose Advanced ➪ Security Settings to open the dialog box shown earlier in this chapter in Figure 26.7.

Click an ID in the Name column to select it and click the Remove ID button to delete an ID. You also have options in the Security Settings dialog box for Exporting Certificates, selecting Usage Options, and viewing certificate details.

Setting usage options

You can create several digital IDs and assign different usage options for each ID. After adding IDs to the Security Settings dialog box, select an ID and open the Usage Options pull-down menu. From the commands shown in Figure 26.12, you have a number of different usage options. Click one of the options shown to assign that option to the selected ID. Click another ID and assign another option. You can only assign one option to an ID. If an option is used with one ID and you apply that option to another ID, the option is removed from the first ID and assigned to your new selection. After assigning options, you'll notice the appearance of the options icons adjacent to the ID names.

FIGURE 26.12

Click an ID in the Security Settings dialog box and select a usage option.

Previewing before signing

Before you sign a document, you can preview the file to determine whether it meets a specification for determining whether dynamic content is included in the file. The document preview for this purpose is handled in the Advanced ➪ Sign & Certify ➪ Preview Document command. When you select the command, a message bar opens at the top of the Document pane as shown in Figure 26.13.

FIGURE 26.13

Select Advanced ⇨ Sign & Certify ⇨ Preview Document to open the message bar.

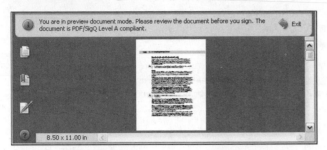

The message bar reports whether the document is PDF/SigQ Level A or Level B. PDF/SigQ Level A indicates that the document contains no dynamic data. When you see this report, you can click the Exit button and go ahead and sign the document without fear of having content that can change the document unaware to the user.

In Figure 26.14, I opened the Preview Document command on a document compliant with the PDF/SigQ Level B specification. Notice the View Report item in the message bar.

FIGURE 26.14

A PDF/SigQ Level B document contains a button to view a report.

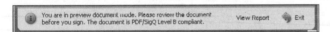

Click the View Report button in the message bar and the PDF/SigQ Conformance Report dialog box opens. This dialog box lists items that contain hidden actions that may not be known to the end user. In the document I examined there are JavaScript actions that control opening, saving, closing the file, executing menu commands, and more, as shown in Figure 26.15. If you find actions in a document that are not intended for use by the end user, you should remove them before singing the document.

Using signature fields

To sign a document containing a signature field, click on the field with the Hand tool. The Sign Document dialog box opens, as shown in Figure 26.16. Choose an ID from the Digital ID pull-down menu. Type your password in the Password text box and select an appearance from the Appearance pull-down menu.

When you click Sign you are prompted to save your file. Locate the folder where you want to save the file and click Save. The document is signed using the Usage Options assigned to the signature.

FIGURE 26.15

Click the View Report button in the message bar on files compliant with PDF/SigQ Level B and a list of items unknown to a user is reported in the PDF/SigQ Conformance Report dialog box.

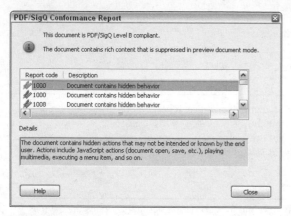

FIGURE 26.16

Select an ID to sign a document from the Digital ID list, type the password for the ID, and choose an appearance setting.

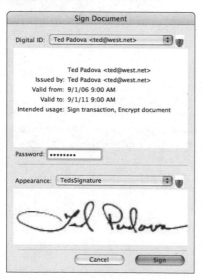

Creating a signature field when signing a document

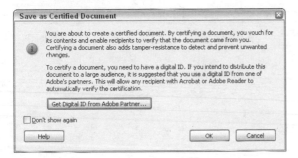 If no signature field appears on a document, you can sign a document by accessing Place Signature from the Sign Task Button pull-down menu. This method of signing prompts you to marquee an area on a page where you want to create a signature field on the document. Click OK in the dialog box informing you what to do and draw a rectangle. When you release the mouse button, the Sign Document dialog box opens. Follow the same steps outlined in the next section.

Certifying a document

You have two choices for certifying a document with a digital ID. You can choose to certify a file with or without a visible signature. From the Sign pull-down menu, select Certify with Visible Signature to have your signature shown on the document. Choose Certify without Visible Signature to add an invisible signature to the file. Using either option opens the Save as Certified Document dialog box shown in Figure 26.17.

FIGURE 26.17

Using either menu command in the Sign task button pull-down menu for certifying documents opens the Save as Certified Document dialog box.

You have choices for acquiring a digital ID you have set up with an Adobe partner or click OK to open the Sign Document dialog box where you apply a signature using the same criteria as when signing with and without signature fields.

A second option exists in the File menu. Select File ➪ Save As Certified Document. The same dialog box opens prompting you to select an ID from an Adobe partner or click OK to open the Sign Document dialog box.

Protect an Adobe PDF File

Enterprises and large institutions are likely candidates for acquiring the Adobe LiveCycle Policy Server. On a per-file basis where an enterprise needs to secure files routinely for many users, the server product from Adobe is a much affordable solution. However, for individual users and small businesses, the Adobe LiveCycle Policy Server may be cost-prohibitive when your needs are securing a few files now and then.

NEW FEATURE Acrobat 8 provides an alternative for individuals and small business that want to take advantage of the benefits of securing files with the Adobe LiveCycle Policy Server without having to purchase the server product. The Create PDF Online feature in Acrobat 8 introduces the Protect an Adobe PDF File with which you can submit files for protection using the Adobe LiveCycle policy Server.

Why are securing files with the Adobe LiveCycle Policy Server a benefit? When you secure PDFs with Acrobat you can secure files for a limited number of people and you can protect files from various types of editing. However, you do not have any control over the validity period in days/weeks/months users can view your PDFs, the time of day a file is accessible to users, whether users can view PDFs online or offline, or track who has viewed, printed, commented on, and/or copied your PDFs. All of these conditions can be controlled using the Adobe LiveCycle Policy Server and securing PDFs with these parameters are now within the reach of individual users.

Access to the Protect an Adobe PDF File using Adobe's online service is made by selecting Advanced ⇨ Adobe Online Services or Adobe Online services from the Secure task button. When you first access the menu command, the Secure Using Adobe online Service dialog box opens in which you set up your account. To start a trial account, click the Register for Trial button if you don't have an account with Adobe Systems. If you do have an account, click the Log In button as shown in Figure 26.18.

FIGURE 26.18

Select Advanced ⇨ Adobe Online Services to start an account or log on.

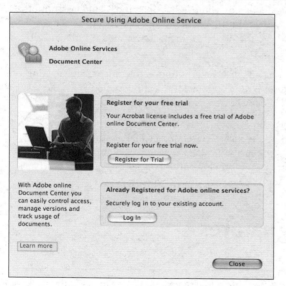

After creating an account or logging on, a preview of the security polices are shown in the Manage Security Policies dialog box. A number of predefined policies are set up for you when you log on as shown in Figure 26.19. You can add new policies and delete policies using the same tools you work with when adding and deleting policies you create using self-signed security.

After creating a trial account or signing up for the service, the Adobe Online Services menu command shows submenu options for Refresh Security Policies which updates any policies you've added, deleted, or edited, and the Manage My Account command. Selecting Manage My Account takes you to Adobe's Web site for account management options.

FIGURE 26.19

The Manage Security Policies dialog box opens when you first use the Adobe Online Service.

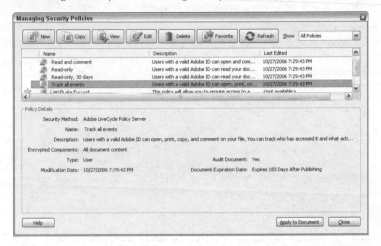

If you want to return to the Manage Security Policies dialog box you need to open the Secure task button menu and select Manage Security Policies (or select Advanced ➪ Security ➪ Manage Security Policies). The Manage Security Policies dialog box is not available from the Adobe Online Services menu command after you initially set up an account or sign up for a trial period.

Select a file in the Manage Security Policies dialog box and click the Edit button to edit a policy. Clicking the button takes you to Adobe's Web site where you set up the options for a security policy. Since these security settings are handled by the Adobe LiveCycle Policy Server, you need to make your edits and changes on Adobe's Web site.

When you want to secure a file using the Protect an Adobe PDF service, open a PDF in Acrobat and open the Manage Security Policies dialog box (Advanced ➪ Security ➪ Manage Security Policies). Select the policy you want to use and click Apply to Document in the Managing Security Policies dialog box. Your file is submitted to Adobe Systems and secured with the Adobe LiveCycle Policy Server.

Working with Digital Signatures and PDF Packages

If you have multiple documents and you combine the files into a PDF Package, all signatures in the package are retained. You might have a series of drawings that need to be signed by different engineers and a cover sheet that is used for signing off on a PDF Package. The package may be comprised of several drawings containing several different signatures or a series of forms in a package with a cover sheet containing an authorizing signature.

In Figure 26.20, a PDF Package is shown with four PDF forms and a cover sheet containing an authorizing signature. Each of the forms in the package was signed before the package was created and the authorized signature appearing on the cover sheet is a valid signature. (Note that PDF Packages can be created using a file in the package as a cover sheet.)

FIGURE 26.20

A PDF Package containing forms all having digital signatures and a cover sheet with a valid signature

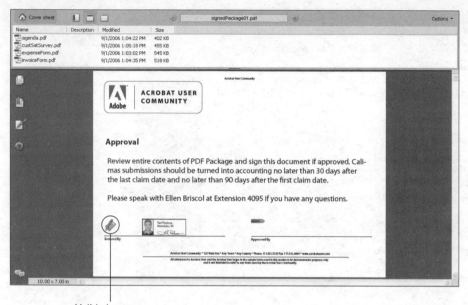

Valid signature

If a document in the package is deleted or an edit is made to any one of the PDFs within the package, Acrobat automatically invalidates the signature on the cover page. Each individual signed page in the file remains with a valid signature and the only signature that is invalidated is the signature on the cover page, as shown in Figure 26.21, after I deleted a form from the package. (The invalidated mark is displayed with a yellow triangle on the signature.)

This behavior provides you assurance that after signing a cover page authorizing or approving the package contents, no tampering with the package contents can be made without alerting you that a change has occurred.

CROSS-REF For more information on creating PDF Packages, see Chapter 12.

FIGURE 26.21

Editing any file within a PDF Package or deleting a file from the package invalidates the signature on the cover page.

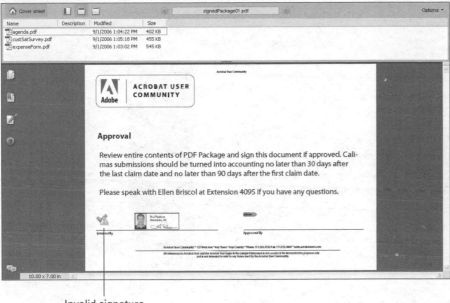

Invalid signature

Using Trusted Identities and Certificate Security

Trusted Identities are added to the Trusted Identities Manager dialog box. The list of Trusted Identities is like an address book where you can add contacts and set certificate properties. You can maintain a contact list of Trusted Identities from people you will do business with or may do business with. Each user listed in Trusted Identities can be used to validate digital signatures and encrypt PDF documents for these users. The Trusted Identities Manager additionally permits you to set levels of trust from the users listed in the contact list.

Using certificate encryption

Encryption using certificates is a means for you to add security for a selected group of users. The advantage of using certificates is you can control the permissions settings individually for each user in the same PDF document. For example, you may want to allow one user to view your document, but restrict printing. For another user you may want to disallow editing, but enable printing. For a third user you may want to allow editing and printing. All these permissions can be set for each user in the same PDF document using the Certificate Security Settings dialog box.

To encrypt a file using certificates, you need access to the public certificate. You can either search for the public certificates which may be located on a network server, or you can collect the public certificates for each user and load them into your Trusted Identities list. Keep in mind, the Trusted Identities Manager is like an address book and merely is a convenient location for where you can store contact and certificate information for users you frequently work with. During encryption you can specify permissions settings individually for each user.

Understanding Encryption, Validation, and the Trusted Identities Manager

In the Manage Trusted Identities dialog box (shown in Figure 26.23), a drop-down menu provides two choices: Contacts and Certificates. Items listed in the menus do not have to match. You can have certificates in the list that are not in the Contacts list. From the Display pull-down menu you can select either Contacts or Certificates and you can Add Contacts or Certificates respective to the menu item you select.

In order to encrypt documents you do *not* have to have a public certificate in your Trusted Identities. For example, a company may have a corporate level security solution in which each employee is issued a certificate that is stored on a network server. You can search certificates on your company's LDAP (Lightweight Directory Access Protocol) server to find someone you want to encrypt for and just use their certificate without adding the certificate to your list of Trusted Identities.

To validate a signature, you do not have to have the public certificate in your Trusted Identities if you've already established a trust with a parent in the chain of trust. For example, you can create a Class 1 certificate for a security partner. So the chain might be Your Company, Inc. ➪ Partner Class 1 ➪ Your Name.

You can then *trust* Your Company, Inc. (the root) and therefore everybody under that chain is automatically trusted by you so you don't need any individual's certificate in your local Trusted Identities for validation. However, if you want to give any user a different trust setting than the trust settings used by the parent, then you do need to add the individual's certificate to your Trusted Identities.

Does an individual need to send you a public certificate? The answer is no, not if the user sends you a file signed with his/her certificate. You can always get the public certificate from a file sent to you.

To acquire a public certificate from a signed document, open a context menu on the signature and select Properties. In the Signature Properties dialog box, click the Show Certificate button. The Certificate Viewer dialog box opens. Click the Export button and you are prompted to save the certificate as a file or e-mail the certificate.

The entire range of possibilities regarding using digital IDs, signing documents, and authenticating signed or certified documents is a very complex subject. In an effort to break it down to a more simplified view, the detail in this chapter assumes you are working in an environment where you are not using a corporate-wide security solution and you're using the self-sign methods of security. If you want the highest levels of security and the most efficient means for securing documents, I encourage you to carefully review the Acrobat Help document and explore all the security information on Web pages hosted by Adobe Systems.

Exporting public certificates

Public certificates are used for validating signatures on documents received and encrypting files which you plan to share. For another user to validate your signature or encrypt a file unique to your profile you need to export your public certificate and share it with other users. Your public certificate does not compromise your password settings or ability to secure your own files. Public certificates are generated from your profile, but do not send along your password to other users.

NOTE   Companies using directory servers to host public certificates do not need to export certificates.

To export a public certificate you need to start with a digital ID you have already created. Choose Advanced ⇨ Security Settings. The Security Settings dialog box shown earlier in Figure 26.7 opens. If you have more than one ID listed in the dialog box, select the ID you want to use and click the Export button. The Data Exchange File – Export Options dialog box opens, as shown in Figure 26.22.

When exporting your certificate, you can choose to save the public certificate as a file or e-mail the certificate to another user.

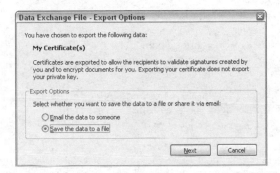

In this dialog box you make a choice for saving your public certificate to disk or e-mailing the certificate directly to another user. If you elect Save the data to a file, you can later attach it to an e-mail message and send it to users as needed. If you select the Email the data to someone radio button and click the Next button, the Compose Email dialog box opens where you add the recipient's e-mail address. Enter an e-mail address and click the Email button and the data file is attached to a new e-mail message. Acrobat supplies a default message in the e-mail note for you providing instructions for the recipient, but you can edit if desired.

Requesting contacts

If you want to add a contact and/or certificate to your list of Trusted Identities, select Advanced ⇨ Manage Trusted Identities to open the Trusted Identities dialog box. Click the Request Contact button and the Email a Request dialog box opens. You add your name, e-mail address and any contact information you want to supply in the text boxes in the Email a Request dialog box. Click the Next button to open the Compose Email dialog box. In this dialog box, you add the recipient e-mail address. A default subject and message appears in the Compose Email dialog box informing the recipient you are requesting a copy of the individual's certificate. Click the Email button and the request is e-mailed to the recipient. Note, you may need to open your default e-mail program and click the Send or Send/Receive button to initiate a send.

When a copy of a certificate is e-mailed back to you, the file appears in a message window as a file attachment. Double-click the attachment and the certificate is automatically added to your list of Trusted Identities after you approve adding the ID or click OK.

Managing Trusted Identities

After you collect public certificates, you need to load the certificates into your Trusted Identities list. To load certificates, choose Advanced ➪ Manage Trusted Identities. The dialog box shown in Figure 26.23 opens.

FIGURE 26.23

You use the Manage Trusted Identities dialog box to add identities from public certificates you collect from other users.

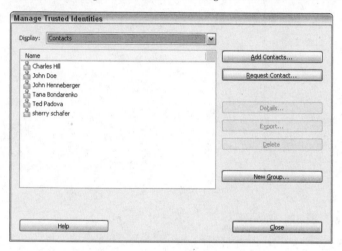

To add a recipient, click the Add Contacts button. The Choose Contacts to Import dialog box shown in Figure 26.24 opens where you can browse your hard drive or network server to locate certificates from other users. When adding identities collected by other users, click the Browse button. The Locate Certificate File dialog box opens where you navigate your hard drive and locate certificates to add to a recipient list. Click Open and the recipient's name appears in the top window of the Choose Contacts to Import dialog box. Select the name of the added contact and click the Import button to add the certificate to the identities list. You use the Search button to search through network servers configured in your Directory Servers.

Add the certificate and return to the Manage Trusted Identities dialog box and continue adding new certificates to your list of recipients.

FIGURE 26.24

Use the Choose Contacts to Import dialog box to add new recipient identities.

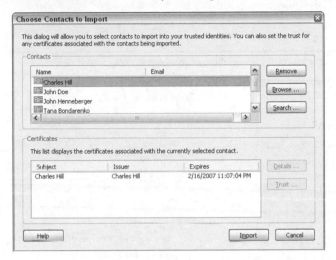

Setting certificate security permissions

One thing to keep in mind is that when you have circumstances that require you to repeat document security for the same set of users or when encrypting documents with the same set of permissions, you'll always want to set up a security policy. In those instances where you intend to secure a document using certificates one time only, you can set permissions without creating a policy. To help simplify the process, this section refers to setting up permissions using certificates for a one-time use.

To secure a document using Certificate Security, open the Document Properties dialog box (File ⇨ Properties). Click the Security tab and select Certificate Security from the Security Method pull-down menu. The Certificate Security Settings Wizard opens. The General settings panel offers you the choice to save your settings as a policy or discard the settings after applying the security. In addition you have options for what you want to encrypt such as the document only or the document and file attachments and the type of encryption you want to apply. In Figure 26.25, you can see the options in the General settings pane. Make a choice for saving your settings as a policy or discarding the settings after applying them. If you choose to create a policy, add a name and description. At the bottom of the General pane make a choice for the type of encryption you want to apply and click Next.

The Select Recipients pane opens, as shown in Figure 26.26. Click Browse and locate the file(s) you want to add. You can add only one file at a time. Keep clicking Browse and add all the files you want to use for this particular Certificate Security. In Figure 26.26, I added several recipients to my list.

Select a recipient in the list and click the Permissions button. The Permissions Settings dialog box opens where you choose individual permissions for a selected recipient, as shown in Figure 26.27. Set permissions for the selected user and click OK. Select another recipient and set permissions for that user. Continue setting permissions for each user.

FIGURE 26.25

Select Certificate Security from the Security Method pull-down menu in the Security tab from the Document Properties dialog box to open the Certificate Security Settings dialog box.

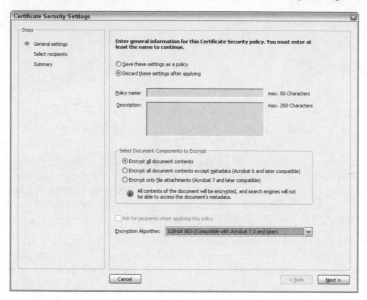

FIGURE 26.26

Several certificates are added to the Select recipients pane in the wizard.

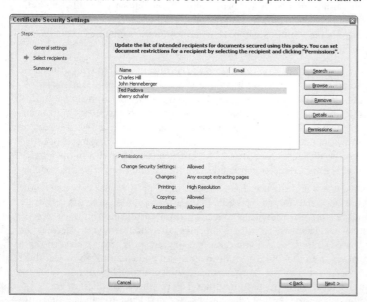

FIGURE 26.27

Select the permissions you want to assign to the selected user and click OK.

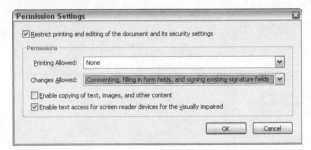

The great strength for using Certificate Security is that all the recipients in your list can be assigned unique permissions. For example, you can prohibit printing for one user, allow low resolution printing for another user and high resolution printing for a third user. In addition, you can protect against a number of different editing options. All of these permissions settings are applied to individual recipients in the same PDF document. Each user needs to open the file using his/her own digital ID and password.

To complete the Certificate Security, click the Next button and the Summary panel opens. A summary for your policy is listed in the panel. If you want to make any changes, click the Back button. To accept the settings you made, click Finish. Save the file and all the permissions assignments to your recipients are encrypted in the document.

Validating Signatures

Digital signatures would be of no value unless you could confirm that a document was signed by the individual claiming to have signed the document. For confirmation purposes you use menu commands and options to validate signatures. There are several options you have when validating signatures and all depends on different circumstances which include:

- If you have established trust with a parent, you don't need the certificate listed in your Trusted Identities. See the "Understanding Encryption, Validation, and the Trusted Identities Manager" sidebar earlier in this chapter. When you open a signed PDF from another person using a third-party security partner certificate, the signature appears as Unknown. Select Properties from a context menu you open on the signature. In the Signature Properties dialog box, click Verify Signature. The signature appears valid without adding to your Trusted Identities. If you want to change the level of trust, you can add the certificate to your Trusted Identities and set the trust in the Manage Trusted Identities dialog box. See the "Managing Trusted Identities" section earlier in this chapter.

- If you open a self-signed document and the user hasn't used a third-party security partner, and you know the document has been sent to you by the PDF author, you can retrieve the certificate from the document without needing the individual to send you the certificate. You might receive files from members of your workgroup where you are confident the document you receive comes from the individual who signed it. In this case, you can open the Signature panel, select the Signature, and select Properties from the Options pull-down menu and click the Show Certificate button in the Signature Properties dialog box. The Certificate Viewer dialog box opens. Click the Trust tab and click the button for Add to Trusted Identities. The certificate is added to your Trusted Identities where you can set the level of trust and use the certificate to validate signatures.

- If you open a document from an anonymous user or one where you question the document authenticity, you can request a certificate. You add the certificate you receive from a PDF author to your Trusted Identities and you can choose to set the level of trust following the same steps outlined in the section "Managing Trusted Identities" earlier in this chapter.

To validate a signature, use the Sign task button or the Signatures pane. Choose Validate All Signatures from either the Sign task button pull-down menu or from the Options menu in the Signatures pane. To validate a single signature, select that signature from the Signatures pane or hover over the signature in the Document pane. Open a context menu and select Validate Signature.

When you open a signed document and view signatures in the Signatures palette, an icon with a question mark may be displayed adjacent to the signature(s). In addition, you'll notice the text below the signature icon often states that the signature validity is unknown. This occurs when the user has not been added to your Trusted Identities list. See the list of options at the beginning of this section.

NOTE Contained in the Security Preferences (Ctrl/⌘+K and click Security in the left pane) is a check box for Verify signatures when the document is opened. If the check box is enabled, the signatures in the document are validated when the document opens. In this case, you do not need to manually access a menu command to validate a signature. You do, however, still need to have a trusted certificate from the individual who signed the document in order to validate upon opening the file. If using external certificate authority, you need to have an active Internet connection to your service to verify signatures. If this box is unchecked, you must manually validate your signatures. Be aware that if your document has more than 10 pages, Acrobat may not validate signatures automatically upon opening the document. This behavior prevents a document from slowing down during open time. If you find documents not certifying signatures at open time, manually review the signatures in the Signatures pane and use the Validate Signature command in the Options pull-down menu.

When you validate a signature, Acrobat opens a dialog box reporting the validation status. If the public certificate is loaded and the validation is true, a dialog box opens reporting the certificate is valid.

If you get UNKNOWN, this certificate is not in your Trusted Identities. Select the Signature Properties button. From the Summary tab select Show Certificate. From the Trust tab, select your Trust Settings and select Add to Trusted Identities. The Import Contact Settings appears when you determine which Trust Settings you desire. Select OK in the Certificate Viewer window. You are returned to Signature Properties. Select Verify Signature. This signature will now be Valid. Select Close to return to the Document pane.

You can view the signature properties by clicking the Signature Properties button to display the Signature Properties dialog box, which reports all the properties of the certificate including the reason for signing, the e-mail address of the person signing the document, and the certificate fingerprint. The Signatures panel reflects a valid signature, as shown in Figure 26.28.

FIGURE 26.28

After a signature is validated, the icon adjacent to the signature name changes to a pen and check mark, and the status is reported as valid.

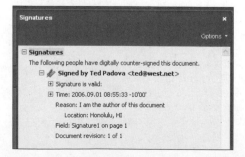

Creating a Security Envelope

Another security option you have in Acrobat is creating a secure envelope adding any file you choose to use as a file attachment. You can create eEnvelopes containing file attachments and secure the PDF and file attachment(s) against unauthorized access. Users of Acrobat or the free Adobe Reader software with access rights can open the PDFs and extract the file attachment(s).

To understand how files are attached in a Secure PDF Delivery workflow, follow these steps.

STEPS: Creating a secure eEnvelope

1. **Open the Create Security Envelope dialog box.** Open the Secure task button pull-down menu and select Create Security Envelope. Note that you do not need to have a document open in Acrobat.

2. **Choose files to include.** The Files to enclose panel in the Create Security Envelope Wizard opens as shown in Figure 26.29. Click the Add File to Send button and the Files to Enclose dialog box opens. Navigate your hard drive, select the file you want to include, and click Open. Note that any file of any type can be added to the security envelope. In my example, I use a Microsoft Word document.

FIGURE 26.29

Click Add File to Send and locate the file to add to your eEnvelope.

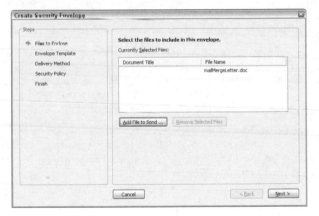

3. **Select a template.** Click Next and the Envelope Template panel opens. You can select from preinstalled templates or click the Browse button to locate a PDF file you want to use for your template. Select a preinstalled template from the list shown in Figure 26.30 and click Next.

FIGURE 26.30

Select a template and click Next.

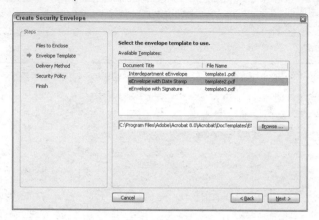

You have templates available for date stamping the envelope and signing the envelope. Choose from template2.pdf to date stamp an envelope and choose template3.pdf to open a template with a digital signature field. All templates have field boxes where you can add addressee information.

4. **Choose a delivery method.** The next panel that opens is the Delivery Method panel. You have two choices for delivering your eEnvelope. Choose from options for sending the envelope later or e-mailing it now from the two radio button options. Select Send the envelope now and click the Next button.

5. **Choose a security policy to apply.** The Security Policy pane opens, as shown in Figure 26.31. Select a policy in the list and click Next.

FIGURE 26.31

Select a security policy and click Next.

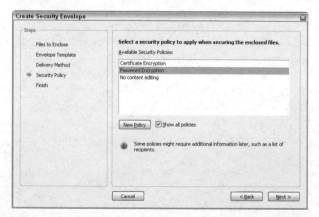

6. **Finish.** The last pane shows the directory path for the selected file. Review the summary and click Next. Click OK and the Security Envelope with the file attachment is attached to a new e-mail message, as shown in Figure 26.32. Edit the message text if you so choose and add a recipient to the To field. Click Send and your Security Envelope is on its way.

FIGURE 26.32

Click Finish and the Security Envelope is attached to a new e-mail message.

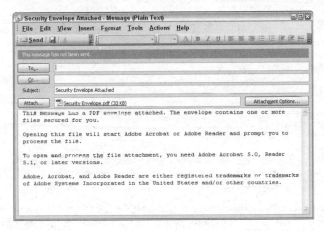

Summary

- PDF documents can be secured with built-in Acrobat Self-Signed Security and security handlers acquired from third-party developers. Files can be secured from users opening documents, editing documents, or for both.

- Different levels of security can prevent users of Acrobat viewers earlier than version 6 from opening files. It is important to know your user audience and what version of Acrobat viewers they use before securing files.

- To digitally sign a document you need to create a digital ID. You create and manage digital IDs via several menu commands and menu options found in the Secure Task Button pull-down menu.

- You can apply appearance settings to your signatures in the form of scanned documents, icons, and symbols from files saved as PDF or other file formats compatible with the Create PDF From File command. You add signature appearances via the Security Preferences dialog box.

- You can digitally sign a document by using an existing signature field or by selecting a menu command where you are prompted to create a signature field.

- You can certify a document using your signature by selecting a menu command to certify the document.

- Trusted Identities are a list of digital ID certificates from people you share information with. You can export your public certificate to a file or attach your public certificate to an e-mail message from within Acrobat. When other users have your public certificate, they can validate your signature or encrypt documents for your use.

■ You can encrypt files for a group of users by using their public certificates stored as Trusted Identities. A single PDF document can be secured for different users and with different permissions for each user.

■ In order to validate a signature, the public certificate for that digital ID needs to be loaded into your Trusted Identities list.

■ Acrobat alerts you when a PDF Package contents has been altered if you add a digital signature to a cover sheet.

■ Any file of any type can be added to a secure envelope. The only way for an end user to access the file attachment is to have the password to open the attached file.

Chapter 27

PDFs and the Web

Throughout this book, I address using PDFs on the Web. As I discussed in Chapter 7, you can download selected Web pages or entire Web sites and have all the HTML pages converted to PDF. In Acrobat 6 and greater you can convert media, animation, and sound to PDFs with the animated pages appearing the same in Acrobat viewers as when you see them on Web sites.

In Chapter 20, I discussed comments and, in Chapter 21, I covered online reviews. Coming ahead in Chapter 30, I talk about eBooks and downloading books as Digital Editions. In Chapter 34, I talk about submitting form data. And in other chapters, you find similar discussions on Acrobat PDFs hosted online. In short, the Web plays a major role with much of your Acrobat activity. In this chapter, I cover more about using PDFs online for viewing in Web browsers and linking to PDF views on Web sites.

IN THIS CHAPTER

Viewing Web-hosted PDFs

Working with Web links

Exporting PDFs to HTML

Setting Up the Environment

To accomplish the tasks in this chapter, you use other authoring applications and set preferences for Acrobat viewers to accommodate viewing PDFs in Web browsers. When creating links and form fields in PDFs designed for Web viewing, you need to open several toolbars.

Open the More Tools window by opening a context menu on the Acrobat Toolbar window and select More Tools or select Tools ➪ Customize Toolbars. In the More Tools window, check the toolbar check boxes for Advanced Editing Toolbar and Forms Toolbar. When creating form fields and links, the Properties Bar can be helpful. To open the Properties Bar, open a context menu on the Toolbar Well and select Properties Bar or press Ctrl/⌘+E.

When the toolbars are opened, open a context menu on the Toolbar Well and select Dock All Toolbars. If the space available in the Document pane is too small

for comfortable editing, you can collapse toolbars by hiding toolbar labels. Right-click in the Toolbar Well and select Show Button Labels ⇨ No Labels. For clarity in this chapter, I keep the tool labels in view.

When viewing PDFs in Web browsers, you may need additional tools depending on what you do in Acrobat sessions related to viewing PDFs on the Web. As you need additional tools when viewing PDFs in a browser window, you can open toolbars through the same context menu opened from the Toolbar Well in the browser window. Rather than setting up the work environment ahead of time with these additional tools, leave the tools used for viewing PDFs online hidden until you need them during a Web-viewing session.

Viewing PDFs in Web Browsers

You open a PDF in a Web browser just as you open a file to view an HTML document. You specify a URL and filename to view the PDF directly in the browser or click on a Web link from within a PDF document to open a URL where a PDF is hosted. For example, logging on to `www.provider.com/file.pdf` results in the display of the PDF page inside the browser window. This type of viewing is referred to as inline viewing, an example of which appears in Figure 27.1.

FIGURE 27.1

Inline viewing of PDFs offers you access to many Acrobat tools, which are available from the Toolbar Well, just as when viewing PDFs in Acrobat.

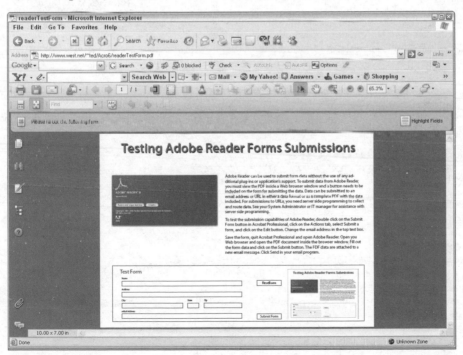

You can also open PDFs on your local hard drive by selecting File ⇨ Open (Windows) or File ⇨ Open File (Macintosh). In the Open dialog box, click Browse (Windows), navigate your hard drive, and select the file you want to open. On the Mac just navigate your hard drive in the Open dialog box and select the file you want to open. Click open and the file opens in the Web browser window. On the Mac, Safari is supported the same as you have available with Microsoft Internet Explorer, as shown in Figure 27.2.

In Figures 27.1 and 27.2, toolbars are open and docked in the Toolbar Well. You have access to tools, commands, and preference settings while viewing PDFs online or locally from your hard drive directly in a browser window. You open toolbars in Web browsers the same way you open them in Acrobat: open a context menu opened from the Toolbar Well and select More Tools. In the More Tools window, check the boxes for the toolbars you want to appear in the browser window.

By default, all Web-hosted PDFs are opened inside your browser. From the browser application you can save a PDF document to your hard drive by choosing File ⇨ Save As.

FIGURE 27.2

PDF files can be opened locally on your hard drive in a browser application. On the Mac, you find Safari supporting inline PDF views just as Windows does.

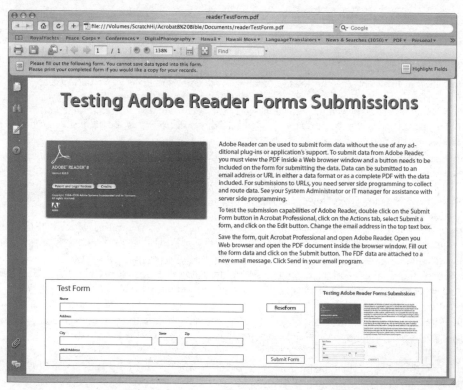

If you prefer to open Web-hosted PDFs in Acrobat, you need to adjust preferences in Acrobat. Preference options provide you choices for viewing PDFs inside your Web browser as an inline view or viewing Web-hosted PDFs inside Acrobat the same as you would view locally hosted PDF documents. To change preferences, choose Edit ➪ Preferences. In the Preferences dialog box, select Internet in the left pane. The viewing preferences appear in the right pane, as shown in Figure 27.3.

To change Web viewing preferences, open the Preferences dialog box and select Internet in the left pane.

Options for handling PDFs on Web sites with Acrobat viewers include the following:

- **Display PDF in browser.** The check box is enabled by default, and PDFs viewed on Web sites are displayed as inline views in browser applications. If you disable the check box as shown in Figure 27.3, PDFs are displayed in Acrobat viewers. The default Acrobat viewer installed on your computer opens if no viewer is currently open and the target document is shown in the Acrobat viewer Document pane.

- **Allow fast web view.** This option speeds up viewing PDFs on Web servers. When this option is enabled, a single page is downloaded to your computer and shown according to how you set your preferences — in the browser window or in an Acrobat viewer window. As you scroll pages in a PDF document, each new page downloads when the page is loaded in the Document pane. If you deselect the check box, the entire PDF document is downloaded to your computer before the first page appears in the browser window or the Acrobat Document pane. You must save the PDF with Fast Web View and the server must be capable of byte-serving for fast Web view to work.

- **Allow speculative downloading in the background.** If you select the preceding Allow fast web view option, and want to continue downloading multiple page PDF documents, check this box. As you view a page, the remaining pages continue to download until the complete PDF is downloaded from a Web site.

- **Connection Speed.** Select the speed of your Internet connection from the pull-down menu choices. This setting applies to viewing Web pages, but also influences the speed selection for viewing multimedia.

- **Internet Settings.** If you click the Internet Settings button, the Internet Properties dialog box opens. In the Internet Properties dialog box you can make choices for configuring your Internet connection, choosing default applications for e-mail, making security settings choices, setting privacy attributes, and other such system-level configurations.

Working with Web links

Web links to PDFs hosted on Web sites occur from within HTML documents and from within PDF files. If using an HTML editor like Adobe GoLive CS or Adobe Dreamweaver, or writing HTML code, you create Web links the same as you link to Web pages. A PDF Web link in HTML might look like http://www.mycompany.com/brochure.pdf — where the link is made to the PDF instead of a document that ends with an .htm or .html extension.

Web addresses contained in the text of a PDF document can be hot links to URLs where PDFs are hosted. In earlier versions of Acrobat you needed the complete URL address including http:// for a Web link to be recognized. In Acrobat 8, a URL like www.adobe.com is recognized as a Web link. Text in PDF documents with URL addresses can be converted to Web links via a menu command. If you distribute PDF files to users of Acrobat 6 or below, you need to add links to the PDF document for the users of these viewers to access Web pages from a PDF.

To create Web links from text in PDF documents, choose Advanced ⇨ Document Processing ⇨ Create Links from URLs. Acrobat opens the Create Web Links dialog box shown in Figure 27.4. In the dialog box you make decisions for the pages where the links are created. Select All to create Web links from all pages in the PDF. The From button enables you to supply page ranges in the two field boxes.

FIGURE 27.4

The Create Web Links dialog box enables you to target pages for creating Web links.

CAUTION Be aware that you don't need to create links in PDF files distributed to Adobe Reader or Acrobat version 7 and above. If you know your audience is using the most recent viewers, don't create the links in your PDF files. Adding links adds unnecessary overhead to the file and the file sizes grow according to the number of links you add.

Acrobat can also globally remove Web links from all pages or a specified page range. To remove Web links, choose Advanced ⇨ Document Processing ⇨ Remove All Links. The same options are available in the Remove Web Links dialog box as those found in the Create Web Links dialog box.

TIP You can create Web links only from text that has been properly identified in the text of the PDF file (either www.Company.com or http://www.company.com). If you need to add a Web link, you can easily create the text in Acrobat without having to return to the authoring program. Select the TouchUp Text tool from the Advanced Editing toolbar. Hold down the Ctrl key (Option key on Macintosh) and click. The text cursor blinks where you click and is ready for you to add new type on the page. Type the URL for the Web link and deselect the text by selecting the Hand tool; and then click in the Document pane. Choose Advanced ⇨ Document Processing ⇨ Create Links from. Acrobat creates the Web link from the URL you added to the document.

Web links in the Organizer

The Organizer behaves like a Web browser Bookmark repository when you're creating links to URLs. You first view a PDF document as an inline view in your Web browser and access the Organizer tool in the Acrobat Toolbar Well within the browser window. The URL for the current viewed document in the Web browser is captured when you add the URL to a collection. After quitting your Web browser, you can access the URL from within Acrobat and the Organizer collections. Opening a document within a collection launches your Web browser and takes you to the URL where the PDF is located. The PDF is then opened inside the browser window, if your viewing preferences remain at the defaults.

CROSS-REF   For more information on using the Organizer, see Chapter 5.

Adding Web links to multiple pages

You may have documents that need Web links created across multiple pages. An example might be a document that has been repurposed from an original design that was created for output to prepress, and then later downsampled and hosted on a Web site. In the original design, you might have a Web link on the cover page, but for the Web-hosted document you may want to create a Web link to an order form or your home page on each page in the brochure document. Where the same URL is specified on each page and the location of the Web link is the same on every page, you can create the Web links in Acrobat after the PDF has been sampled for Web display. The following steps outline a procedure for creating Web links on multiple pages for similar designs or legacy files that don't have Web addresses added in the original authoring application document before a PDF has been created:

CROSS-REF   For information related to repurposing documents and downsampling, see Chapter 18.

STEPS: Creating Web links on multiple PDF pages

1. **Add a header/footer to a multi-page PDF document.** Open the file where the Web links are to be added and choose Document ➪ Header & Footer ➪ Add. In the Add Header & Footer dialog box, create a header or footer and set the type size, the alignment, the color, and the offset distance desired. In this example, I added a footer (center aligned), used Arial 8-point text, and left offsets at the defaults, as shown in Figure 27.5. (In this example, I used an incomplete URL but I started my URL address with *www*.)

FIGURE 27.5

Click on one of the Header or Footer alignment boxes (Left, Center, Right) and add the URL text. Select a font, font size, and offset distance; and then click the OK button.

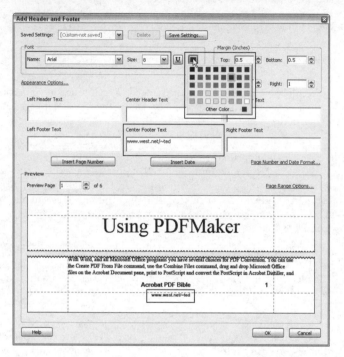

2. **Click OK.**

3. **Save the file and close the document.** When you return to the document pane, the URL links won't be active. You must close the file and reopen it for Acrobat to recognize the links.

4. **Reopen the saved file.** Move the Hand tool to a Web link and a tool tip reports the full URL address as shown in Figure 27.6. Click the link and the file opens in your Web browser.

FIGURE 27.6

When you select the Hand tool and place the cursor over a Web link, the URL appears in a ToolTip.

CROSS-REF For more information on creating headers and footers, see Chapter 16.

TIP If you want Web links to appear rotated along the left or right side of your PDF document, choose Document ➪ Rotate Pages. Add a header or footer as described in the preceding steps. Choose Document ➪ Rotate Pages and select the rotation option that turns the pages back to the original view. Save the document, and the Web links are positioned vertically on each page.

Controlling links view behavior

By default, when you click on a URL link to a PDF document, whether from within your Web browser or from within Acrobat, the resulting view takes you to the same view established in your Initial View properties. Therefore, if your Initial View properties are set to Page Only, Single Page, Fit Page, and Page number 1, the PDF document opens in the Web browser according to these settings just as you would view the file in Acrobat.

The links you create to open different documents and different pages in a PDF file are often unusable when you're viewing PDFs in Web browsers. A link, for example, that opens a secondary PDF won't work in a Web browser unless you modify the link properties and link to the URL where the destination document resides. The Web browser needs URL links to open secondary files. Inasmuch as you may have all links working well for CD-ROM distribution, the links need to have some adjustments made before you can host the PDF documents with usable links on Web servers.

As an example, suppose you want to open page 2 in a PDF file on a Web server. You create a link in one document, direct the link to the URL where the PDF is hosted, and instruct the Web browser or Acrobat viewer to open page 2. To create the link, use either the Link tool or a form field button and enter the following code in an Open Web Link action:

```
http://www.west.net/~ted/pdf/manual.pdf#page=2
```

In this example, the `#page=2` text following the PDF filename is the trigger to open page 2. In addition to accessing user-specified pages, you can control viewing behavior for page layouts, page views, zooms, linking to destinations, and a host of other attributes you assign to the Open Web Link action. Some examples of the code to use following the PDF document name in URL links include the following:

- **Zoom changes:** `#zoom=50`, `#zoom=125`, `#zoom=200`
- **Fit Page view:** `#view=Fit`
- **Destinations:** `#nameddest=Section1`
- **Open Bookmarks palette:** `#pagemode=bookmarks`
- **Open Pages palette:** `#pagemode=thumbs`
- **Collapsing palettes:** `#pagemode=none`
- **Combining viewing options:** `#page=3&pagemode=bookmarks&zoom=125`

TIP More information related to file links on Web hosted documents can be found on Adobe's Web site. Log on to www.adobe.com/education/pdf and type **Web linking** in the Search box. A number of different articles discussing Web links in PDFs are reported in the search results. In addition, you can find several articles covering Web links in PDFs on the Acrobat User Community Web site. Log on to www.acrobatusers.com and visit the blogs and articles sections.

The preceding are some examples for controlling view options when opening PDFs in Web browsers. For each item be aware that you need to use the complete URL address and add one of these options following the location where the PDF document is hosted. Using the page mode example, the complete open action URL might look like http://www.mycompany.com/file.pdf#pagemode=bookmarks.

Converting PDF to HTML

In Chapter 9, I talked about exporting PDFs to a number of different file forms using the Save As command and the new Export task button. In that chapter, you find a summary of the attributes for exporting documents from PDF including exports to HTML. In this chapter, I move forward a little and cover exporting to HTML in a little more depth.

At the onset, let me say that Adobe hasn't done much with the exports to HTML features in Acrobat. With the exception of adding an Export task button in Acrobat 8, the options you have for exporting to HTML in Acrobat 8 are identical to the options you had in Acrobat 6 and 7 Standard and Professional.

Using the export to HTML features in Acrobat can get your PDF content into HTML format, but when exporting images and text together, you'll need to do some polish work in a program designed for authoring Web pages such as Adobe GoLive or Adobe Dreamweaver.

Setting export options

You can control option settings in the Preferences dialog box (Ctrl/⌘+K) by clicking on the Convert from PDF item in the left pane. The right pane displays a list of export formats including HTML 3.2 and HTML 4.01 with CSS 1.0 (Cascading Style Sheets). Click the Edit Settings button and you see a list of options you can edit. These same options are also available to you in the Export dialog box.

Open a PDF document and open the Export task button pull-down menu. Select HTML Web Page from the list and the Save As dialog box opens. The Save as Type (Windows) or Format pull-down menu lets you choose the HTML format you want to export. After selecting the Format, click the Settings button and you see the settings options as shown in Figure 27.7. Again, these options are the same as you have available in the Preferences dialog box. In addition, the Settings options are the same for both HTML formats.

FIGURE 27.7

The Settings adjustments in either the Preferences dialog box or the Save As dialog box are identical.

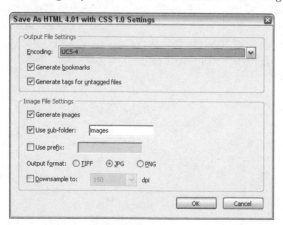

The settings options include:

- **Encoding.** A number of encoding options appear from the pull-down menu. If you have special characters in text use either UTF-8 or UTF-6. If you use an encoding method such as UCS-4, the special characters won't be recognized.

- **Generate Bookmarks.** Links to sections in the HTML document are made from the PDF Bookmarks.

- **Generate tags for untagged documents.** If a document is not tagged, check this box to add tagging for accessibility.

- **Generate images.** If your PDF document has images and you want them converted to a format recognized by HTML, be certain to check this box.

- **Use sub-folder.** All images can be saved to a subfolder nested below the HTML file. Check this box to copy the images to a separate folder. The default folder name is *images*. You can edit the name and provide a name of your choosing for the folder where the images are saved.

- **Use prefix.** If you want a prefix added to your images, check the box and type a prefix name in the text box.

- **Output format.** Choose from the options for the image format you want for the exported images. Use jpg if you have photo images.

- **Downsample to.** Check this box and select an amount to downsample images. The default is 150 ppi. Change this item to 72 ppi for Web viewing.

Converting text documents to HTML

One thing to keep in mind when you convert PDF files to HTML is that the entire PDF document is converted to a single HTML file. If you want separate HTML documents your best option is to first Select Document ➪ Extract Pages. Enter the page numbers you want to extract for one HTML file and click OK. Convert the pages to HTML using the Export ➪ HTML Web Page command. Then return to the original document and extract the pages you want for your second HTML file and convert to HTML, and so on.

CROSS-REF For more information on extracting pages in PDFs, see Chapter 16.

If you have a PDF with Bookmarks, you can convert to HTML with the Bookmarks appearing in the HTML document and linked to the sections of the document that are bookmarked in the original PDF file. To see how to convert a text file with Bookmarks, follow these steps:

STEPS: Converting PDF text only documents to HTML

1. **Open a file containing Bookmarks in Acrobat.** In Figure 27.8, I open a file converted from Microsoft Word. Opening the Bookmarks pane displays the Bookmarks in this file.

2. **Open the Export to HTML dialog box.** Select Export ➪ HTML Web Page. The export dialog box is the Save As dialog box you get when you also select File ➪ Save As.

3. **Adjust Settings.** Click the Settings button in the Save As dialog box and make setting adjustments as described in the "Setting export options" section earlier in this chapter. In this example, I check the box for Generate Bookmarks. Because there are no images in my file, I don't need to address any of the options for exporting images.

FIGURE 27.8

In this example, I use a text document containing Bookmarks.

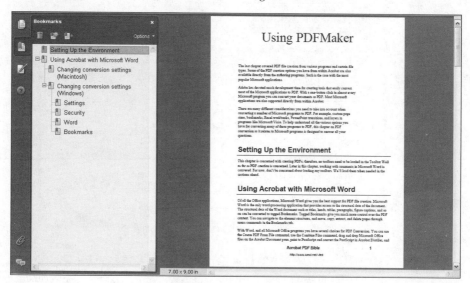

4. **Click OK.** Depending on the size of your file, you may see a progress bar report the export progress or you may just see a flash on your screen. The file is exported without any confirmation dialog box.

5. **View the exported HTML in a Web browser.** Open your Web browser and select File Open. Navigate your hard drive and select the exported file and open it. If you had Bookmarks in the file, they appear as links as shown in Figure 27.9.

FIGURE 27.9

The exported HTML file is opened in a Web browser with links appearing for the Bookmark items that were contained in the PDF file.

Bookmarks converted to links

Exporting PDF files with images to HTML

The process for exporting images is much the same as exporting text files. However, the one option you'll want to edit in the Settings dialog box is the image attributes. To see how PDFs with images are converted to HTML, follow these steps:

STEPS: Converting multi-page PDFs with images to HTML

1. **Open a PDF file with multiple pages and images.**

2. **Select Export ➪ HTML Web Page.**

3. **Adjust Settings options.** Click Settings and select the Output format. In this example, I check the JPG radio button. Click Downsample to and select 72 from the dpi pull-down menu.

4. **Click OK.** The file may take a little time to export depending on the size of your PDF document. When the progress bar finishes, the file is ready to open in your Web browser of HTML editor.

5. **Open the file in your Web browser.** In Figure 27.10, you can see a partial view of my exported file. The original document had two letter and two tabloid pages with several images on each page. This document needs a lot of editing in an HTML editor to format text and graphics for a Web page design.

Figure 27.11 shows the portion of the original PDF document that was exported to HTML.

The best you can hope for with the PDF exports to HTML is a good starting place for editing the HTML in an HTML editor. Acrobat provides you some basic tools to get a PDF document to HTML format. From there, you can expect to do some editing in your favorite HTML editor.

One alternative you have available is to explore using a third-party plug-in designed for exporting PDFs to HTML. A number of different plug-in products are distributed by a number of developers. To find some of the latest plug-ins and obtain some demo copies you can test, visit the PlanetPDF Store. Log on to `www.planetpdf.com/find_software.asp`. On this Planet PDF Web page, you can search for the kind of software you want such as extraction plug-ins. Browse through the contents listed on the Web site after performing a search and look over the products available to you. Before you buy, download a demo copy and test it to see if the product provides you a better solution for your file conversions than you have with Acrobat.

FIGURE 27.10

The HTML file needs a lot of work to polish up the design.

FIGURE 27.11

The original PDF document that was used to export to the HTML file shown in Figure 27.10.

Summary

- PDFs can be viewed inside Web browser windows. When viewed as inline views in Web browsers, Acrobat toolbars and menu options are contained within the browser window.

- You change preferences settings for Web viewing PDFs in Windows in the Acrobat viewer Preferences dialog box.

- To make links from text in PDFs for users of Acrobat 6 and earlier, choose Advanced ➪ Document Processing ➪ Create Links from URLs.

- To create multiple identical Web links across several pages, use the Add Header and Footer dialog box. Type a URL as a header or footer and save the file. Close and re-open the file and the links are active in Acrobat viewers 7 and above.

- By modifying code in the Open Web Link Action properties you can control opening views and override Initial View defaults. Add the code following the URL link to adjust page views, zooms, page modes, and so on.

- You can export PDF to HTML. In most cases you need to polish up the Web page design in an HTML editor after exporting to HTML.

Chapter 28

PDFs and Presentations

Among the many uses for Acrobat PDF files is presentations. Acrobat does not provide the robust features for creating title slides, importing text and graphics in an open PDF document, or creating handouts such as those found in dedicated slide-authoring programs such as Microsoft PowerPoint and Apple's Keynote. However, if you're willing to put in a little work in either designing a slide presentation in a layout program or converting a slide show from PowerPoint or Keynote to PDF, you can explore many other opportunities in Acrobat for making slide presentations dynamic and suitable for any kind of audience through the use of file linking, JavaScripts, and other interactive elements. In this chapter, you learn some helpful methods for producing PDF documents suited for presentations.

Setting Up the Work Environment

Interactivity is one element you'll want to add to documents designed for presentations. To add interactive buttons and fields, open the More Tools window by selecting More Tools from a context menu and check the Advanced Editing toolbar. To create interactive buttons you'll want the Forms tools (Acrobat Professional only). Check the box for the Forms toolbar. For access to all the navigation tools, scroll down to the Page Navigation toolbar and check all the boxes for the Navigation tools and check the Page Navigation toolbar. Click OK and the toolbars open as floating toolbars

When using the Advanced Editing tools or the Forms tools, you'll find the Properties Bar a valuable asset. To open the toolbar, open a context menu from the Toolbar Well and select Properties Bar. After opening the toolbars, open a context menu on the Toolbar Well and select Dock Toolbars.

IN THIS CHAPTER

Using presentation authoring programs

Presentation documents and Adobe PDF Layers

Editing PDF presentation files

Using page transitions

Viewing presentations in Full Screen mode

If you're familiar with the toolbar icons and don't need the tool labels, open a context menu on the Toolbar Well and select Button Labels ⇨ Default Labels. For the figures in this chapter, the toolbar labels are displayed (Button Labels ⇨ All Labels).

Creating Presentation Documents

The first step in creating presentations for viewing in Acrobat is to decide what authoring program you want to use. If you are familiar with either Microsoft PowerPoint or Apple's Keynote, you can create a slide presentation and convert the authoring application file to PDF. For PowerPoint, you'll want to determine whether the PDF conversion is worthwhile. If your slide presentation is about Adobe Acrobat, it makes sense to show the slides in Acrobat. If the presentation is about another topic, you need to determine if it is more beneficial to display the presentation in an Acrobat viewer or directly in PowerPoint. By converting to PDF you make your presentation available to all Adobe Reader users. If you need to pass your presentation through a review committee, you can enable the presentation with Adobe Reader usage rights and provide Adobe Reader users the option for adding comments and notes to your presentation.

CROSS-REF For more information on enabling PDFs with usage rights for Adobe Reader users, see Chapter 19.

If you prefer other author applications to PowerPoint or another dedicated slide application program, conversion to PDF for showing slides in an Acrobat viewer is an ideal solution. Obviously, PDFs offer you more functionality when showing slide presentations than most original authoring applications. Ideally, the best authoring applications to create a slide presentation, if you don't use dedicated slide authoring programs, is a layout program such as Adobe PageMaker, Adobe InDesign, Adobe FrameMaker, or QuarkXPress. These programs offer you the ability to create documents with multiple pages and assign different backgrounds to pages via master pages. In addition, some programs offer you the ability to create text blocks on master pages so the text placement, font sizes, and paragraph properties are identical on each page.

Converting PowerPoint slides to PDF (Windows)

Microsoft PowerPoint files are converted to PDF in much the same way as you convert other Microsoft Office files. The Adobe PDFMaker tool is installed in PowerPoint just as you find with many other Microsoft programs as I described in Chapter 8.

CROSS-REF For more information on conversion to PDF with the PDFMaker tool and Microsoft Office applications, see Chapter 8.

From the Adobe PDF menu, choose Change Conversion Settings to open the Acrobat PDFMaker dialog box shown in Figure 28.1. Select the Adobe PDF Settings you want to use for your file conversion. For presentations without transitions and animations, the Standard Adobe PDF Settings should work sufficiently for showing slides on screens and overheads as well as printing handouts for your audience. If you want to change the compatibility settings, click the Advanced Settings button and you can custom-design Distiller Job Options.

CROSS-REF For more information on changing Adobe PDF settings and using Acrobat Distiller, see Chapter 10. For a description of all the settings you can make in the Acrobat PDFMaker dialog box, see Chapter 8.

As with the other Office applications discussed in Chapter 8, you click the Convert to Adobe PDF tool in the PowerPoint toolbar to convert the slides to a PDF file. Conversion of a PowerPoint slide presentation without adding special features is a relatively easy operation. But let's get a little fancy with our PDF creation and do a little more than just convert a simple PowerPoint presentation to PDF.

FIGURE 28.1

Select Adobe PDF ⇨ Change Conversion Settings to change attributes for the PDF conversion from PowerPoint.

Let me first present a scenario. Suppose you want to create a presentation and after the presentation you want to have your audience participants fill out an evaluation questionnaire. You want the attendees to have a copy of your slide presentation and a PDF form to complete an evaluation. In this scenario you have a few choices. You can add a file link in PowerPoint to the PDF form within PowerPoint, or you can insert the form in the PDF Presentation in Acrobat after converting to PDF, or create a PDF Package after converting the PowerPoint Document to PDF.

Adding forms to presentations makes Acrobat the program of choice for both converting to PDF and attaching or inserting forms in a presentation. To see how we accomplish attaching a PDF form in PowerPoint, look over the following steps.

STEPS: Converting a PowerPoint file with a linked document to PDF

1. **Create a form and enable the form for Adobe Reader users in Acrobat.** Note that this option requires Acrobat Professional. Create a form as described in Chapters 33 and 34. Enable the form by selecting Advanced ⇨ Enable Usage Rights in Adobe Reader.

CROSS-REF For more on forms creation, look over the chapters in Part VI. For more on enabling PDF forms for usage rights in Adobe Reader, see Chapter 19.

2. **Open or create a presentation in PowerPoint.**

3. **Insert an Object.** After creating your presentation in PowerPoint, open a page in the slide presentation where you want a link to the PDF form to appear. Select Insert ⇨ Object and the Insert Object dialog box opens.

4. **Identify the file to be inserted.** Click Create from file in the Insert Object dialog box shown in Figure 28.2. Click Browse to navigate your hard drive and locate the file to be inserted. Select the PDF form in the Browse dialog box and click OK. Back in the Insert Object dialog box, click the Link check box. This is a very important option to enable. If you don't click the Link check box, the PDF will be imported as an object and all form attributes will be lost. Click the Display as icon check box to place an icon on the selected page that will represent a link button. Click OK after making choices in the Insert Object dialog box.

FIGURE 28.2

In PowerPoint, select Insert ⇨ Object to open the Insert Object dialog box.

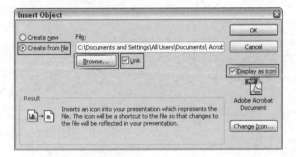

5. **Open the Link Action Settings.** So far you've identified the slide display and associated a linked file with the icon, but PowerPoint still needs to have the link actions added to the presentation or you won't be able to open the linked file. To set the link actions, open a context menu on the link icon. From the menu options, select Action Settings and the Action Settings dialog box opens, as shown in Figure 28.3.

FIGURE 28.3

Open a context menu and select Actions Settings to open the Action Settings dialog box.

6. **Set the link attributes.** In the Action Settings dialog box, leave the default Mouse Click tab in view and click the Hyperlink to radio button. From the pull-down menu below the Hyperlink to radio button select Other File. The Hyperlink to Other File dialog box opens. Locate your PDF form, select it, and click OK. Click OK in the Action Settings dialog box and your file link is complete.

7. **Click the Convert to Adobe PDF tool in PowerPoint.** At this point you're ready to convert to PDF. For this series of steps, you'll use the default Acrobat PDF PDFMaker conversion settings shown earlier in Figure 28.1 so you don't need to bother changing conversion settings

8. **View the PDF in Acrobat.** By default, the slide presentation opens in Acrobat. Locate the page containing your link button.

9. **Examine the link properties.** Click the Select Object tool in the Advanced Editing toolbar and double-click the link rectangle. The Link Properties dialog box opens as shown in Figure 28.4. Notice the object added to the file is a link that can have the properties changed in both Acrobat Standard and Acrobat Professional. The link action is an Execute Menu Item defined to Open a file.

10. **Test the link.** Click Cancel in the Link Properties dialog box and select the Hand tool (or press H on your keyboard when single key accelerators are enabled in the General preferences). Click the link and your PDF file opens in the Acrobat Document pane. The down side of using PowerPoint to create links to PDF files is that when sharing files you need to deploy two separate files and the directory path to the linked file must be preserved in order for the link action to work. You have no option in PowerPoint to embed the PDF document in the presentation or create a file attachment. Once you embed the PDF in PowerPoint all form fields are lost. PowerPoint does support linking to any file. You can use forms created in Acrobat or Adobe Designer. But with the linking limitation, you might find it a better choice to convert the presentation to PDF and then handle your file linking in Acrobat.

FIGURE 28.4
Click Cancel in the Link properties dialog box.

You have many options for linking files in Acrobat. Use of the Link or Button (Acrobat Professional only) tools to open files offers you no more opportunity than PowerPoint. Acrobat provides you additional ways to link files, including the Document ➪ Insert Pages command, the Combine Files task button for either

combining files or creating PDF Packages, and the Attachments pane. For inserting pages and combining files, you're limited to PDFs that don't have any password security, digital signatures, and files created in Adobe Designer. When creating PDF Packages, you can package all types of PDFs together in a single package.

CROSS-REF For more on Inserting Pages, see Chapter 16. For more on combining files, creating PDF Packages, and attaching files, see Chapter 12.

As an example of combining a converted PowerPoint slide presentation and a PDF form into a single PDF document, look over Figure 28.5. The two files appear together. It is much easier to manage the files and share them because you don't have to keep track of two different files. When creating PDF Packages, you won't inadvertently forget to share one file or the other.

FIGURE 28.5

A PDF Package keeps your presentation and form together at all times.

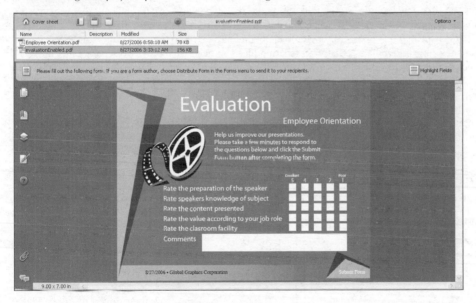

Converting PowerPoint notes and handouts to PDF

If you want to create notes for your audience, then you need to set up PowerPoint properly for printing Notes pages. The setup for printing notes and handouts is handled in the PowerPoint Print dialog box. To print a file with slides and notes, follow these steps.

STEPS: Converting notes to PDF

1. **Open a presentation in PowerPoint.**
2. **Open the Print dialog box.** Choose File ➪ Print in PowerPoint. In the Print dialog box, select the item you want to print. In this example, I chose Notes Pages, as shown in Figure 28.6.

3. **Choose a printer driver.** Make the choice for your printer from the Name pull-down menu. Because you'll want the file set up for conversion to PDF, select the Adobe PDF printer.

FIGURE 28.6

Select Adobe PDF as your target printer and choose Notes Pages from the pull-down menu choices for Print what.

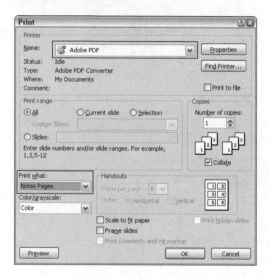

At the bottom of the dialog box, you can make choices for printing a keyline border (Frame slides), scaling if so desired, and including comments if you want to have any PowerPoint comments included in the resulting PDF.

4. **Preview.** To register the settings made in the Print dialog box, click the Preview button and you'll see a page preview of a notes page. The document you end up with contains a slide in the top half of the pages and empty white space on the bottom of each page. If you want to add lines, any graphic elements, and/or a text box after the PDF conversion, you have to handle these edits in Acrobat.

5. **Convert to PDF.** Use the default Acrobat PDFMaker settings and click the Convert to Adobe PDF tool. The PDF opens in Acrobat by default. Your conversion is successful if you see your presentation open in the Document pane.

We've come half the distance for adding notes. You have two choices for note appearances depending on your output needs. If you want to print your handouts, then you'll want to create a template showing lines and a notes section to help your audience take notes. If you distribute your PDF form for electronic viewing, you'll want to create a text field for your audience to add text notes electronically.

Let's look at the second option for adding a text field to your presentation notes for electronic viewing. To start off, let me explain exactly what is to be accomplished. In Figure 28.7 you see the process for creating note pages with a form field. The PDF slide is merged together with a PDF form containing a form field in which users can type notes. These two PDF documents are merged together in Acrobat. The blank page will be used as a template and the template will be spawned as an overlay on all the slide pages. As each page is spawned, a new field name is automatically added to each page. The slide and blank page merged (on the right in Figure 28.7) shows you a sample of a note page with the large text field populated with note comments.

FIGURE 28.7

Two PDF documents are created (slides and a note handout with a text form field) and merged together in Acrobat.

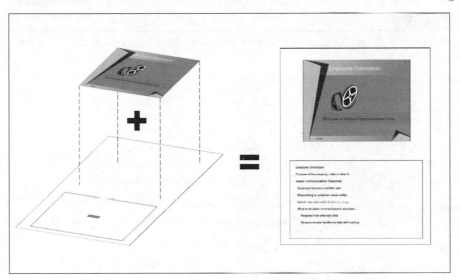

To make this a little easier to understand, look over the summary steps used to follow the process shown in Figure 28.7 before you move on to the actual steps that follow:

1. Create a blank page and save the page as PDF.
2. Add a text field to the blank page.
3. Add a button to the blank page.
4. Add a JavaScript to the button and save the file.
5. Open the PowerPoint file converted to PDF as Notes.
6. Select Document ➪ Insert Pages and insert the blank page with the text field and button as a new page.
7. Create a page template from of the blank page (containing the field and button).
8. The button with the JavaScript appears on the blank page. Click the button and all slides are merged with the template.
9. Delete the template page. Save your file.

Here are the steps to accomplish the task:

1. **Create a blank PDF page.** You can use a number of methods to create a blank page. Insert a blank page from a file you created in another program and exported to PDF. Open the JavaScript Console and type **app.newDoc();** and then press the Num Pad Enter key on your keyboard. By default, Acrobat creates a non-editing text block when you use the Create PDF From Blank Page command. Unfortunately, this page won't work because you can't resize the text block and leaving it at the default will disturb the view of the slide when you add text.

2. **Create a text form field for the template.** If you want to add a text block to each page, you need to do a little editing and create a JavaScript. The first step is to create a template page.

   With the blank page open, create a text form field on the blank page. Format the field as follows:

   - **General tab.** In the Name text box, add any name you want for the field name.

   - **Appearance tab.** Click the Appearance tab and choose a fixed font size. I use 10-point type for my document. Click the Border color swatch to open the Color palette and select a color for a border.

   - **Options tab.** Click the Options tab and check the boxes for Multi-line, Scroll long text, and Allow Rich Formatting.

3. **Click Close in the Text Field Properties dialog box.**

CROSS-REF For more information on formatting text fields, see Chapters 33 and 34.

4. **Create a Button field.** Click the Button tool and drag open a rectangle at the top of the page. (Note Button fields are available only in Acrobat Professional). In the Button properties dialog box, type a name in the General Properties. In my example I use spawnPage. Leave the Appearance settings at default. The default fill color is gray so you'll be able to see the button after creating it. The name option is your choice. Change it in the General tab if you so desire. The text field and the button field on the blank page are shown in Figure 28.8.

FIGURE 28.8

The blank page with a text field and button field

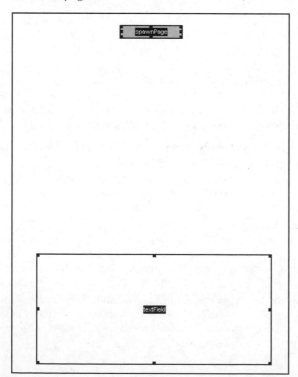

5. **Add a JavaScript.** To automate our process for adding text fields to all pages, we'll use a JavaScript. If you don't use a JavaScript, you'll have to copy and paste a text field and rename each pasted field with a unique field name. Using the Duplicate Fields command won't work because the fields retain all the same names when you use this command. The only way to automate the procedure is to use a JavaScript and let the script provide unique names for all duplicated fields.

Click the Actions tab in the Button Properties dialog box. From the Select Action pull-down menu select Run a JavaScript. Click the Add button and the JavaScript Editor opens. Type the following code in the JavaScript Editor as shown in Figure 28.9.

```
for (var i=0; i<this.numPages-1; i++) {
this.spawnPageFromTemplate ("textTemplate", i, true)
}
this.removeField ("spawnPage").
```

FIGURE 28.9

Type a script in the JavaScript Editor.

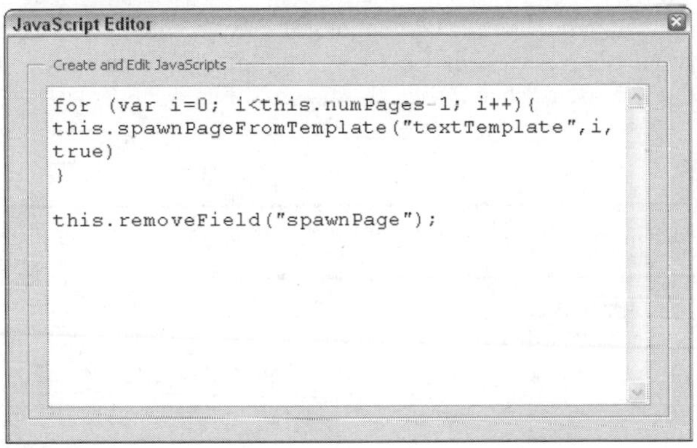

CROSS-REF For now, just add the code as you see it appear here. For a detailed description for what the code means and more on spawning pages from templates, see Chapter 36.

6. **Insert the template page in the notes document.** Click OK in the JavaScript Editor and click Close in the Button Properties window. Save the file to disk.

These steps may appear a bit overwhelming at first, but realize you have to do this only once. If you create a lot of slide presentations in PowerPoint and want to add similar notes pages, you can use the same template file to insert in other PDF Presentations.

7. **Open the Notes PDF document.** From PowerPoint you need to export to PDF a Notes document as described earlier in "Steps: Converting notes to PDF." Open the PDF and select Document ➪ Insert Pages. Locate your blank template file containing the text field and button and insert the file in the notes PDF document. You can insert the file at the beginning or the end of the notes PDF file.

8. **Create a page template.** Be certain the new inserted blank page is in view in the Document pane and select Forms ➪ Page Templates. (Note this menu item is inactive if you don't have at least one form field in the PDF document. If you don't see the page Templates command, select Forms Edit Form in Acrobat).

The Page Templates dialog box opens, as shown in Figure 28.10. Type a name for your template in the name field and click the Add button. Be certain to type the SAME name you used in your JavaScript. In my example the name I used in the JavaScript shown in Step 5 is *textTemplate*. Therefore I name my new Page Template *textTemplate*. The name is case sensitive to be certain to provide a name *exactly* like the name you used in the JavaScript. Click the Add button after typing a name and Acrobat prompts you to confirm adding a page as a template in a dialog box. Click Yes and click Close in the Page Templates dialog box.

FIGURE 28.10

Type a name, click Add, and click Yes in the confirmation dialog box. Click Close and your page is added as a template.

9. **Save the PDF document.** Click the Save tool in the File toolbar and update the notes presentation document.

10. **Click the button on the template page.** You'll notice a text field is added to all pages with unique field names and the button is deleted from the template. Note that the first line of code handled the button deletion so it wouldn't be spawned to all the other pages.

11. **Delete the template page.** Before you move around the document, select Document ➪ Delete Pages. In the Delete Pages dialog box leave the default settings alone and the current page in view will be deleted. Click OK and your template page is removed.

NOTE You can also automate removing templates from PDFs using a JavaScript, but this action takes some more work and more lines of code. In order to include code in your script to remove templates, you need to grant privileges to get around some of the security restrictions in Acrobat. For more information about scripting privileges, see Chapter 36.

12. **Optimize the File.** Select File ➪ Save As to rewrite the file and optimize it for the smallest file size. The completed notes document is shown in Figure 28.11.

If you want a different design for your notes to appear under the slide images, you can create any kind of design in your favorite authoring program and convert to PDF. Use the design as a template and follow the same steps to spawn pages from a template.

TIP   If you want to add page numbers to the notes pages, use the Document ➪ Header & Footer command and add a header or footer with page numbers. To learn more about adding headers and footers in Acrobat, see Chapter 16.

FIGURE 28.11

The completed notes file with the text form field and the button removed.

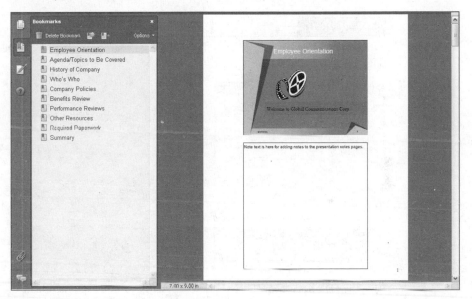

Converting PowerPoint slides to PDF (Mac)

A long-standing problem we've had ever since the introduction of the PDFMakers is that they just don't work well with PowerPoint on the Mac. The PDFMakers work fine in Excel and Word on the Mac, but in PowerPoint it's a turkey shoot and you can watch your computer stand still for hours thinking your presentation is being converted until you finally give up and click the Cancel button. Sometimes it does work, but most of the time it doesn't. Because you have no conversion settings options on the Mac, it's not much of a problem to get around the PDFMaker and use other methods for PDF creation.

Rather than use the PDFMaker in PowerPoint on the Mac, you could use the Print dialog box and print your presentation to PDF. However, the nightmare continues when you try to get the right page size. On Windows you get the exact page size you specify from the default slide page size. On the Mac you get something like a page shown in Figure 28.12.

What's your alternative? If you happen to have a dual core Mac and you run BootCamp, you might look into installing Acrobat on Windows running on your Mac. If you have a friend or colleague using Acrobat and PowerPoint on Windows, you could send your file to your colleague to convert to PDF. Doing so, of course, means that you should both be licensed users of Acrobat. The PowerPoint files are easily transferred between computer platforms as long as you use fonts available on both operating systems.

Finding a workaround will save you much time and aggravation. Do your best to get a little help in converting these files to PDF.

FIGURE 28.12

The Mac PDFMaker from PowerPoint has many problems, among which are producing PDF pages that match the PowerPoint page sizes.

Converting Apple Keynote slides to PDF (Mac)

Another option Mac users have for converting PowerPoint slides to PDF is to open them in Apple's Keynote. Keynote is a dedicated slide presentation authoring application that offers a robust authoring environment providing simplicity and ease in creating slide shows. The charting features in Keynote are easy to use with intuitive palettes for editing chart types and data. Whether you use Keynote to convert PowerPoint slides or use it as your original authoring program, Keynote easily converts presentations to PDF.

Keynote supports file imports for many image formats, video, and sound, and PDF imports that can be sized and scaled. The templates installed with the program are attractive and well designed. After creating a slide show in Keynote, choose File ➪ Export. A dialog box drops down from the application menu bar where you are offered format options for exporting to QuickTime, PowerPoint, or PDF formats. To export directly to PDF format, select the PDF radio button and click Next. Locate the folder where you want the PDF file saved and click the Export button. You won't find Keynote giving you the same problems for matching page sizes between Keynote and PDF.

If you want to attach files to a Keynote presentation, follow the same path as the Windows PowerPoint users. Use the Assemble Files into PDF Package command when you want to add file attachments.

Converting authoring application documents to PDF

Many creative professionals use layout programs for a variety of purposes, including slide presentations. If you use QuarkXPress, Adobe InDesign, Adobe PageMaker, or Adobe FrameMaker for creating a slide presentation, you can export your documents to PDF via the same methods used for PDF exports when preparing files for print. For notes and handouts, you can create master pages in any one of the applications with the graphics, lines, and styles you want, and you can import the PDF document into the layout application. Each of the aforementioned programs supports PDF imports.

CROSS-REF For more information on converting layout program documents to PDF, see Chapter 7.

Depending on the program you use, you can either set up master pages with graphic placeholders or place and size PDF pages individually. In a program such as Adobe InDesign CS, creating Note pages is more work than using PowerPoint, but you can create some workarounds for adding notes to presentations. You begin by creating a master page with the design you want to use for the note handouts. On the master page, add graphic elements such as the lines, text, logo, or other data. Next, create a rectangle with the Rectangle Frame tool. In this example the slide pages need to be sized down to 75 percent; therefore, I created the rectangle and used the Transformation palette to size the rectangle to 75% to accommodate the PDF slide pages.

After creating the template, add pages to the document and assign the template to each page. When it comes time to import the slide file, select File ➪ Place. In the Place dialog box, be certain to select Show Import Options. When the check box is enabled, InDesign opens the Place PDF dialog box, shown in Figure 28.13 where you determine what page is placed.

FIGURE 28.13

To make choices for what page to place in the InDesign file, be certain to enable Show Import Options in the Place dialog box. After clicking OK in the Place dialog box, the Place PDF dialog box opens where you can scroll pages to place the page of choice.

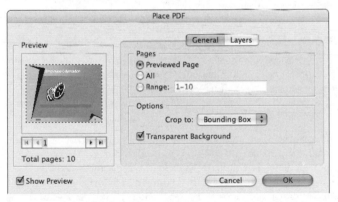

In the Show Import Options dialog box, click the left- or right-pointing arrows to scroll pages. Select a page and click OK. Click the cursor in the area where the rectangle frame was drawn on the master page and the PDF page is placed and sized to the exact fit, including scaling. When the page is placed, move to the next InDesign page and place the next PDF page.

After placing all pages and using a template master for the design layout, select File ⇨ Export. Select Adobe PDF in the Export dialog box and export the file to PDF.

 For more on exporting to PDF from Adobe InDesign, see Chapter 9.

Working with Page Transitions and Effects

Page transitions and effects such as animations can be converted to PDF when you use the PDFMaker in PowerPoint. You also have options for adding transitions directly in Acrobat viewers. Acrobat lacks the ability to provide you animations with text and images such as text flying in or out of a slide, text rotations, fades and dissolves, and so on. However, you can create these kinds of animations in PowerPoint, and when viewed in Full Screen mode, many of the effects are visible in Acrobat.

PowerPoint also supports the import of video, sound, and page transitions, and these imports are also converted to PDF when using the PDFMaker. You can choose to add video and sound imports and page transitions in PowerPoint, or you can use tools in Acrobat Professional to import media and you can create page transitions in any Acrobat viewer including Adobe Reader.

 For more information on working with video and sound in PDFs, see Chapter 23.

Converting animations to PDF from PowerPoint

To convert animations and media to PDF, you need to be certain the right options are enabled in the Acrobat PDFMaker dialog box. The first step in converting files having such content is to select Adobe PDF ⇨ Change Conversion Settings. Be certain the check boxes shown in Figure 28.14 are selected for adding multimedia, saving animations, and saving transitions.

FIGURE 28.14

Check the options for saving media, animations, and transitions in the Acrobat PDFMaker dialog box.

- ☑ Convert Multimedia to PDF Multimedia
- ☑ Save Animations in Adobe PDF
- ☑ Save slide Transitions in Adobe PDF

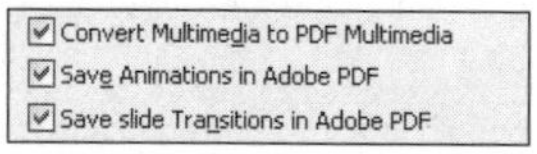

Page transitions are optional. You can bring in transitions from PowerPoint or you can add page transitions in Acrobat. After adjusting the conversion settings in PowerPoint you use the same methods described earlier in "Converting PowerPoint slides to PDF" in this chapter.

Adding page transitions in Acrobat viewers

Page transitions are available in both Edit mode and Full Screen mode in Acrobat. You can set page transitions for all pages in a file or from selected pages in the Pages palette. You can batch-process files and apply transitions on a group of documents with a batch command.

 For more information on creating batch sequences, see Chapter 18.

To set transitions on all pages or a specified range of pages in a document while remaining in Edit mode (as opposed to Full Screen mode) do the following.

STEPS: Adding page transitions to a document

1. **Open a slide presentation in any Acrobat viewer.**

2. **Open the Pages panel by clicking the Pages icon.** Note that in Acrobat Standard and Professional, you can add page transitions using a context menu or a menu command from the Options pull-down menu and selecting Page Transitions. You also have the option of selecting the Advanced ➪ Document Processing ➪ Page Transitions menu command. Note that this command has been moved from the Document menu to the Advanced menu in Acrobat 8.

   You might want to use the Pages panel to access the Set Transitions dialog box because you can easily select a range of pages or a group of noncontiguous pages, or you can make a choice to apply transitions to all pages from selections you make in the Pages panel and then easily access the Page Transitions command.

   If you use Adobe Reader to set page transitions, you don't have access to menu commands from the top-level menu bar or a context menu in the Pages panel. You need to handle page transitions settings in the Full Screen Preferences.

3. **Select pages you want to appear with transitions.** If you want all pages to appear with transitions, skip this step and move to the next step. If you want only a selected range of pages to appear with transitions, click the page thumbnails you want to appear with page transitions. For a noncontiguous selection, press the Ctrl/⌘ key and click each page you want to use.

4. **Open the Set Transitions dialog box.** After selecting pages or when applying transitions to all pages, you can choose Page Transitions from a context menu, the Pages panel Options drop-down menu, or the Advanced ➪ Document Processing submenu. Any one of these choices opens the Set Transitions dialog box shown in Figure 28.15.

FIGURE 28.15

The Set Transitions dialog box offers you a wide range of choices for transition effects you can apply to pages while viewing documents in Edit mode.

5. **Set the transition attributes.** A number of choices are available for applying page transitions. Make some settings adjustments for the following:

   ■ **Transition.** From the Transition pull-down menu, you select the transition effect to be applied for the pages selected either in the dialog box or from the range of pages selected in the Pages panel. Acrobat offers you a total of 16 different choices. One choice is to set No Transition, with the remaining 15 choices being different effects.

   ■ **Direction.** Not all transitions use options in the Direction menu. When an option is available, open the pull-down menu and select a command for the direction you want the transition to move.

   ■ **Speed.** Make a selection for Fast, Medium, or Slow in the Speed pull-down menu.

   ■ **Auto Flip.** If you enable Auto Flip, pages are scrolled at an automatic interval according to the number of seconds you select from the pull-down menu below the Auto Flip check box. Choices for the interval are between −21474833648.000 and +21474833648.000 seconds. You can select fixed interval options or type a value within the acceptable range. If you want to manually scroll pages, leave the check box disabled.

   ■ **Page Range.** If you don't select pages in the Pages tab, use the Set Transitions dialog box to apply transitions to All pages in document, or specify a page range in a contiguous order by clicking on the Pages range and typing in the page From and To field boxes. When you select pages in the Pages panel, the pages become active by default and the transitions are applied to the selected pages.

After setting the effects and page range, click OK and transitions are applied to the pages when you scroll pages in Edit mode.

Although it isn't necessary with all the features in Acrobat 8, you can apply page transitions in authoring applications prior to PDF conversion. If you happen to have an old Acrobat 3 installer CD you'll find a folder on the CD titled Transitions. The Transitions folder contains EPS files with PostScript code to create transitions when pages are scrolled in Edit mode. If you use a layout application to create your slide presentations, place one of the EPS transition effects on a master page in your layout program and convert to PDF. The transitions are applied to all the pages as you scroll through the document. If you elect to use this method, you don't have the flexibility for quickly changing transition effects. The one advantage is that any user of older versions of Acrobat can create PDF documents with transitions by using this method.

Using Full Screen Views

Full Screen mode offers you many different viewing options when you want to show a slide presentation. If your presentation requires a discussion of Acrobat and you want to access tools and menu commands, working in Edit mode is the most obvious choice. When you use Full Screen mode, the menu bar and tools are hidden from view, but the viewing options and alternatives for showing slides in Acrobat are much greater.

Setting Full Screen preferences

The first task in working with Full Screen mode is to set up the environment for showing slides by setting the Full Screen preferences. Choose Edit ➪ Preferences (Acrobat ➪ Preferences on the Macintosh) or press Ctrl/⌘+K. In the left pane, select Full Screen and the preference choices appear, as shown in Figure 28.16.

FIGURE 28.16

To set up the Full Screen view, open the Preferences dialog box and click on Full Screen in the left panel.

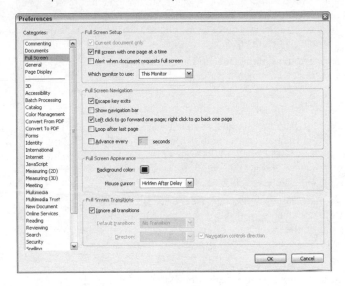

The preference choices include:

- **Current document only.** You can set up Full Screen viewing as a default for all files you view or applied only to the current PDF document. When the check box is disabled, your settings are applied to any file. When the check box is checked, your settings are applied only to the file open in the Document pane.

- **Fill screen with one page at a time.** Sets the page view to the maximum screen coverage by a single page.

- **Alert when document requests full screen.** You may have noticed that if you click a link to open a file or use the Open tool to open a file where the Initial View is saved to open in Full Screen mode, a dialog box, as shown in Figure 28.17, asks if you want to open in Full Screen mode. This preference choice setting controls a dialog box that opens and prompts a user to choose whether to open in Full Screen mode or not. If the user clicks Yes, the file opens in Full Screen mode. If the user clicks no, the file opens, but it opens in edit mode.

FIGURE 28.17

Check the Alert when document requests full screen check box and a dialog box prompting a user to accept viewing in Full Screen mode opens.

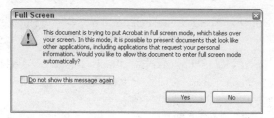

- **Which monitor to use.** From a pull-down menu, you have several choices for monitor viewing. Some of the menu choices are helpful when displaying presentations on projection systems. To find out what menu choice works best for you, change the viewing preference when you prepare a presentation by selecting different menu options before your presentation session and when viewing the presentation on a projection system. When viewing presentations on your own monitor, leave the default setting as This Monitor.

- **Escape key exits.** Entering the Full Screen mode is handled by setting the Initial View options or by pressing Ctrl/⌘+L. If you want to exit Full Screen view you can press the Esc key when this check box is enabled. Be certain to leave the check box at the default switch. If you disable the check box, you need to remember to use Ctrl/⌘+L to exit Full Screen view.

- **Show navigation bar.** When the check box is enabled, icons appear in the lower-left corner of the screen permitting you to go to the previous slide or next slide, or exit Full Screen mode (third icon). In Figure 28.18 the three arrow icons are visible when this preference choice is checked.

FIGURE 28.18

To display navigation buttons while in Full Screen mode, check the Full Screen preference choice for Show navigation bar.

- **Left-click to go forward one page; right-click to go back one page.** When this check box is enabled, you can navigate pages with mouse clicks. For both Windows and Macintosh users who use a two-button mouse, clicking on the left or right button navigates pages in the respective direction.

- **Loop after last page.** Using this option and the next setting for auto advancing, you can set up a kiosk and have the slide presentation continue with auto repetition. After the last page is viewed, the presentation begins again, showing the first page and continuing in an infinite loop.

- **Advance every.** If you enable the check box, the slide presentation automatically scrolls pages at the interval specified in the field box adjacent to the check box. The values permitted for the interval are between 1 and 60 seconds.

- **Background color.** Click on the color swatch and the preset color palette opens where you can make choices for the background color. The background color appears outside the slide pages on all pages that do not fit precisely within the monitor frame. If you want to use a custom color, click on Other Color at the bottom of the palette and select a custom color from your system palette.

- **Mouse cursor.** You have three choices from the pull-down menu for the mouse cursor display while viewing slides in Full Screen mode. You can choose from Always Visible, Always Hidden, or Hidden After Delay. The Hidden After Delay menu choice shows the cursor position when you scroll pages, and then hides it after a short delay (usually a two- to three-second delay).

- **Ignore all transitions.** If you set transitions while in Edit mode and want to eliminate the transition effects while in Full Screen view, enable this check box.

- **Default transition.** From the pull-down menu you have choices for 1 of 16 different transition effects. If you apply a transition in the Full Screen preferences, all pages use the same transition. If you select Random from the menu choices, effects change randomly as you move through slide pages. If you want to use specific transitions that change for selected pages, set the transitions from the Advanced ➪ Document Processing ➪ Page Transitions menu command before opening the Preferences dialog box. Disable Ignore all transitions and the effects you choose for page transitions applied to selected pages in the Pages panel are used when you enter Full Screen mode.

- **Direction.** This is the same option you have when using the Set Page Transitions dialog box. See the section "Adding page transitions in Acrobat viewers" earlier in this chapter.

After setting the Preferences, you can enter Full Screen mode by pressing Ctrl/⌘+L or selecting View ➪ Full Screen Mode.

Saving Initial View options for files opening in Full Screen mode

If you want your PDF document to always open in Full Screen view, you can control the Full Screen view in the Initial View Document Properties dialog box. Settings for initial views are made on a document-by-document basis and the settings you make override an end user's viewing preferences.

To set Initial Views for Full Screen viewing, use the steps that follow

STEPS: Setting the Initial View for Full Screen viewing

1. Open a presentation in Acrobat Standard or Professional.

> **NOTE** You can't change any Document Properties in Adobe Reader even when files are enabled with Reader usage rights.

2. Press Ctrl/⌘+D to open the Document Properties dialog box.

3. Click the Initial View tab.

4. **Check the Open in Full Screen mode check box.** Note that the choices for Navigation tab, Page layout, Magnification, Window Options, and User Interface Options have no effect on files opening in Full Screen mode. If all of the check boxes are selected, as shown in Figure 28.19, the Full Screen view overrides all others.

5. **Save the file.** Before your new settings are applied to the file, you must save the document. Click OK in the Document Properties dialog box and select File ➪ Save As to optimize the file. Click Save and your file is rewritten with optimization and the new Initial View options are saved with the file. You must close and reopen the file to see the new Initial View options take effect.

CROSS-REF For more information on Initial Views, see Chapter 5. For more information on using Save As to optimize file sizes, see Chapter 11.

FIGURE 28.19

Full Screen mode overrides all other preference options selected in the Initial View settings.

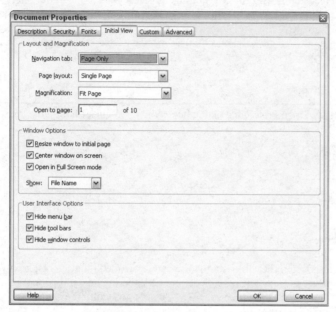

Scrolling pages in Full Screen mode

To advance through slides when in Full Screen mode, you can use the preference setting to scroll pages with mouse clicks. If the preference choice for "Left click to go forward one page; right click to go back one page" is disabled, you scroll pages with keystrokes. Press the Page Down or Page Up keys to move forward and backward through slides. In addition, you can use the up or left arrow keys to move backward and the down or right arrow keys to move forward. Use the Home key to move to the first page and the End key to move to the last page. If you want to move to a specific page without leaving Full Screen mode, press Shift+Ctrl/⌘+N and the Go to Page dialog box opens. Enter the page number to open in the field box and click OK.

Creating interactivity in Full Screen mode

You may have a slide presentation that does not require access to Acrobat menus and tools, but you want to show cross-document links. Perhaps you have a presentation about a company's financial status, economic growth, or projected growth and you want to show a financial spreadsheet, another PDF document, or a scanned image of a memo or report. The slide show created in PowerPoint with the motion objects and viewed in Full Screen view is what you want, but you also want the flexibility for opening other files without leaving Full Screen mode.

Creating links and buttons for cross-document linking

If you want to open a secondary document while in Full Screen mode, you can create links or form field buttons to secondary files. When you click on the link, the link action is invoked. If opening a secondary file, the file link opens in Full Screen mode. After viewing the file, press Ctrl/⌘+W to close the file and return to the last slide view, also in Full Screen mode.

To set up a file link, create a link or form field button and select Open a file in the Select Action pull-down menu. Click the Add button and select the file to open. When the Specify Open Preference dialog box opens, select New window, as shown in Figure 28.20. Click OK and click the Close button. When you view the file in Full Screen mode and click the button, the secondary file opens in Full Screen mode, leaving the slide presentation open in Acrobat.

FIGURE 28.20

Select New window in the Specify Open Preference dialog box. When you click on the link, the secondary file opens in Full Screen mode.

The same behavior exists with other link actions. You can create a URL link to display a Web site while in Full Screen mode by using the Open a web link action. Click on the link and your Web browser opens at the specified URL. When you quit the Web browser, you are returned to the slide presentation in Full Screen mode. If you use PowerPoint effects, the effects are not disturbed.

CROSS-REF   To learn more about setting link actions, see Chapter 22.

Using interactive devices

Another interactivity tool that you can use with Full Screen view is a remote control device. For about $50 to $75 US, you can purchase a handheld remote control. The control comes in two parts. The control device has two buttons used for moving forward and backward in the slide presentation. The companion unit is plugged into a USB port on your laptop or desktop computer. You open the slide presentation in Full Screen view and click the left or right button to navigate slides while you walk across a stage. Some devices also have a button for cursor control. You can remotely move the cursor on a slide and click a button that opens a secondary file, Web link, or other action associated with the button or link.

When using remote devices, be certain to set your Full Screen preferences to "Left click to go forward one page; right click to go back one page." The USB devices have two buttons enabling you to move backward and forward through your slide presentation. When the check boxes are enabled, the back and forward buttons on the handheld device are supported.

Conducting Presentations and Online Meetings

Dynamic and real-time delivery of presentations to workgroups, conference attendees, and expo participants is now extended to online presentations. Adobe's answer to providing an online viewing environment is handled through Acrobat Connect.

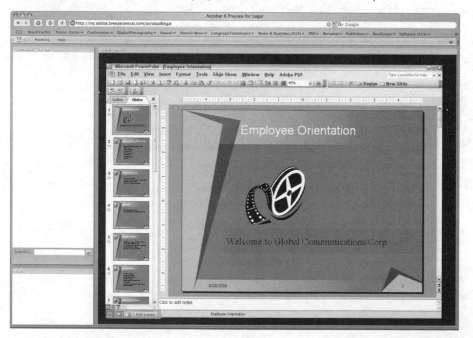

Along with the PDFMaker in all programs supporting Acrobat PDFMaker, you have an additional button installed when you complete your Acrobat installation. The Start Meeting button appears in PowerPoint and all other MS Office programs as well as in Acrobat. Click this button and the Welcome to Start Meeting dialog box opens.

When you log on with your Acrobat Connect account and start a meeting, you can use any application to conduct a slide show. From within PowerPoint, clicking the Start Meeting button opens your personal meeting room where you can share your presentation, as shown in Figure 28.21. All the Acrobat Connect options are available when displaying any file on your computer. You can show the application window or your entire desktop. Audio is handled over the telephone with Acrobat Connect and over the Internet or telephone with Acrobat Connect Professional. You can share your Web cam using either Acrobat Connect or Acrobat Connect Professional.

FIGURE 28.21

Any application document can be displayed in the Acrobat Connect workspace.

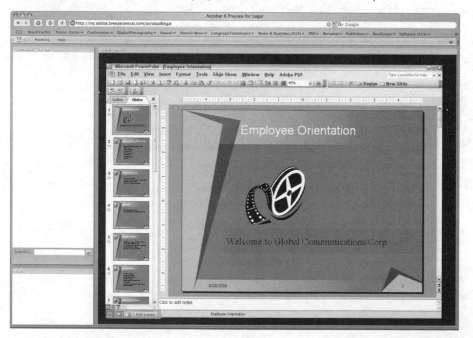

CROSS-REF For more information on hosting and participating in Acrobat Connect online meetings and a description of the differences between Acrobat Connect and Acrobat Connect Professional, see Chapter 29.

Summary

- You convert PowerPoint slides to PDF with the PDFMaker tool.

- To create note handouts from PowerPoint, use the Print dialog box and print the file to the Adobe PDF printer after making the attribute choices in the Print dialog box for the type of handouts you want to create.

- Apple Keynote slides can be exported to PDF and PowerPoint formats. Keynote offers Macintosh users a robust slide creation program with easy, intuitive palettes and tools.

- You can use layout programs to create slide presentations. For creating handout notes, set up a master page with objects and elements to be added to each page. Import the PDF slide presentation and convert to PDF to distribute handouts.

- You apply page transitions to pages individually using the Advanced ⇨ Document Processing ⇨ Page Transitions command or using menu commands in the Pages panel. To apply different transitions to different pages, select pages in the Pages panel and adjust the transitions in the Set Transitions dialog box.

- When using Full Screen mode, open the Preferences dialog box and select Full Screen. Make choices for options used in Full Screen viewing and click OK.

- Full Screen views support file linking with link and button actions, Microsoft PowerPoint animation, and transitions applied to pages with either the Full Screen preferences or the Set Page Transitions command.

- Online presentations can be delivered using Acrobat Connect. You can click the Start Meeting tool in all programs supporting the Acrobat PDFMaker or from Acrobat by clicking the same Start Meeting tool.

Chapter 29

Using Acrobat Connect

IN THIS CHAPTER

Getting familiar with Acrobat Connect

Signing up for an account

Working with Acrobat Connect

Acrobat Connect is a new program provided by Adobe Systems and made accessible from within Acrobat and Adobe Reader. There are two versions of Acrobat Connect designed to satisfy remote meeting needs for large organizations and individual users. Acrobat Connect Professional is a powerful web conferencing program and Acrobat Connect is a personal meeting room.

Through the Connect workspace you can host a meeting complete with screen sharing on your computer. Anyone invited to your Connect meeting can view the meeting using a Web browser on their computer. No special software is required for the Acrobat Connect participants.

In this chapter you learn how to acquire Acrobat Connect Professional and Acrobat Connect and understand some of the Connect features.

Setting Up the Work Environment

The Start Meeting tool appears by default in the Tasks toolbar in all Acrobat viewers. No other tools need to be loaded in Acrobat. To follow along in this chapter, just open a context menu on the Toolbar Well and select Reset Toolbars. The Start Meeting tool remains in the Tasks toolbar, ready for you to use the Connect features.

Understanding Acrobat Connect

If you subscribe to Acrobat Connect (the personal meeting room), your Acrobat/Reader will be automatically configured with your personal meeting room. Why? Because you only have one URL. For Acrobat Connect Professional users, you can create a number of rooms; therefore, you might not configure your preferences for a single room unless you want a default configuration for a specific room.

Acrobat Connect includes features such as sharing a webcam, sharing your monitor screen, and having up to 15 people in your room at one time. Acrobat Connect Professional offers many more features such as sharing a webcam, sharing voice, sharing a screen, file sharing, multiple layouts, and a software development kit to create custom pods. It also allows you to *store* information in your room. With Acrobat Connect Professional you can have up to 2,500 people in your room at one time.

Acrobat Connect is a subscription-only service. Acrobat Connect Professional can be subscription-based, or your company can license the technology to host its own Connect servers.

If you want to collaborate on documents, Acrobat provides you with features such as Shared Reviews, Email-Based Reviews, and Browser-Based Reviews, but when you need to collaborate with *people*, Acrobat Connect can save the day. You can use it collaborate with people *about* documents — bridging the gap for collaboration conversations and workflows.

With Acrobat Connect and Acrobat Connect Professional you can be either a host for a meeting or a participant. To host a meeting with Acrobat Connect, you need to sign up for an Acrobat Connect account and pay fees for the service. As a host, you conduct conference meetings.

As a participant, you do not need any special software to participate in a meeting. You do need to be invited by a host who provides you with logon information that includes a personal meeting room URL, and as an alternative to audio over the Internet, a phone number. An Acrobat Connect Professional user can deliver VoIP (voice over the Internet) where you can hear audio on your computer speakers. If you participate in a personal meeting with an Acrobat Connect user, you need to listen to the audio over a telephone.

As a participant, you just need to supply your name when opening a Web URL. Participants do not need to set up any special configuration and they don't need an Acrobat viewer to participate in a meeting. Log in and viewing activities are handled in your Web browser. Configuration for Acrobat Connect personal meeting rooms is all handled for you when you sign up for an account. No special configuration is needed and you'll be online in no time after signing up for the service.

If you host meetings as an Acrobat Connect Professional user you might subscribe to a regular conference place by editing the Meeting Preference settings in Acrobat. To set up a meeting account, press Ctrl/⌘+K and click Meeting in the left pane. You can also open the Meeting Preferences by clicking the Start Meeting task button and selecting Meeting Preferences from the pull-down menu. Either command opens the Meeting preferences, as shown in Figure 29.1.

When you sign up for an Acrobat Connect personal meeting room, you will receive an e-mail from Adobe that provides information related to your meeting room URL and log-on. When you receive the e-mail, open the preferences and fill in the Meeting Account Settings. Check the Remember my password check box and then each time you click the Start Meeting button in Acrobat or Reader, your personal meeting room opens in your Web browser without having to supply any log-on information.

The text box options in the right pane should be self-explanatory. To set up a meeting account, fill in the text fields. To change your password after initial logon, click the Change Password button. To manage your account, you need to have a meeting URL and an account set up. If you click the Manage Account button without the required account and logon information, Acrobat won't let you proceed.

FIGURE 29.1

Open Preferences and click Meeting in the left pane.

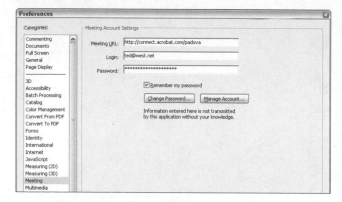

Setting Up an Account

From within Acrobat you can set up an account for Acrobat Connect. The Start Meeting task button has a pull down menu as shown in Figure 29.2. The Meeting Preferences command opens the Preferences window shown earlier in Figure 29.1. "Getting started with meetings" opens the Welcome screen showing information related to Acrobat Connect.

FIGURE 29.2

The Start Meeting pull-down menu shows a few commands for setting preferences, getting help information, and starting a meeting.

If you have no data entered in the Meeting Preferences and you click the Start Meeting menu command, the Welcome to Start Meeting dialog box shown in Figure 29.3 opens. In this dialog box you can create a trial account by clicking the Create Trial Account button. Clicking the button opens a page on Adobe's Web site where you can set up a 15-day trial of Acrobat Connect. On the same Web page, you also find information for setting up an Acrobat Connect Professional account.

Adobe provides several account options for Acrobat Connect Professional users. You may want an account for five users, ten users, or more. Various account tiers are available and easily identified on Adobe's Web site. Pricing for accounts can be on a use base, a monthly fee, or an annual fee.

Acrobat Connect is the lightweight version and pricing is set at $39 US per month or an annual fee of $395 US per year.

FIGURE 29.3

Click Create Trial Account and a Web page opens in your default Web browser where a trial account or other commercial accounts can be set up.

Using Acrobat Connect and Professional Sessions

If you have an Acrobat Connect personal meeting room or an Acrobat Connect Professional account and fill in the Meeting Preferences, click the Start Meeting menu command from the Start Meeting task button and you enter your meeting room as long as you've set up your log-on for Acrobat Connect or credentials for Acrobat Connect Professional in the Meeting Preferences.

If you don't fill in the Meeting Preferences and click Start Meeting, the Welcome to Start Meeting dialog box opens. Click the Log In button and the Start Meeting Log In dialog box opens as shown in Figure 29.4.

After supplying log on information, you enter the meeting as a host. On the host end, the Acrobat Connect Professional product is needed to conduct a meeting. On the participant end, the meeting is viewed through a Web browser where participants enter a meeting usually as a guest.

Acrobat Connect personal meeting users log into their meeting room and the participants log in as a Guest.

One type of meeting that can be conducted is a presentation where the host may show a slide show, demonstrate a product, or point out particular aspects of a document. The entire computer workspace can be displayed in the Acrobat Connect window, as you see in Figure 29.5.

In Figure 29.5, you see a product demonstration of Acrobat 8 Professional displayed in Acrobat Connect. On the left side of the Connect window are comments and questions added by meeting participants and responses from the host assistants.

FIGURE 29.4

Supply log-in information for the Meeting URL, Login (name), and Password.

FIGURE 29.5

Meeting participants can view the entire computer workspace in a Web browser.

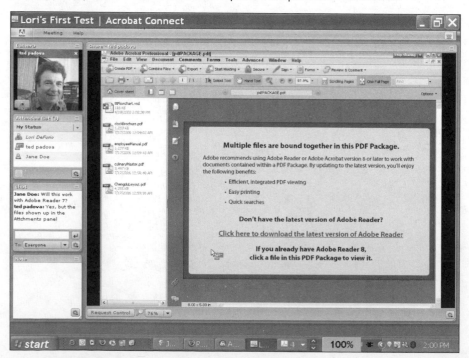

In other Acrobat Connect Professional sessions, you can set up the meeting for audio and video for all meeting participants. All participants can view each participant's video cam and the audio made available for each participant. Users can listen to the audio on computer speakers or by dialing into a conference phone line. To send audio, users need a microphone attached to a computer or they can send audio via a telephone.

For Acrobat Connect users, you can share your screen and your camera. The meeting participants can view the host's screen (via screen sharing), listen to audio via the telephone, and share web cameras and chat.

Summary

- Acrobat Connect Professional and Acrobat Connect are programs designed for conferencing. Pricing is tiered for various levels of meeting participants for the Acrobat Connect Professional. Acrobat Connect is more limited in features. The pricing is set at $39/month or $395/year.

- You can obtain a free 15-day trial for Acrobat Connect by clicking the Create Trial Account button in the Welcome to Meeting dialog box and registering on Adobe's Web site.

- Participants can view a host's computer monitor, send audio and video to all participants, and type questions and comments in the Connect window when a host uses Acrobat Connect Professional. Acrobat Connect users can listen to audio over the telephone.

Chapter 30

PDFs and eBooks

The promise of eBooks has been a roller coaster ride for users, providers, and would-be authors in recent years. The fall of some important content providers, coupled with some not-so-impressive display mechanisms, has slowed down an industry that many thought had a lot of promise. Notwithstanding hardware-display mechanisms and user acceptability, the software used to secure eBooks and make them accessible to every potential consumer was not as robust as viewing documents in Acrobat viewers.

With the introduction of Acrobat 6, Adobe Systems waved good-bye to the Adobe eBook Reader software and offered users, content providers, and content authors a much more attractive means of creation, protection, and delivery of eBooks. In Acrobat 7, the eBook branding was changed to Digital Editions, but the development and delivery for eBooks remained the same in Acrobat 7 as was introduced in Acrobat 6.

Now in Acrobat 8, Adobe has changed the user interface for acquiring and managing Adobe Digital Editions (notice the rebranding of Digital Editions now referred to as *Adobe* Digital Editions). You'll find the new interface to be attractive and intuitive. Adobe Digital Editions are easy to read in the new interface and acquiring new books has been made much easier.

The responsibility for restricting eBook viewing and file exchanging is all within the hands of the content provider using special software to guard and protect eBooks and any other type of PDF document against unauthorized viewing, printing, and file exchanging. In addition, end users can now use an Adobe online service to protect their PDFs without using content providers.

IN THIS CHAPTER

Creating eBooks

Acquiring eBooks

Reading eBooks

Setting Up the eBook Work Environment

The Digital Editions menu commands have changed in Acrobat viewers in version 8. You'll find access to Adobe Digital Editions in Acrobat by selecting Help ➪ Digital Editions. In Adobe Reader 8, look at the File ➪ Digital Editions menu command. No special tools are required for acquiring or reading Adobe Digital Editions. The Adobe Digital Editions reading mode has its own set of tools used for navigating pages, returning to last viewed pages, and opening new books.

Creating eBooks

If you're an end user who purchases content in the form of eBooks and protected files, you really don't need to know much about how the files are created. If you're a content provider, then understanding the options available to you and the restrictions you can apply to eBooks and any other type of PDF file are important to you.

On the user end, you can acquire PDF documents with special encryption that restricts your viewing, exchanging, and terms of use without activating your Acrobat viewer. On the content provider end, you have a very impressive solution available from Adobe in the form of a server-side product that can handle all your Digital Rights Management (DRM) needs.

Adobe Content Server 3

At first view, content providers may feel that Adobe has been fickle in deciding how to handle DRM (Digital Rights management) and restricted use of not only eBooks but also any PDF file. A few generations ago we had the Adobe eBook Reader that was a special software tool designed to view content that was protected against unauthorized distribution and viewing

During the initial life cycle of Acrobat 7, we had the Adobe Content Server software that was used to restrict viewing and distribution through the use of Digital Editions. On November 30, 2004, Adobe discontinued the Adobe Content Server software and introduced the Adobe LiveCycle Policy Server. What has transpired is not a matter of fickle judgment, but rather, an evolution of a very sophisticated solution for any enterprise interested in restricting the viewing of PDF files.

Adobe LiveCycle Policy Server

Adobe LiveCycle Policy Server (www.adobe.com/products/server/policy) is truly a marvelous product. With the Policy Server, an enterprise can track the viewing of any PDF file by any user, set time limits for use, update viewing restrictions, control the online and offline document usage, and revoke use at any time. The entire burden for activation and use is placed on the content provider and the end user merely needs to use the same version of an Acrobat viewer used for any PDF file viewing.

Acquiring Adobe Digital Editions

With just about every upgrade to Acrobat, you also find upgrades to many Adobe server products. With eBooks for example, the previous versions of Acrobat required a content provider to purchase the Adobe Policy Server to encrypt eBooks. With Acrobat 8, Adobe is announcing hosted Adobe Policy Services.

Adobe's new methods for working with eBooks have become much easier in Acrobat 8. Rather than end users needing to configure their security settings in Adobe Reader or Acrobat, an FDF file is sent to a user. No configurations are needed to view the PDF in a protected environment. All security permissions are handled transparent to the end user.

With the introduction of Create Protected PDF Online, you can create a PDF document with the necessary security settings that will protect your content against unauthorized distribution without having to use a content provider or the Adobe Content Sever. You can send the FDF file to the end user complete with the restrictions applied via the Create Protected PDF Online service.

> **TIP** For more information on Adobe Server products and the new Create Protected PDF Online service, select Help ➪ Adobe Online Services.

Adobe has introduced, in conjunction with Acrobat and Reader 8, a new consumer-optimized application for reading and managing eBooks and other digital publications. This new solution, called Adobe Digital Editions, will replace the eBook functionality that had been in Adobe Acrobat and Reader 6 and 7. It is a standalone application (based on Flash Player) that is a 2.5MB download.

As of this writing Adobe Digital Editions is in a public beta program on the Adobe Labs Web site, and by the time this book is published you'll see Adobe Digital Editions moved to the main Adobe Web site. To install the Flash Player and activate Adobe Digital Editions, select Help ➪ Digital Editions in Acrobat or File ➪ Digital Editions in Adobe Reader. You can also log on to `www.adobe.com/go/getdigital editions` to open the Adobe Digital Editions log-on Web page. Selecting any one of the options listed here opens a Web page hosted on Adobe's Web site. The first page provides you information about Adobe Digital Editions and informs you that you need to install the Flash Player application. Click the Download and Install button and the installation proceeds. You arrive at a page that confirms your installation as shown in Figure 30.1. If the installation was not successful you see a message informing you that your computer doesn't have the system requirements to install the Flash Player application.

FIGURE 30.1

After downloading the Flash Player application installer, a Web page reports your successful installation.

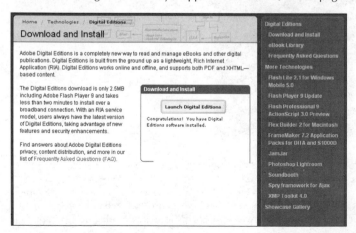

CAUTION   All screen shots taken of Adobe Digital Editions in this chapter are screen shots from the Adobe Digital Editions Beta that has not been finalized as of this writing. When you open Adobe Digital Editions, you may find screens, commands, and features to appear different than is shown in this chapter. The user interface for Adobe Digital Editions is straightforward and intuitive. Therefore you should not have any problems moving around the user interface and discovering how to download digital editions and read them on your computer.

Exploring the Adobe eBook Mall

A number of different eBook providers are listed on Adobe's Web site. You can find eBooks in several languages distributed by a number of different providers. To view Adobe's Web page, select Help ➡ Digital Editions (Acrobat) or File ➡ Digital Editions (Adobe Reader). Your default Web browser opens the Adobe Digital Editions Web page. Click eBook Library in the Adobe Digital Editions (see Figure 30.1) and another Web page opens. A list of free downloads appear on the Web page. Click the Read button appearing adjacent to an eBook to download the file. When the file is downloaded to your computer it appears in your Adobe Digital Editions. In Figure 30.2 you can see the Adobe Digital Editions with several eBooks I downloaded to my computer.

FIGURE 30.2

Check Restore last view settings when reopening documents to view the last page viewed in a document when you reopen Acrobat.

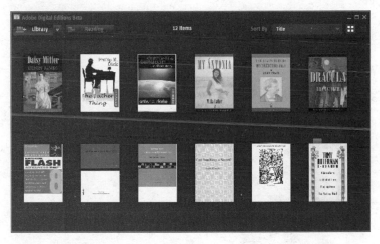

TIP   Among the free downloads you'll find an eBook titled *Inside the Publishing Revolution: The Adobe Story* by Pamela Pfiffer. For an informative essay on how Adobe Systems evolved to become a major influence on how we use computers today and the relationships between the major computing developers, read this book. You'll find many interesting historical events documented and information to help you understand early strategies of the company and where Adobe is headed with the Acrobat family of products and other applications in its product line.

Reading eBooks

After installing the Adobe Digital Editions and downloading some eBooks, just click a publication you see in Figure 30.2 and your book is displayed in a reading mode within the Adobe Digital Edition interface as shown in Figure 30.3.

FIGURE 30.3

Click an eBook in the Adobe Digital Editions window and you can start reading the book.

For books, manuals, and large documents, you might want to look at a preference setting that can help you bookmark pages in the files you read. This type of bookmark is like an analog bookmark you might use to mark the place in a book when you pause and come back later to continue reading from the place you left off.

Open the Preferences dialog box (Ctrl/⌘+K) and click Documents in the left pane. In the right pane, check Restore last view settings when reopening documents, as shown in Figure 30.4. You can choose to open all files on the page last viewed in your Acrobat viewer. For example, if you view a PDF document and quit Acrobat after viewing page 125, and then open Acrobat in another session, the PDF opens to page 125.

FIGURE 30.4

Check Restore last view settings when reopening documents to view the last page viewed in a document when you reopen Acrobat.

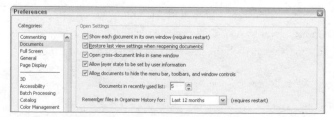

You move around the Adobe Digital Editions window by clicking tools and opening menus. From the Reading menu you can see a list of commands to change the page display and navigate pages as shown in Figure 30.5. The Library menu offers commands to display your book list as with the default thumbnail view or a list view. You also have access to the Help command that opens an FAQ (Frequently Asked Questions) Web page on Adobe's Web site where you can find some help in downloading and viewing eBooks. Another comment in the Library menu enables you to add documents to your library. Select Library ➪ Add Item to Library and a dialog box opens where you can navigate your hard drive and select any PDF file stored locally on your hard drive and add it to your library.

FIGURE 30.5

Open a menu at the top of the Adobe Digital Editions window to select menu commands for viewing, navigation, searching, and accessing help with eBooks.

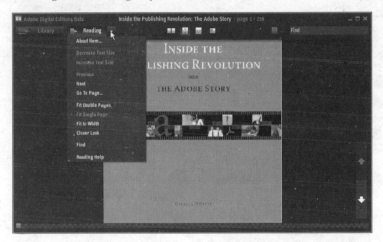

Keep in mind that the screen shots shown here are taken from the beta versions of the Adobe Digital Editions. When the product is out of beta and finally shipped, you may see different menus and menu commands.

Summary

- Any PDF file can be restricted for use with the Adobe LiveCycle Policy Server.
- PDF authors can use the Create Protected PDF Online service to protect eBooks when not using a content provider.
- In order to download and view eBooks you must install the Flash Player application.
- The Adobe LiveCycle Policy Server is a server-side product made available to content providers.
- eBooks and other PDF documents can be opened on the last viewed page when you reopen your Acrobat viewer.
- The Adobe Digital Editions library window provides tools and menu commands for viewing and navigating eBooks.

Chapter 31

Printing to Desktop Color Printers

One of the primary problems many Acrobat users experience is printing files with proper color. Notwithstanding any problems with printing fonts and getting a print out, the most problematic issues with printing PDFs that contain graphic images is accurate reproduction of color. Whether you are a creative professional or a novice to graphic design, some basic issues need to be understood when printing any kind of document containing images or other graphics to a desktop color printer.

This chapter is concerned with printing to local printers of the desktop variety from Acrobat viewers and remarks made in this chapter are not intended for commercial printing. For professional printing and prepress, take a look at Chapter 32.

Setting Up the Work Environment

No special editing tools are required for desktop color printing. There is a special toolbar for Print Production, but you won't need any of the Print Production tools to print to your desktop printer. To maximize your space in Acrobat, reset the toolbars to their default positions. Open a context menu on the Toolbar Well and select Reset Toolbars.

Understanding Color Management

Quite a bit can be said about color management and certainly more attention can be devoted to it than I have room for in this book. Quite simply there are three basic areas you need to address in creating a color-managed workflow:

- **Monitor calibration.** There are software tools on both Windows and the Mac that can help you calibrate your monitor to eliminate color casts and color tints and set the *gamma* (neutral midtone grays) of your

monitor. I won't talk about them because most are useless on LCD type monitors and many people are using LCDs these days. Ideally you would use a calibration device. For low-end color calibration of monitors you can purchase the Pantone Huey (www.pantone.com/products/
products.asp?idArea=2&idProduct=103) or ColorVision Syper2express (www
.colorvision.com/profis/profis_view.jsp?id=581) calibrator for as low as $69 US.
More sophisticated calibrators such as Gretag Macbeth EyeOne 2 calibrators are above $250 US.
I'll leave it up to you as to how far you want to go with calibrating your monitor, but I strongly
recommend that if color output is important to you that you at least purchase one of the low-end
color calibration devices.

- **Color workspace.** Whether you work in Acrobat or in an imaging program like Adobe
Photoshop you need to setup your color workspace. Selections for color workspaces vary with
programs. The two primary workspaces are Adobe RGB (1998) or sRGB. Choices vary according
to the files you prepare and the printing equipment you use.

- **Output color profile.** Each printer and every paper you print on should have a defined color
profile. Color profiles are often installed with your printer. You can also acquire or create custom
color profiles to print to a specific paper on your printer.

NOTE Creating custom printer profiles requires more expensive color calibration equipment. For
a source of calibration equipment, take a look at the Gretag MacBeth Web site at: www
.gretagmacbeth.com.

Don't be concerned yet about which profile to use. More important, try to understand how these three
items interact with each other and what they do. First off, your monitor color profile created with a hardware device adjusts the overall brightness of your monitor. When you print a file, you want to be sure that
the print outputs are not darker or lighter than the images you see on your monitor. A balance needs to be
made between monitor and output so you can safely judge what a print looks like when you print to your
printer.

Color workspace affects how you view color on your monitor. You want to try to get as close to seeing all
the colors that can be reproduced on your printer. This happens when you choose the proper color workspace. You then select a color output profile when it comes time to print your file. Your color is converted
from your workspace color to your printer's colorspace so that all the colors fit within the output space as
closely as possible. Quite simply, if you see a bright red color on your computer monitor and the overall
brightness matches your output, you want to be certain that same color red gets printed on your printer.
This happens when the color is converted from your monitor workspace to your printer's colorspace.

Assuming you can set up your color environment to handle monitor color, workspace color, and output
color, the next thing to understand is how color is managed at print time. You have some choices here. You
can choose to manage color at print time through your printer, by selecting a printer profile, or by printing
a converted color file that requires no color management. This is the one item that is most confusing for
people to grasp — when to manage color at print time and when not to manage color. For the answer and
examples, I'll cover that when we look at printing to specific printers later in this chapter.

Selecting a Color Workspace

Your first step after calibrating your monitor in creating a color managed workflow is to choose your color
workspace. In Acrobat open the Preferences dialog box by pressing Ctrl/⌘+K. In the left pane, click Color
Management and the right pane changes to the view shown in Figure 31.1.

FIGURE 31.1

Click Color Management in the Preferences dialog box to access the Color Management options.

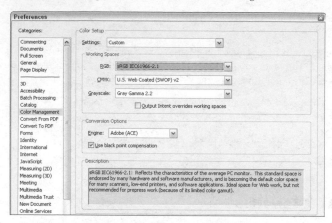

In the Working Spaces section, open the RGB drop-down menu and choose your RGB color workspace. Here you have one of two choices:

- **sRGB.** The name is much longer, as you see in Figure 31.1, but I'll use the abbreviated label and simply call this by the common term — sRGB. Traditionally, this color workspace has been used when files are prepared for screen and Web viewing. This colorspace comes as close as you can get from all the choices available to represent color consistently across all monitors. Of course, there are many variables that prevent you from matching color exactly on all monitors. We'll assume the software engineers are telling us the truth when they say that the best monitor color matching is made by selecting the sRGB colorspace.

  More important, you should be aware that many desktop color printers convert color from sRGB better than other workspaces. Some online photo services and photo service providers may ask you to keep your files in sRGB. For example, if you send photos to a Costco store to print on their Noritsu photo printers, they'd ask you to keep your files in sRGB. At the desktop printer level, you'll need to either run tests or take a look at your printer's user manual to find out if your printer supports sRGB better than other color workspaces.

- **Adobe RGB (1998).** The Adobe RGB colorspace has a wider color gamut than sRGB (meaning you can see a bit more colors in this workspace). If you prepare files for press and commercial printing, you're best off using Adobe RGB. Also, some desktop color printers can take advantage of the wider color gamut, so your printer might give you more accurate color matching when converting your files from Adobe RGB to your printer's color output profile. Again though, you need to run tests or turn to the user manual to see what the manufacturer recommends.

If all your work is designed for output to desktop color printers using an RGB colorspace, you don't need to be concerned about the CMYK choices in the Color Management preferences. If you prepare files for press and commercial printing than CMYK will be a consideration. Make a choice for the color workspace recommended by your commercial printer. If using print shops in the United States, the U.S. Web Coated (SWOP) v2 profile is likely to be your best choice. But be sure to talk to your print shop technicians first.

On Windows, set the Grayscale option to Gray Gamma 2.2 and on the Mac, set the Grayscale to Gray Gamma 1.8. Clear the check box for Output Intent overrides working spaces if your PDF files do not contain embedded Output Intent profiles.

CROSS-REF   For more information on output intent profiles, see Chapter 10.

For the Conversion options, select Adobe (ACE) for the conversion engine. On Windows, you'll have a choice for Adobe (ACE) or Microsoft ICM. On the Mac, you'll have choices for Adobe (ACE) or Apple Colorsync or Apple CMM. Use the Adobe (ACE) color engine for the best results.

Finally, check the box for Use black point compensation. Checking this option gets you closer to a rich black.

Click OK in the Preferences dialog box after you make all your choices and your color settings stay intact until you change them again.

Using Color Output Profiles

Color output profiles come in a number of different flavors. You can use color output profiles supplied by your printer manufacturer that are installed with your desktop printer, use color profiles created by paper manufacturers that are designed for use with specific printers, or create custom profiles for your printer and the papers you use.

NOTE   There are several services available to you for creating custom color output profiles. If you're a creative professional, you might want to look at using a service to prepare a custom profile for your printer and the papers you use. Just go to the Internet and search for custom profiling services. Custom color profiles are offered as low as $25 US. The cost is minimal considering all the consumables you'd waste running tests to get color right on your equipment.

Because most users printing from Acrobat are likely to use printer profiles that were shipped with their desktop printer, I'll stick to talking about these profiles. If you're a creative professional who depends on accurate color proofing, take a look at *Color Correction For Digital Photographers Only* (Wiley Publishing, 2006) or *Color Correction For Digital Photographers For Dummies* (Wiley Publishing, 2007). There's much more to color profiling than can be described here, so a little research can help you get closer to producing accurate color.

When you print your PDF files to your color desktop printer, you make a choice for using a color profile at the time you print your file. You may see a list of color profiles in the Advanced Print Setup dialog box or you may only see the name of your printer. If you see just your printer's name, color profile selection is made automatically by the print driver. Choosing a paper in your print driver options tells the printer what profile to use, hence the color profile choice is automatic.

Regardless of how the color profile is selected, a color conversion takes place from your color workspace to the colorspace of your printer. In essence, the conversion is an attempt to fit all the color you see on your monitor into the printable colorspace on your printer with as close a match as possible.

Some Printing Basics in Acrobat

Before you start printing files to your printer, there are a few toggles and switches you need to verify. If you don't have some options enabled, you may have a more difficult time printing your documents. The essentials for setting up your printing environment and some toggles you should understand are as follows:

■ **Turn Show page thumbnails in Print dialog ON.** A preference choice appears in the General preference settings that controls the print preview in the Print dialog box. A thumbnail preview helps you determine whether the page will print without clipping off edges. As a matter of default, you'll want the print preview enabled. Press Ctrl/⌘+K to open the Preferences dialog box and click General in the left pane. In the right pane, check the box where you see Show page thumbnails in Print dialog, as shown in Figure 31.2. Click OK to dismiss the Preferences dialog box.

FIGURE 31.2

Check Show page thumbnails in Print dialog in the General preferences.

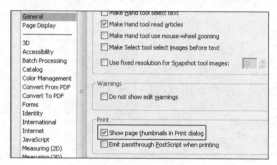

 If you have a lot of different files to print, particularly where color is not an issue, you might want to turn the page preview off. Doing so speeds up opening and working through the Print dialog box.

■ **Set the print attributes.** Several settings in the Print dialog box shown in Figure 31.3 are globally set for all printing on desktop printers. These options are as follows:

▪ **Printer selection.** From the Name drop-down menu, select the printer you want to output your file.

▪ **Comments and Forms.** Above the Preview area you see the section Comments and Forms. For printing composite prints without any comments or markups, select Document from the drop-down menu. For printing with these markups, see the section "Printing Comments, Forms, and Summaries" later in this chapter.

▪ **Page Scaling.** Ideally, you should print files to papers large enough to accommodate your document page size. If your document fits on a standard page size, select None for Page Scaling. If you do need to shrink a document to fit a paper smaller than the document page size, select Shrink to Printable Area or Fit to Printable Area from the Page Scaling drop-down menu. If you need to tile pages, you can make selections for tiling in the same drop-down menu.

▪ **Page Orientation.** Click the Properties button in the top-right corner of the Print dialog box to select either Portrait or Landscape Orientation. Note that you can also select orientation and page size by selecting File ➪ Page Setup before you open the Print dialog box.

▪ **Booklet Printing.** A new feature in Acrobat 8 has been added to the Print dialog box. Open the page Scaling pull-down menu and you find Booklet Printing. Select Booklet printing to print spreads as shown in the Preview Composite in Figure 31.3. You can choose from three additional options for printing booklets. Print Both sides, Front Side Only, or Back Side Only. On desktop printers capable of printing two sides you can run the print first on one side, turn the paper over and print the second side.

FIGURE 31.3

Select your printer from the Name drop-down menu. A new feature in Acrobat 8 permits you to print booklets.

You have some other options in the print dialog box for page range, reversing pages, using auto rotations, choosing a paper source by page size, printing to a file, and so on. All these other options are very similar to printing from other programs and should be familiar to you.

Who's Going to Manage Color?

If you were working in an image editing program such as Adobe Photoshop, you'd have three choices for managing color when printing to your color printer. Your three choices would include:

- **Let the printer manage the color.** When you make this choice in your Print dialog box you enable the printer to choose the color profile. If this choice is selected, you can manage the color in the advanced print settings in your color printer driver.

- **Let the program manage color.** In a program such as Photoshop, you would select a color profile in the Print with Preview dialog box, and enable Photoshop to manage color. In our case, we'll select a color profile and enable Acrobat to manage the color. Making this choice requires you to turn color management off in the advanced print settings of your color printer driver. If you don't turn color management off at the last stage, you wind up with a double profiled print. This results in a severe color shift and color output very different than your monitor view. (See the sidebar in this chapter for more on printing with color shifts.)

■ **No color management.** If you convert an image in a program like Photoshop to your color output profile, the color is ready for output and no further conversion is needed. Because the color is already converted to your printer's color, you need to turn color management off throughout the print process. In Acrobat, you don't have a feature to convert a document's color within the program. Most likely you won't be working with files that have embedded color output profiles in the images, therefore you won't need to worry about printing using this option. If perchance you do work with images that have color converted to a printer profile, you would select Same as Source (No Color Management) in the Advanced Print Setup dialog box from the Profile drop down menu.

CROSS-REF For more information on selecting profiles in the Advanced Print Setup dialog box see the next section "Printing to Desktop Printers."

When printing from Acrobat you have only one of two choices to make. Either enable your printer to determine color, or enable Acrobat to determine color. If you choose to enable your printer to manage the color, you turn color management on. If you enable Acrobat to manage the color, you turn color management off. However, where you turn color on and where you turn color off varies differently between color printers. To demonstrate how color is managed, we need to look at printing Acrobat files from a few different desktop color printers.

Printing to Desktop Printers

Print settings vary according to manufacturers, and I can't hope to cover all printers in this chapter. For a representative sample, I'll use three of the more popular color printers to show you how to print files from Acrobat. To demonstrate how color profiling is handled, I'll use Epson, HP, and Canon printers as examples. If you have a different color printer, you should be able to understand the process and apply similar choices when printing to your color printer.

When you install your printer driver, the installation utility may also install a number of color profiles. In some cases, individual profiles won't be installed—all depends on your printer and the printer driver. If individual color profiles are not installed, then your printer driver contains profile information and makes profile choices within the driver itself. For profiles installed with your printer, you can choose profiles in Acrobat's Advanced Print Setup dialog box and control all the printing using a profile provided by your printer manufacturer.

You have a choice for how these profiles are used. You can choose to select the profile in the Print dialog box, or you can choose an automatic method where the manufacturer created a no-nonsense process of automatic profile selection using your printer driver. The color profile is automatically selected when you choose the paper source.

Printing to Epson printers

For the first example I'll use Epson printers to demonstrate how to print a PDF file from Acrobat using the printer to manage color and using Acrobat to manage color. Because the dialog boxes differ so much between platforms, I'll include printing from Windows and from the Mac in separate descriptions.

Printer profile selection on Windows

In this first example, let's take a look at how to print to an Epson low-end color printer on Windows while allowing the *printer to manage the color*. Depending on the model of your printer, you may see some slight differences in menu names, but the process will follow the same steps.

To print to an Epson printer while enabling the printer to manage the color, follow these steps.

STEPS: Printing from Windows enabling the printer to manage color

1. **Open the Print dialog box.** Select File ➪ Print or press Ctrl/⌘+P to open the Print dialog box shown in Figure 31.3.

   Make all the attribute choices for printing to your printer as was described in the section "Some Printing Basics in Acrobat" for page orientation, page scaling, and so on.

2. **Select your printer.** Open the Name drop-down menu and select your printer as shown earlier in Figure 31.4.

FIGURE 31.4

Select your printer from the Name menu in the Print dialog box.

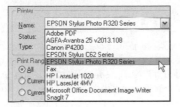

3. **Open the Advanced Print Setup dialog box.** Click Advanced in the Print dialog box.

4. **Select the color profile.** Because we are enabling the printer to determine the color, you select Printer/PostScript Color Management from the Color Profile drop-down menu in the Advanced Print Setup dialog box, as shown in Figure 31.5.

FIGURE 31.5

Select Printer/PostScript Color Management in the Profile drop-down menu.

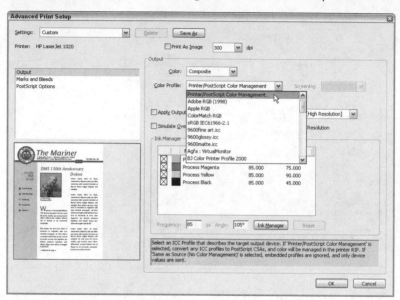

5. **Return to the Print dialog box.** Click OK in the Advanced Print Setup dialog box to return to the Print dialog box.

6. **Open the printer driver dialog box.** At this point we have made all our settings in the Acrobat workspace. Now, we need to make choices in the printer driver to decide how the color is managed. Because we are enabling the printer to manage the color, we'll verify settings to insure that indeed the printer does manage the color.

Click Properties in the Print dialog box to open the Printer Properties dialog box. In this example, I use an Epson Stylus Photo R320 printer and the Epson Stylus Photo R320 Series Properties dialog box opens, as shown in Figure 31.6.

FIGURE 31.6

Select the paper source you use to print your files.

7. **Choose the paper source.** This first choice determines the amount of ink to be used for your print. If printing to a glossy paper more ink is used. If printing to a plain bond paper, less ink is used. From the Type drop-down menu make the paper choice for the paper you use. In this example, I use Premium Glossy Photo Paper as shown in Figure 31.6.

8. **Color manage your output.** Now it's time to color manage your file and this step is critical in your print production workflow. For the Epson printer, you need to click on the Advanced button shown in Figure 31.6 that opens a warning dialog box. Simply click Continue to open the advanced settings dialog box as you see in Figure 31.7.

    A few choices need to be made in this dialog box. The most important are as follows:

    ■ **Select a paper type.** But we selected paper already you say. The second drop down menu in the Paper & Quality section of the dialog box determines what profile the printer uses for its automatic selection. Choose the same paper here as you did back in step 7.

    ■ **Turn color management on.** Because we are enabling the print driver to determine the color, we need to be certain the Color Controls radio button is active. This setting tells the print driver to automatically select a printer profile for the paper type you selected.

    ■ **Set the Color Mode.** Be certain to not use Epson Vivid. This choice produces inferior results on photos. Choose the Epson Standard setting, as shown in Figure 31.7.

    ■ If you frequently print files using the same settings, you can save your settings by clicking the Save Setting button.

9. **Print the photo.** Click OK and OK again in the Print dialog box and your file is sent to your printer. The color is converted automatically from your source workspace of sRGB or Adobe RGB (1998) to the profile the Printer Driver automatically selects for you.

FIGURE 31.7

Click Advanced, and then click Continue to access the advanced settings in the Epson print driver.

Printing from the Macintosh enabling the printer to determine color

On the Macintosh the Epson Printer Driver offers you some different settings although the process is quite similar. Again, we are going to use the automatic method for color conversion and allow the print driver to handle the conversion.

The Acrobat Print dialog box settings and the Advanced Print Setup dialog box settings are identical on the Mac as you find in Windows. You make choices for paper orientation, page scaling, and so on in the Print dialog box and choose Printer/PostScript Color Management in the Advanced Print Setup dialog box just as Windows users. However, on the Mac you don't have a Properties button. All color management choices are made directly in the Acrobat Print dialog box.

To print to an Epson printer when enabling the Printer to manage color, do the following:

1. **Select Print Settings.** Select File ➪ Print and make the same choices as Windows users for print attributes and select Printer/PostScript Color Management in the Advanced Print Setup dialog box.

2. **Select your printer.** At the top of the Acrobat Print dialog box you make a choice for your printer from the Printer drop-down menu, as shown in Figure 31.8.

FIGURE 31.8

Select your printer from the options listed in the Printer drop-down menu.

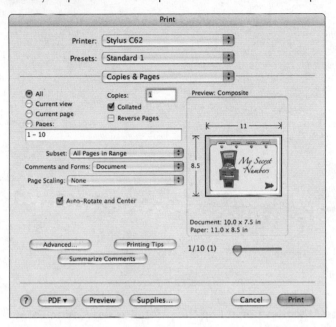

3. **Select the Media Type and Print Quality.** Where you see Copies & Pages, click to open a drop-down menu and select the option for Print Settings. In the Print Settings pane, you make selections for Media Type and Print Quality as shown in Figure 31.9. In this example, I use an Epson Stylus C62 printer and choose Premium Glossy Photo Paper and select Best Photo from the Print Quality drop-down menu.

4. **Choose how to manage the color.** Now it's time to select the color management method. From the drop-down menu where you now see Print Settings, click to open the menu and select Color Management, as shown in Figure 31.10.

   Click Color Controls. Making this choice tells the print driver to manage the color. Select Epson Standard, Photo-Realistic, or other choice you may have other than Epson Vivid from the Mode drop-down menu.

5. **Print the file.** Click Print and the file is printed to your printer with an automatic color conversion from your workspace color to the printer color profile.

FIGURE 31.9

Make choices for Printer, Media Type, and Print Quality in the Acrobat Print dialog box.

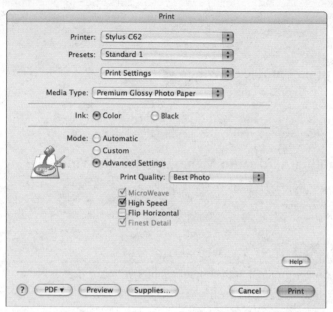

FIGURE 31.10

Click Print Settings to open the drop-down menu and select Color Management.

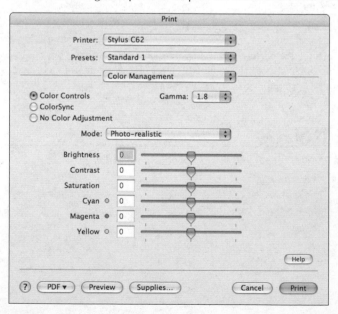

Selecting a printer profile

Your second method for managing color when printing files is to select a printer profile from the available list of color profiles installed with your printers. Whereas the last section used your printer to manage color (when we selected Printer/PostScript Color Management), this time we'll let Adobe Acrobat manage the color. Again, the Windows options and Macintosh commands vary a little so I'll discuss how to print by selecting a profile for each operating system.

Printing using a printer profile on Windows

The steps are the same as those described in printing files for automatic profile selection when setting up the page and selecting a printer. When you select File ➪ Print, you open the Acrobat Print dialog box as described earlier in the previous section. Your steps now change when you enable Acrobat to handle the color conversion and you proceed to move through the Print dialog box as follows:

STEPS: Enabling Acrobat to Manage Color on Windows

1. **Select a color profile.** From the Color Profile drop-down menu in the Advanced Print Setup dialog box, select the color profile designed for use with the paper you have chosen to print your image. In this example, I use a heavyweight matte paper color profile as shown in Figure 31.11.

FIGURE 31.11

Choose a printer profile that matches the paper you use.

2. **Open the printer Properties.** Click Properties and the properties settings for your selected printer driver opens. Check the radio button for Best Photo. From the Type drop-down menu, select the recommended paper choice, as shown in Figure 31.12. Note: If you use a custom color profile, the profile is usually shipped with guidelines for selecting proper paper.

FIGURE 31.12

Select the recommended paper choice under Paper Options.

3. **Manage the color.** Click Advanced and click Continue to arrive at the same dialog box shown earlier in Figure 31.7. The paper choice selection is automatically carried over from the previous properties dialog box (from Step 1). A different setting is in the Color Management section. This time click the ICM (Image Color Management) radio button and click Off (No Color Adjustment), as shown in Figure 31.13. Because you selected the color profile in Step 1, and you are enabling Acrobat to manage the color, you need to be sure that Color Management is OFF. If you don't turn color management off, you end up double profiling your print.

FIGURE 31.13

Click ICM and click Off (No Color Adjustment).

4. **Print the file.** Click OK and click Print to print the file.

Printing using a printer profile on the Macintosh

All the steps to print a file enabling Acrobat to manage color are the same as Windows until you get to the printer driver. On the Mac, do the following to print a PDF document enabling Acrobat to manage color.

STEPS: Enabling Acrobat to Manage Color on the Macintosh

1. **Set the print attributes.** Follow the same steps to make choices for the print attributes and your printer. Go to the Advanced Print Options and select a printer profile for your target paper.

2. **Set the Print Settings.** Use the same settings, as shown earlier in Figure 31.9, to select the Media Type and Print Quality.

3. **Make a choice for Color Management.** Click Print Settings and select Color Management from the drop-down menu in the Print dialog box. This time, because we chose a color output profile and Acrobat is determining the color, we turn color management off. In the Color Management pane, select No Color Adjustment, as you see in Figure 31.14.

4. **Print the file.** Click Print to print the file.

FIGURE 31.14

Select Color Management and click No Color Adjustment.

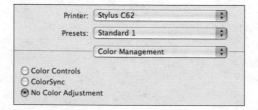

Output with a Magenta Bias

Of Epson printer driver problems, the most common complaint is a magenta shift on prints and it's always the result of a single error during printer driver setup for printing. For reasons not fully understood about the Epson ink sets, either pigment or dye inks, a file converted for Epson output has a strong magenta bias. It seems that an equal mix of all the inks produces a green gray color. The magenta file bias when converted tunes out this green balance of an equal ink mix. That's why a double converted file always has a strong magenta bias.

For creative pros who use Adobe Photoshop, you can preview this magenta bias and discover why some of your prints may appear with a radical color shift when printing to your desktop color printer. To make this observation, in Photoshop, select Edit ➪ Convert to Profile. Select a printer profile from the Profile drop-down menu in the Destination Space area of the Convert to Profile dialog box to convert the color. Your file now has color converted from workspace color to your printer profile.

Next, select File ➪ Save For Web. Since Web graphics are not profile aware, you'll see the same result you would see on an output from your printer using the printer to manage color. Because your file already has color converted to the output profile, letting the printer manage the color ends up double profiling your document. As a result, the color appears with a magenta color shift that you can easily see on your monitor.

Printing to HP inkjet printers

Regardless of the printer you use, the process for printing follows the same logic. Unfortunately each manufacturer uses different dialog boxes and different menu command names that can leave you completely confused if you try to apply steps from printing to one printer to a different printer.

The two methods for managing color (enable the printer driver to determine color by selecting Printer/PostScript Color Management or enable Acrobat to determine color by selecting a specific color profile) are applied to all printers but the dialog boxes, buttons, and menu choices appear differently.

The critical steps you need to be concerned about when printing files is the profile selection, the paper selection, and when to turn color management on or off. If you own an HP printer you probably know where to make your paper selection and your best photo selection. The more obscure setting is likely to be the color management choice. Rather than discuss each detail step for printing to an HP low-end desktop printer, let's take a look how to manage color.

Printing to HP printers on Windows

Again, you have two choices as follows:

- **Let your printer determine color.** Select Printer/PostScript Color Management in the Advanced Print Setup dialog box. Click Properties to open the printer driver properties. Click the Advanced tab when you arrive at the printer driver properties dialog box. Click Graphic and click Image Color Management. From the ICM Method drop-down menu, select ICM Handled by Printer. as shown in Figure 31.15.

- **Let Acrobat determine color.** Select a color profile in the Advance Print Setup dialog box and select ICM Disabled in the Advanced tab in the HP printer driver properties.

FIGURE 31.15

Open Graphic and select ICM Method. Choose ICM Handled by Printer from the drop-down menu.

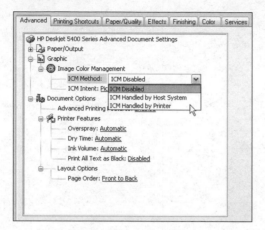

Printing to HP printers on the Macintosh

If there's a way to manage color using one of the HP Deskjet 5400 Series of printers on the Mac, I haven't found it. HP and Windows go together like bread and butter, but HP printers and Macintosh computers leave a lot to be desired. Among the problems with using an HP printer on the Macintosh is the inability to turn color management off. Therefore, the only surefire method of printing to an HP printer on the Mac from an Acrobat viewer is to enable the printer to manage the color. Don't attempt to use a specific color profile.

When you open the Advanced Print Setup dialog box, select Printer/PostScript Color Management, click OK, and click Print. In the HP printer driver dialog box, select the Paper Type/Quality from the drop-down menu below Presets and choose your paper type. Be aware that you'll want to use just HP papers and make a selection for the HP paper type you use, as shown in Figure 31.16.

Because the printer driver determines the options in the Mac OS Print dialog box, you don't have an option for Color Management as you do when using a printer such as an Epson. With the HP printer driver, there are no color management options appearing in the drop-down menu in the Print dialog box.

FIGURE 31.16

Select an HP paper in the Paper Type/Quality dialog box.

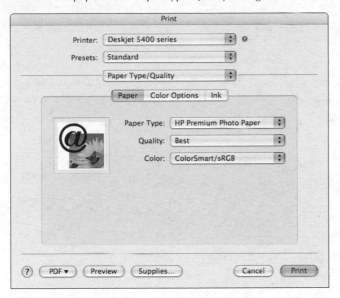

Printing to Canon printers

Again we follow the same logic and choose to either enable or disable color management. With Canon color printers, the area in the print driver dialog box is even more hidden than you find in Epson and HP desktop printers.

Printing to Canon printers on Windows

Using the same two options you control color management as follows:

- **Let your printer determine color.** Select Printer/PostScript Color Management in the Advanced Print Setup dialog box. Click Properties in the Acrobat Print dialog box and click Manual for Color/Intensity in the Main tab, as shown in Figure 31.17.

  Click the Set button to open the Manual Color Adjustment dialog box. Check the box for Enable ICM (Windows Color Management), as shown in Figure 31.18.

- **Let Acrobat determine color.** First select your printer profile in the Advanced Print Setup dialog box and follow the same steps as above. This time uncheck the Enable ICM (Windows Color Management) check box.

FIGURE 31.17

Click the Manual radio button for Color/Intensity.

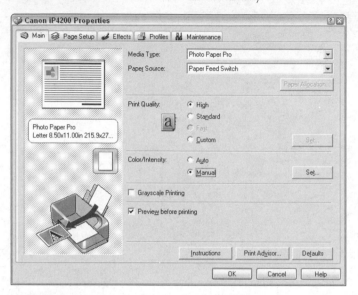

FIGURE 31.18

Check Enable ICM (Windows Image Color Management).

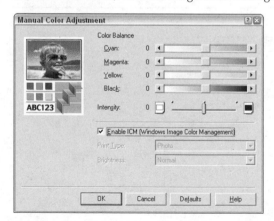

Printing to Canon Printers on the Mac

You make the same choices on the Mac as you do on Windows for how you want to manage color on a Canon printer. Enable the printer to manage the color and make a paper choice in the Quality & Media dialog box, as shown in Figure 31.19.

FIGURE 31.19

Select Quality & Media and select the paper type in the Media Type drop-down menu.

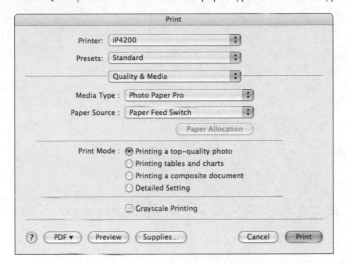

From the drop-down menu below the Presets menu, select Color Options. Here you choose BJ Standard when permitting the printer driver to determine color and None when selecting a printer profile in the Advanced Print Setup dialog box. The options are shown in Figure 31.20.

FIGURE 31.20

Select BJ Standard for printer color management and None when you select a printer profile.

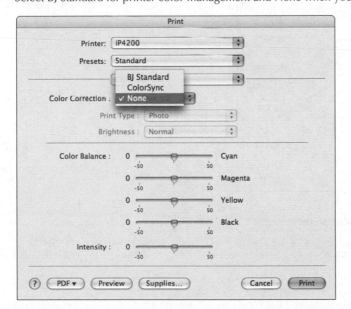

Printing Comments, Forms, and Summaries

You can print document markups as well as form field data from Acrobat viewers. The options are straight-forward and easy to use. However, one limitation you should know about is that comment pop-up notes are not printed and you cannot print the content of a note.

Printing comments

To print comments you need a file that contains some comment notes. To learn more about commenting, see Chapter 20.

To print a file with comments and markups, follow these steps.

STEPS: Printing Document Markups

1. **Open a document containing comments and markups.** You can use the Text Edits tools, Highlight tool, and other comment tools as well as any of the Markup tools such as the Rectangle tool, Cloud tool, Callout tool, and others.

2. **Open the Print dialog box.** Select File ➪ Print.

3. **Select Document and Markups in the Comments and Forms area of the Print dialog box.** When you make the selection for Document and Markups, the page preview in the Preview Composite area of the Print dialog box shows you exactly what elements print, as you see in Figure 31.21.

4. **Click Print.** Your print appears with the comments and markups as was shown in the Preview Composite in the Print dialog box.

FIGURE 31.21

Select Document and Markups from the Comments and Forms drop-down menu.

You have another choice for printing comments. You can choose to print a document with just Stamp comments. From the Comments and Forms drop-down menu, select Document and Stamps. A preview also appears when you choose to print stamp comments. Just make the selection for Document and Stamps and click Print.

Printing form field data

Another option you have is printing just form field data. You can print all form field data with just one exception. Button faces don't print. All the other fields including check boxes, radio buttons, and barcode data print.

To print just the data fields without the background content, select Form fields only in the Print dialog box in the Comments and Forms drop-down menu and print the file.

CROSS-REF For more information on form fields, see Chapter 34.

Printing comment summaries

Yet another option you have when printing PDF documents is creating a comment summary and printing it in one step. Click the Summarize Comments at the bottom of the Print dialog box. The Summarize Options dialog box opens, as shown in Figure 31.22, where you can make a choice for the type of comment summary you want to print. Select an option and click Print Comment Summary. The file that's printed contains just the comments in one of the four summary formats available to you.

CROSS-REF For more information on creating comment summaries, see Chapter 20.

FIGURE 31.22

The Summarize Options dialog box offers choices for using one of four different templates for comment summaries.

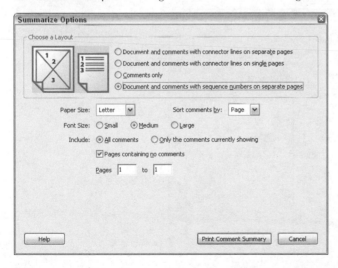

Summary

- A well-managed color workflow requires calibrating your monitor, using a proper workspace color, and printing using a color profile designed for your printer and paper source.

- The two most common methods for managing color with desktop color printers in Acrobat are to enable the printer to manage the color or enable Acrobat to manage the color.

- When you choose to let your printer manage color, you turn color management on in advanced settings in your printer driver.

- When you choose to select a color profile and enable Acrobat to manage color, you turn color management off in your printer driver advanced settings.

- Comment markups can be printed with your document. You choose to print comment markups in the Acrobat Print dialog box in the Comment and Forms drop-down menu.

- You can print form field data without the background PDF design. Choose Form fields only in the Comment and Forms drop-down menu.

- You can create and print comment summaries in one step in the Print dialog box by clicking the Summarize Comments button.

Chapter 32

Commercial Printing and Prepress

At some time or another, the files you output to your desktop printer may be candidates for offset printing. The tools and commands you use for desktop printers, as I explained in Chapter 31, are sufficient for printing to all the printers you have in your office and home. However, when printing PDF documents on commercial printing devices, you must address a number of issues.

For high-end digital prepress and commercial printing, Acrobat Professional includes all the print controls desired by the commercial printing community. Combined with features for previewing color, preflighting jobs, and printing color separations, Acrobat Professional ranks as a strong competitor against any layout or other professional applications designed to serve creative professionals. In this chapter I cover printing from Acrobat Professional using many commercial printing tools.

Setting Up the Work Environment

In Acrobat Professional only, you have a toolbar used specifically for print production. Open a context menu on the Toolbar Well and select Print Production. The Print Production toolbar opens as a floating toolbar, as shown in Figure 32.1.

For printing large documents and when soft proofing files, the Loupe tool is often used. Open a context menu on the Toolbar Well and select More Tools. Scroll down to the Select & Zoom toolbar and select the Loupe Tool check box. Click OK and reopen the same context menu. Select Dock All Toolbars at the bottom of the menu.

NEW FEATURE Adobe Reader 8 and Acrobat Standard 8 now contain both the Loupe tool and the Pan and Zoom tool.

The Print Production toolbar

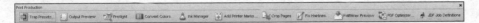

Soft Proofing Color

Soft proofing color refers to viewing color on your monitor with a screen preview of the way color will be printed to hard copy. Rather than print a test proof and consume paper and ink, soft proofing is a digital process whereby you use your computer monitor screen to preview things such as proper color assignments, overprints, separations, transparency, and similar issues that might cause problems on printing devices.

With the exception of previewing overprints, all soft proofing options are contained in Acrobat Professional only. Most of the options you find for soft proofing apply to high-end commercial printing; however, some features can be useful when you're printing to desktop color printers.

Setting up your color management environment

As discussed in Chapter 31, color management is equally important when printing to commercial printing devices and prepress systems. You first begin with monitor calibration and set up your color management preferences. Whereas your workspace color choice is best using the sRGB color space for most desktop printers, the Adobe RGB (1998) color workspace is a better choice for most commercial printing equipment.

CROSS-REF Most of what you need for color management in Acrobat is covered in Chapter 31.

Output Preview

Soft proofing color is handled in the Output Preview dialog box. This dialog box does not provide you options for altering the content. It is used as a viewing tool to diagnose any potential printing problems. From a Preview menu, you select one of two categories in which to preview your document — either Color Warnings or Separations. To open the Output Preview dialog box, click the second tool (Output Preview) in the Print Production toolbar. The Output Preview dialog box opens.

Color Warnings

Click Color Warnings in the Output Preview dialog box. The Color Warnings pane opens, as shown in Figure 32.2.

Several settings in the Color Warnings pane are the same as those found in the Separations pane. The unique options in this pane are the Warnings items. You use this pane to preview any problems that are shown with keylines using the colors in the Warnings areas. If you need more contrast against the background colors, click one of the Warnings color swatches to open a color palette where another color can be selected to display the Warnings keyline borders.

Other areas in the Color Warnings dialog box include the following.

FIGURE 32.2

Open the Output Preview dialog box and click Color Warnings.

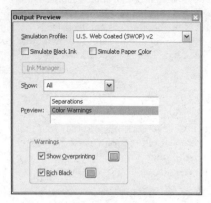

Simulation Profile

Simulation Profile enables you to select from a list of ICC (International Color Consortium) profiles. A number of preset profiles are available from which to choose and you can also create your own custom profiles and add them to the list. You create custom profiles with either software applications such as Adobe Gamma or hardware/software devices that are designed specifically for calibrating monitors and creating ICC profiles. As a profile is created, it is saved as a file to your hard drive.

In order for Acrobat to recognize the ICC profiles you create, you must be certain that the profiles are stored in the proper directory. By default, utilities and commercial devices used for calibrating color save profiles to a directory that makes them accessible to Acrobat. If you want to remove ICC profiles so fewer profiles show up in the Proof Colors dialog box or you have problems getting a profile to the right directory, open the folder where the profiles are stored. On Windows, the path is System32\Spool\Drivers\Color. On Macintosh OS X, look in Macintosh HD:Library:ColorSync:Profiles:Displays. When new profiles are added to the appropriate folder on your computer, you can access the profiles in Acrobat after you quit the program and relaunch it if the profile was added while Acrobat was open.

To select a profile for color proofing, open the Simulation Profile pull-down menu and choose a profile to preview. Selecting the option does not change the color in the document and you can select different profiles from the menu selections without permanently changing color in the file.

From the pull-down menu you'll see a number of different profiles appear in a long list. Select the output device profile you want to simulate. In order to do so, you need to acquire an output profile from your printer or service bureau. For printing on an offset press on coated stock in the United States, use U.S. Web Coated (SWOP) v2 if your printer doesn't have a custom profile to provide you. When you select one of the presets for soft proofing prints, the two check boxes for simulating ink and paper become accessible. (Outside the U.S. you might want to use a Japan or European option available in the CMYK profiles from the CMYK pull-down menu).

> **TIP** To ensure your color proofing uses the same profile each time you view a file onscreen, open a document in Acrobat. Select the profile you want to use as a default from the Simulation Profile pull-down menu. Quit Acrobat and re-launch the program. The last choice you made becomes the new default. You don't need to quit the program to make the profile choice a new default, but if the program crashes during a session, you lose preferences applied in that session. Quitting after making a preference choice ensures that the preference is held in all subsequent Acrobat sessions.

Simulate Black Ink

When the Simulate Black Ink check box is enabled, the preview shows you the dynamic range of the document's profile. Dynamic range is measured in values usually between 0 and 4, although some scanner manufacturers claim dynamic ranges of 4.1, 4.2, or higher. A dynamic range of something like 3.8 yields a wide range of grays between the white point and the black point in a scanned image. If the dynamic range is high, you see details in shadows and highlights. If the dynamic range is low, highlights can get blown out and shadows lose detail. When you enable the Simulate Black Ink check box, look for the distinct tonal differences in the preview and detail in shadows and highlights.

Simulate Paper Color

If the check box for Simulate Paper Color is enabled in the Output Preview dialog box, the preview shows you a particular shade of gray as simulated for the paper color by the profile you choose. You may find that the preview looks too gray or has too much black. This may not be the result of the profile used, but rather the brightness adjustment on your monitor. If your monitor is calibrated properly and the profile accurately displays the paper color, the preview should show you an accurate representation of the document as it is printed on paper.

Warnings

Two different warnings dynamically display potential printing problems. As you select a check box, you can move the Output Preview aside and preview the results in the Document pane. When you select a box and preview the results, the display appears only when the Output Preview dialog box is open. Closing the dialog box returns you to the default view of the document page before you opened the Output Preview.

By default, the options in the Warnings section show potential problems using default colors adjacent to the warning item. You can change the warning colors by clicking on the color swatch and selecting from a preset palette or selecting a custom color from your operating system color palette.

Overprints are often used to *trap* colors when files are intended for printing separations. Trapping a color creates an overlap between colors so any movement of the paper when printed on a printing press prevents printing colors without gaps between the colors. In other cases, overprints may be assigned to colors in illustrations intentionally when a designer wants to eliminate potential trapping problems. For example, you might assign an overprint to text to avoid any trapping problems where black text is printed on top of a background color. In some instances, a designer might unintentionally assign an overprint to a color during the creative process. As a measure of checking overprints for those colors that you properly assign and to review a document for potential problems, you can use Acrobat's Show Overprinting preview to display on your monitor all the overprints created in a file. To view overprints in a PDF document, select the Show Overprinting check box in the Output Preview dialog box.

> **NOTE**   Although you can assign overprints on RGB images/objects in some programs, RGB files won't print with overprints. Overprinting is restricted to CMYK, spot, and gray colors.

To understand what happens with overprints and knockouts, look at Figure 32.3. The composite image is created for printing two colors. These colors are printed on separate plates for two different inks. When the file is separated, the type is *knocked out* of the background, leaving holes in the background. Because the two colors butt up against each other, any slight movement of the paper creates a gap between where one ink color ends and the other begins. To prevent the problem, a slight bit of overprinting is added to the type. In an exaggerated view in Figure 32.3 you can see the stroke around the type character. The stroke is assigned an overprint so its color, which is the foreground color, prints on top of the background color without a knockout.

FIGURE 32.3

If an overprint is assigned to the type, the overprint area of the type color prints on top of the background color. If the paper moves slightly, the overprint prevents any paper color showing through gaps created by the misregistration.

 To carefully examine overprints assigned to type characters, select the Loupe tool in the Zoom toolbar. Move the cursor around the document to preview overprints on small type.

Rich Black

When files are printed with rich black, all the black in the document prints with more density. This is often a common setting used when printing to ink jet printers and commercial oversized printing devices to eliminate any muddy appearance when files contain a substantial amount of black. Select the box to preview how the black will lay down on the printed output. If you see too much density in black, be certain to avoid using rich black when printing the file.

Separations

One of the great features for soft proofing color in Acrobat Professional is the ability to preview a color separation where colors can be viewed individually or in combinations — for example, previewing cyan and magenta instead of previewing all colors. To preview a separation, select Separations from the Preview menu in the Output Preview dialog box. The pane changes to the view shown in Figure 32.4.

If you intend to print a file in four-color process, the Separation Preview dialog box helps you identify any potential problems such as spot colors that may be contained in the file, as in the file used when I opened the Separations preview in Figure 32.4. Likewise, if a spot color only job contains colors not intended to be printed, they also show up.

You can selectively view individual colors by disabling the check boxes adjacent to each color name, viewing selected colors only, and viewing spot colors converted to CMYK. When you click the X in a check box for a color, all image and objects containing a percentage of that color is hidden. Click again and the color displayed.

FIGURE 32.4

The Separations window shows all colors contained in a file.

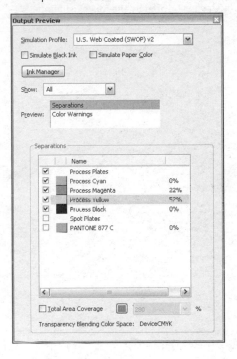

You evaluate color values by moving the cursor around the document with the Separation Preview dialog box open. Notice the percentage values on the far right side of Figure 32.4. These values represent the percent of ink at the cursor position.

Convert Colors

The Convert Colors tool in the Print Production toolbar is truly great whether you soft proof files for commercial printing or you print your PDF documents on your local desktop color printer. Click this tool and the Convert Colors dialog box opens, as shown in Figure 32.5.

Because Acrobat PDF files can have a number of different color profiles assigned to images and objects within the same document, you can easily convert all color in your file to a target printer profile. At the top of the dialog box select a color space containing your document profile. For the Action select Convert and in the Destination space select the output profile you want to use for your printer and paper. At the bottom of the dialog box, you have some options for embedding the converted profile. Select the Embed Profile as Source Color Space check box and the converted color is embedded in the PDF. When you convert color in a document, the color is permanently changed. Select File ➪ Save As and type a new name for the file so you create a backup copy in the event you need to return to your original file.

FIGURE 32.5

Click the Convert Colors tool in the Print Production toolbar to open the Convert Colors dialog box.

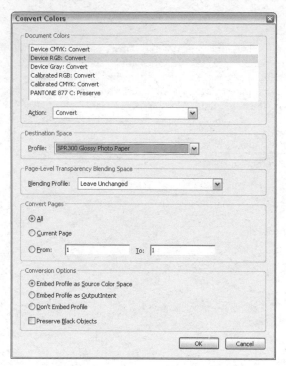

If you convert color for a desktop color printer, be certain to select Same As Source (No Color Management) in your Advanced Print Setup dialog box, as shown in Figure 32.6. If you select a color profile in the Color Profile pull-down menu or you select Printer/PostScript Color Management, you'll end up double-profiling your output.

FIGURE 32.6

Select Same As Source in the Advanced Print Setup if you convert the color space in Acrobat.

CROSS-REF For more information on using output profiles in the Advanced Print Setup dialog box, see Chapter 31.

NOTE Converting color in Acrobat is helpful if you want to soft proof color on your monitor before printing. If you want to bypass soft proofing color, you don't need to worry about converting color in Acrobat. When your file is printed, color conversion happens at print time according to choices you make in the Advanced Print Setup dialog box.

Ink Manager

The Ink Manager dialog box enables you to change ink values and convert colors. Changes you apply to the options aren't saved with the PDF file. If you convert spot colors to CMYK, for example, and save the document, the colors are unaffected when you reopen the file. The changes applied in the Ink Manager take effect only when you print a PDF document. To open the Ink Manager, click the Ink Manager tool in the Print Production toolbar; the Ink Manager dialog box shown in Figure 32.7 opens.

FIGURE 32.7

The Ink Manager enables you to change ink densities and convert color spaces.

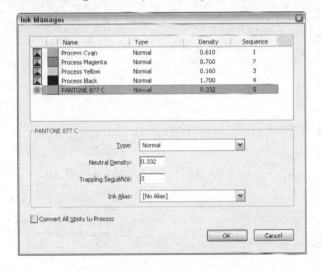

You change density values and the trapping sequence by editing the field box. To alias spot colors, select a spot color and map the color to the same angle and density as a process color. One of the great settings in this dialog box is the check box for Converting All Spots to Process. If you have one or more colors defined as spot colors, you can convert the spot color to process color by checking the box and clicking OK. Another advantage you have with the Ink manager is when you need to remap one spot color value to another. If you have two colors that are supposed to be printed with the same spot values (such as Pantone 185 CVC and Pantone 185 CV), you can map the color so both color names are printed on the same plate.

Transparency Flattener Preview

Transparency creates problems when printing to various PostScript devices because the PostScript RIPs for Level 1, Level 2, and PostScript 3 don't support transparency. For resolving printing problems with transparency, you need to flatten the transparency, which results in files that print successfully on almost any kind of PostScript device. When transparency is flattened in a file the transparent vector objects are converted to non-transparent objects or raster images. Through this conversion, the colors meld together to form a simulated view of transparency. The amount of blending transparent colors needed depends on the amount of transparency you apply to the objects. As you move the Raster/Vector Balance slider to the left to flatten transparency, all vector objects are rasterized. When you move the slider to the right, the transparency flattener maintains as many vector objects as needed in order to successfully print the file.

You can flatten transparency in degrees, and objects in a document are affected according to the degree of transparency flattening you apply. Determining how the other objects are affected is the purpose of the transparency flattener in Acrobat.

When you use the Transparency Flattening tool in the Print Production toolbar, the transparency changes that you make to the PDF are preserved when you save the file. To open the Flattener Preview dialog box, click the Flattener Preview tool in the Print Production toolbar; the options appear as shown in Figure 32.8.

FIGURE 32.8

When the Flattener Preview dialog box opens, click Refresh to see a preview of the document page.

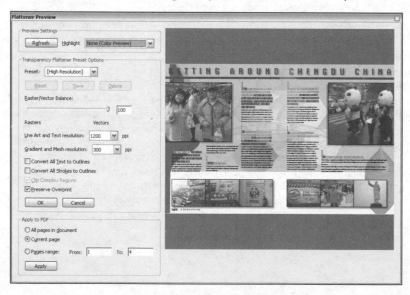

Previews are displayed only for PostScript printing devices. Be certain you have a PostScript printer selected in your Print Setup dialog box before previewing transparency. Beginning with the Highlight pull-down menu you have options for the following:

- **Refresh/Highlight.** Click Refresh when you make attribute changes to see a preview of the results. The Highlight pull-down menu offers selections for areas in the PDF file you can preview.

- **Transparency Flattener Presets.** Select a preset from the pull-down menu. Your options are Low, Medium, and High Resolution. You can reset the preset, save a preset that is added to the menu, and delete a preset after you saved one to the menu.

- **Raster/Vector Balance.** Move the slider left to add more transparency flattening. Click the Refresh button each time you make readjustment of the amount of flattening to see a preview of the results.

- **Gradient and Mesh resolution.** Change values in the field box to edit the resolution you want to apply to gradients and gradient meshes.

- **Convert All Text to Outlines.** If you intend to convert text to outlines, you can see a preview for how text objects are affected in complex regions. When printing a file, you'll want to avoid globally converting text to outlines, as the files are more difficult to print and small text on output devices that print at lower resolutions may appear unsatisfactory.

- **Convert All Strokes to Outlines.** Converts all strokes to outlines. Just as is the case with text converted to outlines, the files will take longer to print if you convert strokes to outlines.

- **Clip Complex Regions.** The boundaries between vector objects and raster objects change as you move the slider. Some objects remain in vector form according to the degree of rasterization you apply. This option ensures the boundaries between the vector and raster objects fall within clipping paths preventing artifacts appearing outside the path boundaries. As with any illustration artwork, the more clipping paths used in a file, the more difficult the printing.

- **Preserve Overprint.** Preserves all overprints assigned in the document.

- **Page Range.** Apply the settings to all pages or select a page range.

- **Apply to PDF.** After making your choices from the various options, click the Apply button. You can save the PDF document and all the transparency flattening is saved with the document.

Trapping Files

You can trap PDF files for commercial printing by applying trap presets from a selection installed as defaults or from custom trap presets you create in Acrobat. The Trap Presets dialog box provides you options for creating custom trap presets, editing a custom preset, assigning presets, and deleting custom presets. Although Acrobat provides you with trapping options, creative professionals should leave the trapping of your files to professional technicians at imaging centers. Unless you completely understand trapping, you can run into trouble by manually trapping your files. Imaging centers either use expensive custom trapping software or In-RIP trapping — both of which are much preferred over what Acrobat provides you with the trapping options.

Fixing hairlines

Before you trap a file, you may need to fix hairline rules. Click the Fix Hairlines tool in the Print Production toolbar to open the Fix Hairlines dialog box. You can adjust a rule when a hairline falls below a specified value to a new value you supply in a field box.

To fix hairlines, click the Fix Hairlines tool in the Print Production toolbar and the Fix Hairlines dialog box opens, as shown in Figure 32.9. In this dialog box you specify the amounts for hairline fixes.

FIGURE 32.9

Click the Fix Hairlines tool in the Print Production toolbar to open the Fix Hairlines dialog box.

Creating trap presets

Make adjustments as needed in the Fix Hairlines dialog box, and then click the Trap Presets tool to open the Trap Presets dialog box shown in Figure 32.10.

FIGURE 32.10

Click the Trap Presets tool to open the Trap Presets dialog box.

The first dialog box that opens enables you to select an existing preset or create a new one. Click the Create button and the New Trap Preset dialog box opens as shown in Figure 32.11. In order to make adjustments in the dialog box you should be familiar with trapping and the acceptable amounts to apply for trap widths, miter adjustments, and attributes assigned to images and thresholds. If you know how to trap a file, you'll know what settings to apply. If you don't know anything about trapping, it's best to leave the job to your commercial printer.

FIGURE 32.11

Set the attributes for the trap preset in the New Trap Preset dialog box.

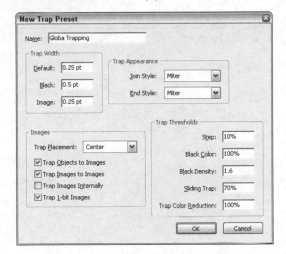

Click OK after providing a name for the new preset and making the adjustments. You are then returned to the Trap Presets dialog box where your new preset is listed in the window. Click the Assign button and the trap values are applied to the document.

Cropping Pages

Two tools appear in the Print Production toolbar for cropping pages in Acrobat. Ideally, you'll want to export to PDF from an authoring program with crop marks at the time you convert to PDF. Acrobat won't retain any bleeds in your document. If you don't have bleeds, then these tools can help you set up the proper page size and add crop marks. A document such as a Microsoft Word file that needs to go to press is an ideal candidate for these tools because you won't find bleeds in Word files.

Adding printer marks

When cropping pages, you'll typically add crop and other printer's marks to the cropped page so you'll know the correct trim size.

 For a description on using the Add Printer Marks tool, see Chapter 8.

Cropping pages

When cropping pages, the thing to remember is to first use the Add Printer Marks tool, and then use the Crop Pages tool in the Print Production toolbar. When you click the Crop Pages tool, the Crop Pages dialog box opens where you set the page size, select the range of pages you want to crop, and view a preview before you exit the dialog box.

After adding crop marks, click OK and the printer marks appear on the page. The process for adding printer marks and using the Crop Pages dialog box is covered in Chapter 8.

 **For a description of using the Crop Pages tool, see Chapter 8.**

PDF Optimizer

PDF Optimizer is a menu command available under the Advanced menu. You can choose Advanced ➪ PDF Optimizer or open the Print Production toolbar and click the PDF Optimizer tool.

When you click the PDF Optimizer tool in the Print Production toolbar, the PDF Optimizer dialog box opens. A number of options appear in several panes for deleting non essential data from files, changing PDF compatibility, and optimizing the file for smaller file sizes. All the options you have in the PDF Optimizer are detailed in Chapter 18.

 **For a description on using PDF Optimizer, see Chapter 18.**

Working with Job Definition Files

You use a Job Definition File (JDF) in production workflows to include information necessary for a production process and information related to the PDF creation.

You assign the information in a JDF file through a collection of dialog boxes that begin with your clicking on the JDF Job Definitions tool at the far-right side of the Print Production toolbar. Click the tool and the JDF Job Definitions dialog box opens, as shown in Figure 32.12.

FIGURE 32.12

Click the JDF Job Definitions tool to open the JDF Job Definitions dialog box.

Click the New button to open the Create New Job Definition dialog box. You make choices for either creating a new definition, using the open document's structure, or applying a definition from another file saved to your hard drive. If you create a new definition, you need to supply a name in the Name field box and click OK, and the Edit JDF Job Definition dialog box opens, as shown in Figure 32.13.

FIGURE 32.13

Create a new JDF Definition and the Edit JDF Definition dialog box opens.

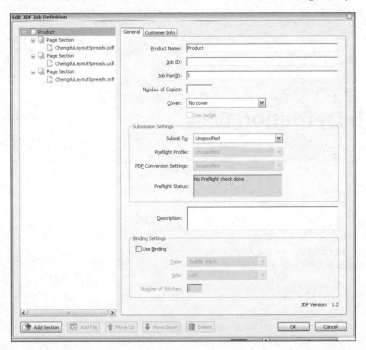

In the default General tab you can define some production information and binding, preflight information, PDF conversion settings, and Job ID information. Click the Customer Info tab and you add contact and identifying information.

The entire process for creating and using JDF files is extensive and beyond the scope of this chapter. For more information about JDF, see the Help document installed with Acrobat.

Preflighting PDF Files

Preflighting is a term used by creative professionals and service technicians to refer to analyzing a file for suitability for printing. A preflight assessment might examine a file for the proper color mode of images, whether images are compressed, whether fonts are accessible either embedded or accessible to the operating system, or any number of other conditions that might interfere with successfully printing a job.

I saved the Preflight tool in the Print Production toolbar to mention last here because preflighting PDF files is a bit complicated and quite complex. In addition to clicking the Preflight tool, you can also open the Preflight dialog box by selecting Advanced ➪ Preflight or pressing Shift+Ctrl/⌘+X. Any one of these actions opens the Preflight dialog box shown in Figure 32.14.

Click the Preflight tool in the Print Production toolbar or select Advanced ➪ Preflight to open the Preflight dialog box.

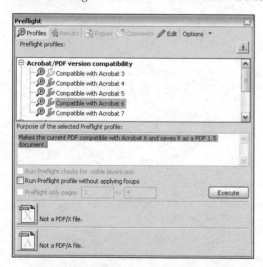

The tools used to preflight files might be stand-alone applications or features built into programs used for printing to commercial printing equipment. Prior to Acrobat 6 you needed to preflight a file before converting to PDF with a standalone product that analyzed the original authoring application file prior to conversion to PDF or a third-party plug-in for Acrobat that performed preflighting on PDF files. Preflighting PDFs from within Acrobat was introduced in Acrobat 6 and has been polished and greatly improved in Acrobat 8.

Preflighting a file

Acrobat requires you to have a file open in the Document pane in order to run a preflight check unless you use a batch sequence or droplet. To preflight a document, be certain a file is open and click the Preflight tool in the Print Production toolbar. The Preflight dialog box shown previously in Figure 32.14 opens. In the top window, you see a number of preinstalled profiles listed with a description for the kind of preflight-ing each profile performs. Use the scroll bar on the right side of the window to display additional profiles.

The Options menu contains a number of menu choices for creating PDF/X- and PDF/A-compliant files, editing profiles, importing and exporting profiles, and creating profile reports that are saved as text files.

CROSS-REF   To learn more about PDF/X and PDF/A, see Chapter 10.

If a profile exists containing the conditions you want to check, select a profile and click the Execute button. If the file you preflight contains errors, a report is displayed in the Preflight window after you execute the preflight. The report is listed in a hierarchy with sub notations listed under parent categories. Click the icon to the left of each category to expand the list, as shown in Figure 32.15.

FIGURE 32.15

If the preflight does not match the conditions of the profile, a report lists the errors in the Preflight window.

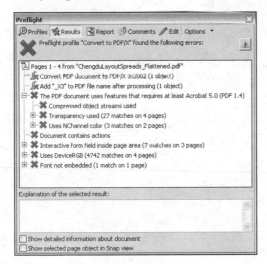

If, after preflighting a file, you see errors reported, as shown in Figure 32.15, you need to fix the problems either in Acrobat using Print Production tools or back in the original authoring program, and recreate the PDF file.

Creating a new profile

If none of the preset profiles do the job of file checking for your workflow, you can create your own custom profiles. Acrobat offers you more than 400 different conditions that you can use in preflighting files. To create a new profile, click the Edit button in the Preflight dialog box; the Preflight: Edit Profile dialog box opens, as shown in Figure 32.16.

FIGURE 32.16

Click the Edit button in the Preflight: Profiles dialog box to open the Preflight: Edit Profiles dialog box.

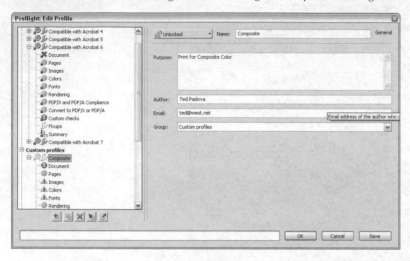

At the bottom of the dialog box, several tools appear for creating and managing profiles.

From left to right, they are as follows:

- **Create a new profile.** Click the icon to create a new profile. The Preflight: Edit Profile pane changes to offer options using field boxes for adding a profile name, a profile description, author name, e-mail address, and a Group where the profile will be nested.

- **Duplicate the selected profile.** Click the icon to duplicate a selected profile. Once it's duplicated, you can edit the profile to change conditions.

- **Delete the selected profile.** Select a profile and click the icon to remove the profile from the list window. You cannot delete the profile if Locked is selected in the Preflight: Edit Profile pane.

- **Import.** Click the Import tool to import a profile created by a vendor or a user in your workgroup.

- **Export.** If you are responsible for creating profiles at a service center or in a company where you want to implement a set of standards, click the Export button. The profile selected when you click this button is exported to a file that you can send to other users who in turn import the profile.

To create a new custom profile, click the Create a new Preflight profile button. Type a name in the dialog box shown in Figure 32.16 and click items in the left pane below your new profile name. As you click each condition, the Preflight: Edit Profile right pane changes to display options for the selected item in the Custom profiles list. From pull-down menus you select options, as shown in Figure 32.17.

FIGURE 32.17

Click an item below your new profile name and click a condition. In the right pane, select the options you want to include for preflighting a file from pull-down menu choices.

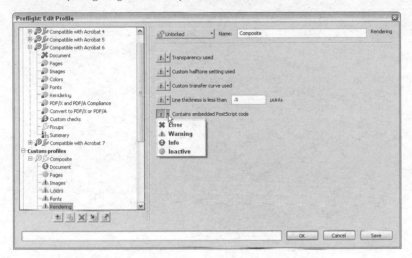

After you create a new custom profile, click the Save button and the new profile is saved to your list of profiles.

Creating reports and comments

Each time you preflight a file, you can create a report of the results. Click the Report button that appears after preflighting a file. The Report button appears at the top of the Preflight dialog box. When you click Report, the Save As dialog box opens. You can save the report in PDF, XML, or Text format by making a choice from the Save as type pull-down menu in the Save As dialog box.

Printing PDFs for Commercial Printing

Acrobat Professional contains all the print controls you need for printing files to commercial devices. To access the options, choose File ➪ Print or click the Print tool in the Toolbar Well. In the Print dialog box, click the Advanced button.

When you select Advanced in the Print dialog box in Acrobat Professional, the Advanced Print Setup dialog box shown in Figure 32.18 opens. There are three categories in the left pane. When you select a category, the right pane changes, just as the Preferences dialog box changes when you select a category.

 You must have a PostScript printer selected in the Print dialog box in order to see all the options in the left pane.

FIGURE 32.18

Click the Advanced button in the Print dialog box to open the Advanced Print Setup dialog box.

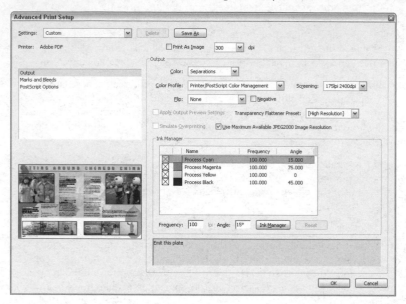

Using Save as PostScript for High-End Printing

Commercial printers should note that although you can successfully print files from the Print dialog box using the Advanced print settings, there are many circumstances where saving a file to PostScript and downloading the PostScript file offers you more options and may be necessary to successfully print a job. For example, to send a PostScript file to other post-processing programs that require DCS (Desktop Color Separation)–compliant PostScript, you are required to download a PostScript file and not use the print path. In addition, PPD (PostScript Printer Description) selection is also provided in the Save As PostScript advanced settings dialog box or by selecting the Export ➪ More Formats ➪ PostScript command from the Export task button. Also those who use imposition software not supporting PDF will need to create a PostScript file to create impositions.

Choosing File ➪ Save As ➪ PostScript (.ps) and assigning attribute choices in the Save as Settings dialog box is the path high-end commercial printers should use instead of printing files directly from the Print dialog box.

For more information on assigning attribute choices in the Save as PostScript dialog box and saving files as PostScript, see Chapter 9.

Imaging centers and creative professionals should look into the next generation of print engines offer by Adobe Systems. The new Adobe PDF Print Engine is a next generation print platform allowing PDF files to be rendered natively and they support newer design features such as full support for transparency. To learn more about the next generation of PDF Print Engines, visit www.adobe.com/products/pdfprintengine.

Output

Output options enable you to set the color and frequency controls for the output. At the top of the dialog box a check box is available for printing the document as an image. For desktop printing when you have trouble printing the file, you can use the Print As Image option as a last resort. Print as Image rasterizes the PDF document and type usually looks poor on the final output. Don't enable the check box for professional printing. This option is also available in the Advanced Print options for Adobe Reader and Acrobat Standard. The remaining items are used for commercial printing and they include the following:

- **Color.** Select from composite or separations. Users with PostScript 3 RIPs can choose either Separations or In-Rip Separations depending on how you set up your RIP defaults. For creative professionals printing separation proofs to desktop printers, select Separations. For composite color, select Composite from the pull-down menu. For printing RC Paper or composite images to film, select Composite Gray.

NOTE If Separations is not available, you don't have a PostScript printer capable of printing separations selected for your printer. If you don't see separations active, cancel out of the dialog box and select the Adobe PDF printer in the Print dialog box; then click on Advanced to return to the Advanced Print Settings.

- **Color Profile.** Select from the pull-down menu items the color profile used in your workflow.

- **Screening.** If you're using the Adobe PDF printer as the printer driver, the screening options won't match the device where you print your job. If you're using a device printer, the screening options for the device are derived from the PPD (PostScript Printer Description). If the frequency is not available from the pull-down menu, you select custom screens and angles from the Ink Manager (discussed later in this list).

- **Flip.** For emulsion control, select horizontal from the Flip pull-down menu to print with emulsion down. You have options for flip vertical and flip vertical & horizontal.

NOTE Adobe's print controls in Acrobat Professional are *almost* perfect. However, one limitation still exists in Acrobat 8. There is no emulsion control for composite printing. Emulsion control is available only when printing separations. Therefore, service centers needing to print emulsion-down composites on LexJet, mylar, transwhite, and other substrates on large format inkjet printers need to flip files prior to PDF creation or by using the Rotation tools in Acrobat.

- **Apply Output Preview Settings.** This setting, in effect, applies the previews you created with other Print Production tools.

- **Simulate Overprinting.** This option, also available for composite, prints only the print results in a proof, showing the results of overprints assigned in the document. This feature emulates the overprinting previews of high-end color proofers, such as what was introduced with the Imation Rainbow printer.

- **Transparency Flattener Preset.** Default and custom presets appear in the pull-down menu. Select a preset if you want to flatten transparency at print time.

- **Use Maximum Available JPEG2000 Image Resolution.** When the check box is enabled, the maximum usable resolution contained in JPEG2000 images is used.

- **Frequency/Angle.** To edit the frequency and angle for each plate, type the desired values in the text boxes. Click each color and edit the Frequency and Angle text boxes.

- **Ink Manager.** Click the Ink Manager button and the Ink Manager dialog box opens providing options the same as those available when you click the Ink Manager tool in the Print Production toolbar. If spot colors are contained in the file, you can convert spot or RGB to CMYK color by selecting the Convert All Spots to Process check box. The spot color converts to CMYK when you check the box.

Marks and Bleeds

Select Marks and Bleeds in the left pane of the Advanced Print Setup dialog box, and the right pane changes to show options for adding printer's marks. All marks added in the Advanced Print Setup dialog box apply only to the printed file. If you want to save a file with printer's marks, use the Add Printer Marks tool in the Print Production toolbar.

Select All to show all printer's marks. If you want individual marks, clear All Marks and select the check boxes individually below the Marks Style pull-down menu. From the pull-down menu options, you can choose Western Style or Eastern Style. Use Eastern Style for printing files in far-eastern countries.

Marks and bleeds are also available for composite proofs as well as separations.

PostScript Options

Click on PostScript Options in the Advanced Print Setup dialog box, and the right pane changes to display options for PostScript attributes as shown in Figure 32.19.

FIGURE 32.19

Click PostScript and the right pane changes to reflect options for PostScript output options.

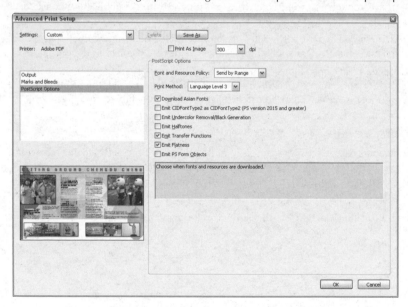

The options include the following:

- **Font and Resource Policy.** Three options are available from the pull-down menu. Select Send at Start to send all fonts to the printer as the print job starts. Select Send by Range to send fonts as they are encountered on the pages as new pages print; the fonts stay in memory until the job finishes printing. Select Send for Each page to conserve memory; the fonts are flushed after each page prints. The last selection takes more time to print but can overcome problems when you are experiencing difficulty in printing a job.

- **Print Method.** Choose from PostScript Level 2 or PostScript 3 depending on the level of PostScript used by the RIP.

- **Download Asian Fonts.** Check the box if Asian characters are in the document and not available at the RIP.

- **Emit CIDFontType2 as CIDFontType2 (PS version 2015 and greater).** Converts TrueType fonts to PostScript font equivalents.

- **Emit Undercolor Removal/Black Generation.** GCR/UCR removal is necessary only if the original file contained embedded settings. Clear the box to remove any embedded settings that might have been inadvertently added and saved in Photoshop. If you want to apply any embedded settings, selecting the box to Emit the settings applies them as if they were embedded in the authoring program.

- **Emit Halftones.** In the event that the PostScript file contained embedded halftones, you can preserve them here, and the frequency assigned in the Output options is used to print the file. Select the box to apply the frequency embedded in a file. You want to preserve halftones when you want an embedded halftone frequency in an image to print at a different frequency than the rest of the job.

- **Emit Transfer Functions.** Clear the box to eliminate any transfer functions that might have been embedded in Photoshop images. If you know you want images to print with embedded transfer functions you may have applied according to instructions provided from a publication house, select the box to preserve the transfer functions.

- **Emit Flatness.** If flatness was exported from files created in Adobe Photoshop with clipping paths or a vector art image has flatness applied, the flatness values are retained in the output.

- **Emit PS Form Objects.** PostScript XObject stores common information in a document, such as backgrounds, headers, footers, and so on. When PostScript XObjects are used, the printing is faster, but it requires more memory. To speed up the printing, select the box to emit PostScript XObjects.

CROSS-REF To understand more about XObjects, see Chapter 10.

You can capture and save the settings you select in the Advanced Print Setup dialog box as a printing profile. Click the Save As button to open the Save Print Settings dialog box. Provide a name and click OK. You select the profiles from the pull-down menu for Settings in the top-left corner of the Advanced Print Setup dialog box.

If you create a setting and want to later delete it from the Settings pull-down menu, select the setting to delete and click the Delete button.

Summary

- You can change page sizes with the Crop Pages tool. You add trim marks with the Add Printer Marks tool in the Print Production toolbar in Acrobat Professional.

- Acrobat Professional provides several tools for soft proofing color, overprints, separation previews, and transparency flattening. Acrobat Standard and Adobe Reader do not support tools used for commercial printing.

- Traps are defined with the Trap Presets tool in Acrobat Professional.

- JDF (Job Definition Files) are defined using the JDF Job Definitions tool in Acrobat Professional.

- Preflighting files is a manner of checking a document for potential errors in printing. Acrobat Professional offers you an extended set of conditions to check files before sending them to pre-press centers and print shops.

- You save PDF/X-compliant files from the Preflight dialog box. Sending PDF/X files to service centers and print shops optimizes your chances for successful output when printing to commercial printing devices.

- A set of preset profiles is installed with Acrobat Professional for preflighting jobs. You can create custom profiles by adding preset conditions in the Preflight dialog box.

- You can import and export profiles. You can acquire profiles from service centers and add them to your profile list for preflighting files.

- The Advanced Print Setup dialog box in Acrobat Professional offers you options for color separations, printer's marks, frequency control, emulsion control, and other print attributes associated with commercial printing.

Part VI

Acrobat PDF and LiveCycle Designer Forms

Chapter 33

Designing PDF Forms (Windows Only)

When it comes to Acrobat and forms, essentially two different types of forms can be created with tools from your Acrobat Professional installation in Windows only. Acrobat Professional lets you create Adobe PDF forms within Acrobat on either Windows or the Macintosh. In Windows, you have another tool installed with Acrobat Professional called Adobe LiveCycle Designer that is a separate executable application. Forms created in Adobe LiveCycle Designer (or simply Designer, or Adobe Designer as I refer to it in this chapter) are an XML Forms Architecture (XML), which is an application of XML for electronic forms.

What's important to remember is that PDF forms created in Acrobat are very different than XML forms created in Adobe Designer. Among other things, you can't edit XML forms in Acrobat and there are some limitations to what you can do with Acrobat PDF forms you edit in Designer.

As a forms development tool, Adobe Designer is one of the best applications you can find to create forms that can be filled out and submitted using any Acrobat viewer. However, Designer is not a panacea for all forms development. You do have many opportunities for impressive forms creation in Acrobat as I explain in the remaining chapters of this book.

For now, we're concerned with Designer and how to use the application to create XML forms. As I stated at the beginning of this book, the *Adobe Acrobat 8 PDF Bible* is not a book on forms and not a book on Adobe Designer. There's much more to Designer than can be covered in this book. When you first open the program you see as much, if not more, tools, menu commands, and features than you have in Acrobat. To cover all the features Designer provides would take a book equal to the size of this one.

What I can hope to do in this chapter is provide a brief introduction to Adobe Designer and talk about some of the neat things you can do with the program. For a much more thorough description of the tools, commands, and features, be certain to look over the Help document provided with your Acrobat installation.

Setting Up the Work Environment

Adobe LiveCycle Designer is a standalone program used to design XML forms. When you create forms in Designer, you cannot edit the form fields in Acrobat. Therefore, the work environment in Acrobat does not require any special tools to edit forms created in Designer. To view and fill out forms in Acrobat use the default toolbar setup. Open a context menu on the Toolbar Well and select Reset Toolbars.

In the Adobe Designer workplace are a number of different options for setting up your work environment. Designer makes extensive use of palettes with fewer tools as in Acrobat; so setting up your workplace is primarily a matter of opening and closing palettes. In Figure 33.1 you can see a number of palettes loaded in palette wells for an editing session.

FIGURE 33.1

The Adobe Designer workplace with a number of palettes loaded in palette wells

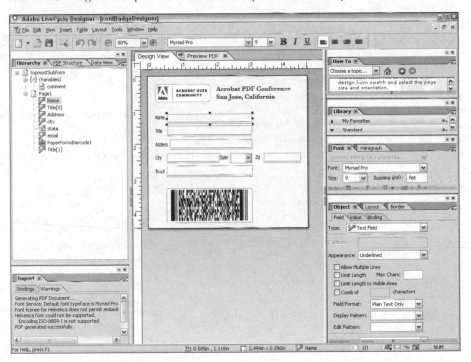

The *Adobification* of Designer

It didn't take a user familiar with Adobe software long to realize that Adobe Designer 7 was like the identified patient in a dysfunctional family. Designer just didn't look and feel quite right compared to other Adobe software. Designer was originally created by another developer and passed through a few other developers before Adobe acquired the product. Adobe didn't build Designer from the ground up. Through continued development Adobe has been enhancing Designer to fall into a more compatible application consistent with other Adobe software.

NEW FEATURE   Designer isn't quite there in terms of appearing much like other Adobe products, but it's get-ting a little closer. One of the first indications to supports this claim is the new feature for cus-tomizing keyboard shortcuts, which is consistent with other Adobe products and actually ahead of Acrobat. You can customize keyboard shortcuts as you can all the Adobe Creative Suite applications. Select Tools ➪ Keyboard Shortcuts and the Keyboard Shortcuts dialog box opens, as shown in Figure 33.2.

FIGURE 33.2

The new Keyboard Shortcuts dialog box lets you custom design keyboard shortcuts to access menu items and palettes.

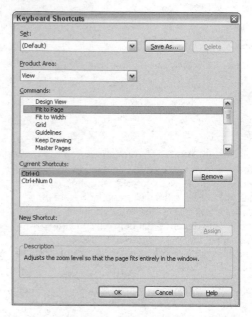

When you open the View menu shortcuts you immediately see the default shortcut keys for Fit Page (Ctrl/⌘+0). You had Ctrl+0 for Fit Page in Designer 7, so this item is no biggie.

NEW FEATURE   Designer 8 offers shortcuts for zooming as you have in Acrobat (Ctrl/⌘++ (plus sign) to zoom in and Ctrl/⌘+- (minus sign) to zoom out). You also have access to the Hand tool by pressing the spacebar, which is a common modifier for all other Adobe programs. Now in Designer 8 you'll find mov-ing around the layout window to be much less frustrating. These shortcuts provide you more freedom of movement in a much-crowded workspace and they're a very welcomed addition to this new release.

To assign a keyboard shortcut, open the Product Area pull-down menu and select the menu where the com-mand appears that you want to assign a keyboard shortcut. As an example, I want to assign Ctrl+W to the File ➪ Close command (can you believe that this isn't a default in the program?). I open the Product Area pull-down menu and select File from the menu list. All the commands in the File menu appear in the Commands window. Click the New Shortcut text box and type the shortcut keys you want to use (in this example I type Ctrl+W). Click the Assign button and the keyboard shortcut appears in the Current Shortcuts list, as you see in Figure 33.3.

FIGURE 33.3

Select a menu choice from the Product Area pull-down menus and type a keyboard shortcut.

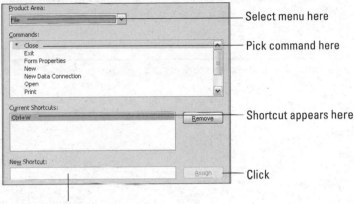

You'll probably gasp when you see the Window ⟿ Workspace command. With great anticipation you move the cursor to the Workspace thinking you're finally going to see a Save Workspace command in an Acrobat product. Unfortunately opening the submenu doesn't provide you the power you have with the Creative Suite applications for saving workspaces. This command has just been renamed in Designer 8 from the Window ⟿ Manage Palettes command in Designer 7. There are a few commands in the submenu for showing/hiding the left and right palettes and showing some floating palettes that help expand your editing space. However, when you begin to work with Designer and realize that most of the editing tasks you do are performed with palettes and menu commands, you'll find that saving workspaces is not as important a feature as it would be in Acrobat.

Designer has a way to go before it gets completely *Adobified* with layers, more keyboard shortcuts consistent with other Adobe programs, and some essential tools such as a Selection Arrow and Hand tool; but a few new commands and a much cleaner palette layout in Designer 8 show that Adobe is headed in the right direction.

Preparing the workspace

Unlike Acrobat in which you engage in very different editing tasks, Designer is all about creating forms. There are some palettes that you won't use in an editing session and others that may be used in some layouts. For example, you might use the Data Connection tools when you want to make a connection to a database file. When designing other forms you might not use the tools. In some forms you may add barcodes, while in other forms you won't need the bar code tools. This is the case for several palettes in Designer.

Regardless of what kind of form you create there are some common palettes needed in almost all form designs and you'll want to set up your work environment with the essential tools first. These palettes are as follows:

- **Object.** The Object palette contains three tabs. The Field tab provides options for assigning appearance attributes to fields. The Value tab contains options for assigning attributes to field values. Among other attributes, the Value tab lets you change field types—something you can't do in Acrobat. The Binding tab lets you set up data connections to bind fields to a database.

■ **Layout.** The Layout tab provides a number of attribute choices for field layouts such as size, margins, captions, and so on.

■ **Border.** The Border tab provides extensive choices for creating field appearances. Acrobat offers a few choices for borders and fills. In Designer, you can format field appearances similar to the way you can format cells in a program such as Microsoft Excel.

■ **Font/Paragraph.** By Default, the Font and Paragraph tabs don't appear in the Designer workspace. If you want to change fonts and set font and paragraph attributes, select Window ➪ Font and both tabs open. Keep this palette open when designing a form. You'll use it often.

■ **Library.** The Library is your repository containing the fields you add to a Designer form. In Acrobat, you click a tool in the Forms toolbar and drag open a rectangle to add a field to a page. Acrobat supports eight different field types. Designer supports 25 different field types/objects in the Library Standard tab alone that you drag from the palette tab to the document page. Among other tabs in the Library palette you also have an option for adding your own custom designed fields that can be reused on many different forms.

NEW FEATURE New in Designer 8 is a My Favorites tab where you can keep frequently used fields in a separate tab.

■ **How To.** Designer's How To tab is similar to the Acrobat How To panel where help information appears in the palette tab. When you first start using Designer, it's a good idea to keep this palette open. After you know your way around the Designer workspace, you can close the palette to make more room for other palettes.

■ **Hierarchy/Data View.** On the left side of the Designer workspace you see the Hierarchy palette. Keep this palette open for all your forms designs. The palette lists all the fields, subforms, master pages, and structure on your design in a hierarchical order. This palette is indispensable and you'll need to use it frequently when creating dynamic forms. The Data View tab is where you make database connections. You may or may not need this tab open depending on the kind of form you design.

■ **Report/Warnings.** The Report tab provides you with information about the form design. The Warnings tab is loaded when you select Window ➪ Report (or Warnings). This tab can be very helpful when creating a new form. The Warnings tab dynamically lists errors and messages for potential problems in your form.

■ **Script Editor.** In Designer 7 the Script Editor opened by default. The Script Editor takes up some precious room at the top of the Designer window and hiding it in Designer 7 always required you adjust the Script Editor to move it out of view. By default, the Script Editor is hidden in Designer 8. If you want to open the Script Editor so that you can write code in FormCalc or JavaScript, select Window ➪ Script Editor. You'll notice in the menu command that you now have a keyboard shortcut to open and close the Script Editor. Press Ctrl+Shift+F5 and the Script Editor opens and closes on the keyboard shortcut. By default, leave the Script Editor hidden to provide you with more room for editing a form and press Ctrl+Shift+F5 when you need to write a script.

■ **Design View/Preview PDF.** The two tabs at the top of the layout area in the Designer window enable you to see the layout (Design view), and a PDF Preview of the form. The Design View and PDF Preview tabs appear by default. To open the Master Pages tab, select View ➪ Master Pages. Additionally, you can add another tab for viewing XML source code. Select View ➪ XML Source to display the tab.

When designing a form you need to view the form in PDF Preview in order to execute actions from fields and fill in data. Be sure to keep the two default tabs open for any design you create. If you lose a tab, look in the View menu to bring it back.

There are additional palettes and tabs you can load from the Window menu. The preceding list covers some of the most essential palettes you need for just about any form design. As you poke around the Window menu a few other palettes that are self-descriptive can be added to your workspace. Be aware, however, that as you add more palettes to the workspace, you reduce the amount of work area you have to lay out your form design.

In addition to palettes, you also have options for displaying a number of hidden tools. By default, Designer opens with a limited tool set. You can add tools and load toolbars by selecting Tools ➪ Customize. The Customize dialog box opens where you can select additional tools and display several toolbars. In addition, you can create a custom toolbar by clicking the New button in the Customize dialog box and add the individual tools you want to use in a toolbar you design.

Understanding the *Why* for Adobe LiveCycle Designer

When you purchase Adobe Acrobat Professional, one of your first thoughts might be, "Why is Adobe providing me with a standalone program to design forms when I can do the job in Acrobat Professional?" This is an important question and you need to understand not only the purpose for using Designer, but also the direction Adobe is moving in terms of PDF form design and deployment.

Adobe Designer is a client-based point-and-click graphical design application that simplifies the creation of forms. IN Acrobat you need to create a form design in another application, convert to PDF, and add form fields in Acrobat. Designer includes the ability to create the form layout as well as the form fields that your form recipient will populate with data, or you may bind a data source to your form and flow the data spawning fields and pages as needed. Forms created with Adobe Designer are intended to be delivered either as PDF or HTML that support user-defined data structures, like XML. In support of standards-based data formatting, such as XML, Adobe is de-emphasizing its proprietary FDF (Form Data Format) as a data exchange format and migrating to XML as an open standard. With tools that help you easily design forms through drag-and-drop methods for handling images and form data fields, Adobe Designer is a tool that simplifies data management and data exchanges.

It's data handling that takes Designer to a level well beyond the capabilities of Adobe Acrobat. Form designers using Adobe Designer can create simple data capture solutions and use the Acrobat products to consolidate data received from clients. The ability to easily transport data to and from other applications via XDP and XML format makes Designer a much less complicated and efficient solution than what you have available using Adobe Acrobat.

As of this writing, Macintosh users are at a disadvantage because Designer is available on Windows only. However, you may expect to eventually see Designer supported on both platforms as development in technology applied to Designer is likely to increase while Adobe still intends to completely support Acrobat PDF form technology. Considering the fact that Adobe is investing as much if not more research and development into Designer as they are devoting to Acrobat, the more you know about Designer today, the better off you'll be when future Acrobat products are released. If you are a serious form designer, you will want to begin using Designer right away.

Getting Started with a New Form Design

Adobe Designer offers you several options for designing forms when you first choose a menu command to create a new form. By default, when you launch Designer by double-clicking the application icon (or use the Start Menu or an application icon alias) you arrive at the Welcome to Adobe LiveCycle Designer Welcome screen. You can choose to dismiss the screen when you launch Designer by removing the check mark in the lower left corner of the Welcome screen where you see Show this Dialog at Startup. If you click New Form in the Welcome screen or you select File ⇨ New, the New Form Assistant Wizard opens as shown in Figure 33.4. Starting a Designer work session when creating a new form usually starts by clicking New Form in the Welcome screen or selecting File ⇨ New. In both cases you start your project by first making a decision for a method to use from options in the New Form Assistant Wizard.

FIGURE 33.4

The New Form Assistant Wizard opens by default when you first launch Adobe Designer.

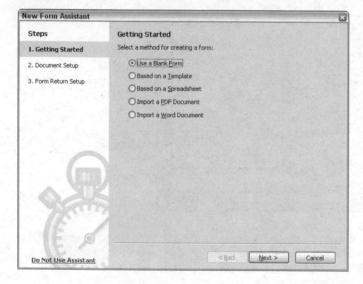

As shown in the New Form Assistant Wizard, you have five different options for creating a form in Designer. These options are as follows:

- **Use a Blank Form.** This option opens a blank page where you add all the design elements on your new form. Essentially you start with a blank page and create the design using tools in Designer for text, graphics, and form fields.

- **Based on a Template.** Unlike Acrobat, you have a number of different preinstalled template files that help you get started in creating a new form design. Click this option and the New Form Assistant changes panes to a view shown in Figure 33.5. From the scrollable list of different preinstalled form designs, select the design most similar to the kind of form you want to create and click Next.

- **Based on a Spreadsheet.** New in Designer 8 you have an option to create a form design from cells in a spreadsheet. You click through the Next buttons assigning different attributes to the form and on the last page in the New Form Assistant Wizard you're prompted to copy cells in a spreadsheet document. You can leave the wizard pane open, launch Microsoft Excel and copy the cells you want to appear as form fields. Close the Excel worksheet and return to Designer. Once data is copied to the Clipboard, the Finish button is active. Click Finish and the copied cells are added to a new form.

FIGURE 33.5

Select a template you want to start with for creating a new design.

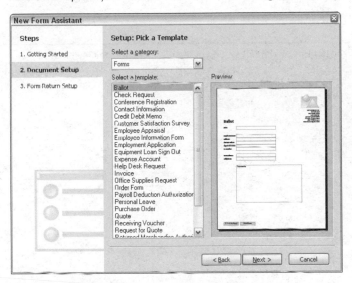

- **Import a PDF Document.** You can create a design in any authoring program and export to PDF. After PDF conversion use the Import a PDF Document option and you can import the PDF into Designer. If you create a form design in Acrobat and import a PDF file containing fields, Designer recognizes the fields created in Acrobat.

When you choose Import a PDF Document and click Next in the New Form Assistant Wizard you identify a PDF document, click Next and arrive at the Setup: Import Options pane shown in Figure 33.6.

Designer needs to know how you want to work with the PDF file. You have two options from the radio buttons in Figure 33.6.

NEW FEATURE Designer 8 supports a new feature called PDF background artwork. When you select Create an Interactive Form with Fixed Pages you are importing the PDF document as a background layer with the background appearing behind form fields (either from a PDF converted with form fields or a PDF with no fields and fields you ultimately add in Designer). PDF background artwork cannot be edited for any content on the background layer. It's important to note that you loose some of the benefits of creating original forms in Designer such as creating dynamic forms, using master pages, and using a grid. However, you have the advantage of maintaining the exact layout of the original PDF including color assignment and font embedding.

The Create an Interactive Form with a Flowable Layout option imports and converts the PDF into an XML template. In this case, you can edit the imported PDF content. If you choose this option you may find much of the original design such as graphics on the PDF layout is not fully translated to the XML form.

- **Import a Word Document.** This option lets you import a Microsoft Word file as a new form design. Designer (like Acrobat 8) has a run form field recognition function that is automatically run when you convert the Word file. All areas on the form design that clearly indicate form field positions such as lines, boxes, and so on are populated with form fields when the file opens in Designer.

FIGURE 33.6

In the Document Setup: Import Options pane, you make a decision for how the PDF will be imported.

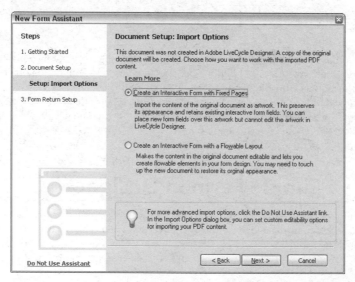

Working with Fonts in Designer

Adobe Designer works similar to the way you might work in page layout programs. You have master pages, page size configurations, ability to import graphics, and many options for setting type. As with layout programs, if you attempt to open a document that contains fonts that are not installed in your system, you wind up with font problems in terms of appearances and improper printing.

If you design a form using a certain font set, be certain the same font family is loaded in your system before opening the file. If you open PDF or Word documents in Designer, you need to have all the fonts contained in the file installed in your system. You may have a huge problem if you work with a number of legacy PDF documents that need to be redesigned in Designer. When fonts are not installed in your system and you open a PDF file in Designer, a Missing Fonts dialog box opens, as shown in the following figure.

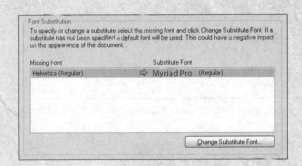

If a font is missing, the font is listed with a caution symbol. To substitute the missing font with a font loaded in your system, click the Change Substitute Font button. The Specify Substitute Font dialog box opens and you select installed system fonts in a scrollable window. Select a font in the list and click OK. You need to repeat the steps for each font appearing with a caution symbol on the Missing Fonts dialog box. After identifying the font substitutions, click OK and the new substituted fonts appear in the document. When you save the file as PDF, the new fonts are embedded in the resultant PDF.

Creating a Simple Form in Designer

You follow several steps to create a form in Adobe Designer whether it is a form from a template, starting with a blank new page, importing a PDF document, converting a Word file, or converting a spreadsheet file. You typically follow steps initially in the New Form Assistant where Designer helps you by providing some options to decide how your form will be deployed and other choices depending on the type of conversion you choose to use.

Creating a blank new page

All the form field attributes are assigned on any kind of form you create in Designer — whether you start from scratch or import a document. Let's start off by creating a simple form in a blank document so you can see how a form is created in Designer. The initial steps follow.

STEPS: Creating a form on a blank page

1. **Launch Adobe Designer.** Note that in Acrobat 7 you could launch Adobe Designer from Acrobat and the New Form Assistant opened where you could make choices for the kind of form you want to create. Now in Acrobat 8, when you select Forms ➪ Create New Form, you don't have an option for creating a form from a blank new document. Your options include Select a template, Start with an electronic document, Import data from a spreadsheet, and Scan from paper. All of the menu commands launch Adobe Designer and start the Create a New Form Wizard, but a blank page is not an option in this wizard.

2. **Click New Form in the Welcome to Adobe LiveCycle Designer Welcome screen.** When you first launch Designer a Welcome screen opens with options for creating a New Form, New from Template, or Open Form. Click the New Form button. (Note that if you want to open Designer without the Welcome screen opening, select the check box where you see Show this Dialog as Startup and remove the check mark).

3. **Select Use a Blank Form in the New Form Assistant Wizard.** After clicking New Form in the Welcome screen, the New Form Assistant Wizard opens. Click Use a Blank Form and click the Next button to open the Document Setup pane in the wizard.

4. **Select a page size.** In the Document Setup pane. select a page size from the Page Size pull-down menu. Select an orientation by clicking either the Portrait or Landscape radio button and select the number of pages you want from the Number of Pages pull-down menu. (Note that the maximum number of pages you can add in the wizard is 10, however, there is no limit to the number of pages that can be dynamically created in Designer.)

5. **Click Next and select the return method.** The final pane in the New Form Assistant Wizard is the Form Return Setup. Here you select a return method. If you want the form e-mailed back to you, select Add an email button. If you want the end user to print the form, select Add a print button. Note that you can choose both options, as shown in Figure 33.7.

FIGURE 33.7

Select both options if you want an e-mail button and a print button to appear on the form.

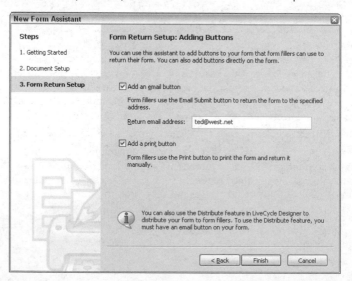

6. **Click Finish and your form opens in the Designer window.** In Figure 33.8, you can see the start of my new form where I selected a 63/4 Envelope with a Landscape orientation for my page size and added an e-mail button and submit button. I hid the left palettes by selecting Window ➪ Workspace ➪ Left Palettes. I also hid the Script Editor for now by pressing Ctrl+Shift+F5.

The start of a new form in the Designer window

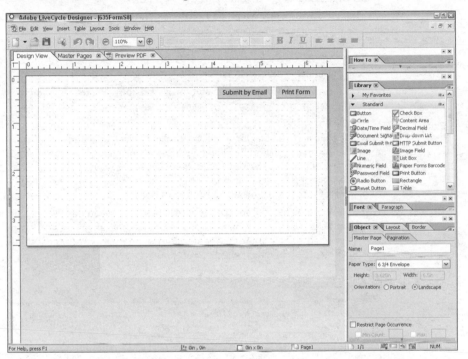

Save your file after you open the document in Designer. Be certain to periodically save the document as you work through additional steps. When you select File ➪ Save (or Save As) the Save dialog box opens. The Save as type pull-down menu offers several options, but for this series of steps, don't bother with all the options now. Select Acrobat 7 (Static) PDF Form (*.pdf). For more information on the other formats, see "Converting Designer XML Forms to Acrobat PDF Forms" later in this chapter.

If you are new to Designer and you're familiar with other Adobe software, your first efforts in Designer are likely to be very frustrating. Adobe is the master of the free form graphic design applications where you can click and grab an object in programs such as Adobe InDesign, Adobe Illustrator, Adobe Photoshop, Adobe GoLive, and even to some degree in Adobe Acrobat. Just click with a selection tool and you have complete freedom of movement without obstruction. This is not the case with Adobe Designer.

There are structured elements in a Designer form and you can't move objects around to the same degree as you can in other Adobe software. Before you add any content to the form, you should familiarize yourself a bit with some of the structural elements.

A Word About Page Sizes

Designer offers you a huge number of fixed page sizes, but another limitation and an obvious indication that Adobe didn't initially create this software product is that you have no option for creating a custom page size — something Adobe has always provided in programs to create freedom in the design environment. This probably won't matter much to the IT-type people, but it surely will drive the graphic design people crazy.

If you want to create a custom page size that doesn't fit within the sizes available in the Page Size pane in the New Form Assistant Wizard, you can create a custom page size in another program and import the file into Designer. Doing so, however, has some limitations.

If you create a blank page in Microsoft Word and import the page from a .doc file format, you can add text, images, and form fields to the document in Designer, but you won't be able to see the design grid.

If you create a blank page and convert it to PDF, you can't see the design grid; you can add form fields, but you cannot add any text or images to the design.

Your best option for creating a new form design is to try to find a page size in the New Form Assistant Wizard Page Size pull-down menu as near as you can to your desired page size. If you must create a custom page size, design your background in a design program with all the background design elements and convert to PDF. Import the PDF file and you can add the form fields in Designer.

Click Master Pages in the Designer window and you see a rectangle appearing as a blue dashed rectangle. Select the rectangle and handles appear at the four corners and four midpoints on each side. This area determines the boundaries of your content. While in the Master Pages view you can click and drag handles to reshape the object. If you click the Design View tab, you see the same rectangle, but you can't resize it while in the Design View mode. Any resizing you do in the Master Pages view restricts all the elements in the Design view to the boundaries of the rectangle on the Master Page. In Figure 33.9, I moved the top side of the Master Page rectangle down, and my two buttons were moved in the layout to stay within the rectangle.

FIGURE 33.9

Moving the rectangle on the Master Page moves all elements in the layout to keep them within the rectangle.

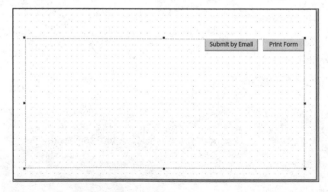

Working with master pages is not unfamiliar to people who create layouts in programs such as Adobe InDesign. Most layout programs offer you many options for creating master pages and placing elements on the master pages without having options to move the master elements on other pages. What's different about Designer is that elements are created for you. Therefore, you need to poke through a design to discover items that you did not create and how they affect the form. This is particularly true when you start working with subforms, as I explain later in the section "Creating Dynamic Forms."

Adding an image

Since you're creating a design from scratch, you'll import graphics as well as add graphic elements with tools in Designer. You can import a variety of different raster image formats including .bmp, .jpg, .gif, .png, and tif into your design.

NEW FEATURE In Designer 8 you now can also import EPS files. This is the first release that has supported .eps documents. Like the image file formats, be certain your image color modes are all RGB. CMYK images won't display properly in Designer. If you have problems importing an EPS file in your design, open the EPS in an image editor such as Adobe Photoshop and rasterize the image. Save the raster image as a TIFF image and you should have no problems.

TIP If you create a Designer form that you will eventually output to press, use RGB images in your Designer form. Import the form in Adobe InDesign and let InDesign convert color from RGB to CMYK plus all the other print controls you need for prepress and commercial printing. Note that you loose many Print Production tools in Acrobat when you open forms created in Designer. As such, you'll find InDesign a much better tool to print files for commercial printing than printing from Acrobat. For more information on printing for prepress and printing, see Chapter 32.

To import images into a Designer form, follow these steps.

STEPS: Importing images into a Designer form

1. **Open the Library palette.** By default, the Library palette opens when you launch Designer. Look for the Standard tab (or Favorites tab) and click the right-pointing arrow so the palette expands.

2. **Drag the Image Object to your document.** The Standard tab in the Library palette contains most of the objects you use in all Designer forms. You have field styles and objects for text and images. Locate the Image Object (not the Image Field Object) and drag it to the document page. When the object appears on the page, drag open the handles to accommodate a rough size for your imported image. The size doesn't have to be precise. You can make adjustments after importing an image.

3. **Select an image to import.** Open a context menu on the object and select Choose image (or simply double-click the object). When you release the mouse button the Browse for Image File dialog box opens. Locate the image to import, select it, and click the Open button. The image appears inside the Image Object, as shown in Figure 33.10.

4. **Size the object.** Drag the handles in or out to accommodate the size of the image without clipping it.

TIP The default cursor in Designer is the Selection Arrow. If you select the Image object or any other tool in any palette and you want to return to the selection arrow, press the Esc key on your keyboard. Designer does not have a separate Tools palette where you can select a tool such as the Selection Arrow.

FIGURE 33.10

Drag the Image Object from the Standard (or Favorites) tab in the Library palette and select Choose image from a context menu (or double-click the Image Object). After the image is imported it appears inside the object.

After selecting the image, the image file appears in the Image Object.

Open the Library pallet and the Standard tab

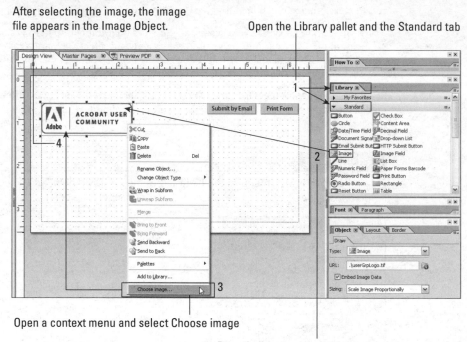

Open a context menu and select Choose image

Drag the image placeholder to the document page

Working with text fields

In Acrobat you draw a text field rectangle open to create a field where text (and numbers that are read as text) is added on a form. The Text Field Properties dialog box offers you a few choices for setting the field appearances such as border and fill colors, insets, embossing, dashes and underlines, and a few different line weights. Adding text fields in Acrobat presumes you have text descriptors in the form design for users to know what data to add to various fields. For example, you might have the text Name appearing in the background layout, and adjacent to the Name text you create a text field where a user types a name.

In Designer, you can add the text descriptors along with the field types (this applies to not only text fields but most of the other field types you have available in the Library tabs). When it comes to appearances, Designer offers options similar to the way you can assign cell appearances in spreadsheet programs. You can control many more field appearances in Designer than you have available in Acrobat.

To learn how to format text fields in Designer, use the following steps.

STEPS: Adding text fields to a form

1. **Drag a Text field from the Standard (or Favorites) tab to the document page.** From the same Library palette you selected an Image object from, click the Text Field object and drag it to the document page. Notice that you have a Text object and a Text Field object in the Standard tab in the Library palette. The text object is used to add text on the page. The Text Field object permits you to add both text and a field to the page. Be certain to drag the Text Field object to the page.

TIP If you want to maximize your workspace or you find it difficult to quickly find objects and fields in the Library palettes, open the View menu and select Standard. From the submenu you can see all the objects/fields in an alphabetical list. Select any item in the submenu and the respective item is added to your document page.

2. **Set the field appearance.** Open the Object palette and click the Field tab. From the Appearance pull-down menu select an appearance option. For my example, I select Underlined from the Appearance menu, as shown in Figure 33.11.

FIGURE 33.11

Open the Appearance menu in the Field tab in the Object palette and select an option for a field appearance.

Note that you also have an option for selecting a Custom appearance in the pull-down menu. Click Custom and the Custom Appearance dialog box opens, as shown in Figure 33.12. From the Edges pull-down menu, you can select Edit Together or Edit individually. The Edit individually option lets you edit each of the four rectangle sides for border options. The corners choices let you modify the corner appearances. The Style menu offers options for creating gradients and pattern fills.

FIGURE 33.12

A number of different appearance options can be selected in the Custom Appearance dialog box.

3. **Set the Value options.** In the Value tab, you have some options for specifying the user requirements for filling in the field. From the Type pull-down menu you can force a field to be filled in by selecting the User Entered – Required option from the menu, as shown in Figure 33.13. Other options shown in the figure include choices for optional, recommended, and calculations. Make a choice for the field value attributes and click the Binding tab.

FIGURE 33.13

Make a choice for user data entry attributes in the Value tab.

4. **Name the field.** Type a name in the Name text box in the Binding tab. If you want to bind the field to a data source, click the icon to the right of the Default Binding text to open a pop-up menu. For a form that you e-mail or submit for printing, the Default Binding is set at Normal, as shown in Figure 33.14.

FIGURE 33.14

Type a name for the field in the Binding tab and leave the default binding at Normal.

NOTE The name you provide in the Binding tab is the field name. Text you type on the form adjacent to the field is a design issue and is not related to the form data.

5. **Add the field caption.** Formatting the data attributes is complete. Now you need to set up the field as it appears on the form. The first item to deal with is typing the text you want to place as the field caption. Click in the default Text Field caption that appears when you first drag a text field to the document page and drag across the text. Type a new name for the text. In my example I used Name, as shown in Figure 33.15, to indicate the end user should type his or her name in the field.

FIGURE 33.15

Type text you want to appear on the form adjacent to the text field.

6. **Size the field.** The default text may be too long or too short in relationship to the field position. You can add more or delete some space between the text you type for the field caption and the field. Move the cursor to the separator bar between the text and the field and drag left or right to size the space occupied by the text. When you move the cursor over the separator bar, the cursor changes appearance, as shown in Figure 33.16.

FIGURE 33.16

Drag the separator bar left to expand the field area.

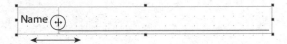

TIP As you work with fields, by default the field appearance has a highlight around the field border. If you want to view the fields without the highlight, select View ⇨ Object Boundaries. The field s will appear the same as when you open the form in an Acrobat viewer.

Formatting Text Fields

When you drag a text field (or other field types) to the document page the field appears with a text caption, by default, on the left side of the actual field, as shown in the following figure.

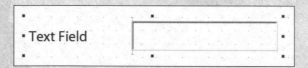

If you're familiar with creating forms in Acrobat, the default appearance of many Designer fields is probably foreign to you. Adobe Designer includes a text caption bound to a field because, unlike Acrobat, Designer is intended to be a design tool as well as a form data creation tool. As such, you need methods for labeling fields in designs you create from blank new pages.

Designer does provide you with a text object tool that enables you to place text near a field to provide a field description or to use the bound text to describe the field. In many cases you'll want to adjust the placement of text relative to the field or you may want to completely get rid of the text. Designer provides you with all the tools you need for modifying the text appearance or eliminating text and reformatting the field, but it may not be completely intuitive.

If you want to eliminate the default formatting and create a field with a rectangle box, you need to visit several palettes. All the options for changing the appearance are not included in a single palette.

If you delete the text caption bound to a field by selecting the text with the cursor and pressing the Delete key, you end up with a field where the field contents are about one-half to two thirds the size of the entire object. You'll immediately notice a large empty space to the left of a field when the field is selected after deleting the text. Designer automatically reserves the space for you to add text. If you want to delete the reserve space, open the Layout palette and open the Position menu in the Caption area and type **0 in**. Note that selecting None when you have a text caption on a field object eliminates the caption and reserve space with one menu selection.

continued

continued

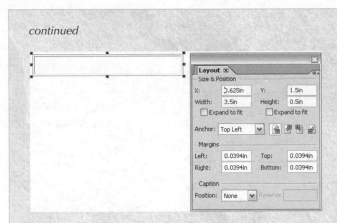

That's one palette down and two more to go. The next issue is the Sunken text appearance. If you want to eliminate that, you need to open the Object palette and click the Field tab. From the Appearance pull-down menu, select None to eliminate the embossed look on the field.

Your final step is to set the appearance to a solid border, underline, or whatever other type of appearance you want. Borders and fills are handled in the Border palette. Open the palette and select Solid from the pull-down menu below the Edges pull-down menu, as shown in the following figure.

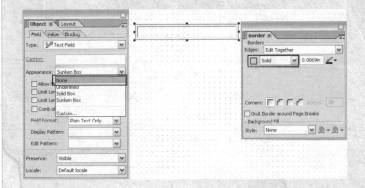

You can minimize your palette selections a bit and set the margins to zero (0) in the Layout palette that substitutes for using the settings in the Object palette, but I find that for almost all designs you continually interact with these three palettes, so they should all be open and accessible when designing any form.

When you want text bound to a field you may wish to relocate the text to a position other than the default at the left side of the field. In the bottom-left corner of the Layout palette is a pull-down menu in which you can reassign the text position. Open the Position pull-down menu in the Caption area of the Layout tab and make a choice for Left, Right, Top or Bottom. The None choice in this menu eliminates the text entirely.

If you do decide to use text with your field, you may want the vertical or horizontal position of the text to be different than the default position that appears as Align Left and Align Top. To change the position alignment, you need to visit yet another palette. Open the Paragraph palette and click the icon for Align Left, Align Center, Align Right, or Justify (the first four icons in the Paragraph palette) and click Align Top, Align Center, or Align Bottom (for vertical alignment from the last three icons in the palette). These icons are shown in the following figure.

Duplicating fields

When you create a form in Acrobat, you can duplicate fields by pressing the Ctrl key and dragging a field to duplicate it (yet another standard Adobe convention). In Designer you approach field duplication in another way. You have the standard Cut/Copy/Paste commands in Designer, but if you create a number of different forms and you want field attributes to appear similar, you can store fields in a custom Library.

To add a Custom Library Group to the Library palette, use the following steps.

STEPS: Creating a custom Library Group

1. **Add a New Group.** Notice the small icon at the top-right corner of each Library tab. Go to the topmost icon in the Library palette and click the mouse button to open a menu. From the menu choices, select Add Group.

2. **Name the new group.** When you select Add Group, the Add Library Group dialog box opens, as shown in Figure 33.17. Type a name for your custom Library Group in the text box and click OK. The new group appears in the Library palette.

FIGURE 33.17

Type a name and click OK in the Add Library Group dialog box to create a custom Library Group.

3. **Drag the field you created on the form to the new group.** Drag the field to the group name you see in the Library palette. Watch for the cursor to change to an arrowhead with a plus symbol, as shown in Figure 33.18. You need to place the cursor over the group name and release the mouse button when you see the cursor change appearance. Click the right arrow to expand the palette and you should see the field within the custom group tab. When you release the mouse button, the Add Library Object dialog box opens.

Drag an object to the new custom library palette.

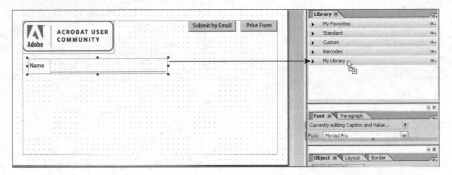

4. **Type a name for your field in the Add Library Object dialog box.** This name is used to merely identify the field in your custom group. It has no value and is not a default text object when you add the field to a page.

   Type a description in the Description text box. Notice a pull-down menu at the bottom of the Add Library Object dialog box in Figure 33.19. You can add an object to any group by selecting a group from the menu. Click OK and your new field is added to your custom library.

Type a name and description in the Add Library Object dialog box.

5. **Add a field to the document page.** Drag the field you added to your custom library to the document page. Position the field as you want it to appear in relation to the first field you created.

6. **Change field attributes.** Edit the text adjacent to the field and edit the name. You can change the name in the Binding tab or open a context menu on the object and select Rename Object. The Rename Object dialog box opens. Type a new name in the dialog box and click OK.

7. **Add additional fields.** Add more fields by dragging the field from your custom library group to the document page and format the fields.

8. **Add multiple fields to your custom library group.** Drag a marquee around the fields to select them and drag the selected fields to your library group. In the Add a Group dialog box add a name and description. I named my group Identifying Information, as you can see in Figure 33.20.

> **TIP** You can alternately add objects to any library group by opening a context menu on a selected object and choosing the Add to Library menu command. The Add Library Object dialog box opens where you can add a name and description, and choose the library where you want the object to be stored.

FIGURE 33.20

Dragging multiple fields to the custom library group adds the fields as a grouped object.

> **TIP** If you don't see the selection arrow for your cursor, you may have a tool selected such as a field tool. To return to the selection arrow when another tool is selected, press the Esc key.

The beauty and the power of using Adobe Designer when it comes to field duplication are in adding multiple fields to a custom library group. When you create new forms, you can drag the grouped item in your custom library group to a document page and all the fields in that group are added to the document.

Adding graphic objects to a form

In the Standard library group you have graphic objects in addition to field objects. The Line object and the Text object are used to draw lines and add text that's not part of a field identifier.

Field Naming Conventions Used by Adobe Designer

When you drag a field from any library group to a document page, Designer automatically adds a field name to your new field. If you add a text field to a page, for example, Designer names the field in the Binding tab TextField1. The next time you drag a text field to the document page, Designer names the next field TextField2, and so on. This naming convention assures you that all fields have a unique field name.

Check boxes also follow the same conventions as other fields. However, radio buttons are named RadioButtonList and additional radio buttons you add to a page are named the same field name. When you open the form in Acrobat and click one radio button it is turned on. Clicking another radio button in the same group turns the other radio buttons off.

Click the Line object in the Standard library group and draw a line on the form. Attributes for a line object are shown in the Object palette. You can edit orientation; line color; and line styles, such as solid, dashed, dotted, and dots with dashes. Draw a line on your form to separate the fields created in all previous steps from the bottom portion of the form.

The Text object is used to add text on a page. You might use text for a group identifier, a column heading, and so on where the text is not bound in any way to a field. Drag the Text object to the document page and click the cursor inside the text. Select the default text and replace it with the text you want to add to the object. If you want to assign attributes to the font and style, open the Window menu and select Font to open the Font tab. In the form I've created thus far I added the text Acrobat User Level.

Working with Tables

Obviously, when you want to create multiple fields in columns and rows, dragging individual fields from a Library tab will take you quite a bit of time. Fortunately, Designer 8 provides you a new feature for creating and editing tables that helps you automate adding tables on your forms. Much like the options we have in Acrobat for duplicating fields, you duplicate columns and rows in Designer using menu commands in the Table menu. However, what Designer has to offer you is much more than is available in Acrobat.

To insert a table, you select Table ⇨ Insert Table. The Insert Table dialog box opens, as shown in the following figure, where you can define columns and rows and add a header and/or footer. Click OK and Designer creates a table automatically without your having to start out with any fields laid down on the page.

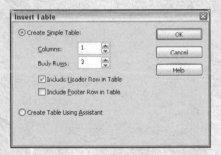

Much more power for designing a table is available in the Table Assistant Wizard, shown in this figure. Click the Create table Using Assistant radio button in the Insert Table dialog box, click OK, and the Table Assistant Wizard opens.

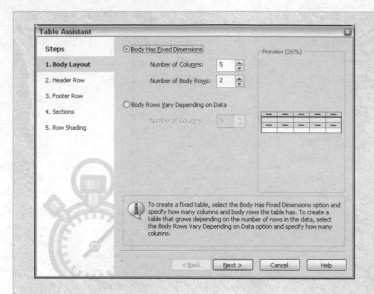

Options available in the Table Assistant are similar to options for creating tables in Adobe InDesign or Microsoft Excel. You can add rows and columns, apply shading to alternating rows, add headers and footers, and divide the table into sections. After creating a table, you can apply edits using the Table menu for adding and deleting rows and columns, merge and split cells, and distribute and group sections.

Adding radio buttons to a form

Radio buttons are intended to be used for either/or circumstances. You might use radio buttons on a form for asking for a credit card type where only one response is acceptable. As a user clicks one radio button all other radio buttons are off. Clicking a second radio button deactivates the first radio button and so on.

By default, Adobe Designer expects you to add radio buttons in this manner. If you want to use radio buttons for multiple responses, you need to set up some custom field attributes. For the sake of staying with standards, let's look over how radio buttons are used with their default values.

STEPS: Adding radio buttons to a form

1. **Drag a radio button from the Standard library group to the designer page.** Continue adding a few more radio buttons by dragging from the Standard library group to the document page. In my example, I added three buttons, as shown in Figure 33.21.

FIGURE 33.21

Drag three radio button fields from the Standard library group to the document page.

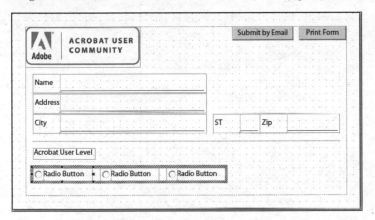

2. **Change the field names.** Click one radio button to select it and open the Binding tab in the Object palette. Type a new name in the Name text box. In my example I used userLevel for the field name, as shown in Figure 33.22. When you change the name of one field in a radio button group, Designer automatically changes all the objects in the same group to the same name. Note that alternately you can select an object and open a context menu. From the menu options select Rename Object. Type a new name in the Rename Object dialog box and click OK. All radio button objects in the same group are renamed.

FIGURE 33.22

Click the Binding tab in the Object palette and change the radio button name. All radio buttons in the same group are renamed.

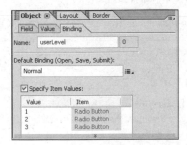

3. **Change the position of the radio button relative to the text.** By default a radio button appears to the left of the default text identifier. To change the position, open the Layout palette. At the bottom of the palette click the Position pull-down menu. Select the position you want for your radio button. In my example, I want the text to appear to the left of the radio button; therefore I select Left in the menu, as shown in Figure 33.23.

FIGURE 33.23

Open the Position drop-down menu and select a position for the caption relative to the field.

4. **Edit the text.** In my example I edited the text for the radio buttons and added Beginning, Intermediate, and Advanced for the three buttons, as shown in Figure 33.24.

FIGURE 33.24

Edit the text for each button to identify the button selection.

Adding a drop-down list to a form

A drop-down list in Designer is the same as a Combo Box in Acrobat terms. The names are different but the attribute assignments are very much the same. Drop-down lists, like combo boxes, can be assigned permissions for custom text entry as well as custom options from a list appearing as a pull-down menu. You add list items in the Field tab in the Object palette and Designer, like Acrobat, offers a choice for sorting the list names.

To learn how to add a drop-down list in Designer, use the following steps.

STEPS: Adding a drop-down list to a form

1. **Drag the Drop-Down List object from the Standard Library tab to the document page.**
2. **Name the field.** Open the Binding tab and type a field name or open a context menu and select Rename Object. In my example, I use the name jobRole.
3. **Set the list attributes.** Open the Field tab in the Object palette and click the + symbol in the List Items area. Type a name for your list and press the Enter key. Continue adding list names.

4. **Sort names.** After you created a list, look it over and see if you want to reorder some of the items. If you want an alpha list and some items are out of order, select an item you want to move and click the up or down arrows to reorder the list, as shown in Figure 33.25.

FIGURE 33.25

Add items to a list and select names in the list, and click the up and down arrows to reorder items.

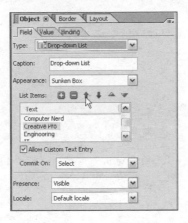

5. **Enable custom text entry.** If you want a user to be able to add custom text, select the box where you see Allow Custom Text Entry.

6. **Add a text caption.** Type the name you want to appear on the form adjacent to the drop-down list.

Other field types available in Designer such as the List Box, the Check Box, and the barcode are also available in Adobe Acrobat Professional. Use of the remaining fields follow similar steps: You rename fields in the Binding tab and assign various attributes in the Field and Value tabs.

CROSS-REF   For more information on creating some additional field types see Chapter 34.

Finishing up a form

I really don't like the default appearances on the Submit by Email and Print Form buttons. As an optional task, open the Border tab and remove the fill from the buttons. Note that you can select both buttons and change the fill in one step.

For the last steps, select File ⇨ Form Properties to open the Form Properties dialog box. Add document title information in the Info properties . In my example, I added the document information you see in Figure 33.26.

Using the Field Editor

Designer 8 introduces a new Field Editor you access by selecting View ⇨ Field Editor. When the Field Editor is on, selected field objects appear with a blue border and pop-up menus. At the top of a field object when the Field Editor is turned on, you can edit field names by clicking in the field box. At the bottom of the field object a menu lists all field object types where you can convert a field object of one type to another. On the lower right corner you can open a pop-up menu where field object attributes can be changed and some commands available in the Edit menu appear.

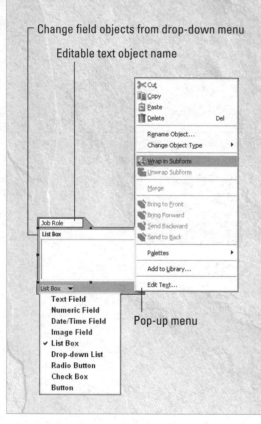

Change field objects from drop-down menu

Editable text object name

Pop-up menu

Click OK and save your file one more time. Click the Preview PDF tab in the Designer window and the file displays as a PDF. Test the form by filling in the fields as shown in Figure 33.27. Be certain to observe the layout and design as much as you assess the field contents. In my example, I need to return to Designer and put a little more space between some of the fields and the text. To return to Designer, close the document in the Acrobat window without saving and select Designer in the Windows Status Bar. Click the Design view and you return to Edit mode where you can fine-tune your design.

FIGURE 33.26

Fill in the document info fields and click OK.

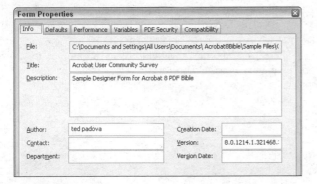

FIGURE 33.27

Fill in the form fields to check the layout. In this form, the text fields for the Address, the State, and the Zip code could use a little polish. These items can be edited back in Designer to modify the form appearance.

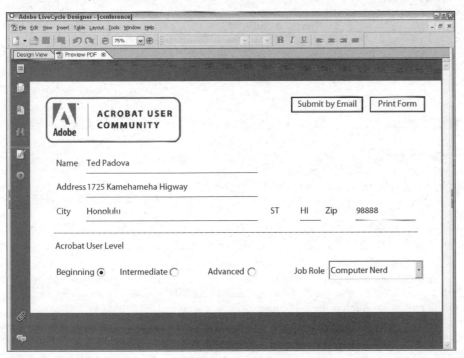

Importing a PDF Document

When you design a form in an authoring program and export to PDF, you make some design decisions for the field appearances. You have essentially two choices. You can design field appearances in your authoring program for field design attributes such as borders, fills, type fonts, and so on, or you can leave the design decisions to Adobe Designer.

There are pros and cons to designing layouts in either program. If you design field appearances in an authoring program and convert to PDF, after adding fields in Designer, you may need to go back to the authoring program to touch up the appearances. This requires you to go back and forth to polish your design because it can be difficult to anticipate the final look of your form while preparing it in the authoring program.

TIP   If you find yourself going back and forth between a layout in Designer and a layout in an authoring program to polish up your design, save the Designer form as a temporary file. After you convert the final layout from an authoring program, you can open the temporary file and copy the fields. Open the final layout in Designer and paste the fields. This saves you time because you don't have to recreate fields each time you update a layout.

If you leave assigning field appearances up to Designer, then you may have problems trying to align fields because Designer doesn't support using grids and snapping fields to a grid when working with PDF Backgrounds.

I find adding the field appearances in Designer to be the best option for me. However, it's a personal choice and you should determine the workflow that best suits your personal preferences. To see how to create a Designer form from a PDF document, let's walk through a series of steps.

Converting a PDF document to a Designer form

Create a layout in your favorite authoring program. I typically use Adobe InDesign or Adobe Illustrator to create form designs, but I'll deviate for this example and create a design in Microsoft Excel. Rather than import the Excel worksheet in Designer, I'll use the PDFMaker and convert to PDF. Excel worksheets can be converted to Designer forms, but when creating more than just numeric cells, the Designer conversion leaves much to be desired. Not all graphic objects get translated properly and your design can appear as a mess if you copy and paste the cells from Excel to Designer.

Figure 33.28 is the layout created in Microsoft Excel that I want to use for my Designer form. On this form I have some numeric fields, a calculation field, and a signature field in addition to some text fields. As yet, no field appearances such as underlines, borders, or fills appear where the fields will fall on the page. I'll add these items in Adobe Designer.

FIGURE 33.28

I started with a form originally created in Microsoft Excel and I converted the Excel file to PDF using the PDFMaker.

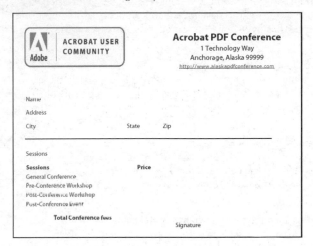

CROSS-REF   For more information on converting Microsoft Excel files to PDF using PDFMaker, see Chapter 8.

To begin the creation, you first need to open the form in Designer. The following steps show you how.

STEPS: Open a PDF Document in Adobe Designer

1. **Create a new document in Designer.** If you launch Designer, the Welcome screen opens. Click the New Form button in the Welcome screen. If you already have Designer open, select File ➪ New or press Ctrl+N. By default, the New Form Assistant Wizard opens. If you have a PDF document open in Acrobat, select Forms ➪ Create New Form. Step through the Create a New Form Wizard and your form opens in Designer.

2. **Select Import a PDF Document in the Getting Started pane.** Click the radio button in the first pane in the New Form Assistant Wizard.

3. **Select the PDF file to import.** Click the Next button in the wizard and you arrive at the Document Setup pane. Click the Browse button and locate your file to import. Select the file and click the Open button.

4. **Choose how you want to work with the PDF file.** Click Next and you arrive at the Setup: Import Options pane. Click the first radio button choice in this pane, as shown in Figure 33.29.

5. **Add an e-mail and print button.** Click Next and you arrive at the last pane in the wizard. By default, the radio buttons are selected for adding an e-mail button and a print button. Leave the radio button selections at the default choice and type your e-mail address in the Return email address text box.

6. **Open the form in Designer.** Click Finish and a new form is created with a PDF background artwork.

7. **Save the file.** Before adding any fields, save the file and routinely press Ctrl+S to update your file as you add new fields.

FIGURE 33.29

Select Create an Interactive Form with Fixed Pages.

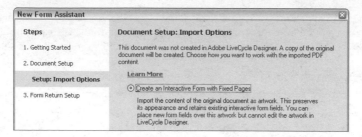

Add text fields

My example form has the same identifying fields as the form I created earlier in this chapter in the section "Working with text fields." In that section I added the identifying fields as a group to my custom library group. Unfortunately, you can't add a group of fields when using a PDF background. The single text field I copied to my custom group, however, can be used.

I drag my single text field from the custom group to the document page and all the attributes previously assigned to the field are copied with the field to the document page. Adding the identifying information is simply a matter of dragging a field from the custom palette, resizing the fields to fit the design, and continuing the steps to populate all the identifying information fields.

> **TIP** Although you can't add a group of fields (with different field objects) to a form with a PDF background, you can copy and paste fields. If you have a design using the same field types and values (except image objects), open the form containing these fields and drag a marquee through the fields to select them. Choose Edit ⇨ Copy and open you new design. Select Edit ⇨ Paste and press the arrow keys on your keyboard to nudge the fields into position. You can press Shift plus an arrow key to move the selected fields 10 points or press one of the arrow keys to move in the respective direction 1 point.

The Submit a Form button and the Print button may need some appearance alterations and placement on your form. Drag the fields to the desired position and open the Object palette. Open the Appearance pull-down menu and select Custom. In the Custom Appearance dialog box choose the appearance options you want for borders and fills. (See Figure 33.12 earlier in this chapter.)

After adding the identifying fields and modifying button appearances, click the Save tool or press Ctrl+S to update the document.

Adding numeric fields

When you create a form in Acrobat, you use text fields for both text and numeric values. In Designer, you have two different field types — a text field and a numeric field. Because Designer has so many more attributes you can assign to fields, having two separate field types makes it much easier to work through the different tabs in the Object palette.

> **NOTE** You can type numeric values in text fields but the data is read as text and not numbers. In order to calculate values, you need to use numeric fields.

To add and configure numeric fields in Designer, use the following steps.

STEPS: Assigning attributes to numeric fields

1. Open the Standard tab in the Library palette and drag a numeric field from the palette to the document page.

2. **Set the field appearance attributes.** Click the Field tab in the Object palette and select an appearance option from the Appearance pull-down menu. In the Display Pattern area, open the pull-down menu and select a display pattern, as shown in Figure 33.30.

FIGURE 33.30

Select an appearance and Display Pattern.

Display patterns are used to format numeric values. A pattern such as $z,zz9.99 results in a figure like $5,432.66. If your total value exceeds the pattern then the result loses the pattern attributes. For example using the same pattern with a number like 10,345 results in 10345 in the field box. Both the currency symbol and the comma are lost. When you format fields, be certain to anticipate the largest value that might be added to a numeric field box and create a pattern to accommodate the largest size.

3. **Name the field.** Click the Binding tab, use the Field Editor, or open a context menu and select Rename Object to change the field name. The default name appears as NumericField1. When we come to calculating fields, this name is a little long to type in the Script Editor. To simplify the job, I name my field "price."

4. **Size and position the field.** Drag the handles to size the field and drag the field to position on the form.

5. **Format the text.** If the text is too large, you can reduce the point size in the Font tab. Click the Paragraph tab and click the Right Justify icon shown in Figure 33.31.

FIGURE 33.31

Click the Right Justify icon in the Paragraph tab.

6. **Add the formatted field to you custom library group.** Drag the field to the custom library group.

7. **Add more numeric fields to the document page.** Drag the numeric field from the custom library group to the document page and populate all the remaining fields that will be summed in a calculation. Don't worry about aligning fields now; you'll take care of that in the next steps.

 In my example, I use just four fields. If I use a larger number of fields in a column or row, I would insert a table to create my fields. (See the sidebar "Working with Tables" earlier in this chapter).

Managing fields

Because you can't use a grid view or snap fields to a grid when working with a PDF background artwork, you need some way to organize your fields in aligned positions, sizes, and distributions. Acrobat provides a number of context menu commands for sizing, aligning, and distributing fields. Fortunately, you have the same options in Adobe Designer through menu commands.

Follow these steps to organize your fields in a precise order.

STEPS: Organizing fields

1. **Select the numeric fields on a form.** Using my example I created four fields that will be used to enter data and the result will be computed in another field. I drag a marquee through the fields and select Layout ⇨ Align.

2. **Align the fields. From the Align submenu select an alignment option.** As shown in Figure 33.32, you have several alignment options. In my example, I chose Layout ⇨ Align ⇨ Left. (Note that all the alignment options in Designer have keyboard shortcuts assigned to the menu commands.)

FIGURE 33.32

Select an alignment option from the Layout ⇨ Align submenu.

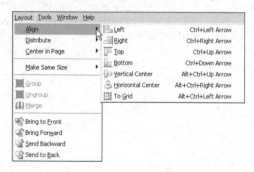

3. **Distribute fields.** The top field in a column should already be in the correct position on the form. If it is not, drag the fields together placing the top field in the proper position. Drag the bottom field to position the field at the bottom of the column. Select Layout ➪ Distribute ➪ Down. This command neatly positions the fields equidistant from each other.

4. **Realign the fields.** One very common use of a modifier in almost all programs is using the Shift key to constrain movement. Unfortunately, Designer doesn't support constraining movement by using a modifier key. If you moved the bottom field down to position the field, you more than likely disturbed the left alignment in Step 2. Realign the fields by selecting Layout ➪ Align ➪ Left.

Calculating fields

Designer supports two different scripting languages — FormCalc and JavaScript. FormCalc is a simple scripting language that follows syntax similar to spreadsheets. JavaScript is similar to the JavaScript you find in Acrobat, but some objects supported in Acrobat are not available in Designer. For example the docTemplate object is not something you have access to in Designer.

Acrobat supports two scripting languages, too — Simplified Field Notation and JavaScript. Simplified Field Notation is also modeled after a spreadsheet language and JavaScript, with the exception of a few limitations, is the same as Designer.

You need to use one of the scripting languages in Designer to calculate data. Because Designer supports two languages, you have to tell Designer which language you want to use to create your calculations. To see how you go about calculating field data in Designer, follow these steps.

STEPS: Calculating field data

1. **Identify the language you want to use for calculations.** You can dynamically switch between the two scripting languages in the Script Editor and make a choice for the language you want to use when you decide to write a script. However, it's always a good idea to set up some form properties when you begin to design a form. Among the properties you can assign to a new design is the default scripting language.

2. **Select File ➪ Form Properties.** The language you identify as your default scripting language is handled in the Defaults tab in the Form Properties dialog box. When the Form Properties dialog opens, click the Defaults tab. From the Default Language pull-down menu, select FormCalc as shown in Figure 33.33. For forms returned to you via e-mail, be certain the Default Run At pull-down menu selection is Client.

FIGURE 33.33

Select FormCalc for the scripting language.

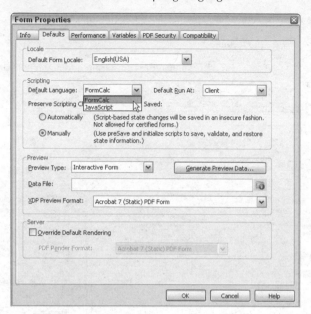

3. **Click OK in the Form Properties dialog box.**

4. **Format the target field.** On my example form I have a field titled total. This field is the target for my calculation. Open the Object palette and click the target field and select Calculated – Read Only in the Value tab from the Type pull-down menu.

5. **Open the Script Editor.** Press Ctrl+Shift+F5 to open the Script Editor window. To reveal more space in the Script Editor, you can open the window by dragging down on the separator bar appearing between the page layout and the Script Editor. (See Figure 33.34.)

6. **Type the calculation script in the Script Editor.** Select calculate from the Show pull-down menu and type the following formula in the Script Editor:

```
Sum (price[*])
```

This simple formula takes all the price number fields and sums them. In Figure 33.34 you can see the steps taken to produce the calculation.

> **TIP** Programmers will tell you that FormCalc is a very easy scripting language, but nothing is truly easy unless you have a fundamental understanding of some basic principles. In regard to scripting languages, the fundamental principles involve knowing key words and how variables are assigned. To understand more about FormCalc, look over some of the templates installed with Designer. On some forms you'll find a few calculation fields. Open the Script Editor and consider how formulas are written in FormCalc. For additional information, look over the online help document. You can also find a manual on FormCalc by visiting http://partners.adobe.com/public/developer/en/xml/formcalc_2.0.pdf.

FIGURE 33.34

Steps taken to produce a calculation for summing a group of fields

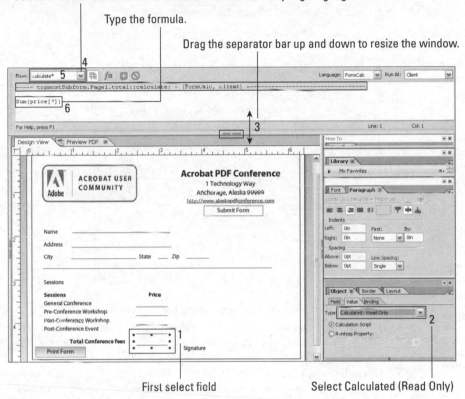

Select Initialize from the Show menu to initialize the scripting language.

Type the formula.

Drag the separator bar up and down to resize the window.

First select field

Select Calculated (Read Only)

Adding a signature field

To complete the form, I'll add a signature field that locks the field data after the form is signed. Follow these steps to complete the form.

STEPS: Adding a signature field

1. **Add a digital signature field.** Open the Standard library tab and drag a Document Signature field to the document page.

2. **Format the appearance attributes.** Open the Object tab and add appearance settings in the Field tab. In my example I added a border to my signature field.

3. **Set the Signature properties.** Click the Document Signature tab and click Lock Fields After Signing. This option renders all fields as Read Only and the fields can't be edited after signing the document.

4. **Set the Signature Handler.** If you don't assign a signature handler, the end user can use any technology they have to sign the form. Skip this step if you want to provide a user the option for using any signature handler they want to use. If you want to force a signature type, click Settings in the Document Signature tab to open the Document Signature Settings dialog box. In the Signature Handler pane shown in Figure 33.35 select Adobe.PPKlite (for example) from the Name pull-down menu. Select 2 for the Version and click OK. Note that this action forces a signature type on the form.

FIGURE 33.35

Select Adobe.PPKLite in the Document Signature Settings.

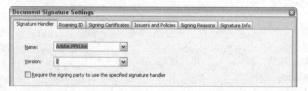

CROSS-REF For more information on Signature Handlers, see Chapter 26.

5. **Test the form.** Save the form to update it and click the Preview PDF tab in the Designer window. Fill-in the form fields to be certain the appearances and calculations work. (See Figure 33.36.)

FIGURE 33.36

Preview the final form in Acrobat and fill in the form fields to be certain the scripts work and the fields are properly aligned.

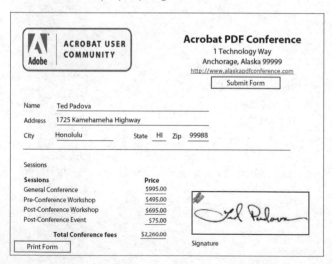

Creating Dynamic Forms

All of what's been covered up to this point falls into the category the Adobe Designer people at Adobe Systems call "static forms." The steps in all preceding pages of this chapter could all be accomplished in Adobe Acrobat as well as with Adobe Designer. The real power of Designer, however, is producing what Adobe calls dynamic forms.

CROSS-REF For information on creating forms in Acrobat, see Chapter 34.

What exactly is a dynamic form? In Adobe Designer terms, a dynamic form is one that, among other things, can adjust itself to accommodate the data supplied by a user or when flowing data in a form from a database file. This is to say that the form fields can grow in size and spawn new fields as dictated by user/database needs on a form. The options for adding more content to a dynamic form are in your hands. The choice to use them rests with the end user or amount of data merged with the form. The magic in this dynamic atmosphere is that the end user can work with any Acrobat viewer to populate a dynamic form — even the Adobe Reader users. Furthermore, no special features need to be added to a PDF document for a Reader user to fill out a dynamic form.

For an example of a dynamic form, take a look at Figures 33.37 and 33.38. In Figure 33.37 I start in Adobe Reader filling in two data fields on a form that was created in Adobe Designer.

FIGURE 33.37

Two data fields are filled in using Adobe Reader.

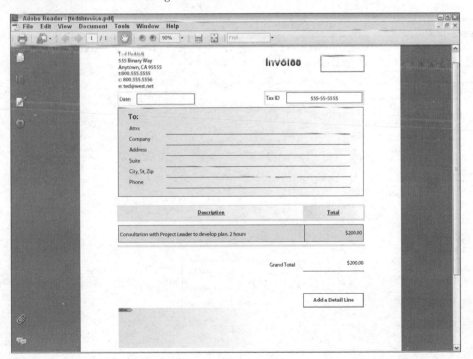

Notice the Add a Detail Line button at the bottom of the form in Figure 33.37. When I click this button, the form spawns two new fields and all the elements below the two fields are moved down to accommodate the added space on the form. In Figure 33.38, you can see that the Description field grows in size to accommodate my need for adding several lines of text by expanding the field as I type. The Grand Total line sums data added to the Total fields.

FIGURE 33.38

Fields are spawned and expanded according to the user needs.

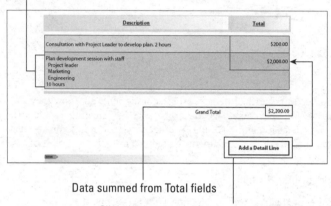

Keep in mind that this form is completed in Adobe Reader and no special usage rights for Reader users have been added to the form. These kinds of dynamic forms can be created for use with printing forms or when managing forms on a server where data streams populate form fields.

ON the CD-ROM You can find a copy of the form shown in Figures 33.37 and 33.38 on the book's CD-ROM in the Chapter 33 folder.

The anatomy of a dynamic form

When you work in Acrobat to create forms, you're working in a static two-dimensional environment. Inasmuch as form fields simulate a layer-type behavior, you lay down the form fields on a flat page. In Designer, you work in a more three-dimensional environment. The distinguishing features in a dynamic form creation environment include the separate areas of the form you have to work with. In Acrobat, you add form fields to a page in a single content area. Anywhere on the page is open territory for your form fields. Designer offers two primary areas where fields and content are added. These two areas include the Content area and Subforms. The various components of a dynamic form are shown in Figure 33.39.

FIGURE 33.39

A dynamic form has several different components.

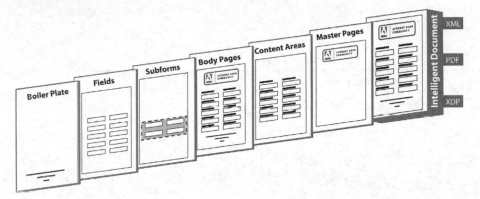

Before you can create a dynamic form, you need to clearly understand these components and how they relate to each other. Whereas you can start tossing fields on a page in Acrobat or when creating a static form in Designer, creating a dynamic form requires precision and planning. You need to know a little bit about what fields are going to be added and what kind of subform treatment the fields require *before* you start editing a form.

The various components of a dynamic form include the following:

■ **Boilerplate.** Boilerplate objects are like headers and footers on PDF documents. If you want to add a page number or some text to your form pages, you use options for creating boilerplate type data.

■ **Fields.** Fields are added to a content area and they are confined to an area defined as the content area. By default, when you create a new document or use one of the other methods to create a PDF form as I explained earlier in the section "Creating a Simple Form in Designer," Designer defines the content area at the full-page size. This content area can be modified. If you inadvertently change the content boundaries and you don't know why you can't get fields to move to an area on your page, it can be very frustrating.

■ **Subforms.** Subforms are the heart of the dynamic form in Designer. A subform is a defined area within the content area where you can add fields and objects. Subforms, among other attributes, can be defined to flow content. Flowing the content is what makes the form shown in Figure 33.38 a dynamic form. The area where you see the Description, Total, and GrandTotal fields was included in a subform in my original design. Without a subform, I wouldn't be able to make the data flow.

It's critical that you completely understand working with and using subforms if you want to create dynamic forms. As I said at the beginning of this chapter, Adobe Designer wasn't developed from the ground up by Adobe Systems. The kind of elements Adobe surely would have included in Designer if Adobe first developed the program would have been layers and modifier keys to easily select nested objects on a page. These tools are simply not in Designer and Designer has its own way of selecting and modifying objects that may be intuitive to the IT people, but surely it will drive the graphic design people crazy.

In Figure 33.40, the body page appears with two areas defined as subforms for this particular design. The dashed lines show the boundaries of the separate subforms.

FIGURE 33.40

Two subforms are used in this dynamic form.

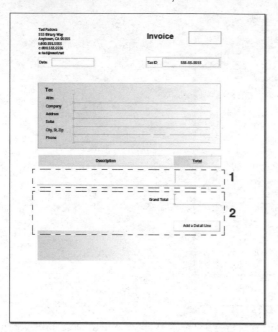

- **Body pages.** Body pages are where you lay out your design integrating components of a master page and content you add to the body page. You can have one or more body pages and one or more master pages in a Designer form. A form doesn't require any content on a master page, but you do need at least one layout on a body page to create a form.

- **Content areas.** Content areas are where you place fields and objects on body pages. Content areas have defined boundaries and you can place fields and objects only within the boundaries. You can have one or more different content areas on a body page.

- **Master pages.** Master Pages in Designer are like master pages in layout programs. You have a separate tab in Designer to open a master page and add content. You might put some text and fields on a master page such as your identifying information, a purchase order or invoice number, and a date. When you click the Body page tab, the master page data is not selectable, just as when working with a layout program such as Adobe InDesign. You can have more than one master page on a form and you can choose which master page to apply to a body page. In Figure 33.41 you can see the master page content in the Master Page view and the defined content area. When you open a body page, no content can be added to the area outside the dashed line.

- **Header and footer rows.** If you are creating a dynamic area (something like a purchase order form) on a form template, you might typically create a table with a header (and optionally a footer) row. If you don't use tables, you create a positioned subform with a header and trailer. The headers and trailers can be dynamic and will appear at the top (and bottom) of each new page that's added to a form to accommodate additional data when imported from a database or filling out a form.

A master page showing objects and fields added to the master page and the dashed line represents the content area.

Setting up the form properties

When you create a blank new form or open a document you want to use as a form, your very first step is to set up the form properties. You'll want to address properties before you start working with the object and field tools in Designer.

To open the Form Properties dialog box, choose File ➪ Form Properties. The default tab in the Form Properties dialog box is the Info tab, as shown in Figure 33.42. Fill in the Title, Description, Author, and Contact fields in this pane.

Add document title information in the Form Properties dialog box.

Form Properties

| Info | Defaults | Performance | Variables | PDF Security | Compatibility |

File: C:\Documents and Settings\All Users\Documents\ Acrobat8Bible\Sample Files\(

Title: Ted's Invoice

Description: Invoice form

Author: Ted Padova   Creation Date:

Contact: ted@west.net   Version:

Department: Version Date:

Click the Defaults tab and you arrive as the Defaults pane. In the Preview section shown in Figure 33.43, open the Preview Type pull-down menu and select Interactive Form. If you have a data file you use with your form for importing XML data, click the icon on the far right of the Data File text box and import your data file (more on that later in the section "Working with XML data"). In the XDP preview Format pull-down menu make a choice for Acrobat compatibility. You can choose to preview your file as Acrobat 6-, 7-, or 8-compatible files in either PDF or XML format.

CROSS-REF For more on Acrobat compatibilities, see Chapter 10.

Other options you have in the Defaults pane are the same as those I talked about in the section "Creating a Simple Form in Designer" earlier in this chapter.

FIGURE 33.43

Choose Interactive Form, import an XML file (optional), and select a preview option in the Defaults tab.

Working with subforms

Perhaps the most difficult part of learning Designer is understanding subforms and the scripting languages. To create dynamic forms, you need some comprehension of both. Subforms are used to make your forms dynamic so you can flow data and populate your forms with new content on demand.

When you first begin to prepare a form for dynamic content you need a mini paradigm for your workflow to understand the direction you want to proceed to create a dynamic form. In a simplified outline here's the order of how you approach creating a dynamic print form.

1. **Set the form properties.** As I've explained already in this chapter, set up the form properties in the Form Properties dialog box.

2. **Create the Master Page layout.** Add all the objects and fields you want to appear on your master page and set the Content area below/above the master page objects.

3. **Create the layout with objects and fields.** For a first effort in Designer, try to lay out the document as you want it to appear when distributed. Notice that you first create the layout here before you start creating subforms.

4. **Add the subforms for your design.** Subforms can be added to your layout as you design a form or after the initial design has been created. If you add subforms while designing a layout, you can easily get confused and it's much more difficult to rearrange elements when you have several subforms on the page.

5. **Add scripts to field objects.** You need all the field objects and the subforms on the page in order to add scripts that invoke actions. This would be the last step in your design process before you preview the form.

When you graduate to binding fields to data, you'll have a good idea for how forms are created in Adobe Designer and you can choose to bind data and when to add subforms to suit your own personal needs. For an introduction to Adobe Designer, try to follow the steps outlined here and practice creating enough dynamic forms so you completely understand all the elements and how to arrange and modify them. Try to get a handle on working with subforms before you begin to delve into binding data to fields and forms.

Adding subforms to a document

There are three locations from which you can add subforms to a document. The most common method is using the Hierarchy palette. (See "Using the Hierarchy palette" later in this chapter.)

Another method is to use the Insert ➪ Standard menu and from the submenu select Subform. This menu command adds a subform to the center of the open document page. Subforms can be added to both Master Pages and Body Pages (Design View).

The other way you can add a subform to a document is to open the Standard library palette and drag the Subform tool to the document page, as shown in Figure 33.44.

FIGURE 33.44

Click the Subform tool and drag a subform to the document page.

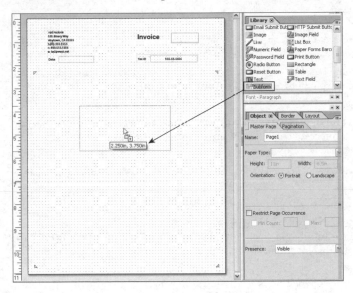

If you start with a subform on a page, you can drag objects and fields within the subform rectangle to bind them to the subform. You can also cut or copy objects and fields, add a subform to the page and resize it by dragging the handles on a selected subform and then paste. When you paste Clipboard data on the page containing a selected subform, the data is pasted into the subform, which also results in binding the data to the subform, as shown in Figure 33.45.

FIGURE 33.45

Two data fields are contained within a subform.

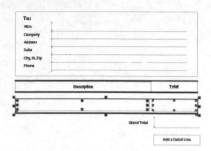

If you add a subform to a page after creating fields and the subform appears on top of the fields, you haven't bound the fields to the subform. Any effort to flow data or work with subform properties respective to the data fields won't be possible.

Using the Hierarchy palette

If there's any gold in Adobe Designer, it's in the Hierarchy palette. This palette dynamically lists all the assets included in your Designer form. Data connections and XML file links are handled in other palettes, but the objects, fields, and subforms you add to a form are all here in the Hierarchy palette.

When you create a new document and open the Hierarchy palette on the left side of the Designer workplace you see the items Designer automatically added to the new blank page. In the Hierarchy palette you see an untitled Subform. If you have more than one page, you'll see an untitled Subform for each page and the subforms are denoted according to page number so they can be easily distinguished from one another.

Click on the "untitled Subform (page 1)" item in the Hierarchy list and you see the content area selected on the blank page, as shown in Figure 33.46. Every Designer document including static forms has at least one *root* subform and a defined content area. If you attempt to delete the subform shown with handles in Figure 33.46, Designer won't let you do it. This is a must when working with Designer.

> **NOTE**   If you use a PDF background artwork, you can't use subforms. Subforms require XML templates which are negated by importing a PDF as background artwork. All forms using PDF background artwork are static forms.

If you reduce the size of the Content area, all the objects, fields, and additional subforms will be confined to your new Content area size. If you find you can't move an object to the edge of your form, go back and check the Content area. Chances are you sized the rectangle to a smaller size than you thought.

Using the Hierarchy palette you can precisely define the sizes of your subforms and bind the elements on your page to the subforms you create. To see how you approach designing a dynamic form with subforms, follow these steps.

FIGURE 33.46

Click untitled Subform (page 1) in the Hierarchy palette and the default Content area is selected.

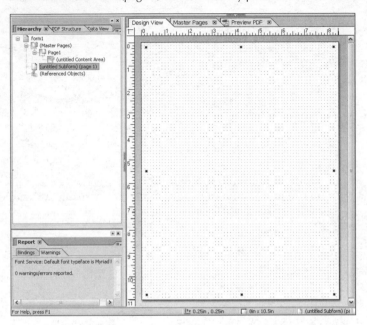

STEPS: Designing a dynamic form

1. **Create a new blank document.** Create a new blank document and set up the Form Properties as mentioned in the section "Setting up the form properties" earlier in this chapter.

2. **Create your layout.** Add fields and objects to a master page and to the body page shown in the Design View using tools covered in the section "Create a Simple Form in Designer" earlier in this chapter. Lay out your form page as precisely as you can. Size fields and objects and place them in the position that you want them to appear in your final layout.

3. **Organize the objects.** Open the Hierarchy palette and move the objects around in an order that will make it easy to group objects together in subforms. The logic should look the same as the final design you want to create.

   The Hierarchy palette works very similar to the Bookmarks panel in Acrobat. You can click and drag items in the list up or down to reorder them. Items can also be nested in parent/child relationships like Acrobat's Bookmarks. The Hierarchy palette for my example form is shown in Figure 33.47.

FIGURE 33.47

The Hierarchy palette is used to organize the content on the form.

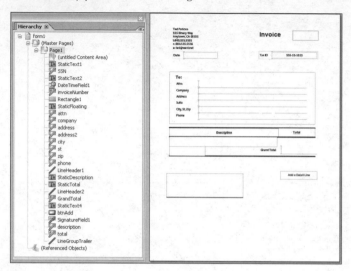

CROSS-REF For more information on working with Bookmarks in Acrobat, see Chapter 22.

CAUTION Be absolutely certain to order the objects together that need to be grouped in a common sub-form and double-check your layout to be certain the design appears as you want before creating a single subform. If you create one or more subforms and then try to move objects around the Hierarchy palette, you'll have a nightmare of a time trying to get the order correct by moving objects on either the document page or in the Hierarchy palette.

4. **Add a subform.** Start at the top of the Hierarchy palette and select items that belong to one subform group. Open a context menu from the selected fields in the Hierarchy palette and choose Wrap in Subform from the menu choices. Your new subform is created with an untitled label. To rename the subform, open a context menu on the new untitled subform and select Rename Object. Type a new name for the subform and press the Enter key on your keyboard.

TIP You can also rename subforms in the Binding tab in the Objects palette.

In my example, I renamed the default root subform "rootSubform" and I added a new subform for the header data and named the subform "HeaderData" as shown in Figure 33.48. My new subform will be added as a child item below the root subform (rootSubform) in the Hierarchy palette.

FIGURE 33.48

I created a new subform for the header data on my form and named it HeaderData.

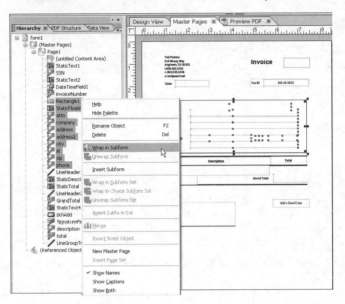

5. **Insert a subform.** I have several content areas that need to flow on my example form. I'll go ahead and create a parent subform without binding any data to the new subform. To do this, I find an empty spot in the Hierarchy palette below all the items in the list and without any object selected I open a context menu and select Insert Subform. This new subform is a child to the root rootSubform. (See Figure 33.49.)

 To clear all items in the Hierarchy palette, click the cursor in an open area on the document page.

6. **Move a subform in the Hierarchy palette.** You reorder subforms in the Hierarchy palette just as you reorder Bookmarks in Acrobat, and the clumsy way Bookmarks are ordered in Acrobat is precisely the way Designer handles moving the subforms around the palette. To nest a subform as a child subform, click and drag up to the subform you want as the parent. When the parent subform is highlighted, release the mouse button and the new subform is nested below the parent as a child subform. To move objects in and out of subforms, you drag around the palette and move horizontally to nest objects below other children in other subforms. At times it can feel a little awkward but a little practice gets you up to speed fast.

On my example form, I moved my new inserted subform below the HeaderData subform but not as a child to the HeaderData. This new subform is a child to the root subform in my document. The position of the new item is shown in Figure 33.49. After moving the new subform, I renamed it "detail."

CROSS-REF For more information on organizing Bookmarks in Acrobat, see Chapter 22.

Create a new subform and nest it under the root subform.

New subform

7. **Nest additional subforms under the inserted subform (now named detail).** On my example form, I have four different groups I want to flow in my document. Later, I'll target the new inserted subform as a Floating subform and the remaining subforms as Content subforms (see "Subform types" coming up next in this chapter). All subforms nested below a flowing subform will flow the content.

   To create the new subforms, I select the objects I want to group in a subform and from a Context menu I select Wrap in Subform. I create four new subforms and name them GroupLeaderSubform, item, GroupTrailer, and GroupTotal. In Figure 33.50 I collapsed the HeaderData subform and my four new subforms according to parent/child relationships are shown with the content grouped for each item.

Create new subforms by selecting data and choose Wrap in Subform from a context menu.

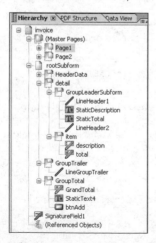

8. **Save the document.** If you find that things get scrambled a little, save your file under a new file-name so you can return to a previous file before you encountered any problems. When your design looks like things are working out as expected, save your edits regularly. If you created a similar type of document as the example shown here, save the file now.

Subform types

Designer provides you two options for setting subform attributes. You can define a subform that flows content or a positioned subform where the content remains static. As you might imagine when you format a subform to flow content, the form takes on dynamic attributes that enable you to create a form that spawns new fields and accommodates sizing fields according to the amount of user data added to a given field. A subform formatted for positioned content doesn't flow on a page within its own subform but may flow according to attributes of the parent subform. If the field attributes are defined to Allow Multiple lines for positioned content, the text exceeding the field borders is set up to be viewed in a scrollable window. In other words, the field doesn't grow to accommodate the text.

When you select a subform in the Hierarchy palette and open the Object palette your options are very different than those you have with other objects and form fields. Using my example file, I click on the detail subform and take a look at the Object palette. This subform is the one I want to format for a data flow. From the Object palette, open the Content pull-down menu, and you see two choices. For my detail subform I want the Flowed option you see in Figure 33.51. The other four fields appearing as children under my detail subform are formatted as Positioned subforms.

FIGURE 33.51

Open the Object palette and click the Subform tab. Select Flowed from the Content pull-down menu.

Below the Content pull-down menu is another pull-down menu for selecting the direction of the flow. The Flow Direction pull-down menu options are available only when formatting the subform to flow text. The first menu item is Top to Bottom. As the name suggests, data is flowed from the top of the page toward the bottom. The second menu choice is Western Text. This option flows data from left to right beginning at the top of the subform and continuing across to the right. The next flow of data is in the second row left to right, and so on. On my example form, I chose the Top to Bottom option for this design.

One more item in the Subform tab in the Object palette is the check box for Allow Page Breaks within Content. Select this box if you want the data to flow across multiple pages.

In the Object palette, you also have another tab that relates specifically to subforms. Click the Pagination tab and you have options for flowing content and handling data overflows. The options you have in this tab are generally applied to flowing data into XML forms from external data sources. In my example file, I left the options at the defaults. as shown in Figure 33.52.

FIGURE 33.52

FIGURE 33.52

Leave the Pagination tab at the default settings.

Calculating data

Another book the size of *Adobe Acrobat 8 PDF Bible* could be written on just the JavaScript and FormCalc scripting languages supported by Adobe Designer. In Chapter 36, I talk about JavaScript and all the code listings in that chapter. With the exception of using the docTemplates object, the JavaScript in Chapter 36 is equally applicable to Designer. To learn more about Acrobat and Designer JavaScript, download the JavaScript Specification manual at:`http://partners.adobe.com/public/developer/en/acrobat/sdk/AcroJSGuide.pdf`.

For more information on FormCalc, a manual is available on Adobe's Web site at:`http://partners.adobe.com/public/developer/en/xml/formcalc_2.0.pdf`. Both the JavaScript and FormCalc manuals should be stored locally on your hard drive when creating forms in either Designer or Acrobat.

CROSS-REF For more information on using JavaScript, see Chapter 36.

In terms of the example form I've used in this section, the form requires only a single short script to complete the design. If you could create the same design in Adobe Acrobat it would take pages of JavaScript to produce the same results. In Designer, you need to add only a few lines of code to complete the design.

The actions for spawning fields and expanding field sizes in Designer are automatic and don't require any special scripting code. If you set up your subforms correctly, Designer handles all you need for managing the data fields on my example form. What you do need, however, is a script to tell your Acrobat viewer to calculate the total data and when you want to spawn new fields. These two scripts belong to the GrandTotal field for summing the data and the btnAdd field on the Add a Detail button.

Here's what to do to add scripts that will sum data and spawn new fields.

STEPS: Add a script to a Designer form

1. **Select the field to sum a total.** Open the Hierarchy palette and click the field where the data sum is calculated. In my example form, I click the GrandTotal field.

2. **Open the FormCalc Script Editor.** Press Ctrl+Shift+F5 to open the script window at the top of the Designer window and select FormCalc from the Language pull-down menu.

3. **Type the code to calculate a sum.** Select calculate from the Show menu and type the following code in the Script Editor window, as shown in Figure 33.53.

   ```
   Sum($form.invoice.#subform[0].detail.item[*].total)
   ```

FIGURE 33.53

Select FormCalc from the Language pull-down menu, select calculate from the Show pull-down menu, and type the code in the Script Editor.

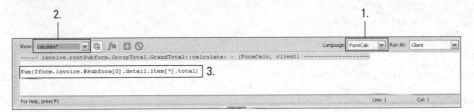

4. Select the btnAdd button in the Hierarchy palette.

5. Type the following script in the FormCalc Editor:

```
detail.item.instanceManager.addInstance();
GroupTotal.GrandTotal.execCalculate();
```

The first line of code adds the instance for spawning new fields and flowing the fields on the form. The second line of code executes the GrandTotal field calculation.

6. **Set the button properties to hide the button when printing.** One last item to deal with before your form is complete is to change the button properties. On my example form I want the Add a Detail item for the btnAdd field to be invisible when the form is printed. The Add a Detail text and the button field are one item. The field has a caption assigned to it for the Add a Detail text. Click the btnAdd field in the Hierarchy palette and open the Field tab in the Object palette. Select Visible (Screen Only) from the Presence pull-down menu, as shown in Figure 33.54.

FIGURE 33.54

Select Visible (Screen Only) to hide the button when the file is printed.

7. Save your form and test it in Acrobat by clicking the Preview PDF button in Designer.

Distributing forms

My example form is designed for use by me and gets distributed only after I fill out the form. The recipient of my form won't be adding any additional form data; therefore, I don't need a submit button on this type of form.

In other cases, you'll want to add an e-mail button to a form so the form data can be returned back to you. If you plan your work ahead of time, the easiest way to add an e-mail button is at the time you create a blank new document. In the New Form Assistant Wizard, the last pane defaults to adding an e-mail button and adding a print button. If you anticipate the end user needing either or both these actions, add the buttons at the time you create a blank new document.

In other cases you may decide after the fact to add a button for e-mailing, printing, or both. You can easily add these buttons to your form at any time during the layout process. In Figure 33.55, I added a print button after completing my form. This was an easy step. I opened the Master Page and selected Insert ⇨ Standard ⇨ Print Button. I then changed the appearance attributes in the Border and Layout tabs. Adding the button didn't disturb my subforms or the scripts I added to my form.

FIGURE 33.55

I added a print button after I completed the layout on my form.

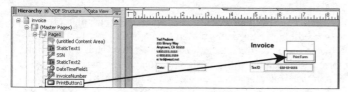

If you add an Email button after the page is created, the button appears with a warning symbol. You need to add an e-mail address after you add the Email Submit Button from either the Insert ⇨ Standard submenu or by dragging an Email Submit Button from the Standard library tab. The e-mail address is edited in the Object palette.

 Assuming you create a form that you want to distribute to recipients, save all your edits, preview the document, and make certain your Email Submit Button appears on the document. As a final step click the Distribute Form tool or select File ⇨ Distribute Form. If you don't have an e-mail submit button Designer informs you in a warning dialog box that you need either a submit button or a JavaScript to proceed. If you have a submit button, Designer switches to Adobe Acrobat where the Form Distribution Options Wizard opens. This wizard walks you through steps to submit your form to recipients. After you complete the final step in the wizard your form is added as an e-mail attachment (when you select Send by email now in the wizard) to a new mail message in your default e-mail program. Click the Send button in your e-mail program and the form is distributed to the recipients you added in the wizard.

CROSS-REF The Distribute Form command appears in both Adobe Designer and Acrobat Professional. You have many new options in Acrobat 8 for distributing forms and collecting form data. For more on using the Distribute Form feature, see Chapter 35.

Run-time events

When you browse the Designer menus you'll notice that the Insert menu lists a number of different commands that always seem to be inaccessible. You may wonder what these commands do and how to make them active. The commands require a little different treatment than the fields and objects you add to pages from other areas in the Insert menu or the Library palette. The items you see grayed out in Figure 33.56 are special properties that are assigned to a few objects and used for run-time events.

FIGURE 33.56

The first eight commands in the Insert menu are used for run-time events.

Run-time is when an application or server retrieves a form design and, among other things, might merge data with the form. In a very simple way, something like executing a mail merge from a word processing program is a run-time event. When you merge the data from a letter, for example, the data is introduced into the letter template merging a data form and a data file with a design producing new pages. A run-time event is also when you open the form in Acrobat. You might want the current date reported on a form when a user opens the form in an Acrobat viewer. Reporting the date when the file opens is also a run-time event.

Designer provides you tools to display certain types of information at run-time. Where and how you insert run-time properties are limited to a few objects. These objects are as follows:

- **Text.** A text object can be used to insert a run-time property.
- **Text Fields.** Text fields can be used to insert a run-time property.
- **Numeric Fields.** Numeric fields can be used to insert run-time properties.

To format a text object with a run-time property, you insert the cursor in the text object, and then open the Insert menu. When the cursor appears inside the text, the grayed out items in Figure 33.56 are all made active. When you want to format a run-time property for a text field or a numeric field, select the field and open the Object palette. From the Type menu you have only one choice to format the field for a run-time property. Select Calculated – Read Only from the menu options. Below the menu, click the Runtime Property radio button and open the pull-down menu to select a run-time event, as shown in Figure 33.57.

Text Fields and numeric fields are formatted for run-time events in the Object palette.

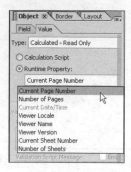

All run-time properties are available to Static Text objects. Text fields can use all properties except the Current Date/Time. Numeric fields can use only properties that report data in numbers such as the Current Page Number, Number of Pages, Current Sheet Number, and Number of Sheets. All other properties are not allowed with this field type.

The options you have for formatting include the following:

- **Floating Field.** You can bind floating fields to data sources. A floating field displays specific text and/or numeric values and requires a text object for this property. You could use a floating field much like a mail merge where the field binds to a data source to render names on a form associated with data — something like sales orders, for example.

- **Current Page Number.** Places the current page number respective to the page where the field properties are assigned.

- **Number of Pages.** You might use this property to report the total pages in a dynamic form that flows data adding new pages until the data is exhausted.

- **Current Date/Time.** Reports the current date and time.

- **Viewer Locale.** This property is used to report the locale for the application that is processing the form. For example, you might design a form in the United States and the form may be processed in India. The field result would report India for the locale.

- **Viewer Name.** Reports the Acrobat viewer name. If the form is run in Adobe Reader, for example, Adobe Reader is reported in the field.

- **Viewer Version.** Reports the Acrobat viewer version (such as 8).

- **Current Sheet Number.** Reports the sheet number. If the form produces 10 sheets of paper and the field is on sheet 10, the number reported is 10.

To understand more about inserting properties for run-time events, follow these steps to report a current date.

STEPS: Assigning run-time properties to a text object

1. **Open a form or create a blank new form.**

2. **Add a static text object to the page.** Select Insert ⇨ Standard ⇨ Text or drag the text object from the Standard library palette. Be certain to use the Text object and not the Text Field object.

3. **Drag across the default text and type the text you want to appear on the form.** In my example I use "This form is completed on:" I'll insert a date that will calculate at run-time.

4. **Insert a date.** While the cursor appears in the text box, select Insert ⇨ Current Date/Time (alternately open a context menu and select Current Date/Time. You'll see the text following the text you type appear as {current date/time} as shown in Figure 33.58.

FIGURE 33.58

With the cursor in the static text field, select Insert ⇨ Current Date/Time.

This form is completed on: {current date/time}

5. **Preview the file in Acrobat.** Click Preview PDF and the file opens in Acrobat. The date is reported as you see in Figure 33.59.

FIGURE 33.59

When opened in Acrobat, the date is reported in date, hours, and minutes.

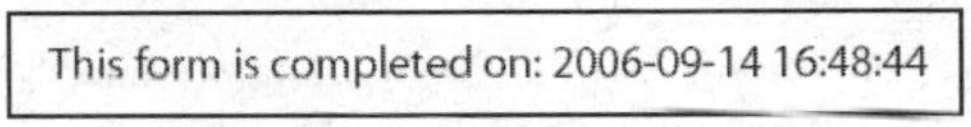

This form is completed on: 2006-09-14 16:48:44

6. **Save the file from Designer.**

7. **Open the file in Acrobat, save it, and close the file.**

8. **Reopen the document in Acrobat.** Wait a few minutes until you're certain the time has changed significantly since you last viewed the file in Acrobat. You'll notice that the date remains fixed to the date stamp when you first opened the file. The field data was created at run-time in Acrobat when you first opened the file. After saving in Acrobat, the field data is static and won't run again.

Converting Designer XML Forms to Acrobat PDF Forms

If you're a Windows user, you have Adobe Designer installed with your Acrobat Professional program. However, if you're a Macintosh user of Acrobat Professional, then you need to use Acrobat Pro to do any kind of form editing. Acrobat Standard users would have no real advantage working with a PDF form since the Form toolbar is not available to Standard users.

CROSS-REF For more information on using the Form toolbar in Acrobat, see Chapter 34.

You might receive a file from a Windows user who wants you to edit a form or change the form design. In order to work on a form in Acrobat, the form needs to be converted to an Acrobat PDF form. Both a static form developed in Designer and a dynamic XML form need to be converted for either a Windows or Mac user to edit the form in Acrobat. When a Designer form is opened in Acrobat, all the Form tools are grayed out and editing features such as those for inserting and replacing pages are not possible.

No commands exist in either Designer or Acrobat specifically for converting an XML form to an Acrobat PDF form. To perform a conversion, you need to use a little workaround. Depending on the type of form you want to convert, you use different methods.

Converting a static form to an Acrobat PDF form

Converting a static form to an Acrobat PDF form on either Windows or the Macintosh is a simple task. Open the form in Acrobat Professional and select Document ➪ Extract Pages as shown in Figure 33.60. Notice in the figure that the form tools to the left of the menu command are grayed out.

The Extract Pages dialog box opens. If you're converting a single-page document, click OK. If you have multiple pages to convert, select the page range and click OK. When the page(s) is extracted, all the form tools and editing features are available to you, as shown in Figure 33.61.

FIGURE 33.60

To convert a static Designer form in Acrobat, select Document ➪ Extract Pages.

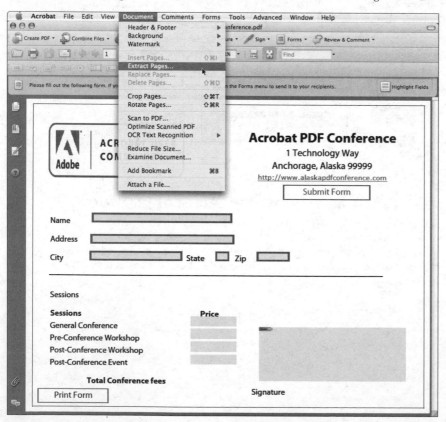

You'll notice that Acrobat reformats field names and you'll find that just about all scripting actions are not converted with the document. If you convert a Designer form, you need to reprogram JavaScripts and button actions. Simple action types such as submitting a form or printing a form from a button action are not converted and need to have the button actions edited in Acrobat. However, field objects are converted and you won't need to create new form fields.

CROSS-REF For more information on adding button actions in Acrobat, see Chapters 22 and 36.

FIGURE 33.61

When a static form is converted to an Acrobat PDF form, the form fields and editing features are all available.

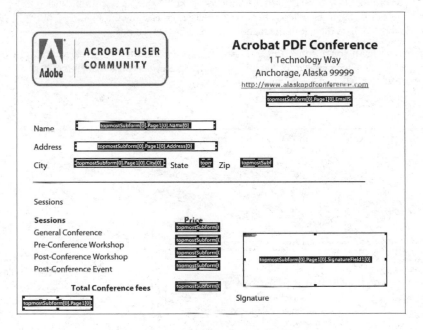

Converting a dynamic XML form to an Acrobat PDF form

If you have a dynamic form saved as an interactive form from Designer you have no options in Acrobat 8 to convert the form to an Acrobat PDF form. The only alternative you have is to use an earlier version of Acrobat. For Macintosh users who want to convert Designer XML forms, you'll want to keep Acrobat 7 loaded on your computer. On the Mac, you can keep both versions of Acrobat on your computer and run Acrobat 7 concurrent with Acrobat 8.

In most cases you would never convert a dynamic form created in Designer to an Acrobat PDF form. Doing so looses all the dynamic attributes of a form. In rare cases where a Macintosh user needs to edit a form that can remain static or if you have a Designer form that was saved as a dynamic form without having dynamic content and you want to edit the form on the Macintosh there is a way to convert the XML form to an Acrobat PDF form.

To convert a Designer interactive XML form to an Acrobat PDF form in Acrobat 7, use the following steps.

STEPS: Converting Designer forms to Acrobat PDF forms in Acrobat 7

1. **Open the form in Acrobat 8.** Your first step is to verify that the form can't be converted using Acrobat 8. Open the Document menu and make sure the Extract pages command is grayed out. If the Extract Pages command is accessible, the form is a static form and you can convert the form using the Extract Pages command.

2. **Launch Acrobat 7.** On the Mac, you can leave Acrobat 8 open while working in Acrobat 7.

3. **Convert the form using Create PDF from Web Page.** Don't open the form in Acrobat 7. Open the Create PDF task button and select From Web Page. Click the Browse button in the Create PDF from Web Page dialog box and locate the file you want to convert in the Browse dialog box. When the file to be converted is selected, click the Create button in the Create PDF from Web Page dialog box shown in Figure 33.62.

FIGURE 33.62

Select the file you want to convert in the Create PDF from Web Page dialog box and click Create.

CROSS-REF For more information on using Create PDF from Web Page, see Chapter 7.

4. **Click the Select Object tool.** After clicking the Create button in the Create PDF from Web Page dialog box, Acrobat works away converting your file. You may need to wait a few minutes for the conversion to be completed. Eventually, the file opens in the Document pane. Click the Select Object tool and you'll see all the form fields in the converted document, as shown in Figure 33.63.

5. **Save the file.** Save the file and quit Acrobat 7. Open the file in Acrobat 8 and you can start editing the document.

FIGURE 33.63

When the file opens in Acrobat 7, click the Select Object tool and you'll see all the form fields converted in the document.

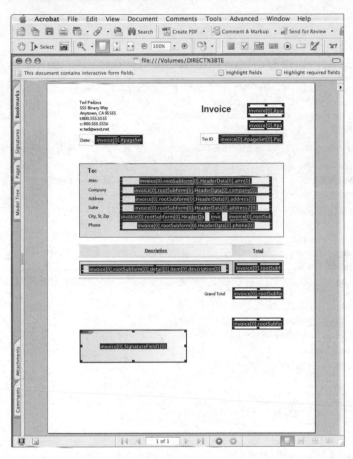

Converting a dynamic form completely destroys all the dynamic attributes of the form. All the scripts are lost and all actions for all fields are lost. This type of conversion is really only a method for converting field objects and editing the form to produce a static document. If you intend to add JavaScripts to the form, you'll find the field name conversions to be tough to work with. Field names are long, as you can see in the converted document in Figure 33.63. Addressing these field names with JavaScripts can be a bit of a chore.

Using Create PDF from Web Page in Acrobat 8

You need to use Acrobat 7 to convert an XML form to an Acrobat PDF form because the Create PDF from Web Page command won't convert the form. Using this command in Acrobat 8 produces a blank page in a PDF with a file attachment. The file attachment is the original PDF document. This behavior is restricted to XML files where Acrobat embeds the XML as a file attachment.

If you use the Create PDF from Web Page command in Acrobat 8 and select a PDF document created in Designer, the Designer form appears as a file attachment, as shown in the following figure.

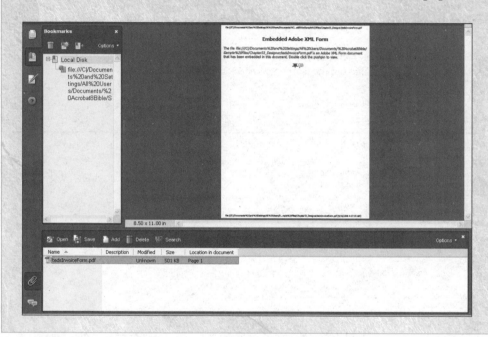

Enabling Forms with Reader Extensions

Adobe Designer has no direct command for enabling PDFs with Adobe Reader extensions. If you select the File ➪ Distribute Form command in Designer, the Form Distribution Options Wizard opens in Acrobat. When you distribute a form, the form is automatically enabled with usage rights for Adobe Reader users. Reader users can fill out the form and save the form data before submitting the form back to you.

Whereas many editing features for static and dynamic Designer forms are lost in Acrobat, the enabling commands are accessible for any kind of Designer form. You can choose to enable a Designer form for Commenting in Adobe Reader using the Comments ➪ Enable for Commenting in Adobe Reader command and you can enable the form for saving field data, commenting, and digital signatures using the Advanced ➪ Enable Usage Rights in Adobe Reader command.

CROSS-REF For more information on enabling documents with usage rights for Adobe Reader, see Chapters 19, 34, and 35.

Creating Data Connections

Binding fields in a form design to a data source is one of the true great features in Adobe Designer. If using Acrobat to bind to data sources you need to have a sophisticated level of JavaScript programming background and a lot of finesse to create the resources that successfully bind data to other sources. With Designer, the process is greatly simplified and the program does much of the mind wrenching work for you.

When binding fields on a form design to a data source, you create an association between the form and some data source that lets you capture, process, output, and print information from the data entries on a form. Designer enables you to bind data either as client-side where you might bind data locally on a hard drive to a backend database file or as server-side binding. Client-side binding enables you to make changes immediately to the data while server-side binding requires you to submit data to a server where changes are made.

You create a new connection to a data source by opening the Data View palette and clicking the icon in the top-right corner of the palette. Clicking the icon opens the New Data Connection Wizard shown in Figure 33.64.

FIGURE 33.64

Click the small icon in the top-right corner of the Data View palette to open the New Data Connection Wizard.

In the New Data Connection Wizard, you make a choice for the type of data connection you want.

XML schema and XML data sources

You can import an XML schema definition into a form design and then bind objects in the form to elements in the XML schema. If you have an XML file and not an XML schema you can bind objects to the XML data form. The process for binding both a schema and a file are similar. The option that differs between the two is selecting which source you want in the New Data Connection Wizard.

To create an XML schema connection, select File ➪ New Data Connection or click the icon in the Data View palette to open the New Data Connection Wizard. In the New Data Connection Wizard, select XML Schema or Sample XML Data. Click Next and click the icon you see with an i appearing over a folder on the far-right side of the Select XML Schema File text box. Browse your hard drive and select the XML schema file. Click OK and the file is added to the Select XML Schema File text box, as shown in Figure 33.65. For connecting to a Sample XML Data File you have the same options for selecting the file in a similar wizard pane.

FIGURE 33.65

Click the icon to the right of the text box to select the XML Schema file.

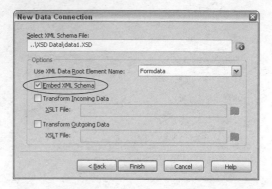

Connecting to OLEDB data sources

OLE Databases (OLEDB) are sets of Component Object Model (COM) interfaces that provide applications with uniform access stored in diverse information sources. In short, these interfaces support DBMS (Database Management Systems) functionality appropriate to the data source that enables it to share data. You might have databases such as Microsoft Access files, Excel spreadsheet files, or other database types that you want to share data with PDF forms. You might have a situation in which you use a single identifying field a user types into a form, such as an employee ID or Social Security number. Using this one piece of data, you can connect to a database to retrieve additional information (or records) associated with this information.

To dynamically edit data in your database file, you make a connection to the database and then bind fields on the form to the corresponding columns in the database.

Designer supports a number of OLEDB drivers. Click the OLEDB radio button in the New Data Connection Wizard and click the Next button. The second pane in the wizard prompts you for the Connection string. Click the Build button and the Data Link Properties dialog box opens, as shown in Figure 33.66. The list in the figure shows you the supported drivers.

You need to name your connection and set up your database connection string. Setting up a database connection string may require you to research your database user manual. From the Provider tab you select the OLE DB provider, and then click the Connection tab to specify the source of the data. A number of different options appear in the Connection, Advanced, and All tabs. In order to make an effective connection, you need to thoroughly understand your database file and the many options you have to specify the properties for the connection.

FIGURE 33.66

Click Build in the New Data Connection Wizard and the Data Link Properties dialog box opens. Select a data connection you want to make from the list of providers.

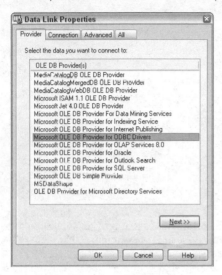

WSDL file

Web Services are applications that run remote over the Web. For example, your form might include a field where the current mortgage rate needs to be calculated. You can connect to a Web Service that determines the daily mortgage rate based on your address. A Web Service Description Language (WSDL) is an XML document (or file) that describes the Web Service and the services and operations (or methods) offered by the service. The connection supports a number of operations. The WSDL file defines the request and response requirements (or syntax) for each operation. Input messages are sent to a server. The server can then reply with an output message. Using Designer you can create and bind fields in a form design to one of many different Web Services.

Aside from connecting to a WSDL via the New Data Connections Wizard, you can:

- Bind one or more operations within one or more Web Services
- Attach fields, subforms, and exclusion groups to the execution of a Web Service operation using a button click event
- Execute a Web Service operation from any event by way of a script
- Enable script access to all returned elements of a Web Service regardless of whether those elements are bound to fields
- Use Simple Object Access Protocol (SOAP) 1.1 style communication
- Exchange data with a Web Service by using doc/literal exchange format SOAP can be either Doc/literal or RPC/encoded. Doc/literal supports drag and drop for automatic population of Data View.
- Write client-side scripts by using the Acrobat SOAP JavaScript Object, which supports RPC/encoded. If you use RPC/encoded you have to do all the connections by hand using JavaScript

To connect to a WSDL service you need to find them on the Internet. You can find lists of WSDL services by visiting www.webservicex.net and www.xmethods.net/. Both these sites post links to WSDL services. To make a connection to a WSDL service and design a form utilizing WSDL data, follow these steps.

STEPS: Binding data to a WSDL service

1. **Create a form design in Adobe Designer.** If you want to test a WSDL connection, you can use a bank new page; otherwise, create a form where you want to introduce the WSDL connection data. Open your form or create a blank new page.

2. **Open a WSDL service in your Web browser.** Use one of the services listing WSDL Web sites (www.webservicex.net or www.xmethods.net) and click a link to a service you want to use. In my example, I use a currency exchange service located at www.webservicex.net/ CurrencyConvertor.asmx?WSDL.

3. **Copy the Web URL from the location bar in your Web browser.**

4. **Open the New Data Connection Wizard.** Switch to Adobe Designer. You can leave your Web browser open and use the Windows Status bar to open your form in Designer.

   Select File ➪ New Data Connection or open the Data View palette and click the icon in the palette to open a pull-down menu and select New Data Connection. In the New Data Connection Wizard, select WDSL as shown in Figure 33.67.

5. **Paste the copied URL in the New Data Connection Wizard.** Click the Next button and paste the copied URL in the text box, as shown in Figure 33.68.

FIGURE 33.67

Open the New Data Connection Wizard and select WSDL File for the connection type.

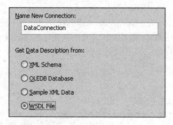

FIGURE 33.68

Paste the copied text in the WSDL File text box.

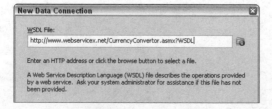

6. **Select an operation.** Click the next box and Designer connects to the WSDL service. In the last wizard pane you'll see a list of operations. Select the first item in the list and click the Finish button, as shown in Figure 33.69. Note that you may have a variety of operations from which to choose. Many services will list duplicated names in the list while others may have unique names for a number of different services. Browse the list box and select the item that suits you needs.

FIGURE 33.69

Select an operation and click Finish.

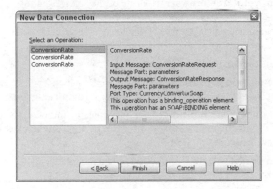

7. **Drag the Data Connection to the form page.** When you click Finish, you'll see a parent item in the Data View palette as the data connection. Below the parent name shown in Figure 33.70 are several child items representing fields and buttons. To add all the items to your form, select the Data Connection parent item and drag it to the form page.

What you see in the Data View is a set of fields for the Request. This is what you need to send to the Web service. You also see a set of fields for the Response. These fields will contain what is returned from the Web service. You also see a button field object that contains the information to connect to the Web service.

FIGURE 33.70

Drag the Data Connection item from the Data View palette to the form page to easily include all elements on your form.

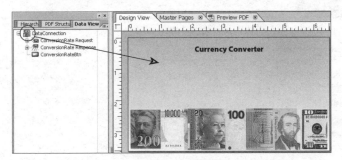

8. **Format the fields.** Move the fields to position and edit any appearance items you want using the Object and Layout tabs.

9. **Save the file.** Select File ➪ Save As and save the file to disk.

10. **Test the form.** Open the form in Acrobat. Add data to the fields for the service you decided to use and click the button to invoke the action. Your Acrobat viewer will make a data connection to the WSDL server and report the results back in your form. In my example I used a currency converter. From the From Currency pull-down menu I select USD for US Dollars and in the To Currency pull-down menu I selected EUR for Euros. After clicking the Conversion Rate Btn, the conversion rate was reported in my form by retrieving the most up-to-date conversion rate from the WSDL server. (See Figure 33.71.)

FIGURE 33.71

My final form reported the results from the WSDL server after I clicked the Conversion Rate Btn.

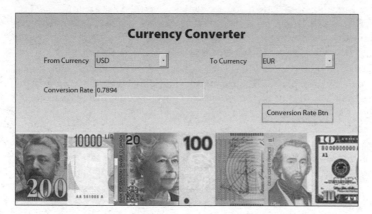

Learning Adobe Designer

If you followed all the steps in this chapter and read it over completely, you know that there's quite a bit to Adobe LiveCycle Designer. I haven't been able to go into all the detail for everything your can do with Designer, so there's quite a bit more than what was covered in the previous pages in this chapter.

If you have a background in programming and database logic, then you may find much of the program to be intuitive and easy to learn. If you don't have skills in programming and understanding database management, then you are likely to have much difficulty getting up to speed in the program. Some people will say that Designer is easy and intuitive. I define easy as something a child or elderly grandparent can learn in 30 minutes time. This program doesn't fall into that category. If someone tells you it's easy to learn, don't believe it! Adobe Designer is complex and tough to learn — especially if you're trying to learn the program from the online guide. You won't become a Designer expert by reading a single chapter in a book on Acrobat. For a good many users, what is needed is some sort of formal training.

If you intend to spend a good part of your workday designing interactive dynamic forms, then you might want to look at a framework for learning the program in detail. Here are some of my recommendations for getting the most out of Adobe Designer:

- **Practice with the program.** Nothing beats practice with a software program than to dive in and start using it. But before you attempt to create some sophisticated forms, try to design static forms. Don't jump into adding subforms and try to create dynamic forms and don't worry about database connections. The more you can become familiar with the different field types and setting field properties, the better off you'll be when it comes time to design more complex forms. Be sure you understand the Library palette, the Object palette and its Value tab, and the Border palette thoroughly. Practice so that it becomes very intuitive and you know exactly where you want to go to change properties for objects and fields. Like any other kind of learning, starting with the basics helps you trim some time off the learning curve.

- **Attend a class.** Some type of formal training is always best when working with a program as complex as Adobe Designer. Search out your local community colleges, universities, and private training centers that offer classes on Designer. But be certain to carefully review the class content before you enroll in a class. If you see classes advertised as "Creating PDF Forms" or "Learning Adobe LiveCycle Designer," make sure that the class instructor and the contents of the class cover creating dynamic forms. An overview of working with fields and creating static PDF forms isn't going to do much more for you than what you can learn by yourself.

   Some private training centers may boast about their credentialed instructors claiming them to be Adobe Certified Experts in Photoshop, Illustrator, InDesign, GoLive, Acrobat, Flash, and a few other programs. My guess is you won't find anyone claiming to have all these certificates to know Designer in depth, at least to the level you need. Look for people who live in the program and do some sort of professional forms design work or are celebrated speakers frequently talking at conferences and expos.

- **Get a video.** This book is written in the early days of Acrobat 8 and we have yet to see if after-market books and videos will appear for Designer. Check regularly on the Internet to see if a video or DVD is released as an instructional tutorial. Videos and DVDs can cover much more territory in less time than reading the online guide.

- **Attend a conference.** One of the best ways to learn features, tips, and workarounds about a program is to attend a conference. There are some extra special benefits to attending a conference. You can attend sessions and sometimes find pre- or post-conference workshops that offer full day courses on Designer. The added benefit is you can gather some e-mail addresses for Adobe employees, speakers, and other conference participants. There's probably not a more valuable asset than having someone to call when you really get stuck on a problem.

- **Be patient.** Learning Designer for the average person is like learning a foreign language. You have to start with basics, add continual reinforcement, and keep practicing. Don't try to create complex forms too quickly. Take your time and learn a little each day. Try to devote some time to concepts and practice many times over so the steps in a process become intuitive and second nature. When you get frustrated, move away from the program and come back the next day. Sometimes a good night's rest can help you solve a problem in a matter of a few minutes that was an all-day burden the day before.

Summary

- You can access Designer from within Acrobat or by opening the program icon.
- Adobe Designer is a point-and-click graphical design application that simplifies creation of form templates intended to be delivered as PDF or HTML.
- Adobe Designer represents a new direction in form design from Adobe Systems. Designer provides Windows users a more sophisticated form designer environment than adding form fields to a PDF document in Adobe Acrobat.
- Adobe Designer supports the use of many different tools, commands and an extensive number of palettes used to create form elements and bind data to external sources.
- You can create new form designs by starting with blank document pages, using PDF background artwork, converting Microsoft Word files, copying spreadsheet data, or using one of many preinstalled templates.
- Form elements are added to a layout from objects in the Library palette or from the Insert menu.
- You can create custom objects and add them to custom libraries complete with scripts and attribute assignments.
- Fields can be grouped in collections and added to custom libraries where they can be reused in subsequent forms.
- Subforms are added to a design to flow data and make the form dynamic where fields and content can be assigned to flow according to user input.
- Field calculations and actions assignments are added in a Script Editor window using either the FormCalc or JavaScript language.
- Designer offers easy access to database connections for fields and forms.
- Designer forms can be enabled with Adobe Reader extensions in Acrobat.
- You can save designer forms as templates, PDF files, and Adobe XML form files.

Chapter 34

Understanding Acrobat Form Tools

In the last chapter, I covered creating forms using Adobe LiveCycle Designer. Unfortunately, Adobe Designer is one of the only features covered in this book that isn't available to Mac people. If you're a Mac person, you may have felt left out while reading Chapter 33. But don't despair. There are plenty of forms features still available for both Macintosh and Windows users in Acrobat 8.

Adobe PDF forms are created in Acrobat Professional using the form tools and many commands for creating a different kind of form. XML forms are created in Adobe Designer and Acrobat PDF forms are created in Acrobat Professional. In some cases, an Acrobat PDF form might be preferred over an XML form. These two forms types are distinctive in both the creation process and for the intended use.

In this chapter, you learn how to use the form tools in Acrobat to create Acrobat PDF forms. The good news is you can create PDF forms in Acrobat on either Windows or the Macintosh.

IN THIS CHAPTER

Defining PDF forms

Filling-in PDF forms

Understanding forms editing

Setting field properties

Managing fields

Creating PDF forms

Working with the Fields panel

NOTE   Creating, modifying, and working with form fields require the use of Acrobat Professional. Acrobat Standard does not support creating or editing PDF forms.

Setting Up the Environment

Working with PDF forms requires the use of the form tools. To open the Forms toolbar, open a context menu on the Toolbar Well and select More Tools to open the More Toolbars window. Scroll the list of Toolbars and check the box for Forms Toolbar. Make sure all form tools are checked. (Note that alternately you have a menu command in the context menu opened from the Toolbar Well to select Forms that opens the Forms toolbar.)

The Select Object tool in the Advanced Editing toolbar is an essential tool to use when creating and editing forms. To gain access to the tool, scroll up the More Toolbars window and check the Advanced Editing toolbar. Within the toolbar

you'll find a number of tools not necessary for forms editing. Clear the Article tool, 3D tool, Crop tool, Sound tool, and TouchUp Reading Order tool.

Scroll down the Window and check the Typewriter toolbar. Click OK and the toolbars open as floating toolbars.

As a last item, return to the context menu on the Toolbar Well and select Properties Bar. When all toolbars are visible in the Document pane, select Dock All Toolbars from a context menu opened from the Toolbar Well.

In addition to tools, a Fields panel offers more options for editing forms. The Fields panel is only accessible when you have a PDF form open in Acrobat. We'll load this panel later in the Chapter when we look at using the Fields panel.

After loading toolbars, your Toolbar Well should look similar to Figure 34.1.

FIGURE 34.1

Tools loaded for a PDF form editing session

What Are Acrobat Forms?

Forms in Acrobat are PDF files with data fields that appear as placeholders for user-supplied data. In Acrobat, you can use text string fields, numeric fields, check boxes, radio buttons, date fields, calculation fields, signature fields, and a variety of custom fields created with JavaScripts. The advantage of using forms in Acrobat is that doing so enables you to maintain design integrity for the appearance of a form while providing powerful control over data management. Rather than using a database manager, which may limit your ability to control fonts and graphics, Acrobat PDFs preserve all the design attributes of a document while behaving like a data manager.

PDF WORKFLOW **Forms are created in Acrobat Professional or Adobe Designer. Form field data can be saved with Acrobat Standard and Professional. You can also save form data with Adobe Reader when the PDF form has been enabled with usage rights for Adobe Reader. When opening PDFs in Adobe Reader that have not been enabled with Reader Extensions you cannot save, import, or export data. In developing PDF workflows for a company or organization, all users expected to design forms in Acrobat need to use the Acrobat Professional software. Corporations and enterprises seeking an affordable solution for extending Adobe Reader to support forms features beyond the licensing limitations of Acrobat 8 Professional, should look at acquiring the Adobe LiveCycle Reader Extensions Server (LRES). For more information about LRES log on to: www.adobe.com/products/server/readerextensions.**

CROSS-REF **See Chapter 19 for more information on enabling PDFs for filling in and saving forms in Adobe Reader, and also for information on licensing restrictions applied to the use of enabling features in Acrobat Professional.**

The non-PDF form

The one thing to keep in mind regarding Acrobat and forms is that a form in the context of PDF is not a paper form scanned as an image and saved as PDF. Tons of these so-called forms are around offices and on the Internet. These documents may have originated as forms, but by the time you understand all of Acrobat's available features, you'll see that these scanned documents can hardly be called forms. Simply put, they're scanned images saved to PDF. The power of Acrobat gives you the tools to create *smart forms*. These forms can be dynamic, intuitive, and interactive, and save both you and the end user much time in providing and gathering information.

Development of a PDF form

In Chapter 33, you learned that forms could be created in Adobe Designer from scratch. Adobe Designer has all the tools you need to create a form design starting with a blank page. Inasmuch as you can create a Blank New Page in Acrobat, PDF forms created in Acrobat usually start out as a document converted to PDF from an authoring program. Programs like Microsoft Office, Adobe InDesign, Adobe Illustrator, or one of you favorite design programs create the layout and background for a PDF form. After the design is created in an authoring program and converted to PDF, you use tools in Acrobat to add form fields and form attributes.

CROSS-REF For information related to PDF creation from authoring programs, see the chapters in Part II.

TIP If you create a design and then add form fields in Acrobat, and then even later decide to change your design, you can edit the design back in your original authoring application. Simply save the design and open the form you created in Acrobat. Select Document ⇨ Replace Pages and select the modified PDF document. Replace the page and your modified design appears without disturbing any added form fields to the original design.

Filling In Forms

When you receive or download a PDF form you will encounter one of two types of forms. The so-called PDF form that was created from a scanned document or a PDF document containing no form fields is one type of form. The other type of form is the PDF document containing form fields. In all Acrobat viewers you can populate form data in either type of form.

Using the Typewriter tool

The Typewriter tool is used to fill in a form containing no form fields. You use the Typewriter tool like a text tool is used in other authoring programs.

To use the Typewriter tools, open a document in an Acrobat viewer and click the Typewriter tool. Click on the page where you want to type text and an I-beam cursor appears. Type the text on a line. This tool was a little clumsy in performance and took a little time to get used to in Acrobat 7, but the performance of the tool has been much improved in Acrobat 8.

You'll notice right away that the default font is Courier and there isn't much paragraph formatting control. If you want to stop typing on one block of text and start a new block, press the Escape (Esc) key. Then click the Typewriter tool and click again on the page in an area where you want to start a new block of text.

The Typewriter tools in the Typewriter toolbar from left to right, as shown in Figure 34.2, include the Typewriter tool, the Text Smaller tool, the Text Larger tool, Decrease Line Spacing tool, and Increase Line Spacing tool. If you want to move a text block after typing, use the Select Object tool.

FIGURE 34.2

Click the Typewriter tool and click on a page to type text. The text defaults to Courier font.

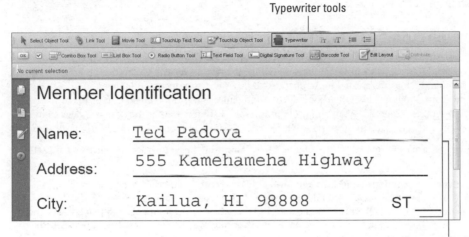

You have a few options for changing font style for text typed with the Typewriter tool by opening a context menu where you can select from Bold, Italic, Underline, Superscript, and Subscript. You can't change font type, but the extra bit of choices for font style gives you more than what we had available with Acrobat 7.

You'll often find that you can't quite get the line spacing right for the form you fill in using the Typewriter tool. However, when you need to fill in a form where no form fields appear on a document, using this tool saves you some time over printing, and hand filling it in, and then faxing the form back to the form author.

TIP If you want more control over type attributes, select the TouchUp Text tool, and then press the Ctrl/Option key and click on a page. The New Text Font dialog box opens where you can choose a type font. After typing text you can add formatting options by opening a context menu and selecting Properties. In the TouchUp Properties dialog box you can edit font size, character spacing, word spacing, horizontal scaling, offsets, font color, and more. Moving text typed with this tool is handled with the TouchUp Object tool.

Filling in forms containing form fields

As you view the form shown in Figure 34.3, notice it contains several text fields, a few combo boxes, a list box, radio buttons, check boxes, and a signature field. To fill out a text field, you need to select the Hand tool, place the cursor over the field, and click the mouse button. When you click, a blinking I-beam cursor appears, indicating that you can add text by typing on your keyboard.

FIGURE 34.3

A form containing many different field types A) Text fields, B) Radio Buttons, C) Checkboxes, D) Combo Box, E) List Box, F) Signature field.

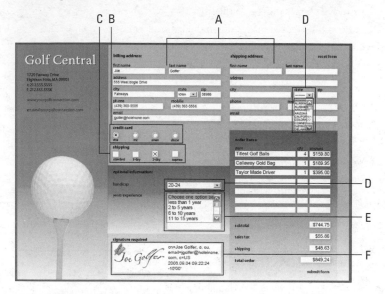

TIP To begin filling in a form, press the Tab key on your keyboard. When the Hand tool is selected and the cursor is not active in any field, pressing the Tab key places the cursor in the first field on the form.

To navigate to the next field for more text entry, you can make one of two choices: Click in the next field or press the Tab key on your keyboard. When you press the Tab key, the cursor jumps to the next field, according to an order the PDF author specified in Acrobat when the form was designed. Be certain the Hand tool is selected and a cursor appears in a field box when you press the Tab key. If you have any other tool selected, you can tab through the fields and type data in the field boxes; however, if you click with the mouse when another tool is selected, you make edits according to the active tool.

When selecting from choices in radio button or check box fields, click in the radio button or check box. The display changes to show a small solid circle or check mark within a box or other kind of user-defined symbol from options you select for button/check box styles. When using a combo box, click the down-pointing arrow in the field and select from one of several pull-down menu choices. List boxes are scrollable fields. Scroll to the choice you want to make using the up and down arrows.

Form field navigation keystrokes

As mentioned in the preceding section, to move to the next field, you need to either click in the field or press the Tab key. Following is a list of other keystrokes that can help you move through forms to complete them:

- **Shift+Tab.** Moves to the previous field.
- **Esc.** Ends text entry.
- **Return.** Ends text entry for single line entries or adds a carriage return for multi-line fields.

- **Double-click a word in a field.** Selects the word.
- **Ctrl/⌘+A.** Selects all the text in a field.
- **Left/right arrow keys.** Moves the cursor one character at a time left or right.
- **Up arrow.** Fielding combo and list boxes moves up the list.
- **Down arrow.** Fielding combo and list boxes moves down the list.
- **Up/down arrow with combo and list boxes selected.** Moves up and down the list. When the list is collapsed, pressing the down-arrow key opens the list.
- **Ctrl/⌘+Tab.** Accepts new entry and exits all fields. The next tab places the cursor in the first field.

Viewing fields

You may open a form in Acrobat where the fields are not clearly visible. Creating form fields on white backgrounds for fields with no border or fill color makes a field invisible when opened in an Acrobat viewer.

If you start to fill in a form and can't see the form fields, click the Highlight Fields button on the Forms Document Message bar. All fields are highlighted with a color specified in the Forms Preferences. In Figure 34.4, the fields are white. When I click the Highlight Fields button in the top right corner of the Forms Document Message bar, the fields are highlighted making it easy to see where each field appears in the form.

FIGURE 34.4

Click Highlight Fields in the Forms Document Message bar to display fields with highlights.

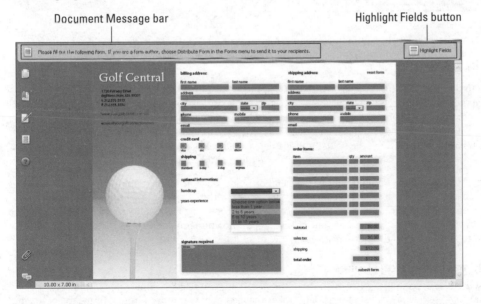

If you don't see the Forms Document Message bar, you need to adjust a preference setting. Press Ctrl/⌘+K to open the Preferences dialog box. Click Forms in the left pane and remove the check mark where you see Always hide forms document message bar. Remove the Always hide forms document message bar check box as shown in Figure 34.5 to display the message bar in the Document pane.

FIGURE 34.5

Remove the Always hide forms document message bar check box to display the message bar in the Document pane.

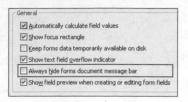

Using Auto-Complete features

While filling in a form, you can enable Acrobat to record common responses you supply in form fields. After recording responses, each time you return to similar fields, the fields are automatically filled in or a list is offered to you for selecting an option for auto-completing fields.

To turn the recording mechanism on, you need to address the Forms preference settings. Open the Preferences dialog box by pressing Ctrl/⌘+K and select Forms in the left pane. In the right-hand pane, open the pull-down menu under the Auto-Complete section of the Forms preferences. You can make menu choices from Off, Basic, and Advanced, as shown in Figure 34.6. Selecting Off turns the Auto-Complete feature off. Selecting Basic stores information entered in fields and uses the entries to make relevant suggestions. Select Advanced from the pull-down menu to receive suggestions from the stored list as you Tab into a field. If a probability matches the list, using the Advanced option automatically fills in the field when you tab into it.

FIGURE 34.6

Click on Forms in the Preferences dialog box and select Basic or Advanced from the Auto-Complete pull-down menu to use the auto-completion feature.

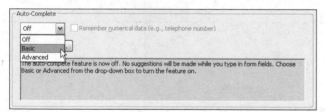

By default, numeric data are eliminated from the data stored for the suggestions. If you want to include numeric data for telephone numbers, addresses, and the like, check the Remember numerical data check box.

The list grows as you complete forms when either the Basic or Advanced choice is enabled in the pull-down menu. You can examine the list of stored entries by clicking the Edit Entry List button; the Auto-Complete Entry List dialog box opens as shown in Figure 34.7. To remove an item from the list, select it and click the Remove button. To remove all entries click the Remove All button.

FIGURE 34.7

To remove entries from your suggestion list, click the Edit Entry List button in the Forms preferences. Select items in the Auto-Complete Entry List and click the Remove button.

In order to record entries, you need to first make the selection for using either the Basic or Advanced Auto-Complete feature. To have suggestions for entries submitted as you type in fields, one of the two menu options needs to be enabled. When you select Off in the pull-down menu, both recording entered data and offering suggestions is turned off.

After selecting either Basic or Advanced in the Forms preferences and editing entries, fill out a form. If you recorded data after filling out one form, the next time you fill out another form you'll see suggestions, as shown in Figure 34.8. The cursor appears just below City and the suggestion (Fairways) is derived from recorded data supplied on another form.

FIGURE 34.8

Enter a field and a data suggestion(s) appears in a drop-down menu.

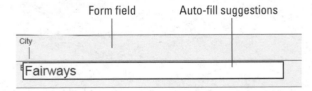

How good is the Auto-Fill feature in Acrobat? When the feature was first introduced several generations ago, it was pretty clumsy. There wasn't much sophistication in controlling what data are recorded and what data are suggested when filling in a form. After several Acrobat revisions, there remain no changes in the Auto-Fill feature. It's still quite clumsy and you'll find sometimes it may work well for you and in other cases, you'll find turning off the Auto-Fill option less distractive when completing a form.

Working in the Forms Editing Environment

As I mentioned at the beginning of the chapter, you use a design application to create a form layout, convert to PDF, and then add the form fields and form features in Acrobat Professional.

NEW FEATURE You'll notice a new Forms menu has been added to Acrobat 8. When you first open a form design you are in Preview mode. Take a look at the Forms menu while in Preview mode and you see commands as shown in Figure 34.9.

FIGURE 34.9

The Forms menu commands when in Preview mode

On the Forms toolbar and in the Forms menu, you have a button command to enter Edit mode. Click the Edit Layout button in the Forms toolbar or select Forms ➪ Edit Form in Acrobat and you enter Edit mode. While in Edit mode, open the Forms menu and you see the addition for four menu items, as shown in Figure 34.10.

FIGURE 34.10

Click the Edit Layout button in the Forms toolbar or select Forms ➪ Edit Form in Acrobat and the Forms menu changes.

The four menu items you see added to the Forms menu while in Edit mode include:

- **Form Tools.** The submenu lists all of the form tools used to create form fields. Select one of the tools from the submenu and the respective tool is activated. If you have the Forms toolbar open, using the menu command to select tools is not necessary.

- **Edit Fields.** The submenu contains items that were formally nested in the Advanced menu in earlier versions of Acrobat. You find commands for setting tab order and field calculation order in the submenu. Additionally, you have commands for duplicating fields and creating tables. (See the section "Understanding Form Fields" later in this chapter for detail on these menu items.)

- **Show Field Properties.** Select one or more fields in a form and this menu item is active. Make the menu choice and the Properties dialog box opens with options enabling you to change common field attributes.

- **Page Templates.** Another command formerly contained in the Advanced menu in earlier versions of Acrobat is the Page Templates command. Select this command for adding and managing page templates.

 For more information on creating page templates, see Chapter 36.

Form Field Recognition

If you create a design in an authoring program with fields clearly defined, you can easily convert your PDF document to a form with populated form fields through the use of a single menu command.

To automate your PDF forms creation, follow these steps.

STEPS: Automatically recognizing form fields

1. **Open a document designed as a form in your favorite authoring application.** Be certain to clearly define form fields with lines, boxes, or other graphic elements.

2. **Convert to PDF.** When converting to PDF, enable adding tags to the PDF document if your PDF export or creation tool supports creating a tagged PDF. Tagged PDFs are not necessary, but they will provide you a little more document integrity particularly when the field names are assigned to the form fields.

3. **Open the file in Acrobat Professional.**

4. **Select Forms ▷ Run Form Field Recognition.** Note that the Run Form Field Recognition command is available in either Edit or Preview mode.

   The surprising thing about running this command in Acrobat 8 is that the form fields are automatically added to the PDF document in record time. It's fast and quite impressive.

5. **Review the help information.** After Acrobat populates your form with fields, the How To panel opens providing links to help information. Click links in the How To panel to review a summary of the form field recognition. In Figure 34.11, I converted a Microsoft Word Document to a PDF form using Run Form Field Recognition.

FIGURE 34.11

Acrobat automatically created form fields after the Run Form Field Recognition command was selected from the Forms menu.

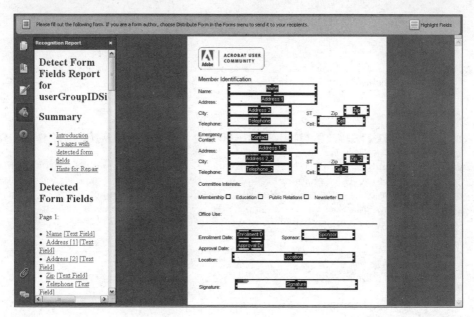

Notice in Figure 34.11, the check box fields were not populated with form fields. The Run Form Field Recognition feature is not perfect, but it does an excellent job of adding text fields. With some forms you'll find radio buttons and check boxes recognized by the Run Form Field Recognition command and in other forms they may be missed. Notice also that the signature field in Figure 34.11 was also created by Run Form Field Recognition. Text clearly identified as a signature creates a signature field.

What kinds of authoring application files can be used with Run Form Field Recognition? Take a look at the brief list of many different original document formats converted to PDF that work well with this command.

- **Microsoft Office.** All Microsoft Office files work well with Run Form Field Recognition. Use the PDFMaker from the Office applications to convert to PDF. (For more on PDFMaker and Microsoft Office applications, see Chapter 8.)

- **Adobe Creative Suite.** Files created in Adobe InDesign and Adobe Illustrator work well with Run Form Field Recognition. Native Adobe Illustrator and Illustrator PDFs are both supported.

- **Adobe Photoshop and scanned forms.** Adobe Photoshop files, also a member of the Adobe Creative Suite, and scanned forms are also supported. After conversion to PDF, you need to run OCR Text Recognition. Select Document ➪ OCR Text Recognition ➪ Recognize Text Using OCR. When you complete the text recognition, select Forms ➪ Run Form Field Recognition. (For more information on using Recognize Text Using OCR, see Chapter 17.)

- **RTF.** From a text editor, save files as RTF (Rich Text Format). Use the Create PDF ➪ From File command to convert to PDF and then Run Form Field Recognition.

- **Web Pages and Adobe GoLive.** There's no need to use Run Form Field Recognition with HTML documents and Web pages. When you use Create PDF ⇨ From Web Page or the PDFMaker in Microsoft Internet Explorer, form fields on Web pages are converted at the time you create the PDF file.

CROSS-REF Form more information on using Run Form Field Recognition with scanned paper forms, see Chapter 17.

If you have other application program files such as Lotus Notes, Corel Draw, WordPerfect, e-mail messages, and so on, most of these file types can also be used with the Run Form Field Recognition command as long as clearly defined form field locations appear on the document.

Preparing files for Run Form Field Recognition

Using the Run Form Field Recognition command does a very good job of recognizing form fields on simple forms. However, when forms become more complex and when you create forms with graphics, gradients, and complex design elements, Run Form Field Recognition falls apart and won't create fields on most graphically intense form designs. For example, take a look at the figure below. When I chose Forms ⇨ Run Form Field Recognition in Acrobat, no fields were recognized on the form.

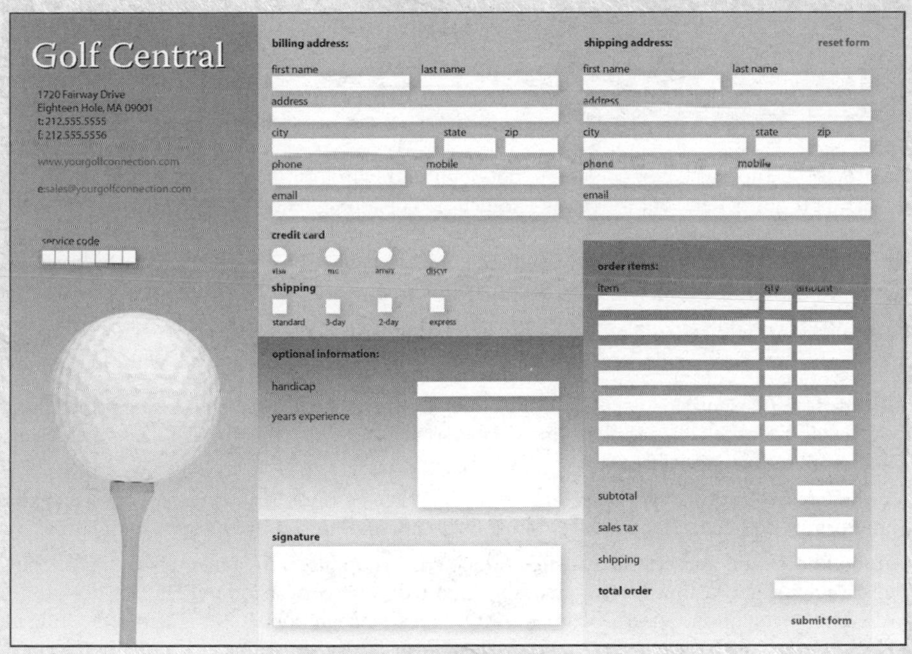

If you use programs like Adobe Illustrator or Adobe InDesign to create forms with complex graphic elements, you can prepare your files for using Run Form Field Recognition by adding an extra layer that you use just for the Run Form Field Recognition command. Using programs like Illustrator or InDesign provide you the benefit for using layers in your design. You can easily create a background with all the graphic elements, a text layer containing all the text in the form, a layer for fields used in the final design, and a separate layer for temporary fields designed for Run Form Field Recognition in Acrobat. An example of such a form I created in Adobe Illustrator is shown below.

If you create a similar form in a program like Adobe Illustrator or Adobe InDesign, save your file to PDF as a PDF version 1.5 or greater document (Acrobat 6 and above compatibility) and check options for creating Adobe PDF Layers. You must save the file as a layered file that appears with Layers in Acrobat. (See Chapter 24 for more on PDFs and Layers.) In Acrobat you can view just the Text and Temp Fields layers, all layers, or any combination of layers. Acrobat won't complain and the Run Form Field Recognition command creates form fields from the Temp Fields layer whether it is visible or not. After using Run Form Field Recognition, my file appeared with the form fields as you see below.

A little polish is needed on the form for sizing some field boxes and adding the radio button and check box fields, but the little time it took to create the temporary layer in the authoring application was a fraction of the time you would need to spend in Acrobat to manually create all the text fields. By using an authoring application supporting layers you can easily create a PDF file that is Run Form Field Recognition–friendly. Planning ahead when designing forms in authoring programs can save you much time when using the Run Form Field Recognition command.

continued

continued

To finish up my form design in Acrobat, I flatten the layers. Be certain to turn off all layers you want discarded and when you select Flatten Layers from the Layers panel Options menu the hidden layers are discarded and the PDF is flattened. All field objects remain undisturbed regardless of what layer views you have on or off.

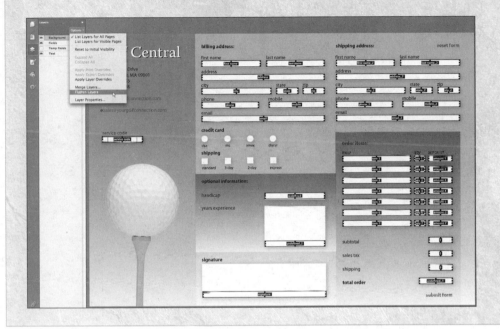

Understanding form fields

Forms contain different types of data fields that hold data, act as buttons that invoke actions, and call scripts to execute a series of actions. Form fields can assume different appearances as well as possess the capability to include graphic icons and images to represent hot links that invoke actions. Acrobat forms are more than a static data filing system — they can be as vivid and dynamic as your imagination.

In Acrobat, the form data fields are created with the form tools. In order to use the form tools, you first need to switch to Edit mode. In addition to clicking the Edit Layout button or select Edit Form in Acrobat from the Forms menu to engage in Edit mode, clicking a form tool in the Forms toolbar also switches from Preview mode to Edit mode. After selecting a tool, draw rectangles using one of the eight form tools to create a field. Upon releasing the mouse button after drawing a field rectangle, the field Properties dialog box opens where attributes are assigned to the field. For an overview of the field types, look over the following list:

■ **Button.** A button is usually used to invoke an action or hyperlink. A button face can be text or a graphic element created in another program that you could apply as an appearance to the button. You can also use different appearance settings in the button properties for adding stroke and fill colors. Buttons are also used to import images.

■ **Check Box.** Check boxes typically appear in groups to offer the user a selection of choices. Yes and no items or a group of check boxes might be created for multiple-choice selections.

■ **Combo Box.** When you view an Acrobat form, you may see a down-pointing arrow similar to the arrows appearing in panel menus. Such an arrow in a PDF form indicates the presence of a combo box. When you click the arrow, a pull-down menu opens with a list of choices. Users are limited to selecting a single choice from combo boxes. Additionally, if designed as such, users can input their own choices.

■ **List Box.** A list box displays a box with scroll bars, much like windows you see in application software documents. As you scroll through a list box, you make a choice of one or more of the alternatives available by selecting items in the list.

■ **Radio Button.** Radio buttons perform the same function in PDF forms as radio buttons do in dialog boxes. Usually you have two or more choices for a category. Forms are usually designed so that when one radio button in a group is turned on, the other buttons in the group are turned off.

■ **Text Field.** Text fields are boxes in which text is typed by the end user to fill out the form. Text fields can contain alphabetical characters, numbers, or a combination of both.

■ **Digital Signature.** Digital signatures can be applied to fields, PDF pages, and PDF documents. A digital signature can be used to lock out fields on a form.

- **Barcode.** The Barcode tool is not a completely new feature in Acrobat 8. Acrobat 7 supported a plug-in to create 2D and 3D Barcodes that was shipped long after the initial release of Acrobat 7.0. Now with Acrobat 8.0, you get the Barcode tool appearing in the Forms toolbar. This tool provides you options for adding barcodes to a PDF form.

Although not form fields per se, a few additional tools also appear in the Forms toolbar. These tools include:

- **Preview.** Acrobat 8 now supports two views when working with PDF forms. You enter an Edit mode to work with form fields and you enter the Preview mode to test your forms. To check your form fields as one might fill in your form, click the Preview button in the Forms toolbar.

- **Edit Layout.** When you need to return to the Edit mode, click the Edit Layout button. You leave preview mode and enter Edit mode where you have additional commands accessible from the Forms menu.

- **Distribute.** This tool is used to start an ad hoc data collection workflow. You can send the form by e-mail or post the form on a Web page, and then you specify a data collection file where the filled in PDF forms are collected by you. For more information on using the Distribute tool, see Chapter 35.

All these form field types and tools are available to you in the Forms toolbar when you create or edit a PDF form in Acrobat.

Assigning Form Field Properties

The process of adding form fields to a form is the same for all fields. You click a form tool in the Forms toolbar, drag open a rectangle on a form, release the mouse button, and a Properties dialog box opens. In the Properties dialog box, you choose options from several different panes. Depending on the field type you create, the panes in the Properties dialog box vary for different field types. Some field properties are common among several fields while other properties are unique to each field type.

To open the Properties dialog box, select a form tool such as the Text Field tool, draw a rectangle, and release the mouse button. The Text Field Properties dialog box opens, as shown in Figure 34.12.

FIGURE 34.12

When you draw a rectangle with any form tool and release the mouse button, the General field properties appear as the default.

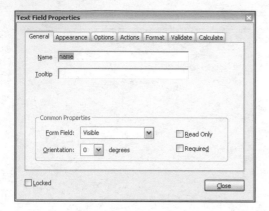

General properties

The General properties tab is the default tab where general properties are assigned. These properties are common to all field types. The properties include:

- **Name.** By default, Acrobat adds a name in the Name field. As a matter of practice you should type a descriptive name in the Name text box. Don't use names with spaces and try to use parent/child names for fields in common groups. A parent/child name might appear as item.1, item.2, item.3 and so on; or you might have client.first, client.last, client.address, and so on.

- **Tooltip.** Type a name and when the cursor is placed over the field in Preview mode, the text appears as a tooltip below the Hand tool cursor.

- **Form Field.** From the pull-down menu, make choices for visibility and printing. By default, the field is visible and prints when the file is printed.

- **Orientation.** A field and a field's contents can be rotated in 90-degree rotations. By default, fields are at a 0 (zero)-degree rotation. Select from 90, 180, and 270 to rotate fields in fixed rotations.

- **Read Only.** When a field is marked as Read Only, the field is not editable. The user is locked out of the field. A Read Only field might be something you use to show fixed price costs where you don't want users changing a fixed purchase price on an order form. Another example is a value that is pre-populated from a database or with fields that show results of other calculated data.

- **Required.** If a field needs to be filled in before the data is submitted, select the Required box.

- **Locked.** Locking a field prevents the field from being moved. You can still type data in the field or make a choice from options for other fields. This item is used to fix fields in position as you edit a form.

Appearance properties

The Appearance tab relates to form field appearances. The rectangles you draw can be assigned border colors and content fills. The text added to a field box or default text you use for a field can be assigned different

fonts, font sizes, and font colors. These options exist in the Appearance properties for all field types except barcode fields (Barcode fields don't have an Appearance tab). Figure 34.13 shows the Appearance properties for a selected text field.

FIGURE 34.13

Click the Appearance tab for any field properties and make choices for the appearance of fields and text.

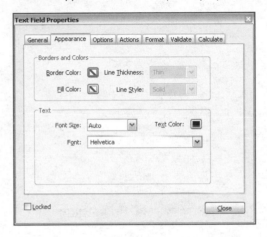

The Appearance options include the following:

- **Border Color.** The keyline created for a field is made visible with a rectangular border assigned by clicking the Border Color swatch and choosing a color.

- **Background Color.** The field box can be assigned a background color. If you want the field box displayed in a color, enable this option, click the color swatch next to it, and choose a color the same way you do for the borders. When the check box is disabled, the background appears transparent.

- **Line Thickness.** Options are the same as those available for link rectangles. Select the pull-down menu and choose from Thin, Medium, or Thick. The pull-down menu is grayed out unless you first select a Border Color.

- **Line Style.** You can choose from five style types from the pull-down menu. The Solid option shows the border as a keyline at the width specified in the Width setting. Dashed shows a dashed line; Beveled appears as a box with a beveled edge; Inset makes the field look recessed; and Underline eliminates the keyline and shows an underline for the text across the width of the field box. See Figure 34.14 for an example of these style types.

- **Font Size.** Depending on the size of the form fields you create, you may have a need to choose a different point size for the text. The default is Auto, which automatically adjusts point sizes according to the height of the field box. Choices are available for manually setting the point size for text ranges between 2 and 300 points.

FIGURE 34.14

Five choices for a border style are available in the Appearance tab when selecting from the Line Style pull-down menu.

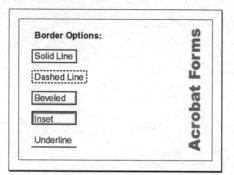

- **Text Color.** If you identify a color for text by selecting the swatch adjacent to Text Color, the field contents supplied by the end user change to the selected color.

- **Font.** From the pull-down menu, select a font for the field data. All the fonts installed in your system are accessible from the pull-down menu. When designing forms for screen displays, try to use sans serif fonts for better screen views.

NOTE When designing forms for cross-platform use, use one of the Base Fonts. Custom fonts loaded in your system may not be available to other users. Base Fonts appear at the top of the font list and are separated from the fonts installed on your system with a space between the Base Fonts and your system fonts. For more information about Base Fonts, see Chapter 8.

The Appearance settings are identical for all field types except Digital Signature fields, Radio Button fields, Check Box fields, and Barcode fields. The Radio Button and Check Box fields use fixed fonts for displaying characters in the field box. You choose what characters to use in the Options tab. When creating Radio Button and Check Box fields, you don't have a choice for Font in the Appearance properties. By default, the Adobe Pi font is used.

Options properties

The Options tab provides selections for specific attributes according to the type of fields you add to a page. Options are available for all fields except the Digital Signatures field. Options tab attributes for the other six field types include options for text, radio buttons, combo and list boxes, and buttons.

Text options

When you use the Text Field tool to create a field and you click on the Options tab, the Properties window appears, as shown in Figure 34.15.

FIGURE 34.15

The Options settings in the Text Field Properties dialog box

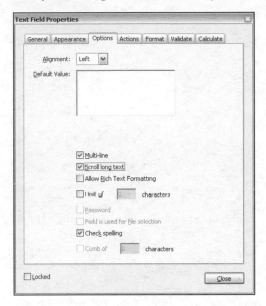

Each of the following attribute settings is optional when creating text fields:

- **Alignment.** The Alignment pull-down menu has two functions. First, any text entered in the Default field is aligned according to the option you specify from the pull-down menu choices. Alignment choices include Left, Center, and Right. Second, regardless of whether text is used in the Default field, when the end user fills out the form the cursor is positioned at the alignment selected from the pull-down menu choices. Therefore, if you select Center from the Alignment options, the text entered when filling out the form is centered within the field box.

- **Default Value.** The Default Value field can be left blank or you can enter text that appears in the field when viewing the form. The Default item has nothing to do with the name of the field. This option is used to provide helpful information when the user fills out the form data. If no text is entered in the Default field, when you return to the form, the field appears empty. If you enter text in the Default field, the text you enter appears inside the field box and can be deleted, edited, or replaced.

- **Multi-line.** If your text field contains more than one line of text, select the Multi-line option. When you press the Return key after entering a line of text, the cursor jumps to the second line where additional text is added to the same field. Multi-line text fields might be used, for example, as an address field to accommodate a second address line.

- **Scrolling long text.** If Multi-line is selected and text entries exceed the height of the field, you may want to add scroll bars to the field. Enable the check box to permit users to scroll lines of text. If the check box is disabled, users won't be able to scroll, but as text is added, automatic scrolling accommodates the amount of text typed in the field.

- **Allow Rich Text Formatting.** When you check this box, users can style text with bold, italic, and bold italic font styles. You may want to enable the check box if you want users to emphasize a field's contents.

- **Limit of [ ] characters.** The box for this option provides for user character limits for a given field. If you want the user to add a state value of two characters, for example, check the box and type 2 in the field box. If the user attempts to go beyond the limit, a system warning beep alerts the user that no more text can be added to the field.

- **Password.** When this option is enabled, all the text entered in the field appears as a series of asterisks when the user fills in the form. The field is not secure in the sense that you must have a given password to complete the form; it merely protects the data entry from being seen by an onlooker.

- **Field is used for file selection.** This option permits you to specify a file path as part of the field's value. The file is submitted along with the form data. Be certain to enable the Scrolling long text option described earlier in this list to enable this option.

- **Check spelling.** Spell checking is available for comments and form fields. When the check box is enabled, the field is included in a spell check. This can be helpful so the spell checker doesn't get caught up with stopping at proper names, unique identifiers, and abbreviations that may be included in those fields.

- **Comb of [ ] characters.** When you create a text field box and enable this check box, Acrobat automatically creates a text field box with subdivision lines according to the value you supply in the Characters field box. Be certain to disable all other check boxes. You can set the alignment of the characters by making a choice from the alignment pull-down menu, but all other check boxes need to be disabled to access the Comb of check box.

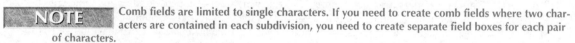 Comb fields are limited to single characters. If you need to create comb fields where two characters are contained in each subdivision, you need to create separate field boxes for each pair of characters.

Check box and radio button options

Check boxes and radio buttons have similar Options attribute choices. When you select either field and click on the Options tab, the settings common to both field types include:

- **Button/Check Box Style.** If a radio button is selected, the title is Button Style. If the field is a check box, the title is listed as Check Box Style as shown in Figure 34.16. From the pull-down menu, you select the style you want to use for the check mark inside the radio button or check box field.

FIGURE 34.16

You can choose various options for radio buttons and check boxes, including those for the style of the check marks or radio buttons.

- **Export Value.** When creating either a check box or radio button, use the same field name for all fields in a common group where you want one check box enabled while all the other check boxes or radio buttons are disabled. To distinguish the fields from each other, add an export value that differs in each field box. You can use export values such as Yes and No or other text, or number values such as 1, 2, 3, 4, and so on.

  The creation of radio buttons and check boxes on Acrobat forms has been confusing to many users and users often inappropriately create workarounds for check boxes and radio buttons to toggle them on and off. To help eliminate confusion, notice the Options properties in Figure 34.16 includes a help message informing you to name fields the same name but use different export values.

- **Button/Check box is checked by default.** If you want a default value to be applied for either field type (for example, Yes), enter the export value and select the box to make the value the default. One distinction appears in the Options dialog box between radio buttons and check boxes. The second check box in the radio button properties is unique to radio buttons.

- **Buttons with the same name and value are selected in unison (applies to radio buttons only).** For data export purposes, you'll want to add a different export value for each radio button and check box. If you don't need to export data to a database with unique export values for each radio button, you can add radio buttons to a page with the same export values and, by default, when a user clicks one radio button all other radio buttons are disabled. If you want all radio buttons to be selected when clicking one button in a group having the same name and export value, check this check box.

The Button/Check Box Style selection from the pull-down menu in both field types provides identical appearances. The styles are shown in Figure 34.17.

FIGURE 34.17

Six icon options are available for check boxes and radio buttons.

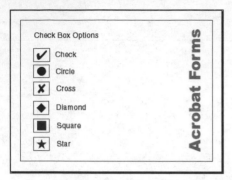

Combo box and list box options

Combo boxes enable you to create form fields with a list of selections appearing in a pull-down window. The user completing a form makes a selection from the menu items. If all items are not visible, the menu contains scroll bars made visible after selecting the down-pointing arrow to open the menu. A list box is designed as a scrollable window with an elevator bar and arrows as you see in authoring application documents, as shown in Figure 34.18.

FIGURE 34.18

View the combo box items by clicking the down arrow. After you open the menu, the scroll bars become visible. List boxes enable users to select multiple items in the scrollable window.

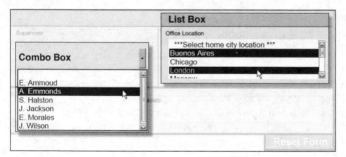

The two field types differ in several ways. First, combo boxes require less space for the form field. The combo box menu drops down from a narrow field height where the menu options are shown. List boxes require more height to make them functional to the point where at least two or three options are in view before the user attempts to scroll the window. Second, you can select only one menu option from a combo box. List boxes enable users to select multiple items. Finally, combo boxes can be designed for users to add text for a custom choice by editing any of the menu items. List boxes provide no option for users to type text in the field box and the menu items are not editable.

The data exported with the file include the selected item from the combo boxes and all selected items for list boxes. The item choices and menu designs for the field types are created in the Options tab for the respective field type. Attributes for list boxes, shown in Figure 34.19, are also available for combo boxes.

FIGURE 34.19

The Options settings for list boxes have common properties also found in combo boxes.

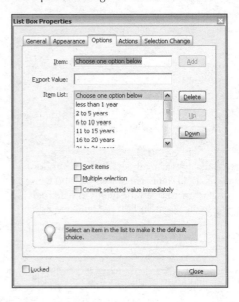

The options include:

- **Item.** You enter the name of an entry you want to appear in the scrollable list in this field.
- **Export Value.** When the data are exported, the name you enter in this field box is the exported value. If the field is left blank, the exported value is the name used in the item description typed in the Item field. If you want different export values than the name descriptions, type a value in this field box. As an example, suppose you created a consumer satisfaction survey form. In that form, the user can choose from list items such as Very Satisfied, Satisfied, and Unsatisfied, and you've specified the export values for these items to be 1, 2, and 3, respectively. When the data are analyzed, the frequency of the three items would be tabulated and defined in a legend as 1=Very Satisfied, 2=Satisfied, and 3=Unsatisfied.
- **Add.** After you enter the Item and Export Values, click the Add button to place the item in the Item List. After adding an item, you can return to the Item field and type a new item in the field box and, in turn, a new export value.
- **Item List.** As you add items, the items appear in a scrollable list window. To edit a name in the list window, delete the item, type a new name in the Item text box, and then click the Add button to add the newly edited item back in the list.
- **Delete.** If an item has been added to the list and you want to delete it, first select the item in the list. Click the Delete button to remove it from the list.

- **Up/Down.** Items are placed in the list according to the order in which they are entered. The order displayed in the list is shown in the combo box or list box when you return to the document page. If you want to reorganize items, select the item in the list and click the Up or Down button to move one level up or down, respectively. To enable the Up and Down buttons, the Sort Items option must be disabled.

- **Sort items.** When checked, the list is alphabetically sorted in ascending order. As new items are added to the list, the new fields are dynamically sorted while the option is enabled.

- **Multiple selection (List box only).** Any number of options can be selected by using modifier keys and clicking on the list items. Use Shift+click for contiguous selections and Ctrl/⌘+click for noncontiguous selections. This option applies only to list boxes.

- **Commit selected value immediately.** The choice made in the field box is saved immediately. If the check box is disabled, the choice is saved after the user exits the field by tabbing out or clicking the mouse cursor on another field or outside the field.

With the exception of the multiple selection item, the preceding options are also available for combo boxes. In addition to these options, combo boxes offer two more items that include:

- **Allow user to enter custom text.** The items listed in the Options tab are fixed in the combo box on the Acrobat form by default. If this check box is enabled, the user can create a custom value. Acrobat makes no provision for some items to be edited, and others are locked out from editing.

- **Check spelling.** Spell checking is performed when a user types in a custom value. As text is typed the spelling is checked.

Button options

Buttons differ from all other fields when it comes to appearance. You can create and use custom icons for button displays from PDF documents or file types compatible with Convert to PDF from File. Rather than entering data or toggling a data field, buttons typically execute an action. You might use a button to clear a form, export data, import data from a data file, or use buttons as navigation links. When you add a button to a page, the Options tab attributes change to those shown in Figure 34.20.

FIGURE 34.20

The Options tab for the Button field properties includes options for button face displays and several different mouse behaviors.

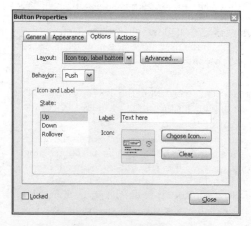

When you create a button, you make choices from the Options tab for the highlight view of the button, the behavior of the mouse cursor, and the text and icon views. The Options attributes for buttons are as follows:

- **Layout.** Several views are available for displaying a button with or without a label, which you add in the Label field described later in this list. The choices from the pull-down menu for Layout offer options for displaying a button icon with text appearing at the top, bottom, left, or right side of the icon, or over the icon. Figure 34.21 shows the different Layout options.

FIGURE 34.21

The Layout options include Label only; Icon only; Icon top, label bottom; Label top, icon bottom; Icon left, label right; Label left, icon right; and Label over icon.

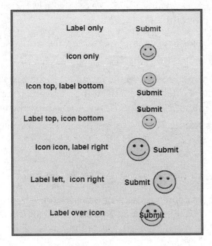

- **Behavior.** The Behavior options affect the appearance of the button when the button is clicked. The None option specifies no highlight when the button is clicked. Invert momentarily inverts the colors of the button when clicked. Outline displays a keyline border around the button, and Push makes the button appear to move in on Mouse Down and out on Mouse Up.

- **Icon and Label State.** Three choices are available in the list when you select Push in the Behavior pull-down menu. Up displays the highlight action when the mouse button is released. Down displays the highlight action when the mouse button is pressed. Rollover changes the icon when a second icon has been added to the rollover option. When the user moves the mouse cursor over the button without clicking, the image changes to the second icon you choose — much like a rollover effect you see on Web pages.

- **Label.** If you've selected a layout type that includes a label, type text in the field box for the label you want to use. Labels are shown when one of the options for the layout includes a label view with or without the icon.

- **Choose Icon.** When you use an icon for a button display, click Choose Icon to open the Select Icon dialog box. In the Select Icon dialog box, use a Browse button to open a navigation dialog box where you locate a file to select for the button face. The file can be a PDF document or a file compatible with converting to PDF from within Acrobat. The size of the file can be as small as the actual icon size or a letter-size page or larger. Acrobat automatically scales the image to fit within the form field rectangle drawn with the Button tool. When you select an icon, it is displayed as a thumbnail in the Select Icon dialog box.

> **TIP** An icon library can be easily created from drawings using a font such as Zapf Dingbats or Wingdings or patterns and drawings from an illustration program. Create or place images on several pages in a layout application. Distill the file to save out as a multiple-page PDF document. When you select an icon to use for a button face, the Select Icon dialog box enables you to scroll pages in the document. You view each icon in the Sample window as a thumbnail of the currently selected page. When the desired icon is in view, click OK. The respective page is used as the icon.

- **Clear.** You can eliminate a selected icon by clicking the Clear button. Clear eliminates the icon without affecting any text you added in the Layout field box.

- **Advanced.** Notice the Advanced button at the top of the Options tab. Clicking the Advanced button opens the Icon Placement dialog box where you select attributes related to scaling an icon. You can choose from icon scaling for Always, Never, Icon is Too Big, Icon is Too Small to fit in the form field. The Scale option offers choices between Proportional and Non-proportional scaling. Click Fit to bounds to ensure the icon placement fits to the bounds of the field rectangle. Sliders provide a visual scaling reference for positioning the icon within a field rectangle.

Barcode options

Barcode fields have unique options designed to work with barcode scanners. You have options from pull-down menus and pop-up dialog boxes opened from buttons, as shown in Figure 34.22. In order to make choices for the items in the Options pane in the Barcode Field Properties dialog box, you need to know what parameters are used by your barcode scanner, fax server, or document scanner. Setting the options requires reviewing the documentation supplied by the hardware used to scan barcodes.

FIGURE 34.22

The Options tab for the Barcodes requires setting options conforming to the tools you use to scan barcodes.

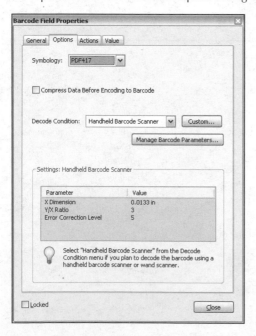

Actions properties

The Actions tab enables you to set an action for any one of the eight field types; the attribute choices are identical for all fields. The same action items available for links, Bookmarks, and page actions are also available to form fields. Click the Actions tab and the pane changes, as shown in Figure 34.23.

CROSS-REF For more information on selecting action types, see Chapter 22.

From the Select Trigger pull-down menu, you make choices for different mouse behaviors that are assigned to invoke the action. From the menu options you have choices for:

- **Mouse Up.** When the user releases the mouse button, the action is invoked.
- **Mouse Down.** When the user presses the mouse button, the action is invoked.
- **Mouse Enter.** When the user moves the mouse cursor over the field, the action is invoked.
- **Mouse Exit.** When the user moves the mouse cursor away from the field, the action is invoked.
- **On Focus.** Specifies moving into the field boundaries through mouse movement or by tabbing to the field. As the cursor enters the field, the action is invoked.
- **On Blur.** Specifies moving away from the field boundaries through mouse movement or by tabbing to the field. As the cursor exits the field, the action is invoked.

Actions assigned to the cursor movements are similar to those in the context of creating links. You first select the trigger, and then select an action type from the Select Action pull-down menu. Click the Add button to add the action to the Actions list.

The action is assigned to the mouse cursor option when you click Add. The default is Mouse Up. When Mouse Up is selected, the action is invoked when the mouse button is released.

FIGURE 34.23

Actions are available for all field types.

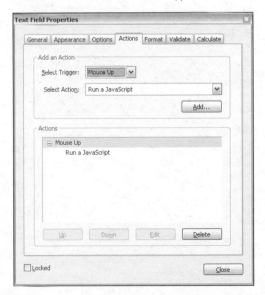

CAUTION Trigger choices other than Mouse Up may sometimes complicate filling in form fields for end users. Just about any program dealing with link buttons has adopted the Mouse Up response to invoke an action. Many users often click down, think about what they are doing, and then move the mouse away without releasing the button. This behavior enables the user to change his/her mind at the last minute. Deviating from the adopted standard might be annoying for a user.

When you click the Add button, a dialog box specific to the action type you are adding opens. The actions listed in this dialog box are the same as those in the Link Properties dialog box discussed in Chapter 22. Turn back to Chapter 22 for examples of how the following action types work. A few of the more important action types used with form fields include importing form data, resetting a form, submitting a form, and showing and hiding a field.

Importing form data

You can export the raw data from a PDF file as a Form Data File (FDF) that can later be imported into other PDF forms. To import data, you use a menu command from the list of action types (Import Form Data) or create a JavaScript. Rather than retyping the data in each form, you can import the same field data into new forms where the field names match exactly. Therefore, if a form contains field names such as First, Last, Address, City, State, and so on, all common field names from the exported data can be imported into the current form. Those field names without exact matches are ignored by Acrobat.

NOTE In earlier versions of Acrobat, you also had an option to Execute a menu item that appears in the Select Action pull-down menu. From the menu items you could select Import (or Export) Data. In Acrobat 8, the Execute a menu item options have been greatly reduced and you can no longer manage data using this action type. For more information on the items available with the Execute a menu item action type, see Chapter 22.

PDF WORKFLOW The Import Data to Form command enables you to develop forms for an office environment or Web server where the same data can easily be included in several documents. When designing forms, using the same field names for all common data is essential. If you import data and some fields remain blank, recheck your field names. You can edit any part of a form design or action to correct errors.

Resetting a form

This action is handy for forms that need to be cleared of data and resubmitted. When the Reset a form action is invoked, data fields specified for clearing data when the field was added are cleared. When you select Reset a form and click the Add button, the Reset a Form dialog box opens. You make choices in this dialog box for what fields you want to clear. Click the Select All button and all data fields are cleared when a user clicks on the button you assign with a Reset a form action. When you use this action, associating it with Mouse Up to prevent accidental cursor movements that might clear the data and require the user to begin over again is best. Reset a form can also be used with a Page Action command. If you want a form to be reset every time the file is opened, the latter may be a better choice than creating a button.

Acrobat's Data Search

When a data file is identified for an import action, Acrobat looks to the location you specified when creating the action. Acrobat also searches other directories for the data. On the Macintosh, Acrobat looks to the Reader and Acrobat User Data directories for the data file. On Windows, Acrobat looks to the Acrobat directory, Reader directory, current directory, Windows directory, and Application Data directory. If Acrobat cannot find the data file, a dialog box opens containing a Browse button to prompt the user to locate the data file.

NEW FEATURE When you design a form and view the form in either Edit or Preview mode, select Forms ⇨ Clear Form to reset a form. Using this command is handy if you have not yet added a Reset button to your form.

CROSS-REF For more information on using page actions, see Chapter 22.

Submitting a form

Form data can be e-mailed or submitted to Web servers. You can design forms so users of the Adobe Reader software can submit data via e-mail or to Web servers. When using the Submit a form action, you have access to options for the type of data format you want to submit.

CROSS-REF For more information on submitting form data, see Chapter 35.

Format properties

The General, Appearance, and Actions tabs are available for all field types. Option attributes are available for all field types except digital signatures. The options vary significantly depending on which field type is used. For a quick glance at the tab differences according to field type, take a look at Table 34.1.

TABLE 34.1

Tab Options for Field Types in the Field Properties Window

Field Type	Appearance	Options	Actions	Format	Validate	Calculate	Selection Change	Signed	Value
Button	X	X	X						
Check Box	X	X	X						
Combo Box	X	X	X	X	X	X			
List Box	X	X	X				X		
Radio Button	X	X	X						
Text	X	X	X	X	X	X			
Signature	X		X					X	
Barcode	X	X	X						X

As shown in Table 34.1, the Format, Validate, and Calculate tab options are only available for Combo Box and Text field types. To access the Format tab, select either of these field types. The Format options are the same for both field types.

When you click the Format tab, you'll find a pull-down menu for selecting a format category. To define a format, open the Select format category and choose from the menu choices the format you want to assign to the Text or Combo Box field. As each item is selected, various options pertaining to the selected category appear directly below the pull-down menu. When you select Number from the menu choices, the Number Options appear as shown in Figure 34.24.

FIGURE 34.24

When you choose either Combo Box or Text as the field type, you can select data format options from the Format tab.

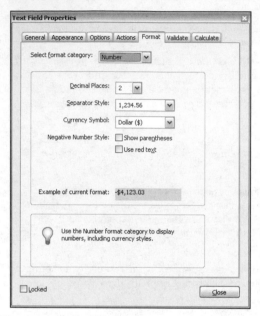

The Select format category menu options include:

- **None.** No options are available when None is selected. Select this item if no formatting is needed for the field. An example of where None applies would be a text field where you want text data such as name, address, and so on.

- **Number.** When you select Number, the Number Options choices appear below the Select format category pull-down menu. The options for displaying numeric fields include defining the number of decimal places, indicating how the digits are separated (for example, by commas or by decimal points), and specifying any currency symbols. The Negative Number Style check boxes enable you to display negative numbers with parentheses and/or red text.

- **Percentage.** The number of decimal places you want to display for percentages is available when you select Percentage from the pull-down menu. The options are listed for number of decimal places and the separator style.

- **Date.** The date choices offer different selections for month, day, year, and time formats.

- **Time.** If you want to eliminate the date and identify only time, the Time category enables you to do so, offering choices to express time in standard and 24-hour units and a custom setting where custom formats are user-prescribed in a field box.

- **Special.** The Special category offers formatting selections for Social Security number, Zip code, extended Zip codes, phone numbers, and an arbitrary mask. When you select Arbitrary Mask, a field box is added where you define the mask. The acceptable values for setting up an arbitrary mask include:

  - **A.** Add *A* to the arbitrary mask field box, and only the alphabetical characters A – Z and a – z are acceptable for user input.

  - **X.** When you add *X* to the arbitrary mask field box, most printable characters from an alphanumeric character set are acceptable. ANSI values between 32 – 166 and 128 – 255 are permitted. (To learn more about what ANSI character values 32 – 166 and 128 – 255 are translated to, search the Internet for ANSI character tables. You can capture Web pages and use the tables as reference guides.)

  - **O.** The letter *O* accepts all alphanumeric characters (A – Z, a – z, and 0 – 9).

  - **9.** If you want the user to be limited to filling in numbers only, enter *9* in the Arbitrary Mask field box.

- **Custom.** Custom formatting is available by using a JavaScript. To edit the JavaScript code, click the Edit button and create a custom format script. The JavaScript Editor dialog box opens where you type the code. As an example of using a custom JavaScript, assume that you want to add leading zeros to field numbers. You might create a JavaScript with the following code:

```
event.value = "000" + event.value;
```

The preceding code adds three leading zeros to all values supplied by the end user who completes the form field. If you want to add different characters as a suffix or prefix, enter the values you want within the quotation marks. To add a suffix, use

```
event.value = event.value + "000";
```

Validate properties

Validate helps ensure proper information is added on the form. If a value must be within a certain minimum and maximum range, select the radio button for validating the data within the accepted values. (See Figure 34.25.) The field boxes are used to enter the minimum and maximum values. If the user attempts to enter a value outside the specified range, a warning dialog box opens, informing the user that the values entered on the form are unacceptable.

FIGURE 34.25

Validate is used with Combo Box and Text field types to ensure acceptable responses from user-supplied values.

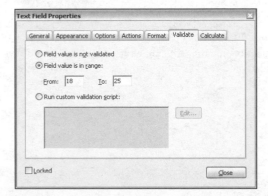

Selecting the Run custom validation script radio button and clicking the Edit button enables you to add a JavaScript. Scripts that you may want to include in this window would be those for validating comparative data fields. A password, for example, may need to be validated. If the response does not meet the condition, the user is denied access to supplying information in the field.

Calculate properties

The Calculate tab (supported in Text and Combo fields) in the Field Properties window enables you to calculate two or more data fields. You can choose from preset calculation formulas or add a custom JavaScript for calculating fields, as shown in Figure 34.26.

FIGURE 34.26

The Calculate tab offers options for calculating fields for summing data, multiplying data, and finding the average, minimum, and maximum values for selected fields. In addition, you can add custom calculations by writing JavaScripts.

The preset calculation formulas are limited to addition, multiplication, averaging, assessing the minimum in a range of fields, and assessing the maximum in a range of fields. For all other calculations you need to select the Simplified field notation or Custom calculation script radio button and click the Edit button. In the JavaScript Editor, you write JavaScripts to perform other calculations not available from the preset formulas. Simplified field notation is written in the JavaScript editor and follows syntax similar to writing formulas in spread sheets. JavaScripts, also written in the JavaScript Editor, require you to know JavaScript as it is supported in Acrobat.

CROSS-REF For more information on calculating data, see Chapters 35 and 36.

Selection Change properties

The Selection Change tab, shown in Figure 34.27, is available for List Box fields only. If a list box item is selected, and then a new item from the list is selected, JavaScript code can be programmed to execute an action when the change is made. As with the other dialog boxes, clicking the Edit button opens the JavaScript Editor dialog box where you create the JavaScript code.

A variety of uses exist for the Selection Change option. You might want to create a form for consumer responses for a given product—something such as an automobile. Depending on information preceding the list box selection, some options may not be available. For example, a user specifies "four-door automobile" as one of the form choices, and then from a list, that user selects "convertible." If the manufacturer does not offer a convertible for four-door automobiles, then through use of a JavaScript in the Selection Change tab, the user is informed that this selection cannot be made based on previous information supplied in the form. The displayed warning could include information on alternative selections that the user could make.

FIGURE 34.27

The Selection Change tab is available only for List Box fields. When using a Selection Change option, you'll need to program JavaScript code to reflect the action when a change in selection occurs.

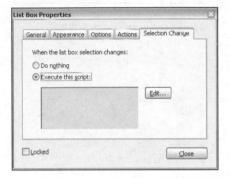

Digital Signature fields properties

The Digital Signature tool enables you to create a field used for electronically signing a document with a digital signature. The Signed tab offers options for behavior with digital signatures as follows:

- **Nothing happens when signed.** As the item description suggests, the field is signed but no action takes place upon signing.

- **Mark as read-only.** When signed, the selected fields are changed to read-only fields, locking them against further edits. You can mark all fields by selecting the radio button and choosing All fields from the pull-down menu. Choose All fields except these to isolate a few fields not marked for read-only, or select Just these fields to mark a few fields for read-only.

- **This script executes when the field is signed.** Select the radio button and click the Edit button to open the JavaScript Editor. Write a script in the JavaScript Editor that executes when the field is signed.

Digital signatures can be used to lock data fields. You can also use them to indicate approval from users or PDF authors, or you may want to display a message after a user signs a form. In Figure 34.28, a JavaScript was added to the Digital Signature Signed Properties.

The script in this example instructs a user to print the form and hand-deliver it to the accounting department. A dialog box opens after the user signs the form.

CROSS-REF For setting up digital signatures and finding out more information related to signing documents, see Chapter 26.

FIGURE 34.28

For custom actions when a user signs a form, use a JavaScript.

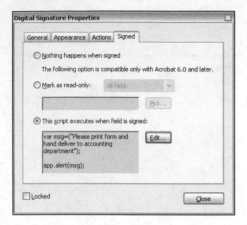

Barcode properties

The unique property settings in the Barcode field are located in the Value tab. Options in this tab are only available with barcode fields, as shown in Figure 34.29. You have options for Encoding from a pull-down menu offering a choice between XML and Tab Delimited data.

FIGURE 34.29

The Value tab appears only in Barcode fields.

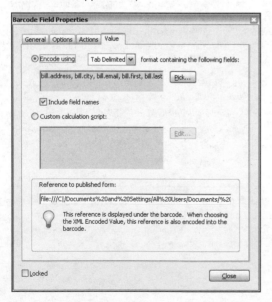

Click the Pick button and the Field Selection dialog box opens as shown in Figure 34.30. You use this dialog box to determine what field data are added to the barcode. Uncheck those items you don't want added, such as buttons that invoke actions, temporary calculation fields, and so on. The Include field names text box offers an option to include field names along with the data in the barcode.

Click Pick and check the items you want to appear as data in the barcode.

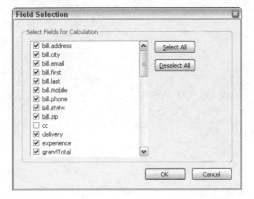

An additional box appears for adding a Custom calculation script. Click the radio button and click Edit to open the JavaScript Editor.

Using the Properties Bar

Many of the appearance attributes you apply in the Field Properties Appearance settings, you can also apply with the Properties Bar. The Properties Bar can be used if the Field Properties window is either opened or closed. As a matter of standard practice, you'll often use the Properties Bar while the Field Properties window is closed. Notwithstanding the options excluded for font selection with check boxes and radio buttons, the options in the Properties Bar are identical for all form tools.

The options available to you include changing field appearances and text. You can make selections for field fills and strokes, line widths, font selection, and font point sizes. To make an appearance change on a field, select the field with the Select Object tool. Make appearance and font changes by clicking buttons in the Properties Bar or making selections from pull-down menus.

Managing fields

For purposes of explanation, I'll use the term *managing fields* to mean dealing with field duplication, deleting fields, and modifying field attributes. After you create a field on a PDF page, you may want to alter its size, position, or attributes. Editing form fields in Acrobat Professional is made possible by using one of several menu commands or returning to the respective Field Properties window.

Organizing fields

To edit a form field's properties, use the Select Object tool or the form tool for the respective field type and double-click the field rectangle. The Properties window opens after you double-click with either tool. You can also use a context-sensitive menu opened from using either tool and clicking on the form field to be edited. At the bottom of the context-sensitive menu, select the Properties command. Also, you can select Forms ⇨ Show Field Properties. Using any one of the menu commands opens the Properties dialog box.

To select multiple fields of different types, you must use the Select Object tool. If you want to select the same field types, use the tool that was used to originally create the fields. Ctrl/Shift+click each field to be selected. You can drag through fields to select them, but you can do so only with the Select Object tool.

When you select multiple fields and choose Properties from the context-sensitive menu, options in the General tab, the Appearance tab, and the Actions tab are available for editing. Specific options for each different field type require that you select only common field types. For example, you can edit the appearance settings for a group of fields where the field types are different. However, to edit something like radio button field options for check mark style, you need to select only radio button fields in order to gain access to the Options tab.

TIP If the fields you want to select are located next to each other or you want to select many fields, use the Select Object tool and drag a marquee through the fields to be selected. When you release the mouse button, the fields inside the marquee and any fields intersected by the marquee are selected. The marquee does not need to completely surround fields for selection — just include a part of the field box within the marquee.

Duplicating fields

You can duplicate a field by selecting it and holding down the Ctrl/Option key while clicking and dragging the field box. Fields can also be copied and pasted on a PDF page, between PDF pages, and between PDF documents. Select a field or multiple fields, and then choose Edit ⇨ Copy. Move to another page or open another PDF document and choose Edit ⇨ Paste. The field names and attributes are pasted together on a new page.

TIP To ensure that field names are an exact match between forms, create one form with all the fields used on other forms. Copy the fields from the original form and paste the fields in other forms requiring the same fields. By pasting the fields, you ensure all field names are identical between forms and can easily swap data between them. If you have JavaScripts at the document level, then use the Document ⇨ Replace Pages command when you want to populate a form having a similar design to an original form.

Moving fields

You can relocate fields on the PDF page by selecting the Select Object tool in the Advanced Editing toolbar, and then clicking and dragging the field to a new location. To constrain the angle of movement, select a field with the Select Object tool, press the Shift key, and drag the field to a new location. For precise movement, use the arrow keys to move a field box left, right, up, or down. When using the arrow keys to move a field, be certain to not use the Shift key while pressing the arrow keys because doing so resizes field boxes as opposed to moving them.

Deleting fields

You delete fields from PDF documents in three ways. Select the field and press the Backspace key (Windows) or Delete key (Macintosh). You can also select the field and then choose Edit ⇨ Delete, or open a context menu and choose Edit ⇨ Delete. In all cases, Acrobat removes the field without warning. If you inadvertently delete a field, you can Undo the operation by choosing Edit ⇨ Undo.

Aligning fields

Even when you view the grids on the PDF page, aligning fields can sometimes be challenging. Acrobat simplifies field alignment by offering menu commands for aligning the field rectangles at the left, right, top, and bottom sides, as well as for specifying horizontal and vertical alignment on the PDF page. To align fields, select two or more fields and then open a context menu and select Align, as shown in Figure 34.31. The alignment options for Left, Right, Top, Bottom, Horizontally, and Vertically appear in a submenu.

FIGURE 34.31

Open a context menu using the Select Object tool on one field in a group of selected fields and choose Align from the menu.

Acrobat aligns fields according to the first field selected (the anchor field appearing with a red highlight). In other words, the first field's vertical position is used to align all subsequently selected fields to the same vertical position. The same holds true for left, right, and top alignment positions. When you use the horizontal and vertical alignments, the first field selected determines the center alignment position for all subsequently selected fields. All fields are center aligned either vertically or horizontally to the anchor field.

TIP   Fields are aligned to an anchor field when multiple fields are selected and you use the align, center, distribute, and size commands. The anchor field appears with a red border whereas the remaining selected field highlights are blue. If you want to change the anchor (the field to be used for alignment, sizing, and so on), click on any other field in the selected group. Unlike other multiple object selections, you don't need to use the Shift key when selecting different fields from among a group of selected fields. All fields remain selected until you click outside the field boundaries of any selected field.

You can distribute fields on a PDF page by selecting multiple fields and choosing Distribute from a context-sensitive menu. Select either Horizontally or Vertically for the distribution type. The first and last fields in the group determine the beginning and ending of the field distribution. All fields within the two extremes are distributed equidistant between the first and last fields.

CROSS-REF   For an example of how to use the Distribute command, see "Creating multiple copies of fields" later in this chapter.

Center alignment is another menu command available from a context menu. When you choose Center ⇨ Vertically or Horizontally from a context menu, the selected field aligns to the horizontal or vertical center of the page. Choose Center ⇨ Both to align a field to the center of a page. If multiple fields are selected, the alignment options take into account the relative positions of the field boxes and center the selected fields as a group while preserving their relative positions.

Sizing fields

Field rectangles can be sized to a common physical size. Once again, the anchor field determines the size attributes for the remaining fields selected. To size fields, select multiple field boxes, and then open a context menu and choose Size ⇨ Height, Width, or Both. Size changes are made horizontally, vertically, or both horizontally and vertically, depending on which menu option you choose. To size field boxes individually in small increments, hold down the Shift key and move the arrow keys. The left and right arrow keys size field boxes horizontally, whereas the up and down arrow keys size field boxes vertically.

Creating multiple copies of fields

To create a table array, select fields either in a single row or single column and open a context menu. From the menu options, select Place Multiple Fields. The Create Multiple Copies of Fields dialog box opens, as shown in Figure 34.32. In the Create Multiple Copies of Fields dialog box, enter a value in the field box for Copy selected fields down (for creating rows of fields) or Copy selected fields across (to create columns of fields). In Figure 34.32, I created three fields and wanted my duplicated fields to be added below the top row. Notice when you make selections in the Create Multiple Copies of Fields dialog box with the Preview check box enabled, you see a dynamic preview in the document for how the fields appear when duplicated.

NOTE You can also create a table array by first creating a single field and selecting options for both Copy Selected Fields down and Copy Selected Fields across.

FIGURE 34.32

To create a table array, select a row or column of fields and open a context menu. Select Place Multiple Fields and make selections in the Create Multiple Copies of Fields dialog box for the number of rows or columns to be duplicated.

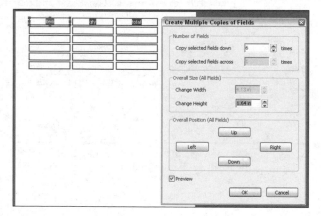

If you want to add both rows and columns, you can supply values in both field boxes for the desired number of columns and rows. The Change Width and Change Height field boxes enable you to adjust the field distance respective to each other — editing the values does not change the physical sizes of the fields. Click the Up/Down buttons for moving all fields vertically or the Left/Right buttons to move fields horizontally. When the preview box is enabled, you'll see a preview of the duplicated rows and columns before you accept the attribute choices by clicking OK.

If, after you click OK, you need to polish the position of the new fields, you can move the top and bottom fields (for aligning single columns), then open a context menu and choose Distribute ⇨ Vertically or Horizontally — depending on whether you're adjusting a row or column.

When using the Distribute command, you can only distribute single rows or columns. If you attempt to select all fields in a table and distribute several rows or columns at once, the results render an offset distribution that most likely creates an unusable alignment.

Duplicating fields

Using the Place Multiple Fields menu command from a context menu enables you to create table arrays or individual columns or rows only on a single page. If you want to duplicate fields either on a page or through a number of pages, another menu command exists for field duplication.

You can use the Duplicate command to duplicate fields, however, in most circumstances when you want to duplicate a field, press the Ctrl/Option key down and click+drag a field. The field and the properties are duplicated. If you need to change the field name, open the properties dialog box and edit the Name in the General properties.

Setting attribute defaults

If you spend time formatting attributes for field appearances, options, and actions, you may want to assign a default attribute set for all subsequent fields created with the same form tool. After creating a field with the attributes you want, open a context menu and select Use Current Properties as New Defaults. The properties options used for the field selected, when you choose the menu command, becomes a new default for that field type. As you change form tools and create different fields, you can assign different defaults to different field types.

Setting field tab orders

You have three options for setting the tab order on a form. This is one item you should address before saving your final edited form. You should be able to press the Tab key to enter the first field on a page and tab through the remaining fields in a logical order to make it easy for the end user to fill in your form. Before deploying your form, be sure to check the tab order.

The fist option you have for setting Tab order is in the Pages panel. Open the Pages panel and open a context menu on the page where you want to set tab order. Select Properties from the menu options and the page Properties dialog box opens, as shown in Figure 34.33. By default the Tab Order pane opens with options for setting tab order by making radio button selections.

FIGURE 34.33

To set tab order, open the Pages panel and open a context menu on the page where you want to edit the tab order. Select Properties from the menu choices and click on Tab Order in the Pages Properties dialog box.

The options for setting tab order include the following:

- **Use Row Order.** Tabs through rows from left to right. If you want to change the direction for tabbing through fields, choose File ⇨ Properties. Click on Advanced in the left pane and select Right Edge from the Binding pull-down menu. When you select Use Row Order and the document binding is set to Right Edge, the tab order moves from right to left.

- **Use Column Order.** Tabs through columns from left to right, or right to left if you change the binding as described in the preceding bullet.

- **Use Document Structure.** When selecting this option, you first need to use a PDF document with structure and tags. The tab order is determined by the structure tree created by the original authoring application when the file was exported to PDF.

- **Unspecified.** The default for all documents you created in earlier versions of Acrobat that you open in Acrobat 6 through 8 have the Unspecified option selected. Unless you physically change the tab order to one of the preceding options, the tab order remains true to the order set in Acrobat 5 or earlier.

The order in which you create fields and add them to a page is recorded. If you happen to create a row of fields, and then change your mind and want to add a new field in the middle of the row, Acrobat tabs to the last field in the row from the last field created. Changing the tab orders in the Page Properties won't help you fix the problem when the fields need to be reordered.

Fortunately, you do have more options for setting tab orders. Select Forms ⇨ Edit Fields ⇨ Set Tab Order and you are prompted in a dialog box to make a choice for setting the tab order, as shown in Figure 34.34.

FIGURE 34.34

Select Forms ⇨ Edit Forms ⇨ Set Tab Order to open a dialog box where you can choose to have Acrobat automatically order the tabs or manually adjust the tab order.

Click Yes in the dialog box and Acrobat makes a best guess for creating the tab order. If you need to manually set the tab order click No and the field tab order arrangement is shown as you see in Figure 34.35.

As shown in Figure 34.35, the numbers in the field boxes show you the current tab order. You can manually adjust tabs by clicking in the fields. When you click on a field, that field becomes the first field in the tab order. Clicking subsequent fields numbers the fields in ascending order.

If you want to start in the middle of a group of fields press Ctrl/Option+click on the field preceding the field you want to reorder. For example, if you want to change a field order from any number to number 6, Ctrl/⌘+click field number five. Move the cursor where you want number 6 to follow. When finished ordering the fields, press the Esc key.

FIGURE 34.35

Numbers on each field show you the current tab order.

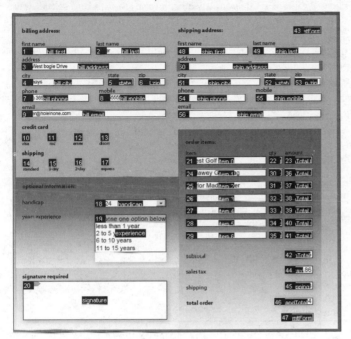

Creating a PDF Form

Forms vary greatly in design and the requirements for field types. It's not possible to develop a standard work-flow that you apply to creating all forms. Sometimes you'll use tools and menu commands on one type of form and on other forms you'll approach the editing a little differently using other tools and menu commands.

As an example for creating a PDF form in Acrobat Professional, let's look at a form containing most of the form fields you have available to you and see how the form, shown earlier in Figure 34.35, is constructed.

This form was created in Adobe Illustrator CS2. Because the form field locations are not clearly defined with lines or boxes, Acrobat can't automatically populate the fields using the Run Form Field Recognition command. The white shapes were created in Illustrator and Acrobat does not interpret them as being form fields. This form needs to be manually constructed using the form tools.

Adding text fields

Starting at the top-left side of the form, I'll add some text fields. Because these fields don't fall in a column or row order, I can't use the Place Multiple Fields menu command. Each field in the billing address area needs to be created manually.

To add fields to the first section in the billing address area, use the following steps.

STEPS: Manually adding text fields to a form

1. **Zoom in to the area where you want to add fields.** Creating forms requires you to zoom in and out a lot. Select the Marquee Zoom tool and zoom into the area you want to work on, as shown in Figure 34.36.

 For more information on page navigation and zooming, see Chapter 5.

2. **Select the Text Field tool and add a text box to the first field position.** The Properties dialog box opens.

3. **Name the field.** By default the General properties appear. Type a name for the first field. In this example, I use a parent/child name and type **bill.first** in the name field, as shown in Figure 34.36. This section of the form relates to billing information, hence, I use bill as my parent name.

FIGURE 34.36

Create a field and type a name in the General properties dialog box.

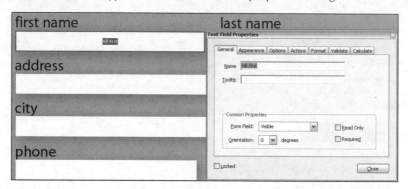

4. **Set Appearances.** Because my design clearly shows the form field positions, I don't need any borders or fills for the fields. In this example, I select None for Border and Fill colors from pull-down menus. For the font size, I typed 10 in the Font Size text box and used the default Helvetica font.

5. **Set Options.** Click the Options tab. For the name fields, I don't need spelling checked and all the check boxes for other items are disabled in the Options pane.

For the text fields in this section, you don't need to address any formatting or calculations. Leave the Properties dialog box open and we'll move to the next step.

Because you've set attributes for one text field, it makes sense to capture those attributes and apply the same attributes to subsequent fields you add to the form requiring the same characteristics. You can handle this in one of two ways. Open a context menu on the selected field and choose Make Current Properties New Defaults or copy the field. Copying a field is a better solution than dragging open new rectangles because you can keep the sizes precisely the same.

NOTE As you work on adding fields to a form, be certain to save your work regularly. Press Ctrl/⌘+S to update your edits.

To continue adding new fields, use the steps that follow.

STEPS: Duplicating fields

1. Press the Ctrl/Option key and click the first field. Press the Shift key and drag the field horizontally to the next position. Adding the Ctrl/Option key duplicates the field. Adding the Shift key constrains movement in the direction you first move the field (in this case horizontally).

 You can have either the Text Field tool or the Select Object tool active to duplicate the field by dragging with the modifier keys.

2. **Size the duplicated field.** The horizontal height should stay fixed at the current size. The width of the field needs to be sized unless your target location matches the horizontal width of the copied field. Move the cursor to the center handle on either side of the rectangle and drag the handle horizontally left or right to size the field.

3. **Edit the field name.** Click the general tab and edit the field name. In this example, I change the name to bill.last keeping my parent/child naming convention the same as the first field.

4. **Duplicate the remaining fields.** Follow the same steps to add the remaining fields in the billing section on the form by Ctrl/Option+click+Shift and drag to position and then resize the fields to sizes on the layout. Be certain to name all fields using the same parent name. (Note that when duplicating some fields you won't want to constrain the movement. Release the Shift key and simply Ctrl/Option+drag to duplicate the field and freely move it to position.)

5. **Edit the telephone fields.** Some additional attributes can be assigned for telephone numbers. After duplicating one field and sizing it to the first telephone number field and editing the field name, click the Format tab. Select Special from the Select format category pull-down menu and choose Special. Click Phone Number in the list, as shown in Figure 34.37.

FIGURE 34.37

Select Phone Number in the Format tab in the Text Field Properties dialog box to format a telephone number.

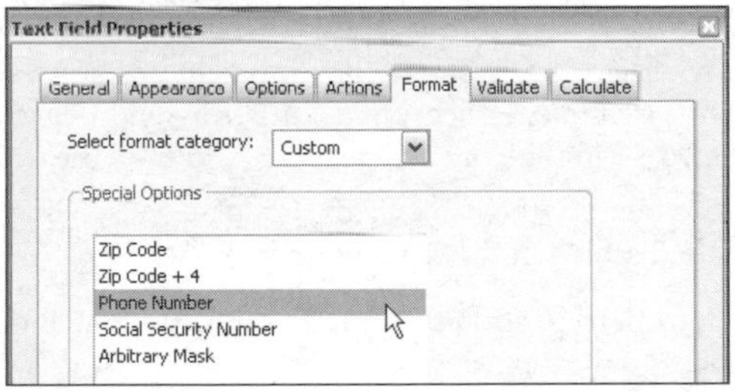

TIP You can visit the bill.state field properties and click Options. Click the Limit of check box and type 2 in the text box to limit the number of characters to 2 characters (for a US state abbreviation). Another option is to copy and paste a field having state or country names in a combo list. You can visit any Web site having a form with a pull-down menu showing all states (and/or countries) and convert the Web page to PDF using the Create PDF ⇨ From Web Page command. Open the PDF in Acrobat and Acrobat recognizes all fields on the HTML converted page. Copy a state field and paste it into your document. Rename the field and set the Appearance attributes.

Another set of fields appears in the order items section. The item, qty, and amount fields are assembled in a table. We can use another method for duplicating fields using the Create Multiple Copies of Fields dialog box.

To use the Create Multiple Fields dialog box, use the following steps.

STEPS: Creating Multiple Copies of Fields

1. **Create the first top row of fields.** Using the Text Field tool create a field for the Item category in the first row. In the Text Field Properties dialog box, don't use a parent/child name. In this example, I used item as the field name. Set the Appearance settings the same as other text fields created thus far and click the Number tab. Because these fields are going to be calculated we have to define the field format as a number. Select Number from the Select format category pull-down menu and format the number with decimal places. Optionally, you can add a currency symbol as shown in Figure 34.38.

FIGURE 34.38

Click Format and set attributes for a number.

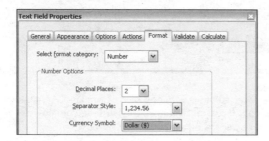

2. **Duplicate the field.** Ctrl/Option+click+Shift and drag to the second field location in the top row. Change the field name to **qty** (abbreviated for quantity). Size the field and duplicate it for the third field position and name that field **total**.

3. **Select the fields.** Click the Select Object tool and drag through all three fields to select them.

4. **Duplicate the fields.** Open a context menu on one of the selected fields and choose Place Multiple Fields. In the Create Multiple Copies of Fields dialog box enter the number of rows to create (note that you need to also include the first row). In my example, I added 7 for the number of rows to duplicate.

   You can make adjustments for positioning the rows in the Create Multiple Copies of Fields dialog box, but you have an easier option using the Distribute command when fields are relatively equidistant from each other. Click OK and the fields are duplicated. Note that Acrobat added child names to all your fields.

5. **Drag the bottom row of fields to position.** Select the three fields in the bottom row by dragging through them with the Select Object tool. Click one of the selected fields, and press the Shift key, and then drag straight down to position in the last row.

6. **Distribute the fields.** Select the first column of fields using the Select Object tool. Open a context menu and select Distribute ⇨ Vertically, as shown in Figure 34.39. Repeat the same steps for each column.

FIGURE 34.39

Select one column of fields and select Distribute ➪ Vertically from a context menu.

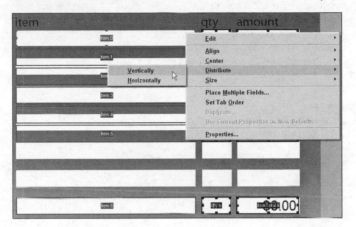

> **NOTE** You can't distribute the three columns with one menu command. Acrobat won't position all three columns in the proper locations. You need to distribute columns and rows individually. After distributing all three columns, the fields fall into the proper positions.

On the example form there are some additional fields used for calculations. You can create the fields and format them using the steps to create a new field or by duplicating a single field. The additional settings you need to make for these fields are in the Calculate tab. For more information on calculating form data, see Chapter 35.

We still have one section on the form needing text fields in addition to the calculation fields, but I'll hold off on those and cover adding the shipping address fields later in this chapter in the section "Using the Fields Panel."

Adding radio buttons and check boxes

Whereas all the text fields, signature fields, combo and list boxes on a form typically require unique field names, radio buttons and check boxes are frequently created using the same field names.

To discover some methods for creating radio buttons and check boxes, follow these steps.

STEPS: Adding radio buttons and check boxes to a form

1. **Zoom in to a target location on your form where you want to add radio buttons.** Continuing with the same example form, I zoom into the credit card and shipping section on the form.

2. **Add a radio button.** Click the radio button tool and draw a rectangle to size for the radio button.

3. **Name the field.** The General properties dialog box opens with the General pane in view. Type a name for your field. In my example, I use cc for the field name for identifying a credit card abbreviation. Note that a parent/child name is not used for this field.

4. **Set the Appearance attributes.** Because my form design clearly indicates the field location, I choose no border and no fill in the Appearance properties. For the type font, the default font uses a symbol and is not editable. For the size of radio buttons and check boxes, leave the Auto setting at the default.

5. **Set the Options.** Click Options in the Radio Button Properties dialog box and type an export value in the Export Value text box. My first radio button is for a Visa card choice so I typed "visa" for the export value, as shown in Figure 34.40.

Type an export value in the Options pane.

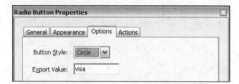

6. **Duplicate the first radio button.** Ctrl/Option+drag with the Shift key to duplicate the button and move it to the second radio button position. Open the Options pane and edit the export value. In this case I change the export value to mc (for MasterCard). Note that you don't change the field name.

7. **Continue duplicating fields and changing export values.** Duplicate the remaining fields and change the export values for each field. I used amex (American Express) and discvr (Discover) for the two remaining fields.

8. **Create a check box.** Select the Check box tool and create a rectangle in the first check box field position. Type a name in the General properties. In my example, I used delivery for the field name. Set the Appearance options and the Options settings the same as those settings made for radio buttons adding unique export values for each field. Create duplicate fields using the same key modifiers when dragging fields to duplicate them.

Adding Combo and List Boxes to a form

Combo and List Boxes are added using the individual tools for each field type. Many of the options you have for both field types are the same. These fields don't require parent/child names. Because there is only one combo box and one list box on the example form, just be certain to name the fields differently.

When you open the Options pane for each field, you type text in the Item text box and click the Add button. You can arrange the list items by selecting them and clicking the Up and Down buttons.

One important consideration with both combo boxes and list boxes is deciding what default value you want each box to display on the form. Whatever you select in the list window for each field type becomes the selected default showing up on the field when the form opens in an Acrobat viewer. If you want a blank field to be the default selection, add a few spaces in the Item text box or type a series of dashed lines and click the Add button. Select the item in the list window and click the Up button to move it to the top. In Figure 34.41, I used a series of dashed lines and moved the item up in the list window. Before closing the Combo Box Properties dialog box, make certain you have the item selected that you want to appear as the default item.

FIGURE 34.41

Select the item you want to appear as the default in a combo or list box; then close the Properties dialog box.

Adding a Button field

One of the last items remaining on my example form is a button field. The text appearing for Reset Form and Submit Form use buttons to invoke actions. To create a Button field, follow these steps.

STEPS: Adding Button fields to a form

1. **Click the Button tool appearing with an OK icon.**

2. **Drag open a rectangle where you want the button to appear.**

3. **Set the name and appearance properties.** For this example, I'll create a button to reset a form. For the name in the General properties, I typed resetForm and in the Appearance properties I chose no border and no fill color. The type is incidental because type won't be added for this field. The text appearing on the document is part of the original design

4. **Select an Action.** Click the Actions tab and select Reset a form from the Select Action pull-down menu. Click the Add button and the Reset a Form dialog box opens.

5. **Select the actions properties.** For the Reset a form action, you pick the fields you want to reset. You can choose to clear all field data or select individual fields for remaining intact while the checked fields are cleared.

   For this form, I want to leave all the billing address fields intact. This way, if the end user adds personal identity information and wants to clear the order data, the user won't need to reenter the personal data.

   Click the Add button after selecting the Reset a form action and the Reset a Form dialog box opens, as shown in Figure 34.42. By default all fields on the form are checked. Scroll the list and uncheck the fields that you don't want cleared.

6. **Click OK.** The button is now set for clearing form data.

The Submit Form button is added very similar to the way you add a reset button. For now, we'll pass this button by and take a look at it in Chapter 35 when we look at handling form data.

On my example form, other than the shipping address fields and the calculations text fields, the only item remaining is the signature field. Select the Signature tool and draw a rectangle at the target location on a form. For this example form, no special formatting was needed other than naming the field and adding Appearance settings, which are similar to the other fields added to the form.

FIGURE 34.42

Uncheck fields you want to remain undisturbed.

Using the Fields Panel

The Fields panel provides you all the same menu commands as you find in menu selections from the Forms menu. The advantage of using the Fields panel lies in some context menu commands available when opening a context menu on a field. If you have difficulty in locating a field when viewing a multi-page form or a form with an extraordinary number of fields, the Fields panel can be very helpful. All fields are listed in alphabetical order that makes it easy to select a field and open the field Properties dialog box using a context menu command. Additionally, you can globally change parent names using the Fields panel that comes in handy on the example form I used in this chapter.

That second set of fields for the shipping address section on my example form still needs to be populated. I could follow the same steps to duplicate fields and set attributes as I did in the "Adding text fields" section earlier in this chapter. However, all the fields in the shipping section are identical in terms of format attributes as the fields I've already created in the billing address section of the form. The easiest way to create the shipping address fields is to duplicate the billing address fields. However, if I copy and paste the billing address fields, I can't globally change the field names for the duplicated set. Attempting to do so will also change the billing address fields and the result will be duplicated fields with the same field names. That means that if you have two fields named lastname and you type text in one field, the text you type is duplicated in the second field having the same field name.

To get around the problem for creating a second set of fields with unique field names, use the Fields panel in the following steps.

STEPS: Renaming fields in the Fields panel

1. **Copy a group of fields.** Open a document containing fields you want to copy and change the field names. For these steps, I use the same example file as mentioned earlier in this chapter.

   Click the Select Object tool and marquee the fields you want to copy. From the Edit menu select Copy. The fields are copied to the clipboard and remain there until you copy something else.

2. **Create a new blank document.** Select File ➪ Create PDF ➪ From Blank Page. A new blank page is created in the Acrobat Document pane and appears in front of your form.

3. **Paste the copied fields.** Select Edit paste and the fields appear selected on the blank page. Leave the fields selected as you continue the steps.

4. **Open the Fields panel.** Select View ➪ Navigation Panels ➪ Fields and the Fields panel opens. The Fields panel opens and displays all the fields in a form. Because I pasted just the billing fields, only those fields are listed in the Fields panel. The fields are listed at the top beginning with the parent name (bill), and then below the parent name are all the fields belonging to that parent, as shown in Figure 34.43. The task at hand is to change just the parent name. In my example, I want to change the parent name from bill to ship so that fields such as bill.first, bill.last, bill.address, and so on are changed to ship.first, ship.last, ship.address, and so on.

FIGURE 34.43

All the fields are listed beginning with the parent name followed by the individual field names.

5. **Rename the fields.** Open a context menu on the parent name. Be certain to open the context menu on the top-most name where you see just the parent name (in my example bill) and not a field with both a parent and child name. From the menu choices, select Rename Field as shown in Figure 34.44.

FIGURE 34.44

Open a context menu on the parent name and select Rename Field.

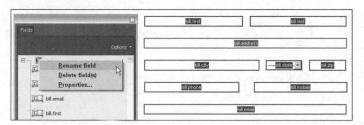

The field name (in this case, the parent name) becomes selected. Type new text and press the Enter key. All field names are changed to the new parent name followed by the same child names as when you copied the fields.

6. **Copy the fields.** With the fields still selected, choose Edit ➪ Copy. The fields with the new names are copied to the clipboard.

7. **Paste the fields into your form.** Click the Close box on the blank page file without saving the document and your original form should appear in the Document pane. Select Edit ➪ Paste and the fields are pasted into your form.

8. **Position the fields.** When the fields are pasted, they remain selected. To keep them selected and easily manageable use the arrow keys on your keyboard to move the fields. Press the Shift key and strike the up-, down-, left-, and right-arrow keys to move the fields together 10 pixels at a time. Release the Shift key and you can nudge the fields into position by moving them 1 pixel at a time.

9. **Save your form.** After you complete editing a form, select File ➪ Save As and overwrite your form to optimize it.

If the edits are complete, you need to perform a little debugging. Double check all the fields with real data and tab through the fields. When you copy/paste fields or use modifier keys to duplicate fields, you'll need to rearrange the tab order. Perform any additional editing that's needed and select File ➪ Save As to overwrite the file again.

Summary

- Acrobat forms are not scanned documents converted to PDF. They are dynamic and can include interactive elements, data fields, buttons, and JavaScripts.

- Automatic form fill-in is enabled in the Preferences dialog box. Form fields can be displayed on PDF pages with a highlight color to help identify field locations.

- Data fields are created from many different field types including text, buttons, combo boxes, list boxes, signatures, check boxes, radio buttons, and barcodes.

- You set all data field attributes in the Field Properties window. Properties can be described for fields by selecting the tabs labeled Appearance, Options, Actions, Calculations, or other tabs associated with specific field types.

- Acrobat 8 has a new Forms menu where you select specific menu commands pertaining to form editing.

- In Acrobat 8, you edit forms in Edit mode and fill in or check form functionality in Preview mode.

- You can edit fields with a context-sensitive menu. Acrobat has several editing commands used for aligning fields, distributing fields, and centering fields on a PDF page.

- Field duplication is handled in a context menu. You can duplicate fields on a page to create tables with the Place Multiple Fields command, or duplicate fields across multiple pages with the Duplicate command.

- The Forms panel dynamically lists all fields created in a PDF file. The panel menus and options can be of much assistance in editing field names and locating fields.

- Field names need to be unique for each field you add to a form. By using root names and extensions, you can reduce the amount of time needed for designing forms and creating calculations.

Chapter 35

Working with Form Data

After you get a handle on creating form fields, as covered in Chapter 34, you'll want to know some things about managing data to help economize your efforts when working with forms and performing routine calculations on data fields. When forms are completed, you have the option of printing a form, compiling form data distributed via e-mails, or sending the data off to a host that processes the field data. In this chapter, I cover data management from calculating field data to importing, exporting, submitting data, and compiling data using the new Distribute Form and Compile Returned Forms features in Acrobat 8.

As is the case with most of the content in Chapter 34, this chapter is also targeted at users who aren't using Adobe Designer. Most of what is covered in this chapter can be handled by Designer. However, if you're a Macintosh user or you want to do some editing in Acrobat Professional, what follows is strictly related to working with data and form fields in Acrobat. Furthermore, the content is restricted to using Acrobat tools and commands for data management. No discussion on using server products, other than a brief explanation about additional products you can acquire, is covered in this chapter.

For Windows users, the best opportunity you have when working with form data is to create your form designs in Adobe Designer as explained in Chapter 33. Designer provides you with XDP, XML, and TXT as export data format options and XDP, XM, and XFD as import format options. With Acrobat form data imports and exports you get FDF, XFDF, XFD, TXT, and a version of XML, which is much different than what is provided with Designer. If you're a serious PDF form designer, Adobe Designer is your best solution for forms creation and handling data.

Setting Up the Environment

As described in the previous chapter, creating form fields requires use of the Forms tools. The same toolbars used in Chapter 34 are used to handle form field editing and field creation. For setting up the Toolbar Well, refer to Chapter 34.

In addition to using form fields, having access to menu commands helps you manage data while working with forms. Nothing specific needs to be opened for menu access. As you move through this chapter, I'll cover the various menu options used for data management and the new menu commands introduced in Acrobat 8.

Calculating Field Data

More often than not, you'll want to create forms that use some kind of calculation for data fields. Calculations might be used for summing data, calculating averages, adding complex formulas, assessing field responses, or many other conditions where results need to be placed in separate fields.

Acrobat offers you a few limited built-in functions for performing math operations. When your needs extend beyond these simple functions, you need to write JavaScripts. Some math operations, as simple as subtracting data or producing a dividend, require use of a JavaScript.

Even though I address JavaScript in some detail in the next chapter, you need to begin learning about JavaScript as it pertains to calculating data. Therefore, I'll start this chapter with some examples on using the built-in functions for calculations in Acrobat and move on, later in this section, to cover some JavaScript basics.

Formatting for calculations

Math operations can be performed on data fields without any formatting applied to either the fields to be calculated or the result field. Although doing so is not required, as a matter of practice applying formats to all fields where calculations are made and to those fields participating in the calculation result is a good idea. As you create a PDF form, you may need to use a particular format that eventually is required either in the formula or for the text appearance in the result field. Rather than going back to the fields and changing the format, you'll save time by supplying proper formats as you create fields.

When creating text fields, open the Format tab in the Text Field Properties window and select the format you want for the field. If Number is the desired format, select Number from the pull-down menu and make choices for the number of decimal places, the display for negative numbers if it applies, and the use of a currency symbol if it applies.

CROSS-REF   For more information on using the Text Field tool, see Chapter 34.

Many times, once you get a field formatted, you want to replicate the attributes on subsequent fields. When you set the attributes for one field, select the field with the Text Field tool or the Select Object tool and open a context menu. Select Use Current Properties as New Defaults. As you create additional fields, the new defaults are applied to all subsequent text fields. If you create a field that needs a different format, you can change the format for the new field without affecting the defaults.

Using the preset calculation formulas

Preset math calculations include sum, product, average, minimum, and maximum. After formatting fields, select the field where you want the result to appear and click the Calculate tab in the Text Field Properties dialog box, as shown in Figure 35.1. For adding a column or row of data, select the *Value is the* radio button. The default is sum (+). Click the down-pointing arrow to open the pull-down menu to make formula choices from the list of other preset formulas.

 NOTE Be certain numeric data is formatted using number format options in the Format tab of the Text Field Properties dialog box when creating form fields.

FIGURE 35.1

To add a preset calculation to a field, click the Calculate tab in the Text Field Properties dialog box. Select the calculation formula from the pull-down menu next to the "Value is the" radio button.

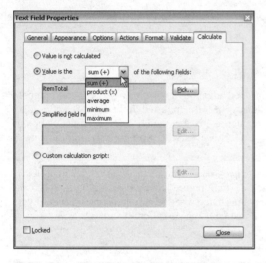

For summing data, leave the default as it appears and click the Pick button. The Field Selection dialog box opens, as shown in Figure 35.2. You can see the fields added to your form and grouped together. To sum a group of fields, select the check box to the left side of each field you want to add to the formula.

Click OK to leave the Field Selection dialog box and return to the Calculate properties. Click Close, and the calculation is ready. In this example, the sum of the data for the selected fields updates as the user enters data in the fields assigned to the calculation.

For performing other preset calculations, you follow the same steps. Select the formula you want to use from the pull-down menu options and select the check boxes for all fields you want to add to the calculation.

 NOTE When using the Average formula, Acrobat averages all fields regardless of whether the fields used in the formula contain data. If you have three fields, but only two have values — for example, 3 and 3 — Acrobat returns a result of 2 ((3+3+0) ÷ 3=2). The preset formula doesn't take into consideration whether or not a field has data in it. To perform an average calculation where you want to average only fields containing a response, you need to write a JavaScript.

FIGURE 35.2

Identify the fields used for the calculation in the Field Selection dialog box by selecting the check box for each field name.

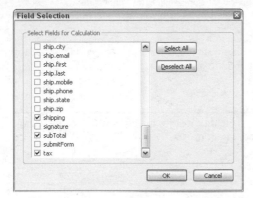

Summing data on parent names

If you've read Chapter 34, you may remember that I mentioned advantages when using parent/child names for form fields. As you can see in Figure 35.2, all the fields in your form are listed in the Field Selection dialog box. If you want to sum data in large tables, clicking on all the boxes in the Field Selection dialog box to select fields for columns or rows in a table can take some time. However, when you use parent/child names, the task is much easier.

In Figure 35.3, the Field Selection dialog box is open and a check mark appears next to the itemTotal field. Notice below this field you have a group of fields using same parent name. The child names 0 through 6 are calculated with just the check box selection made on the parent name when summing fields together. If you write calculation scripts, your scripting is made much easier when using parent/child names.

FIGURE 35.3

If you select the Value is the Sum(+) of the following fields and check a parent name in the Field Selection dialog box, all child field names are added in the calculation.

Imagine a table that contains 25 rows of data with a total field at the bottom of each column; it has 10 columns across the page. By using the parent name in the formula, you can easily create total fields at the bottom of the page by duplicating fields and editing the parent names in the Calculate properties as was described in Chapter 34.

Using hidden fields

Complex formulas can be written in the JavaScript Editor. However, if you aren't up to speed in JavaScript programming or you want to simplify the code you write, you may want to break down a series of calculations and place results in separate fields. For example, suppose you want to calculate the result of A – B * C. If you don't know the code to create the calculation to first subtract two values and multiply the result by another value, you can use separate fields to hold results. In this example, you need a field to hold the result of A – B. In another calculation, you take the result field containing A – B and multiply it by C.

On the PDF form, the result of A – B is not needed for user input — it's simply a container to use as part of the larger formula. To help avoid confusion, you can hide the field. When data are contained in hidden fields, the data can still be used for calculations.

To create such a field, add a text field anywhere on a page and add the calculation in the Calculate properties. In the General properties, select Hidden from the Form Field pull-down menu. If you need to edit a hidden field, you can do so with either the Text Field tool or the Select Object tool.

When using hidden fields, you can create calculations and access the fields in the Field Selection dialog box or use parent names in the Calculate properties as described in the preceding section.

Using Simplified field notation

In addition to enabling you to perform simple calculations and write JavaScripts, the Calculate pane also offers you an option for using Simplified field notation. When you select the radio button for Simplified field notation and click Edit, the JavaScript Editor dialog box opens. In the dialog box you don't write JavaScript code. The code added for this calculation type is based on principles used with spreadsheet formulas.

Simplified field notation can be used in lieu of writing JavaScripts for many different math operations. As an example, suppose you want to calculate a sales tax for a subtotal field. To calculate an 8 percent sales tax with a JavaScript you would open the JavaScript Editor and type the following code:

```
1. var f = this.getField("subtotal");
2. event.value = Math.round(f.value * 8) / 100;
```

As an alternative to using JavaScript, select the Simplified field notation radio button and click the Edit button. In the JavaScript Editor, you type the following code to produce the same sales tax calculation:

```
1. subtotal * .08
```

Notice in the JavaScript code you need to identify each field used in a calculation and assign a variable to the field name. Line 1 of the preceding JavaScript code assigns the variable f to the field subtotal. Notice that in the Simplified field notation the field name does not get assigned to a variable. You simply use all field names as they appear on the form and introduce them in your formulas.

Using JavaScripts

You need to write JavaScripts for all calculations that cannot be made with either the preset formulas or the Simplified field notation method. If you are a novice, you'll find writing simple JavaScripts to be a relatively easy task if you understand a few basic concepts in regard to performing simple calculations, as follows:

- **Variables.** Variables consist of using characters (alphabetical and numeric) to identify a field, a result, or other variable used in the formula. You can use something as simple as a character name or a long descriptive name. Variables might be f, amt, item0grandTotal, Price Amount, and so on.

■ **Identifying fields.** You need to tell Acrobat in the JavaScript code that you want to assign a variable name to a field that exists on your form. The syntax for assigning a field to a variable name might look like

```
var f = this.getField("item");
```

In the preceding code the field name appears in quote marks and the quote marks are contained within parentheses. The variable f is assigned to the field name item on this (the current open) document.

■ **Algebraic formulas.** After identifying the variables, you use standard algebraic notation. Therefore, to divide one value by another (something not available to you with the preset formulas), you might enter the code shown in Figure 35.4 in the JavaScript Editor as follows:

```
1. var f = this.getField("amount");
2. var g = this.getField("itemNumber");
3. event.value = f.value / g.value;
```

FIGURE 35.4

Select Custom calculation script in the Calculation properties and enter the code to perform the calculation in the JavaScript Editor.

The first line assigns the variable f to the field amount. The second line of code assigns the variable g to the field itemNumber. The third line of code is the formula where f is divided by g. The result is placed in the field where you add this script in the JavaScript Editor. The trigger to put the result in the field where the calculation is coded is the event.value item.

Without going into loops and more complex formulas, the beginning Acrobat forms author can do quite a bit by just following the preceding simple example. The code is all case sensitive and your field names need to be identical to the name of the field on the form as you code in the JavaScript Editor.

Managing Form Data

Managing form data, whether it is Acrobat PDF form data or data in the Adobe LiveCycle Designer environment, essentially falls into two categories. One category is industrial strength data management satisfying needs of business enterprises and organizations requiring sophisticated tools beyond Acrobat for collecting and routing data. The other category is local data management you handle using Acrobat and tools within the Acrobat environment for individual and small business needs.

In regard to enterprise data management solutions, you'll find a number of server products developed by Adobe Systems to satisfy the most demanding data management needs. Adobe markets products like Adobe LiveCycle Forms (formerly Adobe LiveCycle Form Server) and about 12 other server products designed to satisfy just about any business need for managing documents and data. All of the Adobe Server products can be found at www.adobe.com/products/server.

Another avenue for enterprise solutions is the Adobe Partner community. Adobe works together with a great number of third party developers to provide an array of solutions satisfying vertical market needs. You can learn more about Adobe partners and the solutions they offer at www.adobe.com/enterprise/partners. In addition to Adobe Systems and Adobe partners, several independent developers provide more server solutions and services to help you define needs and customize your data management requirements. You can find out more about some other developers by searching the Internet.

In short, when it comes to handling data for large scale business transactions you need to look outside Acrobat and find a provider that can deliver the solution that fits your specific needs. One thing to keep in mind is you don't use Acrobat to take form data for invoices and sales receipts for companies such as Sprint, Boeing, and Time-Warner, and expect to write backend code to route data. You need Acrobat and some help from other products designed to work with PDF data.

In terms of local data management, and because this book is about Acrobat and what you can do with the product as it comes out of the box, you have many tools and commands for managing form data. To begin a discovery for handling form data, let's start by looking at how to import and export PDF data in a local environment.

Importing and exporting data

One of the great benefits of importing and exporting data is the ability to eliminate redundancy in recreating common data used in different forms. Among the most common redundant data entries is your personal identifying information. Adding your name, address, phone number, and so on to forms is often a common practice. In an environment where you need to supply your personal identity information, you could keep an FDF (Form Data File) or XML file on your hard drive and load it into different PDF forms, thereby eliminating the need to re-key the data.

> **NOTE** FDF is a legacy format supported by earlier versions of Acrobat prior to version 6. This is a proprietary Adobe format and not a data file you can use with a lot of applications or open the file for editing. XML is a newer format introduced in Acrobat 6 and available in Acrobat 7 and 8. You can open XML files in a text editor and edit the data. You can also view the data in a Web browser. I make references to FDF/XML throughout the chapter for those who need to work with legacy files not supporting XML and for those Acrobat 6 or grater compatible files where XML can be used. If you have a choice when exporting or importing data in Acrobat 6 compatible files or greater, use XML as your default data file format.

In order to swap data between forms, you need to observe one precaution. All data fields used to import FDF/XML data must have identically matched names to the fields from which the data were exported, including case sensitivity. Therefore, the data from a field called Name in a PDF that exports to FDF/XML

cannot be introduced in a PDF with a field called name. Setting up the fields is your first task, and then you can move on to data exports and imports. To clarify this concept further, I first show you how to design forms with common fields, and then export and import data.

Creating common fields

To be certain your field names match exactly between two forms, the easiest and most efficient way to duplicate the fields is to copy fields from one form and paste them into another form. In Figure 35.5, I have a form designed as an annual tournament schedule. Some of the data from my schedule card is identical to some data on a scorecard shown in Figure 35.6.

FIGURE 35.5

A tournament schedule card populated with data

After copying fields from the schedule card and pasting the matching fields into the scorecard, I know I have an exact field match and the data exported from the populated form will find the matching fields in the form shown in Figure 35.6.

TIP If you need to copy all fields on the form, select the Select Object tool and press Ctrl+A (Windows) or ⌘+A (Macintosh) to select all fields. Press Ctrl+C (Windows) or ⌘+C (Macintosh) to copy all the selected fields to the Clipboard.

FIGURE 35.6

The scorecard form uses some of the exact same data as the schedule card.

Exporting FDF/XML data

After the forms have been created with matching fields, complete a form and fill in all the data fields. If you have some fields on one form that have been excluded on a second form, Acrobat ignores any field data where it can't find a matching field name. Therefore, you need not worry about having the same number of fields on both documents.

Exporting data from a PDF file is handled with a menu command. If you want to export the data from a form, choose Forms ⇨ Manage Form Data ⇨ Export Data. A dialog box opens where you name the file and designate a destination for the FDF/XML data.

NOTE   The default export format when you choose Forms ⇨ Manage Form Data ⇨ Export Data is Acrobat FDF (*.fdf* Files). In the Export Form Data As dialog box you can also choose to export data as Acrobat XFDF, XML, or Text formats.

When you select the menu command, the Export Form Data As dialog box opens. By default, the name of your PDF file and an .fdf (or .xml) extension are supplied in the File name field box. This name is used as the FDF/XML filename. If you want to change the name, edit text in the File name field, but be certain to leave an .fdf (or .xml) extension after the filename. Click Save and the file is saved as a Forms Data Format file (or XML file).

The file you save as FDF/XML contains only the data from the form fields. Therefore, the file size is considerably smaller than the PDF that produced the data. The file can be stored on a local disk, network server, or sent as an e-mail attachment to another user. If another user has a PDF with the same field names, the data can be imported with either Acrobat Standard or Acrobat Professional.

Importing FDF/XML data

As with form data exports, importing FDF/XML data in PDF forms is handled with menu commands. Choose Forms ➪ Manage Form Data ➪ Import Data. The Select File Containing Form Data dialog box opens where you can navigate your hard drive and find the FDF/XML file to import.

Select the FDF/XML file to be imported and click the Select button in the dialog box. When you import data from common field names, the fields are populated for all matching fields as shown in my new score-card file after the data import in Figure 35.7. Acrobat ignores all data where no matching fields are found.

FIGURE 35.7

Only data with matching field names is imported. All other data is ignored.

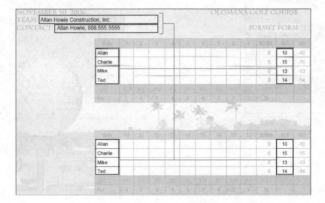

Importing text data

The discussion thus far has been limited to FDF/XML data in Acrobat forms. In addition to using FDF/XML data, you have other options available with different data types. You may receive data files created in database managers or spreadsheets that you want to use in your Acrobat forms. As long as the data exports are properly formatted with text-delimited fields, you can import data saved as text from spreadsheet and database programs.

To understand how Acrobat supports text data, follow these steps.

STEPS: Importing text data

1. **Create a database.** You can use any program capable of exporting data as a text file. In this example, I use Microsoft Excel to create a data file with three records and a row for field names. For the first row in a spreadsheet application, add the exact same names as the field names used in the Acrobat form. All subsequent records (rows) contain the data like the example shown in Figure 35.8.

2. **Add export values for radio buttons and check boxes.** For fields such as check boxes, the data used to denote a checked box is equal to the export value associated with the field in Acrobat. If you use export values like Yes and No, add Yes or No in a data field for the data imported in Check Box fields.

3. **Save the spreadsheet.** Save as text only from your database manager. In this example, I chose File ⇨ Save As and selected Text (tab delimited)(*.txt) in the Microsoft Excel Save As dialog box.

A data file is created in Microsoft Excel (top) with three data records. Each row is a separate record and the cells across each row horizontally represent the field data for the respective record. Row 1 contains the field names that match the PDF form (bottom).

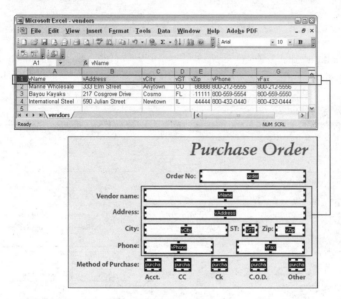

4. **Open the PDF document.** Quit your database manager and open the form to import the data in Adobe Acrobat.

5. **Import the text file.** Choose Forms ⇨ Manage Form Data ⇨ Import Data. The Select File Containing Form Data dialog box opens. From the Objects of type pull-down menu, select Text Files (*.txt). Find the file exported from the database manager and select it. Click the Select button to open the file.

NOTE Each time you use the Forms ⇨ Manage Forms Data ⇨ Import Data menu command, Acrobat defaults to the *.fdf Files of type, expecting you to select an FDF file. Be certain to select Text Files (*.txt) from the Files of type pull-down menu when importing text data. You need to manually access the pull-down menu choice each time you want to import data other than FDF.

6. **Select the data to import.** The Import Data From Delimited Text File dialog box opens. In the dialog box you see the names of the fields appearing at the top of the dialog box. Below the title fields are the records in the database. Only one record can be imported in the form. Therefore, you need to tell Acrobat which record you want to import. Click anywhere in a record row to select the desired record, as shown in Figure 35.9. In this example, the first record data is selected for import.

FIGURE 35.9

Select a record to import by clicking anywhere in the record row you want to import.

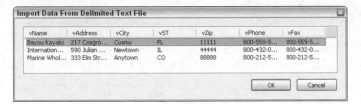

7. **Import the data.** Click OK and the data are imported in the form for all matching field names, as shown in Figure 35.10.

FIGURE 35.10

If your fields are named properly, the data are imported into matching fields in the PDF form.

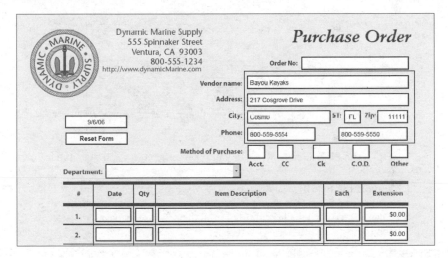

CROSS-REF For more information on using Page Actions and learning more about limitations with the Execute a menu item command, see Chapter 22.

Creating spreadsheets from form data

Exporting data to spreadsheets can be handled in a few different ways. You can select from two different menu commands to export data that can be opened in a program such as Microsoft Excel or you can aggregate form data from multiple forms into a single spreadsheet.

Using Import Buttons and Page Actions

Another method you have available for importing data is to create a button or page action and use the Import form data action type. Create a button or open the Pages panel and select Page Properties from a context menu. In the Page Properties dialog box, shown in the following figure, click the Actions tab and select the Page Open trigger (this menu choice opens by default). From the Select Action pull-down menu, choose Import form data and click the Add button.

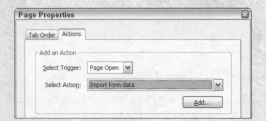

The Select File Containing Form Data dialog box opens. Select the data file you want to import and click the Select button. Save your file and when the document opens on the target page Acrobat automatically imports data from the data file. You might use this method when you prepare forms such as a purchase order form for a vendor where you want your identifying information and the vendor information imported when preparing the order form. If you use a text file containing several vendors, click the vendor you want to use and the respective data are imported.

You'll note that you have no option for exporting data using a button or page action. In earlier versions of Acrobat you could get around the absence of an action type for exporting data by using an Execute a menu item action type. In Acrobat 8, however, the Execute a menu item list is more limiting and you can't select a menu command from the list to export data using a button, Bookmark, link, or page action.

Note that is you add the Import Form Data action to a button, link, bookmark, or page action, the only file format supported by the action type is FDF data. If you want to import other file formats such as TXT or XML, you need to write a JavaScript.

Exporting data to a spreadsheet

Two different menu commands enable you to export PDF data and open the exported data in a spreadsheet. You can open a PDF document and select Forms ⇨ Manage Form Data ⇨ Export. In the Export Form Data As dialog box, open the Save as type (Windows) pull-down menu or Format pull-down menu (Macintosh) and select Text as the file format. Click the Save button and the data can be opened in a spreadsheet program.

A new command in Acrobat 8 enables you to export PDF data to a spreadsheet from a single file or multiple files. Select Forms ➪ Manage Form Data ➪ Merge Data Files Into Spreadsheet. This command works when you want to export data from a single file, but the real power in using the command is when you export data from multiple files. If you have a single PDF document and you use this command, the result is similar to exporting data from the Export command. Using the Export command exports to a text file and using the Merge Data Files Into Spreadsheet command exports to a CSV comma delimited file or XML file. The text file created from the Export command is also a delimited file. As a result, you see very little difference when either file is opened in a program such as Microsoft Excel. All the data fall into rows and columns.

Aggregating data from multiple files into a single spreadsheet

As I mentioned before, the real power in using the Merge Data Files Into Spreadsheet command is when combining data from multiple PDFs into a spreadsheet. To see how this new command in Acrobat 8 works, use the following the steps.

STEPS: Combining data from multiple PDFs into a spreadsheet file

1. **Collect some forms with different data fields.** To follow these steps, start with a form saved as different files having unique data. Save four or five forms to a common folder. In my example I used a simple form, as shown in Figure 35.11. Notice that the fields are highlighted so you can clearly see the form fields. I edited this form and changed the data for three additional forms and saved them all to the same folder.

FIGURE 35.11

Use the same form with different data saving each file to a common folder.

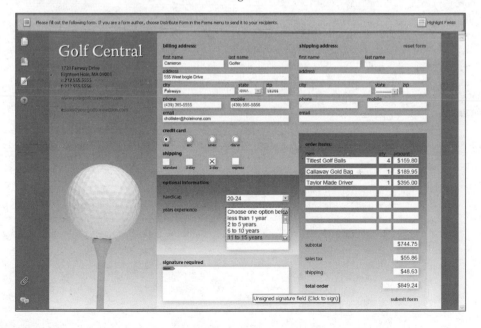

   You can add files from different folders to merge the data into a spreadsheet.

2. **Select Forms ⇨ Manage Form Data ⇨ Merge Data Files into Spreadsheet.** Note that you don't need a document open in the Document pane. If a document is open, the merge command doesn't use the open file. The Export Data From Multiple Files dialog box opens.

3. **Add Files.** Click Add Files and select the files you want to combine together in a single spreadsheet.

   The Select File Containing Form Data dialog box opens. Select the files you want to combine together and click Select. When you return to the Export Data From Multiple Forms dialog box, the files you selected are shown in a window as you can see in Figure 35.12.

4. **Click Export.**

5. **Name and save the file.** When you click the Export button in the Export Data From Multiple Forms dialog box, the Select Folder to Save File dialog box opens. In this dialog box you locate a target folder and type a name for your file. By default the name provided in the File name text box is report. Edit the name and type a descriptive name for the file you save.

6. **Click Export.**

7. **View the file.** In a very short time the Export Progress dialog box opens. Click the View File Now button and Microsoft Excel is launched displaying the merged data as shown in Figure 35.13.

FIGURE 35.12

Selected files are shown in the Export Data From Multiple Forms dialog box.

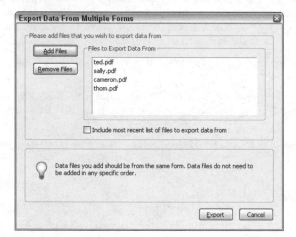

FIGURE 35.13

The aggregated data file opens in Microsoft Excel.

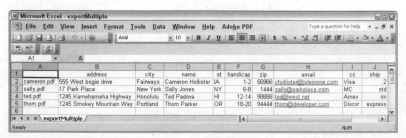

Aggregating FDF/XML data

When you create a Submit button, as I explain in the next section "Submitting and Receiving Data Forms," Adobe Reader users can't submit a PDF document back to you unless the form is enabled with Reader usage rights. If a form is not enabled, Reader users can submit the FDF/XML data back to you (without the PDF document) and you can use the Import Data command to import the FDF/XML data into a PDF form residing on your computer.

If you send files for Reader users and the data are returned to you as FDF/XML, you can aggregate the data in a spreadsheet using the same menu commands as you do when aggregating form data derived from PDF documents. Using the Forms ➪ Manage Form Data ➪ Merge Data Files into Spreadsheet menu command follow the same steps as when merging PDF forms data. When you click Add Files and open the Select File Containing Form Data dialog box, notice the formats supported in the Files of type (Windows) or Format (Macintosh) pull-down menu. You find FDF/XML included as a format as well as XML and XFDF. These file formats are the same formats supported when using the Export Data command.

Submitting and Receiving Data Forms

We've come a long way with data exports, imports, submissions, and retrieval in Acrobat. Several generations ago, back in Acrobat 5, Adobe Reader users needed to view a PDF document inside a Web browser to submit form data. With the last few releases of Acrobat, Adobe Reader users could click a button designed for submitting data on PDF forms inside Acrobat without having to view the PDF in a Web browser. However, one limitation did prevail. Adobe Reader users could only submit form data. The original populated PDF form couldn't be sent back to the PDF author.

CROSS-REF   For more information on viewing PDFs inside Web browsers as inline views, see Chapter 27.

NEW FEATURE   All this has changed in Acrobat 8. Now with the opportunity to enable PDF forms for Reader users, you can create Submit buttons that include the original PDF document along with the form data.

CROSS-REF   For more information on enabling PDF documents with Reader usage rights, see Chapter 19.

Creating a Submit Form button

As you work through several new menu commands for forms handling in Acrobat 8, a dialog box may open and alert you that Acrobat can't find a Submit button. For an example, take a look at Figure 35.14. This dialog box opens when you select the Forms ➪ Distribute Form menu command while attempting to distribute a form that does not have a Submit button that can be detected by Acrobat.

FIGURE 35.14

When a Submit button is required for an action and Acrobat can't detect a Submit button, a warning dialog box opens.

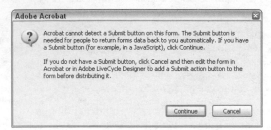

Before you look at using the Distribute Form menu command, you need to know a little something about creating Submit buttons. For a quick and easy way to learn how to create a Submit button, look over the following steps.

STEPS: Adding a Submit button to a PDF document

1. **Open a PDF form with form fields in Acrobat Professional.** You can use a form that has a clearly defined area in the design where the Submit button appears, or set the button attributes to identify the Submit button using a label as a button face. In Figure 35.15, I have text in my form design for a Submit button, but the button has not yet been added to the form.

   Notice also in this form a digital signature field at the bottom of the page. Because I want the recipient to sign the form, the entire PDF file needs to be sent to sender.

FIGURE 35.15

The design of this form has a clear indication for the end user to find a button to submit the form.

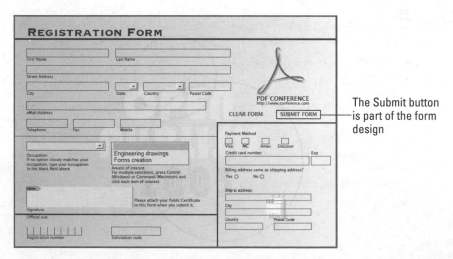

2. **Click the Button tool in the Forms toolbar and create a button on the form.** Draw a rectangle with the Button tool to create a button field.

3. **Name the button.** After drawing a rectangle with the Button tool and releasing the mouse button, the Button Properties dialog box opens. Type a name in the Name text box and press the Enter key to register the name.

TIP   When creating forms on a page, get in the habit of pressing the Enter key on your keyboard after naming a field. This action is optional when you add a single field and either click a tab in the Properties dialog box or click the Close button. However, when duplicating fields and quickly moving around a document, you can sometimes find that a new name is not registered in the Properties dialog box. Clicking the Enter key on your keyboard changes the name before you move on to other tasks.

4. **Set the Appearance properties.** Click the Appearance tab and remove any border or fill from the button appearance. If you don't have a submit icon or name on your design, you'll want to use button text to notify the end user that a Submit button exists. Click the color swatch and select blue for the text color. Blue is something most users will identify as a button because blue text links are commonplace in Web browsers. Set the text attributes so text neatly fits within the button rectangle.

5. **Add text for the button face.** If you have a design element, such as the Submit Form text shown in Figure 35.15, this is optional. If you don't have anything on the page clearly displaying a Submit button, click the Options tab and type Submit Form in the Label text box. Note that the Layout pull-down menu defaults to the Label only menu item that displays the text you type in the Label text box.

6. **Select the Submit a form action.** Click the Actions tab and select Submit a form from the Select Action pull-down menu. Click the Add button and the Submit Form Selections dialog box opens. (See Figure 35.16.)

7. **Enter an e-mail address in the first text box at the top of the page where you see Enter a URL for this link.** In the text box, type: **mailto:<your e-mail address>**. Be certain you have the syntax correct before moving on. (See Figure 35.16.)

8. **Select an Export Format.** Click the "PDF The complete document" radio button, as shown in Figure 35.16.

NOTE   If you want only the FDF/XML data sent back to your e-mail address, click the FDF Include (or XFDF include) button. However, because the form in my example requires a digital signature, the entire PDF needs to be returned.

9. **Click OK to return to the Document pane.**

10. **Enable the PDF with Reader usage rights.** Because you set the attributes for the Submit button to return the PDF document to your e-mail address, you must enable this file or Acrobat won't let you proceed.

   Select Advanced ➪ Enable Usage Rights in Adobe Reader. Click Save when prompted in a dialog box. Your file is now ready to send to users of both Acrobat and Abode Reader. People who receive your form use the Submit button. You can e-mail the form to users or select the new Distribute Form command in Acrobat 8 to send out the form. (See the section "Distributing forms" later in this chapter.)

FIGURE 35.16

Add a return e-mail address using the prefix mailto: and check the radio button to mail back the PDF document.

CROSS-REF For more information on enabling features and using digital signatures in Adobe Reader, see Chapter 19.

The Submit Form Selections dialog box has quite a few options and not all were covered in the preceding steps. Let's take a look at all the options choices you have in this dialog box.

- **Enter a URL for this link.** If you have a data management system or a server product that routes data and manages a database, you can add a URL to the text box. This option requires you to have programming on your server that collects the data when it hits the URL specified in the text box. In you don't have server-side programming to manage the data, your only other option is to add an e-mail address, as shown in Figure 35.16.

- **Export Format.** Along the left side of the dialog box you find several options for the type of export format users can send back to you.

  - **FDF Include.** The FDF data is sent to the server. The three options below the FDF Include item offer you choices for sending the Field data; Comments, which includes any comments created on a form; and Incremental changes to the PDF, which should be used when digital signatures have been used to save updates. Any one or all of the selections can be made for this data type.

  - **HTML.** The data is sent in HTML format. Much as you might create a form on a Web page using HTML and JavaScript, the HTML option processes the same data type.

  - **XFDF Include.** The data are sent in XML format. Two options are available for sending the Field data or the Comments data or both. You cannot submit digital signatures via XFDF.

  - **PDF The complete document.** This option enables you to submit the PDF populated with the field data. This option is useful for Digital Signature workflows or for archiving the complete document. Additionally, if you use bar codes on forms you'll want to have the complete PDF document sent back to you.

■ **Field Selection.** On the right side of the dialog box are options for including all or selected field data in your submission. If fields are to be eliminated, select the Only these button and then click the Select fields button. The Field Selection dialog box opens where you select which fields to use for the data export.

■ **Date Options.** Dates are converted from the format specified on the form to standard date formats when the Date Options check box is enabled.

When the user clicks a Submit button, the form data from the choices you made in the dialog box are sent to the specified URL/e-mail address. Keep in mind that if you do not have the necessary server-side programming, nothing happens to the data and it won't be found on your server. You need intervention from the host to collect and route the data.

TIP If you have a form containing button fields and you want to export the buttons data as well as the text field data, select the Only these radio button in the Submit Form Selections dialog box. The Field Selection dialog box opens after you click the Select Fields button. In the Field Selection dialog box, select the check boxes for all fields you want to submit.

Distributing forms

Deploying PDF forms in Acrobat 7 and earlier has been limited to e-mailing PDFs and using the Submit button for users to mail data back to you. You had to deal with the data on a file-by-file basis without any tools locally on your computer to merge data or display it in a single file source. What was left out of the loop was a method for aggregating data when users returned forms to you — that is, if you don't have a server to manage data.

So far in this chapter, you know there exists a method for aggregating data from PDF forms and exported data using the Merge Data Files into Spreadsheet menu command. But I'm not finished yet. There exists another method in Acrobat 8.

NEW FEATURE The Forms ⬦ Distribute Form command is new in Acrobat 8. When you select this command (or click the Distribute tool in the Forms toolbar or select Distribute Form from the Forms task button pull-down menu) a wizard opens with options similar to what you have available with sharing comments. You follow some steps through several panes and your PDF form is prepared to be distributed to a recipient(s). When the recipient returns the file to you, it again follows similar steps as comments returned to you. Rather than double-click an e-mail attachment to populate a PDF form with comments, double-clicking an e-mail attachment on a distributed form appends the form to a data source where a PDF Package is created.

CROSS-REF For information related to sharing comments, see Chapter 21.

To understand how this marvelous new feature in Acrobat 8 works, let's take a look at the steps involved in distributing a PDF form.

STEPS: Distributing a PDF form

1. **Open a form in Acrobat.** You should start with a blank form that has a Submit button that sends the data back to your e-mail address. (Note that it doesn't matter if you select FDF/XFDF data or the PDF option in the Submit Forms Selection dialog box. The entire PDF document will be returned to you.)

NOTE When you use the Distribute Form command, you don't need to enable the PDF document for Reader users in order for the form to be returned to you.

2. **Open the Distribute Form Wizard.** Select Forms ➪ Distribute Form to open the Form Distribution Options dialog box, as shown in Figure 35.17. This dialog offers two options. You can send the form via e-mail or prepare the form and e-mail it later. Select Send now via email and click OK to open the Distribute Form Wizard.

FIGURE 35.17

Select Send now via email and click OK to open the Distribute Form Wizard.

Note that a link to Adobe's Web site appears in the Form Distribution Options Wizard. Click Check the EULA for details link and a Web page opens where you can review the licensing agreement and the specifics related to the limitations for distributing forms. If in doubt about the distribution restrictions, click the link and review the EULA.

3. **Type your e-mail address in the first pane of the Distribute Form Wizard.** Click the Next button after typing your name and you arrive at the second pane shown in Figure 35.18.

4. **Identify a Data Collection File.** The second wizard pane asks you to identify a Data Collection File. By default, Acrobat creates a file for you in a target location where your original PDF document resides. (See Figure 35.18.) You can click the Browse button to target a new location and create another data file. Leave the settings at the default, but click the Browse button to refresh your memory on where your data collection file resides. Once you are certain to remember the location, click Cancel in the Browse dialog box and click the Next button in the wizard.

FIGURE 35.18

Leave the Data Collection File at the default setting and click Next.

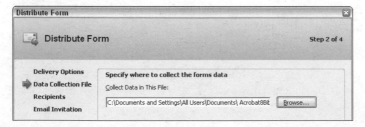

5. **Add recipients.** This pane is similar to the same recipients pane you use with sharing comments. Add e-mail addresses for the recipients in the space provided and click the Next button.

6. **Review the e-mail message.** An automated message appears in the last pane in the wizard. You can edit the message or import a text file. Click Done in the wizard when finished and your file is attached to a new mail message. Click the Send button in your e-mail program and the form is distributed to your recipients.

When a recipient sends a form back to you, it comes back as an e-mail attachment. Double-click the attachment and the Add Completed Form to Data Set dialog box opens, as you see in Figure 35.19.

FIGURE 35.19

Double-click an e-mail attachment from a recipient and the Add Completed Form to Data Set dialog box opens.

The dialog box prompts you to make a decision about where the PDF form is to be saved. You can choose to save the data in the original data collection file created when you first stepped through the Distribute Form Wizard or create a new data set. Leave the default at Add to an Existing Data Set and click OK and your PDF form is added to the data collection. As additional files are received, add the PDF forms to the data collection by double-clicking the e-mail file attachments and clicking OK in the Add Completed Form to Data Set dialog box.

The data collection you append and the one set up for you in the Distribute Form Wizard is a PDF Package. Navigate to the data set file in Acrobat and open it as you would open any PDF document. When the file opens, you see all the returned data on individual forms in a PDF Package, as shown in Figure 35.20.

One difference between the PDF Package created by the Distribute Form Wizard and PDF Packages you created, as explained in Chapter 19, is that the package, shown in Figure 35.20, contains additional tools for Import Data and Export Data. Click the Import Data button and you can append PDFs to the package. Click the Export Data button and you can export the data to a CSV or XML file that you can open in Microsoft Excel with the data combined into a single spreadsheet. Notice the data appearing at the top of Figure 35.20. The data is formatted the same as you see when exporting the data from the PDF Package.

FIGURE 35.20

The data set is a PDF Package. Additional files received from recipients are appended to the package.

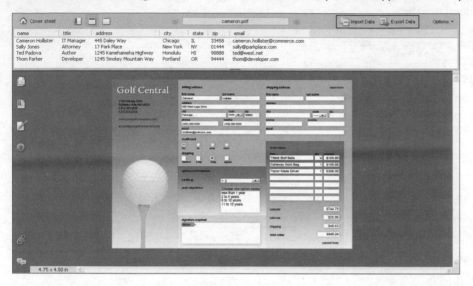

Compiling form data

Suppose you have files that are acquired other than a user clicking a submit button on a form that follows the process described in the "Distributing a PDF Form" steps earlier in this chapter. You might copy files from a flash drive, network server, or have a form e-mailed to you that wasn't part of the invitation you sent to recipients when you chose to Distribute a Form. Can you add these files to your PDF Package?

NEW FEATURE Another new feature in Acrobat 8 is the Compile Returned Forms command appearing in the Forms menu. Select Forms ⇨ Compile Returned Forms (or select the same menu command from the Forms task button) and Acrobat opens the Compile Data dialog box shown in Figure 35.21.

FIGURE 35.21

The Compile Data dialog box enables you to add additional files to a data set.

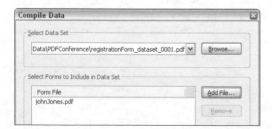

The Compile Data dialog box first asks you to select the data set you want to append to. Click the Browse button and locate the data set created for the forms you are collecting. Click the Add button and locate the files you want to append to the data set. When you click OK, the PDF Package opens in Acrobat showing you the additional files appended to the package.

Using the Forms Tracker

If you have several forms distributed and you're waiting on recipients to send back forms to you, things can quickly get a little disorganized and confusing. What you need is a management system to keep track of the forms currently being reviewed by recipients.

NEW FEATURE   **Fortunately in Acrobat 8 you have a new feature to help you keep your distributed forms organized and tracked. Select Forms ➪ Track Forms and the Forms Tracker opens, as shown in Figure 35.22.**

FIGURE 35.22

The Forms Tracker lists all forms you have distributed and those forms you were asked to fill out.

In the Forms Tracker, you see a list of forms you either distributed to be filled out or forms you were asked to fill out by another user. Click the History button in the left pane and you see a list of all the forms in process. Double-click a file in the list and the original PDF document opens in Acrobat. Click the To Do item in the left pane and you see a list of the files you need to fill out and send back to a PDF author who initiated a distribution session. If you want to search content of the files in the list, type the word(s) you want to search in the text box at the top of the Forms Tracker and press the Enter key on your keyboard. Found results in PDF documents open the respective PDF in the Document pane.

After you've finished a session for collecting forms or submitting them, select a form in the History list and click the Remove button. The form is then deleted from the list.

CROSS-REF   **The Forms Tracker opens in the same window as the Review Tracker. To learn more about the Tracker window, see Chapter 21.**

Summary

- Acrobat offers a few preset calculation formulas used for calculating data. For more sophisticated calculations, you need to use Simplified Notation scripts and JavaScripts.

- When using parent/child names you can easily sum data by adding a parent name in the Calculate properties and selecting the sum (+) menu command.

- Form data can be exported from populated PDF forms to an FDF or XML file. The data can be introduced into any form having matching field names as from where the data were exported.

- To ensure that fields have the same exact names between different forms, copy fields from one document and paste the fields in all other documents.

- Button fields can be created to submit form data from any Acrobat viewer. For Adobe Reader users to submit a PDF with data back to the PDF author, the form needs to be enabled with Adobe Reader usage rights.

- Data can be exported from a PDF document directly to a spreadsheet program.

- A new feature in Acrobat 8 permits you to distribute forms. When the forms are returned to you, you can compile the data in a single PDF document in the form of a PDF Package. Using the Distribute Form menu command does not require you to enable a PDF with usage rights for Adobe Reader users to send the PDF back to you.

- Forms in progress can be managed and organized in the new Acrobat 8 Forms Tracker.

Chapter 36

Understanding JavaScript

With JavaScript you can create dynamic documents for not only forms, but also many other uses such as adding interactivity to files, and viewing options, animation, and similar features not available with Acrobat tools. JavaScript helps you add flare and pizzazz to your PDF files. In Acrobat Standard, you can edit JavaScripts and create JavaScripts using Bookmarks, links, and page actions. However, to get the full range of editing JavaScripts and applying JavaScripts to form fields, you need to use Acrobat Professional.

As with the disclaimer I added in the introduction of this book and in Chapter 33 as it applies to Adobe LiveCycle Designer, this book is also not about JavaScript. It would take another book the size of *Acrobat 8 PDF Bible* to provide complete coverage for all the JavaScript options you have in Acrobat. All I can hope to do in this chapter is provide a starting point in using JavaScript in Acrobat 8 and point you to sources where you can learn more.

For more sophisticated uses and some sound reasoning for coding forms, look at the Acrobat JavaScript Scripting Reference and the Acrobat JavaScript Scripting Guide. Both documents are available from Adobe Systems by logging on to http://partners.adobe.com/asn/acrobat/docs.jsp#javascript.

IN THIS CHAPTER

Getting familiar with JavaScript

Assessing Acrobat viewers and versions

Creating calculations with JavaScript

Adding JavaScripts to document actions

Spawning pages from templates

Working with pop-up menus

Understanding JavaScript and Trusted Functions

Automating JavaScript creation

Setting Up the Environment

As described in Chapter 34, creating form fields requires use of the Forms tools. You also use the same toolbars used in Chapters 34 and 35 to handle form fields where you add JavaScripts. For setting up the Toolbar Well, refer to Chapter 34.

In addition to using form fields, you'll use several menu commands related to writing JavaScripts. As you move through this chapter, the menu options related to accessing and writing JavaScripts are covered.

JavaScripts can be written using an internal editor in Acrobat or an external editor such as WordPad on Windows or TextEdit on the Macintosh. If you write a lot of JavaScript code, open the Preferences dialog box by pressing Ctrl/⌘+K. Click JavaScript in the left pane and check the radio button for Use external JavaScript editor at the bottom of the right pane. Click the Browse button and locate the editor you want to use.

Getting Started with Acrobat JavaScript

Before I begin to explain some coding, let me start by making a few suggestions to the novice user who may find the programming aspects of Acrobat confusing and beyond your reach. For those who haven't coded a single line, you can easily search and find samples of code used in Acrobat forms that you can copy and paste into your designs. Search the Internet and find PDF forms that are not secure, which enables you to examine the code. If, for example, you need a calculation for sales tax, search for one of the many examples of forms where a sales tax calculation is coded in a form field. You can copy and paste fields into your designs and often only need to change a variable name to make it work. Poke around and experiment and you'll find some worthwhile routines in existing PDF forms.

Finding JavaScripts

As you peruse documents searching for JavaScripts either to paste into your own designs or to learn more about using JavaScript in Acrobat, you need to know where scripts are contained. You might copy and paste a script and find that the script doesn't execute properly. One reason is that the script relies on a function contained in another area in the document. Therefore, to gain a complete understanding of how a form works, you need to examine all the potential containers for scripts. As a matter of practice, you'll want to examine several areas in a form where JavaScripts are found.

> **TIP**   If you want a quick glance at JavaScripts contained in a document, select Advanced ⇨ Document Processing ⇨ Edit All JavaScripts. The JavaScript Editor opens and displays all JavaScripts in the document in a scrollable window.

JavaScripts can be contained in the following areas in a PDF document:

- **Field Scripts.** Depending on the field type, you'll find JavaScripts in various tabs in the Field Properties dialog box. For text fields you can find scripts in the Format, Validate and Calculate tabs. Other field types can have scripts contained in tabs specific to the field type.
- **Bookmarks.** JavaScripts can be contained in the Bookmarks Properties in the Actions tab.
- **Links.** Links can have JavaScripts in the Link Properties in the Actions tab.
- **Page Actions.** JavaScripts can be added to Page Open and Page Close actions.
- **Document Level JavaScripts.** JavaScript Functions can be added at the document level/
- **Document Actions.** Document Actions such as saving a file or printing a file can have JavaScripts applied when the action is invoked.

Examining field scripts

The most frequent use of JavaScript in Acrobat forms is when scripts are written for field actions. To examine JavaScripts associated with fields, select the Select Object tool and open the Field Properties. Depending on the field type, there may be several places where a script can be located. The first logical place to look is the Actions tab. Actions can contain JavaScripts for all field types. Click the Actions tab to see what actions are assigned to the field, as shown in Figure 36.1.

CROSS-REF For more information on the different field types in Acrobat 8, see Chapter 34.

FIGURE 36.1

Click the Actions tab to see whether a JavaScript action has been added to the field.

If you see JavaScript assigned to a mouse behavior, click on Run a JavaScript in the Actions list and click the Edit button. Acrobat opens the JavaScript Editor and displays the code written for the script, as shown in Figure 36.2. The code in the JavaScript Editor can be copied from one field and pasted into the editor when you assign a script to another field. In addition, the field can be copied and pasted into another form. When you paste fields with JavaScript in them, the code is preserved in the pasted field.

FIGURE 36.2

Select JavaScript in the Actions tab and click the Edit button. The JavaScript Editor dialog box opens, displaying the code.

JavaScript Editor

Create and Edit JavaScripts

```
this.spawnPageFromTemplate("passwords");
this.pageNum = this.numPages-1;
var r = [588, 454, 648, 474];
var i = this.pageNum++
var f =
this.addField(String(this.pageNum),"text",i,r);
        f.textSize = 12;
        f.alignment = "right";
        f.textColor = color.black;
        f.fillColor = color.transparent;
        f.textfont = font.HelvB;
        f.borderStyle = border.s;
        f.strokeColor = color.transparent;
        f.value = util.printd("mm/dd/yy", new
Date());

app.execMenuItem("NewBookmark");
```

Ln 1, Col 1

OK   Cancel   Go to...

With Text and Combo Box fields you can find JavaScripts in the Actions properties as well as the Format, Validate, and Calculate properties. If you are examining a form to understand how the field actions are executed, be certain to select each of these tabs to see whether any custom formatting or validation is used. Click the Format tab and look for Custom selected in the Select format category pull-down menu, as shown in Figure 36.3. If a JavaScript appears in either the Custom Format Script window or the Custom Keystroke Script window, click the Edit button adjacent to where the script is written. The JavaScript Editor opens in which you can edit the script or copy the text.

FIGURE 36.3

Select the Format tab and click Edit to see a script appear in the dialog box.

The Validate properties offer the same options. Follow the same procedures for finding JavaScripts as described earlier in this section by clicking the Validate tab and clicking Edit where you see a JavaScript in the Run custom validation script window to open the JavaScript Editor dialog box.

Field calculations are often handled in the Calculate properties. When JavaScript produces data calculations, be certain to examine the Calculate properties, as shown in Figure 36.4. However, not all field calculations are assigned to the Calculate properties, so be certain to check the Actions properties as well as Calculate in the event a calculation is performed on an action.

List Boxes offer different properties. If a List Box is used, click the Selection Change tab. A JavaScript can execute when a selection in the List Box changes. If a script appears in the dialog box, click the Edit button to open the JavaScript Edit dialog box.

Digital signatures can also be assigned custom JavaScripts. Click the Signed tab for a Digital Signature field and examine the dialog box for a custom script.

Buttons, Radio Buttons, and Check Boxes can have JavaScripts added only to the Actions properties. When opening these field types, click the Actions tab described earlier.

NEW FEATURE   In Acrobat 8, we have support for creating Barcode fields. The Value tab in the Barcode Properties contains an area where you can add custom JavaScripts similar to scripts you add in the Format and Validate tabs.

FIGURE 36.4

Click the Calculate tab to see whether a custom calculation script has been added to the field. If a script appears in the dialog box, click Edit to open the JavaScript Editor dialog box.

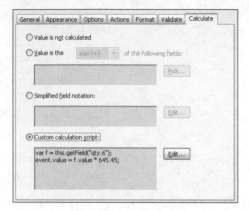

Bookmarks and links

Both Bookmarks and links use the same action types as form fields. You might use a Bookmark for navigating documents rather than creating form field buttons or links on every page to open and close files. When the Bookmarks tab is open, users can click on a Bookmark to open secondary files or perform other actions such as spawning pages from templates.

CROSS-REF For more information on Button Field Properties, see Chapter 22.

To check for JavaScripts contained in Bookmark actions, open the Bookmark Properties dialog box and click the Actions tab. JavaScripts are listed the same as when examining actions for form fields (described in the preceding section). Likewise, when you open Link Properties you can check to see whether a JavaScript has been added as a Link action.

Examining document-level JavaScripts

You may copy a field and paste it into another document and find an error reported when executing the JavaScript action. Notwithstanding variable names that are explained later, you can experience problems like this because the routine in the JavaScript might be calling a JavaScript function or global action that was contained in the original document as a document-level JavaScript. Among your tasks in dissecting a form should be an examination of any document-level JavaScripts. To find document-level JavaScript functions contained in a form, choose Advanced ➪ Document Processing ➪ Document JavaScripts and the JavaScript Functions dialog box opens, as shown in Figure 36.5.

In the JavaScript Functions dialog box, search for any names in the box below the Script Name box. All document-level functions are listed in this dialog box. To examine a script, select the script name and click the Edit button. The JavaScript Editor window, in which you can examine and/or copy the script, opens.

Writing functions and accessing them in JavaScript code written for field actions is much more complex. If you are new to JavaScript you may want to start with simple scripts in form fields until you learn more about how JavaScript is coded and implemented in Acrobat. As you learn more, you can develop more sophisticated routines that include functions.

FIGURE 36.5

Open the JavaScript Functions dialog box by choosing Advanced ➪ JavaScript ➪ Document JavaScripts.

Examining page actions

Page actions execute when a user opens or closes a PDF page. You can assign any action type available from the Select Action types for field actions, including Run a JavaScript. When examining forms, open the Page Properties dialog box by opening a context menu in the Pages tab and selecting Properties. Click on Actions when the Page Properties dialog box opens. If a JavaScript or any other page action is assigned to either the Page Open or the Page Close action, the action types are listed in the Actions window. Notice in Figure 36.6 that both a Page Open and Page Close action appear in the Actions window showing Run a JavaScript for both Page Actions.

CROSS-REF   For more information on Page Actions, see Chapters 16 and 34.

FIGURE 36.6

When you open the Page Properties dialog box and click the Actions tab, both Page Open and Page Close actions are shown in the Actions window.

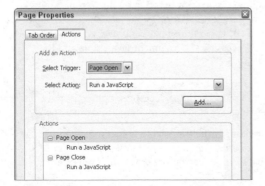

As with the other dialog boxes described earlier in this chapter, click on Run a JavaScript and click the Edit button. The JavaScript Editor window opens where you can view, edit, and/or copy the JavaScript.

Examining document actions

Document actions execute JavaScripts for any one of five different Acrobat functions. On a document close, during a save, after a save, during a print, or after a print, a JavaScript action can be executed. To view any document actions assigned to the PDF document, choose Advanced ➪ Document Processing ➪ Set Document Actions.

CROSS-REF For information on creating JavaScripts on document actions, see "Using Document Actions" later in this chapter.

The Document Actions dialog box opens. If a JavaScript is assigned to a document action, an icon appears adjacent to the action type. You can view a script in the dialog box, as shown in Figure 36.7, or you can open the JavaScript Editor window by selecting the action name and clicking Edit.

FIGURE 36.7

Any document actions assigned to the PDF are displayed with a green circle adjacent to an action type in the Document Actions dialog box.

Searching for page templates

Although not a JavaScript action, page templates can be called upon by JavaScript routines or additional fields can be created from template pages. Because templates can be hidden, the only way to examine JavaScripts on template pages is to first display a hidden template. As a matter of routine, you should search for page templates when examining forms.

To display a hidden template, click the Edit Layout button in the Forms toolbar or select Forms ➪ Edit Form in Acrobat. The Page Templates command is not visible unless you are in edit mode. Select Forms ➪ Page Templates and the Page Templates dialog box opens. If a Page Template is used in the PDF file, a template name appears in a list box in the Page Templates dialog box. If the Page Template is hidden, the square adjacent to the template name appears empty. To show the template page, click on the icon adjacent to the template name. The icon changes to an eye icon inside the square. In Figure 36.8, you see four templates listed in the Page Templates dialog box. Two templates are visible and two templates are hidden.

FIGURE 36.8

Clicking on the icon to the left of a template name for hidden templates makes the template visible in the PDF.

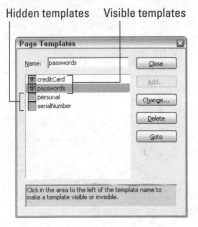

The template likely appears at the end of the document. After you make a template visible, click the GoTo button to navigate to that page. If form fields or links are on the page, you can open them and examine them for JavaScripts.

Using the JavaScript Debugger

All of the aforementioned JavaScript locations can also be found in the JavaScript Debugger. The JavaScript Debugger dialog box enables you to examine JavaScripts from a list in the Scripts window. Press Ctrl/⌘+J or select Advanced ➪ Document Processing ➪ JavaScript Debugger to open the dialog box shown in Figure 36.9. Select an item in the list and click the arrows to open scripts nested in a hierarchical order. When you select the script, the code is shown in the View window.

At the top of the hierarchy in the Scripts window, you'll see all the scripts associated with different actions. Click the right-pointing arrow to expand a listed item. You can expand individual items until you arrive at the action. Select the action, and the code for the item is listed in the lower View window when you select either Script or Script and Console from the pull-down menu options.

The JavaScript Debugger also helps you debug scripts you write. You can set break points that halt routines to help narrow down bugs in your code. To set a break point, click on the left side of each line of code where you want a break to occur. A red circle appears after you set a break point.

FIGURE 36.9

Press Ctrl/⌘+J to open the JavaScript Debugger window.

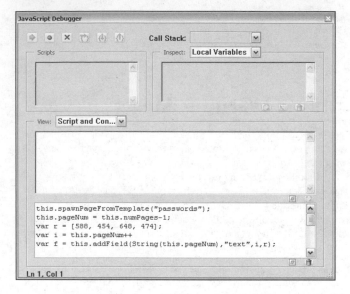

Using the JavaScript Console

The JavaScript Console is a part of the same dialog box where you find the JavaScript Debugger. In the console window you can type a line of code to test it for errors or you can copy code from a field and paste it into the console window. To execute a segment in a routine, select the segment to be tested and press the Num Pad Enter key (or press Ctrl+Enter).

You can also execute a statement by placing the cursor at the beginning of the line to be executed. Press the Enter key on the Num Pad and the routine runs. In Figure 36.10, you see a line of code in the Console in the background. When I press the Num Pad Enter key (or Ctrl/Ctrl+Enter) with the cursor anywhere on the line, the code executes. In this example, an alert dialog box opens as you see in the foreground.

FIGURE 36.10

Press the Enter key on the Num Pad or press Ctrl+Enter (Windows and Mac) with the cursor anywhere on a line of code and the script is executed.

CAUTION   **When testing code in the JavaScript Console, click in a line of code or select several lines of code and press the Num Pad Enter key. If you press the Enter/Return key, you'll add a paragraph return in the console window. If text is selected, the text is deleted when pressing Enter/Return.**

Be certain to check the Preferences dialog box when using the JavaScript Debugger and Console. Open the Preferences dialog box and click on JavaScript in the left pane. On the right side of the dialog box are options for enabling the Debugger and the Console. Be certain these items are enabled before you begin editing scripts.

Creating Viewer Options Warning Alerts

Under some circumstances, it is helpful for users to know the limitations of completing your forms before they attempt filling in data fields. If users open your forms in Adobe Reader, they cannot save the data after filling in the form unless the form is enabled with Adobe Reader usage rights. In other cases, some scripts you add to a form cannot be performed in Adobe Reader. Some examples of such scripts might be transposing data to other forms or spawning a page from a template. These actions require Acrobat. Additionally, new features in Acrobat 8 make some actions unusable for users with viewers earlier than Acrobat 7. Therefore, you may want to assess the viewer type and viewer version when a user opens your forms. If a version or viewer type cannot be used with the form you created, you can alert the user immediately when the file opens.

TIP   **Although some features such as viewing page templates or creating fields are not available in Acrobat Standard, you can often execute JavaScripts in Acrobat Standard that produce actions not available through menu commands. For example, you cannot add templates or write JavaScript code to spawn pages from templates using Acrobat Standard. However, you can write a script for a button to spawn a page from a template in Acrobat Professional. An Acrobat Standard user can open the file, click the button, and a page is spawned via the button action. Before you create viewer version alerts, you need to run all your scripts in Acrobat Standard to determine what scripts cannot be executed in Acrobat Standard. Use viewer version alerts for Acrobat Standard users only when scripts don't execute properly. You can also find a key in the JavaScript Reference Guide that describes which objects and methods work in Acrobat Standard.**

Creating viewer type alerts

A viewer type is the Acrobat viewer used to view the PDF form. Adobe Reader, Acrobat Standard, and Acrobat Professional are the viewer types that are used in filling out PDF forms. Certain actions you add to buttons, page actions, bookmarks, and so on may not be supported by Adobe Reader. To be certain the Reader user is aware that the PDF has limitations and needs to be viewed in Acrobat Standard or Professional, you can add a JavaScript with a viewer type alert. When the PDF is opened in Adobe Reader, an alert dialog box opens if the file is opened in Reader with a message informing the Reader user that the PDF can't be used in the Reader application. If the file is opened in an Acrobat product, the dialog box doesn't open.

To see how you add this type of JavaScript to a document, follow these steps:

STEPS: Adding viewer type alerts

1. **Open the JavaScript Functions dialog box.** Open a PDF and select Advanced ➡ Document Processing ➡ Document JavaScripts to open the JavaScript Functions dialog box. The location for this JavaScript is important. By adding a JavaScript at the document level, the JavaScript is run when the document opens before the first page is displayed. If the viewer type is Adobe Reader, the JavaScript displays a message. All other viewers ignore this message.

2. **Name the JavaScript function.** Type a name for the script in the Script Name text box in the JavaScript Functions dialog box. For this script I use a name such as viewerType, as shown in Figure 36.11.

FIGURE 36.11

Open the JavaScript Functions dialog box and type a name for your new script.

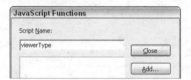

3. **Open the JavaScript Editor.** After typing a name for your script, click the Add button and the JavaScript Editor window opens.

4. **Add a JavaScript.** Enter the following code in the JavaScript Editor dialog box:

```
1. //is Reader (as opposed to Acrobat)
2. if (typeof(app.viewerType)!="undefined")
3.  if(app.viewerType == "Reader")
4.  {
5.    var msg = "Filling out this form requires use of Acrobat
Standard or Acrobat Professional.";
6.    app.alert(msg);
7.  }
```

NOTE The preceding line numbers are for clarification only. The line numbers are not included in the code you write in the JavaScript Editor. The code, as it is written in the JavaScript Editor, appears as shown in Figure 36.12.

The // at the beginning of a line of code is a programmer's comment. The code is not executed. In line 2, the `if` statement assesses the viewer. If the viewer type in line 3 is equal (==) to Adobe Reader (`"Reader"`), then an alert dialog box opens—line 6: `app.alert(msg)`. The variable msg is defined in the line 5 `var msg` statement. Therefore, the variable msg value appears when the alert dialog box opens. If the viewer type is not `Reader`, the warning dialog box does not open.

FIGURE 36.12

Actual code in the JavaScript Editor does not include line numbers. Numbers are used in this chapter to help describe the lines of code.

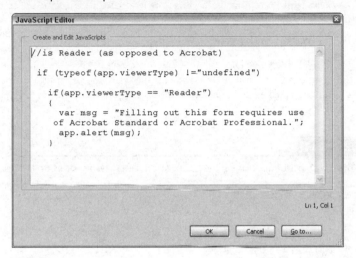

5. **Copy the script.** Press Ctrl/⌘+A to select all and press Ctrl/⌘+C to copy the text to the Clipboard. The text will remain on the Clipboard until you copy something else. We'll use this script to test it in the JavaScript Debugger later.

6. **Click OK in the JavaScript editor.** You return to the JavaScript Functions dialog box where your code is partially shown, as you can see in Figure 36.13.

FIGURE 36.13

Click OK in the JavaScript Editor and you return to the JavaScript Functions dialog box.

7. **Click OK in the JavaScript Functions dialog box.**

8. **Save the file.** Select File ➪ Save or File ➪ Save As and save the file.

9. **Open the JavaScript Debugger.** You can't test the entire script in Acrobat because the viewer type is Acrobat and not Reader, but you can take a look at the dialog box a Reader user will see before you test the script in Reader. Viewing the alert dialog box can help you find any text errors.

10. **Paste the Clipboard text in the JavaScript Debugger.** Press Ctrl/⌘+J to open the JavaScript Debugger window. Click the Trash icon to remove any text in the Console. Press Ctrl/⌘+V to paste the Clipboard text.

11. **Test the script.** Drag the cursor through the text beginning with `var msg` and continuing through `(msg)` : in the second to last line, as you see in Figure 36.14. Press the Num Pad Enter key on your keyboard and the alert dialog box opens, as shown in Figure 36.14.

FIGURE 36.14

Select the text to test and press the Num Pad Enter key on your keyboard.

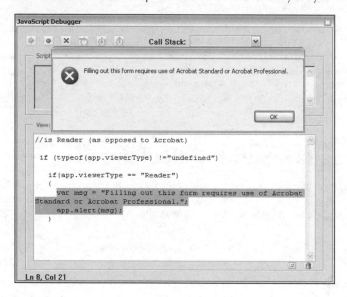

12. **Test the file in Adobe Reader.** To test the entire script and make sure it works properly, open the file in Adobe Reader. When the file opens you should see the alert dialog box open.

Creating viewer version alerts

You may create JavaScripts to perform actions that are not available in earlier versions of Acrobat. The newer Acrobat 8.0 implementation of JavaScript adds more statements and reserved words than earlier versions. If it is essential for a user to complete your form in Acrobat 8, you can add a page action and inform the user in an alert dialog box that Acrobat 8 is needed to complete the form. Follow these steps to assess the viewer version:

STEPS: Create a viewer version alert

1. **Create a JavaScript Function.** Follow the same steps as creating a viewer type alert. Name the script viewerVersion and click the Add button in the JavaScript Functions dialog box to open the JavaScript Editor.

2. **Add a JavaScript.** Type the following code in the JavaScript Editor:

```
1. if (typeof(app.viewerVersion)!="undefined")
2. if(app.viewerVersion < 8.0)
3. {
4. var msg = "Not all features in this document work in Acrobat
viewers lower than version 8.0. Upgrade to Adobe Acrobat Standard 8.0
on Windows or Adobe Acrobat Professional 8.0 on either Windows or
Macintosh before proceeding.";
5. app.alert(msg);
```

In line 2, app.viewerVersion is used instead of the viewer type noted in the earlier example. This routine assesses the current Acrobat viewer version and displays the message in line 4 if the viewer version is less than Acrobat 8.0.

TIP If you're new to JavaScript and you can't seem to remember the code, add both functions to a file. You can use the File ⇨ Create PDF ⇨ From Blank Page command to create a blank new page and add both scripts as Document JavaScripts in your blank document. Add a comment note on the blank page noting the scripts contained in the document. Save the file and add the file in your Organizer in a collection you create for JavaScripts. The next time you need one of the scripts, open the Organizer and locate the file. Open it and copy the script you want to use. Paste the script in a new document and it's ready to go.

Performing JavaScript Calculations

Acrobat provides only a few basic math operations. In the Calculate tab for a text or combo box field, you can choose to sum values or get a product using built-in Acrobat functions. If you want subtraction or division or any other math operations, you need to use one of the two scripting languages — Simplified Field Notation or JavaScript.

CROSS-REF For more information on the built-in math functions in Acrobat, see Chapter 34.

To subtract values using Simplified Field Notation open the Calculate tab in a text or combo box field Properties dialog box and select Simplified Field Notation. Click the Edit button and type the following code:

```
1. total - discount
```

In the previous script a field named discount is subtracted from a field named total. To calculate the same result using JavaScript, click the Custom calculation script radio button in the Calculate tab in the Properties dialog box and click Edit. In the JavaScript Editor, add the following code:

```
1. var f=this.getField("total");
2. var g = this.getField("discount");
3. event.value=f.value - g.value;
```

To divide a field named apples by a field named baskets using Simplified Field Notation, use the following script:

```
1. apples / baskets
```

To perform the same calculation using JavaScript, use the following code:

```
1. var f=this.getField("apples");
2. var g = this.getField("baskets");
3. event.value = f.value / g.value;
```

Sales tax is a common calculation required on many forms. Assuming you have one field for a subtotal and another for a grand total, open the grandTotal field and use the following code to calculate a sales tax using Simplified Field Notation.

```
1. subtotal * .0725
```

For calculating a sales tax using JavaScript, the calculation formula would be:

```
1. var f=this.getField("subTotal");
2. event.value=Math.round(f.value*7.25)/100;
```

The variable name f gets the contents of the subtotal field. The second line of code performs the calculation for variable f to compute sales tax for a tax rate of 7.25 percent. If you want to duplicate the code for one of your forms, change the tax rate accordingly.

In these examples you can quickly see that Simplified Field Notation is a much easier scripting language to work with. Many different math functions are supported with Simplified Field Notation. When you need to add other functions such as creating if/else statements or using loops, then your only choice is JavaScript.

If/else statements

If/else statements are used for conditional items. For example, if one condition is true, do something; otherwise, do something else. A good use for an if/else statement might be eliminating zeros in calculation fields. By default, zeros appear in calculation fields as shown in Figure 36.15. To clear the fields of zeros, you can use an if/else statement.

FIGURE 36.15

A default appearance for calculation fields shows zeros according to the number format selected in the Format properties.

Item ordered	Quantity	Unit	Total
1. Table Alarm Clock		$399.95	$0.00
2. Crafted Alarm Clock		$449.45	$0.00
3. Modern Alarm Clock		$699.99	$0.00
4. Unique Wall Clock		$484.45	$0.00
5. Never on Time Wall Clock		$287.99	$0.00
6. The Grandpa Watch - 25K Gold Plated		$799.99	$0.00
7. The Sportsman Chronograph		$645.45	$0.00

On this form, the total fields are calculated by multiplying the quantity by the fixed unit price. If the total value is zero we want to display the field without any value *else* we want to display the calculated value. Here's the code that eliminates the zeros when the field contents are greater than zero.

```
1. var f=this.getField("quantity");
2. var g=this.getField("unit");
3. if (f=.value!=0)
4. event.value=f.value * g.value;
5. else
6. event.value="";
```

The default for the quantity field is zero and stays that way until a user adds a quantity for purchasing an item. The Unit column contains default values. Therefore, we look at the Quantity field. If the value is not zero, we want the value reported in the Total field. The else statement reports that if the quantity is zero we add nothing to the field (two quote marks with no space between the quotes).

Calculating dates

You can add a date to a form with a simple JavaScript. To add a date to a form, create a text field. Set the attributes for the text appearance and font in the Appearance tab and click the Calculate tab. Add a JavaScript action and enter the following code:

```
1. var d = new Date();
2. console.println(util.printd("mmmm dd, yyyy", d));
```

In the preceding example, the date is reported in the format like January 27, 2007 (or whatever the current date may be). You can change date formats by editing the text within quotes. For example, change the text to read "mmm dd, yyyy", and the date is reported in the format Jul 04, 2007. Change the date to "mm dd, yy" and the date reads 9/24/07.

The date appears in the date field when you open the PDF document. When you open a PDF document on another day, the date changes to reflect the current date. In some instances, you may want the date reported on the day a page was created and not have the date change each time the document opens in Acrobat. You can combine a script to create the date with, for example, spawning a page from a template and add a new date field as the new page is created. (For more on spawning pages from templates, see the section "Spawning a page from a template" later in this chapter.)

In the next example we want to use a JavaScript to create a new field and add a date to the field. Here's how you do it:

STEPS: Add a new date field to a page

1. **Add a button to a page.** To test the script, we'll add a button so when you click the button you can see the result. If you add a date field to a page in conjunction with another action such as spawning a page from a template you would include the script along with the script used to spawn a page.

2. **Open the JavaScript Editor.** Use the same action as covered in previous examples to add a JavaScript action to a button.

3. **Type the script in the JavaScript Editor.** The following code creates a new field and adds a date value to the field:

```
1.    var r = [550, 765, 600, 785];
2.    var i = this.numPages-1
3.    var f = this.addField(myDate,"text",i,r);
```

```
4.   f.textSize = 12;
5.     f.alignment = "right";
6.     f.textColor = color.black;
7.     f.fillColor = color.transparent;
8.     f.textfont = font.HelvB;
9.   f.borderStyle = border.s;
10   f.strokeColor = color.transparent;
11   f.value = util.printd("mm/dd/yy", new Date());
```

4. Click OK in the JavaScript Editor and click Close in the Button Field Properties dialog box.

5. **Test the script.** Click the button with the Hand tool. You should see the field added to the last page in the document.

In Step 3, the first line of code sets a variable to the coordinates (in points) for where the field rectangle will be drawn. In this example the field is drawn in the top right corner on a standard portrait letter size page. Line 2 sets a variable to the last page in the document (remember JavaScript is zero based so the total number of pages minus 1 is the last page in the document). Line 3 is the addField statement adding a "text" field named *myDate* and using the page number (i) and the field coordinates (r).

Lines 4 through 10 set the attributes for the field for alignment, text color, field appearance, and so on. The last line of code creates the date field. When the field is created, it's a date stamp that won't change when the document is opened on a different date.

Using loops

For summing columns of data, you can use the sum + preset formulas where you need results at the end of a column or row. However, at times, summing column or row data with a JavaScript is necessary. You might have a need to multiply an item by a quantity for a subtotal, and then add all the subtotals together to create a grand total. In another situation you might have a form that sums a column of numbers and calculates a sales tax after summing the fields like the example shown in Figure 36.16. In Figure 36.16 the total fields are summed and a sales tax is added to the total in the grand total field at the bottom of the far right column. For summing data in columns, you need to create a loop that loops through all the fields used in the calculation.

FIGURE 36.16

A total field is calculated and a sales tax computed in the same result field.

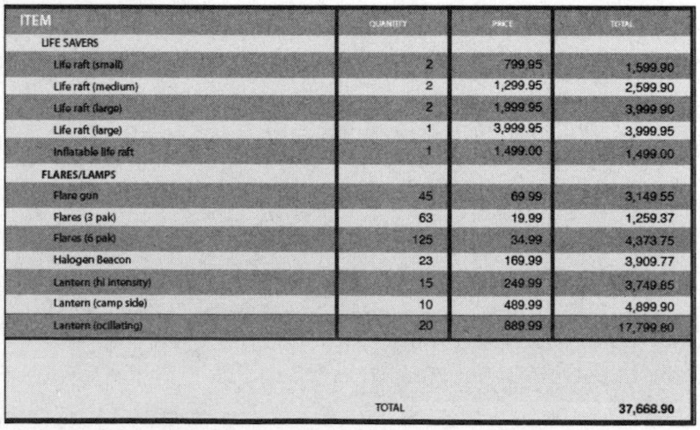

ITEM	QUANTITY	PRICE	TOTAL
LIFE SAVERS			
Life raft (small)	2	799.95	1,599.90
Life raft (medium)	2	1,299.95	2,599.90
Life raft (large)	2	1,999.95	3,999.90
Life raft (large)	1	3,999.95	3,999.95
Inflatable life raft	1	1,499.00	1,499.00
FLARES/LAMPS			
Flare gun	45	69.99	3,149.55
Flares (3 pak)	63	19.99	1,259.37
Flares (6 pak)	125	34.99	4,373.75
Halogen Beacon	23	169.99	3,909.77
Lantern (hi intensity)	15	249.99	3,749.85
Lantern (camp side)	10	489.99	4,899.90
Lantern (ocillating)	20	889.99	17,799.80
		TOTAL	37,668.90

For a simple loop to calculate a row of data, use the following example:

```
1. var f = this.getField("totalItem");
2. var a = f.getArray();
3. var result=0.0;
4. for (i=0; i<a.length; i++) result += a[i].value;
5. event.value = result;
```

Line 1 assigns the variable f to a parent name totalItem. The fields in a column are named totalItem.0, totalItem.1, totalItem.2, totalItem.3, and so on. Line 2 assigns the variable a to an array. Line 3 sets the variable *result* to zero. Line 4 begins the loop and the loop continues through the length of the array summing the result value. Line 5 places the end *result* value in the field.

Using Document Actions

Document actions are actions from JavaScript routines that are implemented when a file is printed, saved, or closed. Rather than using a button to execute an action, Acrobat executes the action during one of five document conditions. A document action is executed when a file is closed, when a file is saved, after a file is saved, when a file is printed, and after a file is printed. There are many uses for executing actions on one of the document action items. You might want to delete unused fields on a form, delete all page templates, or perhaps offer a message to the user after a form has been saved or printed.

As an example, suppose forms need to be completed in an Acrobat viewer and then printed and routed by hand. You can provide instructions on what to do with the form after it finishes printing. In this case, you can set up a document action after a file has finished printing. You are assured the user sees the message because the form needs to be printed as the last step in completing the form.

Follow these steps for creating an alert dialog box with a message to instruct a user what to do with a form after it has printed:

STEPS: Create a document action showing an alert dialog box

1. **Open the Document Actions dialog box.** Open a PDF file and choose Advanced ➪ Document Processing ➪ Set Document Actions. The Document Actions dialog box opens.

2. **Select the Document Did Print action type.** Select one of the five items in the list box for the type of action to be used. In this example, I'll use Document Did Print as the action type.

3. **Open the JavaScript Editor.** Click Edit in the Document Actions dialog box. The JavaScript Editor dialog box opens.

4. **Code the script.** Enter the following code:

   ```
   app.alert("Please submit the printed form to the accounting In box in
   the main office complex.",3)
   ```

5. **Exit the JavaScript Editor.** Click OK in the JavaScript Editor. You return to the Document Actions dialog box where your code appears when the action is selected, as shown in Figure 36.17.

NOTE   The Document Actions dialog box displays an icon adjacent to the action type and the code appears in the window below Execute this JavaScript. If you later want to delete the script, click the Edit button and highlight the text in the JavaScript Editor. Press Delete (Backspace) on the keyboard to eliminate the text.

6. **Print the form.** Print the document to your desktop printer. After the PDF finishes printing, the dialog box opens.

FIGURE 36.17

Select the document action and the JavaScript code is shown in the Execute this JavaScript window.

Working with Page Templates

One very useful tool available to you with page templates and JavaScript is the ability to create new pages from a template page. You can make templates either visible or hidden in your forms. You create new pages from template pages by spawning a page from a template. The spawned pages are duplicates of the template pages, but any fields on spawned pages are created with new field names if desired. The scripts and actions for fields added to template pages are duplicated when you spawn pages from templates. The only changes that occur are field names, so each field in your new document contains unique field names if desired.

Page templates can be spawned to create new pages or you can also use page templates to overlay data on existing pages. For example, a watermark, graphic, text, and so on, as you might add with headers and footers, can be overlaid on pages using page templates.

Creating page overlays was once a very much needed feature in earlier versions of Acrobat, but now with Acrobat 8's more powerful tools for creating headers and footers, the need to overlay pages using JavaScripts is more limited to conditional responses from a user who clicks a button action. For example, if the answer is yes, some content is added to a page from a template. If the answer is no, then either no page is spawned from a template or maybe a different page is spawned. However, for adding overlays to pages such as watermarks, headers, footers, page numbers, and so on, you'll find using the Add Header and Add Footer dialog boxes a better solution. For adding pages to a PDF, the *spawn* object is used (`spawnPageFromTemplate` in older versions of Acrobat) object affords you many uses.

CROSS-REF For more information on creating headers and footers, see Chapter 16.

Creating a page template

To create a page template, open a PDF form in which you want to convert one of the pages to a template. You may have a form where a given user response requires more information, and as a result, a new page is created in the document. You might have a file that creates a summary page after calculating data and the new page is dynamically created with a JavaScript. In another scenario, you might have a document you use for personal record keeping such as a date book, a file organizer, or some other kind of personal data management tool. In these examples, you need to frequently add new pages in a document to add more data. Creating new pages is easily handled by adding a JavaScript to spawn a page from a template. To write such a script, you first need to create a page template.

A page template is a page in a PDF file that you define as a Page Template. You can use an existing page in a document you export to PDF in an authoring program or create a separate PDF document you design for a template and later insert the page in a PDF file.

CROSS-REF For more information on inserting pages in PDF files, see Chapter 16.

In Figure 36.18, I created a page I want to use as a template and inserted the page in a PDF file. The idea behind this page is to use a form to organize my passwords. Each time I acquire a new password for accessing Web sites or documents, I add the pertinent data in my passwords file. Since I'm always adding new passwords, I need to continually create new pages in the PDF file.

To create a Page template, use the steps that follow.

STEPS: Creating a page template

1. **Insert a page in a PDF file or use one of the existing pages in a file you want to use as a Page Template.**
2. **Navigate to the page you want to use for your Page Template.**
3. **Change the Preview mode to Edit mode.** If you are currently in Preview mode you won't see the Page templates command. Click a form tool on the Forms toolbar, select Forms ⇨ Edit Form in Acrobat, or click the Edit Layout button on the Forms toolbar to enter edit mode.

CROSS-REF For more information on using Preview and Edit mode while working on Acrobat PDF forms, see Chapter 34.

4. **Edit the page.** If your template page uses form fields, add all the form fields to the template and test all fields to make sure they work properly. In Figure 36.18, I added a number of fields to my template page.
5. **Open the Page Templates dialog box.** Select Forms ⇨ Page Templates and the Page Templates dialog box opens.
6. **Type a name for your template.** Type a name in the Name text box.
7. **Add the page as a Page Template.** Click the Add button and Acrobat prompts you in a dialog box to confirm adding the page in view in the Document pane as a page template. Click Yes and you return to the Page Templates dialog box.

   If you want your template to be hidden, click the eyeball icon in the Page Templates dialog box. The eyeball disappears, as shown in Figure 36.19, and the Page Template is hidden when you leave the Page Templates dialog box.

FIGURE 36.18

Add a name for the template page and click the eyeball icon to make the template invisible in the document.

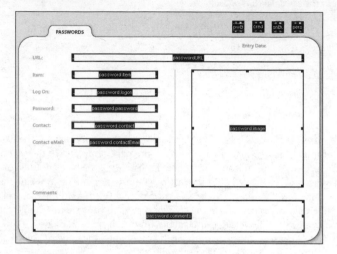

FIGURE 36.19

Add a name for the template page and click the eyeball icon to hide the template page in the document.

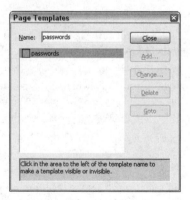

8. **Click Close.** When the Page Templates dialog box closes, the page is added as a Page Template and appears invisible in the PDF file.

NOTE You must have at least one page visible in a PDF. You cannot create a Page Template and hide it if the page template is the only page in the document.

Spawning a page from a template

To create new pages from your template, create a button on the page from which you want the user to spawn a new page. Either a link button or form field can be used. In the link or button properties dialog box, select Run a JavaScript as the action type.

The following code is used to spawn a page from a template.

```
1. var a = this.getTemplate("passwords");
2. a.spawn ({
3.    nPage:this.numPages,
4.    bRename:true,
5.    bOverlay:false
6. })
```

The template name I used is `passwords` as defined in the first line of code. This is the exact same name as you type in the Page Templates dialog box when you create the page template. In the second line of code, the instruction `a.spawn` spawns a page from a template. Lines 3 to 5 set the attributes for the spawned page. In line 3, the spawned page is placed after the last page in the document. You can change the value `this.numPages` to a page number and place the spawned page anywhere in the file. In line 4, any fields contained on the template page are renamed on the spawned page to provide unique field names. If the line is changed to `bRename:false`, all fields are duplicated with duplicate field names. In line 5, the code instructs Acrobat to create a new page in the document. If you change the code to `bOverlay:true`, the spawned page is superimposed over the last page in the file.

Lines 3 through 5 in the preceding script are default values. If you write the script as follows, Acrobat assumes using the defaults without specific notation for the attributes:

```
1. var a = this.getTemplate("passwords");
2. a.spawn();
```

This two-line script works fine in Acrobat 6 through 8; however, there are problems executing the script properly in earlier versions of Acrobat. Be certain to use the script with six lines of code and specify all attributes of the spawned page and you can be certain the script works in all versions of Acrobat.

You can also use an action type to instruct Acrobat to go to the newly created page. By default, spawned pages are created at the end of the PDF document. When pages are spawned, the page containing the button used to spawn a new page remains in view. To help a user navigate to the new spawned page, you can add another line of code to go to the new page. Add the following script after the last line of code used to spawn a page:

```
this.pageNum = this.numPages-1;
```

This line assesses the number of pages in the document, subtracts one from the number and opens the last page. JavaScript is zero based; therefore, the −1 item subtracts one from the total number of pages. In JavaScript terms, page 1 is page 0.

TIP   If you have a document with many pages and need to spawn pages periodically as the user browses the document, use a Bookmark instead of adding buttons on all the pages. A single Bookmark takes up much less memory than button fields added to every page.

You can also add buttons on the template page to spawn pages from a template. In my passwords file, it would be cumbersome to always travel back to the first page to click a button that spawns a page. To make it much easier, I created a button on the template page to spawn additional pages. This way I can search

through my document to see if I have an existing password already created for a given Web site. If not, no matter where I am in the document I can create a new page and add the new password.

Creating Pop-Up Menus

Application pop-up menus can be useful for nesting action items so you can save some space on a form. You might want to have a contents page where a user navigates via menu commands to many different files stored on a CD-ROM or network server. Rather than listing all files on a page or in Bookmarks, you can categorize groups and nest them in submenus for a more economical use of space.

As an example, suppose you want to create links to other PDF documents. You have a small page and don't have enough room to display all the titles of the documents you want the user to access. By creating an application pop-up menu like the one shown in Figure 36.20, you can create categories, subcategories, and links to destinations that assist users in opening files in a relatively small section on a contents page.

FIGURE 36.20

By adding application pop-up menus, you can create lists of destination documents in categorical groups.

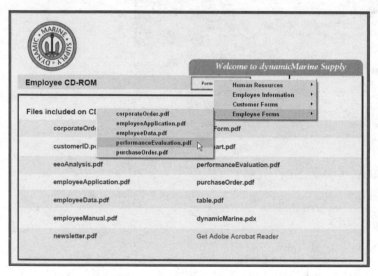

When you select the menu option, the file associated with the link opens in the Document pane. Additionally, you can create application pop-up menus to navigate pages within a document. In Figure 36.21, you can see where a pop-up menu helps out nicely. Designer and Acrobat expert Robert Connolly of pdfPictures.com creates electronic brochures that are viewed in Full Screen mode. To access the huge number of links within the documents while keeping the page design neat and attractive, Bob uses nested pop-up application menus that link to other page views, play video files, print, and navigate the document. To see some examples of the attractive eBrochures designed by Robert Connolly, log on to www .pdfPictures.com where you can download some nicely assembled PDF electronic brochures and take a look at the way application pop-up menus are used in the pdfPictures files.

FIGURE 36.21

Robert Connolly of pdfPictures.com makes extensive use of application pop-up menus to preserve the attractive page designs.

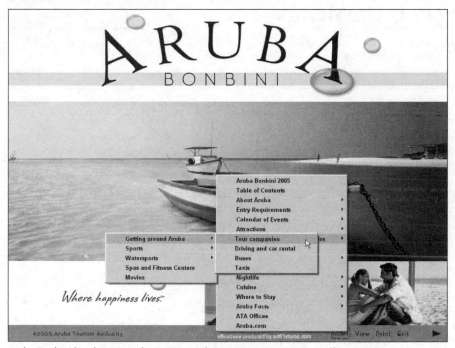

Aruba Bonbini brochure © Aruba Tourism Authority. Reprint permission: pdfPictures.com.

Writing document-level JavaScripts

If you use JavaScript to open and close files, all destination files need to have a document-level JavaScript to make the open actions workable. To open each file being addressed with a JavaScript, you need to add one line of code at the document level.

For each file you want to open from a pop-up menu, open each target document and choose Advanced ➪ JavaScript ➪ Document JavaScripts. In the JavaScript Functions dialog box, type a name for the script in the field box at the top of the dialog box. Click the Add button to open the JavaScript Editor. Delete all the default text in the JavaScript Editor and type the following code:

```
this.disclosed = true;
```

Click OK in the JavaScript Editor to return to the JavaScript Functions dialog box. Click Close and save the file. Repeat the steps for all files you want to open with a JavaScript.

If you don't add the aforementioned code to the document level, the files won't open with a JavaScript. Be certain to verify that all documents contain this one line of code at the document level.

Creating a pop-up menu

After coding functions in the destination documents, create a button field on a form used as a contents page and add the following JavaScript:

```
1. var c = app.popUpMenu
2. (["Category 1", "1a.pdf", "1b.pdf"],
3. ["Category 2", "2a.pdf", "2b.pdf"],
4. ["Category 3", "3a.pdf", "3b.pdf"],);
5. this.slave = app.openDoc((c), this);
```

The first line of code assigns the variable c to the `app.popUpMenu` method. Three categories are in lines 2 to 4. The category name is the first item in quote marks on each line. Following the category names are the filenames that open when the menu item is selected. Line 5 instructs Acrobat to open the selected file.

To create your own pop-up menus, change the category names to menu titles you want to use. Following each category, type the name of the respective document to open. Be certain to begin line 2 with an open parenthesis (and use a closed parenthesis) after the last line of code used to identify the category and filenames (line 4). Each line of code where the categories and filenames appear is contained within brackets.

The code used above works in Acrobat 8, as well as earlier viewers. Updates to the JavaScript implementation in Adobe Acrobat support more refinement for coding application pop-up menus. These newer code listings can be found in the Acrobat JavaScripting Reference Manual for version 8 of Acrobat. An example of a script using an application pop-up menu that opens your default Web browser and takes you to Adobe's Web site where Web pages open for Acrobat and Adobe Reader is coded as follows:

```
1. var aParams = [
2. {cName: "Adobe Web Page", cReturn: "www.adobe.com"},
3. {cName: "-"},
4. {cName: "The Adobe Acrobat family",
5. cReturn: "http://www.adobe.com/products/acrobat/main.html"},
{cName: "Adobe Reader",
cReturn: "http://www.adobe.com/products/acrobat/readstep2.html"}
6. ];
7. // apply the function app.popUpMenuEx to the app object, with an
array
8. // of parameters aParams
9. var cChoice = app.popUpMenuEx.apply( app, aParams );
```

There's much more to creating application pop-up menus and many changes to app.openDoc in version 8 of Acrobat. Be certain to review the Acrobat JavaScripting Reference Manual for code samples using these and other routines you want to implement in Acrobat.

Pop-up menus for page navigation in PDF Packages

The pop-up menus in the previous two sections describe how to navigate pages to open PDF documents and how to open Web pages via pop-up menus. PDF Packages require a different method for navigating through the files from a JavaScript action or a pop-up menu. Unfortunately, you can't use the destinations panel to create destinations in secondary files, and, therefore, it's not possible to target a destination to access a file. Your solution is using a bookmark to create the destination (which is an option for you) and then write a script that uses the bookmark actions properties to open other files within the PDF Package.

For example, take a look at Figure 36.22. In this PDF Package I have a Cover Sheet, a Lesson document, and a Quiz constructed as a PDF form. Each item is a separate PDF document combined together in a PDF Package. If I try to create a destination from one PDF file to target the destination view in another PDF document via the Destinations panel, Acrobat won't let me see the secondary file. Therefore, I need to use another tool to add destinations. Fortunately, the Bookmarks panel let's me accomplish the task for targeting destinations.

FIGURE 36.22

A PDF Package with a Cover Sheet and two PDF files.

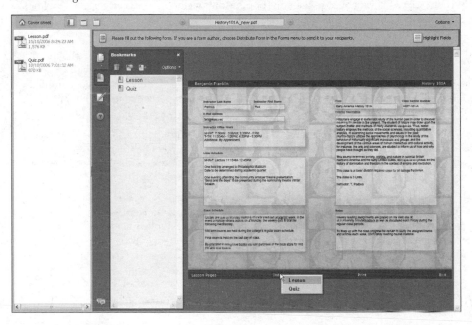

CROSS-REF For more information on using Destinations and creating pop-up menus with destinations, see Chapter 18.

To create the bookmarks, follow these steps:

STEPS: Creating bookmarks in PDF Packages

1. **Open the Bookmarks panel.** Start with the page in view where you want to add a pop-up menu that contains menu commands that will open other PDF files within the PDF Package. Click the Bookmarks icon in the Navigation pane. Note that the Navigation pane is to the right of the files listed in the PDF Package panel.

2. **Create a bookmark.** Press Ctrl/⌘+B or select New Bookmark from the Bookmarks panel to create a new bookmark.

3. **Name the bookmark.** The bookmark is added as an Untitled bookmark and the text is highlighted. Type a descriptive name for your bookmark name. In my example I have two PDF files in addition to the Cover Sheet. The bookmark names I use are Lesson and Quiz. For this first bookmark name, I type *Lesson* to replace the Untitled default text.

4. **Open the Bookmark Properties dialog box.** Open a context menu on the bookmark and select Properties to open the Properties dialog box.

5. **Add an action.** Click the Actions tab and select Go to a page view in the Select Action pull-down menu. Click the Add button shown in Figure 36.23.

FIGURE 36.23

Select Go to a page view and click Add.

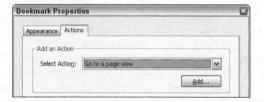

6. **Open the target page.** The Create Go to View dialog box opens. Just leave the dialog box open and click the PDF Package document you want as your target view. In my example, I lick on the Lessons document. The file opens in the Document pane and at this point I click on the Set Link button in the Create Go to View dialog box.

CROSS-REF For more information on using the Go to a page view action and the Create Go to View dialog box, see Chapter 18.

7. **Create additional bookmarks.** Return to the host page where you added the first bookmark if it's not in view and add a second bookmark. In my example I added another bookmark I named *Quiz* and set the link in the Create Go to View dialog box to my second PDF file within my PDF Package.

8. **Save your file.** Click File ➪ Save to save the document and update it within the PDF Package.

At this point you're finished creating the bookmarks that are required to write the script to create a pop-up menu. Your next task is to create a button containing the JavaScript for the pop-up menu. Here's how you do it:

STEPS: Writing a JavaScript to navigate pages in a PDF Package

1. **Open the Forms toolbar and select the Button tool.** Drag open a rectangle to create a button field.

2. **Click Actions and select Run a JavaScript to open the JavaScript Editor.**

3. **Write the following code in the JavaScript Editor:**

```
1. this.gotoNamedDest("target")
2. var cRtn = app.popUpMenu("Lesson","Quiz");
3. if(cRtn != null)
4. {
5.     switch(cRtn)
6.     {
7.         case "Lesson":
8.             this.bookmarkRoot.children[0].execute();
9.             break;
```

```
10.                        case "Quiz":
12.                        this.bookmarkRoot.children[1].execute();
13.                        break;
14.        }
15. }
```

In line 1 the "target" item is a variable. You can use any variable name you wish to use within the quote marks. In line 2 you list the names of your bookmarks. Remember, I used *Lesson* and *Quiz* for my bookmark names, therefore, those names appear listed in line 2. If you have additional bookmarks, the names would follow as bookmarkRoot.children[2], bookmarkRoot.children[3], and so on.

You might think that the pop-up menu used in this example is a bit redundant since you can navigate pages by clicking on the bookmarks you add to the Bookmarks panel. However, there are a few advantages for using pop-up menus over bookmarks. One advantage is easy navigation while in Full Screen mode. You can't see bookmarks when in Full Screen mode; therefore, the bookmarks won't help you in this view. If you create PDF Packages for presentations or other uses where you want the PDFs shown in Full Screen mode, pop-up menus or buttons/links are the only way you can navigate through documents unless you exit Full Screen mode. In Figure 36.24 you can see how a pop-up menu is an advantage in Full Screen mode.

FIGURE 36.24

Pop-up menus are a great advantage for navigating through PDF Packages while in Full Screen view.

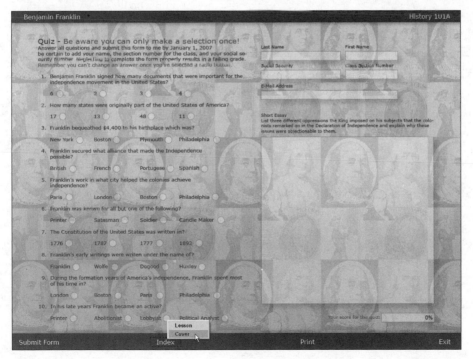

Another advantage is the extra real estate you gain by not having the bookmarks panel open while navigating through documents. You can minimize the PDF Package view but the Bookmarks panel will take up some precious viewing area, especially on smaller monitors.

TIP If you have a form enabled with Adobe Reader usage rights, you cannot edit the form in any way including adding buttons and bookmarks. If you want to add pop-up menus or other items using JavaScripts, first create the PDF Package without an enabled PDF. Save an enabled PDF as a second file. Add all your scripts and test them to be certain everything works correctly. When you're confident no changes need to be made, select Document ➪ Replace Pages and select the enabled file to replace the PDF Package file. All your links buttons, bookmarks, and scripts remain while the enabled PDF document is added to your package.

Working with Trusted Functions

Some Acrobat JavaScript methods have security restrictions. A number of different methods were eliminated from a non-privileged list in Acrobat 7 and continue with more restrictions in Acrobat 8. Using JavaScripts for opening alert dialog boxes, opening files, and navigating pages fall into the category of non-privileged events. Adding page templates, deleting pages, inserting pages, creating new documents, adding bookmarks, and so on fall into privileged events.

One of the ideas behind adding trusted functions to enable privileged events is to protect the end user from changing a document without the user's knowledge. If you create a page action on the second page of a document that deletes pages three through six, for example, the user is clearly unaware that navigating to page two could potentially destroy the document. To protect users from having these kinds of problems, Adobe added Trusted Functions to the Acrobat implementation of JavaScript. In order for privileges to be granted, the end user needs to copy a small JavaScript to the Acrobat JavaScript folder thereby making the user aware that some special treatment of the PDF file is likely to occur.

Creating new documents

When you add a Trusted Function to a document you need two scripts in two different locations. One location is in your document in any one of the areas you can invoke an action to run a JavaScript. The other location is a separate script saved to a text file and placed inside the Acrobat JavaScripts folder.

To make this clearer, let's first look at creating a folder level script in the steps below and then later we'll look at the script you add to a button inside a PDF document.

STEPS: Writing a folder-level script

1. **Open a text editor.** Be certain to use a program such as WordPad or NotePad (Windows) or TextEdit (Macintosh). Don't use a word processing program. Some unexpected results may occur.

2. **Write the following code in your text editor.**

```
1.    var trustedNewDoc = app.trustedFunction( function (nWidth, nHeight)
2.    {
3.    app.beginPriv(); // explicitly raise privilege
4.    app.newDoc( nWidth, nHeight );
5.  app.endPriv();
})
```

3. **Save the file as text only and use a .js extension.**

4. **Copy the file to your JavaScripts folder.** On Windows the directory path is: C:\Program Files\Adobe\Acrobat 8.0\Acrobat\Javascripts.

   On the Mac, open your logon Library folder and open the Acrobat User Data folder. Copy the text file to the JavaScripts folder.

The JavaScript code for this trusted function starts out with assigning the variable `trustedNewDoc` to the function with width and height parameters. In line 3, you see the privileges granted. This is like opening a locked door. The `app.newDoc` object creates a new document at the `nWidth` and `nHeight` values (this is determined in the button script later in Acrobat). The fifth line of code ends the privileges (or locks the door).

The next step is to create the script in Acrobat. In Figure 36.25, you can see where we're headed. I have a document with several predefined page sizes. The Create PDF ⇨ From Blank Page command provides only a few page sizes when creating new blank files. I'd like some more so I created a template with buttons that have scripts to create new pages. Without a Trusted Function, my buttons won't work.

FIGURE 36.25

A document with several predefined page sizes and buttons with JavaScripts that create blank new pages.

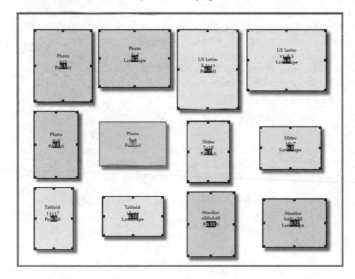

To write the button scripts in Acrobat, follow these steps.

STEPS: Using a Trusted Function in Acrobat

1. **Create a button field.** You can use any one of the locations where JavaScripts are permitted. For this example, I'll use a button field.

2. **Format the field.** Set the format attributes for the field name, appearance, and a button face, as described in Chapter 34.

3. **Add a JavaScript.** Click the Actions tab and add a Run a JavaScript action. In the JavaScript Editor type the following code:

```
1.      trustedNewDoc(432,288);
```

4. **Click OK.**

5. **Test the script.** Click the button with the Hand tool and a blank new document 6x4 inches should appear in the Document pane.

The code in the single line of text calls the Trusted Function (by function name trustedNewDoc) and the values are the measurements of the new page in points. To translate the points to inches divide by 72.

In this example, I added some preset page sizes and used buttons to create the new documents. Another alternative you have available is to create a JavaScript as a New menu item and write the code so a dialog box opens prompting you to add custom page sizes. The script is longer, but follows the same principles by writing a Trusted Function and copying it to the JavaScript folder. When adding a menu item, you don't need a script in a PDF document.

CROSS-REF For example, code for creating a New menu item and scripting a routine that opens a dialog box where custom values for page sizes are added, see the JavaScript 8 Scripting Reference at `http://partners.adobe.com/asn/acrobat/docs.jsp#javascript`. Note that the Web location may change so be certain to search Adobe's Web site if you don't find the document at this URL.

Adding menu commands

Menu items can be added with JavaScripts written as Trusted Functions to customize your Acrobat workplace. You can add menu items for just about any kind of action and position the menu command in any one of the Acrobat menus. For an example of how to add menu items, follow the steps below:

STEPS: Adding menu commands with JavaScript

1. **Launch your text editor.** Be certain to use a text editor and not a word processor.

2. **Write the following code in the text editor:**

```
1.      function totalPages(){
2.   app.alert("Total Pages: " + this.numPages);
3.      }
4.      function totalFields(){
5.   app.alert("Total Fields: "+ this.numFields);
6.      }
7.      function totalTemplates(){
8.   app.alert("Total Page Templates in this file: "+
this.numTemplates);
9.       }
10.  app.addMenuItem ({cName: "Total Pages",
   cParent: "Tools", cExec: "totalPages()"
11. });
12.  app.addMenuItem ({cName: "Number of Fields",
   cParent: "Tools", cExec: "totalFields()"
13. });
14.  app.addMenuItem ({cName: "Page Templates",
   cParent: "Tools", cExec: "totalTemplates()"
15. });
```

3. **Save the text file with a .js extension.**

4. **Copy the file to your Acrobat JavaScripts folder.**

5. **Launch Acrobat.** If Acrobat was open when you added the script to the JavaScripts folder, quit the program and relaunch Acrobat.

6. **Open the Tools menu.** At the bottom of the menu you should see three additional menu commands, as shown in Figure 36.26.

FIGURE 36.26

The Tools menu shows three new menu items produced by the folder level JavaScript.

Three new menu items

Selecting a menu item opens a dialog box reporting the total pages in the open document, the total number of fields in the open document, and the total number of templates in the open document. Particularly useful are the Total Fields and Page Templates commands. Because you don't see any indication in toolbars as to how many fields exist in the document or whether the document contains any page templates, selecting the menu commands quickly reports total fields and page templates found in the document. In Figure 36.27, selecting the Total Fields menu command opened an alert dialog box that reports the total fields in the open PDF file.

FIGURE 36.27

The total number of fields in a document are reported in an application alert dialog box after selecting the Total Fields menu command.

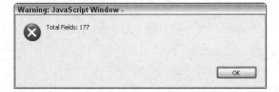

In the JavaScript to create the Tools menu items, the first eight items handle the computations for total pages, total fields, and total templates. Lines 10 through 15 contain the `addMenuItem` objects and attributes for the menu commands locations (Tools menu) and displays.

Using a JavaScript Builder

You can see that as you develop more sophisticated actions from JavaScripts, writing code becomes much more complex and cumbersome. Wouldn't it be nice if you could use a tool to write the JavaScripts for you? Unfortunately, Acrobat doesn't have a built-in JavaScript development tool, but you can acquire a third-party product to install as a plug-in that can save you hours, if not days, of time writing raw code.

CROSS-REF For more information on working with third-party plug-ins, see Chapter 4.

Windjack Solutions, a third-party developer, markets two impressive plug-ins designed specifically for creating all the JavaScript you need to add actions for any field type. As an example, suppose you want to create an application response dialog box. The user clicks a button and a custom dialog box appearing with your company logo opens. If the user clicks OK, the associated action is invoked. If the user clicks Cancel, no action takes place. Windjack Solutions provides you all you need to create a custom user interface code for toolbar buttons.

ON the CD-ROM Windjack Solutions' AcroButtons and AcroDialogs plug-ins are available on the CD-ROM that accompanies this book.

With Windjack Solutions' AcroButtons plug-in, you can easily create custom buttons that can be added to a form and the Acrobat program itself. In Figure 36.28, you see the user interface for creating a custom button. Buttons can be imported from designs you create in illustration, image editing, or other software programs and saved as PDF files.

FIGURE 36.28

The AcroButtons plug-in provides an easy-to-use interface to create custom icons.

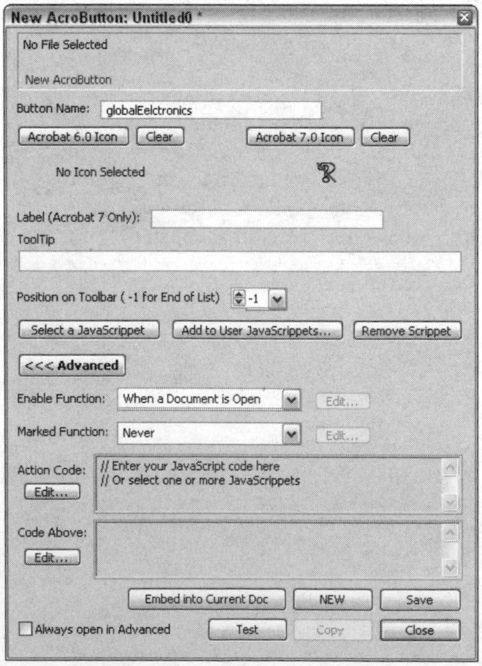

Click either the Acrobat 6 icon or Acrobat 7 icon button in the AcroButtons dialog box and another dialog box prompts you to locate a button design to import. After locating the design and clicking OK, another dialog box opens where you can scale the button, rotate, zoom, add an image mask, and more, as shown in Figure 36.29.

FIGURE 36.29

Buttons can be edited in the AcroButtons plug-in for a number of different image attributes.

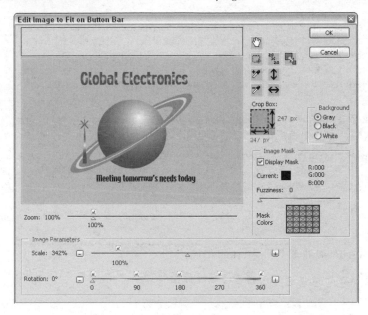

Although AcroButtons and AcroDialogs are two separate programs and can be used independently, this example shows you how to create a custom button that can be introduced in a custom dialog box. After creating a custom button you let AcroDialogs create the dialog box and button actions you want to add to the dialog box. AcroDialogs is a drag-and-drop JavaScript Dialog design application. From the left pane in the AcroDialogs window, you drag buttons or any other field type to a layout pane. Add your assets to the layout, shown in Figure 36.30, and click the Save button.

FIGURE 36.30

AcroDialogs has an easy to use interface that enables you to graphically design your dialog boxes and exports all the JavaScript to create the dialog box for you.

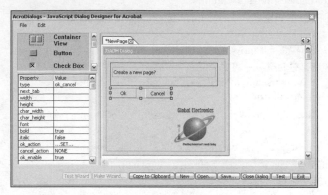

When you click the Save button all the JavaScript is written for you. You can add the JavaScript to any PDF document and reuse the routines each time you want the same actions added to another file. In Figure 36.31, a button is clicked on a form that opens a dialog box created with AcroDialogs. The dialog box has a company logo and actions associated with the OK button. Writing a JavaScript to create the same dialog box in Acrobat could take you days whereas using AcroDialogs takes you about as much time as writing and debugging about ten lines of JavaScript code.

FIGURE 36.31

You create custom dialog boxes in AcroDialogs that take a fraction of the time required to write the code in the JavaScript Editor.

NOTE The warning statement in dialog boxes created with JavaScripts is an Acrobat 8 warning. All custom dialog boxes created with plug-ins or by writing code in the JavaScript Editor appear with this warning statement in Acrobat 8.

If you want to experiment a little with AcroButtons and AcroDialogs, the demo software is available on the book's CD-ROM. Note that AcroButtons and AcroDialogs are supported only on Windows, but the JavaScripts produced by both programs can be run on either platform.

Summary

- One method for learning JavaScript is to examine forms with scripts. You can copy JavaScripts in the JavaScript Editor dialog box or copy form fields and links.

- JavaScripts are found in several places in PDF documents including fields, links, bookmarks, page actions, document-level scripts, and document actions.

- The Edit All JavaScripts command lists all JavaScripts in a document. When you're learning how a form executes JavaScripts, examining all potential areas where scripts are written is a good idea.

- Viewer types and viewer version alerts are used to inform users whether their Acrobat viewer is the correct version and type to complete a form.

- Sums of data in rows and columns are calculated with JavaScripts using loops to gather data through each pass in a loop.

- Document actions are used to execute a JavaScript when a file opens, closes, or prints.

- Pages can be spawned in a document to create new pages from a template page. When pages are spawned, all fields, links, and JavaScripts on the new spawned pages are duplicated from the template page with new field names.

- Pop-up menus can save some space on a form where lists in nested menus are scripted to open pages and/or documents.

- Pop-up menus can be added to PDF Packages for easy page navigation.

- Trusted Functions enable you to grant temporary permissions for executing JavaScripts for privileged methods. These scripts require you to copy the scripts to the JavaScript folder in addition to the scripts you write in Acrobat.

- Some third-party plug-in developers provide tools to help you easily create complex JavaScripts.

Appendix

Using the CD-ROM

This appendix provides information on the contents and system requirements of the CD-ROM that accompanies this book.

System Requirements

The CD is a cross-platform CD and can be read by both Macintosh and Windows computers. Macintosh users need System 10.2 or above. Windows users need Windows XP Service Pack 2 or above.

Installation Instructions

To gain access to the CD-ROM contents, follow these steps:

1. **Insert the CD-ROM in your CD drive.** An autorun program automatically opens a window.
2. **Click the Install button and locate a folder on your hard drive where you want the files installed.**
3. **Click Install and the files are installed in your target folder.**

Contents

The CD contains the following four folders:

- Adobe Reader 8.0 software
- The entire text of this book as a PDF document with an embedded index

APPENDIX
System requirements
Installation instructions
CD-ROM contents
Troubleshooting

- Author-created PDF documents and sample files
- Windows demonstration plug-ins

Adobe Reader 8.0

Double-click the Adobe Reader installer and install the Reader software from the book's CD. Adobe Reader is coded separately for PowerPC Macs and Intel Macs, so be sure to choose the installer appropriate for your computer.

NOTE Before you install Adobe Reader 8 on your computer, check out Adobe's Web site at www .adobe.com/products/acrobat/readermain.html to see if there's a newer version of the Reader software than Adobe Reader 8.0, as you may have purchased this book after Adobe has updated the Reader software. If you find a version later than 8.0 on Adobe's Web site, download that version.

PDF version of the book

The entire text of the *Adobe Acrobat 8 PDF Bible* is available on the CD as a PDF document. Any Acrobat viewer 7.0 and above can open the PDF file and view the contents.

To search the embedded index, open the Search panel by pressing Ctrl/⌘+Shift+F. When the Search panel opens, type a word in the first text box. Acrobat will automatically use the embedded index to find searched words.

CROSS-REF For more options on searching PDF documents, see Chapter 6.

Author-created PDF documents

The authorFiles folder contains tutorial PDF documents and sample files to help you through some of the steps in the text of the book. Not all steps have an associated tutorial document. Files for selected chapters where you may have difficulty creating a similar file are the only files you'll see in the authorFiles folder. This folder contains several subfolders and a welcome PDF file that include:

- **welcome.pdf.** Launch the welcome.pdf file inside the authorFiles folder. On the first page of the welcome.pdf file you'll find a legend describing some navigation methods and a short description of the remaining contents in the document. As you move forward in the file, you'll find links to documents contained in the various subfolders within the authorFiles folder. Click a link to open a PDF or native authoring document. Very little navigation is required at the desktop. Almost all files are opened via links in the welcome.pdf document.

- **Chapters folder.** Inside the Chapters folder you'll find subfolders labeled according to chapter number. See these files for completing steps in the respective chapters. If a chapter folder does not appear for a given chapter, no support files are provided.

- **flashDemos folder.** The flashDemos folder contains several files created with Adobe Captivate and exported as Adobe Flash files. These documents are linked to HTML pages that are included in the same folder. All files can be opened in your default Web browser via links on page 5 in the welcome.pdf document.

  In addition to the Adobe Flash files, several PDF documents are stored that provide some tips using Acrobat. These files are also linked to page 5 in the welcome.pdf document.

- **sampleForms folder.** On page 3 of the welcome.pdf document, you'll find links to sample forms that contain JavaScripts. Examine the fields, bookmarks, page actions, document actions, and document-level JavaScripts in these files as I describe in Chapter 36.

- **URL links.** On page 4 of the welcome.pdf document, you'll find some helpful links to Adobe's Web site for product and services descriptions, links to the Acrobat User Community Web site, and some additional resources where you can find information about Acrobat and PDF. Click any link on page 4 and the respective Web page will open in your default Web browser.

In addition, an electronic brochure courtesy of Robert Connolly of pdfPictures.com (`www.pdfPictures .com`) and Aruba Bonbini is placed in the Chapter 22 folder inside the Chapters folder. This file is available for you to explore how dynamic content and the use of pop-up menus are used in PDF files.

Windows demonstration plug-ins

Two plug-ins are included on the CD for you to experiment with. For additional plug-ins and demonstration downloads, visit `http://store.adobe.com/store/products/plugins/view_by_application .jhtml?id=catPluginsForAcrobat` for a list of the most up-to-date products offered by third-party developers. You can also find a similar list at the Planet PDF Store at `www.planetpdf.com/ find_software.asp`.

To install the AcroButtons and AcroDialogs plug-ins contained on the CD, open the plug_ins folder and double-click each installer. You should install the plug-ins before opening Acrobat. Note that these plug-ins work only with Acrobat Professional on Windows.

Troubleshooting

If you have difficulty installing or using any of the materials on the companion CD, try the following solutions:

- **Turn off any anti-virus software that you may have running.** Installers sometimes mimic virus activity and can make your computer incorrectly believe that it is being infected by a virus. (Be sure to turn the anti-virus software back on later.)
- **Close all running programs.** The more programs you're running, the less memory is available to other programs. Installers also typically update files and programs; if you keep other programs running, installation may not work properly.
- **Reference the ReadMe:** Please refer to the ReadMe file located at the root of the CD-ROM for the latest product information at the time of publication.

Customer care

If you have trouble with the CD-ROM, please call the Wiley Product Technical Support phone number at (800) 762-2974. Outside the United States, call 1(317) 572-3994. You can also contact Wiley Product Technical Support at `http://support.wiley.com`. John Wiley & Sons will provide technical support only for installation and other general quality control items. For technical support on the applications themselves, consult the program's vendor or author.

To place additional orders or to request information about other Wiley products, please call (877) 762-2974.

Index

SYMBOLS AND NUMERICS

Wiley Publishing, Inc.
End-User License Agreement

READ THIS. You should carefully read these terms and conditions before opening the software packet(s) included with this book "Book". This is a license agreement "Agreement" between you and Wiley Publishing, Inc. "WPI". By opening the accompanying software packet(s), you acknowledge that you have read and accept the following terms and conditions. If you do not agree and do not want to be bound by such terms and conditions, promptly return the Book and the unopened software packet(s) to the place you obtained them for a full refund.

1. **License Grant.** WPI grants to you (either an individual or entity) a nonexclusive license to use one copy of the enclosed software program(s) (collectively, the "Software,") solely for your own personal or business purposes on a single computer (whether a standard computer or a work-station component of a multi-user network). The Software is in use on a computer when it is loaded into temporary memory (RAM) or installed into permanent memory (hard disk, CD-ROM, or other storage device). WPI reserves all rights not expressly granted herein.

2. **Ownership.** WPI is the owner of all right, title, and interest, including copyright, in and to the compilation of the Software recorded on the disk(s) or CD-ROM "Software Media". Copyright to the individual programs recorded on the Software Media is owned by the author or other authorized copyright owner of each program. Ownership of the Software and all proprietary rights relating thereto remain with WPI and its licensers.

3. **Restrictions On Use and Transfer.**

   (a) You may only (i) make one copy of the Software for backup or archival purposes, or (ii) transfer the Software to a single hard disk, provided that you keep the original for backup or archival purposes. You may not (i) rent or lease the Software, (ii) copy or reproduce the Software through a LAN or other network system or through any computer subscriber system or bulletin-board system, or (iii) modify, adapt, or create derivative works based on the Software.

   (b) You may not reverse engineer, decompile, or disassemble the Software. You may transfer the Software and user documentation on a permanent basis, provided that the transferee agrees to accept the terms and conditions of this Agreement and you retain no copies. If the Software is an update or has been updated, any transfer must include the most recent update and all prior versions.

4. **Restrictions on Use of Individual Programs.** You must follow the individual requirements and restrictions detailed for each individual program in the About the CD-ROM appendix of this Book. These limitations are also contained in the individual license agreements recorded on the Software Media. These limitations may include a requirement that after using the program for a specified period of time, the user must pay a registration fee or discontinue use. By opening the Software packet(s), you will be agreeing to abide by the licenses and restrictions for these individual programs that are detailed in the About the CD-ROM appendix and on the Software Media. None of the material on this Software Media or listed in this Book may ever be redistributed, in original or modified form, for commercial purposes.

The books you
read to succeed.

**Get the most out of the latest software and leading-edge technologies
with a Wiley Bible—your one-stop reference.**

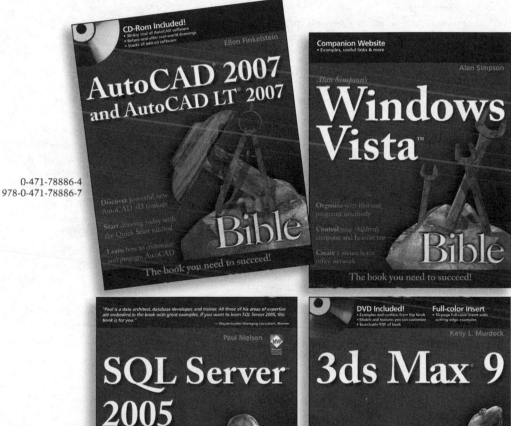

0-471-78886-4
978-0-471-78886-7

0-470-04030-0
978-0-470-04030-0

0-7645-4256-7
978-0-7645-4256-5

0-470-10089-3
978-0-470-10089-9